Beat the Racetrack

Other books by WILLIAM T. ZIEMBA

Stochastic Optimization Models in Finance
Turkish Flat Weaves
Energy Policy Modeling: United States and Canadian Experiences, Vols. I and II
Generalized Concavity in Optimization and Economics

Beat the Racetrack

by William T. Ziemba and Donald B. Hausch

With a Foreword by Edward O. Thorp

E P B M
ECHO POINT BOOKS & MEDIA, LLC
BRATTLEBORO, VERMONT

Published by Echo Point Books & Media
Brattleboro, Vermont
www.EchoPointBooks.com

Beat the Racetrack
ISBN: 978-1-63561-744-3 (paperbound)

Cover design by AnshDeb, Sd Designs

Cover image by babikulesi, courtesy of pixabay

To Rachel, who likes the horses
but loves the popcorn.
—W. T. Z.

To my parents, Robert and Margret Hausch.
—D. B. H.

CONTENTS

Acknowledgments xv

Foreword by Dr. Edward O. Thorp xvii

Introduction xix

1 **Discovery of the Dr. Z System** 1

The lure of racing. The difficulty of actually winning at the racetrack. Putting together the concepts for a winning system.

2 **Betting at the Races** 9

Reading the program and the *Daily Racing Form*. The various types of bets. How the odds are determined: The track take and breakage.

3 **Applying Stock Market Efficiency Concepts to Horse-racing Betting Markets** 17

The crowd is very good at estimating the true probability of winning: Efficiency of the win-betting market. Can you win by betting on only the very best horses? How accurate is the morning line? The need to look for special situations to avoid betting on all races and on inappropriate days.

4 **Finding Profitable Place and Show Bets** 34

Understanding the win, place, and show payoffs. Why place and show betting can yield positive profits. Expected return per dollar bet. Determining when there is an inefficiency in the betting pools and thus a good opportunity to bet. Formulas for determining the expected value per dollar bet.

5 **How Much Should You Bet?** 63

Why you need to have a good money management system. Using the Kelly criterion to maximize the long-run growth of your betting fortune. More on the Kelly criterion: Its desirable properties and limitations. Assumptions of the Dr. Z system. Steps in applying the Dr. Z system. The First Race, Churchill Downs, Louisville, Kentucky, May 6, 1983. The Sixth Race, Hollywood Park, Inglewood, California, June 5, 1982. The King's Favor Purse, Longacres, Renton, Washington, August 14, 1983. The Beat the Racetrack Calculator™.

6 **Using the Dr. Z System at the Racetrack** 100

The Sixth Race and the Triple Bend Handicap, Hollywood Park, Inglewood, California, May 8, 1982. The Whitney Handicap, Saratoga Racetrack, Saratoga, New York, August 1, 1981. The Santa Ynez Stakes, Santa Anita, February 2, 1983. The Seventh Race, Exhibition Park, Vancouver, British Columbia, April 13, 1983. The Kentucky Oaks, Churchill Downs, Louisville, Kentucky, May 6, 1983. The Matinee Handicap, Hollywood Park, Inglewood, California, April 24, 1982. The Longacres Derby, Longacres, Renton, Washington, August 14, 1983.

7 **Using the Dr. Z System in Other Situations** 144

The Belmont Stakes, June 5, 1982: Other-track betting at Golden Gate Fields, Albany, California. The Clout Handicap, Aqueduct, November 12, 1981: A visit to Teletrack, New Haven, Connecticut.

8 **A Great Race: John Henry versus Lemhi Gold in the Oak Tree Invitational at Santa Anita, October 31, 1982** 152

The field. The evolution of the odds. What if Lemhi Gold had been in the money?

9 **Results of Computer Studies Using the Dr. Z System over Long Periods** 164

Exhibition Park: The 1978 summer season. Santa Anita: The 1973/74 winter meeting. Aqueduct: The 1981/82 winter season. How important is the track take? How important is breakage? The 2-minute problem: Bets at Exhibition Park in 1980. Characteristics of Dr. Z system bets.

10 The Kentucky Derby: The Most Exciting Two Minutes in Sports 180

The pageantry. The spectacle. The Dr. Z system bets. Proud Appeal versus Johnny Campo in the 107th Kentucky Derby.

11 Derby Day 1982 206

Alzabella is the first Dr. Z system bet. A late scratch. Baraco in the fifth. The Demolition Derby: The 108th run for the roses. Dual Tracks in the ninth.

12 A Great Day for Canada: Sunny's Halo Wins the Kentucky Derby 222

The Kentucky mood. A Mexican filly is the first Dr. Z system bet. Chris McCarron steals the race. Two Dr. Z system bets in the Bold Forbes. Just call me George. The Dreadnought. The Twin Spires: Almost Derby horses. The 109th Kentucky Derby. It was never like this in Louisiana.

13 Betting on Favorites 255

Betting to win may be profitable with good handicapping. Betting the favorite to place or show. Betting extreme favorites: The Ballerina, Exhibition Park, October 11, 1982. Betting all extreme favorites to place and show. Betting overwhelming favorites in major stakes and futurity races. The Longacres Mile, Longacres, Renton, Washington, August 21, 1983.

14 A Typical Day at the Races: Making the Best Bet in Each Race, Hollywood Park, May 30, 1982 274

Betting on all the races. Useful betting rules. The Results.

15 Minus Pools 296

Eliminating possible minus pools: The Kentucky Oaks at Churchill Downs, May 1, 1981. An extraordinary show pool: The Coaching Club American Oaks at Belmont, June 27, 1981. A typical minus pool: The San Juan Capistrano Invitational Handicap at Santa Anita, April 18, 1982.

16 Refinements to the Basic Dr. Z System 311

Dangers to look for, when not to bet and horses to avoid, conservative versus risky use of the Dr. Z system, and hints on good betting techniques at the racetrack. Regression equations based on differing wealth levels and track handle. Adjusting the optimal bet size for differing track paybacks. Adjustments for coupled entries. Adjustments for making more than one bet. Flow chart of the betting rules. Using fundamental information to improve the Dr. Z system. Recommended handicapping books.

17 Epilogue 329

Why are we making the Dr. Z system public? Will the market become efficient: How much can be bet by all Dr. Z system bettors? Using the Dr. Z system for harness racing. Using the Dr. Z system in England.

Appendix A Thoroughbred racetracks in North America: Seasons, Purses, Betting, and Track Takes. 363

Appendix B Mathematics of the Dr. Z System. 374

Bibliography 383

Index 387

Acknowledgments

In the course of our research and the preparation of this book, we have received the aid and support of a number of colleagues and friends. Without implicating them for any possible errors in this book, we would especially like to thank Mukhtar Ali, Michael Brennan, Brian Canfield, Tom Cover, Bruce Fauman, Peter Griffin, Jay Ritter, Jerry Rosenwald, Mark Rubinstein, Richard van Slyke, Edward O. Thorp, and John Woods. Jenny Russell and Linda Stewart did a marvelous job of typing the various drafts of the manuscript. Sandra Buckingham and Ulrike Hilborn did the artwork. It is our hope that this book will follow proudly in the tradition of Ed Thorp's books *Beat the Dealer* and *Beat the Market* as a scientifically proven system to exploit an existing market inefficiency. We are pleased that Dr. Thorp has written the foreword to the book.

Foreword

The publication of this book is a rare event in the world of gambling because it presents one of the few betting systems ever discovered that really works. It is the only system for betting on horse races which has enough scientific analysis to persuade me that it is valid.

The system is easy to understand and use, which makes it appealing to readers and bettors. The basic ideas behind it are simple ones:

1. The crowd is good at picking a winner—so good, in fact, that the relative amount bet on a horse to win corresponds closely to its actual chances of winning.

2. In the same way, the amount the crowd bets on horses to place and show should be distributed in approximately the same proportions as the amounts bet in the win pool.

3. But sometimes—in about two to four races a day—the place and show pools are considerably "off" from the proportions in the win pool. When that happens, the place and show bets give the player an edge of as much as 20 percent or even more. This phenomenon is an example of an "inefficient market," and it is the basis of the Dr. Z system.

It took two good scientists, Professor William Ziemba and his student Donald Hausch, to back up these ideas with solid analysis. They set out to develop a precise method to measure just how good a bet is, one that would show you both when to bet and how large a bet it should be. Bill Ziemba is an expert in operations research and portfolio management and in the theory and practical applications of gambling. He has long had an active interest in gambling games and systems and has served as a consultant for the Canadian government. His main area of academic expertise, operations research, is concerned with the application of mathematics to the real world. Donald Hausch is an expert economic modeler and computer analyst. All this provides them with the perfect background for what they have done in this book.

Besides the mathematical and scientific analysis, the development of the Dr. Z system required verification using historical data from past races, and it needed to be tested by actual play. The authors did all these things. *And* they won money at the track using their own system. The book presents all the details necessary to make a careful, intelligent, and profitable application of their system. Beyond this, it is also an entertaining introduction to the lore of the track.

This book is for people who want to win. The gambling system it presents is one of the few I have ever seen that I think really works. I am convinced enough to bet my own money on it.

Edward O. Thorp
Newport Beach, California
November 1983

Introduction

This book is about the Dr. Z system, a method that should actually enable you to beat the races. We have used the Dr. Z system at racetracks in California, New York, Kentucky, Washington, and British Columbia. When properly applied, its average profit per dollar wagered is about 10%–20%.

The Dr. Z system is based on an inefficiency in the place- and show-betting markets. The inefficiency is similar to that which occurs in stock option markets and warrant trading, and casino card games such as blackjack. Simply put, the bet or investment will return, on average, substantially more than its purchase price with only a small risk. The inefficiency is large enough to yield profitable bets about two to four times per average racing day. The inefficiency occurs because of the betting habits of the public—in particular, because of their greed for large profits—and because it is difficult for them to estimate the true worth of place and show bets.

We have used a sophisticated mathematical model that selects those profitable bets and determines how much should be wagered to maximize the long-run rate of growth of the bettor's fortune.* The model is solved using a modern electronic computer. To make the Dr. Z system operational at the racetrack, we have developed simple approximations that provide you with easy to follow rules. The rules indicate how good a possible bet is, whether or not it is advisable to place a wager, and how much should be wagered given your particular betting fortune.

Charts and detachable cards are provided in the book for actual application of the Dr. Z system at a racetrack. The Beat the Racetrack Calculator™ is also available for those wishing the simplest, most accurate application of the Dr. Z system.

We have read dozens of books and investigated numerous systems for handicapping and racetrack betting. We believe that the Dr. Z system is the

---

*Some of the research that made this book possible is based in part on stochastic mathematical optimization research supported in part by the Canadian Natural Sciences and Engineering Research Council grant 67-7147.

first scientifically proven method for the average person to obtain consistent horse-race betting profits. Though it is difficult to find hard evidence, no doubt handicapping systems exist that yield profits upon proper application of their methods. These systems, however, usually require extensive knowledge that borders on expert handicapping. The aim of the Dr. Z system is to provide the average nonexpert with a simple, easy-to-use procedure for making modest but substantial profits. To apply the Dr. Z system you need only to follow a few key rules and to be patient, betting only when the wager is really worth making and avoiding the temptation of betting too much or too soon. The Dr. Z system tells you how much of your betting fortune to wager on each profitable situation. You do not have to become an expert handicapper to apply the Dr. Z system and win with it. It should provide slow, steady profits with small risk. At the very least, we hope it will teach you why most racetrack bettors lose and how you can avoid being one of them.

Beat the Racetrack

CHAPTER 1

Discovery of the Dr. Z System

The Lure of Racing

People have been interested in horse races and betting on their outcome for several thousands of years. The Hittites, Greeks, and Romans all had horse races, as well as track-and-field competitions among human athletes.

The horses we call thoroughbreds are descended from three Near East stallions, the Byerly Turk, the Darley Arabian, and the Godolphin Barb, which were bred to English mares in the seventeenth and eighteenth centuries. Of some two hundred sires listed in the first stud book, which was published in 1793, only these three developed breeding lines that exist today. Matchem, foaled in 1748, became the only stallion to continue the Godolphin Barb's line; Herod, foaled in 1758, continued the Byerly Turk's line, which began in 1686; and Eclipse, foaled in 1764, continued the Darley Arabian line. Every thoroughbred racing today is a direct descendent of one of these three lines. It is these thoroughbreds in the North American setting with which we are concerned in this book. However, the Dr. Z system also applies to standardbreds running in harness races, quarter horses, greyhounds, and racing situations involving thoroughbreds in England and other countries (see Chapter Seventeen).

Thoroughbred horse racing is a very popular sport. Indeed, about the same number of people in North America attend the track each year as attend professional and college football and baseball games combined. There are about a hundred thoroughbred tracks in North America, with seasons running from just a few days to nearly half the year. (A current listing of these tracks and their handles appears in Appendix A.) Racetracks are big business: In 1982, 57 million people bet $7.7 billion at racetracks and legalized off-track betting shops in North America. Many more billions were bet with illegal bookies.

People go to the track for several reasons. Among these are the beauty and excitement of the sport. Eight or ten one-thousand-pound animals piloted by hundred-pound jockeys in colorful silks vying to win a race are quite a sight. It is hard to beat the thrill of a horse coming from far off the pace to mount a late charge and nip the leader at the wire. Even more exciting is the challenge of picking the winner. It is a very demanding task, which has its high and low moments. After each race you see countless bettors with long faces tearing up their tickets and rushing to look at the *Daily Racing Form* in an attempt to recoup their losses in the next race. A few winners will be telling their friends about the intricate analysis they used to pick the winner. The longer the odds the horse had, the greater these "bragging rights" are. Then there is the sheer greed of many bettors. They want to pick up easy winnings. For some bets, like the triactor and pick six, payoffs can be in the thousands or even hundreds of thousands of dollars. There is even a chance a big win will change a person's whole life.

Myriad factors can influence the performance of an individual horse and the outcome of a particular race. Some are analyzable and some are due to pure chance. Trying to pick the winners and the in-the-money finishers in a horse race is an intense intellectual challenge that draws the interest and talents of millions of people each year. Their attempts to put together all the relevant factors—the condition of the horses, the track, the skill of the jockeys, the trainers' and owners' intentions, the length of the race, the weights carried by the various horses, and so forth—is an irresistible challenge. One measure of the difficulty of this task is the number of people who can do it successfully. How many people do you know who go to the races? Quite a few, probably. How many win each year? Not many, right? That's what makes it so interesting and challenging.

I have been interested in horse racing for a long time. As a youth I spent many hot summer days at Saratoga analyzing racing forms. Having an analytical mind, I reasoned that I just needed to figure out which factors were really important, and when, in order to have the basis of a winning system. I spent quite a bit of time and energy trying to isolate the factors that determine the chances of a particular horse's winning a given race. One can develop such prediction equations that work reasonably well, but is it possible to beat the races with them? I concluded that you could beat the races with handicapping systems only if you were an expert, one willing to keep abreast daily of all relevant happenings in a given meet.

But I was searching for something simpler that could be applied in a systematic fashion without an intimate knowledge of recent racing results. This required a different approach. Rather than trying to pick the winner and the in-the-money finishers in a given race, I needed to concentrate on how to manage my money and to determine when there are bets that, on average, return significantly more than their costs. I found a good predictor of the actual probability of winning was the amount bet by the crowd.

In aggregate, all the experts and others betting on a particular day generated odds. Those odds, on average, were excellent predictors of the actual chances of each horse's winning. This is not surprising; it is the way most security markets work. Financial analysts call them *efficient markets*. This suggested to me that the really best bets were to place and show.

On the basis of financial markets, I realized that it was best to use the efficiency in the win pools to isolate inefficiencies in the place and show pools. Then I needed to develop sophisticated betting procedures that are easy to use. The idea is to bet more the more advantageous the situation is. That way, your betting fortune grows as fast as possible. Most bettors bet the win pools, since they appear to provide the highest payoff and are the easiest to understand. Place and show betting is considered less profitable and much harder to understand. For example, the exact payoff on place and show bets depends upon which three horses finish in the money. This book is concerned with the use of the Dr. Z system for making bets on outstanding place and show opportunities. Before we begin, let's look at why it is so difficult to win at the racetrack.

The Difficulty of Actually Winning at the Racetrack

Studies of betting behavior show that fewer than one out of every hundred racetrack bettors is actually ahead over a long period of time. Why is it so difficult to win? In the parimutuel system of betting, you must be just a little more clever than the other bettors in the crowd, since you are betting against them. But how much better do you have to be to win? The hidden difficulty is the track commission, which consists of two parts: the *track take* and the *breakage*. The track take is the normal commission that the track subtracts from the total betting pool to make its profit and to pay its expenses. It varies from a low of 14.8% in Ontario and 15% in California and Kentucky to a high of 22.1% in Saskatchewan. The rates tend to be lower in states and provinces where the volume of betting is larger. Table A.6 in Appendix A lists current track takes in the major American states and Canadian provinces. These rates are periodically changed. Call your local jockey club for the latest information if you don't find it listed in the program.

The track take is enormous! In the 1983 Kentucky Derby, 134,444 people bet $5,546,977, so the 15% track take in Kentucky amounted to $832,046—a handsome payoff for the track and a big addition to the total loss of the losers. Over the full day, $11,851,527 was bet, for a commission of $1,777,729.

The second part of the track's commission is the breakage, which is the rounding down of the winnings to common payoff amounts. For example, suppose a horse pays $12.77 for each $2 bet. That $12.77 represents the total bet on all the horses less the track take divided by the number of tickets sold on the winning horse. The actual payoff will be either $12.70 or $12.60, depending on whether the track uses 5¢ or 10¢ breakage to the dollar.

At first glance this 7¢ or 17¢ does not seem like much. After all, with a $2 bet 7¢ is a mere 0.65% of the potential profit, and 17¢ is only 1.58% of the profit. But suppose the parimutuel payoff should be $2.78, with the winning bettors getting $2.70 or $2.60. Now the effect on profits is much more substantial. In the 5¢ case it is 8¢/78¢, or 10.3%, and in the 10¢ case it is 18¢/78¢, or 23.1% of the potential profit. Thus the effect of breakage depends upon the type of bets being made. Ten cent breakage is always at least as large as 5¢ breakage and is often more than double. You can find out which type your track uses by looking at the payoffs in your local newspaper. If all the payoffs are numbers that are multiples of 20¢, like $6.40, $12.80, and $4.20, then it's the 10¢ variety. If you see payoffs that are multiples of 10¢, like $5.10, $8.30, and $13.30, then you are fortunate to have 5¢ breakage. Typically, breakage amounts to an added commission of about 1%–3% on the amount bet for wagers to win. So the total commission of a typical track might be 17% + 2%, or 19%.

Figure 1.1 indicates how two typical bettors, Handicapper Hal and Number-picker Ned, might do in comparison with the average bettor if the total commission is 19%. It is assumed that each bettor begins with $1,000 and bets $20 on average on each of the ten races each day over a twenty-day period.

The average bettor wagers $200 each day and loses $38 (0.19 × $200) plus his or her admission ticket, program, racing form, parking, gas, food, and so forth. So after twenty days his or her $1,000 betting stake has dwindled to $240. Handicapper Hal has studied a number of handicapping books and when he was on vacation in Las Vegas two years ago, he took a one-day seminar that featured several of America's top handicappers. He prides himself on the fact that he knows a lot about speed horses. He always bets each race, although he might double up on horses he thinks are overlays (that is, the odds are better than the chances of winning), and bets less when the race looks very tough. Hal does better than most of his friends who frequently seek out his advice. Hal goes to the track both Saturday and Sunday, since he is too busy driving his cab during the week. He often breaks even or has small winnings. He thinks that if he can eliminate a few more bad bets he will be an overall winner. Hal gets a lot of enjoyment from analyzing the *Daily Racing Form* and he studies it for about two hours the evening before a day's races. The $455 loss that he had over the twenty days was more than compensated for by Hal's enjoyment of the races. He is sure that he will do better next year and likely be ahead at the end of the season.

Ned works as a cashier for a big food market that is several miles from the local racetrack. He likes to go to the track Wednesday evening with several of his pals. On Fridays they play poker. Ned is too busy to spend time studying the racing form. In fact he never buys it. Instead he relies on the picks in the program and often buys one of the tipster's pick sheets. He likes to bet on horses that look good. So gray horses, those with bandaged feet, and those ridden by jockeys he doesn't like are out. He always bets on number 7 in the seventh and number 6 in the ninth, since it was a lucky day when his son was born on the sixth day of September. Ned and his pals sometimes share bets. They like to bet to win and love the exotic pools. One of Ned's friends won $1,400 on the triactor last fall. Ned does not really expect to win, but he thinks that someday he'll get lucky and make a killing. He thinks of his $770 losses this year as an investment and maybe he'll get it all back if he wins the triactor next year.

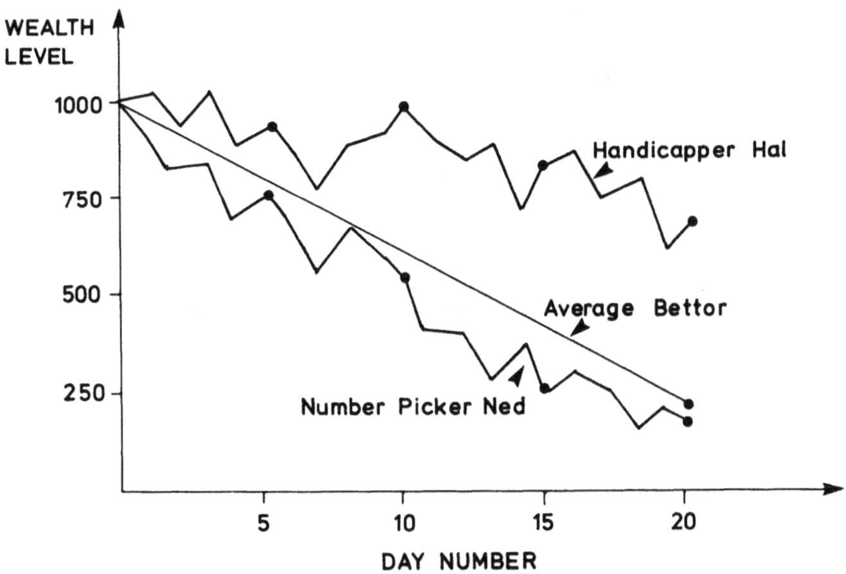

Figure 1.1 Typical behavior of the betting fortunes of three bettors

The crowd is composed of many different types of bettors, although many of them are like Hal and Ned. On average they lose 19% of what they bet because of the track take and breakage. Ned might conceivably win a large triactor and come out ahead, but it is unlikely. Most bettors like Ned will continue to lose a little bit more than the average bettor. Hal is pretty good at handicapping. He might be able to turn himself into a winner. If he can improve his handicapping a little and learn to bet more wisely, maybe this will happen.

But just how much better than the average bettor would Hal have to be to break even? Suppose Hal decides to concentrate on the top horses. Studies show that the top choices of the betting public win about a third of their races. The typical person betting favorites in a nine-race card might pick the winner in three of the races on average. I say on average, because he or she might pick six Monday evening, two Wednesday afternoon, one on Saturday, and so on, to average three per day. These winning horses pay about \$4.86 per \$2 bet, since $\left(\frac{3}{9}\right)x = 0.81$ gives $x = \$2.43$ per dollar bet (the 0.81 is 100% minus the track take and breakage of 19%). To break even, Hal would have to pick 41.2% winners, since $(2.43)y = 1.00$ gives $y = 0.412$. Thus he has to be 23.5% better than the average bettor.

The situation is the same if Hal is picking medium-priced horses that are winning about 15%–20% of the time or longshots that win 5%–10% of their races. Hal simply must be $100/0.81 - 100 = 23.5\%$ better than the average bettor to break even. Hal does not think this will be that difficult. After all he knows so much more than the Neds of the world. Hal will be as surprised as we hope you are when he learns about the efficiency of the win market.

The evidence shows that even though the average bettor is losing 19% of the bet with every wager, he or she is actually quite good at picking winners and establishing fair odds. The average bettor is a composite of experts, those following the consensus, those following the betting patterns, those following their instincts, those who pick gray horses and popular numbers, and so forth. Roughly speaking, on average, their betting odds are a pretty good indication of the true probability of each horse's winning. It will be tougher than Hal thinks. In Chapter Three we take a careful look at this evidence.

Putting Together the Concepts for a Winning System

Beating the races is an intellectual challenge. To have a winning system means that you must be a good handicapper and a good money manager.

You need to have an accurate method of predicting not only the probability that each horse will win a given race, but the probabilities of all possible 1-2-3 finishes. Then you need a way to determine when a given bet will return significantly more, on average, than it costs. Finally, you need to determine how much to bet, taking into account the effect of the bet on the odds, the worthiness of the particular bet, and the amount of betting wealth available for wagering. Since the betting pools and the odds are constantly changing, the procedure must be simple enough for it to be applied quickly just prior to the closing of the mutuel windows and the running of the race. That is the challenge.

We think that we have developed such a system for beating the races. It is called the Dr. Z system, and you should be able to apply it successfully at the racetrack. Although some of the ingredients in the winning mix are complicated, the Dr. Z system is easy to use. You do not have to be an expert handicapper. On the contrary, you need only to follow a few rather simple rules. You need to be patient and bet only when the conditions are right and when the bet is really good enough. To determine whether to bet or not, you'll simply watch the tote board and then use either the detachable cards found inside the back cover of the book or the calculator discussed in Chapter Five.

Before we go on, it's time to tell you how we discovered the various ingredients that make up the Dr. Z system and who your guides are. The emphasis in this book is on the efficiency-of-market approach. It has been used by financial analysts to extract excess returns from various security, financial, and commodity markets whenever this is possible. See Malkiel (1981), Sharpe (1981), and Thorp and Kassouf (1967).* In stock market jargon, it is a technical system based on relative prices rather than on a fundamental system based on intrinsic values. A key to the analysis is the notion that the public, in aggregate, knows pretty well what the chances are of particular horses' winning a given race. However, their greed to make a big killing at the track and the boost to the ego that goes with it make long shots very popular, while favorites are shunned. This makes the favorites relatively better bets. This bias is not enough, however, to produce a winning system for bets to win. But it is a key ingredient in the Dr. Z system for place and show bets.

The efficiency of the win markets has been known for some time. Studies by psychologists, such as Griffith (1949), pointed this out over thirty years ago. We were forcefully reminded of the principles of efficiency win markets by the significant study by Snyder (1978). All that needed to be done was to find a good way to estimate the probability of each horse's winning. And

*We will cite references, which are listed on pages 383–86, by the author's name and year of publication.

that is amazingly simple to do. You need only to find the ratio between two numbers—the amount bet on each horse to win divided by the total win pool. It is quite accurate.

While I was a visiting professor at the University of California at Berkeley in 1978, I had a number of discussions about racetrack market efficiency with Professor Mark Rubinstein. He has a background in financial markets and he, too, was looking for a way to use the tote board information to yield a profitable betting system. He told me about his work with his student King (1978) and the similar ideas of Harville (1973). As you will see in Chapter Five, the Harville formulas combined with the efficiency of the win-market estimates of the probability of winning, generate the probabilities of all possible 1-2-3 in-the-money finishes. This early advice proved invaluable. The key step was to combine these ideas with that of optimal investment over time, a subject in which I have expertise. Doing the actual calculations, developing and testing the Dr. Z system required many refinements. Don Hausch, a former student of mine, and I have been working on this together for the past five years.

Along the way, we have benefited from a number of sources and people mentioned in the acknowledgments. We have also found useful and supportive the work of several people who have investigated ideas associated with the Harville formulas, the favorable favorite bias, or place and show betting. These include Harville (1973), Humber (1981), McCleary (1981), King (1978), Ritter (1978), and Yass (1980). These authors point to possible good bets, although they do not go so far as to tell you when a particular bet is really good enough to bet, nor do they discuss how much the bet should be.

In writing this book, Don and I have drawn on several aspects of our background and expertise. Don is an expert computer analyst, and he developed all the computer programs needed for our work, as well as performed the calculations you will find here. He is also an expert in model formulation and worked closely with me in developing the Dr. Z system. I have been interested in horse racing for over twenty years and have followed it over this period, quite intensely since 1978. I now write a column on racing for a Canadian magazine with the byline of Dr. Z. As a professional researcher and editor in the areas of optimization, financial markets, and investment strategies, I saw the potential of combining the efficiency of the win market and the Harville formulas with proper betting models. Finally, Don and I have been successful appliers of the Dr. Z system at racetracks all over North America.

Let's begin with a general discussion of betting at the races.

CHAPTER 2

Betting at the Races

Reading the Program and the Daily Racing Form

When you go to the racetrack you need to buy a program. It costs about 50¢ to 75¢. The program is published by the racetrack and gives the latest information on which horses are scheduled to run in each race. It also provides you with other useful information, such as the names of the jockeys, owners and trainers, the father (sire) and mother (dam) of each horse running, the morning line odds, the weight carried by each horse, the post positions, the value of the race's purse, the eligibility conditions for entering the race, the track record at this distance, and the colors of the jockeys' silks so that you can recognize the various horses during the running of the race.

A sample program for a mythical dream race involving many famous Kentucky Derby winners appears on page 10. Notice that there are two entries for numbers 1 and 2. Imagine getting Whirlaway and Citation together at 5—1 odds! In the next section we discuss more fully the way the odds are determined, but 5—1 means that if either of these horses was to win, the payoff would be a $5 profit plus the return of the $1 for each dollar bet. So a bet of $10 would return $60. The favorite is the great Secretariat at 3—2, so a winning $10 ticket would pay $25.

Entries are formed when two or more horses are entered from the same stable or by the same trainer. They are coupled to avoid any irregularities arising from the fact that they are running for the same people. The *field*, on the other hand, generally puts weaker horses together so that there are no more than twelve separate bets, since that is all that racetrack totalizator boards can usually accommodate. In races such as the Kentucky Derby, with up to twenty starters, the field may contain as many as nine separate horses.

Each day the track announcer provides additional information regarding such items as late scratches, jockey changes, or overweights. It is easy to mark these changes on your program. Most races have about six to ten horses and do not have entries or fields. In most races if a horse is, for instance, number 3, he will run in post position 3. However, when there are entries or fields, the post position order is usually altered.

The program often provides you with information about the jockey and trainer standings and post position statistics of the current meet. The following reprint is from a 1983 Exhibition Park program.

It is a good idea also to buy the *Daily Racing Form*. It costs around $1.75. It contains a tremendous amount of information about the past performances of the horses running in each race, as well as an analysis of each race by the *Form's* consensus experts. Samples of the *Daily Racing Form's*

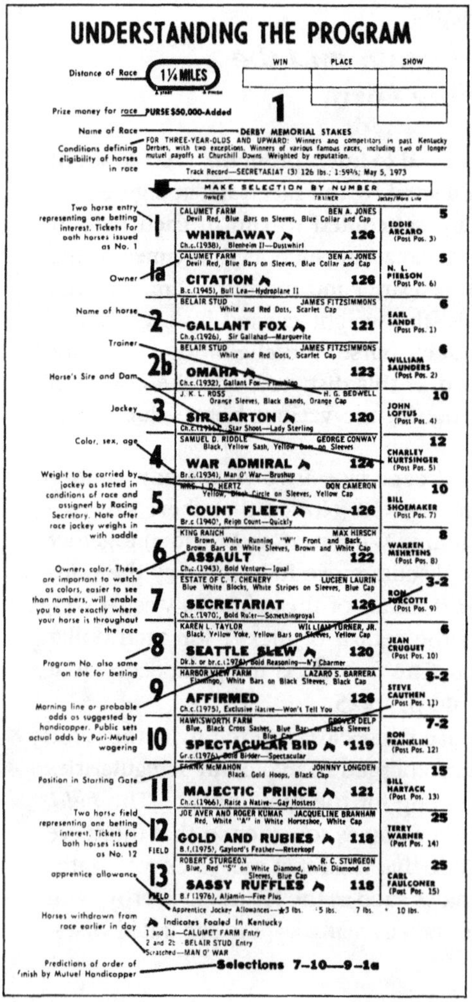

RACING STATISTICS—JOCKEY STANDINGS
(Up to and including May 18)

	Mts.	1st	2nd	3rd	Win%
C. Loseth	150	26	19	16	17.3
M. Walker	137	24	13	22	17.5
S. Krasner	155	23	16	16	14.8
R. Creighton	131	20	14	20	15.2
D. Rycroft	140	17	21	10	12.1
B. Johnson	155	17	15	30	10.9
M. Patzer	141	15	26	11	10.6
K. Skinner	108	12	19	11	11.1
D. Zook	104	8	8	14	7.6
A. Smith	62	7	3	2	11.2
C. Hoverson	70	7	8	7	10.0

TRAINER STANDINGS

	Sts.	1st	2nd	3rd	Win%
H. Barroby	69	18	8	10	26.0
G. Cummins	55	10	9	7	18.1
H. Johnson	59	10	8	8	16.9
H. Clyde	33	8	1	6	24.2
E. Thompson	28	7	4	2	25.0
E. Garcea	34	6	2	7	17.6
R. Crawford	15	5	2	1	33.3
R. Wood	21	5	3	3	23.8
D. Hannah	30	5	2	4	16.6
D. Forster	46	5	8	4	10.8

POST POSITION STATISTICS
(Up to and including May 18)

P.P.	1	2	3	4	5	6	7	8	9	10
Starts	225	223	224	227	224	223	209	188	171	141
Wins	38	28	36	16	31	23	18	14	12	11
% Wins	16.88	12.55	16.07	7.04	13.83	10.31	8.61	7.44	7.01	7.80

consensus selections appear in many places in this book, such as in the discussion of the Kentucky Oaks in Chapter Six beginning on page 123. A guide to reading the *Daily Racing Form* past performances appears on pages 11–12. Try applying this guide to the horses running in the Kentucky Oaks to familiarize yourself with how to read these past performances.

As we have mentioned, the goal of this book is to help you to master the Dr. Z system for beating the racetrack without ever having to become an expert handicapper. We utilize the handicappers' vast knowledge in a very precise way when we discuss the Dr. Z system in Chapters Four and Five. But you will be able to apply the Dr. Z system without referring to the *Daily Racing Form*. The *Form's* main advantage is to give you a deeper understanding and confidence in what you are doing and, most importantly, to provide a quick way to look up information that allows you to eliminate potentially bad bets. We discuss this more fully later in Chapters Five, Fourteen, and Sixteen. For now we suggest that you use extreme caution in betting on horses that have not run recently, are running for the first time, or have extremely mediocre records and whenever the track conditions are not ideal—that is, when the track is not fast. The best bets you can make are those on outstanding horses, when the odds as measured by the Dr. Z system are good, and when the track conditions are ideal. We supply you with numerous examples to study for full details on how to apply the Dr. Z system.

HOW TO READ DAILY RACING FORM PAST PERFORMANCES

Past Performances include cumulative statistics for every horse who has raced on the grass in the U.S. and foreign countries; a symbol Ⓢ pointing out restricted races (not for open company) as well as races for horses bred in a specific state, and a "bullet" ● denoting superior workouts (the best workout of the day at that track for that distance).

FOREIGN-BRED: An asterisk preceding the horse's name indicates he was bred in a foreign country. The country of origin (abbreviated) appears after the breeder's name, as does the state or place and Canadian province of all horses foaled in the United States, Puerto Rico or Canada.

MUD MARKS: One of the following symbols after a horse's name reflects an expert's opinion of his ability on an off track:

✻ Fair Mud Runner   X Good Mud Runner   ⊗ Superior Mud Runner

RECORD OF STARTS AND EARNINGS: Each horse's lifetime statistics are given as well as his complete racing record for the current and prior year, or the last two years in which he competed. The letter M in the current year's record indicates the horse is a maiden. M in the previous year's record indicates the horse was a maiden at the end of that year. TURF RECORD shows his lifetime starts, wins, seconds, thirds and earnings on the grass.

Horse	Mud Mark	Today's Weight	Color Sex Age Pedigree	Today's Claiming Price	Earnings Record					
			Ch. f. 4 by Ridan—Miss Hopes, by Jet Pilot							
Good Hopes	✻	117^{5}	Br. Jones H G (Cal)	$12,000	1981	12	3	2	1	$20,280
Own.—Good Hope Farm			Tr. Jones H G		1980	4	M	0	2	$1,100
			Lifetime 20 3 3 4 $23,600		Turf	4	1	0	1	$6,500

30Jun81-6Hol 6f :22^{4} :46 1:11^{3} ft *6-5e 117^{5} 3^{3} 3^{2} 2^{1} 1no SmithT^{3} Ⓕ Ⓢ c12000 81 GoodHpes,LionTmr,HppyDys 12

Jly 28 Dmr 3f ft :37b   ●Jun 25 Hol 4f ft :46h   ●Jun 30 Hol 3f ft :36^{2}h   May 25 Hol 4f ft :49b

NOTE: Latest workouts are printed under each horse's past performances when they are available. The "bullet" ● indicates it was the best workout of the day at the track and distance.

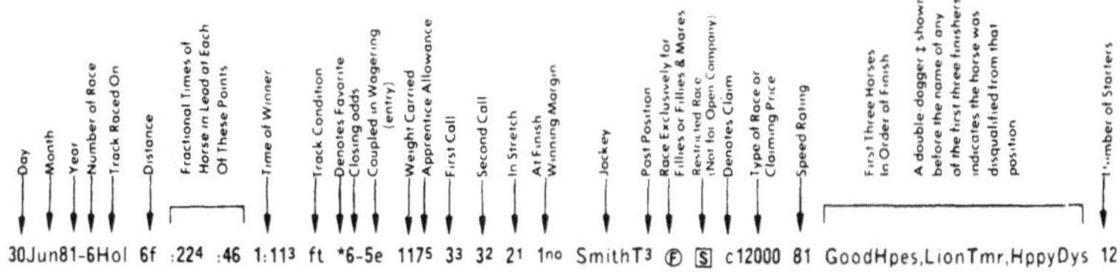

KEY TO SYMBOLS, ABBREVIATIONS IN PAST PERFORMANCES

FOREIGN-BRED HORSES
An asterisk (*) preceding the name of the horse indicates foreign-bred. (No notation is made for horses bred in Canada and Cuba.)

MUD MARKS
✱—Fair mud runner X—Good mud runner
⊗—Superior mud runner

COLOR
B Bay Blk—Black Br—Brown Ch—Chestnut Gr—Gray
Ro Roan Wh—White Dk b or br—Dark bay or brown

SEX
c colt h horse g—gelding rig—ridgling f—filly m—mare

PEDIGREE
Each horse's pedigree lists, in the order named, color, sex, age, sire, dam and grandsire (sire of dam).

BREEDER
Abbreviation following breeder's name indicates the state, Canadian province, place of origin or foreign country in which the horse was foaled.

TODAY'S WEIGHT
With the exception of assigned-weight handicap races, weights are computed according to the conditions of the race. Weight includes the rider and his equipment; saddle, lead pads, etc., and takes into account the apprentice allowance of pounds claimed. It does not include a jockey's overweight, which is announced by track officials prior to the race. The number of pounds claimed as an apprentice allowance is shown by a superior (small) figure to the right of the weight.

TODAY'S CLAIMING PRICE
If a horse is entered to be claimed, the price for which he may be claimed appears in bold face type to the right of the trainer's name.

RECORD OF STARTS AND EARNINGS
The horse's racing record for his most recent two years of competition appears to the extreme right of the name of the breeder and is referred to as his "money lines". This lists the year, number of starts, wins, seconds, thirds, and earnings. The letter "M" in the win column of the upper line indicates the horse is a maiden. If the letter "M" is in the lower line only, it indicates the horse was a maiden at the end of that year.

TURF COURSE RECORD
The horse's turf course record shows his lifetime starts, wins, seconds, thirds and earnings on the grass and appears directly below his money lines.

LIFETIME RECORD
The horse's lifetime record shows his career races, wins, seconds, thirds and total earnings. The statistics, updated with each start, include all his races—on dirt, grass and over jumps—and are located under the trainer's name.

DISTANCE
a—preceding distance (a6f) denotes "about" distance (about 6 furlongs in this instance.)

FOREIGN TRACKS
♦—before track abbreviation indicates it is located in a foreign country.

RACES OTHER THAN ON MAIN DIRT TRACK
⊡—following distance denotes inner dirt course.
Ⓣ—following distance indicates turf (grass) course race.
🅃—following distance indicates inner turf course.
[S]—following distance indicates steeplechase race.
[H]—following distance indicates hurdle race.

TRACK CONDITIONS
ft—fast fr—frozen gd—good sl—slow sy—sloppy
m—muddy hy—heavy
Turf courses, including steeplechase and hurdles:
hd—hard fm—firm gd—good yl—yielding sf—soft

SYMBOLS ACCOMPANYING CLOSING ODDS
• (preceding)—favorite e (following)—entry
f (following)—mutuel field

APPRENTICE OR RIDER WEIGHT ALLOWANCES
Allowance indicated by superior figure following weight—117⁵.

ABBREVIATIONS USED IN POINTS OF CALL
no—nose hd—head nk—neck

DEAD-HEATS, DISQUALIFICATIONS
•—following the finish call indicates this horse was part of a dead-heat (an explanatory line appears under that past performance line).
†—following the finish call indicates this horse was disqualified. The official placing appears under the past performance line. An explanatory line also appears under the past performance of each horse whose official finish position was changed due to the disqualification.
‡—before the name of any of the first three finishers indicates the horse was disqualified from that position.

POST POSITION
Horse's post position appears after jockey's name—Smith T3

FILLY OR FILLY-MARE RACES
Ⓕ—preceding the race classification indicates races exclusively for fillies or fillies and mares.

RESTRICTED RACES
Ⓢ—preceding the race classification indicates races that are not for open company, in addition to those for state-breds.

RACE CLASSIFICATIONS
10000—Claiming race (eligible to be claimed for $10,000). Note: The letter c preceding claiming price (c10000) indicates horse was claimed.
M10000—Maiden claiming race (non-winners—eligible to be claimed).
10000H—Claiming handicap (eligible to be claimed).
º10000—Optional claiming race (entered NOT to be claimed).
10000º—Optional claiming race (eligible to be claimed).
Mdn—Maiden race (non-winners).
AlwM—Maiden allowance race (for non-winners with special weight allowances)
Aw10000—Allowance race with purse value.
HcpO—Overnight handicap race.
SplW—Special weight race.
Wfa—Weight-for-age race.
Mtch—Match race.
A10000—Starter allowance race (horses who have started for claiming price shown, or less, as stipulated in the conditions).
H10000—Starter handicap (same restriction as above).
S10000—Starter special weight (restricted as above). Note: Where no amount is specified in the conditions of the "starters" race dashes are substituted, as shown below:
A—— H—— S——
50000S—Claiming stakes (eligible to be claimed).

STAKES RACES
In stakes races, with the exception of claiming stakes, the name or abbreviation of name is shown in the class of race column. The letter "H" after name indicates the race was a handicap stakes. The same procedure is used for the rich invitational races for which there are no nomination or starting fees. The letters "Inv" following the abbreviation indicate the race was by invitation only.

SPEED RATINGS
This is a comparison of the horse's final time with the track record established prior to the opening of the racing season at that track. The track record is given a rating of 100. One point is deducted for each fifth of a second by which a horse fails to equal the track record (one length is approximately equal to one-fifth of a second). Thus, in a race in which the winner equals the track record (a Speed Rating of 100), another horse who is beaten 12 lengths (or an estimated two and two-fifths seconds) receives a Speed Rating of 88 (100 minus 12). If a horse breaks the track record he receives an additional point for each one-fifth second by which he lowers the record (if the track record is 1:10 and he is timed in 1:09⅘, his Speed Rating is 102). In computing beaten-off distances for Speed Ratings, fractions of one-half length or more are figured as one full length (one point). No Speed Ratings are given for steeplechase or hurdle events, for races of less than three furlongs, or for races for which the horse's speed rating is less than 25.
When Daily Racing Form prints its own time, in addition to the official track time, the Speed Rating is based on the official track time.
Note: Speed Ratings for new distances are computed and assigned when adequate time standards are established.

WORKOUTS
Each horse's most recent workouts appear directly under the past performances. For example, Jly 20 Hol 3f ft :38b indicates the horse worked on July 20 at Hollywood Park. The distance of the work was 3 furlongs over a fast track and the horse was timed in 38 seconds, breezing. A "bullet" ● appearing before the date of a workout indicates that the workout was the best of the day for that distance at that track.
Abbreviations used in workouts:
b—breezing d—driving e—easily g—worked from gate h—handily bo—bore out Ⓣ—turf course Tr—trial race
tr.t following track abbreviation indicates horse worked on training track.

POINTS OF CALL—PAST PERFORMANCES

The points of call in the past performances vary according to the distance of the race. The points of call of the running positions for the most frequently raced distances are:

Distance	1st Call	2nd Call	3rd Call	4th Call
2 Furlongs	Start	—	Stretch	Finish
5/16 Mile	Start	—	Stretch	Finish
3 Furlongs	Start	—	Stretch	Finish
3 1/2 Furlongs	Start	—	Stretch	Finish
4 Furlongs	Start	1/4 Mile	Stretch	Finish
4 1/2 Furlongs	Start	1/4 Mile	Stretch	Finish
5 Furlongs	3/16 Mile	3/8 Mile	Stretch	Finish
5 1/2 Furlongs	1/4 Mile	3/8 Mile	Stretch	Finish
6 Furlongs	1/4 Mile	1/2 Mile	Stretch	Finish
6 1/2 Furlongs	1/4 Mile	1/2 Mile	Stretch	Finish
7 Furlongs	1/4 Mile	1/2 Mile	Stretch	Finish

Distance	1st Call	2nd Call	3rd Call	4th Call
1 Mile	1/2 Mile	3/4 Mile	Stretch	Finish
1 Mi., 70 Yds.	1/2 Mile	3/4 Mile	Stretch	Finish
1 1/16 Miles	1/2 Mile	3/4 Mile	Stretch	Finish
1 1/8 Miles	1/2 Mile	3/4 Mile	Stretch	Finish
1 3/16 Miles	1/2 Mile	3/4 Mile	Stretch	Finish
1 1/4 Miles	1/2 Mile	1 Mile	Stretch	Finish
1 5/16 Miles	1/2 Mile	1 Mile	Stretch	Finish
1 3/8 Miles	1/2 Mile	1 Mile	Stretch	Finish
1 1/2 Miles	1/2 Mile	1 1/4 Miles	Stretch	Finish
1 5/8 Miles	1/2 Mile	1 3/8 Miles	Stretch	Finish
1 3/4 Miles	1/2 Mile	1 1/2 Miles	Stretch	Finish

NOTE: The second call in most races is made 1/4 mile from the finish; the stretch call 1/8 mile from the finish.

The Various Types of Bets

Wagers at the racetrack are of two types, straight bets and so-called exotic, or gimmick, bets. The straight bets are to win, place, and show. It is these bets that we are concerned with in this book. Specifically, the Dr. Z system determines when good place and show bets exist and how much should be bet on them. Exotic bets combine the outcomes of two, three, or six horses. It is unlikely that a given ticket will win, which is why they have such high payoffs. We describe these bets here for your information. There is one important point to remember about them in case you do play them: The track take is generally higher by 2% or more on exotic wagers than on straight bets. Therefore, on average, it is more difficult to beat the racetrack by betting in exotic pools than in straight wagering. Now let's describe the various types of bets.

Type of Bet	You Choose	You Win Only When
Win	One horse	This horse is first.
Place	One horse	This horse is first or second.
Show	One horse	This horse is first, second, or third.
Quinella	Two horses	These two horses finish first and second, in either order.
Exactor (Perfector)	Two horses	These two horses finish first and second in the exact order that you specified.
Triactor (Trifector)	Three horses	These three horses finish first, second, or third in the exact order that you specified.
Daily double	One horse in one race and a second horse in another race (usually races 1 and 2)	Both horses finish first.
Pick six (Sweep six)	One horse in each of six consecutive races	All six horses finish first.

How the Odds Are Determined: The Track Take and Breakage

There are two basic systems for setting the odds in horse races: *fixed* and *parimutuel* odds. Legalized bookmakers may set their own odds. These odds may be different at various points in time as more information and bets are made. Fixed means that once a wager is placed, its odds are specified and will not change, even though one might be able to place another wager later at different odds. For example, months before the Kentucky Derby, such odds are available at various legalized betting establishments for most of the possible contenders and entrants in this race. Since many horses are on the list of Derby hopefuls, a considerable number of which will not even run in the race, these odds are quite high. The 1983 Kentucky Derby winner, Sunny's Halo, went off at 5—2 at Churchill Downs on Derby Day, paying $7 for each $2 bet to win—$5 profit and $2 return of the wager. Sunny's Halo was a 100—1 shot in the Las Vegas winter book. The wife of David Cross, Sunny's Halo's trainer, bet $200 at those odds and received a $20,000 profit plus her $200 bet.

Fixed betting is used very extensively at racetracks in many British Commonwealth countries, such as Australia, Great Britain, and Hong Kong. It is not used at North American racetracks. Here the parimutuel system is used. The essence of the fixed-odds system of betting is that you are wagering against the bookmaker. One of you will lose. He or she must therefore set odds on the various horses that will turn a profit for him or her. To do this the bookmaker sets odds that pay you less than what he or she thinks the true chances of each horse's winning are. For example, if Larry thinks a particular horse has a 25% chance of winning, he might offer you odds of 5—2. Then if the horse wins, he will pay you $7 instead of $8 for your $2 bet. The extra $1 is Larry's expected profit. To make actual profits rather than the expected average profits, he will try to balance the bets so that he has an amount of money inversely proportional to the payout he is giving on each horse. In that way he is assured of making a profit. If too little money is bet on a particular horse, Larry can attempt to generate more bets by raising the odds. This cat-and-mouse game continues until the race is run.

Let us see how it works with an example. For simplicity, suppose there are three horses—A, B, and C. The bookie thinks A has a 50% chance of winning, B has a 30% chance, and C has a 20% chance. True odds are then 1—1 for A, 7—3 for B, and 4—1 for C. These odds are set so that the average return is the amount bet, so there are no profits. For example, with A the average return is $0.5(1 + 1) = 1$. (Recall that with 1—1 odds, the return is the $1 profit plus the return of the original $1 bet.) For B and C it's similar, since $0.3(\frac{7}{3} + 1) = 0.2(4 + 1) = 1$. Hence to make a profit, the bookie might quote 4—5 for A, 2—1 for B, and 7—2 for C. For Larry to be guaranteed a profit, he needs bets roughly in the ratio of 50% bet on A, 30% bet on B, and 20% bet on C. If too little money is bet on A, he might increase the odds to 9—10 or even 1—1. In this way he can balance his books and and still guarantee his profit. He will not be able to do this in all cases. Hence he needs to ensure a reasonable profit by taking a sizable commission. The commission plus his winnings then outweigh his losses. This is where the parimutuel system comes in.

Pierre Oller was a perfume shop owner who played the horses in the 1850s in Paris. After a while he felt that the bookies were taking too much profit. He thought that there should be a better system, so he began to sell different types of perfume for the different horses. For example, Jasmine might be number one and Gardenia number two. The bettors would get small perfume bottles for their bets and Pierre would hold the money. After the race all the perfume bottles were returned, Pierre kept 5% of the money for his profit and expenses, and he distributed the remaining 95% equally among all those who had perfume bottles corresponding to the winning horse. This was the origin of the parimutuel system as Pierre Oller devised it in 1855. It is still used in the same way today except the perfume bottles have been replaced by electronic totalizator tickets. Notice that the key feature in the parimutuel system is that you are betting against all the other bettors and the house is taking a fixed commission. The house plays a passive role—its profit is always the same. In the fixed betting system you are betting against the house, and the commission is not determined in advanced. It can be large or small or even result in a loss for the house.

For example, suppose W_i is the amount bet on horse i to win, Q is the track payback, and there are ten horses. Then the payoff per dollar bet using the parimutuel system if horse number 3 wins is

$$\frac{Q\sum_{j=1}^{10} W_j}{W_3} = \frac{Q(W_1 + W_2 + \cdots + W_{10})}{W_3}.$$

If the track payback is 83%, corresponding to a typical 17% track take, and \$10,000 is bet on all the horses, with \$1,700 bet on horse number 3, the payoff for the typical \$2 bet if number 3 wins will be

$$\frac{0.83(\$10{,}000)(\$2)}{\$1{,}700} = \$9.76.$$

It is awkward to pay \$9.76, so the track takes one more commission, called the breakage. They round the \$9.76 down to either \$9.70 or \$9.60. These are the 5¢ and 10¢ breakages we described in Chapter One. Initially most tracks used 5¢ breakage, but because of inflation and rising costs, more and more are using 10¢ breakage. Breakage amounts to another 1%–3% on your bets, making the average total commission about 17% + 2%, or 19%. Breakage is more important than is commonly realized. We discuss its impact on Dr. Z system bets in Chapter Nine. Suffice it to say that these small amounts cut deeply into profits.

The parimutuel system works in a similar way for place and show bets as well as for exotic bets. We discuss place and show bets in detail in Chapter Four.

PARI-MUTUEL WAGERING

The only permitted wagering is under the pari-mutuel system, employing an electric totalisator. The only wagering pools at Churchill Downs are for WIN, PLACE, SHOW, DAILY DOUBLE and EXACTA, each with separate and independent calculation and distribution.

Under the pari-mutuel system, the wagering patrons establish the odds and the pay-offs in each pool. From each such pool the commission, provided by Kentucky state law, is deducted with the remainder being the net pool for distribution as pay-offs to ticket holders. Each pool is calculated to the dollar with the pay-off to the dime, the resulting breakage going to the racing association, by law.

The number on your ticket is an interest in the pool involved. All horses coupled in an entry or in the "field" are running for the number on your ticket. Example: Horse No. 1, 1A, 1C and/or 1X are all represented by Ticket No. 1. All horses in a "field" entry are represented by Ticket No. 12.

Purchase your ticket by the number on the program. Please call the number of the horse first, then the quantity of tickets desired: Example: "Number seven, two tickets."

In a Win Pool with a single winner, the amount wagered on the winner is deducted from the net pool to give the profit. This is added to the amount wagered to give the pay-off price, which includes the return of the amount wagered with the profit.

In a Place Pool, with two interests, the amount wagered on both interests is deducted from the net pool with the resulting profit divided equally and added to the amount wagered to give two pay-off prices.

In a Show Pool, with three interests, the profit is divided into three equal parts added to the amount wagered for the three pay-off prices.

Daily Double and Exacta wagers are in separate pools and the pay-off prices are figured by the same calculation process as for Win, Place and Show.

If more than the usual number of interests are involved in any pool, i.e., WIN-one, PLACE-two and SHOW-three, the pools are divided so as to give a proportionate profit to each wagering interest.

APPROXIMATE PAY TO WIN

(FOR $2.00) — IF THE ODDS ARE . . .

Odds	Pays	Odds	Pays	Odds	Pays
1-5	$2.40	6-5	$4.40	5-2	$ 7.00
2-5	2.80	7-5	4.80	3	8.00
1-2	3.00	3-2	5.00	7-2	9.00
3-5	3.20	8-5	5.20	4	10.00
4-5	3.60	9-5	5.60	9-2	11.00
1	4.00	2	6.00	5	12.00

CHAPTER 3

Applying Stock Market Efficiency Concepts to Horse-Racing Betting Markets

The Crowd Is Very Good at Estimating the True Probability of Winning: Efficiency of the Win-Betting Market

We have stated that, on average, the crowd is quite a good predictor of the actual probability of each horse's winning. Let us now look at this more carefully. In Figure 3.1 we have plotted the rate of return for win bets at various odds levels for six different data sets. The same data appear in Table 3.1, and Figure 3.2 summarizes it all. These data include a total of 35,285 races involving over 300,000 horses over the 28-year period 1947–75. We have added the track take back to the amounts the track pays to help you understand more fully what is going on and to permit comparisons among the different track takes. Generally speaking, track takes have risen over the years.

Each investigator found that the odds are a fairly good predictor of the actual probability of winning, but that there are biases for low- and high-odds horses; low-odds favorites are underbet. Their true probability of winning is greater than the crowd believes it is. Thus for horses going off at odds around 0.75—1, the rate of return is 9.1% better than chance. It is 6.4% and 6.1% better than chance for horses going off at odds around 1.25—1 and 2.5—1, respectively. To compensate for this bias, horses that have high odds, the so-called long shots, are overbet. Their actual chances of winning are less than the public thinks. For odds around 6—1 to 12—1, this overbetting amounts to 5.2% more than the track take. However, at 15—1 it is a full 10.2%, and at 33—1 it is a whopping 27.7%. Thus if the track take is 19%, you can expect to lose only about 10% by betting extreme

Figure 3.1 Rates of return on win bets at various odds levels for six studies involving 35,285 races during 1947–1975—actual returns: dotted lines; track take added back: solid lines *Source*: Snyder (1978).

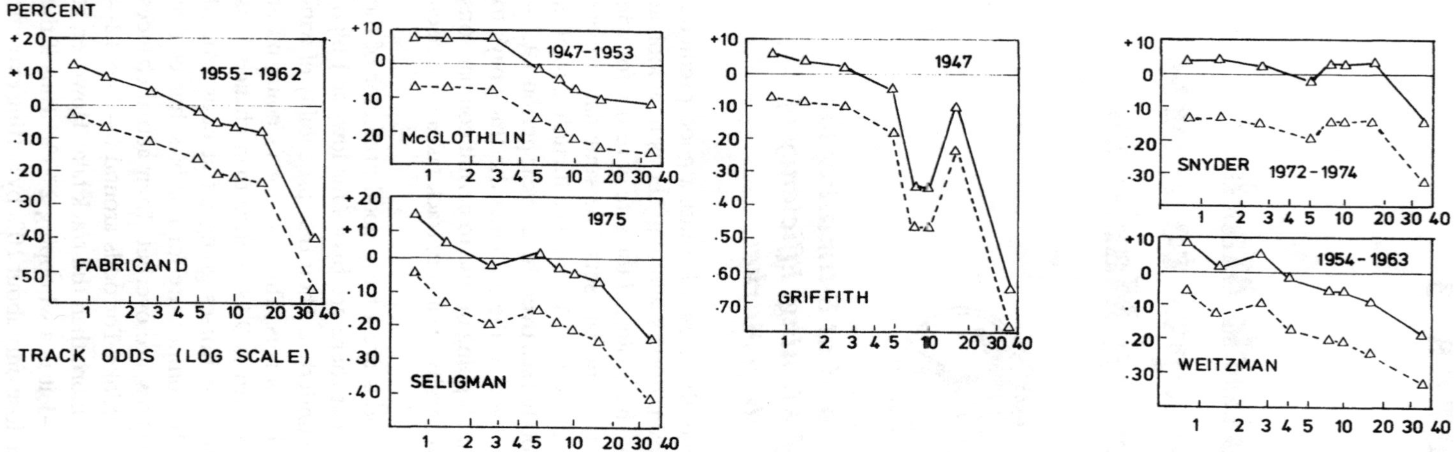

TABLE 3.1 *Summary of six studies comparing the rate of return on win bets at various odds levels*

Study	Date Published	Racing Dates	No. of Races	Rates of Return by Grouped Odds, Take Added Back (Midpoint of Grouped Odds) 0.75	1.25	2.5	5.0	7.5	10.0	15.0	33.0
Griffith	1949	1947	1,124	8.0	4.9	3.1	−3.1	−34.6[a]	−34.1[a]	−10.5	−65.5[a]
McGlothlin	1956	1947–53	9,248	8.0[b]	8.0[a]	8.0[a]	−0.8	−4.6	−7.0[b]	−9.7	−11.0
Weitzman	1965	1954–63	12,000	9.0[a]	3.2	6.8[a]	−1.3	−4.2	−5.1	−8.2[b]	−18.0[a]
Fabricand	1965	1955–62	10,000	11.1[a]	9.0[a]	4.6[a]	−1.4	−3.3	−3.7	−8.1	−39.5[a]
Snyder	1978	1972–74	1,730	5.5	5.5	4.0	−1.2	3.4	2.9	2.4	−15.8
Seligman	1975	1975	1,183	14.0	4.0	−1.0	1.0	−2.0	−4.0	−7.8	−24.2
Combined			35,285	9.1[a]	6.4[a]	6.1[a]	−1.2	−5.2[a]	−5.2[a]	−10.2[a]	−27.7[a]

Source: Adapted from Snyder (1978). [a]Significantly different from zero at 1% level or better. [b]Significantly different from zero at 5% level or better.

favorites going off at odds from 1—2 to 7—5. You will lose about 13% betting on horses with odds about 8—5 to 4—1 and about 24% with the 6—1 to 12—1 horses. Betting the long shots yields very large average losses. At 15—1 the average loss is about 29%, and for horses going off at odds around 25—1 to 40—1, it's nearly half the bet, about 47%.

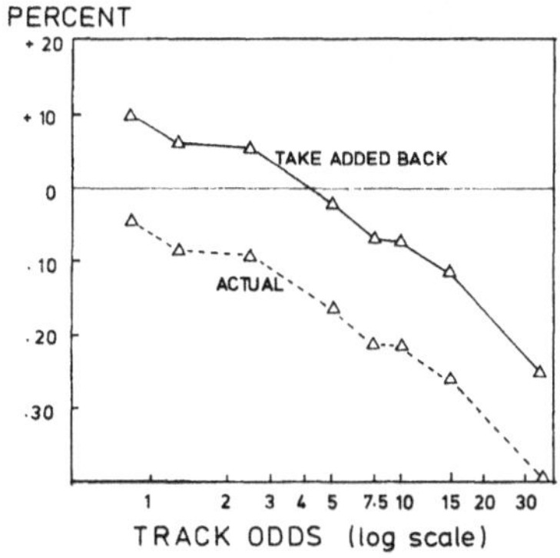

Figure 3.2 Rates of return on win bets at various odds levels: aggregation of six studies involving 35,285 races during 1947–1975 *Source*: Snyder (1978).

Another way to look at the favorite–long-shot bias and the accuracy of the crowd's estimate of the true probability of winning, as reflected in the win odds, is by considering the various levels of favorites. Figure 3.3 shows

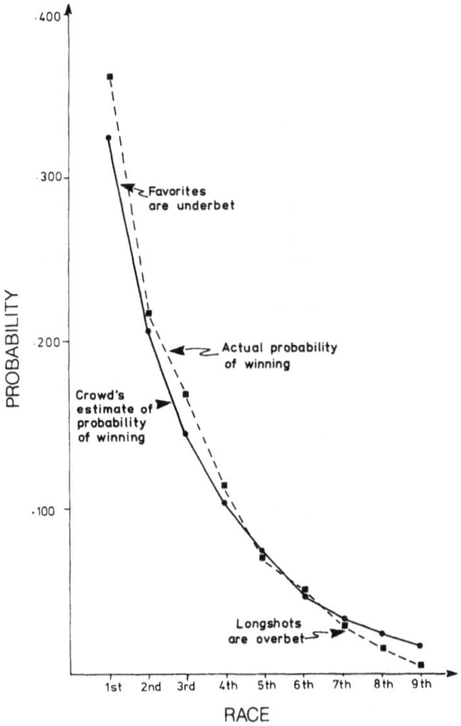

Figure 3.3 Probabilities of the first through the ninth favorites' winning a given race in 729 Atlantic City races involving 5,805 thoroughbred horses in 1978 *Source*: Asch, Malkiel, and Quandt (1982).

the relationship between the actual probability of winning and the crowd's estimate for the first through the ninth favorites in 729 thoroughbred races involving 5,805 horses in 1978 at Atlantic City. These same data also appear in Table 3.2. The data indicate that the first and third favorites are significantly underbet, while the ninth favorite is significantly overbet. For the other favorites these probabilities are equal in a statistical sense. The crowd's estimate of the probability of winning, however, conforms quite well with the actual probability of winning.

TABLE 3.2 *Comparison of the crowd's estimate of the probability of winning with the actual probability of winning for the first through the ninth favorites in 729 Atlantic City races involving 5,805 horses in 1978*

Favorites in Order of Lowest Odds	Number of Races[a]	Actual Probability of Winning	Crowd's Estimate of Probability of Winning	t Statistic[b]
First	729	0.361	0.325	−2.119[c]
Second	729	0.218	0.205	−0.903
Third	729	0.170	0.145	−1.972[c]
Fourth	724	0.115	0.104	−0.961
Fifth	692	0.071	0.072	0.074
Sixth	598	0.050	0.048	−0.279
Seventh	431	0.030	0.034	0.480
Eighth	289	0.017	0.025	1.096
Ninth	165	0.006	0.018	2.095[c]

Source: Asch, Malkiel, and Quandt (1982).

[a]The number of horses declines because many races have only a small number of horses running. The probabilities adjust for the actual number of horses in each race.

[b]The t statistic is used to determine if the actual probability of winning differs from the crowd's estimate so that there is a true favorite–long-shot bias. The formula for t is

$$\frac{\text{Crowd's estimated probability} - \text{actual probability}}{\text{Standard error of actual probability}},$$

where the standard error is $\sqrt{p(1-p)/n}$, p being the actual probability and n the number of races.

[c]Significantly different at the 5% level. That is, we are 95% confident that these probabilities are really different.

In an analogous study involving 20,047 harness races, Ali (1977) found similar results. Once again, as shown in Figure 3.4, the crowd's estimate of the probability of winning tracks the actual probability of winning quite well. The favorite–long-shot bias also occurs in a very consistent fashion. This is shown clearly in Table 3.3. The top favorites are underbet; the second and third choices have equal actual and crowd-generated probabilities of

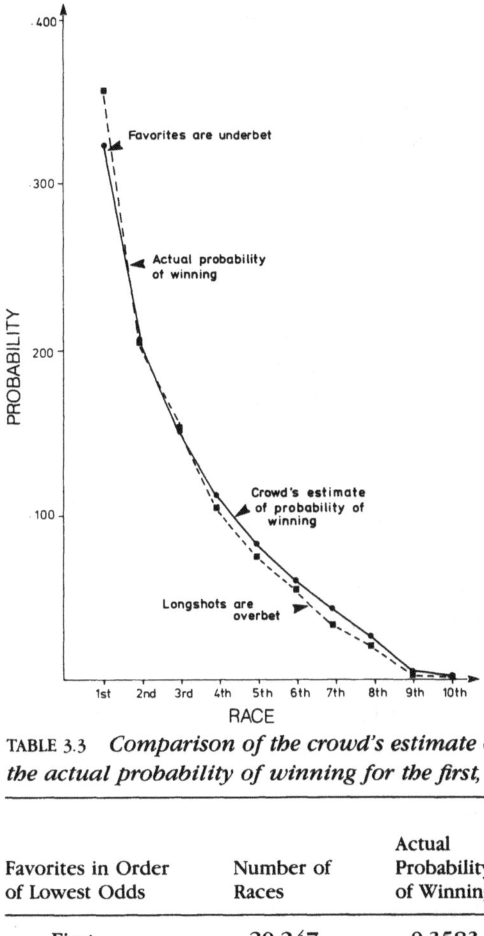

Figure 3.4 Probabilities of first, second, third, . . . , tenth favorites' winning a given race in 20,247 harness horse races at various tracks in 1970–74 *Source*: Ali (1977).

TABLE 3.3 ***Comparison of the crowd's estimate of the probability of winning with the actual probability of winning for the first, second, third, . . . , eighth favorites***

Favorites in Order of Lowest Odds	Number of Races	Actual Probability of Winning	Crowd's Estimate of Probability of Winning	*t* Statistic[a]
First	20,247	0.3583	0.3237	−10.29[b]
Second	20,247	0.2049	0.2077	−0.99
Third	20,247	0.1526	0.1513	−0.52
Fourth	20,247	0.1047	0.1121	3.45[b]
Fifth	20,231	0.0762	0.0827	3.49[b]
Sixth	20,088	0.0552	0.0611	3.01[b]
Seventh	19,281	0.0341	0.0417	5.80[b]
Eighth	15,749	0.0206	0.0276	6.20[b]

Source: Ali (1977).
[a]The *t* statistic is calculated in the same manner as in Table 3.2.
[b]Significantly different at the 5% level.

winning. Finally, the fourth to eighth favorites—the long shots—are overbet. This large sample provides further evidence for the efficiency of the win market and the favorite–long-shot bias. It also indicates that this phenomenon is similar in harness as well as thoroughbred races.

Why do these biases occur? Simple explanations are greed and bragging rights. People simply prefer to bet on horses that will have large payoffs. Not only will they win more, but they can tell their friends about it and reap glory for their cleverness. Bragging rights, a term coined by my colleague Dr. Bruce Fauman, refers to the pleasure one derives from the act of telling one's friends the intricate and clever analysis used to determine a particular winner. Favorites provide little of this ego boosting. There is not much profit or fame derived from betting on a 6—5 favorite who is the best bet of the day in the *Daily Racing Form's* consensus. Hence, the majority of the crowd simply prefers horses with a low probability of a high payoff if they win to those with a high probability of a lower payoff. Snyder states it well:

> There is, of course, no statistical technique which can disentangle the relative importance of "subjective preference for risk" and "increasing marginal utility of money." Every bet also includes, besides a potential monetary gain, the utility derived from all the factors associated with making a bet—analyzing racing forms, pitting one's predictions against others and the elements of luck. These factors are largely absent if one selects a known favorite; there are few players who can skip the challenge of trying to ferret out potential longer-odds winners. Indeed, the main reward of horse betting comes from the thrill of successfully detecting a moderately long-odds winner and thus confirming one's ability to outperform everyone else. Snyder (1978; p. 1113).

The favorite–long-shot bias seems to occur in all reasonably large data sets.* For win bets the bias is not enough to make positive profits by betting on all horses in any odds categories. The best one can do is to bet the favorites and lose about 10% instead of 19%. However, as we shall see, that bias plays an integral role in the winning system for place and show betting that we develop in Chapters Four and Five.

Equally important is the finding that the public's estimate of the probability of winning in various odds groups is a very good estimate of the actual probability of winning. Financial analysts call this phenomenon an *efficient market*. It is similar to conclusions reached by analyses of stock prices indicating that the only way to gain excess returns is to incur additional risk.

---

*Psychologists recognized this phenomenon in the late 1940s. The first seem to have been Preston and Baratta (1948), who investigated subjects in laboratory experiments. This phenomenon is common to many betting and investment situa-

Hence, you can use the following estimate of the probability q_3, that horse 3 will win a given race:

$$q_3 = \frac{W_3}{W}, \qquad (3.1)$$

where W_3 is the amount bet on 3 to win and W is the total amount bet on all the horses to win. Both W_3 and W appear on the tote board. Of course, W_3/W is related to the odds because the odds on horse 3 are simply

$$O_3 = Q\frac{W}{W_3} - 1,$$

where Q is the track payback. The minus one represents the dollar returned per dollar bet if horse 3 actually wins. As an example, suppose \$20,000 is bet on number 3 out of a total win pool of \$80,000. Then the chances that horse 3 wins are about

$$q_3 = \frac{W_3}{W} = \frac{\$20{,}000}{\$80{,}000} = 0.25$$

with odds

$$O_3 = Q\frac{W}{W_3} - 1 = (0.85)\frac{\$80{,}000}{\$20{,}000} - 1 = 2.4,$$

which would be quoted on the totalizator board as 2—1. Equation (3.1) is a good approximation of the true probability of winning. We must always remember, however, that it will overestimate the chance of a long shot's winning and underestimate the chance of a favorite's winning. It is important to notice that just by using equation (3.1) to estimate the probability of each horse's winning, you have a fairly reliable handicapping system. Jeff MacNelly's cartoon Shoe makes the same point. Choice of the favorites will

tions. Epstein (1977) lists as one of the fallacies of betting behavior that the general public tends to overestimate the probability of infrequent events and underestimate the probability of frequent events. The preference for a big payoff drives down the odds on such wagers, so they are in fact very poor bets. For example, for a \$1 bet, gamble A with a 1% chance of receiving \$75 might be preferred to gamble B where you receive only \$3 but win 40% of the time. Gamble A has an average return of 75¢ per dollar bet, so you lose 25% of your bet on average. However, the attractive gamble B has an expected value of \$1.20, for a profitable 20% gain. There is a similar bias in hockey betting (see Ziemba, 1983).

put you above the average in Figure 1.1. Indeed, by betting only on horses with final odds of say 3—1 or less, you will do as well or better than Hal the Handicapper with no handicapping at all.

Can You Win by Betting on Only the Very Best Horses?

We have established that the public tends to overbet long shots and underbet favorites. If the track take is 18%, you can expect to lose about 28% by betting horses at 15—1 and about 12% by betting 2—1 favorites. The key is that in all cases the bettors lose. Since they lose 12% at 2—1 and only about 9% at 1—1, the question arises whether you might not actually turn a profit if you bet on the extreme favorites—those going off at odds like 3—5 or 1—5.

One of the largest studies of the relationship between expected value and odds was that by Fabricand (see Figure 3.1). He considered 10,000 races, and his findings were consistent with the summary of the other studies in Figure 3.2. He also considered horses going off at odds like 2—5, 3—5, 4—5, and 1—1. His results are summarized in Table 3.5. As you can see, the loss is small. In the range 3—5 to 1—1 it is less than 5%. However, at 2—5 there is a small profit of 3.4%.

TABLE 3.5 *Fabricand's study of the comparison of the public's perception of the winning probabilities with the true winning probabilities in 10,000 races during 1955–1962*

Odds	Number of Horses Entered	Number of Winning Horses	Public's Perception of the Winning Probability (%)	True Probability (%)	Public's Estimate of the Expected Number of Winners plus Two Standard Deviations	Expected Profit per Dollar Wagered (¢)
0.40—0.55	129	92	56.9	71.3	73 ± 11	+3.4
0.60—0.75	295	163	50.2	55.3	148 ± 18	−7.1
0.80—0.95	470	241	44.9	51.3	211 ± 22	−3.8
1.00—1.15	615	289	40.6	47.0	250 ± 25	−2.4
1.20—1.35	789	318	37.1	40.3	293 ± 27	−8.1
1.40—1.55	874	331	34.1	37.9	298 ± 28	−6.1
1.60—1.75	954	339	31.5	35.5	301 ± 29	−4.8
1.80—1.95	1,051	325	29.3	30.9	308 ± 30	−10.5
2.00—2.45	3,223	933	26.3	28.9	848 ± 50	−6.5
2.50—2.95	3,623	835	22.8	23.0	826 ± 50	−13.5
3.00—3.45	3,807	797	20.1	20.9	765 ± 50	−11.0
3.50—3.95	3,652	679	18.0	18.6	657 ± 46	−11.6
4.00—4.45	3,296	532	16.2	16.1	534 ± 42	−15.3
4.50—4.95	3,129	486	14.8	15.5	463 ± 40	−10.6
5.00—5.95	5,586	686	13.2	12.3	737 ± 50	−20.1
6.00—6.95	5,154	565	11.4	11.0	588 ± 46	−18.0
7.00—7.95	4,665	460	10.0	9.9	467 ± 41	−16.4
8.00—8.95	3,990	328	9.0	8.2	359 ± 38	−21.8
9.00—9.95	3,617	295	8.1	8.2	293 ± 33	−14.7
10.00—14.95	12,007	717	6.5	6.0	780 ± 54	−20.7
15.00—19.95	7,041	284	4.7	4.0	331 ± 35	−26.4
20.00—99.95	25,044	340	2.5	1.4	626 ± 50	−54.0
TOTALS	93,011	10,035[a]				

Source: Adapted from Fabricand (1965, 1979).
[a]There were 35 dead heats in the 10,000 races.

Let's look more fully at some bets in this odds range. The great horses of the twentieth century often ran at odds in this range. It does not take long for the public to recognize a Secretariat or a Man O' War. As soon as these horses won one or two convincing races, their odds plummeted to even money or less. But were the odds better than they should have been? Table 3.6 gives the results from bets on fourteen of the greatest horses of the twentieth century.

TABLE 3.6 *Rate of return on win bets for extreme favorites: fourteen great twentieth century horses*

Horse	Racing Dates	Wins/ Races	In the Money/ Races	Odds Ranges (wins/races) 1—100 to 1—20	1—15 to 1—7	3—20 to 9—50	1—5 to 2—9
Citation	1947–51	32/45	44/45	1/1	6/6	3/3	5/6
Colin	1907–08	15/15	15/15		3/3		1/1
Count Fleet	1942–43	16/21	21/21	2/2	2/2	1/1	1/2
Equipoise	1930–35	29/51	43/51		4/4	1/2	0/2
Exterminator	1917–24	50/100	84/100	1/1	1/1	1/1	2/2
Forego	1973–78	34/57	50/57	2/2			2/2
Kelso	1959–66	39/63	53/63		1/1	1/1	2/2
Man O' War	1919–20	20/21	21/21	6/6	3/3	1/1	
Nashua	1954–56	22/31	28/31			1/1	3/3
Native Dancer	1952–54	21/22	22/22	3/3	1/1	2/2	3/3
Secretariat	1972–73	16/21	20/21	1/1	4/5		3/3
Swaps	1954–56	19/25	23/25	1/1	1/1	2/2	
Sysonby	1904–05	14/15	15/15	3/3		1/1	
Tom Fool	1951–53	21/30	29/30				
Totals		348/517	468/517	20/20	26/27	14/15	22/26
Percent winners		67.3%	90.5%	100%	96.3%	93.3%	84.6%
Winning payoff				$2.10	$2.20	$2.30	$2.40
Rate of return		1.04 ±0.07[a]		1.05	1.06	1.07	1.02
				1.05 ± 0.06[a]			

Note: The data used to construct this table were obtained from the 1982 Edition of the *American Racing Manual.* In calculating the payoffs and rates of return, it is assumed that breakage is to the nearest 5¢ per dollar wagered. For odds less than 1—20, it is assumed that the payoff is $2.10 per $2 wagered, as is standard for a minus pool (see Chapter Fifteen).

How would you have done betting on these horses? On average, if you bet them only when they were running at 3—5 or less, the average profit would be 3.8%. Moreover, you would be ahead betting in 10 of the 12 odds categories. In addition, the expected return is higher the lower the odds are. The lowest odds were the three races Man O' War won at 1—100. Unfortunately, even though the sample involves 517 races, statistically it is possible that this entire 3.8% is simply due to chance. One must conclude that even with these great horses you cannot be reasonably sure of making a profit. Further complicating the analysis of these extreme favorites is a phenomenon called a *selection bias.* These horses were selected for the

TABLE 3.6 *(continued)*

Odds Ranges (wins/races)							
1—4	3—10 to 1—3	7—20	2—5	9—20	1—2	11—20	3—5
0/2	2/5	1/1	4/5	0/1	0/2		1/1
1/1	1/1	1/1	2/2		1/1		1/1
2/2			1/1		1/2		
2/2	0/1		4/4	0/2	1/2	1/1	3/4
1/1	3/3	1/2		1/3	1/1		3/4
			2/4		1/1		8/12
3/3	6/6		4/7		4/6		1/3
			1/1	1/1	2/2	1/2	1/1
1/1	3/4		2/2		1/1		
2/2	1/1		2/2		1/1		
	2/4		2/2		1/1		
	3/6		1/1				
1/1	1/1		2/2	1/1			1/1
2/2					1/1		
15/17	22/32	3/4	27/33	3/8	15/21	2/3	19/27
88.2%	68.8%	75%	81.8%	37.5%	71.4%	66.7%	70.4%
\$2.50	\$2.60	\$2.70	\$2.80	\$2.90	\$3.00	\$3.10	\$3.20
1.10	0.89	1.01	1.15	0.54	1.07	1.03	1.13
1.04 ± 0.12[a]				1.02 ± 0.13[a]			

[a]These rates of return and those in Table 3.7 are expected values plus or minus two standard deviations. The standard deviation may be estimated by $\sqrt{\Sigma(X_i - \overline{X})^2/(N-1)N}$, where X_i is the return in the ith race out of the N races in each category and $\overline{X}$ is the average return.

list of greatest horses simply because they won most of their races. Horses that ran several races at low odds, then lost their form, don't appear on this list. Proud Appeal, the 1981 Kentucky Derby favorite, was one such horse. His past performances appear on page 202 in Chapter Ten.

To study the matter more fully, we collected data on all the races run at Aqueduct, Belmont Park, and Saratoga in 1980. These data constitute the major races run in New York that year and include about 3,000 races. In 732 of these races a horse went off at odds of even money or less. The results appear in Table 3.7. On average, the rate of return for odds of even money or less was 0.90 or a 10¢ loss per dollar bet. Again, the highest rate

TABLE 3.7 *Rate of return on win bets for extreme favorites: 732 races in New York in 1980*

Track	Racing Dates	Wins/ Races	In the Money/ Races	Odds Ranges (wins/races) 1—10	1—5	3—10
Aqueduct	Jan. 1–Mar. 17, Mar. 19–May 19, Oct. 15–Dec. 31	208/422 (49.3%)	341/417 (81.8%)	0/0	3/3	1/1
Belmont Park	May 21–July 28, Aug. 27–Oct. 13	154/270 (57%)	231/264 (87.5%)	1/1	1/1	10/13
Saratoga	July 30–Aug. 25	21/40 (52.5%)	39/40 (97.5%)	0/0	0/0	0/0
Totals	313 Days	383/732	611/721	1/1	4/4	11/14
Percent winners		52.3%	84.7%	100%	100%	78.6%
Winning payoff				$2.20	$2.40	$2.60
Rate of return		0.90 ±0.04	0.96 ±0.04	1.10	1.20	1.02
				1.06±0.15		

Notes: The data used to construct this table were obtained from *Daily Racing Form's Chart Books* for 1980. Breakage at all three tracks is to the nearest 10¢ per dollar wagered. Thanks are due to Brian Canfield for help in collecting and analyzing this data.

of return was achieved by the lowest-priced horses. For horses going off at 3—10 or less the rate of return was +6%. However, as with the other studies, one cannot conclude that these profits were not due to chance. Indeed, there is no basis to argue that even with these extreme favorites you will do any better than break even.

Readers who are unfamiliar with statistical reasoning, standard deviations, and the like might look at the odds category 9—10. Here the expected return was a meager 0.67, while at 4—5 it was 0.97 and at 1—1 it was 0.96. The statistical analysis shows that, by chance, the returns in this category were quite low. Certainly with a larger sample of races, one would expect the 4—5, 9—10, and 1—1 odds categories to have similar rates of return. Thus, although the sample size of 136 seems quite sizable, it is really too small for definitive conclusions.

In summary, the evidence that we have on extreme favorites is as follows: First, the lower the odds on a horse, the higher the expected return seems to be. Second, extreme favorites going off at odds of 2—5 or less do seem to return a modest profit on average. Finally, even in the odds group of less than 2—5, there is no basis for any definitive statement that you can bet

TABLE 3.7 *(continued)*

Odds Ranges (wins/races)						
2—5	1—2	3—5	7—10	4—5	9—10	1—1
20/31	26/41	19/36	36/70	35/70	29/80	39/90
16/23	17/24	17/28	25/45	29/52	14/44	24/39
1/2	3/5	2/3	4/7	5/6	5/12	1/5
37/56	46/70	38/67	65/122	69/128	48/136	64/134
66.1%	65.7%	56.7%	53.3%	53.9%	35.3%	47.8%
$2.80	$3.00	$3.20	$3.40	$3.60	$3.80	$4.00
0.93	0.99	0.91	0.91	0.97	0.67	0.96
0.94 ± 0.05			0.87 ± 0.04			

The results of place and show bets on these races are discussed in Chapter Thirteen. See Tables 13.2 and 13.3 and the accompanying discussion.

all horses to win at this odds level and make profits. You cannot disprove the hypothesis that you will, at most, simply break even betting these horses to win. To make a definitive statistical statement would require a sample size of at least five years' data in a major racing locality, such as California or New York. At best, even if someone could prove their existence, such profits would be very small anyway. Your attention is better directed to more profitable place and show bets—which is precisely what we do in the rest of this book.

How Accurate Is the Morning Line?

THE MORNING LINE

. . . is an early estimate of probable odds. In the event of scratches or other material changes after the program is printed, a revised Morning Line will be posted. The actual odds on all races are determined by the bettors.

Except for the fact that favorites are overbet and long shots are underbet, the public's estimate of the probability of winning is remarkably close to the actual probability of winning. This analysis is based on the final odds of all the bettors at the racetrack. The question arises about the use of the morning-line odds. Are they more or less accurate? Are they any good at all? Are horses whose actual odds are higher than the morning line more likely or less likely to win? How about those horses that go off at lower odds?

The consensus and evidence are that as a predictor of the probability of winning, the morning odds are much less accurate than the actual final odds. Late bettors are those who bet near the end of the betting period. Winning horses are especially favored by these late bettors and losers are not. Horses that go off at odds less than their morning-line odds are more likely to win than those that go off at odds higher than their morning-line odds. Thus if a horse is 3—1 in the morning line and is going off at 6—1, its actual chance of winning is approximately

$$\frac{\text{Track payback}}{6+1} = \frac{0.84}{7} = 14\% \quad \text{and not} \quad \frac{0.84}{3+1} = 21\%.$$

Similarly, an 8—1 shot in the morning line going off at 2—1 has a chance of winning of about

$$\frac{0.84}{2+1} = 28\% \quad \text{and not} \quad \frac{0.84}{8+1} = 9\%.$$

Table 3.8, based on 792 races at Atlantic City in 1978, illustrates the situation.

Table 3.8 indicates that the horses that win have final odds that are less than the morning line. Horses that do not win and finish second, third, or out of the money have final odds that are larger than their morning-line odds. For example, the second-place finishers have odds 1.16 times the morning-line odds, the third-place finishers 1.22 times the morning-line odds, and the out-of-the-money finishers a whopping 1.59 times the morning-line odds. Moreover, the last two columns of Table 3.8 indicate that people who bet near the end of the betting period are even more accurate predictors of the actual probability of finish. These data are consistent with the notion of "smart money"—those betting in the last few minutes before a race begins are better informed than the general public. They generally bet at this time so as not to tip their hand regarding their bet. Their predictions of the probability of winning are better than those of the general public.

An example of how the final odds may differ from the morning-line odds is provided by the first race at Churchill Downs on May 7, 1983. The morning-line favorite, Modicum at 9—5, went off at 8—5 and won the race.

TABLE 3.8 *Relationship between the final and morning-line odds for all and late bettors for horses finishing in or out of the money*

Horses Finishing	Final Track Odds as a Percentage of Morning-Line Odds	Odds Produced by Bettors in the Last Eight Minutes of Betting as a Percentage of Morning-Line Odds	Odds Produced by Bettors in the Last Five Minutes of Betting as a Percentage of Morning-Line Odds
First	96	82	79
Second	116	106	101
Third	122	117	107
Out of the money	159	163	149

Source: Asch, Malkiel, and Quandt (1982).

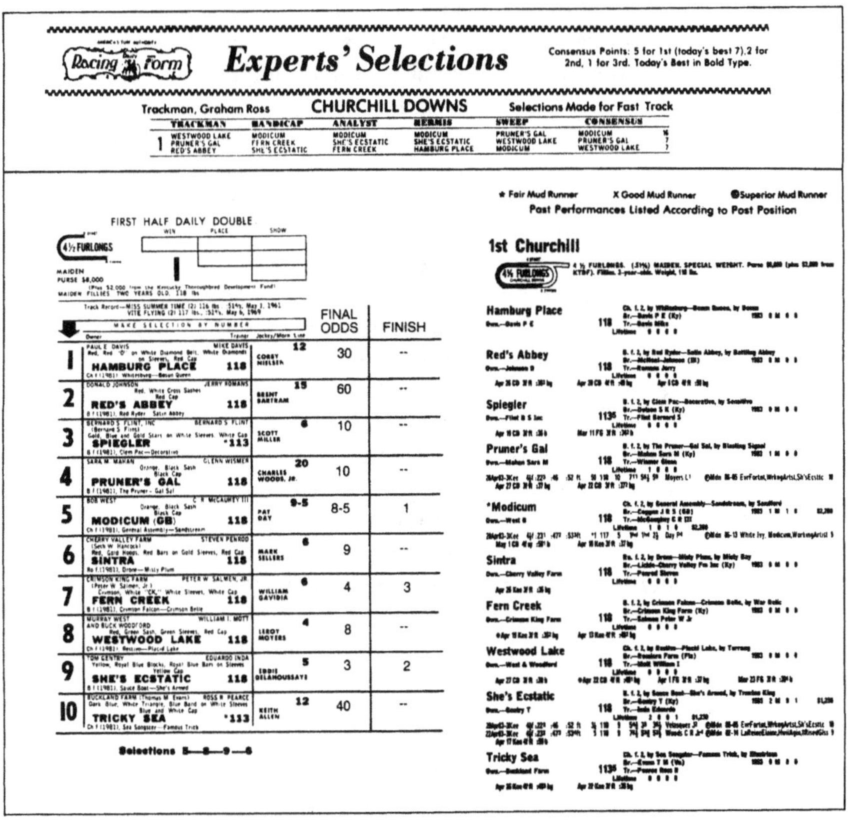
Racing Form **Experts' Selections**

Consensus Points: 5 for 1st (today's best 7), 2 for 2nd, 1 for 3rd. Today's Best in Bold Type.

Trackman, Graham Ross — CHURCHILL DOWNS — Selections Made for Fast Track

	TRACKMAN	HANDICAP	ANALYST	HERMIS	SWEEP	CONSENSUS	
1	WESTWOOD LAKE PRUNER'S GAL RED'S ABBEY	MODICUM FERN CREEK SHE'S ECSTATIC	MODICUM SHE'S ECSTATIC FERN CREEK	MODICUM SHE'S ECSTATIC HAMBURG PLACE	PRUNER'S GAL WESTWOOD LAKE MODICUM	MODICUM PRUNER'S GAL WESTWOOD LAKE	16 7 7

FIRST HALF DAILY DOUBLE — WIN PLACE SHOW

4½ FURLONGS

MAIDEN PURSE $8,000 (Plus $2,000 from the Kentucky Thoroughbred Development Fund) MAIDEN FILLIES TWO YEARS OLD. 118 lbs.

Track Record—MISS SUMMER TIME (2) 116 lbs. :51⅗, May 1, 1961; VITE FLYING (2) 117 lbs., :52⅘, May 6, 1969

MAKE SELECTION BY NUMBER

No.	Owner / Horse / Trainer	Jockey / Morn. Line	FINAL ODDS	FINISH
1	PAUL E DAVIS — MIKE DAVIS Red, Red "D" on White Diamond Belt, White Diamonds on Sleeves, Red Cap HAMBURG PLACE 118 Ch f (1981) Whitesburg—Bosun Queen	COREY NIELSEN 12	30	--
2	DONALD JOHNSON — JERRY ROMANS Red, White Cross Sashes, Red Cap RED'S ABBEY 118 B f (1981), Red Ryder—Satin Abbey	BRENT BARTRAM 15	60	--
3	BERNARD S. FLINT, INC — BERNARD S. FLINT (Bernard S. Flint) Gold, Blue and Gold Stars on White Sleeves, White Cap SPIEGLER *113 B f (1981), Clem Pac—Decorative	SCOTT MILLER 6	10	--
4	SARA M. MAHAN — GLENN WISMER Orange, Black Sash, Black Cap PRUNER'S GAL 118 B f (1981), The Pruner—Gal Sal	CHARLES WOODS, JR. 20	10	--
5	BOB WEST — C. R. McGAUGHEY III Orange, Black Sash, Black Cap MODICUM (GB) 118 Ch f (1981), General Assembly—Sandstream	PAT DAY 9-5	8-5	1
6	CHERRY VALLEY FARM — STEVEN PENROD (Seth W. Hancock) Red, Gold Hoops, Red Bars on Gold Sleeves, Red Cap SINTRA 118 Ro f (1981), Drone—Misty Plum	MARK SELLERS 6	9	--
7	CRIMSON KING FARM — PETER W. SALMEN, JR. (Peter W. Salmen, Jr.) Crimson, White "CK," White Sleeves, White Cap FERN CREEK 118 B f (1981), Crimson Falcon—Crimson Belle	WILLIAM GAVIDIA 6	4	3
8	MURRAY WEST AND BUCK WOODFORD — WILLIAM I. MOTT Red, Green Sash, Green Sleeves, Red Cap WESTWOOD LAKE 118 Ch f (1981), Restivo—Placid Lake	LEROY MOYERS 4	8	--
9	TOM GENTRY — EDUARDO INDA Yellow, Royal Blue Blocks, Royal Blue Bars on Sleeves, Yellow Cap SHE'S ECSTATIC 118 B f (1981), Sauce Boat—She's Armed	EDDIE DELAHOUSSAYE 5	3	2
10	BUCKLAND FARM (Thomas M. Evans) — ROSS R. PEARCE Dark Blue, White Triangle, Blue Band on White Sleeves, Blue and White Cap TRICKY SEA *113 Ch f (1981), Sea Songster—Famous Trick	KEITH ALLEN 12	40	--

Selections 5—8—9—6

★ Fair Mud Runner X Good Mud Runner ●Superior Mud Runner

Past Performances Listed According to Post Position

1st Churchill

4½ FURLONGS

Hamburg Place 118
Red's Abbey 118
Spiegler 113
Pruner's Gal 118
*Modicum 118
Sintra 118
Fern Creek 118
Westwood Lake 118
She's Ecstatic 118
Tricky Sea 113

In doing so he set a track record of $51\frac{2}{5}$ seconds for the $4\frac{1}{2}$-furlong distance, a full $\frac{2}{5}$ second, or about two lengths, off the previous best. She's Ecstatic, number 9, was second at 3—1 odds, down from 5—1 in the morning line. Number 7, Fern Creek, going off at 4—1, down from 6—1, took third.* The tendency for the final odds for horses finishing in the money to fall from those in the morning line and to rise for those finishing out of the money is borne out in this race.

The Need to Look for Special Situations to Avoid Betting on All Races and on Inappropriate Days

The evidence presented in this chapter indicates that the crowd does very well at predicting the actual probability of winning. Late bettors seem to do better than the average, which confirms the notion that their bets really are "smart money." We know from Figure 1.1 and the accompanying discussion that the average bettor is losing about 19% of the money he or she wagers. Just to break even, you must bet on horses that win about 23.5% more often than average. The values in Table 3.8 seem hardly good enough for even these late bettors to win, on average.

We also know that even if you devise a system that will, on average, make a profit, you may still lose by bad luck. A system that, say, wins two out of every five races may still have ten or more straight losses that might bankrupt you. Indeed, in any winning system, you need to add a measure of safety just to overcome this possibility.† We will do this by confining our Dr. Z System bets to those that make back the 19% and indicate a profit of another 14%–18% or more. This should be enough to account for possible bad luck.

The favorite–long-shot bias also indicates that profits are likely to be made betting on the very best horses in top races. Since these horses are traditionally underbet, they are good possibilities to consider. Tables 3.6 and 3.7 indicate, however, that it is unlikely that betting to win will be profitable. But betting to place or show often is. Indeed, many of our best Dr. Z system bets will be on extreme favorites.

---

*Fern Creek was actually a Dr. Z system bet; see the discussion at the end of the section on "The Kentucky Oaks" in Chapter Six.

†An excellent analysis of this bad-luck phenomenon in the context of trying to devise a winning strategy for the Massachusetts Numbers Game appears in Chernoff (November 1980).

In the next two chapters we develop the Dr. Z system. We advise you when a place or show bet is really good enough to bet and how much you should bet on it. You will not have a good bet in every race. To win you must also be careful to select only bets that really appear promising and wager appropriate amounts. Betting on days when the track conditions are not ideal, such as in the mud or on horses that are not in peak form because they have not run recently, adds to the risk. Poor odds, nonideal conditions, and the like rule out many races as profitable betting opportunities. Still, there are usually two to four outstanding Dr. Z system bets per day at a typical track. On average, they will make about 10%–20% profit. We will concentrate on these.

CHAPTER 4

Finding Profitable Place and Show Bets

Understanding the Win, Place, and Show Payoffs

The payoffs to win, as described in Chapter Two, are easy to determine. Consider the 1980 Kentucky Derby, which was run as the ninth race on May 3, 1980, at Churchill Downs in Louisville, Kentucky. The favorite, Rockhill Native, went off at 2.10—1. If he had won, the payoff would have been a \$2.10 profit for each dollar bet, for a \$3.10 total return. Since payoffs are generally based on \$2 bets, the payoff as listed on the tote board would have read \$6.20. The second favorite, Rumbo, at 4—1 thus would have paid \$2(4 + 1), or \$10. The winner was the filly, Genuine Risk, who went off at 13.30—1 and paid \$2(13.30 + 1) = \$28.60. Five weeks later at the Belmont Stakes these three horses met again.

There are many factors that determine the betting patterns leading to the final odds, but recent performance is one of the most important. Rockhill Native's poor Derby performance moved his odds from 2.10—1 to 12.80—1, a sixfold increase. He would have paid \$2(12.80 + 1), or \$27.60. Rumbo's strong second-place finish lowered his odds from 4—1 to 1.90—1. Genuine Risk's win moved her odds from 13.30—1 to 5.10—1, so she should have paid \$2(5.10 + 1) = \$12.20. The invader, Codex, was the favorite at 1.60— 1 and finished seventh. Remember that our discussion in Chapter Three indicates that, on average, these odds give a very good estimate of each horse's true chances of winning.

However, long shots often win races in the mud, making these races the most unpredictable. This race was no exception. The 53.40—1 shot, Tem-

106th Kentucky Derby, May 3, 1980

$339,300 gross value and $45,000 Gold Cup. Net to winner $250,550; second $50,000; third $25,000; fourth $13,750. 293 nominations.

Horse	Eqt	Wt	PP	¼	½	¾	Mile	Str	Fin	Jockeys	Owners	Odds to $1
Genuine Risk		121	10	7^{1hf}	7^{3}	4^{h}	1^{1hf}	1^{2}	1^{1}	J. Vasquez	Mrs. B. R. Firestone	13.30
Rumbo		126	9	13	12^{1hf}	11^{3}	5^{hf}	3^{3}	2^{1}	L. Pincay Jr.	Gayno Stable and Bell	4.00
Jaklin Klugman		126	2	8^{hf}	8^{h}	8^{hf}	4^{2hf}	2^{1hf}	3^{4}	D. McHargue	Klugman-Dominguez	7.10
Super Moment		126	3	10^{1hf}	9^{1hf}	9^{1hf}	9^{3}	5^{hf}	4no	D. Pierce	Elmendorf	8.60
Rockhill Native		126	6	2^{h}	1^{1hf}	2^{h}	2^{hf}	4^{1hf}	5^{nk}	J. Oldham	Harry A. Oak	2.10
Bold 'n Rulling	b	126	1	6^{1hf}	2^{h}	1^{h}	6^{1hf}	7^{3}	6^{2}	P. Valenzuela	Hughes Brothers	68.70
Plugged Nickle		126	11	1^{h}	3^{1hf}	3^{1hf}	3^{1hf}	6^{h}	$7^{3\frac{1}{4}}$	B. Thornburg	John M. Schiff	2.60
Degenerate Jon	b	126	4	9^{2hf}	6^{h}	5^{h}	8^{3}	8^{1hf}	$8^{1\frac{1}{4}}$	R. Hernandez	Barry K. Schwartz	61.70
Withholding		126	12	4^{hf}	10^{1}	10^{1}	11^{2}	9^{2}	9^{2}	M. Morgan	Russell Michael Jr.	64.10
Tonka Wakhan	b	126	5	12^{h}	13	12^{hf}	12^{3}	10^{2}	$10^{2\frac{1}{4}}$	M. Holland	Glenn Bromagen	f-58.90
Execution's Reason		126	13	3^{1hf}	5^{hf}	7^{2hf}	10^{1}	11^{3}	11^{3}	R. Romero	Howard B. Noonan	111.80
Gold Stage		126	7	5^{h}	4^{hf}	6^{h}	7^{hf}	12^{1hf}	12no	A. Cordero	Mrs. Philip B. Hofman	41.50
Hazard Duke	b	126	8	11^{3}	11^{hf}	13	13	13	13	D. Brumfield	Andrew Adams	f-58.90

Time: :24, :48, 1:12-4/5, 1:37-3/5, 2:02. Track fast. Off at 5:39 EDT. Start good. Won driving.

f-Mutuel field

$2 Mutuels paid — Genuine Risk $28.60 straight, $10.60 place, $4.80 show; Rumbo $5.20 place, $3.40 show; Jaklin Klugman $4.40 show.

Winner—Ch.f. by Exclusive Native—Virtuous, by *Gallant Man; trainer LeRoy Jolley; bred in Kentucky by Mrs. G. Watts Humphrey, Jr.

GENUINE RISK settled nicely as the field came away in good order and was reserved behind PLUGGED NICKLE and inside WITHHOLDING around the first turn and early backstretch. She was eased back slightly and moved to the outside smoothly approaching the half-mile pole, gradually raced to the leaders outside four rivals, and took command entering the stretch; was hit once with the whip right-handed, increased her advantage under six well spaced strokes as Vasquez switched to the left, and continued resolutely to the end. RUMBO dropped back last soon after the start and was kept outside rivals, gradually improving position, swerved under right-handed urging after racing wide into the stretch, and gained steadily under heavy left-hand urging in the final furlong. JAKLIN KLUGMAN saved ground behind the first flight, worked between rivals around the final turn, and moved boldly in pursuit of the winner settling into the homestretch, but could not sustain his bid. SUPER MOMENT stayed close to the rail and closed well from the head of the stretch to outfinish the others. ROCKHILL NATIVE had no difficulty taking a clear lead from between rivals entering thee backstretch, but swerved out and was lightly checked for a stride approaching the six-furlong pole, stayed with the pace to the top of the homestretch, and then weakened. BOLD 'N RULLING raced with the pace along the rail for six furlongs, gave way approaching the stretch and drifted out, then held on fairly well in the straightaway, but pulled up lame. PLUGGED NICKLE rated near the lead outside ROCKHILL NATIVE and BOLD 'N RULLING, bore out slightly on the final turn, then raced true while tiring in the homestretch run. DEGENERATE JON was a factor for six furlongs and tired. WITHHOLDING was very wide outside the first flight and tired. TONKA WAKHAN was outrun. EXECUTION'S REASON was used up early. GOLD STAGE also tired early. HAZARD DUKE was not a factor.

THE WINNER'S PEDIGREE AND CAREER HIGHLIGHTS

GENUINE RISK (Chestnut Filly)	Exclusive Native	Raise a Native	Native Dancer
			Raise You
		Exclusive	Shut Out
			Good Example
	Virtuous	*Gallant Man	*Migoli
			*Majideh
		Due Respect II	Zucchero
			Auld Alliance

Year	Age	Sts	1st	2nd	3rd	Won
1979	2	4	4	0	0	$100,245
1980	3	8	4	3	1	503,742
1981	4	3	2	0	1	$ 42,600
TOTALS		15	10	3	2	$646,587

At 2 Years	WON	Tempted, Demoiselle
At 3 Years	WON	Kentucky Derby, Ruffian
	2ND	Preakness, Belmont Stakes, Maskette
	3RD	Wood
At 4 Years	WON	2 Allowances
	3RD	1 Allowance (No Stakes)

perence Hill, was the winner. He paid a whopping $108.80, an amazing payoff in retrospect. Temperence Hill went on to become the eighth-leading thoroughbred money-winner of all time, winning eleven of thirty-one races and $1,567,650.

In each case we know before the race exactly how much each horse will pay to win. It is simply the odds plus one, times two. The situation is quite different for the place and show bets. With these bets you do not know before the race how much the place and show payoffs will be because they

Belmont Stakes

EIGHTH RACE
Belmont
JUNE 7, 1980

1 ½ MILES. (2.24) 112th Running THE BELMONT (Grade I). $200,000 Added. 3–year–olds. By subscription of $100 each to accompany the nomination; $1,000 to pass the entry box; $2,000 to start. A supplementary nomination of $5,000 may be made on Wednesday, June 4 with an additional $15,000 to start, with $200,000 added of which 60% to the winner, 22% to second, 12% to third and 6% to fourth. Colts and geldings 126 lbs.; Fillies 121 lbs. Starters to be named at the closing time of entries. The winning owner will be presented with the August Belmont Memorial Cup to be retained for one year, as well as a trophy for permanent possession and trophies will be presented to the winning trainer and jockey and mementoes to the grooms of the first four finishers. Closed Friday, February 15, 1980 with 247 nominations. Supplementary nominees: Pikotazo, Temperence Hill and Ben Fab.
Value of race $293,700, value to winner $176,220, second $64,614, third $35,244, fourth $17,622. Mutuel pool $1,603,057, OTB pool $2,166,811.

Last Raced	Horse	Eqt.A.Wt	PP	¼	½	1	1¼	Str	Fin	Jockey	Odds $1
31May80 ^{7}Bel^{3}	(S)Temperence Hill	b 3 126	3	7^{hd}	8½	4½	3^{5}	2½	1^{2}	Maple E	53.40
17May80 ^{9}Pim^{2}	Genuine Risk	3 121	1	5½	5½	3½	2^{hd}	1^{hd}	2^{1½}	Vasquez J	5.10
3May80 ^{8}CD^{5}	Rockhill Native	3 126	7	6^{1½}	2½	1^{hd}	1½	3^{5}	3^{2}	Oldham J	12.80
25May80 ^{8}Bel^{1}	Comptroller	3 126	5	1½	1^{hd}	5^{4}	6^{3}	5½	4^{hd}	Encinas R I	26.20
24May80 ^{8}Hol^{1}	Rumbo	3 126	8	9^{hd}	9½	6^{2}	5^{1}	4½	5^{2½}	Shoemaker W	1.90
3May80 ^{8}CD^{4}	Super Moment	3 126	9	10	10	9^{1}	7^{2}	7^{6}	6^{1¼}	Pincay L Jr	13.40
17May80 ^{9}Pim^{1}	Codex	3 126	2	3½	4^{1}	2½	4½	6^{3}	7^{9}	Cordero A Jr	1.60
26May80 ^{9}Bel^{6}	Joanie's Chief	3 126	10	8^{1½}	7½	8^{1½}	8^{8}	8^{14}	8^{12}	Santiago A	101.00
17May80 ^{9}Pim^{5}	Bing	3 126	4	4^{hd}	6^{1}	10	10	10	9no	Cruguet J	119.60
1Jun80 ^{10}Mex^{1}	(S)Pikotazo	3 126	6	2^{1}	3^{1½}	7^{hd}	9^{3}	9½	10	Hernandez R	8.50

(S) Supplementary nomination.

OFF AT 5:39, EDT. Start good, Won driving. Time, :24⅘, :50⅕, 1:15⅕, 1:39⅗, 2:04, 2:29⅘, Track muddy.

$2 Mutuel Prices:

3–(C)–TEMPERENCE HILL	108.80	32.80	15.20
1–(A)–GENUINE RISK		7.80	5.20
7–(G)–ROCKHILL NATIVE			10.40

B. c, by Stop The Music—Sister Shannon, by Etonian. Trainer Cantey Joseph B. Bred by Polk A F Jr (Ky).

TEMPERENCE HILL, unhurried early, moved up outside horses approaching the end of the backstretch, continued his rally into the stretch, caught the leaders with a furlong remaining and proved clearly best under brisk urging. GENUINE RISK, well in hand while saving ground around the first turn, split horses while moving approaching the far turn, gained a brief lead near midstretch but wasn't able to stay with the winner. ROCKHILL NATIVE moved to the leaders from the outside around the first turn, showed speed into the stretch while saving ground and weakened under pressure. COMPTROLLER dueled for the lead into the backstretch, remained prominent to far turn, dropped back while bearing out and lacked a late response. RUMBO, unhurried early, commenced to rally approaching the end of the backstretch, saved ground into the stretch but lacked a further response. SUPER MOMENT was always outrun. CODEX, close up early, made a bid between horses racing into the far turn but was finished after going nine furlongs. JOANIE'S CHIEF failed to be a serious factor. BING gave way soon after going a half. PIKOTAZO stopped badly after racing forwardly into the backstretch. TEMPERENCE HILL raced with mud caulks.

Owners— 1, Loblolly Stable; 2, Firestone Mrs B R; 3, Oak H A; 4, Phipps O; 5, Gayno Stable & Bell Bloodstock Co; 6, Elmendorf; 7, Tartan Stable; 8, Barberino P; 9, Neff B V; 10, Carranza G Z.

Trainers— 1, Cantey Joseph B; 2, Jolley Leroy; 3, Stevens Herbert K; 4, Penna Angel; 5, Bell Thomas R Jr; 6, McAnally Ronald; 7, Lukas D Wayne; 8, Jacobs Eugene; 9, Speck Gordon; 10, Hernandez Claudino.

depend upon which horses finish in the money. You win your place bet if the horse finishes first or second; it does not matter if the horse is first or second. What matters is the relative amounts bet to place on the various horses, in particular on the two horses finishing one-two and on the total pool. You win your show bet if the horse you bet on is first, second, or third. The payoff depends upon how much is bet on the three horses finishing in the money in relation to the total pool.

In the 1980 Kentucky Derby, Genuine Risk and Rumbo placed, and $2 bets on each of them paid $10.60 and $5.20, respectively. For show they paid $4.80 and $3.40. The payoff for the third finisher, Jaklin Klugman, was $4.40. In the 1980 Belmont Stakes, Temperence Hill and Genuine Risk paid $32.80 and $7.80, respectively, to place. For show they paid $15.20 and $5.20, and Rockhill Native paid $10.40. Notice that the place payoffs are quite a bit less than the win payoffs would have been, and the show payoffs are lower yet. This is reasonable, since two horses receive place payoffs and three receive show payoffs, while only one horse wins. These are typical payoffs for horses going off at reasonably long odds.

Let's now look at the situation when the top favorites finish in the money.

In the 1980 Kentucky Oaks, the Kentucky Derby for fillies, the 3—5 favorite, Bold 'n Determined, won and paid $2.40 to place and $2.20 to show. With a large amount bet on Bold n' Determined to place and show, the payoffs on Mitey Lively were $4 and $3, and $3.80 on Honest and True.

In the 1980 Kentucky Oaks, the 27—1 shot, Honest and True, had a show payoff of $3.80, which was less than Genuine Risk's $4.80 at 13.3—1 and Jaklin Klugman's $4.40 at 7.1—1. This payoff was also smaller than Genuine Risk's $5.20 at 5.1—1 and Rockhill Native's $10.40 at 12.8—1 in the 1980 Belmont Stakes. The payoffs depend upon the amounts bet on the various horses in the place and show pools, not on the win odds.

Kentucky Oaks

EIGHTH RACE Churchill MAY 2, 1980 — 1 1/16 MILES. (1.41⅗) 106th Running KENTUCKY OAKS STAKES (Grade I). Purse $100,000 added, Plus $10,000 KTDF. 3-year-old fillies. By subscription of $100 which covers nomination for both the Kentucky Oaks and the La Troienne. All nomination fees to Kentucky Oaks. $200 to pass entry box, $500 additional to start, $100,000 added, of which with subscription fees and all starting fees to be divided 65% to the winner, 20% to second, 10% to third and 5% to fourth. Weight, 121 lbs. Starters to be named through the entry box Wednesday, April 30, at usual time of closing. If race is divided entries of couplings will be divided. The owner of the winner to receive a silver trophy.

Value of race $129,100, value to winner $83,915, second $25,820, third $12,910, fourth $6,455. Mutuel pool $783,880.

Last Raced	Horse	Eqt.	A.	Wt	PP	St	¼	½	¾	Str	Fin	Jockey	Odds $1
5Apr80 ^{9}OP^{1}	Bold 'N Determined		3	121	2	2	1^{1}	1½	1^{hd}	$1^{1\frac{1}{2}}$	$1^{1\frac{1}{2}}$	Delahoussaye E	.60
13Apr80 ^{8}Aqu^{1}	Mitey Lively		3	121	3	4	$3^{3\frac{1}{2}}$	2½	$2^{1\frac{1}{2}}$	$2^{2\frac{1}{2}}$	2½	Velasquez J	6.70
5Apr80 ^{9}OP^{3}	Honest And True	b	3	121	4	1	5^{hd}	5½	5½	3^{2}	3^{3}	Guajardo A	27.00
26Apr80 ^{8}CD^{1}	Ribbon	b	3	121	5	7	7½	7^{2}	$7^{2\frac{1}{2}}$	4½	4^{3}	Ardoin R	14.00
19Apr80 ^{7}Kee^{3}	Lady Taurian Peace		3	121	7	6	$6^{2\frac{1}{2}}$	4^{1}	4^{hd}	5^{3}	$5^{3\frac{1}{2}}$	Day P	64.10
19Apr80 ^{8}Kee^{1}	Sugar And Spice		3	121	6	5	4½	6½	6^{hd}	6^{2}	6¾	Fell J	2.50
19Apr80 ^{7}Kee^{6}	Sweet Audrey		3	121	8	8	8	8	8	7½	7^{6}	Espinoza J C	83.50
19Apr80 ^{8}Kee^{2}	Nice And Sharp		3	121	1	3	2½	$3^{1\frac{1}{2}}$	3^{hd}	8	8	DePass R	62.20

OFF AT 5:30 EDT. Start good, Won driving. Time, :24⅖, :48⅗, 1:13⅗, 1:38⅕, 1:44⅘ Track fast.

$2 Mutuel Prices:

2-BOLD 'N DETERMINED	3.20	2.40	2.20
3-MITEY LIVELY		4.00	3.00
4-HONEST AND TRUE			3.80

B. f, by Bold And Brave—Pidi, by Determine. Trainer Drysdale Neil. Bred by Layton G E (Ky).

The first race at Woodbine on June 5, 1980, is a typical payoff, with the top two favorites in the money. Notice that Jah Man has higher win odds than Aftermath, 2.10—1 versus 1.50—1, yet his show payoff is less, $2.30 versus $2.40.

1st Race Woodbine Jun. 5, 1980

6 FURLONGS. (1.08⅗) 3 & 4-Year-Olds, Bred in Can. Maidens Claiming ($16,000). Purse $5,200. —Canada-bred — Value of race $5,200, value to winner $3,120, second $1,040, third $572, fourth $312, fifth $156. Mutuel pool $45,501.

Last Raced	Horse	Wt.	PP.	½	Str	Fin	Odds $1
25May80 ^{10}WO^{5}	Aftermath	114	6	$1^{1\frac{1}{2}}$	1^{3}	$1^{2\frac{1}{2}}$	1.50
23May80 ^{4}WO^{5}	Social Expression	117	2	2^{2}	$2^{2\frac{1}{2}}$	2¾	7.80
28May80 ^{9}WO^{2}	Jah Man	114	5	6^{hd}	4½	3no	2.10
25May80 ^{10}WO^{9}	Kamarian	115	8	$4^{2\frac{1}{2}}$	3^{2}	4^{2}	9.95
7May80 ^{6}WO^{9}	Irish Taheka	115	7	5½	5^{3}	5^{4}	11.40
28May80 ^{9}WO^{4}	Peterkinooks	114	3	7^{3}	6^{1}	$6^{5\frac{1}{2}}$	16.00
14May80 ^{6}WO^{11}	Truganini	114	4	3^{1}	7^{6}	$7^{2\frac{3}{4}}$	21.80
25Jly79 ^{3}WO^{4}	Lord Treego	114	9	8^{3}	$8^{2\frac{1}{2}}$	8^{3}	9.85
21May80 ^{1}WO^{9}	Skip's Girl	105	1	9	9	9	100.90

Time, :23⅕, :46⅖, 1:12⅕ Track fast. OFF AT 1:31, EDT.

6-AFTERMATH	5.00	3.10	2.40
3-SOCIAL EXPRESSION		5.80	3.00
5-JAH MAN			2.30

In the fifth race at Pimlico on May 19, 1980, the two top favorites finished second and third. There was, however, a dead heat for third between Mexican Red and Series Six. Since the payoff for show had to be split among

5th Race Pimlico May 19, 1980

1 $\frac{1}{16}$ MILES. (1.41) 3-Year-Olds. Allowance. Purse $10,500. —which have never won two races other than maiden or claiming. — Value of race $10,500, value to winner $6,300, second $2,310, thirds $945 each. Mutuel pool $52,014. Exacta Pool $67,605.

Last Raced		Horse	Wt.	PP.	½	Str	Fin	Odds $1
7Apr80	^{6}Pim^{6}	Ashanti Gold	112	1	3^{1}	1^{2}	1^{4}	3.90
10May80	^{7}Pim^{1}	Royal Saim	112	2	6	5^{3}	2^{nk}	2.30
25Apr80	^{7}Pim^{3}	Series Six	113	3	1^{1}	2^{4}	3	DH-2.50
25Apr80	^{7}Pim^{5}	Mexican Red	115	4	5^{8}	3^{2}	3^{7}	DH-6.70
19Apr80	^{6}Pim^{1}	Lambie Boy	117	5	4^{4}	4^{1}	5^{3}	9.20
9May80	^{8}Pim^{6}	Guns O' Va	112	6	2^{6}	6	6	4.80

DH—Dead heat.

Time, :23$\frac{3}{5}$, :46$\frac{4}{5}$, 1:12, 1:38$\frac{1}{5}$, 1:45 Track good. OFF AT 2:52 EDT.

1-ASHANTI GOLD	9.80	4.80	2.20
2-ROYAL SAIM		3.40	2.10
3-DH SERIES SIX			2.10
4-DH MEXICAN RED			2.10

$2 EXACTA 1-2 PAID $31.20.

four horses rather than three, the returns were minimal. Ashanti Gold paid only $2.20 to show, yet he paid $4.80 to place. The other horses returned only $2.10, the minimum payoff.

The eighth race at Greenwood on April 21, 1979, featured a nine-horse field. However, three of the horses—Overskate, Sound Reason, and Royal Sparkle—were coupled to form an entry. These horses were all owned by Stafford Farm and were required to run together. Notice that the post

8th Race Greenwood Apr. 21, 1979

7 FURLONGS. (1.23) JACQUES CARTER. 4-Year-Olds and Up, Bred in Can. . Purse $20,000 Added. Value of race $23,025, value to winner $13,025, second $5,000, third $3,000, fourth $2,000. Mutuel pool $163,964, Minus show pool $90.67.

Last Raced		Horse	Wt.	PP.	½	Str	Fin	Odds $1
4Nov78	^{8}Lrl^{7}	Overskate	126	4	$1^{1\frac{1}{2}}$	$1^{1\frac{1}{2}}$	$1^{\frac{3}{4}}$	a-.35
7Apr79	^{7}Grd^{3}	Maple Grove	120	3	$4^{\frac{1}{2}}$	$2^{1\frac{1}{2}}$	2^{hd}	3.05
14Oct78	^{7}WO^{7}	Sound Reason	126	6	7^{6}	3^{4}	3^{7}	a-.35
7Apr79	^{7}Grd^{8}	Royal Sparkle	115	1	5^{hd}	4^{2}	$4^{2\frac{1}{2}}$	a-.35
25Nov78	^{8}Grd^{3}	Knight's Turn	123	5	$8^{\frac{1}{2}}$	6^{2}	$5^{1\frac{1}{2}}$	23.00
10Apr79	^{7}Grd^{2}	Dancing Relation	120	7	9	7^{4}	$6^{\frac{1}{2}}$	13.20
5Apr79	^{7}Grd^{4}	Forzando	116	8	2^{hd}	5^{1}	7^{6}	53.40
10Apr79	^{6}Grd^{3}	Crafty Money	114	2	$3^{\frac{1}{2}}$	$8^{2\frac{1}{2}}$	$8^{1\frac{1}{2}}$	22.15
13Apr79	^{7}Grd^{1}	Springtide	114	9	6^{hd}	9	9	15.50

a-Coupled: Overskate, Sound Reason and Royal Sparkle.

Time, :23$\frac{3}{5}$, :47$\frac{2}{5}$, 1:12$\frac{3}{5}$, 1:25$\frac{2}{5}$ Track fast. OFF AT 5:09 EST.

1-OVERSKATE (a-entry)	2.70	2.10	2.10
3-MAPLE GROVE		2.40	2.40
1-SOUND REASON (a-entry)	2.70	2.10	2.10

positions did not correspond to the numbers of the horses. This is the usual practice with a race containing an entry. It is common practice to couple horses running for the same owner or trainer to prevent possible irregularities. By betting on the entry, you get three horses for the price of one. It is likely at least one of them will finish in the money. Even at 0.35—1 odds to win, the betting on the entry to place and show was greater than usual. When the entry finished one-three it paid only the minimum $2.10 to place and show. Maple Grove paid $2.40 to place and also to show.

The payoffs for place and show can vary greatly even on successive races at the same racetrack. Compare the fourth and sixth races at Hialeah Park on April 2, 1979. Notice that Divine Davos at 1.70—1 paid more to place and show than Remnant Wave at 2.30—1. Similarly, Kickapoo Creek at 4.60—1 paid more to show than Princess Naskra at 3.10—1.

4th Race Hialeah Park Apr. 2, 1979

ABOUT 1 ⅛ MILES.(turf). (1.47) 4-Year-Olds, Fillies. Maiden Special weights. Purse $8,500. Value of race $8,500, value to winner $5,100, second $1,530, third $935, fourth $425, balance of starters $85 each. Mutuel pool $39,233. Perfecta Pool $30,087. Trifecta Pool $35,646.

Last Raced	Horse	Wt.	PP.	½	Str	Fin	Odds $1
19Mar79 ^{4}Hia^{3}	Remnant Wave	122	6	$3\frac{1}{2}$	2^{1}	$1\frac{3}{4}$	2.30
19Mar79 ^{4}Hia^{7}	Fuzible	122	5	$6^{1\frac{1}{2}}$	3^{2}	2^{hd}	10.90
7Mar79 ^{1}Hia^{10}	Princess Naskra	117	10	$8^{1\frac{1}{2}}$	6^{hd}	$3^{1\frac{1}{4}}$	3.10
19Mar79 ^{4}Hia^{6}	Proud Lina	122	4	10	$7\frac{1}{2}$	$4\frac{1}{2}$	52.50
20Mar79 ^{4}Hia^{9}	Perhaps Barbara	115	9	4^{4}	$5\frac{1}{2}$	5^{hd}	26.30
21Mar79 ^{5}Hia^{8}	Butter Flower	117	8	$9\frac{1}{2}$	$8^{1\frac{1}{2}}$	6^{1}	25.90
21Mar79 ^{12}Hia^{2}	Our Gallant Lady	122	2	1^{3}	$1\frac{1}{2}$	$7^{1\frac{1}{2}}$	3.70
19Mar79 ^{4}Hia^{8}	Our Prissy	122	7	$5\frac{1}{2}$	9^{4}	8^{hd}	34.60
19Mar79 ^{4}Hia^{4}	Canyon Ride	122	1	7^{1}	$4\frac{1}{2}$	9^{5}	3.00
21Mar79 ^{5}Hia^{7}	Aphaia	122	3	$2^{1\frac{1}{2}}$	10	10	87.20

Time, 1:51 Course firm. OFF AT 1:59 EST.

6-REMNANT WAVE	6.60	3.80	2.60
5-FUZIBLE		10.00	4.80
10-PRINCESS NASKRA			3.00

$2 PERFECTA 6-5 PAID $64.20. $2 TRIFECTA 6-5-10 PAID $184.60.

6th Race Hialeah Park Apr. 2, 1979

7 FURLONGS. (1.20⅗) 4-Year-Olds and Up, Fillies and Mares. Claiming ($7,500 to $6,500). Purse $4,500. Value of race $4,500, value to winner $2,700, second $810, third $450, fourth $180, balance of starters $45 each. Mutuel pool $44,731. Perfecta Pool $33,538. Trifecta Pool $38,892.

Last Raced	Horse	Wt.	PP.	½	Str	Fin	Odds $1
12Mar79 ^{6}Hia^{5}	Divine Davos	116	2	4^{3}	$2\frac{1}{2}$	$1^{1\frac{1}{2}}$	1.70
15Mar79 ^{2}Hia^{6}	Gay Du Nord	116	9	$3^{1\frac{1}{2}}$	$1\frac{1}{2}$	$2\frac{3}{4}$	5.40
12Mar79 ^{6}Hia^{10}	Kickapoo Creek	120	10	2^{hd}	3^{3}	3^{2}	4.60
15Mar79 ^{2}Hia^{4}	Let It Rock	116	11	$6\frac{1}{2}$	5^{3}	$4^{1\frac{1}{2}}$	3.70
5Mar79 ^{10}GP	Step Out Fancy	109	8	1^{hd}	$4\frac{1}{2}$	5^{1}	43.80
23Mar79 ^{3}Hia^{3}	Wouldn't She Tho	107	3	7^{2}	6^{2}	6^{1}	22.20
28Mar79 ^{1}Hia^{6}	True Exchange	114	1	10^{2}	8^{4}	$7^{3\frac{1}{2}}$	129.00
27Mar79 ^{10}Hia^{10}	North WindDancer	111	7	8^{3}	$7\frac{1}{2}$	8^{3}	7.60
9Mar79 ^{8}FD^{4}	Ms. Jackie Blue	114	5	$11^{1\frac{1}{2}}$	$9^{1\frac{1}{2}}$	9^{6}	15.80
2Jan79 ^{6}Crc^{8}	Cap's Cissy	106	6	9^{2}	11^{5}	$10\frac{1}{2}$	83.50
11Dec78 ^{7}Key^{8}	I'm For Triggs'z	116	12	$5\frac{1}{2}$	10^{1}	11^{8}	28.70
20Mar79 ^{7}FD^{5}	Anitas Hat	120	4	12	12	12	54.40

Time, :23⅕, :46⅘, 1:13⅕, 1:26⅘ Track fast. OFF AT 3:00, EST.

2-DIVINE DAVOS	5.40	4.00	3.20
9-GAY DU NORD		6.60	4.20
10-KICKAPOO CREEK			3.40

$2 PERFECTA 2-9 PAID $30.80. $2 TRIFECTA 2-9-10 PAID $147.00.

Why Place and Show Betting Can Yield Positive Profits

How can we take advantage of these discrepancies? No such discrepancies occur for win bets, since the win odds are essentially efficient, but they do occur in the place and show pools. A discrepancy or inefficiency occurs when a much lower proportion of the place or show pool is bet on a particular horse than this horse's proportion of the win pool. The Dr. Z system is a method to exploit these inefficiencies in a precise manner. We develop the basic ideas in this and the succeeding chapter. Our focus now is first to get a feel for when these inefficiencies occur so that they can be easily recognized. As an example, suppose the tote board is as follows:

	Horse							
	#1	#2	#3	#4	#5	#6	#7	Totals
Odds	4—5	14—1	6—1	5—2	16—1	11—1	33—1	
Win	8,293	1,009	2,116	4,212	885	1,251	457	18,223
Place	2,560	660	1,386	2,610	696	903	399	9,214
Show	1,570	495	1,860	1,881	543	712	287	6,558

The place pool is about half the win pool, 9,214/18,223, so ***you need to find a horse where relatively much less than half is bet to place.*** Less than a third, 2,560/8,293, is bet on horse 1 to place, while for all the other horses, there is more than half as much bet to place as to win. The show pool is about a third the win pool, 6,558/18,223, so you would like to find a horse where relatively much less is bet to show. For horses 2 to 7, the ratio between show bet and win bet is more than a third. For example, horse 2 has

$$\frac{\text{Show bet}}{\text{Win bet}} = \frac{495}{1{,}009} = 0.491.$$

Disregard bets like these. However, horse 1 looks promising. It has

$$\frac{\text{Show bet}}{\text{Win bet}} = \frac{1{,}570}{8{,}293} = 0.185,$$

which is much less than $\frac{1}{3} = 0.333$.

Thus, horse 1 may well be a good bet to place and/or to show. Three key questions must now be answered: (1) How good is the bet? (2) Is the bet really good enough? (3) How much should you bet? We answer question

(1) later in this chapter and questions (2) and (3) in Chapter Five.

Let us first look at how the place and show mutuel payoffs are determined. Let Q be the track payback. This is usually about 83%. If P_i is the amount bet on horse i to place, and $P = \sum_{i=1}^{n} P_i$, where P is the place pool and n the number of possible horses, then the payoff per dollar bet on horse i to place is

$$\begin{cases} 1 + \dfrac{PQ - P_i - P_j}{2P_i} & \text{if} \begin{cases} i \text{ is first and } j \text{ is second or} \\ j \text{ is first and } i \text{ is second} \end{cases} \\ 0 & \text{if } i \text{ is not first or second.} \end{cases} \tag{4.1}$$

Thus if horses i and j are first and second, each bettor on i (and also j) to place first receives the amount of his or her bet. The remaining amount in the place pool, after the track take, is then split evenly among the place bettors on i and j. The payoff to horse i to place is independent of whether i finishes first or second, but it is dependent on which horse finished with it. A bettor on horse i to place hopes that a long shot, not a favorite, will finish with it.

Let S_i be the amount bet on horse i to show and $S = \sum_{i=1}^{n} S_i$ be the total show pool. The payoff per dollar bet on show is then

$$\begin{cases} 1 + \dfrac{SQ - S_i - S_j - S_k}{3S_i} & \text{if} \begin{cases} i \text{ is first, second, or third} \\ \text{and finishes with } j \text{ and } k \end{cases} \\ 0 & \text{if } i \text{ is not first, second, or third.} \end{cases} \tag{4.2}$$

To understand equations (4.1) and (4.2), let's suppose horse 1 is in the money with horse 2 for a place bet. The payoff per dollar bet to place on horse 1 is

$$1 + \frac{9{,}214(0.83) - 2{,}560 - 660}{2(2{,}560)} = \$1.86.$$

If horse 4 finishes with horse 1, then 1's payoff for place per dollar bet is

$$1 + \frac{9{,}214(0.83) - 2{,}560 - 2{,}610}{2(2{,}560)} = \$1.48.$$

For show, suppose horse 1 finishes in the money with the long shots 2 and 7. Then the payoff for show per dollar bet on horse 1 is

$$1 + \frac{6{,}558(0.83) - 1{,}570 - 495 - 287}{3(1{,}570)} = \$1.66.$$

If 1 finishes in the money with the other favorites, 3 and 4, then the show payoff drops to

$$1 + \frac{6{,}558(0.83) - 1{,}570 - 1{,}860 - 1{,}881}{3(1{,}570)} = \$1.03.$$

At an actual racetrack, the values would be adjusted for breakage, \$2 bets, and \$2.10 minimum payout. With 5¢ on the dollar, \$1.86 becomes \$3.70, \$1.48 becomes \$2.90, \$1.66 becomes \$3.30, and \$1.03 becomes \$2.10. So the payoffs are much larger when relative long shots rather than favorites finish in the money. Notice that as less is bet to place or show on horse 1, the payoff is improved in two ways. For example, with place there is less taken off than \$2,560 and likewise less than \$2,560 is divided. With proportionally less bet to place or show, the payoff becomes much larger.

Let us now look at some more actual race results to determine the type of situations for which you are looking, so that you can learn to recognize them easily. An extreme case occurs when the place payoff actually exceeds the win payoff, as with Chocolate Lover in the ninth race at Hollywood Park on December 11, 1982. This makes for an outstanding bet.

6207—NINTH RACE. Mile and one-sixteenth. 3-year-olds & p. Top claiming price \$20,000. Purse \$10,000.

6189	Chocolate Lover, Sibille	121	12	4	5^{1}	2^{hd}	$1^{\frac{1}{2}}$	1^{2}	$1^{3\frac{1}{2}}$	1.10
6144	Hanalei Prince, Steiner	x111	1	2	4^{2}	$5^{3\frac{1}{2}}$	3^{4}	3^{2}	2^{hd}	12.00
6135	Royal Earl, Ortega	121	9	10	$10^{\frac{1}{2}}$	9^{5}	$5^{\frac{1}{2}}$	4^{3}	$3^{1\frac{1}{2}}$	5.10
——	Apache Scout, Guzman	116	5	12	12	12	8^{hd}	5^{4}	$4^{1\frac{1}{2}}$	8.30
——	Dancing Casanova, Vinzla ...	116	11	3	3^{1}	1^{1}	$2^{1\frac{1}{2}}$	2^{1}	5^{3}	19.00
6055	Game Of Spies, Bombek	114	7	6	8^{2}	8^{hd}	4^{hd}	$6^{\frac{1}{2}}$	$6^{2\frac{1}{2}}$	116.80
6144	Mity Busy, Pedroza	114	10	8	11^{5}	$11^{\frac{1}{2}}$	$9^{2\frac{1}{2}}$	7^{hd}	7no	18.10
——	Count By Five, Lipham	114	8	11	9^{hd}	10^{hd}	11^{1}	8^{hd}	8^{1}	43.00
6153	Bold Taste, Cruz	116	6	7	7^{3}	6^{1}	7^{3}	9^{2}	$9^{3\frac{1}{2}}$	111.70
6153	California Fig, Dihssye	116	2	0	6^{hd}	7^{2}	6^{hd}	10^{8}	10^{7}	7.60
6046	Mel's Victory, McHargue	115	3	5	1^{hd}	3^{hd}	10^{2}	11^{3}	11^{3}	33.30
6101	Amazing Career, Frazier	121	4	1	2^{1}	4^{hd}	12	12	12	11:60

Scratched—K's Vindicator, Bidadoon, China Blast.

CHOCOLATE LOVER	**4.20**	**4.40**	**3.00**
HANALEI PRINCE		**8.40**	**5.20**
ROYAL EARL....			**3.40**

Time—:23, .46 3/5, 1:11 1/5, 1:37 2/5, 1:44 1/5. Winner—b.g.4 Illustrious—Khal Me Fancy. Trained by s. Morguelan. Mutuel pool \$107,821. Exacta Pool \$259,487. Attendance—13,801. Total handle \$3,175,962.

Claimed—Apache Scount by S. Rahe, trainer G. Lewis, for \$10,000. Royal Earl by Lewis Potter, trainer G. Lewis, for \$10,000. Chocolate Lover by J. M. Orman, trainer D Vienna, for \$10,000.

\$5 EXACTA (12-1) PAID \$115.00

The extreme inefficiency required to have the place payoff exceed the win payoff is rare, however. It usually occurs when a seemingly unbeatable horse is bet at extremely low odds to win, while the place (and possibly also the show) betting is simply overlooked. The crowd feels that the payoff will be too small to warrant the risk. They could not be more wrong! A typical example of this was the 1983 Florida Derby, where Copelan, a 1—5 shot, paid $3.00 to place and $2.60 to show. His win payoff had he won, would have been $2.40.

11th One and one-sixteenth miles. Three-year-olds and up. Claiming $4,000. Purse $3,900.

Horse	Jockey	Wt	P	½	¾	Str	Fin	Odds
Dollar Power	Spencer	113	5	1-5	1-3	1-5	1-5	12.60
Duffus Castle	Wrayton	101	8	6-½	4-1	2-h	2-1	4.30
Tagy	Rycroft	115	10	10	9-1	5-½	3-1	17.60
Pertock	Krasner	109	3	8-½	6-½	4-2	4-3½	2.85
Here To Shine	Creighton	113	9	3-1	2-2	3-2	5-no	11.10
Glen Magic	Mena	113	7	4-2	5-2	6-h	6-1	4.30
Individual Boy	L'siere	108	1	9-2½	8-1½	8-5	7-1½	6.05
North Lane	Patzer	117	6	2-2½	2-2½	2-½	3-h	6.75
Concilliator	Adcock	116	4	5-½	10	9-4	9-7	8.90
Silver Ducat	Johnson	113	2	7-2	7-h	10	10	8.00

Time—:47.4, 1:14.1, 1:42, 1:49.1.
Winner: Command Module-Miss Hot Shot.
Trainer: Delores Hehn

DOLLAR POWER	**27.20**	**14.20**	**9.60**
DUFFUS CASTLE		**15.80**	**9.30**
TAGY			**11.50**

Triactor (5,8,10) paid $3,657.50

GULFSTREAM PARK
Florida Derby
Time 1:49 4/5

Croeso	172.00	35.80	12.40
Copelan		3.00	2.60
Law Talk			5.60

Also ran in order — My Mac, Chumming, Blink, Current Hope, Princilian, Pure Grit, Caveat, Bet Big, El Cubanoso, Thalassocrat.
Jockeys—Olivares, Pincay, Hernandez.
Perfecta (10-5) paid $366.20

This behavior often occurs in the last race or two when many bettors are looking only to the exotics and the win pools for a big payoff to get back to even. This was the case in the eleventh race at Exhibition Park on July 27, 1983. Duffus Castle, at 4.30—1, paid a whopping $15.80 to place and $9.30 to show. If he had won, his payoff would have been only $10.60.

Many observers consider the greatest performance of all time by a thoroughbred to be Secretariat's win in the 1973 Belmont Stakes by an amazing thirty-one lengths. He broke the track record for the $1\frac{1}{2}$-mile distance by a full two seconds, ten lengths better than any previous horse. Equally impressive is the fact that, at 1—10 win odds, his place payoff profits were double those for win. A $2.40 place payoff in a five-horse field with a 1—10 shot is a truly amazing bet.

The mighty Kelso, who was horse of the year for an unprecedented five consecutive years from 1960 to 1964, often returned more to place than win as the two following race charts indicate.

Such payoffs occur frequently on the very best horses. John Henry was the horse of the year in 1981, and he is the all-time leading money winner, with earnings of over $4 million. In the 1983 running of the Arlington Million, he was the favorite of the crowd at 7—5. He lost the race to the 38—1 shot, Tolomeo. His place payoff, however, was $4.80, the same as he would have paid to win had he won.

Place and also show payoffs almost as good occur frequently with odds-

Belmont Stakes

EIGHTH RACE Bel June 9, 1973 1½ MILES. (2:26$\frac{3}{5}$). One Hundred-fifth running BELMONT. SCALE WEIGHTS. $125,000 added. 3-year-olds. By subscription of $100 each to accompany the nomination; $250 to pass the entry box; $1,000 to start. A supplementary nomination may be made of $2,500 at the closing time of entries plus an additional $10,000 to start, with $125,000 added, of which 60% to the winner, 22% to second, 12% to third and 6% to fourth. Colts and geldings. Weight, 126 lbs.; fillies, 121 lbs. The winning owner will be presented with the August Belmont Memorial Cup to be retained for one year, as well as a trophy for permanent possession and trophies will be presented to the winning trainer and jockey. Closed Thursday, Feb. 15, 1973, with 187 nominations.
Value of race $150,200. Value to winner $90,120; second, $33,044; third, $18,024; fourth, $9,012.
Mutuel Pool, $519,689. Off-track betting, $688,460.

Last Raced	Horse	EqtAWt	PP	¼	½	1	1¼	Str	Fin	Jockeys	Owners	Odds to $1
5-19-73^8 Pim^1	Secretariat	b3 126	1	1^h	1^h	1^7	1^{20}	1^{28}	1^{31}	RTurcotte	Meadow Stable	.10
6- 2-73^6 Bel^4	Twice a Prince	3 126	4	4^5	4^{10}	3^h	2^h	3^{12}	$2\frac{1}{2}$	BBaeza	Elmendorf	17.30
5-31-73^6 Bel^1	My Gallant	b3 126	3	3^3	3^h	4^7	3^2	2^h	3^{13}	ACorderoJr	A I Appleton	12.40
5-28-73^8 GS^2	Pvt. Smiles	b3 126	2	5	5	5	5	5	$4\frac{3}{4}$	DGargan	C V Whitney	14.30
5-19-73^8 Pim^2	Sham	b3 126	5	2^5	2^{10}	2^7	4^8	$4^{1\frac{1}{2}}$	5	LPincayJr	S Sommer	5.10

Time, :23$\frac{3}{5}$, :46$\frac{1}{5}$, 1:09$\frac{4}{5}$, 1:34$\frac{1}{5}$, 1:59, 2:24 (new track record) (against wind in backstretch). Track fast.

$2 Mutuel Prices:			
2-SECRETARIAT	2.20	2.40	...
5-TWICE A PRINCE		4.60	...

(NO SHOW MUTUELS SOLD)

Ch. c, by Bold Ruler—Somethingroyal, by Princequillo. Trainer, L. Laurin. Bred by Meadow Stud, Inc. (Va.). **IN GATE—5:38. OFF AT 5:38 EASTERN DAYLIGHT TIME. Start good. Won ridden out.**

SECRETARIAT sent up along the inside to vie for the early lead with SHAM to the backstretch, disposed of that one after going three-quarters, drew off at will rounding the far turn and was under a hand ride from Turcotte to establish a record in a tremendous perfomance. TWICE A PRINCE, unable to stay with the leaders early, moved through along the rail approaching the stretch and outfinished MY GALLANT for the place. The latter, void of early foot, moved with TWICE A PRINCE rounding the far turn and fought it out gamely with that one through the drive. PVT. SMILES showed nothing. SHAM alternated for the lead with SECRETARIAT to the backstretch, wasn't able to match stride with that rival after going three-quarters and stopped badly. **Scratched—Knightly Dawn.**

SEVENTH RACE Aqu 18251 October 19, 1963 2 MILES. (Kelso, Oct. 29, 1960, 3:19$\frac{2}{5}$, 3, 119.) Forty-fifth running JOCKEY CLUB GOLD CUP. Weight for age. $100,000 added. 3-year-olds and upward. By subscription of $100 each, which shall accompany the nomination; $1,000 additional to start, with $100,000 added. The added money and all fees to be divided 65 per cent to the winner, 20 per cent to second, 10 per cent to third and 5 per cent to fourth. 3-year-olds, 119 lbs.; older, 124 lbs. The Jockey Club will present a Gold Cup to the owner of the winner and trophies will be presented to the winning trainer and jockey. Closed Tuesday, Oct. 1, with 19 nominations.
Value of race $108,900. Value to winner $70,785; second, $21,780; third, $10,890; fourth, $5,445.
Mutuel Pool, $391,933.

Index	Horses	Eq't A Wt	PP	¼	½	1	1½	Str	Fin	Jockeys	Owners	Odds to $1
18014Aqu^1	—Kelso	6 124	1	$4^{\frac{1}{2}}$	2^3	1^1	1^2	1^6	1^4	I Vanlez'ela	Bohemia Stable	.15
18170Aqu^5	—Guadalcanal	5 124	2	6^4	5^4	5^8	5^{10}	4^6	2^5	B Sorensen	R L Dotter	17.75
18170Aqu^3	—Garwol	5 124	6	$3^{1\frac{1}{2}}$	3^1	$3^{1\frac{1}{2}}$	$4^{1\frac{1}{2}}$	3^h	$3^{3\frac{1}{2}}$	J Sellers	Harbor View Farm	19.75
18170Aqu^2	—Will I Rule	3 119	5	2^h	1^h	$2^{1\frac{1}{2}}$	2^2	$2^{1\frac{1}{2}}$	4^{10}	J Ruane	F E Dixon Jr	10.50
18170Aqu^7	—Sensitivo	6 124	3	5^5	4^4	4^3	3^1	5^6	5^8	S Hern'dez	R F Bensinger	30.45
18180Aqu^2	—Left Hook	b 3 119	7	7	6^6	6	6	6	6	W Boland	Hobeau Farm	41.30
18170Aqu^4	—Mr. Consistency	b 5 124	4	1^h	7	Saddle slipped.				J Vasquez	Ann Peppers	9.30

Time, :25, :48$\frac{2}{5}$, 1:12$\frac{4}{5}$, 1:39, 2:30, 2:55$\frac{1}{5}$, 3:22 (with wind in backstretch). Track fast.

$2 Mutuel Prices:			
1-KELSO	2.30	2.40	2.10
2-GUADALCANAL		6.20	3.00
6-GARWOL			2.40

Dk. b. or br. g, by Your Host—Maid of Flight, by Count Fleet. Trainer, C. H. Hanford. Bred by Mrs. R. C. duPont. **IN GATE—4:50. OFF AT 4:50 EASTERN DAYLIGHT TIME. Start good. Won easily.**

KELSO, steadied when caught between horses during the initial quarter-mile, took command after three-quarters and, establishing a long lead in the upper stretch, won with speed in reserve. GUADALCANAL saved ground while outrun early and finished determinedly in the middle of the track but was unable to threaten KELSO, although much the best of the others. GARWOL, forwardly placed and in hand to the last half-mile, made a mild challenge entering the stretch and tired. WILL I RULE, forwardly placed until inside the stretch, had nothing left. SENSITIVO moved up boldly near the upper turn but failed to stay. LEFT HOOK, never close, had no mishap. MR. CONSISTENCY was pulled up near the three-quarters mile pole after the rider's saddle had slipped.

on favorites, such as in the 1977 Kentucky Derby with Seattle Slew, the 1981 Blue Grass Stakes at Keeneland with Proud Appeal, and the E.P. Taylor Stakes at Woodbine with De La Rose. Later in the chapter you will learn how to evaluate how good these payoffs really are.

SEVENTH RACE
Sar 21296
August 27, 1964

1 1-8 MILES (turf). (Shield Bearer, Aug. 9, 1961, 1:47, 6, 117.) Mechanicville Purse. Allowances. Purse $9,500. 3-year-olds and upward which have not won three races of $2,925 in 1964. 3-year-olds, 116 lbs.; older, 123 lbs. Non-winners of two races of $3,575 at a mile or over since May 30 allowed 3 lbs.; of two such races since April 22, 5 lbs.; of such a race since then, 7 lbs. (Maiden, claiming, optional and starter races not considered.)

Value to winner $6,175; second, $1,900; third, $950; fourth, $475. Mutuel Pool, $106,000.

Index	Horses	Eq't	A	Wt	PP	St	1/4	1/2	3/4	Str	Fin	Jockeys	Owners	Odds to $1
20996Aqu5	—Kelso		7	118	4	3	$2^{1\frac{1}{2}}$	2^{1}	2^{1}	$1^{\frac{1}{2}}$	$1^{2\frac{1}{2}}$	I Valenz'ela	Bohemia Stable	.30
21261Sar2	—Knightsboro	b	5	116	1	1	$1^{2\frac{1}{2}}$	$1^{2\frac{1}{2}}$	1^{h}	$2^{1\frac{1}{2}}$	$2^{1\frac{1}{2}}$	R Turcotte	N Hellman	15.90
21242Sar5	—Rocky Thumb	b	4	120	8	8	6^{3}	6^{6}	$4^{1\frac{1}{2}}$	$3^{\frac{1}{2}}$	3^{5}	J Combest	E B Ryan	27.85
21208Sar1	—Flag		4	118	5	2	3^{h}	$3^{1\frac{1}{2}}$	3^{3}	4^{3}	4^{1}	R Ussery	R C Kidder	5.15
21157Sar4	—Jay Dee		5	116	6	7	5^{3}	5^{h}	6^{3}	5^{h}	5^{3}	H Gustines	J M Schiff	53.85
21171Sar2	—Swift Sands	b	6	116	7	4	4^{3}	4^{3}	5^{3}	6^{1}	6^{h}	J Ruane	Mrs V Adams	14.85
21242Sar6	—Dusky Damion	b	7	116	3	5	7^{1}	7^{1}	7^{3}	7^{6}	7^{6}	D Pierce	Swiftsure Stable	11.70
21162Ran5	—Shop		5	116	2	6	8	8	8	8	8	J L Rotz	B Ferrari	75.70

Time, 1:46⅗ (with wind in backstretch). Track hard. NEW COURSE RECORD. EQUALS AMERICAN RECORD.

$2 Mutuel Prices:			
4-KELSO	2.60	2.70	2.30
1-KNIGHTSBORO		6.30	4.10
8-ROCKY THUMB			4.90

Dk. b. or br. g, by Your Host—Maid of Flight, by Count Fleet. Trainer, C. Hanford. Bred by Mrs. R.C. duPont, Jr.

IN GATE—5:08. OFF AT 5:08 EASTERN DAYLIGHT TIME. Start good. Won handily.

KELSO, forwardly placed from the start, took command from KNIGHTSBORO after entering the stretch and drew clear while under mild urging. KNIGHTSBORO, away fast, set the pace until inside the stretch but was unable to stay with KELSO. ROCKY THUMB, reserved early, moved to the inside at the final turn but could not better his position when set down in the drive. FLAG, caught between horses and checked slightly approaching the stretch, failed to respond when clear. JAY DEE had no excuse. SWIFT SANDS tired after showing early speed. DUSKY DAMION and SHOP, never close, had no mishaps.

Scratched—21242Sar Grand Applause.

NINTH—1¼ miles, main turf, 3-year-olds up, ARLINGTON MILLION:

Horse and Jockey	PP	1/4	3/4	1M	Str.	Fin.	$1
Tolomeo [Eddery]	5	2^{hd}	$3^{\frac{1}{2}}$	3^{hd}	$3^{1\frac{1}{2}}$	1^{nk}	38.20
John Henry [McCarron]	13	$3^{\frac{1}{2}}$	$2^{1\frac{1}{2}}$	2^{1}	2^{1}	$2^{\frac{1}{2}}$	1.40
Nijinsky's Secret [Velez]	7	1^{1}	1^{hd}	$1^{\frac{1}{2}}$	$1^{\frac{1}{2}}$	3^{2}	10.30
Thunder Puddles[Cordero]	9	$6^{\frac{1}{2}}$	6^{1}	$6^{1\frac{1}{2}}$	6^{1}	4^{nk}	13.10
a—Erins Isle [Pincay]	2	$8^{1\frac{1}{2}}$	8^{1}	8^{2}	8^{4}	5^{nk}	2.40
Hush Dear [Vasquez]	6	9^{1}	5^{hd}	4^{hd}	4^{1}	6^{2}	19.90
f—Bold Run [Starkey]	8	$4^{\frac{1}{2}}$	4^{hd}	$5^{\frac{1}{2}}$	5^{hd}	7no	36.60
Muscatite [Fires]	3	5^{1}	7^{hd}	7^{hd}	7^{hd}	$8^{\frac{3}{4}}$	24.00
Trevita [Velasquez]	4	7^{hd}	$11^{1\frac{1}{2}}$	11^{1}	10^{5}	$9^{2\frac{1}{2}}$	38.30
Rossi Gold [Day]	1	$11^{\frac{1}{2}}$	13^{4}	13^{2}	13^{1}	10^{1}	21.90
Be My Native [Piggott]	11	12^{hd}	10^{1}	9^{hd}	$9^{\frac{1}{2}}$	$11^{2\frac{1}{4}}$	17.40
Majesty's Prince [Maple]	12	14	14	14	11^{2}	12^{10}	10.40
a—The Wonder [Shoemaker]	14	13^{4}	$9^{\frac{1}{2}}$	$10^{\frac{1}{2}}$	14	13^{nk}	2.40
f—Noble Player [Cauthen]	10	$10^{\frac{1}{2}}$	$12^{1\frac{1}{2}}$	12^{2}	12^{2}	14	36.60

$2 mutuels paid:

Tolomeo	78.40	33.20	17.00
John Henry		4.80	3.40
Nijinsky's Secret			6.00

Time—:24 2/5, :50 3/5, 1:41 3/5, 2:04 2/5. Winner BC 3 by Lypheor-Almagest by Dike. Owned by Carlo d'Alessio. Trained by Luca M. Cumani. Mutuel pool $645,542. Perfecta pool $229,567.

Perfecta [5-11] $439.20

Some outstanding show bets are on pages 47–52. These include Harry Caray in a claiming race at River Downs, Lamerok in the Bougainvillea Handicap, Noble Nashua and Maudlin in the Jerome Handicap, Perfect Remedy in the HITS Parade Invitational Futurity, Fearless Miss in a maiden race at Beulah, I'm Smokin in an allowance race at Santa Anita, Foolish Girl in an allowance race at Hollywood Park, Ballysadare in a maiden race at Hialeah, Spectacular Nashua and Sunny And Clear in a claiming race at Woodbine, Honey Fox in the Black Helen Handicap at Hialeah, J. Burns in

103rd Kentucky Derby, May 7, 1977

$267,200 gross value and $15,000 Gold Cup. Net to winner $214,700; second $30,000; third $15,000; fourth $7,500. 297 nominations.

Horse	Eqt Wt	PP	¼	½	¾	1	Str	Fin	Jockeys	Owners	Odds to $1
Seattle Slew	126	4	2^{1}	2^{4}	2^{4}	1^{h}	1^{3}	$1^{1\frac{3}{4}}$	J. Cruguet	Karen L. Taylor	.50
Run Dusty Run ..	126	8	$4\frac{1}{2}$	4^{3}	4^{1}	3^{1}	2^{3}	2^{nk}	D. McHargue	Golden Chance Farm	a-5.50
Sanhedrin	b 126	1	$12^{1\frac{1}{2}}$	10^{1}	12^{2}	8^{2}	$4^{1\frac{1}{2}}$	$3^{3\frac{1}{4}}$	J. Velasquez	Darby Dan Farm	14.60
Get the Axe	126	5	9^{2}	$9^{1\frac{1}{2}}$	9^{h}	9^{h}	7^{2}	4no	W. Shoemaker	Bwamazon Farm	27.90
Steve's Friend ...	b 126	11	$7^{1\frac{1}{2}}$	$7^{1\frac{1}{2}}$	$5^{1\frac{1}{2}}$	4^{2}	$5\frac{1}{2}$	5no	R. Hernandez	Kinship Stable	29.20
Papelote	b 126	14	$5^{1\frac{1}{2}}$	6^{2}	$8^{1\frac{1}{2}}$	$7^{1\frac{1}{2}}$	6^{2}	$6^{2\frac{1}{4}}$	M. A. Rivera	Marvin L. Warner	f-42.80
Giboulee	b 126	13	12^{2}	$8\frac{1}{2}$	10^{h}	$13^{1\frac{1}{2}}$	$9^{1\frac{1}{2}}$	7^{h}	J. Fell	J. L. Levesque	40.20
For the Moment ..	b 126	10	$1\frac{1}{2}$	1^{h}	1^{1}	2^{3}	$3\frac{1}{2}$	$8\frac{3}{4}$	A. Cordero, Jr.	Gerald Robins	7.00
Affiliate	b 126	7	$10\frac{1}{2}$	12^{2}	11^{h}	$6\frac{1}{2}$	$8\frac{1}{2}$	$9^{1\frac{3}{4}}$	L. Pincay, Jr.	Harbor View Farm	38.20
Flag Officer	126	6	15	$11\frac{1}{2}$	$13\frac{1}{2}$	10^{1}	$10^{1\frac{1}{2}}$	$10\frac{1}{2}$	L. Ahrens	Nasty Stable	46.90
Bob's Dusty	126	3	3^{3}	3^{5}	3^{2}	5^{2}	12^{2}	11^{nk}	J. C. Espinoza	R. N. Lehmann	a-5.50
Sir Sir	126	2	$6\frac{1}{2}$	5^{1}	6^{2}	12^{2}	11^{h}	12^{2}	J. J. Rodriguez	La Luna Stable	f-42.80
Nostalgia	b 126	15	$13^{1\frac{1}{2}}$	$14\frac{1}{2}$	14^{1}	14^{3}	13^{6}	13^{3}	L. Snyder	W. S. Farish III	40.00
Western Wind	126	9	$14^{1\frac{1}{2}}$	15	15	15	14^{7}	14^{10}	R. Turcotte	J. M. Roebling	31.10
Best Person	b 126	12	8^{3}	$13\frac{1}{2}$	7^{1}	11^{1}	15	15	G. Patterson	W. C. Partee	f-42.80

Time: :23, :45-4/5, 1:10-3/5, 1:36, 2:02-1/5. Track fast. Off at 5:41 EDT. Start good. Won ridden out.

Coupled: a-Run Dusty Run and Bob's Dusty. f-Mutuel field.

$2 mutuels paid—Seattle Slew $3.00 straight, $2.80 place, $2.80 show; Run Dusty Run $3.40 place, $3.20 show; Sanhedrin $4.60 show.

Winner—Dk. b. or br. c, by **Bold Reasoning—My Charmer, by Poker, trainer William H. Turner, Jr.; bred in Kentucky by Ben S. Castleman.**

SEATTLE SLEW swerved sharply to the outside into GET THE AXE, after failing to break smartly, was rushed to the leaders early placing SIR SIR in slightly close quarters, continuing through tight quarters nearing the end of the opening quarter. SEATTLE SLEW forced his way through moving FLAG OFFICER, AFFILIATE and BOB'S DUSTY out. Continuing in full stride, SEATTLE SLEW engaged FOR THE MOMENT at that point to duel for the lead from the outside to the top of the stretch at which stage he disposed of that one when put to extreme pressure, drew off with a rush and prevailed under intermittent urging. RUN DUSTY RUN broke well to gain a forward position, rallied along the outside on the final turn, continued willingly only to lug in through the closing stages and could not reach the winner. RUN DUSTY RUN survived a claim of foul lodged by the rider of SANHEDRIN for alleged interference in the closing stages. The latter, unhurried early while racing along the inner railing, came out for the drive and finished full of run. GET THE AXE closed some ground in his late bid but could not seriously threaten. STEVE'S FRIEND, unhurried early, moved up gradually along the outside on the second turn to loom boldly a furlong away but lacked a further response. PAPELOTE saved ground to no avail. FOR THE MOMENT, away sharply to make the pace, saved ground while dueling with SEATTLE SLEW to the top of the stretch at which point he succumbed suddenly. FLAG OFFICER was outrun. BOB'S DUSTY showed forwardly for three-quarters and retired. SIR SIR was caught in close quarters after the start.

THE WINNER'S PEDIGREE AND CAREER HIGHLIGHTS

SEATTLE SLEW (Dark Bay or Brown Colt)	Bold Reasoning	Boldnesian	Bold Ruler
			Alanesian
		Reason to Earn	Hail to Reason
			Sailing Home
	My Charmer	Poker	Round Table
			Glamour
		Fair Charmer	Jet Action
			Myrtle Charm

Year	Age	Sts	1st	2nd	3rd	Won
1976	2	3	3	0	0	$ 66,669
1977	3	7	6	0	0	641,370
1978	4	7	5	2	0	473,006
Totals		17	14	2	0	$1,208,726

At 2 Years	**WON**	**Champagne**
At 3 Years	**WON**	**Kentucky Derby, Flamingo, Wood, Preakness, Belmont Stakes**
	UNP	**Swaps**
At 4 Years	**WON**	**Marlboro Cup, Woodward, Stuyvesant**
	2ND	**Patterson, Jockey Club Gold Cup**

an allowance race at Arlington,* Glorious Song in the Beldame Stakes at Belmont and the 1978 triple crown winner Affirmed in the Charles H. Strub Stakes at Santa Anita in February 1979.

---

*Perplext's payoff of $8.20 for show at 10.3—1 was good, but not outstanding. Such long shots are typically overbet to win and here to place as well.

Blue Grass Stakes

SEVENTH RACE
Keeneland
APRIL 23, 1981

1 ⅛ MILES. (1.47⅗) 57th Running THE BLUE GRASS STAKES (Grade I). $150,000 Added. For 3-year-olds. By subscription of $75 each w'.ich shall accompany the nomination, $750 to pass the entry box and $750 additional to start, with $150,000 added (plus $15,000 KTDF), of which 65% of all monies to the owner of the winner, 20% to second, 10% to third, and 5% to fourth. Colts and geldings. Weights: colts and geldings, 121 lbs.; fillies, 116 lbs. In the event the number of starters requires the race to be run in more than one division, it will be drawn in accordance with the rules of racing, and not less than 75% of the added purse will be offered in each division. Starters to be named through the entry box by the usual time of closing. The owner of the winner to receive a gold julep cup. No Supplementary Nominations. (In the event the field exceeds twelve and the race is not divided, the race will start at the eighth pole and finish at the sixteenth pole). Closed with 243 nominations.
Value of race $186,975, value to winner $120,559, second $37,095, third $20,047, fourth $9,274. $13,500 Reverts to the KTDF. Mutuel pool $504,694.

Last Raced	Horse	Eqt.A.Wt	PP	St	¼	½	¾	Str	Fin	Jockey	Odds $1
5Apr81 ^{8}Aqu^1	Proud Appeal	3 121	6	3	$1^{1½}$	$1^{½}$	1^{hd}	1^2	1^3	Fell J	a-.50
29Mar81 ^{9}FG^{11}	Law Me	3 121	5	7	6^2	4^1	3^1	3^3	$2^{¾}$	Day P	85.60
14Apr81 ^{7}Kee^3	Golden Derby	3 121	9	4	2^1	$2^{1½}$	2^4	$2^{2½}$	3^{hd}	Espinoza J C	a-.50
28Mar81 ^{9}Hia^3	Double Sonic	3 121	3	11	11	10^{hd}	$8^{1½}$	$5^{1½}$	$4^{1½}$	Thornburg B	16.60
29Mar81 ^{9}FG^3	Beau Rit	b 3 121	10	6	$7^{1½}$	6^1	6^{hd}	8^6	5^6	Rubbicco P	12.10
14Apr81 ^{7}Kee^2	Sportin' Life	3 121	2	9	9^3	7^{hd}	7^5	6^3	$6^{6½}$	Velasquez J	10.30
14Apr81 ^{7}Kee^8	Habano	3 121	4	2	3^2	3^1	$4^{1½}$	7^2	7^2	McHargue D G	48.10
6Apr81 ^{5}Aqu^1	Shahnameh	3 121	1	1	5^{hd}	5^3	5^1	4^1	$8^{2½}$	Asmussen C B	45.10
18Mar81 ^{9}Hia^7	Cinnamon's Choice	3 121	7	10	10^{hd}	11	11	9^6	9^{12}	Brumfield D	5.90
14Apr81 ^{7}Kee^1	Swinging Light	b 3 121	8	8	8^{hd}	9^3	9^2	10^8	10^{15}	Delahoussaye D J	9.60
16Apr81 ^{8}Kee^1	Bysantine	b 3 121	11	5	$4^{½}$	$8^{1½}$	10^{hd}	11	11	Delahoussaye E	69.00

a-Coupled: Proud Appeal and Golden Derby.

OFF AT 4:49, EST. Start good, Won ridden out. Time, :23⅗, :47⅗, 1:11⅗, 1:38, 1:51⅗ Track sloppy.

$2 Mutuel Prices:				
	1-PROUD APPEAL (a-entry)	3.00	3.00	2.80
	6-LAW ME		30.00	11.20
	1-GOLDEN DERBY (a-entry)	3.00	3.00	2.80

Dk. b. or br. c, by Valid Appeal—Proud N' Happy, by Proudest Roman. Trainer Hough Stanley M. Bred by Camp P & Yewell R (Fla).

PROUD APPEAL, away alertly and quickly in command, made all the pace, shook off a challenge by GOLDEN DERBY approaching the lane, responded to intermittent left-handed urging in upper stretch, ducked out slightly just before the furlong marker and again before the sixteenth pole but was straightened away to increase the margin under a hand ride late. LAW ME, allowed to settle early, rallied with left-handed pressure when set down for the drive and was up to gain the place while no threat to the winner. GOLDEN DERBY prompted the early pace, challenged approaching the lane, could not match the winner and weakened in the final strides. DOUBLE SONIC, devoid of early foot, found best stride late. BEAU RIT had no rally. SPORTIN' LIFE had no speed. HABANO had speed for a half and gave way steadily. SHAHNAMEH never launched a serious bid. CINNAMON'S CHOICE was always far back. SWINGING LIGHT never threatened. BYSANTINE flashed brief foot.

Owners— 1, Winfield M H; 2, Whittaker E; 3, Gaines & Lehmann; 4, Elias F & L; 5, Roussel Carol; 6, Farish W S III; 7, Coello M A; 8, Manhasset Stable; 9, Calumet Farm; 10, Zantker E; 11, Saron Stable.

Trainers— 1, Hough Stanley M; 2, McClain Edward T; 3, Adams William E; 4, Krnjaich George; 5, Roussel Louis III; 6, Carroll Del W; 7, Gonzalez Francisco; 8, Picou James E; 9, Veitch John M; 10, Conway James P; 11, Drysdale Neil.

Scratched—Tap Shoes (28Mar81 ^{9}Hia^1).

E. P. Taylor Stakes

NINTH RACE
Woodbine
OCTOBER 17, 1981

1 ¼ MILES.(inner-turf). (2.01⅗) *26th Running E P TAYLOR STAKES (Grade III). $100,000 added. Fillies and Mares. 3-year-olds and up. By subscription of $100 each which shall accompany the nomination and an additional $1,000 when making entry; with $100,000 added, plus all fees to be divided 60% to winner, 20% to second, 11% to third, 6% to fourth and 3% to fifth. 3-year-olds. Weight 118 lbs. (53 1/2 kg); older, 124 lbs. (56 kg) (European Scale). (No Canadian-bred allowances). Final entries to be made through the entry box at the closing time then in effect for overnight events. A trophy will be presented to the winning owner. ($35,000 of this purse has been provided through the Province of Ontario's thoroughbred racing and breeding improvement program). Nominations closed Tuesday, September 8, 1981 with 50 nominations). *Formerly run as the Nettie Stakes.
Value of race $115,000, value to winner $69,000, second $23,000, third $12,650, fourth $6,900, fifth $3,450. Mutuel pool $192,126.

Last Raced	Horse	Eqt.A.Wt	PP	¼	½	¾	1	Str	Fin	Jockey	Odds $1
12Oct81 ^{8}Bel^1	De La Rose	3 118	4	$8^{3½}$	$8^{3½}$	$8^{½}$	2^1	$1^{3½}$	$1^{2½}$	Maple E	.30
4Oct81 ^{5}Fra^{13}	Sangue	3 118	7	$6^{1½}$	$4^{1½}$	4^{hd}	$6^{2½}$	2^2	2^2	Lequeux A	a-6.55
30Sep81 ^{5}Fra^2	Sajama	3 118	1	$7^{½}$	7^{hd}	9	9	4^{hd}	$3^{1½}$	Stahlbaum G	a-6.55
3Oct81 ^{9}WO^2	Turnablade	4 124	9	9	9	5^1	5^{hd}	$5^{1½}$	4^{nk}	Hosang G	b-5.90
3Oct81 ^{9}WO^3	Lady Face	3 118	2	4^2	3^{hd}	6^{hd}	7^{hd}	6^{hd}	$5^{1½}$	Penna D	25.55
31Aug81 ^{4}Eng^2	Viendra	3 118	6	3^{hd}	5^{hd}	7^1	$8^{½}$	8^1	6^1	Swatuk B	24.90
10Oct81 ^{9}WO^6	Regent Miss	3 118	8	5^{hd}	6^1	2^{hd}	$4^{½}$	9	7no	Grubb R	30.65
3Oct81 ^{9}WO^4	Suave Princess	3 118	5	1^{hd}	$2^{1½}$	3^1	$3^{½}$	$7^{½}$	8^{hd}	Dennie D	b-5.90
2Oct81 ^{6}Med^2	Fair Davina	5 124	3	2^2	1^{hd}	$1^{½}$	1^{hd}	$3^{½}$	9	Beckon D	12.80

a-Coupled: Sangue and Sajama; b-Turnablade and Suave Princess.

OFF AT 5:01 EDT. Start good, Won handily. Time, :25⅗, :49⅗, 1:15⅗, 1:41⅕, 2:05⅗ Course firm.

$2 Mutuel Prices:				
	5-DE LA ROSE	2.60	2.30	2.50
	1-SANGUE (a-entry)		3.60	5.00
	1-SAJAMA (a-entry)		3.60	5.00

B. f, by Nijinsky II—Rosetta Stone, by Round Table. Trainer Stephens Woodford C. Bred by Miller & West Mr-Mrs R S (Ky).

Owners— 1, DeKwiatkowski H; 2, Nahas N; 3, Nahas N; 4, Sikura J; 5, Hyde E G; 6, Sangster R E; 7, Whispering Hills; 8, Sikura J; 9, Irish Acres Farm.

Trainers— 1, Stephens Woodford C; 2, Zilber Maurice; 3, Zilber Maurice; 4, Mattine T; 5, Merrill Frank H; 6, Hills Barry W; 7, Nemett G S; 8, Allain Emile M; 9, Hickey P Noel.

Scratched—Condessa (4Oct81 ^{4}Fra^{10}).

SECOND RACE
River Downs
APRIL 25, 1983

6 FURLONGS. (1.08⅗) CLAIMING. Purse $2,800. 3-year-olds and upward which have not won three races in 1982–83. Weight, 3-year-olds, 111 lbs.; older, 124 lbs. Non-winners of two races in 1983 allowed 3 lbs.; a race in 1983, 6 lbs. Claiming price $3,000.
Value of race $2,800, value to winner $1,680, second $560, third $280, fourth $140, fifth $84, sixths $28 each. Mutuel pool $17,013. Quinella pool $14,135.

Last Raced	Horse	Eqt.A.Wt	PP	St	¼	½	Str	Fin	Jockey	Cl'g Pr	Odds $1
16Apr83 ^{7}Beu^7	Big Hock	b 8 116	7	1	$2^{½}$	2^3	1^5	1^{10}	Neff S	3000	8.30
25Mar83 ^{2}OP^{12}	Harry Caray	7 116	8	5	6^1	$7^{½}$	$5^{½}$	2no	Ouzts P W	3000	1.10
16Mar83 ^{7}Lat^9	Market Bagger	9 116	3	9	8^1	$8^{½}$	6^1	3^1	Henson J R	3000	5.60
30Dec82 ^{6}Lat^{10}	Joey R. Boy	5 116	1	8	$7^{1½}$	5^1	$3^{1½}$	$4^{1½}$	Henry W T	3000	13.40
10Mar83 ^{6}Lat^9	Red Mirage	b 9 116	12	4	3^{hd}	3^1	7^2	$5^{½}$	Arnold M W	3000	45.40
7Apr83 ^{2}Beu^4	DH In My Prime	6 116	5	2	$1^{2½}$	1^1	2^1	6	Matias R R	3000	19.00
9Apr83 ^{1}Beu^3	DH Bad Billy	9 111	6	12	12	11^2	9^4	$6^{1½}$	Wade R M Jr^5	3000	4.70
2Apr83 ^{10}Lat^6	Money Layne	5 116	2	7	$4^{1½}$	4^{hd}	4^{hd}	8no	Crews W	3000	17.40
29Mar83 ^{4}Lat^4	Reconvene	6 116	10	6	9^5	9^5	$8^{½}$	$9^{4½}$	Marte I	3000	12.90
31Mar83 ^{2}Lat^{11}	Hurrian's Blizzard	5 116	4	10	10^{hd}	10^{hd}	11^4	$10^{½}$	Costa A J	3000	41.10
29Mar83 ^{3}Lat^8	Edward Norman	5 116	11	3	5^{hd}	6^{hd}	10^3	$11^{3½}$	Adkins R M	3000	80.80
14Apr83 ^{9}Beu^7	Mr. Hurry	b 7 116	9	11	11^1	12	12	12	Eyerman M J	3000	68.90

DH—Dead heat.

OFF AT 2:29. Start good. Won ridden out. Time, :22⅗, :47⅕, 1:13⅗ Track fast.

$2 Mutuel Prices:				
	7-BIG HOCK	18.60	7.00	5.60
	8-HARRY CARAY		3.00	3.60
	3-MARKET BAGGER			5.80
	$3 QUINELLA (7-8) PAID $17.40.			

B. h, by Caribbean Line—Lotta Rhythm, by Rhymiss. Trainer Arnold Leo C. Bred by Olson S (Ky).

BIG HOCK raced close up early, came outside of IN MY PRIME to gain a clear lead entering the stretch, then increased his margin through the drive while ridden out. HARRY CARAY outsprinted early rallied along the inside to gain the place but did not menace. MARKET BAGGER improved his position but did not menace. JOEY R. BOY saved ground but did not threaten. IN MY PRIME and BAD BILLY finished in a dead heat for sixth.

Owners— 1, Arnold L C; 2, Danner W J; 3, Dykema C C; 4, Piepmeyer Deborah; 5, Yinger Marti & A; 6, Edwards W H; 7, Neil R; 8, Carr D; 9, Davis Jr & Held; 10, Bauer G; 11, Norman E R Jr; 12, Eyerman L J.

Harry Caray was claimed by Isaacs G; trainer, Isaacs George.

Scratched—Cathy's Good Taste (13Apr83 ^{9}Beu^7); Wild and Wooley (6Apr83 ^{3}Lat^7); Bo's Brick (6Apr83 ^{9}Beu^8); Lil Kicker (18Mar83 ^{4}Tam^8).

Bougainvillea Handicap

(2nd Division)

TENTH RACE
Hialeah Park
APRIL 9, 1983

1 $\frac{1}{16}$ MILES.(turf). (1.51⅗) 30th Running BOUGAINVILLEA HANDICAP (2nd Div) (Grade II). $40,000 Added. 3-year-olds and upward. By subscription of $150 each, which shall accompany the nomination, $750 to pass the entry box, Starters to pay $750 additional with $40,000 added. The added money and all fees to be divided 60% to the winner, 20% to second, 11% to third, 6% to fourth and 3% to fifth. Weights: Monday, April 4, 1983. Starters to be named through the entry box by the usual time of closing. Trophy to winning owner. Closed with 52 nominations.
Value of race $64,900, value to winner $38,940, second $12,980, third $7,139, fourth $3,894, fifth $1,947. Mutuel pool $165,400. Perfecta Pool $91,448.

Last Raced	Horse	Eqt.A.Wt	PP	St	¼	½	¾	Str	Fin	Jockey	Odds $1
30Mar83 ^{7}Hia^{1}	Lamerok	b 4 118	10	5	2½	2½	2^{1}	1^{hd}	1^{1}	Vasquez J	1.50
21Mar83 ^{7}Hia^{2}	Fray Star	5 112	11	9	5½	4^{hd}	4^{hd}	3^{1}	2^{2}½	Santiago J A	25.90
7Mar83 ^{9}GP^{2}	Tonzarun	5 110	6	7	4^{2}	3^{1}½	3½	7^{2}½	3^{hd}	Soto S B	21.40
21Mar83 ^{7}Hia^{10}	Pin Puller	b 4 110	12	14	14	14	13½	9½	4no	Velez J A Jr	11.80
7Mar83 ^{9}GP^{3}	Dhausli	6 114	2	2	6^{3}	5½	5^{1}½	5½	5no	St Leon G	20.00
21Mar83 ^{7}Hia^{3}	Gleaming Channel	b 5 113	14	8	1^{2}	1^{4}	1½	2^{3}½	6^{hd}	Fann B	19.10
21Mar83 ^{9}Hia^{4}	DH Reimbursement	b 4 110	4	1	13^{1}½	13^{3}	8½	4^{hd}	7	Smith A Jr	10.30
21Mar83 ^{9}Hia^{8}	DH Hail Victorious	b 4 110	1	3	9½	10^{1}½	9^{hd}	6^{hd}	7^{2}	Pennisi F A	f-28.10
21Mar83 ^{7}Hia^{7}	Nihoa	4 109	7	4	8^{1}½	7^{1}½	7^{2}	8½	9½	Samyn J L	20.80
14Mar83 ^{8}Hia^{1}	Unknown Lady	4 113	13	12	12^{1}½	11^{hd}	11^{1}	10^{3}	10^{2}	Perret C	3.00
7Mar83 ^{9}GP^{10}	Current Blade	b 5 114	5	13	11^{1}½	12^{1}	14	11^{hd}	11½	Bailey J D	16.50
21Mar83 ^{9}Hia^{3}	Sabr Ayoub	4 111	9	11	10½	9^{hd}	12^{3}	12^{6}	12^{6}	Hernandez C	9.20
28Mar83 ^{9}Hia^{3}	Irish Pete	4 112	3	6	3½	6^{5}	6^{1}½	13^{3}	13^{2}	Fires E	f-28.10
15Mar83 ^{3}Hia^{5}	Pimpont	6 108	8	10	7^{hd}	8^{2}	10^{hd}	14	14	Shelton R L	f-28.10

DH—Dead heat.
f—Mutuel field.

OFF AT 5:52. Start good, Won driving. Time, 1:53 Course firm.

$2 Mutuel Prices:			
7–LAMEROK	5.00	3.80	3.80
8–FRAY STAR		12.40	11.80
4–TONZARUN			10.60

$2 PERFECTA 7–8 PAID $69.60.

B. c, by Round Table—Flying Buttress, by Exclusive Native. Trainer Jolley Leroy. Bred by Brant P M (Ky).

LAMEROK was unhurried when outrun early, joined GLEAMING CHANNEL on the second turn, gained the advantage in midstretch, opened a clear lead and proved best. FRAY STAR raced forwardly between horses and was gaining on the winner at the finish. TONZARUN a factor from the outset, was shuffled back at the head of the stretch, then was gaining slowly at the finish. PIN PULLER was outrun to the head of the stretch, then finished with good energy along the outside. DHAUSLI well-placed continued on well to the finish. GLEAMING CHANNEL quickly sprinted clear, but weakened inside the final eighth. REIMBURSEMENT moved up steadily to reach contention in midstretch, but hung late to finish in a dead-head with HAIL VICTORIOUS. The latter raced along the outside and finished on even terms with REIMBURSEMENT. NIHOA lacked a closing response. UNKNOWN LADY failed to be a serious threat. CURRENT BLADE was outrun. SABR AYOUB was finished after a half. IRISH PETE was a factor for six-furlongs, then gave way. PIMPONT had some early speed.

Owners— 1, Brant P M; 2, Bucare & Stelcar Stables Inc; 3, Everett Don; 4, Heardsdale; 5, Gleis & Grod; 6, Centennial Farms; 7, Glusman Stables; 8, Allen H; 9, Polk A F; 10, Helman O; 11, Buckland Farm; 12, Moubarak A; 13, Drinkhouse M F; 14, Luro Frances W.

Overweight: Fray Star 1 pound; Tonzarun 1; Dhausli 2; Hail Victorious 4; Unknown Lady 4; Irish Pete 5.

Jerome Handicap

EIGHTH RACE
Belmont
AUGUST 29, 1981

1 MILE. (1.33⅗) 112th Running JEROME HANDICAP (Grade II). $100,000 added. To be run Saturday, August 29, 1981. 3-year-olds. By subscription of $200 each which should accompany the nomination; $800 to pass the entry box, with $100,000 added. The added money and all fees to be divided 60% to winner, 22% to second, 12% to third and 6% to fourth. Weights Monday, August 24. Starters to be named at the closing time of entries. Trophies will be presented to the winning owner, trainer and jockey and mementos to the grooms of the first four finishers. Nominations close Wednesday, August 12, 1981. Closed with 27 nominations.
Value of race $115,000, value to winner $69,000, second $25,300, third $13,800, fourth $6,900. OTB pool $364,582.

Last Raced	Horse	Eqt.A.Wt	PP	St	¼	½	¾	Str	Fin	Jockey	Odds $1
15Aug81 ^{8}Sar^{4}	Noble Nashua	3 120	3	8	8^{1}½	5½	3^{2}	2^{4}	1^{3}½	Asmussen C B	3.10
2Aug81 ^{5}Sar^{1}	Maudlin	3 112	7	3	1½	1^{1}½	1^{1}½	1½	2^{3}½	Cordero A Jr	3.90
15Aug81 ^{1}Sar^{4}	Sing Sing	b 3 109	9	11	11	11	7^{hd}	6^{2}	3^{1}¾	Venezia M	62.10
14Aug81 ^{7}Sar^{1}	Red Wing Prince	3 107	2	6	4½	8^{2}	5^{2}	4^{hd}	4^{1}½	Credidio A Jr	24.10
19Jly81 ^{8}Bel^{2}	Proud Appeal	3 126	8	9	5½	3^{hd}	4^{1}½	5^{hd}	5^{1}	Fell J	2.20
9Aug81 ^{6}Sar^{2}	Pass The Tab	3 113	10	1	3^{1}	2^{1}½	2^{1}½	3^{3}	6¾	Vasquez J	13.20
15Aug81 ^{8}Sar^{1}	Willow Hour	3 123	4	4	6½	6^{hd}	6^{hd}	8^{3}	7^{hd}	Maple E	7.10
2Aug81 ^{8}Sar^{3}	Silver Supreme	b 3 114	5	10	10^{4}	9^{1}	8^{4}	7^{hd}	8^{3}	Migliore R	19.60
15Aug81 ^{8}Sar^{7}	Lemhi Gold	3 117	11	2	9^{1}½	10^{1}	9^{1}	9^{8}	9^{11}	Velasquez J	11.60
15Aug81 ^{1}Sar^{6}	Swinging Light	b 3 111	6	7	7^{1}	7½	11	11	10^{1}	Martens G	82.90
15Aug81 ^{1}Sar^{1}	Face the Moment	3 112	1	5	2^{1}	4^{1}	10^{3}	10½	11	MacBeth D	27.10

OFF AT 5:04, EDT. Start good, Won ridden out. Time, :22⅗, :44⅘, 1:08⅘, 1:33⅕ Track fast.
New track record.

$2 Mutuel Prices:			
3–(C)–NOBLE NASHUA	8.20	4.20	4.40
7–(G)–MAUDLIN		5.20	5.60
10–(J)–SING SING			13.80

Dk. b. or br. c, by Nashua—Noble Lady, by Vaguely Noble. Trainer Martin Jose. Bred by Grousemont Farm (Ky).

Owners— 1, Flying Zee Stable; 2, Tartan Stable; 3, Sugartown Stable; 4, Daybreak Farm; 5, Meadow Bay Stable; 6, Villareal L; 7, Schott Marcia W; 8, Berry M; 9, Jones Aaron U; 10, Zantker E; 11, Mangurian H T Jr.

Trainers— 1, Martin Jose; 2, Nerud Jan H; 3, Nickerson Victor J; 4, Fernandez Floreano; 5, Hough Stanley M; 6, Barrera Albert S; 7, Picou James E; 8, DeStasio Richard T; 9, Barrera Lazaro S; 10, Conway James P; 11, Root Thomas F Jr.

Overweight: Maudlin 4 pounds; Swinging Light 3.

Scratched—Master Tommy (17Aug81 ^{10}Wat^{2}).

HITS Parade Invitational Futurity

NINTH RACE
Fair Grounds
DECEMBER 26, 1981

6 FURLONGS. (1.09) 2nd Running HITS PARADE INVITATIONAL FUTURITY. $100,000 Guaranteed. For foals of 1979 auctioned off at the Hits Parade Invitational Two-Year Olds In Training Sale of April 26, 1981. Weight, Fillies 117 lbs. Colts and Geldings 120 lbs. Winners of $50,000 or more to carry 3 lbs. additional. Non-winners of a stakes allowed 3 lbs. Non-winners of two races allowed 5 lbs. Maidens allowed 7 lbs. No apprentice allowance. No supplemental nominations. Those Fillies, having paid all nomination, sustaining, qualifying and entry fees to the Hits Parade Invitational Futurity, have the option of paying a $50 nomination fee and running in a $25,000 Added Filly Hits Parade Invitational Futurity.
Value of race $119,020, value to winner $71,412, second $23,804, third $13,092, fourth $7,141, fifth $3,571. Mutuel pool $111,964. Exacta Pool $134,645.

Last Raced	Horse	Eqt.	A.	Wt	PP	St	¼	½	Str	Fin	Jockey	Odds $1
17Dec81 ^{8}FG^{4}	Real Dare		2	113	11	6	2^{hd}	$1^{1\frac{1}{2}}$	1^{6}	1^{13}	Franklin R J	b-4.50
17Dec81 ^{4}FG^{1}	Perfect Remedy	b	2	115	3	4	5^{hd}	$3^{1\frac{1}{2}}$	3^{4}	2^{5}	Ardoin R	.90
17Dec81 ^{6}FG^{1}	Kin of Kingley	b	2	117	7	7	1^{hd}	2^{3}	2^{hd}	$3^{1\frac{1}{2}}$	Patin B C	17.70
17Dec81 ^{8}FG^{3}	To Tall Tara		2	114	5	8	$10^{\frac{1}{2}}$	9^{2}	6^{4}	4^{hd}	Copling D	12.60
17Dec81 ^{4}FG^{5}	Native Ben		2	115	12	11	$9^{1\frac{1}{2}}$	8^{hd}	$4^{\frac{1}{2}}$	5no	Frazier R L	33.00
17Dec81 ^{8}FG^{2}	Miss Pro Teen	b	2	114	2	9	6^{hd}	6^{hd}	5^{hd}	6^{4}	Guidry R D	7.90
17Dec81 ^{4}FG^{6}	Positive Dream		2	113	13	14	$12^{\frac{1}{2}}$	$11^{1\frac{1}{2}}$	$8^{1\frac{1}{2}}$	$7^{1\frac{1}{2}}$	Breen R	b-4.50
17Dec81 ^{4}FG^{4}	Caesar's Conquest		2	113	14	1	13^{6}	13^{4}	9^{3}	8^{2}	Gell V D	a-50.60
17Dec81 ^{4}FG^{2}	Quebec Dancer		2	115	4	5	$7^{\frac{1}{2}}$	5^{hd}	7^{hd}	$9^{1\frac{1}{2}}$	Romero R P	11.40
17Dec81 ^{4}FG^{3}	Stiletto		2	115	10	2	3^{hd}	7^{hd}	10^{2}	$10^{2\frac{1}{2}}$	Herrera C	32.10
17Dec81 ^{6}FG^{4}	Steve Mission	b	2	115	8	10	8^{1}	12^{hd}	11^{1}	11^{1}	Munster L	9.00
17Dec81 ^{6}FG^{2}	Lil Billy Boy	b	2	115	6	12	11^{hd}	10^{hd}	$12^{1\frac{1}{2}}$	$12^{1\frac{1}{2}}$	Barbazon D S	54.50
17Dec81 ^{8}FG^{5}	Royce's Pride		2	113	1	3	$4^{1\frac{1}{2}}$	4^{hd}	13^{hd}	13^{nk}	Barrow T	a-50.60
17Dec81 ^{8}FG^{6}	City Judge		2	115	9	13	14	14	14	14	Guajardo A	133.00

a–Coupled: Caesar's Conquest and Royce's Pride; b–Real Dare and Positive Dream.
OFF AT 4:36 CST. Start good, Won easily. Time, :22⅖, :46, 1:11⅖ Track fast.

$3 Mutuel Prices:

2–REAL DARE (b–entry)	16.50	7.80	6.90
4–PERFECT REMEDY		5.10	5.10
8–KIN OF KINGLEY			11.10

$3 EXACTA 2–4 PAID $51.90.

B. g, by Beau Groton—Big Dare, by Kentucky Pride. Trainer Dorignac J P III. Bred by Dorignac J P Jr (La).
Owners— 1, Dorignac J P Jr; 2, Franks J; 3, Robert R J; 4, Huffman D; 5, Rollins B; 6, Williams A; 7, Dorignac Margaret; 8, Bader Paula; 9, Trotter W E II; 10, Broussard J E; 11, Faldon M L; 12, Roberts M; 13, Bader Paule; 14, Roberts R F.
Trainers— 1, Dorignac J P III; 2, Marshall Louis G; 3, Calais Ralph; 4, Huffman Don; 5, Gelpi David A; 6, Mabry John C; 7, Dorignac J P III; 8, Fox William I; 9, McKean Clyde Sr; 10, Broussard Joseph E; 11, Dettwiller Dan; 12, Alleman Joe; 13, Fox William I; 14, Alleman Joseph.
Overweight: Stiletto 2 pounds.
Scratched—Knight of Truth (17Dec81 ^{8}FG^{7}).

SECOND RACE
Beulah
APRIL 27, 1983

6 FURLONGS. (1.09⅘) MAIDEN. SPECIAL WEIGHT. Purse $5,400 (includes $2,000 from the OTF). Fillies. 3 and 4–year–olds, Ohio–bred. Weight, 3–year–olds, 112 lbs.; 4–year–olds, 122 lbs.
Value of race $5,400, value to winner $3,240, second $1,080, third $540, fourth $270, fifth $162, sixth $108. Mutuel pool $14,772. Quinella Pool $15,163.

Last Raced	Horse	Eqt.	A.	Wt	PP	St	¼	½	Str	Fin	Jockey	Odds $1
	Fearless Miss		4	122	5	5	$2^{2\frac{1}{2}}$	1^{hd}	1^{1}	$1^{4\frac{1}{2}}$	Matias R R	2.20
13Dec82 ^{9}Tdn^{8}	Alice Sugar		3	114	9	1	1^{hd}	2^{5}	2^{5}	2^{7}	Gehri D L	6.60
	She's My Partner		3	114	8	9	$6^{1\frac{1}{2}}$	4^{hd}	3^{2}	3^{4}	Sosa R	17.50
20Apr83 ^{3}Beu^{4}	Papila Fair		3	116	11	8	7^{hd}	6^{1}	6^{1}	$4^{3\frac{1}{2}}$	Rice D R Jr	12.10
20Apr83 ^{3}Beu^{3}	Victoria Velvet		3	114	2	10	8^{3}	8^{4}	$7^{2\frac{1}{2}}$	$5^{\frac{1}{2}}$	Perrotta M	3.10
20Apr83 ^{3}Beu^{6}	Blinda	b	3	114	6	6	4^{1}	5^{3}	4^{2}	6^{4}	Jimenez M A	42.70
	Rullah Mae	b	3	118	4	7	$5^{\frac{1}{2}}$	$7^{\frac{1}{2}}$	8^{3}	7^{1}	Lang D D	4.00
13Apr83 ^{2}Beu^{8}	Enthusiastic Lady		3	112	7	4	3^{hd}	3^{hd}	5^{hd}	$8^{2\frac{1}{2}}$	Delaura K A	6.50
13Apr83 ^{2}Beu^{9}	Bold Nova		3	114	3	12	12	12	10^{5}	$9^{2\frac{1}{2}}$	Diehl C	96.30
20Apr83 ^{3}Beu^{7}	Mojo Work'n		3	114	12	3	10^{3}	9^{1}	$9^{\frac{1}{2}}$	10^{5}	Alicea M	64.90
20Apr83 ^{3}Beu^{10}	Evermoor		3	113	1	11	11^{hd}	11^{hd}	$11^{1\frac{1}{2}}$	11^{2}	Spickard M A	48.50
20Apr83 ^{3}Beu^{11}	Bell Dawn		3	112	10	2	$9^{1\frac{1}{2}}$	$10^{\frac{1}{2}}$	12	12	Schwing C	60.70

OFF AT 2:27. Start good. Won ridden out. Time, :22⅘, :46⅖, 1:12⅘ Track fast.

$2 Mutuel Prices:

5–FEARLESS MISS	6.40	3.40	3.60
9–ALICE SUGAR		6.40	5.00
8–SHE'S MY PARTNER			6.80

$3 QUINELLA (5–9) PAID $40.50.

Ch. f, by Bold Gun—Gala Lege, by Johns Joy. Trainer Cook Robert L. Bred by Green Meadows Farm (Ohio).
FEARLESS MISS was bumped leaving the gate then drove up to prompted the early pacesetter from the outside, took over near the stretch, and drew off in the final furlong under mild urging. ALICE SUGAR sprinted clear from the gate and angled to the rail, continued well into the midstretch, but could not match the winner late. SHE'S MY PARTNER was best of the rest. VICTORIA VELVET was bumped leaving the gate. RULLAH MAE was bumped into the winner leaving the gate. ENTHUSIASTIC LADY was finished early. BOLD NOVA broke out sharply then came in.
Owners— 1, Ryper & Routsong; 2, Sugar J J; 3, Gutheil P A; 4, Miller D L; 5, Sheets M E; 6, Horn, Harmon & McGregor; 7, Slaughter R Jr; 8, Winning Way Farm; 9, Williams J Sr; 10, Wolfe Lavaunne; 11, Group Evermore; 12, McGinnis Esther.
Overweight: Alice Sugar 2 pounds; She's My Partner 2; Papila Fair 4; Victoria Velvet 2; Blinda 2; Rullah Mae 6; Bold Nova 2; Mojo Work'n 2; Evermoor 1.
Scratched—Unruffled Sail (28Oct82 ^{3}Beu^{11}); Anarctic Queen; Gin and Boogie (22Dec82 ^{3}Lat^{5}); Lynda's Babe (17Apr83 ^{2}Beu^{12}).

SANTA ANITA PARK, NOVEMBER 1, 1982

5730—FIFTH RACE. Six furlongs. Classified allowance. 3-year-olds & up. Purse $34,000.

3490	Mr. Prime Minister, Vinzle	117	4	6	$3^{1/2}$	$3^{2 1/2}$	-	$3^{2 1/2}$	1no	5.70
3689	I'm Smokin, Shoemaker	117	3	4	$2^{2 1/2}$	1^{hd}	-	1^{1}	2^{nk}	1.50
5651	Stand Pat, Hansen	114	2	9	9	9	-	$8^{1 1/2}$	$3^{1/2}$	31.90
1133	Murrtheblurr, Harris	115	7	2	1^{hd}	$2^{2 1/2}$	-	$2^{2 1/2}$	$4^{1/2}$	13.80
5651	Double Discount, Castaneda	115	5	5	6^{2}	$6^{1 1/2}$	-	$5^{1/2}$	5no	3.80
1008	Priority, Pincay	117	9	1	4^{hd}	4^{1}	-	4^{hd}	$6^{1 1/2}$	7.30
1689	Kangroo Court, Steiner	x109	1	7	$8^{1 1/2}$	8^{2}	-	$6^{1/2}$	7^{nk}	40.20
3063	Egg Toss, Winland	x109	6	8	$7^{1 1/2}$	7^{1}	-	7^{hd}	$8^{3 1/2}$	5.50
3751	Foyt's Ack, McHargue	116	8	3	$5^{1 1/2}$	$5^{1/2}$	-	9	9	22.50

No scratches

MR. PRIME MINISTER 13.40 6.40 5.80
I'M SMOKIN 3.20 3.80
STAND PAT 10.40

Time—:21 3/5, :43 4/5, :56, 1:08 4/5. Winner—b.g.5. Command Module—Janet Dear Trained by M. Millerick. Mutuel pool $230,757. Exacta pool $480,359.

$5 EXACTA (4-3) PAID $125.00

HOLLYWOOD PARK, NOVEMBER 21, 1982

6075—THIRD RACE. Mile and one-sixteenth. 3-year-olds & up, fillies & mares. Allowance. Purse $22,000.

Index	Horse and jockey—	Wt.	PP.	ST.	¼	½	¾	Str.	Fin.	To $1
5784	Foolish Girl, Castaneda	114	7	5	4^{2}	3^{hd}	3^{1}	1^{1}	$1^{2 1/2}$	2.00
5784	Dazzlingly, McCarron	116	4	3	2^{hd}	2^{1}	2^{1}	2^{2}	2^{6}	3.60
5784	Joan's Lady, Delahoussaye	116	8	6	6^{1}	6^{1}	4^{hd}	$3^{1/2}$	$3^{2 1/2}$	11.70
5784	Delightedly, Hawley	116	2	7	$5^{1/2}$	5^{2}	$6^{3 1/2}$	5^{3}	4^{1}	1.10
5511	Jewel's Charity, Ortega	113	6	2	$1^{3 1/2}$	1^{3}	$1^{1/2}$	$4^{2 1/2}$	5^{3}	54.70
5608	Petite Maid, Sibille	115	5	8	8	8	7^{2}	$6^{1/2}$	6^{1}	37.30
5707	A Star Attraction, Pierce	115	3	1	3^{2}	$4^{2 1/2}$	$5^{1/2}$	7^{3}	$7^{2 1/2}$	30.70
5773	Ocean Sunset, Campas	115	1	4	7^{1}	7^{hd}	8	8	8	65.50

No scratches.

FOOLISH GIRL 6.00 3.40 4.20
DAZZINGLY 4.60 4.20
JOAN'S LADY 5.00

Time—:23, :46 4/5, 1:12, 1:37, 1:43 2/5. Winner—ch.f. Foolish Pleasure—Millie Ouis. Trained by G. Jones. Mutuel pool $213,470. Exacta pool $339,865.

HIALEAH PARK
TUESDAY, APRIL 26, 1983

WEATHER CLEAR.. TRACK HARD.

10th Hia— About $1\frac{1}{16}$ Miles. Turf. 3 & 4-Year-Olds. Maidens Claiming ($32,000 to $28,000). Purse $8,500. Value to winner $5,100.

2-Ballysadare(Cruguet J 113) 11.40 4.20 5.40
11-Jubilance(Alvarado V 113) 3.20 2.40
10-Marechal Neigh(Fires E 113) 4.40

$2 PERFECTA 2-11 PAID $112.60. $2 TRIFECTA 2-11-10 PAID $865.60.

Time, 1:43. Course Hard. Off at 5:32.

Also ran—Boston Broker, Black And Blue, Proud And Crafty, Utopia Grey, Erd The Third, Friendly Bet, Elton's Song, Charlie's Mercedes and Derby Dream.

4th Race Woodbine Jun. 11, 1980

5 FURLONGS. (.57⅗) 2-Year-Olds, Fillies, Bred In Can. Claiming ($16,000 to $14,000). Purse $5,200. —Canada-bred — Value of race $5,200, value to winner $3,120, second $1,040, third $572, fourth $312, fifth $156. Mutuel pool $39,289. Exactor Pool $71,713.

Last Raced	Horse	Wt.	PP.	⅜	Str	Fin	Odds $1
	SpectacularNashu	117	1	1^{hd}	1^{2}	1^{2}	2.00
29May80 $^{2}WO^{3}$	Sunny And Clear	117	2	2^{hd}	2^{hd}	$2\frac{1}{2}$	1.50
29May80 $^{2}WO^{5}$	TwentyThreeSouth	114	8	3^{3}	3^{3}	$3\frac{3}{4}$	b-13.40
	Elegant Display	112	4	$6^{2}\frac{1}{2}$	4^{hd}	$4\frac{1}{2}$	a-5.85
4Jun80 $^{1}WO^{3}$	Run Sheba	111	6	4^{hd}	5^{4}	5^{3}	10.20
29May80 $^{2}WO^{4}$	Suspicious Rose	112	7	7^{hd}	7^{8}	$6^{1}\frac{1}{2}$	a-5.85
4Jun80 $^{1}WO^{2}$	Zulu Princess	117	3	5^{hd}	6^{1}	7^{8}	4.70
29May80 $^{2}WO^{8}$	Brownie T.	114	5	8	8	8	b-13.40

a-Coupled: Elegant Display and Suspicious Rose; b-Twenty Three South and Brownie T..

Time, :23⅗, :48, 1:01⅘ Track fast. OFF AT 2:48 EDT.

3-SPECTACULAR NASHUA 6.00 2.80 3.40
4-SUNNY AND CLEAR 2.50 2.60
2-TWENTY THREE SOUTH (b-entry) 4.30
$2 EXACTOR 3-4 PAID $20.10.

8th Race Arlington Jun. 12, 1980

6 FURLONGS. (1.08⅖) 3-Year-Olds and Up. Allowance. Purse $20,000. —which have not won two races of $9,200 in 1979-80. — Value of race $20,000, value to winner $12,000, second $4,000, third $2,200, fourth $1,200, fifth $600. Mutuel pool $144,149.

Last Raced	Horse	Wt.	PP.	½	Str	Fin	Odds $1
10Apr80 $^{9}OP^{3}$	J. Burns	122	10	$4^{1}\frac{1}{2}$	$1\frac{1}{2}$	1^{1}	1.00
5Jun80 $^{8}AP^{6}$	Perplext	115	6	2^{1}	2^{2}	$2^{2}\frac{1}{4}$	10.30
31May80 $^{7}AP^{9}$	Sippin Charter	114	1	8^{hd}	$6\frac{1}{2}$	3no	54.50
26May80 $^{7}AP^{4}$	Arcadia Type	117	8	$5\frac{1}{2}$	$3^{1}\frac{1}{2}$	4^{hd}	26.90
28Jly79 $^{8}AP^{3}$	Liberal	110	9	9^{10}	5^{hd}	$5^{2}\frac{3}{4}$	31.30
5Jun80 $^{8}AP^{4}$	Cregan's Cap	119	3	1^{hd}	4^{1}	6^{1}	3.20
2Jun80 $^{5}AP^{3}$	Razorback	112	5	$6\frac{1}{2}$	7^{1}	$7\frac{3}{4}$	7.20
26May80 $^{7}AP^{3}$	Manifest Victory	115	7	4^{1}	8^{5}	$8^{3}\frac{1}{2}$	24.70
5Jun80 $^{8}AP^{3}$	Third And Lex	122	2	10	9^{6}	9^{10}	6.60
22Jly79 $^{3}LaD^{2}$	Doc's First Volley	115	4	7^{4}	10	10	74.50

Time, :22⅖, :45, :57⅕, 1:09⅘ Track fast. OFF AT 5:01 1/2 CDT.

10-J. BURNS 4.00 3.40 3.40
6-PERPLEXT 8.00 8.20
1-SIPPIN CHARTER 10.60

Black Helen Handicap

NINTH RACE
Hialeah Park
MARCH 5, 1982

1 ⅛ MILES.(turf). (1.45⅗) 40th Running BLACK HELEN HANDICAP (Grade II) $100,000 added. Fillies and Mares. 3-year-olds and up. By subscription of $200 each, which shall accompany the nomination, $1,000 to pass the entry box, starters to pay $1,000 additional with $100,000 added. The added money and all fees to be divided 60% to the winner, 22% to second, 11% to third, 5% to fourth and 2% to fifth. Weights Saturday, Feb. 27, 1982. Starters to be named through the entry box by the usual time of closing. Trophy to winning owner. Nominations closed Fri., Feb. 19, 1982. Closed with 24 nominations.
Value of race $121,800, value to winner $73,080, second $26,796, third $13,398, fourth $6,090, fifth $2,436. Mutuel pool $100.276. Perfecta Pool $120.050.

Last Raced	Horse	Eqt.A.Wt	PP	St	¼	½	¾	Str	Fin	Jockey	Odds $1
15Feb82 9Hia1	Honey Fox	5 123	1	5	$5^{1½}$	$4^{½}$	$4^{½}$	3^{3}	$1^{¾}$	Samyn J L	1.80
15Feb82 9Hia5	Endicotta	6 113	4	3	$1^{1½}$	$1^{1½}$	$1^{1½}$	2^{hd}	$2^{1¼}$	Fires E	40.30
15Feb82 9Hia3	Shark Song	4 112	2	1	2^{4}	$2^{1½}$	2^{3}	$1^{½}$	$3^{½}$	Migliore R	14.00
15Feb82 9Hia2	De La Rose	4 124	3	8	7^{3}	7^{6}	6^{3}	$4^{½}$	$4^{2½}$	Maple E	.60
15Feb82 9Hia4	Wings of Grace	4 112	6	2	3^{2}	3^{2}	3^{hd}	$5^{1½}$	5no	Velasquez J	18.00
16Feb82 8Hia1	Anti Lib	4 114	5	4	4^{1}	$5^{½}$	5^{1}	6^{6}	6^{4}	Vasquez J	11.30
26Feb82 8Hia3	Friendly Frolic	b 5 109	7	6	8	8	8	8	$7^{½}$	Espinoza J C	118.20
15Feb82 9Hia6	Lady Face	b 4 111	8	7	6^{2}	6^{1}	7^{5}	7^{1}	8	Penna D	73.10

OFF AT 5:12 Start Good, Won driving. Time, 1:47 Course firm.

$2 Mutuel Prices:				
	1–HONEY FOX	5.60	4.00	7.00
	4–ENDICOTTA		14.80	12.60
	2–SHARK SONG			15.00

$2 PERFECTA 1–4 PAID $116.80.

B. m, by Minnesota Mac—War Sparkler, by Fort Salonga. Trainer Schulhofer Flint S. Bred by Hartigan J H (Fla).
Owners— 1, Torsney J M; 2, Asbury T; 3, Tikkoo R N; 4, de Kwiatkowski H; 5, Darby Dan Farm; 6, Pen-Y-Bryn Farm; 7, Cashman Mary Lou; 8, Hyde E G.
Trainers— 1, Schulhofer Flint S; 2, Rieser Stanley M; 3, Howe Peter M; 4, Stephens Woodford C; 5, Rondinello Thomas L; 6, Whiteley David A; 7, Vanier Harvey L; 8, Merrill Frank H.
Scratched—Blue Wind (20Feb82 10Hia7).

Beldame Stakes

EIGHTH RACE
Belmont
OCTOBER 11, 1981

1 ¼ MILES. (2.00) 43rd Running THE BELDAME (Grade I). Purse $200,000 added. Fillies and Mares, 3-year-olds and upward at weight for age. By subscription of $500 each, which should accompany the nomination; $1,500 to pass the entry box, with $200,000 added The added money and all fees to be divided 60% to the winner, 22% to second, 12% to third and 6% to fourth. Weight for age. 3-year-olds, 118 lbs. Older, 123 lbs. Starters to be named at the closing time of entries. Mrs John E. Cowdin has donated a perpetual cup to be held by the owner of the winner for one year. A permanent trophy will be presented to the owner of the winner and trophies to the winning trainer and jockey and mementoes to the grooms of the first four finishers. Closed with 13 nominations Wednesday, September 23, 1981.
Value of race $218,500, value to winner $131,100, seconds $37,145 each, fourth $13,110. Mutuel pool $180,340, OTB pool $154,050.

Last Raced	Horse	Eqt.A.Wt	PP	¼	½	¾	1	Str	Fin	Jockey	Odds $1
27Sep81 8Bel2	Love Sign	4 123	6	$1^{1½}$	$1^{1½}$	$1^{½}$	$1^{½}$	$1^{2½}$	1^{7}	Shoemaker W	2.30
27Sep81 8Bel3	DH Jameela	5 123	2	$3^{½}$	5^{hd}	$6^{1½}$	$3^{½}$	3^{4}	2	Fell J	4.10
19Sep81 8Bel7	DH Glorious Song	5 123	4	7	3^{hd}	2^{1}	2^{4}	$2^{1½}$	$2^{5½}$	Velasquez J	1.70
27Sep81 8Bel4	Discorama	3 118	3	4^{1}	6^{1}	$5^{½}$	$4^{1½}$	4^{4}	4^{5}	Hernandez R	15.70
1Oct81 1Bel1	Anti Lib	3 118	5	$6^{½}$	4^{1}	$3^{½}$	6^{5}	5^{2}	5^{10}	Vasquez J	17.20
18Sep81 6Med1	Prismatical	3 118	1	2^{2}	$2^{½}$	4^{2}	$5^{½}$	6^{6}	$6^{2½}$	Cordero A Jr	4.80
26Sep81 8Key7	Real Prize	3 118	7	$5^{½}$	7	7	7	7	7	Maple E	25.10

DH—Dead heat.
OFF AT 5:14 EDT. Start good, Won ridden out. Time, :24⅖, :48⅖, 1:12⅕, 1:37, 2:01⅘ Track fast.

$2 Mutuel Prices:				
	7–(G)–LOVE SIGN	6.60	2.60	2.40
	2–(B)–DH JAMEELA		2.40	2.80
	4–(D)–DH GLORIOUS SONG		2.20	3.00

Ch. g, by Exclusive Native—Courtly Dee, by Never Bend. Trainer Watters Sidney Jr. Bred by Eaton Farm Inc & Red Bull Stable (Ky).
Owners— 1, Clark S C Jr; 2, Miron Julie; 3, Dogwood Stable; 4, Gasparri R P; 5, Federico J; 6, Hellston Stable; 7, Wildenstein Stable.
Trainers— 1, Watters Sidney Jr; 2, Fernandez Floreano; 3, Alexander Frank A; 4, Morgan Victor; 5, DeStasio Richard T; 6, Johnson Philip G; 7, Penna Angel.
Scratched—Winter's Tale (1Aug81 8Sar2).

Charles H. Strub Stakes

EIGHTH RACE
Santa Anita
FEBRUARY 4, 1979

1 ¼ MILES. (1.58⅘) 17th Running CHARLES H STRUB STAKES. $200,000 Added. (Grade I). 4–year–olds. (Foals of 1975). By subscription of $100 each, to accompany the nomination; $500 to pass the entry box and $2,000 additional to start; with $200,000 added, of which $40,000 to second, $30,000 to third, $15,000 to fourth and $5,000 to fifth. Supplementary nominations made by Tuesday, January 30, by payment of $7,500. Weight, 114 lbs.; with 1 lb. additional for each total of $40,000 in accumulated first monies won as a three–year–old and four–year–old to $160,000; then 1 lb. additional for each accumulated total of $50,000 in first monies won to $360,000; then 1 lbs. for each additional accumulated total of $60,000 to $600,000. Winners of $300,000 or more as two–year–olds to carry no less than 120 lbs., regardless of later winnings. Starters to be named through the entry box by the closing time of entries. A trophy will be presented to the owner of the winner. CLOSED FRIDAY, DECEMBER 1, 1978 WITH 91 NOMINATIONS. SUPPLEMENTARY NOMINATIONS CLOSE TUESDAY, JANUARY 30, 1979.

TIONS CLOSE TUESDAY, JANUARY 30, 1979. ONE MILE AND ONE–QUARTER.

Value of race $232,500, value to winner $142,500, second $40,000, third $30,000, fourth $15,000, fifth $5,000. Mutuel pool $923,079.

Last Raced	Horse	Eqt.	A.	Wt	PP	¼	½	¾	1	Str	Fin	Jockey	Odds $1
20Jan79 $^{8}SA^{2}$	Affirmed		4	126	8	2^{1}	$3^{1\frac{1}{2}}$	3^{2}	1^{1}	1^{2}	1^{10}	Pincay L Jr	.90
21Jan79 $^{8}SA^{5}$	Johnny's Image		4	115	4	3^{hd}	2^{hd}	$2^{\frac{1}{2}}$	2^{4}	2^{5}	2^{4}	Hawley S	13.90
20Jan79 $^{8}SA^{5}$	Quip		4	115	5	6^{1}	$5^{\frac{1}{2}}$	$5^{\frac{1}{2}}$	5^{5}	3^{2}	3^{7}	Cordero A Jr	79.80
18Jan79 $^{5}SA^{1}$	El Fantastico	b	4	114	2	7^{hd}	8^{4}	$8^{\frac{1}{2}}$	7^{2}	5^{2}	4^{3}	Shoemaker W	11.10
20Jan79 $^{8}SA^{1}$	Radar Ahead		4	120	7	4^{2}	4^{4}	4^{5}	4^{2}	4^{2}	5^{hd}	McHargue D G	1.50
27Jan79 $^{5}SA^{1}$	Thin Slice		4	114	9	9	9	9	$8^{\frac{1}{2}}$	$7^{\frac{1}{2}}$	6^{1}	Maple E	53.50
20Jan79 $^{8}SA^{4}$	Noble Bronze	b	4	116	3	8^{3}	6^{hd}	6^{hd}	$6^{\frac{1}{2}}$	6^{2}	7^{5}	Toro F	13.30
20Jan79 $^{8}SA^{6}$	Syncopate		4	115	1	5^{2}	$7^{3\frac{1}{2}}$	7^{4}	9	$8^{\frac{1}{2}}$	8^{8}	Pierce D	87.40
24Jan79 $^{5}SA^{1}$	Quilligan Quail	b	4	114	6	$1^{1\frac{1}{2}}$	1^{1}	$1^{\frac{1}{2}}$	3^{hd}	9	9	McCarron C J	56.70

OFF AT 4:38 PST. Start good for all but RADAR AHEAD, Won handily. Time, :23, :47, 1:10⅘, 1:35⅗, 2:01 Track good.

$2 Mutuel Prices:				
	10–AFFIRMED	3.80	3.20	3.40
	4–JOHNNY'S IMAGE		7.40	4.80
	5–QUIP			9.80

Ch. c, by Exclusive Native—Won't Tell You, by Crafty Admiral. Trainer Barrera Lazaro S. Bred by Harbor View Farm (Fla).

AFFIRMED broke alertly then showed his speed nearing the first turn to prompt the pace, raced out in the middle of the track while behind the leader, raced on his own courage to the five sixteenth pole, responded to some left handed urging while disposing of JOHNNY'S IMAGE and drew away in the final furlong. JOHNNY'S IMAGE broke in stride to show speed, forced the pace on the rail, continued inside to battle the winner to the stretch then could not match strides thereafter. QUIP outrun early, kept to his task to improve his position in the drive. EL FANTASTICO had no early speed. RADAR AHEAD broke off balance, moved up behind the winner into the first turn, gave way wide and gradually weakened. NOBLE BRONZE failed to response. SYNCOPATE saved ground for nothing. QUILLIGAN QUAIL set the pace to the half then stopped.

Owners— 1, Harbor View Farm; 2, Tanz Meryl Ann; 3, Tartan Stable; 4, Bradley & Peters; 5, Vail S H; 6, Vanderbilt A G; 7, Breliant W; 8, Elmendorf; 9, Fell & Good & Kessler & Lewis.

Trainers— 1, Barrera Lazaro S; 2, Frankel Robert; 3, Lukas D Wayne; 4, Whittingham Charles; 5, Jones Gary; 6, Burch William; 7, Bucalo John; 8, McAnally Ronald; 9, Alvarez Fernando.

Overweight: Syncopate 1 pound.

Scratched—Little Reb (20Jan79 $^{8}SA^{3}$); Wrangle (20Jan79 $^{9}SA^{4}$).

Expected Return per Dollar Bet

You now have good evidence that horses underbet to place and show may be outstanding bets. What you really need to know is how good they really are and how to compare various possible bets. You will learn that the payoffs do not have to be as good as most of those shown previously. Indeed, each day there will be two to four such Dr. Z system bets at a typical track.

Let us now evaluate horses on the basis of their expected return per dollar bet. This is the average return you would expect if this or similar bets were made many times. For example, suppose the dollar bet can return either $2.00, $1.50, or nothing. If the probabilities of these payoffs are 0.4, 0.3, and 0.3, respectively, then the expected return is

$$0.4(\$2.00) + 0.3(\$1.50) + 0.3(\$0) = \$1.25.$$

So, on average, you would expect to make 25¢ per dollar bet, or a 25% profit. Of course, in any particular race you will receive either $2.00, $1.50, or nothing, so that even though, on average, you make 25% on such bets, you still can lose. However, as you make more and more similar bets, the chance of being behind is less and less. For example, with one race the chance of being behind is 30%—losing the race. With two races it is 27%—losing both races, (0.3)(0.3); plus losing the first race and winning the small prize in the second race, also (0.3)(0.3); and winning the small prize in the first race and losing the second race, also (0.3)(0.3). With three races you have to lose at least two of the three races to be behind, so the probability of being behind drops to 21.6%. With eight races, the probability of being behind is 18.3%; after twenty races it is 9.3%; fifty races, 1.83%; and only 0.15% after one hundred races. Generally, then, if you have a sequence of profitable wagers you will come out ahead as long as the wagers are not too risky and you bet appropriate amounts.

Determining When There Is an Inefficiency in the Betting Pools and Thus a Good Opportunity to Bet

To calculate the exact expected value of a dollar bet to place or show on a particular horse requires that we know (1) the probability of all possible in-the-money finishes and (2) the place or show payoff in each case. This we do in our computer model.* For actual use this is too cumbersome, as there can be more than one hundred possible in-the-money finishes. Instead, we utilize simple approximate formulas that require only two sets of figures: the amounts bet to place or show on the horse in question and the total pools. The expected value per dollar bet to place is

$$\text{EX} \quad \text{Place} = 0.319 + 0.559\frac{W_i/W}{P_i/P}, \tag{4.3}$$

where P_i and W_i are the amounts bet to place and show, respectively, on horse i, and P and W are the place and win pools. So with the example on page 40, the expected value per dollar bet to place on horse 1 is

*Those interested in these mathematical details may consult Appendix B. This knowledge is not required for a full understanding of the Dr. Z system. The equations presented in this section and the constants, such as 0.319 and 0.559 in equation (4.3), were first derived by Hausch, Ziemba, and Rubinstein (1981) and Hausch and Ziemba (October 1983).

$$\text{EX} \quad \text{Place} = 0.319 + 0.559\left(\frac{8{,}293/18{,}223}{2{,}560/9{,}214}\right) = 1.20.$$

Thus, on average, you would expect to make a profit of 20% betting horse 1 to place.

The expected value per dollar bet to show is

$$\text{EX} \quad \text{Show} = 0.543 + 0.369\frac{W_i/W}{S_i/S} \tag{4.4}$$

where S_i is the amount bet on horse i to show out of the total show pool S and W_i and W are as described previously. For the example on page 40, the expected value-per-dollar bet to show on horse 1 is

$$\text{EX} \quad \text{Show} = 0.543 + 0.369\left(\frac{8{,}293/18{,}223}{1{,}570/6{,}558}\right) = 1.24.$$

So, on average, one would expect to make a profit of 24% betting horse 1.

Figures 4.1 and 4.2 graphically display the place and show expected-value-per-dollar-bet equations (4.3) and (4.4), respectively. To use them read W_i/W on the horizontal axis and P_i/P for place or S_i/S for show on the vertical axis, respectively. The line where the two values intersect gives the expected value per dollar bet. For example, for the show bet on horse 1, $W_1/W = 8{,}293/18{,}223 = 0.455$ and $S_1/S = 1{,}570/6{,}558 = 0.239$. These numbers intersect on the 1.24 expected-value line.

Formulas for Determining the Expected Value per Dollar Bet

Formulas (4.3) and (4.4) for computing the expected value per dollar bet to place and show, respectively, were based on a track take of 17.1%. This was the track take at Exhibition Park when these equations were developed.

Other tracks will have different takes, and even at the same track the take will vary over time. For example, at Exhibition Park it is now 16.3%. Hence we need to have equations for the expected value per dollar bet to place and show for any track take. They are

$$\text{EX} \quad \text{Place} = 0.319 + 0.559\frac{W_i/W}{P_i/P} + \left(2.22 - 1.29\frac{W_i}{W}\right)(Q - 0.829) \tag{4.5}$$

$$\text{EX Show} = 0.543 + 0.369\frac{W_i/W}{S_i/S} + \left(3.60 - 2.13\frac{W_i}{W}\right)(Q - 0.829). \quad (4.6)$$

These equations are just the Exhibition Park equations (4.3) and (4.4) with an adjustment to account for the fact that the track take Q differs from 0.829.

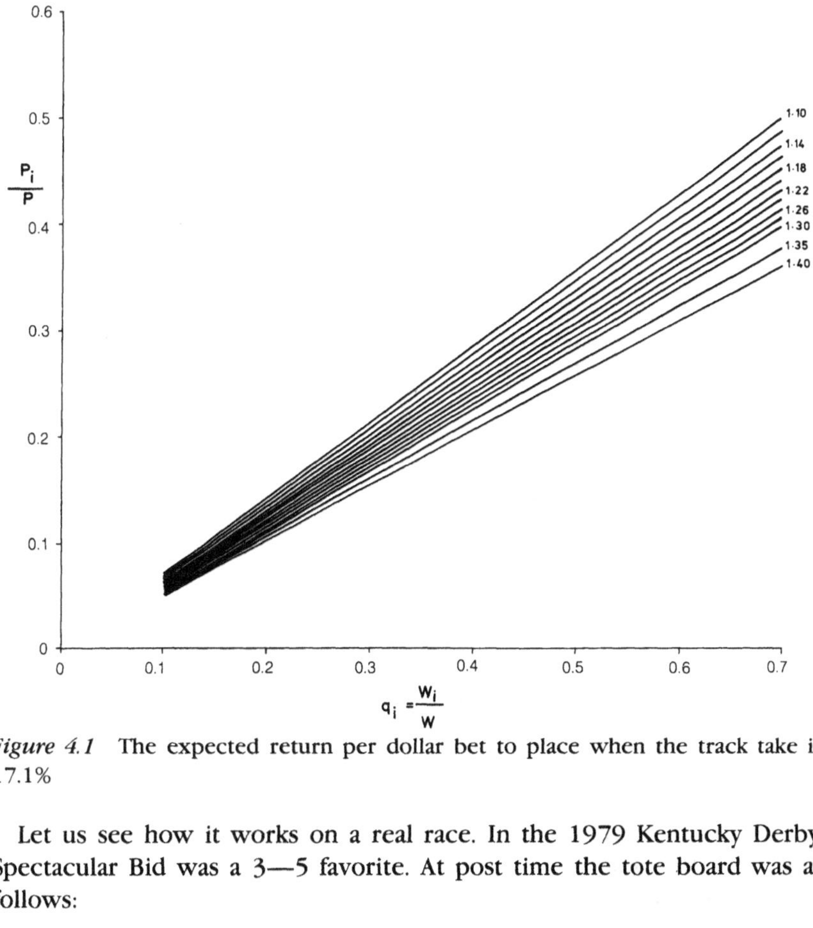

Figure 4.1 The expected return per dollar bet to place when the track take is 17.1%

Let us see how it works on a real race. In the 1979 Kentucky Derby, Spectacular Bid was a 3—5 favorite. At post time the tote board was as follows:

	Totals	#3 Spectacular Bid	Percent of Bet on Spectacular Bid
Odds		3—5	
Win	2,307,288	1,164,220	50.5
Place	949,999	339,277	37.5
Show	749,274	195,419	26.1

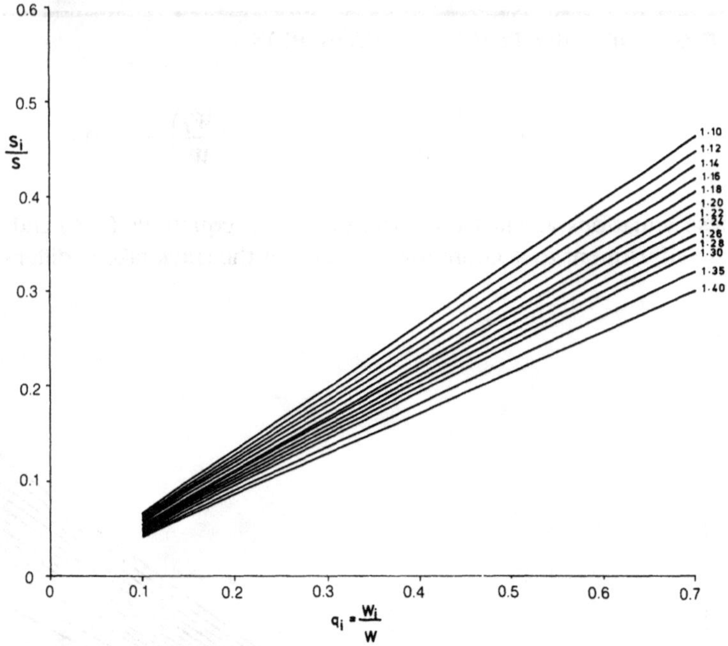

Figure 4.2 The expected return per dollar bet to show when the track take is 17.1%

Much less was bet on Spectacular Bid to place and show, relative to the total pools, than to win. For show it was only about half as much.

The track take in Kentucky is 15%, so the expected value per dollar bet to place on Spectacular Bid was

$$\begin{aligned} \text{EX} \quad \text{Place} &= 0.319 + 0.559\left(\frac{1{,}164{,}220/2{,}307{,}288}{339{,}277/949{,}999}\right) \\ &\quad + \left[2.22 - 1.29\left(\frac{1{,}164{,}220}{2{,}307{,}288}\right)\right](0.85 - 0.829) \\ &\quad + 1.10 + 0.03 \\ &= 1.13. \end{aligned}$$

So the expected value was 1.13, or a 13% profit, on average, per dollar bet. The correction amounts to 3%.

For show the expected value per dollar bet was

$$\begin{aligned} \text{EX} \quad \text{Show} &= 0.543 + 0.369\left(\frac{1{,}164{,}220/2{,}307{,}288}{195{,}419/749{,}274}\right) \\ &\quad + \left[3.60 - 2.13\left(\frac{1{,}164{,}220}{2{,}307{,}288}\right)\right](0.85 - 0.829) \\ &= 1.26 + 0.05 \\ &= 1.31. \end{aligned}$$

The expected value of 1.31 to show on Spectacular Bid thus represented an average profit of 31%. The correction amounts to 5%.

Figures similar to Figures 4.1 and 4.2 for the calculation of the expected value per dollar bet to place and show using equations (4.5) and (4.6), respectively, appear in Chapter Five. They are set up there to indicate simply *bet* or *do not bet* in any particular possible betting situation.

The chart of the race was as follows:

105th Kentucky Derby, May 5, 1979

$317,400 gross value and $18,000 Gold Cup. Net to winner $228,650; second $50,000; third $25,000; fourth $13,750. 299 nominations.

Horse	Eqt	Wt	PP	¼	½	¾	1	Str	Fin	Jockeys	Owners	Odds to $1
Spectacular Bid		126	3	7^2	6^h	$4\frac{1}{2}$	$2^{1\frac{1}{2}}$	$1^{1\frac{1}{2}}$	$1^{2\frac{3}{4}}$	R. J. Franklin	Hawksworth Farm	.60
General Assembly		126	6	1^h	2^5	2^h	1^h	2^5	2^3	L. Pincay Jr.	B. P. Firestone	a-11.10
Golden Act		126	1	$8^{1\frac{1}{2}}$	9^h	8^h	7^4	3^h	$3^{1\frac{3}{4}}$	S. Hawley	W. Oldknow-R. Phipps	19.20
King Celebrity	b	125	7	$6^{1\frac{1}{2}}$	7^4	$5\frac{1}{2}$	5^3	$4\frac{1}{2}$	$4^{2\frac{1}{2}}$	C. B. Asmussen	Che-Bar Stable	112.40
Flying Paster	b	126	9	3^h	4^h	3^h	3^1	5^4	$5^{3\frac{1}{2}}$	D. Pierce	B. J. Ridder	2.20
Screen King		126	5	10	8^1	7^4	6^h	$6\frac{1}{2}$	$6^{3\frac{1}{4}}$	A. Cordero Jr.	Flying Zee Stable	9.80
Sir Ivor Again		126	8	9^h	10	9^5	9^{15}	8^3	$7^{1\frac{1}{4}}$	D. MacBeth	Mrs. T. Christopher	a-11.10
Shamgo		126	4	2^h	$1\frac{1}{2}$	1^h	4^h	7^5	$8^{4\frac{1}{4}}$	F. Olivares	Rogers Red Top Inc.	102.20
Lot o' Gold		126	10	4^3	$3^{1\frac{1}{2}}$	$6\frac{1}{2}$	8^h	9^{20}	9^{25}	D. Brumfield	F. E. Lehmann	50.90
Great Redeemer	b	126	2	$5^{1\frac{1}{2}}$	5^3	10	10	10	10	R. DePass	Mr-Mrs. J. Mohamed	78.70

Time: :24-1/5, :47-2/5, 1:12-2/5, 1:37-3/5, 2:02-2/5. Track fast. Off at 5:39 EDT. Start good. Won driving.

Coupled: a-General Assembly and Sir Ivor Again.

$2 Mutuels paid—Spectacular Bid $3.20 straight, $3.00 place; $2.80 show; General Assembly $5.80 place, $3.40 show; Golden Act $4.20.

Winner—Gr. c. by Bold Bidder-Spectacular, by Promised Land, trainer G. G. (Bud) Delp; bred in Kentucky by Mrs. William Jason and Mrs. William Gilmore.

SPECTACULAR BID ducked in slightly leaving the gate and was settled well off the pace, moved slightly outside on the initial turn, rallied strongly after five-eighths staying well wide to be clear, ranged up outside GENERAL ASSEMBLY with FLYING PASTER inside entering the last turn and was bumped by FLYING PASTER when that one was forced out slightly by GENERAL ASSEMBLY. He responded when roused righthanded leaving the last turn, moved clear nearing the eighth pole but was roused steadily five times left-handed to draw out. GENERAL ASSEMBLY sprinted up on the pace between rivals entering the first turn, shook off SHAMGO and continued gamely when joined by SPECTACULAR BID and FLYING PASTER. He drifted out slightly entering the last turn and gradually gave way. GOLDEN ACT brushed by GREAT REDEEMER leaving the gate, stayed inside to commence his bid after a mile and finished with good courage. KING CELEBRITY moved boldly to the pace inside but was blocked with a half mile left, got clear between rivals entering the stretch and hung. FLYING PASTER broke sharply, rallied inside SPECTACULAR BID and was floated by GENERAL ASSEMBLY entering the last turn and weakened. SCREEN KING pinched back at start, moved widest to launch his bid after 6 furlongs and had nothing left. SIR IVOR AGAIN could only pass tiring rivals. SHAMGO sprinted to the pace inside, maintained a slight advantage for three-quarters of a mile and tired. LOT o' GOLD stayed in striking position for a half, then retired. GREAT REDEEMER stopped badly.

THE WINNER'S PEDIGREE AND CAREER HIGHLIGHTS

SPECTACULAR BID (Gray Colt)	Bold Bidder	Bold Ruler	*Nasrullah
			Miss Disco
		High Bid	To Market
			Stepping Stone
	Spectacular	Promised Land	Palestinian
			Mahmoudess
		Stop On Red	To Market
			Danger Ahead

Year	Age	Sts	1st	2nd	3rd	Won
1978	2	9	7	1	0	$ 384,484
1979	3	12	10	1	1	1,279,183
1980	4	9	9	0	0	1,117,790
TOTAL		30	26	2	1	$2,781,607

At 2 Years	WON	World's Playground, Champagne, Young America, Laurel Futurity, Heritage
	2ND	Dover Stakes
At 3 Years	WON	Kentucky Derby, Preakness Stakes, Flamingo, Blue Grass, Florida Derby, Hutcheson, Fountain of Youth, Marlboro Cup.
	2ND	Jockey Club Gold Cup
	3RD	Belmont Stakes
At 4 Years	WON	Malibu, San Fernando, Charles H. Strub, Santa Anita Handicap, Mervyn Leroy Handicap, California Stakes, Washington Park Stakes, Amory Haskell, *Woodward Stakes. *Walkover.

Only time Spectacular Bid was out of the money was in the 1978 Tyro Stakes when he finished fourth.

Spectacular Bid won the race easily and paid \$3.20 to win, \$3.00 to place, and \$2.80 to show. The bet to place was excellent. The bet to show was fantastic. To get \$2.80 to show with a 3—5 shot when the second favorite is 2.20—1 and the next best rated horse is 9.8—1 is a bettor's dream.

With 1.13 as the expected value to place and 1.33 to show, you would expect to receive \$2.26 and \$2.66 on average, respectively. The actual payoff when you win, of course, must be higher to compensate for the times you lose. In this case the payoffs were even higher because the second favorite, Flying Pastor, finished out of the money.

If there is a coupled entry one other correction is needed in the calculation of the expected value per dollar bet to place or show. Occasionally two or three horses are run as a single coupled entry, or simply entry, because an owner or trainer enters these horses in the same race, or there are more horses than the tote board can accommodate. The latter case is usually called a field. In the Kentucky Derby, with up to twenty starters and twelve totalizator positions, the field can contain as many as nine horses. The entry wins, places, or shows if any one of the horses wins, places, or shows. If the horses in the entry come first and second, all the place pool goes to the place tickets on the entry. If two of the three in-the-money horses are the entry then two-thirds of the show pool profits goes to the holders of tickets on the entry rather than the usual third.* Finally, the entry gets all the show pool money if the entry has three horses and they finish one-two-three. Hence you have an advantage betting on an entry. To correct for this, equations (4.5) and (4.6) for expected value per dollar bets to place and show, respectively, are modified as follows:

$$\text{EX Place} = \underbrace{0.319 + 0.559\frac{W_i/W}{P_i/P}}_{\text{Ordinary expected value}} + \Big(\underbrace{2.22 - 1.29\frac{W_i}{W}}_{\text{Correction for track-take departures from 17.1\%}}\Big)(Q - 0.829)$$

$$+ \underbrace{0.867\frac{W_i}{W} - 0.857\frac{P_i}{P}}_{\text{Correction because the bet is on an entry}} \qquad (4.7)$$

*This is the usual split. However, at some tracks the split is 50-50, so every betting opportunity gets the same portion of the profit.

$$\text{EX Show} = \underbrace{0.543 + 0.369\frac{W_i/W}{S_i/S}}_{\text{Ordinary expected value}} + \left(3.60 - \underbrace{2.13\frac{W_i}{W}}_{\substack{\text{Corrections for track-take}\\ \text{departures from 17.1\%}}}\right)(Q - 0.829)$$

$$+ \underbrace{0.842\frac{W_i}{W} - 0.810\frac{S_i}{S}}_{\substack{\text{Correction because the}\\ \text{bet is on an entry}}} \tag{4.8}$$

We illustrate the use of these formulas with the following race. Suppose 1 is the entry of horse 1 and horse 1A, that there are six other starters, and that the tote board at post time is as follows:

	Horse							
	#1	#2	#3	#4	#5	#6	#7	Totals
Odds	2—1	10—1	5—2	8—1	4—1	14—1	4—1	
Win	6,772	2,054	6,021	2,521	4,426	1,517	4,222	27,533
Place	2,825	1,274	3,392	1,591	3,123	1,098	3,123	16,335
Show	1,632	744	1,740	835	1,782	600	2,398	9,731

Suppose that the track take is 16%, so $Q = 0.84$, and that we have 10¢ breakage. The expected return per dollar bet to place using equation (4.7) is then

$$\text{EX Place} = \underbrace{0.319 + 0.559\left(\frac{6{,}772/27{,}533}{2{,}825/16{,}335}\right)}_{\text{Ordinary expected value}}$$

$$+ \underbrace{\left[(2.216 - 1.288)\left(\frac{6{,}772}{27{,}533}\right)\right](0.84 - 0.829)}_{\substack{\text{Correction for track-take}\\ \text{departures from 17.1\%}}}$$

$$\underbrace{+\ 0.867\left(\frac{6{,}772}{27{,}533}\right) - 0.857\left(\frac{2{,}825}{16{,}335}\right)}_{\text{Coupled-entry correction}}$$

$$= 1.114 + 0.021 + 0.065 = 1.20.$$

Thus the track-take correction is 0.021 and the coupled-entry correction is 0.065. This 0.086 added to the ordinary expected value makes the expected value per dollar bet on the 1-1A entry 1.20, which, as we will see in Chapter Five, would qualify it as a Dr. Z system bet. One would then expect to make 20% profit, on average, by betting on horse 1.

Similarily, the expected return per dollar to show using equation (4.8) is

$$\text{EX Show} = \underbrace{0.543 + 0.369\left(\frac{6{,}772/27{,}533}{1{,}632/9{,}731}\right)}_{\text{Ordinary expected value}}$$

$$+ \underbrace{\left[3.60 - 2.13\left(\frac{6{,}772}{27{,}533}\right)\right](0.84 - 0.829)}_{\text{Track-take correction}}$$

$$+ \underbrace{0.842\left(\frac{6{,}772}{27{,}533}\right) - 0.810\left(\frac{1{,}632}{9{,}731}\right)}_{\text{Coupled-entry correction}}$$

$$= 1.084 + 0.034 + 0.071 = 1.19.$$

Thus the track-take correction is 0.034 and the coupled-entry correction is 0.071. The correction of 0.105 makes the expected value per dollar bet on the entry of horse 1-1A equal to 1.19. This would give an average profit of 19% and qualify it as a Dr. Z system bet to show.

Hence the entry of 1-1A is a good bet to place and to show. The actual payoff depends upon whether or not 1 or 1A, or both, are in the money and the amounts bet on the other horse or horses that also finish in the money.

For example, if the finish is 1-5-3 then the payoff will be

1	6.80	5.20	3.80
	5	5.00	3.60
		3	3.60

In this case, horse 1 at 2—1 receives \$5.20 to place and \$3.80 to show, which is slightly more than the payoffs on either horse 5 at 4—1 or horse 3 at 5—2. The computation of these payoffs is analogous to those given earlier in this chapter.

If 1 and 1A both finish in the money then the show payoff increases because 1-1A get two-thirds of the show profit rather than one-third. With a finish of 1-5-1A the payoffs will be

1	6.80	5.20	5.80
5		5.00	3.60
1A			5.80

The payoffs for horse 5 to place and show remain the same, as does the place payoff for horse 1. However, the show payoff on horse 1 now becomes $5.80 instead of $3.80, exceeding the place payoff.

If the finish is 1-1A-5, the payoffs will be

1	6.80	9.60	5.80
1A		9.60	5.80
5			3.60

The show profits remain the same on horses 1 and 5, since it is the total amounts bet and not the order of the finish that matters. However, horse 1 now gets the entire place profit and the payoff becomes $9.60, which exceeds the win payoff of $6.80. This is not surprising, because the expected value per dollar bet on horse 1 to win is simply the track payback of 0.86, while the expected return per dollar bet on 1 to place is 1.20. Thus with the favorable outcome of 1 winning and 1A coming in second, the place payoff exceeds the win payoff.

To summarize, equations (4.3) and (4.4) will give you the expected value per dollar bet to place and show, respectively, when the track take is 17.1% or close to this. When the track take differs from 17.1%, equations (4.5) and (4.6) will give you the place and show expected returns, respectively. These equations are the ones you will use most of the time. Figures 5.7–5.10 in Chapter Five provide a shorthand way to determine whether or not a given horse is a Dr. Z system bet or not.

On occasion there will be an entry that is a possible Dr. Z system bet. In this case you need to use equations (4.7) and (4.8) to compute the expected value per dollar bet to place and show, respectively. We have assumed that the entry contains exactly two horses and that there is no other entry. Our calculations indicate that there is generally little change in the expected value when there are three or more horses in the entry or when you are betting on some horse, be it an entry or a single horse, and there is another entry in the race. Generally, the expected value rises slightly when you have an entry of three or more horses rather than just two horses. Similarly, the expected value generally falls slightly when an entry is present and you are not betting on it. Our recommendation is that you keep these matters in mind but simply use equations (4.7) and (4.8). They will give you quite accurate estimates of the true expected value to place and show, respectively.

Now that we have discussed how you can calculate the expected value per dollar bet to place and show on possible Dr. Z system bets, we can turn to the question of how much you should bet and provide further details about the Dr. Z system.

CHAPTER 5

How Much Should You Bet?

Why You Need to Have a Good Money Management System

We know from our discussion in Chapter Four that there are situations where bets can be made to place and show that have expected value in the range 1.15–1.30 or higher. Thus, on average, we expect our profit rates to be 15%–30% or higher. We also know that if we do not bet too much, we can be reasonably sure of being ahead with such bets when they are placed over a fairly long period of time. But how much should we bet?

We can compare various betting systems by seeing how they measure up against several reasonable criteria. Four such criteria are: (1) How much does it gain on average? (2) How fast does it accumulate profits? (3) How long does it take to reach a specified goal of a specific amount of profit? (4) How risky is the system—are you taking a big chance of losing most or all of your betting fortune at one blow?

Despite its reasonableness, the first criterion will not help us separate the good systems from the bad ones. The reason is that all betting systems have the same expected profit per dollar wagered—assuming our bets do not influence the odds, which is the case unless our bets get very large. We need to focus on the other three criteria.

To get an idea of what constitutes a good system let's look at some possible betting strategies. In the *Martingale*, or *doubling-up*, system you begin with a bet, say $1, and bet $1 again if the bet is won, but bet $2 if it is lost. If you lose again, you bet $4, then $8, $16, and so on. The idea is to have a good chance of making the $1 profit on each sequence of bets. Let's see how it works.

Win	Win	Loss	Win	Total	Loss	Loss	Loss	Win	Total
+1	+1	−1	+2	+1	−1	−2	−4	+8	+1

So in these cases, $1 is won on each sequence of bets. Trouble arises when you get a sequence like the following:

Loss	Loss	Loss	Loss	Loss	Loss	Loss	Loss	Total
−1	−2	−4	−8	−16	−32	−64	−128	−255

In this case you need to start betting huge sums just to win the $1. You may run out of money first. It may also be difficult to bet so much; suppose your $1's are really $100 bets. Moreover, in the context of horse racing, large bets can greatly influence the odds. With a high bet one simply gets poorer odds. A situation with a good expected value will become less favorable and possibly even unfavorable with a large bet. Betting along the Martingale lines leads to a number of wins of $1 and then a huge loss. Let's put aside this and all other doubling-up strategies. Doubling up after wins is just as bad.

In *pyramid* systems, also known as *d'Alembert* or *progression* systems, you up the bet with a win and decrease it with a loss. For example, you can bet $5 per race and add or subtract $1 with a win or a loss, respectively. The idea is to bet more when you are winning and less when you are losing. The amount of the bet looks like a sequence of pyramids, such as the following:

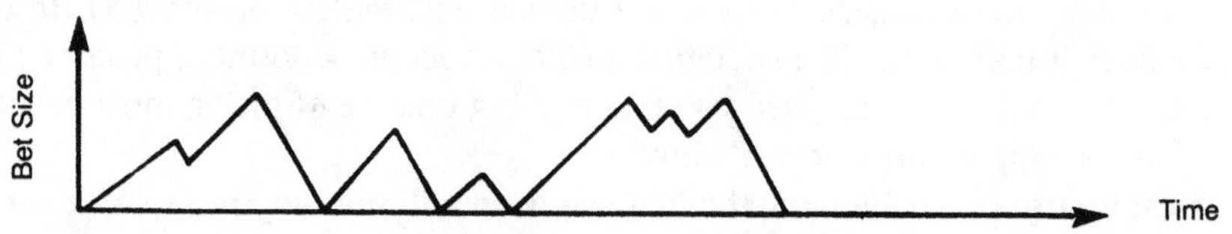

Of course, you can invert this system and bet more when you are losing, so you get a sequence of inverted pyramids or an upside-down image of the preceding graph. Again, these betting systems are arbitrary. They do not consider how good the bet is. We certainly want to bet more when the bet is more attractive. We also want to take into account the fact that as our bet becomes larger, the very act of placing such a bet lowers the worth of the bet, since the odds become less favorable.

None of these systems offers what we want: a good way to make our betting resources grow at a fast rate with low risk, while taking into account the facts that (1) we would like to bet more when the bet, not our previous wins or losses, is more favorable and (2) the size of our bet will influence the odds.

There are several possible systems that we might employ that have such desirable properties.* The basic trade-off is growth versus risk. We can look for the most conservative system, the one with the least risk of losing our betting fortune that still provides modest growth in that fortune. Alternatively, we might strive for a strategy with the largest growth rate. It will be more risky, but in the long run we most likely will have a much higher fortune. We will take the latter route and utilize the Kelly criterion betting system.

Using the Kelly Criterion to Maximize the Long-Run Growth of Your Betting Fortune

John L. Kelly, Jr. was an engineer with the Bell Telephone Company in 1956 when he discovered the betting system that carries his name. His main interest was efficient transmission of electrical signals. Little did he know that his discovery would make him world famous because of its use as the basis of a superb way to invest in securities and to gamble in games like blackjack and horse racing.†

The criterion is simple: Go for the gold! More specifically, the Kelly criterion is to invest so that *the long-run rate of growth of your betting fortune is the highest possible.*

How does it stack up against our three remaining reasonable criteria for evaluating possible betting systems: (1) How fast does it accumulate profits? (2) How long does it take to reach a specified goal of some designated amount of profit? and (3) How risky is the system—are you taking a big

---

*Those with mathematical backgrounds who would like to delve deeper into this topic might consult Epstein (1977).

†Those who would like to read more on the Kelly criterion might consult the papers by Breiman, Hakansson, and Thorp in Ziemba and Vickson (1975), as well as those by Bell and Cover (1980), Ethier and Tavare (1983), Finkelstein and Whitley (1981), Friedman (1981), Griffin (1983), and McLean, Ziemba, and Blazenko (1983). Thorp (1975) is especially lucid. These papers are highly mathematical. Although Kelly has received most of the credit, it was Breiman who really showed how attractive the Kelly criterion was around 1960. Thorp and others have used it to develop successful investment strategies. The discussion in this section contains the properties of the Kelly criterion pertinent to the Dr. Z system.

chance of losing most or all of your betting fortune? Very well, indeed! Since it is based on the first criterion, it accumulates profits faster than any other system. Indeed, it has been proved mathematically that the Kelly criterion has the following property:

> Suppose two people are wagering on the outcome of the same series of favorable betting opportunities; one uses the Kelly criterion and the other uses an essentially different betting strategy. Then the ratio of the Kelly bettor's fortune to that of the other bettor's fortune becomes increasingly large as time goes on, with higher and higher probability. After a long time the Kelly bettor will have infinitely more wealth than the other bettor with a probability approaching one. In fact, if a Kelly bettor at the racetrack also has access to fair casino bets, he is more likely to be ahead even after the first bet.

The Kelly betting system is also the best-possible wagering system in terms of the second criterion of reaching a specified goal as soon as possible. It has the following property:

> Suppose that a bettor is wagering on the outcome of a sequence of favorable betting opportunities and that he or she has a goal of reaching a fortune of $\$M$ as soon as possible. By betting according to the Kelly criterion, his or her expected time to reach M will be lower than with any other betting system, provided that M is sufficiently large.

Our third criterion is safety. What is the chance of losing all or a major portion of your betting fortune? Since the Kelly criterion is based on growth, it is riskier than some other possible betting systems. However, an adjustment of the Kelly betting amount can be made to make the system as safe as desired. We can make a trade and accept less growth in return for more security. We can do this by adopting a fractional Kelly betting system.

Figures 5.1–5.6 illustrate three possible betting situations that mirror what you are likely to encounter with some typical Dr. Z system bets. We suppose that the expected value per dollar bet is 1.20 so that you have a 20% profit on average. Let's consider three possible bets:*

---

*These examples are merely illustrative. The calculations are made using the methods in MacLean, Ziemba, and Blazenko (1983). However, they typify possible Dr. Z system bets. The betting amounts suggested as a fraction of your betting fortune are accurate for small bets that do not influence the odds too much. For larger fortunes and bets, the optimal wagers are kept down in order to reflect the effect of our bet on the possible payoffs. In actual Dr. Z system bets, the possible payoffs are numerous rather than having just one possible outcome as supposed here. But these simplified cases generate the same conclusions as would the actual bets.

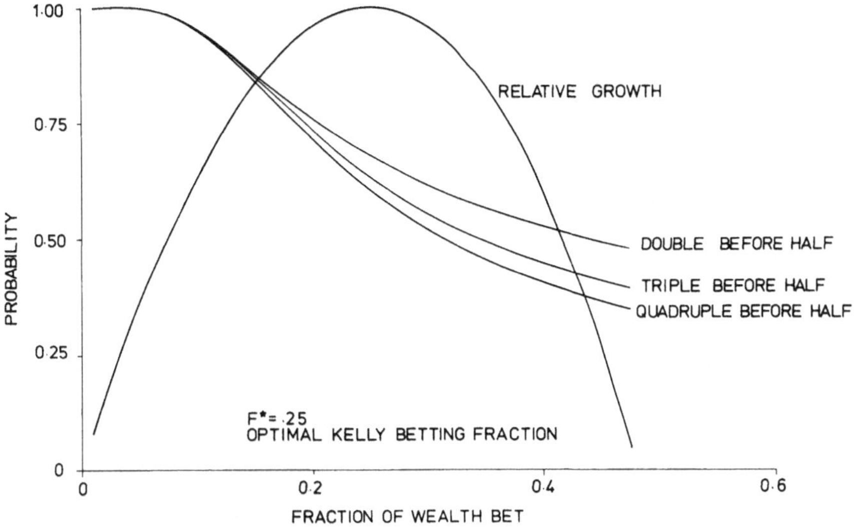

Figure 5.1 Relative growth and probabilities of doubling, tripling, and quadrupling initial wealth for various fractions of wealth bet for the gamble win $2 with probability 0.4 and lose $1 with probability 0.6

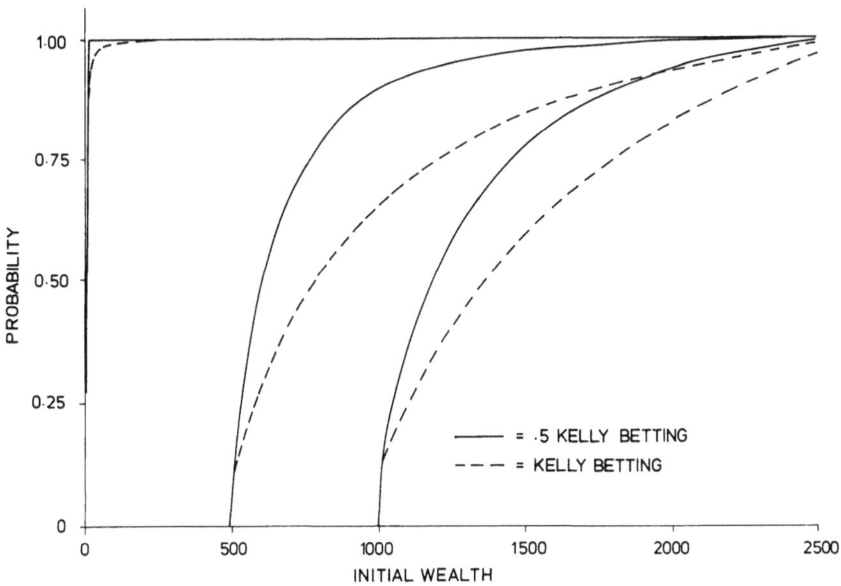

Figure 5.2 Probability of reaching $2,500 before falling to 0, $500, and $1,000 with various initial wealth levels with Kelly and 0.5-Kelly betting strategies for the gamble win $2 with probability 0.4 and lose $1 with probability 0.6

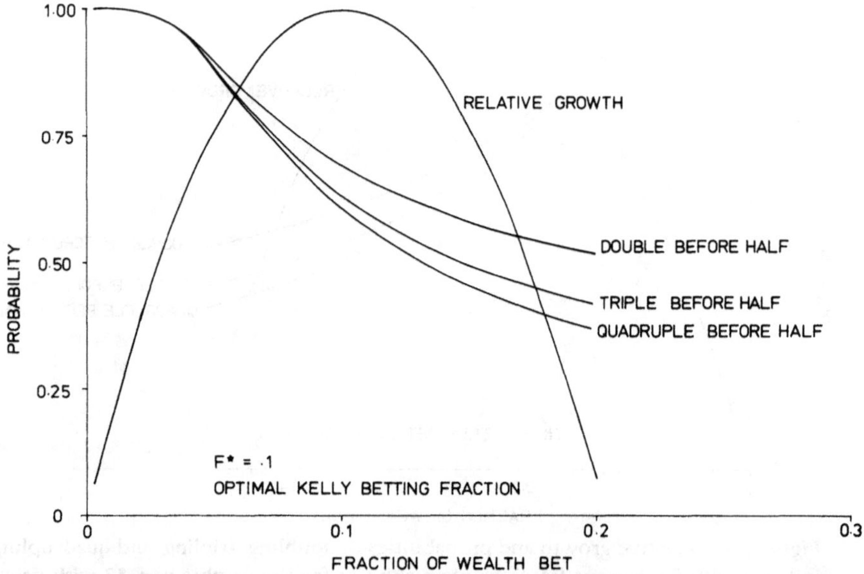

Figure 5.3 Relative growth and probabilities of doubling, tripling, and quadrupling initial wealth for various fractions of wealth bet for the gamble win $1 with probability 0.625 and lose $1 with probability 0.375

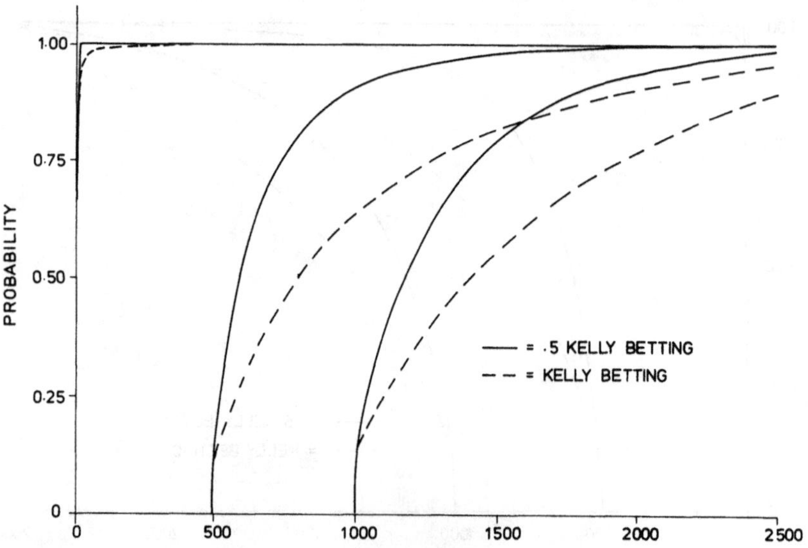

Figure 5.4 Probability of reaching $2,500 before falling to 0, $500, and $1,000 with various initial wealth levels with Kelly and 0.5-Kelly betting strategies for the gamble win $1 with probability 0.625 and lose $1 with probability 0.375

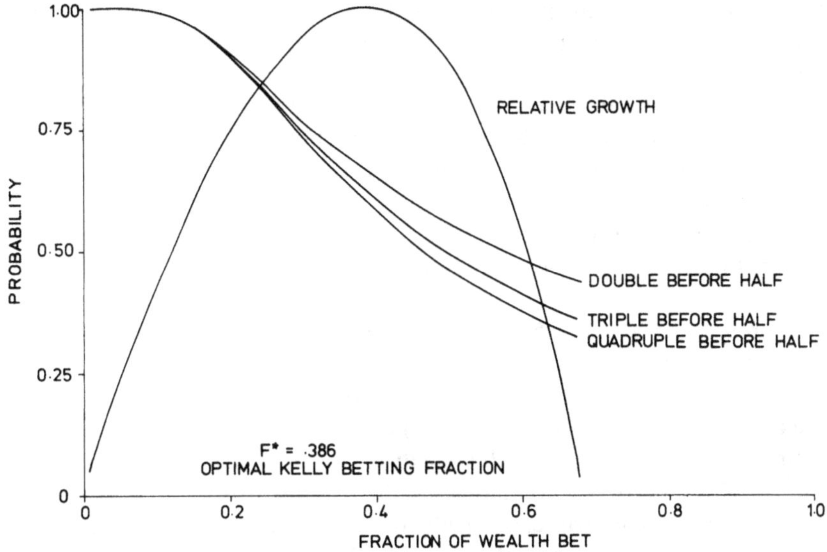

Figure 5.5 Relative growth and probabilities of doubling, tripling, and quadrupling initial wealth for various fractions of wealth bet for the gamble win $0.594 with probability 0.771 and lose $1 with probability 0.229

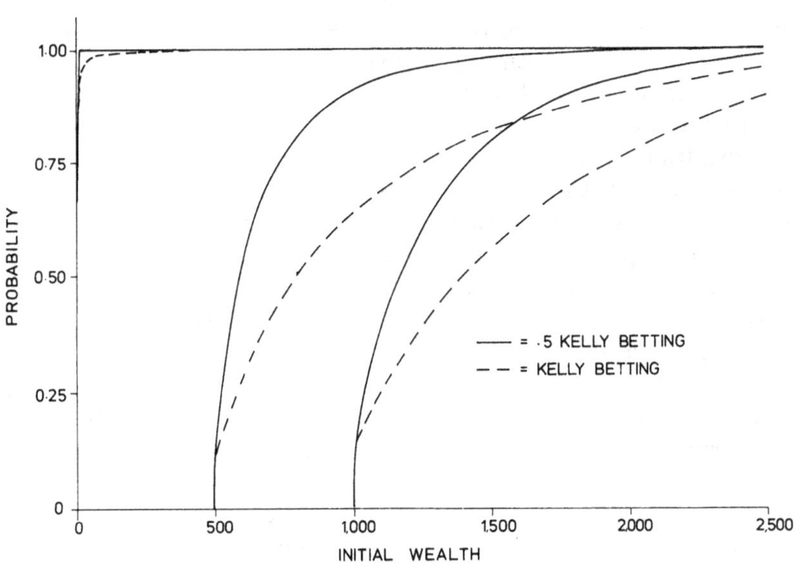

Figure 5.6 Probability of reaching $2,500 before falling to 0, $500, and $1,000 with various initial wealth levels with Kelly and 0.5-Kelly betting strategies for the gamble win $0.594 with probability 0.771 and lose $1 with probability 0.229

1. You win $2 with probability 0.4 and lose $1 with probability 0.6, assuming a place bet on a reasonably long-priced horse. In this case the optimal Kelly criterion bet is to wager 10% of your money on each race.
2. You win $1 with probability 0.625 and lose $1 with probability 0.375, assuming a place bet on a favorite or a show bet on a longer-priced horse. In this case the optimal Kelly criterion bet is to wager 25% on each race.
3. You win $0.594 with probability 0.771 and lose $1 with probability 0.229, assuming a show bet on a favorite. The optimal bet is to wager 38.6% of your betting fortune on each race.

Figures 5.1, 5.3, and 5.5 display the relative growth rates for bets 1, 2, and 3, respectively. Notice that as you bet more or less than the optimal Kelly fraction of your initial wealth, the growth rate declines. Eventually, if you bet very small amounts or very large amounts, the growth rate becomes virtually zero. To maintain high growth you need to make bets close to the optimal Kelly betting amounts. These figures also display the probability that you will double, triple, or quadruple your initial betting wealth before it falls to one-half. For example, in Figure 5.1, which corresponds to bet 1, the optimal Kelly bet is 10% of your betting wealth. This maximizes the rate of growth of your betting fortune. The chance of doubling before halving is about 70%, tripling before halving about 65%, and quadrupling before halving about 60%.

There is never any reason to bet any more than the optimal Kelly bet, since both the relative growth and the security decrease. By betting less than the Kelly bet, the relative growth decreases but the security improves. For example, if you bet half the optimal Kelly bet, or 5% of your wealth, the growth rate drops to about 78% of the maximum. But the chances of doubling, tripling, and quadrupling are all around 85%. Figures 5.3 and 5.5 show similar results for the safer bets 2 and 3. In these cases the optimal Kelly bets are larger because the risk of losing is much less. The probabilities of doubling, tripling, and quadrupling your fortune before losing half of it when you bet the optimal Kelly amount are similar to those in Figure 5.1. However, these probabilities are much higher if you make bets in the 5%–10% range, as in situation 1.

Figures 5.2, 5.4, and 5.6 give the probabilities that you will reach a goal of $2,500 before dropping to $1,000, $500, or $0 for situations 1, 2, and 3. The graphs give the optimal Kelly-bet values, as well as half the optimal Kelly-bet values, for various levels of initial wealth. For example, in Figure 5.2 the chance of going to $0 is almost negligible if you have a betting fortune of at least $100 or more.* Starting with an initial wealth of $1,500,

*In our actual calculations we have used $1 as the bankruptcy point, as the minimum bet at racetracks is $2.

the chance of reaching \$2,500 before falling to \$1,000 is about 0.60 and 0.80 with full-Kelly and 0.5-Kelly betting, respectively. Similarly, the chances of reaching \$2,500 before falling to \$500 are about 0.83 and 0.95, respectively, for full-Kelly and 0.5-Kelly betting strategies. Figures 5.4 and 5.6 provide a similar analysis for the safer cases of 2 and 3.

AN IMPORTANT OBSERVATION: In this book we advocate using the Kelly criterion. It has the property that the long-run rate of growth of your betting fortune is maximized. As we just discussed and as is shown in Figures 5.1–5.6, this entails some risk, since some of the bets made can be quite large. Those who wish to lower this risk (and also the corresponding growth rate) can simply use a fractional-Kelly betting system. Figures 5.1, 5.3, and 5.5 will give you advice regarding what fraction is appropriate for your particular preference for trade-offs between growth and risk. There will be no change in the way you decide whether to bet or not as described in the following section, "Steps in Applying the Dr. Z System." However, the amount bet should be decreased. For example, if the Kelly optimal bet is \$100 and your preferred fraction is 0.6, then you bet \$60. Professional blackjack teams use fractional-Kelly strategies of from 0.2 to 0.8. This is advisable since their edge is about 2%, and the risks of losing are quite high. In our Dr. Z system bets, the edge is considerably higher—at least 14%. It is our opinion that using the ordinary Kelly criterion rather than a fractional-Kelly betting system is preferable.

More on the Kelly Criterion: Its Desirable Properties and Limitations

We believe that the Kelly criterion is the best possible betting system for use on place and show bets and we utilize it in the Dr. Z system. It has many good properties and a few bad properties.

Good Properties

1. The Dr. Z system can be used on a race-by-race basis. For example, you don't need to worry about what races might come up later in the day or what happened in earlier races. All you need to know to make the optimal bet on a particular race is your betting fortune and the characteristics of the bet in question.
2. The more attractive the betting situation, the more the Kelly criterion tells you to bet. For example, in coin-tossing bets where you win \$1 with probability p and lose \$1 with probability $1 - p$, you simply bet that fraction of your fortune that equals your edge. So if your fortune is \$100 and $p =$

0.55 and $1 - p = 0.45$, you bet the fraction $0.55 - 0.45 = 0.10$, or $10.* For more complicated bets, such as those to place and show, the optimal bet is also a fraction of your wealth. However, if the amount of the bet is so large that it influences the odds, the optimal bet is not a fraction of your wealth. In all cases, the amount bet is larger the more preferable the betting situation.

3. The Kelly criterion allows you to take into account the effect of your bets on the odds. The optimal bet is made by considering all bets by the crowd, as well as the track take.

4. You can never really go broke with the Kelly criterion system of betting. Since you are generally wagering an amount proportional to your betting wealth, you simply will bet less when you are losing. So if your betting fortune becomes quite small, your bets will be smaller yet. Figures 5.2, 5.4, and 5.6 illustrate this clearly.

5. The Kelly criterion tells you to bet more when you are winning because your betting wealth is higher.

Bad Properties

1. The Kelly-criterion bets tend to be quite high whenever the bets look especially attractive. Thus in an extended losing streak, your betting fortune will drop off considerably. If that happens it will take quite a while to recoup these losses.

2. If you have two identical betting opportunities in successive races and win one of the bets and lose the other, you will wind up behind. For example, suppose you are betting 10% of your fortune of $100. If you win, your fortune becomes $100 + $10 = $110. Then you bet $11, and if you lose your fortune becomes $99. Conversely, if you lose first, your fortune becomes $100 − $10 = $90. Then you bet $9, and if you win you have $99. In either case, you will end up with $99, which is less than your original stake of $100.

3. Related to (2), the average rate of return of a Kelly-criterion bettor is not as large as with some other betting systems. Remember that the average return per dollar bet is the same for all betting systems. This means that some systems bet in such a way that their average profits are more than the Kelly criterion will provide. The Kelly criterion sacrifices average rates of return for high growth.

---

*If the horse has odds of O—1 and wins with probability p and loses with probability $q = 1 - p$, then the optimal fraction becomes $(pO - q)/O$. So for a 3—1 shot who wins with probability 0.4, you bet 20% of the current betting fortune, since $[0.4(3) - 0.6]/3 = 0.2$.

*Assumptions of the Dr. Z System**

There are three basic assumptions that underlie the Dr. Z system.

First, it is assumed that the market for win bets is efficient. Specifically, we suppose that the probability that a given horse wins the race in question is equal to the fraction of money bet on that horse to win. So if W_i is bet on horse i to win and the total win pool is W, then the probability that horse i wins the race is

$$q_i = \frac{W_i}{W}. \tag{5.1}$$

For example, if the win pool is $10,000 and $2,500 is bet on horse 4, then $q_4 = 0.25$, so horse 4 as a 25% chance of winning.

We know from our discussion in Chapter Three that equation (5.1) is quite accurate except for the favorite–long-shot bias. It serves us well as a working hypothesis. The errors in overestimating long shots' chances of winning and underestimating favorites' chances of winning are not a problem.†

Second, it is assumed that the Harville (1973) formulas can be used to estimate the probability of all possible win, place, and show finishes. They are based on the following reasonable idea: Suppose a race has four horses with probabilities of winning of $\frac{1}{3}$, $\frac{1}{2}$, $\frac{1}{12}$, and $\frac{1}{12}$. Now if horse 1 wins, then the probability that horse 2 is second is

$$\frac{\frac{1}{2}}{1-\frac{1}{3}} = \frac{3}{4}$$

and the probability that horse 3 is second is

$$\frac{\frac{1}{12}}{1-\frac{1}{3}} = \frac{1}{8}.$$

The probabiity that horse 4 is second is also $\frac{1}{8}$.

The idea is that the relative chances of winning of the various horses left in the race remain the same. It is as if horse 1 were eliminated from the race and 2 and 3 are vying to win the next position, that is, to come in second.

---

*This section contains some discussion that is more mathematical than the rest of the text. Understanding it is not required to use the Dr. Z system, the steps of which are explained in detail in the following section.

†Readers with mathematical backgrounds can find more on this in Appendix B.

The Harville formula for place is as follows: Let q_i be the probability that i wins the race as determined by equation (5.1) and q_j be the probability that j wins the race. Then the probability that i wins the race and j is second is

$$q_{ij} = \underbrace{(q_i)}_{\substack{\text{Probability}\\ \text{that } i \text{ is}\\ \text{first}}} \underbrace{\left(\frac{q_j}{1 - q_i}\right)}_{\substack{\text{Probability}\\ \text{that } j \text{ is}\\ \text{second once}\\ \text{it is known}\\ \text{that } i \text{ is first}}}. \tag{5.2}$$

So for our example, with $q_1 = \frac{1}{3}$, $q_2 = \frac{1}{2}$, $q_3 = \frac{1}{12}$, and $q_4 = \frac{1}{12}$, the probability that 1 is first and 2 is second is

$$q_{12} = \underbrace{(q_1)}_{\substack{\text{Probability}\\ \text{that 1 wins}}} \underbrace{\left(\frac{q_2}{1 - q_1}\right)}_{\substack{\text{Probability}\\ \text{that 2 is}\\ \text{second if 1}\\ \text{wins}}} = \left(\frac{1}{3}\right)\left(\frac{\frac{1}{2}}{1 - \frac{1}{3}}\right) = \frac{1}{4}.$$

Similarly, the probability that 4 is first and 1 is second is

$$q_{41} = \underbrace{(q_4)}_{\substack{\text{Probability}\\ \text{that 4 wins}}} \underbrace{\left(\frac{q_1}{1 - q_4}\right)}_{\substack{\text{Probability}\\ \text{that 1 is}\\ \text{second if 4}\\ \text{wins}}} = \left(\frac{1}{12}\right)\left(\frac{\frac{1}{3}}{1 - \frac{1}{12}}\right) = \frac{1}{33}.$$

The Harville formula for show follows. We now consider the possibility that three horses are in the money and call them i, j, and k. Then the probability that i wins the race, j is second, and k is third is

$$q_{ijk} = \underbrace{(q_i)}_{\substack{\text{Probability} \\ \text{that } i \text{ wins}}} \underbrace{\left(\frac{q_j}{1 - q_i}\right)}_{\substack{\text{Probability} \\ \text{that } j \text{ is} \\ \text{second if} \\ i \text{ wins}}} \underbrace{\left(\frac{q_k}{1 - q_i - q_j}\right)}_{\substack{\text{Probability} \\ \text{that } k \text{ is} \\ \text{third if } i \text{ wins} \\ \text{and } j \text{ is second}}} \tag{5.3}$$

So for our example, with $q_1 = \frac{1}{3}$, $q_2 = \frac{1}{2}$, $q_3 = \frac{1}{12}$, and $q_4 = \frac{1}{12}$ the probability that 1 is first, 2 is second, and 3 is third is

$$q_{123} = \underbrace{(q_1)}_{\substack{\text{Probability} \\ \text{that 1 wins}}} \underbrace{\left(\frac{q_2}{1 - q_2}\right)}_{\substack{\text{Probability} \\ \text{that 2 is} \\ \text{second if} \\ \text{1 wins}}} \underbrace{\left(\frac{q_3}{1 - q_1 - q_2}\right)}_{\substack{\text{Probability} \\ \text{that 3 is} \\ \text{third if 1 wins} \\ \text{and 2 is second}}}$$

$$= \left(\frac{1}{3}\right)\left(\frac{\frac{1}{2}}{1 - \frac{1}{3}}\right)\left(\frac{\frac{1}{12}}{1 - \frac{1}{3} - \frac{1}{2}}\right) = \frac{1}{8}.$$

Similarly, the probability that 4 is first, 1 is second, and 2 is third is

$$q_{412} = \underbrace{(q_4)}_{\substack{\text{Probability} \\ \text{that 4 wins}}} \underbrace{\left(\frac{q_1}{1 - q_4}\right)}_{\substack{\text{Probability} \\ \text{that 1 is} \\ \text{second if} \\ \text{4 wins}}} \underbrace{\left(\frac{q_2}{1 - q_4 - q_1}\right)}_{\substack{\text{Probability} \\ \text{that 2 is} \\ \text{third if 4 wins} \\ \text{and 1 is second}}}$$

$$= \left(\frac{1}{12}\right)\left(\frac{\frac{1}{3}}{1 - \frac{1}{12}}\right)\left(\frac{\frac{1}{2}}{1 - \frac{1}{12} - \frac{1}{3}}\right) = \frac{2}{77}.$$

The Harville formulas are used in the Dr. Z model to estimate the probabilities of all possible finishes so that we can get an overall worth of any possible bet once we know how much is bet to win, place, and show on the various horses. They are also useful in the analysis of other bets, such as those occurring in minus pools, which we discuss in Chapter Fifteen.*

PARIS ROAD, ch. g. 1975, by Jungle Road-Made In Paris, by Succession

Owner: R. J. McCance. Trainer: Robert McCance. 1980. 5 3 0 0 $5.985 **114**
Breeder: Mr. and Mrs. R. W. Hall (B.C., Canada). $6,250 1979 5 2 0 0 $3,204

21Jun80	5EP	1 1/16	:491	1:142	1:48	ft	16	115	41¾	2½	12	1½	WlknsnW2	5000	71	ParisRoad115	Gail'sPunch	10
4Jun80	5EP	6½ f	:23	:464	1:20	sy	25	116	42½	32½	2½	1h	WlksonW1	4000	78	ParisRoad116	TicketCount	9
23May80	6EP	6½ f	:222	:454	1:19	ft	20	114	1013	612	812	814	MelansnG9	4000	69	Ionion Sea 117	Hacker	10
2May80	1EP	6½ f	:222	:463	1:203	ft	20	119	85¾	52¾	12	12¼	MelansnG6	3200	75	ParisRoad119	FireBall	10
18Apr80	6EP	6 f	:232	:473	1:134	sy	40	115	812	810	610	711	WlknsnW9	4000	72	KakaDeHrt114	Citizen'sAwrd	10
14Jly 79	4EP	1 1/16	:474	1:124	1:464	ft	31	113	911	1012	913	913	FrazierD8	3000	64	ElliesBoy113	RoyalTruce	10
30Jun79	4EP	6½ f	:224	:463	1:194	gd	14	119	75½	67½	512	59¼	BrayR10	3200	70	SuperWin114	BowHunter	10
16Jun79	4EP	1 1/16	:484	1:144	1:49	sy	6	116	812	810	714	719	BrayR6	4000	49	Kevin'sAw?rd114	PlmThePea	8
30May79	1EP	6½ f	:224	:463	1:194	ft	3¾*	122	53¼	33½	2½	12½	BrayR10	2500	79	ParisRoad122	CoolArtic	10
16May79	1EP	6½ f	:223	:463	1:194	ft	23	115	75	53½	1½	12	BrayR1	2500	79	ParisRoad115	LaBelleMichell	10

The Harville formulas are based on the concept that the relative chance that each of several horses will finish first is not changed when one of them is eliminated. However, the acid test is how well they predict real races. As a test, we used them to compute the expected values using races over 110 days at Exhibition Park in 1978 and seventy-five days at Santa Anita in 1973/74.† The object was to compare the Harville formulas' estimates of the expected values with the observed expected values. Naturally, we were interested primarily in situations where the expected value was greater than one, since that is when profits are made. We therefore compared the expected values when the Harville formulas indicated that the expected value was at least 1.04 so that we could expect a 4% profit or more.

The results appear in Table 5.1. It is supposed that we bet $10 on every horse whose expected value was at least 1.04, as estimated by using the Harville formulas in conjunction with the efficient-win-market assumption (5.1). The results were quite encouraging because the estimated expected return was reasonably close to the actual average return. Indeed, even wagering such equal bets you would make a nice profit. Of course, we will want to bet more when the odds, as measured by the expected return, are higher and the measured probability of the risk of losing is lower. We do this with the Kelly-criterion betting system, the third key assumption of the Dr. Z system.

*Although very useful and accurate most of the time, the Harville formulas overestimate the probability of coming in second or third for Silky Sullivan–type horses. Those are late chargers that either have that burst of speed in the stretch to overtake several horses and win the race or they do not and finish quite far back. For these horses the probability of finishing second or third is virtually zero. The record of Paris Road, who had this characteristic while racing at Exhibition Park in 1981, follows. This overestimation does not cause us any difficulty, for we recommend that in the rare instance when you encounter such a horse you simply do not bet on the horse for place or show.

†The actual formulas used to do this are quite complex and appear in Appendix B. These data are discussed more fully in Chapter Nine.

TABLE 5.1 ***Results of betting $10 to place or show on horses with expected returns of at least* E *at Exhibition Park in 1978 and Santa Anita in 1973/74***

	Details of Bets											
	Exhibition Park 1978						Santa Anita 1973/74					
Expected Return Is at Least *E*	Number of Bets to Place	Total Net Profit ($)	Net Rate of Return (%)	Number of Bets to Show	Total Net Profit ($)	Net Rate of Return (%)	Number of Bets to Place	Total Net Profit ($)	Net Rate of Return (%)	Number of Bets to Show	Total Net Profit ($)	Net Rate of Return (%)
1.04	225	51	2.3	612	332	5.4	103	123	11.9	307	−180	−5.9
1.08	126	−101	−8.0	386	535	13.9	52	128	24.6	162	69	4.3
1.12	69	111	16.1	223	408	18.3	22	92	41.8	89	30	3.4
1.16	40	51	12.8	143	263	18.4	7	23	32.9	46	124	27.0
1.20	18	53	29.4	95	217	22.8	3	−13	−43.3	27	62	23.0
1.25	11	−27	−24.5	44	112	25.5	0	0	—	9	60	66.7
1.30	3	−30	−100.0	27	108	40.0	0	0	—	5	51	102.0
1.50	0	0	—	3	60	200.0	0	0	—	0	0	—

	Summary								
	Exhibition Park			Santa Anita			Totals		
Expected Return Is at Least *E*	Number of Bets to Place and Show	Total Net Profit ($)	Net Rate of Return (%)	Number of Bets to Place and Show	Total Net Profit ($)	Net Rate of Return (%)	Number of Bets to Place and Show	Total Net Profit ($)	Net Rate of Return ($)
1.04	837	383	4.6	410	−57	−1.4	1247	326	2.6
1.08	512	434	8.5	214	197	9.2	726	631	8.7
1.12	292	519	17.8	111	122	11.0	403	641	15.9
1.16	183	314	17.2	53	147	27.7	236	461	19.5
1.20	113	270	23.9	30	49	16.3	143	319	22.3
1.25	55	85	15.5	9	60	66.7	64	145	22.7
1.30	30	78	26.0	5	51	102.0	35	129	36.9
1.50	3	60	200.0	0	0	—	3	60	200.0

The third major assumption underlying the Dr. Z system is that we bet according to the Kelly criterion. As we discussed in the preceding sections of this chapter, this strategy provides the maximum rate of growth of your betting fortune.

The actual mathematical model underlying the Dr. Z system considers the effect of our bets on all the possible payoffs for place and show.* It then calculates the optimal bets for place and show, taking into account the track take and the relative amounts bet to win, place, and show on the various horses. To make the Dr. Z system easy to use at racetracks, we have made approximations of the true optimal solutions, enabling you easily to estimate the expected value per dollar bet to place or show on any given horse and to determine how much you should wager out of your betting fortune.

The expected-value equations appeared in Chapter Four; the equations for the optimal amount to bet for place and show follow. In the following section, we provide you with detailed steps in applying the Dr. Z system, including charts that indicate when a bet is a Dr. Z system bet and how much you should bet. To obtain the maximum accuracy, different equations are necessary for different wealth levels and sizes of the track's betting pools. All these equations appear in Chapter Sixteen; they were used to calculate the charts that appear in the following section.

Equations for place and show betting with a betting wealth of $500 follow. The place-betting equation is appropriate when the place pool is between $10,000 and $150,000 and the show-betting equation is appropriate for a show pool between $6,000 and $100,000. These equations are to be used only if the expected-value equations from Chapter Four indicate that a bet should be made.†

$$\text{Place bet} = \left[505q_i + 527q_i^2 - \left(\frac{386q_iP_i}{q_iP - 0.60P_i}\right)\right]\left(\frac{P - 10{,}000}{140{,}000}\right) + \left[375q_i + 525q_i^2 - \left(\frac{271q_iP_i}{q_iP - 0.70P_i}\right)\right]\left(\frac{150{,}000 - P}{140{,}000}\right) \tag{5.4}$$

$$\text{Show bet} = \left[131 + 2{,}150q_i^2 - 1{,}778q_i^3 - \left(\frac{150S_i}{q_iS - 0.70S_i}\right)\right]\left(\frac{S - 6{,}000}{94{,}000}\right) + \left[86 + 1{,}516q_i^2 - 968q_i^3 - \left(\frac{90.7S_i}{q_iS - 0.85S_i}\right)\right]\left(\frac{100{,}000 - S}{94{,}000}\right) \tag{5.5}$$

*Mathematical details of the model appear in Appendix B.

†These formulas for optimal place and show bets assume a track payback Q of 0.829. For other values of Q we have developed a correction factor for the optimal bet sizes. It is similar to the correction factors for expected value to place and show in equations (4.5) and (4.6). This feature is discussed in Chapter Sixteen.

Recall that $q_i = W_i/W$, where W_i is the win bet on i and the win pool is W, P_i is the place bet on i, P is the place pool, S_i is the show bet on i, and S is the show pool.

We illustrate these equations in the examples later in the chapter. Now let's go over the full steps in applying the Dr. Z system.

Steps in Applying the Dr. Z System

Full details on how to apply the Dr. Z system follow. First, there is a set of rules indicating when you should consider not betting. Second, there are some useful hints and cautions that you should keep in mind in selecting your bets. Finally, there are the steps in the evaluation of a possible Dr. Z system bet, including charts to determine whether to bet or not and, if so, how much you should bet. Detailed examples of three actual races using these procedures are then provided. More examples appear in succeeding chapters.

We recommend that you *do not bet* in any of the following situations:

1. On days when the track is not fast. This especially means heavy, sloppy, or muddy tracks, but also includes tracks listed as in fair or good condition. Horses' performances are extremely variable on such tracks.

2. When there is a minus pool and some horse or horses are bet so heavily to place or show that the payoff on all horses will be $2.10 if this horse or any of the entry horses are in the money. Minus pools and exceptions to this rule are discussed in detail in Chapter Fifteen.

3. When the horse in question is going off at odds of more than 8—1. Since these long shots are traditionally overbet, the possible payoff that you might get is not sufficient to justify the risk involved.

4. When the horse in question is a Silky Sullivan-type runner. These are horses whose records indicate that they are late chargers who come from far off the pace and either win the race or finish out of the money. You can recognize these horses by consulting the past performances. If a horse has run that kind of race in its last ten outings, don't bet it to place or show.

5. When the expected return per dollar bet is less than 1.14 for the top tracks and 1.18 for other tracks. The tracks with sufficiently large betting pools and superior horses to warrant the 1.14 expected-value cutoff are as follows:

Arlington Park, Illinois
Aqueduct, New York
Belmont Park, New York
Churchill Downs, Kentucky
Del Mar, California
Golden Gate, California
Gulfstream Park, Florida
Hawthorne, Illinois
Hialeah, Florida
Hollywood Park, California
Keeneland, Kentucky
Los Alamitos, California
Louisiana Downs, Louisiana
Longacres, Washington
Meadowlands, New Jersey
Monmouth Park, New Jersey
Oaklawn Park, Arkansas
Pimlico, Maryland
Santa Anita Park, California
Saratoga, New York
Sportsman's Park, Illinois
Woodbine, Ontario

At all other tracks use an expected value cutoff of 1.18. Figures 5.7–5.10 can be used for this purpose.

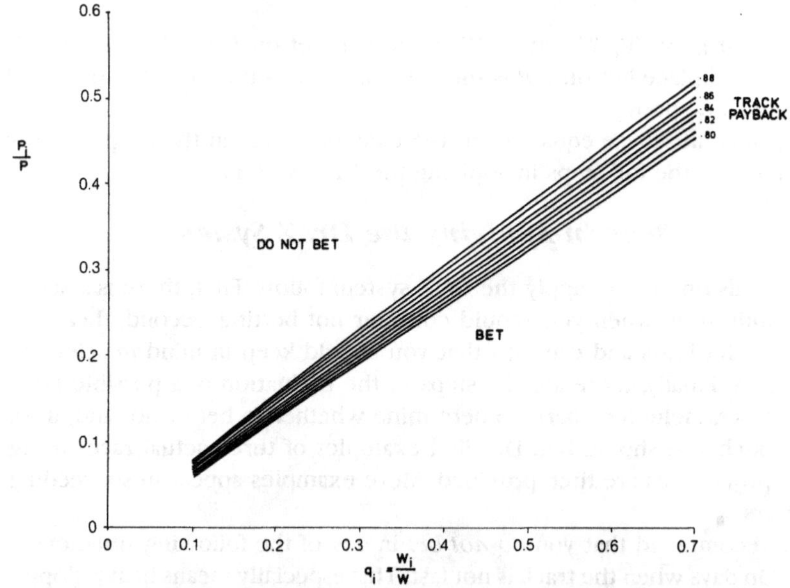

Figure 5.7 Graphs to indicate whether or not to make a place bet when the expected-value cutoff is 1.14 and the track payback varies from 0.80 to 0.88—*bet* if value is on or below the appropriate line; *do not bet* otherwise

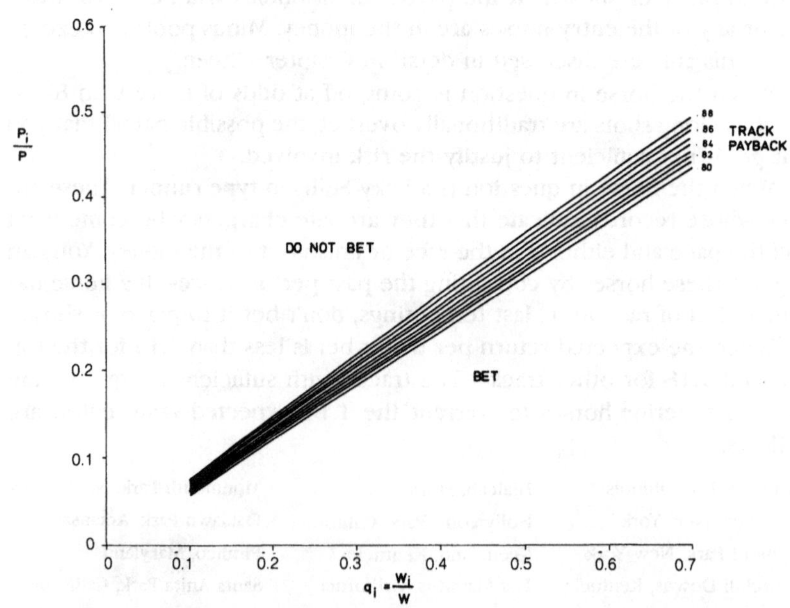

Figure 5.8 Graphs to indicate whether or not to make a place bet when the expected-value cutoff is 1.18 and the track payback varies from 0.80 to 0.88—*bet* if value is on or below the appropriate line; *do not bet* otherwise

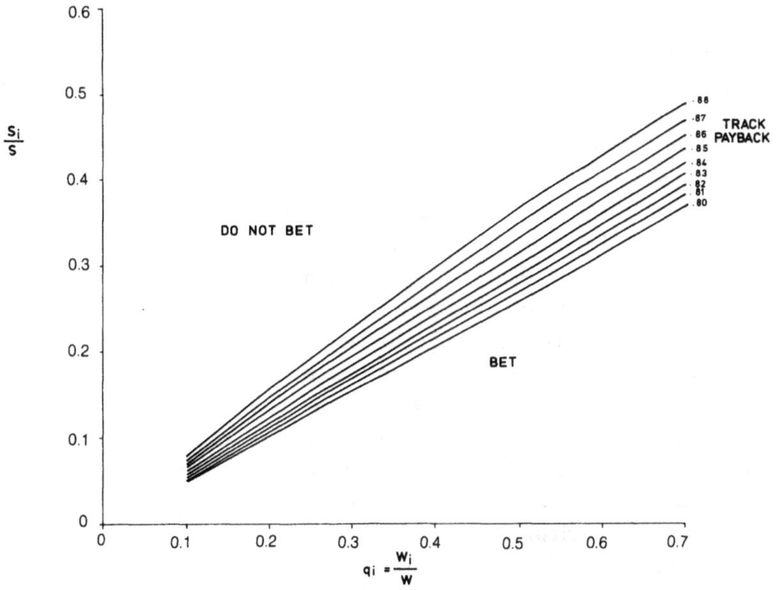

Figure 5.9 Graphs to indicate whether or not to make a show bet when the expected-value cutoff is 1.14 and the track payback varies from 0.80 to 0.88—***bet*** if value is on or below the appropriate line; ***do not bet*** otherwise

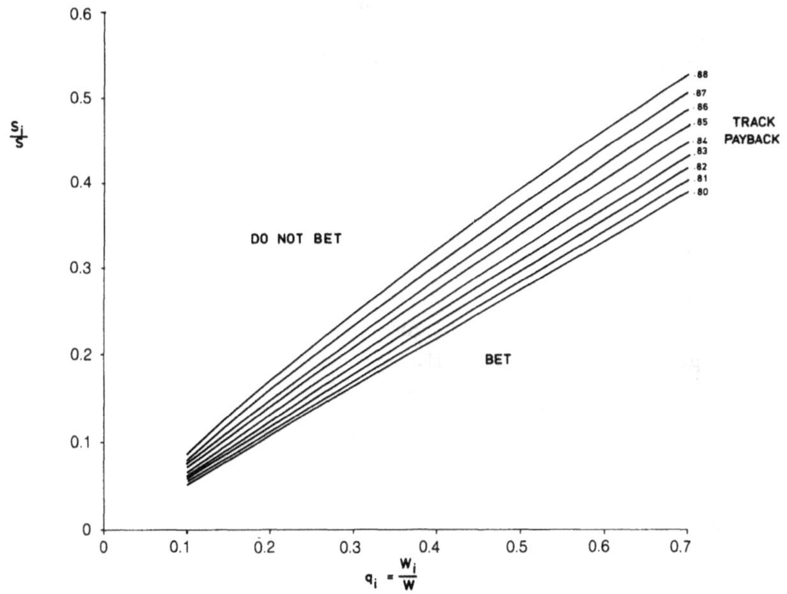

Figure 5.10 Graphs to indicate whether or not to make a show bet when the expected-value cutoff is 1.18 and the track payback varies from 0.80 to 0.88—***bet*** if value is on or below the appropriate line; ***do not bet*** otherwise

We recommend that you *display caution* in the following circumstances:

1. It may be advisable not to bet on horses coming off a long layoff. A particularly dangerous situation is the standout who, for example, last year won six of eight starts and was second in the other two races. He has not run this year. Now it is August and he is made a prohibitive favorite in a long race, all on the basis of his past record and some excellent recent workouts at short distances. There is a good chance this horse will die in the stretch and finish out of the money. In general you have to use some judgment in these long-layoff situations. If you want to be cautious, do not bet on any horse that has not run in the last two to three months.

2. You should be cautious betting on first-time starters. Super workouts are no substitute for actual racing experience. Bet on them only if the conditions seem ideal otherwise and the odds are excellent.

3. We argued in Chapters Three through Five that the win odds generated by the crowd can be used with the Harville formulas to generate good predictors of a horse's chances of finishing second or third, so we bet when the expected payoff was large in comparison with fair odds. This was done without reference to the horses' and jockeys' actual records. There is no doubt, however, that a person feels more comfortable when the bet is on a horse that is frequently in the money, at today's distance, running against similar quality horses, and with his regular jockey—ideally one of the top jockeys at the current meet. When the situation is not so comfortable as all that, you may wish to lower your bet. On average, this caution should provide you with the greater security you wish and only slightly less growth in your betting fortune.

Expected-Value Cutoff

Size of Place Pool ($)	1.14	1.18
Small 2,000–9,999	Use Figure 5.11	Use Figure 5.14
Medium 10,000–49,999	Use Figure 5.12	Use Figure 5.15
Large 50,000+	Use Figure 5.13	Use Figure 5.16

Size of Show Pool ($)	1.14	1.18
Small 1,200–5,999	Use Figure 5.17	Use Figure 5.20
Medium 6,000–29,999	Use Figure 5.18	Use Figure 5.21
Large 30,000+	Use Figure 5.19	Use Figure 5.22

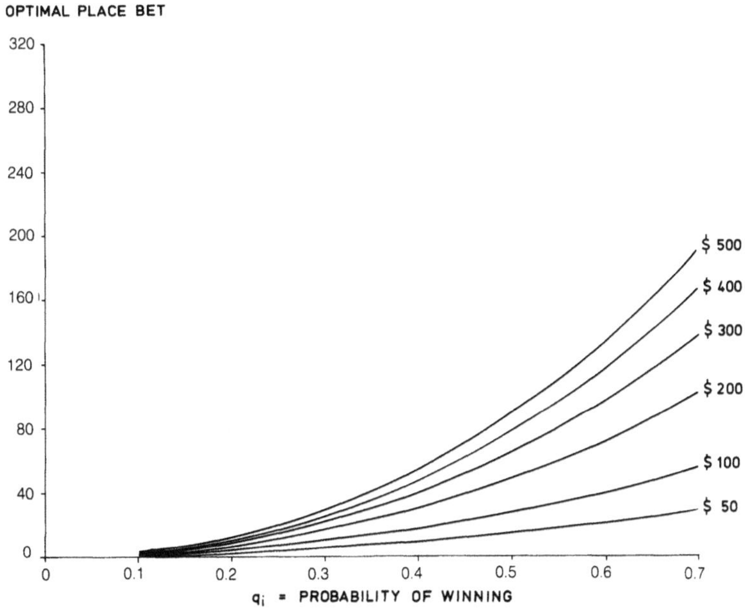

Figure 5.11 Optimal place bet for various q_i and betting-wealth levels when the expected return is 1.14 and the place pool is small ($2,000–$9,999)

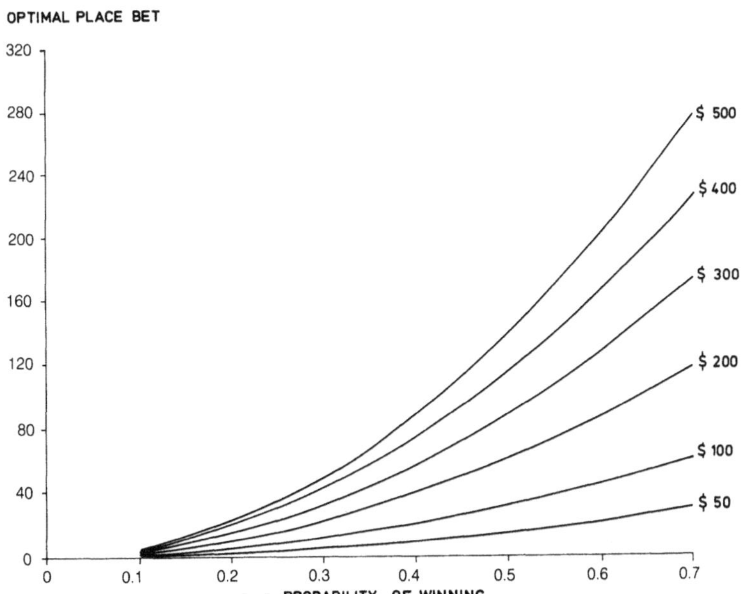

Figure 5.12 Optimal place bet for various q_i and betting-wealth levels when the expected return is 1.14 and the place pool is medium ($10,000–$49,999)

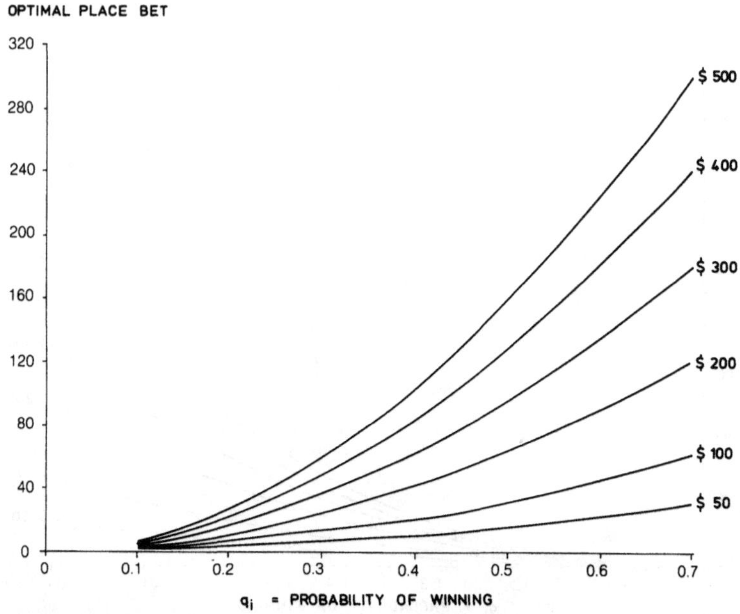

Figure 5.13 Optimal place bet for various q_i and betting-wealth levels when the expected return is 1.14 and the place pool is large ($50,000+)

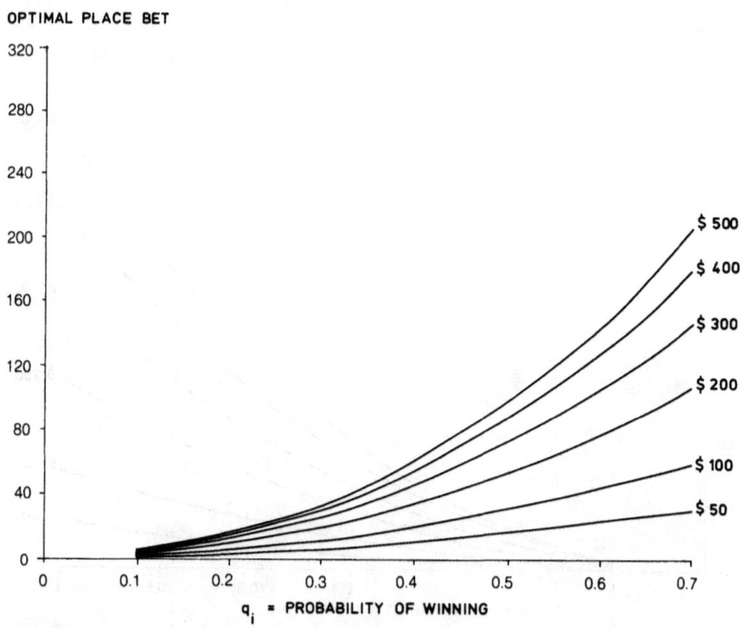

Figure 5.14 Optimal place bet for various q_i and betting-wealth levels when the expected return is 1.18 and the place pool is small ($2,000–$9,999)

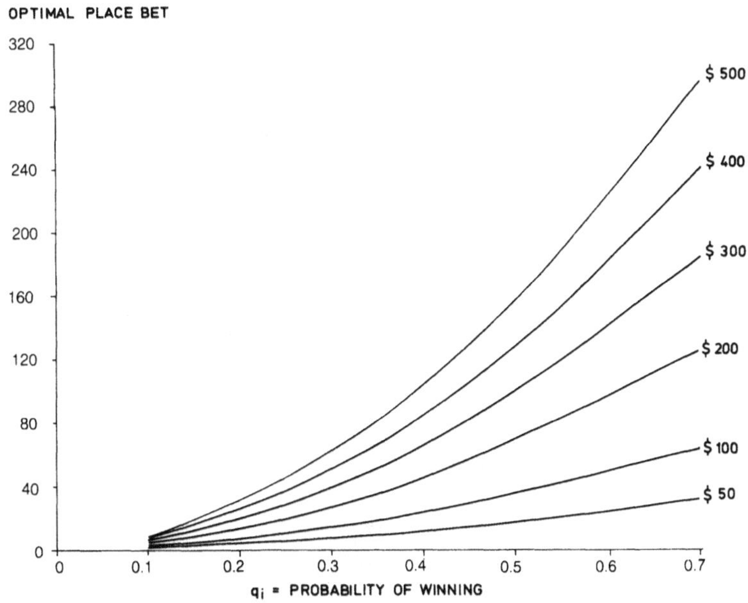

Figure 5.15 Optimal place bet for various q_i and betting-wealth levels when the expected return is 1.18 and the place pool is medium ($10,000–$49,999)

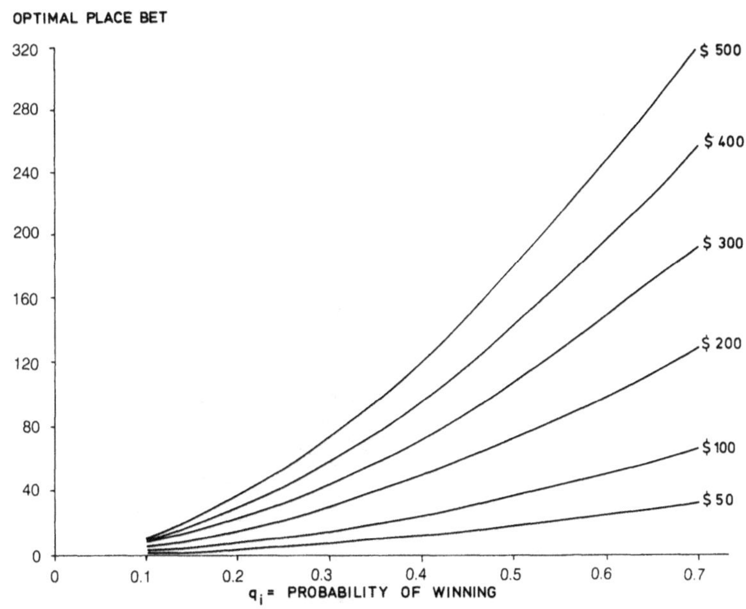

Figure 5.16 Optimal place bet for various q_i and betting-wealth levels when the expected return is 1.18 and the place pool is large ($50,000 +)

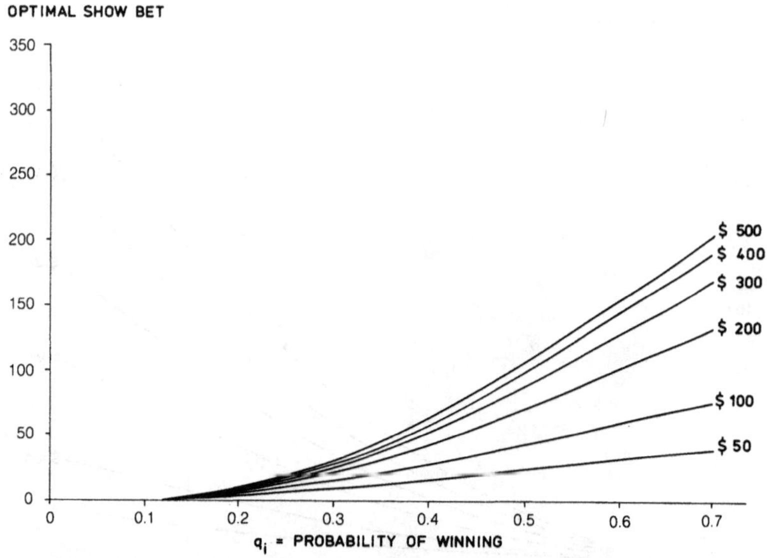

Figure 5.17 Optimal show bet for various q_i and betting-wealth levels when the expected return is 1.14 and the show pool is small ($1,200–$5,999)

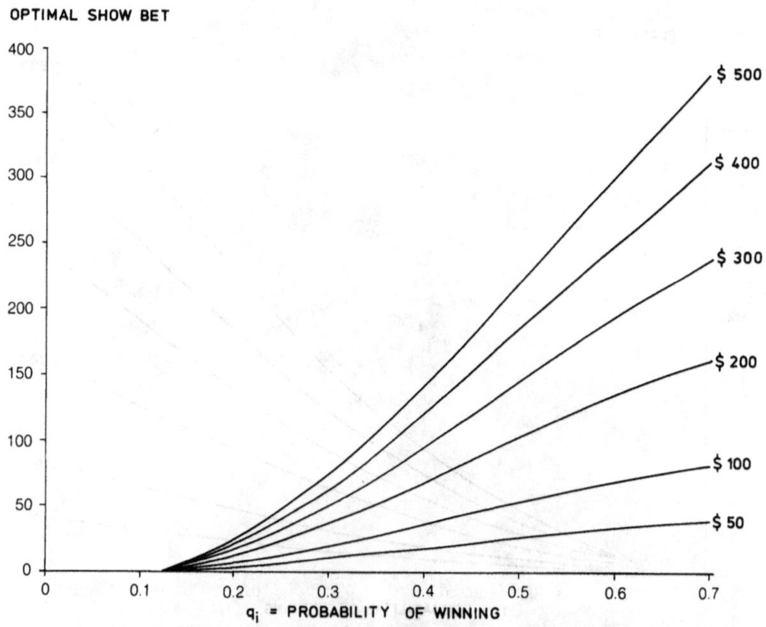

Figure 5.18 Optimal show bet for various q_i and betting-wealth levels when the expected return is 1.14 and the show pool is medium ($6,000–$29,999)

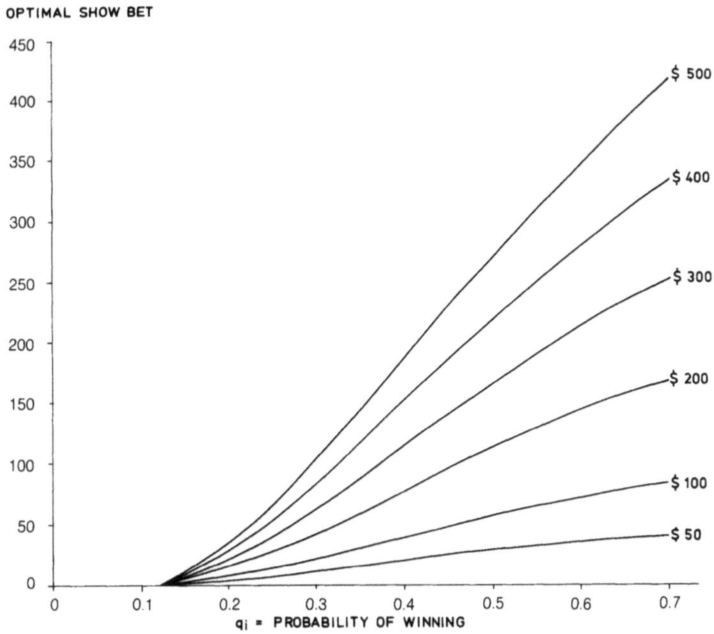

Figure 5.19 Optimal show bet for various q_i and betting-wealth levels when the expected return is 1.14 and the show pool is large ($30,000+)

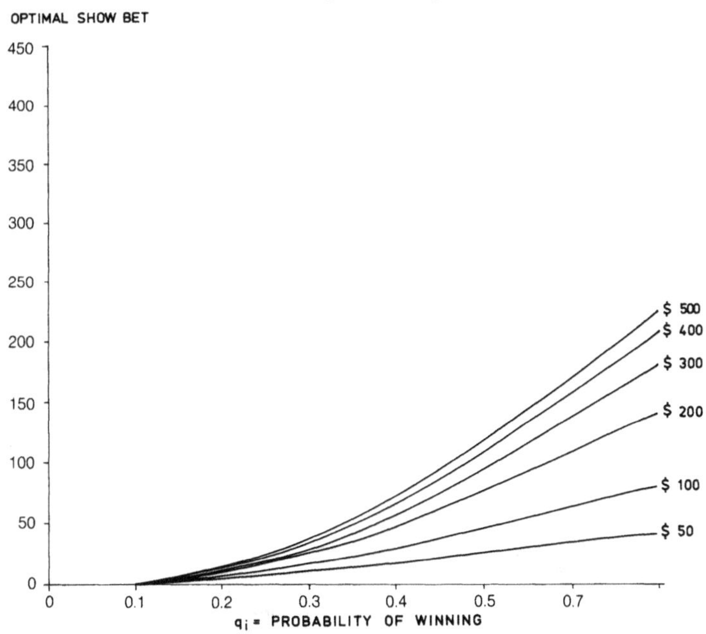

Figure 5.20 Optimal show bet for various q_i and betting-wealth levels when the expected return is 1.18 and the show pool is small ($1,200–$5,999)

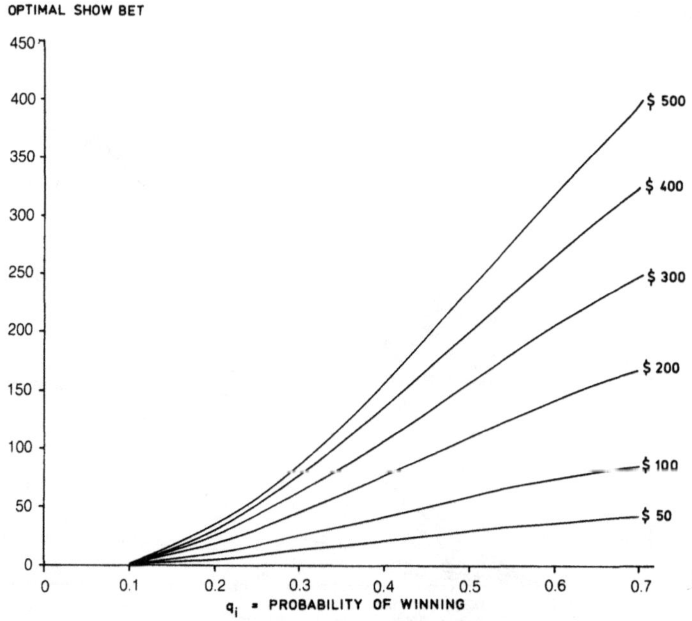

Figure 5.21 Optimal show bet for various q_i and betting-wealth levels when the expected return is 1.18 and the show pool is medium ($6,000–$29,999)

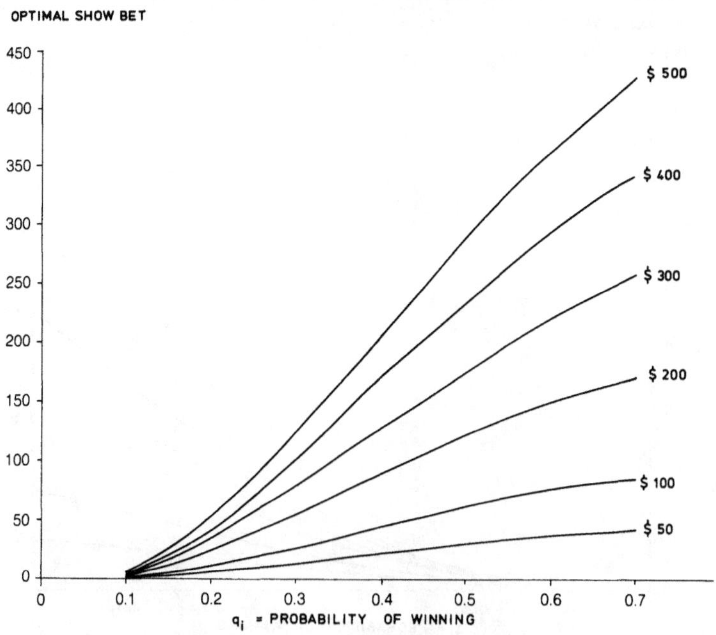

Figure 5.22 Optimal show bet for various q_i and betting-wealth levels when the expected return is 1.18 and the show pool is large ($30,000+)

We recommend the following betting procedure for determining and placing Dr. Z system bets.

1. Situate yourself so that you have a clear view of the tote board mutuels and are in a position to be able to place a bet near the end of the betting period. Most tracks have two or more tote boards. The one that is best to use is often the one farthest away from the finish line. Check to see how long the lines are in a few races so that you can judge how late you can wait before betting. The lines may be shorter in the clubhouse. If you are with a friend, one of you can be watching the tote board and the other holding a place in the betting-window lineup.

2. Start looking for possible Dr. Z system bets four to six minutes before post time or even earlier. Use the following charts to see how good a promising bet really is before you bet. Recheck it when you are ready to bet. Do not bet any sooner than necessary.

3. Figures 5.7–5.10 may be used to determine whether or not you should bet. If there is a possible place or show bet, you will need to look at only one figure. If you are considering a place bet and a show bet you will need to look at two figures. If you are at a top track with an expected-value cutoff of 1.14, use Figure 5.7 for place and Figure 5.9 for show. If you are at another track, use Figure 5.8 for place and Figure 5.10 for show.

To use these figures evaluate W_i/W for the horizontal axis and P_i/P or S_i/S for the vertical axis for place and show, respectively. If the point where the values intersect is *on or below the line* corresponding to the track payback of your track, then bet. If it is *above the line, do not bet.*

For example, consider a possible show bet on horse 3 at Churchill Downs. The expected-value cutoff is 1.14, so we use Figure 5.9. The track take is 15%, so the track payback is 0.85. Suppose $W_3 = \$50{,}000$ is bet on 3 to win, out of a total win pool of $W = \$100{,}000$, and $S_3 = \$20{,}000$ is bet on 3 to show, out of a show pool of $S = \$50{,}000$. Then $W_3/W = 0.5$ and $S_3/S = 0.4$. Since these numbers cross above the $Q = 0.85$ line, you do not bet. If instead $S_3 = \$15{,}000$, the $S_3/S = 0.3$, and you should bet since the numbers now cross below the $Q = 0.85$ line.

Now consider a possible place bet on horse 5 at Exhibition Park. The expected-value cutoff is 1.18, so we use Figure 5.8. The track take is 16.3%, so the track payback is about 0.84. Suppose $W_5 = \$10{,}000$, $W = \$30{,}000$, $P_5 = \$2{,}000$, and $P = \$12{,}000$. Then $W_5/W = 0.333$ and $P_5/P = 0.167$. Since these numbers cross below the $Q = 0.84$ line, you should bet.

4. Figures 5.11–5.22 may be used to determine how much you should bet. Again, you consult one figure for each possible bet.

To use these figures, first evaluate $q_i = W_i/W$ for the horizontal axis then read off the optimal Kelly bet on the vertical axis corresponding to the amount of your betting wealth. For example, for the show bet on horse 3 at Churchill Downs with an expected-value cutoff of 1.14 and a large show pool of \$50,000, we use Figure 5.19. Since $q_3 = W_3/W =$ \$50,000/\$100,000 = 0.5, the optimal bet with a betting fortune of \$300 is about \$170; with a fortune of \$500 it is about \$275.

For the place bet on horse 5 at Exhibition Park, with an expected-value cutoff of 1.18 and a medium-sized place pool of \$12,000, we use Figure 5.15. Since $q_5 = W_5/W =$ \$10,000/\$30,000 = 0.333, the optimal bet with a betting fortune of \$200 is \$36; with a fortune of \$50 it is \$10.

Let's now look at some Dr. Z system bets on real races.

The First Race, Churchill Downs, Louisville, Kentucky, May 6, 1983

The actual payoff that you will receive from a Dr. Z system bet can vary greatly. Our main premise is that you should bet when the odds are favorable for you—that is, when the expected return per dollar bet is sufficiently high, say at least 1.14. In this and the next two sections, we show how the Dr. Z system was used when the payoff was expected to be (1) medium, as on Fern Creek in the first race at Churchill Downs on May 6, 1983; (2) small, as on C'est Moi Cheri in the sixth race at Hollywood Park on June 5, 1982; and (3) relatively large, as on B.C. Place in the King's Favor Purse at Longacres on August 14, 1983. All these were outstanding bets. It is important that you understand that the expected return and not the expected payoff is the crucial concept for selecting good bets.

Fern Creek was a typical Dr. Z system bet. The program, past performances, experts' selections, and chart of this race appear in the section "How Accurate is the Morning Line?" on page 31 in Chapter Three. The tote boards were as follows:

	Totals	#7 Fern Creek	Expected Value per Dollar Bet on Fern Creek to Show[a]	Optimal Bet to Show on Fern Creek[a]
With six minutes to post time				
Odds		4—1		
Win	96,028	15,563		
Show	37,193	3,549	1.24	
With two minutes to post time				
Odds		4—1		
Win	118,803	19,230		
Show	45,209	4,163	1.26	28

[a]Since the track take in Kentucky is 15% for thoroughbreds, the expected value per dollar bet on Fern Creek to show using equation (4.6) is ►

With the detachable cards, a quick check of Figure 5.9 (the track take in Kentucky is 15%) with $q_i = 0.1619$ and $S_i/S = 0.092$ indicates a Dr. Z bet should be made. Figure 5.22 suggests a bet of \$24.* The final tote board values were

*The detachable cards give the optimal bet when the expected return to show is 1.14 or 1.18. Fern Creek, however, has an expected return of 1.26. This difference explains why the "true" optimal bet using equation (5.5) is higher than the "conservative" optimal bet from the cards. When one is using a 1.14 cutoff and the expected value greatly exceeds this value, it is better to use the 1.18 card instead—it will give a more accurate bet. By keeping to the 1.14 card, your bet will be more conservative and smaller.

$$\text{► EX Show Fern Creek} = \underbrace{0.543 + 0.369\left(\frac{19{,}230/118{,}803}{4{,}163/45{,}209}\right)}_{\text{Ordinary expected value}}$$

$$+ \underbrace{(3.60 - 2.13)\left(\frac{19{,}230}{118{,}803}\right)(0.85 - 0.829)}_{\text{Correction for track-take departure from 17.1\%}}$$

$$= 1.19 + 0.07$$

$$= 1.26.$$

This indicates that we expect to make 26%, on average, by betting on Fern Creek to show.

With our betting fortune of \$500 the optimal bet was \$28. This bet can be calculated using equation (5.5), as follows:

$$\text{Show bet} = \left[131 + 2{,}150q_i^2 - 1{,}778q_i^3 - \left(\frac{150}{q_iS/S_i - 0.70}\right)\right]\left(\frac{S - 6{,}000}{94{,}000}\right) + \left[86 + 1{,}516q_i^2 - 968q_i^3 - \left(\frac{90.7}{q_iS/S_i - 0.85}\right)\right]\left(\frac{100{,}000 - S}{94{,}000}\right). \quad (5.5)$$

For Fern Creek, $q_i = 19{,}230/118{,}803 = 0.1619$, $S_i = 4{,}163$, and $S = 45{,}209$. Hence

$$\text{Show bet} = \left[131 + 2{,}150(0.1619)^2 - 1{,}778(0.1619)^3 - \left(\frac{150}{(0.1619)(45{,}209)/(4{,}163) - 0.70}\right)\right]\left(\frac{45{,}209 - 6{,}000}{94{,}000}\right)$$

$$+ \left[86 + 1516(0.1619)^2 - 968(0.1619)^3 - \left(\frac{90.7}{(0.1619)(45{,}209)/(4{,}163) - 0.85}\right)\right]\left(\frac{100{,}000 - 45{,}209}{94{,}000}\right)$$

$$= (131 + 56.4 - 7.6 - 141.8)(0.417) + (86 + 39.7 - 4.1 - 99.9)(0.583)$$

$$= 15.8 + 12.7$$

$$= \$28.50.$$

	Totals	#7 Fern Creek	Expected Value per Dollar Bet on Fern Creek to Show	Optimal Bet to Show on Fern Creek ($)
Odds		4—1		
Win	133,999	21,397		
Show	50,569	4,677	1.25	24

Obviously, it would be best to do all our calculations on the final tote board figure, since then we would not have to worry about the odds changing after we bet. Unfortunately, the best we can do is base our calculations on the tote board one or two minutes before all betting ends. For this race the "two-minute problem" is no problem at all, since on the basis of the final tote board we have

$$\text{EX Show Fern Creek} = 1.25$$

and

$$\text{Show bet} = \$24.$$

These two values are very close to those calculated. The two-minute problem is discussed in more detail in Chapter Nine.

As mentioned in Chapter Three, the favorite, Modicum, won the race, setting a new track record for $4\frac{1}{2}$ furlongs. She's Ecstatic finished second, and Fern Creek took third. The chart of the race was as follows:*

FIRST RACE
Churchill
MAY 6, 1983

4 ½ FURLONGS. (.51⅗) MAIDEN. SPECIAL WEIGHT. Purse $8,000 (plus $2,000 from KTDF). Fillies. 2-year-olds. Weight, 118 lbs. 6TH DAY. WEATHER CLEAR. TEMPERATURE 79 DEGREES.

Total purse $10,000. Value of race $8,700, value to winner $5,200, second $2,000, third $1,000, fourth $500. ($1,300 reverts to the KTDF). Mutuel pool $251,926.

Last Raced	Horse	Eqt.A.Wt	PP	St	¼	Str	Fin	Jockey	Odds $1
20Apr83 3Kee2	Modicum	2 118	5	5	$1^{\frac{1}{2}}$	1^{2}	1^{4}	Day P	1.70
28Apr83 3Kee3	She's Ecstatic	2 118	9	8	3^{hd}	3^{2}	2^{3}	Delahoussaye E	3.40
	Fern Creek	b 2 118	7	6	2^{2}	$2^{1\frac{1}{2}}$	3^{nk}	Gavidia W	4.20
	Sintra	2 118	6	10	$9^{1\frac{1}{2}}$	6^{3}	4^{3}	Sellers M S	9.90
	Spiegler	2 113	3	3	$6^{\frac{1}{2}}$	$4^{\frac{1}{2}}$	$5^{2\frac{1}{2}}$	Miller S E5	10.00
28Apr83 3Kee5	Pruner's Gal	2 118	4	4	4^{2}	$5^{\frac{1}{2}}$	6^{4}	Woods C R Jr	18.40
	Westwood Lake	2 118	8	7	7^{3}	7^{1}	$7^{\frac{1}{2}}$	Moyers L	8.10
	Tricky Sea	2 113	10	9	5^{hd}	8^{3}	8^{3}	Allen K K5	43.20
	Hamburg Place	2 118	1	1	8^{hd}	9^{5}	9^{8}	Neilson C	33.20
	Red's Abbey	2 118	2	2	10	10	10	Bartram B E	60.00

OFF AT 1:52. Start good. Won handily. Time, :22, $:45\frac{1}{5}$, $:51\frac{3}{5}$ Track fast.
(New track record.)

Official Program Numbers

$2 Mutuel Prices:			
5-MODICUM	5.40	2.80	2.40
9-SHE'S ECSTATIC		3.40	2.60
7-FERN CREEK			3.40

Ch. f, by General Assembly—Sandstream, by Sandford. Trainer McGaughey C R III. Bred by Coggan J R S (GB).

MODICUM, hustled to the lead just after the start, made all the pace and increased the margin in the lane with a hand ride. SHE'S ECSTATIC, always well placed, was no match for the winner but finished strongly to be easily second best. FERN CREEK prompted the early pace but had no late rally. SINTRA lacked the needed response.

Owners— 1, West B; 2, Gentry T; 3, Crimson King Farm; 4, Cherry Valley Farm; 5, Flint B S Inc; 6, Mahan Sara M; 7, West & Woodford; 8, Buckland Farm; 9, Davis P E; 10, Johnson D.

The $3.40 show payoff on Fern Creek returned $40.80 for the $24 bet, for a profit of $16.80.

*We actually bet the $28 value indicated on our calculator for a return of $47.60 and profit of $19.60.

The Sixth Race, Hollywood Park, Inglewood, California, June 5, 1982

C'est Moi Cheri was a Dr. Z system bet in the sixth race at Hollywood Park on June 5, 1982. Near post time the tote board was as follows:

	Totals	#7 C'est Moi Cheri	Expected Value per Dollar Bet on C'est Moi Cheri to Show[a]	Optimal Bet to Show on C'est Moi Cheri[a] ($)
Odds		1—1		
Win	335,698	136,125		
Show	56,841	12,284	1.29	213

[a]From equation (4.6), the expected value per dollar bet to show on C'est Moi Cheri is

$$\begin{aligned}\text{EX Show C'est Moi Cheri} &= 0.543 + 0.369\left(\frac{136{,}125/335{,}698}{12{,}284/56{,}841}\right)\\ &\quad + (3.60 - 2.13)\left(\frac{136{,}125}{335{,}698}\right)(0.85 - 0.829)\\ &= 1.23 + 0.06\\ &= 1.29.\end{aligned}$$

Thus with California's 15% track take, we expect to make 29%, on average, betting on C'est Moi Cheri. The optimal bet using equation (5.5) is

$$\begin{aligned}\text{Show bet C'est Moi Cheri} &= \Bigg[131 + 2{,}150(0.4055)^2 - 1{,}778(0.4055)^3\\ &\quad - \left(\frac{150}{(0.4055)(56{,}841)/(12{,}284) - 0.70}\right)\Bigg]\left(\frac{12{,}284 - 6{,}000}{94{,}000}\right)\\ &\quad + \Bigg[86 + 1516(0.4055)^2 - 968(0.4055)^3\\ &\quad - \left(\frac{90.7}{(0.4055)(56{,}841)/(12{,}284) - 0.85}\right)\Bigg]\left(\frac{100{,}000 - 12{,}284}{94{,}000}\right)\\ &= \$213,\end{aligned}$$

since $q_i = 136{,}125/335{,}698 = 0.4055$, $S = 56{,}841$, and $S_i = 12{,}284$.

Figure 5.9, with $q_i = 136{,}125/335{,}698 = 0.4055$ and $S_i/S = 12{,}284/56{,}841 = 0.2161$, indicates that a Dr. Z bet should be made. Since $q_i = 0.4055$, Figure 5.19 indicates that the optimal bet with a betting wealth of $500 is $184. (Using Figure 5.22 with the 1.18 cutoff, we get an optimal bet of $208.)

C'est Moi Cheri was a wire-to-wire winner, beating the second-place finisher Kiss 'Em Goodbye by $4\frac{1}{2}$ lengths. Visual Emotion took third. The

Experts' Selections

Consensus Points: 5 for 1st (today's best 7), 2 for 2nd, 1 for 3rd. Today's Best in Bold Type.

Daily Racing Form

Trackman, Warren Williams **HOLLYWOOD PARK** Selections Made for Fast Track

	TRACKMAN	HANDICAP	ANALYST	HERMIS	SWEEP	CONSENSUS	
6	NAN'S DANCER	NAN'S DANCER	C'EST MOI CHERI	NAN'S DANCER	C'EST MOI CHERI	NAN'S DANCER	19
	C'EST MOI CHERI	C'EST MOI CHERI	NAN'S DANCER	C'EST MOI CHERI	NAN'S DANCER	C'EST MOI CHERI	16
	JUNE THREE	KISS 'EM GOODBYE	JUNE THREE	KISS 'EM GOODBYE	JUNE THREE	JUNE THREE	3

Analyst's Hollywood Comment

SIXTH RACE
1—C'Est Moi Cheri
2—Nan's Dancer
3—June Three

C'EST MOI CHERI is a half sister to the quick Cheri Meri and she seems to have inherited that ability to ramble. She's had 14 works since Jan. 28, the best being 1:00 4/5, :35 3/5b, :59, :58 2/5, :34 1/5, 1:00hg, 1:10 2/5, 1:11 1/5 and 1:00. She'll be tough to catch at first asking. NAN'S DANCER found her running legs last out when she was beaten a neck by the promising Miss Elea in 1:22 3/5 for 7 panels. If the top filly needs the outing she'll be extremely hard to handle. Mandella debuts JUNE THREE, and the trainer has a good percentage of wins with first-timers.

6th Hollywood

6 FURLONGS. (1.07⅘) MAIDEN. Purse $17,000. Fillies and mares. 3-year-olds and upward. Weights, 3-year-olds, 115 lbs.; older, 122 lbs.

Golden Lady Belle — Ch. f. 3, by Golden Eagle II—Baffi's Lady, by Petrone
Own.—Di Baffi Stable 115 Br.—Pernicano G J (Cal) 1982 0 M 0 0
Tr.—Rose Larry 1981 0 M 0 0
Lifetime 0 0 0 0
Jun 4 Hol 3f ft :36 hg May 29 Hol 5f ft 1:02 hg May 19 Hol 5f ft 1:04 hg May 11 Hol 5f ft 1:01 h

Visual Emotion — Ch. f. 3, by King Emperor—Join the Waves, by Sailor
Own.—Jones B C 115 Br.—Jones B C (Ky) 1982 1 M 0 0
Tr.—Russell John W 1981 0 M 0 0
Lifetime 1 0 0 0
29May82-6Hol 6f :21 :45 1:10ft 26 114 8 9½ 9 16 9 10 10 12 ShoemakerW10 ⒻMdn 73 RiseDePie,FoxyTmmie,BellePrleus 10
May 25 Hol 5f ft 1:01 h May 19 Hol 6f ft 1:18 h May 13 Hol 5f ft 1:01 hg May 7 Hol 6f ft 1:14 h

Real Notion — B. f. 3, by Torsion—Bekky's Star, by Dark Star
Own.—Groves F N (Lessee) 115 Br.—McLean-Robbins-Fonzone (Ky) 1982 7 M 1 0 $6,450
Tr.—Sullivan John 1981 3 M 0 0 $800
Lifetime 10 0 1 0 $7,250
22May82-4Hol 7f :22 :45 1:22ft 25 114 4 1½ 3 1½ 3 3 4 7½ Castaneda M4 ⒻMdn 77 MissElea,Nn'sDncer,LedingAdvocte 7
9May82-4Hol 1 1/16 :46 1:11 1:43ft 12 114 7 5 6 5 6 7¾ 7 17 DelahoussyeE6 ⒻMdn 61 Broadtail,Fndngerin,VoodooQueen 10
21Apr82-6SA 1 1/16 :46 1:11 1:43ft 47 117 8 7½ 7 5½ 5 5½ 4 9½ Valenzuela PA4 ⒻMdn 78 Nncy'sBby,BillyKnockn,Complbilty 12
10Apr82-4SA 1 1/16 :46 1:11 1:43ft 24 117 2½ 3 1 5 2½ 7 6½ Valenzuela PA3 ⒻMdn 75 GreySusan,‡Compatability,Fostoria 9
13Feb82-4SA 1 1/16 :47 1:12 1:44ft 10 117 6 5¾ 7 8 6 11 7 12 DelahoussyeE2 ⒻMdn 65 Permeability,HastyNijinsky,Celind 12
31Jan82-3SA 6f :21 :44 1:09ft 3¾ 117 7 8½ 7 7½ 6 9½ 5 7¾ DelahoussyeE4 ⒻMdn 82 SweetMystery,Celinda,HwiinShke 12
17Jan82-3SA 6f :21 :45 1:11ft 8¾ 117 8 5¾ 5 4¾ 3nk 2nk DelahoussyeE4 ⒻMdn 82 RgingStorm,RelNotion,SlutToLov 12
9Dec81-6Hol 6f :22 :46 1:12 ft 7 117 5 4½ 5 3 5 8½ 5 8½ Toro F4 ⒻMdn 68 Melinda's Plum, Visto,CitizenKate 11
14Nov81-3SA 6f :22 :44 1:10ft 43 116 6 5½ 6 4¾ 6 3½ 5 3½ DelahoussyeE1 ⒻMdn 84 Vihava,Marie'sFastLass,HwiinShke 8
2Oct81-6SA 6f :22 :45 1:11ft 86 115 9 8 8 11 8 11 8 12 DelahoussyeE7 ⒻMdn 70 EnglishGirl,PyOrPly,GloriousGren 11
May 31 Hol 4f ft :51 h May 19 Hol 4f ft :52 h May 7 Hol 4f ft :48 h May 1 Hol 4f ft :47 h

My Native Princess — B. f. 3, by Our Native—Marching Melody, by Go Marching
Own.—Littlest Ranch Inc 115 Br.—Backer J W (Ky) 1982 1 M 0 0
Tr.—Brunson Sam 1981 0 M 0 0
Lifetime 1 0 0 0
29May82-6Hol 6f :21 :45 1:10ft 81 115 5 5¾ 5 6½ 6 5 7 5¾ Aragon J4 ⒻMdn 79 RiseDePie,FoxyTmmie,BellePrleus 10
May 22 Hol 5f ft 1:02 hg ●May 5 EP 4f ft :48 hg ●Apr 27 EP 6f ft 1:16 hg

Kiss 'em Goodbye — B. f. 3, by Annihilate 'em—Free Guess, by Correlation
Own.—Magee Mr or Mrs R W 115 Br.—Greathouse L F (Ky) 1981 1 M 0 0
Tr.—Taliaferro Charles L
Lifetime 1 0 0 0
18Nov81-6Hol 6f :22 :45 1:10ft 14 117 4 3½ 5 4 7 13 6 9 Sibille R9 ⒻMdn 75 FilomenGle,IrishBild,Melind'sPlum 9
Jun 3 Hol 3f ft :35 hg May 29 Hol 6f ft 1:13 h May 22 Hol 6f ft 1:15 h May 18 Hol 5f ft 1:03 h

June Three — Dk. b. or br. f. 3, by Ramsinga—June Too, by Fleet Nasrullah
Own.—Sifton J 115 Br.—Stoneacres Farm (Man-C) 1982 0 M 0 0
Tr.—Mandella Richard 1981 0 M 0 0
Lifetime 0 0 0 0
Jun 1 Hol 4f ft :48 h May 26 Hol 7f ft 1:28 hg May 19 Hol 6f ft 1:16 hg ●May 11 GD tr.t 6f ft 1:13 hg

C'Est Moi Cheri — Dk. b. or br. f. 3, by Don B—Oui Oui Cheri, by Bar le Duc
Own.—Kirkorian B & Lynn 115 Br.—Warton J (Fla) 1982 0 M 0 0
Tr.—Cleveland Gene 1981 0 M 0 0
Lifetime 0 0 0 0
May 30 Hol 5f ft 1:00 h May 25 Hol 3f ft :35 b May 9 Hol 5f ft :59 h ●May 4 Hol 5f ft :58 h

Nan's Dancer — B. f. 3, by Marshua's Dancer—Film Festival, by Spring Double
Own.—Bolas G A 115 Br.—Tackett P (Ky) 1982 2 M 1 0 $3,825
Tr.—Rettele Loren 1981 0 M 0 0
Lifetime 2 0 1 0 $3,825
22May82-4Hol 7f :22 :45 1:22ft 3½ 114 2hd 1hd 1hd 2nk McCarron C J1 ⒻMdn 84 MissElea,Nn'sDncer,LedingAdvocte 7
15May82-6Hol 6f :21 :44 1:10ft 27 115 11 13 10 15 7 8¾ 5 3½ Black K7 ⒻMdn 82 Native Gal, RiseDePie,FallenAngel 12
Jun 3 Hol 3f ft :36 h May 29 Hol 5f ft :59 h May 11 Hol 6f ft 1:12 h May 5 Hol 5f ft 1:01 h

payoff for show for C'est Moi Cheri was a smashing $3.40. She paid $3.60 to place and $4.00 to win. The bet of $208 returned $353.60, for a profit of $145.60.* The chart of the race was as follows:

*Our actual bet of $213 returned $362.10, for a $149.10 profit.

SIXTH RACE **6 FURLONGS. (1.07⅘) MAIDEN. Purse $17,000. Fillies and mares. 3-year-olds and upward. Weights, 3-year-olds, 115 lbs.; older, 122 lbs.**

Hollywood

JUNE 5, 1982

Value of race $17,000, value to winner $9,350, second $3,400, third $2,550, fourth $1,275, fifths $212.50 each. Mutuel pool $521,071.

Last Raced	Horse	Eqt	A	Wt	PP	St	¼	½	Str	Fin	Jockey	Odds $1
	C'Est Moi Cheri		3	115	7	4	1^{1}	$1^{3\frac{1}{2}}$	$1^{3\frac{1}{2}}$	$1^{4\frac{1}{2}}$	Sibille R	1.00
18Nov81 ^{6}Hol^{6}	Kiss 'em Goodbye		3	116	5	1	4^{2}	$3^{\frac{1}{2}}$	3^{4}	2^{hd}	Black K	10.90
29May82 ^{6}Hol^{10}	Visual Emotion		3	115	2	5	$3^{\frac{1}{2}}$	2^{1}	2^{2}	$3^{4\frac{1}{2}}$	Olivares F	52.60
22May82 ^{4}Hol^{2}	Nan's Dancer		3	115	8	7	7^{6}	$6^{\frac{1}{2}}$	4^{1}	4^{hd}	McCarron C J	1.50
22May82 ^{4}Hol^{4}	DH Real Notion	b	3	115	3	3	$6^{\frac{1}{2}}$	7^{3}	7^{2}	5	Castaneda M	18.20
29May82 ^{6}Hol^{7}	DH My Native Princess		3	115	4	6	5^{hd}	5^{hd}	5^{hd}	5^{3}	McHargue D G	25.80
	Golden Lady Belle		3	115	1	8	8	8	8	7^{nk}	Ortega L E	59.60
	June Three	b	3	115	6	2	2^{1}	4^{2}	6^{1}	8	Toro F	8.80

DH—Dead heat.

OFF AT 4:46. Start good. Won handily. Time, :22, :44⅘, :57, 1:10 Track fast.

$2 Mutuel Prices:

7–C'EST MOI CHERI	4.00	3.60	3.40
5–KISS 'EM GOODBYE		7.60	5.00
2–VISUAL EMOTION			9.80

Dk. b. or br. f, by Don B—Oui Oui Cheri, by Bar le Duc. Trainer Cleveland Gene. Bred by Warton J (Fla).

C'EST MOI CHERI sprinted clear without need of urging, drew away to a long lead into the stretch, was reminded of her task with one crack of the whip at midstretch, and steadily drew away in hand. KISS 'EM GOODBYE, well-placed throughout, was no match for the winner but closed gamely to edge VISUAL EMOTION for the place. The latter moved nearest the winner at the far turn and flattened out in the final furlong. NAN'S DANCER stayed to the outside around the far turn and showed little punch from the middle of the track. REAL NOTION showed nothing. MY NATIVE PRINCESS lugged in throughout and finished on even terms with REAL NOTION. GOLDEN LADY BELLE was outrun. JUNE THREE tired badly.

Owners— 1, Kirkorian B & Lynn; 2, Magee Mr or Mrs R W; 3, Jones B C; 4, Bolas G A; 5, Groves F N (Lessee); 6, Littlest Ranch Inc; 7, Di Baffi Stable; 8, Sifton J. **Overweight:** Kiss 'em Goodbye 1 pound.

The King's Favor Purse, Longacres, Renton, Washington, August 14, 1983

B. C. Place was a Dr. Z system bet in the seventh race, the King's Favor Purse at Longacres on August 14, 1983. One minute before post time the tote board was as follows:

	Totals	#4 B. C. Place	Expected Value per Dollar Bet on B. C. Place[a]	Optimal Bet to Show on B. C. Place[a] ($)
Odds		7—2		
Win	31,422	5,583		
Show	16,101	1,785	1.17	9

[a]From equation (4.6), the expected value per dollar bet on B. C. Place was

$$\text{EX Show B. C. Place} = 0.543 + 0.369\left(\frac{5{,}583/31{,}422}{1{,}785/16{,}101}\right) + \left[(3.60 - 2.13)\left(\frac{5{,}583}{31{,}422}\right)\right](0.84 - 0.829)$$

$$= 1.13 + 0.04$$

$$= 1.17.$$

Thus with Washington's 16% track take we expect to make 17%, on average, betting on B. C. Place. The optimal bet for a betting wealth of $500 calculated using equation (5.5) is $9, since q_i = 5,583/31,422 = 0.1777, S = 16,101, and S_i = 1,785.

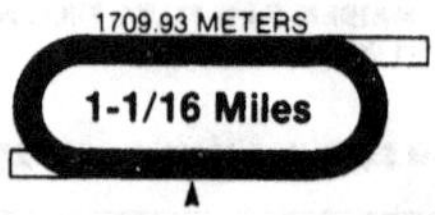

WIN PLACE SHOW

SEVENTH

KING'S FAVOR PURSE

PURSE $7,000. FOR THREE-YEAR-OLDS. 120 lbs. Non-winners since April 26, 3 lbs. Non-winners in 1983, 6 lbs. **Claiming price $20,000.** (Races for $16,000 or less not considered).

Track Record—EAGLE CREST (4) 114—1:39 4/5 ONE MILE AND ONE-SIXTEENTH

	OWNER	TRAINER	JOCKEY
1	G. M. Stable Flame orange, black sash GM on front, flame orange cap **TUSA** **120** Ch. c. 3 Kentuckian—Shesarunner (WA)	Eugene Zeren	6 Mike James
2	Larry Schneider Silver, white sleeves, matching cap **MOONSHINE WAY** **114** Br. g. 3 Noholme Way—She Shine (WA)	Brad Taylor	3 Gary Baze
3	Ben Harris Red & white, H on back, red & white cap **SATUS WAY** **114** Br. g. 3 Noholme Way—Satus Lady (WA)	Owner	20 Dale Baze
4	C. A. Roberts Black, pink ROBERTS on back, black cap **B. C. PLACE** **117** B. c. 3 Mark Place—Sex Place (CAN)	Cy Anderson	6 Paul Nicolo
5	Corky VanOsten Royal blue, blue diamond in white star, gold trim, matching cap **RUSHIN' IN** **114** Ch. g. 3 Sibirri—Daurna (WA)	Eugene Stallings	20 J. W. Mills
6	K & L Stables Orange, K & L shield on back, orange cap **PREDICATION** **120** Br. c. 3 Pretense—Madame Axe (CA)	Craig Roberts	8/5 Martin Pedroza
7	Dr. & Mrs. W. W. Lien White, multicolored polka dots, matching cap **COUNT ON ZU** **114** B. g. 3 Zulu Tom—Count on Sue (WA)	N. E. Norton	15 Gary Stevens
8	W. L. Hooper Light blue, multicolored polka dots, light blue cap **COLONEL JERRY** **114** Ch. g. 3 Big Stir—Feathers Sue (WA)	Ladonna Damron	4 Jerry Pruitt

Declared: RIP ADHEM

Latest Workout: TUSA—Aug. 13, 3/8, :37 Lga Ft.

CLOCKER'S SELECTION: 6-2-8

```
7th Lga    1 1-16 MILES. (1:39⅘). CLAIMING. Purse, $7,000. 3-year-olds. Weight, 120 lbs. Non-
           winners since April 26 allowed 3 lbs.; non-winners in 1983, 6 lbs. (Races for $16,000
           or less not considered.) Claiminy price, $20,000.

Tusa                          120  Ch. c, 1980, by Kentuckian—Shesarunner, by Your Host.
                                   Breeder, Plemmonston Stud (Wash.).          1983. 4 1 1 1   $4,275
Owner, G. M. Stable. Trainer, Eugene Zeren.              $20,000               1982. 0 M 0 0   ——
15Jly83 1Lga   1 1/16 :473 1:131 1:453ft  2 *120  89½ 54½ 2h 1nk  JmsM5  M20000 71 Tusa 120          Think Fresh 9
22Jun83 2Lga   1 1/16 :463 1:121 1:461sy  8½ 120  1017 812 57½ 21 JmsM9  M16000 67 Military Merit 120  Tusa 10
3Jun83 4Lga    6½f :222 :454 1:173ft  19 120  54 56½ 36 38   StvnG7 M20000 73 RipAdhem120    MilitaryMerit 9
25May83 3Lga   6f :221 :454 1:113ft  10 1155 1114 1115 919 716 NlsnM8 M16000 62 DetermindFire120 LittleMike 11
     July 10 Lga 5f ft 1:04⅘b        May 18 Lga 3f ft :36⅘bcg        May 4 Lga 5f ft 1:03⅕bgc

Moonshine Way                 114  Dk. b. or br. g, 1980, by Noholme Way—She Shine, by Pilot John.
                                   Breeder, Mr.-Mrs. Guy C. Roberts (Wash.).   1983. 7 2 1 2   $9,060
Owner, Larry Schneider. Trainer, Brad Taylor.            $20,000               1982. 2 M 0 1   $485
                                                     LIFETIME (thru 1982)       2 M 0 1   $485
6Aug83 8Lga    6½f :22 :451 1:164ft  5½ 119  78½ 76½ 63½ 21½  BazeG3   20000 83 ShortSocks120  MoonshneWay 8
30Jly83 7Lga   1 1/16 :473 1:121 1:442ft  4¾*119  64½ 63¾ 44½ 44  BazeG8  20000 73 C. W. Moss 114  John Day 12
20Jly83 7Lga   6½f :213 :442 1:154ft  6½ 122  87¼ 87½ 613 65½  PierceL4  25000 84 Saber Ben 119 Just Cavorting 11
26Jun83 4Lga   6½f :214 :443 1:16 ft  4 114  89 78½ 67½ 32  StevnsG3  25000 87 RipAdhem119  FortiethPrince 9
15Jun83 7Lga   6f :22 :452 1:103ft  18 114  1113 1011 56½ 11½  StevenG4  16000 83 MoonshneWy114  NoteofHope 12
2Jun83 2Lga    6½f :213 :444 1:184ft  2¼*122  45 78½ 35 15  PiercL2  M12500 75 MoonshinWay122  OuttaCache 12
11May83 2Lga   6f :223 :462 1:12 ft  3¾ 121  31½ 32½ 45½ 34  PrcL10  M10000 72 FriendlyAtom115  LittleClinkr 11
21Oct82 4Lga   6½f :213 :45 1:174sy  5 120  610 58½ 46 32  PiercL8  M16000 78 LetsGoDtch120  MorningEagle 12
6Aug82 4Lga    5½f :223 :462 1:053ft  20 120  96¾ 99¾ 811 88  CperB3  M20000 76 Deblynton 120  Taiwocondo 9
     May 30 Lga 3f ft :36⅘b        MAY 8 LGA 3F M :36HG        May 4 Lga 4f ft :51⅘b

Satus Way                     114  Dk. b. or br. g, 1980, by Noholme Way—Satus Lady, by Happy Trail.
                                   Breeder, Mr.-Mrs. Ben Harris (Wash.).       1983. 5 0 0 0   $755
Owner, Ben Harris. Trainer, Ben Harris.                  $20,000               1982.10 2 2 2   $17,680
                                                     LIFETIME (thru 1982)      10 2 2 2   $17,680
30Jly83 7Lga   1 1/16 :473 1:121 1:442ft  14 114  31½ 42½ 1117 1120  FrazirB9  20000 57 C. W. Moss 114  John Day 12
14Jly83 9Lga   1 1/16 :464 1:122 1:451m  17 114  1121 1017 915 713  PruittJ11  32000 60 RedBrnRtrns120  Lyon'sShdw 11
11Jun83 9Lga   1 1/16 :46 1:11 1:443ft  5¾ 1105  613 812 820 722  BrnsVJ5  40000 54 Ourteshun117  FlyingBob 8
27May83 9Lga   6½f :22 :453 1:18 ft  12 1095  916 913 78¾ 43½  BrnesVJ9  32000 75 ShortSocks119  Lyon'sShadow 9
14May83 7Lga   6f :22 :45 1:094ft  11 114  814 813 712 616  PruittJ4  40000 71 SplndorBoy120  DancgDrctor 8
27Nov82 9YM    1 :50 1:16 1:44 sl 6-5 *121  1011 76 42 1½  PruittJ9  HcpS 56 Satus Way 121  Fleet Spud 10
31Oct82 9YM    1 1/16 :461 1:11 1:43 ft  17 114  97½ 73¾ 24 23  PruittJ9  AlwS 97 Table Sean 119  Satus Way 10
10Oct82 7Lga   1 :481 1:144 1:421sl  5 120  69¾ 64½ 56 42½  PrittJ4  Aw6500 56 Tubafor 120  Pic O'Morn 6
29Sep82 8Lga   1 :484 1:15 1:44 hy  4¼ 116  69 65½ 79¼ 33½  PrittJ1  Aw6500 45 ExclusivBiddr118  DynamoDoc 8
19Sep82 9Lga   1 :46 1:103 1:364ft  25 118  32 33 57 510  PruittJ7  HcpS 75 Dave's Reality 122  Tubafor 10
4Sep82 5Lga    6f :213 :45 1:111m  3½ 120  47½ 44½ 21 16½  PruittJ1  Mdn 90 SatusWay120  MilitaryMerit 7
     Aug 11 Lga 5f ft 1:02⅕b        JULY 24 LGA 5F FT 1:00H        July 7 Lga 4f ft :54⅕b

B. C. Place                   117  B. c, 1980, by Mark's Place—Sextant, by Ship Leave.
                                   Breeder, McDonald Farms Ltd (B.C.-C.).      1983.12 1 2 2   $12,066
Owner, C. A. Roberts. Trainer, Cy Anderson.              $20.000               1982. 1 M 0 0   $1,000
                                                     LIFETIME (thru 1982)       1 M 0 0   $1,000
1Aug83 8EP     1 1/16 :24 :482 1:472ft  7½ 113  54¾ 4¾ 2½ 2½  MenaJG6  25000 73 Troika111  B.C.Place 8
24Jly83 9EP    1 3/8 :474 1:41 2:203ft  46 122  44 41½ 410 49½  MenaJG6  SplW 71 TimelyOne  VictoriousLd 7
17Jly83 7EP    1 1/16 :473 1:13 1:452ft  8½ 114  43 42½ 612 411  LosethC5  23000 73 ScotT.N.Me  Maj'sPromise 8
10Jly83 8EP    6½f :224 :462 1:184ft  24 115  42 63¾ 814 912  ZookDJ9  25000 72 SelCove  Elit'sCommand 10
     10Jly83—Wide
1Jly83 7EP     1 1/16 :482 1:141 1:473gd  5 116  72¾ 95 79½ 77½  ZookDJ7  25000 65 Gus'sLittleBuddy  CriASmile 10
25Jun83 2EP    1 1/16 :48 1:13 1:462ft 6-5 *114  2h 13 16 16  ZkDJ5  M23000 79 B.C.Place  StrChllenger 6

Rushin' In                    114  Ch. g, 1980, by Sibirri—Daurna, by Equinaut.
                                   Breeder, Rainier Stables (Wash.).           1983. 7 2 0 0   $5,775
Owner, Corky Van Osten. Trainer, Eugene Stallings.       $20,000               1982. 3 1 0 0   $1,200
                                                     LIFETIME (thru 1982)       3 1 0 0   $1,200
30Jly83 7Lga   1 1/16 :473 1:121 1:442ft  19 114  1110 1111 811 89½  JamesM4  20000 67 C. W. Moss 114  John Day 12
20Jly83 7Lga   6½f :213 :442 1:154ft  43 114  65 77¼ 819 812  JamesM7  25000 78 Saber Ben 119 Just Cavorting 11
3Jly83 5Lga    1 1/16 :471 1:121 1:454ft  41 114  68½ 56 22½ 1½  GslvFA10  16000 70 Rushin' In 114  I'm Cricket 12
19Jun83 4Lga   6f :22 :453 1:103ft  29 114  1010 1011 1012 99¼  GnlvsFA3  20000 74 DerBingo121  FortiethPrince 11
29May83 3Lga   6f :214 :453 1:111ft  4¼ 114  44 56½ 69½ 68¼  HnnMA3  c16000 72 Crash Cache 114  Der Bingo 7
6May83 6Lga    6f :22 :453 1:114m 9-5 *117  22 22 12½ 1½  AragonJ5  12500 77 Rushin'sIn117  SunDrcThundr 9
30Apr83 2Lga   6f :214 :45 1:111ft  21 117  54¼ 44½ 712 74½  HnnMA9  20000 75 Prime Fire 117  Proxy's Boy 9
7Nov82 1PM     6f :223 1:131ft  8½ 118  2½ 2½ 2h 1h  VnsW4  M20000 81 Rushin'In118  BrokersLark 9
14Oct82 4Lga   6f :214 :45 1:10 ft  26 120  3½ 32½ 35 68¾  PrittJ7  M12500 77 Proxy's Boy 120  Teepee Rings 12
1Sep82 4Lga    6f :22 :461 1:124ft  9 120  78 919 1120 1017  LsthC9  M12500 55 Whatsup 120  Anahuy 12
     Aug 7 Lga 5f ft 1:02⅕b        July 28 Lga 3f m :38⅘b        July 16 Lga 4f ft :48h

Predication                   120  Dk. b. or br. c, 1980, by Pretense—Madame Axe, by The Axe II.
                                   Breeder, Wood River Ranch (Calif.).         1983.10 2 4 1   $10,080
Owner, K-L Stables. Trainer, Craig Roberts.              $20,000               1982. 3 M 0 0   ——
                                                     LIFETIME (thru 1982)       3 M 0 0   ——
3Aug83 8Lga    6f :22 :451 1:094ft  9½ 119  64¾ 67¼ 916 912  BazeMB4  25000 75 ShootngClam114  CouponTycn 9
14Jly83 9Lga   1 1/16 :464 1:122 1:451m  7¾ 119  79¾ 1118 1121 1120  BazeG8  32000 53 RedBrnRtrns120  Lyon'sShdw 11
     14Jly83—Checked sharply on second turn.
2Jly83 6Lga    1 1/16 :484 1:132 1:453ft  3½ 114  2½ 2h 31 23  FrazrB5  c25000 68 RedBaronRtrns117  Predction 8
22Jun83 6Lga   6½f :221 :453 1:164sy 9-5 *114  22 21½ 33 1½  FrzierB7  20000 85 Predcatin114  RedBaronRetrn 7
26May83 7Lga   6f :222 :46 1:112ft  4¼ 120  1½ 11 1h 22½  FrazirB7  20000 76 Nativistic 122  Predication 8
13May83 8Lga   6f :22 :453 1:103ft  7¼ 120  64½ 67 611 412  StevenG4  20000 71 Phil E. B. Jon 117  John Day 12
30Apr83 1Lga   6f :222 :462 1:12 ft  2¼*120  53 42½ 34½ 1h  StvnG6  M16000 76 Predication 120  Barb's Boy 12
5Mar83 2PM     6f :223 :464 1:13 sy 9-5 120  21 1h 1½ 25  StevensG9  Mdn 77 FlyingBob120  Predication 12
19Feb83 5PM    6f :222 :462 1:13 gd 3-4 *120  12½ 12 1h 33  GnslvsFA4  Mdn 79 BridgeTender120  FlyingBob 6
5Feb83 2PM     6f :222 :461 1:122ft  2¼*120  11½ 11½ 22½ 26½  StevensG9  Mdn 78 PrairieBreakr120  Prediction 12
20Dec82 2Hol   6½f :214 :444 1:18 ft  9¾ 118  64½ 67½ 69¾ 612  VzlaP7  M32000 68 DarkAce116  Elated 12
     Aug 1 Lga 4f ft :51⅕b        JULY 12 LGA 4F SY :48⅘H        June 12 Lga 5f ft 1:05b
```

```
Count On Zu               114  B. g, 1980, by Zulu Tom—Count On Sue, by Eastern Flier.
                               Breeder, Dr.-Mrs. Wm. W. Lien (Wash.).   1983. 6 2 0 1   $7,095
Owner, Dr.-Mrs. W. W. Lien. Trainer, N. E. Norton.        $20,000       1982. 5 M 0 1     $830
                                                   LIFETIME (thru 1982)       5 M 0 1     $830
30Jly 83 7Lga   1 1/16 :4731:1211:442ft 10  114 1210109¾ 711 69  StevnsG1 20000 68 C. W. Moss 114  John Day 12
17Jly 83 5Lga   6½f :213 :4421:163ft 27  114 129 1213109 62½ StvnsG10 20000 83 Nuncio 114  Der Bingo 12
8Jun83 6Lga     1 1/16 :4641:1311:47 ft 2½ 114 59½ 42¼ 22 1h  StevenG3 16000 64 Count On Zu 114  C. W. Moss 7
3Jun83 5Lga     1 1/16 :4731:1331:47 ft 5  114 48½ 34 41¾ 1no StevenG1 12500 64 Count On Zu 114  I'm Cricket 8
  3Jun83—Bumped in stretch.
19May83 3Lga    6½f :221 :4531:182ft 3¼*120 1010 710 610 35½ AgnJ12 M12500 71 CatchAFool121  LittleClinker 12
4May83 4Lga     5½f :221 :4641:06 ft 7  120 85¼ 88¼ 88¾ 62¾ ArgnJ1 M12500 81 Gulf King 120  Venture Bay 12
  4May83—Steadied at 7-16 pole.
21Oct82 4Lga    6½f :213 :45 1:174sy 12 120 1017 819 612 45  KwlsL5 M16000 75 LetsGoDtch120  MornngEagle 12
7Oct82 4Lga     1 :4811:1431:431m 20 120 76¾ 57 46 33  KnwlL5 M16000 50 WhereWasIt120  ExtraExclsiv 10
29Sep82 4Lga    1 :5011:18 1:464hy 10 120 912 811 66¾ 63½ KnwlL9 M12500 31 Whirlin Sterlin 120  R. Jesson 10
16Sep82 4Lga    6½f :222 :4541:193ft 14 120 11131017 713 64 KnwlL11 M8000 67 Battlestr120  PalouseLautrec 12
    Aug 12 Lga 4f m :48⅗h          JULY 7 LGA 5F FT 1:00H          June 29 Lga 5f ft 1:02bc

Colonel Jerry             114  Ch. g, 1980, by Big Stir—Feathers Sue, by Feathers.
                               Breeder, Mr.-Mrs. G. E. Morrison (Wash.).  1983. 9 0 3 2   $4,822
Owner, W. L. Hooper. Trainer, LaDonna Damron.              $20,000       1982.11 1 2 1   $3,672
                                                   LIFETIME (thru 1982)      11 1 2 1   $3,672
30Jly 83 7Lga   1 1/16 :4731:1211:442ft 7¼ 114 96¼ 74¾ 54¾ 32½ PruittJ2 20000 74 C. W. Moss 114  John Day 12
24Jly 83 3Lga   1 1/16 :4731:1211:441ft 5½ 114 33½ 3nk 11 2½ PruittJ5 16000 77 C.W. Moss 120  Colonel Jerry 9
  24Jly83—Steadied at start.
10Jly 83 7Lga   6½f :213 :4431:16 ft 14  114 89 107¾ 815 77  WalesH2 25000 82 Hot Drums 120  Cookie Shoes 12
2Jly 83 8Lga    6f :222 :4531:102ft 33  117 52 41¾ 76¼ 76¾ PrttJ9 Aw8000 77 More Action 120  Vitez 9
3Jun83 6Lga     6½f :22 :4611:171ft 7  114 68 57½ 56 56½ PruittJ2 25000 76 DncngDirctr120  HoHoCharlie 7
19May83 9Lga    6f :213 :4441:101ft 50  117 1012111211171115 PrittJ2 Aw8500 70 Steel Prince 117  Dr. Sea 12
29Apr83 9Lga    6f :22 :4521:111ft 5¼ 117 57 49 38 32¼ PrittJ4 Aw8000 78 Just For Bill 118  Dr. Sea 9
24Apr83 9YM     6f :234 :4831:17 hy 9¾ 117 32 3½ 32 21½ HngwhR6 HcpS 56 Pic O'Morn 117  Colonel Jerry 7
17Apr83 8YM     5½f :221 :4531:04 ft 13 117 42½ 21½ 22 23½ HlwtR2 Aw1600 91 Muckledeedun120  ColonlJerry 6
27Nov82 9YM     1 :50 1:16 1:44 sl 30  123 75¼ 42½ 53 814 Dahlqst1 HcpS 42 Satus Way 121  Fleet Spud 10
20Nov82 9YM     6f :22 :47 1:153m9-5 *122 75¼ 45 65 612 DlqtT4 Aw1200 55 JudgesLast117  InnBallofFire [illegible]
    Aug 10 Lga 5f ft 1:01⅗b        July 22 Lga 3f ft :35⅘hc        June 29 Lga 5f ft 1:01⅗b
```

Figure 5.9, with $q_i = 0.1777$ and $S_i/S = 1{,}785/16{,}101 = 0.1109$, indicates that a show bet should be made. Since $q_i = 0.1777$, Figure 5.18 indicates that the optimal bet with a betting wealth of $500 is $15.

At post time the tote board was as follows:

	Totals	#4 B. C. Place	Expected Value per Dollar Bet on B. C. Place
Odds			7—2
Win	38,816	6,886	
Show	19,172	2,286	1.13

Colonel Jerry grabbed the early lead and was a wire-to-wire winner. Rushin' In took second, and B. C. Place was third. The show payoff of $4.40 on B. C. Place resulted in a return of $33 for the $15 bet, or an $18 profit.* The chart of the race was

*Our $9 returned $19.80, for a $10.80 profit. In most cases the charts give conservative betting values slightly less than the true optimal value. However, for some small bets the charts indicate a slightly larger bet.

SEVENTH RACE
Lga
Aug. 14, 1983

1 1-16 MILES. (1:39⅘). CLAIMING. Purse, $7,000. 3-year-olds. Weight, 120 lbs. Non-winners since April 26 allowed 3 lbs.; non-winners in 1983, 6 lbs. (Races for $16,000 or less not considered.) Claiming price, $20,000.

Value to winner, $3,850; second, $1,330; third, $1,015; fourth, $630; fifth, $175. Mutuel Pool, $82,525. Exacta Pool, $143,738.

Last Raced	Horses	EqtAWt	PP	St	¼	½	¾	Str	Fin	Jockeys	Owners	Odds to $1
30Jly 83 ^{7}Lga^{3}	Colonel Jerry	b3 114	8	4	$4^{3\frac{1}{2}}$	2^{3}	1^{2}	1^{5}	1^{4}	PruittJ	W L Hooper	3.60
30Jly 83 ^{7}Lga^{8}	Rushin' In	3 114	5	2	2^{2}	$3^{1\frac{1}{2}}$	3^{1}	2^{4}	$2^{6\frac{1}{2}}$	MillsJW	C Vanosten	24.80
1Aug83 ^{8}EP^{2}	B. C. Place	3 117	4	3	3^{h}	$4^{1\frac{1}{2}}$	4^{3}	$4^{1\frac{1}{2}}$	$3^{2\frac{1}{2}}$	NicoloP	C A Roberts	3.70
15Jly 83 ^{1}Lga^{1}	Tusa	3 120	1	8	8	8	7^{h}	7^{5}	4^{1}	JamesM	G M Stable	6.20
30Jly 83 ^{7}Lga^{6}	Count On Zu	3 114	7	6	$6^{1\frac{1}{2}}$	6^{5}	6^{4}	$6^{\frac{1}{2}}$	$5^{\frac{1}{2}}$	StevensG	Dr-Mrs W W Lien	14.75
6Aug83 ^{8}Lga^{2}	Moonshine Way	3 119	2	5	5^{4}	$5^{1\frac{1}{2}}$	$5^{\frac{1}{2}}$	3^{1}	6^{4}	BazeG	L Schneider	2.55
3Aug83 ^{8}Lga^{9}	Predication	3 120	6	1	$1^{2\frac{1}{2}}$	1^{h}	$2^{1\frac{1}{2}}$	5^{h}	$7^{\frac{3}{4}}$	PedrozaMA	K-L Stables	4.10
30Jly 83 ^{7}Lga^{11}	Satus Way	b3 116	3	7	7^{2}	7^{1}	8	8	8	BazeD	B Harris	20.25

OFF AT 4:54. START GOOD. WON EASILY. Time, :23⅗, :47⅗, 1:12, 1:38⅕, 1:44⅘. Track fast.

$2 Mutuel Prices			
8—COLONEL JERRY	9.20	4.10	3.20
5—RUSHIN' IN		16.60	8.10
4—B.C. PLACE			4.40

$5 EXACTA (8-5) PAID $326.50.

Ch. g, by Big Stir Feathers Sue, by Feathers. Trainer, Ladonna Damron. Bred by Mr.-Mrs. G. E. Morrison (Wash.).

The Beat the Racetrack Calculator™

At the racetrack, Figures 5.7 to 5.10 can be used to determine whether or not a given bet to place or show has an expected value of at least 1.14 or 1.18 and thus qualifies as a Dr. Z system bet. For a place bet one simply computes the ratios W_i/W and P_i/P for the horse in question and determines if the intersection of these numbers is above (do not bet) or on or below (bet) the appropriate track-take line. For a show bet you use W_i/W and S_i/S. Similarly, Figures 5.11 to 5.22 can be used to determine how much to bet to place or show with 1.14 or 1.18 the expected-value cutoffs. From the horizontal axis you read off the optimal bet corresponding to a given probability of winning $q_i = W_i/W$ and your betting-wealth level, using the figure corresponding to the mutuel pool size where the race is being run. These values are approximate, but quite usable. When they err, it is usually on the conservative side, suggesting slightly lower bets than is optimal.

The Beat the Racetrack Calculator™ automatically takes into account factors such as your betting wealth, the track take, the size of the mutuel pools, and whether an entry is present. The aim of the Beat the Racetrack Calculator™ is to enable you to perform the calculations you need to evaluate a possible bet as quickly, accurately, and simply as possible. You are then free to watch the tote board and evaluate possible bets as post time nears. Your evaluation of a particular bet should take less than a minute.

The BTR calculator is a plug-in ROM for use with the Hewlett Packard HP41C, HP41CV, or HP41CX calculator. the ROM and HP41C calculator and instructions are available in selected outlets for $295.00 ($369.00 Canadian)—prices valid through 1985. For information write to: Dr. Z Investments, Inc., P.O. Box 35334, Los Angeles, CA 90045. For those who already have an HP41 series calculator, the ROM and instructions are available for $140.00 ($175.00 Canadian). (The publisher makes no warranties concerning this offer. Please refer all inquiries to the address noted above.)

CHAPTER 6

Using the Dr. Z System at the Racetrack

Now that you have a basic understanding of our approach to winning at the racetrack using Dr. Z system bets, we can show you how it is used in typical betting situations. We describe eight races at six different tracks in California, British Columbia, New York, Kentucky, and Washington.

I was at the track when these races were run. This is the usual application of the Dr. Z system. However, betting on races being run in other locales is becoming more and more popular. We discuss this type of betting in Chapter Seven.

Most of the Dr. Z system bets are on horses to show. There are occasional place bets. In some situations you make bets to show on two different horses or to place and show on the same horse. A race at Exhibition Park and the Santa Ynez Stakes at Santa Anita described here provide examples of the latter situations. (Chapter Nine provides details on the relative distribution of the various types of Dr. Z system bets.)

The Sixth Race and the Triple Bend Handicap, Hollywood Park, Inglewood, California, May 8, 1982

Southern California boasts three of the nation's top tracks: Santa Anita Park in Arcadia near the Pasadena Rose Bowl, Del Mar near San Diego, and

Hollywood Park in Inglewood near the Forum sports arena just south of the city. These tracks alternate their seasons, so top quality racing is available all year to the millions of racing fans in the area. Top jockeys, such as Chris McCarron, Sandy Hawley, Eddie Delahoussaye, Bill Shoemaker, Walter Guerra, Darrell McHargue, and Laffit Pincay, Jr., ride there regularly for the nation's highest purses on extraordinary, high-quality thoroughbreds. The fair weather brings huge crowds to the tracks and the relative wealth of the area results in extremely high betting pools. For example, typically 30,000 people bet over $5 million daily at Santa Anita Park. On opening day and occasions with major stakes races, the crowd can swell to well over 50,000 and the handle to nearly $10 million.

Such conditions are very good for Dr. Z system bettors. The track is usually fast. The quality of horses and jockeys is such that there is a large percentage of races that are run true-to-form—that is, more or less as expected. The large pools mean that Dr. Z system bets placed near the end of the betting period can be made in substantial amounts without depressing the place or show odds too much.

In May 1982, I was a visiting professor at UCLA. Since Hollywood Park was only a scant half-hour drive on the San Diego freeway from our home in West Los Angeles, it was easy to visit. Most Saturdays and Sundays have major races with purses of $50,000 or more. These draw the top horses and both the spectacle and the investment possibilities make for a very enjoyable afternoon.

Saturday, May 8, 1982, was clear and warm and featured the $50,000 added Triple Bend Handicap. It was a good day to visit Hollywood Park. On that day there were two Dr. Z system bets, and they both won. As we have previously stated, two to four Dr. Z system bets per day is about typical. On average, Dr. Z system bets win about 60% of the time. Chapter Nine provides a more detailed discussion of these win rates.

The sixth race was a maiden race for three-year-olds and upward for a purse of $18,000. Maiden races are for horses that have never won a race in their career and hence are largely unproven. One must use extreme caution in betting on such races. Swing Till Dawn was making his first start, a situation that calls for even more caution. However, his pedigree and workouts were outstanding. This colt had the promise to be something special. The rest of the field was quite weak except for the second and third choices of the crowd: The Hague and Colonialism. Chris McCarron, the meet's leading jockey, was in the irons of Swing Till Dawn. Chris's consistency and winning ways added a measure of confidence to the information provided by the consensus group of experts and the outstanding workouts.

Swing Till Dawn did look like a top prospect, but I would bet only if the odds were good enough! They were. With one minute to post time the tote board was as follows:

	Totals	#4 Swing Till Dawn	Expected Value per Dollar Bet on Swing Till Dawn
Odds		7—5	
Win	339,272	116,637	
Place	131,740	33,380	1.11
Show	69,682	15,621	1.17

The expected value per dollar wagered on Swing Till Dawn was 1.11 to place and 1.17 to show. My betting fortune that day was $1,000, so I did not bet to place, but wagered $222 to show.*

At post time the situation was similar, and the final tote board was

	Totals	#4 Swing Till Dawn	Expected Value per Dollar Bet on Swing Till Dawn
Odds		7—5	
Win	350,246	119,896	
Place	137,398	34,816	1.11
Show	73,113	16,543	1.16

These values gave expected values to place and show of 1.11 and 1.16, respectively.

As expected, Swing Till Dawn won the race, followed by the long shot Beau Glacier. This provided a handsome $4 place payoff on the 7—5 favorite, Swing Till Dawn. However, it was still not quite good enough to qualify as a Dr. Z system bet. The betting public's second choice, The Hague, finished third. The fairly heavy betting to show on The Hague dropped Swing Till Dawn's show payoff to $2.80, which was still better than a typical show payoff for a 7—5 favorite. My bet of $222 to show returned $310.80, for a profit of $88.80. The chart of the race was

*You may determine these expected values and optimal bet sizes in several ways. The equations given in Chapters Four, Five, and Sixteen or the calculator discussed on page 99 will calculate them exactly. The charts provided in Chapters Four and Five may be used to determine fairly accurate expected values and betting amounts. Detachable cards of these charts appear in the back of the book.

SIXTH RACE

Hollywood

MAY 8, 1982

1 1/16 MILES. (1.39) MAIDEN. Purse $18,000, 3-year-olds and upward. Weights, 3-year-olds, 114 lbs.; older, 124 lbs.

Value of race $18,000, value to winner $9,900, second $3,600, third $2,700, fourth $1,350, fifth $450. Mutuel pool $560,757.

Last Raced	Horse	Eqt.	A.	Wt.	PP	St	1/4	1/2	3/4	Str	Fin	Jockey	Odds $1
	Swing Till Dawn		3	114	4	1	1-1	1-1	1 ½	2-4	1hd	McCarron C J	1.40
2Apr82 6SA 4	Beau Glacier		4	124	10	6	5-2½	4 ½	2-3½	1hd	2hd	Hawley S	27.60
20Apr82 2SA 2	The Hague	b	3	117	7	9	6hd	6-3½	5-2½	3-3½	3-3½	Pincay L Jr	2.20
20Apr82 2SA 9	Falardeau		3	114	9	11	11-4	10-1½	6-2	4-4	4-4½	Valenzuela P A	29.20
1May82 6Hol 6	Wajima San		3	115	5	12	12	12	9-2	7 ½	5hd	Pierce D	77.10
23Apr82 6Hol 2	Jasmine Prince		4	124	6	10	10-3	8-1	7-2½	8-2	6-5	Guerra W A	7.70
25Apr82 6Hol 7	Crimson Axe	b	3	109	12	7	7-5	7-2½	8-2	9-6	7 ½	Steiner J J-5	138.10
25Apr82 6Hol 5	Discerner	b	3	114	2	8	4hd	5-2½	4 ½	6hd	8-1½	Black K	61.90
25Apr82 6Hol 3	Colonialism		3	115	8	2	3-2	3hd	3-1	5hd	9-3½	Sibille R	5.30
	Le Fur	b	3	114	1	4	9hd	9hd	10-1	10-3	10-5	Olivares F	16.00
4Apr82 3SA 12	Center Rural	b	3	115	3	3	8 ½	11-2½	12	11-3	11	McHargue D G	44.50
21Mar82 6SA	Rakkasan	b	3	114	11	5	2hd	2 ½	11-3	12	-	Diaz A L	154.10

Rakkasan, Eased.
OFF AT 4:40. Start good. Won driving. Time, :23 2/5, :47 2/5, 1:12, 1:37 1/5, 1:44 Track fast.

$ 2 Mutuel Prices:				
4-	SWING TILL DAWN	4.80	4.00	2.80
10-	BEAU GLACIER		14.40	6.40
7-	THE HAGUE			2.80

Gr. c, by Grey Dawn II-Swinging Lizzie, by The Axe II. Trainer Marikian Charles M. Bred by Jonabell Farm (Ky).

SWING TILL DAWN outsprinted rivals for the early lead, drew clear while rated down the backstretch, lost the lead to BEAU GLACIER in the upper stretch but came on again under strong handling and prevailed narrowly. The latter, unhurried early, moved up to force the issue outside the winner at the far turn, got the lead in the upper stretch but weakened slightly near the end. THE HAGUE, unhurried early, responded outside horses when roused on firrl turn, closed strongly in the middle of the track in the final sixteenth and just missed. FALARDEAU also rallied on the outside around the final turn but did not menace in the last sixteenth. JASMINE PRINCE was never dangerous. COLONIALISM was finished after six furlongs. CENTER RURAL was very wide. RAKKASAN was finished early and was eased when hopelessly beaten in the stretch.

Owners- 1, McClure & Reagan; 2, Daniels Mrs T L; 3, Elmendorf; 4, Cashman E C; 5, Lauro-Arico-Chartier et al; 6, Blum Maribel; 7, Fkde-Schltz-Shy-Stle; 8, Hunt N B; 9, Smma St-Vly Brdng-Ynk et al;10, Baker H J;11, Nakamura K;12, Major Acres.

Trainers- 1, Marikian Charles M; 2, Cofer Riley S; 3, Mandella Richard; 4, Sullivan John; 5, Cole Peter; 6, Winick Randy; Bunn Thomas M Jr; 8, Rettele Loren; 9, Wheeler Lin;10, Knight Chay R;11, Doyle A T;12, Hofmans David.

Overweight: The Hague 3 pounds; Wajima San 1; Colonialism 1; Center Rural 1.

Scratched- Quack Attack(9Apr82 6SA 8); Iron Axe(17Apr82 6SA 7); Timberjack(20Mar82 6SA 5).

8th Hollywood

7 FURLONGS
HOLLYWOOD PARK

7 FURLONGS. (1.19⅘) 4th Running of THE TRIPLE BEND HANDICAP. $50,000 added. 3-year-olds and upward. By subscription of $50 each, which shall accompany the nomination, $500 additional to start, with $50,000 added, of which $10,000 to second, $7,500 to third, $3,750 to fourth and $1,250 to fifth. Weights, Monday, May 3. Starters to be named through the entry box by closing time of entries. A trophy will be presented to the owner of the winner. Closed Wednesday, April 28, 1982, with 15 nominations.

Never Tabled

Dk. b. or br. h. 5, by Never Bend—Table Flirt, by Round Table

Own.—Wygod M J — **112**

Br.—Wygod M J (Ky) — 1982 3 2 1 0 $24,200

Tr.—Mandella Richard — 1980 0 M 0 0

Lifetime 3 2 1 0 $24,200

2May82-3Hol	6f	:22^{3}	:44^{4}	1:08^{4}ft	*2-5	120	3^{1½}	2^{2}	2^{2½}	2no	McCarronCJ^{2}	Aw22000	93	Jenny'sDvid,NeverTbled,StrikItBig	5
15Apr82-7SA	6f	:21^{4}	:44^{4}	1:09 ft	*1	120	2½	2^{hd}	1^{2}	1^{5½}	McCarronCJ^{7}	Aw19000	93	Never Tabled, Santir,TonysLanding	9
2Apr82-6SA	6f	:21^{4}	:45	1:10^{1}ft	2¾	118	3^{2}	3^{1}	1^{2½}	1^{8}	Pincay L Jr^{2}	Mdn	87	NeverTbled,Hwkire,SpnishNugget	10

●Apr 26 SA 6f ft 1:11^{2} h   Apr 11 SA 5f ft 1:02^{1} h   Mar 31 SA 4f ft :50^{2} b   Mar 25 SA 7f ft 1:25 h

Fingal *

B. g. 8, by Gaelic Dancer—Moog, by Noor

Own.—Mevorach & Vallone — **113**

Br.—Claiborne Farm (Cal) — 1982 6 3 1 0 $56,500

Tr.—Frankel Robert — 1981 14 6 2 1 $144,250

Lifetime 50 20 8 5 $344,513 — Turf 10 4 1 1 $70,200

21Apr82-5SA	a6½f	(T):21^{1}	:43^{3}	1:13 fm	3	115	3^{1½}	3^{2½}	3^{3}	1no	DelahoussayeE^{4}	75000	94	Fingal, Tellaround, Gray Dandy	12
4Apr82-2SA	6½f	:21^{4}	:44^{3}	1:15^{2}ft	*4-5	115	5^{4}	4^{2½}	1^{hd}	1^{2½}	DelahoussayeE^{5}	60000	93	Fingal, Amen Brother, Tellaround	8
21Mar82-1SA	6f	:21^{4}	:44^{4}	1:09^{1}ft	*1	116	5^{5½}	4^{3}	3^{2}	1^{1}	DelahoussayeE^{5}	50000	92	Fingal, Incorporator, Beach Walk	8
21Feb82-5SA	a6½f	(T):21^{2}	:43^{1}	1:13 fm	*1-2	116	2^{hd}	2^{1}	3^{4}	4^{6}	DelahoussayeE^{4}	62500	88	FrndlyUncAln,Incorprtr,AmnBrthr	11
6Feb82-5SA	a6½f	(T):21	:43^{1}	1:12^{3}fm	*4-5	115	6^{3½}	6^{7}	3^{4½}	2^{3½}	DelahoussayeE^{4}	70000	92	Gray Dandy, Fingal, Steelinctive	10
30Jan82-4SA	6f	:21^{2}	:43^{4}	1:08^{2}ft	*4-5e	118	9^{8}	9^{10}	6^{6}	4^{2¾}	DelahoussayeE^{2}	62500	93	MinstrelGrey,MrbleCourt,Tellround	9
25Oct81-5SA	a6½f	(T):21^{1}	:43^{3}	1:14 fm	*4-5	120	3^{4}	3^{5}	3^{1}	5^{4½}	McCarron C J^{4}	70000	85	Tellaround, Dandy Wit, Gray Dandy	8
11Oct81-7SA	6f	:22	:45^{1}	1:10 ft	*1	121	2^{1}	2^{1½}	2^{1½}	1^{nk}	McCrronCJ^{10}	Aw32000	88	Fingal, Marble Court, Sham'sFool	10
2Oct81-5SA	6½f	:22	:44^{3}	1:15^{4}ft	*3-2	117	3^{2½}	3^{2}	2^{hd}	1^{2}	McCarronCJ^{3}	Aw34000	91	Fingal, Double Discount, Parsec	5
22Aug81-7Dmr	1 1/16	(T):46^{3}	1:11	1:42^{1}fm	*3	116	1^{hd}	1^{hd}	2^{3}	7^{7}	DelahoussayeE^{1}	80000	91	Sosegado, Me Good Man, Partout	10

May 6 Hol 3f ft :37^{1} b   Apr 30 Hol 4f ft :47^{1} h   Apr 15 SA 4f ft :49^{1} h   Mar 29 SA 4f gd :48^{4} h

Remember John

B. g. 3, by The Irish Lord—Yoweee, by Crozier

Own.—Sheridan Mr-Mrs J — **110**

Br.—Valenti P (Cal) — 1982 4 3 1 0 $92,750

Tr.—Vienna Darrell — 1981 6 1 2 1 $52,900

Lifetime 10 4 3 1 $145,650

1May82-7Hol	6f	:22	:44^{2}	1:08^{3}ft	*3-5	122	2^{hd}	1^{hd}	1^{1}	1½	McCrronCJ^{4}	Debonair	94	RemmbrJohn,ArtDirctor,RingProud	5
31Mar82-8SA	6½f	:21^{3}	:44^{1}	1:15^{1}ft	3	117	1½	1^{hd}	1½	1¾	DelhoussyeE^{1}	Baldwin	94	RmmbrJohn,TmToExplod,CrystlStr	7
21Mar82-4SA	6½f	:21^{2}	:44	1:15^{2}ft	*2-3	115	1½	1^{1}	1^{3}	1^{5}	DelhoussyeE^{1}	Aw20000	93	RemembrJohn,ClticSbr,EstrSrmon	6
17Feb82-8SA	6f	:21^{2}	:43^{4}	1:08^{3}ft	20	117	1^{hd}	2^{1}	2^{2½}	2^{3}	DlhoussyE^{6}	Blsa Chca	92	TmToExplod,RmmbrJohn,JornytS	10
9Sep81-8Dmr	1	:45^{3}	1:11^{1}	1:37^{2}ft	10	117	1^{hd}	1^{hd}	5^{1½}	9^{7½}	McCarronCJ^{8}	Dmr Fut	73	GatoDelSol,TheCaptain,RingProud	10
26Aug81-8Dmr	1	:45^{4}	1:10^{3}	1:36^{4}ft	6½	117	1½	1^{1½}	2^{hd}	5^{5½}	Toro F^{6}	Balboa	78	TheCaptain,DistantHeart,GtoDelSol	9
12Aug81-8Dmr	6f	:22	:45	1:11 ft	*4-5	120	1^{hd}	1½	1^{hd}	3^{1}	McCarronCJ^{5}	De Anza	82	King'sFinder,Heln'sBu,RmmbrJohn	5
29Jly81-8Dmr	6f	:22^{1}	:45^{2}	1:10^{4}ft	*4-5	114	1½	1½	1^{2½}	1^{1¾}	McCrrCJ^{5}	[S]Gradution	84	RemmbrJohn,King'sFindr,DistntHrt	9
18Jly81-8Hol	6f	:21^{3}	:44^{4}	1:10^{2}ft	19	115	2^{hd}	2^{hd}	1½	2^{hd}	Toro F^{10}	Hol Juv	85	TheCptin,RememberJohn,Hln'sBu	12
5Jly81-6Hol	6f	:22	:45^{3}	1:11^{2}ft	*6-5e	116	6^{9}	5^{7½}	3^{4}	2^{2¾}	Toro F^{7}	[S]Mdn	77	SwetndNturl,RmmbrJohn,Wicklow	11

Apr 29 Hol 3f ft :36^{3} h   Apr 27 Hol 5f ft 1:01^{2} h   Apr 24 SA 6f ft 1:13^{3} h   Apr 19 SA 5f ft :58 h

Rock Softly

B. g. 4, by Rock Talk—Softly, by Sole Landing

Own.—Byrn-Dvis-Glsn-Nvk-Rsnbrg **115**

Br.—Retler Mr-Mrs R H (Md)	1982	9	1	2	3	$107,250
Tr.—Newsom Jesse C	1981	21	4	5	1	$138,625
Lifetime 35 5 7 6 $251,675	Turf	13	1	3	1	$66,725

18Apr82-7SA	1	:453	1:10	1:343ft	3½	120	33	2½	2½	1no	McCarronCJ5	Aw40000	96	Rock Softly, Sir Dancer, Tell Again	8
28Mar82-7SA	1 1/16	:451	1:084	1:411ft	*8-5	117	37½	59½	47½	34½	DelhoussyeE4	Aw35000	98	Sunshine Swag, A Run, RockSoftly	8
20Mar82-8GG	1	(T):48	1:122	1:364yl	9½	117	31½	86¼	1014	1021	LamanceC8	S F Mle H	62	Silveyville, Visible Pole, ASureHit	10
6Mar82-7SA	1⅛	(T):452	1:094	1:463fm	4½	119	57	54	42½	22	DelhoussyeE4	Aw45000	92	Lake City, Rock Softly, Braughing	7
28Feb82-6SA	1 1/16	:47	1:104	1:412ft	*2½	117	2hd	2hd	31½	2nk	DelhoussyeE6	Aw40000	94	Egg Toss, Rock Softly, Western	6
21Feb82-8SA	1¼	(T):434	1:34	1:591fm	18	116	68	44	46½	67¾	Black K10	Sra Nvda H	83	HighCounsel,HndsomeOn,IrishHrt	11
7Feb82-8SA	1¼	:451	1:344	2:002ft	51	115	56½	54	47	37	Black K8	C H Strub	80	It's the One, Dorcaro, Rock Softly	8
17Jan82-8SA	1⅛	:452	1:092	1:473ft	36	114	66½	54½	32	35¾	Black K5	Sn Frndo	85	It's the One, Princelet, Rock Softly	9
3Jan82-8SA	7f	:221	:454	1:26 hy	13	114	89½	813	716	416	Black K2	Malibu	54	Island Whirl, Shanekite, It'stheOne	8
20Dec81-7Hol	7f	:22	:444	1:22 ft	3½	121	62¾	3½	11	1¾	Black K3	Aw32000	87	RockSoftly,LaughingBoy,DustyHul	8

May 5 Hol 4f ft :493 hg   Apr 25 Hol 5f ft 1:054 h   Apr 16 Hol tr.t 4f ft :523 h   Apr 10 Hol tr.t 4f ft :52 h

Laughing Boy

B. c. 4, by Shecky Greene—Pomade, by Prince John

Own.—Elmendorf **112**

Br.—Elmendorf Farm (Ky)	1982	6	1	3	0	$31,100
Tr.—Stidham Michael	1981	12	2	2	0	$37,975
Lifetime 21 4 5 0 $76,150	Turf	3	0	1	0	$7,100

29Apr82-8Hol	6f	:22	:443	1:082ft	*3-2	114	31½	2½	1½	12½	McCarronCJ2	Aw26000	95	LaughingBoy,BeachWalk,Redoutble	7
17Apr82-6SA	a6½f	(T):212	:44	1:132fm	10	114	34½	32½	2½	22¼	Hansen R D1	Aw32000	90	Captain Nick,LaughingBoy,Isopach	9
11Apr82-5SA	6½f	:22	:451	1:17 sy	*9-5	115	65¼	65½	64¼	73¼	Toro F6	Aw26000	82	Tellround,Redoutble,He'sSomthing	7
26Feb82-7SA	6f	:22	:444	1:084ft	9½	115	74½	52½	11½	2no	Toro F1	Aw26000	94	MisterWilder,LughingBoy,Tllround	7
13Feb82-5SA	6½f	:213	:442	1:161ft	7	115	88¼	79½	55½	2nk	Toro F4	Aw26000	89	Kearney,LaughingBoy,Mari'sBook	10
28Jan82-7SA	6½f	:212	:434	1:153ft	6	113	55½	45	42½	65½	Guerra W A1	Aw26000	86	Tooovrprim,MistrWildr,Cloonwillin	7
28Dec81-7Hol	7f	:22	:444	1:22 ft	4¾	114	52¾	41½	41½	2¾	McCarronCJ1	Aw32000	86	RockSoftly,LaughingBoy,DustyHul	8
9Dec81-7Hol	6½f	:221	:45	1:154ft	17	114	54½	32½	42½	42½	McCarronCJ8	Aw25000	88	PompeiiCourt,KngrooCourt,Dorcro	8
13Nov81-7Hol	6f	:22	:443	1:084ft	26	115	65½	53	52	54½	Rivera M A4	Aw26000	88	Hcwind,KngrooCourt,PompiiCourt	8
29Oct81-7SA	6f	:22	:443	1:09 ft	16	114	42¾	45½	66¾	68¼	ValenzuelPA4	Aw34000	85	Shnekite,ImportntMemo,NtivFishr	7

Apr 25 Hol 4f ft :482 h   Apr 7 SA 4f ft :474 h   Apr 3 SA 5f ft 1:02 h   Mar 29 SA 4f gd :481 h

Gifted Dancer

Ch. c. 4, by L'Enjoleur—Second Coming, by Sir Gaylord

Own.—Roden W F **117**

Br.— C T Chenery Estate (Va)	1982	4	3	1	0	$47,700
Tr.—Russell John W	1981	8	1	5	1	$34,950
Lifetime 15 5 7 1 $84,620	Turf	5	2	2	0	$39,450

23Apr82-7Hol	6f	:221	:444	1:092ft	*9-5	118	41½	2hd	1hd	2nk	Pincay L Jr5	Aw35000	90	PirateLw,GiftedDncer,MisterWilder	7
26Mar82-5SA	a6½f	(T):213	:44	1:141fm	*2½	117	22½	1hd	1½	11	Pincay L Jr6	Aw32000	88	GftdDncr,AnswrtoMusc,SRullhRn	12
7Mar82-5SA	a6½f	(T):211	:433	1:14 fm	*7-5	120	63¾	42½	2½	1¾	Pincay L Jr6	Aw23000	89	GftdDncr,RnOfDmonds,Hostd'Oro	11
24Feb82-6SA	6f	:213	:441	1:09 ft	*2	117	44½	41¾	3nk	12¾	Pincay L Jr7	Aw19000	93	GiftedDncer,RglFlcon,VikingHustlr	7
31Dec81-5SA	6½f	:224	:462	1:192hy	*2¾	113	2hd	32½	21½	22½	ShoemkerW3	Aw18000	70	Tuff to Beat, Gifted Dancer, Mufti	7
16Dec81-3Hol	6f	:222	:452	1:101ft	3¾	117	32½	22½	22½	1½	Pincay L Jr2	50000	86	GiftedDncer,MsterJono,Logrhythm	6
13Jun81-9Hol	1 1/16	(T):461	1:103	1:414fm	3¾	115	34½	31	42	75½	McHrgueDG6	Aw22000	84	MasterThatch,RegalSport,Enhnce	12
29May81-8Hol	1 1/16	(T):473	1:12	1:424fm	3	115	1hd	1hd	1hd	2nk	McHrgueDG6	Aw24000	85	MsterJono,GiftedDncer,MsterThtch	9
15May81-9Hol	6f	:214	:443	1:094ft	3½	115	52¾	54¼	33	34½	McHrgueDG3	Aw22000	83	Menswer,Jeff'sEncore,GiftedDncer	7
8May81-7Hol	6½f	:222	:45	1:162ft	3	115	2hd	2hd	2hd	2hd	Toro F1	Aw22000	88	Fair Hint, Gifted Dancer, Breached	6

May 6 Hol 5f ft 1:033 h   May 1 Hol 5f ft 1:012 h   Apr 17 SA 6f ft 1:144 h   Apr 11 SA 6f ft 1:181 h

Pompeii Court

B. h. 5, by Tell—Port Damascus, by Damascus

Own.—Lewyk & Crowe **116**

Br.—Keck H B (Ky)	1982	4	2	0	1	$46,800
Tr.—Anderson Laurie N	1981	16	5	5	3	$45,954
Lifetime 24 9 7 4 $97,634						

7Mar82-3SA	1	:443	1:083	1:342ft	*2½	116	2½	1½	1½	1hd	Hawley S1	Aw40000	97	PompCort,KngrooCort,SonofDodo	7
18Feb82-7SA	1	:451	1:09	1:333ft	11	114	1½	11	13	14½	Hawley S2	Aw32000	101	PompeiiCourt,QuntumLep,Western	8
5Feb82-7SA	6½f	:212	:433	1:15 ft	11	115	42½	42½	43	33¾	Sibille R5	Aw32000	91	VictorySmpl,BondRullh,PompCourt	8
20Jan82-5SA	7f	:214	:45	1:244sy	4¾	115	2hd	1hd	1hd	42	Sibille R1	Aw32000	74	Gristle,QuntumLep,AnswertoMusic	5
18Dec81-7Hol	6f	:214	:443	1:095ft	9	115	3nk	3nk	32	55	Sibille R6	Aw30000	84	Hacwind,BennyBob,CrestoftheWve	7
9Dec81-7Hol	6½f	:221	:45	1:154ft	5½	116	1hd	1½	12	11¼	Sibille R2	Aw25000	91	PompeiiCourt,KngrooCourt,Dorcro	8
27Nov81-7Hol	6½f	:223	:453	1:183sy	*3	115	1hd	11½	21½	2¾	Sibille R4	Aw25000	76	DndyWit,PompiiCourt,Sli'sRoylDrm	8
13Nov81-7Hol	6f	:22	:443	1:084ft	15	115	1hd	2½	2½	34¼	Sibille R1	Aw26000	89	Hcwind,KngrooCourt,PompiiCourt	8
17Oct81-8StP	6f	:222	:451	1:101ft	*9-5	118	55½	54¼	35	44	Garcia C1	Aw6500	94	Kinlin, Flashys Champ,ThreeforYou	7
30May81-9NP	1 1/16	:472	1:113	1:43 ft	2¾	119	11	1hd	2hd	3nk	Hedge R2	Cont'ntal H	100	MisterCountry,Ky.Alt,PompiiCourt	7

May 3 Hol 6f ft 1:131 h   Apr 23 SA 6f ft 1:121 h   Apr 16 SA 4f ft :483 h   Mar 31 SA 5f ft 1:012 h

Shanekite B. c. 4, by Hoist Bar—Win Shane, by Anyoldtime
Br.—Udko Selma (Cal) 1982 4 0 2 0 $30,000
Own.—Udko Selma 117 Tr.—Landers Dale 1981 10 6 0 0 $161,000
Lifetime 20 8 4 0 $213,125 Turf 1 0 1 0 $12,000
17Apr82-8SA a6½f ⓣ:21 :4311:13 fm 7½ 118 65½ 62¾ 3½ 21½ Hawley S1 Sn Simn H 92 Shagbark, Shanekite, Belfort 8
24Mar82-8SA 5½f :213 :442 1:021ft 4½ 118 — — — — HawleyS6 El Conejo H — ToB.OrNot,Belfort,Terresto'sSinger 8
24Mar82—Lost rider
9Jan82-8SA 7f :213 :434 1:204ft 3½ 119 43½ 41½ 89 812 Hawley S6 Sn Crlos H 84 Solo Guy, ‡King Go Go, Smokite 8
3Jan82-8SA 7f :221 :454 1:26 hy *8-5 120 51½ 1½ 2½ 26 Hawley S6 Malibu 64 Island Whirl, Shanekite, It'stheOne 8
19Dec81-8Hol 7f :212 :434 1:219ft *4-5 117 41½ 41½ 11 12½ Hawley S4 Yuletide H 89 Shanekite, FlyingChick,IslandWhirl 5
28Nov81-8Hol 1 :48 1:13 1:384m 3½ 113 1hd 1½ 3½ 42½ Hawley S4 Ntv Dvr.H 69 Syncopate, King Go Go, Wickerr 6
11Nov81-8Hol 6f :213 :441 1:081ft 2¾ 114 52½ 11 14 12½ HawieyS8 Sprnt Chmp 96 Shanekite,Syncopte,BigPresenltion 8
11Nov81—Run in two divisions, 8th & 9th races.
29Oct81-7SA 6f :22 :443 1:09 ft *4-5 118 22½ 22½ 2hd 15 Hawley S1 Aw34000 93 Shnekite,ImportntMemo,NtivFishr 7
4Sep81-8Dmr 1 1/16 :453 1:092 1:41 ft 8 117 34 45½ 46 511 Hawley S6 El Cajon 84 Island Whirl, Rock Softly, Damas 9
24Aug81-8Dmr 1 :452 1:101 1:363ft *3-2 117 31½ 22 22 43½ Pincay L Jr4 Aw30000 81 AtYourPlesure,Sli'sRoylDrem,Dscro 6
Apr 30 Hol 6f ft 1:142 h Apr 24 SA 4f ft :494 h Apr 13 SA ⓣ 5f yl 1:04 h (d) Apr 5 SA HC 5f gd 1:041 h (d)

The feature race of the day was the 7-furlong $50,000 added Triple Bend Handicap. It featured such top horses as Shanekite, Remember John, Never Tabled, Fingal, Laughing Boy, Rock Softly, and Pompeii Court. Never Tabled had two wins and a second in three recent local starts. He had not run until he was a five-year-old, but his brief record was quite impressive. Fingal was a strong horse who had won nearly $350,000 in the fifty races of his career. He came into the Triple Bend off three consecutive impressive victories at Santa Anita. As the favorite in four previous races, however, he had failed to win and twice had been out of the money.

Remember John was the only three-year-old scheduled to be in the race. His record of three victories and one second in four 1982 races was quite impressive. He was consistently running under 1:09 for 6 furlongs. Despite this blinding speed, fear of the older horses or some other reason caused his owner to scratch Remember John. Rock Softly was moving up in class. His 96 speed rating in a recent 1-mile victory at Santa Anita made him a definite threat. Laughing Boy was similar. He appeared to be outclassed, but a convincing 6-furlong victory at Hollywood the previous week in $1{:}08^2$ meant that he could not be ruled out. Gifted Dancer had four wins and two seconds in his last six races. However, today's competition was much stronger than he had previously faced. Pompeii Court had just run two smashing mile-race victories at Santa Anita. In one of them as an 11—1 shot, he had broken the track record by running a $1{:}33^3$ mile, a sizzling time. The final horse in the race was Shanekite, who had a brilliant but erratic record. In 1981, he had six wins in ten outings and finished out of the money in the remaining four races. He had not won in 1982 and had even lost his rider, Sandy Hawley, in one of these races. However, if sharp, he could run 6 furlongs in 1:08 flat and could handle this competition. This was a classic match.

The noted handicapper and Harvard dropout Andy Beyer believes thoroughbred handicapping is the supremely challenging intellectual activity. This race presented such a challenge for talented handicappers. We, of course, have argued in this book that you should leave such handicapping to these experts. You have to be very good to beat them, but you can rely on their skills to establish fair win odds and then use this information to select a place or show bet if one is good enough.

Shanekite was made an even-money favorite of the crowd. The tote board 1 minute before post time was as follows:

	Totals	#8 Shanekite	Expected Value per Dollar Bet on Shanekite
Odds		1—1	
Win	398,851	155,321	
Place	131,018	40,952	1.05
Show	59,163	14,585	1.18

These values provided an expected value per dollar bet of 1.05 to place and 1.18 to show. Thus Shanekite was a Dr. Z system bet to show but not good enough to bet to place. My betting fortune was $1,088, reflecting my earlier win in the sixth race. The optimal Dr. Z system bet was $310 to show on Shanekite. The totals at post time were similar:

	Totals	#8 Shanekite	Expected Value per Dollar Bet on Shanekite
Odds		1—1	
Win	407,589	158,523	
Place	139,217	42,739	1.06
Show	60,030	15,108	1.17

Never Tabled won the race, followed by Shanekite and Pompeii Court. The chart of the race was as follows:

EIGHTH RACE
Hollywood
MAY 8, 1982

7 FURLONGS. (1.19 2/5) 4th Running of THE TRIPLE BEND HANDICAP. $50,000 added. 3-year-olds and upward. By subscription of $50 each, which shall accompany the nomination. $500 additional to start, with $50,000 added, of which $10,000 to second, $7,500 to third, $3,750 to fourth and $1,250 to fifth. Weights, Monday, May 3. Starters to be named through the entry box by closing time of entries. A trophy will be presented to the owner of the winner. Closed Wednesday, April 28, 1982, with 15 nominations.

Value of race $54,250, value to winner $31,750, second $10,000, third $7,500, fourth $3,750, fifth $1,250. Mutuel pool $606,836.

Last Raced		Horse	Eqt.	A.	Wt.	PP	St	1/4	1/2	Str	Fin	Jockey	Odds $1
2May82	3Hol 2	Never Tabled		5	112	1	3	1½	1-1	1-1½	1-2	McCarron C J	4.90
17Apr82	8SA 2	Shanekite	b	4	117	7	6	6-5	5½	3-3½	2hd	Hawley S	1.10
7Mar82	3SA 1	Pompeii Court		5	116	6	1	3hd	2hd	2hd	3-2½	Shoemaker W	3.30
18Apr82	7SA 1	Rock Softly		4	117	3	7	7	7	5-2	4-3	Pincay L Jr	6.40
29Apr82	8Hol 1	Laughing Boy	b	4	115	4	5	5½	6-6	4hd	5-8	McHargue D G	10.70
21Apr82	5SA 1	Fingal		8	113	2	4	2hd	4-3	7	6hd	Valenzuela P A	13.30
23Apr82	7Hol 2	Gifted Dancer		4	117	5	2	4-6	3hd	6-1	7	Guerra W A	29.40

OFF AT 5:48. Start good. Won ridden out. Time, :21 4/5, :44, 1:08 2/5, 1:21 Track fast.

$ 2 Mutuel Prices:				
1-	NEVER TABLED	11.80	5.00	3.40
8-	SHANEKITE		3.20	2.60
7-	POMPEII COURT			2.80

Dk. b. or br. h, by Never Bend-Table Flirt, by Round Table. Trainer Mandella Richard. Bred by Wygod M J (Ky).

NEVER TABLED got the lead soon after the start, drew clear on the turn and maintained a safe margin through the final furlong. SHANEKITE lacked early speed, stayed wide throughout but rallied strongly through the stretch. POMPEII COURT in close contention while four-wide to the stretch, responded in the drive but could not overtake the winner. ROCK SOFTLY, sluggish at the start, gradually made up ground in the drive but did not threaten. LAUGHING BOY, shuffled back after the start, was never dangerous. FINGAL tired in the stretch. GIFTED DANCER was finished after five furlongs.

Owners- 1, Wygod M J; 2, Udko Selma; 3, Lewyk & Crowe; 4, Bymn-Dvis-Glsn-Nvk-Rsnbrg; 5, Elmendorf; 6, Mevorach & Vallone; 7, Roden W F.

Trainers- 1, Mandella Richard; 2, Landers Dale; 3, Anderson Laurie N; 4, Newsom Jesse C; 5, Stidham Michael; 6, Frankel Robert; 7, Russell John W.

Overweight: Rock Softly 2 pounds; Laughing Boy 3.

Scratched- Remember John(1May82 7Hol 1); Belfort(17Apr82 8SA 3).

The payoff for show for Shanekite was $2.60. This was a little poorer than expected for an even-money favorite with an expected value of 1.17. One might hope to get at least $2.80 or possibly $3.00. However, because the top three choices out of the small seven-horse field had finished in the money, Shanekite's payoff was lowered, so with breakage it became $2.60. Despite the fact that the place payoff of $3.20 on Shanekite seems quite high, it was still not a Dr. Z system bet. My show bet of $310 returned $403, for a profit of $93—a 30% return on investment.

The Whitney Handicap, Saratoga Racetrack, Saratoga, New York, August 1, 1981

The fifty-sixth running of the Whitney Handicap at Saratoga featured a strong card of horses vying for their share of the $150,000 added purse. Amber Pass was the consensus favorite, followed by Winter's Tale and Glorious Song. The race was also to include such strong horses as The Liberal Member, Ring of Light, Temperence Hill, and Noble Nashua. A series of minor colds and other ailments as well as strategy for upcoming races led to the scratching of four horses: Amber Pass, Glorious Song, Temperence Hill, and Classic Trail. This left eight starters. Winter's Tale was established as a 3—2 favorite of the betting public. He had his regular jockey, Jeffrey Fell, in the irons and the number 1 post position. In twelve starts he had finished first or second on ten occasions and as a favorite was always in the money. An upset possibility was Fio Rito, who had performed brilliantly at low odds against much weaker competition.

DOUBLE WAGERING ON 8th & 9th RACES

1⅛ MILES

EIGHTH RACE
THE WHITNEY HANDICAP
(56 RUNNING)
$150,000 ADDED
(Grade I)

FOR THREE-YEAR-OLDS AND UPWARD. By subscription of $300 each, which should accomany the nomination; $1,200 to pass the entry box, with $150,000 added. The added money and all fees to be divided 60% to the winner, 22% to second, 12% to third and 6% to fourth. Trophies will be presented to the winning owner, trainer and jockey and mementoes to the grooms of the first four finishers.

(Closed (Wednesday, July 15, 1981 with 37 nominatons)

Track Record—1:47; TRI JET (5), 123 lbs.; August 3, 1974.

MAKE SELECTION BY NUMBER

No.	Owner / Colors / Horse / Breeding	Trainer	Weight	Jockey	Morn. Line
1	ROKEBY STABLES; Dark Gray, Yellow Braids, Sleeves and Cap; **WINTER'S TALE**; Ro.g.5, Arts and Letters—Christmas Wind by Nearctic	MacK. MILLER	121	JEFFREY FELL	3-1
2	PETER BARBERINO; Royal Blue, Gold Braces and Emblem, Gold Chevrons on Sleeves, Gold Cap; **JOANIE'S CHIEF**; B.c.4, Ack Ack—Merry Madeline by Fleet Host	EUGENE JACOBS	108	JEAN-LUC SAMYN	15-1
3	RAYMOND J. LeCESSE; Orange, Lilac Yoke, Lilac and Orange Halved Sleeves, Orange Cap; **FIO RITO** (NY); Gr.h.6, Dreaming Native—Seagret by Sea Charger	M. FERRARO	113	LESLIE HULET	20-1
4	FRANK STRONACH; Light Blue, Black Diamond Frame, Black Hoop on Sleeves, Blue and Black Cap; **GLORIOUS SONG**; B.m.5, Halo—Ballade by Herbager	J. CAIRNS	118	ROBIN PLATTS	4-1
5	CALUMET FARM; Devil's Red, Blue Collar, Two Blue Hoops on Sleeves, Blue Cap; **RIVALERO**; B.g.5, Riva Ridge—Dictates by Bold Ruler	J. M. VEITCH	112	JACINTO VASQUEZ	15-1
6	LOCUST HILL FARM; White, Cherry Hoop, Cherry Sleeves, White Cap; **BLUE ENSIGN**; Gr.c.4, Hoist the Flag—Laughter by Bold Ruler	D. W. CARROLL	109	JACK KAENEL	10-1
7	OGDEN PHIPPS; Black, Cherry Cap; **The Liberal Member**; Ch.g.6, Bold Reason—Lady Pitt by Sword Dancer	A. PENNA	113	ANGEL CORDERO, JR.	5-1
8	VIOLA SOMMER; Green, Gold Diamond Hoop, Gold Sleeves, Green Cap, Gold Tassel; **RING OF LIGHT**; B.g.6, In Reality—Due Dilly by Sir Gaylord	F. MARTIN	114	RUBEN HERNANDEZ	8-1
9	LOBLOLLY STABLE; Yellow and Chocolate Brown Diagonal Quarters, Yellow Sleeves, Brown Hoop, Yellow Cap; **TEMPERENCE HILL**; B.c.4, Stop the Music—Sister Shannon by Etonian	J. B. CANTEY	127	DONALD MacBETH	6-1
10	HARRY T. MANGURIAN, JR.; Beige, Blue Sash, Two Blue Hoops on Sleeves, Blue Cap; **CLASSIC TRIAL**; B.h.5, In Reality—Desert Trial by Moslem Chief	T. F. ROOT, SR.	106	RICHARD MIGLIORE	20-1
11	FLYING ZEE STABLES; Light Blue, White Yoke and "ZZ," White Blocks on Sleeves, Blue Cap, White Tassel; **NOBLE NASHUA**; B.c.3, Nashua—Noble Lady by Vaguely Noble	J. MARTIN	114	EDDIE MAPLE	6-1

Change of Equipment: TEMPERENCE HILL—Blinkers On.

SCRATCHED—AMBER PASS

The odds on Winter's Tale were reasonably good throughout the betting period. An expected value of 1.15 just two minutes before post time qualified Winter's Tale as a Dr. Z system bet. The tote board was as follows:

	Totals	#1 Winter's Tale	Expected Value per Dollar Bet to Show on Winter's Tale
Odds		3—2	
Win	424,370	131,021	
Show	52,609	11,011	1.15

With an initial wealth of $2,500, the optimal bet to show on Winter's Tale was $270. At post time the odds to show had dropped slightly.

	Totals	#1 Winter's Tale	Expected Value per Dollar Bet to Show on Winter's Tale
Odds		3—2	
Win	486,875	159,273	
Show	57,957	14,313	1.09

The expected value per dollar bet to show on Winter's Tale was now 1.09.

•*Sweep's* *Saratoga Analysis*

EIGHTH RACE
1—Amber Pass
2—Winter's Tale
3—Glorious Song

Recently restored to his best form, AMBER PASS gets a slight nod to capture the nine-furlong Whitney. The Pass Catcher colt impressed in Delaware but will have to be at his best to handle WINTER'S TALE. This veteran also seems to have reached his form of last year, a possibility that makes him the one to beat. GLORIOUS SONG is at her best and her best makes her eligible to handle the males in this event.

SELECTIONS • GRADED ENTRIES
Saratoga

Consensus Totals Based on 5 points for First (7 for Best Bet), 2 for 2nd, 1 for 3rd. Best Bet in **Bold Type. Clocker Selections not included in Consensus.**

	TRACKMAN	HANDICAP	ANALYST	HERMIS	SWEEP	CLOCKER	CONSENSUS	
8	Amber Pass	Glorious Song	Amber Pass	Winter's Tale	Amber Pass	Winter's Tale	Amber Pass	21
	Winter's Tale	Amber Pass	The Liberal Member	Amber Pass	Winter's Tale	Amber Pass	Winter's Tale	15
	Glorious Song	Winter's Tale	Temperence Hill	Temperence Hill	Glorious Song	The Liberal Memoer	Glorious Song	7

8 SARATOGA

1⅛ MILES
SARATOGA
Start & Finish

1 ⅛ MILES. (1.47) 54th Running THE WHITNEY HANDICAP (Grade I). $150,000 Added. 3-year-olds and upward. By subscription of $300 each, which should accompany the nomination; $1,200 to pass the entry box, with $150,000 added. The added money and all fees to be divided 60% to the winner, 22% to second, 12% to third and 5% to fourth. Weights Monday, July 27. Starters to be named at the closing time of entries. Trophies will be presented to the winning owner, trainer and jockey and mementoes to the grooms of the first four finishers. Closed with 37 nominations.

Winter's Tale

B. g. 5, by Arts And Letters—Christmas Wind, by Nearctic
Br.—Mellon P (Va)
Tr.—Miller Mack
Own.—Rokeby Stable

121

	St.	1st	2nd	3rd	Amt.
1981	5	1	3	0	$48,170
1980	7	5	1	0	$462,880

19Jly81- 7Bel	fst	1 1/16	:46⅕	1:10	1:40⅘	3↑ Allowance	3	5	55	51½	1½	12½	Fell J	b 115	*.60	98-12	Winter's Tale 1152½ Niteange 115¾ Far Out East 1152¾	Handily	6
4Jly81- 8Bel	sly	1¼	:47⅗	1:36	2:02	3↑ Suburban H	7	2	21	67½	711	711	Fell J	123	3.80	79-20	TemperenceHill127hdRingofLight115¾HighlandBlde113nk	Faltered	8
13Jun81- 8Bel	fst	1⅛	:46⅗	1:10	1:46⅗	3↑ Nassau Cty H	3	3	2½	2½	24	24	Fell J	125	*.50	90-14	Fool'sPrayer1124Winter'sTale1252¾HerbWter1123½	Best of others	5
6Jun81- 1Bel	fst	1	:46⅖	1:10⅖	1:34⅘	3↑ Allowance	5	3	33	21½	21½	21½	Fell J	122	*.60	92-14	Amber Pass 1151½ Winter's Tale 1225½King'sWish1156	Stmbld st.	5
15May81- 8Bel	fst	7f	:23⅕	:46⅖	1:23⅗	Allowance	2	4	32	21	25	2¾	Fell J	122	*.60	83-19	Rivalero 122¾ Winter's Tale 122hd Tax Holiday 1053	Gamely	6
6Sep80- 7Bel	fst	1⅛	:45	1:09⅖	1:47	3↑ Marlboro H	8	3	32	3nk	12	14½	Fell J	123	3.30	92-15	Winter'sTle1234½GloriousSong117nkJklinKlugmn1183½	Ridden out	8
2Aug80- 8Sar	fst	1⅛	:46	1:09⅗	1:48⅕	3↑ Whitney	7	7	79	88	711	714	Fell J	126	3.70	80-10	State Dinner 120½ Dr. Patches 114½ Czaravich 1232½	Outrun	8
19Jly80- 8Bel	fst	1½	:51⅗	2:05	2:28⅗	3↑ Brooklyn H	4	3	21	11½	13	15	Fell J	120	3.40	77-20	Winter's Tale 1205 State Dinner1213½RingofLight1142	Ridden out	5
4Jly80- 8Bel	fst	1¼	:47⅘	1:36	2:00⅗	3↑ Suburban H	1	2	1½	2½	11	1hd	Fell J	114	2.70	97-14	Winter's Tale 114hd State Dinner 117hd Czaravich 1271½	Driving	7
15Jun80- 8Bel	fst	1⅛	:46⅗	1:10⅖	1:47⅕	3↑ Nassau Cty H	8	1	1½	11	14	17¾	Venezia M	111	3.90e	91-17	Winter's Tale 1117¾ Crow's Nest1095DewanKeys114nk	Ridden out	8

LATEST WORKOUTS Jly 25 Bel 4f fst :47 h Jly 16 Bel [T] 6f fm 1:13⅖ h (d) Jly 14 Bel 4f fst :49⅖ b Jly 10 Bel 4f fst :47⅗ b

Joanie's Chief *

B. c. 4, by Ack Ack—Merry Madeline, by Fleet Host
Br.—Hillbrook Farm (Ky)
Tr.—Jacobs Eugene
Own.—Barberino P

108

Turf Record

St.	1st	2nd	3rd
6	1	0	0

	St.	1st	2nd	3rd	Amt.
1981	12	2	3	4	$96,081
1980	16	1	2	2	$38,780

19Jly81- 9Del	fst	1 1/16	:46	1:10	1:41⅘	3↑ Wm Dupont Jr	7	9	816	86¾	710	44¾	Samyn J L	111	14.40	94-12	Amber Pass 119nk Phleming 118hd Herb Water 1084½	Mild rally	10
3Jly81- 8Bel	my	6f	:22⅕	:45	1:09	3↑ True North H	4	6	78	75	52¼	11¼	Samyn J L	109	23.70	97-16	Jonie'sChief1091¼ProudAppel117nkGuiltyConscience1133½	Driving	7
27Jun81- 6Bel	fst	6f	:22⅖	:45	1:09⅖	3↑ Allowance	6	5	33	47½	46½	35	Cordero A Jr	119	4.40	90-16	Engine One 1131½ Pikotazo 1193½ Joanie's Chief 119no	Wide	6
6Jun81- 7Bel	fst	1	:46⅕	1:10⅖	1:35⅗	3↑ Allowance	6	5	33	34½	25	25	Cordero A Jr	117	2.10	85-14	GuiltyConscienc1155Joni'sChif1171½PrincCrimson115½	Lugged in	10
1May81- 8Aqu	fst	6f	:23⅕	:46	1:10⅕	Allowance	7	4	54	34	32½	21½	Cordero A Jr	119	*.80	88-26	IrishSwords1191½Joanie'sChief1192¼SpartnEmperor1153½	Gamely	7
20Apr81- 8Aqu	fst	6f	:23	:46⅖	1:11⅕	Allowance	5	3	34	33½	21	12½	Cordero A Jr	116	2.60	85-30	Joanie's Chief 1162½Miroman119hdTrafficBreaker115¾	Ridden out	7
21Mar81-10Hia	fst	1⅛	:46⅘	1:10⅕	1:48⅗	3↑ Seminole H	3	5	66¼	68½	711	68¾	Velez R I	106	23.50	80-19	Boyne Valley 1101¾ Land of Eire 1111 Poor Dad115no	No menace	9
14Mar81- 8Hia	fst	1⅛	:48	1:12⅕	1:48⅖	Allowance	4	3	21	2hd	11½	2½	Velez R I	115	*1.30	89-09	Sailor Talk 119½ Joanie's Chief 1158½ Bing 115no	Game try	7
28Feb81- 9GP	fst	1¼	:48	1:36⅘	2:03⅕	3↑ Gulf Park H	3	6	55½	88¼	811	87¼	Velez R I	105	19.20	73-18	Hurry Up Blue 1191 YosiBoy1111ImperialDilemma113¾	No excuse	9
14Feb81- 9GP	fst	1⅛	:48⅗	1:12	1:49	3↑ Donn H	2	4	43	47	33	35	Velez R I	107	8.80	82-20	Hurry Up Blue 1162½ Tunerup 1262½Joanie'sChief1072	Bid, evenly	5

LATEST WORKOUTS Jly 29 Sar 5f sly 1:03⅖ b Jly 18 Bel tr.t 3f fst :37⅖ b Jly 11 Bel tr.t 5f fst 1:02 b Jly 2 Bel tr.t 3f gd :37⅕ b

Amber Pass

B. c. 4, by Pass Catcher—Amberina, by Somerset
Br.—DiLibero E M (Fla)
Tr.—Hine Hubert
Own.—Entremont

116

	St.	1st	2nd	3rd	Amt.
1981	5	3	1	1	$130,490
1980	10	3	2	4	$199,097

19Jly81- 9Del	fst	1 1/16	:46	1:10	1:41⅘	3↑ Wm Dupont Jr	3	7	59	55	22	1nk	Asmussen C B	b 119	*.80	99-12	Amber Pass 119nk Phleming 118hd Herb Water 1084½	Driving	10
6Jun81- 1Bel	fst	1	:46⅖	1:10⅖	1:34⅘	3↑ Allowance	2	2	1hd	11½	11½	11½	Asmussen C B	b 115	1.60	94-14	Amber Pass 1151½ Winter's Tale 1225½ King's Wish 1156	Driving	5
25May81- 8Bel	fst	1	:44⅕	1:08⅗	1:33⅘	3↑ Metropol'n H	1	2	11	1½	31½	33½	Hernandez R	b 115	5.10	95-22	Fappiano 1152¾ Irish Tower 127¾ Amber Pass 1157½	Weakened	7
2May81- 8Aqu	gd	7f	:22⅖	:45⅕	1:23	3↑ Carter H	6	1	31½	2hd	22	1½	Maple E	b 114	5.60e	86-19	Amber Pass 114½ GuiltyConscience1111Dunham'sGift1161	Driving	7
18Apr81- 6Pim	fst	6f	:23	:45⅗	1:10⅗	Allowance	4	4	2hd	1hd	2hd	2nk	McCauley W H	b 114	*.90	93-18	Rex Imperator 119nkAmberPass11410FoolsDance1124	Drifted out	5
6Sep80- 7Bel	fst	1⅛	:45	1:09⅖	1:47	3↑ Marlboro H	5	2	2hd	1hd	69	716	MacBeth D	b 116	11.00	76-15	Winter'sTl1234½GloriousSong117nkJklinKlugmn1183½	Speed 6 fur.	8
16Aug80- 8Sar	fst	1¼	:45⅘	1:36⅕	2:02⅘	Travers	9	2	2hd	13	1hd	31½	MacBeth D	b 126	12.50	84-13	TmprncHll1261½FrstAlbrt126noAmbrPss1266¾	Drifted out,bumped	9
2Aug80- 9Mth	fst	1⅛	:46⅘	1:10⅘	1:49⅖	Mth Invit H	1	3	42½	41¾	43	32¾	MacBeth D	b 121	2.10e	85-18	Thanks to Tony 111½ Superbity 1242¼ Amber Pass 121nk	Mild bid	8
20Jly80- 8Hol	fst	1¼	:45⅖	1:35	2:00⅘	Swaps	8	2	22	12½	14	2hd	MacBeth D	b 123	4.70	87-14	First Albert 123hd Amber Pass 1234 Mr. Mud 1142½	Sharp	11
5Jly80- 8Bel	fst	1⅛	:45⅕	1:09⅕	1:49	Dwyer	3	2	22	21½	13	11	MacBeth D	b 114	4.00	82-17	Amber Pass 1141 Temperence Hill 129hd Comptroller1193	Driving	8

LATEST WORKOUTS ●Jly 17 Pim 3f fst :34 h Jly 12 Pim 7f fst 1:28 h ●Jly 7 Pim 7f gd 1:28⅖ h ●Jly 1 Pim 5f fst :59 h

Fio Rito *

Gr. h. 6, by Dreaming Native—Seagret, by Sea Charger
Br.—LeCesse R (NY)
Tr.—Ferraro Michael

113

Turf Record					St.	1st	2nd	3rd	Amt.
St.	1st	2nd	3rd	1981	5	4	1	0	$58,772
2	0	0	0	1980	12	9	2	0	$192,309

Own.—LeCesse R

20Jly81- 8Bel sly 1 :45⅗ 1:09⅗ 1:35 3↑ [S]EvanShipman 4 4 1hd 2hd 1½ 12½ Hulet L b 117 *.30 93–15 Fio Rito 1172½ Sir Ack 121¾ Naskra's Breeze 117nk Drew Clear 7
4Jly81- 9FL fst 170 :47⅕ 1:11 1:40⅗ 3↑ [S]Gen.sullivan 2 3 2hd 16 16 18½ Hulet L b 120 *.10e 98–17 Fio Rito 1208½ Sea Bourne 1172 D. J.'s Nitecap 1144 Easily 5
13Jun81- 8FL fst 170 :47⅖ 1:11 1:40⅕ 3↑ [S]Allowance 3 2 11 18 18 111 Hulet L b 118 *.20 114–10 Fio Rito 11811 Holiday Chip 118nk Publisher 1101 Ridden out 7
7Jun81- 6FL fst 6f :22 :45 1:09⅘ 3↑ Allowance 5 2 43½ 33½ 2hd 17 Hulet L b 114 *.20 105–08 Fio Rito 1147 Mari Juno 1041½ Lake Placid 1145 Drew clear 5
25May81- 9FL fst 6f :23⅕ :46⅕ 1:10⅗ 3↑ [S]Williamson 1 5 51¾ 33 33 31½ Hulet L b 115 *.10e 99–12 [D]Sea Bourne 119¾ Al's Sky Lab 119¾ Fio Rito 1157 Rallied 5
25May81-Placed second through disqualification
28Dec80- 8Aqu fst 1⅛ [•]:48⅖ 1:13⅘ 1:46⅖ 3↑ [S]Alex M. Robb 6 3 1hd 2hd 32 22 Saumell L b 126 *.50 80–18 Sir Ack 1192 Fio Rito 126nk Quintessential 123hd Gamely 8
10Dec80- 8Aqu fst 6f [•]:22⅖ :45⅗ 1:10⅕ 3↑ [S]Joe Palmer 5 2 43½ 42¼ 42 1nk Saumell L b 126 *1.00 93–11 Fio Rito 126nk Kim's Chance 122no Sir Ack 1193½ Wide, just up 5
27Nov80- 8Aqu fst 1⅜ :48⅘ 1:12⅘ 1:56 3↑ Queens Cty H 4 1 11½ 1hd 35½ 58½ Hulet L b 120 *2.60 73–24 Fool'sPryer1121¼RingofLight1155½Pictursqu1141¼ Unruly, slow st. 7
9Nov80- 8FL sly 1¼ :48⅗ 1:39⅖ 2:07⅖ 3↑ [S]Wadsworth H 6 1 12 11½ 13 15½ Hulet L b 138 *.20e 93–17 Fio Rito 1385½ Green Parade 1144½ Captain Pat 126nk Easily 7
6Oct80- 8Bel fst 1⅛ :46 1:11 1:51⅖ 3↑ [S]Bongard H 5 2 11 11 11 11¾ Hulet L b 126 *.70 70–26 Fio Rito 1261¾ Kim's Chance 1243 Sir Ack 117no Driving 5

Glorious Song

B. m. 5, by Halo—Ballade, by Herbager
Br.—Taylor E P (Can)
Tr.—Cairns John

118

Turf Record					St.	1st	2nd	3rd	Amt.
St.	1st	2nd	3rd	1981	6	2	2	0	$180,485
5	3	1	0	1980	11	6	4	1	$525,617

Own.—Stronach F

1Jly81- 9WO fst 1⅛ :46⅗ 1:10⅘ 1:48 3↑ Dom Day H 2 3 31½ 2½ 14½ 15½ Platts R 125 *.35 102–14 Glorious Song 1255½ DrivingHome1262½ByeByeTony112hd Handily 9
26Apr81- 8Hol fst 1 :46⅕ 1:11⅖ 1:36⅖ 3↑ M'vy Leroy H 6 4 53¾ 32 1hd 2nk Toro F 121 *1.70 84–21 ElvnStitchs115nkGloriousSong1212½SummrTmGuy1145½ Sharp try 8
8Mar81- 8SA fst 1¼ :45⅖ 1:34⅕ 1:59⅗ S Anita H 11 8 89¼ 66½ 57 55½ McHargue D G 119 10.30 86–11 John Henry 1281 King Go Go 1171¼ Exploded 115no Wide 11
22Feb81- 8SA fst 1⅛ :44⅘ 1:08⅘ 1:47⅕ (F)S Margar'a H 6 4 47 44½ 31 2nk McCarron C J 130 *1.10 93–12 Princess Karenda 118nkGloriousSong1301¼Ack'sSecret1222 Sharp 10
31Jan81- 8SA gd 1 1/16 :46⅖ 1:10⅘ 1:43⅕ (F)S Maria H 1 3 32 2hd 12½ 12 McCarron C J 127 *.50 85–23 GlorosSong1272TrckRbbry1175MssHntngtn11310 Eased final yds. 4
10Jan81- 8SA fst 7f :21⅘ :43⅘ 1:20⅕ San Carlos H 1 7 75½ 63 46 46½ Hawley S 120 4.50 92–10 FlyingPstr1243¼ToB.OrNot1232DoublDiscount1151¼ Flattened out 8
6Sep80- 7Bel fst 1⅛ :45 1:09⅖ 1:47 3↑ Marlboro H 4 7 710 63¾ 22 24½ Velasquez J 117 *1.70 87–15 Winter'sTale1234½GloriousSong117nkJklinKlugmn1183½ Went well 8
16Aug80- 9Mth fst 1⅛ :46⅘ 1:11⅕ 1:48 3↑ A Haskell H 2 5 75¾ 4nk 2½ 21¾ Velasquez J 117 6.70 93–15 SpctclrBd1321¾GlorsSng1171¼ThClVrgnn1124 DriftedOut,brushed 8
12Jly80- 9WO fm 1¼ (T):45⅗ 1:37⅕ 2:01⅗ [S]Maturity 2 4 35½ 11½ 13 13½ Leblanc J B 121 *.25 99–09 Glorious Song 1213½ Great State 1261 Nice Idea 1211 Handily 6
1Jly80- 7WO fst 1⅛ :48 1:11⅘ 1:50⅕ 3↑ Dom Day H 2 5 54¾ 3nk 11½ 11 Leblanc J B 123 *.30 91–13 Glorious Song 1231 Maple Grove 1184 Knight'sTurn1181½ Handily 8

LATEST WORKOUTS Jly 25 Sar 5f fst 1:00⅗ b Jly 18 WO 1 fst 1:40⅕ b Jly 13 WO 5f fst :58⅗ b Jun 28 WO 4f fst :48⅘ b

Rivalero *

B. g. 5, by Riva Ridge—Dictates, by Bold Ruler
Br.—Stokes R G (Va)
Tr.—Veitch John M

112

Turf Record					St.	1st	2nd	3rd	Amt.
St.	1st	2nd	3rd	1981	6	2	0	1	$50,904
1	0	0	0	1980	14	4	1	3	$140,149

Own.—Calumet Farm

19Jly81- 8Bel fst 7f :22⅗ :45 1:21⅕ 3↑ Tom Fool 5 5 69 66½ 34½ 34½ Vasquez J 119 12.00 91–12 Rise Jim 1191¾ ProudAppeal1212¾Rivalero119hd Lckd Lt.response 6
4Jly81- 5Bel sly 1 1/16 :47 1:11 1:42⅕ 3↑ Allowance 1 4 42 2½ 2hd 11½ Vasquez J 119 3.40 91–20 Rivalero 1191½ Dr. Tipton 1152½ Voodoo Rhythm 1171 Ridden out 6
6Jun81- 1Bel fst 1 :46⅖ 1:10⅗ 1:34⅘ 3↑ Allowance 4 5 45 46 49½ 413 Vasquez J 115 9.10 81–14 Amber Pass 1151½ Winter's Tale 1225½ King's Wish 1156 Evenly 5
25May81- 8Bel fst 1 :44⅕ 1:08⅗ 1:33⅗ 3↑ Metropol'n H 3 6 610 611 614 619 Saumell L 115 26.00 80–22 Fappiano 1152¾ Irish Tower 127¾ Amber Pass 1157½ Outrun 7
15May81- 8Bel fst 7f :23⅕ :46⅖ 1:23⅗ Allowance 6 6 54½ 43 35½ 1¾ Vasquez J 122 9.80 84–19 Rivalero 122¾ Winter's Tale 122hd Tax Holiday 1053 Driving 6
7May81- 8Bel fst 7f :23⅕ :46⅖ 1:22⅗ Allowance 7 7 63½ 53 48 412 Fell J b 122 4.20 77–21 Fappiano 1224 Miroman 119no Dynamite Cap 1157½ Off slowly 7
16Oct80- 5Med fst 1¼ :47⅕ 1:35⅖ 2:00⅖ 3↑ Med Cup H 11 7 98½ — — — Fell J b 116 14.10 — — Tunerup 1176 Dr. Patches 1168 Dewan Keys 115no Bled 12
4Oct80- 6Bel yl 1 1/16 [T]:47⅕ 1:11 1:44⅖ 3↑ Handicap 5 3 35 47½ 511 511 Fell J b 115 1.60 67–22 Not Tomorrow 1103½ No Neck 1131½ [DH]T. V. Series 112 Tired 5
6Sep80- 6Med fst 1 1/16 :45⅗ 1:10⅗ 1:44 3↑ Jrsy Blues H 6 4 38 62½ 43 41¼ Fell J b 119 *1.20 88–21 Tunerup 112no Dewan Keys 1141 Foretake 114nk Brushed 8
16Aug80- 5Sar fst 1 3/16 :46⅗ 1:10⅗ 1:56⅕ 3↑ Allowance 4 4 412 37½ 1hd 1hd Fell J b 119 *.70 96–13 Rivalero 119hd Pianist 1154¾ Picturesque 115hd Driving 6

LATEST WORKOUTS Jly 27 Sar 4f sly :47⅗ h Jly 17 Bel 3f fst :36⅕ b Jly 13 Bel 4f fst :47⅗ h Jly 3 Bel 3f sly :36 b

The Liberal Member

Ch. g. 6, by Bold Reason—Lady Pitt, by Sword Dancer
Br.—Phipps O (Ky)
Tr.—Penna Angel
Own.—Phipps O

113

Turf Record St.	1st	2nd	3rd		Year	St.	1st	2nd	3rd	Amt.
					1981	2	0	1	1	$54,910
8	1	1	1		1979	9	3	1	1	$166,149

Date/Race	Track	Dist.		Fractions			Race	PP	St	1st call	2nd call	Str	Fin	Jockey	Wt	Odds	Speed	Comment		Field
18Jly81- 8Bel	fst	1½		:49⅖	2:01⅗	2:26	3↑Brooklyn H	2	7	6^{7}	$2^{\frac{1}{2}}$	$2^{1\frac{1}{2}}$	2^{4}	Cordero A Jr	113	5.40	86–15	Hechizado 116^{4} The Liberal Member113$^{\frac{3}{4}}$PeatMoss111$^{3\frac{1}{4}}$	2nd best	10
11Jly81- 7Bel	fst	1		:45⅖	1:09⅘	1:35⅖	3↑Allowance	1	6	4^{2}	3^{1}	$3^{\frac{1}{2}}$	$3^{\frac{1}{2}}$	Cordero A Jr	115	8.00	90–16	NearEast115$^{\frac{1}{2}}$DiplomaticNote115^{hd}TheLiberalMember115^{3}	Evenly	8
15Dec79- 8Aqu	fst	1⅝	⊡	:48⅕	2:04⅗	2:43⅗	3↑Gallant Fx H	3	10	7^{10}	$5^{6\frac{1}{2}}$	6^{9}	6^{11}	Encinas R I	126	*2.30	97–15	Identical 110^{6} Ethnarch 118$^{2\frac{1}{2}}$ Land of Eire 114$^{\frac{1}{2}}$	Outrun	12
1Sep79- 8AP	fm	1½	Ⓣ	:48	2:06⅕	2:32⅕	3↑Arlington H	10	8	8^{22}	$7^{8\frac{1}{4}}$	$3^{6\frac{1}{2}}$	4^{13}	Encinas R I	117	2.70	65–28	Bowl Game 124$^{4\frac{1}{2}}$ Young Bob110^{8}Liveinthesunshine105$^{\frac{1}{2}}$	Bid,tired	14
12Aug79- 8Sar	my	1⅛		:47⅗	1:12⅖	1:51⅘	3↑B Baruch H	4	6	6^{10}	6^{10}	5^{16}	5^{22}	Encinas R I	117	*2.10	54–25	Overskate 128$^{\frac{3}{4}}$ Timbo 108$^{\frac{3}{4}}$ Native Courier 115$^{3\frac{1}{4}}$	Outrun	7
4Aug79- 8Sar	fst	1⅛		:48⅕	1:10⅘	1:47⅗	3↑Whitney	6	6	4^{1}	4^{1}	3^{nk}	$3^{1\frac{1}{4}}$	Encinas R I	120	7.00	96–12	Star DeNaskra120$^{\frac{3}{4}}$Cox'sRidge117$^{\frac{1}{2}}$TheLiberalMember120$^{\frac{1}{2}}$	Rallied	6
21Jly79- 8Bel	fst	1½		:50⅗	2:03⅗	2:28⅘	3↑Brooklyn H	4	4	$3^{2\frac{1}{2}}$	1^{3}	$1^{1\frac{1}{2}}$	$1^{\frac{3}{4}}$	Encinas R I	114	6.10	76–24	The LiberalMember114$^{\frac{3}{4}}$BowlGame119^{hd}StateDinner123$^{2\frac{3}{4}}$	Driving	5
11Jly79- 6Bel	fst	1½		:48⅖	2:02⅘	2:28⅗	3↑Handicap	4	6	$5^{7\frac{1}{2}}$	1^{8}	1^{14}	1^{15}	Encinas R I	114	*.80	77–17	The LiberalMember114^{15}Framarco109$^{2\frac{3}{4}}$Yamasaki112^{6}	Ridden out	7
30Jun79- 6Bel	fm	1⅜	[T]	:49⅕	1:36⅖	2:14	3↑Allowance	4	5	$4^{2\frac{1}{2}}$	2^{hd}	1^{2}	$1^{2\frac{3}{4}}$	Encinas R I	115	2.20	99–07	TheLiberlMember115$^{2\frac{3}{4}}$IvoryHunter115$^{5\frac{1}{2}}$Metphor115$^{\frac{3}{4}}$	Ridden out	5
17Jun79- 4Bel	fm	1¼	[T]	:49⅕	1:38⅘	2:01⅘	3↑Allowance	8	7	$6^{7\frac{1}{2}}$	3^{1}	4^{2}	$3^{1\frac{1}{2}}$	Encinas R I	117	4.30	83–15	NonCommercil113$^{1\frac{1}{2}}$[D]SndroTsc112^{hd}ThLibrlMmbr117$^{1\frac{1}{2}}$	Impeded	11

17Jun79-Placed second through disqualification

LATEST WORKOUTS Jly 31 Sar 4f fst :50 b — Jly 17 Bel 4f fst :47⅗ b — Jly 7 Bel 4f fst :47⅗ h — Jun 30 Bel 5f fst 1:01 b

Ring of Light *

B. g. 6, by In Reality—Due Dilly, by Sir Gaylord
Br.—Chenery C T Estate of (Va)
Tr.—Martin Frank
Own.—Sommer Viola

114

Year	St.	1st	2nd	3rd	Amt.
1981	12	4	4	1	$221,074
1980	21	7	2	5	$340,959

Date/Race	Track	Dist.		Fractions			Race	PP	St	1st call	2nd call	Str	Fin	Jockey	Wt	Odds	Speed	Comment		Field
4Jly81- 8Bel	sly	1¼		:47⅗	1:36	2:02	3↑Suburban H	2	1	1^{1}	1^{2}	1^{3}	2^{hd}	Asmussen C B	115	16.80	90–20	TemperenceHill127^{hd}RingofLight115$^{\frac{3}{4}}$HighlndBld113^{nk}	Just failed	8
21Jun81-10Suf	fst	1⅛		:47	1:11⅕	1:49⅖	3↑Mass H	8	7	$8^{5\frac{1}{4}}$	4^{3}	$5^{5\frac{1}{2}}$	$4^{8\frac{1}{2}}$	Maple E	119	*1.20e	85–15	Soldier Boy 114$^{2\frac{1}{2}}$ Niteange 108^{2} Driving Home 114^{4}	Rallied	9
7Jun81- 9Suf	fst	6f		:22⅖	:45⅖	1:10⅗	3↑Suf Downs H	3	10	10^{11}	$8^{6\frac{3}{4}}$	$5^{3\frac{1}{2}}$	1no	Maple E	116	3.30e	88–29	Ring of Light 116no Dave's Friend 128$^{1\frac{3}{4}}$ Triocala 112$^{1\frac{1}{2}}$	Driving	10
30May81- 6Bel	fst	7f		:23⅖	:46	1:22⅖	3↑Handicap	2	6	5^{6}	$5^{5\frac{1}{2}}$	$2^{1\frac{1}{2}}$	$2^{2\frac{1}{2}}$	Maple E	120	*1.30	87–17	Rise Jim 122$^{2\frac{1}{2}}$ Ring of Light 120$^{1\frac{1}{2}}$ Dr. Patches 118^{nk}	2nd best	6
17May81- 8Bel	fst	6f		:22⅗	:45⅗	1:09⅘	3↑Roseben H	5	8	8^{11}	8^{8}	$4^{1\frac{1}{2}}$	$1^{\frac{3}{4}}$	Maple E	113	7.00e	93–22	Ring of Light 113$^{\frac{3}{4}}$ Guilty Conscience112^{1}Convenient114$^{\frac{1}{2}}$	Driving	8
11Apr81- 8Aqu	fst	1¼		:47⅖	1:35⅗	2:00⅘	3↑Excelsior H	3	2	$2^{1\frac{1}{2}}$	2^{4}	2^{5}	$2^{4\frac{3}{4}}$	Asmussen C B	113	9.60	87–22	Irish Tower 127$^{4\frac{3}{4}}$ Ring of Light 113$^{\frac{1}{2}}$ Relaxing 125^{1}	Held place	6
4Apr81- 7Aqu	fst	1⅛		:47⅕	1:11	1:49⅘	Allowance	5	4	$3^{3\frac{1}{2}}$	1^{hd}	1^{6}	1^{5}	Cordero A Jr	122	*.40	86–25	RingofLight122^{5}CreativePlan114^{3}DegenerateJon117$^{3\frac{1}{2}}$	Ridden out	6
28Mar81- 8Aqu	fst	1		:45	1:09⅕	1:35	3↑Westchster H	4	6	$4^{4\frac{1}{2}}$	$3^{2\frac{1}{2}}$	$2^{\frac{1}{2}}$	2no	Fell J	114	6.70	91–20	Dunham's Gift 115no Ring ofLight114^{nk}Dr.Blum124$^{\frac{1}{2}}$	Sharp effort	6
14Mar81- 8Aqu	fst	6f	⊡	:23⅕	:46⅖	1:11⅕	3↑Toboggan H	4	4	$4^{4\frac{1}{2}}$	$4^{3\frac{1}{4}}$	4^{5}	$4^{5\frac{1}{4}}$	Lovato F Jr	114	3.50	83–18	Dr.Blum123$^{2\frac{1}{4}}$GuiltyConscience115^{no}Dunham'sGift118$^{2\frac{3}{4}}$	No factor	4
6Mar81- 8Aqu	sly	1 1/16	⊡	:48⅕	1:14⅕	1:47⅗	Allowance	6	3	3^{2}	$1^{\frac{1}{2}}$	1^{3}	$1^{2\frac{1}{2}}$	McCarron G	117	*1.80	76–37	Ring of Light 117$^{2\frac{1}{2}}$ Contare 108$^{3\frac{3}{4}}$ Hasty Tam 115$^{7\frac{3}{4}}$	Easily	8

LATEST WORKOUTS ●Jly 30 Sar 4f sly :45⅗ h — ●Jly 25 Bel tr.t 6f fst 1:14 b — ●Jly 12 Bel tr.t 5f fst :59 h — ●Jun 30 Bel tr.t 6f fst 1:12 h

Temperence Hill *

B. c. 4, by Stop The Music—Sister Shannon, by Etonian
Br.—Polk A F Jr (Ky)
Tr.—Cantey Joseph B
Own.—Loblolly Stable

127

Turf Record St.	1st	2nd	3rd		Year	St.	1st	2nd	3rd	Amt.
					1981	6	3	1	0	$368,090
3	0	0	1		1980	17	8	3	1	$1,130,452

Date/Race	Track	Dist.		Fractions			Race	PP	St	1st call	2nd call	Str	Fin	Jockey	Wt	Odds	Speed	Comment		Field
18Jly81- 8Bel	fst	1½		:49⅖	2:01⅗	2:26	3↑Brooklyn H	5	6	7^{7}	8^{10}	7^{13}	8^{17}	Maple E	128	2.30	73–15	Hechizado 116^{4} TheLiberalMember113$^{\frac{3}{4}}$PeatMoss111$^{3\frac{1}{4}}$	No factor	10
4Jly81- 8Bel	sly	1¼		:47⅗	1:36	2:02	3↑Suburban H	1	4	4^{9}	4^{5}	$3^{3\frac{1}{2}}$	1^{hd}	MacBeth D	127	3.20	90–20	TmprncHill127^{hd}RingofLght115$^{\frac{3}{4}}$HghlndBld113^{nk}	Brushed, driving	8
14Jun81- 8Hol	fst	1¼		:45⅗	1:34⅘	2:00⅖	3↑Gold Cup H	2	4	$5^{5\frac{1}{4}}$	$7^{5\frac{3}{4}}$	$5^{6\frac{3}{4}}$	5^{6}	Maple E	129	3.20	83–16	[D]Ctermn120^{hd}ElevenStitchs122$^{2\frac{1}{2}}$SuprMomnt117^{nk}	Lacked room	10
25May81- 8Hol	fst	1⅛		:45⅖	1:10⅕	1:48⅖	3↑Californian	3	4	4^{11}	$5^{2\frac{1}{2}}$	$3^{2\frac{1}{2}}$	2^{hd}	Maple E	130	*1.60	87–15	Eleven Stitches 122^{hd} Temperence Hill 130^{nk} Kilijaro123$^{3\frac{3}{4}}$	Sharp	12
10Apr81- 9OP	fst	1 1/16		:46⅘	1:11⅖	1:43⅖	Oaklawn H	4	5	4^{3}	1^{hd}	$1^{\frac{1}{2}}$	1^{2}	Maple E	126	*.60	91–18	Temperence Hill126^{2}SunCatcher123$^{1\frac{3}{4}}$Uncool114$^{2\frac{1}{2}}$	Brushed, clear	5
28Mar81- 9OP	fst	1 1/16		:49	1:13	1:44⅕	Razorback H	1	5	$5^{6\frac{1}{2}}$	3^{1}	2^{hd}	1^{nk}	Maple E	124	*.40	87–21	Temperence Hill 124^{nk} Blue Ensign113^{3}Belle'sRuler112$^{4\frac{1}{2}}$	Driving	6
25Oct80- 8Aqu	sf	1½	Ⓣ	:51⅘	2:13	2:39⅗	3↑Turf Classic	5	4	3^{3}	6^{8}	7^{11}	7^{16}	Maple E	121	2.40	27–57	Anifa 123^{3} Golden Act 126^{5} John Henry 126^{nk}	Tired	8
18Oct80-10LaD	gd	1¼		:49⅕	1:39⅗	2:06⅗	Super Derby	3	4	2^{5}	$1^{\frac{1}{2}}$	1^{3}	$1^{5\frac{1}{2}}$	Maple E	126	*.50	92–19	Temperence Hill 126$^{5\frac{1}{2}}$ First Albert 126$^{\frac{1}{2}}$CactusRoad126^{no}	Driving	8
4Oct80- 8Bel	fst	1½		:49⅘	2:05⅕	2:30⅕	3↑J C Gold Cup	1	3	4^{3}	$1^{\frac{1}{2}}$	1^{3}	$1^{5\frac{1}{2}}$	Maple E	121	2.30	69–19	TemperenceHill121$^{5\frac{1}{2}}$JohnHenry126^{2}IvoryHunter126$^{3\frac{1}{2}}$	Ridden out	7
6Sep80- 7Bel	fst	1⅛		:45	1:09⅖	1:47	3↑Marlboro H	6	8	8^{11}	$7^{4\frac{1}{4}}$	5^{5}	5^{12}	Maple E	119	6.20	80–15	Winter'sTale123$^{4\frac{1}{2}}$GloriousSong117^{nk}JklinKlugmn118$^{3\frac{1}{2}}$	No factor	8

LATEST WORKOUTS Jly 31 Sar 3f fst :26⅕ b — Jly 17 Bel 3f fst :36⅗ h — Jly 13 Bel 6f fst 1:15 b — Jly 3 Bel 3f sly :38⅘ b

Classic Trial

B. h. 5, by In Reality—Desert Trial, by Moslem Chief
Br.—Mangurian H T Jr (Fla)
Tr.—Root Thomas F Sr

Own.—Mangurian H T Jr

106

	Turf Record					St.	1st	2nd	3rd	Amt.
St.	1st	2nd	3rd		1981	15	2	0	2	$27,559
6	1	0	1		1980	4	1	0	1	$7,430

29Jly81- 4Sar sly 1⅛ :47⅗ 1:12⅕ 1:50 3↑Allowance 1 1 13 13 15 17 Hernandez R b 119 10.20 85-18 ClassicTril1197NephewScott1173½OurCptinWillie1162½ Ridden out 8
23Jly81- 9Crc fst 1 :47⅗ 1:13⅘ 1:41⅘ 3↑Allowance 7 7 613 58½ 46½ 42½ Puckett H5 b 114 *1.40 76-25 Cherokee Sky 1001½ End of Lent 110½ Four Lane 117½ Rallied 7
11Jly81- 8Crc fm 1 1/16 Ⓣ:47⅘ 1:12 1:43⅘ 3↑Allowance 3 6 53¾ 810 56½ 44½ Cardone E b 121 *2.60 81-14 Tax Haven 1102½ Nataniel 1172 Golden Jackpot 117hd Blocked 10
4Jly81- 9Crc fst 1⅛ :47⅖ 1:13 1:52⅖ 3↑American H 9 9 814 88½ 610 47½ Cardone E b 110 25.50 78-19 Poking 1154 Noble Warrior 1193 Roogh Lord 114½ Rallied 10
27Jun81- 7Crc fst 170 :47⅗ 1:12⅘ 1:43⅘ 3↑Allowance 7 6 65 47½ 47 38 Cardone E b 122 6.90 85-16 Court Of Flags 1183GleamingChannel1135ClassicTrial1224 Rallied 7
13Jun81- 8Crc fm *1 1/16 Ⓣ 1:45⅖ 3↑Allowance 3 8 86½ 55½ 31 13 Cardone E b 119 5.30 88-12 ClssicTril1193BrodwyHys1192½BrveYoungMench1153½ Drew clear 9
30May81- 8Crc fst 7f :22⅗ :45⅘ 1:26⅘ 3↑Allowance 6 10 1117 1115 97½ 82½ Cardone E b 120 28.30 80-11 NocturnlPhntom109½ChiefMgistrte114nkTrilAppel109hd No factor 12
18May81- 7Hia fst 1 1/16 :47 1:12⅖ 1:47⅖ 3↑Allowance 1 4 411 48 65½ 42½ Cardone E b 118 8.50 64-30 Fast Summer 110hdEndofLent1112OverDeposited104nk Weakened 6
9May81- 6Hia gd *1 1/16 Ⓣ 1:44⅕ 3↑Allowance 2 7 75 44 43½ 35½ Cardone E b 118 18.80 72-21 Gleaming Channel 1094½ Mini Pie 1181 Classic Trial 1183 Rallied 8
11Mar81-10Hia fm 1⅛ Ⓣ 1:49 Allowance 5 4 48½ 87½ 912 810 Cardone E b 116 25.40 79-10 Ransom Ozzie 1161½Roustabout1161½MortalFriends116½ Fell back 10

LATEST WORKOUTS Jun 25 Crc 3f sly :36⅗ b Jun 21 Crc 4f fst :50 b

Noble Nashua

Dk. b. or br. c. 3, by Nashua—Noble Lady, by Vaguely Noble
Br.—Grousemont Farm (Ky)
Tr.—Martin Jose

Own.—Flying Zee Stable

114

	St.	1st	2nd	3rd	Amt.
1981	9	5	0	1	$269,755
1980	4	2	1	0	$62,007

19Jly81- 8Hol fst 1¼ :45 1:35⅗ 2:01⅕ Swaps 6 6 611 22½ 1½ 12½ Pincay L Jr 123 *2.30 85-20 Noble Nashua 1232½ Dorcaro 1157 Stancharry 123¾ Handily 7
5Jly81- 8Bel fst 1⅛ :46⅘ 1:11⅗ 1:49⅕ Dwyer 3 4 31½ 41½ 11½ 12¾ Asmussen C B 119 4.70 81-23 Noble Nashua 1192¾ TapShoes1264SilverExpress1141¾ Drew clear 10
18Jun81- 7Bel fst 7f :22⅗ :44⅘ 1:21⅘ 3↑Allowance 1 3 1hd 2hd 2hd 1hd Maple E 112 2.20 93-17 NobleNashua112hdFiveStarFlight1144½[DH]WestOnBrod111 Driving 6
25May81- 9Key fst 1⅛ :46⅗ 1:10⅖ 1:49 Penn Derby 4 1 12½ 1½ 3nk 55¾ Asmussen C B b 122 3.90 84-16 Summing1221½Sportin'Lif1221½ClssicGoGo1221¾ Brushed, bore in 9
2May81- 8CD fst 1¼ :45⅕ 1:36 2:02 Ky Derby 9 14 1311 1311 108¾ 911 Asmussen C B 126 71.70 76-12 Pleasant Colony 126¾ Woodchopper 1263 Partez 1262½ No threat 21
18Apr81- 9Aqu fst 1⅛ :45⅘ 1:10⅖ 1:49⅗ Wood Mem'l 6 2 2½ 22 49 414 Cordero A Jr 126 5.50 73-23 Pleasant Colony 1263 Highland Blade1265CuretheBlues1266 Tired 6
5Apr81- 8Aqu fst 1 :45 1:08⅘ 1:33⅗ Gotham 1 3 32 34½ 36 38½ Cordero A Jr 123 3.40 89-19 ProudAppeal123noCuretheBlues1268½NobleNashua1235½ Steadied 6
25Feb81- 8Aqu gd 1 1/16 ⊡:47 1:12⅕ 1:43 Whirlaway 4 1 12 11 14 19½ Cordero A Jr 119 *.40 99-20 Noble Nashua 1199½ Royal Pavilion 1194½ Summing 1196 Easily 5
6Feb81- 9Tam fst 6f :22⅖ :46⅖ 1:12⅗ Allowance 5 3 43 32½ 2½ 15½ Cordero A Jr 116 *.10 82-24 Noble Nashua 1165½ Rit Cat 113no Sible Sue 11410 Drew out 7
25Oct80- 9Lrl sly 1 1/16 :46⅕ 1:11⅗ 1:44⅖ Lrl Futurity 2 2 23 22½ 310 414 Cordero A Jr 122 3.50 72-19 Cure the Blues 1226½ Matching Gift 1226KanReason1221 Bumped 7

LATEST WORKOUTS Jly 29 Sar 5f sly 1:00⅖ h Jly 2 Bel tr.t 5f gd :59⅘ h ●Jun 26 Bel tr.t 6f fst 1:14⅗ b Jun 15 Bel tr.t 4f my :48⅖ h (d)

Fio Rito took to the lead and held off Winter's Tale's late charge to steal the race. The payoff to show on Winter's Tale was $2.80, a reasonable payoff for a 3—2 shot, most of whose main opposition was scratched. My $270 bet returned $378, for a profit of $108. The chart of the race was as follows:

Whitney Handicap

EIGHTH RACE
Saratoga
AUGUST 1, 1981

1 ⅛ MILES. (1.47) 54th Running THE WHITNEY HANDICAP (Grade I). $150,000 Added. 3-year-olds and upward. By subscription of $300 each, which should accompany the nomination; $1,200 to pass the entry box, with $150,000 added. The added money and all fees to be divided 60% to the winner, 22% to second, 12% to third and 5% to fourth. Weights Monday, July 27. Starters to be named at the closing time of entries. Trophies will be presented to the winning owner, trainer and jockey and mementoes to the grooms of the first four finishers. Closed with 37 nominations.

Value of race $175,500, value to winner $105,300, second $38,610, third $21,060, fourth $10,530. Mutuel pool $265,447, OTB pool $414,227.

Last Raced	Horse	Eqt.	A.	Wt	PP	St	¼	½	¾	Str	Fin	Jockey	Odds $1
20Jly81 ^{8}Bel^{1}	Fio Rito	b	6	113	3	4	1^{hd}	1½	1½	1^{1}	1^{nk}	Hulet L	10.20
19Jly81 ^{7}Bel^{1}	Winter's Tale	b	5	121	1	8	$4^{1\frac{1}{2}}$	5½	5^{hd}	3^{hd}	2^{1}	Fell J	1.50
4Jly81 ^{8}Bel^{2}	Ring of Light		6	114	7	5	$3^{1\frac{1}{2}}$	3^{1}	2^{1}	2½	3^{hd}	Hernandez R	6.80
18Jly81 ^{8}Bel^{2}	The Liberal Member		6	114	6	3	5^{hd}	4^{hd}	6^{2}	4^{1}	4½	Cordero A Jr	3.00
19Jly91 ^{9}Del^{4}	Joanie's Chief		4	108	2	2	7½	7^{1}	8	$6^{1\frac{1}{2}}$	5½	Samyn J L	19.50
19J:y81 ^{8}Hol^{1}	Noble Nashua		3	114	8	6	6½	6^{hd}	4^{1}	$5^{1\frac{1}{2}}$	$6^{1\frac{1}{4}}$	Maple E	4.20
19Jly81 ^{8}Bel^{3}	Rivalero		5	114	4	7	8	8	7½	$7^{1\frac{1}{2}}$	7^{2}	Vasquez J	12.70
19Jly81 ^{9}Del^{8}	Blue Ensign	b	4	109	5	1	$2^{1\frac{1}{2}}$	2^{1}	3½	8	8	Kaenel J L	51.00

OFF AT 5:45 EDT. Start good, Won driving. Time, :23⅖, :46⅘, 1:10, 1:34⅘, 1:48 Track fast.

$2 Mutuel Prices:				
	3-(D)-FIO RITO	22.40	6.20	3.80
	1-(A)-WINTER'S TALE		4.00	2.80
	8-(I)-RING OF LIGHT			4.20

Gr. h, by Dreaming Native—Seagret, by Sea Charger. Trainer Ferraro Michael. Bred by LeCesse R (NY).

FIO RITO broke through before the start, went right after the leaders, raced well out from the rail while making the pace, responded readily when challenged by RING OF LIGHT approaching the stretch and, after gaining a clear advantage with a furlong remaining, was all out to turn back WINTER'S TALE. The latter, never far back, moved up along the inside approaching the far turn, continued to save ground into the stretch and finished with good courage. RING OF LIGHT, reserved behind the early leaders into the backstretch, made a run from the outside at the far turn, remained prominent into the stretch but wasn't good enough. THE LIBERAL MEMBER, reserved early, rallied between horses after entering the stretch but failed to sustain his bid. JOANIE'S CHIEF, outrun early while saving ground, angled out entering the stretch and finished with good energy. NOBLE NASHUA, taken back early, commenced to rally while racing wide approaching the end of the backstretch, loomed a threat leaving the far turn but lacked a late response. RIVALERO was always outrun. BLUE ENSIGN, a forward factor to the far turn, drifted out while weakening.

Owners— 1, LeCesse R; 2, Rokeby Stable; 3, Sommer Viola; 4, Phipps O; 5, Barberino P; 6, Flying Zee Stable; 7, Calumet Farm; 8, Locust Hill Farm.

Trainers— 1, Ferraro Michael; 2, Miller Mack; 3, Martin Frank; 4, Penna Angel; 5, Jacobs Eugene; 6, Martin Jose; 7, Veitch John M; 8, Carroll Del W.

Overweight: The Liberal Member 1 pound; Rivalero 2.

Scratched—Amber Pass (19Jly81 ^{9}Del^{1}); Glorious Song (1Jly81 ^{9}WO^{1}); Temperence Hill (18Jly81 ^{8}Bel^{8}); Classic Trial (29Jly81 ^{4}Sar^{1}).

The Santa Ynez Stakes, Santa Anita, February 2, 1983

The first national conference on thoroughbred handicapping was held in Los Angeles, February 1–3, 1983. It was a great opportunity for us to hear the latest theories and experiences of many of America's top handicappers.* Also, we could combine the trip with a visit to Santa Anita on February 2.

*For those interested in the latest in handicapping, see our guide to this literature in Chapter Sixteen.

Set at the foot of the San Gabriel mountains in Arcadia, California, Santa Anita is one of America's most beautiful tracks. The warm southern California climate and the enormous Los Angeles population base contribute to the huge betting crowds. With its average daily handle of over $5 million and large purses, Santa Anita draws an unusually high standard of jockeys, trainers, and thoroughbreds. Saturday and Sunday cards often contain races with purses worth several hundred thousand dollars. During the weekdays the purses and crowds are smaller but still considerable. For example, on Wednesday, February 2, the purses ranged from $12,000–$75,000 (added) with most races in the $15,000–$30,000 range.

It was a cold, wet day; the track condition was listed as muddy. Such off-tracks are usually a signal that the bettor should be cautious or not bet at all. The poor track condition can yield races that are not run true to form. In such cases long shots often replace favorites in the winner's circle, and the races are run in slow times. The grounds crew at Santa Anita, however, is famed for its handling of the track. The members of the crew knew that they needed to seal the track before the rain came. It was sealed by rolling the dirt track hard so that there would be a firm backing, even though the topsoil was muddy. The success of their work was apparent all day long when fractional and winning times were just about typical for a fast track. The muddy track gave a slight edge to strong front-runners, which, because of the efficiency in the win pool, was presumably reflected in the odds.* Dr. Z system bettors should be cautious on such days unless they have confidence that the horses are more or less running true to form.

Although we felt that the track would be all right for our Dr. Z system bets, we carefully monitored the situation throughout the day. In your own betting we recommend that you exercise caution or even stay home on off-track days until and unless you feel confident about your analysis of the situation. For your first few visits, try to select days when conditions are ideal: beautiful, sunny weekend days with the best horses and large pools.

The feature race of the day was the Santa Ynez Stakes with a $75,000 added purse ($83,550 total) for three-year-old fillies. The race was run over 7 furlongs and featured some top sprinters. The standout in the race, Fabulous Notion, had a perfect record with five strong wins in five outings.

*There is very little published evidence that the bettors do actually adjust their betting to reflect such track biases. Academics believe that the market for win bets remains efficient. Many handicappers no doubt believe that it does not remain efficient and that track biases are one of the key places to look for so-called overlays. One of the major track biases is that of post position. The advantage varies from track to track and by the length of the race. We are currently studying the effect of these biases on win, place, show, and exotic bets at Exhibition Park in 1982. The results will appear in Canfield, Fauman, and Ziemba (March 1984).

Her speed ratings were in the 90s for the sprint races and 83 in her only route race, which she won by six lengths.* All her wins were convincing. Today she had her steady jockey, Donald Pierce, a good post position, and strong recent workouts. Minor drawbacks were the additional weight assignment to 124 pounds and a month's layoff since her convincing win in the California Breeder's Championship Stakes on December 30, 1982. Fabulous Notion was the top choice of all the Santa Anita handicappers and the *Daily Racing Form's* consensus best bet of the day. The second choice was A Lucky Sign, who had a strong record of three wins in five starts. Her speed ratings were outstanding and very consistent. She would be guided in the irons by the great Chris McCarron, who had led her to two consecutive wins at Santa Anita recently.† Today she was picking up weight to start at 121 and was assigned the outside post position in the number 9 slot. Other strong horses were the undefeated Autumn Magic and Sophisticated Girl.

Experts' Selections

Consensus Points: 5 for 1st (today's best 7), 2 for 2nd, 1 for 3rd. Today's Best in Bold Type.

Daily Racing Form

Trackman, Warren Williams **SANTA ANITA PARK** Selections Made for Fast Track

	TRACKMAN	HANDICAP	ANALYST	HERMIS	SWEEP	CONSENSUS	
8	FABULOUS NOTION	**FABULOUS NOTION**	FABULOUS NOTION	**FABULOUS NOTION**	FABULOUS NOTION	**FABULOUS NOTION**	29
	A LUCKY SIGN	A LUCKY SIGN	SOPHISTICATED GIRL	A LUCKY SIGN	A LUCKY SIGN	A LUCKY SIGN	9
	SOPHISTICATED GIRL	TIME OF SALE	A LUCKY SIGN	SOPHISTICATED GIRL	SOPHISTICATED GIRL	SOPHISTICATED GIRL	5

ANALYST'S *Santa Anita Comment*

EIGHTH RACE

1—Fabulous Notion
2—Sophisticated Lady
3—A Lucky Sign

FABULOUS NOTION has yet to taste defeat and appears headed for her sixth straight win today despite giving away chunks of weight to her rivals. She must give 10 pounds to SOPHISTICATED GIRL, who won her last gamely and ran champion Landaluce to two lengths in the Oak Leaf here last fall. The weight factor could easily tell in this spot. A LUCKY SIGN has won two stakes here at the meet, but will be stretching out an extra furlong today off strictly speed breeding. AUTUMN MAGIC has won her lone two starts but gets the acid test today. She can't be overlooked.

---

*A speed rating of 100 equals the track record at this distance. For every 1/5 second off the track record, one point is deducted. Hence a rating of 83 indicates that the race was run 3-2/5 seconds slower than the track record. Speed ratings above 80 are good; those above 90 are outstanding.

†As usual, Chris McCarron and Laffit Pincay, Jr. were locked in a duel for top jockey of the meet. As indicated by the following table, Pincay and McCarron were running 1-2 considerably above the other jockeys.

ABOUT 1,400 METERS

EIGHTH RACE

SANTA YNEZ STAKES (Grade II)

$75,000 Added

For fillies three years old. (Foals of 1980). **By subscription of $50 each to accompany the nomination, $100 to pass the entry box and $750 additional to start, with $75,000 added, of which $15,000 to second, $11,250 to third, $5,625 to fourth and $1,875 to fifth. 121 lbs. Winners of $50,000 twice in 1982-83, 3 lbs. additional; of $50,000 three times in 1982-83, 5 lbs. Non-winners of two races of $25,000 since December 25 or two of $25,000 or one of $50,000 at any time allowed 2 lbs.; of a race of $25,000 since December 25 or two of $15,000 or one of $25,000 at any time, 4 lbs.; of a race of $12,000, 7 lbs. A trophy will be presented to the owner of the winner. Closed Wednesday, January 26, 1983, with 18 nominations.**

SANTA YNEZ RECORD—TERLINGUA (3) 121 lbs. 1979 1:21⅕

Track Record—SPECTACULAR BID (4) 126 lbs, January 5, 1980 1:20

MAKE SELECTIONS BY NUMBER — PROBABLE ODDS

No.	Owner / Colors / Horse / Breeding	Trainer	Weight	Jockey	Probable Odds
1	Claudia H. & Morey Mirkin Red, white interlocking horseshoes on back, white cuffs, red cap **AUTUMN MAGIC** B.f. '80, Proud Clarion—Autumn Amber Breeders—Brereton C. Jones & Louise I. Humphrey (Kentucky)	Gary Jones	114	Fernando Toro	6
2	Golden Eagle Farm Burgundy, gold eagle on back, gold sleeves, burgundy and gold cap **SOPHISTICATED GIRL** Br.f. '80, Stop the Music—Close Control, by Dunce Breeders—Dr. & Mrs. G. G. Meredith (Maryland)	Gary Jones	114	Eddie Delahoussaye	8
3	Pine Meadow Thoroughbred Pink, dark green and light green inverted sashes, light green cuffs, pink cap **FABULOUS NOTION** B.f. '80, Somethingfabulous—Careless Notion Breeder—Ray Stark (California)	James Jordan	124	Donald Pierce	7/5
4	Hanson Stock Farm White, red and white emblem on back, red sleeves, red and white cap **EASTERN BETTOR** Br.f. '80, Out of the East—Happy Bettor Breeder—Owner (California)	Loren Rettele	119	Patrick Valenzuela	15
5	Fred W. Hooper Blue, white circle "H", white shoulder straps, red sleeves, blue and red cap **FLYING LASSIE** Br.f. '80, Tri Jet—Delta Flight, by Delta Judge Breeder—Owner (Florida)	L. R. Fenstermaker	117	Terry Lipham	15
6	Poyer & Steinmann Blue and green diagonal halves, green and blue "HL" on back, blue sleeve, green sleeve, blue and green cap **O'HAPPY DAY** Br.f. '80, Cojak—Holiday Greetings, by Best Turn Breeder—Ron M. Linton (Maryland)	Loren Rettele	114	Sandy Hawley	12
7	Demeter & Oatlands Stable White, light blue sashes, light blue sleeves, white cuffs, white and blue cap **D'ARQUES** Br.f. '80, Crystal Water—Real Effort, by Sailor Breeders—Ron Stolich & Fran Aebi (California)	John Canty	114	William Shoemaker	20
8	Northwest Farms White, red and white emblem on back, red and white checked sleeves, red cap **TIME of SALE** Br.f. '80, Drum Fire—Run Tara Run Breeder—Owner (Washington)	C. R. Knight	119	Laffit Pincay, Jr.	15
9	Headley, Johnston, Johnston & Elizabeth Johnston (trustee) Red, white belt and bar on sleeves, red cap **A LUCKY SIGN** B.f. '80, Lucky Mike—Zealous Sally, by In Zeal Breeder—Old English Rancho (California)	Bruce Headley	121	Chris McCarron	5/2

EQUIPMENT CHANGE—Flying Lassie races with blinkers.

8th Santa Anita

7 FURLONGS. (1.20) 32nd Running of THE SANTA YNEZ STAKES (Grade II). $75,000 added. Fillies. 3-year-olds. (Allowance). By subscription of $50 each to accompany the nomination, $100 to pass the entry box and $750 additional to start, with $75,000 added, of which $15,000 to second, $11,250 to third, $5,625 to fourth and $1,875 to fifth. Weight, 121 lbs. Winners of $50,000 twice in 1982–83, 3 lbs. additional; of $50,000 three times in 1982–83, 5 lbs. Non-winners of two races of $25,000 since December 25 or two of $25,000 or one of $50,000 at any time allowed 2 lbs.; of a race of $25,000 since December 25 or two of $15,000 or one of $25,000 at any time, 4 lbs.; of a race of $12,000, 7 lbs. Starters to be named through the entry box by the closing time of entries. A trophy will be presented to the owner of the winner. Closed Wednesday, January 26, 1983 with 18 nominations.

Autumn Magic

B. f. 3, by Proud Clarion—Autumn Ember, by Gallant Man
Br.—Jones B & Humphrey Louise (Ky) 1983 1 1 0 0 $11,000
Own.—Mirkin Claudia H & M **114** **Tr.—Jones Gary** 1982 1 1 0 0 $9,350
Lifetime 2 2 0 0 $20,350

14Jan83-7SA 1 1/16 :46 1:103 1:424ft *8-5 115 43 31½ 1hd 1½ Toro F2 ⒻAw20000 87 AutumnMgic,‡ChicNtiv,OrintlChmp 9
26Dec82-3SA 6f :214 :444 1:092ft 11 117 86¼ 64 22½ 12 Toro F5 ⒻMdn 91 Autumn Magic, Toga, SpruceSong 10
Jan 25 SA 4f m :484 h Dec 16 SA 4f ft :473 h Dec 9 SA 6f ft 1:13 h Dec 2 SA 6f ft 1:141 h

Sophisticated Girl

Dk. b. or br. f. 3, by Stop the Music—Close Control, by Dunce
Br.—Meredith Dr-Mrs C G (Md) 1982 5 2 1 0 $86,391
Own.—Golden Eagle Farm **114** **Tr.—Jones Gary**
Lifetime 5 2 1 0 $86,391

30Dec82-5SA 1 1/16 :454 1:11 1:441ft *2-5 117 712 57 2hd 11½ DlhoussyE3 ⒻAw20000 80 SophstctdGrl,HcklbrryHony,Mrznrs 9
28Nov82-6Hol 1 1/16 :46 1:104 1:422ft *6-5e120 87¼ 74¼ 77½ 59¾ DlhossyE6 ⒻHol Strlt 73 FbulosNoton,O'HppyDy,StphnBryn 9
23Oct82-8SA 1 1/16 :454 1:094 1:414ft 18 115 46¼ 35 24 22 DlhossyE1 ⒻOak Leaf 90 Landluce,SophistictedGirl,GrnjRein 7
11Oct82-6SA 1 :461 1:113 1:383ft 3 117 67¼ 52¾ 31½ 12½ DelahoussyeE4 ⒻMdn 75 SophisticatedGirl,Mnznres,MuyJup 8
1Oct82-4SA 6f :211 :442 1:10 ft 10 117 1111 911 912 43½ DelahoussyeE5 ⒻMdn 84 Osage Lady, Tiptopper, Loan 12
Jan 25 SA 5f m 1:03 h Jan 19 SA 4f gd :474 h Jan 12 SA 5f ft 1:002 h Jan 7 SA 4f ft :50 h

Fabulous Notion

B. f. 3, by Somethingfabulous—Careless Notion, by Jester
Br.—Stark R (Cal) 1982 5 5 0 0 $378,368
Own.—PineMeadowsThoroughbreds **124** **Tr.—Jordan James**
Lifetime 5 5 0 0 $378,368

30Dec82-8SA 7f :211 :442 1:22 ft *2-3 122 32½ 21 12 14 PiercD9 ⒻⓈCal Brdrs 90 FblosNoton,EstrnBttor,I'mPrstgs 10
28Nov82-8Hol 1 1/16 :46 1:104 1:422ft 8¾ 120 2hd 1hd 14 16 Pierce D3 ⒻHol Strlt 83 FbulosNoton,O'HppyDy,StphnBryn 9
5Nov82-10LA 6f :22 :452 1:102ft *1-2 120 1½ 11 11 1½ PncLJr1 ⒻSaddleback 93 FbulosNoton,EstrnBttor,LonForgnr 7
13Oct82-6SA 6f :214 :45 1:093ft *3-5 118 22 2½ 1½ 12½ Pincay LJr6 ⒻAw20000 90 FabulousNotion,Infantes,OsageLdy 6
3Oct82-3SA 6f :211 :442 1:091ft *3-5 117 1½ 12 14 16½ Pincay L Jr4 ⒻⓈMdn 92 FabulousNotion,Castlelnd,Ally'sLdy 7
Jan 31 SA 4f ft :47 h ●Jan 25 SA 6f m 1:143 h Jan 20 SA 5f ft 1:002 h ●Jan 15 SA 5f ft :58 h

Eastern Bettor

Dk. b. or br. f. 3, by Out of the East—Happy Bettor, by Crazy Kid
Br.—Hanson Stock Farm (Cal) 1983 1 0 0 0 $4,500
Own.—Hanson Stock Farm **119** **Tr.—Rettele Loren** 1982 8 3 3 0 $75,108
Lifetime 9 3 3 0 $79,608

12Jan83-8SA 6f :211 :44 1:093ft 5½ 119 96¼ 89 56¼ 46½ McHrDG4 ⒻPasadena 83 ALuckySign,LotusDncer,PstryCun 12
30Dec82-8SA 7f :211 :442 1:22 ft 7 120 53½ 54½ 45½ 24 SibillR6 ⒻⓈCal Brdrs 86 FblosNoton,EstrnBttor,I'mPrstgs 10
26Nov82-8BM 6f :224 :462 1:124gd 2½ 116 33½ 22 2hd 13 Hall D C2 ⒻⓈCrtshp 76 EstrnBttor,LuckyLksd,MkThSnshn 7
17Nov82-8Hol 6½f :213 :442 1:161ft 4 115 74¾ 65 714 610 VlenzulPA8 ⒻTrlingua 79 LuckyLkesid,I'mPrstigious,Cstllnd 10
5Nov82-10LA 6f :22 :452 1:102ft 5 120 33½ 31½ 31 2½ VlnlPA7 ⒻSaddleback 92 FbulosNoton,EstrnBttor,LonForgnr 7
24Oct82-4SA 6f :213 :442 1:094ft 26 114 31½ 2½ 1hd 11¼ VlenzulPA5 ⒻAw20000 89 EstrnBttor,ALuckySign,LonForignr 7
15Oct82-3SA 6f :22 :451 1:11 ft 4¼ 117 42 53¾ 42¾ 12 Sibille R7 ⒻM32000 83 EsternBettor,KnitTwo,HonyDon't 12
11Jun82-4Hol 5f :214 :443 :572ft 13 116 1011 918 918 812 McHargue DG4 ⒻMdn 80 Barzell, Lituya Bay, Body Talk 10
16May82-4AC 2f :223ft 4¼ 115 5 32 21½ Vilches A4 Mdn — ArticultdProof,EstrnBttor,Fbld'mq 9
Jan 26 SA 5f sl 1:013 h Jan 20 SA 5f ft 1:01 h Jan 6 SA 5f ft 1:02 h Dec 25 SA 5f ft :584 h

O'Happy Day

Dk. b. or br. f. 3, by Cojak—Holiday Greetings, by Best Turn
Br.—Linton R M (Md) 1982 8 2 2 0 $132,345
Own.—Poyer & Steinmann **114** **Tr.—Rettele Loren** Turf 1 0 0 0 $2,250
Lifetime 8 2 2 0 $132,345

18Dec82-8BM 1 1/16 :47 1:122 1:462ft *1 115 65¼ 2½ 21½ 2½ BazeRA4 ⒻB M Lassie 66 BabyDoon,O'HppyDy,AmbitiousGl 14
8Dec82-8Hol 1 1/16 Ⓣ:462 1:114 1:43 fm 3½ 117 2½ 2hd 21½ 45 HwleyS9 ⒻTrksh Trsrs 79 LituyaBay,GoldSpruce,GranjaReina 9
28Nov82-8Hol 1 1/16 :46 1:104 1:422ft 28 120 65½ 64¼ 45 26 Hawley S9 ⒻHol Strlt 77 FbulosNoton,O'HppyDy,StphnBryn 9
5Nov82-7Hol 1 :464 1:113 1:381ft 9½ 118 1hd 2hd 1hd 1no Hawley S4 ⒻAw20000 75 O'HappyDy,GrnjRein,DoubleSmoke 7
21Oct82-6SA 1 1/16 :462 1:112 1:443ft 3½ 117 21 2hd 1½ 1¾ Sibille R8 ⒻMdn 78 O'HppyDy,CsSh'sALdy,ContnntlGrl 8
1Oct82-4SA 6f :211 :442 1:10 ft 54 117 43½ 55¾ 56¾ 63¾ Sibille R3 ⒻMdn 84 Osage Lady, Tiptopper, Loan 12
4Sep82-6Dmr 6f :214 :45 1:102ft 23 117 65½ 511 57¼ 412 Sibille R3 ⒻMdn 74 OlympicSkis,NtliB.Frindly,RdEmbr 12
25Aug82-6Dmr 6f :222 :452 1:102ft 12 117 74¾ 812 813 512 Sibille R12 ⒻMdn 74 MissBigWig,DncingGust,IsbllD'Est 12
Jan 31 SA 4f ft :473 h Jan 26 SA 5f sl 1:013 h Jan 17 SA 6f ft 1:123 h Jan 12 SA 5f ft :593 h

```
D'Arques                              Dk. b. or br. f. 3, by Crystal Water—Real Effort, by Sailor
                                      Br.—Stolich R & Aebi Fran (Cal)        1983 1 1 0 0     $9,350
Own.—Demeter & Oatlands Stable   114  Tr.—Canty John                         1982 8 M 3 0    $13,025
                                Lifetime   9 1 3 0   $22,375
12Jan83-4SA  6f :212 :443 1:103ft *6-5 117  63  65  3nk 1½   ShoemkrW10 Ⓕ[S]Mdn 85 D'Arques, Agigael, Shesqueennow 11
29Dec82-4SA  6f :214 :45  1:10 ft *6-5 117  2hd 1½  11½ 22   ShoemkerW3 Ⓕ[S]Mdn 86 PstryQueen,D'Arques,Shesquennow 9
18Nov82-6Hol 6f :221 :451 1:102ft *6-5 117  31  3½  2hd 2no  Sibille R2 Ⓕ[S]Mdn 85 BlueJetSet,D'Arques,Casey'sPoona 9
28Oct82-6SA  6f :213 :442 1:093ft  11  117  51½ 46½ 32  21¼  ShoemkerW3 Ⓕ[S]Mdn 89 I'mPrstigious,D'Arqus,StphniBryn 10
16Oct82-3SA  6f :212 :443 1:084ft  11  117  34½ 35  36  49½  ShoemkerW6 Ⓕ[S]Mdn 84 ALuckySign,Vivaciously,ChiquitGt 12
27Aug82-4Dmr 6f :22  :451 1:11 ft  15  117  2hd 65½ 811 1015 Diaz A L9  Ⓕ[S]Mdn 68 WickedFall,KookieKper,LdeirGrnd 11
11Aug82-4Dmr 6f :22  :454 1:113ft  6¾  117  12½ 12½ 23½ 49½  Diaz A L8  Ⓕ[S]Mdn 70 GrnjRein,OlympicBronze,NtlieN'Me 9
 1Aug82-4Dmr 6f :221 :454 1:122ft  4½  117  1hd 56  54½ 45½  Diaz A L4  Ⓕ[S]Mdn 70 ShowMeDeer,NtliN'M,Ms.Spllbindr 6
27May82-4Hol 5f :22  :451  :573ft  15  116  42½ 45½ 513 614  Olivares F10  ⒻMdn 77 JustLikeHelen,SlewMnet,LdirGrnd 10
   Jan 28 SA 6f sl 1:173 h     Jan 6 SA 5f ft 1:004 h     Dec 20 SA 6f ft 1:133 h

Time Of Sale                          Dk. b. or br. f. 3, by Drum Fire—Run Tara Run, by Run for Nurse
                                      Br.—Northwest Farms (Wash)             1983 1 1 0 0    $12,100
Own.—Northwest Farms             119  Tr.—Knight Chay R                      1982 6 2 1 1    $66,949
                                Lifetime   7 3 1 1   $79,049
21Jan83-7SA  6½f:213 :443 1:163ft  2¼  121  21½ 21½ 11½ 1nk  McCrrnCJ6 ⒻAw22000  87 TimeOfSle,LonForignr,ShriliBrown 6
23Oct82-8SA  1 1/16:454 1:094 1:414ft 27 115 2hd 45½ 617 723 CstnedM3 ⒻOak Leaf 69 Landluce,SophistictedGirl,GrnjRein 7
11Oct82-8SA  7f :222 :45  1:214ft  14  120  1hd 22  28  311  McCrrnCJ1 ⒻAnoakia  80 Landaluce, Rare Thrill, TimeOfSale 8
18Sep82-9Lga 1  :461 1:121 1:381ft  *1  121  21  31  610 716  LiphmT9 ⒻMrcr Grl H 62 Pretencia, Theonia First, Aunt Iva 10
 5Sep82-9Lga 6½f:22  :45  1:181ft  *2¾ 118  41¼ 42½ 44  2½   LiphamT7 [S]Gtstn Fut 77 Big Flyer, Time Of Sale, Thurman 12
16Aug82-8Dmr 1  :46  1:11 1:382ft  16  113  52¼ 42¾ 52¾ 1½   ShomkrW8 ⒻSorrento  78 Time Of Sale,SharlliBrown,Infantes 8
30Jly82-6Dmr 6f :221 :454 1:114ft  22  1105 31½ 22½ 22½ 1½   CapitineNM3 ⒻM35000 79 TimeOfSale,Blanquit,Nvonod'sStr 12
   Jan 30 SA 4f gd :493 h     Jan 20 SA 3f ft :35 h     Jan 16 SA 5f ft :592 h     Jan 5 SA 6f ft 1:133 hg

A Lucky Sign                          B. f. 3, by Lucky Mike—Zealous Sally, by In Zeal
                                      Br.—Old English Rancho (Cal)           1983 1 1 0 0    $42,250
Own.—Hdly-Jhnstn-ElzJhnstn(Trst) 121  Tr.—Headley Bruce                      1982 4 2 1 0    $54,825
                                Lifetime   5 3 1 0   $97,075
12Jan83-8SA  6f :211 :44  1:093ft *2¼  119  42  22½ 2hd 12   McCrrCJ2 ⒻPasadena   90 ALuckySign,LotusDncer,PstryCun 12
29Dec82-8SA  6f :211 :434 1:094ft *9-5 118  2hd 2½  1½  1½   McCrrCJ5 ⒻLa Cntnla  89 ALuckySign,LotusDncr,OrintlChmp 8
24Oct82-4SA  6f :213 :442 1:094ft *2-3 118  11½ 1½  2hd 21¼  Pincay LJr6 ⒻAw20000 88 EstrnBttor,ALuckySign,LonForignr 7
16Oct82-3SA  6f :212 :443 1:084ft *6-5 117  1½  12½ 16  17   McCarronCJ5 Ⓕ[S]Mdn 94 ALuckySign,Vivaciously,ChiquitGt 12
 3Oct82-3SA  6f :211 :442 1:091ft  6¼  117  2½  32  46½ 412  McCarronCJ6 Ⓕ[S]Mdn 80 FabulousNotion,Castlelnd,Ally'sLdy 7
   Jan 7 SA 5f ft 1:00 h     Dec 23 SA 5f sl 1:00 h     ●Dec 17 SA 5f ft :583 h     ●Dec 9 SA 6f ft 1:102 hg
```

The leading jockeys at Santa Anita Park from December 26, 1982–January 30, 1983

Jockey	Mounts	First	Second	Third	Winning Percentage	In-the-Money Percentage
McCarron, C. J.	166	41	27	19	25	52
Pincay, L. Jr.	141	37	26	12	26	53
Delahoussaye, E.	173	24	27	19	14	41
Shoemaker, W.	96	15	12	11	16	40
Black, K.	110	14	10	8	13	29
Valenzuela, P. A.	159	13	16	20	08	31
Hawley, S.	130	12	16	15	09	33
Steiner, J. J.[a]	120	12	11	13	10	30
Romero, R. P.	126	11	13	18	09	33
Toro, F.	119	10	11	20	08	35

[a]Apprentice.

Both Fabulous Notion and A Lucky Sign looked like outstanding horses, with Fabulous Notion the top choice. Either one seemed like a good bet if the odds to place or show were good enough. A Lucky Sign was about a

3—1 shot to win throughout the betting period, and her place and show odds were never favorable. However, Fabulous Notion was an outstanding show bet and a good place bet. The evolution of the odds, betting pools, and optimal betting amounts was as follows:

		#3 Fabulous Notion	Expected Return per Dollar Bet on Fabulous Notion	Optimal Bet on Fabulous Notion	Totals ($)
	Odds	4—5			
	Win bet	21,010			49,084
12 min	Place bet	7,502	0.99	0	19,955
to post	Show bet	1,048	1.60	334	6,617
	Odds	1—1			
	Win bet	24,315			57,123
9 min	Place bet	8,842	0.99	0	23,518
to post	Show bet	1,166	1.70	335	8,142
	Odds	4—5			
	Win bet	28,713			67,145
7 min	Place bet	11,032	0.98	0	28,825
to post	Show bet	1,485	1.67	343	10,080
	Odds	4—5			
	Win bet	42,157			97,510
5 min	Place bet	13,397	1.08	0	40,261
to post	Show bet	2,357	1.67	366	15,892
	Odds	1—1			
	Win bet	46,491			110,022
4 min	Place bet	14,550	1.10	0	46,040
to post	Show bet	3,142	1.48	358	17,762
	Odds	1—1			
	Win bet	70,673			166,666
1 min	Place bet	19,631	1.17	99	67,792
to post	Show bet	5,763	1.31	282	26,155
	Odds	4—5			
	Win bet	95,726			209,713
	Place bet	23,415	1.21	187	79,062
Final	Show bet	8,387	1.25	303	32,493

With one minute to post time, the expected value to place was 1.17 and to show 1.31. Our betting fortune was $1,000. The optimal betting equations programmed into our calculator indicated a place bet of $99 and a show bet of $282 on Fabulous Notion. As the following chart of the race indicates, A Lucky Sign won the race, followed by Sophisticated Girl, and Fabulous Notion was third. Thus we won our show bet and lost our place bet. Our profit was $(282)(0.4) - 99 = 112.80 - 99 = 13.80$.

EIGHTH RACE
Santa Anita
FEBRUARY 2, 1983

7 FURLONGS. (1.20) 32nd Running of THE SANTA YNEZ STAKES (Grade II). $75,000 added. Fillies. 3-year-olds. (Allowance). By subscription of $50 each to accompany the nomination, $100 to pass the entry box and $750 additional to start, with $75,000 added, of which $15,000 to second, $11,250 to third, $5,625 to fourth and $1,875 to fifth. Weight, 121 lbs. Winners of $50,000 twice in 1982–83, 3 lbs. additional; of $50,000 three times in 1982–83, 5 lbs. Non-winners of two races of $25,000 since December 25 or two of $25,000 or one of $50,000 at any time allowed 2 lbs.; of a race of $25,000 since December 25 or two of $15,000 or one of $25,000 at any time, 4 lbs.; of a race of $12,000, 7 lbs. Starters to be named through the entry box by the closing time of entries. A trophy will be presented to the owner of the winner. Closed Wednesday, January 26, 1983 with 18 nominations.

Value of race $82,800, value to winner $49,050, second $15,000, third $11,250, fourth $5,625, fifth $1,875. Mutuel pool $321,268.

Last Raced	Horse	Eqt.	A.	Wt	PP	St	¼	½	Str	Fin	Jockey	Odds $1
12Jan83 ^{8}SA^{1}	A Lucky Sign	b	3	121	8	4	2^{1}	$1\frac{1}{2}$	$1^{1\frac{1}{2}}$	$1^{\frac{3}{4}}$	McCarron C J	3.00
30Dec82 ^{5}SA^{1}	Sophisticated Girl	b	3	116	2	7	7^{1}	7^{3}	$3^{\frac{1}{2}}$	$2^{\frac{3}{4}}$	Delahoussaye E	10.10
30Dec82 ^{8}SA^{1}	Fabulous Notion	b	3	124	3	8	$6^{\frac{1}{2}}$	4^{2}	$2^{2\frac{1}{2}}$	$3^{4\frac{1}{2}}$	Pierce D	.80
12Jan83 ^{8}SA^{4}	Eastern Bettor		3	119	4	5	$3^{1\frac{1}{2}}$	$3^{1\frac{1}{2}}$	4^{3}	$4^{2\frac{1}{2}}$	Valenzuela P A	14.60
18Dec82 ^{8}BM^{2}	O'Happy Day	b	3	114	5	2	5^{3}	$5^{\frac{1}{2}}$	$5^{1\frac{1}{2}}$	$5^{\frac{1}{2}}$	Hawley S	28.90
14Jan83 ^{7}SA^{1}	Autumn Magic		3	115	1	6	8	8	7^{2}	6^{6}	Toro F	6.10
21Jan83 ^{7}SA^{1}	Time Of Sale	b	3	119	7	1	1^{hd}	$2^{1\frac{1}{2}}$	6^{2}	$7^{8\frac{1}{2}}$	Pincay L Jr	22.50
12Jan83 ^{4}SA^{1}	D'Arques		3	114	6	3	$4^{\frac{1}{2}}$	6^{1}	8	8	Shoemaker W	38.30

OFF AT 4:00. Start good for all but FABULOUS NOTION. Won driving. Time, :22⅕, :44⅘, 1:10, 1:23⅘ Track sloppy.

$2 Mutuel Prices:				
	9–A LUCKY SIGN	8.00	3.60	3.40
	2–SOPHISTICATED GIRL		7.00	3.80
	3–FABULOUS NOTION			2.80

B. f, by Lucky Mike—Zealous Salty, by In Zeal. Trainer Headley Bruce. Bred by Old English Rancho (Cal).

A LUCKY SIGN, engaged for the lead at once, disposed of TIME OF SALE in the upper stretch and held SOPHISTICATED GIRL safe. The latter lacked early speed, rallied strongly on the outside around the turn and was gaining on the winner at the end. FABULOUS NOTION broke in the air and was off behind her field, rallied on the outside around the turn, then weakened slightly in the final sixteenth. EASTERN BETTOR went evenly. AUTUMN MAGIC was never a factor. TIME OF SALE vied for the early lead inside the winner and tired in the stretch. D'ARQUES had brief early speed and also tired badly in the stretch. All starters except O'HAPPY DAY wore mud calks.

Owners— 1, Hdly-Jhnstn-Eliz Jhnstn(Trstee); 2, Golden Eagle Farm; 3, Pine Meadows Thoroughbreds; 4, Hanson Stock Farm; 5, Poyer & Steinmann; 6, Mirkin Claudia H & M; 7, Northwest Farms; 8, Demeter & Oatlands Stable.

Overweight: Sophisticated Girl 2 pounds; Autumn Magic 1.

Scratched—Flying Lassie (12Jan83 ^{8}SA^{6}).

The Seventh Race, Exhibition Park, Vancouver, British Columbia, April 13, 1983

The seventh race on the card Wednesday, April 13, 1983, was an allowance race for three-year-olds with a purse of $6,400. The 6-furlong race featured two standouts, Intoxicator and Highly Rumored, running against four considerably weaker horses. It was the second day of the 1983 meet and this race was the first of the year for all six starters. They all had spent their racing careers at Exhibition Park and had not run since the late summer of 1982.

It was a beautiful, clear night with Vancouver's springtime view of the mountains and ocean coast at its best. The track was fast. I was anxious to see what changes the new season had brought and to get organized for the summer betting. I knew, as well, that the early part of any new meet is a time to be cautious; it is wise to wait until the horses' forms become well established. Hence I kept my betting fortune to a modest $300.

Both Intoxicator and Highly Rumored looked quite promising. They were ridden by two top local jockeys, Kenny Skinner and Chris Loseth. Both Skinner and Loseth were former Exhibition Park jockey champions who were returning from riding stints in the United States to be in Vancouver for the summer meet.

Intoxicator was purchased for $105,000, a handsome sum for a Vancouver-based thoroughbred, and has been lightly raced. The *Daily Racing Form's* consensus of experts thought that he was ready for a big race and installed Intoxicator as an overwhelming favorite. The impressive rating of 33 out of 35 in the consensus made him the best bet for the day. Highly Rumored was expected to give Intoxicator a good run for the money but to be outclassed. Since both Intoxicator and Highly Rumored had not run much during 1982, had failed at low odds, and would be starting for the first time this season, I was cautious. I liked them both but would bet only if the odds were good.

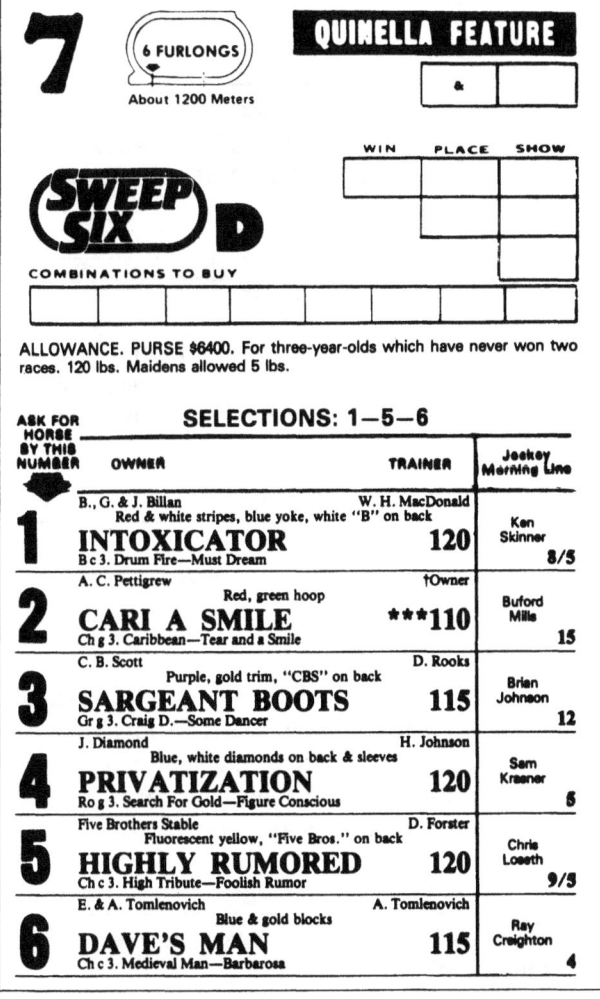

7 6 FURLONGS About 1200 Meters

QUINELLA FEATURE &

WIN PLACE SHOW

SWEEP SIX D

COMBINATIONS TO BUY

ALLOWANCE. PURSE $6400. For three-year-olds which have never won two races. 120 lbs. Maidens allowed 5 lbs.

SELECTIONS: 1—5—6

ASK FOR HORSE BY THIS NUMBER	OWNER / TRAINER	Jockey / Morning Line
1	B., G. & J. Billan — W. H. MacDonald Red & white stripes, blue yoke, white "B" on back **INTOXICATOR** 120 B c 3. Drum Fire—Must Dream	Ken Skinner 8/5
2	A. C. Pettigrew — †Owner Red, green hoop **CARI A SMILE** ***110 Ch g 3. Caribbean—Tear and a Smile	Buford Mills 15
3	C. B. Scott — D. Rooks Purple, gold trim, "CBS" on back **SARGEANT BOOTS** 115 Gr g 3. Craig D.—Some Dancer	Brian Johnson 12
4	J. Diamond — H. Johnson Blue, white diamonds on back & sleeves **PRIVATIZATION** 120 Ro g 3. Search For Gold—Figure Conscious	Sam Krasner 5
5	Five Brothers Stable — D. Forster Fluorescent yellow, "Five Bros." on back **HIGHLY RUMORED** 120 Ch c 3. High Tribute—Foolish Rumor	Chris Loseth 9/5
6	E. & A. Tomlenovich — A. Tomlenovich Blue & gold blocks **DAVE'S MAN** 115 Ch c 3. Medieval Man—Barbarosa	Ray Creighton 4

Exhibition

COMMENT

SEVENTH RACE

INTOXICATOR came up a touch short in that stakes attempt last July but is again prepping well for his seasonal bow and will take some beating. HIGHLY RUMORED showed much promise last year and has also been lively in the mornings. PRIVATIZATION showed nothing after that impressive debut but may be ready for better things now.

Racing Form **EXPERTS' SELECTIONS**

Consensus Points: 5 for 1st (best 7), 2 for 2d, 1 for 3d. Best in CAPITALS.

Trackman, Tim Toon — EXHIBITION PARK — Selections Made for Fast Track

RACE	TRACKMAN	HERMIS	HANDICAP	ANALYST	SWEEP	CONSENSUS	
7	INTOXICATOR Highly Rumored Sargeant Boots	Intoxicator Highly Rumored Sargeant Boots	INTOXICATOR Sargeant Boots Highly Rumored	INTOXICATOR Highly Rumoured Privatization	INTOXICATOR Highly Rumored Privatization	INTOXICATOR Highly Rumored Sargeant Boot	33 9 4

Throughout the betting period the odds on both Intoxicator and Highly Rumored were good and both looked like Dr. Z system bets.

With one minute to post time the tote board was as follows:

	Totals	#1 Intoxicator	#5 Highly Rumored
Odds		3—5	7—5
Win	22,814	11,006	7,850
Show	4,564	1,408	950

The optimal bets were $90 on Intoxicator and $50 on Highly Rumored.* The expected values per dollar bet were 1.14 and 1.18, respectively. The last-minute betting was concentrated on Highly Rumored to win and Intoxicator to show. This reinforced the Highly Rumored show bet and made the Intoxicator show bet not quite so good. The tote board at post time was

*The calculation of the optimal wagers when there are two different bets is discussed in Chapter Sixteen.

	Totals	#1 Intoxicator	#5 Highly Rumored
Odds		4—5	6—7
Win	28,486.00	13,044.00	10,170.00
Show	6,637.00	2,016.00	1,358.00
Expected value		1.12	1.21
Optimal bet		$90	$50

The race was run true to form. Intoxicator was a wire-to-wire winner by nine lengths over Highly Rumored. The 40—1 longshot, Cari A Smile, finished third. The chart of the race and mutuel payoffs were as follows:

7th Six furlongs. Three-year-olds. Claiming Allowance. Purse $6.400.

Horse	Jockey	Wt	P	¼	½	Str	Fin	Odds
Intoxicator	Skinner	120	1	1-2	1-3	1-5	1-9	.80
Highly Rumored	Loseth	120	5	3-4	2-3	2-5	2-3½	1.35
Cari A Smile	Mills	110	2	4-4	4-2	4-2	3-2	41.20
Sargeant Boots	Johnson	115	3	6	5-4	5-4	4-nk	19.95
Dave's Man	Creighton	115	6	2-h	3-4	3-1	5-2	9.45
Privatization	Krasner	120	4	5-1½	6	6	6	17.80

Time — :22.4, :45.4, 1:11.
Winner: Drum Fire-Must Dream.
Trainer: W. MacDonald.

INTOXICATOR	**3.60**	**2.50**	**2.50**
HIGHLY RUMORED		**2.60**	**2.80**
CARI A SMILE			**4.40**

Intoxicator paid as much to show as to place, and Highly Rumored paid more. This happens often with Dr. Z system bets. My bets of $90 on Intoxicator and $50 on Highly Rumored returned $112.50 and $70, respectively, for a $42.50 profit.

The Kentucky Oaks, Churchill Downs, Louisville, Kentucky, Friday, May 6, 1983

The Kentucky Oaks is the Kentucky Derby for fillies. It is run each year the Friday before the first Saturday in May, which is the day the Derby is run, and features the top three-year-old fillies. The $1\frac{1}{8}$-mile race is for a $150,000 added purse. In the 1940s and 1950s, the Kentucky Oaks, the Pimlico Oaks, and the Coaching Club American Oaks at Belmont were referred to as the triple crown for fillies. In recent years the triple crown usually refers to three races all run at Belmont: the Acorn Mile, the Mother Goose, and the Coaching Club American Oaks. Davona Dale won the Kentucky Oaks, the Black Eyed Susan Stakes at Pimlico (formerly the Pimlico Oaks) and the triple crown in 1979, an impressive record over the brief two month period in May and June when these five races were held.

We had been in Chicago for a Management Science Conference, where I participated in sessions on options pricing, efficient markets, and the mathematics of gambling. During the week preceding the race, while I was doing research at the Keeneland racetrack library in Lexington for this book, the spring rains had been continual and extremely heavy.* Fortunately, the rain ended on Wednesday, and by the end of the day on Thursday, the track even had to be watered. On Friday the weather was sunny, and the track was blazing fast. In the first race, Modicum, running in his second career start, broke the $4\frac{1}{2}$-furlong track record by $\frac{2}{5}$ second to win the race in $51\frac{2}{5}$ seconds. A description of this race appeared in Chapter Five.

Princess Rooney was an overwhelming favorite to win the 1983 Kentucky Oaks. She had nine previous races and had won them all by margins of three, four, eight, ten, twelve and even eighteen lengths. In only one race was the outcome in doubt. She held on for a half-length victory in a $30,000 allowance race. She had run recently, winning her two races at the Keeneland meet by a total of $19\frac{1}{2}$ lengths.

Many observers had hopes that her owner, Paula Tucker, and trainer, Frank Gomez, could be persuaded to enter Princess Rooney in the 1983 Kentucky Derby. No doubt she would have been one of the favorites, along with Sunny's Halo and Marfa. Since a filly had won the Kentucky Derby only twice in 108 runnings, the chance of such a victory was appealing to many observers ever since Genuine Risk won in 1980. It is well known that the Derby, with its 20 starters and intense competition, is a very demanding and difficult race. Many horses never recover from a Derby race. For a stallion whose value might escalate by $10 million as a result of a Derby victory, such a risk is well worth taking. But for a filly there is not much money to be gained in breeding. The risks of the race may well dominate the possible added prestige and breeding value. As Princess Rooney's trainer summed it up, ". . . you would not have Chris Evert play Jimmy Connors at Wimbledon."

So Princess Rooney was in the Oaks. The rest of the field was reasonably strong and would give Princess Rooney her toughest test to date. The main competition was from the Tom Gentry filly, Rosy Spectre, who had finished first or second in each of her five career starts. The *Daily Racing Form's* consensus gave Princess Rooney a perfect 35/35 rating, since she was rated the best bet of the day by all five of their expert selectors. She had the advantageous post position, number 1, and was ridden by the veteran jockey Jacinto Vasquez. The 1—5 morning-line odds in the program and the *Daily*

*The Keeneland library on the grounds of the Keeneland Racetrack has a wonderful collection of books and materials on all aspects of thoroughbred racing. Their materials date to the eighteenth century. It is open to the public and has a very courteous and helpful staff.

Racing Form's expert selection's best bet of the day seemed justified. Weekend Surprise, Number 6, was scratched, so the field had seven starters.

Last Race Exacta Wagering Now Available

WIN	PLACE	SHOW

1⅛ MILES

START FINISH

STAKE

Purse $150,000-Added

8

THE KENTUCKY OAKS

(One Hundred and Ninth Running)

FILLIES, THREE YEARS OLD. By subscription of $100 each: $750 to pass the entry box; $750 additional to start with $150,000 added of which 65% of all monies to the owner of the winner, 20% to second, 10% to third and 5% to fourth. Weight, 121 lbs. Closed Tuesday, February 15, 1983 with 187 Nominations. A silver trophy to the winning owner.

Track Record—AEROFLINT (3) 116 lbs.; 1:48²/₅; Nov. 18, 1961
LAS OLAS (4) 111 lbs.; 1:48²/₅; Nov. 21, 1959

MAKE SELECTION BY NUMBER

No.	Owner / Trainer	Jockey/Morn. Line
1	PAULA TUCKER — FRANK GOMEZ Light Blue, White Dots, White Chevrons on Sleeves Light Blue Cap **PRINCESS ROONEY** 121 Gr.f.(1980), Verbatim—Parrish Princess by Drone Bred in Kentucky by Ben and Tom Roach	1-5 JACINTO VASQUEZ
2	MRS. V. LEVAN, MRS. B. WALTERS AND L. WESTON — ADRIAN J. MAXWELL Pink, Grey Blocks, Pink Cap **BRIGHT CROCUS** 121 Ch.f.(1980), Clev er Tell—Bold Saffron by Bold Hour Bred in Kentucky by T. I. Harkins	8 SANDY HAWLEY
3	EVERETT LOWRANCE — JAMES ECKROSH Orange, Green "L," Green Bars on Sleeves Orange Cap **FIFTH QUESTION** 121 Gr.f.(1980), Fifth Marine—Little Divy by Royal Cap Bred in Oklahoma by Everett Lowrance	10 PAT DAY
4	WHITE FOX FARM (Dewey White) — ELWOOD McCANN Maroon, Silver Hoops, Mar. Chev. on Silver Slvs., Silv. Cap **SHAMIVOR** 121 Dk.b. or br.f.(1980), Sham—Ivorie II by Sir Ivor Bred in Florida by Waldemar Farms, Inc. & Gerald R Robins	15 DON BRUMFIELD
5	TOM GENTY — EDUARDO INDA Yellow, Royal Blue Blocks, Royal Blue Bars on Sleeves Yellow Cap **ROSY SPECTRE** 121 Ch.f.(1980), Nijinsky II—Like a Charm by Pied d'or Bred in Kentucky by Tom Gentry	15 EDDIE DELAHOUSSAYE
6	W. S. KILROY AND W. S. FARISH — DEL W. CARROLL II Green, Yellow Chevrons, Green Cap **Weekend Surprise** 121 B.f.(1980), Secretariat—Lassie Dear by Buckpasser Bred in Kentucky by W. S. Farish III & W. S. Kilroy	20 CHRIS McCARRON
7	RYEHILL FARM (James P. Ryan) — WOODFORD C. STEPHENS Navy, Gold Belt, Gold Blocks on Sleeves, Gold Cap **BEMISSED** 121 Ch.f.(1980), Nijinsky II—Bemis Heights by Herbager Bred in Maryland by Ryehill Farm	20 FRANK LOVATO, JR.
8	WANAJA FARM & B. T. ENERGY (Janie Martin and Don Ball) — JACK VAN BERG Gold, Purple "V," Purple Sleeves, Purple Cap **BRINDY BRINDY** 121 Ch.f.(1980), Grand Revival—Belle Of Caledon by Bull Vic Bred in Kentucky by John McGarrah	12 KENNETH JONES

Indicates Foaled In Kentucky

Selections 1—2—3—8

Racing Form

Experts' Selections

Consensus Points: 5 for 1st (today's best 7), 2 for 2nd, 1 for 3rd. Today's Best in Bold Type.

Trackman, Graham Ross — **CHURCHILL DOWNS** — Selections Made for Fast Track

8	PRINCESS ROONEY	PRINCESS ROONEY	PRINCESS ROONEY	PRINCESS ROONEY	PRINCESS ROONEY	PRINCESS ROONEY	35
	WEEKEND SURPRISE	SHAMIVOR	ROSY SPECTRE	BRIGHT CROCUS	ROSY SPECTRE	ROSY SPECTRE	4
	FIFTH QUESTION	BRINDY BRINDY	FIFTH QUESTION	WEEKEND SURPRISE	BRIGHT CROCUS	WEEKEND SURPRISE	3

8th Churchill

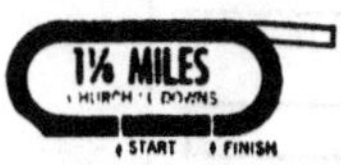

1⅛ MILES. (1.48⅘) 109th Running KENTUCKY OAKS (Grade I). $150,000 added. Fillies. 3-year-olds. By subscription of $100 each; $750 to pass the entry box; $750 additional to start with $150,000 added of which $65% of all monies to the owner of the winner, 40% to second, 10% to third and 5% to fourth. Weight, 121 lbs. Starters to be named through the entry box Wednesday, May 4, by the usual time of closing. If the race is divided entries or couplings will be divided. A silver trophy to the winning owner. Closed with 187 nominations.

Princess Rooney — **Gr. f. 3, by Verbatim—Parrish Princess, by Drone**
Br.—Roach B & T (Ky) — 1983 3 3 0 0 $110,333
Own.—Tucker Paula — **121** — **Tr.—Gomez Frank** — 1982 6 6 0 0 $223,815
Lifetime 9 9 0 0 $334,148

```
23Apr83-7Kee  1 1/16 :463 1:113 1:452sy  *1-5 121  1hd 1hd 12½ 19½  Vasquez J4  (F)Ashland  79-24 PrincessRooney,Shamivor,Decision 6
13Apr83-7Kee  a7f  1:272ft  *1-3 123  21 2hd 13 110  Vasquez J8  (F)Aw28000  86-21 PrincessRooney,FiestyBll,SilvrdSilk 8
5Mar83-7GP  7f :221 :45 1:234ft  *1-5 114  31½ 3½ 1½ 1½  Vasquez J2  Aw30000  85-19 PrncssRoony,Mrgnmrgnmrgn,Alchs 8
23Oct82-6Med  1 1/16 :471 1:11 1:43 ft  *1-3 121  1½ 12 17 111  Vasquez J6 (F)Gardenia  94-11 PrncssRoony,FrOnc'nMyLf,GldSprc 7
10Oct82-8Bel  1 :461 1:113 1:39 ft  *6-5 119  1hd 11½ 16 18  Fell J2  (F)Frizette  70-29 PrncssRny,WnnngTck,WkndSrprs 13
11Sep82-9Crc  7f :222 :454 1:234ft  *1-5 116  11 12½ 18 112  PnnisFA7 (F)Melaleuca  97-14 PrincssRoony,Hiusonso,Rin'sMissy 8
1Sep82-9Crc  7f :222 :46 1:251ft  *4-5 116  1½ 11½ 110 118  Pennisi FA1 (F)Aw10000  90-18 PrncssRoony,CortUnn,FlwlssDmnd 5
7Jun82-7Crc  5f :223 :463 :593ft  *6-5 114  1½ 11½ 13 14  Pennisi F A1 (F)Aw9500  94-15 PrncssRoony,Ishudhdtht,RoyltyMss 6
22May82-3Crc  5f :224 :47 1:002ft  *2 115  3nk 1hd 12 13  Pennisi F A9  (F)Mdn  90-14 Princess Rooney, Rilia, Marie V. 9
    May 2 CD 6f gd 1:16 b    Apr 21 Kee 5f ft 1:002 b    Apr 12 Kee 3f gd :36 b    ●Apr 8 Kee 5f sy 1:023 b (d)
```

Bright Crocus — **B. f. 3, by Clev Er Tell—Bold Saffron, by Bold Hour**
Br.—Harkins T I (Ky) — 1983 4 1 1 0 $87,809
Own.—Levan-Waters-Weston — **121** — **Tr.—Maxwell Adrian J** — 1982 8 3 1 1 $48,764
Lifetime 12 4 2 1 $136,573 — Turf 8 3 1 1 $48,764

```
16Apr83-10Hia  1⅛ :471 1:12 1:494ft  *1 121  52½ 63½ 48½ 511  Hawley S1 (F)Poinsetta  72-23 Thinghatab,Overreaction,BuffloGl 15
    16Apr83—Crowded, st'd
26Mar83-10FG  1 1/16 :472 1:124 1:454gd  6 121  55 53½ 2hd 15½  Hawley S2 (F)Fg Oaks  83-24 Bright Crocus, MissMolly,Shamivor 6
28Feb83-9GP  1 1/16  1:452ft  31 114  85¾ 23 25 36¼  VsqzJ7 (F)Bonnie Miss  68-24 Unccompnd,‡MssMolly,BrghtCrcs 12
    28Feb83—Placed second through disqualification
7Feb83-9GP  7f :221 :451 1:232gd  14 114  82½ 63¾ 910 912  McBtD8 (F)ForwardGal  75-21 Unccompnid,Lis'sCpitl,QuxotcLdy 15
23Sep82◆3Ascot(Eng)  1  1:471gd  *2 128  (T) 8  PgttL (F)HooverFilliesMile(Gr.3)  Acclimatise, DancingMeg,Alligatrix 8
9Sep82◆6Doncaster(Eng)  1  1:391gd  6 119  (T) 15  PiggottL  (F)May Hill Stks  BrghtCrocs,SlkPyjms,GoodbyShlly 8
7Aug82◆4Newmarket(Eng)  7f  1:293gd  3½ 128  42  PggttL  (F)Sweet Solera Stks  Flamenco, Acclimatise, Montervie 8
24Jly82◆2Ascot(Eng)  6f  1:152gd  3½ 127  (T) 32½  PgttL  (F)PrincessMargaretStk  RöylHroin,HnrysScrt,BrightCrocus 6
6Jly82◆4Newmarket(Eng)  6f  1:121gd  2 125  (T) 43¾  PttL (F)CherryHintonStks(Gr.3)  CrimeofPassion,Crolside,SilkPyjms 8
26Jun82◆1Newmarket(Eng)  6f  1:154gd*1-2 125  (T) 11  PgttL  (F)Dance In Time Stk  BrghtCrocs,KyTThMnstrl,HntrsGrv 5
    May 4 CD 4f m :50 b    ●May 1 CD 5f sy 1:014 h    Apr 13 Hia 4f ft :502 b    Apr 8 Hia 4f ft :50 b
```

Fifth Question — **Gr. f. 3, by Fifth Marine—Little Divy, by Royal Cap**
Br.—Lowrance Everett (Okla) — 1983 6 2 1 2 $101,635
Own.—Lowrance E — **121** — **Tr.—Eckrosh James** — 1982 2 2 0 0 $21,003
Lifetime 8 4 1 2 $122,638

```
23Apr83-7Kee  1 1/16 :463 1:113 1:452sy  4¼ 116  48½ 613 512 532  Day P5  (F)Ashland  47-24 PrincessRooney,Shamivor,Decision 6
9Apr83-9OP  1 1/16 :473 1:123 1:443ft  3¼ 115  75½ 64 23½ 2½  Day P9  (F)Fantasy  84-21 BrndyBrndy,FfthQston,ChsAPrtnr 11
    9Apr83—Bothered
30Mar83-9OP  170 :462 1:122 1:43 ft  3 118  68½ 47½ 21 16  Day P1  (F)Aw30000  81-23 FfthQstn,BrndyBrndy,FrOnc'nMyLf 7
18Mar83-9OP  6f :224 :462 1:13 ft  4¼ 118  1211 106¾ 75½ 3½  Day P11  (F)Magnolia  79-22 Lt.Prl,ForOnc'nMyLif,FifthQuston 12
21Feb83-9OP  6f :221 :463 1:131sy  *1 118  64½ 55½ 46½ 35½  Day P3  (F)M Wash  73-27 Lt.Perle,ElgntExprinc,FifthQustion 7
11Feb83-7OP  5½f :224 :48 1:082gd  8¼ 116  89½ 68 55¾ 1½  HghtwrTW3 (F)Aw25000  76-28 FifthQuestion,Lt.Perl,BrindyBrindy 9
26Dec82-8Haw  1 1/16 :48 1:122 1:452ft  3 114  2hd 11½ 11½ 12  HghtwrTW3 (F)Durazna  71-23 Fifth Question, O Yoko,SheWillTell 5
8Dec82-2Haw  6½f :222 :454 1:19 ft  16 119  1115 812 31 1hd  HightowerTW7 (F)Mdn  78-22 FifthQuestion,SuprDot,SrtogRvlry 11
    May 3 CD 5f sy 1:052 b    Apr 21 Kee 4f ft :52 b    Apr 7 OP 5f ft 1:053 b    Mar 28 OP 4f sl :54 b
```

```
Shamivor                              Dk. b. or br. f. 3, by Sham—Ivoire II, by Sir Ivor
                                      Br.—Waldomar Fms Inc&RobinsG (Fla)   1983  6 2 3 1   $60,410
Own.—White Fox Farm             121   Tr.—McCann Elwood Sr                 1982  4 2 0 0   $10,300
                                 Lifetime  10  4  3  1   $70,710
23Apr83-7Kee  1 1/16:463 1:113 1:452sy  12 114  2hd 2hd 22½ 29½  BrumfildD3 (F)Ashland   69-24 PrincessRooney,Shamivor,Decision 6
26Mar83-10FG  1 1/16:472 1:124 1:454gd  3¾ 115  13  12  1hd 37½  RomeroRP3 (F)Fg Oaks    75-24 Bright Crocus, MissMolly,Shamivor 6
 5Mar83-9FG   140:491 1:143 1:43 ft     3-2 117  12  11½ 11½ 2hd  Ardoin R1 (F)Dava Dale  78-21 Duped, Shamivor, Juliet's Pet 5
20Feb83-9FG   140:464 1:124 1:423ft    *4-5 120  1hd 13  12½ 14½  EspinozJC7 (F)Aw11000   80-25 Shamivor,MadamNorm,YellowBow 8
13Feb83-9FG   6f :22   :46  1:121ft     4¾ 117  32  31½ 41  23   EspinozaJC7 (F)Thelma   81-20 Duped, Shamivor, Sally Stride 8
14Jan83-7FG   140:47  1:133 1:432ft    *8-5 119  11½ 16  15  14½  EspinozJC2 (F)Aw10000   76-19 Shamivor,Tani'sNuPearl,Kristy'sFir 9
23Dec82-8FG   6f :221  :463 1:13 ft      3 119  117½ 62¾ 31 11   McKnight J7 (F)Aw9000   80-21 Shmivor,WinterWitch,CityPrincss 11
16Dec82-6FG   6f :223  :47  1:133ft    *9-5 119  12  13  13  17   McKnight J10 (F)Mdn     77-22 Shmivor,RobbngAround,LdyBrtrm 11
27Nov82-9FG   6f :222  :472 1:133m      65 112  3nk 2hd 66  816  McKhtJ10 (F)Pontalba     61-25 Duped, How Clever, Distant Mom 11
17Nov82-2CD   6f :222  :462 1:114ft     27 120  42  21½ 42  47½  Maple S10 (F)Mdn        79-23 Shea Lee,I'mDriven,JamacianSpell 12
    Apr 22 Kee 3f ft :35 b     ●Apr 18 Kee 5f ft 1:00 h     Apr 12 Kee 6f ft 1:122 h     Mar 25 FG 4f ft :52 b
```

```
Rosy Spectre                          Ch. f. 3, by Nijinsky II—Like A Charm, by Pied d'Or
                                      Br.—Gentry T E (Ky)                  1983  4 2 2 0   $22,920
Own.—Gentry T E                 121   Tr.—Inda Eduardo                     1982  1 M 1 0    $2,400
                                 Lifetime  5  2  3  0   $25,320
27Apr83-5Kee  1 1/16:49  1:133 1:472ft *6-5 115  83¾ 63¾ 31½ 1½   Day P9 (F)Aw15700       69-18 RosySpectre,BroadwayDolcie,Exult 9
19Apr83-2Kee  a7f             1:292ft  *2-3 118  41  53  3nk 2no  Day P8 (F)Aw14600       76-18 Plchee,RosySpectre,BrodwyDolcie 11
 8Apr83-4Kee  a7f             1:283sy  *4-5 118  45½ 32  13  15   Romero R P6 (F)Mdn      80-14 RosySpectr,Mrdith'sMomnt,ClvrRn 8
26Mar83-5Hia  7f :224  :46  1:26 ft    *3-2 119  64¾ 44½ 22½ 22½  Vasquez J10 (F)Mdn      70-17 YoWon'tBSorry,RsySpctr,PcktLnr 12
15Aug82-4Dmr  6f :22   :45  1:103ft     17 117  89  713 59  23½  McHargue DG9 (F)Mdn     81-12 BrillintMove,RosySpctr,AdriticGirl 10
    May 4 CD 4f m :493 b     Apr 25 Kee 4f gd :51 b     Apr 16 Kee 4f gd :50 b     Apr 3 Kee 5f ft 1:001 b
```

```
Weekend Surprise                      B. f. 3, by Secretariat—Lassie Dear, by Buckpasser
                                      Br.—Farish III & Kilroy (Ky)         1983  2 0 0 1    $3,730
Own.—Kilroy & Farish III        121   Tr.—Carroll Del W II                 1982  9 5 1 2  $190,588
                                 Lifetime  11  5  1  3   $194,318
 2May83-8CD   7f :233  :47  1:252sy    *9-5 121  87  75¾ 65  31½  Day P8 (F)La Troien     79-18 HowClever,SuperBell,WkndSurpris 8
13Apr83-7Kee  a7f             1:272ft     5 123  64½ 65¼ 79  716  BrumfildD3 (F)Aw28000   70-21 PrincessRooney,FiestyBll,SilvrdSilk 8
25Nov82-8CD   1 1/16:492 1:141 1:47 gd *2-5e119  31  42  31  1½   Day P1 (F)Gold Rod      73-23 WekndSurpris,NtionlBnnr,QurrlOvr 6
11Nov82-8CD   1  :471 1:12  1:374ft     *1 122  41½ 41  1½  13¼  BrumfldD6 (F)Pcahonts   80-20 WeekendSurprise,Dcision,QurrlOvr 9
      11Nov82—Run in two divisions, 6th and 8th races
 4Nov82-7CD   7f :232  :463 1:25 ft    *1-2 121  57  54½ 1hd 11½  Day P1 (F)Aw13700       82-24 WkndSrprs,PrttyPrfct,YKy'sLdyKt 6
10Oct82-8Bel  1  :461 1:113 1:39 ft      9½ 119  76½ 69  49  312  VelasquezJ4 (F)Frizette 58-29 PrncssRny,WnnngTck,WkndSrprs 13
18Sep82-7Bel  7f :23   :461 1:24 ft      5½ 119  513 512 48½ 34½  Velasquez J2 Matron     77-17 WngsofJov,ShrThFntsy,WkndSrprs 5
29Aug82-8Sar  6f :221  :453 1:094ft      2½ 119  59½ 54¾ 33½ 56¼  VelsquzJ1 (F)Spinaway   85-15 ShrThFntsy,SngngSsn,MdnghtRptr 6
 4Aug82-8Sar  6f :221  :452 1:11 ft    3-2e114   710 611 45½ 11   VlsqzJ7 (F)Schuylervile 85-13 WkndSurpris,ShrThFntsy,FlyingLss 7
 2Jun82-8Bel  5½f:223  :454 1:041ft      2¾ 116  65  53½ 54¼ 22   VelsquezJ7 (F)Rosedale  92-11 GlJubil,WkndSurpris,SubvrsivChick 7
    May 1 CD 3f sy :384 b     Apr 25 Kee 5f gd 1:012 b     Apr 19 Kee 4f ft :503 b     Apr 12 Kee 3f gd :362 b
```

```
Bemissed                              Ch. f. 3, by Nijinsky II—Bemis Heights, by Herbager
                                      Br.—Ryehill Farm (Md)                1983  4 0 0 1   $27,423
Own.—Ryehill Farm               121   Tr.—Stephens Woodford C              1982  9 4 1 2  $254,432
                                 Lifetime  13  4  1  3   $281,855          Turf  5 3 0 2  $111,969
23Apr83-8Pim  1 1/16(T):50 1:1611:50 yl  3¼ 110  55  43  32½ 31   LtFJr5 (F)Gallorette H  60-39 WeddingPrty,SunnySprkler,Bmissd 8
 9Apr83-9OP   1 1/16:473 1:123 1:443ft    17 121  54½ 31½ 44  45   Lovato FJr4 (F)Fantasy  80-21 BrndyBrndy,FfthQston,ChsAPrtnr 11
30Mar83-9OP   170:462 1:122 1:43 ft       *1 115  711 612 512 417  Maple E7 (F)Aw30000     64-23 FfthQstn,BrndyBrndy,FrOnc'nMyLf 7
14Feb83-9GP   7f :231  :462 1:234ft        8 117  43  52½ 67½ 611  MapleE7 Golden Grass    74-21 Cast Party, Smart Style, Reap 9
      14Feb83—Run in two divisions 7th & 9th races
14Nov82-8Aqu  1⅛ :491 1:14  1:52 ft    *1-2e121  24  42  45  46   LovtFJr3 (F)Demoiselle  69-23 OnlyQueens,GoldSpruce,NtionlBnnr 7
30Oct82-8Lrl  1 1/16:471 1:121 1:44 ft    2e122  33½ 2hd 12½ 13¼  Lovato F Jr7 (F)Selima  88-15 Bemissed, Icy Time, No BodyElse's 9
21Oct82-8Aqu  1⅛(T):4821:13 1:514fm      2e121  36½ 32½ 1hd 1no  LovtFJr5 (F)Miss Grillo 85-15 Bemissed, Cryptic, Magnifique 8
16Oct82-8Bow  7f :222  :443 1:243ft      6¾ 119  55½ 46½ 43  42¾  LtFJr3 (F)[S]Kindergrtn 79-25 SngngSsn,NorthrnStng,NoBdyEls's 8
19Sep82-9WO   1  [T]:4811:14 1:403yl      *1 112  65¼ 3nk 1hd 11¾  LovatoFJr6 (F)Natalma   75-25 Bemissed,HoldMClosr,DonnsFncy 13
 3Sep82-8Bel  1  (T):4741:1221:381yl   *4-5e112  32½ 2½  22  33½  MpleE9 (F)Evening Out   70-26 Cryptic, NationalBanner,Bemissed 11
    May 2 CD 5f gd 1:04 b     Apr 7 OP 4f ft :49 b     Mar 27 OP 5f ft 1:024 b     Mar 20 Hia 3f ft :35 h
```

```
Brindy Brindy                         Ch. f. 3, by Grand Revival—Belle of Caledon, by Bull Vic
                                      Br.—McGarrah John (Ky)               1983  5 1 1 1  $179,880
Own.—Wanaja Fm & Energy B T     121   Tr.—Van Berg Jack C                  1982  6 4 0 1   $40,998
                                 Lifetime  11  5  1  2   $220,878
 9Apr83-9OP   1 1/16:473 1:123 1:443ft    59 115  11  11½ 13½ 1½   Jones K3 (F)Fantasy     85-21 BrndyBrndy,FfthQston,ChsAPrtnr 11
30Mar83-9OP   170:462 1:122 1:43 ft       30 112  12  15  11  26   Jones K2 (F)Aw30000     75-23 FfthQstn,BrndyBrndy,FrOnc'nMyLf 7
18Mar83-9OP   6f :224  :462 1:13 ft      14e118   3nk 3½  64  88   Jones K1 (F)Magnolia    72-22 Lt.Prl,ForOnc'nMyLif,FifthQuston 12
21Feb83-9OP   6f :221  :463 1:131sy      5¼ 115  21  44  512 515  EspinozJC5 (F)M Wash    64-27 Lt.Perle,ElgntExprinc,FifthQustion 7
11Feb83-7OP   5½f:224  :48  1:082gd      *2 116  31½ 22  23  31¾  Day P9 (F)Aw25000       74-28 FifthQuestion,Lt.Perl,BrindyBrindy 9
11Nov82-6CD   1  :46  1:104 1:381ft       6 117  1hd 1½  11½ 12½  EspnzJC3 (F)Pcahonts    78-20 BrndyBrndy,Rbrt'sDll,IsssN'Answrs 7
      11Nov82—Run in two divisions, 6th and 8th races
27Oct82-5Kee  6½f:231  :462 1:172ft      8½ 115  1½  1½  15  15   EspinozJC4 (F)Aw14600   90-18 BrindyBrindy,SwziGirl,Don'tTellDd 6
19Oct82-4Kee  6f :222  :454 1:104ft       8 112  11½ 2½  31½ 32¼  EspinozJC7 (F)Aw14600   86-18 DoblThCont,PrttyPrfct,BrndyBrndy 7
22Aug82-6ElP  5½f:222  :454 1:051ft      7½ 119  1½  1½  1½  1hd  EspinozaJC8 (F)Aw8400   94-11 BrindyBrindy,CongnilJni,HilltopSis 8
14Aug82-6FP   5½f:222  :472 1:064ft       6 116  2½  21½ 2hd 46   Evans RD10 (F)Juvenile  77-26 SilveredSilk,SusieCircle,Arlecchin 10
      14Aug82—Run in two divisions, 6th and 8th races
    ●Apr 26 Kee 5f ft 1:012 b     Apr 6 OP 5f sl 1:06 b     Mar 26 OP 5f ft 1:043 b     Mar 14 OP 4f ft :494 b
```

I expected that Princess Rooney would be heavily bet to win and that there likely would be a Dr. Z bet to place or to show or both. To my amazement, the first reading of the tote board with about twenty-three minutes to post time was as follows:

	Totals	#1 Princess Rooney
Odds		1—9
Win	61,214	44,920
Place	27,930	14,808
Show	268,441	257,150

The 1—9 win odds did not surprise me. I figured the win odds would rise to about 1—5 at post time. When I looked at the show pools it was clear to me that someone or some group of individuals had bet about $250,000 to show on Princess Rooney. Out of the show pool of $268,441, the bet on Princess Rooney was $257,150. Since the show bet is usually less than the place bet, $18,441 seemed like the bet of the early bettors. The quarter-million-dollar bet dominated the show pool and made it six times as large as the win pool—quite a reversal from the usual situation where the show pool is a half or a third or even less of the win pool.

Why would someone make such a large bet? Presumably they figured that Princess Rooney was virtually unbeatable and it was extremely unlikely that she would not be in the money and finish at least third. Such huge bets on one or more horses cause what is known as a *minus pool.* The minus means that if the horse or horses come in, then the track actually loses money.

Let us see how it would work in this case. With a 15% track take for expenses, taxes, and the like, there would be only

$$(0.85)(\$268{,}441) = \$228{,}175$$

to pay back to bettors who have wagered $257,150 to show on Princess Rooney. So even if nothing was bet on the other two horses finishing in the money with Princess Rooney, the payoff per $2 bet would be

$$\$2\left(\frac{\$228{,}175}{\$257{,}150}\right) = \$1.77.$$

Now you cannot pay someone $1.77 when they bet $2 and the horse wins. So instead, a minimum payment is made, which is usually $2.10. In Chapter Fifteen, where minus pools are discussed, we argue that when this is the case you should generally not bet on any horses. There are possible exceptions but they are rare. However, according to Kentucky State law the minimum payoff is $2.20, not $2.10. This changed the situation considerably, since the possible payoff was doubled from a 5% profit to one of 10%. In fact, as we show later, this was a good bet.

Let us now look at the evolution of the betting pools and the odds and observe what happened here so that we can determine whether or not there was a Dr. Z system bet to place or show on Princess Rooney or on some other horse.

With nineteen minutes to post time the show pool was as follows:

	Totals	#1	#2	#3	#4	#5	#6	#7	#8
Show	349,530	328,730	2,778	4,725	1,557	2,820	—	1,893	7,027

The minus pool on Princess Rooney was still very strong. The show betting on all the other horses was 2% or less of that bet on the favorite.

The tote board was as follows:

	Totals	#1 Princess Rooney
With eleven minutes to post time		
Odds		1—5
Win	145,041	99,919
Place	85,618	40,263
Show	450,401	408,145
With seven minutes to post time		
Odds		3—10
Win	212,365	138,700
Place	136,645	59,579
Show	574,561	501,401
With three minutes to post time		
Odds		3—10
Win	286,185	184,515
Place	211,798	104,052
Show	661,941	561,447
With one minute to post time		
Odds		3—10
Win	316,312	205,230
Place	233,221	112,657
Show	687,849	580,667

I hope by now that you have noticed that the best bet on Princess Rooney was to place, not show, and that it was good enough to qualify as a Dr. Z system bet. Only about half the place pool was bet on Princess Rooney, while about two-thirds was bet on Princess Rooney to win. At one minute to post time, the expected value of a place bet on Princess Rooney dipped to 1.10, which made it a Dr. Z system bet, although just barely.* Since our betting wealth was $1,500, the optimal bet to place was $665.

What about betting on Princess Rooney to show as well? The payoff would be $2.20 if she finished in the money, so in order to analyze the situation we needed the probability of her finishing in the money. The probability that Princess Rooney would win the race was about 0.692 and 0.224 that she would finish second.† Hence she would place in the race with a probability of 0.916. The probability that Princess Rooney would be third was 0.061. Thus the chance that she would show was 0.977. Hence the expected value per dollar bet to show on Princess Rooney was

$$\text{EX Show} = \underbrace{0.977(\$1.10)}_{\text{Win}} + \underbrace{0.023(0)}_{\text{Loss}} = \$1.075.$$

*An expected value of 1.10 is justified here because of the very high quality of horses, the size of the mutuel pool, and the strong favorite bias discussed in Chapter Four.

†With one minute to post time, Princess Rooney was a 3—10 shot. According to the discussion concerning the underbetting of extreme favorites in Chapter Three (see in particular Table 3.7), the expected value of a win bet on Princess Rooney would be at least 0.9. Thus her chance of winning was about $p = 0.692$, since $p(\$2.60) = 0.9(\$2)$. There were six other horses in the race, each with a chance of winning of about 0.051. From the Harville formulas, equations (5.2) and (5.3), the probability that Princess Rooney would come in second was about

$$\frac{nq_j q_1}{1 - q_j} = \frac{6(0.051)(0.692)}{1 - 0.051} = 0.224,$$

and third, about

$$\frac{n(n-1)q_j q_k q_1}{1 - q_j - q_k} = \frac{6(5)(0.051)^2(0.692)}{1 - 2(0.051)} = 0.061.$$

Thus the probability of placing was 0.692 + 0.224 = 0.916, and the probability of showing was 0.916 + 0.061 = 0.977.

The quarter-million-dollar bet thus looked quite good. About 98% of the time the big bettor would win $25,000. Two percent of the time he or she would lose the $250,000. So, on average, he or she would make a profit of 7.5%, or $18,750, with very little risk. Hence this was one case where it was a good idea to bet in a minus pool. The $2.20 minimum payoff made the expected return of 1.075 a handsome figure, considering the risk. With a $2.10 minimum payoff, the expected return would drop to about 1.025 and the return would not be high enough to justify the risk. In conclusion, the show bet was a good one and similar bets are to be encouraged as long as the conditions are ideal: fast track, proper weighting of horse, post position, recent races, and so forth. However, the place bet with an expected value of 1.10 was still the preferred bet.

Princess Rooney took the lead and won wire to wire. In the stretch several horses challenged her, but she was able to pull away from them to a comfortable win. Bright Crocus took second, and Bemissed was third. Rosy Spectre was never a factor. Our bet of $665 returned $798 for a profit of $133.

At post time the tote board was as follows:

	Totals	#1 Princess Rooney	#2 Bright Crocus	#7 Bemissed
Odds		1—5	13—1	24—1
Win	361,955	238,957	20,401	11,842
Place	258,807	130,649	17,640	10,780
Show	718,936	601,892	11,682	10,320

The chart of the race was as follows:

EIGHTH RACE
Churchill
MAY 6, 1983

1 ⅛ MILES. (1.48⅘) 109th Running KENTUCKY OAKS (Grade I). $150,000 added. Fillies. 3-year-olds. By subscription of $100 each; $750 to pass the entry box; $750 additional to start with $150,000 added of which $65% of all monies to the owner of the winner, 40% to second, 10% to third and 5% to fourth. Weight, 121 lbs. Starters to be named through the entry box Wednesday, May 4, by the usual time of closing. If the race is divided entries or couplings will be divided. A silver trophy to the winning owner. Closed with 187 nominations.
Value of race $179,950, value to winner $116,968, second $35,990, third $17,995, fourth $8,997. Mutuel pool $1,339,698, Minus show pool $82,377.16.

Last Raced	Horse	Eqt.A.Wt	PP	St	¼	½	¾	Str	Fin	Jockey	Odds $1
23Apr83 ^{7}Kee^1	Princess Rooney	3 121	1	2	1^{hd}	1^1	1^1	$1^{1\frac{1}{2}}$	$1^{1\frac{1}{4}}$	Vasquez J	.20
16Apr83 ^{10}Hia^5	Bright Crocus	3 121	2	5	7	7	$6^{\frac{1}{2}}$	4^5	2^2	Hawley S	13.90
23Apr83 ^{8}Pim^3	Bemissed	3 121	6	7	4^1	4^1	3^{hd}	$2^{\frac{1}{2}}$	$3^{\frac{1}{2}}$	Lovato F Jr	24.60
27Apr83 ^{5}Kee	Rosy Spectre	3 121	5	4	5^2	6^2	5^1	3^{hd}	$4^{6\frac{1}{2}}$	Delahoussaye E	16.50
23Apr83 ^{7}Kee^5	Fifth Question	3 121	3	6	6^{hd}	5^{hd}	7	5^3	$5^{5\frac{3}{4}}$	Day P	8.50
9Apr83 ^{9}OP^1	Brindy Brindy	3 121	7	1	2^1	$3^{3\frac{1}{2}}$	$4^{1\frac{1}{2}}$	6^{hd}	6^{nk}	Jones K	8.10
23Apr83 ^{7}Kee^2	Shamivor	3 121	4	3	3^4	$2^{\frac{1}{2}}$	2^3	7	7	Brumfield D	34.50

OFF AT 5:37. Start good. Won driving. Time, :23⅘, :47, 1:12, 1:37⅗, 1:50⅘ Track fast.

$2 Mutuel Prices:				
	1–PRINCESS ROONEY	2.40	2.40	2.20
	2–BRIGHT CROCUS		5.80	2.20
	7–BEMISSED			2.20

Gr. f, by Verbatim—Parrish Princess, by Drone. Trainer Gomez Frank. Bred by Roach B & T (Ky).

PRINCESS ROONEY, racing in uncharcteristic uneven fashion, broke alertly and smoothly came around BRINDY BRINDY to secure the lead completing the opening quarter-mile, but raced with head turned toward the inside while apparently trying to bear out after settling into the backstretch, and bobbled at the three-eights pole and again approaching the quarter-pole. The drived slightly into the stretch, responded to intermittent right hand urging, and held BRIGHT CROCUS clear while swerving slightly near the wire. BRIGHT CROCUS brushed several times with FIFTH QUESTION while being taken under restraint in the run to the clubhouse turn, was eased to the outside completing six furlongs, willingly raced to the leaders and appeared briefly threatening inside the last sixteenth, but was not gaining at the end. BEMISSED, rated forwardly, moved outside PRINCESS ROONEY for the stretch drive and responded gamely, although no match for the top two. ROSY SPECTRE had room along the rail to loom a threat in the drive and then hung. FIFTH QUESTION brushed with BRIGHT CROCUS early and was outrun. BRINDY BRINDY was lightly raced after she was displaced by PRINCESS ROONEY and tired after six furlongs. SHAMIVOR was used up racing outside the first flight. Equipment: No blinkers.

Owners— 1, Tucker Paula; 2, Levan-Waters-Weston; 3, Ryehill Farm; 4, Gentry T E; 5, Lowrance E; 6, Wanaja Fm & Energy B T; 7, White Fox Farm.

Scratched—Weekend Surprise (2May83 ^{8}CD^3).

As a check on our regression estimate of the expected value to place on Princess Rooney, we found that if Princess Rooney were to pay exactly \$2.40 then

$$\text{EX Place} = \$2.40(0.916)/\$2 = 1.10,$$

which agreed with our 1.10 estimate from equation (4.6) and our calculator. It was likely that Princess Rooney would pay \$2.40 to place if she finished first or second, although it was possible, depending on the pools, for the payoff to be \$2.20 or \$2.60. The estimates here are a little on the conservative side, since the expected value of a win bet might exceed 0.90. With a higher win probability, the placing and showing probabilities, and expected values, would be slightly higher. The analysis and conclusion remain the same.

The Matinee Handicap, Hollywood Park, Inglewood, California, April 24, 1982

The late races of each day's card often contain Dr. Z system bets. They generally feature better, more consistent horses running for larger purses. Even more importantly, by then most of the crowd have lost a lot of money and want to find some bets that will allow them to recoup their loses. Betting to place or show, especially on low-priced horses, does not interest them much. Indeed, they are more interested in wagering on longer-priced win bets and in the exotic pools. Thus from the seventh race on, there is a good chance of locating one or more outstanding Dr. Z system bets.

The ninth, and final, race at Hollywood Park on April 24, 1982, provided an outstanding Dr. Z system bet. The $1\frac{1}{16}$-mile race on the turf was the \$40,000 added second division of the Matinee Handicap. Whenever the number of entries exceeds about twelve, many handicaps are run in two divisions. The two divisions can be thought of simply as different races. They are usually run on different days.

The favorite in the race was Tacora, a Chilean horse, who was to be ridden by the great jockey Chris McCarron. Tacora had a strong and consistent record and deserved his favorite position. Other strong horses in the race were Sweet Maid, Granja Deseo, and Viendra.

Experts' Selections Daily Racing Form

Consensus Points: 5 for 1st (today's best 7), 2 for 2nd, 1 for 3rd. Today's Best in Bold Type.

Trackman, Warren Williams **HOLLYWOOD PARK** Selections Made for Fast Track

	TRACKMAN	HANDICAP	ANALYST	HERMIS	SWEEP	CONSENSUS	
9	TACORA	COAX ME HOME	VIENDRA	TACORA	GRANJA DESEO	TACORA	14
	SWIFT BIRD	TACORA	CHATEAU DANCER	CHATEAU DANCER	SWEET MAID	GRANJA DESEO	6
	GRANJA DESEO	CHATEAU DANCER	TACORA	VIENDRA	TACORA	VIENDRA	6

ANALYST'S *Hollywood Comment*

NINTH RACE
1—Viendra
2—Chateau Dancer
3—Tacora

VIENDRA was fourth to Star Pastures in a Group III event in England and was a forward contender in other highly regarded events in Britain. She connected in her third start in the U.S. over a fine field. Lipham handles her nicely and looks well placed to continue her winning ways. CHATEAU DANCER seems to be improving with each race and Russell appears to have her razor sharp right now. Guerra takes over the controls. TACORA has won three of seven turf starts and was second to Manzanera Feb. 26. McCarron got acquainted with her last start. COAX ME HOME seems to enjoy the turf and usually gives a good account of herself. With Pat V. aboard she may be sent to the lead along with I FELL IN LOVE.

9th Hollywood

1 $\frac{1}{16}$ MILES. (TURF). (1.39⅗) 4th Running of THE MATINEE HANDICAP (2nd Division). $40,000 added. Fillies and mares. 3-year-olds and upward, which have not won $24,000* other than claiming or starter since December 25, 1981. By subscription of $50 each, which shall accompany the nomination, $500 additional to start, with $40,000 added, of which $8,000 to second, $6,000 to third, $3,000 to fourth and $1,000 to fifth. Weights, Monday, April 19. Starters to be named through the entry box by closing time of entries. A trophy will be presented to the owner of the winner. *A race worth $24,000 to the winner. Closed Wednesday, April 14, 1982 with 36 nominations.

Swift Bird — B. m. 5, by Northern Dancer—Flood Light, by Bold Lad
Own.—Nakamura K — **114** — Br.—Belair Farm Ltd (Ky) — Tr.—Doyle A T

Lifetime	39	6	4	10	$191,450
1982	6	0	0	2	$15,250
1981	16	3	2	3	$110,500
Turf	10	2	0	3	$46,825

17Apr82-7SA	1	:45^{1} 1:09^{4} 1:35 ft	3½	115	$2^{\frac{1}{2}}$	3^{1}	$4^{5\frac{1}{2}}$	6^{7}	DlhossyE^{7}	(F)B Thghtfl	87	Contrefaire, Aduana, Track Jester	11
10Apr82-8SA	1$\frac{1}{16}$	:45^{4} 1:09^{4} 1:42 ft	18	115	$5^{4\frac{1}{2}}$	$5^{4\frac{1}{2}}$	5^{2}	$5^{\frac{1}{2}}$	CastnedM^{1}	(F)St Lca H	90	Si, Coax Me Home, Sweet Maid	8
17Mar82-9SA	1$\frac{1}{16}$	:47^{1} 1:12^{2} 1:47 sy	5	114	4^{3}	$3^{1\frac{1}{2}}$	$3^{\frac{1}{2}}$	$3^{3\frac{1}{2}}$	ShmrW^{2}	(F)La Merced	62	Miss Huntington, Si, Swift Bird	7
19Feb82-8SA	a6½f (T)	:21^{2} :43^{4} 1:14^{2} fm	9	114	$6^{2\frac{3}{4}}$	$5^{4\frac{1}{2}}$	$6^{3\frac{3}{4}}$	$5^{3\frac{1}{4}}$	VlenzulPA^{2}	(F)Aw35000	84	ExcitableLady,PlentyO'Toole,Sison	6
24Jan82-9SA	1$\frac{1}{16}$	:47^{1} 1:11 1:42^{2} ft	17	114	$2^{\frac{1}{2}}$	2^{hd}	1^{1}	3^{1}	GuerraWA^{3}	(F)Aw40000	88	Balletomane, Tangaroa, Swift Bird	7
14Jan82-8SA	6½f	:21^{3} :44^{1} 1:15^{2} ft	28	116	$6^{5\frac{1}{2}}$	$7^{7\frac{1}{2}}$	9^{11}	8^{7}	ShoemkrW^{9}	(F)Aw40000	86	Mtching,PstForgtting,StopDncing	10
25Nov81-8Hol	1$\frac{1}{16}$	:45^{3} 1:09^{3} 1:41^{3} ft	6	117	2^{6}	$4^{4\frac{1}{2}}$	$6^{9\frac{1}{2}}$	6^{11}	PincyLJr^{3}	(F)Prncsnsn	76	BScout,ImptintLss,MissHuntington	8
4Nov81-8SA	1$\frac{1}{16}$	:45^{4} 1:09^{4} 1:41^{1} ft	4	117	3^{2}	$3^{2\frac{1}{2}}$	3^{3}	6^{6}	PincayLJr^{1}	(F)Manta H	89	HppyGuess,MissHuntington,BScout	7
30Sep81-8SA	a6½f (T)	:21^{3} :44 1:13^{4} fm	13	113	$7^{5\frac{3}{4}}$	6^{9}	7^{12}	$5^{9\frac{1}{4}}$	DlhssE^{6}	(F)Atmn Dys H	81	Kilijro,Ack'sSecret,MissHuntington	9
30Sep81—Run in two divisions, 8th & 9th races.													
8Aug81-8Dmr	1 (T)	:47^{2} 1:11^{1} 1:35^{2} fm	13	115	3^{1}	3^{1}	$6^{4\frac{1}{4}}$	$7^{5\frac{3}{4}}$	ShmrW^{2}	(F)Palomar H	91	Kilijaro, Lisawan, Satin Ribera	9

Apr 4 SA 1 ft 1:41^{2} h — Mar 29 SA tr.t 6f gd 1:16^{1} h — Mar 24 SA 6f ft 1:12^{2} h — Mar 13 SA 6f sl 1:16^{2} h

Sweet Maid — B. m. 5, by Proud Clarion—Honor Maid, by Prince John
Own.—Elmendorf — **114** — Br.—Elmendorf Farm (Ky) — Tr.—McAnally Ronald

Lifetime	31	6	6	3	$154,191
1982	1	0	0	1	$9,750
1981	11	2	2	1	$72,026
Turf	8	0	1	1	$10,000

10Apr82-8SA	1$\frac{1}{16}$	:45^{4} 1:09^{4} 1:42 ft	34	114	$6^{7\frac{1}{2}}$	$8^{6\frac{1}{2}}$	7^{3}	3^{nk}	AsssnCB^{5}	(F)St Lca H	91	Si, Coax Me Home, Sweet Maid	8
10Oct81-6Bel	1	:47 1:10^{4} 1:36 ft	27	115	$7^{7\frac{1}{2}}$	$7^{7\frac{1}{2}}$	5^{6}	$5^{8\frac{1}{4}}$	SantiagoA^{2}	(F)Aw35000	80	ExprssivDnc,DmMystrius,TinTnToo	7
20Sep81-1Bel	1$\frac{1}{16}$	:48 1:13^{1} 1:45^{4} gd	6½	119	$4^{3\frac{1}{2}}$	4^{4}	3^{9}	3^{13}	Venezia M^{2}	(F)HcpO	60	WaywardLass,Nora'sLss,SweetMid	4
16Aug81-8Sar	1⅛ (T)	:47^{4} 1:12^{4} 1:50^{3} yl	51	111	7^{16}	$7^{7\frac{1}{4}}$	5^{7}	5^{13}	Venezia M^{7}	(F)Diana H	61	DeLaRose,RokebyRose,Euphrosyne	8
29Jly81-6Sar	7f	:23^{1} :46^{3} 1:24^{2} sy	4½	119	$6^{9\frac{1}{4}}$	6^{9}	3^{6}	$2^{7\frac{1}{4}}$	Venezia M^{5}	(F)Aw35000	73	Love You Dear,SweetMaid,Avenare	6
3Jly81-7Bel	1$\frac{1}{16}$ (T)	:47^{2} 1:11^{1} 1:43^{3} yl	8¼	117	$6^{7\frac{1}{2}}$	$6^{8\frac{3}{4}}$	$5^{6\frac{1}{2}}$	$4^{7\frac{3}{4}}$	Venezia M^{3}	(F)Aw35000	70	StephniLigh,MovItNow,Mrs.Robrts	7
22Jun81-8Bel	1	:46^{1} 1:11^{1} 1:35^{4} ft	23	118	6^{9}	6^{5}	4^{6}	5^{6}	VnzM^{6}	(F)Tw'lght Tear	83	Jameela,ChainBracelet,IslandChrm	6
22Mar81-7Aqu	1⅛	:48^{4} 1:13^{3} 1:53^{2} ft	2	120	$6^{6\frac{1}{2}}$	$6^{4\frac{1}{2}}$	2^{1}	1^{nk}	Venezia M^{3}	(F)HcpO	68	SweetMaid,Skagerrak,Nalee'sFntsy	6
11Mar81-8Aqu	170 [•]	:49^{1} 1:14^{3} 1:46^{1} sy	*6-5	122	$5^{4\frac{1}{2}}$	$5^{2\frac{3}{4}}$	$6^{7\frac{1}{2}}$	6^{11}	Venezia M^{6}	(F)HcpO	60	Cinto Tora, General J., Ms. Balding	6
8Feb81-8Aqu	1⅛ [•]	:47 1:11^{4} 1:51^{3} sy	6¼	113	7^{15}	7^{10}	4^{8}	4^{11}	VnzM^{5}	(F)Rare Treat H	77	Pinkton,EnglishTrifle,I'llBeAround	9

Apr 20 SA 4f ft :50^{4} h — Apr 4 SA 1 ft 1:43^{4} h — ●Mar 29 SA 6f gd 1:13^{2} h — ●Mar 24 SA 1 ft 1:38 h

Coax Me Home *

Ch. m. 5, by Windy Sands—Carry Me Home, by Coursing

Br.—Old English Rancho (Cal) 1982 5 1 1 1 $27,240

Own.—Johnston-Johnston Est et al 115 Tr.—Warren Donald 1981 9 4 1 2 $75,750

Lifetime 19 6 4 3 $116,590 Turf 5 2 0 1 $28,540

10Apr82-8SA 1 1/16 :454 1:094 1:42 ft 16 115 33 33 31 2nk Sibille R3 ⒻSt Lca H 91 Si, Coax Me Home, Sweet Maid 8

25Mar82-8SA 1⅛Ⓣ:4741:1211:481fm 2½ 114 11 1½ 11½ 5nk Hawley S5 ⒻAw40000 86 BScout,MssHuntngton,PlntyO'Tool 6

26Feb82-8SA 1⅛Ⓣ:4531:10 1:473fm 6½ 117 22 2hd 2½ 43¾ Pincay LJr5 ⒻAw40000 85 Manzanera,Tacor,MissHuntington 10

14Feb82-10TuP 1 1/16Ⓣ:4821:1341:461fm 3½ 123 31½ 1hd 1hd 32 PowllJP6 ⒻSns Grl H 86 Bttlewind,ElevenPlicns,CoxMHom 11

3Jan82-10TuP 1 Ⓣ:48 1:1411:41 fm *1 122 32 31½ 3½ 1½ PowllJP7 Chrs Evrt H 86 CoaxMeHome,DeRuci,SunsetStrip 11

3Jan82—Run in two divisions, 8th & 10th races.

25Sep81-11Pom 1 1/16 :473 1:12 1:442ft *1-2e 117 55 45½ 46½ 35 MenaF8 ⒻLs Mdrns H 85 ConkyJohnston,LRegl,CoxMeHome 9

3Sep81-9Dmr 1 1/16 :453 1:103 1:44 ft *4-5 117 22½ 21½ 2hd 2nk PincyLJr3 ⒻJun Drlng 80 Bishop Again, CoaxMeHome,Nuera 5

3Sep81—Run in two division, 8th & 9th races.

7Aug81-7Dmr 7½fⓉ:224 :46 1:292fm 10 117 1½ 2hd 1½ 1nk Pincay LJr5 ⒻAw26000 94 CoaxMeHome,MiQuimer,BerryBush 9

11Apr81-8SA 1 1/16 :452 1:10 1:414ft 18 116 42 43 45 410 VlnzulPA1 ⒻSt Lca H 82 Finance Charge, Si, Swift Bird 10

26Mar81-9SA 1 1/16 :461 1:112 1:43 ft 14 119 27 21 1½ 1nk Hawley S9 ⒻAw32000 86 CoaxMeHome,Flordelisada,Tangaro 9

Apr 19 SA Ⓣ 5f fm 1:023 h (d) Apr 4 SA 5f ft :592 h Mar 21 SA 5f ft 1:002 h Mar 13 SA 5f sl 1:041 h

Granja Deseo

B. m. 5, by Astray—Marimacho, by Lake Erie

Br.—Granja Vista del Rio (Cal) 1982 7 1 0 1 $33,875

Own.—Granja Vista del Rio Stable 116 Tr.—Palma Hector O 1981 19 2 5 4 $76,150

Lifetime 38 4 7 6 $126,450 Turf 19 3 3 3 $93,075

3Apr82-8SA 1¼ :461 1:353 2:003ft 16 115 710 711 713 612 Pierce D7 ⒻSta Brb H 74 Ack'sSecret,Lndresse,PlentyO'Tool 8

25Mar82-8SA 1⅛Ⓣ:4741:1211:481fm 6½ 119 68½ 65½ 32½ 4hd ShoemkrW4 ⒻAw40000 86 BScout,MssHuntngton,PlntyO'Tool 6

13Mar82-8SA 1½Ⓣ:4842:0222:272gd 12 112 713 713 715 411 ShomkrW7 Sn Mrno H 67 LemhiGold,Exploded,ChnceyBidder 8

13Mar82—Run in two divisions, 8th & 9th races.

26Feb82-8SA 1⅛Ⓣ:4531:10 1:473fm 11 121 921 916 98½ 76 Sibille R2 ⒻAw40000 83 Manzanera,Tacor,MissHuntington 10

18Feb82-8SA 1⅛Ⓣ:4641:1121:483fm 16 115 712 75 43½ 33½ Sibille R2 ⒻAw40000 80 BerryBush,SatinRibera,GranjDeseo 7

5Feb82-8SA 1⅛Ⓣ:4531:0941:47 fm 14 115 718 714 54¼ 53¼ Sibille R7 ⒻAw45000 89 Daeltown, Lisawan, Berry Bush 7

15Jan82-8SA 1⅛Ⓣ:4821:1231:494fm 5 115 87½ 84¼ 2½ 1½ Sibille R1 ⒻAw35000 78 Granja Deseo, Balletomane,Gracias 8

4Dec81-8Hol 1 1/16Ⓣ:4721:1121:42 fm 7¾ 118 912 97½ 54¾ 31 Sibille R2 ⒻAw27000 88 Saharet, Tap DancerII,GranjaDeseo 9

5Nov81-8SA 1⅛Ⓣ:4611:1021:48 fm 5½ 1155 514 612 47½ 42½ WnlndWM1 ⒻAw34000 84 Battlewind, Syria, Forseek 9

28Oct81-7SA 1⅛Ⓣ:4721:1241:503fm 2½ 1135 65½ 64½ 31½ 1hd WnlndWM2 ⒻAw28000 74 Granja Deseo, Colacka, Grasiosa 6

Apr 21 SA 4f ft :472 h Apr 15 SA 5f ft 1:001 h Mar 21 SA 5f ft 1:014 h Mar 6 SA 6f ft 1:131 h

I Fell in Love

B. f. 4, by Somethingfabulous—Selection, by T V Lark

Br.—Ring Connie M (Cal) 1982 3 1 0 0 $20,750

Own.—Ring Mrs Connie M 114 Tr.—Clapp Roger E 1981 11 3 1 2 $52,725

Lifetime 17 5 1 2 $82,075 Turf 6 2 0 0 $28,600

1Apr82-8SA 1 :47 1:112 1:364sy 3¾ 1095 11½ 13 15 16½ Steiner J J3 ⒻAw35000 85 I Fell in Love, Viga,WesternStarlet 6

3Mar82-8SA 6½f :213 :44 1:142ft 28 114 54 59½ 57½ 610 SteinrJJ3 ⒻLs Cngs H 88 ExctblLdy,‡QnfCrnll,Pppy'sLckyGrl 7

3Mar82—Placed fifth through disqualification

13Jan82-5SA a6½f Ⓣ:213 :4431:154fm *2¼ 114 85 56 35 107¼ AsmssnCB4 ⒻAw32000 73 Chuck O Luck, Que Appeal, Larla 11

29Dec81-7SA 1 1/16 :463 1:104 1:421ft 6½ 1095 31½ 32½ 33 33½ Steiner J J4 ⒻAw35000 87 ImptintLss,MssHuntngton,IFllnLov 6

25Nov81-4Hol 1 :453 1:103 1:362ft *1 117 22½ 2½ 21½ 23½ Pincay LJr3 ⒻAw26000 80 TrckJester,IFellinLove,Spokswomn 5

18Oct81-7SA 6½f :221 :451 1:153ft 7¼ 117 54 66 46 32½ Pincay LJr6 ⒻAw32000 89 Rosy Cloud, La Pistola, IFellinLove 7

30Sep81-9SA a6½f Ⓣ:213 :4331:141fm 16 117 1012 1011 99 77¼ PcLJr2 ⒻAtmn Dys H 81 Save WildLife,Disconiz,IGotSpeed 11

30Sep81—Run in two divisions, 8th & 9th races.

29Aug81-8Dmr 1 1/16 :46 1:102 1:421ft 9 116 49½ 45 36 58¾ Hawley S4 ⒻTory Pns 80 NorthernFble,GlittrHittr,Rj'sDlight 6

9Aug81-5Dmr 1 Ⓣ:4631:1111:363fm 9 112 11½ 11½ 12 1nk McCrrCJ10 ⒻAw24000 91 I Fell in Love,Nuera,Movin'Money 10

29Jly81-7Dmr 1 1/16Ⓣ:4641:12 1:444fm 40 1075 12 12 45½ 1114 WnlndWM9 ⒻAw24000 71 Reinstate, Rihuana, Jctssean 12

●Apr 21 SA 3f ft :33 h Apr 11 SA 5f ft 1:003 h Mar 28 SA 1 ft 1:402 h Mar 22 SA 3f ft :343 h

Viendra

Ch. f. 4, by Raise a Native—Friendly Relations, by Nearctic

Br.—Harcourt H (Fla) 1982 2 1 0 0 $13,750

Own.—Sangster R E 113 Tr.—Gosden John H M 1981 8 1 2 0 $25,247

Lifetime 10 2 2 0 $38,997 Turf 10 2 2 0 $38,997

15Apr82-5SA 1⅛Ⓣ:48 1:1241:491fm 11 114 65½ 31 1½ 1¾ Lipham T3 ⒻAw25000 81 Viendra, Sangue, Coral Dance 11

4Mar82-5SA 1¼Ⓣ:4711:37 2:011fm 8¼ 113 78¾ 34 38½ 612 Lipham T10 Aw21000 69 Rostropovich, Garibi, Latrone 10

17Oct81-9WO 1¼[T]:4921:4112:052fm 25 118 53¼ 84¾ 88¾ 67½ SwtukB6 ⒻE P Taylor 72 De La Rose, Sangue, Sajama 9

31Aug81◆4Newcastle(Eng) 1¼ 2:09 fm 2¼ 119 Ⓣ 23 Hide E ⒻVirginia Vielle, Viendra, Docklands 4

18Aug81◆4York(Eng) 1½ 2:351gd 11 126 Ⓣ 9 CthnS ⒻYorkshire Oaks(Gr1) Condessa, Leap Lively, Fiesta Fun 11

1Aug81◆2Goodwood(Eng) 1¼ 2:093gd 7 117 Ⓣ 42¾ CuthenS ⒻNassau(Gr2) Go Leasing, Vielle, Strigida 11

8Jly81◆3Newmarket(Eng) 1 1:403gd 20 115 Ⓣ 43¾ CauthenS ⒻChild(Gr3) Star Pastures, Tolmi, Seasurf 10

24May81◆4Longchamp(Fra) a1¼ 2:15 gd 10 128 Ⓣ 715 CuthnS ⒻPrix St Alary(Gr1) Tootens, Tropicaro, Last Love 10

15May81◆3Newbury(Eng) 1¼ 2:11 gd 4 119 Ⓣ 2hd CuthenS ⒻSr Chas Clre Strigida, Viendra, Leah 8

6May81◆1Chester(Eng) a7½f 1:374sf 3½ 123 Ⓣ 12½ CuthnS ⒻSefton(Mdn) Viendr,WhtHeven,CoptHllPrincess 10

Apr 10 SA Ⓣ 1 fm 1:414 h (d) Apr 5 SA Ⓣ 5f gd 1:021 h (d) Mar 31 SA 4f ft :51 h Mar 25 SA Ⓣ 7f fm 1:29 h

Chateau Dancer — Ch. f. 4, by Giacometti—Delray Dancer, by Chateaugay
Br.—Smth-Stvns-Mhlstn-Mfrd (Ky) 1982 2 0 1 1 $14,200
Own.—Pegasus Stud & St George 115 Tr.—Russell John W 1981 6 0 0 3 $15,328
Lifetime 14 2 3 5 $55,775 Turf 13 2 3 5 $55,250
27Mar82-8SA a6½f Ⓣ:213 :4411:143fm 12 117 3½ 32½ 2½ 31 PncLJr2 ⒻMonrovia H 85 CatGirl,ExcitableLady,ChteuDncer 10
28Feb82-7SA a6½f Ⓣ:214 :4431:142fm 2¾ 117 73¾ 32½ 2hd 21½ Pincay LJr3 ⒻAw26000 85 Vocalist,ChateauDancer,BrightLdy 10
9Dec81-8Hol 1 1/16 Ⓣ:4831:1231:424fm 11 112 2hd 2hd 2½ 32¼ ShmkrW7 ⒻMorgaise 83 Saison, Kell MyPet,ChateauDancer 9
4Dec81-8Hol 1 1/16 Ⓣ:4721:1121:42 fm *2½ 113 54½ 53¾ 65¼ 65½ ShoemkrW9 ⒻAw27000 83 Saharet, Tap DancerII,GranjaDeseo 9
20Nov81-8Hol 1 Ⓣ:48 1:12 1:36 fm 4¾ 114 76½ 95¾ 53¾ 31 CastnedM6 ⒻAw28000 88 Syria,VelvetChieftain,ChteuDncer 10
7Sep81-5Dmr 6f :214 :443 1:093ft 5¾ 115 44½ 45 58 59 McHrgDG3 ⒻAw21000 81 La Pistola, Matching, Track Jester 5
21Aug81-8Dmr 7½f Ⓣ:223 :4541:294fm *3 109 66¼ 11 2hd 32¾ ShoemkrW4 ⒻAw24000 89 ElevenPelicans,Rihun,ChteuDncer 10
10Apr81♦4Newbury(Eng) a7¼f 1:324sf 3½ 126 Ⓣ 47½ PiggottL ⒻFred Darling Marwell, Star Pastures, FastFriend 9
13Sep80♦5Doncaster(Eng) 1 1:422gd 4½ 124 Ⓣ 35½ Eddery P ⒻMay Hills ExclusivlyRisd,SilknKnot,ChtuDncr 8
12Jly80♦2York(Eng) 6f 1:15 gd *6-5 129 Ⓣ 13 PggttL ⒻJohn Courage ChtuDncr,MrstonMgn,DiscoDncing 7
Apr 20 SA 6f ft 1:14 h Apr 14 SA 5f ft 1:012 h Apr 6 SA 5f ft 1:00 h ●Mar 9 SA 5f ft :582 h

***Tacora** — B. m. 5, by Mr Long—Temuquita, by Nipigon
Br.—Alamos P B (Chile) 1982 3 1 1 0 $32,000
Own.—Maggio C J 116 Tr.—Rossi Lee J 1981 7 0 3 0 $23,200
Lifetime 13 4 4 0 $70,432 Turf 7 3 1 0 $25,632
20Mar82-8SA 1⅛ :454 1:094 1:471ft 11 114 64 64 45½ 47¾ McCrrCJ3 ⒻSta AnaH 85 TrackRobbery,Mnzner,Ack'sSecret 8
26Feb82-8SA 1⅛ Ⓣ:4531:10 1:473fm 14 118 45½ 41¼ 31 21¾ GuerraWA8 ⒻAw40000 87 Manzanera,Tacor,MissHuntington 10
5Feb82-4SA 1 1/16 :452 1:103 1:431ft 9-5 115 59½ 42 21 11½ McHrgDG2 ⒻAw30000 85 Tacora, Astrious, Katsura 6
21Oct81-9SA 1 :45 1:091 1:36 ft *1 115 47 23 22½ 2¾ CastnedM6 ⒻAw34000 88 Impatient Lass, Tacora, Forseek 9
1Oct81-8SA 1 1/16 :472 1:112 1:423ft 3¼ 117 53½ 54½ 33 2½ Pincay LJr4 ⒻAw40000 87 Tangaroa, Tacora, Happy Guess 6
13Sep81-11Dmf 1 1/16 :462 1:11 1:43 ft 33 112 53½ 41½ 11½ 11¾† OrtgLE4 ⒻEncinitas H 85 ‡Tacora, Satin Ribera, Battlewind 7
†13Sep81—Disqualified and placed second
17Jun81-9Hol 1 1/16 Ⓣ:4641:1121:414fm 3¾ 117 1019 1016 98¾ 86¾ Pincay LJr2 ⒻAw30000 83 RomnProspct,BshpAgn,Glc'sFntsy 10
25May81-8GG 1⅜ Ⓣ:4931:3842:154fm 16 110 77½ 65½ 710 88¾ LinnceC7 ⒻYba Bna H 80 MrzyDots,PrncssKrnd,PrncssToby 10
29Apr81-9Hol 1 1/16 Ⓣ:4641:1121:42 fm 7 115 811 87½ 53¾ 43 McHrgDG3 ⒻAw32000 86 Soft Reply, Spiffy Laree, Jetssean 9
26Mar81-9SA 1 1/16 :461 1:112 1:43 ft 12 115 — — — — DlhoussyE7 ⒻAw32000 — CoaxMeHome,Flordelisada,Tangaro 9
26Mar81—Lost rider
Apr 18 SA 1 ft 1:392 h. Apr 13 SA 4f ft :483 h Apr 5 SA 1 ft 1:413 h Mar 13 SA 5f sl 1:044 h

Throughout the betting period, Viendra was an outstanding Dr. Z system bet. At 5—1 he was going off at odds less than his morning line, which as we argued in Chapter Three is a good sign. Viendra's rider, Terry Lipham, was not one of Hollywood's top jockey's. However, he had guided Viendra to a victory on the turf in his last start, recently run at neighboring Santa Anita. Viendra was tied for the second pick in the *Daily Racing Form's* consensus and was the Analyst's top choice. The day was a typical clear southern California day and the track was fast. In short, there was nothing to rule him out as a possible Dr. Z system bet if the odds were good.

At the end of the betting period the tote board was as follows:

	Totals	#6 Viendra
Odds		5—1
Win	129,233	16,353
Show	27,488	1,149

About one-eighth of the money in the win pool was bet on Viendra, (16,353/129,233 = 1/7.9), but only about one twenty-fourth of the show pool was bet on Viendra, (1,149/27,488 = 1/23.9). Thus three times less money, relatively, was bet on Viendra to show than to win. Viendra looked like an outstanding Dr. Z system bet. But how good was the bet?

Since the track take in California is 15%, the expected value per dollar bet to show on Viendra using equation (4.6) is

$$\text{EX Show Viendra} = 0.543 + 0.369\left(\frac{16{,}353/129{,}233}{1{,}149/27{,}488}\right) + \left[3.60 - (2.13)\left(\frac{16{,}353}{129{,}233}\right)\right](0.85 - 0.829)$$

$$= 1.66 + 0.07$$

$$= 1.73.$$

The expected value of 1.73 meant that, on average, we should expect to make a profit of 73% by betting on Viendra to show. The optimal bet was \$52.* Alternatively, with an expected-value cutoff of 1.14 at Hollywood Park, Figure 5.9 indicated that a bet should be made. From Figure 5.21 a bet of about \$15 was suggested. Again, because the expected value was so much higher than 1.18 the bet was quite conservative.

*The expected value of 1.73 was so high that there were problems using equation (5.5) to indicate the optimal bet. This was because equation (5.5) is the result of a statistical regression using data that had a maximum expected return to place or show of 1.40 plus the adjustment for track takes that differ from 17.1%. This was a reasonable methodology, since occurrences of expected returns greater than 1.40 are rare. What should be done when one of those outstanding occurrences, like Viendra, occurs? The approach we suggest is to pretend that the expected return is not really 1.73, but rather to determine the optimal bet with equation (5.5) on the premise that the expected return is 1.40. This is done by pretending that the public's show bet on Viendra is not really \$1,149, but a larger value that will yield an expected return of 1.40. From equation (4.4) we can calculate this larger value, for adjusted S_i, as $\tilde{S}_i = q_i S/2.32 = (0.1265)(27{,}488)/2.32 = \$1{,}498$ for Viendra. Using $q_i = 0.1265$, $S = 27{,}488$, and $\tilde{S}_i = 1{,}498$ in equation (5.5) yields the suggested bet of \$52. This approach indicates a lower bet than is optimal, but usually it is close. The use of equations (5.4) and (5.5) in such situations is discussed further in Chapter Sixteen. For Viendra, $q_i = 16{,}353/129{,}233 = 0.1265$, $S = 27{,}488$, and the adjusted $\tilde{S}_i = 1{,}498$. From equation (4.6), EX Show Viendra = 1.40 + 0.07 = 1.47, and from equation (5.5),

$$\text{Show bet Viendra} = \left[131 + 2{,}150(0.1265)^2 - 1{,}780(0.1265)^3 - \left(\frac{150}{(0.1265)(27{,}488)/1{,}498 - 0.70}\right)\right]\left(\frac{27{,}488 - 6{,}000}{94{,}000}\right)$$
$$+ \left[86 + 1{,}516(0.1265)^2 - 968(0.1265)^3 - \left(\frac{90.7}{(0.1265)(27{,}488)/1{,}498 - 0.85}\right)\right]\left(\frac{100{,}000 - 27{,}488}{94{,}000}\right) = \$52.$$

Viendra ran a strong race but was beaten by the favorite, Tacora. I Fell in Love took third. Because the Dr. Z system bet was so good, Viendra at 5—1 paid $8.80 to place and a whopping $9.40 to show. What a bet! My $52 bet to show returned $244.40, for a profit of $192.40. The chart of the race was as follows:

NINTH RACE
Hollywood
APRIL 24, 1982

1 1/16 MILES. (TURF) (1.39 4/5) 4th Running of THE MATINEE HANDICAP (2nd Division). $40,000 added. Fillies and mares. 3-year-olds and upward, which have not won $24,000* other than claiming or starter since December 25, 1981. By subscription of $50 each, which shall accompany the nomination, $500 additional to start, with $40,000 added, of which $8,000 to second, $6,000 to third, $3,000 to fourth and $1,000 to fifth. Weights, Monday, April 19.
Starters to be named through the entry box by closing time of entries. A trophy will be presented to the owner of the winner. *A race worth $24,000 to the winner. Closed Wednesday, April 14, 1982 with 36 nominations.

Value of race $44,900, value to winner $26,900, second $8,000, third $6,000, fourth $3,000, fifth $1,000. Mutuel pool $206,780. Exacta Pool $428,516.

Last Raced			Horse	Eqt.	A.	Wt.	PP	St	1/4	1/2	3/4	Str	Fin	Jockey	Odds $1
20Mar82	8SA	4	Tacora	b	5	116	8	5	3 ½	3hd	5-1	4-2½	1 ¾	McCarron C J	2.40
15Apr82	5SA	1	Viendra		4	113	6	7	6 ½	7-3	6-1	3hd	2hd	Lipham T	5.70
1Apr82	8SA	1	I Fell in Love	b	4	114	5	3	1-1	1 ½	1hd	1-1	3-2½	Steiner J J	10.60
3Apr82	8SA	6	Granja Deseo		5	116	4	8	8	8	8	6-2	4hd	Shoemaker W	4.70
10Apr82	8SA	2	Coax Me Home		5	115	3	1	2hd	4 ½	3hd	2 ½	5-1½	Valenzuela P A	4.50
10Apr82	8SA	3	Sweet Maid		5	114	2	4	5hd	6hd	7-2	7 ½	6 ½	Asmussen C B	8.30
17Apr82	7SA	6	Swift Bird	b	5	115	1	2	4 ½	2-1½	2-1	5 ½	7-4	McHargue D G	12.80
27Mar82	8SA	3	Chateau Dancer		4	115	7	6	7-3	5-1½	4 ½	8	8	Guerra W A	7.50

OFF AT 6:07. Start good. Won driving. Time, :23 1/5, :47 3/5, 1:11 3/5, 1:35 2/5, 1:41 2/5 Course firm.

$ 2 Mutuel Prices:				
8-	TACORA	6.80	3.80	3.00
6-	VIENDRA		8.80	9.40
5-	I FELL IN LOVE			7.80

$5 EXACTA 8-6 PAID $169.00.

B. m, by Mr Long-Temuquita, by Nipigon. Trainer Rossi Lee J. Bred by Alamos P B (Chile).

TACORA, in contention from the outset, responded for the final drive, found room between horses in the upper stretch and outfinished VIENDRA. The latter, unhurried for six furlongs, went outside to rally entering the stretch and finished strongly. I FELL IN LOVE, used up making the early pace, weakened in the final furlong. GRANJA DESEO, devoid of early speed, rallied wide and did not threaten. COAX ME HOME lodged a bid near the rail entering the stretch but weakened in the final furlong. SWIFT BIRD forced the early pace outside of I FELL IN LOVE and tired in the stretch. CHATEAU DANCER, in good position between horses for six furlongs, tired in the stretch.

Owners- 1, Maggio C J; 2, Sangster R E; 3, Ring Mrs Connie M; 4, Granja Vista del Rio Stable; 5, Johnston-Johnston Est et al; 6, Elmendorf; 7, Nakamura K; 8, Pegasus Stud & St George.

Trainers- 1, Rossi Lee J; 2, Gosden John H M; 3, Clapp Roger E; 4, Palma Hector O; 5, Warren Donald; 6, McAnally Ronald; 7, Doyle A T; 8, Russell John W.

Overweight: Swift Bird 1 pound .

Scratched- Vocalist(23Apr82 8GG 1).

Attendance 30,386. Total Mutuel Pool $4,784,784.

The Longacres Derby, Longacres, Renton, Washington, August 14, 1983

Longacres is one of America's top tracks, serving the metropolitan Seattle area. A top race brings out a huge crowd. One of the major races of the year was the forty-sixth running of the Longacres Derby. It was a $100,000 added race over $1\frac{3}{16}$ miles for three-year-olds. The $73,000 winner's share of the purse drew a number of strong horses, including Junction Road, Mythically, Lifaregal, and Dynamic Doc. The overwhelming favorite, however, was Prairie Breaker. With eight wins, a second, and a third in eleven starts against tough competition in 1983, Prairie Breaker certainly was the horse to beat.

The crowd established Prairie Breaker as a 4—5 favorite. In the best stakes races, top horses going off at less than even money are often Dr. Z system bets. An especially appealing situation, often leading to outstanding payoffs, arises when there are no other top choices and the betting is spread

WIN	PLACE	SHOW

NINTH

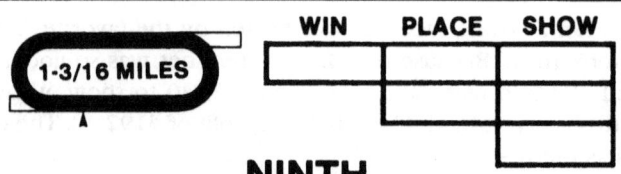

LONGACRES DERBY (46th Running)

PURSE $100,000 ADDED. FOR THREE-YEAR-OLDS. By subscription of $150, which shall accompany the nomination, $500 to pass the entry box, $1,000 additional to start with $100,000 added, of which $20,000 to second, $15,000 to third and $10,000 to fourth and $3,000 to fifth. All nominations, entry and starting fees to the winner. Closed with 44 nominations.

Track Record—REGALBERTO (3) 122—1:54 ONE MILE AND THREE-SIXTEENTH

	OWNER	TRAINER	JOCKEY
1	Tri Star Stable, R. Tsang & W. Bowie Chinese red, gold stars on back, red cap **JUNCTION ROAD** Br. c. 3 Junction—Cycool (KY)	Dave Forster **115**	6 **Kenneth Skinner**
2	Osborne Farm Yellow, brown cross sashes, brown stripe on sleeves, yellow cap **ALLOWANCE** Ch. c. 3 Champagne Supper—Fund (WA)	Howard Belvoir **106**	50 **Gallyn Mitchell**
3	Marvin Pietila & Estate of Waino Pietila Blue, white band, blue cap **PRAIRIE BREAKER** B. g. 3 Sir Paulus—Addie O Lea (WA)	Dick Wilkinson **124**	4/5 **Gary Stevens**
4	Mr. & Mrs. Peter J. Whiting Yellow, brown sash, yellow cap **MYTHICALLY** B. c. 3 Run of Luck—Never Vain (CA)	L. Shoemaker **118**	9/2 **Paul Nicolo**
5	Loto Can, Inc. Red & black stripes, red & black cap **COUNTRY BORN** B. g. 3 Native Born—Runnun Tell (WA)	Gary Vickery **110**	30 **Mike James**
6	Selvin, Siegel, Wellman et al Beige, bulldog on back, matching cap **LIFAREGAL** B. c. 3 President—Regal Key (FRA)	Jim Penney **117**	5 **Martin Pedroza**
7	Poor Four Stable White, red flame & yellow emblem on back, red & yellow cap **SABER BEN** Ch. c. 3 Champagne Supper—Saber Deb (WA)	Howard Belvoir **108**	50 **Basil Frazier**
8	Rimrock Stable & Edwards Bloodstock Dark blue, blue & gray checks on sleeves, gray E on back, matching cap **DYNAMO DOC** Br. c. 3 Bold Commander—Little Girl Lost (KY)	Ed Walsh **115**	10 **Danny Sorenson**
9	Heather Dedomenico Yellow, brown cross sashes, brown stripe on sleeves, D on back, yellow cap **HEATHER ALA RONI** Br. f. 3 Theologist—Scarlet Heather (WA)	Dan Kenney **110**	15 **Jerry Taketa**
10	Vaughan Stable Orange, blue sleeves & sash, orange cap **RED BARON RETURNS** Ch. c. 3 Mateor—T. V. Return (WA)	Kay Vaughan **110**	50 **J. W. Mills**

CLOCKER'S SELECTION: 3-4-6

9th Lga

1 3-16 MILES. (1:54). 46TH RUNNING OF THE LONGACRES DERBY. Purse, $100,000-added. 3-year-olds. By subscription of $150, which shall accompany the nomination, $500 to pass the entry box, $1,000 additional to start with $100,000-added, of which $20,000 to second, $15,000 to third, $10,000 to fourth and $3,000 to fifth. All nominations, entry and starting fees to the winner. High weights preferred. Closed Friday, July 15 with 44 nominations.

Junction Road **115** Dk. b. or br. c, 1980, by Junction—Cycool, by Cyane.
Breeder, Morris-O'Brien (Ky.). 1983. 8 3 2 2 $31,062
Owner, Tri Star Stable-R. Tsang-W. Bowie. Trainer, Dave Forster. 1982. 0 M 0 0 ——
31Jly 83 9Lga 1⅛ :4541:0941:494ft 9 117 515 49½ 44½ 32½ SkinnrK8 HcpS 82 PrairieBreaker124 Mythically 8
16Jly 83 9EP 1 1/16 :4731:1241:444ft 9-5 *116 41¾ 1h 12½ 13 SkinnrK3 HcpS 87 JunctionRoad116 PhylThBses 8
3Jly 83 8Lga 6½f :222 :45 1:144ft 5½ 117 42½ 21½ 33 28 SkrK5 Aw10000 87 ExclusivBiddr119 JnctinRoad 9
25Jun83 9Lga 1 1/16 :4631:1121:424ft 2½ 122 76¾ 43 44½ 58¾ PlrcL4 Aw10000 76 Dynamo Doc 117 Ourteshun 8
25Jun83—Wide.
15Jun83 9Lga 6½f :221 :4431:16 ft 2½*120 42½ 43 44½ 31¾ RycftC8 Aw9400 87 PicO'Morn120 ExclusiveBddr 8
18May83 9EP 6½f :214 :4521:182ft 6-5 *120 69½ 75¾ 51½ 1½ RyctD7 Aw6400 86 JnctionRoad120 MoneySprgs 9
30Apr83 6EP 6½f :22 :4521:18 ft 1-2 *120 35 24 13 15 RycrftD6 Mdn 88 JunctionRoad VictoriousLd 9
16Apr83 7EP 6f :23 :4631:114ft 2-3 *120 21 2h 1½ 2¾ RycrftD3 Mdn 92 ThroghAndClr JunctionRoad 9
16Apr83—Jumped gate trks st
Aug 11 EP 5f ft 1:03⅗b June 13 Lga 4f ft :47⅕h June 8 EP 5f ft 1:03h

Allowance **106** Ch. c, 1980, by Champagne Supper—Fund, by Speak John.
Breeder, Osborne Farm (Wash.). 1983. 6 0 1 1 $4,116
Owner, Osborne Farm. Trainer, Howard Belvoir. 1982. 11 2 0 3 $10,210
LIFETIME (thru 1982) 11 2 0 3 $10,210
7Aug83 9Pla 1 :46 1:11 1:364ft 3¾ 118 34 34½ 45½ 45¾ ColtonR4 HcpS 87 MissMackee121 Wnd'emHgh 7
27Jly 83 6Lga 1 1/16 :4611:11 1:437sy 4½ 119 36½ 1½ 2h 2½ BazeMB4 25000 81 Bold Treaty 116 Allowance 7
7Jly 83 9Lga 6f :222 :4441:082ft 39 117 63¾ 79 1020 918 MhGV6 Aw8500 76 DncingDirctr119 FortithPrnc 11
30Jun83 8Lga 6f :214 :4421:09 ft 34 111 712 712 614 79¾ MtchlGV6 40000 81 DancngDirectr120 TudrRmmr 10
28Jan83 1SA 1 :4711:1331:421sl 9 116 716 819 pulled up ToroF8 32000 BranBey DarkAce 8
14Jan83 9SA 1 1/16 :4741:12 1:434ft 5 116 52 32½ 33½ 32 ToroF1 32000 80 Bick'sAKick DarkAce 9
29Dec82 2SA 1 :4521:1031:372ft 3½*116 810 86½ 64½ 75 SmkrW5 32000 76 DarkAce MoorsMountain 10
23Dec82 5Hol 1 1/16 :4721:1321:471sl 4¾ 115 57 66 611 64 ShkrW7 50000 55 SterlingSilva Brazenesian 8
19Nov82 1Hol 6f :22 :4521:111gd 21 115 94½ 54 58 31 BlackK8 40000 80 AllTheBest FuzzyFreeze 9
10Oct82 9Lga 1 1/16 :4721:1341:482sl 26 122 91510151023 1021 LosthC12 SpwS 36 Dave's Reality 122 Chirp 13
19Sep82 9Lga 1 :46 1:1031:364ft 6¾ 120 79½ 89½ 610 613 BazMB10 HcpS 72 Dave's Reality 122 Tubafor 10
5Sep82 7Lga 6½f :22 :45 1:173ft 25 120 55 44½ 36 12 BzMB1 Aw7500 81 Allowance 120 Sailalong 9
JULY 19 LGA 3F FT :35⅖B June 22 Lga 5f ft 1:02⅘bc June 14 Lga 5f ft 1:01⅘bc

Prairie Breaker **124** B. g, 1980, by Sir Paulus—Addie O. Lea, by Orazio.
Breeder, Waino-Marvin Pietila (Wash.). 1983. 11 8 1 1 $85,793
Owner, Marvin Pietila-Estate of Waino Pietila. Tr., D. Wilkinson. 1982. 0 M 0 0 ——
31Jly 83 9Lga 1⅛ :4541.0941:494ft 3-5 *124 615 510 34 12 StevenG7 HcpS 84 PrairieBreaker124 Mythically 8
17Jly 83 9Lga 1 1/16 :4531:1011:431ft 4-5 *122 512 38¾ 2h 15½ StevenG7 HcpS 83 PrairiBreakr122 SonofSibirri 7
3Jly 83 9Lga 1 :4541:1041:362ft 4¾ 119 88¾ 32½ 11 11½ StevenG8 HcpS 87 PrairiBreakr119 DynamoDoc 8
18Jun83 9Lga 6½f :214 :4411:142ft 2¾ 120 77 78½ 67 45 StvnsG10 HcpS 92 King Alphonse 124 Sailalong 11
29May83 9Lga 6f :212 :4411:094ft 3 116 78½ 79½ 48 11½ StevnsG4 HcpS 87 Prairie Breaker116 Sailalong 8
8May83 9Lga 5½f :213 :45 1:04 m 7¾ 122 98½ 711 714 32 StvnsG11 AlwS 90 NoTheologian120 Intoxicator 11
24Apr83 9PM 1 1/16 :4811:1241:442ft 1-2 *123 54 2h 12 13 StevnsG5 HcpS 94 PrairiBreakr123 RahRahRah 5
14Apr83 9PM 6f :223 :46 1:103ft 1-5 *121 21½ 3½ 2h 1½ StvnsG5 Aw3000 94 PrairieBreaker121 JustFrBill 5
20Mar83 9PM 1 :4741:1321:384ft 3-5 *117 36½ 2h 15 112 StvsG1 Aw3100 87 PrairieBreakr117 ScappsBay 7
20Feb83 9PM 1 1/16 :4631:1241:474gd 6-5 *120 26 26 22 22½ BazeG3 HcpS 74 Boss C. 121 Prairie Breaker 12
5Feb83 2PM 6f :222 :4611:122ft 8 120 21½ 21½ 12½ 16½ BazeG12 Mdn 85 PrairieBreakr120 Prediction 12
AUG 11 LGA 5F FT 1:00⅕B JULY 14 LGA 5F M 1:00⅗H June 16 Lga 4f ft :50b

Mythically **118** B. c, 1980, by Run of Luck—Never Vain, by Prince Tenderfoot.
Breeder, Mr.-Mrs. P. J. Whiting (Calif.). 1983. 8 2 5 0 $36,490
Owner, Mr.-Mrs. P. J. Whiting. Trainer, Leonard Shoemaker.
31Jly 83 9Lga 1⅛ :4541:0941:494ft 3¾ 120 38½ 36½ 23 22 NicoloP2 HcpS 82 PrairieBreaker124 Mythically 8
9Jly 83 11Pln 1 1/16 :47 1:1131:44 ft 1 *119 31 2h 1h 21½ NicoloP5 HcpS 83 IdealMoment114 Mythically 8
19Jun83 8GG Ⓣ1 1/16 :4621:1121:45 fm 4½ 114 11 11 11 2nk NicoloP2 HcpS 77 BrianKe Mythically 11
10Jun83 6GG 1 1/16 :46 1:1041:432ft 3½ 120 21½ 1h 13 16 NclP2 Aw13000 86 Mythically HundrdollrJo 8
21May83 6GG 1 1/16 :47 1:1111:44 ft 2½*112 12 13 16 17 NicoloP9 Mdn 83 Mythically Exhibit 10
7May83 1GG 1 1/16 :4611:11 1:45 ft 8-5 *118 2½ 2½ 3½ 2¾ NicoloP4 Mdn 77 HonoredOne Mythically 9
7May83—Lugged out, bumped stretch.
23Apr83 2GG 6f :223 :4631:13 sy 7-5 *118 43½ 52½ 41 21 †NicoloP6 Mdn 73 Blck'Shrrod Mythically 10
†Disqualified and placed fifth.
8Apr83 7GG 6f :223 :4641:113ft 3 118 83¾ 74¾ 33½ 2nk NcloP5 M25000 81 Interim Mythically 10
8Apr83—Bumped hard break, lacked room 3 1-2.
Aug 11 Lga 5f ft 1:02⅖b JULY 23 GG 7F FT 1:27⅘H JULY 2 GG 7F FT 1:25⅗h

Country Born ✱ **110** B. g, 1980, by Native Born—Runnun Tell, by Tell.
Breeder, L & M Farms, Inc (Wash.). 1983. 6 1 2 1 $9,965
Owner, Loto Can, Inc. Trainer, Gary Vickery. 1982. 5 2 1 0 $30,656
LIFETIME (thru 1982) 5 2 1 0 $30,656
10Aug83 8Lga 1 1/16 :4621:11 1:434ft 5½ 118 11 13 13 15½ BzMB8 Aw8500 80 CountryBorn118 Lyon'sShadw 12
27Jly 83 7Lga 1 1/16 :4741:12 1:443sy 3½ 119 11 11½ 13 2½ BzMB4 Aw8500 75 Lyon'sShadow117 CountryBrn 7
14Jly 83 9Lga 1 1/16 :4641:1221:451m 3½*119 15 14 11½ 31¾ BazeMB7 32000 71 RedBrnRtrns120 Lyon'sShdw 11
15Jun83 9Lga 6½f :221 :4431:16 ft 5½ 120 2½ 3½ 32½ 44¾ BzMB6 Aw9400 84 PicO'Morn120 ExclusiveBddr 8
15Jun83—Wide.
25May83 9Lga 6f :222 :4541:103ft 3 *119 42 32½ 31 22½ BzMB1 Aw8500 80 PhilE.B.Jon122 CountryBorn 11
8May83 9Lga 5½f :213 :45 1:04 m 4¾ 120 53½ 55 57½ 66 BazeMB9 AlwS 86 NoTheologian120 Intoxicator 11
8May83—Wide on turn.
10Oct82 9Lga 1 1/16 :4721:1341:482sl 7¾ 122 31½ 33 1229 1340 BazeMB3 SpwS Dave's Reality 122 Chirp 13
26Sep82 9Pla 6½f :222 :4611:19 m 4¾ 121 11½ 15 15 112 BazMB6 SpwS 89 CountryBorn121 PicO'Morn 12
5Sep82 9Lga 6½f :22 :45 1:181ft 3½ 121 31 31½ 913 129½ HowgR8 SpwS 68 Big Flyer 121 Time of Sale 12
21Aug82 4Lga 6f :221 :46 1:113ft 8-5 *120 1h 1h 12 16 HowgR9 Mdn 78 CountryBorn120 ShotABid 11
July 8 Lga 7f ft 1:24h June 9 Lga 7f ft 1:28b MAY 21 LGA 6F FT 1:13⅘H

***Lifaregal** **117** B. c, 1980, by President—Regal Key, by Royal and Regal.
Breeder, M. Desandre (Fra.). 1983. 5 1 0 0 $15,700
Owner, Selvin-Siegel-Wellman et al. Trainer, Edwin Gregson. 1982. 8 2 4 1 $23,714
LIFETIME (thru 1982) 8 2 4 1 $23,714

24Jly 83 8Hol 1¼ :463 1:351 2:01 ft 35 114 77½ 66 611 68½ MezaRQ6 AlwS 77 Hyperborean115 MyHabitony 9
19Jun83 8GG Ⓣ1 1/16 :462 1:112 1:45 fm 4 118 88½ 87½ 54½ 74 MenaF7 HcpS 73 BrianKe Mythically 11
11Jun83 8Hol Ⓣ1 1/16 :49 1:133 1:43 fm 18 115 96¼ 94½ 51¼ 53 PierceD9 HcpS 81 BaronO'Dublin TanksBridge 9
21May83 8Hol Ⓣ1 1/16 :461 1:102 1:412 fm 4¼ 118 914 128 1210 129¾ ShkrW13 HcpS 82 Barberstown LovrBoy 13
30Apr83 9Hol 1 1/16 :482 1:132 1:463 gd 4¼ 115 35½ 34 31½ 1nk TroF2 Aw24000 62 Lifaregal O'HappyDay 6
13Nov82 3Marseill(Fra) Ⓣa1¼ sf 122 15 GoudotB Px Dlahnte Lifaregal HatTrick MyWinter 10
13Nov82—No time taken; no wagering.
16Oct82 1Lyon(Fra) Ⓣa1 1/16 sf 128 42¼ GoudotB Px D Rouvrs RoyaldeLuze OretDiamant MisWn 11
16Oct82—No time taken; no wagering.
29Sep82 1Marseill(Fra) Ⓣa1⅛ gd 121 11 BlscG PxMsAndn(Mdn) Lifaregal Royal deLuze Cargy 9
29Sep82—No time taken; no wagering.
AUG 8 DMR 1M FT 1:37⅘H Aug 1 Dmr 5f ft 1:00b July 19 Hol 5f ft :59⅘h

Saber Ben **108** Ch. c, 1980, by Champagne Supper—Saber Deb, by Saber Charge.
Breeder, Osborne Farms (Wash.). 1983. 4 1 0 0 $4,235
Owner, Poor Four Stable. Trainer, Howard Belvoir. 1982. 6 1 3 0 $8,655
LIFETIME (thru 1982) 6 1 3 0 $8,655

31Jly 83 9Lga 1⅛ :454 1:094 1:494 ft 37 111 821 815 713 512 FrazierB1 HcpS 72 PrairieBreaker124 Mythically 8
20Jly 83 7Lga 6½f :213 :442 1:154 ft 26 119 1010 1011 46 1¾ BazeMB8 25000 90 Saber Ben 119 Just Cavorting 11
7Jly 83 9Lga 6f :222 :444 1:082 ft 64 122 106½ 1015 918 815 PiercL8 Aw8500 79 DncingDirctr119 FortithPrnc 11
30Jun83 8Lga 6f :214 :442 1:09 ft 27 113 1015 1016 924 917 StevenG2 40000 74 DancngDirectr120 TudrRmmr 10
14Dec82 6BM 6f :223 :454 1:104 ft 9 114 97 108½ 79¼ 88½ LncC1 Aw12000 77 SportingBlood NIN'Shn 10
14Dec82—Lacked racing room in backstretch.
30Nov82 6BM 6f :24 :49 1:15 sy 8-5 *113 42 31 22 22½ LmcC5 Aw12000 62 DistantMan SaberBen 5
19Nov82 8BM 6f :222 :453 1:113 sy 3½ 113 69½ 48 37 24 LmcC4 Aw12000 78 NoTheologian SaberBen 6
31Oct82 9PM 6f :214 :45 1:114 ft 10 120 812 918 48½ 24½ BazeMB6 HcpS 83 Kim Como 117 Saber Ben 12
24Oct82 9Lga 1⅛ :47 1:114 1:513 m 21 116 1214 1215 1427 1429 MrcVV11 HcpS 46 Yuma Queen 114 Tubafor 14
8Oct82 5Lga 6f :223 :464 1:13 m 14 120 65½ 67¼ 41½ 15 BzMB2 M25000 71 Saber Ben 120 Noodle Roni 8
Aug 10 Lga 5f ft 1:01⅕b June 22 Lga 5f ft 1:02⅗bc June 14 Lga 5f ft 1:00⅗h

Dynamo Doc **115** Dk. b. or br. c, 1980, by Bold Commander—Little Girl Lost, by Tudor
Grey. Breeder, Jim Eagle (Ky.). 1983. 7 2 1 0 $17,220
Owner, Rimrock Stable-Edwards Bloodstock. Tr., Ed Walsh. 1982. 10 1 3 3 $21,460
LIFETIME (thru 1982) 10 1 3 3 $21,460

3Jly 83 9Lga 1 :454 1:104 1:362 ft 8½ 119 78¼ 54½ 53½ 21½ SornsnD4 HcpS 85 PrairiBreakr119 DynamoDoc 8
3Jly83—Wide on second turn.
25Jun83 9Lga 1 1/16 :463 1:112 1:424 ft 2¼ *117 89¾ 53¼ 2h 16 SrnD5 Aw10000 85 Dynamo Doc 117 Ourteshun 8
19Jun83 9Lga 6½f :214 :441 1:142 ft 32 120 108½ 109¼ 77 56½ PierceL7 HcpS 90 King Alphonse 124 Sailalong 11
29May83 9Lga 6f :212 :441 1:094 ft 12 120 810 810 612 67¼ PierceL3 HcpS 80 Prairie Breaker116 Sailalong 8
23Apr83 7GG 1 1/16 :471 1:114 1:511 ft 56 112 fell SornsnD4 AlwS ParisPrince119 TanksBrigade 12
14Apr83 8GG 1 :501 1:144 1:392 ft 6 113 67½ 610 58 46 SrnD5 Aw13000 65 TanksBrigade Thurman 6
14Apr83—Broke in tangle
22Mar83 6GG 6f :231 :464 1:123 m 4½ 113 66½ 66¾ 55½ 1no SrnD5 Aw11000 76 DynamoDoc AuntieRose 6
22Mar83—Bobbled at break
24Oct82 9Lga 1⅛ :47 1:114 1:513 m 4¾ 119 812 78¼ 34 511 PierceL1 HcpS 64 Yuma Queen 114 Tubafor 14
10Oct82 9Lga 1 1/16 :472 1:134 1:482 sl 7½ 122 1117 813 47 36¾ PiercL11 SpwS 50 Dave's Reality 122 Chirp 13
29Sep82 8Lga 1 :484 1:15 1:44 hy 5¾ 120 818 712 66¼ 21 PiercL5 Aw6500 48 ExclusivBiddr118 DynamoDoc 8
19Sep82 9Lga 1 :46 1:103 1:364 ft 8¼ 120 69 57 47 46½ PierceL2 HcpS 78 Dave's Reality 122 Tubafor 10
AUG 11 LGA 4F FT :47⅗H Aug 7 Lga 7f ft 1:28⅘b Aug 1 Lga 5f ft 1:01⅗b

Heather Ala Roni × **110** Dk. b. or br. f, 1980, by Theologist—Scarlet Heather, by Cold
Command. Br., Paskey Dedomenico (Wash.). 1983. 3 2 0 0 $20,750
Owner, Heather Dedomenico. Trainer, Dan Kenney. 1982. 4 1 1 0 $22,467
LIFETIME (thru 1982) 4 1 1 0 $22,467

30Jly 83 9Lga 1 1/16 :453 1:11 1:434 ft 2¼ *116 23 1h 34½ 513 FrazirB3 HcpS 67 ⒻStllrPrfrmr118 WindyJnny 9
9Jly 83 9Lga 1 :463 1:111 1:363 gd 3¾ 113 21 1h 1h 11 FrazirB5 HcpS 86 ⒻHthrAlaRni113 StlrPrfrmr 11
9Jly83—Bumped at 1-2 pole.
23Jun83 8Lga 6f :22 :453 1:103 m 4 117 21½ 21 13 19 FrzirB5 Aw8000 83 ⒻHeathrAlaRni117 LttlGngr 7
23Jun83—Carried wide on turn.
24Oct82 9Lga 1⅛ :47 1:114 1:513 m 9½f 119 23½ 2h 913 1222 FrazirB13 HcpS 53 Yuma Queen 114 Tubafor 14
3Oct82 9Lga 1 1/16 :474 1:132 1:471 m 16 119 12 11 2h 23½ FrazerB2 SpwS 59 ⒻFlagDeLune119 HthrAlaRni 14
17Sep82 3Lga 6½f :214 :451 1:174 ft 6¾ 118 1h 12 13 18 BazG11 M20000 80 ⒻHeatherAlaRoni118 Garvin 11
28Aug82 3Lga 6f :214 :454 1:111 ft 12 118 65½ 45 56 414 SorensnD2 Mdn 66 ⒻThoniaFrst118 UnitdFeatre 7
JULY 25 LGA 4F FT :46⅗H July 19 Lga 1m ft 1:37⅖h July 4 Lga 5f ft 1:02⅘b

Red Baron Returns **110** Ch. c, 1980, by Mateor—T.V. Return, by Flying Lark.
Breeder, O'Harrow-Vaughan (Wash.). 1983. 10 3 1 1 $15,185
Owner, Vaughan Stable. Trainer, Kay Vaughan. 1982. 7 2 0 2 $6,510
LIFETIME (thru 1982) 7 2 0 2 $6,510

10Aug83 8Lga 1 1/16 :462 1:11 1:434 ft 5¼ 120 1218 1014 612 57¾ MJW10 Aw8500 72 CountryBorn118 Lyon'sShadw 12
27Jly 83 7Lga 1 1/16 :472 1:12 1:443 sy 2½ *120 79 76¾ 57½ 33½ MllJW2 Aw8500 72 Lyon'sShadow117 CountryBrn 7
14Jly 83 9Lga 1 1/16 :464 1:122 1:451 m 5¼ 120 1015 711 47½ 11½ MillsJW6 32000 73 RedBrnRtrns120 Lyon'sShdw 11
2Jly 83 6Lga 1 1/16 :484 1:132 1:453 ft 6¾ 117 42 31 2h 13 MillsJW4 25000 71 RedBaronRtrns117 Predction 8
22Jun83 6Lga 6½f :221 :453 1:164 sy 2½ 117 34 31½ 2h 2½ MillsJW2 20000 84 Predcatin114 RedBaronRetrn 7
15Jun83 6Lga 6½f :221 :444 1:154 ft 6¼ 117 67 613 79¾ 69¼ SornsnD1 25000 81 Candy Patch 120 Hot Drums 8
3Jun83 6Lga 6½f :22 :451 1:171 ft 16 117 711 714 610 43½ SornsnD5 25000 79 DncngDirctr120 HoHoCharlie 7
3Jun83—Veered in, steadied at start.
14May83 7Lga 6f :22 :45 1:094 ft 9½ 114 712 710 610 515 StevnsG8 40000 72 SplndorBoy120 DancgDrctor 8
24Apr83 9YM 6f :234 :483 1:17 hy 3-2e *124 64 65¼ 711 721 MlgrinT1 HcpS 37 Pic O'Morn 117 Colonel Jerry 7
2Apr83 9YM 5f :222 :453 1:013 gd 5¾ 117 59 59½ 53¾ 13 MgrnTM7 HcpS 72 RedBarnRetrns117 ShotABid 9
22Sep82 8Lga 6½f :223 :462 1:183 ft 3-2 *120 74¼ 31 1h 12 BazeG1 20000 76 RedBaronRetrns120 C.W.Mss 8
Aug 3 Lga 5f ft 1:00⅖h July 21 Lga 5f ft 1:00⅖h JULY 9 LGA 5F SY 1:00H

fairly evenly among the rest of the field. That seemed to be the case in this race. With one minute to post time, the tote board was as follows:

	Totals	#3 Prairie Breaker	Expected Value per Dollar Bet to Place and Show on Prairie Breaker
Odds		4—5	
Win	104,409	47,510	
Place	59,752	16,655	1.25
Show	43,936	11,950	1.19

The expected values to place and show with Longacres 16% track take, using equations (4.5) and (4.6), were then

$$\begin{aligned}\text{EX Place Prairie Breaker} &= 0.319 + 0.559\left(\frac{47{,}510/104{,}409}{16{,}655/59{,}752}\right)\\ &\quad + \left[2.22 - 1.29\left(\frac{47{,}510}{104{,}409}\right)\right](0.84 - 0.829)\\ &= 1.23 + 0.02\\ &= 1.25.\end{aligned}$$

$$\begin{aligned}\text{EX Show Prairie Breaker} &= 0.543 + 0.369\left(\frac{47{,}510/104{,}409}{11{,}950/43{,}936}\right)\\ &\quad + \left[3.60 - 2.13\left(\frac{47{,}510}{104{,}409}\right)\right](0.84 - 0.829)\\ &= 1.16 + 0.03\\ &= 1.19.\end{aligned}$$

Hence Prairie Breaker was a Dr. Z system bet to place, as well as to show.

Equations (5.4) and (5.5) suggested bets of \$155 to place and \$221 to show on Prairie Breaker:

$$\begin{aligned}\text{Place bet Prairie Breaker} &= \Bigg[505(0.4550) + 527(0.4550)^2\\ &\quad - \left(\frac{386(0.4550)(16{,}655)}{(0.4550)(59{,}752) - (0.60)(16{,}655)}\right)\Bigg]\left(\frac{59{,}752 - 10{,}000}{140{,}000}\right)\\ &\quad + \Bigg[375(0.4550) + 525(0.4550)^2\\ &\quad - \left(\frac{271(0.4550)(16{,}665)}{(0.4550)(59{,}752) - (0.70)(16{,}665)}\right)\Bigg]\left(\frac{150{,}000 - 59{,}752}{140{,}000}\right)\\ &= \$155.\end{aligned}$$

Show bet

$$\text{Prairie Breaker} = \left[131 + 2{,}150(0.4550)^2 - 1{,}778(0.4550)^3 - \left(\frac{150(11{,}950)}{(0.4550)(43{,}936) - (0.70)(11{,}950)}\right)\right]\left(\frac{43{,}936 - 6{,}000}{94{,}000}\right)$$

$$+ \left[86 + 1{,}516(0.4550)^2 - 968(0.4550)^3 - \left(\frac{90.7(11{,}950)}{(0.4550)(43{,}936) - (0.85)(11{,}950)}\right)\right]\left(\frac{100{,}000 - 43{,}936}{94{,}000}\right)$$

$$= \$221.$$

However, these equations were developed assuming that there was only one bet to be made to place or show, but not both. When the two bets are on the same horse, the total amount recommended to be bet is too large and needs to be scaled down according to the following formulas:

$$\text{Optimal place bet} = \text{minimum}\left[\begin{matrix}\text{place bet from} \\ \text{equation (5.4)'}\end{matrix}\quad 1.59\left(\begin{matrix}\text{Place bet from} \\ \text{equation (5.4)}\end{matrix}\right) - 0.639\left(\begin{matrix}\text{show bet from} \\ \text{equation (5.5)}\end{matrix}\right)\right] \tag{6.1}$$

$$\text{Optimal show bet} = 0.907\left(\begin{matrix}\text{show bet from} \\ \text{equation (5.5)}\end{matrix}\right) - 0.134\left(\begin{matrix}\text{place bet from} \\ \text{equation (5.4)}\end{matrix}\right)$$

Hence

Optimal place bet

$$\text{Prairie Breaker} = \text{minimum}\{\$155, 1.59(\$155) - 0.639(\$221)\}$$

$$= \text{minimum}\{\$155, \$105\}$$

$$= \$105 \text{ and}$$

Optimal show bet

$$\text{Prairie Breaker} = 0.907(\$221) - 0.134(\$155)$$

$$= \$179.$$

We made these bets on Prairie Breaker. When the horses were going into the starting gate, however, Junction Road acted up and it was decided to scratch him. The odds on Prairie Breaker then dropped to 3—5, and further betting was allowed for a few minutes. Track management likes to have refunded money due to a scratch bet on other horses so their take is not diminished. Fortunately for us, the expected value per dollar bet to place and show on Prairie Breaker remained high enough to qualify it as a Dr. Z system bet. When the race began, the final tote board was as follows:

	Totals	#3 Prairie Breaker	Expected Value per Dollar Bet on Prairie Breaker
Odds		3—5	
Win	134,897	63,997	
Place	77,600	25,622	1.14
Show	57,805	18,208	1.13

As Charlie Brown might have predicted, the 53—1 long shot, Red Baron Returns, stole the race from Prairie Breaker. Mythically took third. Our payoffs were outstanding, since Prairie Breaker paid a whopping $3.40 to place and a substantial $2.50 to show. The $3.40 was more than the $3.20 Prairie Breaker would have paid to win had he won. Since he was a Dr. Z system bet, the payoff was likely to be large. When the extreme long shot, Red Baron Returns, finished in place money, Prairie Breaker's return skyrocketed to the $3.40. Mythically was reasonably heavily bet to show, so the show payoff on Prairie Breaker was lowered to the $2.50. Our bets of $105 to place and $179 to show returned $178.50 and $223.75, respectively, for a profit of $118.25. The chart of the race was as follows:

NINTH RACE
Lga
Aug. 14, 1983

1 3-16 MILES. (1:54). 46TH RUNNING OF THE LONGACRES DERBY. Purse, $100,000-added. 3-year-olds. By subscription of $150, which shall accompany the nomination, $500 to pass the entry box, $1,000 additional to start with $100,000-added, of which $20,000 to second, $15,000 to third, $10,000 to fourth and $3,000 to fifth. All nominations, entry and starting fees to the winner. High weights preferred. Closed Friday, July 15 with 44 nominations.

Value of race, $120,600. Value to winner, $72,600; second, $20,000; third, $15,000; fourth, $10.000; fifth, $3,000. Mutuel Pool, $270,302.

Last Raced	Horses	EqtAWt	PP	St	¼	½	¾	Str	Fin	Jockeys	Owners	Odds to $1
10Aug83 ^{8}Lga^{5}	Red Baron Returns	3 113	9	8	$8^{1\frac{1}{2}}$	$8^{1\frac{1}{2}}$	8^{h}	$5^{3\frac{1}{2}}$	$1^{2\frac{1}{2}}$	MillsJW	Vaughan Stable	53.10
31Jly 83 ^{9}Lga^{1}	Prairie Breaker	3 124	2	6	$4\frac{1}{2}$	6^{4}	5^{2}	3^{h}	2^{4}	StevensG	Pietila-Estat ofWPtila	.75
31Jly 83 ^{9}Lga^{2}	Mythically	3 118	3	2	3^{1}	$3^{1\frac{1}{2}}$	3^{3}	1^{1}	3^{nk}	NicoloP	Mr-Mrs P J Whiting	3.95
7Aug83 ^{9}Pla^{4}	Allowance	3 106	1	3	5^{h}	$5\frac{1}{2}$	7^{4}	7^{1}	$4^{1\frac{1}{2}}$	MitchellGV	Osborne Farms	45.45
31Jly 83 ^{9}Lga^{5}	Saber Ben	3 109	6	7	$7^{2\frac{1}{2}}$	7^{4}	6^{h}	8^{2}	5^{2}	FrazierB	Poor Four Stable	57.75
24Jly 83 ^{8}Hol^{6}	Lifaregal	3 117	5	5	6^{5}	4^{1}	4^{h}	4^{h}	6^{nk}	PedrozaMA	Selvin-Siegel-Wellmn	7.40
10Aug83 ^{8}Lga^{1}	Country Born	b3 111	4	1	$2^{1\frac{1}{2}}$	2^{3}	$2^{1\frac{1}{2}}$	6^{2}	7^{1}	JamesM	Loto Can, Inc	15.35
30Jly 83 ^{9}Lga^{5}	Heather Ala Roni	3 112	8	4	$1\frac{1}{2}$	$1^{1\frac{1}{2}}$	1^{1}	2^{h}	$8^{2\frac{1}{2}}$	TaketaJ	H Dedomenico	47.85
3Jly 83 ^{9}Lga^{2}	Dynamo Doc	b3 115	7	9	9	9	9	9	9	SorensonD	RmrckStabl-E Bldsck	4.95

OFF AT 6:08. START GOOD. WON DRIVING. Time, :22$\frac{4}{5}$, :46$\frac{3}{5}$, 1:11, 1:37$\frac{3}{5}$, 1:47$\frac{3}{5}$. Track fast.

$2 Mutuel Prices

10—RED BARON RETURNS	108.20	20.60	6.00
3—PRAIRIE BREAKER		3.40	2.50
4—MYTHICALLY			2.90

Ch. c, by Mateor—T. V. Return, by Flying Lark. Trainer, Kay Vaughan. Bred by O'Harrow-Vaughan (Wash.).

RED BARON RETURNS, permitted to settle in stride early, gradually worked his way forward on the final turn, drove between horses in the upper stretch to run down the leaders with a rush and won going away. PRAIRIE BREAKER raced within striking distance early, was sent up along the outside going into the far turn, raced wide into the stretch and closed strongly in the final furlong. MYTHICALLY was forwardly placed from the beginning, ran down the leaders to take command briefly in the upper stretch but lacked the needed closing kick. ALLOWANCE saved ground while being outrun early, responded when settled for the drive and finished willingly. LIFAREGAL raced within striking distance early, but could not sustain his bid in the drive. COUNTRY BORN prompted the pace for six furlongs and gave way. HEATHER ALA RONI went to the front at once, saved ground while setting the pace and gave way in the drive. DYNAMO DOC was always outrun. **JUNCTION ROAD FLIPPED IN THE GATE AND WAS ORDERED SCRATCHED WITH ALL WAGERS ON HIM BEING REFUNDED.**

Overweight—Country Born, 1 pound; Heather Ala Roni, 2; Red Baron Returns, 3; Saber Ben, 1.
Scratched—Junction Road.

CHAPTER 7

Using the Dr. Z System in Other Situations

We now turn to using the Dr. Z system when you are not at the track where the race is run. Usually the race is shown on closed-circuit TV monitors and there is local betting. However, as long as you have access to the win, place, and show mutuel pools, you can apply the Dr. Z system. We describe two such instances: piping in an important national race, such as the Belmont Stakes, which may go to twenty or more different racetracks and viewing a whole card from a nearby racetrack in a theaterlike atmosphere, as is done with New York State racing cards at the Teletrack facility in New Haven, Connecticut.

The Belmont Stakes, June 5, 1982: Other-Track Betting at Golden Gate Fields, Albany, California

The Belmont Stakes is the third and final jewel in the Triple Crown. In 1982, for the first time, betting on both the Preakness and the Belmont Stakes was allowed at several other tracks, including Golden Gate Fields in Albany, California and Los Alamitos Race Course in Los Alamitos, California. Each of these tracks had separate betting pools and betting closed just before the actual race at the home track. The race was then viewed on closed-circuit television or on the infield screen if there was one. With separate betting pools, all the tracks paid different amounts to win, place, and show for the horses in the money. The idea of other-track betting is gaining popularity, and in the future we will probably see more and more such races.

The Belmont field included the highly touted Linkage, as well as the Kentucky Derby and Preakness winners, Gato Del Sol and Aloma's Ruler. These three horses were all ridden by their regular jockeys, Bill Shoemaker, Eddie Delahoussaye, and Jack Kaenel. The other leading contender was Conquistador Cielo, who had impressive Eastern wins but was running on only four days' rest. His regular jockey, Eddie Maple, was unable to ride because of an injury and had been replaced by Laffit Pincay, Jr. Delahoussaye, Pincay, and Shoemaker flew in from California to ride the race. It is common for top jockeys such as these to fly across the country to ride in an important race. They usually return immediately to their home track so they miss only one day's races there.

The final tote board betting amounts at Golden Gate were:

	#1	#2	#3	#4	#5	#6
Odds	4—1	80—1	60—1	9—1	30—1	10—1
Win	28,027	1,717	2,371	13,755	4,234	13,303
Place	9,311	721	1,040	6,851	2,529	7,185
Show	5,034	703	962	2,931	1,729	3,356

	#7	#8	#9	#10	#11	Totals
Odds	8—5	20—1	40—1	8—1	7—2	
Win	56,629	5,917	3,565	15,759	30,301	175,578
Place	24,353	2,598	2,035	6,512	8,653	71,788
Show	11,491	1,639	1,339	3,051	3,658	35,893

A quick scan of the tote board pointed to a possible show bet on number 11, Conquistador Cielo. From equation (4.6), the expected return on a dollar bet to show was 1.24. For different wealth levels, the optimal bets were*

Wealth level	100	500	1,000	2,500	5,000	10,000
Optimal bet	5	25	38	76	99	145

Conquistador Cielo won the race by an impressive fourteen lengths, breaking the track record at Belmont for $1\frac{1}{2}$ miles on an off track. He was followed by Gato Del Sol and Illuminate, who finished third.

*These bets were computed using the equations in Tables 16.3 and 16.4.

The mutuel payoffs at Golden Gate were as follows:

11	9.80	6.80	5.60
	1	6.60	4.60
		8	10.20

Compare these mutuel payoffs with those in the chart of the race at Belmont that follows:

Belmont Stakes

EIGHTH RACE
Belmont
JUNE 5, 1982

1½ MILES. (2.24) 114th Running THE BELMONT STAKES (Grade I). Purse $200,000 added. 3-year-olds. By subscription of $100 each to accompany the nomination; $1,000 to pass the entry box; $2,000 to start. A supplementary nomination of $5,000 may be made on Wednesday, June 2 with an additional $15,000 to start, with $200,000 added of which 60% to the winner, 22% to second, 12% to third and 6% to fourth. Colts and Geldings, 126 lbs. Fillies, 121 lbs. Starters to be named at the closing time of entries. The winning owner will be presented with the August Belmont Memorial Cup to be retained for one year, as well as a trophy for permanent possession and trophies will be presented to the winning trainer and jockey and mementoes to the grooms of the first four finishers. Closed Tuesday, February 16, 1982 with 332 nominations.

Value of race $266,200, value to winner $159,720, second $58,564, third $31,944, fourth $15,972. Mutuel pool $1,201,491, OTB pool $2,248,366.

Last Raced	Horse	Eqt.	A.	Wt	PP	¼	½	1	1¼	Str	Fin	Jockey	Odds $1
31May82 ^{8}Bel^{1}	Conquistador Cielo		3	126	11	$2^{\frac{1}{2}}$	$1^{1\frac{1}{2}}$	1^{hd}	1^{4}	1^{10}	1^{14}	Pincay L Jr	4.10
1May82 ^{8}CD^{1}	Gato Del Sol		3	126	1	$9^{1\frac{1}{2}}$	8^{3}	5^{1}	4^{2}	2^{1}	2^{4}	Delahoussaye E	6.40
23May82 ^{8}Bel^{3}	Illuminate		3	126	8	8^{hd}	11	8^{1}	$6^{1\frac{1}{2}}$	5^{4}	$3^{3\frac{3}{4}}$	Velasquez J	11.20
15May82 ^{8}Pim^{2}	Linkage		3	126	7	5^{2}	3^{1}	3^{5}	2^{hd}	$3^{\frac{1}{2}}$	$4^{\frac{1}{2}}$	Shoemaker W	2.20
15May82 ^{8}Key^{3}	High Ascent		3	126	3	$4^{1\frac{1}{2}}$	5^{4}	$2^{2\frac{1}{2}}$	3^{3}	4^{hd}	$5^{5\frac{3}{4}}$	Lovato F Jr	40.90
24May82 ^{7}Bel^{2}	Lejoli		3	126	9	11	9^{hd}	9^{4}	5^{hd}	6^{2}	$6^{1\frac{3}{4}}$	Samyn J L	23.80
24May82 ^{7}Bel^{1}	Estoril	b	3	126	6	$6^{\frac{1}{2}}$	$6^{1\frac{1}{2}}$	6^{3}	7^{3}	7^{8}	7^{13}	Fell J	9.20
28May82 ^{7}Bel^{1}	Royal Roberto	b	3	126	4	$10^{\frac{1}{2}}$	$10^{\frac{1}{2}}$	7^{2}	9^{10}	9^{12}	$8^{1\frac{1}{4}}$	Cordero A Jr	7.20
15May82 ^{8}Pim^{1}	Aloma's Ruler		3	126	10	$3^{1\frac{1}{2}}$	$4^{\frac{1}{2}}$	4^{hd}	8^{4}	8^{hd}	9^{13}	Kaenel J L	7.30
22May82 ^{1}Bel^{4}	Anemal		3	126	2	1^{1}	2^{3}	10^{10}	10^{16}	10	10	Martens G	44.10
15May82 ^{8}Pim^{3}	Cut Away	b	3	126	5	7^{3}	7^{3}	11	11	—	—	Bailey J D	25.70

Cut Away, Eased.

OFF AT 5:39, Start good, Won ridden out. Time, :23⅘, :47⅕, 1:12, 1:37⅖, 2:03⅕, 2:28⅕, Track sloppy.

$2 Mutuel Prices:				
	11-(K)-CONQUISTADOR CIELO	10.20	7.40	6.80
	1-(A)-GATO DEL SOL		8.00	6.40
	8-(H)-ILLUMINATE			6.40

B. c, by Mr Prospector—K D Princess, by Bold Commander. Trainer Stephens Woodford C. Bred by Iandoli L E (Fla).

CONQUISTADOR CIELO, very wide into the first turn, opened a clear advantage while racing well out in the track nearing the backstretch, continued wide while making the pace, responded readily when challenged by HIGH ASCENT, shook off that rival before going nine furlongs and drew off steadily under a hand ride. GATO DEL SOL, reserved early, moved up outside horses midway of the far turn, continued very wide into the stretch but was no match for the winner while besting the others. ILLUMINATE, badly outrun for a mile, saved ground into the stretch while rallying but lacked a further response. LINKAGE, never far back while under light restraint, rallied while racing well out in the track racing into the far turn, remained a factor to the stretch and gave way. HIGH ASCENT, well placed into the backstretch, made a run along the inside to engage CONQUISTADOR CIELO approaching the end of the backstretch, remained a factor until near the stretch but had nothing left. LEJOLI, badly outrun early, made up some ground approaching the stretch but lacked a further response. ESTORIL had no apparent excuse. ROYAL ROBERTO saved ground to no avail. ALOMA'S RULER, away alertly, was allowed to follow the leader into the backstretch and was finished at the far turn. ANEMAL, hustled to the front along the inside at the first turn, stopped badly. CUT AWAY wasn't able to keep up through the run down the backstretch and was eased during the late stages. LEJOLI raced with mud caulks.

Owners— 1, deKwiatkowski H; 2, Peters L J; 3, Humphrey G W Jr; 4, Christiana Stable; 5, Buckland Farm; 6, Peskoff S D; 7, Seeligson A A Jr; 8, Key West Stable; 9, Scherr N; 10, Pappas D J; 11, Allen H.

Trainers— 1, Stephens Woodford C; 2, Gregson Edwin; 3, Kay Michael; 4, Clark Henry S; 5, Campo John P; 6, Blusiewicz Leon; 7, Doyle A T; 8, Iselin James H; 9, Lenzini John J Jr; 10, Gullo Thomas J; 11, Jacobs Eugene.

Los Alamitos Race Course also had other-track betting on the Belmont Stakes. Their final tote board figures and payoffs help show the large differences in the public opinions in different locations.

At Los Alamitos they were as follows:

	#1	#2	#3	#4	#5	#6
Odds	5—2	99—1	99—1	11—1	40—1	8—1
Win	10,877	217	342	3,350	955	4,565
Place	4,340	116	140	1,701	438	2,507
Show	1,725	108	103	702	323	1,493

	#7	#8	#9	#10	#11	Totals
Odds	1—1	40—1	99—1	12—1	6—1	
Win	19,388	862	394	3,197	5,428	49,575
Place	7,238	263	221	1,362	1,986	20,312
Show	3,222	234	194	653	877	9,634

11	15.40	7.40	6.00
	1	4.40	4.00
		8	17.20

There was no Dr. Z system bet at Los Alamitos.

The efficient win-market hypothesis discussed in Chapter Three suggests that the win odds should have been approximately the same across all the tracks. The bettors at Belmont, however, had considerably more information than the bettors at the other tracks. They knew how the horses had been running, how the jockeys were doing, what the track conditions were, how the horses looked in the paddock and the parade to post, and so on. Therefore, we would expect (1) different odds at the different tracks and (2) the odds at Belmont to be the most accurate odds. Since the Belmont odds are the best estimate of each horse's winning probability, Dr. Z system bettors away from Belmont would actually prefer to use the Belmont Park win figures against their own track's place and show figures when looking for possible bets. This would be possible if Belmont's tote board figures were displayed over the closed-circuit televisions. For example, if you were at Los Alamitos, the following Belmont Park win figures were displayed (these are the actual final tote board figures for the on-track betting at Belmont Park, page 148):

	#1	#2	#3	#4	#5	#6
Odds	6—1	70—1	60—1	12—1	40—1	10—1
Win	94,915	8,829	9,825	51,938	15,127	60,191
	#7	#8	#9	#10	#11	Totals
Odds	9—5	18—1	25—1	7—1	5—2	
Win	231,728	35,788	22,656	86,085	189,160	806,242

These figures indicate that the Belmont Park bettors had a higher opinion of Conquistador Cielo than the bettors at the other tracks. At Los Alamitos, you could scan these win figures and the place and show pools shown at your track. These would indicate a possible place and show bet on number 11, Conquistador Cielo. The values to isolate would then be:

	#11 Conquistador Cielo	Totals	
Win	189,160	806,242	from Belmont
Place	1,986	20,312	from Los Alamitos
Show	877	9,634	from Los Alamitos

The expected return on a place bet was then 1.70 and 1.56 on a show bet.
For different wealth levels the optimal bets were then

Wealth level	100	500	1,000	2,500	5,000
Optimal place bet	9	47	94	229	294
Optimal show bet	18	84	102	154	177

Note that Belmont had Conquistador Cielo at 5—2 odds, while Los Alamitos had him at 6—1, so it would seem there existed an overlay in the win pool, as well as for place and show, at Los Alamitos. Whether to make a win bet and how much to bet are beyond the scope of this book, but the attractiveness of the betting possibility should be apparent to the reader.*

*We have since analyzed this problem. Readers with technical backgrounds might wish to refer to Hausch and Ziemba (December 1983).

The Clout Handicap, Aqueduct, November 12, 1981: A Visit to Teletrack, New Haven, Connecticut

The Teletrack facility in New Haven, Connecticut, provides a new concept in horse-race observation and wagering. Since there are no racetracks in Connecticut and many in neighboring New York, it is natural for the races in New York to be used for Connecticut betting. The facility resembles a movie theater where the races are shown live. During the year, thoroughbred races from Aqueduct, Belmont, and Saratoga, and harness races from Roosevelt and Yonkers are featured. The odds, win, place, and show pools, as well as the projected features payoffs, are flashed on the screen as the betting proceeds. Although the Teletrack pools are separate from the track's pools, they also include the bets from about 180 off-track betting shops in

Turf Course

SEVENTH RACE

PURSE $18,000

THE CLOUT

FOR THREE-YEAR-OLDS AND UPWARD WHICH HAVE NEVER WON TWO RACES OTHER THAN MAIDEN, CLAIMING OR STARTER. Three-year-olds, 120 lbs.; older, 122 lbs. Non-winners of a race other than maiden or claiming over a mile and a furlong since October 15 allowed 3 lbs.; of such a race since October 1, 5 lbs.

If the Stewards consider it inadvisable to run this race on the turf course it will be run on the main track at one mile and three furlongs.

ONE MILE AND THREE FURLONGS (Turf Course)
Track Record—2:14⅗: FLUORESCENT LIGHT (4), 115 lbs.; November 7, 1978.

MAKE SELECTION BY NUMBER

No.	Owner	Trainer	Jockey/Morn. Line
1	WALTER HAEFNER Blue and White Stripes, Blue Sleeves, White Chevrons, Blue Cap **IVANOFF (Ire.) 117** Ch.c.4, Connaught—True Rocket by Roan Rocket	V. J. NICKERSON	**6-1** **JEAN-LUC SAMYN**
2	BROWN BADGETT Brown and Green Diamonds, Green Sleeves, Brown Hoop, Green Cap, Brown Visor **NATOMAS BREEZE *112** Ch.c.4, Secretariat—Spanish Breeze by Windy City 2nd	WAYNE MURTY	**4-1** **RICHARD MIGLIORE**
3	CALUMET FARM Devil's Red, Blue Collar, Two Blue Hoops on Sleeves, Blue Cap **COME RAIN OR SHINE 117** Ch.c.4, Nijinsky 2nd—Sign Of The Times by Francis S.	J. M. VEITCH	**3-1** **ANGEL CORDERO, JR.**
4	ARCHIE R. DONALDSON Maroon, Light Blue Ball, Blue Sleeves, Two Maroon Hoops, Maroon and Blue Cap **THE MESSANGER 117** Dk b or br.c.4, Big Spruce—Taratan by Summer Tan	K. E. JENSEN	**6-1** **LARRY SAUMELL**
5	AUGUSTIN STABLES White and Green Halves, White Sleeves, Green Cap **STATE OF SIEGE 115** Ch.g.3, Damascus—Herbalesian by Herbager	J. E. SHEPPARD	**20-1** **DARYL MONTOYA**
6	CAESAR P. KIMMEL Orange, Black Cross Sashes, Black Diamonds on Sleeves, Orange and Black Cap **ON THE GRASS *112** Ch.c.4, Vaguely Noble—Bellevarde by Herbager	J. J. TONER	**15-1** **Constantino Hernandez**
7	SANTO LUCA Red, Blue Diamond Hoop, Blue Diamonds on Sleeves, Red Cap, Blue Tassel **SANTO'S JOE 119** Gr.c.4, Northern Jove—Maria L. by Mystic 2nd	OWNER	**5-1** **EDDIE MAPLE**
8	ARCADY STABLE Kelly Green, Light Green Sash and "A," Kelly Green and Light Green Halved Sleeves, Light Green Cap **ICEBOX CAKE 112** Gr.f.3, Iceapade—Ore to Grow On by Lucky Debonair	F. I. WRIGHT	**15-1** **JEFFREY FELL**
9	STEPHEN C. CLARK, JR. Yellow, Blue Braid, Sleeves and Cap **COUNTRY CORNER *112** B.g.4, One For All—Dance by Native Dancer	S. WATTERS, JR.	**10-1** **VICTOR MOLINA**
10	MRS. DION K. KERR Light Blue, Green Sash, Green Hoop on Sleeves, Blue Cap **ERIN'S TIGER 115** Ch.c.3, Terrible Tiger—Irish Exchange by Swaps	R. NIEMINSKI	**6-1** **CASH ASMUSSEN**

Change of Equipment: ICEBOX CAKE—Blinkers On.

SCRATCHED—DANGEROUS MISSION, LOTHIAN, KITCHEN COMMANDER, BEYOND RECALL, AIRBUS

Connecticut. The total handle is small, averaging about $400,000 per day and reaching as high as $650,000 on Saturdays. The take at Teletrack was 17% plus 10¢ breakage, for a total commission of about 20%. The track take in New York was 14%. Except for the small pools and relatively high commission, the facility allows for easy adaptation of the Dr. Z system. The flashing pools let you stand near or even in a betting line, so a bet can be made very close to post time.

I was in the East giving lectures in the finance seminars at New York and Yale Universities on efficient market ideas in horse-racing betting markets. I took the opportunity to visit Teletrack, which like Yale is in New Haven. That afternoon, November 12, 1981, races from Aqueduct were being featured.

Come Rain or Shine, number 3 in the seventh race, was a 3—1 morning-line favorite ridden by Angel Cordero, Jr., the leading jockey at Aqueduct, with an in-the-money percentage of 57%. He was a Dr. Z system bet throughout the betting period. With two minutes to post time the betting pools were

	Totals	#3 Come Rain or Shine
Odds		5—2
Win	10,463	2,313
Show	837	115

The expected value per dollar bet to show on Come Rain or Shine was thus 1.14, as may be calculated using equation (4.4). Since the show pools were so small, I decided to be cautious and make a flat bet of $20. The show pools of $115 and $837 were so small that one or two sizable bets would greatly affect the show odds. During the final betting, the win odds on Come Rain or Shine rose to 3—1. My bet and the others had lowered the expected value per dollar bet to show on Come Rain or Shine to 1.12—1. The final mutuels were

	Totals	#3 Come Rain or Shine
Odds		3—1
Win	12,032	2,471
Show	1,312	174

3	8.00	3.80	3.40
2		3.20	2.60
4			7.00

Come Rain or Shine easily won the race and paid $3.40 to show. Hence my $20 bet produced a profit of $14. The payoffs at Teletrack are shown above; the chart of the race is on page 151. Notice that these payoffs were different and that Come Rain or Shine was not a Dr. Z system bet to show at Aqueduct.

SEVENTH RACE

Aqueduct

NOVEMBER 12, 1981

1 3/8 MILES. (TURF) (2.14 1/5) ALLOWANCE. Purse $18,000. 3-year-olds and upward, which have never won two races other than Maiden, Claiming or Starter. Weights, 3-year-olds, 120 lbs. Older, 122 lbs. Non-winners of a race other than maiden or claiming over a mile and a furlong since October 15, allowed 3 lbs. Of such a race since October 1, 5 lbs.

Value of race $18,000, value to winner $10,800, second $3,960, third $2,160, fourth $1,080. Mutuel pool $123,881, OTB pool $128,000. Exacta Pool $186,984. OTB Exacta Pool $174,465.

Last Raced	Horse	Eqt.	A.	Wt.	PP	1/4	1/2	3/4	1	Str	Fin	Jockey	Odds $1
11Oct81 9Bel 5	Come Rain or Shine	b	4	117	3	5 ½	5 ½	4 ½	2 ½	1 ½	1-1½	Cordero A Jr	2.10
20Oct81 8Lrl 8	Natomas Breeze		4	112	2	8-3	8 ½	7-1½	4 ½	4 ½	2 ½	Migliore R-5	1.80
6Aug81 9Sar 7	The Messanger		4	117	4	6-1½	6-4	5-1	3hd	3-3	3 ¾	Saumell L	29.40
30Oct81 7Aqu 5	Santo's Joe	b	4	119	7	1 ½	2-1	1-1½	1-2	2-2	4 ½	Maple E	7.60
29Oct81 7Aqu 6	Country Corner		4	112	9	7-4	7 ½	8 ½	7-6	5-3	5-3¾	Molina V H-5	17.40
11Oct81 9Bel 9	Ivanoff		4	117	1	9	9	9	6-1	6-3	6-5	Samyn J L	6.30
8Oct81 7Bel 4	Icebox Cake	b	3	114	8	2-1½	3-1½	3 ½	5-2	7-12	7-16	Fell J	10.90
23Oct81 9Med 3	State of Siege	b	3	115	5	3-3	4-3	6-2	8	8	8	Montoya D	27.20
25Oct81 5Aqu 5	On the Grass	b	4	112	6	4-4	1-2	2-2	-	-	-	Hernandez C-5	17.50

On the Grass, Bolted.

OFF AT 3:27 EST. Start good, Won driving. Time, :23, :47 2/5, 1:15, 1:41 3/5, 2:08, 2:20 4/5, Course firm.

$ 2 Mutuel Prices:				
3-	COME RAIN OR SHINE	6.20	3.00	2.40
2-	NATOMAS BREEZE		2.80	2.20
4-	THE MESSANGER			5.80

$2 EXACTA 3-2 PAID $14.40.

Ch. c, by Nijinsky II-Sign of the Times, by Francis S. Trainer Veitch John M. Bred by Calumet Farm (Ky).

COME RAIN OR SHINE, reserved early, rallied racing into the far turn, moved through inside SANTO'S JOE to take over near the final furlong and proved clearly best. NATOMAS BREEZE, outrun early, moved up outside horses approaching the end of the backstretch, continued wide into the stretch and was going well at the finish. THE MESSANGER rallied racing into the far turn, moved to the inside for the drive and continued on with good energy. COUNTRY CORNER failed to seriously menace with a mild rally. INVANOFF moved within striking distance at the far turn but lacked a late response. ICEBOX CAKE tired badly. STATE OF SIEGE tired badly. SANTO'S JOE gained a clear lead when ON THE GRASS bolted, made the pace into the stretch while racing well out in the course but had nothing left. ON THE GRASS moved away to a clear lead while bearing out approaching the second turn and bolted entering the backstretch.

Owners- 1, Calumet Farm; 2, Badgett B; 3, Donaldson A R; 4, Luca S; 5, Clark S C Jr; 6, Haefner W; 7, Arcady Stable; 8, Augustin Stables; 9, Kimmel C P.

Overweight: Icebox Cake 2 pounds.

Scratched- Dangerous Mission(26Oct81 2Aqu 1); Lothian(14Sep81 6Bel 2); Kitchen Commander(7Nov81 5Aqu 5); Erin's Tiger (30Oct81 7Aqu 8); Beyond Recall(3Nov81 6Aqu 6); Airbus(29Oct81 7Aqu 5).

CHAPTER 8

A Great Race: John Henry versus Lemhi Gold in the Oak Tree Invitational at Santa Anita, October 31, 1982

The Field

It was a classic matchup: John Henry versus Lemhi Gold. John Henry had won the Oak Tree the previous two years enroute to garnering horse-of-the-year honors in 1981. The future of the seven-year-old gelding was clouded because a minor ankle injury had kept him on the sidelines for most of the 1982 season. Running recently at Santa Anita in the Burke Handicap as a warmup, he had managed a credible race, but finished fourth, out of the money. He was the sentimental favorite of the record 55,031 fans, yet the fact that he had won only one of his last four races, and that on a disqualification, tempered their enthusiasm. He had his usual jockey, the great Bill Shoemaker. Was he ready? Lemhi Gold, on the other hand, was coming extraordinarily sharp after demolishing the best horses on the East coast in the Marlboro Cup and the Jockey Cup Gold Cup at Belmont. He was also returning to the scene of one of his greatest triumphs, his victory over Perrault in the San Juan Capistrano Invitational in April (see pages 301–310 for a discussion of this race). Chris McCarron, who rode Lemhi Gold in the Capistrano, was in the irons again for the Oak Tree. A convincing win would likely give the four-year-old horse-of-the-year honors for 1982.

As was to be expected, the betting was heavy, especially on the two top choices but also on other strong horses in the field, such as Pelerin and Craelius. There were outstanding Dr. Z system bets to place and show on John Henry. The discussion of these bets focuses on the evolution of the odds, betting pools, and the expected value of various bets as post time approached. It is in this fashion that we suggest you approach the Dr. Z system, always watching the board from about six minutes to post time until you actually bet with about a minute or two to go. Your task is to watch the board and let the expert handicappers establish the win odds.

As we discussed in Chapter Three, on average, these odds closely represent the true probability of each horse's winning. So you need not worry whether Lemhi Gold or John Henry is the better horse. You are simply looking for a good bet. The discussion of this race also gives us a good opportunity to consider three important aspects of the mutuel payoffs: (1) how the payoffs are calculated, (2) the effect on these payoffs of which horses finish in the money, and (3) the effect on these payoffs of breakage.

Experts' Selections

Consensus Points: 5 for 1st (today's best 7), 2 for 2nd, 1 for 3rd. Today's Best in Bold Type.

Daily Racing Form

Trackman, Warren Williams — **SANTA ANITA PARK** — Selections Made for Fast Track

	TRACKMAN	HANDICAP	ANALYST	HERMIS	SWEEP	CONSENSUS	
8	JOHN HENRY LEMHI GOLD CRAELIUS	JOHN HENRY LEMHI GOLD CRAELIUS	**LEMHI GOLD** **JOHN HENRY** **CRAELIUS**	JOHN HENRY LEMHI GOLD **MAIPON**	LEMHI GOLD JOHN HENRY PELERIN	JOHN HENRY LEMHI GOLD CRAELIUS	19 16 3

ANALYST'S *Santa Anita Comment*

EIGHTH RACE

1—Lemhi Gold
2—John Henry
3—Craelius

LEMHI GOLD returns home after a very successful Eastern invasion where he accounted for several prestigious races in New York and is in line for Horse of the Year honors, but not until he gets past last year's top horse, JOHN HENRY. These two warriors engage in their first meeting and it could result in one of the best features of the season. LEMHI GOLD has developed by leaps and bounds during the fall and must be given the edge over the comebacking JOHN HENRY. The latter had his outing in the Burke, a race he obviously needed and, had to give chunks of weight away to his rivals. He's much better prepared today. CRAELIUS is coming to around very nicely now, running second in the Burke, and had a :59 2/5 work Thursday. PELERIN can't be discounted off one dull effort.

EXACTA RACE

EIGHTH RACE

THE OAK TREE
$300,000

For three-year-olds and upward. By invitation, with no nomination or starting fees. The winner to receive $180,000, with $60,000 to second, $36,000 to third, 18,000 to fourth and $6,000 to fifth. Three-year-olds, 122 lbs.; older, 126 lbs. A trophy will be presented to the owner of the winner.

OAK TREE RECORD—CZAR ALEXANDER (Cordero) 1969 2:23⅗

Course Record—FIDDLE ISLE (5) 124 March 21, 1970 2:23

MAKE SELECTIONS BY NUMBER — PROBABLE ODDS
OWNER — TRAINER — JOCKEY

1 Doherty & Snowden — Charles Whittingham — **4**
Black, green sash, sleeves and cap
PELERIN (Fr) **126** — Laffit Pincay, Jr.
B.h. '77, Sir Gaylord—Padrona, by St. Paddy
Breeder—Sir Philip Oppenheimer (France)

2 Mrs. Howard B. Keck — Charles Whittingham — **8**
Blue, coral pink hoop, sleeves and cap
CRAELIUS **122** — Ray Sibille
B.c. '79, Avatar—Nas-Mahal, by Nasrullah
Breeder—Howard B. Keck (Kentucky)

3 Naji Nahas — Jean-Pierre Dupuis — **30**
Red, royal blue sleeves, red and blue cap
BUCHANETTE **119** — Alain Lequeux
B.f. '79, Youth—Duke's Little Gal
Breeder—Nelson B. Hunt (Kentucky)

4 Aaron U. Jones — L. S. Barrera — **6/5**
White, red cross sashes, red bar on sleeves, white and red cap
LEMHI GOLD **126** — Chris McCarron
Ch.c. '78, Vaguely Noble—Belle Marie
Breeder—Owner (Kentucky)

5 Walter Harris — Eldon Hall — **30**
Yellow, black stripes, yellow and black "HHH" on white ball on back, yelow cap
REGALBERTO **126** — Fernando Toro
B.c. '78, Roberto—Every Evening, by Roi Dagobert
Breeder—Red Oak Farm (Florida)

6 Dotsam Stable — Ronald McAnally — **7/5**
Brown, blue hoop, blue bar on sleeves, brown and blue cap
JOHN HENRY **126** — William Shoemaker
B.g. '75, Ole Bob Bowers—Once Double
Breeder—Golden Chance Farm, Inc. (Kentucky)

7 C. L. Hirsch — Warren Stute — **30**
Black, gold diamonds on sleeves, gold cap
MAIPON (Chi) **126** — Marco Castaneda
Ch.h. '77, Tantoul—Doninda, by Cardinal 2nd
Breeder—Haras Dadinco (Chile)

JOCKEY STANDINGS
(Through Saturday, October 30, 1982)

Jockey	Mts.	1st	2nd	3rd	Win Pct.	In Money Pct.
Laffit Pincay, Jr.	156	31	21	22	19.8	47.4
Patrick Valenzuela	147	26	22	15	17.7	42.9
Sandy Hawley	130	22	22	14	16.9	44.6
Ray Sibille	160	21	12	20	13.1	33.1
Chris McCarron	116	20	16	17	17.2	45.7
Eddie Delahoussaye	126	17	14	20	13.5	40.5
Kenny Black	102	17	7	14	16.7	37.3
Terry Lipham	95	12	6	7	12.6	26.3
Darrel McHargue	89	10	11	3	11.2	27.0
Marco Castaneda	128	6	15	12	4.7	25.8
William Shoemaker	75	6	12	12	8.0	40.0
Donald Pierce	53	6	6	4	11.3	30.2

8th Santa Anita

1½ MILES. (TURF). (2.23) 14th Running of THE OAK TREE INVITATIONAL (Grade I). Purse $300,000. (Weight for age). 3-year-olds and upward. By invitation, with no nomination or starter fees. The winner to receive $180,000, with $60,000 to second, $36,000 to third, $18,000 to fourth and $6,000 to fifth. Weights, 3-year-olds, 122 lbs.; older, 126 lbs. The Oak Tree Racing Association will invite a representative field of horses to compete. The field will be drawn by the closing time of entries. A trophy will be presented to the owner of the winner. Invitations Thursday, October 21, 1982.

*Pelerin

B. h. 5, by Sir Gaylord—Padrona, by St Paddy
Br.—Oppenheimer Sir P (Fra) 1982 3 0 1 0 $8,000
Own.—Doherty & Snowden **126** **Tr.—Whittingham Charles** 1981 6 4 0 0 $172,007
Lifetime 19 5 2 0 $229,996 **Turf 19 5 2 0 $229,996**

```
17Oct82-8SA   1¼Ⓣ:4711:3431:583fm 2½ 122  66¾ 66 66¼ 65¼ PincayLJr3 C F Brk H 89 Mehmet, Craelius, It's the One 7
8Oct82-8SA    1⅛Ⓣ:4611:10 1:462fm*6-5 117  87 65½ 53½ 2nk Pincay L Jr3 Aw40000 95 Tell Again, Pelerin, Dare You II 8
6Sep82-7Dmr   1 1/16Ⓣ:4741:1131:422fm 4 120  810 811 812 74¾ Pincay L Jr2 Aw32000 92 DareYouII,GoldenFlak,RustyCnyon 8
4Oct81♦4Longchamp(Fra) a1½ 2:351sf 33 130  Ⓣ 1721 HideE Arc de Triomphe (Gr1) Gold River, Bikala, April Run 24
6Sep81♦5BadenBaden(Ger) a1½2:273gd*7-5 130  Ⓣ 12 StrkG GrssrPr vn Bdn (Gr1) Pelerin, Hohritt, Maivogel 8
25Jly81♦4Ascot(Eng) 1½ 2:352gd 7½ 133  Ⓣ 511 TylrB Kng Geo VI-Q Elz (Gr1) Shergar, Madam Gay, Fingals Cave 7
19Jun81♦2Ascot(Eng) 1½ 2:381fm 7 124  Ⓣ 13 TaylorB Hardwick (Gr2) Pelerin, Light Cavalry, Lancastrian 9
7May81♦2Chester(Eng) a1⅝ 2:584gd*7-5 130  Ⓣ 11½ TaylorB Ormonde (Gr3) Pelerin, Billbroker, Shaftsbury 5
11Apr81♦4Newbury(Eng) 1½ 2:441sf 16 120  Ⓣ 1hd TaylorB John Porter (Gr2) Pelerin, Cracaval, Shining Finish 9
20Aug80♦4York(Eng) 1½ 2:344gd 11 119  Ⓣ 413 Reid J Grt Voltgeur (Gr2) Prince Bee, Light Cavalry, Saviour 5
  Oct 28 SA Ⓣ5f fm 1:00 h (d)   Oct 23 SA Ⓣ3f fm :36 h (d)   Oct 15 SA Ⓣ4f fm :481 h (d)   Oct 4 SA Ⓣ6f fm 1:153 h (d)
```

Craelius

B. c. 3, by Avatar—Nas-Mahal, by Nasrullah
Br.—Keck H B (Ky) 1982 11 4 5 0 $142,525
Own.—Keck Mrs H B **122** **Tr.—Whittingham Charles** 1981 2 M 0 0 $425
Lifetime 13 4 5 0 $142,950 **Turf 7 2 4 0 $95,775**

```
17Oct82-8SA   1¼Ⓣ:4711:3431:583fm 13 114  41½ 31½ 2hd 2hd McCrrnCJ4 C F Brk H 94 Mehmet, Craelius, It's the One 7
3Oct82-8SA    1⅛Ⓣ:46 1:1011:461fm*9-5e118  88½ 85¾ 33 22½ ShomkrW5 Volante H 93 Lamerok, Craelius, Sari's Dreamer 9
3Sep82-8Dmr   1 1/16:461 1:101 1:414ft *3-2e117  86 62¾ 42½ 1nk ShoemkerW4 El Cajon 91 Craelius, Poley, Kerlan 10
22Aug82-8Dmr  1⅛Ⓣ:4631:1111:49 fm 5¾e116  119 82¾ 43½ 73¾ ShmkrW9 Dmr Dby H 89 GiveMStrngth,WtrBnk,TkThFloor 13
8Aug82-9Dmr  1 Ⓣ:4641:1111:353fm *1 116  53½ 31½ 2hd 2½ ShmrW7 La Jla Mle H 94 TakeTheFloor,Craelius,SwordBlade 8
     8Aug82—Run in two divisions, 8th & 9th races.
21Jly82-9Dmr  7½fⓉ:223 :4621:304fm *1 114  88 85¼ 5¾ 12½ ShomkrW6 Oceanside 85 Crelius,TkeTheFloor,SwingTillDwn 8
    21Jly82—Run in two divisions, 8th & 9th races.
8Jly82-8Hol   1 1/16Ⓣ:4621:1021:403fm 3½e114  64½ 52½ 1½ 21 Shoemaker W7 Wstwd 95 Sun Worship, Craelius, Ask Me 11
26Jun82-8Hol  1⅛:463 1:102 1:464ft 6 113  99 89 826 828 HawleyS1 Silvr Scrn H 67 Journey at Sea, Cassaleria,Guachan 9
26May82-9Hol  1 1/16Ⓣ:4621:1111:421fm*3-5 120  42½ 1½ 1½ 12 McCarronCJ8 Aw22000 88 Craelius, SwingTillDawn,Reconfirm 8
16May82-4Hol  1 1/16:472 1:114 1:421ft *1 114  1hd 1hd 12 15 McCarron C J3 Mdn 84 Crelius,Pleztobefirst,SlickNSneky 10
  ●Oct 28 SA Ⓣ5f fm :592 h (d)  Oct 23 SA Ⓣ3f fm :36 h (d)   Oct 14 SA Ⓣ5f fm 1:013 h (d)   Sep 21 SA 6f ft 1:13 h
```

*Buchanette

B. f. 3, by Youth—Duke's Little Gal, by Duke of Dublin
Br.—Hunt N B (Ky) 1982 9 2 1 1 $47,944
Own.—Nahas N **119** **Tr.—Dupuis Jean-Pierre** Turf 9 2 1 1 $47,944
Lifetime 9 2 1 1 $47,944

```
18Oct82♦5StCloud(Fra) a1 5/16 2:274sf 7½ 121  Ⓣ 1hd DbrcqG ⒻPx de Flore (Gr 3) Buchntt,DoublingTm,UnknownLdy 13
12Oct82♦4Longchamp(Fra) a1¼ 2:192sf 2½ 120  Ⓣ 44¾ DbrcqG Px du Ranelagh WelshTerm,AlfredsChoic,Tompkins 7
27Sep82♦5MLaffitte(Fra) a1¼ 2:091gd 15 113  Ⓣ 4nk KsssJL La Cpe d'Mlfftte(Gr3) Coquelin,ByllytheKid,BeMyNative 13
13Sep82♦5Evry(Fra) a1½ 2:392gd*6-5 120  Ⓣ 2nk DbrcqG Px Mrice de Nexn Rubino, Buchanette, Blau 7
21Aug82♦5Deauville(Fra) a1 11/16 3:011gd 9 120  Ⓣ 12 DbrcG ⒻPx de Pomone(Gr2) Zalataia, Akiyda, April Run 13
2Aug82♦5Vichy(Fra) a1½ 2:35 gd 5 111  Ⓣ 45½ KsssJL Gr Px de Vchy(Gr3) Karkour, No Attention, Palikaraki 12
27Jun82♦2Longchamp(Fra) a1¼ 2:102gd 4¼ •123  Ⓣ 33½ SmniH ⒻPx de Mileret(Gr2) Grease, Parannda, Buchanette 7
13Jun82♦4Chantilly(Fra) a1 5/16 2:164sf 21 128  Ⓣ 68¼ SmniH ⒻPx de Diane(Gr1) Harbour, Akiyda, Paradise 14
16May82♦1Longchamp(Fra) a1 5/16 2:191gd 4 123  Ⓣ 12 DbrcG ⒻPx La Ce(Mdn) Buchnette,LuckyProspctor,Shnnky 9
```

Lemhi Gold — Ch. c. 4, by Vaguely Noble—Belle Marie, by Candy Spots
Br.—Jones A U (Ky) — 1982 11 6 2 1 $1,060,375
Own.—Jones A U — 126 — Tr.—Barrera Lazaro S — 1981 7 2 1 0 $50,070
Lifetime 18 8 3 1 $1,110,445 — Turf 7 5 1 0 $480,305

9Oct82-8Bel 1½:473 2:04 2:311ft 2¼ 126 28 14 15 14½ McCrrCJ2 J C Gld Cp 64 LmhiGold,SilvrSuprm,ChristmsPst 10
18Sep82-8Bel 1¼:473 1:36 2:01 ft 7½e115 31 11 15 18¾ VsquzJ2 Mrlbro Cup H 93 LemhiGold,SilverSuprem,PirofDucs 8
29Aug82-8AP 1¼Ⓣ:4621:35 1:584fm 3¼ 126 85¾ 52¼ 44½ 45¼ McCrrCJ5 Bud Million 120 Perrault, Be My Native, Motavato 14
7Aug82-8Sar 1⅛:472 1:11 1:474ft 5¾ 117 47 45 56¼ 45¾ McCrrnCJ1 Whitney H 90 Silver Buck,Winter'sTale,TapShoes 6
10Jly82-8Bel 1½Ⓣ:4912:0142:26 fm *1 126 13 1½ 1hd 1nk McCrrCJ2 SwordDncr 94 Lemhi Gold, Erins Isle, Field Cat 5
31May82-8Hol 1½Ⓣ:4922:0132:251fm*3-5 123 32 3½ 1hd 22½ Guerra WA6 Hol Inv H 91 Exploded, Lemhi Gold, The Bart 6
18Apr82-8SA a1¾ Ⓣ:46 2:453fm 3 121 43½ 1hd 12½ 17 GurrWA4 S J Cp Iv H 99 Lemhi Gold, Exploded, Perrault 9
13Mar82-8SA 1½Ⓣ:4842:0222:272gd 2¼ 119 12½ 12½ 15 15 GuerrWA4 Sn Mrno H 78 LemhiGold,Exploded,ChnceyBidder 8
13Mar82—Run in two divisions, 8th & 9th races.
25Feb82-8SA 1⅛Ⓣ:4641:1111:48 fm*8-5 113 42 41½ 1½ 11¼ Guerra W A8 Aw35000 87 LemhiGold,Fingal'sCave,Essenbee 10
15Feb82-8SA 1 1/16:462 1:10 1:41 ft 3½ 114 43 31½ 33½ 31¼ Guerra WA1 El Monte 95 WoodlandLad,SirDncer,LemhiGold 10
Oct 28 SA Ⓣ 5f fm 1:013 b (d) ●Oct 23 SA Ⓣ 5f fm :593 h (d) Oct 6 Bel 5f ft 1:022 b Sep 29 Bel 5f ft :591 h

Regalberto — B. c. 4, by Roberto—Every Evening, by Roi Dagobert
Br.—Red Oak Farm (Fla) — 1982 9 3 2 3 $128,070
Own.—Harris W — 126 — Tr.—Hall Eldon — 1981 13 6 2 1 $163,200
Lifetime 30 10 9 5 $346,400 — Turf 9 2 2 2 $76,625

10Oct82-8BM 1 Ⓣ:4621:1031:36 fm*8-5 123 32 45 66 87½ Toro F9 Mrks Plce H 92 Silveyville,MountainMrine,Cinnpo 10
6Sep82-8Dmr a1¼:463 1:344 1:57 ft 14 119 11½ 11 2hd 22 Toro F9 Dmr Inv H 90 Muttering, Regalberto, Exploded 9
26Aug82-8Dmr 1 1/16Ⓣ:4921:13 1:432fm 14 119 21 2½ 2hd 12 Toro F2 Aw30000 92 Regalberto, Island Whirl, Monarch 6
11Jly82-11Pln 1⅛:47 1:11 1:51 ft *3-5 125 42 43¼ 2½ 24½ AndrsJR1 Alamedan H 76 Sir Optimist, Regalberto, Kilty 9
27Jun82-8GG 1⅛:461 1:10 1:502ft *6-5 123 47 46 31½ 32½ SrnsD2 [S]Citatn Inv H 78 SenstionlGuy,HllowdEnvoy,Rglbrto 8
6Jun82-8GG 1⅜Ⓣ:4831:3822:163fm 6¼ 117 2hd 11 3½ 3¾ SornsonD6 Rlng Grn H 84 DonRoberto,CptinGenerl,Reglbrto 11
31May82-8GG 1 1/16Ⓣ:4841:1221:441fm*4-5 123 32 32 31 31¾ SorensonD5 Nor Iva H 79 SensationalGuy,JunBrrer,Reglberto 5
17Mar82-8GG 1 1/16:472 1:114 1:432sy 2¼ 123 43 42 1hd 14½ SrnsnD4 [S]Sky Sl Iv H 86 Reglbrto,ExcutivCounsl,PlsntPowr 6
6Mar82-6GG 1 :463 1:103 1:352ft *1-2 117 69¾ 43½ 3½ 11¼ Sorenson D3 Aw17000 91 Reglberto,KobukCountry,Foyt'sAck 7
18Sep81-11Bmf 1 1/16:452 1:093 1:412ft *2-3 124 32½ 1hd 11½ 14 Baze R A1 Sn Mteo H 92 Regalberto, Chiaroscuro,Silveyville 6
Oct 29 SA 5f ft 1:00 h ●Oct 23 BM 1 ft 1:37 h ●Oct 16 BM 5f ft :584 h Oct 9 BM 3f ft :36 h

John Henry — B. g. 7, by Ole Bob Bowers—Once Double, by Double Jay
Br.—Golden Chance Farm Inc (Ky) — 1982 3 1 0 1 $356,300
Own.—Dotsam Stable — 126 — Tr.—McAnally Ronald — 1981 10 8 0 0 $1,798,030
Lifetime 66 30 12 7 $3,379,110 — Turf 37 21 8 4 $2,212,962

17Oct82-8SA 1¼Ⓣ:4711:3431:583fm*4-5 129 31½ 42 42¾ 41¾ ShomkrW6 C F Brk H 92 Mehmet, Craelius, It's the One 7
28Mar82-8SA 1½Ⓣ:4622:00 2:24 fm*1-2 126 33 33 43½ 34¾ ShoemkrW3 Sn Ls Ry 90 Perrault, Exploded, John Henry 5
7Mar82-8SA 1¼:45 1:342 1:59 ft *6-5 130 913 51¾ 2½ 2no Shoemaker W9 S A H 94 ‡Perrault, John Henry, It'stheOne 11
7Mar82—Placed first through disqualification
6Dec81-8Hol 1½Ⓣ:49 2:03 2:264fm*2-5 126 12 11 3½ 42 ShomkrW5 Hol Trf Cp 84 ProvidntiII,QuntoConqur,Goldiko 10
8Nov81-8SA 1½Ⓣ:4721:5932:232fm*2-5 126 1½ 1½ 2hd 1nk ShoemkrW4 Oak Tree 98 John Henry, Spence Bay, The Bart 7
10Oct81-8Bel 1½:48 2:021 2:282ft *3 126 42½ 21 11½ 1hd ShomkrW8 J C Gld Cp 78 John Henry, Peat Moss, Relaxing 11
30Aug81-6AP 1¼Ⓣ:5011:4222:073sf *1e126 86½ 56 31 1no ShmkrW12 Arl Million — John Henry, The Bart, MadamGay 12
11Jly81-8Bel 1½Ⓣ:4942:03 2:264fm*1-3 126 31½ 11 11½ 13½ ShmkrW3 Swd Dancer 90 John Henry,PassingZone,PeatMoss 5
14Jun81-8Hol 1¼:453 1:344 2:002ft *6-5 130 66¼ 65¾ 46½ 42¾ PcLJr7 Hol Gd Cup H 86 ‡Ctermn,ElevnStitchs,SuprMomnt 10
17May81-8Hol 1½Ⓣ:5112:04 2:274fm*2-5 130 2½ 2½ 1½ 1¾ Pincay LJr5 Hol Inv H 81 John Henry, Caterman,GalaxyLibra 7
Oct 26 SA 6f ft 1:141 b ●Oct 16 SA 3f ft :342 b Oct 10 SA Ⓣ 1⅛ fm 1:47 h Oct 5 SA 1⅛ ft 1:522 h

***Maipon** — Ch. h. 5, by Tantoul—Doninda, by Cardanil II
Br.—Haras Dadinco (Chile) — 1982 11 2 4 1 $128,900
Own.—Hirsch C L — 126 — Tr.—Stute Warren — 1981 5 1 2 0 $10,778
Lifetime 23 6 6 4 $173,854 — Turf 19 6 5 4 $171,680

22Oct82-8SA 1⅛Ⓣ:4611:10 1:461fm 3¾ 120 22 22½ 2½ 1¾ McHrgueDG6 Aw40000 96 Maipon,Ptti'sTriumph,RustyCnyon 7
10ct82-8SA a6½f Ⓣ:22 :4431:134fm 7¼ 122 44½ 32 42¼ 22½ McHrgueDG6 Aw40000 87 Shagbark, Maipon, J. D. Quill 8
26Aug82-8Dmr 1 1/16Ⓣ:4921:13 1:432fm 3½ 119 46 54 42¾ 44½ ShoemkerW1 Aw30000 87 Regalberto, Island Whirl, Monarch 6
15Aug82-8Dmr 1⅛Ⓣ:4841:1211:482fm 20 117 1½ 32 53 65¼ McHrguDG7 E Read H 91 Wickerr, Spence Bay, Perrault 7
6Aug82-8Dmr 1 1/16Ⓣ:4911:13 1:43 fm*8-5 118 41¾ 31½ 32 21¼ McHargue D G1 HcpO 93 Wild Surf, Maipon, Buen Chico 6
20Jun82-8Hol 1 1/16Ⓣ:4611:0941:401fm 58 115 53½ 53¼ 31½ 1no McHrguDG5 Inglwd H 98 Maipon, Spence Bay, Wickerr 11
12Jun82-5Hol 1⅛Ⓣ:48 1:1141:471fm 4¼ 115 45 42 2½ 2¾ Toro F1 Aw35000 93 Tell Again, Maipon, Le Duc de Bar 6
22May82-5Hol 1 1/16Ⓣ:4721:1111:404fm 15 115 53½ 53¼ 62¼ 42¼ Toro F2 Aw40000 93 CaptainNick,PirteLw,Ptti'sTriumph 8
7May82-8Hol 1 1/16:46 1:102 1:413ft 7 115 2½ 2hd 35½ 69¾ McHrgueDG4 Aw35000 77 Haughty But Nice, A Run, Baltanas 6
25Apr82-7Hol 1 1/16Ⓣ:4711:1031:404fm 4½ 115 31½ 42¼ 31½ 33¾ McHrgueDG5 Aw35000 91 Captain Nick, Bold East, Maipon 9
Oct 28 SA 5f ft :592 h Oct 19 SA 5f ft 1:013 h Oct 14 SA Ⓣ 1⅛ fm 1:563 h (d) ●Oct 8 SA 1 ft 1:383 h

The Evolution of the Odds

The tote board was as follows:

	#4 Lemhi Gold	Expected Return per Dollar Bet on Lemhi Gold	#6 John Henry	Expected Return per Dollar Bet on John Henry	Totals
With thirteen minutes to post time					
Odds	1—1		6—5		
Win pool	65,479		55,997		158,188
Place pool	31,689	Less than 1	11,471	1.42	61,500
Show pool	9,590	1.04	3,589	1.61	27,681
With six minutes to post time					
Odds	1—1		3—2		
Win pool	107,579		84,224		253,450
Place pool	38,062	Less than 1	17,086	1.30	87,180
Show pool	12,576	1.15	5,327	1.61	43,988
With two minutes to post time					
Odds	1—1		6—5		
Win pool	134,946		116,897		327,850
Place pool	41,809	Less than 1	22,037	1.29	103,162
Show pool	18,943	1.08	8,667	1.51	59,641
With one minute to post time					
Odds	1—1		6—5		
Win pool	155,771		134,642		374,383
Place pool	43,616	0.95	25,381	1.24	112,130
Show pool	24,618	1.03	10,917	1.45	69,772

Throughout the betting period, John Henry, horse number 6, remained an outstanding place and show bet with expected values way above the 1.14 cutoff for Dr. Z system bets that we suggested for top tracks in Chapter Five. There never was a possible bet on Lemhi Gold to place, since the expected value stayed under 1 throughout the betting period. The show betting indicated a possible bet, although not high enough to warrant a bet near the end of the betting period. The optimal betting amounts on John Henry for various wealth levels were* (see page 158)

*The expected returns given here were computed using equations (4.5) and (4.6). The betting amounts were calculated using the equations in Chapter Sixteen. You can estimate these values using the charts in Chapter 5.

Initial wealth	50	250	500	1,000	5,000	10,000
Place bet	3	17	33	73	374	739
Show bet	18	95	192	335	1,224	2,147
Total bet	21	112	225	408	1,598	2,886
Place profit	3.30	18.70	36.30	80.30	374.00	739.00
Show profit	16.20	85.50	153.60	268.00	979.20	1,502.90
Total profit	19.50	104.20	189.90	348.30	1,353.20	2,241.90

The tote board at post time was as follows:

	#2 Craelius	#4 Lemhi Gold	Expected Return per Dollar Bet on Lemhi Gold	#5 Regalberto
Odds	13—1	4—5		35—1
Win pool	24,785	183,551		9,082
Place	14,673	48,446	0.96	6,469
Show	9,040	29,009	1.04	6,205

	#6 John Henry	Expected Return per Dollar Bet on John Henry	Totals
Odds	7—5		
Win pool	149,879		425,976
Place	27,894	1.22	122,847
Show	14,007	1.34	79,645

The chart of the race was as follows:

Oak Tree Invitational

EIGHTH RACE
Santa Anita
OCTOBER 31, 1982

1 ½ MILES.(turf). (2.23) 14th Running THE OAK TREE. $300,000 Added. (Grade I). 3-year-olds and upward. By invitation, with no nomination or starting fees. The winner to receive $180,000, with $60,000 to second, $36,000 to third, $18,000 to fourth and $6,000 to fifth. Weight, 3-year-olds, 122 lbs. Older, 126 lbs. The Oak Tree Racing Association will invite a representative field of horses to compete. The field will be drawn by the closing time of entries. A trophy will be presented to the owner of the winner. Invitations Thursday, October 21.
Value of race $300,000, value to winner $180,000, second $60,000, third $36,000, fourth $18,000, fifth $6,000. Mutuel pool $628,468. Exacta Pool $477,157.

Last Raced	Horse	Eqt.	A.	Wt	PP	¼	½	1	1¼	Str	Fin	Jockey	Odds $1
17Oct82 ^{8}SA^{4}	John Henry		7	126	6	$4^{1\frac{1}{2}}$	4^{1}	4^{1}	2^{2}	$2^{2\frac{1}{2}}$	$1^{2\frac{1}{2}}$	Shoemaker W	1.40
17Oct82 ^{8}SA^{2}	Craelius	b	3	122	2	3^{1}	$3^{1\frac{1}{2}}$	1^{hd}	$1^{1\frac{1}{2}}$	$1^{\frac{1}{2}}$	$2^{1\frac{1}{2}}$	Sibille R	13.60
10Oct82 ^{8}BM^{8}	Regalberto		4	126	5	$2^{1\frac{1}{2}}$	$2^{2\frac{1}{2}}$	3^{hd}	$4^{2\frac{1}{2}}$	$3^{\frac{1}{2}}$	3^{2}	Toro F	38.80
17Oct82 ^{8}SA^{6}	Pelerin		5	126	1	$5^{\frac{1}{2}}$	7	7	$6^{\frac{1}{2}}$	6^{4}	$4^{1\frac{1}{4}}$	Pincay L Jr	8.10
9Oct82 ^{8}Bel^{1}	Lemhi Gold		4	126	4	$1^{\frac{1}{2}}$	1^{hd}	2^{hd}	3^{hd}	4^{3}	5^{4}	McCarron C J	.90
18Oct82 ^{5}Fra^{1}	Buchanette		3	119	3	7	5^{1}	$5^{4\frac{1}{2}}$	5^{3}	$5^{\frac{1}{2}}$	6^{10}	Lequeux A	55.60
22Oct82 ^{8}SA^{1}	Maipon		5	126	7	$6^{\frac{1}{2}}$	$6^{\frac{1}{2}}$	6^{hd}	7	7	7	Castaneda M	27.50

OFF AT 4:24 Start good, Won driving. Time, :24$\frac{2}{5}$, :47$\frac{2}{5}$, 1:10$\frac{3}{5}$, 1:35$\frac{1}{5}$, 1:59$\frac{3}{5}$, 2:24, Course firm.

$2 Mutuel Prices:

6–JOHN HENRY	4.80	4.20	3.80
2–CRAELIUS		6.20	4.80
5–REGALBERTO			6.00

$5 EXACTA 6–2 PAID $102.00.

B. g, by Ole Bob Bowers—Once Double, by Double Jay. Trainer McAnally Ronald. Bred by Golden Chance Farm Inc (Ky).

JOHN HENRY, taken in hand after the start, remained unhurried outside horses for seven furlongs, moved up to challenge outside of CRAELIUS at the far turn, wore down that one under strong handling in the final furlong and drew clear near the end. CRAELIUS, reserved in good position along the rail for a mile, moved suddenly inside of LEMHI GOLD to take the lead nearing the far turn, resisted gamely when challenged by JOHN HENRY but weakened in the closing yards. REGALBERTO forced the early pace outside of LEMHI GOLD, dropped back a bit on the final turn but rallied gamely outside the leaders through the stretch drive. PELERIN failed to seriously threaten. LEMHI GOLD darted to the lead at once, maintained a short advantage for a mile and gradually tired thereafter. BUCHANETTE brushed with PELERIN entering the front stretch the first time, raced within easy striking distance of the leaders for a mile, took up inside of LEMHI GOLD at the far turn and did not threaten in the drive. Lequeux, aboard BUCHANETTE, lodged a claim of foul against LEMHI GOLD but, after reviewing the videotapes, the stewards allowed the order of finish to stand.

Owners— 1, Dotsam Stable; 2, Keck Mrs H B; 3, Harris Walt; 4, Doherty & Snowden; 5, Jones Aaron U; 6, Nahas N; 7, Hirsch C L.

Trainers— 1, McAnally Ronald; 2, Whittingham Charles; 3, Hall Eldon; 4, Whittingham Charles; 5, Barrera Lazaro S; 6, Dupuis Jean-Pierre; 7, Stute Warren.

The bets on John Henry were extremely good ones. With a final expected value of 1.22 to place and 1.34 to show, you would expect a reasonably good payoff. However, with Lemhi Gold finishing out of the money, the payoff was outstanding.

The payoffs were computed as follows. For place, total profit to be shared by backers of John Henry and Craelius equals total place pool minus track take minus dollar bets returned to John Henry and Craelius backers

$$= 122{,}847 - \underbrace{0.15(\$122{,}847)}_{\substack{\text{15\% take in} \\ \text{California,} \\ \text{or \$18,427.05}}} - \$27{,}894 - \$14{,}673$$

$$= \$61{,}852.95.$$

$$\text{Share to John Henry's backers} = \frac{\$61{,}852.95}{2} = \$30{,}926.48.$$

$$\text{Payoff per dollar bet} = \underbrace{\$1}_{\text{Return of bet}} + \underbrace{\frac{\$30{,}926.48}{\$27{,}894}}_{\text{Profit}} = \$2.1087.$$

$$\text{Payoff per \$2 ticket} = 2(\$2.1087) \text{ less breakage} = \$4.20.$$

In this case breakage, or rounding down to the nearest 20¢ on a $2 ticket, amounted to 1.74¢, about 1% of the amount bet. The share to Craelius backers was also $30,926.48, but since there were fewer of them, the payoff was higher.

$$\text{Payoff per dollar bet} = \$1 + \frac{\$30{,}926.48}{\$14{,}673} = \$3.1077.$$

$$\text{Payoff per \$2 ticket} = 2(\$3.1077) \text{ less breakage} = \$6.20.$$

The breakage was 1.54¢, about 1% of the amount bet.

The payoffs to place were $4.20 on John Henry and $6.20 on Craelius, the latter reflecting the fact that more money was bet on John Henry. Throughout the betting period, John Henry was a system bet to place, with an expected value of over 1.20, which ended up at 1.22, so you would have expected, on average, to make a profit of 22¢ for each dollar wagered. Since it was certainly possible for John Henry to finish out of the money, to make a real profit you have to receive more when he is in the money. In this case, the actual profit was $2.20 per $2 ticket, or 110%. The payoff was this high on the 7—5 shot John Henry because the relative long shot Craelius, who went off at 13—1, came in second.

What If Lemhi Gold Had Been in the Money?

Clearly, if Lemhi Gold had come in second, the payoff on John Henry would have been lower. But how much less?

The total profit to be shared would have been

$$\underbrace{\$122{,}847}_{\text{Total place pool}} - \underbrace{\$18{,}427.05}_{\text{Track take}} - \underbrace{\$27{,}894}_{\text{Dollar bets on John Henry}} - \underbrace{\$48{,}446}_{\text{Dollar bets on Lemhi Gold}} = \$28{,}079.05,$$

which is considerably less than the \$61,852.95 with Craelius. John Henry's share would be \$28,079.95/2 = \$14,039.98.

The payoff per \$2 ticket on John Henry would have been

$$2\left(\frac{\$14{,}039.98}{\$27{,}894.00} + \$1\right) \text{less breakage} = \$3.00$$

and on Lemhi Gold,

$$2\left(\frac{\$14{,}039.98}{\$48{,}446} + \$1\right) \text{less breakage} = \$2.40.$$

The breakage on Lemhi Gold would have been 17.96¢, or about 9% of the amount bet, which, added to the 15%, would have made a startling 24% commission! The results show that the payoff to John Henry would still have been quite good, while Lemhi Gold would have paid only \$2.40.

Thus with the Dr. Z system bet on John Henry, the payoff would be good if the other favorite came in and outstanding if he did not. Over the long run, with many bets of this kind, on average you should make about the 10%–20% indicated for Dr. Z system bets in Chapter Nine. The key is to get good payoffs, when the horse actually comes in, that more than compensate for when he finishes out of the money.

The situation with show betting is much the same. Let us now go through the analysis both to be sure that the message is clear and to discover any important differences.

Total profit to be shared by backers of John Henry, Craelius, and Regalberto = total show pool minus track take minus dollar bets returned to John Henry, Craelius, and Regalberto backers

$$= \$79{,}645 - \underbrace{0.15(\$79{,}645)}_{\$11{,}946.75} - \$14{,}007 - \$9{,}040 - \$6{,}205$$

$$= \$38{,}446.25$$

Thus each of the three horses' backers would have received \$38,446.25/3 = \$12,815.42 profit.

The payoffs on John Henry per \$2 ticket were

$$2\left(\frac{\$12{,}815.42}{\$14{,}007} + \$1\right) \text{less breakage} = \$3.80;$$

on Craelius,

$$2\left(\frac{\$12{,}815.42}{\$9{,}040} + \$1\right) \text{less breakage} = \$4.80;$$

and on Regalberto,

$$2\left(\frac{\$12{,}815.42}{\$6{,}205} + \$1\right) \text{less breakage} = \$6.00.$$

Breakage amounted to 2.99¢ for John Henry, 3.53¢ for Craelius, and 13.1¢ for Regalberto on each $2 ticket.

Now how would these payoffs have been affected if Lemhi Gold had finished in the money? Let us suppose that John Henry, Lemhi Gold, and Craelius were in the money. As we know, the order of their finish does not matter. What counts is how much is bet on each of the horses finishing in the money.

The total profit to be shared would have been

$$\underbrace{\$79{,}645}_{\text{Total show pool}} - \underbrace{\$11{,}946.75}_{\text{Track take}} - \underbrace{\$14{,}007}_{\text{Dollar bets on John Henry}} - \underbrace{\$9{,}040}_{\text{Dollar bets on Craelius}} - \underbrace{\$29{,}009}_{\text{Dollar bets on Lemhi Gold}} = \$15{,}642.25.$$

Each horse's share would have been $15,642.25/3 = $5,214.08; thus the payoffs on John Henry per $2 ticket would have been

$$2\left(\frac{\$5{,}214.08}{\$14{,}007} + \$1\right) \text{less breakage} = \$2.60;$$

on Craelius,

$$2\left(\frac{\$5{,}214.08}{\$9{,}040} + \$1\right) \text{less breakage} = \$3.00;$$

and on Lemhi Gold,

$$2\left(\frac{\$5{,}214.08}{\$29{,}009} + \$1\right) \text{less breakage} = \$2.20.$$

Breakage would have amounted to 14.4¢ for John Henry, 15.4¢ for Craelius, and 15.9¢ for Lemhi Gold for each \$2 bet. Thus \$2.744 was rounded to \$2.60, \$3.154 to \$3.00, and \$2.359 to \$2.20. As you can see, breakage mounts up! It is a considerable additional cost. Adding it to the track take often makes the total track commission over 20% of the amount bet. It is an even higher percentage of the profits. In this case it would have been

$$\frac{15.4¢}{60¢ + 15.4¢}(100) = 20.4\%$$

just for breakage on John Henry. On Lemhi Gold it would have been

$$\frac{15.9¢}{20¢ + 15.9¢}(100) = 44.3\%.$$

Breakage is such an important aspect of betting that we discuss it more thoroughly, including its effect on Dr. Z system bets, in Chapter Nine. However it is clear that (1) breakage is more important for show betting than place betting, since the payoffs are generally lower; and (2) it is a very significant cost, especially when the payoffs are low and the exact payoff is just below the next breakage level—for example, a \$2.59 payoff becomes \$2.40 rather than \$2.60.

The exercise of assuming that Lemhi Gold was in the money taught us that (1) the payoff amounts on all the horses become much smaller when a favorite with a heavy amount bet to place or show on it finishes in the money; (2) the payoff on the Dr. Z system bet horse becomes lower but still can be reasonably good; and (3) the effect is usually greater on show bets than place bets, since less is generally bet to show than place, with the result that a large amount bet on the favorite has more of an impact on the payoffs. In conclusion, John Henry was a great bet to place and show. When the favorite finished out of the money, the payoffs were very high. Even if Lemhi Gold had come in the money, the payoffs to John Henry would have been quite reasonable considering he was a 7—5 shot.

CHAPTER 9

Results of Computer Studies Using the Dr. Z System over Long Periods

In this chapter we show you how the Dr. Z system performs over long periods. To do this we collected data for entire meetings at three different major tracks during different years. These include the 1978 summer meeting at Exhibition Park involving 9,037 horses, running in 1,065 races over 110 days; the 1973/74 winter meeting at Santa Anita involving 5,895 horses, running in 627 races over 75 days; and the 1981/82 winter meeting at Aqueduct involving 3,470 horses, running in 380 races over 43 days. In all three cases, use of the Dr. Z system resulted in substantial profits.

We also investigate three crucial issues: the importance of the track take, breakage, and the fact that you must make bets a minute or two before the race is run. The combined effect of the track take and breakage is very large indeed, which means you should be aware of how much these commissions are at your local track; they have a considerable effect on profits. The evidence shows that the last-minute betting can reduce the attractiveness of some Dr. Z system bets. In most such cases, however, the bets remain good ones. Bets placed two minutes before the horses run usually do lead to substantial profits. We also look at some other characteristics of Dr. Z system bets, such as How large are they? How often do you make them? What happens on non-fast-track days?

Exhibition Park: The 1978 Summer Season

Exhibition Park has one long racing season each year. It runs from early April through October. There are usually four racing cards per week, each of about ten races. The horses running at Exhibition Park are of good quality and the betting in this wealthy seaport city is quite high, averaging over $1 million per day. Much of this money is bet on such features as the daily double, quinella, exactor, sweep six, and triactor. The win, place, and show pools remain quite high as well.

The 1978 season ran for 110 days and involved 9,037 horses running in the 1,065 races. We collected data on the win, place, and show pools for every one of these horses in all these races. The track take was 18.1% (it is now 16.3%), and Exhibition Park has 5¢ breakage. We calculated the expected value per dollar bet for place and show for all 9,037 horses using equations similar to (4.3) and (4.4). Whenever the expected value was 1.20 or better, we would place a Dr. Z system bet. The amount of the bet was determined by equations similar to (5.5) and (5.6).* Using an initial wealth of $2,500, our wealth over the season, if we bet on every Dr. Z system bet, regardless of weather, grew to $7,698, yielding a profit of $5,198. The history of our betting fortune over the season appears in Figure 9.1. The average bettor starting with a $2,500 fortune would have lost it all by the 32nd day. Our fortune generally moved up along the typical jagged line that represents

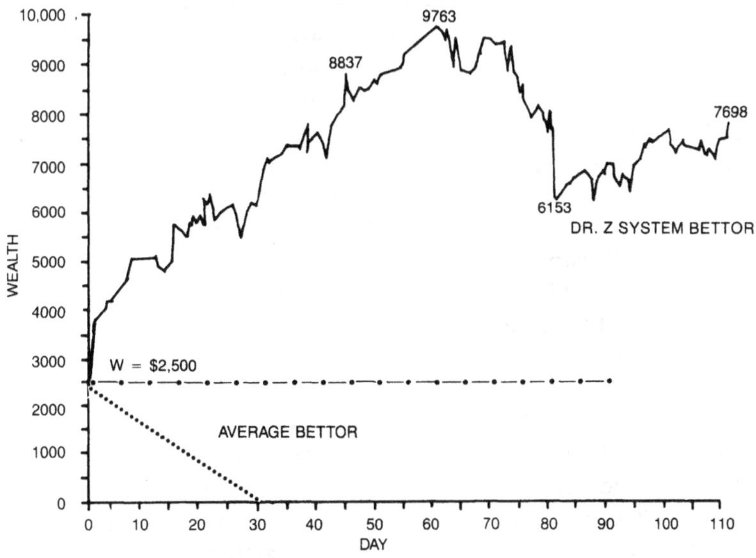

Figure 9.1 Betting-wealth-level history for Dr. Z system bets at the 1978 summer meeting at Exhibition Park using an expected-value cutoff of 1.20

*This study was done by Hausch, Ziemba, and Rubinstein (1981). Since that time we have developed even more exact equations to calculate both the expected returns and the amount to bet. These differences are minor, however, although the results from the new equations would most likely lead to slightly higher profits.

actual win and losses. It peaked once at $8,837 on the 44th day, then at $9,763 on the 62nd day. From about the 70th to the 80th day, there was a substantial losing streak.

The data in Figure 9.1 include every Dr. Z system bet regardless of track condition. As we discussed in Chapter Five, we recommend that you do not bet when the track is not fast. Of the eighty-seven days on which we placed Dr. Z system bets, using the conservative 1.20 expected-value cutoff,* the track was fast on fifty-seven days, and it was slow, muddy, heavy, wet, or sloppy on thirty days. The results reveal that on the fifty-seven fast-track days, we bet $32,501 and received $38,364, a profit of $5,863, or 18%. However, on the other thirty days we bet $17,501 and received $16,535, a loss of $645, or 3.7%. If we had eliminated these non-fast-track days, our profit for the year would have been $5,863 on our $2,500 investment.

Santa Anita: The 1973/74 Winter Meeting

Southern California has three major thoroughbred racetracks: Del Mar, where the "turf meets the surf" 25 miles north of San Diego; Hollywood Park, in Inglewood, situated near the Los Angeles International Airport and adjacent to the Forum, home of the Lakers and Kings; and Santa Anita in Arcadia, near the foot of the San Gabriel mountains and not far from the Rose Bowl in Pasadena. Thoroughbred racing is very active in southern California and the three tracks alternate seasons, resulting in year-round quality racing. Santa Anita has two seasons: The Oak Tree meeting usually runs from early October to early November, and the winter meeting typically begins the day after Christmas and runs until early April. Mark Rubinstein, with the aid of Michael Alhadeff of Longacres Racetrack, collected data on the win, place, and show mutuels for the 5,895 horses running in 627 races over seventy-five days in the 1973/74 winter meeting at Santa Anita.

The horses running at Santa Anita are of unusually high quality and include some of America's finest bloodstock. The betting pools are large, averaging over $5 million per day. The win, place, and show pools are very large. It takes a large bet to have much influence on the odds. The track take was 17.5% (it is now 15%), and Santa Anita has 10¢ breakage.

As with our Exhibition Park bets, we calculated the expected value per dollar bet using equations similar to (4.3) and (4.4). Because of the higher-quality horses and larger betting pools, we utilized a 1.16 expected-value cutoff for our Dr. Z system bets. Using an initial wealth of $2,500, our wealth over the season—if we bet on every Dr. Z system bet whose expected value

*Recall from Chapter Five that we now recommend 1.18 as the preferred expected-value cutoff for tracks like Exhibition Park.

to place or show was at least 1.16*—grew to $5,337, for a profit of $2,837. The history of our betting fortune over the season appears in Figure 9.2. The average bettor starting with $2,500 is bankrupt by the twenty-fourth day. The Dr. Z system bets at Santa Anita were large, which led to considerable swings in our betting fortune. We peaked out at $4,635 on the thirty-fifth day, then at $6,559 on the seventy-first day. Although there were several losing streaks, the overall trend was a substantial increase in wealth over time. The calculations of the optimal place and show bets were calculated using the equations in Chapter Sixteen.

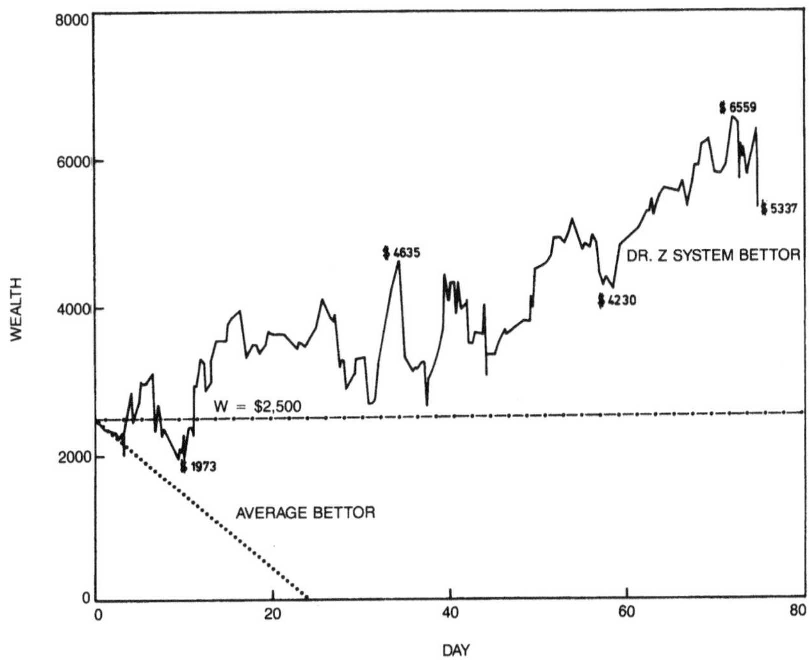

Figure 9.2 Betting-wealth-level history for Dr. Z system bets at the 1973/74 winter meeting at Santa Anita using an expected-value cutoff of 1.16

Aqueduct: The 1981/82 Winter Season

Aqueduct is one of the three major thoroughbred racing tracks in New York State. The others are Belmont and Saratoga. Between them and the Mead-

*Since it rarely rains in Arcadia, we did not worry about eliminating non-fast-track days, since there would be so few. We recommend, however, that you do not bet at Santa Anita on non-fast-track days. We now recommend an expected value cutoff of 1.14 for top quality tracks such as Santa Anita.

owlands in New Jersey, they provide top quality racing for the millions in the New York metropolitan area throughout the year. Aqueduct's racing season typically runs from mid-October to mid-May and Belmont's in the summer except for August, which is reserved for beautiful Saratoga near Albany.

Richard van Slyke collected the win, place, and show mutuels for us for the forty-three-day period December 27, 1981–March 27, 1982. During this period, 3,470 horses ran in 380 races. In New York the betting occurs off-track as well as at the racetrack. The off-track betting mutuels are then combined with the on-track values a few minutes before post time. Because the off-track bettors do not know the actual mutuel pools and because their bets amount to about half of the total pools and because this money enters the tote board of the track in one fell swoop, more Dr. Z system bets occur. The track take in New York was 15%. Aqueduct has 10¢ breakage. We calculated the expected value per dollar bet to place and show for all 3,470 horses using equations (4.5) and (4.6). Whenever the expected value per dollar bet was at least 1.14, we would make a Dr. Z system bet, whose amount was determined using equations in Chapter Sixteen. From an initial wealth of $2,500, our wealth over the season grew to $6,292, for a profit of $3,792. The history of our betting fortune over the season appears in Figure 9.3. The average bettor would have lost his fortune by the 148th

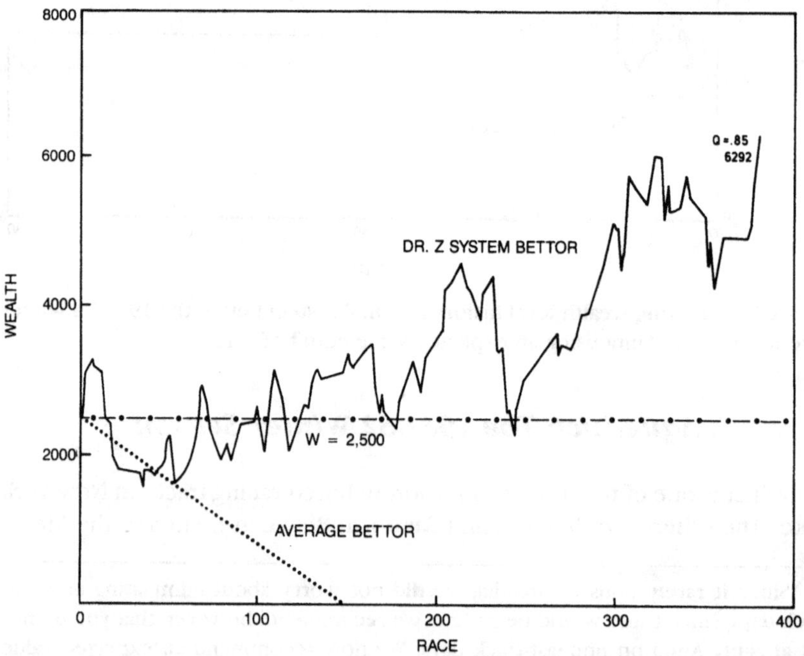

Figure 9.3 Betting-wealth-level history for Dr. Z system bets at the 1981/82 Aqueduct winter meeting using an expected-value cutoff of 1.14

race. As with the Exhibition Park and Santa Anita data, there is a jagged look to the line tracing our wealth level that reflects both individual wins and losses and winning and losing streaks.

How Important Is the Track Take?

The track take amounts to a commission of 14%–22% on every dollar wagered. It pays for purses, taxes, and expenses, and it also provides profits for the racetrack owners. An additional 1% or 2% makes a large difference in the payoffs and especially in the profits you make with a winning system. This effect is illustrated in Table 9.1, which provides payoff figures for track takes of 14% to 18%. On a bet that would return $9.83 without track take (and breakage), $1.38 is lost to a track that has a 14% track take. After that, about 10¢ is lost for each percentage increase in the track take. At 17%, that means 29¢. With a payoff of $6.51, 92¢, or nearly a dollar is lost—even with a low track take of 14%. Another $6\frac{1}{2}$¢ is lost for each percentage increase in the track take. For a 17% track take, that means another 19¢, or $1.11 in total. For a small payoff, such as $3.85, the percentage effect is the same, but the actual dollar costs are less. A 14% track take amounts to 54¢, and 17% to 65¢.

TABLE 9.1 *Effect on payoffs of 14%, 15%, 16%, 17%, and 18% track takes*

Payoff of a $2 Bet before Track Take ($)	Payoff after Track Take But before Breakage with Varying Track Takes ($)				
	14%	15%	16%	17%	18%
9.83	8.45	8.35	8.26	8.16	8.06
6.51	5.59	5.53	5.46	5.40	5.34
3.85	3.31	3.27	3.23	3.20	3.16

The effect on profits is even more dramatic. You lose not only because there are additional costs in each race, but also because your betting wealth is less, which means the actual bets you make are smaller. During the 1981/82 season, Aqueduct had a 15% track take. Dr. Z system bets yielded a final wealth of $6,292, for a profit of $3,792. Aqueduct recently increased the track take to 17%; prior to 1981/82 it was 14%. Figure 9.4 shows what the effect would have been on both our betting wealth and profits if this higher track take had been operative in 1981/82, and it also shows how much better we would have done with a 14% track take. With a 17% track take our final betting wealth would have fallen to $5,058. Our profit of $3,792 would have dropped by $1,234 to $2,558—nearly a third of the profits—

due to a 2% increase in the track take. With a track take of 14%, the final betting wealth would have grown to $7,090, for a profit of $4,590, or $798 more than with the 15% track take. As a rule of thumb, you may assume that each 1% increase in the track take eats up about a sixth of the profits. At a track take of 20% or more, there simply would not be many Dr. Z system bets, and total profits would likely be quite small.

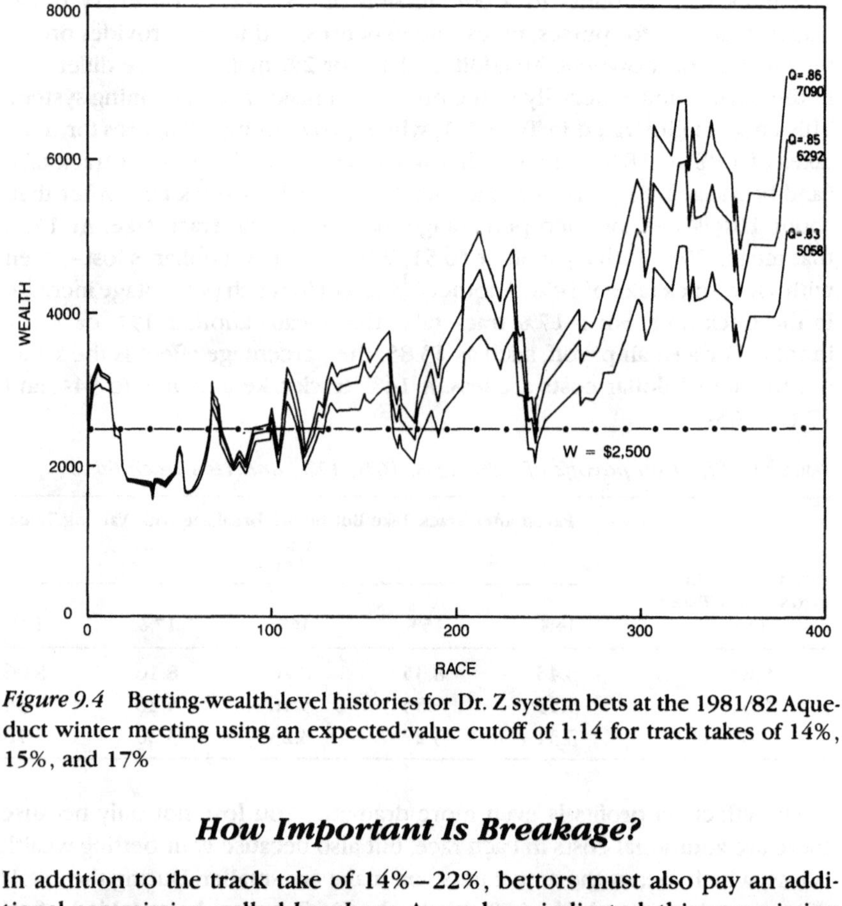

Figure 9.4 Betting-wealth-level histories for Dr. Z system bets at the 1981/82 Aqueduct winter meeting using an expected-value cutoff of 1.14 for track takes of 14%, 15%, and 17%

How Important Is Breakage?

In addition to the track take of 14%–22%, bettors must also pay an additional commission, called *breakage*. As we have indicated, this commission refers to the funds not returned to the betting public because the payoffs are rounded down to the nearest 10¢ or 20¢ on a $2 bet. For example, a payoff net of the track take of $6.39 would pay $6.30 or $6.20, respectively. Breakage occurs in the win, place, and show as well as in the exotic pools. We refer to rounding down to the nearest 10¢ on a $2 bet as 5¢ breakage, that is, 5¢ per dollar, and rounding down to the nearest 20¢ on a $2 bet as 10¢ breakage. Initially, most tracks utilized a 5¢ breakage. In recent years, however, more and more tracks have switched to 10¢ breakage. It amounts to a substantial additional commission and more profits for the track. Table 9.2 illustrates the difference between these two types of breakage and their effect on total payoff and total profits.

TABLE 9.2 *Effect of 5¢ and 10¢ breakage on payoff and profit*

Payoff on a $2 Bet after Track Take But before Breakage ($)	Payoff after 5¢ Breakage ($)	Payoff after 10¢ Breakage ($)	Percentage of Payoff Lost to 5¢ Breakage
10.35	10.30	10.20	0.48
8.57	8.50	8.40	0.82
6.39	5.30	6.20	1.41
4.61	4.60	4.60	0.22
3.87	3.80	3.80	1.81
2.95	2.90	2.80	1.69
2.68	2.60	2.60	2.99
2.39	2.30	2.20	3.91
2.26	2.20	2.20	2.65
2.08	2.10	2.10	−0.96

TABLE 9.2 (*Continued*)

Percentage of Payoff Lost to 10¢ Breakage	Percentage of Profit Lost to 5¢ Breakage	Percentage of Profit Lost to 10¢ Breakage
1.45	0.60	1.80
1.75	1.07	2.59
2.97	2.09	4.32
0.22	0.38	0.38
1.81	3.74	3.74
5.08	5.26	15.79
2.99	13.33	13.33
7.94	23.08	48.72
2.65	23.08	23.08
−0.96	−25.00	−25.00

As Table 9.2 shows, the 10¢ breakage is never less than 5¢ breakage and usually is considerably more. As a percentage of the payoff, breakage usually increases as the payoff becomes smaller, unless the payoff is close to the breakage round-off amount. An exception is the minus pool; in that case $2.10 must be paid even if the payoff before breakage is only $2.08. In

Kentucky, the minimum payoff is $2.20. Minus pools are discussed in Chapter Fifteen.

Our calculations indicate that, on average, bettors using the Dr. Z system lose about 1.79% of the total payoff on their bets to 5¢ breakage and 3.14% to 10¢ breakage. Adding these amounts to the track take gives the total commission. For example, at Churchill Downs in Louisville, Kentucky, the 15% track take becomes about 18% with their 10¢ breakage, and at Exhibition Park in Vancouver, British Columbia, the 16.3% track take also becomes about 18% with their 5¢ breakage. To determine the true commission at a given racetrack, you must take into account both the breakage and the track take. A table of track takes for various U.S. states and Canadian provinces appears in Appendix A.

The full extent of the effect of breakage is shown in what it does to profits. Using the 1978 Dr. Z system bets for Exhibition Park without breakage, an initial wealth of $2,500 would leave you with $8,319 at the end of the year. With 5¢ breakage you would have $7,521,* and with 10¢ breakage, $6,918. The effect of breakage throughout the 1978 season is shown in Figure 9.5. In addition to taking money away from total wealth, breakage has the additional effect of lowering the bet size, since a lower betting wealth means

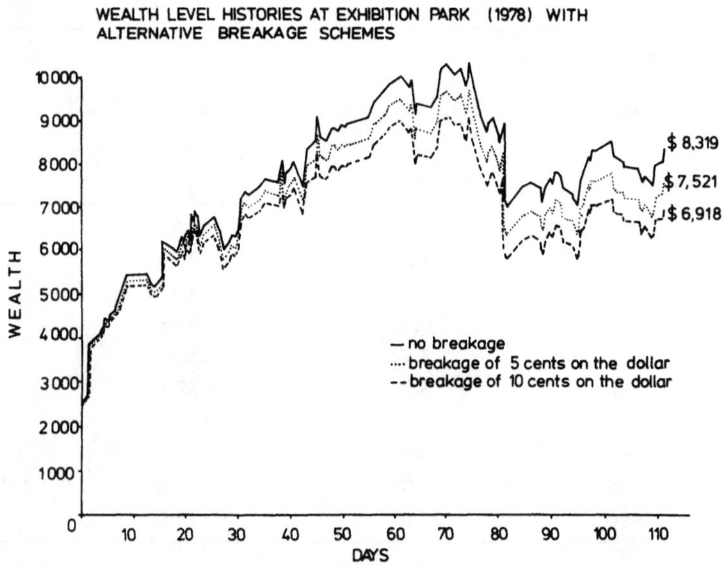

Figure 9.5 Wealth-level histories of Dr. Z system bets at Exhibition Park in 1978 with alternative breakage schemes

*This $7,521 final wealth is different from the $7,698 in Figure 9.1, because Figure 9.5 used a 1.18 expected-value cutoff and Figure 9.1 used a 1.20 expected-value cutoff.

smaller bets and lower future profits. These calculations indicate that 5¢ breakage averages 13.7% of profits, and 10¢ breakage averages 24.1% of profits on Dr. Z system bets.

To summarize, breakage, especially the very common 10¢ variety, is a very substantial cost. The costs are highest when you are making bets on short-odds horses. Unfortunately, this is an unavoidable aspect of the Dr. Z system.

The Two-Minute Problem: Bets at Exhibition Park in 1980

The computer studies described in this chapter for the races at Exhibition Park in 1978, Santa Anita in 1973/74, and Aqueduct in 1981/82 give convincing evidence of the validity of using the Dr. Z system over extended periods. These studies were based on the win, place, and show mutuel pools at the end of the betting period. In practice, it takes thirty seconds or so to determine your optimal bet and a minute or so actually to make the bet. Even with the charts in Chapter Five or with some appropriate way of determining the optimal bet size, you need to utilize the betting information one to two minutes before the end of the betting period.

You need to find out just when the betting stops at any particular racetrack you are attending. This may be exactly at the listed post time or possibly a few minutes later. The key is to watch where the horses are. When they get close to the starting gate, you know that the totalizator machines will be closed soon. An exception occurs when there is a late scratch or an incident among the horses. Then the betting can go on for several more minutes. In a recent race at Exhibition Park, the final one on the card, which features the heavily bet triactor, there were three late scratches. Management, wanting to make sure that their commission would not be lost, held up the race for over thirty minutes so that the refunded money could be rebet.

In the rest of this book, the betting described used the tote values as they stood one or two minutes before the end of the betting period, that is, when we made our actual bets. On occasion, a bet is a Dr. Z system bet with two minutes to go, but as a result of the late betting, it is no longer a good bet at post time. This difficulty does not seem to happen very often, and has not proved to be a serious problem for us.

To study the possible effects of the two-minute problem, we did a computer analysis of this phenomenon. On nine days during July and August 1980, during which ninety races were run, we went to Exhibition Park and recorded data at two minutes before post time and then at thirty-second intervals until the race was run. We utilized a betting fortune of $2,500 and

TABLE 9.3 *Results from summer 1980 Exhibition Park betting: twenty-two Dr. Z system bets during ninety races over ten days*

Date	Race	Regression Estimate of Expected Return per Dollar, Two Minutes before End of Betting	Regression Estimate of Expected Return per Dollar, at the End of Betting	Regression Estimate of Optimal Bet Two Minutes before End of Betting ($)	Finish	Net Return Based on Final Data with Consideration of Our Bets Affecting Odds	Final Wealth ($)
							$2,500
July 2	9	120	122	19,SHOW ON 4	5-6-7	− $19	2,481
"	10	120	123	72,SHOW ON 8	8-1-2	72	2,553
July 9	7	121	110	292,SHOW ON 1	2-7-1	131	2,684
"	10	135	122	248,PLACE ON 1	1-6-2	260	2,944
July 16	6	131	122	487,PLACE ON 9 }	9-8-6	536 } 682	3,626
		139	117	292,SHOW ON 9 }		146 }	
"	7	125	127	7,SHOW ON 1	5-2-8	−7	3,619
July 23	3	149	149	30,SHOW ON 2	2-10-7	92	3,711
"	4	139	134	573,SHOW ON 10	6-10-4	201	3,912
July 30	8	121	111	215,PLACE ON 4	4-1-5	129	4,041
"	9	123	125	591,SHOW ON 6	8-1-5	−591	3,450
Aug 6	6	128	112	39,SHOW ON 4	4-3-1	59	3,509
"	9	124	103	51,SHOW ON 2	4-1-3	−51	3,458
Aug 8	1	121	132	87,SHOW ON 1	1-10-4	139	3,597
"	3	127	111	635,SHOW ON 3	3-4-7	127	3,724
"	4	126	113	126,SHOW ON 2	2-7-1	82	3,806
Aug 11	8	121	112	94,SHOW ON 8	8-6-2	113	3,919
"	9	131	130	688,SHOW ON 5	5-3-4	138	4,057
Aug 13	3	128	106	33,SHOW ON 2	1-6-7	−33	4,024
"	6	131	122	205,SHOW ON 5	5-8-4	144	4,168
"	7	134	133	511,SHOW ON 6	8-5-9	−511	3,657
"	10	123	109	108,SHOW ON 5	3-5-1	59	3 716

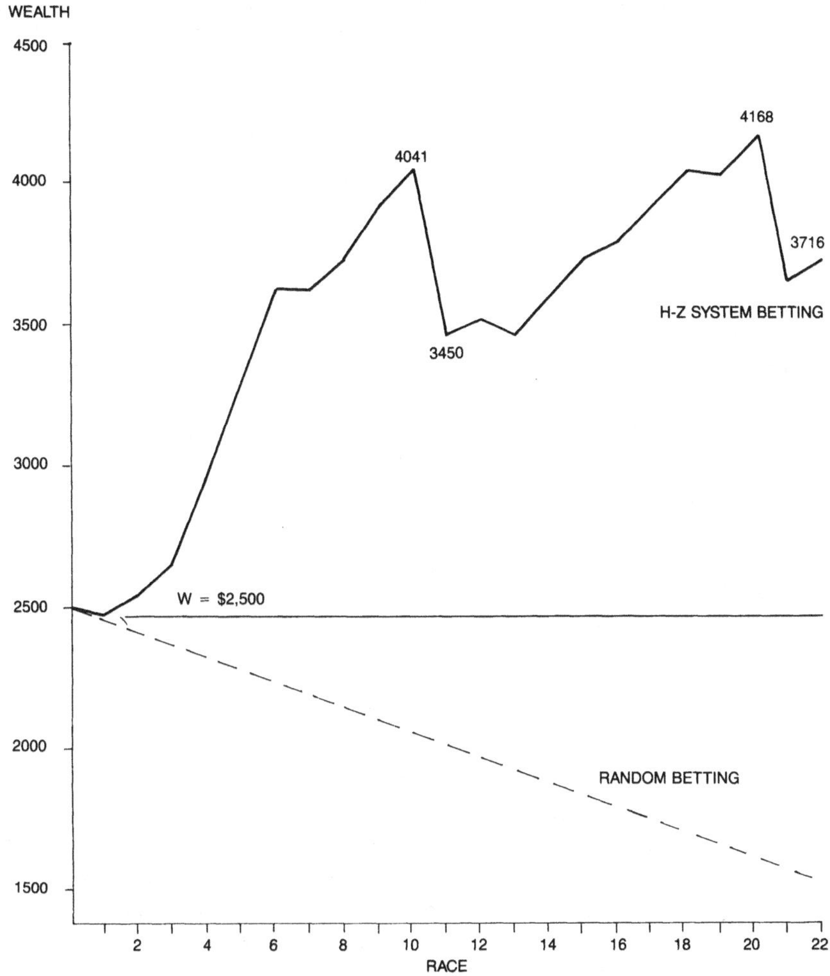

Figure 9.6 Results from summer 1980 Exhibition Park betting: twenty-two Dr. Z system bets during ninety races over ten days

made our Dr. Z system bets using the win, place, and show pools two minutes before the race. We then based our results on the final win, place, and show pools. There were twenty-two Dr. Z system bets at the two-minute mark, using our conservative cutoff of 1.20 expected value. The results appear in Table 9.3 and Figure 9.6.

Our $2,500 grew to $3,716, for a profit of $1,216, or 48.6%, on our initial investment. The twenty-two bets were for a total of $5,304, so our rate of return was 22.9%. Since we were choosing only bets with an expected value of at least 1.20 with two minutes to the race, we expected an average rate of return within this range. The expected value at post time was often less than it was with two minutes to go. However, it never fell to less than 1.00, breaking even, and only three times to less than 1.10. It increased five times in the twenty-two races. On most of the days, there were two Dr. Z system bets. One day had three, another four. Nineteen of the bets were to show and only three to place. In one race we bet to place and show on the same horse. *We won sixteen of the twenty-two bets, or* 72.7%. *Weighting by the amount bet, we won* 77.1% *of the time.* We made bets ranging from $7 to $688. Two of the largest bets were lost: $511 and $591. In one of these cases, the bet was on a horse that had not run recently; of course, we do not recommend such a bet in the Dr. Z system. Figure 9.6 shows that the general trend of our betting wealth was up, at the 22.9% average growth rate per dollar bet, but our fortune went up and down significantly when there were several big wins or a large loss. With random betting, a $2,500 betting fortune would have dwindled to about $1,500, so we were about $2,200 ahead of the typical bettor. In Appendix B we have calculated that the probability that we could have done this much better than the average bettor simply by chance is negligible: three chances in one hundred thousand. Similarly, the probability that we were ahead in our bets after the twenty-two Dr. Z system bets simply by chance is only 5.4%. The results, then, do seem to represent true exploitation of a market inefficiency.

Characteristics of Dr. Z System Bets

Table 9.5 summarizes results of the Dr. Z system bets made at Aqueduct in 1981/82, Santa Anita in 1973/74, Exhibition Park in 1978 and 1980, and at Churchill Downs on the 1981, 1982, and 1983 Kentucky Derby Days. The data sets for Aqueduct, Santa Anita, and 1978 Exhibition Park were collected after each racing season was completed. The 1980 Exhibition Park and Kentucky Derby Days data sets were collected race by race at the track. In all cases an initial betting wealth of $2,500 was assumed.

The expected-value cutoffs used were 1.10 on the Derby Days, reflecting the superior quality of horses; 1.14 at Aqueduct and Santa Anita, reflecting the overall high quality of horses; and 1.20 at Exhibition Park.* These cutoff values were determined from Table 5.1 and from other calculations we made. We worked on the basis of an expected 20% rate of return on the first dollar bet. Obviously this 20% would drop when we started betting larger amounts, since our bets would begin to affect the odds.

The most common Dr. Z system wager is a show bet on a favorite. Good show and place bets occur about 85% and 15% of the time, respectively. The percent of bets won is about 59%, while the percent of bets won when weighted by the size of the bet is 71%. This difference arises from the fact that the large bets are on favorites which often finish in-the-money, while

*We recommend 1.18 as the best cutoff at tracks like Exhibition Park.

small bets are placed on longer-odds horses, which finish in the money less often. At a track like Santa Anita with large betting pools, our bets did not affect the odds very much and our average bet was about 7% of our wealth. The average bet dropped to about 5% of our wealth at tracks with smaller betting pools. In the course of these thousands of races and hundreds of Dr. Z system bets, the total amount wagered was $162,477.

The size distribution of our bets at Exhibition Park in 1978 and Aqueduct in 1981/82 appears in Table 9.4.* The track take amounted to $26,035. Our profit was $18,505, an 11.4% rate of return on dollars wagered. Higher rates of return were achieved for races where we were actually at the track, when we were able to skip rainy days and avoid horses that did not meet the simple handicapping qualifications mentioned in Chapter Five. The lower rates of return, as expected, were at the tracks where we had no information other than the win, place, and show mutuel pools.

TABLE 9.4 ***Distribution of bet sizes with initial wealth of $2,500 at Exhibition Park in 1978 and Aqueduct in 1981/82***

	Exhibition Park 1978		Aqueduct 1981/82		Totals	
Bet Size ($)	Number of Bets	Percentage of Bets	Number of Bets	Percentage of Bets	Number of Bets	Percentage of Bets
0–50	22	13	18	14	40	13
51–100	37	21	10	8	47	16
101–200	35	20	20	16	55	19
201–400	39	22	42	34	81	27
401–600	16	9	12	10	28	9
601–1,000	19	11	17	14	37	12
1,001+	6	4	5	3	10	3
Totals	174	100	124	100	298	100

Finally, the average payout per $2 bet ranged from $2.97 to $3.33 at the various tracks, with an average value of $3.12. This value was actually a relatively high show return, considering that the Dr. Z system often picks heavy favorites.

*For comparison with higher betting wealths, see Table 9.6, which shows an initial betting wealth of $10,000 at Exhibition Park in 1978 and Santa Anita in 1973/74.

TABLE 9.5 *Summary statistics on Dr. Z system bets made at Aqueduct in 1981/82, Santa Anita in 1973/74; Exhibition Park in 1978 and 1980; and at the 1981, 1982, and 1983 Kentucky Derby days with an initial betting wealth of $2,500*

Track and Season	Number of Races	Track Take ($	Expected-Value Cutoff	Number of Dr. Z System Bets	Number of Bets Won	Percentage of Bets Won
Aqueduct 1981/82	380	15	1.14	124	68	55
Santa Anita 1973/74	627	15	1.14	192	114	59
Exhibition Park 1978	1,065	18.1	1.20	174	97	56
Exhibition Park 1980	90	17.1	1.20	22	16	73
Kentucky Derby Days[a] 1981, 1982, 1983	30	15	1.10	19	17	89
Totals and weighted averages	2,192	—	—	531	312	59

Track and Season	Percentage of Bets Won Weighted by Size of Bet	Total Money Wagered ($)	Track Take ($)	Total Profits ($)	Average Payout per $2 Bet ($)	Rate of Return on Bets Made ($)
Aqueduct 1981/82	65	42,686	6,403	3,792	3.33	8.9
Santa Anita 1973/74	69	51,631	7,745	2,837	3.16	5.5
Exhibition Park 1978	72	49,991	9,048	5,198	3.08	10.4
Exhibition Park 1980	77	5,403	924	1,216	3.18	22.5
Kentucky Derby Days[a] 1981, 1982, 1983	96	12,766	1,915	5,462	2.97	42.8
Totals and weighted averages	71	162,477	26,035	18,505	3.12	11.4

[a]The size of the Derby Day bets here are different from those in Chapters Ten, Eleven, and Twelve, because these optimal bets were calculated on the basis of an initial betting wealth of $2,500.

TABLE 9.6 ***Size distribution of Dr. Z system bets with $10,000 initial betting wealth at Santa Anita in 1973/74 and Exhibition Park in 1978***

	Santa Anita				Exhibition Park			
	Place		Show		Place		Show	
Size ($)	% of Bets	% of $Bet	% of Bets	% of $Bet	% of Bets	% of $Bet	% of Bets	% of $Bet
0–50	7.1	0.3	2.6	0.1	29.4	3.6	17.0	1.0
51–100	0	0	1.3	0.1	23.5	6.7	13.8	2.8
101–200	0	0	3.9	0.4	5.9	2.9	22.3	9.3
201–300	21.4	6.1	5.2	1.0	5.9	4.4	14.9	10.3
301–500	7.1	3.2	9.1	2.6	23.5	30.6	8.5	9.1
501–700	14.3	10.3	13.0	5.7	0	0	6.4	10.5
701–1,000	14.3	14.4	7.8	4.8	0	0	7.4	17.5
1,001 +	35.8	65.7	57.1	85.3	11.8	51.8	9.7	39.5
	n = 14	$11,932	n = 77	$104,142	n = 17	$4,954	n = 94[a]	$33,507

Total place bets — Total show bets

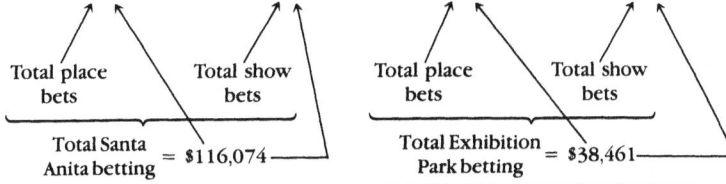

Total Santa Anita betting = $116,074

Total place bets — Total show bets

Total Exhibition Park betting = $38,461

[a]Two of these bets had $EX_s^l \geq 1.20$ and $s_l^* = 0$.

CHAPTER 10

The Kentucky Derby: The Most Exciting Two Minutes in Sports

The Pageantry

The Kentucky Derby is the world's most famous horse race. It is called the most exciting two minutes in sports. Since 1875, the country's best three-year-old thoroughbreds "run for the roses" at Churchill Downs in Louisville, Kentucky, on the first Saturday in May. The Derby is the first jewel of the triple crown of horse racing; it is followed by the Preakness and the Belmont Stakes. The winner receives a rose garland of some five hundred dark red roses, which, since 1932, has been hand sewn by Mrs. Kingsley Walker. The winning horse, jockey, trainer, and owner also share the substantial purse and racing immortality. The tradition and prestige of the race are immense, although hard to grasp fully without a visit to the Derby. The intensity of excitement builds as the prospects of the favorites for the Derby are evaluated in the early months of the year and culminates during Derby Week. For a full week, Louisville is alive with activities and enthusiasm much like those of football bowl games. There are parties, parades, Ohio river cruises, awards, and hundreds of reporters jostling amid the more than one hundred thousand visitors enjoying the atmosphere of mint juleps, fine weather, and lush surroundings, while they discuss the pros and cons of the various Derby hopefuls.

As many as twenty horses enter the $1\frac{1}{4}$-mile race. Many more would like to enter. The field is kept down by limiting it to the horses with the highest earnings from previous races. The legendary Secretariat in 1973 ran the fastest Derby and set the Churchill Downs track record of $1{:}59^2$ for $1\frac{1}{4}$ mile. In fact, Secretariat is the only horse ever to have won the Derby in less than two minutes. Northern Dancer ran the course in two minutes flat in 1964. Figure 10.1 shows the ten fastest Derby races and how the horses might have finished. Remember that one-fifth of a second roughly equals one length. The times of different races are not really comparable, since track conditions are so variable. However, the Secretariat time is still a most remarkable feat.*

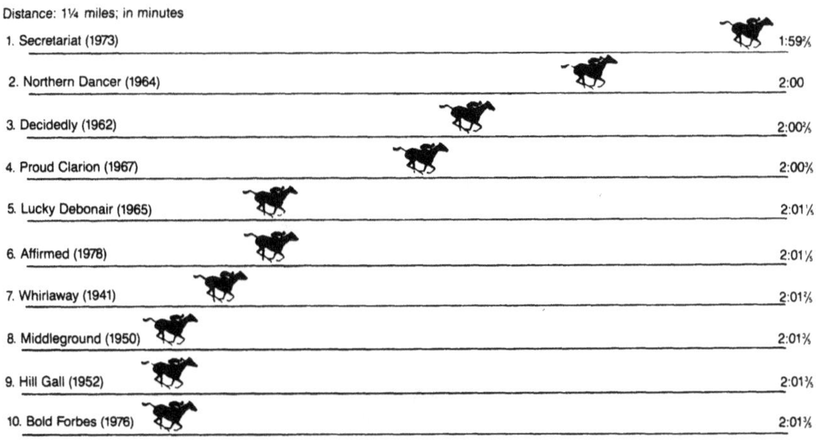

Figure 10.1 The ten fastest runnings of the Kentucky Derby

The usual starting gate with stalls for twelve horses is supplemented with a second gate to accommodate all twenty starters. This mass of horseflesh thundering in front of the stands for the first time is quite a sight. The huge number of starters means hard work for the jockeys, who try to angle for good positions. As a result of the difficulty of achieving good position and the intense competition, many prerace favorites falter badly in the Derby.

*Secretariat's performance in the Derby was the start of perhaps the greatest sequence of outstanding stakes victories in the history of thoroughbred racing. He broke the track record in the Preakness and Belmont Stakes, the latter by a full two seconds. He then broke two other track records. In all, he set records at five different distances at five different tracks. The chart of his Belmont Stakes victory appears in Chapter Four on page 44. Charts of the other races in 1973 appear in Quinn (1983; pp. 177 ff.).

Kentucky Derby Winners

YEAR	WINNER	OWNER
1875	Aristides, ch. c.	H. P. McGrath
1876	Vagrant, br. g.	William Astor
1877	Baden-Baden, ch. c.	Daniel Swigert
1878	Day Star, ch. c.	T. J. Nichols
1879	Lord Murphy, b. c.	Geo. W. Darden & Co.
1880	Fonso, ch. c.	J. S. Shawhan
1881	Hindoo, b. c.	Dwyer Bros.
1882	Apollo, ch. g.	Morris & Patton
1883	Leonatus, b. c.	Chinn & Morgan
1884	Buchanan, ch. c.	W. Cottrill
1885	Joe Cotton, ch. c.	J. T. Williams
1886	Ben Ali, br. c.	J. B. Haggin
1887	Montrose, b. c.	Labold Bros.
1888	Macbeth II, b. g.	Chicago Stable
1889	Spokane, ch. c.	Noah Armstrong
1890	Riley, b. c.	Edward Corrigan
1891	Kingman, b. c.	Jacobin Stable
1892	Azra, b. c.	Bashford Manor
1893	Lookout, ch. c.	Cushing & Orth
1894	Chant, b. c.	Leigh & Rose
1895	Halma, blk. c.	Byron McClelland
1896	Ben Brush, b. c.	M. F. Dwyer
1897	Typhoon II, ch. c	J. C. Cahn
1898	Plaudit, br. c.	J. E. Madden
1899	Manuel, b. c.	A. H. & D. H. Morris
1900	Lieut. Gibson, b. c.	Charles H. Smith
1901	His Eminence, b. c.	F. B. VanMeter
1902	Alan-a-Dale, ch. c	T. C. McDowell
1903	Judge Himes, b. c.	C. R. Ellison
1904	Elwood, b. c.	Mrs. C. E. Durnell
1905	Agile, b. c.	S. S. Brown
1906	Sir Huon, b. c.	George J. Long
1907	Pink Star, b. c.	J. Hal Woodford
1908	Stone Street, b. c.	C. E. Hamilton
1909	Wintergreen, b. c.	J. B. Respess
1910	Donau, b. c.	William Gerst
1911	Meridian, b. c.	R. F. Carman
1912	Worth, br. c.	H. C. Hallenbeck
1913	Donerail, b. c.	T. P. Hayes
1914	Old Rosebud, b. g.	H. C. Applegate
1915	Regret, ch. f.	H. P. Whitney
1916	George Smith, blk. c.	John Sanford
1917	*Omar Khayyam, ch. c.	Billings & Johnson
1918	Exterminator, ch. g.	W. S. Kilmer
1919	Sir Barton, ch. c.	J. K. L. Ross
1920	Paul Jones, br. g.	Ral Parr
1921	Behave Yourself, b. c.	E. R. Bradley
1922	Morvich, br. c.	B. Block
1923	Zev, br. c.	Rancocas Stable
1924	Balck Gold, blk. c.	Mrs. R. M. Hoots
1925	Flying Ebony, blk. c.	G. A. Cochran
1926	Bubbling Over, ch. c.	Idle Hour Stock Farm
1927	Whiskey, b. c.	H. P. Whitney
1928	Reigh Count, ch. c.	Mrs. J. D. Hertz
1929	Clyde Van Dusen, ch. g.	H. P. Gardner
1930	Gallant Fox, b. c.	Belair Stud
1931	Twenty Grand, b. c.	Greentree Stable
1932	Burgoo King, ch. c.	E. R. Bradley
1933	Brokers Tip, br. c.	E. R. Bradley
1934	Cavalcade, br. c.	Mrs. Dodge Sloane
1935	Omaha, ch. c.	Belair Stud
1936	Bold Venture, ch. c.	M. L. Schwartz
1937	War Admiral, br. c.	Glen Riddle Farm
1938	Lawrin, b. c.	Woolford Farm
1939	Johnstown, b. c.	Belair Stud
1940	Gallahadion, b. c.	Milky Way Farm
1941	Whirlaway, ch. c.	Calumet Farm
1942	Shut Out, ch. c.	Greentree Farm
1943	Count Fleet, br. c.	Mrs. John D. Hertz
1944	Pensive, ch. c.	Calumet Farm
1945	Hoop, Jr., b. c.	F. W. Hooper
1946	Assault, ch. c.	King Ranch
1947	Jet Pilot, ch. c.	Maine Chance Farm
1948	Citation, ch. c.	Calumet Farm
1949	Ponder, dk. b. c.	Calumet Farm
1950	Middleground, ch. c.	King Ranch
1951	Count Turf, b. c.	J. J. Amiel
1952	Hill Gail, b. c.	Calumet Farm
1953	Dark Star, br. c.	Cain Hoy Stable
1954	Determine, gr. c.	A. J. Crevolin
1955	Swaps, ch. c.	R. C. Ellsworth
1956	Needles, b. c.	D. & H. Stable
1957	Iron Liege, b. c.	Calumet Farm
1958	Tim Tam, dk. b. c.	Calumet Farm
1959	*Tomy Lee, b. c.	Fred Turner, Jr.
1960	Venetian Way, ch. c.	Sunny Blue Farm
1961	Carry Back, br. c.	Mrs. Katherine Price
1962	Decidedly, gr. c.	El Peco Ranch
1963	Chateaugay, ch. c.	Darby Dan Farm
1964	*Northern Dancer, b. c.	Windfields Farms
1965	Lucky Debonair, b. c.	Mrs. Ada L. Rice
1966	Kauai King, dk. b. c.	Michael J. Ford
1967	Proud Clarion, b. c.	Darby Dan Farm
1968	**Forward Pass	Calumet Farm
1969	Majestic Prince, ch. c.	Frank McMahon
1970	Dust Commander, ch. c.	Robert Lehmann
1971	Canonero II, b. c.	Edgar Calbett
1972	Riva Ridge, b. c.	Meadow Stable
1973	Secretariat, ch. c.	Meadow Stble
1974	Cannonade, b. c.	John M. Olin
1975	Foolish Pleasure, b. c.	John L. Greer
1976	Bold Forbes, dk. b. c.	E. R. Tizol
1977	Seattle Slew, dk. b. c.	Karen L. Taylor
1978	Affirmed, ch. c.	Harbor View Farm
1979	Spectacular Bid, gr. c.	Hawksworth Farm
1980	Genuine Risk, ch. f.	Mrs. Bertram Firestone
1981	Pleasant Colony, dk. b. c.	Buckland Farm
1982	Gato Del Sol, gr. c.	Hancock & Peters
1983	*Sunny's Halo, ch. c	D. J. Foster Stable

*Indicates an imported horse.
**Awarded first place after disqualification of winner.

Derby Details

1875—Aristides' time of 2:37¾ was the fastest mile and a half ever run in the United States by a three-year-old carrying 100 pounds.

1877—The official measurement of the track was one mile and seventeen inches around.

1886—Bookmakers did not operate at the track because of failure to reach a license agreement with the management.

1892 and 1905—The smallest fields that ever started a Derby went to the post — 3.

1895—On the west side of the track, the new grandstand with its twin spires was completed.

1896—The first Derby at a mile and a quarter distance was run.

1904—Mrs. Charles Elwood Durnell of Missouri was the first woman to own a Derby winner.

1913—Donerail, the longest-priced winner of a Derby, paid $184.90 straight.
Thomas P. Hayes of Lexington, Kentucky, was the last man to breed, own, and train a Derby winner.

1915—Regret won and is the first filly to have this distinction. She carried 112 pounds.

1917—Omar Khayyam (England) was the first imported horse to win a Derby. Tomy Lee (England) won in 1959. Northern Dancer (1964) was foaled in Canada but is not considered an imported horse.

1919—Sir Barton won the Derby and became the first of America's Triple Crown winners.

1920—This is the first year that all colts and geldings carried 126 pounds and fillies, 121.

1924—The Golden Jubilee Derby. The 14-karat gold cup, valued at $5,000, was presented for the first time. Lemon & Son, jewelers, designed the cup.

1926—Radio Station WHAS broadcast the Derby locally for the first time.

1929—1.19 inches of rain fell making this the wettest Derby on record.
Clyde Van Dusen was the first son of Man o' War to win a Derby. In 1937, War Admiral was the second and last.
The first coast-to-coast broadcast of the Derby was heard over the National Broadcasting Company network.

1932—Since the use of the starting gate, the field was at the post for the longest time — 15½ minutes.

1933—Colonel E. R. Bradley won his fourth Derby with Brokers Tip. The trainer of the four winners was H. J. "Dick" Thompson. The names of all Bradley horses began with a "B".

1941—Whirlaway ran the Derby distance in 2:01⅖, a record that stood for twenty-one years.

1945—Due to wartime restrictions, all racing was banned in the United States on January 3. With victory in Europe on VE Day, May 8, racing was resumed. The Derby was held on June 9. Only once before, April 29, 1901, was the Derby not run in May.

1948—Citation became the eighth Triple Crown winner and the first Thoroughbred to win over a million dollars in purses.

1952—The Derby was televised, live, nationally for the first time.
Eddie Arcaro won his fifth Derby on Hill Gail, a record for one jockey and since tied by Bill Hartack.
Ben A. Jones trained his sixth winner, also a record.

1964—Northern Dancer set a new track record for a mile and a quarter Derby — 2:00.

1969—Richard M. Nixon, 37th President, was first man in this office to attend the Derby.

1973—Secretariat, enroute to the first Triple Crown Championship in 25 years, wins the Derby in track record time of 1:59⅖.

1974—100th Derby won by Cannonade, who earned $274,000, the largest Derby purse in history.

1976—Bold Forbes defeats Honest Pleasure, the first horse ever to have more than $1 million bet on him to win.

1977—Seattle Slew, at $.50 to the dollar, wins the Derby and later a Triple Crown Championship.

1978—Steve Cauthen rides his first Derby and wins on Harbor View Farm's AFFIRMED, the second Triple Crown winner in as many years.

1979—Spectacular Bid, second horse to pass $2 million in winnings (March 1980), wins Derby at $.60 to the dollar.

1980—Genuine Risk, paying $28.60, became the first filly in 65 years to win the Derby.

DERBY FACTS

RECORD GROSS PURSE — $550,100 in 1982.

RECORD WINNER'S SHARE — $428,850 to Gato del Sol in 1982.

LARGEST FIELD — 23 in 1974.

SMALLEST FIELD — Three in 1892 and 1905.

FASTEST RUNNING — Secretariat, 1:59 2/5 in 1973.

SLOWEST RUNNING — Stone Street, 2:15 1/5 in 1908.

SHORTEST-PRICED WINNERS — Count Fleet (1943) and Citation (1948, coupled with Coaltown), $2.80.

LONGEST-PRICED WINNER — Donerail (1913), $184.90.

MOST WINS, OWNER — Calumet Farm with eight (Whirlaway, 1941; Pensive, 1944; Citation, 1948; Ponder, 1949; Hill Gail, 1952; Iron Leige, 1957; Tim Tam, 1958; Forward Pass, 1968).

MOST WINS, TRAINER — Ben A. Jones with six (Lawrin, 1938; Whirlaway, 1941; Pensive, 1944; Citation, 1948; Ponder, 1949; Hill Gail, 1952).

MOST WINS, JOCKEY — Five apiece by Eddie Arcaro (Lawrin, 1938; Whirlaway, 1941; Hoop Jr., 1945; Citation, 1948; Hill Gail, 1952) and Bill Hartack (Iron Leige, 1957; Venetian Way, 1960; Decidedly, 1962; Northern Dancer, 1964; Majestic Prince, 1969).

FOREIGN-BRED WINNERS — English-bred Omar Khayyam (1917) and Tomy Lee (1959), Canadian-bred Northern Dancer (1964) and Sunny's Halo (1983).

WINNERS — 100 colts, seven geldings, two fillies (Regret, 1915, and Genuine Risk, 1980).

The Kentucky Derby Trophy

The gold cup presented to the winner of the Kentucky Derby was first designed for Churchill Downs president Matt Winn to commemorate the 50th anniversary of the race in 1924. Designed and produced by Lemon & Son, a prominent Louisville jeweller, the trophy has been given to every Derby winner's owner ever since.

The trophy is manufactured in New England from Lemon & Sons molds. The cup is 14k gold on a marble base. It is housed in a silk-lined mahogany case especially built to display the trophy.

To commemorate the 100th Kentucky Derby in 1974, a special version of the Derby cup was created. The horseshoe on the front face of the cup was studded with diamonds and emeralds, bringing the trophy's value to over $16,000. Today with rising gold prices, the trophy without jewels is valued at nearly $45,000.

At the Derby, the trophy, along with smaller silver replicas for the winning jockey and trainer, stands on the infield presentation stand above the winners circle. At the conclusion of the race the trophies are presented by the Governor of Kentucky and Churchill Downs president Lynn Stone.

The cups are left in Louisville for engraving and then are presented permanently to the winning owner, trainer and jockey. Prior to 1924, other types of trophies were given at the Kentucky Derby, generally pieces of antique silver. Today the Kentucky Derby trophy has become a familiar symbol of the greatest two minutes in sports.

For many of them, their careers never regain their prerace promise.

Despite this hazardous aspect, owners, trainers, and jockeys are willing year after year to try their best to have a Derby winner. In addition to the prestige and the nearly half-million-dollar purse, the owner can expect to see the value of his Derby-winning horse increasing by millions. Inflation and rising expectations have pushed the value of the best bloodstock to astronomical heights. Although the breeding performance of a stallion may be influenced significantly by his racing performance, his price reacts dramatically to this record, often quite out of proportion to its true importance.

Secretariat was syndicated in 1972 as a two-year-old for what was then a record $6.08 million. The performances of this Triple Crown winner's sons and daughters have not yet measured up to their sire's brillance. The average earnings of those of his offspring actually racing have been only $25,485. Still, Secretariat's stud fee is a reputed $80,000 for each of the approximately fifty-three mares he services each year. Half of this fee is paid in advance and half is paid when a live foal is delivered. Since he produced forty-seven live foals in 1982, three of which are the customary fee to Claiborne Farms in Paris, Kentucky, where he lives and breeds, Secretariat's annual gross income is about $80,000 times 44, or about $3.5 million. Although expenses such as insurance, a whopping 4%–5% or more of his value each year, are high and taxes and depreciation complicated, it is clear that the return is impressive. The stud fee is kept up by the bidding for the yearlings as they are sold at auction. Secretariat's yearlings averaged $240,654 for his first five crops, although the price dropped to $175,389 in 1982. Still, these prices may well justify the fee, especially if there is a glimmer of a hope of producing a new Secretariat.*

The Spectacle

Our first visit to Kentucky for the Derby was in 1981 for the 107th running of this classic race. The city of Louisville was one massive jam of cars and

*The 1982 horse of the year, Conquistador Cielo, was syndicated for $36.4 million and commands a reputed $150,000 stud fee. The famous thoroughbred breeding farms, such as Claumet, Claiborne, Elmendorf, Gainesway, Spendthrift, Tom Gentry, and others, are located in the Lexington, Kentucky, area, a scant two hours' drive away from Churchill Downs. Except for Calumet, these farms are generally open to the public by appointment. A good information guide is *The Complete Guide to Kentucky Horse Country,* Classic Publishers, Prospect, Kentucky 40059. A good guide for information on all aspects of the 108 runnings of the Derby up to 1982 is *The Kentucky Derby: Churchill Downs* 1875–1983, available at no cost from the Kentucky Thoroughbred Owners and Breeders Association, Box 4158, Lexington, Kentucky 40544.

people. All the hotels within 70 miles were full, even at two to five times their normal rates. Churchill Downs begins to fill up early in the morning, and racing begins at 11:30. About 46,000 people have the cherished reserved seats. Such seats are difficult to come by for newcomers, since most seats are reserved from year to year. The rest of the fans are allowed to roam the grounds and congregate in the field. They come by the thousands from all over the United States and Canada. Here are the Kentucky Derby statistics for 1983. They give you an idea of the current scope of the spectacle.

DETAILED BETS ON THE DERBY

	Win	Place	Show	Total
Slew O' Gold	$ 237,766	$100,751	$79,622	$418,139
Play Fellow	221,075	95,093	72,065	388,233
Balboa Native, Total ... Departure, Marfa (entry)	755,833	293,365	250,790	1,299,988
Chumming, Caveat (entry)	341,888	153,585	119,569	615,042
Desert Wine	156,182	73,181	49,583	278,946
Country Pine	54,466	20,255	20,543	95,264
Freezing Rain, Highland Park (entry)	107,732	46,352	51,069	205,153
Sunny's Halo	745,524	262,382	179,758	1,187,664
Current Hope	136,137	56,017	52,330	244,484
Parfaitement	62,467	26,526	28,376	117,369
Pax In Bello	103,898	47,250	37,251	188,399
Law Talk, Explosive .... Wagon, My Mac, Paris . Prince, Luv A Libra .... (field)	220,701	118,561	169,034	508,296
Totals	$ 3,143,669	$1,293,318	$1,109,990	$5,546,977

DETAILED BETS ON ALL RACES DERBY DAY

	Win	Place	Show	Total
First Race	$ 147,291	$69,932	$62,113	$279,336
Second Race	213,562	117,077	104,080	434,719
Third Race	314,811	164,875	141,625	621,311
Fourth Race	403,105	206,773	180,904	790,782
Fifth Race	447,119	235,323	195,902	878,344
Sixth Race	482,830	234,357	191,848	909,035
Seventh Race	520,042	274,738	240,612	1,035,392
Eighth Race (Derby)	3,143,669	1,293,318	1,109,990	5,546,977
Ninth Race	328,700	140,126	94,398	563,224
Tenth Race	332,499	116,186	74,033	522,718
Totals	$ 6,333,628	$2,852,705	$2,395,505	$11,581,838
Daily Double				269,689
Grand Total				$11,851,527

DERBY DAY STATISTICS 1983

Derby souvenir glasses sold — 100,000
Mint juleps sold — 80,000
Bourbon for juleps — 8,000 quarts
Ice for juleps — 60 tons
Mint for juleps — 150 bushels
Soft drinks sold — 4,000 gallons
Shrimp sold in clubhouse — 1,000 pounds
Price for a platter of shrimp on Millionaires' Row — $80
Hot dogs sold — 7 miles (73,920 dogs at 6 inches each)
Price for a hot dog — $1.50
Beer sold — 1,500 16-gallon kegs (two-thirds in the infield)
Total commodes and urinals — 890:
In the grandstand — 230
In the clubhouse — 300
On Millionaires' Row — 60
In the infield — 250
Portable units — 50 (half in the infield)
Trash cans — 500
Trash — 21.6 truckloads (975 cubic yards)
Post-Derby clean-up workers — 300
Tulip blossoms — 14,000
Daily Racing Forms sold — 20,000
Spires — 1 pair
Men wearing hats with twin spires — 1
Betting windows — 1,000
Betting windows for wagers of at least $50 — 50
Average total betting per person for Derby Day — $41.25
Average winnings per person — $6.19
Anti-gambling evangelists outside the Downs — 2
Length of ABC-TV broadcast — 90 minutes
ABC-TV cameras covering the race — 24
Passes for "working" press — 1,625
Band members playing "My Old Kentucky Home" — 130
Time to play "My Old Kentucky Home" — 2:30
Millionaires on Millionaires' Row — 2,336
Total Downs seating — 45,094
Former presidents, Republican — 1
Former presidents, Democrat — 1
Vice presidents — 1
Democratic governors from out of state — 6
Democratic governors from Kentucky — 1
Republican governors — 0
Members of Congress — 6
Famous sports figures (not linked to horse racing) — 7
Members of royalty — 2
Actors — 11
Ex-Yippies — 1

On May 2, 1981, despite rather cool weather in the 50s, 144,000 were in attendance. It was a great event for us. But could we apply the Dr. Z system? We knew the pools would be astronomical, so last-minute betting would not affect the odds much. But could we get near the windows to place a bet just before each race was run? We were quite pleased and surprised to find that despite the huge crowd, conditions were amazingly good for the Dr. Z system. There were the usual infield tote boards, which people from the stands use to follow the betting activities. There also is a convenient tote board in the back of the grandstand. It is near the paddock area where the horses appear with their jockeys, trainers, and owners to discuss last-minute strategy prior to each race. Opposite the tote board and paddock is a small row of ticket windows. Since this area is far away from the track, it clears out prior to each race when the patrons scramble to get a good view of the race on nearby closed-circuit TV sets. With such a huge crowd the area did not completely clear out, but we had the enviable opportunity to stand in short, two- to five-deep lines and watch the tote board. Thus we could easily make bets well within one minute of post time, and we were routinely making them with fifteen to thirty seconds to go.

Churchill Downs

Sweep's Graded Handicap

FIRST RACE–5 Furlongs. **11:30 EDT**

2-Year-Olds, Colts and Geldings. Maiden Special weights. Purse $8,400.

P.P.	Horse	Jockey	Wgt	Odds
1	Good n' Dusty	No Rider	122	
3	Big Sandy Magnet	Gonzlaez R Jr	122	
8	Don's First Bid	Tauzin L	122	
2	Rash Investment	Sayler B	122	
4	Richwood Lad	Breen R	122	
5	The Great Upheave	Bullard B A	[5]117	
6	Big J B	Wirth B	[7]115	
7	Bronze N' Bold	Romero R P	122	
9	Shilling	Melancon L	122	
10	The Big E.	Espinoza J C	122	
11	Sunset Mark	Sayler B	122	

COUPLED-Rash Investment and Sunset Mark; Big Sandy Magnet and The Great Upheave; Richwood Lad and Shilling.

SECOND RACE–6 Furlongs. **12:15 EDT**

3-Year-Olds. Claiming ($15,000 to $13,000). Purse $8,900.

1	English Squire	No Rider	117	1-1
7	Bloomer Ridge	Tauzin L	113	4-1
4	Good Grip	Sipus E J	113	6-1
5	Pleasure Man	Romero R P	117	8-1
8	Tru Touch	McKnight J	117	8-1
2	Grandpa's Jamie	Bullard B A	[5]108	15-1
9	Lid	Morgan M R	113	15-1
3	Captain J. J.	Ramos A	113	30-1
6	Twibil	Nicolo P	117	30-1

COUPLED-Grandpa's Jamie and Lid.

THIRD RACE–6 Furlongs. **1:00 EDT**

4-Year-Olds and Up. Claiming ($10,000 to $9,000). Purse $7,800.

1	Lavalier	Delahoussaye E	118	3-1
3	Jeffervescent	Lively J	117	4-1
9	Cosmic Jove	No Rider	117	6-1
13	Bridgets Boy	Foster D E	117	5-1
6	Navajo Warrior	Bullard B A	[5]112	8-1
12	Revised	Whited D E	117	8-1
14	Play Havoc	Breen R	117	8-1
5	Barrister Sib	No Rider	117	10-1
8	Seven Diplomats	Wirth K	117	15-1
10	Big Hock	Day P	117	15-1
11	Jimminey Crockett	Melancon L	117	15-1
4	Master Smart	No Rider	117	20-1
2	Rapid Trace	Beech J Jr	113	30-1
7	Another Ali	Burns C W	117	30-1
15	Breezy Jester	Whited D E	117	8-1

COUPLED-Revised and Breezy Jester.

FOURTH RACE–$1\frac{1}{16}$ Miles. **1:50 EDT**

4-Year-Olds and Up. Claiming ($18,000 to $16,000). Purse $10,500.

9	Bag of Fish	Romero R P	117	4-1
12	Bordeaux Native	Sipus E J	113	5-1
11	Most Decidedly	Ledezma C	117	6-1
4	Mister Guy	No Rider	117	6-1
1	Easy Diggin	Melancon L	117	8-1
3	Bright Desi	Whited D E	117	10-1
6	Marileo	Espinoza J C	117	10-1
8	Snow Seed	Whited D E	117	10-1
10	Torsions Lad	Snyder L	113	10-1
2	Judy's Joker	No Rider	113	15-1
5	Peremptory	Cordero A Jr	110	20-1
7	Mark Him Great	Warner T	117	30-1

COUPLED-Bright Desi and Snow Seed.

FIFTH RACE–6 Furlongs. **2:40 EDT**

3 & 4-Year-Olds. Allowance. Purse $9,900.

1	Illhandleit	Romero R P	110	3-1
2	Ixtapan	Melancon L	110	4-1
4	Manny T.	Whited D E	113	4-1
7	Super Ridge	Delahoussaye E	120	5-1
6	Greek Minstrel	No Rider	113	8-1
5	A Toast to Harry	Wirth K B	110	10-1
3	Shot N' Missed	Foster D E	120	12-1
9	Big Bragger	No Rider	110	20-1
8	Lagnaf	Bowlds M A	110	30-1

SIXTH RACE–5 Furlongs. **3:30 EDT**

81st Running DEBUTANTE STAKES ALLOWANCE. 2-Year-Olds, Fillies. . Purse $25,000 Added.

3	Cypress Bay	Dellie D	119	5-2
4	Mystical Mood	Velasquez J C	119	3-1
10	Miss Preakness	Espinoza J C	119	5-1
1	Shoo Fly Shecky	Romero R P	114	6-1
9	Priceless Hero	McKnight J	119	8-1
12	Top Canary	Cordero A Jr	119	8-1
11	Pure Platinum	Day P	119	15-1
2	Ali's Oolah	Sayler B	114	20-1
5	Trunk Line	Martinez L J	114	15-1
6	Amazing Love	No Rider	114	6-1
7	Betty Money	Sayler B	114	20-1
8	Kirby	Melancon L	114	20-1

COUPLED-Shoo Fly Shecky and Amazing Love; Ali's Oolah and Betty Money; Trunk Line and Pure Platinum.

SEVENTH RACE–$1\frac{1}{16}$ Miles. **4:20 EDT**

3-Year-Olds. Allowance. Purse $50,000.

4	Mythical Ruler	Wirth K B	122	4-5
2	Master Tommy	Lively J	117	2-1
5	What It Is	Espinoza J C	119	10-1
3	Marion Frances	Breen R	113	12-1
7	Cornish Music	No Rider	113	12-1
6	Poona's Stage	No Rider	113	15-1
1	Fast Earl	No Rider	113	20-1

EIGHTH RACE–1¼ Miles. **5:38 EDT**

107th Running KENTUCKY DERBY SCALE WEIGHT (Grade I). 3-Year-Olds. . Purse $200,000 Added.

5	Proud Appeal	Fell J	126	2-1
7	Pleasant Colony	Velasquez J	126	4-1
16	Cure the Blues	Shoemaker W	126	4-1
19	Tap Shoes	Hernandez R	126	6-1
15	Bold Ego	Lively J	126	8-1
1	Splendid Spruce	McHargue D M	126	15-1
11	Woodchopper	Delahoussaye E	126	20-1
13	Classic Go Go	Black A S	126	12-1
2	Golden Derby	Espinoza J C	126	2-1
12	Well Decorated	MacBeth D	126	30-1
4	Double Sonic	Thornburg B	126	12-1
9	Noble Nashua	Asmussen C B	126	30-1
10	Hoedown's Day	Chapman T M	126	12-1
3	Partez	Hawley S	126	12-1
17	Beau Rit	Rubbicco P	126	12-1
18	Television Studio	Whited D E	126	12-1
8	Pass the Tab	Pincay L Jr	126	30-1
6	Habano	Feliciano B R	126	12-1
14	Top Avenger	Snyder L	126	50-1
20	Wayward Lass	Asmussen C B	121	30-1

COUPLED-Golden Derby and Proud Appeal; Noble Nashua and Wayward Lass.

NINTH RACE–6 Furlongs. **6:50 EDT**

4-Year-Olds and Up. Allowance. Purse $13,500.

4	Rossi Gold	Day P	119	8-5
6	Samoyed	Shoemaker W	119	3-1
5	Conge	Romero R P	122	4-1
3	Sun Czar	Whited D E	117	8-1
2	Mountain Native	Melancon L	115	8-1
1	Iron Pegasus	No Rider	119	15-1
7	Phillip J. C.	Marino A G	115	15-1
8	Straight and Smart	White R D	[7]112	20-1

TENTH RACE–$1\frac{1}{16}$ Miles. **7:35 EDT**

3 & 4-Year-Olds. Allowance. Purse $10,500.

12	Lothian	Hernandez R	120	2-1
5	Sorroto	No Rider	120	4-1
6	Hard Silver	Pincay L Jr	123	6-1
9	Tan U Tell	No Rider	110	8-1
2	Wolfgang Grr	Martinez L J	110	10-1
4	D. J. Road	Delahoussaye E	113	10-1
3	Mr. Bobeva	Delahoussaye E	110	10-1
8	Goat Burchett	Feliciano B R	120	15-1
11	Clearly Proud	Melancon L	110	15-1
1	Crimson Spruce	Day P	110	20-1
7	Salad King	Sayler B	110	20-1
10	Right J. G.	Whited D E	110	20-1

COUPLED-Mr. Bobeva and D. J. Road.

Jockey Standings

Jockey	Starts	1st	2nd	3d
Pincay, L. Jr.	503	119	105	61
Gall, D.	540	106	93	93
Sibille, R.	515	105	82	70
Baze, R. A.	511	99	93	79
Delahoussaye, E.	506	90	84	74
Pettinger, D. R.	485	89	72	67
Migliore, R.	517	88	79	57
Vigliotti, M. J.	487	87	75	60
Fell, J.	451	85	67	59
Cooksey, P. J.	506	84	70	53

(January 1 through April 28, inclusive.)

Racing Form **Experts' Selections**

Consensus Points: 5 for 1st (today's best 7), 2 for 2nd, 1 for 3rd. Today's Best in Bold Type.

Trackman, Graham Ross — **CHURCHILL DOWNS** — Selections Made for Fast Track

	TRACKMAN	HANDICAP	ANALYST	HERMIS	SWEEP	CONSENSUS	
1	BIG SANDY MAGNET GOOD N' DUSTY BRONZE N' BOLD	GOOD N' DUSTY BRONZE N' BOLD RASH INVESTMENT	GOOD N' DUSTY BRONZE N' BOLD THE BIG E.	GOOD N' DUSTY BIG SANDY MAGNET DON'S FIRST BID	GOOD N' DUSTY BIG SANDY MAGNET DON'S FIRST BID	GOOD N' DUSTY BIG SANDY MAGNET BRONZE N' BOLD	22 9 5
2	TRU TOUCH BLOOMER RIDGE LID	ENGLISH SQUIRE GOOD GRIP TRU TOUCH	ENGLISH SQUIRE TRU TOUCH PLEASURE MAN	**ENGLISH SQUIRE** TRU TOUCH GOOD GRIP	ENGLISH SQUIRE BLOOMER RIDGE GOOD GRIP	ENGLISH SQUIRE TRU TOUCH BLOOMER RIDGE	22 10 4
3	COSMIC JOVE LAVALIER JEFFERVESCENT	LAVALIER BIG HOCK BARRISTER SIB	BIG HOCK LAVALIER BARRISTER SIB	BARRISTER SIB COSMIC JOVE REVISED	LAVALIER JEFFERVESCENT COSMIC JOVE	LAVALIER COSMIC JOVE BIG HOCK	14 8 7
4	PEREMPTORY JUDY'S JOKER BAG OF FISH	JUDY'S JOKER MISTER GUY BAG OF FISH	BAG OF FISH EASY DIGGIN BORDEAUX NATIVE	JUDY'S JOKER MISTER GUY BAG OF FISH	BAG OF FISH BORDEAUX NATIVE MOST DECIDEDLY	BAG OF FISH JUDY'S JOKER PEREMPTORY	13 12 5
5	GREEK MINSTREL ILLHANDLEIT MANNY T.	GREEK MINSTREL ILLHANDLEIT SUPER RIDGE	MANNY T. SUPER RIDGE GREEK MINSTREL	MANNY T. GREEK MINSTREL IXTAPAN	ILLHANDLEIT IXTAPAN MANNY T.	GREEK MINSTREL MANNY T. ILLHANDLEIT	13 12 9
6	MYSTICAL MOOD MISS PREAKNESS PRICELESS HERO	CYPRESS BAY MISS PREAKNESS BETTY MONEY	CYPRESS BAY MYSTICAL MOOD MISS PREAKNESS	CYPRESS BAY MISS PREAKNESS MYSTICAL MOOD	CYPRESS BAY MYSTICAL MOOD MISS PREAKNESS	CYPRESS BAY MYSTICAL MOOD MISS PREAKNESS	20 10 8
7	**MYTHICAL RULER** WHAT IT IS POONA'S STAGE	**MYTHICAL RULER** MASTER TOMMY WHAT IT IS	**MYTHICAL RULER** MASTER TOMMY WHAT IT IS	MYTHICAL RULER WHAT IT IS MASTER TOMMY	**MYTHICAL RULER** MASTER TOMMY WHAT IT IS	**MYTHICAL RULER** WHAT IT IS MASTER TOMMY	33 7 7
8	PLEASANT COLONY PROUD APPEAL DOUBLE SONIC	PROUD APPEAL SPLENDID SPRUCE BOLD EGO	PROUD APPEAL CURE THE BLUES PLEASANT COLONY	PROUD APPEAL CURE THE BLUES TAP SHOES	PROUD APPEAL PLEASANT COLONY CURE THE BLUES	PROUD APPEAL PLEASANT COLONY CURE THE BLUES	22 8 5
9	SUN CZAR IRON PEGASUS ROSSI GOLD	ROSSI GOLD CONGE IRON PEGASUS	CONGE ROSSI GOLD IRON PEGASUS	ROSSI GOLD SUN CZAR CONGE	ROSSI GOLD SAMOYED CONGE	ROSSI GOLD CONGE SUN CZAR	18 9 7
10	LOTHIAN WOLFGANG GRR MR. BOBEVA	LOTHIAN CRIMSON SPRUCE D. J. ROAD	SORROTO LOTHIAN MR. BOBEVA	LOTHIAN WOLFGANG GRR MR. BOBEVA	LOTHIAN SORROTO HARD SILVER	LOTHIAN SORROTO WOLFGANG GRR	22 7 4

The Dr. Z System Bets

The first Dr. Z system bet occurred in the third race on Jeffervescent. He was a California horse with a reasonably good record, having finished in the money in eleven of his twenty-two starts. He was dropping in class and coming off a layoff, with this his first start of 1981.

Betting a horse that is coming off a substantial layoff is always a great risk, so we were cautious regarding Jeffervescent and would not make a large bet. At the end of the betting, the tote board stood as follows:

	Totals	#4 Jeffervescent
Odds		7—2
Win	317,312	58,621
Show	139,742	15,825

6 FURLONGS (START / FINISH)

WIN	PLACE	SHOW

3

CLAIMING

PURSE $7,800

FOUR-YEAR-OLDS AND UPWARD, 122 lbs. Non-winners of two races since April 1 allowed 3 lbs. of a race since then, 5 lbs. Claiming Price $10,000 for each $500 to $9,000, 2 lbs. (Races where entered for $8,000 or less not considered.)

Track Record—BENEDICTO (6) 117 lbs.; 1:09 1/5; May 13, 1961
AMBER BREAK (6) 116 lbs.; 1:09 1/5; Nov. 25, 1970
BARBIZON STREAK (3) 122 lbs.; 1:09 1/5; May 22, 1971

MAKE SELECTION BY NUMBER

No.	Owner	Trainer	Jockey/Morn. Line
1	HEIDI HO STUD (W. W. Hopkins) Orange, Brown "HH" Orange Cap **REVISED** 117 Dk.b. or br.g.(1977), Toga Mio—Glow Lady Glow	D. R. VANCE	6 DAVID WHITED (Post Pos. 10) $10,000
1a	HEIDI HO STUD (W. W. Hopkins) Orange, Brown "HH" Orange Cap **BREEZY JESTER** 117 Dk.b. or br.g.(1976), Venetian Jester—Breezy X	D. R. VANCE	6 DAVID WHITED (Post Pos. 12) $10,000
2	T. D. ACKEL Green, Green "AAA" on White Triangle, Green Chevrons on White Sleeves, Green Cap **LAVALIER** 117 Gr.g.(1977), Gage Line—Scissile	OWNER	3 EDDIE DELAHOUSSAYE (Post Pos. 1) $10,000
3	JAMES CARSON Flamingo, Black "C," Black Bars on Sleeves Black Cap **RAPID TRACE** 113 B.g.(1975), Royal Trace—Better Sister	OWNER	20 JOHN BEECH, JR. (Post Pos. 2) $9,000.
4	ROBERT SULLIVAN Red, White Flying "F" Red Cap **JEFFERVESCENT** 117 B.g.(1975), Windy Sands—Cliche With Love	W. H. FIRES	8 JOHN LIVELY (Post Pos. 3) $10,000
5	HOWARD PRIDDY AND DELORIS MEREDITH White, Green Stripes, Yellow Sleeves, Green Cap **MASTER SMART** 117 B.g.(1977), El Bat—Lucy Flew	J. E. HIKES	9-2 DARRELL FOSTER (Post Pos. 4) $10,000
6	J. H. RUTTER White, Black "R" on Gold Crown, Black Bars on Sleeves White Cap **BARRISTER SIB** 117 B.g.(1974), Somebody II—Holme's Rough	W. I. MOTT	8 ALBERTO RAMOS (Post Pos. 5) $10,000
7	J. E. SOWARDS Red, White Bar "S," Blue Stars on White Sleeves Red Cap **NAVAJO WARRIOR** *112 Dk.b. or br.g.(1977), Navajo—Salad	OWNER	20 BRENT BULLARD (Post Pos. 6) $10,000
8	C. V. QUEEN Green, White "Q," White Bars on Sleeves Green Cap **SEVEN DIPLOMATS** 117 B.g.(1977), Diplomat Way—Overton Miss	JERRY BURKHART	20 KEVIN B. WIRTH (Post Pos. 7) $10,000
9	C. B. BENJAMIN Orange, White Hoops White Cap **COSMIC JOVE** 117 Gr.g.(1976), Northern Jove—Cosmic Motion	T. W. KELLEY	5 RANDY ROMERO (Post Pos. 8) $10,000
10	HASSI SHINA & LEO ARNOLD Navy, Yellow Belt, Yellow Bars on Orange Sleeves Navy Cap **BIG HOCK** 117 B.h.(1975), Caribbean Line—Lotta Rhythm	LEO ARNOLD	8 PAT DAY (Post Pos. 9) $9,500.
11	J. C. CRAIG Purple, Orange "JCC," Orange Bars on Sleeves Purple Cap **PLAY HAVOC** 117 B.g.(1976), Winning Hit—Tracy Brite	JAMES TULLY	8 ROBERT BREEN (Post Pos. 11) $10,000

1 and 1a—HEIDI HO STUD Entry
Scratched—ANOTHER ALI, JIMMINEY CROCKETT, BRIDGETS BOY

Selections 2—5—9—1

The track take is 15% in Kentucky. Using equation (4.4), we calculated the expected value per dollar bet at 1.21. Our betting fortune was $1,000, which indicated a bet of $62. Jeffervescent won the race and paid a handsome $5.20 to show. This provided a $99.20 profit for our $62 bet. The chart of the race was as follows:

THIRD RACE — 6 FURLONGS. (1.09 1/5) CLAIMING. Purse $7,800. 4-year-olds and upward. Weight, 122 lbs. Non-winners of two races since April 1 allowed 3 lbs.; of a race since then, 5 lbs. Claiming price $10,000; for each $500 to $9,000 allowed 2 lbs. (Races where entered for $8,000 or less not considered.)

Churchill

MAY 2, 1981

Value of race $7,800, value to winner $5,070, second $1,560, third $780, fourth $390. Mutuel pool $624,643.

Last Raced		Horse	Eqt.	A.	Wt.	PP	St	1/4	1/2	Str	Fin	Jockey	Cl'gPr	Odds $1
11Aug80	10Dmr 7	Jeffervescent	b	6	117	3	6	2-2	1-1½	1-1½	1-1¾	Lively J	10000	3.50
10Apr81	10OP 12	Play Havoc	b	5	117	11	2	6hd	2 ½	2-2	2-2½	Breen R	10000	8.20
25Apr81	5CD 9	Master Smart		4	117	4	4	1-1	3hd	3-1	3hd	Foster D E	10000	6.70
23Mar81	5Hia 3	Cosmic Jove	b	5	117	8	7	7hd	7-1	5-1	4-1½	Romero R P	10000	8.80
7Apr81	5OP 3	Revised		4	117	10	11	12	9 ½	8-3	5no	Whited D E	10000	a- 11.40
25Apr81	5CD 7	Big Mock	b	6	117	9	3	10-2	8 ½	7hd	6nk	Day P	9500	13.20
2Apr81	5FG 2	Barrister Sib	b	7	117	5	12	8hd	6-4	4hd	7-2½	Ramos A	10000	5.30
14Apr81	2Kee 6	Seven Diplomats	b	4	117	7	8	5-1	4 ½	6hd	8-1½	Wirth K	10000	42.60
13Feb81	8FG 8	Lavalier		4	117	1	10	3hd	5 ½	9-2	9-2½	Pincay L Jr	10000	3.00
25Apr81	3CD 5	Breezy Jester		5	117	12	1	4hd	10-1	10 ½	10 ¾	Chapman T M	10000	a- 11.40
22Apr81	1Kee 4	Navajo Warrior	b	4	112	6	5	9 ½	12	11-2	11-2½	Bullard B A-5	10000	31.30
18Apr81	4Beu 4	Rapid Trace		6	114	2	9	11-1	11hd	12	12	Beech J Jr	9000	43.00

a-Coupled: Revised and Breezy Jester.

OFF AT 1:01 EDT. Start good. Won ridden out. Time, :22, :45 2/5, :57 4/5, 1:11 Track fast.

$ 2 Mutuel Prices:					
	4-	JEFFERVESCENT	9.00	5.80	5.20
	11-	PLAY HAVOC		10.60	7.20
	5-	MASTER SMART			6.00

B. g, by Windy Sands-Cliche With Love, by Four-and-Twenty. Trainer Fires William H. Bred by Linehan W J (Cal).

JEFFERVESCENT, hustled up to prompt the early pace, took command approaching the lane and was ridden out to the wire. PLAY HAVOC, allowed to settle early, came up to challenge entering the lane, could not match the winner but was clearly second best. MASTER SMART, away alertly and quickly in command, dropped back approaching the lane and had no late rally. COSMIC JOVE lacked the needed response. BIG MOCK raced wide. BARRISTER SIB could not sustain a bid in the lane. LAVALIER had brief speed, as did BREEZY JESTER.

Owners- 1, Sullivan Robert; 2, Craig J C; 3, Priddy Howard & Meredith Delores; 4, Benjamin C B; 5, Heidi Ho Stud; 6, Arnold L & Shina M; 7, Rutter J M; 8, Queen C V; 9, Ackel Thad D;10, Heidi Ho Stud;11, Sowards J E;12, Carson James.

Corrected weight: Lavalier 117 pounds. Overweight: Rapid Trace 1 pound .

Jeffervescent was claimed by Schmidt H C ; trainer, Casse Mark; Play Havoc was claimed by Allen W M ; trainer, Loyd Jack C; Cosmic Jove was claimed by Miller W R ; trainer, Chalk Ted W; Revised was claimed by Isaacs George ; trainer, same; Big Mock was claimed by Hopkins W W ; trainer, Vance David R; Lavalier was claimed by Davis Paul ; trainer, Davis Mike.

Scratched- Another Ali(1May80 9CD 6); Jimminey Crockett(25Apr81 5CD 8); Bridgets Boy(31Mar81 6Lat 2).

The fifth race was an allowance race for three-year-olds who had never won a race other than a maiden or a claiming. Hence it was filled both with horses with mediocre records and those who were upcoming horses. Shot N' Missed had finished second in his only race and was awarded first place through a disqualification. His speed rating of 90 in the short $4\frac{1}{2}$-furlong race was reasonably good for this group.

6 FURLONGS

ALLOWANCE
PURSE $9,900

WIN | PLACE | SHOW

5

THE REFLECTED GLORY
(Plus $2,800 from the Kentucky Thoroughbred Development Fund)
THREE AND FOUR-YEAR-OLDS WHICH HAVE NEVER WON A RACE OTHER THAN MAIDEN OR CLAIMING. Three-year-olds, 113 lbs.; four-year-olds, 123 lbs. Non-winners of a race other than claiming since April 3 allowed 3 lbs.

Track Record BENEDICTO (6) 117 lbs.; 1:09¹ s., May 13, 1961
AMBER BREAK (6) 116 lbs.; 1:09¹ s., Nov. 25, 1970
BARBIZON STREAK (3) 122 lbs.; 1:09¹ s.; May 22, 1971

MAKE SELECTION BY NUMBER

No.	Owner	Trainer	Colors	Horse	Wt.	Breeding	Jockey	Morn. Line
1	A. M. STALL, EARL BURKE AND J. R. QUERBES	FRANK BROTHERS	White, Blue Diamond Frames, Blue Cap	ILLHANDLEIT	110	Dk.b. or c.(1978), Hold Your Peace—Flo Mar	RANDY ROMERO	7-2
2	A. J. FOYT, JR.	A. J. FOYT III	Orange, White "AJ," Black and White Blocked Sleeves, Orange Cap	IXTAPAN	110	B.g.(1978), Nalees Man—Reverse English	LARRY MELANCON	9-2
3	MRS. CONNIE PATTON	THOMAS PATTON	Orange, Black Diamond, Black Bars on Sleeves, Orange Cap	SHOT N' MISSED	120	B.g.(1977), Naskra—Guest Shot	DARRELL FOSTER	15
4	DAN LASATER	D. R. VANCE	Red, White "L," Yoke and Sleeves, Red Cap	MANNY T.	113	B.c.(1978), What A Pleasure—Honky Star	DAVID WHITED	5-2
5	T. E. WETTERER	KENNETH BURKHART	Red, Red "W" on Black Ball, Black Dots, Red Cap	A TOAST TO HARRY	110	B.g.(1978), Bravest Roman—Tropical Eve	KEITH F. WIRTH	6
6	CARMINE-ESPO STABLE (Carmine Oliverio and Richard Esposito)	G. T. POOLE III	Green, Wh. Circ. "CE," Grn. Diam. on Wh. Slvs., Grn. Cap	GREEK MINSTREL	113	B.c.(1978), Tudor Grey—Pretty Poesy	TOMMY BARROW	10
7	W. G. CLARK	W. H. FIRES	White, Brown Sash, White Cap	SUPER RIDGE	120	B.c.(1977), Riva Ridge—Midnight Madrigal	EDDIE DELAHOUSSAYE	5
8	J. P. BOWLDS	OWNER	Black, White Cross Sashes, Red Sleeves, Black Cap	LAGNAF	110	B.g.(1978), Captain Lex—Belle Echo	MICHAEL BOWLDS	20
9	T. A. Grissom Stable (T. A. Grissom)	Stig Rasmussen	White, Red "G," Gold Cuffs, Red Cap	BIG BRAGGER	110	B.c.(1978), Cougar II—Boasting	WILLIAM SHOEMAKER	20

Selections 4—1—2—7

Near post time the expected value on Shot N' Missed was 1.31, which indicated a bet of $197. The tote board at post time was

	Totals	#3 Shot N' Missed
Odds		5—2
Win	474,181	108,367
Show	206,585	25,760

Ixtapan won the race, followed by Lagnaf, and Shot N' Missed took third. The show payoff on Shot N' Missed was a substantial $4.40 for a 5—2 shot. The 1.28 expected value, plus the fact that the favorite in the race, Manny T., finished out of the money, while two longer-priced horses were in the money, caused the high payoff. Our bet of $197 returned $433.40, for a profit of $236.40.

FIFTH RACE

Churchill

MAY 2, 1981

6 FURLONGS. (1.09 1/5) ALLOWANCE. Purse $9,900 (plus $2,800 from KTDF). 3- and 4-year-olds which have never won a race other than maiden or claiming. Weight, 3-year-olds, 113 lbs.; 4-year-olds, 123 lbs. Non-winners of a race other than claiming since April 3 allowed 3 lbs.

Value of race $12,280, value to winner $8,255, second $2,540, third $990, fourth $495. $420 reverts to the KTDF. Mutuel pool $911,308.

Last Raced	Horse	Eqt.	A.	Wt.	PP	St	1/4	1/2	Str	Fin	Jockey	Odds $1
9Apr81 4OP 1	Ixtapan		3	112	2	9	5 ½	6 ½	3-3	1-1¾	Melancon L	5.10
16Apr81 8Kee 6	Big Bragger	b	3	110	9	3	9	9	5 ½	2nk	Shoemaker W	24.30
21Mar81 3Grd 1	Shot N' Missed	b	4	120	3	5	1-1	1hd	1-1	3-1	Foste: D E	2.80
25Apr81 6CD 2	Manny T.	b	3	113	4	8	6hd	3hd	2hd	4-2¾	Whited D E	2.50
25Apr81 6CD 7	Super Ridge		4	120	7	1	8-5	7hd	4hd	5-2½	Delahou:saye E	9.20
4Apr81 5Kee 6	Illhandleit	b	3	113	1	4	3hd	5hd	6hd	6 ½	Romero R F	6.10
25Apr81 6CD 11	Lagnaf		3	110	8	2	7hd	4hd	7-4	7-4½	Bowlds M A	72.20
10Apr81 4Kee 2	Greek Minstrel	b	3	116	6	7	4-2	8-2	8-4	8-10	Barrow T	7.70
25Apr81 4CD 3	A Toast to Harry	b	3	115	5	6	2-3	2-2	9	9	Wirth K B	11.10

OFF AT 2:40 EDT. Start good. Won driving. Time, :21 4/5, :45 1/5, :58, 1:10 4/5 Track fast.

$ 2 Mutuel Prices:

2-	IXTAPAN	12.20	5.80	4.00
9-	BIG BRAGGER		14.20	5.70
3-	SHOT N' MISSED			4.40

B. g, by Nalees Man-Reverse English, by Reverse. Trainer Foyt Anthony J III. Bred by Jones B C (Ky).

IXTAPAN, off last and unhurried early, launched a bold bid when set down for the drive and was up in the final furlong to draw clear. BIG BRAGGER, void of early foot, found best stride in the lane and was just up for the place. SHOT N' MISSED made the pace most of the way and weakened against the top two in the late stages. MANNY T. LAUNCHED a bid upper stretch but could not sustain it. A TOAST TO HARRY prompted the early pace and gave way.

Owners- 1, Foyt A J Jr; 2, T A Grissom Stable; 3, Patton Mrs C; 4, Lasater Dan; 5, Clark W G; 6, Stall A M et al; 7, Bowlds James P; 8, Carmine-Espo Stable; 9, Wetterer Tom.

Overweight: Ixtapan 2 pounds; Illhandleit 3; Greek Minstrel 3; A Toast to Harry 5.

The sixth race was the eighty-first running of the $25,000 added Debutante Stakes for two-year-old fillies. It featured a two-horse entry and eight other starters after Ali's Oolah and Trunk Line were scratched. The ten starters all had brief racing careers. Most of them were running only their second race. Six of them had won their only race. The favorites were Cypress Bay, Top Canary, Mystical Mood, and Miss Preakness. Cypress Bay looked the best, winning her only start as a 3—2 favorite by seven lengths, with a 94 speed rating. She seemed like a reasonable bet if the odds were good and they were.

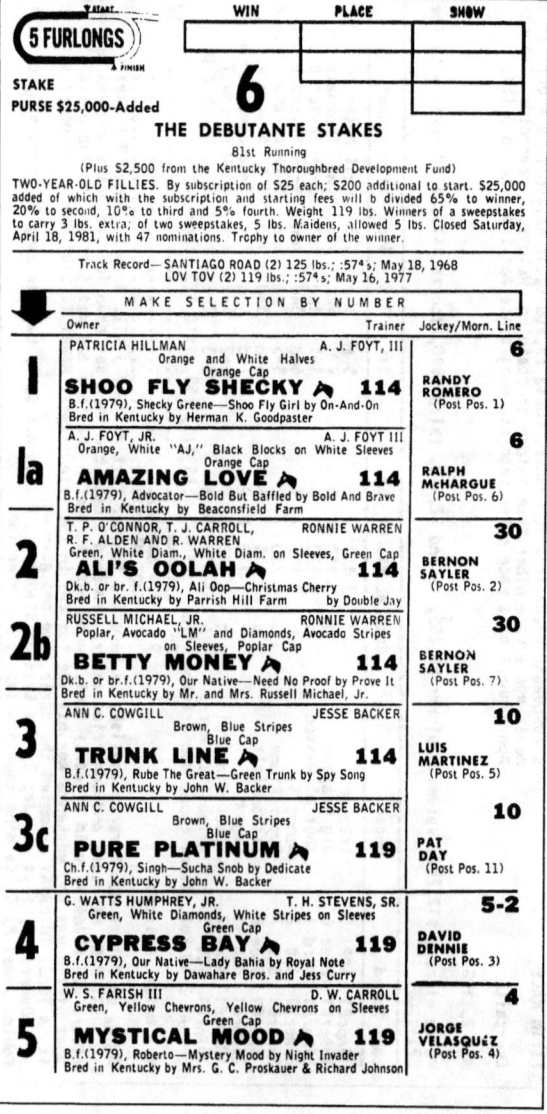

START 5 FURLONGS FINISH

WIN	PLACE	SHOW

STAKE
PURSE $25,000-Added

6

THE DEBUTANTE STAKES

81st Running

(Plus $2,500 from the Kentucky Thoroughbred Development Fund)

TWO-YEAR-OLD FILLIES. By subscription of $25 each; $200 additional to start. $25,000 added of which with the subscription and starting fees will b divided 65% to winner, 20% to second, 10% to third and 5% fourth. Weight 119 lbs. Winners of a sweepstakes to carry 3 lbs. extra; of two sweepstakes, 5 lbs. Maidens, allowed 5 lbs. Closed Saturday, April 18, 1981, with 47 nominations. Trophy to owner of the winner.

Track Record—SANTIAGO ROAD (2) 125 lbs.; :57⁴⁄₅; May 18, 1968
LOV TOV (2) 119 lbs.; :57⁴⁄₅; May 16, 1977

MAKE SELECTION BY NUMBER

No.	Owner	Trainer	Colors	Horse	Wt.	Breeding	Jockey	Morn. Line
1	PATRICIA HILLMAN	A. J. FOYT, III	Orange and White Halves, Orange Cap	**SHOO FLY SHECKY**	114	B.f.(1979), Shecky Greene—Shoo Fly Girl by On-And-On. Bred in Kentucky by Herman K. Goodpaster	RANDY ROMERO (Post Pos. 1)	6
1a	A. J. FOYT, JR.	A. J. FOYT III	Orange, White "AJ," Black Blocks on White Sleeves, Orange Cap	**AMAZING LOVE**	114	B.f.(1979), Advocator—Bold But Baffled by Bold And Brave. Bred in Kentucky by Beaconsfield Farm	RALPH McHARGUE (Post Pos. 6)	6
2	T. P. O'CONNOR, T. J. CARROLL, R. F. ALDEN AND R. WARREN	RONNIE WARREN	Green, White Diam., White Diam. on Sleeves, Green Cap	**ALI'S OOLAH**	114	Dk.b. or br. f.(1979), Ali Oop—Christmas Cherry by Double Jay. Bred in Kentucky by Parrish Hill Farm	BERNON SAYLER (Post Pos. 2)	30
2b	RUSSELL MICHAEL, JR.	RONNIE WARREN	Poplar, Avocado "LM" and Diamonds, Avocado Stripes on Sleeves, Poplar Cap	**BETTY MONEY**	114	Dk.b. or br.f.(1979), Our Native—Need No Proof by Prove It. Bred in Kentucky by Mr. and Mrs. Russell Michael, Jr.	BERNON SAYLER (Post Pos. 7)	30
3	ANN C. COWGILL	JESSE BACKER	Brown, Blue Stripes, Blue Cap	**TRUNK LINE**	114	B.f.(1979), Rube The Great—Green Trunk by Spy Song. Bred in Kentucky by John W. Backer	LUIS MARTINEZ (Post Pos. 5)	10
3c	ANN C. COWGILL	JESSE BACKER	Brown, Blue Stripes, Blue Cap	**PURE PLATINUM**	119	Ch.f.(1979), Singh—Sucha Snob by Dedicate. Bred in Kentucky by John W. Backer	PAT DAY (Post Pos. 11)	10
4	G. WATTS HUMPHREY, JR.	T. H. STEVENS, SR.	Green, White Diamonds, White Stripes on Sleeves, Green Cap	**CYPRESS BAY**	119	B.f.(1979), Our Native—Lady Bahia by Royal Note. Bred in Kentucky by Dawahare Bros. and Jess Curry	DAVID DENNIE (Post Pos. 3)	5-2
5	W. S. FARISH III	D. W. CARROLL	Green, Yellow Chevrons, Yellow Chevrons on Sleeves, Green Cap	**MYSTICAL MOOD**	119	B.f.(1979), Roberto—Mystery Mood by Night Invader. Bred in Kentucky by Mrs. G. C. Proskauer & Richard Johnson	JORGE VELASQUEZ (Post Pos. 4)	4

6	MARCIE WEST — J. O. KEEFER Green, White Sash Green Cap **KIRBY** 114 B.f.(1979), Inverness Drive—Gold Idol by Don B. Bred in Kentucky by Verne H. Winchell	**20** LARRY MELANCON (Post Pos. 8)
7	TAYHILL STABLE — E. K. CLEVELAND, JR. (Karen Lee Taylor) White, Green Twin Spires, White Cap **PRICELESS HERO** 119 B.f.(1979), Our Hero—Pricelyn by Joe Price Bred in Washington by Wooden Horse Investments	**8** JIM McKNIGHT (Post Pos. 9)
8	GOLDEN CHANCE FARM, INC. — W. E. ADAMS (Verna Lehmann) Gold, Red "GCF," Red Chevron on Sleeves, Gold Cap **MISS PREAKNESS** 119 Ch.f.(1979), Master Derby—Running Beauty by Double Jay Bred in Kentucky by Golden Chance Farm, Inc.	**6** JULIO ESPINOZA (Post Pos. 10)
9	KINGHAVEN FARM — JOHN TAMMARO (D. G. Willmot) Navy, Wh. Halves, Wh. Bars on Slvs., Wh. Dots on Blue Cap **TOP CANARY** 119 Ch.f.(1979), Accipiter—Caliphs Canary by No Robbery Bred in Kentucky by Vintage Farms, Inc.	**3** ANGEL CORDERO, JR. (Post Pos. 12)

Indicates Foaled In Kentucky

1 and 1a—PATRICIA HILLMAN—A. J. FOYT, JR. Entry
2 and 2b—T. P. O'CONNOR, T. J. CARROLL, R. F. ALDEN & RONNIE WARREN—RUSSELL MICHAEL, JR. Entry
3 and 3c—ANN C. COWGILL Entry

Selections 4—9—5—8

One minute before post time the tote board was as follows:

	Totals	#4 Cypress Bay
Odds		1—1
Win	522,550	204,439
Show	213,710	51,883

This gave an expected value of 1.19. With our betting fortune of $1,335.60, a bet of $510 to show on Cypress Bay was suggested.

At post time the odds were similar:

	Totals	#4 Cypress Bay	Expected Value per Dollar Bet on Cypress Bay	Optimal Bet on Cypress Bay ($)
Odds		1—1		
Win	535,218	209,225		
Show	219,930	53,287	1.20	510

Pure Platinum, part of the number 2 entry, won the race, followed by Miss Preakness. Cypress Bay held on for third and paid $3. Our $510 bet returned $765, for a $255 profit. The chart of the race was as follows:

SIXTH RACE — Churchill — MAY 2, 1981

5 FURLONGS. (.57 4/5) 81st Running DEBUTANTE STAKES ALLOWANCE. $25,000 Added. Fillies. 2-year-olds. By subscription of $25 each; $200 additional to start. $25,000 added of which with the subscription and starting fees wil be divided 65% to the winner, 20% to second, 10% to third and 5% to fourth. Weight, 119 lbs. Winners of a sweepstakes to carry 3 lbs. additional; of two sweepstakes, 5 lbs. additional. Maidens allowed 5 lbs.. Starters to be named through the entry box Thursday, April 30, at the time of closing. If the race is divided, entries or couplings will be divided. A trophy to the owner of the winner. (Closed with 47 nominations.)

Value of race $30,675, value to winner $19,939, second $6,135, third $3,068, fourth $1,533. Mutuel pool $996,427.

Last Raced	Horse	Eqt.	A.	Wt.	PP	St	3/16	3/8	Str	Fin	Jockey		Odds $1
24Apr81 3Kee 1	Pure Platinum		2	119	9	5	3-1	2-1	2 ½	1-1½	Day P		35.40
3Apr81 3Kee 1	Miss Preakness		2	119	8	4	1-1	1 ½	1 ½	2 ¾	Espinoza J C		9.50
11Apr81 3Kee 1	Cypress Bay		2	119	2	2	7-2	6hd	6 ½	3-1	Dennis D		1.00
7Apr81 3Kee 2	Betty Money		2	114	5	8	5-1	3hd	4-1½	4-1^	Sayler B		35.40
27Apr81 3CD 3	Shoo Fly Shecky		2	114	1	1	2hd	5-1	3-1	5nk	Romero R P	a-	8.30
7Apr81 3Kee 1	Mystical Mood		2	119	3	9	6 ½	7-1	7-1	6-1½	Velasquez J		4.00
	Amazing Love		2	114	4	7	4hd	4 ½	5hd	7nk	McHargue D G	a-	8.30
19Mar81 3Hia 1	Top Canary		2	119	10	10	10	8-1	8-4	8-2½	Cordero A Jr		5.60
27Apr81 3CD 1	Priceless Hero		2	119	7	6	9-4	9hd	9hd	9 ¾	McKnight J		13.30
24Apr81 3Kee 4	Kirby	b	2	114	6	3	8-1	10	10	10	Melancon L		36.90

a-Coupled: Shoo Fly Shecky and Amazing Love.
OFF AT 3:31 EDT. Start good. Won driving. Time, :22 4/5, :45 4/5, :58 4/5 Track fast.

$ 2 Mutuel Prices:

3-	PURE PLATINUM	72.80	24.00	8.40
8-	MISS PREAKNESS		9.00	4.60
4-	CYPRESS BAY			3.00

Ch. f, by Singh-Sucha Snob, by Dedicate. Trainer Backer Jesse L. Bred by Backer John W (Ky).

PURE PLATINUM, just behind the early leaders, came up to prompt the pace approaching the lane, took command at the sixteenth pole and drew clear late under a strong hand ride. MISS PREAKNESS, away alertly and quickly in command made the pace, could not withstand the winner late but held the place. CYPRESS BAY lacked the needed reponse. BETTY MONEY, well placed early, had no rally. SHOO FLY SHECKY showed early speed, dropped back approaching the lane, launched a second bold bid along the rail in midstretch but could not sustain it in the final sixteenth.MYSTICAL MOOD never threatened. AMAZING LOVE had speed until the stretch. TOP CANARY had no speed. KIRBY flashed brief foot, checked leaving the backstretch and raced wide in the lane.

Owners- 1, Cowgill Ann C; 2, Golden Chance Farm Inc; 3, Humphrey G Watts Jr; 4, Michael Russell Jr; 5, Hillman Patricia; 6, Farish W S III; 7, Foyt A J Jr; 8, Kinghaven Farms; 9, Tayhill Stable;10, West Marcie.

Scratched- Ali's Oolah(7Apr81 3Kee 7); Trunk Line(22Apr81 3Kee11).

The seventh race—the Twin Spires, a $50,000 allowance for three-year-olds—was to feature the standout Mythical Ruler. Mythical Ruler won all his races during 1981 and three of five in 1980, always finishing in the money. When he was scratched and so could run in the Derby, the top choices became Master Tommy and What It Is. Master Tommy was a Dr. Z system bet throughout the betting period.

1 1/16 MILES

START FINISH

ALLOWANCE
PURSE $50,000

WIN	PLACE	SHOW

7

THE TWIN SPIRES
(Plus $7,000 from the Kentucky Thoroughbred Development Fund)

THREE-YEAR-OLDS, 122 lbs. Non-winners of a race of $15,000 at a mile or over allowed 3 lbs.; of $15,000 at any distance, 5 lbs.; of $9,750 at any distance, 7 lbs.; of $6,200 at a mile or over in 1981, 9 lbs. (Maiden, claiming and starter races not considered.)

Track Record—YES SIR (5) 110 lbs.; $1:41\frac{3}{5}$; Nov. 25, 1970

MAKE SELECTION BY NUMBER

	Owner	Trainer	Jockey/Morn. Line
1	CAROLYN WELCH Yellow, Black "WJW" on Yellow Diamonds Black Cap **FAST EARL** 113 B.c.(1978), Sir Earl—Fast Fountain	WILLIAM WELCH	30 RICHARD ADKINS
2	CARL SWAN White, Red Swan, Red Bars on Sleeves White Cap **MASTER TOMMY** 117 B.c.(1978), Master Derby—Tall Corn	T. J. WALKER	4-5 JOHN LIVELY
3	G. S. BROMAGEN Red, White Horns, White Sleeves Red Cap **MARION FRANCES** 113 Ch.c.(1978), Hard Work—Brashness	T. W. KELLEY	10 ROBERT BREEN
4	N. E. CASSE Black, Red Cardinal Red Cap **WHAT IT IS** 119 B.c.(1978), Tell—Major Anne	MARK CASSE	8-5 JULIO ESPINOZA
5	AL LEVINSON Orange, Blue Sunburst Blue Cap **POONA'S STAGE** 113 B.g.(1978), Stage Director—Poona's Day	JUDITH ZOUCK	15 RALPH McHARGUE
6	DAN LOGAN White, Green Bar "L" White Cap **CORNISH MUSIC** 113 Dk.b. or br.c.(1978), Stop The Music—Spicy Life	MITCH SHIROTA	10 WILLIAM SHOEMAKER

Indicates Foaled In Kentucky

Scratched—MYTHICAL RULER

Selections 2—4—3—6

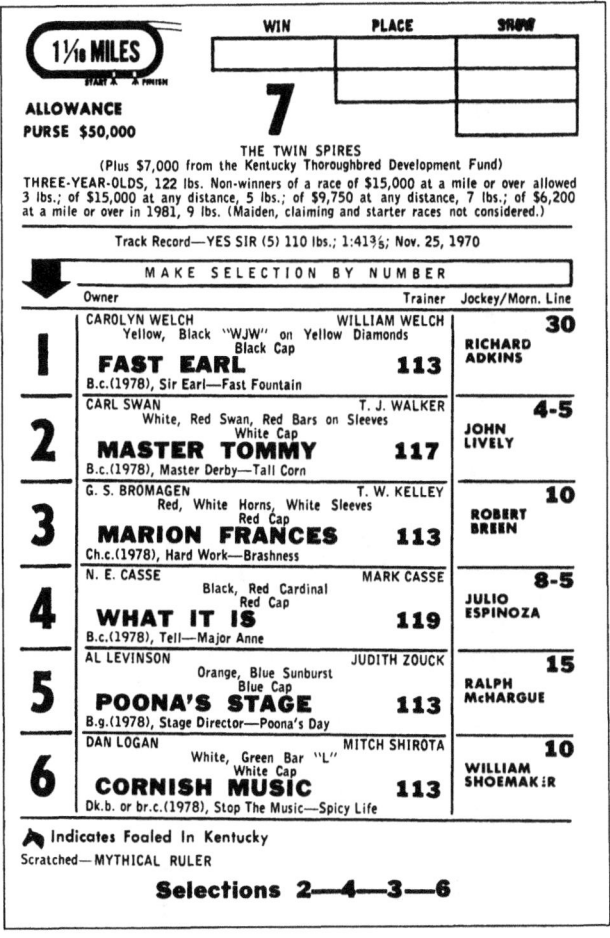

The final tote board was

	Totals	#2 Master Tommy
Odds		4—5
Win	548,084	245,308
Show	186,601	50,924

This gave an expected value of 1.20 and an optimal bet of $781 with our fortune of $1,590.60.

What It Is won the race, beating Master Tommy. Cornish Music took third. The chart of the races was as follows:

SEVENTH RACE — Churchill — MAY 2, 1981

1 1/16 MILES. (1.41 3/5) ALLOWANCE. Purse $50,000 (plus $7,000 from KTDF). 3-year-olds. Weight, 122 lbs. Non-winners of a race of $15,000 at a mile or over allowed 3 lbs.; of $15,000 at any distance, 5 lbs.; of $9,750 at any distance, 7 lbs.; of $6,200 at a mile or over in 1981, 9 lbs. (Maiden, claiming and starter races not considered.)

Total purse $57,000. Value of race $55,600, value to winner $37,050, second $10,000, third $5,700, fourth $2,850. ($1,400 reverts to the KTDF). Mutuel pool $986,791.

Last Raced	Horse	Eqt.	A.	Wt.	PP	St	1/4	1/2	3/4	Str	Fin	Jockey	Odds $1
28Apr81 8CD 1	What It Is	b	3	119	4	3	2-2	1-1	1-1½	1-1½	1no	Espinoza J C	2.90
11Apr81 9OP 5	Master Tommy	b	3	117	2	1	3hd	4-5	3-6	2-3	2-3	Lively J	.80
28Apr81 8CD 3	Cornish Music	b	3	113	6	6	6	5 ½	4-2	4-6	3-3½	Shoemaker W	2.80
15Apr81 6Kee 8	Marion Frances	b	3	113	3	5	4-4	3 ½	2 ½	3-1	4-6	Breen R	11.30
25Apr81 6CD 8	Poona's Stage		3	113	5	2	1hd	2-1½	5-5	5-6	5-13	McHargue D G	30.10
25Apr81 6CD 12	Fast Earl	b	3	113	1	4	5 ½	6	6	6	6	Adkins R M	31.70

OFF AT 4:20 EDT. Start good. Won driving. Time, :24 3/5, :47 4/5, 1:12 1/5, 1:38, 1:44 4/5 Track fast.

$ 2 Mutuel Prices:				
4-	WHAT IT IS	7.80	3.20	2.20
2-	MASTER TOMMY		2.80	2.20
6-	CORNISH MUSIC			2.20

B. c, by Tell—Major Anne, by B Major. Trainer Casse Mark. Bred by Rogers W H (Ky).

WHAT IT IS, away alertly, pressed the early pace, took clear command going down the backstretch and withstood the late bid of MASTER TOMMY while kept to left-handed pressure. The latter, allowed to settle early, rallied with left-handed urging in the final furlong but could not get up in time. CORNISH MUSIC had no speed but rallied to best the others. MARION FRANCES had no rally. POONA'S STAGE made or forced the early pace and gave way.

Owners- 1, Casse N E; 2, Swan C W; 3, Logan D; 4, Bromagen G S; 5, Levinson Al; 6, Welch Carolyn.

Scratched- Mythical Ruler(25Apr81 7CD 1).

Despite the 1.20 expected value per dollar bet to show on Master Tommy, which qualified it as a Dr. Z system bet, the payoff was only $2.20. Given the fact that there were only six starters, when the other favorite, What It Is, finished in the money with a substantial show bet, the show pool yielded a $2.20 payoff for all in-the-money finishers. This is one of the difficulties of playing a Dr. Z system bet with few starters and two or more major favorites. If all the favorites are in the money, the payoff will be small. If, of the favorites, only the horse you have bet is in the money, then the show payoff will be more substantial.

Our bet of $781 returned $859.10 for a profit of $78.10. Our betting fortune was now $1,668.70.

Proud Appeal versus Johnny Campo in the 107th Kentucky Derby

The eighth race was the 107th running of the Kentucky Derby. The favorite was Proud Appeal. He had won nine of his ten starts and was to be ridden by his steady jockey, Jeffrey Fell. Races like his recent $1{:}33^3$ with a 98 speed rating in the Gotham Stakes at Aqueduct made him look exceptionally strong. The other top horses were Pleasant Colony, Cure the Blues, Bold Ego, and Tap Shoes. Pleasant Colony had a mediocre record, but he was coming off a convincing win in the recent Wood Memorial at Aqueduct. Moreover, his colorful trainer, Johnny Campo, had gone on record that Pleasant Colony was the best horse and would win the race. Cure the Blues had been soundly beaten by eight lengths by Pleasant Colony in the Wood Memorial. The rest of his record was impeccable—loss by a nose to Proud Appeal in the Gotham and six straight convincing victories. Bold Ego had won ten of his thirteen starts and was coming off three straight victories, including the Arkansas Derby. He was ridden by his regular jockey, John Lively. Tap Shoes had just won the Flamingo Stakes and had won five of his nine starts. He had had only one bad race and was being ridden as usual by Ruben Hernandez.

It is romantic to win the Kentucky Derby, so I bet $50 on my favorite horse, Proud Appeal, to win. Pleasant Colony turned out to be a Dr. Z system bet. At post time the tote board was as follows:

	Total	#4 Pleasant Colony
Odds		7—2
Win	2,614,993	480,510
Show	950,079	132,845

The expected value per dollar bet on Pleasant Colony to show was 1.09, so with our fortune of $1,668.70, we bet $342.

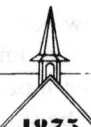

107th Running
KENTUCKY DERBY
EIGHTH RACE

1875 — 1981

$200,000 ADDED — ONE MILE and ONE-QUARTER — TRACK RECORD—SECRETARIAT (3), 126 lbs., 5-5-73, 1:59-2/5
(Plus $20,000 from the Kentucky Thoroughbred Development Fund)

For three-year-olds. By subscription of $100 each which covers nomination for both The Kentucky Derby and Derby Trial. All nomination fees to Derby winner. $4,000 to pass entry box. $3,500 additional to start. $200,000 added, of which $50,000 to second, $25,000 to third, $12,500 to fourth. $100,000 guaranteed to winner (to be divided equally in the event of a dead heat). Weight 126 lbs. The owner of the winner to receive a gold trophy. Closed Tuesday, February 17, 1981, with 432 nominations.

USE THESE NUMBERS FOR BUYING PARI MUTUEL TICKETS

No.	Owner	Trainer	Colors	Horse	Wt.	Breeding	Jockey	Morning Line	P.P.
1	FREDERICK E. LEHMANN & GAINESWAY (John R. Gaines)	W. E. ADAMS	Blue, Green Pine Tree, Blue Cap	GOLDEN DERBY ▲	126	Ro c, 1978, Master Derby—Old Goldie by Young Emperor. BRED IN KENTUCKY BY FREDERICK E. LEHMANN	JULIO ESPINOZA	2	(P. P. 2)
1a	M. H. WINFIELD, ROBERT ENTENMANN, JOHN R. GAINES & STANLEY M. HOUGH	STANLEY M. HOUGH	Black, Tan "W" and Braces, Tan Chevrons on Sleeves, Tan Cap	PROUD APPEAL	126	Dk b or br c, 1978, Valid Appeal—Proud N' Happy by Proudest Roman. BRED IN FLORIDA BY R. YOWELL & P. CAMP	JEFF FELL	2	(P. P. 5)
2	FLYING ZEE STABLE (Carl Lizza, Jr. & Herbert Hockreiter)	JOSE MARTIN	Light Blue, White "ZZ" and Yoke, White Cap	NOBLE NASHUA ▲	126	Dk b or br c, 1978, Nashua—Noble Lady by Vaguely Noble. BRED IN KENTUCKY BY GROUSEMONT FARM	CASH ASMUSSEN	30	(P. P. 9)
2b	FLYING ZEE STABLE (Carl Lizza, Jr. & Herbert Hockreiter)	JOSE MARTIN	Light Blue, White "ZZ" and Yoke, White Cap	WAYWARD LASS	121	Dk b or br f, 1978, Hail The Pirates—Young Mistress by Third Martini. BRED IN FLORIDA BY H. A. LURO	CASH ASMUSSEN	30	(P. P. 20)
3	SURF & TURF STABLE (Earl Shultz & Alan Yasukochi)	C. R. KNIGHT	Yellow, Yellow Seahorse on Green Ball, Yellow Bars on Green Sleeves, Yellow and Green Cap	SPLENDID SPRUCE ▲	126	B c, 1978, Big Spruce—Splendid Spree by Damascus. BRED IN KENTUCKY BY LILLIE F. WEBB	DARREL McHARGUE	15	(P. P. 1)
4	BUCKLAND FARM (Thomas M. Evans)	JOHN P. CAMPO	Dark Blue, White Triangle, Dark Blue Bars on White Sleeves, Blue and White Cap	PLEASANT COLONY	126	Dk b or br c, 1978, His Majesty—Sun Colony by Sunrise Flight. BRED IN VIRGINIA BY T. M. EVANS	JORGE VELASQUEZ	4	(P. P. 7)
5	LEOPOLDO VILLAREAL	ALBERT BARRERA	Royal Blue, Royal Blue "V" on Light Blue Ball, Light Blue Stripes on Royal Blue Sleeves, Royal Blue Cap	PASS THE TAB	126	Gr c, 1978, Al Hattab—Dantina by Gray Phantom. BRED IN CALIFORNIA BY LEOPOLDO VILLAREAL	LAFFIT PINCAY, JR.	30	(P. P. 8)
6	GREENTREE STABLE (John Hay Whitney)	J. M. GAVER, JR.	Pink, Black Stripes on Sleeves, Pink Cap	WOODCHOPPER ▲	126	Gr c, 1978, Hatchet Man—Musical Chairs by Swaps. BRED IN KENTUCKY BY GREENTREE STUD INC.	EDDIE DELAHOUSSAYE	30	(P. P. 11)
7	HERBERT ALLEN	EUGENE JACOBS	White, Red Cross Sashes, Red Blocks on Sleeves, White Cap	WELL DECORATED	126	Dk b or br c, 1978, Raja Baba—Paris Breeze by Majestic Prince. BRED IN FLORIDA BY HERBERT ALLEN	DON MacBETH	30	(P. P. 12)
8	DOUBLE B RANCH (J. D. Barton) & JOSEPH KIDD	JACK VAN BERG	Light Blue, White "B" in Horseshoe, Light Blue Cap	BOLD EGO	126	Dk b or br c, 1978, Bold Tactics—Coya's Ego by Bullin. BRED IN NEW MEXICO BY J. D. BARTON	JOHN LIVELY	8	(P. P. 15)
9	BERTRAM R. FIRESTONE	LE ROY JOLLEY	Green, White Diamond Frame, White Diamonds on Sleeves, Green Cap	CURE THE BLUES	126	B c, 1978, Stop the Music—Quick Cure by Dr. Fager. BRED IN VIRGINIA BY MR. & MRS. BERTRAM R. FIRESTONE	WILLIAM SHOEMAKER	9-2	(P. P. 16)
10	ARTHUR B. HANCOCK III & LEONE J. PETERS, et al	HORATIO A. LURO	White, Purple Star, Purple Band on Sleeves, White Cap	TAP SHOES ▲	126	Ch c, 1978, Riva Ridge—Bold Ballet by Bold Bidder. BRED IN KENTUCKY BY LEONE J. PETERS & ARTHUR HANCOCK III	RUBEN HERNANDEZ	6	(P. P. 19)
11	ULF JENSEN, KARL HOLMAN, RAYMOND RONCARI & EDMUND DiGIULIO	LARRY S. BARRERA	White, Red Heart, White Bars on Red Sleeves, Red Cap	FLYING NASHUA ▲	126	B c, 1978, Nashua—Joys Will by Yes You Will. BRED IN KENTUCKY BY FREEMAN & PERKINS	ANGEL CORDERO, JR.	30	(P. P. 22)
12 FIELD	MR. & MRS. HENRY GREENE & ELIZABETH DAVIS	D. WAYNE LUKAS	Lavender, Purple Chevrons, Purple Circled "DG," Purple Sleeves, Lavender Cap	PARTEZ ▲	126	B c, 1978, Quack—Lady Marguery by Tim Tam. BRED IN KENTUCKY BY H. B. NOONAN & RUNNYMEDE FARM INC.	SANDY HAWLEY	8	(P. P. 3)
13 FIELD	FRED & LOU ELIAS	GEORGE P. KRNJAICH	Orange, Black "EB" in Black Diamond Frame, Orange Cap	DOUBLE SONIC	126	Ro c, 1978, Nodouble—Eloquent Es by Palestinian. BRED IN FLORIDA BY ELIAS BROTHERS FARM	BUCK THORNBURG	8	(P. P. 4)
14 FIELD	MARCO A. COELLO	FRANCISCO GONZALEZ	Grey, Red Panel, Blue Sleeves, Grey Cap	HABANO	126	Dk b or br c, 1978, Ferrol—Miss Tepeji by Breezy Lane. BRED IN MEXICO BY ESTEVEZ M. GUILLERMO	BENNY FELICIANO	8	(P. P. 6)
15 FIELD	JO ANN DOMINGUEZ, MARIE FREIDEL & CHRIS THATCHER	ROGER DOMINGUEZ	Blue, Gold "R&R" in Gold Diamond Frame, Blue Bars on Gold Sleeves, Blue Cap	HOEDOWN'S DAY	126	B c, 1978, Bargain Day—Miss Hoedown by Dance Lesson. BRED IN CALIFORNIA BY MR. & MRS. ROGER DOMINGUEZ	TOMMY CHAPMAN	8	(P. P. 10)
16 FIELD	V. W. WINCHELL	J. C. MEYER	Maroon, White Circled "VHW," White Stripes on Sleeves, White Cap	CLASSIC GO GO ▲	126	Dk b or br c, 1978, Pago Pago—Classic Perfection by Never Bend. BRED IN KENTUCKY BY V. W. WINCHELL	ANTHONY BLACK	8	(P. P. 13)
17 FIELD	W. P. BISHOP	DWIGHT VIATOR	Blue, White "B," Blue Stars on White Sleeves, Blue Cap	TOP AVENGER	126	B c, 1978, Staunch Avenger—Atop by Dunce. BRED IN TEXAS BY W. P. BISHOP	LARRY SNYDER	8	(P. P. 14)
18 FIELD	CAROLE R. ROUSSEL	LOUIE ROUSSEL III	Light Blue, Cerise Dots, Light Blue Cap	BEAU RIT	126	B g, 1978, Lord Rebeau—Rit N Rough by Rough 'N Tumble. BRED IN FLORIDA BY EARLY BIRD STUD	PHIL RUBBICCO	8	(P. P. 17)
19 FIELD	BWAMAZON FARM (M. A. Waldheim)	ANTHONY BASILE	White, Blue Hoops, Blue Stripes on Sleeves, Blue Cap	TELEVISION STUDIO ▲	126	B g, 1978, Within Hail—Put On T.V. by T.V. Lark. BRED IN KENTUCKY BY BWAMAZON FARM	DAVID WHITED	8	(P. P. 18)
20 FIELD	AL RISEN, JR. & PAXTON PRICE	FRED WIRTH	Gold, Red Cross Sashes, Red Bars on Sleeves, Red Cap	MYTHICAL RULER ▲	126	Ro c, 1978, Ruritania—Our Nanny by Victorian Era. BRED IN KENTUCKY BY OSCAR PENN	KEVIN WIRTH	8	(P. P. 21)

▲ Indicates Foaled in Kentucky.

1-1a—Frederick E. Lehmann & John R. Gaines—M. H. Winfield, Robert Entenmann, John R. Gaines & Stanley M. Hough Entry

2-2b—Flying Zee Stable Entry

FIELD—12-13-14-15-16-17-18-19-20

Selections—1a-4-9-10

107th-Kentucky Derby-107th

Route the *Field Will Travel*

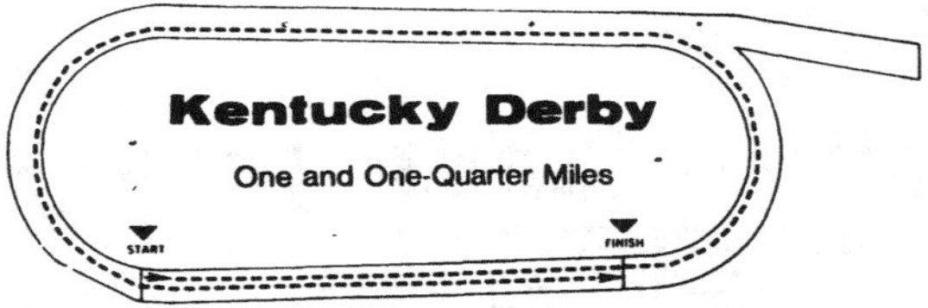

8th Churchill

1 ¼ MILES. (1.59⅗) 107th Running KENTUCKY DERBY SCALE WEIGHT (Grade I). $250,000 Added (plus $20,000 from KTDF). 3-year-olds. By subscription of $100 which covers nomination for both the Kentucky Derby and Derby Trial. All nomination fees to Derby winner. $4,000 to pass entry box Thursday, April 30, $3,500 additional to start. $250,000 added, of which: $50,000 to second, $25,000 to third, $12,500 to fourth. $100,000 guaranteed to the winner (to be divided equally in the event of a dead heat.) Weight, 126 lbs. Starters to be named through the entry box Thursday, April 30, at the time of closing. The maximum number of starters for the Kentucky Derby will be limited to twenty. In the event more than twenty entries pass through the entry box at the usual time of closing, the twenty starters will be determined at that time with preference given to those that have accumulated the highest earnings. For those that enter and are eliminated under this condition, the nomination fee and the fee to pass through the entry box, will be refunded. The owner of the winner to receive a gold trophy. (Closed with 432 nominations.)

Coupled—Golden Derby and Proud Appeal; Noble Nashua and Wayward Lass.

Splendid Spruce

B. c. 3, by Big Spruce—Splendid Spree, by Damascus
Br.—Webb Lillie F (Ky) — 1981 6 2 1 0 $219,100
Own.—Surf and Turf Stable — 126 — Tr.—Knight Chay R — 1980 5 2 1 0 $23,500

12Apr81-8SA	1⅛	:453	1:101	1:49 ft	15	120	65¾	52½	2½	1½	McHrguDG2	S A Dby	84	SplnddSprc,JhnlN'Hrld,Hdwn'sDy	13
28Mar81-8SA	1 1/16	:46	1:10	1:42 ft	48	116	21	21	2½	2nk	McHrDG3	SanFelipeH	91	Stnchrry,SplndidSpruc,FlyingNshu	12
18Mar81-7SA	1 1/16	:462	1:13	1:474sy	2½	117	27	11½	18	120	Pincay L Jr5	Alw	62	SplendidSpruce,Prtez,GelicNvonod	6
12Feb81-8SA	1 1/16	:47	1:111	1:422ft	6½	117	44½	58½	67½	64¾	Pincay L Jr5	Alw	84	Litigator, Gaelic Navonod, Seafood	6
31Jan81-7SA	1 1/16	:471	1:114	1:444gd	8½	116	31	3½	41	54½	Shoemaker W1	Alw	72	Jetzier, Heavy Hand, Tell Again	7
17Jan81-7SA	1	:462	1:103	1:351ft	5½	117	54	74½	54½	47½	Shoemaker W3	Alw	85	Stnchrry,InvincibleDooley,TellAgin	7
10Sep80-8Dmr	1	:462	1:11	1:361ft	*2½	114	119	910	610	78½	ShmrW3	Del Mar Fut	78	BoldAndGold,LooksLikRin,SrDncr	12
27Aug80-8Dmr	1	:46	1:111	1:372ft	3½	115	54½	43½	43½	21½	ShoemakerW5	Balboa	79	BoldAndGold,SplndidSpruc,SirDncr	7
18Aug80-7Dmr	1	:461	1:12	1:382ft	*8-5	117	42	1hd	1½	11½	Shoemaker W6	Alw	76	SplendidSpruc,Dgn,LongLivThKing	8
19Jly80-8Hol	6f	:212	:442	1:10 ft	11	122	95½	1110	1110	107½	LphT5	Hol Juv Chmp	79	Loma Malad, Motivity, Bold Ego	13
3Jly80-1Hol	6f	:221	:451	1:102ft	*9-5	116	64	57½	2hd	1½	Shoemaker W9	Mdn	85	Splendid Spruce, Thriver, Partez	11

●Apr 29 CD 5f ft :592 h — Apr 24 CD 7f gd 1:292 h — ●Apr 18 SA 4f ft :462 h — Apr 9 SA 5f ft :592 h

*Habano

Dk. b. or br. c. 3, by Ferrol—Miss Tepeji, by Breezy Lane
Br.—Gillermo Estevez M (Mex) — 1981 3 1 0 0 $33,479
Own.—Coello M A — 126 — Tr.—Gonzalez Francisco — 1980 9 8 1 0 $167,645

23Apr81-7Kee	1⅛	:472	1:113	1:512sy	48	121	32	45	713	718	McHrDG4	Blue Grass	62	ProudAppeal,LawMe,GoldenDerby	11
14Apr81-7Kee	1 1/16	:464	1:103	1:441ft	6½	118	21½	63½	811	826	Cordero A Jr2	Alw	59	SwingingLght,Sportn'Lf,GoldnDrby	8
6Mar81-8Mex	7f	:231	:463	1:272ft	*1-9e	117	32½	33	21	1½	CordroAJr4	Qutzlcotl	79	Habano, Distinct Lover, Offset	11
14Dec80-10Mex	1	:483	1:152	1:441ft	*1-3e	117	32½	2hd	2½	1½	Soto S B2	Fut	62	Habano, Consolapa, Linea Maginot	8
29Nov80-10Mex	7f	:232	:471	1:262ft	*1-9e	117	21	2½	11½	18	Soto S B5	Cudad	84	Habano, Linea Maginot,SenorRicky	6
16Nov80-10Mex	6½f	:232	:461	1:192ft	*1-2e	117	41	31½	2hd	13½	Mercado F3	Alw	86	Habano, Senor Ricky, Henares	7
30Aug80-10Mex	7f	:23	:471	1:254gd	*4-5	117	75	62½	12	110	Soto S B15	Anhuac	87	Habano, Alvertido, Jereba	15
19Aug80-9Mex	6½f	:224	:463	1:203ft	*1-2	117	31½	2hd	1hd	2hd	Cervantes J G2	Alw	80	Jereba, Habano, Don Nicho	6
2Aug80-10Mex	6½f	:222	:461	1:202m	*2-3e	117	42½	42	1hd	1nk	CrvntsJG9	Cuhtemoc	81	Habano, Definido, Linea Maginot	12
19Jly80-10Mex	6f	:222	:461	1:123ft	*6-5e	117	52	31½	2½	14	CervantesJG7	Cridors	88	Habáno, Definado, Senor Ricky	14
10Jun80-7Mex	5f	:23	:462	:584ft	8-5	117	1½	1hd	11	13	Cervantes J G5	Alw	95	Habano, Senor Ricky, Fly Victory	8
27May80-1Mex	5f	:224	:462	:592ft	36	117	1hd	1hd	15	14½	Cervantes J G5	Mdn	92	Habano, Impresor, Cascabelillo	10

Apr 20 Kee 1 1/16 sy 1:58 b — Apr 12 Kee 1 1/16 ft 1:59 b

Pleasant Colony

Dk. b. or br. c. 3, by His Majesty—Sun Colony, by Sunrise Flight
Br.—Evans T M (Va) — 1981 3 1 1 0 $114,179
Own.—Buckland Farm — 126 — Tr.—Campo John P — 1980 5 2 1 0 $87,900
Turf 1 0 1 0 $12,040

18Apr81-9Aqu	1⅛	:454	1:102	1:493ft	*13	126	413	37	13	13	Fell J5	Wood Mem'l	87	PlsntColony,HighlndBld,CurthBlus	6
8Mar81-9GP	1⅛	:47	1:111	1:502ft	4	122	1118	911	57	513	BrcclleVJr6	Fla Derby	67	Lord Avie, Akureyri, Linnleur	11
16Feb81-9GP	1 1/16	:48	1:121	1:442ft	17	122	813	86	3nk	2no	BrcclVJr8	YouthStks	79	Akureyri, PleasantColony,LordAvie	9
9Nov80-8Aqu	1⅛	:474	1:123	1:501ft	5½	116	710	64¾	32	2½	BraccileVJr5	Remsen	83	‡Akureyri,PlsntColony,FoolishTnnr	8

9Nov80—Placed first through disqualification

27Oct80-8Aqu	1⅛ (T)	:484	1:144	1:544sf	43	115	1314	1213	57½	2¾	BraccileVJr12	Pilgrim	69	Akureyri, Pleasant Colony, Jetzier	14
13Oct80-8Bow	7f	:224	:453	1:25 ft	6½	113	75	75½	74	52½	BrfldD10	Mar Nursery	78	John'sRoll,PintdShild,MtchingGift	11

13Oct80—Run in Two Divisions 8th & 9th Races.

22Sep80-2Med	1 70	:471	1:132	1:443ft	4½	118	711	49	13	10½	Asmussen C B8	Mdn	78	PlsntColony,CmmntyIntrst,SldCrdt	8
1Sep80-4Bel	7f	:223	:461	1:243ft	28	118	3½	42	613	616	Brumfield D7	Mdn	63	Summing, Academy H., Bay Ridge	7

Apr 29 CD 4f ft :481 h — Apr 15 Bel tr.t 4f gd :494 h — ●Apr 11 Bel tr.t 1 ft 1:393 h — Apr 6 Bel tr.t 1 gd 1:40 h (d)

Pass the Tab

Gr. c. 3, by Al Hattab—Dantina, by Gray Phantom
Br.—Villareal L (Cal) — 1981 3 0 2 0 $38,000
Own.—Villareal L — 126 — Tr.—Barrera Albert S — 1980 6 6 0 0 $129,287

18Apr81-8Spt	1⅛	:462	1:122	1:493ft	*3½	126	22	3½	3nk	2½	Rivera M A11	Ill Dby	97	Paristo, Pass the Tab, Bitterrook	13
9Apr81-8Aqu	1	:444	1:09	1:351ft	*4-5	119	1½	2½	11½	23	Cordero A Jr3	Alw	87	Cdt High, Pass The Tab,Mr.Wilford	7
7Mar81-8Aqu	6f	[•]:224	:464	1:112sy	2	126	32	32	47	515	Nicolo P3	Swift	72	Proud Appeal,Triocala,BuffaloLuck	5
31Aug80-11SFe	6½f	:221	:442	1:161ft	*1-5	118	2hd	13	18	113	KillnM7	S Fe Futur'y	99	PssTheTb,Shlli'sDnsr,DrconicSpok	10
22Aug80-6SFe	6½f	:221	:44	1:161ft	*1-5	118	2hd	13	16	113	Killen M9	SplW	99	PassTheTb,DrconicSpoke,FirstAwy	9
17Jly80-7Aks	6f	:223	:454	1:123m	*2½	122	98½	98½	32½	14	Killen M5	Aks Juv	74	Pass The Tab, Louis S.,CrossFlags	12
22Jun80-10LaM	4½f	:223	:451	:511ft	*1-3	119	2	32½	1nk	10½	KllnM4	Switch Frsom	100	Pass The Tab, Sir L. J., Little Art	10
14Jun80-9LaM	4½f	:232	:464	:523ft	*1-3	119	4	1½	11	16½	Killen M3	Alw	93	PssThTb,BouncngArond,KngHoopr	9
18May80-3SFe	4½f	:222	:45	:513ft	*3-2	118	1	11½	13	115	Killen M4	Mdn	98	PassTheTab,MgicPrter,TheRipper	10

Apr 28 CD 7f ft 1:26 h — Apr 3 Bel tr.t 4f ft :474 h — Mar 28 Bel tr.t 5f ft 1:00 b — ●Mar 15 Aqu 5f ft 1:00 h

Noble Nashua

Dk. b. or br. c. 3, by Nashua—Noble Lady, by Vaguely Noble
Br.—Gromemont Farm (Ky) — 1981 4 2 0 1 $54,576
Own.—Flying Zee Stable — 126 — Tr.—Martin Jose — 1980 4 2 1 0 $62,807

18Apr81-9Aqu	1⅛	:454	1:102	1:493ft	5½	126	2½	22	49	414	CrdrAJr6	WoodMem'l	73	PlsntColony,HighlndBld,CurthBlus	6
5Apr81-8Aqu	1	:45	1:084	1:333ft	3½	123	32	34½	38	38½	Cordero AJr1	Gotham	89	ProudAppel,CuretheBlus,NoblNshu	6
25Feb81-8Aqu	1 1/16	[•]:47	1:121	1:43 gd	*2-5	119	12	11	14	19½	CordrAJr4	Whirlaway	99	NobleNashua,RoylPvilion,Summing	5
6Feb81-9Tam	6f	:222	:462	1:123ft	*1-9	116	43	32½	2½	15½	Cordero A Jr5	Alw	82	Noble Nashua, Rit Cat, Sible Sue	7
25Oct80-9Lrl	1 1/16	:461	1:113	1:442sy	3½	122	23	22½	310	414	Cordero A Jr2	Lrl Fut	72	CuretheBlues,MtchingGift,KnRson	7
12Oct80-8Bel	1	:461	1:113	1:371ft	4½	122	32	1hd	11	22½	CrdrAJr8	Champagne	80	Lord Avie, Noble Nashua, Sezyou	9
29Sep80-7Bel	6½f	:224	:454	1:164ft	*2-3	122	31	32	2½	1nk	Pincay L Jr1	Alw	92	NobleNashua,ReallySmrt,JiggsAlrm	6
18Sep80-6Bel	6f	:223	:462	1:103ft	3	118	67	42½	1hd	15	Pincay L Jr9	Mdn	89	Noble Nashua,SambaBoy,HaveOne	10

Apr 14 Bel tr.t 6f ft 1:161 b — Apr 1 Bel tr.t 4f ft :481 b — ●Mar 25 Bel tr.t 5f ft :593 h — ●Mar 18 Bel tr.t 5f ft :593 b

Golden Derby

Ro. c. 3, by Master Derby—Old Goldie, by Young Emperor
Br.—Lehmann Frederick E (Ky) 1981 3 0 0 2 $23,067
Own.—Lehmann F E & Gaines J R 126 Tr.—Adams William E 1980 7 3 0 2 $78,292

23Apr81-7Kee 1⅛ :47² 1:11³ 1:51²sy *1-2e 121 2½ 2hd 2² 33¾ EspnzJC⁹ Blue Grass 76 ProudAppeal,LawMe,GoldenDerby 11
14Apr81-7Kee 1 1/16 :46⁴ 1:10³ 1:44¹ft 16 113 11½ 11½ 1hd 33½ Espinoza J C¹ Alw 81 SwingingLght,Sportn'Lf,GoldnDrby 8
28Mar81-8Lat 1 :46 1:11 1:38 ft 2½ 122 33½ 511 828 838 Hawley S³ Spiral 53 MythiclRuler,ClssicGoGo,IronGem 10
6Sep80-8AP 7f :22¹ :44⁴ 1:23⁴ft 3½e 122 64¾ 35 68½ 814 HwleyS⁸ Arl Was Fut 69 WellDcortd,LordAvi,FirwyPhntom 15
20Aug80-8AP 6f :22² :46 1:13 gd *2-3e 124 1½ 1hd 2½ 31½ Espnz.JC¹ Arch Ward 75 FirwyPhntom,Linnleur,GoldenDrby 9
21Jly80-8Bel 6f :22² :46 1:11²ft 3½ 122 2¹ 1hd 11½ 1hd McHrguDG¹ Tremont 85 GoldenDerby,GrtProspctor,LordAvi 9
28Jun80-8CD 5½f :22 :44⁴ 1:04¹ft 4½ 125 2½ 2½ 12½ 1½ EspinozaJC³ Jeff Cup 102 GoldenDerby,PlinSpking,BoldTyson 7
31May80-8CD 5f :22¹ :45⁴ :59 ft 5½ 117 2½ 2½ 11½ 1no EspnJC⁵ Bshfrd Man 94 GoldnDrby,WrongImprssion,Stublm 9
7May80-7Spt 4f :21² :45³ft 7½ 112 5 2½ 3³ 3⁴ SpencrSA³ Spt Jvnle 92 FullofDrive,BoldTyson,GoldenDrby 7
23Apr80-7Kee 4½f :22² :46² :53 ft 7½ 116 6 1hd 3½ 56¾ EspinozJC⁶ Lafayette 83 FirmBoss,BndthTims,SilvrDollrBoy 7

Apr 29 CD 4f ft :51 b Apr 22 Kee 3f ft :38⁴ b Apr 20 Kee 4f sy :49² b Apr 13 Kee 3f ft :38 b

Partez

B. c. 3, by Quack—Lady Marguery, by Tim Tam
Br.—Noonan-Runnymede Farm (Ky) 1981 5 1 2 0 $27,900
Own.—Davis E & Greene Mr-Mrs H 126 Tr.—Lukas D Wayne 1980 9 2 1 2 $77,821
Turf 1 1 0 0 $16,500

12Apr81-8SA 1⅛ :45³ 1:10¹ 1:49 ft 9½ 120 53½ 62¾ 55½ 67 McCrronCJ¹ S A Dby 77 SplnddSprc,JhnlN'Hrld,Hdwn'sDy 13
5Apr81-4SA 1⅛ ①:45¹ 1:09 1:47¹fm *7-5 114 13½ 13½ 13 19 Hawley S² Alw 91 Partez, Tell Again, Quantum Leap 6
21Mar81-6SA 1 1/16 :46¹ 1:11¹ 1:43³gd 3½ 114 4³ 3nk 3nk 2¹ Hawley S² Alw 82 Seafood, Partez, Table Torch 8
15Mar81-8SA 1 :45³ 1:10³ 1:36 ft 16 116 98½ 813 812 714 LiphamT⁸ San Rafael 75 JohnlN'Hrold,MingsotChif,ARun 10
1Mar81-7SA 1 1/16 :46² 1:13 1:47⁴sy 3½ 120 313 36½ 2⁸ 220 Lipham T¹ Alw 42 SplendidSpruce,Prtez,GelicNvonod 6
15Nov80-8SA 1 1/16 :46³ 1:11 1:43⁴ft *2½ 118 4² 31½ 42½ 31½ Lipham T⁷ Norfolk 81 Sir Dancer, Chiaroscuro, Partez 8

15Nov80—Run in two divisions 8th & 9th races.

29Oct80-8SA 7f :21⁴ :44⁴ 1:23 ft 6½ 117 54½ 5⁶ 52½ 1½ LiphmT² Sunny Slope 85 Partez, Chiaroscuro, Loma Malad 7
17Oct80-7SA 1 :45⁴ 1:11² 1:38 ft *9-5 120 2³ 2½ 1½ 2hd McHargueD G¹ Alw 79 Dialect, Partez, Table Torch 9
18Sep80-8Dmr 1 :46² 1:11 1:36¹ft 22 114 97 64½ 44½ 44 LiphmT⁴ Del Mar Fut 83 BoldAndGold,LooksLikRin,SrDncr 12
27Aug80-8Dmr 1 :46 1:11¹ 1:37²ft 6½ 115 3½ 5⁴ 59½ 911 Lipham T⁶ Balboa 70 BoldAndGold,SplndidSpruc,SirDncr 7
3Aug80-1Dmr 1 :47⁴ 1:12¹ 1:37⁴ft 8-5 118 3² 44½ 2½ 1¹ Lipham T⁶ Mdn 79 Partez,SprkOfBlue,SportingBrother 9
3Jly80-1Hol 6f :22¹ :45¹ 1:10²ft 15 116 1hd 1½ 1hd 31¾ Valenzuela P A¹ Mdn 83 Splendid Spruce, Thriver, Partez 11
24May80-1Hol 5f :22¹ :45³ :57³ft 5 115 42½ 4¹ 5⁶ 5⁷ Lipham T⁶ Mdn 85 Fair Hint, GreatGame,FAbulousToo 7

Apr 29 Kee 5f sy 1:01¹ b ●Apr 10 SA 3f ft :34² h Apr 3 SA 3f ft :35³ hg Mar 31 SA ① 6f fm 1:01¹ h (d)

Double Sonic

Ro. c. 3, by Nodouble—Eloquent Es, by Pyjestinian
Br.—Elias Brothers Farm (Fla) 1981 5 1 0 1 $114,087
Own.—Elias F & L 126 Tr.—Krajnick George 1980 12 4 2 1 $53,801

23Apr81-7Kee 1⅛ :47² 1:11³ 1:51²sy 17 121 1013 813 58½ 43¾ ThrnbrgB³ Blue Grass 76 ProudAppeal,LawMe,GoldenDerby 11
28Mar81-9Hia 1⅛ :47 1:10⁴ 1:49¹ft 6½ 122 6⁷ 67½ 6⁸ 3⁵ ThornbrgB³ Flamingo 81 TpShoes,WellDecorted,DoublSonic 7
8Mar81-9GP 1⅛ :47 1:11¹ 1:50²ft 12 122 1017 1011 46½ 411 SmithAJr¹¹ Fla Derby 69 Lord Avie, Akureyri, Linnleur 11
4Feb81-9GP 7f :22³ :45² 1:23²ft 14 122 312 416 58½ 44 SmithAJr⁶ Hutcheson 83 Lord Avie, Spirited Boy, Linnleur 7
3Jan81-9Crc 1 1/16 :47² 1:12¹ 1:46²ft 14 121 1321 914 51½ 1¹ SthAJr¹¹ TrpParkDby 87 DoubleSonic,Akureyri,MightBHom 14
20Dec80-9Crc 1 1/16 :47 1:12³ 1:46²ft 14 117 914 7⁵ 58½ 3² SthAJr⁷ Whtaplesure 85 Akureyri, ‡Linnleur, Double Sonic 9

20Dec80—Placed second through disqualification

6Dec80-9Crc 1 1/16 :48⁴ 1:13³ 1:46⁴ft 3½ 117 108½ 714 612 58½ CrdnE⁶ Cty Of Miami 76 CatchThatPass,BearCt,RoylPruner 12
15Nov80-9Crc 170 :47² 1:13² 1:46²ft *3-5 119 68½ 58½ 46 22½ CrdonE⁸ J H Bright 75 Bear Cat, Double Sonic,MalcolmW. 6
1Nov80-9Crc 170 :46⁴ 1:13³ 1:45³ft *½ 116 717 77½ 46½ 37½ CrdnE⁶ Ponce Deleon 74 RoughLord,MlcolmW.,DoubleSonic 7
11Oct80-7Crc 1 :48 1:13⁴ 1:41⁴ft *3-2 114 510 4⁷ 31½ 1¾ CrdoneE³ F Pleasure 79 DoblSonc,StotHrtdMn,GovrnorBob 7

11Oct80—Run in Two Divisions: 7th & 9th Races.

1Oct80-7Crc 1 :48² 1:14 1:42 ft 3½ 114 44½ 411 43½ 1² Cardone E⁴ Alw 78 DoblSonc,Mry'sKngdom,IncrdblJhn 5
8Sep80-9Crc 170 :49¹ 1:15³ 1:47¹ft 6 116 52½ 63½ 1hd 13½ Cardone E⁴ Alw 74 DoublSonic,RinBouRunnr,ZmbziWy 6
29Aug80-8Crc 6f :22⁴ :46¹ 1:12 ft 7½ 118 8⁷ 6⁹ 516 514 Jimenez I J⁵ Alw 78 StoutHertedMn,Hrry'sHze,ErlyBob 8
20Aug80-8Crc 6f :22² :46¹ 1:13¹ft 20 118 80¾ 711 613 49¾ Jimenez I J⁶ Alw 76 Spirited Boy,CraftyEd,MalcolmW. 11
2Aug80-3Crc 6f :22³ :47 1:13³ft 22 117 98½ 98½ 3² 2nk Jimenez I J⁵ Mdn 84 ‡StoutHrtdMn,DoublSonc,VldDncr 12

2Aug80—Place first through disqualification.

23Jly80-5Crc 5f :23 :46⁴ :59³sy 17 116 1011 915 815 817 Cardone E¹⁰ Mdn 80 SpiritdBoy,‡GovrnorBob,GlicPnny 12
12Jly80-6Crc 5f :23¹ :47³ 1:01²ft 28 116 911 811 6⁶ 64¾ Jimenez I J⁷ Mdn 83 MlcolmW.,Tigirish,PickersDelight 11

Apr 22 Kee 3f ft :36⁴ b Apr 16 Kee 1 ft 1:42 b Mar 27 Crc 3f ft :37³ b Mar 21 Crc 1 ft 1:43 b

Proud Appeal ×

B. c. 3, by Valid Appeal—Proud N Happy, by Proudest Roman
Br.—Camp & Yowell (Fla) 1981 5 5 0 0 $269,230
Own.—Winfield M H et al 126 Tr.—Hough Stanley M 1980 4 3 0 0 $72,737

23Apr81-7Kee 1⅛ :47² 1:11³ 1:51²sy *1-2e 121 1½ 1hd 1² 1³ Fell J⁶ Blue Grass 80 ProudAppeal,LawMe,GoldenDerby 11
5Apr81-8Aqu 1 :45 1:08⁴ 1:33³ft 9-5 123 1½ 1½ 1hd 1no Fell J³ Gotham 98 ProudAppel,CuretheBlus,NoblNshu 6
22Mar81-8Aqu 7f :22 :44³ 1:22¹ft *1-3 121 1hd 1½ 1⁵ 14½ Fell J¹ Bay Shore 90 ProudAppl,WillowHour,RoylPvilion 4
7Mar81-8Aqu 6f ⊡:22⁴ :46⁴ 1:11²sy *4-5 126 2hd 2hd 1hd 1³ Fell J⁵ Swift 87 Proud Appeal,Triocala,BuffaloLuck 5
22Feb81-8Aqu 6f ⊡:22 :45¹ 1:09⁴sy 1e 117 3½ 2hd 1hd 1¾ Fell J¹ Woodhaven 95 Proud Appeal,Triocala,BuffaloLuck 5
29Jly80-9Mth 5½f :22² :46¹ 1:05¹sy *4-5 122 77½ 68¾ 48½ 410 Fell J¹ Tyro 79 Khrtoum,TrvellingMusic,JohnnyKs 8
30Jun80-8Bel 5½f :23² :46³ 1:04²ft *3-5 122 2½ 2hd 1½ 11½ Fell J⁶ Great Amer 93 ProudAppeal,IncredibleLuck,KidKs 7
16Jun80-8Bel 5½f :22² :46¹ 1:05¹ft 4 117 32½ 3² 11½ 1⁸ Fell J⁴ Youthful 89 Proud Appeal, Kid Kas, Lockjaw 9
17May80-3Crc 5f :23 :47 :59⁴ft 9-5 115 1² 11½ 1⁴ 16½ Guerra W A⁶ Mdn 96 Proud Appeal,Hypnotized,CraftyEd 8

●Apr 19 Kee 5f ft :58⁴ h Apr 1 Bel tr.t 4f ft :46³ h Mar 18 Bel tr.t 4f ft :48³ h ●Mar 3 Bel tr.t 4f ft :47³ h

Hoedown's Day

B. c. 3, by Bargain Day—Miss Hoedown, by Dance Lesson
Br.—Dominguez Mr-Mrs Roger (Cal) 1981 3 1 1 1 $100,200
Own.—Dominguez-Freidel-Thatcher 126 Tr.—Dominguez Roger 1980 8 4 2 0 $64,525

12Apr81-8SA 1⅛ :45³ 1:10¹ 1:49 ft 39e 120 41¾ 32½ 3² 32¾ ChapmnTM⁵ S A Dby 81 SplnddSprc,JhnlN'Hrld,Hdwn'sDy 13
7Mar81-8GG 1 1/16 :47⁴ 1:13¹ 1:47⁴sl 3 122 2³ 2⁴ 3⁶ 212 ChpnTM⁵ Calif Derby 52 AlwaysACinch,Hoedown'sDy,Okubo 6
21Feb81-8GG 1 :45² 1:09⁴ 1:35²ft 6½e 119 1hd 1¹ 1³ 11½ ChpnTM⁸ Gold Rush 91 Hdwn'sDy,AlysACnch,SnppyBrgn 13
1Nov80-8BM 1 1/16 :45 1:09⁴ 1:42¹ft 6 117 2² 2³ 11½ 2¾ ChpTM⁴ Elcam'oReal 87 ChrgngStr,Hodown'sDy,SnshnSwg 13
17Oct80-8BM 1 :45² 1:09⁴ 1:36 ft 3½e 115 11½ 11½ 1hd 2hd Munoz E⁸ San Mateo 88 AlysACnch,Hdw'sDy,LngLvThKng 10
30Oct80-8BM 6f :22² :45 1:09⁴ft 3-2 119 31½ 4³ 45½ 46½ MnozE⁷ Francis Drak 84 MkeHimFmous,LomMld,DressyNtiv 7
29Aug80-11Sac 1 :46¹ 1:10⁴ 1:36³ft *2-3 119 11½ 1² 12½ 1⁶ MnozE⁵ S Fjuvchamp 93 Hoedown'sDy,JdRing,AndrwThoms 8
30Jly80-11Bmf 6f :22² :45³ 1:11²ft 6-5 122 41¾ 3² 1½ 1² Munoz E⁴ Mid Pen 83 Hoedown'sDay,Reglberto,Soderling 5
3Jun80-8GG 5½f :22¹ :45⁴ 1:04³ft 5 117 1½ 1² 1³ 13½ Munoz E⁵ Tanforan 90 Hodown'sDy,Rglbrto,BlowngSnow 11
29Apr80-8GG 5f :22 :45³ :58³ft 3½ 118 3² 54¾ 6⁸ 6⁷ Winick D¹¹ Juvenile 84 D. Aminoil, Hematite,BlowingSnow 8
16Apr80-4GG 5f :22¹ :45³ :57³ft *8-5 118 1hd 11½ 1² 1⁵ Winick D¹⁰ Mdn 96 Hoedown'sDy,SirEchelon,Hemtite 12

Apr 25 CD 7f ft 1:30 h Apr 21 CD 4f ft :48 b ●Apr 10 SA 4f ft :45³ h Apr 4 GG 5f ft :59³ hg

Woodchopper

Gr. c. 3, by Hatchet Man—Musical Chairs, by Swaps
Br.—Greentree Stud Inc (Ky) 1981 5 3 0 2 $100,185
Own.—Greentree Stable 126 Tr.—Gaver John M Jr 1980 1 M 0 0

11Apr81-9OP 1⅛ :47¹ 1:11² 1:50²ft 2½ 123 98½ 85½ 6⁷ 33¾ ShomkrW⁸ Aks Derby 87 BoldEgo,TopAvenger,Woodchopper 9
28Mar81-9FG 1⅛ :46² 1:11³ 1:50⁴ft 6 113 1012 97½ 4⁵ 1¹ VelasquezJ⁴ La Derby 90 Woodchopper, A Run, Beau Rit 13
13Mar81-9FG 1 40 :48 1:13³ 1:42 ft *8-5 119 811 5⁸ 3½ 12½ McKnight J⁷ Alw 83 Woodchopper,ExctlyE.,MotorCop 10
5Mar81-5FG 1 1/16 :47³ 1:13⁴ 1:46³ft *8-5 119 613 54½ 12½ 1³ McKnight J⁸ Mdn 79 Woodchopper,LitningInBottle,Rust 8
19Feb81-4FG 6f :22¹ :47¹ 1:12¹ft 17 119 108½ 119½ 710 37½ McKnight J⁷ Mdn 76 LiutantCorly,LssSon,Woodchoppr 12
23Aug80-4Sar 6f :22⁴ :46² 1:11²ft 12 118 1112 1111 1013 1014 Gonzalez M A⁴ Mdn 69 JungleJove,Summing,CountrAttck 12

Apr 28 CD 1 ft 1:38 h Apr 10 OP 3f ft :37 b Apr 7 OP 6f ft 1:14⁴ b Mar 27 FG 4f ft :49 h

Well Decorated

Dk. b. or br. c. 3, by Raja Baba—Paris Breeze, by Majestic Prince
Br.—Allen H (Fla) 1981 3 1 1 0 $81,686
Own.—Allen Herbert 126 Tr.—Jacobs Eugene 1980 8 3 0 1 $208,887

14Apr81-7Kee 1 1/16 :46⁴ 1:10³ 1:44¹ft *1-2 113 4³ 53½ 4⁸ 43½ MacBeth D⁶ Alw 81 SwingingLght,Sportn'Lf,GoldnDrby 8
28Mar81-9Hia 1⅛ :47 1:10⁴ 1:49¹ft 3½ 122 1½ 1hd 1² 2¹ MacBethD³ Flamingo 85 TpShoes,WellDecorted,DoublSonic 7
9Mar81-9Hia 7f :22² :44⁴ 1:22¹ft 5½ 119 32½ 3⁴ 2hd 1no MacBeth D¹ Bahamas 92 WellDecorted,DshO'Plesure,TpShos 8
25Oct80-8Lrl 1 1/16 :46¹ 1:11³ 1:44²sy 6 122 46½ 38½ 413 516 AsmussenCB³ Lrl Fut 70 CuretheBlues,WchingGift,KnRson 7
12Oct80-8Bel 1 :46¹ 1:11³ 1:37¹ft 2½ 122 2¹ 2hd 3² 4⁸ ‡PncyLJr⁶ Champagne 74 Lord Avie, Noble Nashua, Sezyou 9

‡12Oct80—Dead heat

6Sep80-8AP 7f :22¹ :44⁴ 1:23⁴ft 6 122 77¾ 57½ 3nk 1² PncLJr⁴ Arl Was Fut 83 WellDcortd,LordAvi,FirwyPhntom 15
23Aug80-8Sar 6½f :22² :45³ 1:17 ft 4½ 122 1hd 1hd 2² 3⁸ Venezia M³ Hopeful 79 Tap Shoes,LordAvie,WellDecorated 9
4Aug80-8Sar 6f :22 :45 1:10¹ft 4½ 117 1¹ 1² 1⁴ 14½ VeneziaM⁶ Sar Spec'l 88 WellDecorated,TapShoes,Motivity 10
24Jly80-5Bel 6f :22² :46 1:11¹ft 1¾ 118 1¹ 1hd 1¹ 1nk Venezia M⁴ Mdn 85 WellDecorated,JungleJove,CutHigh 9

Apr 21 Kee 4f ft :48 bg ●Apr 11 Kee 4f sy :47 b ●Mar 25 GP 5f ft :58² h Mar 21 GP 1 ft 1:38 h

Classic Go Go

B. c. 3, by Pago Pago—Classic Perfection, by Never Bend
Br.—Winchell V H (Ky) 1981 10 7 2 0 $287,383
Own.—Winchell V H 126 Tr.—Meyer Jerome C 1980 5 1 1 1 $10,300

25Apr81-7CD 1 :47² 1:11⁴ 1:37⁴ft *1 122 2² 2¹ 2¹ 2⁴ Delahoussaye E¹ Alw 76 MythclRulr,ClsscGoGo,TlrsonStudo 4
16Apr81-7Kee 7f :23 :45⁴ 1:24 ft *2-5 121 3½ 1hd 1² 11½ Black A S¹ Alw 86 ClssicGoGo,WthCaton,Contorsonst 6
28Mar81-8Lat 1 :46 1:11 1:38 ft *3-5 122 44½ 3³ 2⁴ 28½ Black A S² Spiral 82 MythiclRuler,ClssicGoGo,IronGem 10
18Mar81-8Pim 6f :22⁴ :45⁴ 1:10¹gd *3-5 122 44½ 4⁶ 48½ 4⁹ Black A S⁴ H Jacobs 86 Century Prince, J. D.Quill,IrishKing 5
28Feb81-9Bow 1 1/16 :47¹ 1:12² 1:46⁴ft *1-3 122 69½ 3⁴ 12½ 1⁶ Black A S⁹ Bowie 72 ClssicGoGo,HonorbleMn,BostonTe 10
16Feb81-9Bow 7f :23 :46 1:23¹ft 8-5 122 64¾ 53½ 2hd 1³ Fann B⁶ Gen. George 89 ClsscGoGo,ThrtyEghtPcs,AztcCrwn 9
7Feb81-8Aqu 1⅛ ⊡:47³ 1:12 1:50³ft 5½ 117 56¾ 4⁶ 2hd 11½ Fann B¹ Lucky Draw 93 ClassicGoGo,RoyalPavilion,Triocala 7
1Feb81-8Key 6f :22² :45⁴ 1:11²ft 3½ 122 6⁸ 42½ 2hd 11½ Black A S² Alw 85 ClssicGoGo,HoldOnPto,Rock'NRdy 6
14Jan81-7Aqu 1 1/16 ⊡:48³ 1:14 1:45¹ft 4½ 109 43½ 2hd 1hd 1nk Migliore R³ HcpO 88 ClssicGoGo,SwpforPowr,MornngHz 9
10Jan81-5Aqu 1 1/16 ⊡:47² 1:13⁴ 1:46³ft 23 115⁷ 2² 2hd 1⁴ 1⁷ Migliore R⁵ Alw 81 ClssicGoGo,RoylPvilion,EverNoble 10
29Dec80-3Med 1 1/16 :50² 1:16¹ 1:48⁴ft *7-5 113⁵ 53½ 3¹ 1hd 1¾ Kaenel J L⁴ Mdn 65 ClassicGoGo,TurnAngle,HastyScott 7
19Dec80-4Med 6f :23 :47² 1:14²ft 2½ 118 4³ 44½ 42½ 32½ Lovato F Jr⁷ Mdn 68 JeffreyH.,Standpoint,ClassicGoGo 12
11Dec80-4Med 6f :23 :46⁴ 1:13 ft 3½ 120 85½ 42½ 21½ 2½ Fann B¹⁰ Mdn 77 Bitterrook,ClssicGoGo,PssingAge 11
3Dec80-3Med 170 :48¹ 1:13³ 1:43³ft 8½ 118 2¹ 2½ 3³ 43½ MacBeth D³ Mdn 80 Main Stem,GreyTiger,MorningHaze 8
6Nov80-4Med 6f :22³ :46 1:12 ft 67 118 108½ 1017 915 811 Chatman H G⁹ Mdn 72 GreekMinstrel,Simbari,SuperHawk 10

Apr 12 Kee 5f ft 1:01² b ●Mar 27 Lat 3f sy :36³ h Mar 10 Bow 6f ft 1:12¹ h

Top Avenger

B. c. 3, by Staunch Avenger—Atop, by Dunce
Br.—Bishop W P (Tex) 1981 3 1 1 0 $75,720
Own.—Bishop W P 126 Tr.—Viator Dwight 1980 5 5 0 0 $93,620

11Apr81-9OP 1⅛ :47¹ 1:11² 1:50²ft 20 120 2½ 2½ 21½ 21½ Snyder L⁵ Aks Derby 90 BoldEgo,TopAvenger,Woodchopper 9
28Mar81-9FG 1⅛ :46² 1:11³ 1:50⁴ft 5 123 4⁸ 41½ 5⁸ 713 TrosclirAJ⁵ La Derby 77 Woodchopper, A Run, Beau Rit 13
13Feb81-8OP 6f :22 :46¹ 1:12 ft *1 121 41¾ 4¾ 2hd 11¾ Trosclair A J⁶ HcpO 85 Top Avenger, Lockjaw, KanofSpots 9
31Dec80-9FG 6f :22¹ :46¹ 1:11¹ft *2-5 124 11½ 1hd 1hd 1no TrosclairAJ⁷ Sugar Bl 89 TopAvenger,Contorsionist,GlassStr 9
30Nov80-9FG 6f :21⁴ :45⁴ 1:11 ft *1 122 46½ 3½ 1² 14½ TrsclrAJ¹² OldHckory 90 Top Avenger,GlassStar,SilentBasis 14
7Sep80-10EvD 6f :22⁴ :46 1:13 ft *3-5 120 2¹ 2¹ 1¹ 1⁵ TrosclrAJ¹¹ Lfyte Fty 83 TopAvenger,CjunMoccsin,LLStev 12
21Aug80-6EvD 6f :23² :47 1:13¹ft *1-2 120 4nk 2hd 1¹ 14½ Trosclair A J⁶ Trials 82 Top Avenger, Rust, Honey Pro 9
25Jly80-5LaD 5f :22⁴ :47³ 1:00 ft 3 120 2½ 1½ 1¹ 1⁴ Trosclair A J² Mdn 95 Top Avenger, Dr. No, Dr. Spanky 12

Apr 29 CD 4f ft :51³ b ●Apr 25 CD 6f ft 1:13² h Apr 21 CD 5f ft 1:03² b ●Mar 24 FG 1 ft 1:39⁴ h

Bold Ego

Dk. b. or br. c. 3, by Bold Tactics—Coya's Ego, by Bullin
Br.—Barton J D (NM) 1981 5 3 0 0 $205,990
Own.—Double B Ranch & Kidd J 126 Tr.—Van Berg Jack 1980 8 7 0 1 $176,686

11Apr81-9OP 1⅛ :471 1:112 1:502ft *2-3 123 1½ 1½ 11½ 11¼ Lively J9 Aks Derby 91 BoldEgo,TopAvenger,Woodchopper 9
14Mar81-9OP 170 :462 1:114 1:412ft 3 122 11 11 15 15¾ Lively J4 Rebel H 89 BoldEgo,CatchThtPss,ChpelCreek 10
28Feb81-9OP 6f :214 :46 1:114sy 3½ 117 11 1½ 14 16¾ Lively J4 HcpO 86 Bold Ego, Lockjaw, Vodika Collins 8
13Feb81-8OP 6f :22 :461 1:12 ft 4 120 2hd 2hd 42½ 56¾ Lively J5 HcpO 79 Top Avenger, Lockjaw, KanofSpots 9
21Jan81-8SA 6f :213 :441 1:094ft 5¼ 122 11 1hd 2½ 59 Jones K1 San Miguel 81 Motivity, Royal Forbes, Torso 6
14Sep80-10Alb 6f :214 :451 1:112ft *2-5 118 2hd 1½ 13 15¼ CshnJL9 N. Mex Futy 86 Bold Ego, Bin ABattle,ColonelDay 10
6Sep80-18Alb 6f :221 :454 1:131m *1-3 118 31 3nk 31 11 Cushing J L6 SplW 77 BoldEgo,Draconic'sLdy,IrishEye's 10
19Jly80-8Hol 6f :212 :442 1:10 ft 8¼ 122 1hd 1hd 1½ 33¼ CshJL2 Hol JuvChmp 83 Loma Malad, Motivity, Bold Ego 13
8Jun80-10Rui 4f :23 :47 ft *2-3 120 1 2hd 1hd 12¾ CshJL3 [S]R Gr' DeFut 88 Bold Ego, Dr. Me Up, First Away 10
30May80-7Rui 4f :223 :473ft *1-5 120 1 11 12 14¾ Cushing J L1 SplW 85 BoldEgo,CowboyLoving,AlaskanStr 8
4May80-11Sun 5f :22 :451 :572ft *6-5 120 1hd 1hd 11 12¾ CushingJL1 R Allison 96 BoldEgo,ElegantLaura,SquawBred 11
25Apr80-12Sun 5f :22 :452 :573ft *6-5 120 1hd 1hd 12 14 Cushing J L8 SplW 95 BoldEgo,ElegntLur,CcheInvestmnt 8
29Mar80-5Sun 4f :223 :453ft 15 118 3 1hd 12 14½ Cushing J L6 Mdn 96 BoldEgo,JohnnyDark,Casey'sImge 10
Apr 25 CD 1⅛ ft 1:56 b ●Apr 19 CD 7f ft 1:29 h ●Apr 4 OP 1 sy 1:42 b Mar 29 OP 7f sy 1:263 h

Cure the Blues ✕

B. c. 3, by Stop the Music—Quick Cure, by Dr Fager
Br.—Firestone B R Mr-Mrs (Va) 1981 3 1 1 1 $47,004
Own.—Firestone B R 126 Tr.—Jolley Leroy 1980 5 5 0 0 $131,102

18Apr81-9Aqu 1⅛ :454 1:102 1:493ft *1-5 126 1½ 12 23 38 VsquzJ1 Wood Mem'l 79 PlsntColony,HighlndBld,CurthBlus 6
5Apr81-8Aqu 1 :45 1:084 1:333ft *2-3 126 2½ 2½ 2hd 2no Vasquez J6 Gotham 98 ProudAppel,CuretheBlus,NoblNshu 6
26Mar81-9Hia 7f :23 :453 1:23 sy *1-9 122 22½ 1hd 14 15 Vasquez J1 Alw 88 CurethBlus,GovrnorBob,LPromnur 6
25Oct80-9Lrl 1 1/16 :461 1:113 1:442sy *1-2 122 13 12½ 16 16½ Turcotte R L1 Lrl Fut 86 CuretheBlues,MtchingGift,KnRson 7
13Oct80-9Bow 7f :223 :442 1:232ft *1-3 116 2hd 13 16 15 TrcttRL1 MarNursery 88 CuretheBlus,CnturyPrinc,JunglJov 6
13Oct80—Run in Two Divisions 8th & 9th Races.
6Oct80-8Bow 6f :223 :452 1:10 ft *1-5 113 13 13 15 17 Passmore W J3 Alw 90 CuretheBlues,SilentBsis,Viky'sChrg 6
20Sep80-7Bow 7f :231 :462 1:244ft *2-5 115 2½ 1hd 18 110 Turcotte R L3 Alw 81 CurthBlus,DoublWhmmy,HighJump 7
16Apr80-3Pim 5f :24 :472 :584ft *3-5 120 11½ 12 15 110 Turcotte R L1 Mdn 91 CurthBlus,PlyfulChstr,RunBoldRun 6
Apr 15 Aqu 5f gd :593 h ●Apr 2 Aqu 4f m :47 b Mar 25 Hia 2f ft :243 b ●Mar 19 Hia 6f ft 1:093 h

Beau Rit

B. g. 3, by Lord Rebeau—Rit-n-Rough, by Rough'n Tumble
Br.—Early Bird Stud (Fla) 1981 6 3 1 1 $96,100
Own.—Roussel Carole 126 Tr.—Roussel Louie III 1980 2 1 1 0 $6,000

23Apr81-7Kee 1⅛ :472 1:113 1:512sy 12 121 67 67½ 815 55¼ RbbccP10 Blue Grass 75 ProudAppeal,LawMe,GoldenDerby 11
29Mar81-9FG 1⅛ :462 1:113 1:504ft 11 126 810 63½ 33 33 RubbiccoP6 La Derby 87 Woodchopper, A Run, Beau Rit 13
14Mar81-9FG 1 1/16 :472 1:124 1:45 ft *8-5 122 44 32 21½ 2no RbbccoP6 La Dby Trl 87 SenateChairmn,BeuRit,Andy'sWish 9
8Feb81-9FG 1 1/16 :471 1:124 1:461ft *8-5 119 58½ 35½ 11½ 1hd RbbccP10 HPradeDby 81 BeuRit,BoysNiteOut,CircleofSteel 13
25Jan81-8FG 1 1/16 :47 1:131 1:463ft 8-5 119 39 2½ 11½ 11 RbbccP9 H P DbyTrls 79 Beau Rit, Nobubble, Contorsionist 9
9Jan81-5FG 140 :48 1:14 1:424ft *1-2 119 21 2½ 1hd 11 Rubbicco P7 Alw 79 Beau Rit, Nobubble, Hurricane Bay 7
24Dec80-4FG 6f :224 :471 1:124m *2-5 119 1hd 1hd 15 15 Rubbicco P2 Mdn 81 Beau Rit, Rust, Effy Says 11
4Dec80-4FG 6f :224 :481 1:112ft 23 119 2½ 2hd 2½ 21 Rubbicco P8 Mdn 87 Bold Ivor, Beau Rit, Captense 12
Apr 22 Kee 3f ft :36 b ●Apr 16 Kee 5f ft 1:001 h Mar 21 FG 5f ft 1:023 b Mar 13 FG 3f ft :38 b

Television Studio

B. g. 3, by Within Hail—Put on T V, by T V Lark
Br.—Bwamazon Farm (Ky) 1981 2 0 0 1 $2,560
Own.—Bwamazon Farm 126 Tr.—Basile Anthony 1980 11 3 2 3 $101,106

25Apr81-7CD 1 :472 1:114 1:374ft 11 122 310 46 45½ 37 Day P3 Alw 73 MythclRulr,ClsscGoGo,TlvsonStudo 4
3Apr81-6Kee a7f 1:26 ft 2½ 123 74¼ 77¼ 69½ 621 Brumfield D8 Alw 72 Sportin'Lif,MronFrncs,CrwfordSpcl 8
22Nov80-8CD 1 1/16 :49 1:14 1:47 ft 6¾ 119 56 52¾ 23 1nk BrumfldD2 Ky Jky Cb 73 TelevisionStudio,Linnleur,BrCrkDm 8
1Nov80-7CD 1 1/16 :49 1:143 1:483ft 8-5 117 43½ 31 11 14 Brumfield D4 Alw 65 TlvisionStudio,TwstnAlong,Skyclon 6
21Oct80-4Kee 1 1/16 :483 1:144 1:481ft *6-5 117 58 51¼ 3nk 2hd Brumfield D4 Mdn 65 ‡BcksGlor,TlvsonStdo,RmnSttsmn 12
21Oct80—Placed first through disqualification
11Oct80-3Kee 1 1/16 :483 1:144 1:493ft 3 117 1012 74½ 3½ 2½ Haire D8 Mdn 57 MrinEist,TlvsonStudo,RldndChrg 12
15Sep80-3AP 7f :233 :474 1:291sl 2½ 122 62¾ 63¼ 34½ 24¾ Patterson A8 Mdn 51 FllLine,TlvisionStudio,WstrnBufflo 8
18Aug80-5AP 6f :224 :464 1:141sl 16 122 87¾ 79½ 56 55¼ Patterson A7 Mdn 66 Corsicana, King Pali, Global Jet 8
8Aug80-4AP 5½f :222 :462 1:051ft 17 122 85¾ 67¼ 54¼ 47¾ Patterson A4 Mdn 81 IntrpdHttr,MsssspRbl,RldndChrg 11
21Jly80-3AP 5½f :224 :472 1:07 sy 3¾ 122 87¼ 89¾ 412 414 Patterson A9 Mdn 66 Broadway Raider, MannyT.,FallLine 9
27May80-3AP 5f :224 :454 :574ft 4½ 122 78 77 611 314 Patterson A2 Mdn 83 ThRzzul,Buck'sLstDrm,TlvsonStdo 8
16May80-3AP 5f :223 :454 :58 ft *7-5e 122 57 44½ 46 39¾ Patterson A5 Mdn 86 MontryGift,ThRizzuli,TlvisionStudo 9
15Apr80-3Kee 4½f :223 :46 :52 gd 4-5 121 7 812 611 318 Morgan M R7 Mdn 77 RodgrRnhrt,Prnr'sEdg,TlvsonStdo 10
●Apr 20 Kee 6f sy 1:15 h Apr 10 Kee 5f ft 1:053 b Apr 2 Kee 3f ft :363 b Mar 29 Kee 7f ft 1:30 b

Tap Shoes

Ch. c. 3, by Riva Ridge—Bold Ballet, by Bold Bidder
Br.—Hancock A III & Peters L J (Ky) 1981 2 1 0 1 $110,592
Own.—Peters L & Hancock III et al 126 Tr.—Luro Horatio A 1980 7 4 1 1 $197,084

28Mar81-9Hia 1⅛ :47 1:104 1:491ft *3-5 122 43 31 22 11 HernndezR6 Flamingo 86 TpShoes,WellDecorted,DoublSonic 7
9Mar81-9Hia 7f :222 :444 1:221ft *9-5 122 78¾ 711 43 3nk HernndezR6 Bahamas 92 WellDecorted,DshO'Plesure,TpShos 8
12Oct80-8Bel 1 :461 1:113 1:371ft *3-2 122 54 53¾ 65½ 611 HrnndR1 Champagne 71 Lord Avie, Noble Nashua, Sezyou 9
13Sep80-8Bel 7f :223 :452 1:234ft *1-2 122 2hd 1hd 11 11¾ HernandezR1 Futurity 83 TapShoes,DashO'Plesure,McCrcken 6
23Aug80-8Sar 6½f :222 :453 1:17 ft 2½ 122 62¾ 42 12 12 HernandezR5 Hopeful 87 Tap Shoes,LordAvie,WellDecorated 9
13Aug80-8Sar 6f :213 :443 1:10 ft 5½ 115 89½ 88 45 11¾ HernandezR3 Sanford 90 Tap Shoes, Triocala,PaintedShield
4Aug80-8Sar 6f :22 :45 1:101ft 21 117 61¾ 32 34½ 24½ HernndzR9 Sar Spec'l 84 WellDecorated,TapShoes,Motivity 10
4Jly80-8Suf 5½f :222 :463 1:053ft *9-5 114 56 54½ 42 34½ O'DrscllJ4 Mayflower 91 And More, Lockjaw, Tap Shoes 12
16Jun80-3Bel 5½f :221 :473 1:052ft 4½ 113 52½ 41½ 11½ 16½ Hernandez R10 Mdn 83 Tap Shoes, Chapel Creek, Behold 10
Apr 22 Kee 3f ft :394 b Apr 18 Kee 1 1/16 ft 1:453 h Apr 11 Hia 5f ft 1:01 b Apr 6 Hia 5f ft 1:00 h

Mythical Ruler

Ro. c. 3, by Ruritania—Our Nanny, by Victorian Era
Br.—Penn O (Ky) 1981 3 3 0 0 $53,660
Own.—Risen Al Jr & Price Paxton 122 Tr.—Wirth Fred 1980 5 3 1 1 $17,520

25Apr81-7CD 1 :472 1:114 1:374ft 2½ 122 12 11 11 14 Wirth K B4 Alw 80 MythclRulr,ClsscGoGo,TlvsonStudo 4
28Mar81-8Lat 1 :46 1:11 1:38 ft 10 114 13 13 14 16½ Wirth K1 Spiral 89 MythiclRuler,ClssicGoGo,IronGem 10
20Mar81-8Lat 1 :464 1:121 1:401ft 3 115 2hd 12 12½ 14 Wirth K4 Alw 78 MythiclRulr,MgicDust,RgingBufflo 7
13Sep80-5Lat 6f :221 :461 1:122ft *2-5 1157 36½ 31½ 31½ 2hd Wirth B2 Alw 86 Magic Dust,MythicalRuler,GiGiBear 6
16Aug80-9ElP 6f :224 :46 1:112ft 7-5 116 15 12 12 11¾ WrthB7 J C Elp Mem 93 Mythical Ruler, Iron Gem,GiGiBear 7
8Aug80-8ElP 5½f :222 :46 1:062ft *1-2 1137 2hd 2hd 11 12 Wirth B5 Alw 88 MythicalRuler,GiGiBear,I'mforNavy 6
26Jly80-3ElP 5f :224 :46 :583ft 3 10910 1½ 14 15 19½ Wirth B10 Mdn 98 Mythical Ruler, Mr.D.H.S.,SeaCzar 11
●Apr 18 CD 6f ft 1:14 h

Pleasant Colony did indeed win the race, followed by Woodchopper and Partez. Proud Appeal was in the race until the mile pole, then faltered badly and finished eighteenth. He also became one of the horses whose career was essentially destroyed by the Derby. Never regaining his earlier form, he was quickly retired to stud, where he now stands for Gainesway Farms.

Pleasant Colony paid $4.40 to show, so our bet of $342 returned $752.40, for a profit of $410.40.

It was a great day for us. In addition to the fun we had had, all four of our Dr. Z system bets had been winners. Our only loss was the win bet on Proud Appeal. Our $2,079.10 stake grew to $2,531. We vowed to come back to try it again the following May.

EIGHTH RACE
Churchill
MAY 2, 1981

1 ¼ MILES. (1.59⅖) 107th Running KENTUCKY DERBY SCALE WEIGHT (Grade I). $200,000 Added (plus $20,000 from KTDF). 3-year-olds. By subscription of $100 which covers nomination for both the Kentucky Derby and Derby Trial. All nomination fees to Derby winner. $4,000 to pass entry box Thursday, April 30, $3,500 additional to start. $200,000 added, of which: $50,000 to second, $25,000 to third, $12,500 to fourth. $100,000 guaranteed to the winner (to be divided equally in the event of a dead heat.) Weight, 126 lbs. Starters to be named through the entry box Thursday, April 30, at the time of closing. (This provision waived, by court order, permitting Flying Nashua and Mythical Ruler to start). The maximum number of starters for the Kentucky Derby will be limited to twenty. In the event more than twenty entries pass through the entry box at the usual time of closing, the twenty starters will be determined at that time with preference given to those that have accumulated the highest earnings. For those that enter and are eliminated under this condition, the nomination fee and the fee to pass through the entry box, will be refunded. The owner of the winner to receive a gold trophy. (Closed with 432 nominations.)
Total purse $424,700. Value of race $413,450, value to winner $317,200, second $55,000, third $27,500, fourth $13,750. ($11,250 reverts to KTDF.) Mutuel pool $4,566,179.

Last Raced	Horse	Eqt.	A.	Wt	PP	¼	½	¾	1	Str	Fin	Jockey	Odds $1
18Apr81 ^{9}Aqu^{1}	Pleasant Colony		3	126	7	17^{1}	16^{hd}	$15^{\frac{1}{2}}$	$4^{\frac{1}{2}}$	$1^{1\frac{1}{2}}$	$1^{\frac{3}{4}}$	Velasquez J	3.50
11Apr81 ^{9}OP^{3}	Woodchopper		3	126	11	$20^{\frac{1}{2}}$	19^{2}	$19^{1\frac{1}{2}}$	$11^{\frac{1}{2}}$	5^{hd}	2^{3}	Delahoussaye E	34.20
12Apr81 ^{8}SA^{6}	Partez	b	3	126	3	12^{1}	12^{1}	10^{1}	2^{2}	2^{1}	$3^{2\frac{1}{2}}$	Hawley S	f-7.90
25Apr81 ^{7}CD^{2}	Classic Go Go		3	126	13	$19^{\frac{1}{2}}$	$18^{2\frac{1}{2}}$	17^{hd}	9^{2}	7^{hd}	4no	Black A S	f-7.90
25Apr81 ^{7}CD^{3}	Television Studio	b	3	126	18	21	20^{hd}	$20^{\frac{1}{2}}$	10^{2}	8^{1}	$5^{1\frac{1}{2}}$	Whited D E	f-7.90
18Apr81 ^{8}Spt^{2}	Pass the Tab		3	126	8	11^{1}	10^{1}	$7^{\frac{1}{2}}$	3^{1}	$6^{\frac{1}{2}}$	6^{nk}	Pincay L Jr	31.10
12Apr81 ^{8}SA^{1}	Splendid Spruce	b	3	126	1	10^{1}	$9^{\frac{1}{2}}$	$9^{\frac{1}{2}}$	$5^{\frac{1}{2}}$	4^{hd}	7^{nk}	McHargue D G	13.60
12Apr81 ^{8}SA^{4}	Flying Nashua	b	3	126	21	18^{hd}	15^{3}	16^{hd}	15^{hd}	9^{3}	$8^{2\frac{3}{4}}$	Cordero A Jr	48.00
18Apr81 ^{9}Aqu^{4}	Noble Nashua		3	126	9	14^{2}	13^{hd}	$13^{1\frac{1}{2}}$	13^{1}	$10^{2\frac{1}{2}}$	9no	Asmussen C B	71.70
11Apr81 ^{9}OP^{1}	Bold Ego		3	126	15	2^{1}	2^{hd}	2^{hd}	1^{hd}	3^{1}	$10^{2\frac{3}{4}}$	Lively J	9.90
23Apr81 ^{7}Kee^{4}	Double Sonic		3	126	4	16^{1}	21	21	17^{1}	11^{1}	$11^{2\frac{3}{4}}$	Thornburg B	f-7.90
12Apr81 ^{8}SA^{3}	Hoedown's Day		3	126	10	$6^{1\frac{1}{2}}$	7^{1}	$11^{1\frac{1}{2}}$	$12^{1\frac{1}{2}}$	$12^{\frac{1}{2}}$	12^{nk}	Chapman T M	f-7.90
23Apr81 ^{7}Kee^{5}	Beau Rit	b	3	126	17	15^{hd}	$17^{1\frac{1}{2}}$	18^{1}	$18^{\frac{1}{2}}$	13^{hd}	13^{nk}	Rubbicco P	f-7.90
28Mar81 ^{9}Hia^{1}	Tap Shoes		3	126	19	13^{1}	14^{3}	$14^{1\frac{1}{2}}$	$14^{\frac{1}{2}}$	14^{6}	14^{7}	Hernandez R	7.60
18Apr81 ^{9}Aqu^{3}	Cure the Blues	b	3	126	16	$8^{1\frac{1}{2}}$	6^{hd}	8^{hd}	$16^{\frac{1}{2}}$	15^{2}	15^{2}	Shoemaker W	4.70
14Apr81 ^{7}Kee^{4}	Well Decorated		3	126	12	$4^{\frac{1}{2}}$	4^{hd}	4^{hd}	$6^{\frac{1}{2}}$	$16^{\frac{1}{2}}$	$16^{\frac{1}{2}}$	MacBeth D	65.10
25Apr81 ^{7}CD^{1}	Mythical Ruler	b	3	126	20	5^{1}	$5^{1\frac{1}{2}}$	5^{hd}	$7^{\frac{1}{2}}$	17^{2}	$17^{2\frac{1}{2}}$	Wirth K B	f-7.90
23Apr81 ^{7}Kee^{1}	Proud Appeal		3	126	5	$3^{\frac{1}{2}}$	$3^{1\frac{1}{2}}$	3^{2}	8^{hd}	18^{3}	18^{2}	Fell J	a-2.30
11Apr81 ^{9}OP^{2}	Top Avenger		3	126	14	1^{hd}	1^{1}	1^{hd}	19^{1}	19^{3}	$19^{4\frac{1}{2}}$	Snyder L	f-7.90
23Apr81 ^{7}Kee^{7}	Habano		3	126	6	9^{hd}	11^{1}	12^{2}	$20^{1\frac{1}{2}}$	20^{4}	20^{5}	Feliciano B R	f-7.90
23Apr81 ^{7}Kee^{3}	Golden Derby		3	126	2	$7^{\frac{1}{2}}$	$8^{2\frac{1}{2}}$	$6^{2\frac{1}{2}}$	21	21	21	Espinoza J C	a-2.30

a-Coupled: Proud Appeal and Golden Derby.
f—Mutuel field.

OFF AT 5:41 EDT. Start good. Won ridden out. Time, :21⅗, :45⅕, 1:10⅕, 1:36, 2:02 Track fast.

$2 Mutuel Prices:

4-PLEASANT COLONY	9.00	5.60	4.40
6-WOODCHOPPER		23.40	13.00
12-PARTEZ (f-field)			4.00

Dk. b. or br. c, by His Majesty—Sun Colony, by Sunrise Flight. Trainer Campo John P. Bred by Evans T M (Va).

PLEASANT COLONY, taken in reserve leaving the gate and then patiently and well ridden, was under good control by the jockey while rapidly working into contention through the field on the final turn and settled outside the leaders for the drive at the head of the stretch. He raced past PARTEZ with authority and Velasquez using the whip four times left-handed and once on the right, and was ridden out by hand to hold WOODCHOPPER safe. WOODCHOPPER, also held in reserve the first half-mile, threaded between horses and closed resolutely from the top of the top of the stretch to be gradually increasing his advantage over the others. PARTEZ, reserved just off of the first flight for a half-mile, reached the front between calls in the early stretch but offered no resistance to the winner, relaxed when Hawley mis-judged the finish line and rose in the irons at the sixteenth pole as he was relinquishing second to WOODCHOPPER, then finished evenly with the jockey riding him out the final yards. CLASSIC GO GO, another reserved off of the fast early pace, advanced steadily on the final turn and into the last furlong, then was hanging at the end. TELEVISION STUDIO, last from the gate and well back into the far turn, lost ground circling horses and finished determinedly near the center of the track. PASS THE TAB briefly appeared threatening on the stretch turn and tired. SPLENDID SPRUCE raced on the inside and lacked a closing response. FLYING NASHUA was in traffic most of the race and lacked a rally. NOBLE NASHUA did not threaten. BOLD EGO was lightly rated with a fast early pace, responded to take command on the stretch turn but had little left the final quarter-mile. DOUBLE SONIC made up ground the last half-mile without threatening. HOEDOWN'S DAY tired. BEAU RIT saved ground. TAP SHOES was in close traffic at the first turn. CURE THE BLUES was kept wide and tired. WELL DECORATED was a factor for a mile and faltered. MYTHICAL RULER was extremely wide. PROUD APPEAL bid for the lead along the rail in the backstretch and stopped. TOP AVENGER was used up with the fast early pace. HABANO was used up early. GOLDEN DERBY was shuffled back along the rail at the first turn, recovered to race forwardly placed but stopped in the drive.

Owners— 1, Buckland Farm; 2, Greentree Stable; 3, Davis E & Greene Mr-Mrs H; 4, Winchell V H; 5, Bwamazon Farm; 6, Villareal L; 7, Surf and Turf Stable; 8, Digiulio & Holman & Jensen & Ronca; 9, Flying Zee Stable; 10, Double B Ranch & Kidd J; 11, Elias F & L; 12, Dominguez-Freidel-Thatcher; 13, Roussel Carole; 14, Peters L & Hancock III et al; 15, Firestone B R; 16, Allen Herbert; 17, Risen Al Jr & Price Paxton; 18, Winfield M H et al; 19, Bishop W P; 20, Coello M A; 21, Lehmann F E & Gaines J R.

Scratched—Wayward Lass (1May81 8CD3).

THE WINNER'S PEDIGREE AND CAREER HIGHLIGHTS

PLEASANT COLONY (Dark Bay or Brown Colt)	His Majesty	*Ribot	Tenerani
			Romanella
		Flower Bowl	*Alibhai
			Flower Bed
	Sun Colony	Sunrise Flight	Double Jay
			Misty Morn
		*Colonia	Cockrullah
			Naiga

Year	Age	Sts	1st	2nd	3rd	Won
1980	2	5	2	1	0	$87,968
1981	3	9	4	2	1	877,415
TOTALS		14	6	3	1	$965,383

At 2 Years	WON	*Remsen
	2nd	Pilgrim
	UNP	Maryland Nursery
		*Placed first through disqualification.
At 3 Years	WON	Kentucky Derby, Wood, Preakness, Woodward
	2nd	Fountain of Youth, Travers
	3rd	Belmont Stakes
	UNP	Florida Derby, Marlboro Cup

CHAPTER 11

Derby Day 1982

Bill was busy with his classes at UCLA and unable to make the trip to Kentucky, so I went alone. I arrived at the track well before the first race, joining the tens of thousands passing through the turnstiles. It's a great deal of fun to watch the diversity of people attending the Derby, from the celebrities and wealthy horse owners who arrive in chauffeur-driven limousines to the party-loving infielders, many of whom never see a horse all day. I positioned myself at the tote board in the back of the grandstand, which was, as we had learned at Derby '81, the most convenient location to watch the tote board and bet.

Racing Form **Experts' Selections**

Consensus Points: 5 for 1st (today's best 7), 2 for 2nd, 1 for 3rd. Today's Best in Bold Type.

Trackman, Graham Ross — **CHURCHILL DOWNS** — Selections Made for Fast Track

	TRACKMAN	HANDICAP	ANALYST	HERMIS	SWEEP	CONSENSUS	
1	DOOR KING NATIVE NASHUA A TOAST TO HARRY	TONIMAROW BARRISTER SIB VERACITY	TONIMAROW BARRISTER SIB VERACITY	TONIMAROW VERACITY M. J'S GLORY	TONIMAROW BARRISTER SIB VERACITY	TONIMAROW BARRISTER SIB DOOR KING	20 6 5
2	PRETTY MA AMI LOVE WAY COME ON CAMILLA	ALZABELLA COME ON CAMILLA ARTANIA	LIBRELLA ALZABELLA LOVE WAY	LOVE WAY ALZABELLA COME ON CAMILLA	LOVE WAY JAY'S PROMISE ALZABELLA	LOVE WAY ALZABELLA PRETTY MA AMI	13 10 5
3	FOUR CHAMP'S LE BON MAN BIRDBRAIN	STAR DRONE BIRDBRAIN LADYS SAMSON	STAR DRONE FOUR CHAMP'S BIRDBRAIN	STAR DRONE ALIAS JAKE BIRDBRAIN	STAR DRONE BIRDBRAIN FOUR CHAMP'S	STAR DRONE FOUR CHAMP'S BIRDBRAIN	20 8 7
4	SUPER RIDGE EXCLUSIVE ROMEO GI GI BEAR	ROSSI GOLD EXCLUSIVE ROMEO BACKSTABBER	**ROSSI GOLD** NO BAY BACKSTABBER	**ROSSI GOLD** NO BAY SUPER RIDGE	**ROSSI GOLD** SUPER RIDGE BACKSTABBER	ROSSI GOLD SUPER RIDGE EXCLUSIVE ROMEO	26 8 4
5	AM JOY DUST OFF THE MAT POP'S LITTLE MAN	STOLEN GOODS ORANGEVILLE BARACO	DUST OFF THE MAT AM JOY STOLEN GOODS	BARACO ORANGEVILLE STOLEN GOODS	STOLEN GOODS BARACO ORANGEVILLE	STOLEN GOODS BARACO AM JOY	12 8 7
6	WHAT IT IS OIL CITY TIM'S MARKFIVE	WHAT IT IS D. J. ROAD MIROMAN	WHAT IT IS D. J ROAD OIL CITY	MIROMAN TIM'S MARKFIVE EXECUTION'S REASON	OIL CITY D. J. ROAD WHAT IT IS	WHAT IT IS OIL CITY D. J. ROAD	16 8 6
7	**LISTCAPADE** SOY EMPEROR JOHNNY CAN HOP	LISTCAPADE CUT AWAY NOTED	LISTCAPADE NOTED SOY EMPEROR	LISTCAPADE SOY EMPEROR NOTED	LISTCAPADE SOY EMPEROR NOTED	**LISTCAPADE** SOY EMPEROR NOTED	27 7 5
8	MUTTERING EL BABA ROYAL ROBERTO	**EL BABA** MUTTERING AIR FORBES WON	EL BABA AIR FORBES WON MUTTERING	EL BABA AIR FORBES WON MUTTERING	EL BABA AIR FORBES WON MUTTERING	EL BABA MUTTERING AIR FORBES WON	24 10 7
9	DOUBLE THREES ENDEMONIADO LUDICROUS	AVATOIL DUAL TRACKS ARGONAFTIS	ARGONAFTIS GENUINE MAGIC AVATOIL	AVATOIL ARGONAFTIS DOUBLE THREES	ARGONAFTIS GENUINE MAGIC DUAL TRACKS	ARGONAFTIS AVATOIL DOUBLE THREES	13 11 6
10	AVIONIC OLD HUNDRED ROYAL NIN	AVIONIC BRAD SHY OMAR	AVIONIC NO SAD NEWS DASH AND C.	AVIONIC NO SAD NEWS NATIVE DIGGER	AVIONIC OLD HUNDRED NO SAD NEWS	AVIONIC NO SAD NEWS OLD HUNDRED	25 5 4

Alzabella Is the First Dr. Z System Bet

The first Dr. Z system bet was in the second race for three-year-old maiden fillies.

6½ FURLONGS

MAIDEN
PURSE $8,500

WIN	PLACE	SHOW

2

(Plus $2,200 from the Kentucky Thoroughbred Development Fund)
MAIDEN FILLIES THREE YEARS OLD, 119 lbs.

Track Record—DOGOON (5) 121 lbs.; 1:16; Nov. 5, 1957

MAKE SELECTION BY NUMBER

No.	Owner / Trainer	Jockey/Morn. Line
1	S. HUBERT MAYES, JR. AND FLETCHER CLEMENT — RICHARD B. MATTINGLY Red & Blk. Hal., Wh. Sash, Rd & Blk. Dots on Slvs., Rd. Cp.. **ARTANIA** *114 Gr.f.(1979), Ruritania—Arctic Actress	12 TRAVIS HIGHTOWER
2	MARTIN-WEIR STABLE (Gary Weir and Polly Martin) — JERRY CALVIN Blue, Red & White Dia., Red Dia. on Wh. Slvs. Blue Cap **COME ON CAMILLA** 119 B.f.(1979), Winds Of Thought—Song Of Nashua	15 JOHN LIVELY
3	JAMES A. ARATA — FORREST KAELIN Maroon, White Circled "A," White Sleeves Maroon Cap **LIKE A PICASSO** 119 Gr.f.(1979), Sr. Diplomat—Empress Erin	30 TOMMY BARROW
4	DUNTREATH FARM (James Grissom) — MICHAEL J. GRISSOM White, Red "G," Red Collar, Red Cuffs, Red Cap **LOVE WAY** 119 Ro.f.(1979), Drone—Betty Spur	4 EDDIE DELAHOUSSAYE
5	LOBLOLLY STABLE (John E. Anthony) — C. R. McGAUGHEY III Yellow, Brown Triangle, Brown Triangle on Slvs., Yellow Cap **LIBRELLA** 119 Dk.b. or br.f.(1979), Roberto—Fiesta Libre	10 EDDIE MAPLE
6	LESLIE COMBS II AND FRANCIS KERNAN — RAY LAWRENCE, JR. Orange, Blue Bars on Sleeves, Blue Cap **SANS PAREIL** ***109 B.f.(1979), Quack—Joans Paris	5 JAMES WELLMAN
7	H. J. SNAVELY — DIANNE CARPENTER Blue, Silver Sash, Silver Stripes on Sleeves Blue Cap **ERUDITE ROAD** 119 Ch.f.(1979), Barbs Delight—Cedar Road	30 JULIO ESPINOZA
8	JOHN W. FLOYD — WAYNE MURTY White, Black "JWF," Gold Bars on Sleeves White Cap **ALZABELLA** 119 Ch.f.(1979), Top Command—Alza	3 JORGE VELASQUEZ
9	440 RANCH (Norman Blankenship) — JACK VAN BERG White, Green Twin Spires, White Cap **SUE'S MASTER** 119 Dkb. or br.f.(1979), Master Hand—Sue's Susie	10 DARRELL HAIRE
10	ROBERT G. KLUENER AND TAYLOR ASBURY — NEIL J. HOWARD White, Orange Dots, Orange Cap **DON'T DELAY BABE** 119 B.f.(1979), Naskra—Within Limits	30 JIM McKNIGHT
11	WARREN KING — D. E. HUGHES Silver, Black "KK," Silver Bars on Black Sleeves Black Cap **JAY'S PROMISE** 119 B.f.(1979), Fabled Monarch—Passions Promise	4 ANTHONY RINI
12	ARCHIE DONALDSON — J. J. SARNER, JR. Maroon, Maroon Bars on Blue Sleeves Maroon Cap **CARO'S DESIGN GIRL** 119 Gr.f.(1979), Caro—Beautiful Design	12 RANDY ROMERO

Scratched—PRETTY MA AMI, LADY JACK, ALL BRAVE, LOVIN HAWAIIAN

Selections 8—4—11—6

Two minutes before post time, the mutuels on the lightly raced Alzabella were

	Totals	#8 Alzabella	Expected Value per Dollar Bet on Alzabella
Odds		2—1	
Win	220,845	60,820	
Show	96,105	15,716	1.23

SECOND RACE

Churchill

MAY 1, 1982

6 1/2 FURLONGS. (1.16) MAIDEN. SPECIAL WEIGHT. Purse $8,500 (plus $2,200 from the KTDF). Fillies. 3-year-olds. Weight, 119 lbs.

Total purse $10,700. Value of race $10,590, value to winner $6,955, second $2,140, third $1,070, fourth $425. ($110 reverts to the KTDF). Mutuel pool $465,680.

Last Raced			Horse	Eqt.	A.	Wt.	PP	St	1/4	1/2	Str	Fin	Jockey	Odds $1
28Feb82	4SA	3	Alzabella		3	119	8	6	4hd	2 ½	1-3	1-5	Velasquez J	1.90
			Librella		3	119	5	11	9 ½	7hd	2-1	2-2½	Maple E	9.00
9Apr82	4GP	7	Sans Pareil		3	109	6	12	10-1	8-3	5-2	3no	Wellman J-10	12.90
16Apr82	3Kee	5	Come On Camilla	b	3	119	2	5	6-2	6hd	4-1½	4 ½	Lively J	31.80
22Apr82	2Kee	2	Jay's Promise	b	3	119	11	1	5hd	3-3	3hd	5-2½	Rini A	3.20
29Mar82	6OP	10	Sue's Master	b	3	119	9	3	2 ½	1 ½	6-3	6-2½	Haire D	35.30
			Caro's Design Girl		3	119	12	2	12	12	8-3	7-1½	Romero R P	33.80
14Apr82	2Kee	3	Love Way		3	119	4	10	7hd	10-2	7hd	8-4	Delahoussaye E	2.50
8Apr82	4OP	5	Artania		3	114	1	4	1hd	4 ½	10-3	9hd	Hightower T W-5	33.20
22Apr82	2Kee	6	Like a Picasso		3	119	3	9	11-2	11-1½	9hd	10-3½	Barrow T+	64.80
24Apr82	5CD	11	Erudite Road	b	3	119	7	7	3-1½	5hd	11hd	11no	Espinoza J C	69.50
21Apr82	2Kee	9	Don't Delay Babe	b	3	119	10	8	8-1	9hd	12	12	McKnight J	67.60

OFF AT 12:17. Start good for all but JAY'S PROMISE. Won handily. Time, :22 4/5, :46 2/5, 1:11 1/5, 1:17 3/5 Track fast.

$ 2 Mutuel Prices:				
8- ALZABELLA....................................	5.80	4.00	3.80
5- LIBRELLA.....................................		8.00	5.80
6- SANS PAREIL..................................			5.60

Ch. f, by Top Command-Alza, by Olden Times. Trainer Murty Wayne. Bred by Floyd J W (Ky).

ALZABELLA, just behind the early leaders, came up to challenge entering the lane, drew off in upper stretch and increased the margin under a hand ride. LIBRELLA, allowed to settle, rallied to be clearly second best but was no threat to the winner. SANS PAREIL, unhurried, lacked running room when launching a bid in the lane. COME ON CAMILLA lacked the needed response. JAY'S PROMISE broke fastest but bobbled leaving the gate and tired in the lane. SUE'S MASTER vied for the lead until the stretch and gave way. LOVE WAY had no rally. ARTANIA made the pace briefly and gave way. ERUDITE ROAD had brief speed.

Owners- 1, Floyd J W; 2, Loblolly Stable; 3, Combs II & Kernan; 4, Weir-Martin Stable; 5, King W; 6, 440 Ranches; 7, Donaldson A; 8, Duntreath Farm; 9, Mayes Jr & Clement;10, Arata J;11, Snavely H J;12, Klumer R & Asbury T.

Trainers- 1, Murty Wayne; 2, McGaughey C R III; 3, Lawrence Ray Jr; 4, Calvin Jerry; 5, Hughes Donald E; 6, Van Berg Jack C; 7, Sarner Jerome J Jr; 8, Grissom Michael J; 9, Mattingly Richard B;10, Kaelin Forrest;11, Carpenter Dianne;12, Howard Neil J.

+ Apprentice allowance waived: Like a Picasso 5 pounds.

Scratched- Pretty Ma Ami(10Apr82 2Kee 8); Lady Jack(15Feb82 3SA 11); All Brave(28Oct81 6Aqu 6); Lovin Hawaiian (29Mar82 5OP 5).

With Kentucky's track take of 15%, equation (4.4) indicated that the expected value per dollar bet to show was 1.23. With my betting fortune of $400, the optimal bet was $88. With Jorge Velasquez in the saddle, Alzabella ran an excellent race, winning by five lengths. She paid $3.80 to show, so my $88 bet returned $167.20, for a profit of $79.20. The chart of the race is on page 208.

A Late Scratch

The fourth race was an allowance race involving horses at least four years old. For three of the seven horses, this was their first outing of 1982. The class of the field was Rossi Gold, with earnings of $500,608 and a lifetime record of 20 in-the-money finishes in 26 races. He was the "best pick of the day" by three of the five *Daily Racing Form's* experts and was the favorite of the crowd.

START
6½ FURLONGS
FINISH

WIN	PLACE	SHOW

ALLOWANCE
PURSE $15,000

4

(Plus $3,700 from the Kentucky Thoroughbred Development Fund)
FOUR-YEAR-OLDS AND UPWARD WHICH HAVE NOT WON $3,250 TWICE SINCE HALLOWEEN OTHER THAN MAIDEN, CLAIMING OR STARTER, 121 lbs. Non-winners of $9,750 twice in 1981-82 allowed 3 lbs.; $9,750 in 1982, 6 lbs. $6,500 twice in 1981-82, 9 lbs. (Races where entered for $30,000 or less not considered.)

Track Record—DOGOON (5) 121 lbs.; 1:16; Nov. 5, 1957

MAKE SELECTION BY NUMBER

No.	Owner	Trainer	Colors	Horse	Weight	Breeding	Jockey	Morn. Line
1	WILLIAM G. CLARK	WILLIAM H. FIRES	White, Chocolate Cross Sashes, Chocolate Cap	SUPER RIDGE	115	B.h.(1977), Riva Ridge—Midnight Madrigal	JOHN LIVELY	15
2	MRS. JAMES H. RUTTER	WILLIAM I. MOTT	White, Black "R" on Gold Crown, Black Bars on Sleeves, White Cap	BACKSTABBER	121	Dk.b. or br.g.(1976), Cutlass—Shower Of Flowers	RONALD ARDOIN	7-2
3	SHAMROCK HILL FARM (M. P. Ryan)	E. W. REYNOLDS	Green, White Sleeves, Green Cap	NO BAY	115	Dk.b. or br.g.(1978), Mo Bay—Queen Em	RANDY ROMERO	5
4	W. P. THOMPSON	DEWEY SMITH	Pink, Black "T", Pink Cap	EXCLUSIVE ROMEO	121	Ch.h.(1977), Gallant Romeo—Baby Louis	DARRELL HAIRE	6
5	LESLIE COMBS II	RAY LAWRENCE, JR.	Orange, Blue Bars on Sleeves, Blue Cap	ROSSI GOLD	121	B.g.(1976), Taj Rossi—Rock Gold	PAT DAY	4-5
6	BETTY CONRAD AND NONA RODRIQUEZ	JOSE T. RODRIQUEZ	Green, White "MO," Green Cap	GI GI BEAR	112	B.c.(1978), Slade—Amy Jo	PHILLIP RUBBICCO	30
7	440 RANCH (Norman Blankenship)	JACK VAN BERG	Green, White Twin Spires, Green Cap	BILLBOARD	112	B.h.(1977), Crimson Satan—Poster Girl	JEFF FELL	15

Selections 5—2—3—4

One minute to post time, the tote board was as follows:

	Totals	#5 Rossi Gold	Expected Value per Dollar Bet on Rossi Gold
Odds		3—5	
Win	388,375	184,016	
Show	163,553	43,207	1.26

An expected value per dollar bet to show of 1.26 on a heavy favorite such as Rossi Gold suggests a large Dr. Z system bet. With my betting wealth now $479.20, the optimal bet was $294. I bet just as the horses were entering the starting gate. Unfortunately, at that moment, Exclusive Romeo, the number 4 horse, injured himself at the gate and was scratched. This meant a delay of the race for five minutes while the public was allowed to collect their refunds on Exclusive Romeo and rebet. This also meant the Dr. Z system bet on Rossi Gold could turn sour if there was heavy betting on him to show due to the delay. Fortunately this was not the case, as the final tote board indicated:

	Totals	#5 Rossi Gold	Expected Value per Dollar Bet on Rossi Gold
Odds		3—5	
Win	387,974	193,574	
Show	155,275	46,062	1.22

Rossi Gold won with a strong finish and paid $2.40 to show, a good payoff considering a six-horse field and a 3—5 favorite. My $294 bet returned $352.80, for a profit of $58.80. The chart of the race was as follows:

FOURTH RACE
Churchill
MAY 1, 1982

6 1/2 FURLONGS. (1.16) ALLOWANCE. Purse $15,000 (plus $3,700 from the KTDF). 4-year-olds and upward, which have not won $3,250 twice since October 31 other than maiden, claiming or starter. Weight, 121 lbs. Non-winners of $9,750,; twice in 1981-82, allowed 3 lbs.; of $9,750 in 1982, 6 lbs.; of $6,500 twice in 1981-82, 9 lbs. (Races where entered for $30,000 or less not considered).

Total purse $18,700. Value of race $17,960, value to winner $12,155, second $3,000, third $1,870, fourth $935. ($740 reverts to the KTDF.) Mutuel pool $744,562.

Last Raced			Horse	Eqt.	A.	Wt.	PP	St	1/4	1/2	Str	Fin	Jockey	Odds $1
18Oct81	8MO	13	Rossi Gold		6	121	4	5	5-2	5-1	3-1	1-2½	Day P	.60
28Mar82	9FG	3	Backstabber		6	121	2	4	3-2	3-3	2-1½	2-2	Ardoin R	3.00
6Apr82	8OP	3	Billboard		5	114	6	2	2-1½	1hd	1-1	3-2½	Fell J	33.30
21Apr82	8Kee	4	Super Ridge	b	5	115	1	6	6	6	6	4-3½	Lively J	5.30
20Apr82	8Kee	5	Gi Gi Bear		4	112	5	1	4-5	4-1	5½	5-1½	Rubbicco P	23.40
4Dec81	9FG	3	No Bay	b	4	115	3	3	1-1½	2-1½	4-1½	6	Romero R P	7.00

OFF AT 1:53. Start good. Won ridden out. Time, :22 2/5, :40, 1:10 1/5, 1:16 2/5 Track fast.

$ 2 Mutuel Prices:				
5-	ROSSI GOLD	3.20	2.40	2.40
2-	BACKSTABBER		3.00	2.60
7-	BILLBOARD			4.20

B. g, by Taj Rossi-Rock Gold, by Fleet Nasrullah. Trainer Laurence Raymond Jr. Bred by Spendthrift Farm (Ky).

ROSSI GOLD, unhurried, rallied on the outside when set down for the drive and drew clear late while ridden out to the wire. BACKSTABBER, allowed to settle, was no match for the winner when challenged but continued willingly to be clearly second best. BILLBOARD prompted the early pace, gained the advantage entering the lane but could not stay with the top two. SUPER RIDGE had no speed. NO BAY, away alertly, made the early pace and gave way. EXCLUSIVE ROMEO INJURED HIMSELF WHEN BEING LOADED IN THE STARTING GATE AND WAS ORDERED SCRATCHED BY THE STEWARDS ON THE ADVICE OF THE TRACK VETERINARIAN. ALL WAGERS ON HIM WERE ORDERED REFUNDED.

Owners- 1, Combs L II; 2, Rutter Mrs J H; 3, 440 Ranches; 4, Clark W G; 5, Conrad & Rodriquez Mmes; 6, Shamrock Hill Farm.

Trainers- 1, Laurence Raymond Jr; 2, Mott William I; 3, Van Berg Jack C; 4, Fires William H; 5, Rodriquez Jose T; 6, Reynolds Edward W.

Overweight: Billboard 2 pounds.

Scratched- Exclusive Romeo(17Aug81 8AP 5).

Baraco in the Fifth

The fifth race, for three-year-olds, also had a small field of only seven horses. The consensus of the *Daily Racing Form's* experts gave the nod to Stolen Goods, but the public preferred the front-running Baraco. The public, however, overlooked the show bet on Baraco.

START
6½ FURLONGS
FINISH

WIN PLACE SHOW

ALLOWANCE
PURSE $15,000

5

(Plus $3,700 from the Kentucky Thoroughbred Development Fund)
THREE-YEAR-OLDS WHICH HAVE NOT WON $6,825 THREE TIMES OTHER THAN MAIDEN OR CLAIMING, 122 lbs. Non-winners of $9,750 twice in 1982 allowed 3 lbs.; $7,800 in 1982, 6 lbs.; $6,500 twice, 10 lbs. (Maiden, claiming or starter races not considered in allowances.)

Track Record—DOGOON (5) 121 lbs.; 1:16; Nov. 5, 1957

MAKE SELECTION BY NUMBER

No.	Owner / Trainer	Jockey/Morn. Line
1	MARVIN WARNER — WILLIAM SWEENEY White, White "W" on Red Ball, Red Stripes on Sleeves White Cap **BARACO** 119 B.c.(1979), Barachois—Cohasset	5-2 CHARLES WOODS, JR.
2	GEORGE A. ZIMMERMAN — JAMES E. MORGAN White, Blue Sash, Blue Bars on Sleeves White Cap **DUST OFF THE MAT** 112 B.c.(1979), Run Dusty Run—Somersault	4 TOMMY MEYERS
3	JACK E. SOWARDS — OWNER Red, White Bar "S," Blue Stars on White Sleevs Red Cap **THE GREAT UPHEAVE** 112 Ch.c.(1979), Novaya—Nursing	30 EDDIE DELAHOUSSAYE
4	BETTY CONRAD AND NONA RODRIQUEZ — JOSE T. RODRIQUEZ Green, White "MO," Green Cap **AM JOY** 112 Dk.b. or br.c.(1979), Slade—Amy Jo	10 PHILLIP RUBBICCO
5	FARID SEFA — LARRY. D. EDWARDS Red, Yellow "S" Red Cap **ORANGEVILLE** ***102 Ch.g.(1979), Get Araction—Naked Kiss	12 BRENDA HILL
6	BAYARD SHARP — DEL W. CARROLL Purple, Gold Sash, Gold Bars on Sleeves Purple Cap **STOLEN GOODS** 119 B.g.(1979), Dewan—Sweet Robbery	8-5 RANDY ROMERO
7	JOHN FRANKS — ROBERT HOLTHUS Green, Orange "JF" on White Ball, Orange and White Halved Sleeves, Green Cap **POP'S LITTLE MAN** 119 Ch.c.(1979), Billy Rogell—Touch of Midas	5 DARRELL HAIRE

With two minutes to post time the tote board read as follows:

	Totals	#1 Baraco	Expected Value per Dollar Bet on Baraco
Odds		7—5	
Win	432,641	152,413	
Show	179,553	40,439	1.18

With my current betting wealth of $538, the optimal bet was $167. The final tote board, which follows, remained much the same:

	Totals	#1 Baraco	Expected Value per Dollar Bet on Baraco
Odds		6—5	
Win	441,870	157,536	
Show	182,503	41,956	1.17

Baraco took the lead from the starting gate, but could not outrun Am Joy in the stretch. He did hang on for second, beating Orangeville by a neck. The payoff to show was $3.00, for a return of $250.50 and a profit of $83.50. My betting fortune was now $621.50. The chart of the race was as follows:

FIFTH RACE
Churchill
MAY 1, 1982

6 1/2 FURLONGS. (1.16) ALLOWANCE. Purse $15,000 (plus $3,700 from the KTDF). 3-year-olds, which have not won $6,825 three times other than maiden or claiming. Weight, 122 lbs. Non-winners of $9,750 twice in 1982 allowed 3 lbs.; of $7,800 in 1982, 6 lbs.; of $6,500 twice, 10 lbs. (Maiden, claiming and starter races not considered in allowances).

Total purse $18,700. Value of race $17,590, value to winner $12,155, second $3,000, third $1,500, fourth $935. ($1,110 reverts to the KTDF). Mutuel pool $841,848.

Last Raced		Horse	Eqt.	A.	Wt.	PP	St	1/4	1/2	Str	Fin	Jockey	Odds $1
15Apr82	7Kee 6	Am Joy	b	3	112	4	2	2-1	2-3	1½	1½	Rubbicco P	11.00
3Apr82	7Kee 3	Baraco	b	3	119	1	4	1hd	1hd	2-1	2nk	Woods C R Jr	1.30
23Apr82	6Kee 7	Orangeville		3	105	5	1	4-2½	3-1½	3-2½	3-3	Hill B M-10	12.20
16Apr82	8Kee 7	Dust Off the Mat		3	113	2	3	3-1½	4-3	4-3	4-1½	Meyers T	9.80
23Apr82	6Kee 5	The Great Upheave	b	3	115	3	5	5½	5-3	5-2½	5-2	Delahoussaye E	27.80
15Apr82	7Kee 9	Pop's Little Man	b	3	119	7	7	7	7	7	6no	Haire D	4.10
20Apr82	5Kee 1	Stolen Goods		3	119	6	6	6-5	6-2	6hd	7	Romero R P	2.50

OFF AT 2:40. Start good. Won driving. Time, :22 4/5, :46, 1:11 3/5, 1:18 3/5 Track fast.

$ 2 Mutuel Prices:				
4-	AM JOY	24.00	7.20	4.60
1-	BARACO		3.60	3.00
5-	ORANGEVILLE			4.20

Dk. b. or br. c, by Slade-Amy Jo, by Sir Mango. Trainer Rodriquez Jose T. Bred by Rodriquez M & Conrad B (Ky).

AM JOY settled away nicely after an alert beginning, responded to strong urging and outfinished BARACO. The latter moved up quickly along the rail to take a slight lead over AM JOY and was not good enough in the stretch drive. ORANGEVILLE, well placed behind the top pair, loomed boldly within the last furlong and was hanging slightly at the finish. DUST OFF THE HAT lacked a closing response. THE GREAT UPHEAVE had no mishap. POP'S LITTLE MAN and STOLEN GOODS were outrun.

Owners- 1, Conrad & Rodriquez Mmes; 2, Warner M L; 3, Sefa F; 4, Zimmerman G A; 5, Sowards J E; 6, Franks J; 7, Sharp B.

Trainers- 1, Rodriquez Jose T; 2, Sweeney William; 3, Edwards Larry D; 4, Morgan James E; 5, Sowards Jack E; 6, Holthus Robert E; 7, Carroll Del W.

Overweight: Orangeville 4 pounds; Dust Off the Mat 1; The Great Upheave 3.

The Demolition Derby: The 108th Run for the Roses

The list of no-shows at the 1982 Kentucky Derby was more impressive than the entrants. The race had been nicknamed the "Demolition Derby," since many of the outstanding three-year-olds were sidelined because of injuries. Timely Writer, the impressive winner of the Flamingo Stakes and the Florida Derby, had required emergency abdominal surgery in late April. Deputy Minister, the 1981 two-year-old champion, had been injured in Florida. Conquistador Cielo, who later won the Belmont Stakes and horse-of-the-year honors, and Aloma's Ruler, who later won the Preakness Stakes, were both recovering from minor ailments. Stalwart had been retired. Lets Don't Fight had died. Hostage, the Arkansas Derby winner, was injured during a workout at Churchill Downs. Linkage was also missing. He was fit, but after three hard races in five weeks—winning both the Blue Grass Stakes by an impressive five lengths only nine days before, and the Forerunner Purse, and placing in the Louisiana Derby—he needed a rest and was skipping the Derby for the Preakness.

Despite the missing horses there were some impressive starters. The crowd's favorite was Air Forbes Won, to be ridden by Angel Cordero, Jr. In 1976, Cordero rode Air Forbes Won's sire, Bold Forbes, to victory in the 102nd Kentucky Derby. Air Forbes Won was undefeated in four starts in 1982, including the Wood Memorial and the Gotham Stakes, both at Aqueduct. The second favorite was El Baba, to be ridden by Don Brumfield. In ten starts the only horses who had beaten El Baba were Linkage and Hostage, both no-shows in the Derby. Another contender was Muttering, who four weeks earlier had won the Santa Anita Derby. Laffit Pincay, Jr. aboard Muttering would be trying for his first Kentucky Derby victory in nine attempts. Other contenders included Star Gallant with the great Bill Shoemaker, Royal Roberto, Laser Light, the one-eyed Cassaleria, Water Bank, Rockwall, and Gato Del Sol. Rock Steady had been scratched, leaving nineteen starters.

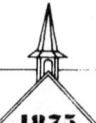

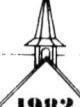

108th Running
KENTUCKY DERBY
EIGHTH RACE

1875 — 1982

$250,000 ADDED — ONE MILE and ONE-QUARTER — TRACK RECORD—SECRETARIAT (3), 126 lbs., 5-5-73, 1:59 2/5

Plus $25,000 from the Kentucky Thoroughbred Development Fund

For three-year-olds. By subscription of $200 each. All nomination fees to Derby winner. $5,000 to pass entry box, $5,000 additional to start. $250,000 added, of which $60,000 to second, $30,000 to third, $15,000 to fourth. $150,000 guaranteed to winner to be divided equally in the event of a dead heat. Weight 126 lbs. The owner of the winner to receive a gold trophy.
Closed Tuesday, February 16, 1982, with 388 nominations.

USE THESE NUMBERS FOR BUYING PARI MUTUEL TICKETS

OWNER — TRAINER — JOCKEY and Morning Line

1 ELMENDORF (Max Gluck) — RON McANALLY — 20
Gold, Royal Blue Sash, White Dots on Blue Sleeves, Gold Cap
WATER BANK ♞ 126 — MARCO CASTANEDA
B c, 1979, Naskra—Summertide by Crewman (P. P. 14)
BRED IN KENTUCKY BY ELMENDORF FARM

1a 20 20 STABLE (James Brady, Tom Gentry & Ron McAnally, et al) — RON McANALLY — 20
Green and White Triangular Thirds, Green Cap
CASSALERIA ♞ 126 — DARREL McHARGUE
Dk b or br c, 1979, Pretense—Special Charm by Verbatim (P. P. 18)
BRED IN KENTUCKY BY BRADYLEIGH FARMS & EDWIN BRADY

2 LEN MAYER — JACK VAN BERG — 15
Purple, Pink, Orange and Green Chevrons, Pink, Orange and Green Chevrons on Sleeves, Purple Cap
BOLD STYLE ♞ 126 — JEFF FELL
B c, 1979, Bold Commander—Marianna Trench by Pago Pago (P. P. 2)
BRED IN KENTUCKY BY LEN MAYER

3 MRS. JOE W. BROWN — DEWEY SMITH — 5-2
White, Black "B" and Stars, Red Cap
EL BABA ♞ 126 — DON BRUMFIELD
B c, 1979, Raja Baba—Hail To El by Hail To All (P. P. 4)
BRED IN KENTUCKY BY CHARLES GARTRELL

4 KEY WEST STABLE (Mitchell D. Wolfson) — JAMES ISELIN — 20
Yellow, White Diamonds, White Bars on Sleeves, Yellow Cap
ROYAL ROBERTO 126 — M. A. RIVERA
Dk b or br c, 1979, Roberto—Princess Roycraft by Royal Note (P. P. 5)
BRED IN NEW YORK BY KEY WEST STABLE

5 JOHN, JR., JOHN & DAVID GREATHOUSE — GEORGE R. ARNOLD II — 15
Gold, Green Yoke, Green Chevrons on Sleeves, Gold Cap
Wavering Monarch ♞ 126 — RANDY ROMERO
B c, 1979, Majestic Light—Uncommitted by Buckpasser (P. P. 6)
BRED IN KENTUCKY BY GLENCREST

6 EDWARD ANCHEL — FRANK LaBOCCETTA — 7-2
Blue and White Triangular Thirds, Blue Cap
AIR FORBES WON 126 — ANGEL CORDERO, JR.
B c, 1979, Bold Forbes—Bronze Point by Tobin Bronze (P. P. 7)
BRED IN OHIO BY HOWARD B. NOONAN

7 LIVE OAK PLANTATION (Mrs. Charlotte Weber) — PATRICK J. KELLY — 30
White, Red Dots, Black Sleeves, Red Cap
LASER LIGHT 126 — EDDIE MAPLE
B c, 1979, Majestic Light—Peaceful Union by Royal Union (P. P. 8)
BRED IN FLORIDA BY LIVE OAK STUD

8 TARTAN STABLE (Mrs. James Binger) — D. WAYNE LUKAS — 4
Red, Tartan Sash, Red Cap
MUTTERING 126 — LAFFIT PINCAY, JR.
Ro c, 1979, Drone—Malvine by Gamin (P. P. 11)
BRED IN FLORIDA BY TARTAN FARMS CORPORATION

9 NELSON BUNKER HUNT — VINCENT CLYNE — 30
Light Green, Dark Green Blocks, Light Green Sleeves, Light Green Cap
ROCKWALL ♞ 126 — HERIBERTO VALDIVIESO
B c, 1979, Cannonade—Fiddling Jimmer by Jimmer (P. P. 15)
BRED IN KENTUCKY BY NELSON BUNKER HUNT

10 BUCKRAM OAK FARM (Mahmoud Fustok) — LEONARD IMPERIO — 8
Green, Red Sash, Red Band on Sleeves, Red Cap
STAR GALLANT 126 — WILLIAM SHOEMAKER
Dk b or br c, 1979, My Gallant—Liza Star by Bold Hitter (P. P. 17)
BRED IN FLORIDA BY ROMA STABLE

11 A. B. HANCOCK III & LEONE J. PETERS — EDWIN J. GREGSON — 10
Grey, Yellow Sash, Yellow Sleeves, Yellow Cap
GATO DEL SOL ♞ 126 — EDDIE DELAHOUSSAYE
Gr c, 1979, Cougar II—Peacefully by Jacinto (P. P. 19)
BRED IN KENTUCKY BY A. B. HANCOCK III & LEONE J. PETERS

12 FIELD — RI-MA-RO STABLE (Roberto Perez & Robert DeFilippis) — ALFREDO CALLEJAS — 8
Yellow, Red Diamond Frame, Red Diamonds on Sleeves, Red Cap
CUPECOY'S JOY 121 — ANGEL SANTIAGO
B f, 1979, Northerly—Lady Abla by Alsina (P. P. 1)
BRED IN NEW YORK BY ROBERTO PEREZ

13 FIELD — HERBERT ALLEN — EUGENE JACOBS — 8
White, Red Cross Sashes, Red Blocks on Sleeves, Red Cap
NEW DISCOVERY ♞ 126 — JERRY BAILEY
B c, 1979, Arts and Letters—Synphonos by Le Fabuleux (P. P. 3)
BRED IN KENTUCKY BY MRS. WILLIAM duPONT III

14 FIELD — CARROLL W. GLASER, R. L. ELLETT, E. C. CAMP & L. C. MEHAFFEY — TOMMIE T. MORGAN — 8
Blue, Red "M" on White Ball, Red Sleeves, Blue Cap
MUSIC LEADER 126 — PAT DAY
Ch c, 1979, Scout Leader—Harp Music by Stage Door Johnny (P. P. 9)
BRED IN FLORIDA BY DR. & MRS. E. C. HART & TOWN & COUNTRY FARMS LTD.

15 FIELD — HARBOR VIEW FARM (Louis D. Wolfson) — STANLEY M. HOUGH — 8
Flamingo, White Bars on Black Sleeves, Black Cap
REINVESTED 126 — DON MacBETH
Ch c, 1979, Irish Castle—Crafty Alice by Crafty Admiral (P. P. 10)
BRED IN FLORIDA BY REGAL OAK FARM

16 FIELD — J. E. JUMONVILLE, SR. — JOHN MABRY — 8
Red, White "JIM" in White Diamond Frame, White Sleeves, Red Cap
REAL DARE 126 — RICHARD GUIDRY
B g, 1979, Beau Groton—Big Dare by Kentucky Pride (P. P. 12)
BRED IN LOUISIANA BY J. P. DORIGNAC, JR.

17 FIELD — RUSSELL MICHAEL, JR. & ANTHONY J. KNAPP — RONNIE G. WARREN — 8
Poplar, Avocado "LM" and Diamonds, Avocado Stripes on Sleeves, Poplar Cap
ROCK STEADY ♞ 126
Dk b or br c, 1979, Raise A Bid—Roccoco Miss by Lucky Debonair (P. P. 13)
BRED IN KENTUCKY BY EUGENE C. CASHMAN

18 FIELD — WOLFIE & SEYMOUR COHEN & RICHARD KUMBLE — HOWARD TESHER — 8
Blue, Light Blue Yoke, White "WC," Light Blue Band on Sleeves, Blue Cap
WOLFIE'S RASCAL 126 — JORGE VELASQUEZ
B c, 1979, London Company—Daisy Trimmer by Bold Discovery (P. P. 16)
BRED IN FLORIDA BY RAY AMLUNG

19 FIELD — JOHN D. MARSH — JOSEPH B. CANTEY — 8
Yellow, Purple Panel, Yellow Bars on Purple Sleeves, Purple Cap
MAJESTY'S PRINCE 126 — RUBEN HERNANDEZ
Ch c, 1979, His Majesty—Pied Princess by Tom Fool (P. P. 20)
BRED IN VIRGINIA BY JOHN D. MARSH

♞ Indicates Foaled In Kentucky.

1-1a—Elmendorf—20 20 Stable Entry

FIELD—12-13-14-15-16-17-18-19

Selections—3-6-8-10

108th-Kentucky Derby-108th

Route the Field Will Travel

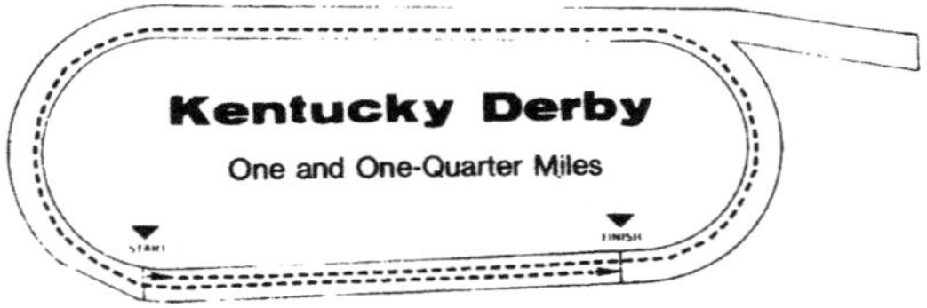

8th Churchill

1¼ MILES. (1.59⅘) 108th Running KENTUCKY DERBY Scale Weight (Grade I) $250,000 added (plus $25,000 from the KTDF). 3-year-olds. By subscription of $200. All nomination fees to winner. $5,000 to pass entry box Thursday, April 29, $5,000 additional to start. $250,000 added, of which $60,000 to second, $30,000 to third, $15,000 to fourth. $150,000 guaranteed to winner (to be divided equally in the event of a dead heat). Weight, 126 lbs. Fillies 121, lbs. Starters to be named through the entry box Thursday, April 29, at time of closing. The maximum number of starters for The Kentucky Derby will be limited to twenty. In the event more than twenty entries pass through the entry box at the usual time of closing, the twenty starters and up to eight also-eligibles will be determined at that time with preference given to those that accumulated the highest earnings. Should any entry(ies) be withdrawn from the starting field prior to 4 P.M. scratch time, Friday, April 30, vacancies will be filled from the also-eligible list and placed in the outside post position(s) in order of preference. For those that pass the entry box and are eliminated under this condition, the entry fee will be refunded. The owner of the winner to receive a gold trophy. Nominations close Tuesday, February 16. (Closed with 388 nominations.)

Coupled—Water Bank and Cassaleria.

Cupecoy's Joy

Own.—Ri-Ma-Ro Stables 121
B. f. 3, by Northerly—Lady Abla, by Alsina
Br.—Perez R (NY) 1982 6 2 3 1 $121,606
Tr.—Callejas Alfredo L 1981 8 2 2 3 $91,814
Lifetime 14 4 5 4 $213,420

Entered 30Apr82- 8 CD
27Mar82-9Lat 1 1/16 :463 1:113 1:443ft 9¼ 115 2hd 23 25 35 SntgoA10 Jim B Spiral 82 Goodn'Dusty,FstGold,Cupcoy'sJoy 12
17Mar82-8Aqu 6f :224 :46 1:11 gd 8-5 115 31 31½ 32 2nk Santiago A5 ⓈCatskill 86 PayorPly,Cupecoy'sJoy,FdedPoster 7
20Feb82-8Aqu 6f ⊡:223 :4541:11 ft *2 121 2hd 1hd 14 2hd Santiago A4 ⒻCicada 89 Bold Ribbons,Cupecoy'sJoy,Adept 11
3Feb82-8Aqu 6f ⊡:221 :4641:144sy *2-3 121 — — 13 1nk SntA2 ⒻⓈSag Harbor 70 Cupecoy'sJoy,HstyDmscn,LdyHoot 7
3Feb82—Running positions omitted because of weather conditions.
6Jan82-8Aqu 6f ⊡:221 :4511:101ft 3½ 114 1hd 1½ 2hd 1no SantigoA8 ⓈMontauk 93 Cpcoy'sJoy,AskMhmmd,Jn'sKnsmn 8
1Jan82-8Aqu 6f ⊡:23 :4731:133sy 5¾ 115 32½ 31½ 21 21¼ SantiagoA4 ⒻRosetown 75 NncyHung,Cupcoy'sJoy,ScrltBgoni 8
6Dec81-8Aqu 6f ⊡:224 :47 1:13 ft 13 122 2hd 3½ 21½ 32 Santiago A3 ⒻTreetop 77 Trove, Larida, Cupecoy's Joy 6
29Nov81-8Aqu 7f :231 :464 1:253ft 19 119 51¾ 41½ 55½ 711 SantigoA14 ⓈA T Cole 62 AskMuhmmd,ScrltBgon,GlfordLd 15
18Nov81-8Aqu 7f :223 :46 1:251m 6¾ 115 13 11½ 12 12¼ SntgA1 ⒻⓈEast View 75 Cupecoy'sJoy,DamLittle,KeyStark 12
28Oct81-1Aqu 7f :231 :463 1:244m 2 116 11 1hd 35½ 38¾ SntigoA1 ⒻⓈAw22000 68 ScrletBegoni,FreePss,Cupcoy'sJoy 6
18Oct81-8Aqu 7f :23 :46 1:243ft 5 114 11½ 11 2hd 31½ SantigoA3 ⓈD Runyon 76 GuilfordLd,MjesticKt,Cupecoy'sJoy 7
2Sep81-8Bel 6f :222 :454 1:112ft *3-2 114 1hd 1½ 2hd 22¼ SntigoA6 ⒻⓈMohawk 83 PetitMurill,Cupcoy'sJoy,PrmirWho 7
14Aug81-8Sar 6f :223 :454 1:112ft 5¼ 116 11½ 14 14 21 Santiago A5 ⓈEmpire 82 SluteMeSir,Cupecoy'sJoy,BrightRx 9
13Jly81-4Bel 6f :23 :464 1:122ft 3½ 117 14 15 16 18 Santiago A10 ⒻⓈMdn 80 Cupecoy'sJoy,GrndOldFlg,DmLittl 13
●Apr 25 CD 5f ft :59 h ●Mar 25 Lat 4f ft :464 h ●Mar 12 Bel tr.t 4f ft :464 h Mar 6 Bel tr.t 1 ft 1:46 b

Wavering Monarch

Own.—Greathouse Family 126
B. c. 3, by Majestic Light—Uncommitted, by Buckpasser
Br.—Glencrest Farm (Ky) 1982 3 2 0 1 $36,948
Tr.—Arnold George R II 1981 0 M 0 0
Lifetime 3 2 0 1 $36,948

22Apr82-7Kee 1⅛ :463 1:10 1:48 ft 5½ 121 32 21 22½ 36 RomroRP9 Blue Grass 91 Linkage,GtoDelSol,WveringMonrch 9
14Apr82-8Kee a7f 1:261ft *3-5 117 1hd 1½ 12 110 Romero R P2 Aw14500 92 WvrngMonrch,PopcrnCssrl,Frl'sJt 10
2Apr82-4Kee a7f 1:28 ft *1 116 52½ 3nk 12 17½ Romero R P6 Mdn 83 WvrngMonrch,PocktflfHp,BtthTms 8
Apr 29 CD 4f ft :484 b Apr 21 Kee 3f ft :354 b ●Apr 11 Kee 4f ft :48 b Apr 8 Kee 5f ft :59 h

Air Forbes Won

Own.—Anchel E 126
B. c. 3, by Bold Forbes—Bronze Point, by Tobin Bronze
Br.—Noonan H B (Ohio) 1982 4 4 0 0 $173,880
Tr.—LaBoccetta Frank 1981 0 M 0 0
Lifetime 4 4 0 0 $173,880

17Apr82-8Aqu 1⅛ :472 1:112 1:51 ft *3-5 126 2½ 21½ 2½ 1nk CordrAJr2 Wood Mem 88 AirForbesWon,Shimtoree,LsrLight 10
3Apr82-8Aqu 1 :442 1:083 1:353gd 2½ 114 54½ 2hd 1½ 13¼ Venezia M7 Gotham 88 AirForbesWon,Shimtor,BigBrvRock 8
20Mar82-5Aqu 7f :232 :462 1:234ft *1-5 122 32½ 32½ 1hd 13 Cordero AJr4 Aw16000 82 AirForbesWon,Illuminate,MjorFrnk 7
4Mar82-4Aqu 6f ⊡:23 :4641:111ft *3-5 122 21½ 2hd 13 17½ Cordero A Jr12 Mdn 88 AirForbsWon,SilvrPik,ElvtorShos 12
●Apr 26 CD 7f sy 1:292 h ●Apr 12 Aqu 7f ft 1:26 b ●Mar 29 Aqu 6f ft 1:123 h ●Mar 18 Aqu 4f gd :461 h (d)

Laser Light

Own.—Live Oak Plantation 126
B. c. 3, by Majestic Light—Peaceful Union, by Royal Union
Br.—Live Oak Stud (Fla) 1982 3 0 0 2 $22,844
Tr.—Kelly Patrick J 1981 5 2 2 0 $207,580
Lifetime 8 2 2 2 $230,424

17Apr82-8Aqu 1⅛ :472 1:112 1:51 ft 6½ 126 89¼ 56 33 32½ Maple E8 Wood Mem 77 AirForbesWon,Shimtoree,LsrLight 10
3Apr82-9GP 1⅛ :471 1:111 1:493ft 16 122 32 46 715 720 Maple E7 Fla Derby 64 TimelyWriter,StarGallnt,OurEscpde 7
18Mar82-9GP 1 1/16 :47 1:114 1:434ft *6-5 119 712 55 35 34¾ Maple E5 Aw14000 77 Hostage, Nor Bee, Laser Light 7
29Nov81-8Hol 1 1/16 :481 1:141 1:474sl 3½ 121 1011109 916 920 Maple E3 Hol Fut'y 36 Stalwart, Cassaleria, Header Card 12
14Nov81-8Aqu 1⅛ :481 1:131 1:504ft *2-3e 113 54½ 11½ 15 15 Maple E8 Remsen 81 LserLight,RelTwister,Wolfie'sRscl 11
5Nov81-6Med 1 1/16 :471 1:113 1:443ft *9-5 119 1212 98¾ 45½ 23 MapleE9 Yng America 83 DeputyMinister,LsrLight,RlTwistr 14
24Oct81-8Lrl 1 1/16 :47 1:122 1:443gd 6¾ 122 56 4¾ 21½ 2no Montoya D5 Lrl Fut'y 85 DeputyMinistr,LsrLight,‡CgyCougr 8
12Oct81-4Bel 1 :48 1:124 1:372ft 9¼ 118 76½ 51¾ 11½ 12¼ Maple E3 Mdn 81 LsrLight,LWshingtonin,TidsOfChnc 7
Apr 26 CD 6f sy 1:153 h Apr 14 Bel 5f ft 1:001 b Apr 10 Hia 3f ft :37 b ●Mar 30 Hia 5f sy 1:00 hg

Music Leader

Own.—Glaser C W 126
Ch. c. 3, by Scout Leader—Harp Music, by Stage Door Johnny
Br.—Hart E C & Town&CntryFm (Fla) 1982 5 1 0 1 $10,942
Tr.—Morgan T T 1981 14 4 2 4 $116,957
Lifetime 19 5 2 5 $127,898 Turf 1 1 0 0 $20,430

10Apr82-7OP 170 :47 1:131 1:431ft 6 116 43½ 41½ 44 66¾ Whited D E6 Aw35000 73 DropYourDrawers,HiPi,Listcapade 10
29Mar82-9OP 170 :474 1:132 1:454ft *2 115 3½ 4nk 31½ 35½ Whited D E6 Aw25000 61 UnoRoberto,JudoJima,MusicLeader 8
20Mar82-9OP 170 :46 1:122 1:434ft 32 113 49½ 33 34 41¾ Whited D E4 Rebel H 75 BoldStyle,Mjesty'sPrince,LostCrek 8
13Mar82-9FG 1 1/16 :472 1:12 1:442ft 46 114 714 714 618 628 Poyadou B E8 Dby Trl 62 Linkage, El Baba,SpoonfulofHoney 8
7Feb82-8DeD 6½f :241 :492 1:233ft *2-5 117 1hd 1½ 13 12¼ Cahanin J T3 Aw5500 80 MusicLeder,JukboxCindrll,NtivSbr 10
31Dec81-9FG 6f :222 :454 1:113ft 12 118 97¾105½ 89¾ 810 Ardoin R8 Sgr Bowl H 77 El Baba, Talk oftheTimes,TuninIn 13
19Dec81-5FG 6f :222 :462 1:124ft *3-5e 115 65½ 46 56½ 52¼ Ardoin R2 Aw11500 79 ToughImp,GrayJohn,InevitbleLeder 8
29Aug81-9AP 7f :222 :461 1:291sy 18e 122 65½ 56 34½ 31¼ ArdonR7 Ap Wash Fty 55 LtsDontFight,TropicRulr,MuscLdr 15
21Aug81-8LaD 6½f :224 :454 1:18 ft 8-5 122 3nk 3nk 1½ 12 Ardoin R6 Aw16000 92 MusicLeder,InevitbleLdr,SwordDvil 8
1Aug81-7LaD a7½f Ⓣ:232 :4721:313fm*8-5 114 53½ 31 1hd 13½ Ardoin R3 Grady Mad 89 MusicLedr,JustinScott,MissMolki 11
23Jly81-8Aks 6f :221 :441 1:09 ft 30 116 84½ 53½ 33 23 Howard D L5 Juvenile 89 CruznDud,MusicLdr,LtsDontFight 11
11Jly81-5LaD 6f :222 :454 1:122ft 17 114 65¾ 68¾ 54½ 31¾ Poyadou B E6 Envoy 85 CruzenDude,CherokCircl,MusicLdr 8
13Jun81-9LaD 5f :221 :462 :592ft 11 114 11111113 85 59 Ardoin R2 Carousel 85 CruzenDud,HommdLovin,RosJudg 13
3May81-11Sun 5f :221 :461 :583gd 5 118 97 98½ 88½ 68½ BrossetteAD6 R A Fut 80 PluckyHussy,RlSpculton,InvtblLdr 12
24Apr81-6Sun 5f :223 :47 :591m 2½ 118 21½ 22 12 13½ Brossette A D6 SplW 86 Music Leader, T. Dykes,Johu'sMary 9
29Mar81-10DeD 4f :222 :48 ft 6½e 118 8 89¼ 79¼ 34 BrsstlAD1 JeanLafFut 89 UminAreDens,RglAvngr,MusicLdr 10
20Mar81-7DeD 4f :231 :484ft 5½ 118 4 4nk 32½ 22 BrossetteAD9 Fut Trls 87 GryJohn,MusicLeder,HommdLovin 9
27Feb81-3DeD 4f :24 :492ft 4½ 122 2 11½ 12 1hd Brossette A D2 Mdn 86 MusicLeader,GrayJohn,BuzzinBebe 9
15Feb81-3DeD 2½f :281ft 3½ 116 4 53¾ 34½ Lyda R4 Mdn — CcheKing,Tmie'sBndit,MusicLedr 10
Apr 27 CD 1 gd 1:422 h Apr 6 OP 5f ft 1:02 b

Bold Style
B. c. 3, by Bold Commander—Marianna Trench, by Pago Pago
Own.—Mayer L 126 Br.—Mayer Len (Ky) 1982 4 3 0 1 $98,870
Tr.—Van Berg Jack C 1981 7 1 2 2 $21,331
Lifetime 11 4 2 3 $120,201 Turf 1 1 0 0 $10,020
10Apr82-9OP 1⅛ :474 1:123 1:513ft 12 123 11 21 33½ 33 SnyderL1 Arknsas Dby 82 Hostage, El Baba, Bold Style 10
20Mar82-9OP 170 :46 1:122 1:434ft 3 116 34½ 2½ 1hd 1no Snyder L2 Rebel H 77 BoldStyle,Mjesty'sPrince,LostCrek 8
12Mar82-8OP 170 :471 1:123 1:434ft *3-2 114 1hd 12½ 14 14½ Snyder L2 Aw15000 77 Bold Style, Hidden Image, Railin 12
23Jan82-10TuP a7½f ①:231 :48 1:35 fm*3-2 118 63¾ 73¾ 41½ 12 MrtinzFIII1 Phoenix H — Bold Style, Many More, Briskoric 12
27Dec81-10TuP 6½f :213 :433 1:151ft 13 120 86¾ 710 58½ 58½ WhtdDE6 Ariz Para Ft 86 Tropic Ruler,JungleBlade,Intrigue 12
16Dec81-8TuP 6½f :224 :444 1:16 ft 3 120 32 42½ 21½ 24 Snyder L4 Fut Trl 87 Jungle Blade, Bold Style, Big Sam 10
28Nov81-3CD 6f :221 :453 1:12 ft 9 118 73½ 22 21 1hd Snyder L9 Mdn 86 BoldStyl,ForbiddnPlsur,ShsRchOn 12
9May81-11TuP 5f :212 :442 :563ft 21 119 66½ 1014 37 36 StllsWE11 PhoenixFut 88 ClassyCraft,Orphan'sArt,BoldStyle 12
29Apr81-9TuP 4½f :222 :452 :512ft 7½ 119 6 31½ 2hd 22½ Stallings W E2 SplW 92 Gusto Gal, Bold Style,PepperSpeed 9
13Apr81-3TuP 4½f :223 :46 :523ft 5½ 118 8 67 47 44¾ Stallings W E10 Mdn 84 KhalitDusty,GentilPersoon,JoJulie 10
1Apr81-4TuP 4½f :222 :454 :521ft 5 118 3 47½ 57 33 Stallings W E3 Mdn 88 Cintolove, A Jolla Wind,BoldStyle 10
Apr 27 CD 1 gd 1:422 h Apr 19 CD 7f ft 1:29 h ●Mar 30 OP 6f ft 1:15 b Mar 18 OP 5f ft 1:013 h

New Discovery
B. c. 3, by Arts and Letters—Symphonos, by Le Fabuleux
Own.—Allen H 126 Br.—DuPont Mrs W III (Ky) 1982 6 1 2 1 $85,398
Tr.—Jacobs Eugene 1981 11 M 1 4 $49,156
Lifetime 17 1 3 5 $134,554
22Apr82-7Kee 1⅛ :463 1:10 1:48 ft 14 121 710 814 720 725 VelsquezJ7 Blue Grass 72 Linkage,GtoDelSol,WveringMonrch 9
3Apr82-9GP 1⅛ :471 1:111 1:493ft 12 118 510 510 612 513 Vasquez J6 Fla Derby 71 TimelyWriter,StarGallnt,OurEscpde 7
6Mar82-10Hia 1⅛ :462 1:104 1:493sy 14 122 107½ 63½ 34½ 23½ VelsquezJ12 Flamingo 80 TimelyWriter,NewDiscovry,LDnsur 16
13Feb82-10Hia 1⅛ :461 1:102 1:484ft 7½ 112 48½ 44½ 2hd 21½ VlsquzJ3 Everglades H 86 RoylRobrto,NwDiscovry,VictorinLn 8
30Jan82-10Hia 6f :222 :454 1:112ft 5½ 120 88½ 810 41 12½ Velasquez J6 Mdn 86 NwDscovry,PrncWstport,TThPnny 12
16Jan82-6Hia 6f :222 :461 1:113ft 2½ 120 1012 911 99¾ 37½ Velasquez J4 Mdn 77 GllntWind,TnciousLdr,NwDiscovry 12
14Nov81-8Aqu 1⅛ :481 1:131 1:504ft 24 114 119 109 1015 816 Fell J9 Remsen 65 LserLight,RelTwister,Wolfie'sRscl 11
5Nov81-6Med 1 1/16 :471 1:113 1:443ft 16 119 96½ 88¾ 1112 1012 CrdrAJr8 Yng America 74 DeputyMinister,LsrLight,RlTwistr 14
24Oct81-8Lrl 1 1/16 :47 1:122 1:443gd 7¾ 116 12 2hd 57 513 Lovato F Jr7 Lrl Fut'y 72 DeputyMinistr,LsrLight,‡CgyCougr 8
10Oct81-7Bel 1 :464 1:111 1:362ft 35e 122 84½ 53¾ 54½ 37¾ SamynJL5 Champagne 78 TimelyWritr,BforDwn,NwDiscovry 13
26Sep81-8Bel 7f :222 :452 1:234ft 43 115 911 86 54¾ 36 McHargueDG4 Cowdin 77 NtiveRj,TimelyWriter,NewDiscovry 9
17Sep81-6Bel 7f :224 :461 1:243m 8-5 118 2½ 11 2½ 44½ Vasquez J4 Mdn 74 Bid'sMjestic,TidsOfChng,Bmbolino 8
22Jly81-8Bel 6f :222 :452 1:102ft 31 113 95½ 64½ 73¾ 73 AsmssnCB10 Tremont 87 ReglSton,MincdWords,RingProud 11
10Jly81-4Bel 5½f :23 :462 1:053ft *1 118 1hd 1½ 13 3nk Fell J9 Mdn 87 Pavrotti,NewDiscovery,BronzeCup 10
21Jun81-8Bel 5½f :22 :452 1:043ft 9 113 58 56 55 44½ Fell J4 Gr. American 87 FullVntur,Hrschiwlkr,ShippngMgnt 8
8Jun81-8Bel 5½f :22 :453 1:044ft 17 115 610 67 55½ 35½ Fell J2 Youthful 86 DeputyMinister,Ringro,NwDiscovry 6
18May81-4Bel 5f :231 :464 :591ft 4½ 118 33 43 54¾ 38¾ Fell J7 Mdn — Hrschiwlkr,PrncWstport,NwDscvry 8
Apr 27 CD 1 gd 1:413 b Apr 17 GP 5f ft 1:01 b ●Mar 31 GP 6f ft 1:133 b ●Mar 24 GP 1 ft 1:42 b

El Baba
B. c. 3, by Raja Baba—Hail to El, by Hail to All
Own.—Brown Mrs J W 126 Br.—Gartrell C & Farish W S III (Ky) 1982 5 3 2 0 $233,860
Tr.—Smith Dewey 1981 5 5 0 0 $151,003
Lifetime 10 8 2 0 $384,863
10Apr82-9OP 1⅛ :474 1:123 1:513ft *1 126 31 41½ 23 22 BrmfldD8 Arknsas Dby 83 Hostage, El Baba, Bold Style 10
28Mar82-10FG 1⅛ :464 1:112 1:503ft 2¼ 123 34 21½ 1hd 1¾ Brumfield D1 La Dby 91 El Baba, Linkage,SpoonfulofHoney 8
13Mar82-9FG 1 1/16 :472 1:12 1:442ft *2-3 125 22½ 21½ 22½ 24 Brumfield D6 Dby Trl 86 Linkage, El Baba,SpoonfulofHoney 8
27Feb82-9OP 6f :222 :47 1:123m *1-3 124 22½ 2hd 12 13 Brumfield D7 HcpO 82 El Baba, Moro, Johnny B. Fast 7
12Feb82-8OP 6f :223 :463 1:121gd *4-5 123 61¾ 21½ 1½ 1½ Brumfield D5 HcpO 84 ElBaba,LostCreek,DropYourDrwers 8
31Dec81-9FG 6f :222 :454 1:113ft *1-2 122 21½ 1hd 2hd 1hd BrmfldD1 Sgr Bowl H 87 El Baba, Talk oftheTimes,TuninIn 13
21Nov81-8CD 1 1/16 :473 1:123 1:451ft *6-5 119 1½ 11½ 11½ 13½ RomroRP4 Ky Jky Clb 82 El Baba,CrowntheKing,TalentTown 9
11Nov81-7CD 7f :232 :47 1:244ft *2-5 114 21½ 41½ 2hd 12 Brumfield D2 Aw18500 83 El Baba, Am Joy, Broad Minded 6
31Oct81-2Kee 6f :222 :462 1:112ft *1 121 2hd 1½ 15 19 Brumfield D8 Aw14500 85 El Baba, Dreamtide, Kings Dusty 12
24Oct81-2Kee 6f :224 :463 1:114gd *2 118 1½ 13 16 116 Brumfield D10 Mdn 83 El Baba, Birdbrain, Stiletto 12
Apr 29 CD 4f ft :483 b ●Apr 24 CD 1 ft 1:391 h Apr 6 OP 5f ft 1:024 b ●Mar 25 FG 4f ft :48 h

Royal Roberto
Dk. b. or br. c. 3, by Roberto—Princess Roycraft, by Royal Note
Own.—Key West Stable 126 Br.—Key West Stable (NY) 1982 7 1 2 1 $71,085
Tr.—Iselin James H 1981 2 2 0 0 $18,600
Lifetime 9 3 2 1 $89,685 Turf 1 1 0 0 $7,800
24Apr82-8CD 1 :45 1:093 1:361ft 3½ 122 813 58½ 44½ 31½ RiverMA9 Derby Trial 86 Listcapade,StarGlint,RoylRoberto 10
15Apr82-7Kee 7f :222 :451 1:224ft 8¾ 120 98¾ 89½ 32½ 2½ Rivera M A7 Aw30200 91 Linkage, Royal Roberto, CenterCut 9
3Apr82-9GP 1⅛ :471 1:111 1:493ft 11 122 613 612 47 411 Samyn J L4 Fla Derby 73 TimelyWriter,StarGallnt,OurEscpde 7
6Mar82-10Hia 1⅛ :462 1:104 1:493sy 4½ 122 1512 1211 77 65¾ Samyn J L16 Flamingo 78 TimelyWriter,NewDiscovry,LDnsur 16
13Feb82-10Hia 1⅛ :461 1:102 1:484ft 4½ 114 613 59½ 3nk 11½ Fell J7 Everglades H 88 RoylRobrto,NwDiscovry,VictorinLn 8
5Feb82-8Hia 1 1/16 :48 1:121 1:44 ft *1 116 85½ 67 34½ 21½ Fell J3 Aw15000 82 Bold'nCold,RoyalRoberto,OurBoss 10
12Jan82-8Hia 7f :23 :453 1:234ft 4½ 116 1113 817 76 41¾ Fell J11 Aw14000 82 ShootngDuck,H'sAnAngl,ShrpFutr 12
14Nov81-5Med 170 ①:481 1:13 1:421gd*8-5 117 810 68 43 1no Perret C8 Aw13000 79 RoylRoberto,RedBrigde,JsonThRcr 8
15Oct81-4Aqu 6f :23 :464 1:123ft 4 118 106½ 73¾ 51½ 11¼ Fell J12 Ⓢ Mdn 78 RoylRoberto,CtchMe,QuitOldFrind 12
Mar 31 GP 4f ft :51 b Mar 18 GP 4f ft :503 b Mar 4 GP 4f ft :51 b

Reinvested
Ch. c. 3, by Irish Castle—Crafty Alice, by Crafty Admiral
Own.—Harbor View Farm 126 Br.—Regal Oak Farm (Fla) 1982 8 3 2 0 $61,180
Tr.—Hough Stanley M Turf 1 1 0 0 $7,800
Lifetime 8 3 2 0 $61,180
17Apr82-8Aqu 1⅛ :472 1:112 1:51 ft 20 126 79 710 67½ 55 MiglorR10 Wood Mem 75 AirForbesWon,Shimtoree,LsrLight 10
20Mar82-10Tam 1 1/16 :47 1:113 1:451ft 11 114 86½ 3½ 1hd 11½ Luhr RD10 Tampa Dby 93 Reinvested,StgeReviewer,RlTwistr 12
11Mar82-7GP 1 1/16 :474 1:12 1:44 ft *6-5 122 1hd 1½ 1hd 1no Brumfield D7 Aw13000 81 Rinvstd,DoYourDncing,SldConqust 8
22Feb82-3Hia 1 1/16 :482 1:131 1:444ft *1 118 2hd 1½ 2½ 21 Brumfield D2 Aw14000 78 Star Choice, Reinvested, Pavarotti 7
13Feb82-10Hia 1⅛ :461 1:102 1:484ft 6¾e 114 2½ 21 67½ 616 BrfldD6 Everglades H 72 RoylRobrto,NwDiscovry,VictorinLn 8
3Feb82-7Hia 1⅛ :47 1:11 1:514ft *8-5 120 43 33 1½ 2no Fell J3 Aw14000 73 Moore Dusty,Reinvested,CatchVilla 8
22Jan82-6Hia 1⅛ ① 1:51 fm 4 120 67½ 45 2½ 1½ Fell J12 Mdn 79 Reinvested, Phaedra, GuidingRule 12
9Jan82-4Hia 7f :232 :463 1:251ft *1 120 105¾ 86¾ 65¾ 79¾ Vasquez J2 Mdn 67 Limrick,I'mPurGold,PrvtEncountr 12
●Apr 29 CD 4f ft :48 h Apr 15 Bel tr.t 4f ft :481 b ●Apr 9 Bel tr.t 1 gd 1:39 h Mar 31 Hia 4f ft :482 h

Muttering
Ro. c. 3, by Drone—Malvine, by Gamin
Own.—Tartan Stable 126 Br.—Tartan Farms Corp (Fla) 1982 2 1 1 0 $208,800
Tr.—Lukas D Wayne 1981 7 3 1 0 $108,429
Lifetime 9 4 2 0 $317,229
4Apr82-4SA 1⅛ :453 1:094 1:473ft 5 120 33 31½ 1½ 1no Pincay L Jr6 Sa Derby 91 Muttring,PrncSpllbound,JournyAtS 9
6Mar82-8SA 1 :443 1:091 1:342ft 9½ 121 610 43 42 2½ McCrrnCJ9 San Rafael 96 PrincSpllbound,Muttring,Unprdctbl 9
23Dec81-8Hol 1 1/16 :471 1:113 1:431ft 5½ 117 31 1hd 11 13 PncLJr7 Auld Lg Syne 79 Muttering, King's Finder,Cassaleria 9
31Oct81-8SA 1 1/16 :461 1:103 1:421ft 8½ 118 75½ 75½ 65½ 43½ Pincay L Jr2 Norfolk 87 Stalwart, Racing Is Fun,GatoDelSol 9
14Oct81-8SA 1 1/16 :462 1:113 1:433ft 3 120 41 52½ 1hd 23½ PincayLJr6 El Rio Rey 79 PrincSpllbound,Muttrng,SpdBrokr 10
4Oct81-4SA 1 :463 1:113 1:373ft 3 117 3½ 2½ 2½ 1½ Pincay L Jr5 Aw21000 81 Muttering,MillStrm,Smugglr'sGold 6
15Aug81-4Dmr 1 :462 1:12 1:391ft 2¼ 117 1hd — — — McHrgueDG3 Aw18000 — Spiritino, Carrie's Ten, Far Niente 6
15Aug81—Eased
18Jly81-8Hol 6f :213 :444 1:102ft 14 117 84¾ 1112 1114 1015 Lipham T6 Juv Champ 70 TheCptin,RememberJohn,Hln'sBu 12
10Jly81-6Hol 6f :22 :452 1:111ft 5½ 116 43 31½ 2½ 1½ Delahoussaye E1 Mdn 81 Muttering,LuckyLegnd,Mggi'sBst 12
●Apr 23 Kee 6f ft 1:13 b ●Apr 15 Kee 5f ft :591 h Mar 31 SA 3f ft :354 b ●Mar 23 SA 6f ft 1:103 h

Real Dare
B. g. 3, by Beau Groton—Big Dare, by Kentucky Pride
Own.—Jumonville J E Sr 126 Br.—Dorignac J P Jr (La) 1982 8 6 0 1 $108,069
Tr.—Mabry John C 1981 2 1 0 0 $72,012
Lifetime 10 7 0 1 $180,081
24Apr82-6JnD 7f :24 - :483 1:292sy *1-3 123 65¾ 25 1hd 12½ Guidry RD6 Ⓢ Aw10000 73 RelDre,AnothrDoctor,ElctronicDvic 6
28Mar82-10FG 1⅛ :464 1:112 1:503ft 6 126 76 64 814 828 Cauthen S7 La Dby 63 El Baba, Linkage,SpoonfulofHoney 8
6Mar82-9FG 1 1/16 :483 1:14 1:473sy *1-3 119 52½ 41½ 3½ 31¼ FrlRJ4 Ⓢ Cres Cty Dby 73 Gnilrew, Long Traffic, Real Dare 9
27Feb82-9FG 1 1/16 :483 1:14 1:463gd *1-9 123 12 13 18 113 FrnlRJ9 Ⓢ Hit Par Inv 79 RelDre,PmsProvOut,KnightofTruth 9
18Feb82-9FG 1 1/16 :48 1:134 1:461ft *1-9 123 15 16 18 117 FrnlnRJ1 Ⓢ Hit Par Trl 81 RelDre,Cesr'sConqust,PmsProvOut 7
31Jan82-9FG 6f :23 :464 1:11 ft *2-5 120 22 2½ 11½ 19 FrnlnRJ6 Ⓢ Gentilly H 90 RelDre,FirstCowboy,ExclusiveMstr 8
16Jan82-7FG 6f :223 :463 1:113ft *1-2 112 22 2hd 13 110 FranklinRJ4 Ⓢ Aw16000 87 Real Dare,FirstCowboy,TommyBolo 7
6Jan82-8FG 6f :223 :463 1:123ft *1-3 116 31 13 15 15 Franklin R J7 Aw9500 82 RealDre,TwiceBurned,LeedsCreek 10
26Dec81-9FG 6f :222 :46 1:112ft 4½e 113 2hd 11½ 16 113 FrnlRJ11 Hts Prde Fty 88 RelDre,PerfectRemdy,KinofKingly 14
17Dec81-8FG 6f :223 :471 1:141sy 7 113 1211 1211 87 43¼ Walker B J Jr7 Fut Trl 71 DesertMirge,MissProTeen,ToTllTr 12
Apr 14 JnD 4f ft :46 h Mar 20 FG 1 ft 1:424 h

Rock Steady
Dk. b. or br. c. 3, by Raise a Bid—Roccoco Miss, by Lucky Debonair
Own.—Knapp & Michael Jr 126 Br.—Cashman E C (Ky) 1982 5 1 0 0 $5,883
Tr.—Warren Ronnie 1981 7 2 1 1 $14,428
Lifetime 12 3 1 1 $20,311
24Apr82-8CD 1 :45 1:093 1:361ft 29e 113 35½ 46½ 33 41¼ RomroRP5 Derby Trial 86 Listcapade,StarGlint,RoylRoberto 10
16Apr82-8Kee 7f :224 :46 1:231ft 32 112 84½ 87¾ 86½ 511 Melancon L4 Aw18100 79 Deep Freeze, LeadAstray,JudoJima 8
26Mar82-8Lat 6f :231 :471 1:121sl *4-5 114 41½ 3½ 15 16 Solomon G2 Aw6600 83 RockStdy,Micky'sBans,BloomrRidg 7
6Feb82-9FG 6f :223 :451 1:103ft 15e 111 82½ 87 712 717 NemtiW8 Black Gld H 75 Linkage, Cagey Cougar,TalentTown 8
16Jan82-5FG 140 :474 1:131 1:422ft 2¾ 116 43 53½ 65½ 56½ Elmer D2 Aw9700 74 Mid Yell, Enlightenment,BostonZip 8
31Dec81-9FG 6f :222 :454 1:113ft 9½e 114 86½ 94¾ 912 910 ImprtoJ10 Sgr Bowl H 77 El Baba, Talk oftheTimes,TuninIn 13
16Dec81-5FG 6f :223 :471 1:132gd *3-2 119 33 32 1hd 14 Melancon L5 Aw9500 78 RockStedy,Orngeville,TwiceBurnd 10
18Nov81-6CD 6f :221 :453 1:11 ft 3 115 51½ 52¾ 36½ 23¾ Melancon L4 Aw12300 87 Tunin In, RockSteady,DeepFreeze 12
2Nov81-5CD 7f :24 :48 1:263ft 6¼ 120 1hd 11 13 14 Melancon L2 Mdn 74 RockStdy,RunJohnnyRun,TopBrick 9
3Sep81-4Bel 7f :231 :463 1:251ft 5 118 31 62¾ 44 45¾ Maple E3 M60000 70 Wolfie'sRascal,ClearMn,ChpterOne 9
3Aug81-9FE 4½f :224 :462 :524ft 5 120 5 66 33½ 33½ Sayler B3 Mdn 93 PublicImage,NearWillie,RockStedy 9
13Jun81-2CD 5f :223 :462 1:001ft 14 122 109½ 1011 1011 1013 Sayler B8 Mdn 75 Bronzn'Bold,EnglishCoin,MistyBid 12

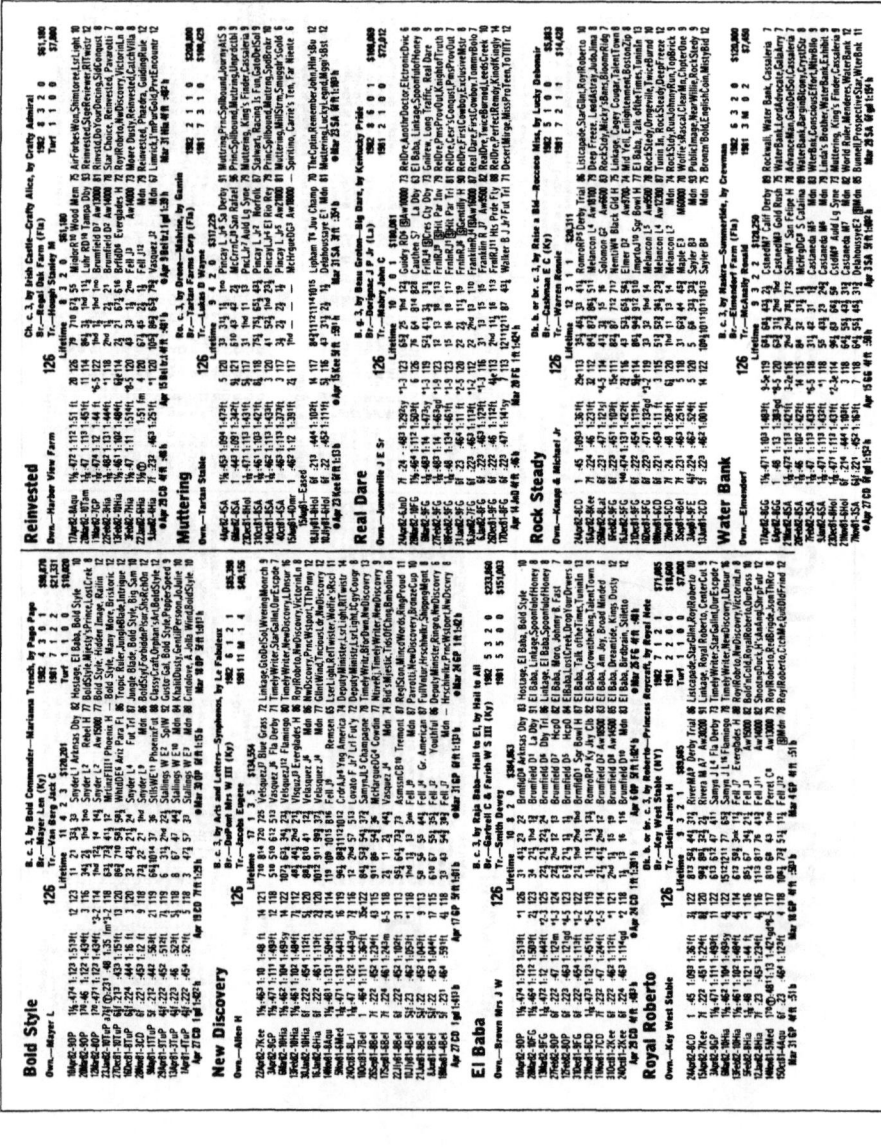

Water Bank
B. c. 3, by Naskra—Summertide, by Crewman
Own.—Elmendorf 126 Br.—Elmendorf Farm (Fla) 1982 6 3 2 0 $120,800
Tr.—McAnally Ronald 1981 3 M 0 2 $7,450
Lifetime 9 3 2 2 $128,250
17Apr82-8GG 1⅛ :471 1:103 1:483ft 9-5e 119 68½ 68½ 43½ 2½ CstnedM7 Calif Derby 89 Rockwall, Water Bank, Cassaleria 7
6Apr82-8GG 1 :48 1:13 1:383gd *8-5 120 63¾ 31½ 2hd 1hd CastnedM3 Gold Rush 75 WaterBank,LordAdvocate,GalaArry 7
21Mar82-8SA 1 1/16 :472 1:113 1:421ft 3-2e 116 2hd 2hd 78¼ 712 ShmrW1 San Felipe H 78 AdvanceMan,GatoDelSol,Cassaleria 7
20Feb82-8SA 1 1/16 :46 1:102 1:422ft 14 115 84 32 31½ 1½ McHrgDG8 S Catalina 89 WaterBank,BarginBlcony,CrystlStr 8
7Feb82-3SA 1 1/16 :47 1:113 1:433ft *6-5 118 31½ 42 31 1¾ Castaneda M5 Mdn 83 WterBnk,ConsciousEffort,NtivBllo 9
9Jan82-6SA 1 1/16 :471 1:113 1:432ft *1 118 55 43½ 23 24¾ Castaneda M6 Mdn 79 Linda's Brother,WaterBank,Exhibit 9
23Dec81-8Hol 1 1/16 :471 1:113 1:431ft *2-3e 114 96½ 83 66½ 56 CstdM9 Auld Lg Syne 73 Muttering, King's Finder,Cassaleria 9
21Nov81-6Hol 6f :214 :444 1:103ft 3 118 64½ 55½ 43½ 31¾ Castaneda M7 Mdn 82 World Ruler,Menderes,WaterBank 12
7Nov81-3SA 6½f :221 :452 1:163ft 7 118 64½ 55½ 45½ 31¾ DelahoussyeE2 Ⓢ Mdn 85 Bunnell,ProspectiveStar,WterBnk 11
●Apr 27 CD 6f gd 1:152 h Apr 15 GG 4f ft :50 h Apr 3 SA 5f ft 1:002 h Mar 28 SA 6f gd 1:154 h

Rockwall

B. c. 3, by Cannonade—Fiddling Jimmer, by Jimmer
Br.—Hunt N B (Ky) 1982 2 1 1 0 $133,400
Own.—Hunt N B 126 Tr.—Clyne Vincent 1981 4 1 0 1 $13,125
Lifetime 6 2 1 1 $146,525

17Apr82-8GG 1⅛ :471 1:103 1:483ft 41 112 3½ 1hd 11½ 1½ VldvsHA2 Calif Derby 90 Rockwall, Water Bank, Cassaleria 7
4Apr82-6SA 1 1/16 :453 1:103 1:424ft 12 117 79¼ 41½ 32 22½ Sibille R7 Aw21000 84 Tell Don, Rockwall, Penngrove 9
27Dec81-4SA 1 :471 1:12 1:362ft 8 120 77½ 76 55 46¼ Sibille R8 Aw20000 81 BargainBlcony,Botrell,AlmoStrnger 8
20Dec81-6Hol 1 :463 1:123 1:39 ft 3 117 811 76¼ 52¼ 11¼ Sibille R5 Mdn 71 Rockwall,FirstLarry,Linda'sBrother 9
12Dec81-6Hol 1 1/16 :46 1:12 1:452ft *2¼ 117 89¾ 2hd 21 32 Sibille R4 Mdn 66 LimoJohn,ChrgeBetween,Rockwll 10
29Nov81-6Hol 1 :494 1:16 1:422sl 21 117 614 66 45 42¼ Ramirez O3 Mdn 52 Botrell, Native Bello, Hell's Island 6
●Apr 29 CD 5f ft 1:01 h Apr 25 CD 1 ft 1:464 b Apr 15 SA 3f ft :352 h Apr 10 SA 1 ft 1:374 h

Wolfie's Rascal

B. c. 3, by London Company—Daisy Trimmer, by Bold Discovery
Br.—Amlung R (Fla) 1982 6 2 1 0 $72,662
Own.—Cohen, Cohen, Kumble 126 Tr.—Tesher Howard M 1981 6 2 0 1 $39,395
Lifetime 12 4 1 1 $112,057

17Apr82-8Aqu 1⅛ :472 1:112 1:51 ft 21 126 55½ 46 43 42½ VelsquzJ5 Wood Mem 77 AirForbesWon,Shimtoree,LsrLight 10
27Mar82-9Lat 1 1/16 :463 1:113 1:443ft *8-5 120 85¾ 814 614 612 BrcclVJr8 Jim BSpiral 75 Goodn'Dusty,FstGold,Cupcoy'sJoy 12
6Mar82-10Hia 1⅛ :462 1:104 1:493sy 14 122 119 85 66 55½ BrcclieVJr11 Flamingo 78 TimelyWriter,NewDiscovry,LDnsur 16
24Feb82-8Aqu 1⅛ ⊡:4721:1221:511ft 2¼ 117 31½ 1hd 1hd 11¾ BrcclVJr6 Lucky Draw 90 Wolfi'sRscl,AskMuhmmd,FstGold 11
12Feb82-8Aqu 1 1/16 ⊡:4741:1231:441ft *2 119 2hd 1hd 2½ 21 SantiagoA3 Whirlaway 91 AskMuhmmd,Wolfie'sRscl,FstGold 7
13Jan82-8Aqu 170 ⊡:4811:1321:424ft *9-5 119 42½ — 11½ 12½ Santiago A2 Aw18000 88 Wolfie'sRscl,SkinDncr,Shy'sRbllion 6
13Jan82—Running positions omitted because of weather conditions.
7Dec81-7Aqu 1 1/16 ⊡:4741:1231:462ft 3 117 2½ 2hd 1½ 13½ Santiago A7 Aw17000 82 Wolfie'sRscl,ClssHero,MortggeMn 12
22Nov81-8Aqu 1 :46 1:11 1:364ft 5½e 114 84½ 77 68 68½ Santiago A6 Nashua 74 Our Escapade,John'sGold,Hostage 10
14Nov81-8Aqu 1⅛ :481 1:131 1:504ft 54 113 33 43½ 38 39¾ Santiago A3 Remsen 71 LserLight,RelTwister,Wolfie'sRscl 11
26Oct81-5Aqu 1 :464 1:122 1:383sy 7½ 117 32½ 64¾ 77½ 79¾ Velasquez J6 Aw17000 63 LiftOneA.,SealedConquest,RedRng 8
3Sep81-4Bel 7f :231 :463 1:251ft 8½ 114 41½ 1hd 12½ 14¾ Velasquez J7 M55000 76 Wolfie'sRascal,ClearMn,ChpterOne 9
13Aug81-5Crc 6f :231 :47 1:134ft 11 116 62¾ 55½ 56½ 56¾ Guerra W A4 M50000 76 Drakus Here, Fitz's Night,IrishPete 6
Apr 13 Aqu 6f ft 1:15 h Apr 5 Kee 6f ft 1:142 h ●Mar 23 Lat 6f ft 1:132 h Mar 13 Hia 7f ft 1:292 b

Star Gallant

Dk. b. or br. c. 3, by My Gallant—Liza Star, by Bold Hitter
Br.—Roma Stable (Fla) 1982 4 2 2 0 $124,600
Own.—Buckram Oak Farm 126 Tr.—Imperio Leonard 1981 2 2 0 0 $41,760
Lifetime 6 4 2 0 $166,360

24Apr82-8CD 1 :45 1:093 1:361ft *1-3 122 1½ 15 11½ 21¼ Hawley S4 Derby Trial 87 Listcapade,StarGllnt,RoylRoberto 10
3Apr82-9GP 1⅛ :471 1:111 1:493ft 6-5 122 11½ 12 1hd 22 Hawley S1 Fla Derby 82 TimelyWriter,StarGallnt,OurEscpde 7
22Mar82-9GP 1 1/16 :471 1:111 1:431ft 2¼ 117 11½ 11 11 14 Hawley S5 Ftn Youth 85 StarGallant,DistinctivePro,CutAwy 9
16Feb82-9Hia 7f :223 :443 1:23 ft *1-3 116 22 1hd 11 14 Hawley S7 Aw14000 88 Star Gallant, CutAway,Rex'sProfile 7
23Dec81-8Aqu 6f ⊡:214 :4531:111gd *2-3 113 53¾ 2hd 13 12¼ Hernandez C3 Alsab 88 StrGllnt,FoxmorFlght,WndFrmThS 7
10Dec81-4Aqu 6f ⊡:224 :47 1:11 ft *9-5 1117 42½ 2hd 12 16 Hernandez C10 Mdn 89 Star Gallant,Shimatoree,Joy'sMac 14
●Apr 22 CD 3f ft :343 h ●Mar 30 GP 4f gd :47 b ●Mar 15 Hia 6f ft 1:102 h ●Mar 7 Hia 4f ft :457 h

Cassaleria

Dk. b. or br. c. 3, by Pretense—Special Charm, by Verbatim
Br.—Bradyleigh FarmsInc&Brady (Ky) 1982 4 1 0 2 $121,600
Own.—20/20 Stable 126 Tr.—McAnally Ronald 1981 8 2 2 4 $234,070
Lifetime 12 3 2 6 $355,670

17Apr82-8GG 1⅛ :471 1:103 1:483ft 9-5e 122 56½ 47½ 33½ 3½ McHrDG3 Calif Derby 89 Rockwall, Water Bank, Cassaleria 7
4Apr82-4SA 1⅛ :453 1:094 1:473ft 8 120 912 85 54½ 65¼ ShoemkrW7 Sa Derby 86 Multring,PrncSpllbound,JournyAtS 9
21Mar82-8SA 1 1/16 :472 1:113 1:421ft 3-2e 123 3½ 4¾ 2½ 3¾ McHrDG5 San FelipeH 89 AdvanceMan,GatoDelSol,Cassaleria 7
6Feb82-8BM 1 1/16 :461 1:102 1:424ft *2-3 120 711 78¾ 45 1½ McHrDG3 El CamReal 85 Cassaleria, CrystalStar,TropicRuler 9
23Dec81-8Hol 1 1/16 :471 1:113 1:431ft *2-3e 120 63½ 41¾ 32 33 McHrDG5 AuldLgSyne 76 Muttering, King's Finder,Cassaleria 9
29Nov81-8Hol 1 1/16 :481 1:141 1:474sl 4½ 121 79¼ 57 2½ 2½ McHrguDG8 Hol Fut'y 55 Stalwart, Cassaleria, Header Card 12
14Nov81-8BM 1 1/16 :451 1:101 1:413gd *8-5 115 610 31½ 11 13½ McHrDG2 ElCamoReal 91 Cassaleria, Songhay, Lucky Ship 9
18Oct81-2SA 1 1/16 :464 1:114 1:424ft *7-5 118 43½ 31 13 110 Castaneda M3 Mdn 87 Cassaleria,ChargeBetween,BisonBy 7
7Oct81-4SA 1 :463 1:113 1:37 ft 3¾ 118 47 33 31½ 3nk Ortega L E2 Mdn 84 Stalwart,CompanyChairman,Cssleri 9
23Aug81-6Dmr 1 :463 1:113 1:374ft 4½ 117 52½ 42 33½ 35½ Ortega L E3 Mdn 73 OkieCityLd,StndupComedin,Cssleri 9
1Aug81-6Dmr 6f :224 :454 1:104ft 4 118 79 47 35½ 37 Ortega L E5 Mdn 77 ExplosiveTwist,SpeedBroker,Csslri 8
26Jun81-6Hol 5½f :223 :464 1:054ft 21 116 97 78½ 46 22 Castaneda M6 M50000 90 Spiritino, Cassaleria, Convince Me 12
●Apr 27 CD 6f gd 1:152 b Apr 13 SA 5f ft 1:001 h

Gato Del Sol

Gr. c. 3, by Cougar II—Peacefully, by Jacinto
Br.—Hancock III & Peters (Ky) 1982 4 0 2 1 $86,365
Own.—Hancock III & Peters 126 Tr.—Gregson Edwin 1981 8 2 1 3 $220,828
Lifetime 12 2 3 4 $307,193

22Apr82-7Kee 1⅛ :463 1:10 1:48 ft 3¾ 121 46 46 34½ 25½ DlhossyE3 Blue Grass 91 Linkage,GtoDelSol,WveringMonrch 9
4Apr82-4SA 1⅛ :453 1:094 1:473ft 7½ 120 812 98 67 43¼ DelhoussyE4 Sa Derby 88 Multring,PrncSpllbound,JournyAtS 9
21Mar82-8SA 1 1/16 :472 1:113 1:421ft 4¾ 118 76½ 75¼ 43 2nk DlhssyE6 San Felipe H 90 AdvanceMan,GatoDelSol,Cassaleria 7
25Feb82-7SA 6½f :221 :45 1:152ft 9-5 115 67¾ 68¼ 65½ 33¼ DelhoussyeE5 Aw22000 90 LuckyLegend,RcingIsFun,GtoDlSol 6
29Nov81-8Hol 1 1/16 :481 1:141 1:474sl 5¾ 121 89¼ 77½ 711 714 DelhoussyE6 Hol Fut'y 42 Stalwart, Cassaleria, Header Card 12
14Nov81-8Hol 7f :211 :432 1:22 ft 3½ 122 511 59½ 33½ 2½ DlhossyE5 Hol Prevue 86 Sepulveda,GatoDelSol,DesertEnvoy 6
31Oct81-8SA 1 1/16 :461 1:103 1:421ft 3¾ 118 911 86¼ 55½ 32½ DelhoussyeE3 Norfolk 87 Stalwart, Racing Is Fun,GatoDelSol 9
9Sep81-8Dmr 1 :453 1:111 1:372ft 3¾ 114 1012 105¼ 73¼ 1hd DelhoussyE2 Dmr Fut 81 GatoDelSol,TheCaptain,RingProud 10
26Aug81-8Dmr 1 :454 1:103 1:364ft 5¼ 115 79 46 54½ 33½ DelahoussyeE7 Blaboa 80 TheCaptain,DistantHeart,GtoDelSol 9
14Aug81-6Dmr 1 :47 1:124 1:39 ft *8-5 117 3nk 11½ 13 17 McCarron C J5 Mdn 73 Gato Del Sol, Kell's Boy, ClubFlush 8
10Jly81-6Hol 6f :22 :452 1:111ft *2½e 116 66 67¼ 67 77 Valenzuela P A2 Mdn 74 Muttering,LuckyLegnd,Mggi'sBst 12
28Jun81-6Hol 5½f :221 :461 1:051ft 5½e 116 79¾ 69 55¾ 33½ Delahoussaye E5 Mdn 81 Irisher, Zanyo, Gato Del Sol 12
Apr 29 CD 4f ft :483 b Apr 18 Kee 4f sy :504 b ●Apr 12 Kee 6f ft 1:133 b ●Apr 3 SA 3f ft :342 h

Majesty's Prince

Ch. c. 3, by His Majesty—Pied Princess, by Tom Fool
Br.—Marsh J D (Va) 1982 3 1 1 0 $37,512
Own.—Marsh J D 126 Tr.—Cantey Joseph B 1981 8 2 3 2 $71,849
Lifetime 11 3 4 2 $109,361 Turf 4 2 2 0 $47,264

10Apr82-9OP 1⅛ :474 1:123 1:513ft 5e 117 1016 109¾ 811 56¼ KenelJL2 Arknsas Dby 79 Hostage, El Baba, Bold Style 10
20Mar82-9OP 170 :46 1:122 1:434ft 4½e 115 718 59 46 2no Kaenel J L6 Rebel H 77 BoldStyle,Mjesty'sPrince,LostCrek 8
5Mar82-7OP 6f :222 :471 1:13 ft 6 114 77½ 65 3½ 1½ Kaenel J L11 Aw15000 80 Mjesty'sPrince,Hvgrtdt,HrfordMn 12
14Nov81-8Aqu 1⅛ :481 1:131 1:504ft 5½ 115 65 1113 1117 917 MacBeth D1 Remsen 64 LserLight,RelTwister,Wolfie'sRscl 11
24Oct81-8Lrl 1 1/16 :47 1:122 1:443gd 9-5 122 67½ 65¾ 47 49 Maple E1 Lrl Fut'y 76 DeputyMinistr,LsrLight,‡CgyCougr 8
24Oct81—Placed third through disqualification
1Oct81-8Bel 1 1/16 Ⓣ:4741:1111:43 fm *9-5 117 31 3nk 2hd 2hd Maple E5 Prince John 81 Gnom'sGld,Mjsty'sPrnc,DncngSchl 7
14Sep81-8Bel 1 Ⓣ:4531:1021:351fm *2-5 115 2½ 2hd 21½ 24¾ Maple E4 Cascade H 84 DncngSchool,Mjsty'sPrnc,BbyDuck 8
4Sep81-3Bel 1 Ⓣ:48 1:1231:384gd *2-3 119 12½ 13½ 13½ 15¾ Maple E3 Aw20000 71 Mjsty'sPrnc,DncngSchool,OrEscpd 6
20Aug81-2Sar 6f :23 :462 1:104ft 4e 122 31½ 51½ 3½ 2nk Maple E4 Aw19000 86 TalcPlot,Mjesty'sPrince,IrishMrtini 8
6Aug81-4Sar 1 ⊡:4831:1431:39 gd 2¼ 118 11 11 11½ 13¾ Maple E4 Mdn 81 Mjsty'sPrnc,ClssHro,Who'sFrDnnr 10
20Jly81-6Bel 6f :224 :461 1:123sy 14 118 1023 1021 616 36 Maple E6 Mdn 73 JtlingPlsur,BronzCup,Mjsty'sPrnc 10
Mar 31 OP 6f gd 1:152 b Mar 1 OP 5f gd 1:034 h

Throughout the eighty minutes between the seventh race and the Derby, the best bet was Air Forbes Won to show, as indicated by the final tote board figures:

	Totals	#1 Air Forbes Won	Expected Value per Dollar Bet on Air Forbes Won
Odds		5—2	
Win	2,853,976	641,476	
Show	1,006,969	129,486	1.25

With my betting fortune now up to $621.50, the optimal bet was $99.

Gato Del Sol, ridden by Eddie Delahoussaye, ran an impressive race to win the Churchill classic by $2\frac{1}{2}$ lengths over Laser Light and Reinvested. Gato Del Sol, a 21—1 shot, was the last horse away from the gate and stayed near the rear until the backstretch. Then he picked up ground outside the final turn and ran strongly until the finish. Delahoussaye had planned this late charge on the outside ever since he had come in second on Woodchopper in the 1981 Kentucky Derby. Woodchopper had been trapped inside, which had probably cost him the race, and Delahoussaye was determined not to repeat that strategy. El Baba and Air Forbes Won ran second and third for most of the race, but both weakened in the final stretch and finished eleventh and seventh, respectively. The $99 loss dropped my betting fortune to $522.50.

The chart of the race was as follows:

108th Kentucky Derby, May 1, 1982

$550,100 gross value and $40,000 Gold Cup. Net to winner $428,850; second $60,000; third $30,000; fourth $15,000. 388 nominations.

Horse	Eqt	Wt	PP	¼	½	¾	Mile	Str	Fin	Jockeys	Owners	Odds to $1
Gato Del Sol		126	18	19	19	10½	5½	1½	$1^{2\frac{1}{2}}$	E. Delahoussaye	Hancock & Peters	21.20
Laser Light		126	8	18^{hd}	17^{hd}	18½	10^{1}	9^{hd}	2^{nk}	E. Maple	Live Oak Plantation	18.20
Reinvested		126	10	$16^{1\frac{1}{2}}$	16½	14^{1}	7^{1}	2½	$3^{2\frac{1}{2}}$	D. MacBeth	Harbor View Farm	f-8.90
Water Bank		126	13	$14^{1\frac{1}{2}}$	$12^{1\frac{1}{2}}$	$16^{1\frac{1}{2}}$	8^{2}	5^{hd}	4¾	M. Castaneda	Elmendorf	a-12.60
Muttering		126	11	4^{hd}	5½	4½	4^{hd}	4^{hd}	5^{3}	L. Pincay	Tartan Stable	4.20
Rockwall	b	126	14	12^{1}	9^{1}	$5^{1\frac{1}{2}}$	6^{1}	$7^{1\frac{1}{2}}$	6¾	H. Valdivieso	Nelson B. Hunt	47.80
Air Forbes Won		126	7	3^{hd}	3^{3}	3^{2}	3^{3}	3^{hd}	$7^{1\frac{1}{4}}$	A. Cordero	Edward Anchel	2.70
Star Gallant		126	16	6^{1}	7½	9^{hd}	9^{1}	10^{1}	8no	W. Shoemaker	Buckram Oak Farm	15.70
Majesty's Prince		126	19	13^{hd}	13½	17^{1}	14^{2}	11½	9^{hd}	R. Hernandez	John D. Marsh	f-8.90
Cupecoy's Joy		121	1	$1^{1\frac{1}{2}}$	$1^{3\frac{1}{2}}$	1^{4}	1½	8^{hd}	10½	A. Santiago	Ri-Ma-Ro Stable	f-8.90
El Baba		126	4	2½	2^{3}	2^{2}	2^{hd}	6^{hd}	11^{1}	D. Brumfield	Mrs. Joe W. Brown	3.30
Wavering Monarch		126	6	11^{2}	10^{hd}	11^{hd}	11½	12^{2}	$12^{1\frac{1}{4}}$	R. Romero	Greathouse family	39.50
Cassaleria		126	17	15^{hd}	15^{hd}	15^{hd}	13½	13½	13^{nk}	D. McHargue	20/20 Stable	a-12.60
Royal Roberto		126	5	17^{1}	18½	19	17½	14½	14½	M. Rivera	Key West Stable	9.30
Music Leader	b	126	9	$8^{1\frac{1}{2}}$	8½	8^{hd}	$12^{1\frac{1}{2}}$	15^{hd}	$15^{2\frac{1}{2}}$	P. Day	Glaser-Ellett, et al	f-8.90
Bold Style	b	126	2	7^{2}	4^{hd}	7^{hd}	15½	16½	16^{nk}	J. Fell	Len Mayer	29.30
Wolfie's Rascal		126	15	5½	6^{hd}	6½	16^{2}	17^{3}	$17^{1\frac{1}{2}}$	J. Velasquez	Cohen-Cohen-Kumble	f-8.90
New Discovery		126	3	10½	11^{hd}	13^{hd}	$18^{1\frac{1}{2}}$	18^{4}	18^{6}	J. Bailey	Herbert Allen	f-8.90
Real Dare		126	12	9^{1}	14^{1}	$12^{1\frac{1}{2}}$	19	19	19	R. Guidry	J. E. Jumonville, Sr.	f-8.90

Time: :23, :46-1/5, 1:10-4/5, 1:37-1/5, 2:02-2/5. Track fast. Off at 5:40 EDT. Start good. Won driving.

f-mutuel field. A-coupled Water Bank and Cassaleria.

$2 mutuels paid — Gato Del Sol $44.40 straight; $19.00 place; $9.40 show, Laser Light $17.00 place; $9.20 show; Reinvested (field) $4.40 show.

Winner — Gr. c, by *Cougar II — Peacefully, by Jacinto. Trainer Edwin Gregson. Bred in Kentucky by Hancock III & Peters.

GATO DEL SOL came away relaxed in last position and clear of horses, advanced on the outside under his own courage in the backstretch, picked up the field with a strong run completing the turn to take command before the furlong pole, was unaffected by REINVESTED leaning on him briefly and drew clear under strong right hand use of the whip into the final yards. LASER LIGHT also relaxed in the early running, followed GATO DEL SOL around horses leaving the backstretch and was wide straightening away for the final stretch drive, loomed boldly but could not sustain his bid while gamely besting REINVESTED for the place. REINVESTED, intimidated by WATER BANK leaving the half-mile marker and bothering CASSALERIA, swung slightly out on that rival getting room on the outside to follow GATO DEL SOL approaching mid-stretch, leaned in briefly under right hand urging and hung. WATER BANK saved ground early, found room between rivals with a stretch bid and hung. MUTTERING, well placed from the beginning, made a bid between horses entering the stretch and weakened slightly. ROCKWALL finished well without being a threat. AIR FORBES WON responded with a strong run to reach the leaders completing the final turn and weakened late. STAR GALLANT was never a serious factor. MAJESTY'S PRINCE bore out slightly while tiring. CUPECOY'S JOY set the pace in comfortable fashion into the stretch turn before giving way. EL BABA, well situated closest to the pace, drew on even terms for the lead entering the stretch and weakened suddenly. CASSALERIA was being outrun when bothered by REINVESTED in the backstretch and never became a factor. ROYAL ROBERTO was outrun at all stages. BOLD STYLE saved ground racing forwardly placed for six furlongs and tired. WOLFIE'S RASCAL lost ground and dropped back early. NEW DISCOVERY gave a dull effort. REAL DARE tired badly.

Scratched: Rock Steady

THE WINNER'S PEDIGREE AND CAREER HIGHLIGHTS

GATO DEL SOL Grey Colt	*Cougar II	Tale of Two Cities	Tehran Menda II
		Cindy Lou II	Madara Maria Bonita
	Peacefully	Jacinto	Bold Ruler Cascade II
		Morning Calm	Hail to Reason Yellow Mist

Year	Age	Sts	1st	2nd	3rd	Won
1981	2	8	2	1	3	$220,828
1982	3	9	2	3	1	$588,779
TOTALS		17	4	4	4	$809,607

At 2 Years	WON	Del Mar Futurity
	2nd	Hollywood Revue
	3rd	Balboa Stakes
At 3 Years	WON	Kentucky Derby
	2nd	San Felipe, Blue Grass Stakes
	3rd	
	UNP	Santa Anita Derby

Dual Tracks in the Ninth

The final Dr. Z system bet of the day was on Dual Tracks in the ninth race. With two minutes to post time the tote board was

	Totals	#3 Dual Tracks	Expected Value per Dollar Bet on Dual Tracks
Odds		3—1	
Win	397,004	75,441	
Show	110,222	11,621	1.28

1 1/16 MILES (START / FINISH)

WIN | PLACE | SHOW

9

CLAIMING

PURSE $10,000

FOUR-YEAR-OLDS AND UPWARD, 123 lbs. Non-winners of three races at a mile or over since February 5 allowed 2 lbs.; two such races since March 17, 4 lbs.; one such race since April 1, 6 lbs. Claiming Price $25,000; for each $1,000 to $20,000, 1 lb. (Races where entered for $10,000 or less not considered.)

Track Record—YES SIR (5) 110 lbs.; 1:41 3/5; Nov. 25, 1970

MAKE SELECTION BY NUMBER

No.	Owner	Trainer	Colors	Horse	Weight	Breeding	Jockey	Morn. Line	Claiming Price
1	MASON RUDD	WALTER BINDNER, JR.	Blue, White Circled "MR," White Bars on Sleeves Blue Cap	ENDEMONIADO (Arg)	117	Dk.b. or br.h.(1977), Dairey—Francachela	GENE SOLOMON	15	$25,000.
2	DARREL E. HOUT	DAVID M. WALSH	Purple, Gold "DH," Gold Dots Purple Cap	BEFORE THE BENCH	117	B.g.(1975), Advocator—Landing Derby	LEROY TAUZIN	20	$25,000.
3	ALBERT M. STALL AND EARL BURKE	WILLIAM I. MOTT	White, Blue Diamond Frames, White Cap	DUAL TRACKS	117	B.g.(1975), Central Paris—Rose Duel	RONALD ARDOIN	5-2	$25,000
4	HAWKSWORTH FARM (Harry, Teresa and Tom Meyerhoff)	JUDITH ZOUCK	Blue, Black Cross Sashes, Blue Bars on Blk Slvs., Blue Cap	AVATOIL	117	Ch.c.(1978), Avatar—Toll No More	LARRY MELANCON	4	$25,000.
5	W. C. PARTEE	LYNN WHITING	Orange, White Dots Orange Cap	ARGONAFTIS	119	B.h.(1977), My Swallow—Artistically	PAT DAY	7-2	$25,000.
6	JOHN FRANKS	ROBERT HOLTHUS	Green, Orange "JF" on White Ball, Orange and White Halved Sleeves, Green Cap	LUDICROUS	112	B.g. (1975), Droll Role—Wild Note	RANDY ROMERO	6	$20,000
7	WESLEY GUY	OWNER	Brown, White Blocks Brown Cap	SCARLET GUY	115	Ro.h.(1976), Peace Corps—Scarlet Request	TERRY WARNER	20	$23,000
8	BLACKTHORN STABLE (P. F. Lenihan and M. J. Schnurr)	GREG FOLEY	Black, Gold Belt, Gold Bars on Sleeves, Black Cap	GENUINE MAGIC	117	Dk.b. or br.h.(1975), Nalees Man--Smart Smart	MARK SELLERS	5	$25,000
9	BERNARD FLINT, INC. (Bernard S. Flint)	BERNARD S. FLINT	Gold, Blue & Gold Stars on White Sleeves, White Cap	MOLTO BENE	*112	B.g.(1977), Northern Challenge—Unchopped	TRAVIS HIGHTOWER	10	$25,000.

Scratched—CHARLIES FINALE, DOUBLE THREES, BELLE'S RULER, BELL SWINGER, BAL BAY

Selections 3—5—4—8

With my betting fortune now $522.50, the optimal bet was $67. Dual Tracks made his move in the stretch, but could only grab third behind Avatoil and Genuine Magic. But with a show bet, a third is as good as a win! He paid $3.80 to show, for a return of $127.30 and a profit of $60.30. The chart of the race is on page 221.

NINTH RACE 1 1/16 MILES. (1.41 3/5) CLAIMING. Purse $10,000, 4-year-olds and upward. Weight, 123 lbs. Non-winners of three races at a mile or over since February 5 allowed 2 lbs.; two such races since March 17, 4 lbs.; one such race since April 1, 6 lbs. Claiming price $25,000; for each $1,000 to $20,000 allowed 1 lb. (Races where entered for $18,000 or less not considered.)

Churchill

MAY 1, 1982

Value of race $10,000, value to winner $6,500, second $2,000, third $1,000, fourth $500. Mutuel pool $688,145.

Last Raced		Horse	Eqt.	A.	Wt.	PP	St	1/4	1/2	3/4	Str	Fin	Jockey	Cl'gPr	Odds $1
14Apr82	1Kee 1	Avatoil		4	119	4	4	5-2	5-2	1-1½	1-3	1-2	Melancon L	25000	2.90
22Apr82	8Kee 2	Genuine Magic		7	117	9	5	3hd	2hd	2hd	2-1½	2-1½	Sellers M S	25000	3.10
10Apr82	8Kee 5	Dual Tracks		7	117	3	6	8-1	8-2	6 ½	5-2	3-1½	Ardoin R	25000	3.40
10Apr82	5OP 1	Argonaftis		5	119	5	2	1 ½	4-1½	5-1	3hd	4-1½	Day P	25000	3.80
22Apr82	8Kee 4	Ludicrous		7	112	6	3	2-1	3hd	4hd	4hd	5-5	Romero R P	20000	8.60
26Apr82	7CD 7	Molto Bene	b	5	112	9	9	4-1½	1 ½	3-1	6-3	6nk	Hightower T W-5	25000	10.90
24Apr82	6CD 6	Scarlet Guy		6	115	7	8	9	9	9	7-1	7-3½	Warner T	23000	51.50
10Apr82	8Kee 9	Before the Bench		7	117	2	1	6hd	7-1	7hd	9	8nk	Tauzin L	25000	54.80
22Apr82	8Kee 7	Endemoniado		5	117	1	7	7-1½	6hd	8-4	8hd	9	Solomon G	25000	26.20

OFF AT 6:51. Start good. Won driving. Time, :25 3/5, :49 1/5, 1:13 2/5, 1:38 2/5, 1:44 4/5 Track fast.

$ 2 Mutuel Prices:				
4-	AVATOIL	7.80	4.40	3.60
8-	GENUINE MAGIC		4.20	3.20
3-	DUAL TRACKS			3.80

Ch. c, by Avatar-Toil No More, by Grand Central. Trainer Zouch Judith. Bred by Skara Glen Stables (Ky).

AVATOIL, allowed to settle, commenced a rally leaving the backstretch, took clear command entering the lane, held sway while kept to urging. GENUINE MAGIC, always with the leaders, could not withstand the winner but continued willingly to be second best. DUAL TRACKS, void of speed, rallied to best the others. ARGONAFTIS made the pace briefly and gave away. LUDICROUS prompted the early pace but had no late rally. MOLTO BENE, just off the early pace, took command after a half but could not sustain the bid.

Owners- 1, Hawksworth Farm; 2, Black Thorn Stable; 3, Burice & Stall; 4, Partee W C; 5, Franks J; 6, Flint B S; 7, Guy W; 8, Hout D E; 9, Rudd M.

Trainers- 1, Zouch Judith; 2, Foley Greg; 3, Mott William I; 4, Whiting Lynn; 5, Holthus Robert E; 6, Flint Bernard S; 7, Guy Wesley; 8, Walsh David M; 9, Bindner Walter Jr.

Argonaftis was claimed by Schlansky Leslie ; trainer, Flint Bernard.

Scratched- Charlies Finale(20Apr82 8Kee 2); Double Threes(3Apr82 5OP 2); Belle's Ruler(22Apr82 8Kee 5); Bell Swinger (10Apr82 5OP 3); Bal Bay(13Apr82 10GP 5).

The Dr. Z system had won four races out of five for the day. Churchill Downs had once again been good to me. It had built my betting wealth to $582.80 from an initial $400, a 46% rate of return for the day. I was already looking forward to Derby '83.

CHAPTER 12

A Great Day for Canada: Sunny's Halo Wins the Kentucky Derby

The Kentucky Mood

We had been in Chicago for the semiannual joint meetings of the Operations Research Society of America and the Institute of Management Sciences. I had organized several sessions dealing with the latest theory and practice of trading stock options and with the mathematics of gambling. We had also read some research papers and I had a number of meetings involved with my activities as finance editor of the journal *Management Science*.

One of my UBC students, Brian Canfield, who was keen to learn more about stock market activities and horse-race betting, came along as well. When Don went back to Northwestern, Brian and I drove to Kentucky. Don flew down later for Derby Day. It takes about six hours to reach the Kentucky border, and the mood suddenly changes from industrial towns and rolling farm country to beautifully kept bluegrass horse farms with their white board fences. It had been two years since my last visit, and we had a whole week before the Derby to explore the farms in the Lexington area and do research for this book at the Keeneland and Churchill Downs racetracks and at the Keeneland racing library. The first few days brought an unbelievable amount of heavy spring rain. Finally, at midweek, the weather cleared and remained pleasant throughout our stay. It took the track at Churchill Downs only about a day to dry out, and the sun was so strong that the track had to be watered only two days after the torrential drenching it took.

This area of Kentucky has the greatest assembly of horse farms in the world and much of the finest bloodstock. As I mentioned in Chapter Ten, most of the farms allow visitors with appointments, and I highly recommend that you visit them. The highlight for us was a visit to Claiborne farms in Paris, Kentucky. This 3,200-acre farm supports twenty-eight major stallions and about five hundred mares, yearlings, and other horses. It was a rare treat to see such great horses as Secretariat, Spectacular Bid, Nijinski II, Riva Ridge, Conquistador Cielo, Coastal, Drone, Damascus, and Mr. Prospector close up. The investment side of racing involves a fantastic set of investment gambles. Horses' values can vary by millions of dollars as the result of a single event—for instance, a convincing victory in an important race or a minor injury. The price of the best bloodstock has reached astronomical levels. The twenty-eight stallions at Claiborne include some of the world's best. Their total value is several hundred million dollars.

The most important auction of yearlings takes place at Keeneland. At the July, 1983, sale, 301 yearlings sold for an average price of $501,495, or over $150 million in total. These are amazing sums for horses that have never run a race. The competitive bidding among racing's elite millionaires, each hoping to obtain the best bloodstock, drives the prices to these unheard-of sums. Prices are dependent on the horse's pedigree, the fame and performance of his sire and dam and their heritage, and on the physical appearance of the young animal.

Northern Dancer, the 1964 Derby winner in what was then the record time of two minutes flat, has been the star of the show of late. His offspring have proved to be outstanding runners and even better sires. His stud fee of as much as $700,000 with no guarantee of a live foal may sound outrageously expensive. However, it has certainly paid off, and if the chemistry is right, the returns can be smashing. At this sale, one filly yearling of his sold for $2.5 million and a yearling colt for $10.2 million. These prices were paid by Sheikh Mohammed ibn Rashid al Maktoum of the oil-rich United Arab Emirate state of Dubai, who outbid Robert Sangster, the British sports pool magnate. Their personal grudge match, spurred on because Sangster had won the auction in the previous two years, is money in the bank for consigners of Northern Dancer's offspring. It is hard to imagine that at such prices these yearlings are wise investments. The purchases are a bit like giving the good looking five-year-old son of a top baseball star married to a former Olympic-medal-winning daughter of a famous distance runner a contract for $2 million per year when he turns eighteen. In total, thirteen Northern Dancer yearlings were sold at the 1983 Keeneland and Saratoga sales for a total of $26,110,000, or $2,008,462 each. All told, his offspring have sold at auction for over $87 million. Not bad for a twenty-two-year-old horse who as a colt drew no interest when offered for sale for $25,000. He still services about thirty-five mares each year.

The breeding of top thoroughbreds has become a giant pyramid, with prices dependent on how much the offspring might be sold for after a brief racing career, rather than on a horse's real earnings potential. Despite the current recession and lower track attendance and despite modest prices for medium- and lower-quality thoroughbreds, the best are flying high for now at least.*

Derby Day brought good weather, although there was a threat of showers late in the day that might have affected the Derby. We situated ourselves near the paddock area behind the grandstands, where we could watch the tote board and make bets near post time. There was no trouble making bets within one minute of post time. And we knew that with the size of the pools, the conditions were good for application of the Dr. Z system.

Racing Form — **Experts' Selections**

Consensus Points: 5 for 1st (today's best 7), 2 for 2nd, 1 for 3rd. Today's Best in Bold Type.

Trackman, Graham Ross — **CHURCHILL DOWNS** — Selections Made for Fast Track

	TRACKMAN	HANDICAP	ANALYST	HERMIS	SWEEP	CONSENSUS	
1	ERUDITE ROAD STREET URCHIN HIS KNOCKERS	HUSTLIN BARB ERUDITE ROAD BEAUTIFUL BAY	BEAUTIFUL BAY HUSTLIN BARB LUMINARIA G.	**HUSTLIN BARB** LUMINARIA G. BEAU VOU	HUSTLIN BARB BEAU VOU BEAUTIFUL BAY	HUSTLIN BARB ERUDITE ROAD BEAUTIFUL BAY	19 7 7
2	FOXFIRE COVE ATENSHEIS IRON SKILLET	MY DAY DREAM IRON SKILLET APPLE JENNIE	RAJ UT TULLE'S FOOLY IRON SKILLET	BAIL ME OUT TULLE'S FOOLY RAJ UT	TULLE'S FOOLY IRON SKILLET RARE PICTURE	TULLE'S FOOLY RAJ UT IRON SKILLET	9 6 6
3	**BIRDBRAIN** SAME SEA TRADERS JET	GREAT BALANCE BIRDBRAIN LOOKS LIKE DAD	LOOKS LIKE DAD GREAT BALANCE DOLFINAIR	DOLFINAIR GREAT BALANCE LOOKS LIKE DAD	**GREAT BALANCE** LOOKS LIKE DAD DOLFINAIR	GREAT BALANCE BIRDBRAIN LOOKS LIKE DAD	16 9 9
4	FLAG ADMIRAL SLASH AND CUT CLUB SHOOTER	FLAG ADMIRAL GRINDSTONE TURN CLEVER ENCOUNTER	FLAG ADMIRAL SOUTHERN BOY CLEVER ENCOUNTER	SOUTHERN BOY FLAG ADMIRAL GRINDSTONE TURN	FLAG ADMIRAL SOUTHERN BOY GRINDSTONE TURN	FLAG ADMIRAL SOUTHERN BOY GRINDSTONE TURN	22 9 4
5	HEAD GAMES FOLLOW DUSTY JACK SLADE	FIGHTIN HILL HEAD GAMES STRAIGHT SHOT	HEAD GAMES CHIDESTER GREAT POSSIBILITY	CHIDESTER JACK SLADE HEAD GAMES	HEAD GAMES CHIDESTER JACK SLADE	HEAD GAMES CHIDESTER FIGHTIN HILL	18 9 5
6	CAN'THOLDMEBACK LIBERTY LANE OIL CITY	BACKSTABBER LIBERTY LANE OIL CITY	**LIBERTY LANE** BAYOU BLACK CELTIC SABER	BAYOU BLACK LIBERTY LANE CELTIC SABER	LIBERTY LANE BAYOU BLACK CELTIC SABER	LIBERTY LANE BAYOU BLACK BACKSTABBER	18 9 5
7	LE COU COU HIGH HONORS SAVERTON	HIGH HONORS LE COU COU THALASSOCRAT	HIGH HONORS CUCKOLD LE COU COU	CUCKOLD HIGH HONORS COMMON SENSE	CUCKOLD HIGH HONORS COMMON SENSE	HIGH HONORS CUCKOLD LE COU COU	16 12 8
8	SUNNY'S HALO SLEW O' GOLD HIGHLAND PARK	**SUNNY'S HALO** MARFA PLAY FELLOW	SUNNY'S HALO MARFA PAX IN BELLO	MARFA SUNNY'S HALO CAVEAT	SUNNY'S HALO MARFA CAVEAT	**SUNNY'S HALO** MARFA SLEW O' GOLD	24 11 2
9	MAJOR RUN BROADWAY REVIEW DUST OFF THE MAT	BROADWAY REVIEW BAL BAY DAVRICK	SORROTO SWAY BAL BAY	SWAY MAJOR RUN SORROTO	SWAY SORROTO MAJOR RUN	SWAY SORROTO MAJOR RUN	12 8 8
10	OLD HUNDRED MATTI BABES TOM LIGHTFOOT	MATTI BABES CAPTAIN PHIL TO THE PENNY	TO THE PENNY CAPTAIN PHIL HARD UP	CAPTAIN PHIL TO THE PENNY TOM LIGHTFOOT	CAPTAIN PHIL TO THE PENNY TOM LIGHTFOOT	CAPTAIN PHIL TO THE PENNY MATTI BABES	14 10 7

A Mexican Filly Is the First Dr. Z System Bet

The first Dr. Z system bet occurred in the first race, a $6\frac{1}{2}$-furlong race for four-year-old and older fillies and mares. The morning-line favorites were Hustlin Barb, Luminaria G., and Beautiful Bay. None of the horses had outstanding records, but each had shown flashes of brilliance. Hustlin Barb was

*Readers who would like to learn more about the breeding industry and keep up with the latest events in racing might consult the BLOOD-HORSE. It is a beautifully produced weekly magazine that is also a very useful source of information (Box 4038, Lexington, Kentucky 40544, $2 per issue).

dropping sharply in class to the $7,500 claiming level, which installed her as the favorite despite a poor 1983 season with only one in-the-money finish in five starts. Beautiful Bay did not show much except for a win and a second in February against weaker competition. Luminaria G. was a Mexican horse who was claimed in her first race in the United States. She was moving back to the $7,500 claiming level, where she had won convincingly, after a disappointing fourth-place finish as the favorite in her last start. The crowd made Luminaria G. the favorite.

FIRST HALF DAILY DOUBLE

6½ FURLONGS

WIN PLACE SHOW

1

CLAIMING

PURSE $5,500

FILLIES AND MARES FOUR YEARS OLD AND UPWARD, 121 lbs. Non-winners of two races since March 15 allowed 3 lbs.; two races since February 11, 6 lbs.; a race since April 8, 9 lbs. Claiming Price, $7,500. (Races where entered for $6,000 or less not considered.)

Track Record—DOGOON (5) 121 lbs.; 1:16; Nov. 5, 1957

MAKE SELECTION BY NUMBER

No.	Owner / Trainer	Horse	Weight	Jockey	Morn. Line
1	LOYD FORD / RICK HILES; Yellow, Black "F," Black Bars on Sleeves, Black Cap	BEAUTIFUL BAY; B.m.(1977), Barbizon Streak—Rip N Roll	*107	KEITH ALLEN	5
2	Sundance Stable (Dianne Carpenter) / Dianne Carpenter; Orange, Gold Rising Sun, Gold Yoke, Gold Band on Sleeves, Gold Cap	ERUDITE ROAD; Ch.f.(1979), Barbs Delight—Cedar Road	112	LEROY MOYERS	15
3	CARL C. DYKEMA / W. E. ADAMS; Black and White Blocks, Red Windmill, Black Cap	QUASARITA; B.f.(1979), Tara Road—Sea Leopard	112	MICHAEL MORAN	8
4	THOMAS L. LANG / DONALD E. HUGHES; Blue, White "TL," White Sleeves, Blue Cap	BEAU VOU; B.m.(1977), I Want You—His Babu Lark	112	PATRICK JOHNSON	6
5	BILLY G. ASHABRANER / OWNER; Orange, White "A," White Sleeves, Orange Cap	LUMINARIA G. (Mex); Ch.f.(1979), Going Around—Permisa	112	GENE SOLOMON	7-2
6	BIG TEN STABLE (Earl C. Shackleford) / JAMES BEMISS; Blue, Yellow "X," Yellow Bars on Sleeves, Blue Cap	STREET URCHIN; Ch.m.(1977), Bold Street—Plucky Pixie	112	CHARLES WOODS, JR.	15
7	FARID SEFA / LARRY D. EDWARDS; Red, Yellow "S", Red Cap	HUSTLIN BARB; B.f.(1979), Hustlin Greek—Delightful Barb	*107	WILLIAM TROILO	2
8	RAMON COTO & NORMAN E. CASSE / MARK CASSE; Black, Red Cardinal, Red Bars on Sleeves, Red Cap	IRISH BREEZE (Fr); B.m.(1977), Sea Break—In Spe	112	JIM McKNIGHT	8
9	SARA NIEMANN / CHARLES W. STONE; Blue and White Halves, Blue and White Stripes on Sleeves, Blue Cap	HIS KNOCKERS; Ch.f.(1979), His B.—Nancy Knox	112	MARK SELLERS	12

Selections 7—5—1—4

Luminaria G. looked like a possible Dr. Z system bet to show. The tote board was as follows:

	Totals	#5 Luminaria G.	Expected Value per Dollar Bet on Luminaria G.
With four minutes to post time			
Odds		8—5	
Win	105,272	31,967	
Show	50,087	9,852	1.17

	Totals	#5 Luminaria G.	Expected Value per Dollar Bet on Luminaria G.
With two minutes to post time			
Odds		8—5	
Win	119,144	37,003	
Show	53,218	10,699	1.17
With one minute to post time			
Odds		8—5	
Win	130,255	41,577	
Show	57,643	12,210	1.16

With our betting fortune of $1,000 we bet $159 to show on Luminaria G. At post time the tote board stood as follows:

	Totals	#5 Luminaria G.	Expected Value per Dollar Bet on Luminaria G.
Odds		7—5	
Win	147,291	50,374	
Show	62,113	13,728	1.17

Luminaria G. won the race, followed by Beautiful Bay and Beau Vou. Hustlin Barb finished out of the money. The chart of the race was as follows:

FIRST RACE
Churchill
MAY 7, 1983

6 ½ FURLONGS. (1.16) CLAIMING. Purse $5,500. Fillies and mares. 4-year-olds and upward. Weight, 121 lbs. Non-winners of two races since March 15 allowed 3 lbs.; two races since February 11, 6 lbs.; a race since April 8, 9 lbs. Claiming price, $7,500. (Races where entered for $6,000 or less not considered.) 7TH DAY. WEATHER CLEAR. TEMPERATURE 77 DEGREES.

Value of race $5,500, value to winner $3,575, second $1,100, third $550, fourth $275. Mutuel pool $279,336.

Last Raced	Horse	Eqt.A.Wt	PP	St	¼	½	Str	Fin	Jockey	Cl'g Pr	Odds $1
30Mar83 ^{9}Lat^{4}	Luminaria G.	4 114	5	5	$1^{1\frac{1}{2}}$	1^{2}	$1^{3\frac{1}{2}}$	$1^{6\frac{1}{2}}$	Solomon G	7500	1.40
5Apr83 ^{4}OP^{4}	Beautiful Bay	6 107	1	4	$3^{\frac{1}{2}}$	3^{1}	$2^{1\frac{1}{2}}$	2^{nk}	Allen K K^{5}	7500	4.40
20Apr83 ^{1}Kee^{3}	Beau Vou	b 6 112	4	7	7^{2}	$6^{1\frac{1}{2}}$	3^{3}	3^{2}	Johnson P A	7500	8.20
9Dec82 ^{8}Lat^{4}	His Knockers	4 112	8	1	2^{1}	$2^{1\frac{1}{2}}$	$4^{\frac{1}{2}}$	4^{1}	Sellers M S	7500	16.20
28Apr83 ^{1}Kee^{8}	Street Urchin	b 6 112	6	3	$5^{\frac{1}{2}}$	5^{1}	5^{2}	$5^{2\frac{1}{2}}$	Woods C R Jr	7500	27.80
30Mar83 ^{5}OP^{6}	Hustlin Barb	b 4 107	7	2	6^{1}	$4^{\frac{1}{2}}$	6^{3}	6^{5}	Troilo W D^{5}	7500	2.40
20Apr83 ^{1}Kee^{4}	Quasarita	4 115	3	8	8	8	7^{2}	$7^{6\frac{1}{2}}$	Moran M T	7500	22.20
28Apr83 ^{1}Kee^{7}	Erudite Road	b 4 112	2	6	4^{1}	7^{2}	8	8	Moyers L	7500	14.10

OFF AT 11:33. Start good. Won driving. Time, :23⅕, :46⅘, 1:11⅘, 1:18⅕ Track fast.

Official Program Numbers

$2 Mutuel Prices:			
5-LUMINARIA G.	4.80	3.40	2.80
1-BEAUTIFUL BAY		4.60	3.20
4-BEAU VOU			3.60

Ch. f, by Going Around—Permisa, by Bal Musette. Trainer Ashabraner Billy G. Bred by Mora D Cardenas (Mex).

LUMINAIRIA G., hustled to the lead just after the start, made all the pace but was kept to pressure when drawing off in the lane. BEAUTIFUL BAY, well placed early, could not stay with the winner but continued willingly to gain the place. BEAU VOU made a mild bid to clearly best the others. HIS KNOCKERS prompted the early pace and gave way. HUSTLIN BARB never menaced.

Owners— 1, Ashabraner B G; 2, Ford L; 3, Lang T L; 4, Niemann Sara; 5, Big Ten Stable; 6, Sefa F; 7, Dykema C C; 8, Sundance Stable.

Overweight: Luminaria G. 2 pounds; Quasarita 3.

Luminaria G. was claimed by Sutton H E; trainer, Fires William H.

Scratched—Irish Breeze (22Apr83 ^{2}Kee^{8}).

Luminaria G.'s $2.80 payoff gave us a profit of $63.60 on our $159 bet.

Chris McCarron Steals the Race

The third race was a claiming race for four-year-old horses and older horses who had not won two recent races. Nine horses were competing in the 6-furlong race. The consensus favorite was Great Balance. Dolfinar, Superstep, Traders Jet, Steel Britches, Birdbrain, and Looks Like Dad were the competition. Dolfinar and Traders Jet had strong records with numerous wins. Traders Jet was also lightweighted at 112 pounds and was ridden by the great Chris McCarron, who had flown in from California to ride Desert Wine in the Derby. As usual, Chris was in a head-to-head competition with Laffit Pincay, Jr. as the nation's top-money-winning jockey. Table 12.1 shows the earnings of the top jockeys and trainers in 1983. Going into Derby Day, Pincay and McCarron had a considerable edge both in earnings and place percentage over their California colleague Eddie Delahoussaye and two New York–based jockeys, Angel Cordero, Jr. and Jorge Velasquez. The colorful Californian Laz Barrera was comfortably in first place among the trainers. Traders Jet's recent races showed little, and he was dropping sharply in

TABLE 12.1 *The 1983 money-leading jockeys and trainers going into Derby Day*

	Money Leaders				
Jockey	Mounts	Winners	Seconds	Place Percentage	Purses Won ($)
Pincay	474	112	81	40.7	2,847,202
C. McCarron	508	124	82	40.6	2,838,763
Delahoussaye	455	61	80	31.0	2,220,685
Cordero	426	86	65	35.4	1,977,782
Velasquez	373	73	46	31.9	1,930,844
Day	483	96	85	37.5	1,700,726
Davis	516	88	62	29.1	1,440,435
Alvarado	498	66	75	28.3	1,423,979
Valenzuela	428	53	55	25.2	1,333,447
Hawley	372	51	44	25.5	1,301,919
Trainers	Starts	Winners	Seconds	Place Percentage	Purses Won ($)
Barrera	109	39	17	51.3	1,431,305
Lukas	167	21	21	25.2	1,209,207
Van Berg	505	55	56	22.0	1,163,514
Whittingham	127	29	12	32.3	1,149,980
Gosden	97	20	12	33.0	887,660
Palma	191	29	31	31.4	670,370

class. Great Balance had the best lifetime earnings and an impressive $2,000+ winnings per start. Twice he had been claimed while winning at claiming prices in the $18,000–$20,000 range. After little success running against $25,000 claimers, he was returning to run against these cheaper horses again.

START
6 FURLONGS
FINISH

WIN	PLACE	SHOW

CLAIMING
PURSE $7,500

3

FOUR-YEAR-OLDS AND UPWARD, 122 lbs. Non-winners of two races since March 7 allowed 2 lbs.; a race since then, 4 lbs.; two races since January 7, 6 lbs. Claiming Price $18,000; for each $500 to $16,000, 1 lb. (Races where entered for $14,000 or less not considered.)

Track Record—BENEDICTO (6) 117 lbs.; 1:09⅘; May 13, 1961
AMBER BREAK (6) 116 lbs.; 1:09⅘; Nov. 25, 1970
BARBIZON STREAK (3) 122 lbs.; 1:09⅘, May 22, 1971

MAKE SELECTION BY NUMBER

No.	Owner / Trainer	Jockey / Morn. Line
1	WENDELL KETCHUM — FORREST KAELIN Red, Black Stripes on Yellow Sleeves Red Cap **DOLFINAR** 120 B.g.(1974), Lucky Debonair—Dolphin's Girl	4 TOMMY BARROW $18,000
2	MICHAEL REAVIS, et al — MICHAEL REAVIS Red, White "MR" Red Cap **SUPERSTEP** 116 B.g.(1978), Walker's—Tatty II	8 JUVENIAL L. DIAZ $18,000.
3	J. C. KIRK — OWNER Blue, Gold Blocks Blue Cap **TRADERS JET** 112 B.g.(1979), Trader Ed—Daisey Jet	6 CHRIS McCARRON $16,000.
4	ALDO MARROCCO — WILLIAM I. MOTT Green, White and Red Thirds, Black "M," White Sleeves Red Cap **GREAT BALANCE** 120 B.g.(1977), Jeff D.—Bette's Gold	5-2 LEROY MOYERS $18,000.
5	ERIC BACHELOR — WILLIAM G. MITCHELL Green, Black "B," Black Stars, Black Bars on Sleeves Green and Black Cap **STEEL BRITCHES** 116 B.g.(1979), High Steel—Pokey Britches	6 MARK SELLERS $18,000.
6	MJAKA STABLE — C. R. McGAUGHEY III (Jane Meyer and Elizabeth Lavin) Black, White Diamond Belt, Red Sleeves, Red Cap **BIRDBRAIN** *111 B.g.(1979), Accipter—Matriculation	8 KEITH ALLEN $18,000.
7	RONALD & SUE STINSON AND JAMES ADAIR — EDWIN H. DAVIS, JR. Red, White Yoke, White Bars on Black Sleeves, Red Cap **PORTUGUESE PICNIC** 116 Dk.b. or br.h.(1977), The Pruner—Successfully Yours	15 CHARLES WOODS, JR. $18,000.
8	JAMES C. CRAIG — JAMES R. TULLY Purple, Orange "JCC," Orange Bars on Purple Sleeves Purple Cap **LOOKS LIKE DAD** 116 Ch.g.(1979), Dare to Command—Coras Pride	7-2 DON BRUMFIELD $18,000
9	FRANCIS LINK — JERRY BURKHART Green, White Circled "L," White Dots Green Cap **SAME SEA** 116 Gr.g.(1979), North Sea—La Meme Chose	20 DARRELL FOSTER $18,000.

Selections 4—8—1—3

The tote board pointed to Great Balance as a possible Dr. Z system bet to show.

	Totals	#4 Great Balance	Expected Value per Dollar Bet on Great Balance
With one minute to post time			
Odds		5—2	
Win	292,291	63,973	
Show	135,425	19,178	1.18

Our betting fortune of $1,063.60 suggested a bet of $78. At post time the tote board stood as follows:

	Totals	#4 Great Balance	Expected Value per Dollar Bet on Great Balance
Odds		5—2	
Win	314,811	68,376	
Show	141,625	22,799	1.11

Chris McCarron stole the race and led Traders Jet for a victory and an $18.80 win payoff. Great Balance held on for second, and Superstep took third. With Dolfinar and Looks Like Dad out of the money and Traders Jet and Superstep relative long shots, the show payoff on Great Balance was a smashing $4. Our $78 bet was doubled. The chart of the race was as follows:

THIRD RACE
Churchill
MAY 7, 1983

6 FURLONGS. (1.09⅗) CLAIMING. Purse $7,500. 4–year–olds and upward. Weight, 122 lbs. Non–winners of two races since March 7 allowed 2 lbs.; a race since then, 4 lbs.; two races since January 7, 6 lbs. Claiming price, $18,000; for each $500 to $16,000 allowed 1 lb.(Races where entered for $14,000 or less not considered.)

Value of race $7,500, value to winner $4,875, second $1,500, third $750, fourth $375. Mutuel pool $621,311.

Last Raced	Horse	Eqt.	A.Wt	PP	St	¼	½	Str	Fin	Jockey	Cl'g Pr	Odds $1
11Mar83 ^{10}FG^{9}	Traders Jet		4 112	3	1	1^{hd}	2^{hd}	1½	1no	McCarron C J†	16000	8.40
15Apr83 ^{4}OP^{5}	Great Balance	b	6 120	4	4	4^{hd}	3^{hd}	2^{1½}	2^{4}	Moyers L	18000	2.80
16Apr83 ^{10}FP^{4}	Superstep	b	5 116	2	3	3^{1½}	5^{hd}	3^{2}	3^{2½}	Diaz J L	18000	10.20
16Mar83 ^{8}OP^{7}	Portuguese Picnic		6 116	7	5	8^{1½}	6^{1½}	5^{hd}	4^{1½}	Woods C R Jr	18000	41.50
8Apr83 ^{8}OP^{5}	Looks Like Dad	b	4 116	8	7	5^{1½}	4^{hd}	4^{1½}	5^{nk}	Brumfield D	18000	2.60
4Mar83 ^{10}OP^{11}	Birdbrain		4 111	6	6	7^{3}	8^{2}	6^{1½}	6^{4}	Allen K K^{5}	18000	7.80
9Apr83 ^{5}OP^{1}	Dolfinair		9 116	1	9	9	9	7^{2}	7^{3}	Barrow T	18000	4.80
20Apr83 ^{5}Kee^{9}	Steel Britches		4 116	5	2	2^{hd}	1½	8^{2}	8^{nk}	Sellers M S	18000	6.70
17Dec82 ^{7}FG^{11}	Same Sea	b	4 116	9	8	6½	7^{1½}	9	9	Foster D E	18000	32.80

OFF AT 1:01. Start good. Won driving. Time, :22, :45, :57⅗, 1:10⅗ Track fast.

$2 Mutuel Prices:			
3-TRADERS JET	18.80	7.60	5.40
4-GREAT BALANCE		4.80	4.00
2-SUPERSTEP			6.20

B. g, by Trader Ed—Daisy Jet, by Bronze Jet. Trainer Kirk James C. Bred by Mills P D (Pa).

TRADERS JET broke in stride to make or force the pace throughout and narrowly outgamed GREAT BALANCE in the final furlong. The latter was always well placed, challenged the winner throughout the lane, could not catch that one but was easily second best. SUPERSTEP vied for the lead most of the way but had no late rally. PORTUGESE PICNIC had no speed. LOOKS LIKE DAD was shuffled back shortly after the start, recovered to launch a bid entering the lane but could not sustain it. STEEL BRITCHES dueled for the early lead and stopped.

Owners— 1, Kirk J C; 2, Marrocco A; 3, Reavis M L et al; 4, Stinson R W el al; 5, Craig J C; 6, Mjaka Stable; 7, Ketchum W; 8, Bachelor E; 9, Link F.

† **Apprentice allowance waived:** Traders Jet 7 pounds. **Corrected weight:** Great Balance 120 pounds.

Great Balance was claimed by Hyman Carol; trainer, Kirk James C.

Two Dr. Z System Bets in the Bold Forbes

The fourth race was a 1-mile allowance race for three-year-olds. The favorites were Southern Boy and Flag Admiral, and they were to be ridden by California's two top jockeys, Chris McCarron and Laffit Pincay, Jr. Like McCarron, Pincay had flown in for the Derby and was to ride Caveat. Southern Boy had just run in the Arkansas Derby and was completely outclassed by the likes of Sunny's Halo and Caveat. He had had some good races early in the year, but his recent record was mediocre. Flag Admiral was coming off a convincing win in the mud at Keeneland. His previous three starts were disasters. Despite their undistinguished records, Southern Boy and Flag Admiral did seem to outclass the rest of the field. They had proved themselves much faster, at least whenever they ran a strong race. Fellow Californian jockeys Terry Lipham and Eddie Delahoussaye were riding Bill Hicks and Clever Encounter, respectively, to warm up for their mounts on Paris Prince and Sunny's Halo, respectively, in the Derby. Both Bill Hicks and Clever Encounter had had good recent races, but they appeared to be outclassed by the favorites.

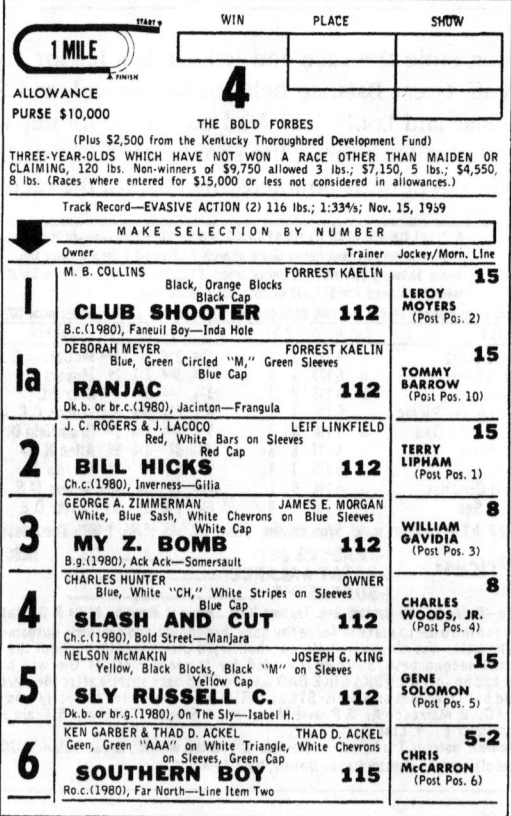

START
1 MILE
FINISH

WIN PLACE SHOW

ALLOWANCE
PURSE $10,000

4

THE BOLD FORBES

(Plus $2,500 from the Kentucky Thoroughbred Development Fund)

THREE-YEAR-OLDS WHICH HAVE NOT WON A RACE OTHER THAN MAIDEN OR CLAIMING, 120 lbs. Non-winners of $9,750 allowed 3 lbs.; $7,150, 5 lbs.; $4,550, 8 lbs. (Races where entered for $15,000 or less not considered in allowances.)

Track Record—EVASIVE ACTION (2) 116 lbs.; 1:33⅘; Nov. 15, 1959

MAKE SELECTION BY NUMBER

	Owner / Trainer	Jockey/Morn. Line
1	M. B. COLLINS — FORREST KAELIN Black, Orange Blocks Black Cap **CLUB SHOOTER** 112 B.c.(1980), Faneuil Boy—Inda Hole	15 LEROY MOYERS (Post Pos. 2)
1a	DEBORAH MEYER — FORREST KAELIN Blue, Green Circled "M," Green Sleeves Blue Cap **RANJAC** 112 Dk.b. or br.c.(1980), Jacinton—Frangula	15 TOMMY BARROW (Post Pos. 10)
2	J. C. ROGERS & J. LACOCO — LEIF LINKFIELD Red, White Bars on Sleeves Red Cap **BILL HICKS** 112 Ch.c.(1980), Inverness—Gilia	15 TERRY LIPHAM (Post Pos. 1)
3	GEORGE A. ZIMMERMAN — JAMES E. MORGAN White, Blue Sash, White Chevrons on Blue Sleeves White Cap **MY Z. BOMB** 112 B.g.(1980), Ack Ack—Somersault	8 WILLIAM GAVIDIA (Post Pos. 3)
4	CHARLES HUNTER — OWNER Blue, White "CH," White Stripes on Sleeves Blue Cap **SLASH AND CUT** 112 Ch.c.(1980), Bold Street—Manjara	8 CHARLES WOODS, JR. (Post Pos. 4)
5	NELSON McMAKIN — JOSEPH G. KING Yellow, Black Blocks, Black "M" on Sleeves Yellow Cap **SLY RUSSELL C.** 112 Dk.b. or br.g.(1980), On The Sly—Isabel H.	15 GENE SOLOMON (Post Pos. 5)
6	KEN GARBER & THAD D. ACKEL — THAD D. ACKEL Geen, Green "AAA" on White Triangle, White Chevrons on Sleeves, Green Cap **SOUTHERN BOY** 115 Ro.c.(1980), Far North—Line Item Two	5-2 CHRIS McCARRON (Post Pos. 6)

7	TOM GENTRY — EDUARDO INDA Yellow, Royal Blue Blocks, Royal Blue Bars on Sleeves Yellow Cap **FLAG ADMIRAL 117** B.c.(1980), Hoist the Flag—Lord's Lady	**7-2** LAFFIT PINCAY, JR. (Post Pos. 7)
8	MR. & MRS. JOSEPH C. WOLFMAN — ANGEL MONTANO Red, Silver Sleeves Red Cap **GRINDSTONE TURN 112** Gr.c.(1980), Turn To Reason—Rose Rondeau	**6** LARRY MELANCON (Post Pos. 8)
9	FRANK JONES, JR. — JERRY ROMANS Orange, Brown "FJ," Brown Dots Orange Cap **GASTGEBER 112** B.g.(1980), Within Hail—Votre Hotesse	**15** BRENT BARTRAM (Post Pos. 9)
10	IZZIE PROLER — BILLY S. BORDERS Blue, Green Triangle, Blue Band on Green Sleeves Blue Cap **CLEVER ENCOUNTER 112** B.c.(1980), Clev Er Tell—Boston Pocket	**5** EDDIE DELAHOUSSAYE (Post Pos. 11)

1 and 1a—M. B. COLLINS—DEBORAH MEYER Entry

Selections 6—7–10—8

Both Southern Boy and Flag Admiral were favorites of the betting public and relatively overlooked to show. The tote board read as follows:

	Totals	#6 Southern Boy	Expected Value per Dollar Bet on Southern Boy	#7 Flag Admiral	Expected Value per Dollar Bet on Flag Admiral
With four minutes to post time					
Odds		6—5		2—1	
Win	312,797	116,195		87,134	
Show	150,399	36,980	1.16	26,753	1.18
With one minute to post time					
Odds		6—5		9—5	
Win	358,410	134,508		100,908	
Show	167,613	42,721	1.14	30,011	1.19

We bet $300 on Southern Boy to show and $200 on Flag Admiral to show. At post time the tote board was as follows:

	Totals	#6 Southern Boy	Expected Value per Dollar Bet on Southern Boy	#7 Flag Admiral	Expected Value per Dollar Bet on Flag Admiral
Odds		1—1		9—5	
Win	403,104	155,710		113,712	
Show	180,904	48,779	1.13	32,047	1.19

Flag Admiral won the race, followed by Clever Encounter, and Southern Boy took third. With the two top choices finishing in the money, the show payoffs were slightly depressed, but not as much as usual, since they both were Dr. Z system bets. Flag Admiral paid $2.80 and Southern Boy $2.40. Our bets of $300 and $200 on Southern Boy and Flag Admiral, respectively, paid $360 and $280 for a profit of $140. The chart of the race was as follows:

FOURTH RACE
Churchill
MAY 7, 1983

1 MILE. (1.33⅘) ALLOWANCE. Purse $10,000 (plus $2,500 from KTDF). 3–year–olds, which have not won a race other than maiden or claiming. Weight, 120 lbs. Non–winners of $9,750 allowed 3 lbs.; $7,150, 5 lbs.; $4,550. (Races where entered for $15,000 or less not considered in allowances.)

Total purse $12,500. Value of race $12,375, value to winner $8,125, second $2,500, third $1,250, fourth $500. ($125 reverts to the KTDF). Mutuel pool $790,782.

Last Raced	Horse	Eqt.A.Wt	PP	St	¼	½	¾	Str	Fin	Jockey	Odds $1
23Apr83 ^{4}Kee^{1}	Flag Admiral	3 117	7	5	$6^{1\frac{1}{2}}$	$2^{1\frac{1}{2}}$	$1^{1\frac{1}{2}}$	1^{3}	$1^{7\frac{1}{2}}$	Velasquez J	1.90
16Apr83 ^{8}Kee^{3}	Clever Encounter	3 115	11	1	$10^{1\frac{1}{2}}$	11	8^{3}	3^{5}	2^{2}	Delahoussaye E	5.00
16Apr83 ^{9}OP^{9}	Southern Boy	3 115	6	7	3^{hd}	$5^{1\frac{1}{2}}$	$2^{1\frac{1}{2}}$	2^{2}	3^{7}	McCarron C J	1.10
22Apr83 ^{6}Kee^{3}	Grindstone Turn	b 3 112	8	3	5^{1}	$6^{1\frac{1}{2}}$	$4^{\frac{1}{2}}$	4^{1}	$4^{\frac{3}{4}}$	Melancon L	23.50
30Apr83 ^{4}Det^{2}	Gastgeber	b 3 112	9	4	$7^{\frac{1}{2}}$	7^{hd}	6^{1}	$5^{\frac{1}{2}}$	5^{4}	Bartram B	49.90
28Apr83 ^{8}Kee^{4}	My Z. Bomb	b 3 114	3	9	$2^{1\frac{1}{2}}$	3^{hd}	$3^{1\frac{1}{2}}$	$7^{1\frac{1}{2}}$	$6^{\frac{1}{2}}$	Gavidia W	27.10
2May83 ^{2}CD^{8}	Club Shooter	3 112	2	10	8^{hd}	$9^{\frac{1}{2}}$	10^{2}	9^{4}	$7^{\frac{3}{4}}$	Moyers L	a-30.10
30Apr83 ^{3}RD^{1}	Bill Hicks	3 112	1	6	$1^{1\frac{1}{2}}$	1^{1}	$5^{1\frac{1}{2}}$	$6^{1\frac{1}{2}}$	8^{2}	McKnight J	50.60
15Apr83 ^{2}Kee^{8}	Sly Russell C.	b 3 114	5	11	$9^{1\frac{1}{2}}$	$8^{1\frac{1}{2}}$	7^{hd}	8^{hd}	9^{7}	Solomon G	45.40
30Apr83 ^{6}CD^{4}	Slash And Cut	b 3 112	4	8	4^{hd}	$4^{\frac{1}{2}}$	9^{hd}	10^{2}	10^{3}	Woods C R Jr	15.80
24Mar83 ^{6}OP^{9}	Ranjac	b 3 115	10	2	11	10^{3}	11	11	11	Barrow T	a-30.10

a–Coupled: Club Shooter and Ranjac.

OFF AT 1:51. Start good. Won ridden out. Time, :22⅘, :46, 1:10⅗, 1:35⅗ Track fast.

$2 Mutuel Prices:

7–FLAG ADMIRAL	5.80	3.60	2.80
10–CLEVER ENCOUNTER		4.40	2.80
6–SOUTHERN BOY			2.40

B. c, by Hoist The Flag—Lord's Lady, by Sir Gaylord. Trainer Inda Eduardo. Bred by Gentry T (Ky).

FLAG ADMIRAL, just behind the early leaders, came up to challenge leaving the backstretch, took clear command approaching the lane and increased the margin steadily while ridden out to the wire. CLEVER ENCOUNTER, void of early foot, commenced a rally approaching the lane, continued willingly when set down for the drive and was up to gain the place. SOUTHERN BOY, well placed early, had no rally. GRINDSTONE TURN lacked the needed response. MY Z. BOMB prompted the early pace and gave way. BILL HICKS made the early pace and stopped. SLASH AND CUT had speed for a half.

Owners— 1, Gentry T; 2, Proler I; 3, Ackel & Garber; 4, Wolfman Mr-Mrs J C; 5, Jones F Jr; 6, Zimmerman G A; 7, Collins M B; 8, Lacoco & Rogers; 9, McMakin N; 10, Hunter C; 11, Meyer Deborah.

Overweight: Clever Encounter 3 pounds; My Z. Bomb 2; Sly Russell C. 2; Ranjac 3.

Just Call Me George

The fifth race was the Pleasant Colony, an allowance race for three-year-olds. Head Games, Chidester, and Fightin Hill were the top choices. Jorge Velasquez, the great Panamanian jockey (who likes to be called "George" rather than "Horgay"), Eddie Maple, Jean Cruguet, and Don Brumfield were using the race as a warmup before their Derby mounts on Marfa, Chumming, Play Fellow, and Highland Park, respectively. The top three choices along with Great Possibility, Straight Shot, and Jack Slade all looked like possible winners. The odds on Head Games were the best. He had also finished first or second in five of his six career starts (see page 233).

With one minute to post time, the tote board was as follows:

	Totals	#1 Head Games	Expected Value per Dollar Bet on Head Games
Odds		2—1	
Win	415,685	103,216	
Show	182,613	32,715	1.12

1 1/16 MILES

START — FINISH

ALLOWANCE

PURSE $12,000

WIN	PLACE	SHOW

5

THE PLEASANT COLONY

(Plus $3,000 from the Kentucky Thoroughbred Development Fund)

THREE-YEAR-OLDS WHICH HAVE NOT WON TWO RACES OTHER THAN MAIDEN OR CLAIMING, 121 lbs. Non-winners of $9,750 twice allowed 3 lbs.; $7,800 twice, 6 lbs.; $5,850 twice, 9 lbs. (Races where entered for $20,000 or less not considered in allowances.

Track Record—YES SIR (5) 110 lbs.; 1:41⅗; Nov. 25, 1970

MAKE SELECTION BY NUMBER

No.	Owner / Trainer / Colors / Horse / Weight / Breeding	Jockey/Morn. Line
1	PATRICIA BLASS — WILLIAM H. FIRES Pink, Green Dots Pink and Green Cap **HEAD GAMES** 118 B.c.(1980), Clev er Tell—Princess Connie	3 JORGE VELASQUEZ
2	DAN LASATER — LARRY D. EDWARDS Red, White Yoke, White "L," Red Bars on White Sleeves Red Cap **FIGHTIN HILL** 112 Dk.b. or br.c.(1980), Nodouble—Hat Brim	6 EDDIE MAPLE
3	ROBERT N. LEHMANN — W. E. ADAMS Blue, White Horseshoe, White Sash, Red Sleeves Blue Cap **FOLLOW DUSTY** 112 Ch.c.(1980), Bob's Dusty—Rigbie Charm	10 MICHAEL MORAN
4	THOMAS L. LANG — DONALD E. HUGHES Blue, White "TL," White Sleeves Blue Cap **TWIST THE GOODS** 112 B.g.(1980), Twist The Axe—Got The Goods	20 WILLIAM GAVIDIA
5	STRAPRO STABLE — BILLY S. BORDERS (Joseph Strauss, Sr. and Izzie Proler) Orange, White Star, Orange Stars on White Slvs., Orange Cap **GREAT POSSIBILITY** 112 B.c.(1980), Soy Numero Uno—Kateri	4 JULIO ESPINOZA
6	RICHARD GARTIN — JOHN D. EVANS III Purple, Pink Triangular Panel Purple Cap **STRAIGHT SHOT** 112 Dk.b. or br.c.(1980), Norcliffe—Princess Jamie	8 JEAN CRUGUET
7	JAMES C. CRAIG — JAMES G. ARNETT Purple, Orange "JCC," Orange Bars on Sleeves Purple Cap **CHIDESTER** 112 Ch.c.(1980), Graustark—Nalees Folly	5 GARTH PATTERSON
8	ANDREW ADAMS — DAVID C. KASSEN Gold, Black Cross Sashes, Black Stripes on Sleeves Gold Cap **JACK SLADE** 112 B.c.(1980), Big Spruce—Holding	5 DON BRUMFIELD
9	MARY M. ZIMMERMAN — GLENN WISMER Orange, Blue Lightning "Z" Orange Cap **FANCY FRIEND** 112 Dk.b. or br.c.(1980), Steve's Friend—Fancy Gloves	10 LEROY MOYERS

Selections 1—5—7—8

With our betting fortune of $1,281.60 a bet of $33 to show on Head Games was suggested. At post time the tote board was

	Totals	#1 Head Games	Expected Value per Dollar Bet on Head Games
Odds		2—1	
Win	447,119	112,623	
Show	195,902	39,257	1.07

Unfortunately, Head Games finished out of the money, so we lost our $33 bet, leaving our betting fortune as $1,248.60. The chart of the race was as follows:

FIFTH RACE
Churchill
MAY 7, 1983

1 $\frac{1}{16}$ MILES. (1.41$\frac{3}{5}$) ALLOWANCE. Purse $12,000 (plus $3,000 from KTDF). 3-year-olds, which have not won two races other than maiden or claiming. Weight, 121 lbs. Non-winners of $9,750 twice allowed 3 lbs.; $7,800 twice, 6 lbs.; $5,850 twice, 9 lbs. (Races where entered for $20,000 or less not considered in allowances.)
Total purse $15,000. Value of race $12,450, value to winner $7,800, second $2,400, third $1,500, fourth $750. ($2,550 reverts to the KTDF.) Mutuel pool $878,344.

Last Raced	Horse	Eqt.A.Wt	PP	St	¼	½	¾	Str	Fin	Jockey	Odds $1
6Apr83 ^{9}Hia^{2}	Straight Shot	3 112	6	2	$1^{\frac{1}{2}}$	$1^{\frac{1}{2}}$	$1^{\frac{1}{2}}$	1^{1}	1^{nk}	Cruguet J	6.60
30Apr83 ^{6}CD^{1}	Fightin Hill	b 3 114	2	7	7^{1}	$6^{2\frac{1}{2}}$	$3^{1\frac{1}{2}}$	$2^{\frac{1}{2}}$	2^{2}	Maple E	5.50
16Apr83 ^{8}OP^{3}	Chidester	3 112	7	3	$2^{1\frac{1}{2}}$	$2^{3\frac{1}{2}}$	2^{3}	3^{3}	$3^{2\frac{1}{2}}$	Patterson G	3.20
27Apr83 ^{8}Kee^{2}	Follow Dusty	b 3 115	3	5	$5^{2\frac{1}{2}}$	4^{hd}	4^{2}	4^{3}	4^{1}	Moran M T	18.10
16Apr83 ^{2}OP^{1}	Head Games	b 3 118	1	4	3^{2}	3^{2}	$5^{1\frac{1}{2}}$	$5^{2\frac{1}{2}}$	5^{4}	Velasquez J	2.30
27Apr83 ^{8}Kee^{5}	Fancy Friend	3 112	9	6	6^{1}	$8^{1\frac{1}{2}}$	7^{3}	6^{hd}	6^{nk}	Moyers L	30.50
28Apr83 ^{8}Kee^{1}	Jack Slade	3 114	8	8	$8^{1\frac{1}{2}}$	9	8^{4}	8^{8}	$7^{\frac{1}{2}}$	Brumfield D	5.00
27Apr83 ^{8}Kee^{6}	Twist The Goods	3 114	4	9	9	7^{2}	$6^{1\frac{1}{2}}$	$7^{1\frac{1}{2}}$	8^{11}	Gavidia W	59.60
22Apr83 ^{6}Kee^{1}	Great Possibility	3 112	5	1	4^{hd}	$5^{\frac{1}{2}}$	9	9	9	Espinoza J C	8.70

OFF AT 2:41. Start good. Won driving. Time, :24$\frac{4}{5}$, :48$\frac{1}{5}$, 1:12$\frac{1}{5}$, 1:37$\frac{4}{5}$, 1:44$\frac{1}{5}$ Track fast.

$2 Mutuel Prices:			
6-STRAIGHT SHOT	15.20	7.80	4.80
2-FIGHTIN HILL		7.00	5.00
7-CHIDESTER			3.80

Dk. b. or br. c, by Norcliffe—Princess Jamie, by Prince John. Trainer Evans John D III. Bred by Davis W R (Fla).

STRAIGHT SHOT, taken under a rating hold after quickly taking the lead, saved ground into the final turn, gradually came out to meet the challenge of FIGHTIN HILL and held that one safe. FIGHTIN HILL, in close and taken in hand leaving the gate, advanced between horses after a half-mile, loomed boldly on the outside in the stretch drive and was not quite good enough. CHIDESTER raced lapped outside the winner into the early stretch, was carried out just slightly and weakened. FOLLOW DUSTY saved ground to no avail. HEAD GAMES raced wide throughout. JACK SLADE was not a serious factor. GREAT POSSIBLITY raced wide.

Owners— 1, Gartin R; 2, Lasater D; 3, Craig J C; 4, Lehmann R N; 5, Blass Patricia; 6, Zimmerman Mary M; 7, Adams A; 8, Lang T L; 9, Strapro Stable.

Overweight: Fightin Hill 2 pounds; Follow Dusty 3; Jack Slade 2; Twist The Goods 2.

The Dreadnought

The sixth race was the Dreadnought, a 7-furlong allowance race with a purse of $14,000. The top choices were Bayou Black, Liberty Lane, the entry of Backstabber and Can'tholdmeback, and Oil City. Bayou Black looked very sharp, with five consecutive in-the-money finishes, all but one with speed ratings in the 90s. He also had the services of jockey Eddie Delahoussaye. Liberty Lane was also a very consistent horse with nearly as good a record. The bet was on Bayou Black.

7 FURLONGS

START / FINISH

ALLOWANCE

PURSE $14,000

WIN	PLACE	SHOW

6

THE DREADNOUGHT

(Plus $3,500 from the Kentucky Thoroughbred Development Fund)

FOUR-YEAR-OLDS AND UPWARD, WHICH HAVE NOT WON $4,875 TWICE SINCE JUNE 26 OTHER THAN MAIDEN, CLAIMING OR STARTER, 121 lbs. Non-winners of $10,400 since April 8 allowed 3 lbs.; $9,750 since January 7, 6 lbs.; $8,450 since October 8, 9 lbs. (Maiden, claiming and starter races not considered in in allowances.)

Track Record—OLDEN TIMES (6) 124 lbs.; 1:21⅖; April 30, 1964

MAKE SELECTION BY NUMBER

	Owner	Trainer	Jockey/Morn. Line
1	JAMES H. RUTTER White, Black "R" on Gold Crown, Black Bars on Sleeves White Cap **BACKSTABBER** 115 Dk.b. or br.g.(1976), Cutlass—Shower Of Flowers	WILLIAM I. MOTT	4 LEROY MOYERS (Post Pos. 2)
1a	JAMES H. RUTTER White, Black "R" on Gold Crown, Black Bars on Sleeves White Cap **CAN'THOLDMEBACK** 115 Dk.b. or br.h.(1976), Pallasgreen—Sunday Vollie	WILLIAM I. MOTT	4 LEROY MOYERS (Post Pos. 5)
2	PRESTON MADDEN AND ROGERS RED TOP, INC. (Walter Mullady) White, Red Top, Red Sleeves, White Cap **NOTED** 112 B.g.(1979), Buffalo Lark—Wild Note	THOMAS H. STEVENS, SR.	8 MARK SELLERS (Post Pos. 1)
3	ALBERT M. STALL AND EARL BURKE White, Blue Diamond Frames, White Cap **BAYOU BLACK** 112 Dk.b. or br.h.(1976), Droll Role—Dymond Island	FRANK BROTHERS	9-5 EDDIE DELAHOUSSAYE (Post Pos. 3)
4	W. C. PARTEE Orange, White Dots Orange Cap **OIL CITY** 118 Dk.b. or br.g.(1977), Pia Star—Sapose Speed	LYNN WHITING	4 JORGE VELASQUEZ (Post Pos. 4)
5	J. C. WATSON & RICKY HIGGS Green, White "W," White Sleeves Green Cap **DEUCES ARE LOOSE** 115 B.c.(1979), Zen—Cruise Director	RICKY HIGGS	20 CHARLES WOODS, JR. (Post Pos. 6)
6	DRAVO FOLEY Red, Red "F" on White Diamond, White Diamonds on Sleeves Red Cap **LIBERTY LANE** 112 Dk.b. or br.h.(1978), Great Sun—Barbs Compact	GREG FOLEY	5-2 DON BRUMFIELD (Post Pos. 7)
7	TOM GENTRY Yellow, Royal Blue Blocks, Royal Blue Bars on Sleeves Yellow Cap **CELTIC SABER** 112 Ch.c.(1979), Blade—Celtic Lyn	EDUARDO INDA	12 LAFFIT PINCAY, JR. (Post Pos. 8)

1 and 1a—JAMES H. RUTTER Entry

Scratched—THIRD AND LEX

Selections 3—6–1a—4

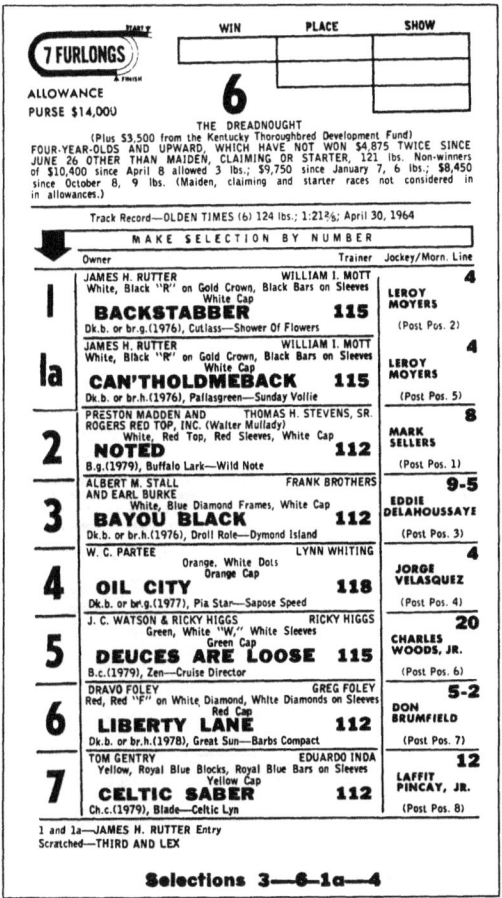

The tote board was as follows:

	Totals	#3 Bayou Black	Expected Value per Dollar Bet on Bayou Black
With three minutes to post time			
Odds		8—5	
Win	407,823	131,439	
Show	165,867	30,306	1.25
With one minute to post time			
Odds		8—5	
Win	469,967	149,753	
Show	188,358	37,275	1.20

With our betting fortune of $1,248.60, a bet of $317 to show on Bayou Black was suggested.

	Totals	#3 Bayou Black	Expected Value per Dollar Bet on Bayou Black
At post time			
Odds		8—5	
Win	482,830	154,423	
Show	191,848	38,018	1.20

Bayou Black won the race, followed by Noted and Liberty Lane. The show payoff on Bayou Black was $3, so we made a profit of $158.50 on our $317 bet. The chart of the race was as follows:

SIXTH RACE
Churchill
MAY 7, 1983

7 FURLONGS. (1.21$\frac{3}{5}$) ALLOWANCE. Purse $14,000 (plus $3,500 from KTDF). 4-year-olds and upward, which have not won $4,875 twice since June 26 other than maiden, claiming or starter. Weight, 121 lbs. Non-winners of $10,400 since April 8 allowed 3 lbs.; $9,750 since January 7, 6 lbs.; $8,450 since October 8, 9 lbs. (Maiden, claiming and starter races not considered in allowance.)

Total purse $17,500. Value of race $16,625, value to winner $11,375, second $2,800, third $1,750, fourth $700. ($875 reverts to the KTDF). Mutuel pool $909,035.

Last Raced	Horse	Eqt.A.Wt	PP	St	¼	½	Str	Fin	Jockey	Odds $1
30Mar83 ^{9}FG^{2}	Bayou Black	7 115	2	1	$2^{3\frac{1}{2}}$	1^{1}	$1^{2\frac{1}{2}}$	$1^{2\frac{1}{4}}$	Delahoussaye E	1.60
26Apr83 ^{7}Kee^{2}	Noted	4 112	1	5	$6^{2\frac{1}{2}}$	6^{7}	3^{2}	2^{4}	Sellers M S	13.20
28Apr83 ^{6}Kee^{3}	Liberty Lane	5 114	6	6	$4^{\frac{1}{2}}$	3^{1}	2^{1}	3^{1}	Brumfield D	2.30
16Apr83 ^{6}OP^{6}	Oil City	6 118	3	3	5^{1}	5^{2}	$4^{1\frac{1}{2}}$	$4^{2\frac{1}{2}}$	Velasquez J	7.30
16Apr83 ^{6}Kee^{2}	Can'tholdmeback	b 7 115	4	4	3^{hd}	$4^{3\frac{1}{2}}$	5^{2}	5^{5}	Moyers L	4.90
16Apr83 ^{8}FP^{1}	Deuces Are Loose	4 115	5	2	1^{hd}	$2^{2\frac{1}{2}}$	6^{6}	6^{2}	Woods C R Jr	20.40
20Apr83 ^{5}Kee^{2}	Celtic Saber	b 4 117	7	7	7	7	7	7	Pincay L Jr	8.10

OFF AT 3:30. Start good. Won handily. Time, :23$\frac{3}{5}$, :45$\frac{4}{5}$, 1:09$\frac{4}{5}$, 1:23 Track fast.

$2 Mutuel Prices:			
3-BAYOU BLACK	5.20	4.00	3.00
2-NOTED		9.20	5.20
6-LIBERTY LANE			2.80

Dk. b. or br. h, by Droll Role—Dymond Island, by Drone. Trainer Brothers Frank L. Bred by Stall A M (Ky).

BAYOU BLACK was rated confidently from the beginning, saved ground disposing of DEUCES ARE LOOSE on the turn and finished out handily. NOTED came outside horses for the stretch drive, was no match for the winner but clearly bested the rest. LIBERTY LANE responded when called upon to loom briefly menacing outside the winner in the early stretch and weakened. OIL CITY gave an even eoofrt. CAN'THOLDMEBACK tired. DEUCES ARE LOOSE was used up after a half mile.

Owners— 1, Stall & Burke; 2, Rogers Red Top Farm & Madden; 3, Foley D; 4, Partee W C; 5, Rutter J H; 6, Watson & Higgs; 7, Gentry T E.

Corrected weight: Bayou Black 112 pounds. **Overweight:** Bayou Black 3 pounds; Liberty Lane 2; Celtic Saber 5.

Scratched—Backstabber (19Apr83 ^{5}Kee^{4}); Third and Lex (28Apr83 ^{6}Kee^{8}).

The Twin Spires: Almost Derby Horses

The Twin Spires was a $50,000 added stakes race for three-year-olds over a $1\frac{1}{8}$-mile distance. The top choices were High Honors, Le Cou Cou, Common Sense, and Daring Diabolo. These horses and the rest of the field had run against the likes of Derby horses Caveat, Total Departure, Pax In Bello, Sunny's Halo, Slew O' Gold, Parfaitement, Current Hope, Chumming, Marfa, Desert Wine, Highland Park, and Freezing Rain. These were the horses not quite good enough to be in the Derby. By convention, the top twenty nominated horses rated in terms of earnings are allowed in the race. As horses are scratched, more places become available, but at twenty-fourth and twenty-ninth on the earnings list, Le Cou Cou and High Honors did not make the final twenty. The top thirty earners of 1983 appear in Table 12.2 on page 240.

High Honors had had six strong races out of seven, including a third-place finish in the Wood Memorial behind Slew O' Gold and Parfaitement. Le Cou Cou had a history of finishing close whenever he had started at astronomical odds. He was a scant three lengths off the pace at 102—1 in the Derby Trial, beaten only by Caveat, Total Departure, and Pax In Bello. The crowd made High Honors, who was ridden by Jorge Velasquez, an odds-on favorite. He was also a Dr. Z system bet for show.

1⅛ MILES
START FINISH

STAKE
Purse $50,000-Added

7

WIN PLACE SHOW

THE TWIN SPIRES

THREE-YEAR-OLDS, 121 lbs. $250 to pass the entry box with $50,000 added of which 65% to the owner of winner; 20% to second; 10% to third and 5% to fourth. Trophy to the winning owner.

Track Record—AEROFLINT (3) 116 lbs.; 1:48⅖; Nov. 18, 1961
LAS OLAS (4) 111 lbs.; 1:48⅖; Nov. 21, 1959

MAKE SELECTION BY NUMBER

No.	Owner / Trainer	Jockey/Morn. Line
1	GOLDEN CHANCE FARM — W. E. ADAMS (Verna Lehmann) Gold, Red "GCF," Red Chevron on Sleeves, Gold Cap **ASKED TO RUN** 121 B.c.(1980), Naskra—Running Beauty by Double Jay Bred in Kentucky by Golden Chance Farm, Inc.	12 PHILLIP RUBBICCO (Post Pos. 6)
1a	GOLDEN CHANCE FARM — W. E. ADAMS (Verna Lehmann) Gold, Red "GCF," Red Chevron on Sleeves, Gold Cap **DERBY DOUBLE** 121 Ch.c.(1980), Master Derby—Double Intent by Double Jay Bred in Kentucky by Golden Chance Farm, Inc.	12 MICHAEL MORAN (Post Pos. 10)
2	DUANE B. CLARK — JAMES G. ARNETT Green, White "DC," Green Bars on White Sleeves Green Cap **LE COU COU** 121 Gr.c.(1980), Zen—Bold Summer by Ballydonnell Bred in Illinois by Duane B. Clark	3 DONALD HOWARD (Post Pos. 1)
3	DANIEL M. GALBREATH — THOMAS L. RONDINELLO Brown and White Diamonds, White Sleeves Brown Cap **HIGH HONORS** 121 B.c.(1980), Graustark—Cum Laude Laurie by Hail to Reason Bred in Kentucky by Daniel M. Galbreath	8-5 JORGE VELASQUEZ (Post Pos. 2)
4	BROWNELL COMBS II — RAY LAWRENCE, JR. Blue, Orange Bars on Sleeves Orange Cap **CUCKOLD** 121 B.c.(1980), Circle Home—Night of Nights by Johns Joy Bred in Kentucky by Michael L. Cerone	10 EDDIE DELAHOUSSAYE (Post Pos. 3)
5	HOWARD P. WILSON — ROGER LAURIN Maroon, White Yoke Maroon Cap **THALASSOCRAT** 121 Dk.b. or br.c.(1980), Mr. Leader—Gracious Betty by Degage Bred in Kentucky by Howard P. Wilson	12 DONALD MacBETH (Post Pos. 4)
6	LINDA & FLETCHER CLEMENT — RICHARD B. MATTINGLY Black and Red Halves, White Sash, Red and Black Dots on White Sleeves, Red Cap **WEED EATER** 121 B.g.(1980), Hearts of Lettuce—Cats Kitten by Tronado Bred in Arkansas by Fletcher B. Clement	30 LEROY MOYERS (Post Pos. 5)
7	J. & L. STABLE — DENNIS J. MANNING (Joseph Taibbi and Laurence Palumbo) Black, Or. "JL," Or. Braces, Or. Diam. on Slvs., Or. Cap **COMMON SENSE** 121 Dk.b. or br.c.(1980), Fire Dancer—Prompt Jackie by Smiling Jack Bred in Florida by Ceedoubless Farm	4 JACK PENNEY (Post Pos. 7)

8	MARY M. ZIMMERMAN GLENN WISMER Orange, Blue Lightning "Z" Orange Cap **SAVERTON** **121** Ch.c.(1980), Dike—More Gloves by White Gloves II Bred in Florida by Mrs. Mary Zimmerman	**12** **CHARLES WOODS, JR.** (Post Pos. 8)
9	DIABOLO STABLE JERRY CALVIN (Gary Weir and John McDaniel) Blue, Red Stars on White Sash, Wh. Band on Slvs., Blue Cap **DARING DIABOLO** **121** B.c.(1980), Diabolo—Delicate Fame by Sensitivo Bred in Kentucky by J. Smreker and C. Young	**8** **DON BRUMFIELD** (Post Pos. 9)

Indicates Foaled In Kentucky
1 and 1a—GOLDEN CHANCE FARM Entry
Selections 3—2—7—9

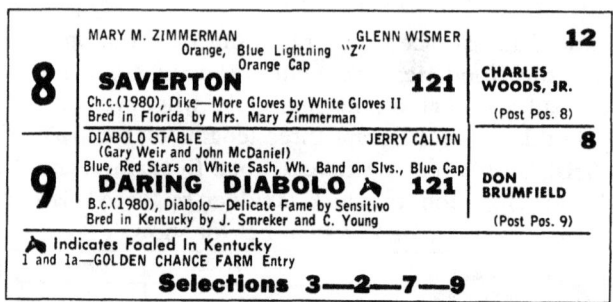

The tote board was as follows:

	Totals	#3 High Honors	Expected Value per Dollar Bet on High Honors
With two minutes to post time			
Odds		4—5	
Win	463,915	217,972	
Show	222,910	70,409	1.15
With one minute to post time			
Odds		3—5	
Win	495,324	237,351	
Show	231,893	74,281	1.15

We bet $688 to show on High Honors. At post time the tote board was

	Totals	#3 High Honors	Expected Value per Dollar Bet on High Honors
Odds		3—5	
Win	520,042	250,319	
Show	240,612	78,267	1.14

High Honors crossed the finish line first. Then Donald Howard, the jockey of the second horse, Le Cou Cou, lodged a claim of foul against Jorge Velasquez, who rode High Honors. A flashing INQUIRY sign is not good for one's blood pressure, but since, at worst, High Honors would be knocked down to second, we calmly waited for the decision of the stewards. The claim was allowed, and High Honors was taken down. So the official order of finish was Le Cou Cou first, High Honors second, and Common Sense third. Our show bet on High Honors paid $2.40, so we made a profit of

\$137.60 on our \$688 bet. Of course, High Honors' show payoff would be the same whether he finished first or second. The payoff would have changed only if one or more horses had been disqualified out of the money. The chart of the race was as follows:

SEVENTH RACE
Churchill
MAY 7, 1983

1 ⅛ MILES. (1.48⅘) 1st Running TWIN SPIRES STAKES. SPECIAL WEIGHT. \$50,000 Added. 3-year-olds. Weight, 121 lbs. \$250 to pass the entry box with \$50,000-added of which 65% goes to the winner, 20% to second, 10% to third, and 5% to fourth.

Value of race \$52,500, value to winner \$34,125, second \$10,500, third \$5,250, fourth \$2,625. Mutuel pool \$1,035,392.

Last Raced	Horse	Eqt.	A.	Wt	PP	St	¼	½	¾	Str	Fin	Jockey	Odds \$1
23Apr83 ^{8}Aqu^{3}	[D]High Honors	b	3	121	2	5	3^{hd}	3½	2^{hd}	1^{hd}	1^{nk}	Velasquez J	.70
30Apr83 ^{9}CD^{4}	Le Cou Cou	b	3	121	1	1	1^{hd}	1^{1}	1^{1}	2½	2^{1½}	Howard D L	4.70
23Apr83 ^{7}Aqu^{4}	Common Sense	b	3	121	7	3	6^{1½}	4^{1½}	4^{1½}	3^{3}	3^{3}	Penney J C	8.20
28Apr83 ^{7}Kee^{11}	Thalassocrat		3	121	4	6	7^{1½}	7^{1½}	7^{1½}	4^{5}	4^{9}	MacBeth D	15.90
27Apr83 ^{8}Kee^{1}	Cuckold	b	3	121	3	8	8^{1½}	8^{1½}	8^{2}	7^{hd}	5^{5}	Delahoussaye E	16.50
30Apr83 ^{9}CD^{12}	Saverton		3	121	8	4	4^{1}	5½	5^{hd}	5^{hd}	6^{hd}	Woods C R Jr	9.80
30Apr83 ^{9}CD^{11}	Derby Double	b	3	121	10	7	5^{hd}	6^{hd}	6^{hd}	6^{hd}	7^{hd}	Moran M T	a-18.30
16Apr83 ^{9}OP^{11}	Daring Diabolo		3	121	9	9	10	10	9^{hd}	9^{2}	8^{2}	Brumfield D	16.50
30Apr83 ^{9}CD^{14}	Asked To Run	b	3	121	6	2	2^{1½}	2^{1}	3^{hd}	8^{1½}	9^{2}	Rubbicco P	a-18.30
30Apr83 ^{6}CD^{8}	Weed Eater	b	3	121	5	10	9^{1}	9^{hd}	10	10	10	Moyers L	53.10

[D]-High Honors Disqualified and placed second.
a-Coupled: Derby Double and Asked To Run.
OFF AT 4:21. Start good. Won driving. Time, :23⅘, :47⅗, 1:11⅘, 1:36⅗, 1:49⅗ Track fast.

\$2 Mutuel Prices:			
2-LE COU COU	11.40	3.60	3.00
3-HIGH HONORS		2.80	2.40
7-COMMON SENSE			3.20

Le Cou Cou—Gr. c, by Zen—Bold Summer, by Ballydonnell. Trainer Arnett James G. Bred by Clark Duane B (Ill).

HIGH HONORS, always well placed, drifted in with right handed pressure in midstretch brushed with LE COU COU before taking command at the furlong marker and proved best. Following a stewards' inquiry and an objection by the rider of LE COU COU for interference in the stretch run, HIGH HONORS was disqualified an placed second. LE COU COU broke in stride to make the early pace, began to drift out after the three-sixteenths pole, brushed with the winner just before the eighth pole and could not match that one late. COMMON SENSE, never far back, lacked the needed response against the top two. THALASSACRAT improved position in upper stretch. SAVERTON had brief speed. ASKED TO RUN prompted the early pace and gave way.

Owners— 1, Galbreath D M; 2, Clark D B; 3, J & L Stable; 4, Wilson H P; 5, Combs B II; 6, Zimmerman Mary M; 7, Golden Chance Farm Inc; 8, Diabolo Stable; 9, Golden Chance Farm Inc; 10, Clement F B & Linda.

The 109th Kentucky Derby

The eighth race of the day was the Kentucky Derby. The full field of twenty horses contained no super horses. It was a wide-open race. The writers' choices for the winner, as displayed in Table 12.2, included Marfa, Slew O'Gold, Caveat, Play Fellow, Sunny's Halo, and Explosive Wagon. In addition, Chumming, Highland Park, Desert Wine, Current Hope, Parfaitement, Pax In Bello, and Paris Prince each had a genuine chance to win. But the center of attention was Marfa. You can see why by consulting his past-performance chart. He had a tendency to lug, that is, to move laterally without reason during a race. Hence he was in constant trouble. So far this behavior had only led to one disqualification, which had occurred in his last race, the Blue Grass Stakes at Keeneland. Copeland, the leading money earner among Derby hopefuls (see Table 12.2) had been injured in that race and was out of Derby contention. It was not clear if Marfa had been involved. Marfa's running style also hampered him and possibly other horses in at least four

TABLE 12.2 *1983 Kentucky Derby prospects' earnings and the racing writers' picks*

Here's the way racing writers pick the finish

Billy Reed, Courier-Journal: 1. Marfa. 2. Sunny's Halo. 3. Current Hope. 4. Chumming. Time 2:01⅘.

Bob Adair, Courier-Journal: 1. Slew O' Gold. 2. Caveat. 3. My Mac. 4. Parfaitement. Time 2:02⅘.

Richard Sowers, Courier-Journal: 1. Caveat. 2. Marfa. 3. Highland Park. 4. Play Fellow. Time 2:03⅗.

Dale Austin, Baltimore Sun: 1. Play Fellow. 2. Parfaitement. 3. Caveat. 4. Marfa. Time: 2:00.

Bill Christine, Los Angeles Times: 1. Sunny's Halo. 2. Caveat. 3. Balboa Native. 4. Marfa. Time 2:02⅖.

Russ Harris, New York Daily News: 1. Sunny's Halo. 2. Caveat. 3. Marfa. 4. Pax In Bello. Time 2:02⅖.

Mike Barry, Louisville Times: 1. Play Fellow. 2. Marfa. 3. Current Hope. 4. Sunny's Halo. Time 2:02⅗.

Jim Bolus, Louisville Times: 1. Play Fellow. 2. Sunny's Halo. 3. Slew O' Gold. 4. Caveat. Time 2:02.

Rich Bozich, Louisville Times: 1. Sunny's Halo. 2. Play Fellow. 3. Desert Wine. 4. Marfa. Time 2:02⅘.

Dave Koerner, Louisville Times: 1. Slew O' Gold. 2. Play Fellow. 3. Pax In Bello. 4. Parfaitement. Time 2:01⅘.

Graham Ross, Daily Racing Form: 1. Sunny's Halo. 2. Slew O' Gold. 3. Play Fellow. 4. Highland Park. Time 2:01⅗.

Bob Roesler, New Orleans Times-Picayune/States Item: 1. Sunny's Halo. 2. Caveat. 3. Play Fellow. 4. Desert Wine. Time 2:01⅘.

Ed Schuyler, Associated Press: 1. Caveat. 2. Sunny's Halo. 3. Marfa. 4. Highland Park. Time 2:02⅗.

Steven Crist, New York Times: 1. Explosive Wagon. 2. Pax In Bello. 3. Marfa. 4. Balboa Native. Time 2:01⅖.

Andrew Beyer, Washington Post: 1. Marfa. 2. Play Fellow. 3. Caveat. 4. Sunny's Halo. Time 2:03.

Derby prospects' unofficial earnings

1.	Copelan	$569,090
2.	Desert Wine	527,315
3.	Sunny's Halo	481,019
4.	Marfa	386,943
5.	Highland Park	382,858
6.	Total Departure	378,868
7.	Current Hope	263,537
8.	Pax in Bello	256,473
9.	Caveat	238,337
10.	Luv a Libra	232,818
11.	Paris Prince	231,940
12.	My Mac	207,197
13.	Bounding Basque	201,322
14.	Balboa Native	177,625
15.	Play Fellow	166,787
16.	Slew o' Gold	158,940
17.	Parfaitement	157,088
18.	Chumming	151,826
19.	Explosive Wagon	151,110
20.	Elegant Life	148,854
21.	Coax Me Matt	137,053
22.	* Noble Home	132,500
23.	* Hail to Rome	119,660
24.	Le Cou Cou	107,793
25.	Dixieland Band	96,867
26.	Freezing Rain	89,325
27.	Country Pine	74,158
28.	Law Talk	68,107
29.	High Honors	46,940
30.	Saverton	29,123

* Includes only original purse awards for Spiral Stakes.

other races. He was also a controversial starter in the Spiral Stakes because of some irregularities in his earnings record. A day before the race, it was discovered that he was about $2,000 short to qualify. Since he was the top horse in the race, so the story goes, he was allowed to run. He ran a smashing 98 to win by eight lengths. The gray colt was a brilliant but erratic and possibly dangerous runner. He was to be ridden by Jorge Velasquez, who had just been disqualified in the previous race. Win or lose, he seemed to be the horse to determine the outcome of the race. The entry of Marfa,

TABLE 12.3 *Previous day's preliminary wagering on the 1983 Kentucky Derby*

Horse	Odds	Win ($)	Place ($)	Show ($)
1. Balboa Native, Total Departure, and Marfa	5—2	68,469	18,760	13,171
2. Chumming and Caveat	5—1	36,245	14,994	9,424
3. Freezing Rain and Highland Park	17—1	13,189	4,854	4,497
4. Slew O' Gold	10—1	21,341	8,181	4,953
5. Play Fellow	12—1	17,720	7,757	4,035
6. Desert Wine	18—1	12,766	4,567	3,165
7. Country Pine	50—1	4,286	1,368	938
8. Sunny's Halo	5—2	63,329	20,783	12,106
9. Current Hope	13—1	17,562	6,528	3,282
10. Parfaitement	60—1	3,570	1,323	1,063
11. Pax In Bello	25—1	8,171	3,232	2,054
12–16. Law Talk, Paris Price, My Mac, Explosive Wagon, and Luv A Libra	8—1	25,877	13,382	13,817
		293,525	105,729	72,505

Balboa Native, and Total Departure was installed as the race favorite at 5—2.

The second choice, listed at 5—1 in the morning line, but the consensus choice and best bet of the day, was the Canadian horse, Sunny's Halo. In the preliminary betting (see Table 12.3) he was also going off at 5—2. Sunny's Halo had a strong record as a two-year-old at Woodbine in Toronto. He had done poorly in two summer races in New York. His trainer, David Cross, eliminated thirty-two of his stable of thirty-five horses to concentrate on Sunny's Halo, who he thought was possibly the horse of a lifetime. Sunny's Halo responded with a win in the Rebel Handicap at Oaklawn Park in Arkansas. Cross was then looking to the Derby. His wife had bet $200 at 100—1 odds in the Las Vegas winter book that the colt would take the Derby. With 405 nominations, the odds on any nonprominent horse are quite large. Cross wanted a rider with proven Derby experience. Who could be better than the 1982 winner, Eddie Delahoussaye? Eddie had been scheduled earlier in the year to ride Roving Boy, the 1982 Eclipse award champion for a juvenile colt or gelding, and a possible super horse. Unfortunately, he had been injured in January at Santa Anita. Delahoussaye was glad to ride for Cross. He had led Sunny's Halo to a four-length victory in the Arkansas Derby with a 96 speed rating. He looked strong; however, tradition was not on his side. No Arkansas Derby winner had ever won the Kentucky Derby, and no horse since Jet Pilot in 1947 had won the Derby with only two starts as a three-year-old.

I liked quite a few horses in the race as possible long-shot winners. Marfa and Sunny's Halo certainly were the class, but Marfa was risky and Sunny's Halo lightly raced. I would bet on them, especially Sunny's Halo, if they were Dr. Z system bets. I was still hoping to bet on a winner in the Derby. Since there were so many strong horses, I diversified my bet of $50 over seven top contenders going off at relatively long odds. I bet $10 to win on number 2, the entry of Chumming and Caveat; on number 3, the entry of Freezing Rain and Highland Park; on number 4, Slew O' Gold; on number 5, Play Fellow; and on number 6, Desert Wine.

The Dr. Z system bet, if there was to be one, seemed to be on Sunny's Halo. The tote board was as follows:

	Totals	#8 Sunny's Halo	Expected Value per Dollar Bet on Sunny's Halo
With fifty-four minutes to post time			
Odds		5—2	
Win	2,155,976	482,703	
Show	768,057	119,245	1.14
With thirty-four minutes to post time			
Odds		5—2	
Win	2,564,483	592,960	
Show	930,971	142,078	1.16
With twenty minutes to post time			
Odds		5—2	
Win	2,879,256	668,880	
Show	1,026,474	160,470	1.15
With eight minutes to post time			
Odds		5—2	
Win	3,041,257	711,776	
Show	1,077,595	170,164	1.15
With one minute to post time			
Odds		5—2	
Win	3,099,808	729,747	
Show	1,098,076	175,643	1.14

With our betting fortune of $1,494.70 reflecting my $50 win bet, we bet $87 to show on Sunny's Halo.

	Totals	#8 Sunny's Halo	Expected Value per Dollar Bet on Sunny's Halo
At post time			
Odds		5—2	
Win	3,143,669	745,524	
Show	1,099,990	179,758	1.14

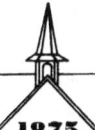

109th Running
KENTUCKY DERBY
EIGHTH RACE

1875 — 1983

$250,000 ADDED — **ONE MILE and ONE-QUARTER** — **TRACK RECORD—SECRETARIAT (3), 126 lbs., 5-5-73, 1:59-2/5**

For three-year-olds. By subscription of $200 each. All nomination fees to the winner. $5,000 to pass entry box, $5,000 additional to start. $250,000 added, of which $60,000 to second, $30,000 to third, $15,000 to fourth, (to be divided equally in the event of a dead heat). Weight 126 lbs. The owner of the winner to receive a gold trophy.

Closed Tuesday, February 15, 1983, with 405 nominations.

USE THESE NUMBERS FOR BUYING PARI MUTUEL TICKETS

No.	OWNER	TRAINER	Colors	Horse	Wt.	Breeding	JOCKEY	Morning Line	P. P.
1	ROBERT H. SPREEN	D. WAYNE LUKAS	Yellow, Brown "RS," Brown Bars on Sleeves, Yellow Cap	BALBOA NATIVE ♞	126	Ch c, 1980, Native Royalty—Diamond Till by Model Fool. BRED IN KENTUCKY BY R. E. OWENS	SANDY HAWLEY	5-2	(P. P. 3)
1a	REBALOT STABLE (Stephen V. Lyons & Jay Templeman)	D. WAYNE LUKAS	Copper and Yellow Diamond Quarters, Yellow Bars on Copper Sleeves, Copper Cap	TOTAL DEPARTURE	126	B c, 1980, Greek Answer—Life Style by Manifesto. BRED IN FLORIDA BY JOHN H. HARTIGAN	PAT VALENZUELA	5-2	(P. P. 9)
1x	L. ROBERT FRENCH, JR., BARRY BEAL & D. WAYNE LUKAS	D. WAYNE LUKAS	Forest Green, White Dots, Forest Green Cap	MARFA ♞	126	Gr c, 1980, Foolish Pleasure—Gray Matter by Stratmat. BRED IN KENTUCKY BY TOM GENTRY	JORGE VELASQUEZ	5-2	(P. P. 18)
2	HICKORY TREE STABLE (James P. Mills)	WOODFORD C. STEPHENS	Green, Yellow Sash, Yellow Blocks on Sleeves, Green Cap	CHUMMING	126	Dk b or br c, 1980, Alleged—Gulls Cry by Sea-Bird. BRED IN VIRGINIA BY NEWSTEAD FARM	EDDIE MAPLE	5	(P. P. 4)
2b	AUGUST BELMONT IV, et al	WOODFORD C. STEPHENS	Scarlet, Maroon Sleeves, Black Cap	CAVEAT	126	Dk b or br c, 1980, Cannonade—Cold Hearted by The Axe II. BRED IN MARYLAND BY RYEHILL FARM	LAFFIT PINCAY, JR.	5	(P. P. 20)
3	BWAMAZON FARM (Millard A. Waldheim)	ANTHONY BASILE	White, Royal Blue Hoops, Royal Blue Stripes on Sleeves, Royal Blue Cap	FREEZING RAIN ♞	126	Ch c, 1980, It's Freezing—All's Well by Well Mannered. BRED IN KENTUCKY BY BWAMAZON FARM	WILLIAM GAVIDIA	15	(P. P. 8)
3c	BWAMAZON FARM (Millard A. Waldheim) & BRERETON C. JONES	ANTHONY BASILE	White, Royal Blue Hoops, Royal Blue Stripes on Sleeves, Royal Blue Cap	HIGHLAND PARK ♞	126	Ch c, 1980, Raise a Native—Old Goat by Olden Times. BRED IN KENTUCKY BY BWAMAZON FARM	DON BRUMFIELD	15	(P. P. 19)
4	EQUUS EQUITY STABLE (Delmar L. Pearson, Jr. Lessee)	SIDNEY WATTERS, JR.	Black, Silver Yoke, Silver Bars on Sleeves, Silver Cap	SLEW O' GOLD ♞	126	B c, 1980, Seattle Slew—Alluvial by Buckpasser. BRED IN KENTUCKY BY CLAIBORNE FARM	ANGEL CORDERO, JR.	6	(P. P. 1)
5	NANCY VANIER, CARL LAUER & ROBERT VICTOR	HARVEY L. VANIER	Yellow, Blue Sash, Yellow Cap	PLAY FELLOW ♞	126	B c, 1980, On The Sly—Play For Keeps by Run For Nurse. BRED IN KENTUCKY BY MR. & MRS. PAUL BAKEWELL III	JEAN CRUGUET	4	(P. P. 2)
6	T90 RANCH (Dan J. Agnew) & CARDIFF STUD (Fred Sahadi)	JERRY FANNING	Red, Red "T90" on White Ball, White Cap	DESERT WINE ♞	126	B c, 1980, Damascus—Anne Campbell by Never Bend. BRED IN KENTUCKY BY BRERETON C. JONES & WARNERTON FARMS	CHRIS McCARRON	15	(P. P. 5)
7	DANIEL M. GALBREATH	THOMAS L. RONDINELLO	Brown and White Diamonds, White Sleeves, Brown Cap	COUNTRY PINE ♞	126	B c, 1980, His Majesty—Mountain Sunshine by Vaguely Noble. BRED IN KENTUCKY BY DANIEL M. GALBREATH	MICHAEL VENEZIA	20	(P. P. 7)
8	DAVID J. FOSTER RACING STABLE (David J. Foster, et al)	DAVID C. CROSS, JR.	Orange, White Stripes, Orange Cap	SUNNY'S HALO	126	Ch c, 1980, Halo—Mostly Sunny by Sunny. BRED IN CANADA BY DAVID J. FOSTER	EDDIE DELAHOUSSAYE	5	(P. P. 10)
9	ROBERT BAKER & HOWARD KASKEL	ROGER LAURIN	Orange, White Sash, White Stripes on Sleeves, Orange Cap	CURRENT HOPE ♞	126	Ro c, 1980, Little Current—Kahoolawe by Warfare. BRED IN KENTUCKY BY MR. & MRS. J. C. MABEE	ALEXIS SOLIS	12	(P. P. 12)
10	MRS. BERNARD DANEY	J. WILLIAM BONIFACE	Red, Black Cross Sashes, Black Band on White Sleeves, White Cap	PARFAITEMENT	126	Ch c, 1980, Halo—Double Axle by The Axe II. BRED IN PENNSYLVANIA BY BLACK GATE NURSERY TRUST	HERBERT McCAULEY	20	(P. P. 13)
11	MR. & MRS. ARNOLD A. WILLCOX	STEVEN T. JERKENS	Crimson, Black Collar and Cuffs, Gold Sleeves, Crimson Cap	PAX IN BELLO	126	B c, 1980, Hold Your Peace—Chicanery by Pretense. BRED IN FLORIDA BY MR. & MRS. ARNOLD A. WILLCOX	JEFFREY FELL	15	(P. P. 14)
12 FIELD	BUCKRAM OAK FARM (Mahmoud Fustok)	LEONARD IMPERIO	Green, Red Sash, Red Band on Sleeves, Red Cap	LAW TALK	126	B c, 1980, Wardlaw—Tellinoid by Captain's Gig. BRED IN FLORIDA BY S. L. HAYMAN & ELLIOTT FUENTES	CARLOS MARQUEZ	30	(P. P. 6)
13 FIELD	PEGGY McREYNOLDS	GENE C. NORMAN	Green, Pink Stripes, Pink Sleeves, Green Cap	EXPLOSIVE WAGON	126	Ch c, 1980, Explodent—Gypsy Wagon by Conestoga. BRED IN FLORIDA BY WINDY CITY STABLE	CHARLES MUELLER	30	(P. P. 11)
14 FIELD	ARONOW STABLE (Donald J. Aronow)	NEWCOMB GREEN	Red, White "A," White Braces, White Bars on Sleeves, Red Cap	MY MAC	126	Dk b or br g, 1980, Minnesota Mac—My Mom Nullah by My Dad George. BRED IN FLORIDA BY ROYAL WAY FARM	DONALD MacBETH	30	(P. P. 15)
15 FIELD	DOLLY GREEN	LAZARO S. BARRERA	Red, Gold Yoke, Gold Bars on Sleeves, Red Cap	PARIS PRINCE ♞	126	Ch c, 1980, Exclusive Native—Dancers Countess by Northern Dancer. BRED IN KENTUCKY BY HOLTSINGER, INC.	TERRY LIPHAM	30	(P. P. 16)
16 FIELD	VIVIANNE DeCOSTA & STANLEY YAGODA	HELIODORO GUSTINES	Gold, Purple Triangular Panel, Gold and Purple Diagonal Quartered Sleeves, Gold and Purple Cap	LUV A LIBRA	126	B c, 1980, Diplomat Way—Lip Talk by Assegai. BRED IN FLORIDA BY FARNSWORTH FARM	JULIO ESPINOZA	30	(P. P. 17)

♞ Indicates Foaled In Kentucky.

1-1a-1x—Robert H. Spreen—Rebalot Stable—L. Robert French, Jr., Barry Beal & D. Wayne Lukas Entry

2-2b—Hickory Tree Stable—August Belmont IV, et al Entry

3-3c—Bwamazon Farm—Bwamazon Farm & Brereton C. Jones Entry

FIELD—12-13-14-15-16

Selections—1x-5-8-2b

109th-Kentucky Derby-109th

8th Churchill

1 ¼ MILES. (1.59⅖) 109th Running KENTUCKY DERBY (Grade I). $250,000 added. 3-year-olds. By subscription of $200 each. All nomination fees to the winner. $5,000 to pass the entry box, $5,000 additional to start, with $250,000 added of which $60,000 to second, $30,000 to third and $15,000 to fourth (to be divided equally in the event of a dead heat). Weight 126 lbs. Starters to be named through the entry box Thursday, May 5, at usual time of closing. The maximum number of starters for the Kentucky Derby will be limited to twenty. In the event more than twenty entries pass through the entry box at the time of closing, the twenty starters and up to eight also eligibles will be determined at that time with preference given to those horses that have accumulated the highest earnings. Should any entry(ies) be withdrawn from the starting field prior to 4 P.M. scratch time, Friday, May 6, vacancies will be filled from the also eligible list and placed in the outside post positions in order of preference. For those that pass the entry box and are eliminated under this condition the entry fee will be refunded. Gold trophy to the winning owner. Closed with 405 nominations Tuesday, February 15, 1983.

Coupled—Balboa Native, Total Departure and Marfa; Chumming and Caveat; Freezing Rain and Highland Park.

Mutuel Field—Law Talk, Luv A Libra, Paris Prince, Explosive Wagon, My Mac.

Route the *Field* Will Travel

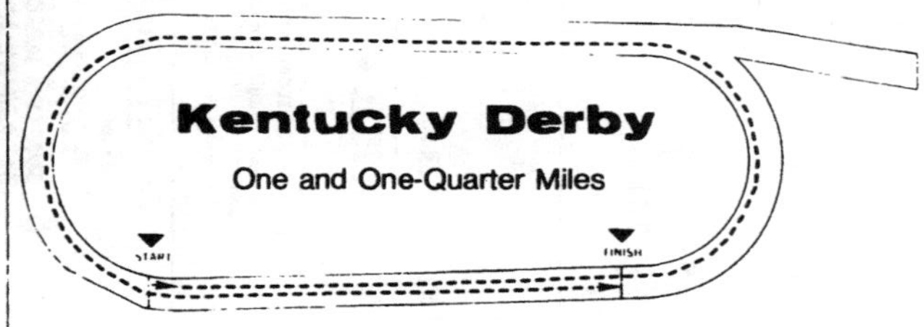

Slew O' Gold — B. c. 3, by Seattle Slew—Alluvial, by Buckpasser
Br.—Claiborne Farm (Ky) — 1983 4 2 1 1 $136,740
Own.—Equusequity Stable — 126 — Tr.—Watters Sidney Jr — 1982 3 2 0 0 $22,200
Lifetime 7 4 1 1 $158,940

23Apr83-8Aqu 1⅛ :48^1 1:12^1 1:51 ft *6-5 126 5^2 4$^{1\frac{3}{4}}$ 1^{hd} 1^{nk} Maple E^1 Wood Mem 80-24 SlewO'Gold,Prfitement,HighHonors 7
23Apr83—Run in two divisions 7th & 8th races
13Apr83-1Aqu 1⅛ :48^3 1:12^3 1:50^{4}ft *1 117 1^{hd} 1^1 1^6 1$^{7\frac{3}{4}}$ Cordero AJr^4 Aw23000 81-19 Slew O' Gold, Law Talk, El Cubano 6
19Mar83-10Tam 1$\frac{1}{16}$:48 1:13 1:47^{1}ft 2¾ 118 4$^{2\frac{1}{2}}$ 4$^{3\frac{1}{2}}$ 2^3 2$^{\frac{3}{4}}$ RiverHJr^2 Tampa Bay 82-21 Morgnmrgnmrgn,SlwO'Gld,QckDp 14
19Mar83—Steadied, checked
5Mar83-10Tam 1$\frac{1}{16}$:47^4 1:13^2 1:47^{2}ft *2-5 118 8$^{6\frac{3}{4}}$ 4^3 3$^{2\frac{1}{2}}$ 3$^{3\frac{3}{4}}$ MolnVH^4 Sam F Davis 78-23 Sverton,TwoTurnsHome,SlwO'Gold 8
13Nov82-8Aqu 1⅛ :48^2 1:12^4 1:50^{1}gd *9-5e 115 5$^{2\frac{1}{2}}$ 5^3 6^{10} 6^{12} Lovato F Jr^{11} Remsen 72-20 PxInBllo,Chumming,PrimitivPlsur 11
23Oct82-9Aqu 1 :47 1:12^1 1:37^{2}ft 3¾ 117 2$^{\frac{1}{2}}$ 1^{hd} 1$^{1\frac{1}{2}}$ 1$^{1\frac{3}{4}}$ Lovato F Jr^8 Aw20000 79-21 Slew O' Gold, Last Turn,Chumming 9
15Oct82-3Aqu 6½f :23^2 :47 1:18^{4}ft *3-5 118 2$^{\frac{1}{2}}$ 2$^{\frac{1}{2}}$ 1$^{\frac{1}{2}}$ 1^{nk} Cordero A Jr^8 Mdn 81-26 SlewO'Gold,Countertrde,MjestyCov 8
May 5 CD 4f ft :48 h — Apr 30 CD 6f sy 1:14 h — ●Apr 20 Bel tr.t 5f sy :59^2 h — ●Apr 10 Bel tr.t 6f sy 1:13^1 h (d)

Play Fellow ✻ — B. c. 3, by On the Sly—Play for Keeps, by Run for Nurse
Br.—Bakewell Mr–Mrs P III (Ky) — 1983 6 3 1 1 $153,568
Own.—Vanier Nancy&Lauer&Victor — 126 — Tr.—Vanier Harvey L — 1982 4 1 3 0 $13,220
Lifetime 10 4 4 1 $166,788

28Apr83-7Kee 1⅛ :46^4 1:11 1:49^{2}sy 19 121 8^{12} 4$^{5\frac{1}{2}}$ 1^{hd} 1no Cruguet J^3 Blue Grass 90-16 Play Fellow, ‡Marfa, Desert Wine 12
2Apr83-10Hia 1⅛ :47^1 1:11^1 1:49^{2}ft 4¾ 118 13$^{9\frac{1}{4}}$ 12$^{8\frac{3}{4}}$ 11^7 10$^{3\frac{3}{4}}$ Cruguet J^1 Flamingo 81-18 CurrntHop,Chmmng,Gn'lPrcttonr 14
2Apr83—Wide, brushed
19Mar83-10Hia 1⅛ :45^3 1:09^3 1:48^{4}ft *6-5 112 10$^{8\frac{3}{4}}$ 6^8 5^5 3$^{\frac{1}{2}}$ Cruguet J^9 Everglades 87-18 Gn'lPrcttnr,OhMyWndlnd,PlyFllw 12
28Feb83-7GP 7f :22^2 :45 1:23^{2}ft *1 122 6^7 6^7 3$^{1\frac{1}{2}}$ 1$^{5\frac{1}{2}}$ Cruguet J^5 Aw21000 87-24 PlayFellow,SmartStyle,GunCarrige 8
9Feb83-8GP 7f :22 :44^4 1:23^{3}ft *8-5 119 10^9 9$^{9\frac{1}{4}}$ 3^{nk} 1^2 Cruguet J^9 Aw14000 86-24 Play Fellow, Tarmoud,HighHonors 12
26Jan83-8GP 6f :22 :45 1:09^{4}ft 6½ 119 9$^{5\frac{1}{4}}$ 6^6 2^4 2$^{2\frac{1}{2}}$ Cruguet J^2 Aw14000 87-20 JusticeSnders,PlyFellow,ElPerico 10
23Nov82-3CD 7½f :23^1 :46^3 1:34 m *9-5 118 2^{hd} 1^2 1^1 2$^{2\frac{3}{4}}$ Gallitano G^3 Aw11200 72-35 Jenkins Ferry, PlayFellow,Ida'sSon 6
13Nov82-4CD 7f :23^3 :47^2 1:26^{3}ft *8-5 118 3$^{\frac{1}{2}}$ 2$^{\frac{1}{2}}$ 2$^{\frac{1}{2}}$ 2$^{\frac{1}{2}}$ Gallitano G^8 Aw11200 73-22 DarkSuce,PlyFellow,NibbleOnDrrell 8
3Nov82-5CD 6f :22^3 :46^3 1:12^{4}gd *1e 121 4$^{1\frac{1}{2}}$ 3$^{2\frac{1}{2}}$ 1$^{\frac{1}{2}}$ 1$^{3\frac{1}{4}}$ Gallitano G^{11} Mdn 82-26 Play Fellow, Great Boy, Lazaro 12
22Oct82-3Kee 6½f :22^2 :45^4 1:19 ft 3 120 5$^{5\frac{1}{2}}$ 1$^{1\frac{1}{2}}$ 1^2 2$^{1\frac{1}{4}}$ Haire D^1 Mdn 81-18 NturllyBlu,PlyFllow,GrndstonTurn 12
●Apr 20 Kee 7f ft 1:25^2 h — Apr 16 Kee 5f gd 1:01 b — Mar 31 Hia 4f sy :48 b — Mar 26 Hia 5f ft 1:03 b

Country Pine — B. c. 3, by His Majesty—Mountain Sunshine, by Vaguely Noble
Br.—Galbreath D M (Ky) — 1983 7 2 1 1 $63,958
Own.—Galbreath D M — 126 — Tr.—Rondinello Thomas L — 1982 2 1 0 0 $10,200
Lifetime 9 3 1 1 $74,158

23Apr83-7Aqu 1⅛ :48^1 1:12^2 1:51^{2}ft 3¾ 126 5^5 3$^{\frac{1}{2}}$ 2^{hd} 2no Bailey JD^8 Wood Mem 78-24 BoundingBsque,CountryPin,AztcRd 8
23Apr83—Run in two divisions 7th & 8th races; Wide
2Apr83-10Hia 1⅛ :47^1 1:11^1 1:49^{2}ft 13e 118 9^5 4^3 7$^{3\frac{1}{4}}$ 8$^{2\frac{1}{4}}$ Bailey J D^2 Flamingo 83-18 CurrntHop,Chmmng,Gn'lPrcttonr 14
2Apr83—Steadied
23Mar83-5Hia 7f :23 :45^3 1:22 ft *4-5 118 3^2 2^{hd} 1$^{\frac{1}{2}}$ 1^2 Bailey J D^6 Aw11000 93-16 Country Pine, Luv ALibra,Tarmoud 7
21Feb83-10GP 1$\frac{1}{16}$:47^4 1:12 1:43^{3}ft 3½ 113 6$^{7\frac{1}{4}}$ 4^5 6^8 4$^{7\frac{1}{4}}$ Fell J^2 Ftn Youth 76-24 Copelan, Current Hope, Blink 8
21Feb83—Run in two divisions 9th & 10th races
9Feb83-9GP 7f :22^1 :45 1:22^{4}ft 3½ 112 10^5 8$^{4\frac{3}{4}}$ 5$^{3\frac{1}{4}}$ 3$^{\frac{3}{4}}$ VelsquezJ^8 Hutcheson 89-24 CurrntHop,HighlndPrk,CountryPn 13
18Jan83-5GP 6f :22^2 :45^4 1:10^{1}ft *1 122 2^2 1^3 1^5 1^9 Velasquez J^8 Aw14000 88-18 CountryPine,Stn'sChrger,SlickRulr 9
8Jan83-6GP 6f :21^4 :44^3 1:10^{4}sy 3½ 122 10$^{6\frac{3}{4}}$ 10^{14} 6$^{9\frac{1}{2}}$ 5$^{4\frac{1}{2}}$ Velasquez J^2 Aw14000 81-17 Sligh Jet, Unreal Zeal, Pure Grit 12
28Nov82-4Aqu 7f :22^4 :46^1 1:25 ft *6-5 118 2$^{\frac{1}{2}}$ 2^1 1^2 1$^{2\frac{1}{2}}$ Velasquez J^4 Mdn 76-28 CountryPine,ThWholTickt,QutiGold 9
11Nov82-4Aqu 6f :22^2 :46 1:10^{4}ft 6¼ 118 3^1 9$^{5\frac{3}{4}}$ 7$^{6\frac{3}{4}}$ 5$^{7\frac{1}{4}}$ Velasquez J^1 Mdn 80-19 Jeff'sCompnion,JungleDust,Nevdo 13
May 5 Bel 4f ft :49 b — May 1 Bel 4f ft :48^2 b — Apr 22 Bel 3f ft :38 b — Apr 17 Bel tr.t 6f gd 1:13^2 h

Freezing Rain *

Ch. c. 3, by It's Freezing—All's Well, by Well Mannered
Br.—Bwamazon Farm (Ky) 1983 5 2 1 0 $64,640
Own.—Bwamazon Farm 126 Tr.—Basile Anthony 1982 5 3 0 2 $24,685
Lifetime 10 5 1 2 $89,325

28Apr83-7Kee 1⅛ :46^{4} 1:11 1:49^{2}sy 2¾e 121 10^{12} 6^{9} $5^{5\frac{1}{4}}$ $5^{9\frac{1}{2}}$ Gavidia W^{1} Blue Grass 80-16 Play Fellow, ‡Marfa, Desert Wine 12
21Apr83-7Kee 7f :22^{4} :45^{1} 1:23^{4}ft *2-3 120 $8^{9\frac{1}{4}}$ $8^{9\frac{1}{4}}$ $3^{3\frac{1}{2}}$ 2^{1} Solomone M^{2} Aw28000 86-15 DerbyDouble,FrezingRin,Hrry'NBill 9
9Apr83-7Kee 6f :22^{1} :45^{1} 1:11^{1}sy *4-5 118 9^{6} $7^{5\frac{3}{4}}$ $3^{3\frac{1}{2}}$ 1½ BrumfieldD^{4} Lafayette 86-25 Freezing Rain, Harry'NBill,Hamlet 11
5Mar83-9GP 7f :22^{2} :45^{2} 1:23^{3}ft *4-5 119 $6^{6\frac{1}{4}}$ $7^{3\frac{1}{2}}$ $5^{2\frac{3}{4}}$ $5^{3\frac{1}{2}}$ Brumfield D^{9} Aw30000 82-19 Slewpy,Victorious,Gen'lPrctitioner 9
8Jan83-9GP 6f :22 :44^{3} 1:10 sy 4½e 114 $7^{7\frac{1}{4}}$ $5^{6\frac{1}{2}}$ 3^{3} 1¾ BrmfldD^{7} Spect'ul Bid 89-17 FreezingRin,WriteOff,TotlDeprture 9
27Nov82-4CD 7f :24 :48 1:25^{4}m *1 115 3^{2} $4^{1\frac{3}{4}}$ 2^{hd} 1^{nk} Brumfield D^{6} Aw15700 78-29 FreezingRain,BrshBrother,DrkSuce 8
10Nov82-6CD 6f :22 :45^{3} 1:11^{1}ft *6-5 115 $6^{2\frac{1}{4}}$ $3^{1\frac{1}{2}}$ 1½ 1^{4} Brumfield D^{3} Aw11200 90-22 FreezingRin,ShrpTimes,SlyRussllC. 9
22Oct82-4Kee 6½f :22^{3} :46 1:18^{1}ft *4-5 115 $9^{3\frac{1}{2}}$ 6^{5} $5^{3\frac{3}{4}}$ 3^{2} Day P^{10} Aw13500 84-18 Admirl'sGin,SoringTims,FrzingRin 12
13Oct82-4Kee 6f :22^{1} :46 1:11^{2}ft *2-3 115 $9^{6\frac{3}{4}}$ $7^{5\frac{1}{4}}$ 4^{4} 3^{1} Day P^{3} Aw13500 84-16 DerbyDouble,HndStnd,FrezingRin 12
20May82-5AP 5f :23^{1} :46^{4} :58^{4}ft *3-5 122 2^{2} 2½ 2½ 1^{nk} Day P^{4} Mdn 92-29 Freezing Rain, Spare Card, Dakota 9
May 5 CD 4f ft :48 h Apr 16 Kee 5f gd 1:03^{2} b Apr 7 Kee 4f ft :49^{2} b Apr 2 Kee 7f ft 1:28^{4} b

Balboa Native *

Ch. c. 3, by Native Royalty—Diamond Till, by Model Fool
Br.—Owens R E (Ky) 1983 5 2 0 2 $141,000
Own.—Spreen R H 126 Tr.—Lukas D Wayne 1982 7 1 1 2 $36,625
Lifetime 12 3 1 4 $177,625

16Apr83-9OP 1⅛ :46^{2} 1:11^{3} 1:49^{2}ft *3 123 14^{25} 14^{18} 10^{16} 7^{11} Velasquez J^{1} Ark Dby 85-19 Sunny's Halo, Caveat, Exile King 14
27Mar83-11FG 1⅛ :47^{4} 1:12^{3} 1:50^{3}ft 3½ 118 7^{11} 7^{7} 4^{4} 1½ Velasquez J^{7} La Dby 91-19 BalboNtive,FoundPerlHrbor,Slewpy 8
27Mar83—Wide.
5Mar83-8SA 1 :46 1:10^{3} 1:35^{3}ft 16 116 7^{13} $7^{9\frac{3}{4}}$ 5^{8} $3^{6\frac{1}{2}}$ DlhossyE^{1} San Rafäel 83-16 Desert Wine, Naevus, BalboaNative 7
5Mar83—Fanned wide into stretch
6Feb83-5SA 1 1/16 :47 1:12^{1} 1:44^{4}m 4 118 9^{16} 8^{16} 5^{7} $1^{1\frac{1}{2}}$ Pincay L Jr^{9} Aw20000 77-19 BlboNtive,FletScrmmr,BrodwyHrry 9
9Jan83-2SA 1 1/16 :45^{3} 1:10^{1} 1:41^{3}ft *2½ 118 $8^{8\frac{1}{2}}$ $8^{9\frac{1}{2}}$ $4^{7\frac{1}{2}}$ $3^{6\frac{1}{2}}$ Toro F^{4} Aw20000 86-10 Debt, Fleet Naskra, Balboa Native 8
3Dec82-5Hol 1 1/16 :45^{1} 1:10^{1} 1:42^{4}ft 4½ 117 10^{13} $7^{5\frac{1}{2}}$ 4¾ 3^{2} Pincay L Jr^{4} Aw19000 79-20 SprDmond,DomntngDooly,BlbNtv 10
30Oct82-3SA 1 :45^{2} 1:09^{4} 1:35^{2}ft 4 117 4^{11} 4^{8} $4^{6\frac{1}{2}}$ $4^{5\frac{1}{2}}$ Romero R P^{2} Aw23000 85-10 RollANaturl,GlemMchine,SweetMn 5
16Oct82-7Kee 1 1/16 :47^{1} 1:11^{2} 1:43^{3}ft 23 121 $9^{8\frac{3}{4}}$ 9^{13} 10^{12} 9^{25} Meza R Q^{5} Brdrs' Fut 63-17 HighlandPark,Caveat,BrightBaron 12
8Sep82-8Dmr 1 :46^{1} 1:12^{2} 1:38^{4}sl 12 114 9^{13} 7^{11} 5^{10} 3^{12} VlnlPA^{9} Dmr Futurity 62-30 RovingBoy,DesertWine,BalboNtive 9
28Aug82-6Dmr 1 :46^{1} 1:11^{2} 1:37 ft 3½ 117 3½ $3^{1\frac{1}{2}}$ 3^{7} 1^{2} Valenzuela P A^{9} Mdn 83-13 Balboa Native, Brian Ke, Adolfo 10
21Aug82-6Dmr 6f :22^{3} :46 1:11^{1}ft 13 118 $5^{2\frac{1}{2}}$ $5^{3\frac{1}{4}}$ 6^{3} 2^{1} Valenzuela P A^{11} Mdn 81-12 MonsiurExcitmnt,BlboNtiv,Subsdz 12
1Aug82-6Dmr 1 :47^{3} 1:13^{1} 1:38^{2}ft 2¾ 116 2^{1} $7^{8\frac{3}{4}}$ 7^{10} 7^{18} Lipham T^{4} Mdn 58-14 TnksBriqd,Morry'sChmp,DbonirHrc 8
Apr 23 Kee 4f ft :49 b Apr 19 SA 5f m 1:04 h (d) Apr 10 SA 4f ft :48^{1} h

Chumming

Dk. b. or br. c. 3, by Alleged—Gulls Cry, by Sea-Bird
Br.—Newstead Farm (Va) 1983 6 1 1 1 $166,316
Own.—Hickory Tree Stable 126 Tr.—Stephens Woodford C 1982 4 2 1 1 $361,000
Lifetime 10 3 2 2 $527,316 Turf 1 0 0 0 $160

30Apr83-9CD 1 :46^{2} 1:11 1:37^{4}m *3-2e 116 $12^{8\frac{1}{2}}$ $11^{6\frac{1}{2}}$ $6^{7\frac{1}{2}}$ $5^{9\frac{1}{4}}$ Maple E^{12} Dby Trl 71-28 Caveat,TotalDeparture,PaxInBello 14
2Apr83-10Hia 1⅛ :47^{1} 1:11^{1} 1:49^{2}ft 9¼ 118 $6^{4\frac{1}{4}}$ 7^{5} $6^{2\frac{3}{4}}$ 2^{nk} Maple E^{9} Flamingo 85-18 CurrntHop,Chmmng,Gn'lPrcttonr 14
2Apr83—Altered course
5Mar83-11GP 1⅛ :48^{1} 1:11^{3} 1:49^{4}ft 5¾ 118 $2^{1\frac{1}{2}}$ $3^{4\frac{1}{2}}$ $4^{5\frac{1}{2}}$ $5^{6\frac{1}{4}}$ CordrAJr^{8} Flordia Dby 77-19 Croeso, Copelan, Law Talk 13
21Feb83-9GP 1 1/16 :48^{1} 1:12 1:44^{3}ft 3½ 114 $4^{3\frac{1}{4}}$ 6^{3} $5^{2\frac{1}{4}}$ 3½ Maple E^{8} Ftn Youth 77-24 HighlandPark,Thlssocrt,Chumming 9
21Feb83—Brushed; Run in two divisions 9th & 10th races
11Feb83-7GP 1 1/16 :48^{1} 1:12^{2} 1:43^{3}ft *6-5 119 3^{1} 1^{hd} 1^{1} 1½ Maple E^{7} Aw16000 83-21 Chumming, Law Talk, GameDancer 7
19Jan83-5GP a1 Ⓣ 1:37^{2}fm 6-5 119 9^{11} $7^{6\frac{1}{2}}$ $6^{6\frac{1}{2}}$ $6^{8\frac{1}{4}}$ Maple E^{2} Aw16000 84-13 Reap, Cancun, Smart Style 10
13Nov82-8Aqu 1⅛ :48^{2} 1:12^{4} 1:50^{1}gd 2¾ 115 1½ 1½ 2½ $2^{1\frac{3}{4}}$ Maple E^{1} Remsen 82-20 PxInBllo,Chumming,PrimitivPlsur 11
2Nov82-7Aqu 1 :45^{4} 1:10^{4} 1:36 ft *4-5 122 $4^{2\frac{1}{2}}$ 1½ $1^{1\frac{1}{2}}$ $1^{2\frac{3}{4}}$ Maple E^{8} Aw20000 86-16 Chumming,RisingRaj,Nshu'sHidewy 8
23Oct82-9Aqu 1 :47 1:12^{1} 1:37^{2}ft *2¾ 122 6^{3} 6^{5} $5^{5\frac{1}{2}}$ $3^{4\frac{1}{2}}$ Bailey J D^{2} Aw20000 74-21 Slew O' Gold, Last Turn,Chumming 9
8Oct82-4Bel 1 :47 1:13 1:39^{4}ft 6 118 $3^{3\frac{1}{2}}$ 3^{nk} 2^{hd} 1½ Maple E^{7} Mdn 66-25 Chumming,MomentofJoy,Tnyosho 11
May 5 CD 4f ft :48^{1} b Apr 28 CD 4f ft :48^{4} b Apr 23 Bel 1 ft 1:41 h Apr 12 OP 5f ft 1:03^{3} b

Desert Wine *

B. c. 3, by Damascus—Anne Campbell, by Never Bend
Br.—Jones B-Warnerton Farms (Ky) 1983 4 2 1 0 $166,315
Own.—Cardiff StudFarm&T90Ranch 126 Tr.—Fanning Jerry 1982 8 3 3 1 $361,000
Lifetime 12 5 4 1 $527,315

28Apr83-7Kee 1⅛ :46^{4} 1:11 1:49^{2}sy 4 121 2½ $2^{1\frac{1}{2}}$ $4^{3\frac{1}{4}}$ $3^{7\frac{1}{2}}$ McCrrnCJ^{5} Blue Grass 82-16 Play Fellow, ‡Marfa, Desert Wine 12
28Apr83—Placed second through disqualification, steadied near 3/16 pole
10Apr83-4SA 1⅛ :46 1:10^{2} 1:49^{2}ft *4-5 120 $6^{3\frac{1}{4}}$ $4^{2\frac{1}{2}}$ $7^{7\frac{1}{2}}$ $6^{9\frac{1}{4}}$ McCrrCJ^{10} S A Derby 73-19 Marfa, My Habitony, Naevus 10
10Apr83—Wide 7/8 turn
27Mar83-8SA 1 1/16 :45^{4} 1:09^{4} 1:41^{3}ft *2-3 124 1½ 1^{hd} 2^{hd} 2^{hd} McCrrCJ^{6} SanFelipeH 93-13 ‡Naevus, Desert Wine,FifthDivision 6
27Mar83—Placed first through disqualification; Bumped in stretch
5Mar83-8SA 1 :46 1:10^{3} 1:35^{3}ft *6-5 119 1½ $1^{1\frac{1}{2}}$ 1^{2} $1^{2\frac{1}{2}}$ McCrrnCJ^{3} San Rafael 90-16 Desert Wine, Naevus, BalboaNative 7
12Dec82-8Hol 1 1/16 :45^{4} 1:10^{1} 1:41^{4}ft 6½e 121 2^{hd} 3^{nk} 2^{hd} 2^{nk} McCrronCJ^{3} Hol Fut'y 86-20 RovingBoy,DesertWin,FifthDivision 9
27Nov82-8Hol 7f :21^{4} :43^{4} 1:21^{2}ft 3 122 4^{3} $4^{2\frac{1}{4}}$ 3^{4} 3^{3} OlivaresF^{2} Hol Prevue 87-14 Copelan, R. Awacs, Desert Wine 8
30Oct82-8SA 1 1/16 :45 1:09^{1} 1:41^{3}ft 3e 118 2^{hd} 1^{hd} $2^{1\frac{1}{2}}$ $2^{4\frac{1}{2}}$ Lipham T^{2} Norfolk 88-10 Roving Boy, Desert Wine, Aguila 9
6Oct82-8SA 7f :21^{4} :44^{2} 1:22^{3}ft *3-5 124 $2^{1\frac{1}{2}}$ 2^{1} 1^{hd} 1½ ShmrW^{4} Sunny Slope 87-15 Desert Wine, Aguila, Crispen 4
8Sep82-8Dmr 1 :46^{1} 1:12^{2} 1:38^{4}sl 9-5e 120 1^{3} 1½ 1½ 2½ ShmrW^{5} Dmr Futurity 73-30 RovingBoy,DesertWine,BalboNtive 9
25Aug82-8Dmr 1 :45^{4} 1:09^{4} 1:35^{2}ft *4-5 117 $2^{1\frac{1}{2}}$ 3^{2} 4^{5} — Olivares F^{5} Balboa — — Roving Boy, Encourager,FullChoke 5
25Aug82—Lost rider
17Jly82-8Hol 6f :21^{2} :44^{1} 1:09^{3}ft 2½ 116 $3^{1\frac{1}{2}}$ 3^{2} 1^{hd} $1^{6\frac{1}{2}}$ OlvrsF^{4} Hol Juv Chmp 89-10 Desert Wine, Ft. Davis, Full Choke 6
27Jun82-4Hol 5½f :22^{1} :45^{1} 1:04 ft *4-5 116 $2^{1\frac{1}{2}}$ $2^{2\frac{1}{2}}$ 2½ $1^{1\frac{1}{2}}$ Olivares F^{7} Mdn 91-12 Desert Wine,SonOfSong,BlueSeas 11
●Apr 22 Kee 5f ft :59^{4} h Apr 5 SA 6f ft 1:12^{3} h Mar 24 SA 5f ft :59^{2} b Mar 19 SA 6f ft 1:12^{4} h (d)

Law Talk

B. c. 3, by Wardlaw—Tellinoid, by Captain's Gig
Br.—Hayman & Fuentes (Fla) 1983 5 1 2 2 $52,207
Own.—Buckram Oak Farm **126** Tr.—Imperio Leonard 1982 5 1 0 2 $15,900
Lifetime 10 2 2 4 $68,107

13Apr83-1Aqu 1⅛ :483 1:123 1:504ft 2 117 67 33½ 26 27¾ Smith A Jr3 Aw23000 73-19 Slew O' Gold, Law Talk, El Cubano 6
2Apr83-8Aqu 1 :463 1:11 1:363ft *4-5 114 42 32 32½ 35¾ Samyn J L3 Gotham 77-23 Chas Conerly, ElegantLife,LawTalk 6
2Apr83—Run in Two Divisions: 7th & 8th Races; Lacked room, std
5Mar83-11GP 1⅛ :481 1:113 1:494ft 18 118 65 44½ 33½ 34¾ HrnndzC1 Flordia Dby 78-19 Croeso, Copelan, Law Talk 13
11Feb83-7GP 1$\frac{1}{16}$:481 1:122 1:433ft 3 122 65½ 32½ 21 2½ Samyn J L5 Aw16000 82-21 Chumming, Law Talk, GameDancer 7

Parfaitement

Ch. c. 3, by Halo—Double Axle, by The Axe II
Br.—Black Gates Nursery Trust (Pa) 1983 3 2 1 0 $86,058
Own.—Daney Mrs Bernard **126** Tr.—Boniface J William 1982 6 5 1 0 $71,030
Lifetime 9 7 2 0 $157,088

23Apr83-8Aqu 1⅛ :481 1:121 1:51 ft 3 126 2½ 1hd 2hd 2nk McClWH7 Wood Mem 80-24 SlewO'Gold,Prfitement,HighHonors 7
23Apr83—Run in two divisions 7th & 8th races
15Apr83-8Aqu 1 :462 1:103 1:37 ft 2½ 107 2hd 1½ 11½ 12½ Davis R G2 HcpO 81-29 Parfaitement,MouseCorps,Tumrshu 5
2Apr83-9Grd 6½f :234 :48 1:201ft *6-5 119 1hd 1hd 14 15¾ McClWH4 Woodstock 85-18 Parfitement,BgO'Bucks,NleesPoint 6
26Dec82-8Key 1$\frac{1}{16}$:482 1:133 1:471ft *2-3 119 21½ 2½ 12½ 1½ McClyWH1 Allegheny 68-30 Parfaitement, BalaGala,Jane'sPoise 6
4Dec82-8Key 6f :22 :452 1:104ft *4-5 121 34 31½ 2½ 22 Agnello A5 Dragoon 85-22 TwoDavids,Parfitement,OnionJuice 8
20Nov82-8Key 7f :222 :451 1:24 ft *2-3 122 31½ 2½ 11 18 Wilson R8 Ⓢ Pa Futy 87-21 Parfaitement,Jne'sPoise,RoylDuel 10
7Nov82-8Key 7f :224 :453 1:241ft 2½ 117 2½ 21 12 11½ Agnello A6 Freetex 86-23 Parfaitement, Jane'sPoise,BalaGala 6
23Oct82-7Key 6f :223 :462 1:13 ft *6-5 120 2hd 2hd 13 11½ Agnello A8 Aw10000 76-29 Prfitement,ChocolteDncer,GoosGrs 8
12Oct82-3Key 6f :224 :463 1:122ft 11 120 43½ 2½ 13 110 Terry J5 Ⓢ Mdn 79-29 Prfitement,JzzMster,ChckbookBrkr 7
●Mar 26 Pim 6f ft 1:14 h

Pax In Bello

B. c. 3, by Hold Your Peace—Chicanery, by Pretense
Br.—Willcox Mr-Mrs A A (Fla) 1983 3 1 1 1 $18,635
Own.—Willcox Mrs A A **126** Tr.—Jerkens Steven T 1982 9 3 3 1 $243,923
Lifetime 12 4 4 2 $262,558

30Apr83-9CD 1 :462 1:11 1:374m 2½ 122 31½ 32 2½ 3nk Fell J13 Dby Trl 80-28 Caveat,TotalDeparture,PaxInBello 14
11Apr83-9Hia 1$\frac{1}{16}$:471 1:111 1:424ft *1-9 125 12½ 14 1½ 21¾ Fell J5 ⓈD. Chappel H 87-22 Saverton, Pax InBello,FancyFriend 6
11Apr83—Wide
21Mar83-5Hia 7f :224 :451 1:224ft *2-5 118 22 2hd 12½ 12¾ Fell J5 Aw13000 89-20 PxInBello,SuperRolfe,MyBestChoic 6
13Nov82-8Aqu 1⅛ :482 1:124 1:501gd 5 113 84 42½ 1½ 11¾ Fell J9 Remsen 84-20 PxInBllo,Chumming,PrimitivPlsur 11
23Oct82-8Lrl 1$\frac{1}{16}$:463 1:123 1:45 ft 18 122 45 73¼ 44½ 21 Perret C5 Lrl Futurity 82-21 CstPrty,PxInBello,PrimitivePlesur 11
23Oct82—Blocked
16Oct82-7Med 6f :221 :453 1:103ft *4-5 116 41½ 33 22 22¾ Miranda J4 Comet 87-15 Bet Big,PaxInBello,GeminiDreamer 7
12Sep82-8Bel 7f :23 :461 1:241ft 7½ 122 53¾ 64½ 33½ 35¼ Miranda J4 Bel Fut 76-19 Copelan,Satan'sCharger,PaxInBello 6
12Sep82—Very wide
28Aug82-8Sar 6½f :221 :444 1:163ft 4½ 122 3½ 65½ 67 44½ Miranda J4 Hopeful 85-13 Copelan, Victorious, Aloha Hawaii 9
28Aug82—Jumped a shadow
14Aug82-6Sar 6f :222 :46 1:10 ft 4½ 119 41½ 1½ 13 12¾ Miranda J5 Aw19000 90-11 Pax In Bello, Thalassocrat, Savour 7
30Jly82-4Bel 5½f :223 :462 1:051ft 2½ 118 41¾ 31½ 12 11½ Miranda J8 Mdn 89-16 PaxInBello,RisingRaja,TimelyHitter 9
11Jun82-3Mth 5f :221 :453 :58 ft 2½e118 1hd 1½ 1hd 2no Lopez C5 Mdn 96-18 Truby, Pax In Bello, Dashing Duke 9
1Jun82-5Mth 5f :222 :453 :581ft 8 118 41¾ 44½ 48 59¾ Perret C8 Mdn 85-15 Pappa Riccio, Dashing Duke, Truby 8
Apr 28 CD 5f ft :594 h Apr 24 Bel 1 gd 1:46 b Apr 21 Bel tr.t 5f ft :59 h Apr 17 Bel tr.t 6f gd 1:16 b

My Mac

Dk. b. or br. g. 3, by Minnesota Mac—My Mom Nullah, by My Dad George
Br.—Royal Way Farm (Fla) 1983 5 1 0 0 $134,895
Own.—Aronow Stable **126** Tr.—Green Newcomb 1982 15 5 5 2 $72,302
Lifetime 20 6 5 2 $207,197 Turf 1 0 0 0 $2,052

16Apr83-9OP 1⅛ :462 1:113 1:492ft 5½ 123 710 46½ 67½ 58¾ MacBeth D14 Ark Dby 87-19 Sunny's Halo, Caveat, Exile King 14
2Apr83-10Hia 1⅛ :471 1:111 1:492ft 16 122 116 85½ 52¾ 72¼ MacBeth D6 Flamingo 83-18 CurrntHop,Chmmng,Gn'lPrcttonr 14
2Apr83—Steadied, blocked
5Mar83-11GP 1⅛ :481 1:113 1:494ft 14 122 118½1010 57 44¾ McBthD13 Flordia Dby 78-19 Croeso, Copelan, Law Talk 13
21Feb83-9GP 1$\frac{1}{16}$:481 1:12 1:443ft 8½ 122 85 32½ 42 4¾ MacBethD6 Ftn Youth 77-24 HighlandPark,Thlssocrt,Chumming 9
21Feb83—Run in two divisions 9th & 10th races. Wide
5Jan83-9Crc 1$\frac{1}{16}$:474 1:13 1:463ft 8½ 121 76 53½ 11 1½ McBethD8 Trp Pk Dby 86-19 My Mac, Caveat, Blink 11
18Dec82-9Crc 170 :472 1:122 1:422ft 6½ 117 79½ 410 33 22¾ MrqzC6 What A Pleas 95-13 WorldAppel,MyMc,SunnyLooking 11
30Nov82-9Crc 170 :49 1:14 1:441ft *6-5 119 33½ 21½ 21 21¼ Marquez C3 Aw14000 88-14 Sunny Looking, My Mac, Blink 5
11Nov82-9Crc a1$\frac{1}{16}$ Ⓣ 1:474fm*3-2 119 55 43 32½ 51¾ MarquezC9 Cty Miami 74-24 Blink,Disstistction,‡JudgMyBudgt 11
11Nov82—Placed fourth through disqualification
3Nov82-9Crc 1 :463 1:131 1:402ft *9-5 119 35 31½ 2hd 1nk Marquez C5 Aw20000 86-21 MyMc,Bobbi'sPlesure,FleetL'Hurux 8
16Oct82-10Crc 1$\frac{1}{16}$:474 1:134 1:473ft 15 115 65½ 41¾ 12½ 1½ MrquezC4 Fool'sh Plsr 81-20 My Mac, Blink, Judge My Budget 11
23Sep82-7Crc 6f :222 :453 1:114ft *6-5 116 2½ 1hd 12½ 11¾ Marquez C4 Aw11000 93-16 My Mac, Royality Miss,Devil'sPawn 5
13Sep82-9Crc 1 :484 1:133 1:401ft 2½ 112 32½ 31 42½ 44 Velez J A Jr6 Aw13000 83-20 Bobbi's Pleasure, Luv ALibra,Blink 6
18Aug82-9Crc 6f :221 :462 1:123ft 9-5 1077 43½ 32 33¾ 32¾ Feriole M F1 Aw10000 86-18 HelloHndsome,Bobbi'sPlsur,MyMc 5
30Jly82-8Crc 6f :22 :454 1:124ft 4¾ 1057 61½ 33 1½ 14½ Feriole M F3 Aw9500 88-17 My Mac, Gloversville, High Tracy 12
21Jly82-7Crc 5½f :222 :463 1:063ft 8½ 112 51¾ 41½ 31½ 2½ Velez J A Jr4 Aw9500 91-17 Dr. Butcher, My Mac, Top Case 7
2Jly82-5Crc 5½f :23 :471 1:064ft *8-5 114 1hd 1hd 1hd 2no Velez J A Jr1 40000 91-15 High Tracy, My Mac, Here's toPaul 6
14Jun82-5Crc 5f :224 :471 1:003ft *8-5 118 12 13 12 2½ Rocco J1 30000 88-16 What What,MyMac,FleetL'Heureux 7
7Jun82-2Crc 5f :224 :473 1:01 ft 5¾ 115 42¾ 2½ 1½ 1¾ Rocco J4 M25000 87-15 MyMac,MarkJilyne,StrikingPrince 11
28May82-4Crc 5f :233 :484 1:022sy 7 115 43½ 32 31½ 42 Baltazar C6 M25000 78-22 KeenBluffer,FncyFrind,‡TudorGnrl 9
28May82—Placed third through disqualification
20May82-3Crc 5f :232 :481 1:02 ft *6-5 115 34 34 35 46 Rocco J1 M30000 76-17 Sailor's Lad, Tudor General, Fort 7
May 2 CD 6f gd 1:132 h Mar 26 Hia 7f ft 1:282 h Mar 21 Hia 5f ft 1:032 b Mar 17 Crc 4f sy :494 h (d)

Paris Prince *

Own.—Green Dolly **126**

Ch. c. 3, by Exclusive Native—Dancers Countess, by Northern Dancer
Br.—Holtsinger Inc (Ky) 1983 5 1 1 0 $145,925
Tr.—Barrera Lazaro S 1982 7 3 1 0 $86,015
Lifetime 12 4 2 0 $231,940 Turf 1 0 0 0 $3,324

23Apr83-7GG	1⅛ :471	1:114	1:511sl	6	119	65¼	32	11	1¾	Lipham T7	Cal Derby	77-27	ParisPrince,TanksBrigade,BillyBll	12
10Apr83-4SA	1⅛ :46	1:102	1:492ft	18e	120	88¼	75¾	55	58¾	Lipham T3	S A Derby	73-19	Marfa, My Habitony, Naevus	10
23Mar83-8SA	6½f :22	:442	1:151ft	11	117	4nk	34	33	26	DelhoussyeE4	Baldwin	88-19	TotlDprtur,PrisPrinc,Morry'sChmp	9
23Feb83-8SA	6f :214	:442	1:093ft	4	120	62¼	44	41¾	58¼	DlhossyE2	Bolsa Chica	82-19	Dedicata, Maariv, Hyperborean	6
12Feb83-8SA	7f :223	:452	1:222ft	12	119	63¼	63¼	47½	45¼	DlhssyE7	San Vicente	83-14	Shecky Blue, Full Choke, Naevus	7
12Feb83—Wide throughout														
27Nov82-8Hol	7f :214	:434	1:212ft	3½	119	53½	64¼	57½	67½	PincyLJr1	Hol Prevue	82-14	Copelan, R. Awacs, Desert Wine	8
17Nov82-3Hol	6f :222	:451	1:091ft	*3-2	120	2½	2hd	11½	14	Pincay L Jr5	Aw21000	91-17	PrisPrince,RollANturl,‡SterlingSilv	7
30Oct82-8SA	1 1/16 :45	1:091	1:413ft	4	118	811	912	710	49¼	Pincay L Jr6	Norfolk	84-10	Roving Boy, Desert Wine, Aguila	9
20Oct82-8SA	1 1/16 :464	1:113	1:433ft	*7-5	117	1½	1hd	1½	12½	PincayLJr5	El Rio Rey	83-16	ParisPrince,WildAgin,Morry'sChmp	8
7Oct82-8Bel	1 1/16 Ⓣ:474	1:113	1:42 fm	3½	113	2hd	54	55½	46	VelsquzJ3	Prince John	80-14	Caveat, Fortnightly, Nivernay	7
16Sep82-8Bel	6½f :223	:461	1:181ft	13	122	21	32	31	2½	Graell A5	Aw19000	84-19	Cast Party, ParisPrince,SmartStyle	9
28Aug82-5Sar	6f :22	:453	1:113ft	*8-5	118	1hd	1hd	1½	11	Graell A2	Mdn	82-13	ParisPrince,StopCrd,ClssicMoment	8

May 5 CD 4f ft :483 b   Apr 17 SA Ⓣ 4f fm :494 h   Apr 3 SA 4f ft :474 h   Mar 18 SA 5f ft 1:00 h

Total Departure

Own.—Rebalot Stable **126**

B. c. 3, by Greek Answer—Life Style, by Manifesto
Br.—Hartigan J H (Fla) 1983 5 1 1 1 $75,569
Tr.—Lukas D Wayne 1982 8 4 0 0 $315,469
Lifetime 13 5 1 1 $391,038

30Apr83-9CD	1 :462	1:11	1:374m	3¾	122	51¾	21	1½	2hd	Velasquez J11	Dby Trl	80-28	Caveat,TotalDeparture,PaxInBello	14
10Apr83-4SA	1⅛ :46	1:102	1:492ft	3½e	120	1hd	11½	11	46¾	Pincay LJr2	S A Derby	75-20	Marfa, My Habitony, Naevus	10
23Mar83-8SA	6½f :22	:442	1:151ft	*2	117	2hd	1½	13	16	Pincay L Jr9	Baldwin	94-19	TotlDprtur,PrisPrinc,Morry'sChmp	9
19Jan83-9GP	7f :22	:443	1:232ft	*2	123	11	11½	21½	69	Fires E1	[S]Floridian H	78-20	Pure Grit, Sunny Looking, Bet Big	9
8Jan83-9GP	6f :22	:443	1:10 sy	*2-3	122	12	2hd	21	32	Fires E1	Spect'ul Bid	87-17	FreezingRin,WriteOff,TotlDeprture	9
30Oct82-8SA	1 1/16 :45	1:091	1:413ft	7	118	1hd	2hd	47½	716	McCarron CJ8	Norfolk	77-10	Roving Boy, Desert Wine, Aguila	9
9Oct82-7Bel	1 :452	1:102	1:374ft	8	122	1hd	21½	36	59¾	Fell J8	Champagne	66-25	Copelan, PappaRiccio,ElCubanaso	13
29Sep82-8Bel	7f :223	:451	1:242ft	*8-5	122	2½	2½	33½	72½	Fires E10	Cowdin	77-18	What'sDat,PappaRiccio,CastParty	11
28Aug82-8AP	7f :22	:45	1:233ft	*7-5	122	11½	12½	13½	16	Fires E3	Arlwashfut	84-21	TotlDeprture,CoxMMtt,HighlndPrk	8
11Aug82-8AP	6f :223	:46	1:111ft	7-5	124	12½	13½	13	13¾	Fires E6	Arch Ward	86-17	TotlDeprture,HighlndPrk,PssingBs	8
28Jly82-8AP	5½f :22	:454	1:044ft	*4-5	115	2½	2hd	12½	13	Fires E8	Joliet	91-24	TotalDeparture,SpreCrd,PrePlnned	9
5Jly82-8AP	5½f :214	:452	1:042ft	*3-5	115	31½	31	43½	47¾	Fires E5	Primer	85-14	GreatHunter,PssingBse,HighlndPrk	6
21Apr82-3GP	5f :223	:46	:581ft	8-5	122	13	15	17	111	Fires E12	Mdn	95-20	TotlDprtr,ProspctvFlsh,NtTwTms	12

Apr 6 SA 5f ft 1:012 h   Mar 31 SA 6f ft 1:124 h

Sunny's Halo *

Own.—D J Foster Stable **126**

Ch. c. 3, by Halo—Mostly Sunny, by Sunny
Br.—Foster D J (Ont-C) 1983 2 2 0 0 $245,190
Tr.—Cross David C Jr 1982 11 5 2 1 $235,829
Lifetime 13 7 2 1 $481,019

16Apr83-9OP	1⅛ :462	1:113	1:492ft	*3	126	15	15	14	14	DelhoussyE13	Ark Dby	96-19	Sunny's Halo, Caveat, Exile King	14
26Mar83-9OP	170 :462	1:121	1:421gd	2½	121	41¾	51¼	1hd	13	Snyder L2	Rebel H	85-15	Sunny's Halo, Sligh Jet,LeCouCou	11
26Mar83—Boxed in stretch turn														
4Nov82-6Med	1 1/16 :454	1:093	1:432ft	30	122	31	34½	47½	69	PennaD10	Yng Amer'a	83-14	Slewpy, Bet Big, El Cubanaso	11
23Oct82-8Lrl	1 1/16 :463	1:123	1:45 ft	*2¼	122	1hd	42	811	916	BrcclVJr9	Lrl Futurity	67-21	CstPrty,PxInBello,PrimitivePlesur	11
11Oct82-9WO	1⅛ :472	1:122	1:533sy	*1-4	122	14	16	16	17½	PnnD3	[S]Coro'n Fut'y	72-29	Snny'sHlo,RsngYongStr,HlbrtnHsk	8
25Sep82-9WO	1 1/16 :472	1:124	1:452sy	*1-3	123	11½	13	15	16½	Penna D1	Grey	82-28	Snny'sHlo,RsngYngStr,HrdScrmblr	9
12Sep82-9WO	7f :233	:462	1:234ft	*4-5	122	1½	11½	13½	17½	Penna D4	Swynford	90-20	Sunny'sHlo,ScrtWrd,RsngYoungStr	6
18Aug82-8Sar	6f :22	:443	1:102ft	2½	122	42½	42	55	57½	Fell J5	Sanford	80-15	Copelan, Smart Style, Safe Ground	5
21Jly82-8Bel	6f :224	:453	1:101ft	*8-5	122	33½	33½	33	32	Fell J3	Tremont	89-17	Laus'Cause,RulingGold,Sunny'sHlo	6
4Jly82-9WO	6f :221	:453	1:102ft	*6-5	114	43	3½	15	110	Penna D3	Colin	91-12	Snny'sHlo,SqrCornwll,‡MyrnsRssn	10
19Jun82-7WO	5½f :22	:454	1:053sy	2¾	115	31½	34	34½	21¾	Penna D1	[S]Clarendon	87-19	SvnStons,Sunny'sHlo,SqurCornwll	10
24May82-9WO	5f :22	:452	:581ft	2¾	117	57	411	28	28½	Penna D5	Victoria	86-18	Flying Pocket, Sunny'sHalo,Snazee	7
9May82-4WO	5f :231	:483	1:014ft	4½	120	76¼	68	44	1hd	Penna D7	[S]Mdn	77-25	Sunny'sHalo,TugO'Nr,RiseARegent	9

May 1 CD 1 sy 1:413 h   ●Apr 26 CD 1 ft 1:433 b   Apr 10 OP 1 ft 1:40 h   Apr 5 OP 6f sy 1:183 b

Explosive Wagon *

Ch. c. 3, by Explodent—Gypsy Wagon, by Conestoga

Br.—Windy City Stable (Fla) — 1983 6 3 0 1 $68,460

Own.—McReynolds Peggy — **126** — **Tr.—Norman Gene** — 1982 9 6 2 1 $82,650

Lifetime 15 9 2 2 $151,110

23Apr83-9LaD 1$\frac{1}{16}$:48^{4} 1:13^{4} 1:45^{2}sl *2-5 124 4^{nk} 1^{hd} 1^{4} 1^{4} MuellrC^{2} Hldy In Dxie 85-22 ExplosvWgon,Emprr'sClths,Hrrwgt 7

27Mar83-11FG 1⅛ :47^{4} 1:12^{3} 1:50^{3}ft *6-5 123 6^{4½} 6^{4} 5^{4} 5^{5½} Mueller C^{8} La Dby 85-19 BalboNtive,FoundPerlHrbor,Slewpy 8

27Mar83—Rank early, carried out first turn

12Mar83-10FG 1$\frac{1}{16}$:48^{2} 1:13 1:43^{4}ft *4-5 119 5^{1¾} 3^{1½} 1^{1½} 1^{5½} Mueller C^{2} Dby Trl 93-14 ExplosvWgon,HlToRom,TmrtyPrnc 7

19Feb83-10FG 1$\frac{1}{16}$:47^{2} 1:11^{4} 1:45 ft 13 116 7^{6¾} 5^{5½} 2^{hd} 1^{3} MuellrC^{8} Le Comte H 87-19 ExplosvWgon,FndPrlHrbr,PrntFrl 11

5Feb83-9FG 6f :21^{4} :45^{3} 1:11 ft 9-5 120 1^{3} 1^{2} 3^{1} 5^{6¾} Mueller C^{6} Blk Gold H 83-17 ProntoForli,OnForAunti,WillowDriv 7

15Jan83-9FG 6f :22 :45^{4} 1:11^{1}ft *1-3 122 2^{½} 1^{½} 2^{hd} 3^{4} Mueller C^{5} HcpO 85-18 ProntoForl,WllowDrv,ExplosvWgon 9

31Dec82-9FG 6f :21^{3} :45^{4} 1:11^{2}ft 2½ 119 6^{4¼} 5^{2¾} 1^{1½} 1^{4} MullrC^{3} Sugar Bowl H 88-22 ExplosvWgn,ErnstLck,Mndbgglng 10

12Dec82-5FG 6f :22^{2} :46 1:12^{2}gd *4-5 116 1^{hd} 1^{½} 1^{hd} 1^{½} Mueller C^{2} Aw11000 83-22 ExplosiveWagon,Hmlet,ChnceALot 9

17Oct82-4LaD 6½f :22^{1} :44^{3} 1:16^{1}ft *8-5 122 2^{½} 2^{hd} 1^{hd} 1^{8} Mueller C^{6} Aw17000 101-07 ExplosvWgon,ChncALot,HlToRom 12

2Oct82-9LaD 6½f :22^{3} :45^{3} 1:17 ft 9¼ 122 2^{½} 1^{1} 1^{3½} 1^{3} Mueller C^{4} Aw18000 97-09 ExplosiveWagon,WildAgin,JoeJoe 12

24Sep82-6LaD 6f :23 :46^{2} 1:12 ft *9-5 122 4^{1¼} 3^{nk} 2^{½} 1^{nk} Mueller C^{5} Aw14000 89-15 ExplosvWgon,MomntOfRlty,DblLn 12

3Sep82-9LaD 6f :23 :46^{1} 1:12 ft 2¼ 120 2^{½} 2^{2} 2^{2½} 2^{1} Mueller C^{2} Aw14000 88-12 ChncALot,ExplosvWgon,ChrlyKrk 10

27Aug82-7LaD 6f :22^{2} :45^{3} 1:12 ft 4½ 122 4^{1¼} 2^{hd} 1^{1½} 3^{2} Perrodin E J^{4} Aw15000 87-10 Mr.Stormn,Soy'sHop,ExplosvWgn 10

6Aug82-6LaD 6f :22^{3} :45^{4} 1:11^{1}ft *8-5 120 4^{1¾} 3^{3} 3^{4} 2^{4} Mueller C^{4} Aw12500 89-10 TmrtyPrnc,ExplsvWgn,SnbrndBby 11

22Jly82-5LaD 6f :22^{2} :45^{4} 1:13^{1}ft 4 120 1^{4} 1^{6} 1^{6} 1^{4½} Mueller C^{7} Mdn 83-16 ExplosvWgn,OcnKngdm,LndngChf 12

●May 5 CD 5f ft 1:00^{1} h — Apr 21 LaD 4f ft :47^{3} b — Apr 16 LaD 5f ft :58 b — Mar 25 FG 4f ft :49^{2} b

Current Hope

Ro. c. 3, by Little Current—Kahoolawe, by Warfare

Br.—Mabee Mr-Mrs J C (Ky) — 1983 5 3 1 0 $213,293

Own.—Baker & Kaskel — **126** — **Tr.—Laurin Roger** — 1982 8 2 0 2 $50,244

Li.etime 13 5 1 2 $263,537

2Apr83-10Hia 1⅛ :47^{1} 1:11^{1} 1:49^{2}ft 37 122 14^{9¼} 6^{4} 1^{½} 1^{nk} Solis A^{11} Flamingo 85-18 CurrntHop,Chmmng,Gn'lPrcttonr 14

2Apr83—Wide, driving

5Mar83-11GP 1⅛ :48^{1} 1:11^{3} 1:49^{4}ft 10 122 9^{7¾} 7^{8¼} 7^{9} 7^{10} VlsquzJ^{10} Flordia Dby 73-19 Croeso, Copelan, Law Talk 13

21Feb83-10GP 1$\frac{1}{16}$:47^{4} 1:12 1:43^{3}ft 4¼ 117 4^{5½} 2^{3} 2^{½} 2^{2¼} MacBethD^{7} Ftn Youth 81-24 Copelan, Current Hope, Blink 8

21Feb83—Run in two divisions 9th & 10th races

9Feb83-9GP 7f :22^{1} :45 1:22^{4}ft 9½ 114 13^{11} 9^{4¾} 1^{hd} 1no Solis A^{11} Hutcheson 90-24 CurrntHop,HighlndPrk,CountryPn 13

9Feb83—Lost whip

15Jan83-7GP 7f :22^{2} :45 1:23^{3}ft 3½ 114^{5} 7^{7½} 7^{7¼} 1^{3} 1^{6} Solis A^{2} Aw15000 86-20 CurrentHope,ElCubno,DerbyDouble 9

27Nov82-8Aqu 1 :46^{1} 1:12 1:37^{3}ft 13 114 8^{9¾} 4^{4} 5^{4} 6^{9¼} Fell J^{8} Nashua 69-29 IEnclose,LoosCnnon,MomntofJoy 11

4Nov82-6Med 1$\frac{1}{16}$:45^{4} 1:09^{3} 1:43^{2}ft 33 119 9^{16} 8^{11} 6^{8½} 5^{8¾} Fell J^{1} Yng Amer'a 83-14 Slewpy, Bet Big, El Cubanaso 11

23Oct82-8Lrl 1$\frac{1}{16}$:46^{3} 1:12^{3} 1:45 ft 31 122 10^{7¾} 2^{hd} 3^{2} 4^{6¾} Fell J^{8} Lrl Futurity 76-21 CstPrty,PxInBello,PrimitivePlesur 11

16Oct82-3Aqu 7f :23^{1} :47 1:24^{4}ft *6-5 117 1^{1½} 1^{1½} 1^{5} 1^{3} Cordero AJr^{1} Aw19000 77-26 CurrentHope,ProudCapitl,Ski'sHert 7

29Sep82-6Bel 7f :22^{4} :45^{3} 1:23^{3}ft 2½ 117 5^{5} 5^{2¾} 3^{2} 3^{5½} Russ M L^{3} Aw19000 78-18 WhiteBirch,GlxyGuide,CurrentHope 8

29Sep82—Forced wide

7Jly82-7Bel 5½f :22^{1} :46 1:05^{3}ft 7 115 3^{5} 3^{4½} 4^{2½} 5^{3½} Russ M L^{1} Juvenile 84-18 Victorious,NorthernIce,Laus'Cause 7

24Jun82-4Bel 6f :23 :46^{1} 1:10^{3}ft 11 118 1^{1½} 1^{1} 1^{2} 1^{4} Russ M L^{9} Mdn 89-12 CrrntHop,LgndryWlth,FlonosFllw 10

3Jun82-4Bel 5f :22^{2} :45^{3} :57^{4}ft 3½ 117 2^{2} 2^{2} 2^{4} 3^{8¼} Russ M L^{3} Mdn 97-12 What's Dat, Sluggard,CurrentHope 8

May 5 CD 4f ft :48 h — Apr 30 CD 1 sy 1:46^{4} b — Apr 25 Kee 6f gd 1:16^{3} b — Apr 18 Bel tr.t 5f ft :59^{4} h

Luv A Libra

B. c. 3, by Diplomat Way—Lip Talk, by Assagai

Br.—Farnsworth Farm (Fla) — 1983 5 0 2 0 $19,180

Own.—DeCosta Viviann & Yagoda — **126** — **Tr.—Gustines Heliodoro** — 1982 15 2 5 3 $213,638

Lifetime 20 2 7 3 $232,818

30Apr83-9CD 1 :46^{2} 1:11 1:37^{4}m 15 122 10^{8} 7^{4½} 7^{7¾} 7^{12} Fires E^{6} Dby Trl 68-28 Caveat,TotalDeparture,PaxInBello 14

2Apr83-10Hia 1⅛ :47^{1} 1:11^{1} 1:49^{2}ft 69 122 8^{4¾} 9^{6} 8^{3½} 4^{2} Fires E^{4} Flamingo 83-18 CurrntHop,Chmmng,Gn'lPrcttonr 14

2Apr83—Shuffled back

23Mar83-5Hia 7f :23 :45^{3} 1:22 ft 2½ 115 4^{2} 1^{hd} 2^{½} 2^{2} Vasquez J^{4} Aw11000 91-16 Country Pine, Luv ALibra,Tarmoud 7

12Mar83-6Hia 6f :22^{2} :45^{4} 1:11^{1}ft 4¾ 115 4^{¾} 4^{4½} 4^{1¾} 2^{hd} Alvarado V^{1} Aw11000 87-14 Sylvia's Time, Luv A Libra, Truby 8

12Mar83—Taken up

5Jan83-9Crc 1$\frac{1}{16}$:47^{4} 1:13 1:46^{3}ft 54 121 8^{7} 11^{9½} 10^{10} 10^{12} Lee M A^{2} Trp Pk Dby 74-19 My Mac, Caveat, Blink 11

18Dec82-9Crc 1^{70} :47^{2} 1:12^{2} 1:42^{2}ft 10 120 4^{6½} 6^{15} 8^{19} 9^{24} RssML^{2} What A Pleas 74-13 WorldAppel,MyMc,SunnyLooking 11

13Nov82-8Aqu 1⅛ :48^{2} 1:12^{4} 1:50^{1}gd 33 122 3^{1} 2^{½} 4^{7} 4^{9¾} Vergara O^{5} Remsen 74-20 PxInBllo,Chumming,PrimitivPlsur 11

4Nov82-6Med 1$\frac{1}{16}$:45^{4} 1:09^{3} 1:43^{2}ft 75 122 7^{11} 7^{11} 8^{16} 8^{15} Maple E^{3} Yng Amer'a 77-14 Slewpy, Bet Big, El Cubanaso 11

9Oct82-7Bel 1 :45^{2} 1:10^{2} 1:37^{4}ft 26 122 10^{12} 9^{18} 9^{17} 8^{17} Lee M A^{6} Champagne 59-25 Copelan, PappaRiccio,ElCubanaso 13

25Sep82-9Crc 1$\frac{1}{16}$:48^{1} 1:13^{4} 1:47^{4}ft 7 120 6^{3¾} 5^{3¼} 2^{1½} 1^{nk} LeeMA^{1} [S]Fla Stallion 80-15 Luv A Libra, Blink, El Kaiser 14

13Sep82-9Crc 1 :48^{4} 1:13^{3} 1:40^{1}ft *1 112 2^{½} 2^{½} 2^{hd} 2no Aviles O B^{4} Aw13000 87-20 Bobbi's Pleasure, Luv ALibra,Blink 6

28Aug82-9Crc 6f :21^{2} :45^{2} 1:12 ft 21 118 8^{7½} 5^{9} 5^{4¾} 2^{3½} LeeMA^{2} [S]Fla Stallion 88-10 El Kaiser, Luv A Libra, Blink 11

20Aug82-9Crc 6f :22^{1} :46^{1} 1:12^{4}ft *6-5 114 5^{4½} 4^{4½} 4^{1¾} 2^{1} Lee M A^{4} Aw9500 87-19 King Billy, Luv A Libra, Top Case 7

31Jly82-9Crc 5½f :22^{1} :46^{1} 1:05^{3}ft 46 116 8^{6¾} 9^{7¾} 6^{6¾} 5^{6½} LeeMA^{6} [S]Fla Stallion 90-15 ElKiser,NightMover,HelloHndsom 13

10Jly82-9Crc 5½f :22 :45^{4} 1:05 ft 24 113 5^{7½} 5^{7¼} 5^{3¼} 3^{5¼} Lee M A^{2} Criterium 95-11 El Kaiser, Night Mover, LuvALibra 6

28Jun82-5Crc 5½f :22^{4} :47^{3} 1:07^{3}ft 2¾e 115 5^{4} 3^{2½} 1^{2} 1^{4½} Lee M A^{2} Mdn 87-20 LuvALibr,MonsieurNsty,‡DrvishHro 9

9Jun82-4Crc 5f :22^{4} :46 1:00 ft 10 115 5^{3} 4^{6} 4^{5¼} 2^{6½} Danjean R^{7} Mdn 85-24 NightMover,LuvALibr,Gloversville 10

27May82-2Crc 5f :22^{4} :47^{1} 1:01^{1}sy *3-5 115 3^{4½} 3^{6} 3^{5} 2^{½} Aviles O B^{6} M40000 85-20 CrowningWish,LuvALibr,Km'sDlvry 7

17May82-6Crc 5f :22^{4} :47^{3} 1:01^{1}ft *2½ 115 3^{3} 4^{5½} 4^{2} 3^{1½} Danjean R^{1} Mdn 84-17 Bobbi'sPlesur,Glovrsvill,LuvALibr 12

30Apr82-3GP 5f :23 :47 :59^{2}gd 6 122 2^{½} 2^{hd} 2^{1½} 3^{3½} Londono O J^{3} Mdn 85-18 Cordon, Gun Carriage, Luv A Libra 8

May 5 CD 4f ft :50^{2} b — Apr 29 CD 3f sy :38^{1} b — Apr 24 Hia 5f sy :59^{2} b — Apr 20 Hia 6f ft 1:13^{3} h

Marfa *

Gr. c. 3, by Foolish Pleasure—Gray Matter, by Stratmat
Br.—Gentry T (Ky) 1983 9 3 3 0 $384,544
Own.—French Jr, Beal & Lukas 126 Tr.—Lukas D Wayne 1982 2 M 0 1 $2,400
Lifetime 11 3 3 1 $386,944

28Apr83-7Kee 1⅛ :464 1:11 1:492sy *3-2 121 69½ 56 2hd 2no† VelsquezJ7 Blue Grass 90-16 Play Fellow, ‡Marfa, Desert Wine 12
†28Apr83—Disqualified and placed fourth, bore in upper stretch
10Apr83-4SA 1⅛ :46 1:102 1:492ft 3½e120 78¼ 65½ 31½ 13 VelsquezJ7 S A Derby 82-19 Marfa, My Habitony, Naevus 10
26Mar83-9Lat 1 1/16 :461 1:103 1:422ft *3½ 120 46 31½ 1hd 18 Velasquez J10 Spiral 98-24 Marfa, Noble Home, Hail ToRome 12
26Mar83—Daily Racing Form Time 1:44 1/5; Lugged in
16Mar83-8SA 1 1/16 :461 1:104 1:423ft *2 117 84¾ 84½ 56½ 45½ PincayLJr7 S Catalina 82-17 FastPassge,Hyperboren,MyHbitony 8
16Mar83—Forced wide 7/8 turn, lugged in through stretch
6Mar83-5SA 1 1/16 :46 1:104 1:433ft 5½ 120 76¾ 54¼ 2hd 2nk Toro F7 Aw20000 83-17 Silent Fox, Marfa,LouisvilleSummit 9
6Mar83—Wide 3/8 turn lugged in through stretch; Broke slowly
13Feb83-6SA 1 1/16 :463 1:112 1:432ft 4 118 43 11 15 13½ Toro F10 Mdn 84-12 Marfa, Blue Seas, Gato Montes 12
13Feb83—Off poorly wide
30Jan83-4SA 7f :221 :451 1:244gd 2¼ 118 35 31½ 2½ 2no Toro F4 Mdn 76-22 Added Feature, Marfa, Flint Fire 7
9Jan83-6SA 1 1/16 :461 1:104 1:414ft 3¼ 118 66½ 53½ 55¼ 56 Toro F8 Mdn 86-09 Major Henry, Fast Screen,BlueSeas 8
1Jan83-4SA 6f :213 :444 1:094ft 7¼ 118 912 911 75¼ 22 Pincay L Jr3 Mdn 87-11 Fast Passage, Marfa, Viron 10
7Nov82-6Hol 1 1/16 :471 1:114 1:44 ft 7¼ 118 52¼ 31½ 32 34½ Pincay L Jr2 Mdn 70-20 EminentLad,RightOnCenter,Marfa 10
17Oct82-6SA 1 1/16 :461 1:104 1:422ft 4¼ 117 51¾ 53¾ 710 825 Pincay L Jr7 Mdn 64-09 FfthDvson,SomthngByond,Estpnd 10
Apr 22 Kee 5f ft 1:001 b Apr 4 SA 5f ft 1:013 h

Highland Park *

Ch. c. 3, by Raise a Native—Old Goat, by Olden Times
Br.—Bwamazon Farm (Ky) 1983 4 2 1 0 $76,648
Own.—Bwamazon Farm & Jones 126 Tr.—Basile Anthony 1982 11 6 2 3 $306,210
Lifetime 15 8 3 3 $382,858

28Apr83-7Kee 1⅛ :464 1:11 1:492sy 2¾e121 33½ 34½ 68¼ 715 BrumfldD6 Blue Grass 75-16 Play Fellow, ‡Marfa, Desert Wine 12
19Apr83-7Kee 1 1/16 :471 1:112 1:444ft *1-3 123 32 2hd 1hd 1no Vasquez J3 Aw28000 82-18 HighlandPrk,PssingBse,RomnForce 8
21Feb83-9GP 1 1/16 :481 1:12 1:443ft *2-3 122 2hd 2hd 1½ 1nk BrumfildD9 Ftn Youth 78-24 HighlandPark,Thlssocrt,Chumming 9
21Feb83—Run in two divisions 9th & 10th races
9Feb83-9GP 7f :221 :45 1:224ft *9-5 122 61 31½ 2hd 2no BrumfildD9 Hutcheson 90-24 CurrntHop,HighlndPrk,CountryPn 13
20Nov82-8CD 1 1/16 :50 1:143 1:47 sy *3-5 122 22 22 21½ 13¼ BrumfildD2 Jcky Club 73-26 Highland Park,CoaxMeMatt,Caveat 5
6Nov82-8CD 1 :464 1:112 1:381ft *2-5 122 31 2½ 11½ 16 Brumfield D7 Iroquois 78-24 HighlandPark,CoxMeMtt,WhiteFig 8
16Oct82-7Kee 1 1/16 :471 1:112 1:433ft 2¾ 121 3½ 2hd 2hd 1no Lively J10 Brdrs' Fut 88-17 HighlandPark,Caveat,BrightBaron 12
9Oct82-6Kee a7f 1:283sy *6-5 123 1hd 11 12 14½ Brumfield D2 Aw28200 80-22 HighlndPrk,WillowDrv,RunForGrco 6
28Aug82-8AP 7f :22 :45 1:233ft 9½ 122 52¼ 43½ 35½ 36½ RomrRP8 Ap Wsh Fut 77-21 TotlDeprture,CoxMMtt,HighlndPrk 8
11Aug82-8AP 6f :223 :46 1:111ft 3 124 33 35 23 23¾ RomroRP3 Arch Ward 82-17 TotlDeprture,HighlndPrk,PssingBs 8
23Jly82-8Aks 6f :22 :45 1:11 ft *7-5 113 42 2½ 1½ 12½ Romero R P6 Juvenile 82-20 HighlandPark,HandStand,TriSwps 10
5Jly82-8AP 5½f :214 :452 1:042ft 2½e115 52¼ 52¼ 22 3¾ Romero R P3 Primer 92-14 GreatHunter,PssingBse,HighlndPrk 6
30May82-3AP 5f :223 :463 :591ft 9-5 122 11 11½ 12½ 17 Fires E3 Mdn 90-23 HighlandPark,SpareCard,FinalFight 7
20Apr82-3Kee 4½f :223 :454 :52 ft 2 118 4 2hd 21 23 Brumfield D2 Mdn 92-05 BoldUprsng,HghlndPrk,KntnLndng 8
3Apr82-3Kee 4½f :222 :464 :531gd *6-5 119 4 52¼ 32 31¾ Brumfield D5 Mdn 87-11 It'sDewn,HppinessRod,HighlndPrk 11
May 5 CD 4f ft :48 h Apr 25 Kee 5f gd 1:013 b ●Apr 18 Kee 3f ft :35 h ●Apr 14 Kee 1 ft 1:422 h

Caveat *

Dk. b. or br. c. 3, by Cannonade—Cold Hearted, by The Axe II
Br.—Ryehill Farm (MD) 1983 7 1 3 0 $144,458
Own.—Belmont A et al 126 Tr.—Stephens Woodford C 1982 11 3 3 3 $133,432
Lifetime 18 4 6 3 $277,890 Turf 5 3 2 0 $78,656

30Apr83-9CD 1 :462 1:11 1:374m *3-2e122 138¾137 43½ 1hd Pincay L Jr9 Dby Trl 80-28 Caveat,TotalDeparture,PaxInBello 14
16Apr83-9OP 1⅛ :462 1:113 1:492ft 8¾ 120 1319 1012 35½ 24 Maple E11 Ark Dby 92-19 Sunny's Halo, Caveat, Exile King 14
16Apr83—Bumped soundly at 3/8 pole
6Apr83-9OP 1 1/16 :482 1:141 1:45 ft 8-5 116 44 43 2hd 2hd Maple S3 Aw30000 83-26 Exile King, Caveat, Sligh Jet 5
19Mar83-10Hia 1⅛ :453 1:093 1:484ft 4¾ 114 64½ 43½ 42 41 Maple E1 Everglades 87-18 Gn'lPrcttnr,OhMyWndlnd,PlyFllw 12
19Mar83—Hit by whip
5Mar83-11GP 1⅛ :481 1:113 1:494ft 22 122 1210 1112 913 1016 Maple E11 Flordia Dby 67-19 Croeso, Copelan, Law Talk 13
21Feb83-10GP 1 1/16 :474 1:12 1:433ft 3½ 117 57 65¼ 46 58½ Maple E6 Ftn Youth 74-24 Copelan, Current Hope, Blink 8
21Feb83—Bumped; Run in two divisions 9th & 10th races
5Jan83-9Crc 1 1/16 :474 1:13 1:463ft 4 121 1010 96¾ 43 2½ Maple E9 Trp Pk Dby 85-19 My Mac, Caveat, Blink 11
29Dec82-9Crc 7f :222 :453 1:253ft *2-5 119 65 57½ 37½ 35¼ Brumfield D2 Aw20000 83-17 Gn'lPrcttonr,Morgnmorgnmrgn,Cvt 7
27Nov82-8Lrl 1 1/16 :474 1:134 1:451ft *1 122 86 64½ 21 31¼ MplE4 Ⓢ Maryland Juv 81-26 DixielndBnd,DeputedTestmony,Cvt 9
20Nov82-8CD 1 1/16 :50 1:143 1:47 sy 7-5 122 43 33 32 36 Maple E3 Jcky Club 67-26 Highland Park,CoaxMeMatt,Caveat 5
25Oct82-8Aqu 1⅛ Ⓣ:502 1:162 1:573sf *3-2 122 87 62 2hd 2hd Maple E1 Pilgrim 56-56 Fortnightly,Cavet,DomintingDooley 8
16Oct82-7Kee 1 1/16 :471 1:112 1:433ft 2 121 84¾ 63¼ 1hd 2no Maple E2 Brdrs' Fut 88-17 HighlandPark,Caveat,BrightBaron 12
7Oct82-8Bel 1 1/16 Ⓣ:474 1:113 1:42 fm 2¾ 117 53 31½ 1½ 12 Maple E1 Prince John 86-14 Caveat, Fortnightly, Nivernay 7
10Sep82-9Bel 1 Ⓣ:461 1:111 1:35 fm *9-5 119 64 41 2½ 1no Maple E7 Aw20000 90-12 Caveat,LoverBoyLeslie,ElCubanso 11
10Aug82-9Sar 1 Ⓣ:502 1:152 1:404yl *2 118 85½ 2hd 14 19 Maple E4 Mdn 72-28 Caveat, Sobieski, So Intent 10
16Jly82-4Bel 7f Ⓣ:231 :462 1:252fm 3½e118 41½ 43½ 2½ 2nk Bailey J D6 Mdn 77-18 Bartow, Caveat, Upper Court 12
9Jly82-4Bel 6f :224 :463 1:113ft 4e118 1½ 41½ 68½ 614 Maple E1 Mdn 70-22 CthdrlAsl,DomntngDly,NghtTmBg 11
18Jun82-4Bel 5f :223 :462 :591ft 2¼ 118 54¼ 53¾ 53 56 Cordero A Jr7 Mdn 92-15 PrimitivePlesure,CthdrlAisl,Lutyns 8
May 5 CD 4f ft :493 b Apr 28 CD 4f ft :51 b Apr 23 Bel 6f ft 1:114 h ●Apr 13 OP 4f sy :474 h

The chart of the race was as follows:

109th Kentucky Derby

EIGHTH RACE
Churchill
MAY 7, 1983

1 ¼ MILES. (1.59$\frac{2}{5}$) 109th Running KENTUCKY DERBY (Grade I). Purse $250,000 added. 3-year-olds. By subscription of $200 each. All nomination fees to the winner, $5,000 to pass the entry box, $5,000 additional to start, with $250,000 added of which $60,000 to second, $30,000 to third and $15,000 to fourth (to be divided equally in the event of a dead heat). Weight 126 lbs. Starters to be named through the entry box Thursday, May 5, at usual time of closing. The maximum number of starters for the Kentucky Derby will be limited to twenty. In the event more than twenty entries pass through the entry box at the time of closing, the twenty starters and up to eight also eligibles will be determined at that time with preference given to those horses that have accumulated the highest earnings. Should any entry be withdrawn from the starting field prior to 4 p.m. scratch time, Friday, May 6, vacancies will be filled from the also eligible list and placed in the outside post positions in order of preference. For those that pass the entry box and are eliminated under this condition the entry fee will be refunded. Gold trophy to the winning owner. Closed with 405 nominations Tuesday, February 15, 1983.
Value of race $531,000, value to winner $426,000, second $60,000, third $30,000, fourth $15,000. Mutuel pool $5,546,977.

Last Raced	Horse	Eqt.	A.	Wt	PP	¼	½	¾	1	Str	Fin	Jockey	Odds $1
16Apr83 ^{9}OP^{1}	Sunny's Halo		3	126	10	2^{hd}	$2^{\frac{1}{2}}$	$1^{\frac{1}{2}}$	1^{hd}	$1^{\frac{1}{2}}$	1^{2}	Delahoussaye E	2.50
28Apr83 ^{7}Kee^{2}	Desert Wine		3	126	5	$3^{1\frac{1}{2}}$	3^{3}	3^{hd}	$2^{1\frac{1}{2}}$	$2^{2\frac{1}{2}}$	2^{nk}	McCarron C J	15.90
30Apr83 ^{9}CD^{1}	Caveat	b	3	126	20	$16^{2\frac{1}{2}}$	$17^{1\frac{1}{2}}$	15^{1}	11^{hd}	$7^{1\frac{1}{2}}$	3^{1}	Pincay L Jr	b-6.70
23Apr83 ^{8}Aqu^{1}	Slew O' Gold		3	126	1	$7^{\frac{1}{2}}$	7^{2}	6^{2}	7^{hd}	3^{hd}	4^{nk}	Cordero A Jr	10.10
28Apr83 ^{7}Kee^{4}	Marfa	b	3	126	18	$13^{\frac{1}{2}}$	14^{2}	$14^{1\frac{1}{2}}$	8^{1}	$4^{1\frac{1}{2}}$	5^{1}	Velasquez J	a-2.40
28Apr83 ^{7}Kee^{1}	Play Fellow	b	3	126	2	11^{2}	10^{hd}	$10^{\frac{1}{2}}$	6^{1}	$5^{\frac{1}{2}}$	6^{2}	Cruguet J	10.90
30Apr83 ^{9}CD^{3}	Pax In Bello		3	126	14	8^{hd}	$9^{1\frac{1}{2}}$	$8^{\frac{1}{2}}$	$9^{1\frac{1}{2}}$	6^{hd}	7^{hd}	Fell J	24.40
23Apr83 ^{7}Aqu^{2}	Country Pine		3	126	7	12^{1}	$12^{1\frac{1}{2}}$	$11^{1\frac{1}{2}}$	$10^{\frac{1}{2}}$	$9^{2\frac{1}{2}}$	$8^{2\frac{1}{2}}$	Venezia M	47.40
16Apr83 ^{9}OP^{7}	Balboa Native	b	3	126	3	$19^{\frac{1}{2}}$	16^{hd}	18^{1}	$18^{1\frac{1}{2}}$	14^{hd}	9^{nk}	Hawley S	a-2.40
23Apr83 ^{7}GG^{1}	Paris Prince	b	3	126	16	$9^{1\frac{1}{2}}$	8^{hd}	7^{1}	5^{1}	$8^{1\frac{1}{2}}$	10^{2}	Lipham T	f-10.90
2Apr83 ^{10}Hia^{1}	Current Hope		3	126	12	$18^{\frac{1}{2}}$	20	19^{hd}	17^{1}	$10^{1\frac{1}{2}}$	11^{nk}	Solis A	18.30
30Apr83 ^{9}CD^{5}	Chumming		3	126	4	20	18^{1}	20	19^{1}	13^{2}	12^{nk}	Maple E	b-6.70
28Apr83 ^{7}Kee^{5}	Freezing Rain		3	126	8	17^{2}	$19^{\frac{1}{2}}$	17^{1}	$16^{1\frac{1}{2}}$	$16^{2\frac{1}{2}}$	13^{hd}	Gavidia W	c-23.50
16Apr83 ^{9}OP^{5}	My Mac	b	3	126	15	14^{hd}	15^{3}	16^{1}	15^{hd}	$11^{\frac{1}{2}}$	14^{4}	MacBeth D	f-10.90
23Apr83 ^{9}LaD^{1}	Explosive Wagon		3	126	11	10^{hd}	$11^{1\frac{1}{2}}$	12^{1}	14^{2}	15^{2}	15^{1}	Mueller C	f-10.90
23Apr83 ^{8}Aqu^{2}	Parfaitement		3	126	13	$6^{1\frac{1}{2}}$	6^{1}	$5^{\frac{1}{2}}$	$4^{\frac{1}{2}}$	$12^{\frac{1}{2}}$	16^{2}	McCauley W H	41.20
28Apr83 ^{7}Kee^{7}	Highland Park	b	3	126	19	5^{hd}	5^{2}	$4^{1\frac{1}{2}}$	$3^{1\frac{1}{2}}$	17^{1}	17^{hd}	Brumfield D	c-23.50
30Apr83 ^{9}CD^{7}	Luv A Libra		3	126	17	4^{hd}	4^{hd}	9^{1}	12^{1}	19^{6}	18^{2}	Espinoza J C	f-10.90
13Apr83 ^{1}Aqu^{2}	Law Talk		3	126	6	15^{2}	13^{hd}	13^{1}	13^{1}	$18^{1\frac{1}{2}}$	19^{15}	Marquez C	f-10.90
30Apr83 ^{9}CD^{2}	Total Departure		3	126	9	$1^{\frac{1}{2}}$	$1^{1\frac{1}{2}}$	2^{1}	20	20	20	Valenzuela P A	a-2.40

a–Coupled: Marfa, Balboa Native and Total Departure; b–Caveat and Chumming; c–Freezing Rain and Highland Park. f—Mutuel field.

OFF AT 5:40. Start good, Won driving. Time, :23$\frac{4}{5}$, :47$\frac{1}{5}$, 1:11$\frac{4}{5}$, 1:36$\frac{4}{5}$, 2:02$\frac{1}{5}$ Track fast.

$2 Mutuel Prices:			
8–SUNNY'S HALO	7.00	4.80	4.00
6–DESERT WINE		12.20	9.80
2–CAVEAT (b–entry)			5.20

Ch. c, by Halo—Mostly Sunny, by Sunny. Trainer Cross David C Jr. Bred by Foster D J (Ont–C).

SUNNY'S HALO, rating kindly from the beginning, assumed command on his own courage in the backstretch, drew away from DESERT WINE under a hand ride in the upper stretch and maintained his margin under steady right-hand urging the final furlong. DESERT WINE stalked SUNNY'S HALO from the outside, could not stay with SUNNY'S HALO after drawing on even terms with him just before the quarter-pole, but continued resolutely under left-hand urging and held off CAVEAT's late bid for the place. CAVEAT, taken in hand and eased toward the inside for a saving of ground after the start, was forced extremely wide rallying around CURRENT HOPE into the stretch and closed steadily in a very good effort. SLEW O' GOLD, bothered slightly by PLAY FELLOW at the start, saved ground most of the way and bested MARFA in a duel with that rival through the homestretch. MARFA relaxed outside horses off of the pace, maintained a straight course under a left-hand whip in the stretch drive and lacked a sufficient response. PLAY FELLOW, in good position behind the first flight, was hanging when jockey Cruguet misjudged the finish line and rose for a stride at the sixteenth marker, and finished out evenly. PAX IN BELLO had a clear run at the leaders along the rail for the drive and failed to respond. COUNTRY PINE gave an even effort. BALBOA NATIVE made up some ground belatedly. PARIS PRINCE stayed outside rivals and tired. CURRENT HOPE was steered very wide for the stretch run. CHUMMING gave a dull effort. FREEZING RAIN was not a serious factor. MY MAC was outrun. EXPLOSIVE WAGON tired. PARFAITEMENT lost ground outside the first flight and faltered. HIGHLAND PARK stayed outside SUNNY'S HALO and DESERT WINE into the final turn before giving way. LUV A LIBRA was used up early. LAW TALK showed nothing. TOTAL DEPARTURE, brushed by SUNNY'S HALO at the start, stopped after going three-quarters in a race remarkably free of trouble for the size of the field.

Owners— 1, D J Foster Racing Stable; 2, Cardiff Stud & T 90 Ranch; 3, Belmont A et al; 4, Equusequity Stable; 5, Beal & French Jr & Lukas; 6, Vanier Nancy & Lauer & Victor; 7, Willcox Mrs A A; 8, Galbreath D M; 9, Spreen R H; 10, Green Dolly; 11, Baker & Kaskel; 12, Hickory Tree Stable; 13, Bwamazon Farm; 14, Aronow Stable; 15, McReynolds Peggy; 16, Daney Mrs Bernard; 17, Bwamazon Farm & Jones; 18, DeCosta Viviann & Yagoda; 19, Buckram Oak Farm; 20, Rebalot Stable.

Delahoussaye ran a perfect race with Sunny's Halo and beat the fading Desert Wine by two lengths. Sunny's Halo won the $426,000 first prize and racing immortality. It was a great day for trainer Cross and the owner, Toronto stockbroker Pud Foster. Mrs. Cross won $20,000 on her bet. Desert Wine held on for second, just edging out the late-charging Caveat and Slew O' Gold. Marfa had a charge at the mile pole but was unable to challenge the leaders. He was never a factor in the race. It is interesting that the top five finishers were ridden by the top five jockeys listed in Table 12.1. The three California leaders, Pincay, McCarron, and Delahoussaye, finished three-two-one. Delahoussaye had turned in a rare double, complementing his win in 1982 with Gato Del Sol. He also had a second on the 34—1 shot Woodhopper in 1981. Sunny's Halo paid a handsome $4.00 to show, so our bet of $87 was doubled. With my $50 win bet subtracted, our profit was $37.

It Was Never like This in Louisiana

The ninth race was a $1\frac{1}{16}$-mile claiming race for four-year-olds and upward for a purse of $10,000. The field of eight horses included the entry of Dust Off the Mat and Broadway Review. Although Sway, Sorroto, and Major Run were the top choices, the field was wide open. The remaining starters, Bal Bay, Davrick, and Bell Swinger, as well as the entry, looked like tough competition. The extent of the competition and the evenness of the field were borne out by the fact that the morning-line odds varied only within the narrow range of 5—2 to 8—1.

Sway appealed to me. He had won the most money per career start; was recently claimed twice; had finished second in his last start at this distance, running against $50,000 claimers who were superior to today's $35,000 claimers; and he was a very consistent horse, having finished in the money in his last eleven starts and twenty-seven times out of thirty-two career starts. Although consistent, his speed ratings were not really superior to his competition. For example, at Keeneland both Broadway Review and Sorroto had recently run 85s at today's distance, while Sway's second at Oaklawn Park was an 82. It is, of course, difficult to compare speed ratings across days and tracks, but the message was clear: Sway looked good and he liked to be in there close, but I would bet only if the odds were good. They were.

WIN	PLACE	SHOW

1 1/16 MILES

START ▲ ▲ FINISH

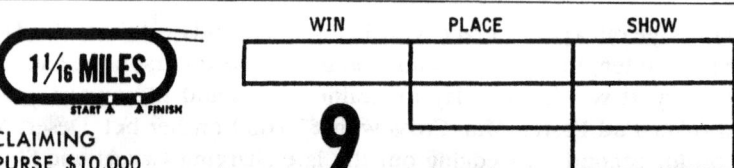

CLAIMING
PURSE $10,000

9

FOUR-YEAR-OLDS AND UPWARD, 123 lbs. Non-winners of two races at a mile or over since March 7 allowed 2 lbs.; one such race since April 7, 4 lbs.; two such races since January 7, 6 lbs. Claiming Price, $35,000; for each $1,000 to $30,000, 1 lb. (Races where entered for $27,500 or less not considered.)

Track Record—YES SIR (5) 110 lbs.; 1:41 3/5; Nov. 25, 1970

MAKE SELECTION BY NUMBER

No.	Owner / Silks / Horse / Weight / Breeding	Trainer	Jockey/Morn. Line
1	GEORGE A. ZIMMERMAN White, Blue Sash, White Chevrons on Blue Sleeves White Cap **DUST OFF THE MAT** 121 B.g.(1979), Run Dusty Run—Somersault	JAMES E. MORGAN	4 WILLIAM GAVIDIA (Post Pos. 2) $35,000
1a	MRS. W. L. LYONS BROWN Turquoise and White Quarters, Turquoise Band on White Sleeves, Turquoise Cap **BROADWAY REVIEW** 121 Ch.c.(1978), Reviewer—Veroushka	JAMES E. MORGAN	4 WILLIAM GAVIDIA (Post Pos. 8) $35,000
2	FARID SEFA Red, Yellow "S" Red Cap **BAL BAY** 117 B.g.(1975), Vertex—Marsh Harbour	LARRY D. EDWARDS	5 DON BRUMFIELD (Post Pos. 1) $35,000
3	GOLDEN CHANCE FARM (Verna Lehmann) Gold, Red "GCF," Red Chevron on Sleeves, Gold Cap **MAJOR RUN** 117 B.g.(1977), Lt. Stevens—Running Beauty	W. E. ADAMS	8 GERLAND GALLITANO (Post Pos. 3) $35,000
4	DONAMIRE FARM (Don Ball) White, Black Circled "DM," Black Yoke, White Bars on Black Sleeves, White Cap **SORROTO** 117 Dk.b. or br.h.(1977), Going Straight—Jeroy	MIKE BALL	7-2 JULIO ESPINOZA (Post Pos. 4) $35,000
5	W. C. PARTEE Orange, White Dots Orange Cap **SWAY** 117 Ch.g.(1977), High Tribute—Miss Sway	LYNN WHITING	5-2 GARTH PATTERSON (Post Pos. 5) $35,000
6	HERVE RACEVITCH Orange, Black Sash Black Cap **DAVRICK** 117 Ch.g.(1979), Groshawk—Tally	JUDITH ZOUCK	8 LEROY MOYERS (Post Pos. 6) $35,000
7	A. J. FOYT, JR. Orange, White "AJ," Black Blocks on White Sleeves Orange Cap **BELL SWINGER** 117 Ch.h.(1978), His Majesty—Brilliant Thought	A. J. FOYT III	5 LARRY MELANCON (Post Pos. 7) $35,000

1 and 1a—GEORGE A. ZIMMERMAN—MRS. W. L. LYONS BROWN Entry

Selections 5—4—1a—2

Sway was made an 8—5 favorite, and the tote board read as follows:

	Totals	#5 Sway	Expected Value per Dollar Bet on Sway
With five minutes to post time			
Odds		8—5	
Win	263,172	82,933	
Show	78,790	18,477	1.10
With one minute to post time			
Odds		8—5	
Win	309,244	87,900	
Show	96,649	20,194	1.11

With our betting fortune of $1,531.70, we bet $91 on Sway to show.

	Totals	#5 Sway	Expected Value per Dollar Bet on Sway
At post time			
Odds		8—5	
Win	328,700	94,398	
Show	102,009	22,468	1.09

Derby Day brings out individuals of many types searching for a day of excitement, some fun, and (hopefully) some winnings. Many want to make a big killing. Close to where we were standing, a fellow from Louisiana was talking about his troubles that day. Going into the ninth race he was about $5,000 behind in his bets. The entry of Dust Off the Mat and Broadway Review at 5—2 looked like it would get him even with a $2,000 win bet. With two good horses, it seemed to be a good bet, so he made it. Things looked good for him when Broadway Review, number 1A, crossed the finish line first. Unfortunately for the man from Louisiana, Don Brumfield, the jockey on the second-place finisher, Bal Bay, claimed foul, and the claim was allowed. It was the second time that day a winner had been disqualified, and he complained that he had had both of them. This reversal did not sit well with the man from Louisiana, who saw his big gain back to even go up in smoke. He rushed out of the track quite angry over his $7,000 loss on the day, yelling that the races were fixed in Kentucky and vowing to never return.

Sway did manage to take third and pay $2.80 for show, so we won our Dr. Z system bet. The chart of the race was as follows:

NINTH RACE
Churchill
MAY 7, 1983

1 $\frac{1}{16}$ MILES. (1.41⅗) CLAIMING. Purse $10,000. 4-year-olds and upward. Weight, 123 lbs. Non-winners of two races at a mile or over since March 7 allowed 2 lbs.; one such race since April 7, 4 lbs.; two such races since January 7, 6 lbs. Claiming price, $35,000; for each $1,000 to $30,000 allowed 1 lbs. (Races where entered for $27,500 or less no considered.)

Value of race $10,000, value to winner $6,500, second $2,000, third $1,000, fourth $500. Mutuel pool $563,224.

Last Raced	Horse	Eqt.	A.	Wt	PP	St	¼	½	¾	Str	Fin	Jockey	Cl'g Pr	Odds $1
28Apr83 ^{4}Kee^{1}	[D]Broadway Review		5	121	8	8	8	8	8	3^{hd}	1^{hd}	Gavidia W	35000	a-2.90
19Mar83 ^{10}OP^{7}	Bal Bay		8	117	1	6	5^{4}	5^{3}	$4^{\frac{1}{2}}$	5^{2}	2^{hd}	Brumfield D	35000	7.70
16Apr83 ^{5}OP^{2}	Sway		6	117	5	3	2^{hd}	$2^{\frac{1}{2}}$	$1^{1\frac{1}{2}}$	1^{hd}	$3^{\frac{3}{4}}$	Patterson G	35000	1.70
19Apr83 ^{8}Kee^{2}	Sorroto	b	6	117	4	4	$3^{\frac{1}{2}}$	3^{2}	$2^{1\frac{1}{2}}$	$2^{1\frac{1}{2}}$	4^{1}	Espinoza J C	35000	3.60
15Apr83 ^{7}Kee^{3}	Bell Swinger		5	117	7	7	7^{3}	7^{3}	$6^{1\frac{1}{2}}$	$4^{1\frac{1}{2}}$	5^{3}	Melancon L	35000	8.10
19Apr83 ^{8}Kee^{6}	Davrick	b	4	117	6	5	4^{4}	4^{2}	$5^{\frac{1}{2}}$	7^{6}	$6^{2\frac{1}{2}}$	Moyers L	35000	18.20
28Apr83 ^{4}Kee^{2}	Major Run	b	6	117	3	2	1^{hd}	1^{hd}	$3^{\frac{1}{2}}$	6^{hd}	7^{13}	Gallitano G	35000	12.00
19Apr83 ^{8}Kee^{4}	Dust Off the Mat		4	121	2	1	$6^{1\frac{1}{2}}$	$6^{1\frac{1}{2}}$	$7^{1\frac{1}{2}}$	8	8	McKnight J	35000	a-2.90

[D]–Broadway Review Disqualified and placed second.
a–Coupled: Broadway Review and Dust Off the Mat.

OFF AT 6:50. Start good. Won driving. Time, :25⅕, :49, 1:13⅖, 1:39⅘, 1:46⅗ Track sloppy.

$2 Mutuel Prices:			
2–BAL BAY	17.40	6.40	3.60
1–BROADWAY REVIEW (a–entry)		4.20	2.80
5–SWAY			2.80

Bal Bay—B. g, by Vertex—Marsh Harbour, by First Landing. Trainer Edwards Larry D. Bred by Red Oak Farm Inc (Fla).

BROADWAY REVIEW, void of early foot, commenced a rally when set down for the drive, cut over on BAL BAY near the eighth pole, drew clear briefly but was all out to withstand BAL BAY at the wire. Following an objection by the rider of BAL BAY for interference in the stretch run, BROADWAY REVIEW was disqualified and placed second. BAL BAY, allowed to settle, challenged when set down for the drive, was bothered by BROADWAY REVIEW in midstretch but recovered to come again and just missed. SWAY pressed the early pace, took clear command approaching the lane but could not withstand the top two. SORROTO, well placed early, had no late rally. DAVRICK had brief speed. MAJOR RUN made the early pace and gave way. DUST OFF THE MAT tired after a half.

Owners— 1, Brown Mrs W L Lyons; 2, Sefa F; 3, Partee W C; 4, Donamire Farm; 5, Foyt A J Jr; 6, Racevitch H; 7, Golden Chance Farm; 8, Zimmerman G A.

Corrected weight: Broadway Review 121 pounds; Dust Off the Mat 121.

Derby Day again was an excellent day for us. We made nine Dr. Z system bets, all to show, in eight races, and all but one finished in the money to win for us. Taking into account the $50 loss on our win bets on the Derby, our $1,000 initial stake grew to $1,568. Typically, on an average day at the track, there are two to four Dr. Z system bets. In some cases, there are as few as one or even none. Over the three years on Derby Day we had five, five, and now nine Dr. Z system bets. The reason for the large number of Dr. Z system bets was likely due to the massive crowd and the many rich visitors who were, as usual, looking for the big killing and felt it to be in the win pools. Their betting behavior led to a substantial opportunity for good profits by Dr. Z system bettors. We were also using a fairly risky cutoff of 1.10 to reflect the very high quality of horses running on Derby Day.

CHAPTER 13

Betting on Favorites

Betting to Win May Be Profitable with Good Handicapping

In Chapter Three we presented considerable evidence that favorites are underbet to win by about 7% (see Tables 3.1 and 3.5 and Figures 3.1 and 3.2). Thus if the track take is 15%, as it is at Santa Anita, then the strategy of betting all favorites to win would likely lose about 8%, plus breakage of about 3% (with Santa Anita's 10¢ breakage), for a total loss of about 11%. Presumably, good handicapping would eliminate some of the losers and also horses that are poor bets (that is, those going off at lower odds than their chance of winning), so a modified system would actually achieve profits. Since it is not our intention in this book to discuss handicapping methods in detail (although some hints appear in Chapters Fourteen and Sixteen), we will not pursue this possibility here either. But we mention it here for those readers who are skilled in handicapping and who wish to develop such procedures. We now turn our attention to place and show betting on the favorite.

Betting the Favorite to Place or Show

An interesting and easy strategy to follow is always to bet the favorite of the crowd to place or show. Generally, this will be a *losing* strategy. As with win bets, the favorites are underbet, so the actual average loss will generally be about 5%–10% less than the track take plus breakage. However, if you restrict your bets to horses that have good *odds* for place or show, then it can be a winning strategy.

Table 13.1 provides details on such bets over 1,080 races, on 120 days

TABLE 13.1 *Rate of return versus expected value for favored horses in 1,080 races on 120 days in 1981/82 at Keystone Race Track, Bensalem, Pennsylvania*

Expected Value of a $1 Bet[a]	Place: Number of Bets[b]	Place: Total Profit ($)	Place: Rate of Return (%)	Show: Number[b] of Bets	Show: Total Profit ($)	Show: Rate of Return (%)	Total Number of Bets	Total Profit ($)	Rate of Return (%)
0.85 or less	104	−39.60	−38.1	9	−3.40	−37.8	113	−43.00	−38.1
0.86–0.90	175	−30.70	−17.5	44	−14.20	−32.3	219	−44.90	−20.5
0.91–0.95	264	−59.90	−22.7	131	−23.70	−18.8	395	−83.60	−21.2
0.96–1.00	219	1.50	+0.7	252	−28.05	−11.1	471	−26.55	−5.6
1.01–1.05	151	−15.70	−10.4	214	−17.70	−8.3	365	−33.40	−9.2
1.06–1.10	80	−4.40	−5.5	188	−30.80	−11.1	268	−25.20	−9.4
1.11–1.17	44	−1.50	−3.4	129	−5.30	−4.1	173	−6.80	−3.9
1.18–1.20	15	7.50	+50.5	33	3.50	+10.6	48	+11.00	+22.9
1.21–1.25	16	−2.40	−15.0	35	7.60	+21.7	51	+5.20	+10.2
1.26–1.30	8	3.70	+46.3	20	10.80	+54.0	28	+14.50	+51.9
1.31–1.35	—	—	—	9	−3.00	−33.3	9	−3.00	−33.3
1.36–1.40	1	1.40	+140.4	5	3.60	+72.0	6	+5.00	+83.3
1.41–1.45	—	—	—	3	3.80	+126.7	3	+3.80	+126.7
1.46 or more	1	−1.00	−100.0	3	2.90	+36.7	4	+1.90	+47.5
Totals	1,078	−141.1	−13.1	1,075	−83.95	−7.8	2,153	−225.05	−10.5
				Summary					
1.00 or less	762	−128.7	−16.9	436	−69.35	−15.9	1,198	−198.05	−16.5
1.01–1.17	275	−21.60	−7.9	531	−43.80	−8.3	806	−65.40	−8.1
1.18 or more	41	9.20	22.4	108	29.20	27.0	149	38.40	25.8

[a]Computed using the Exhibition Park regression equations (4.3) and (4.4).
[b]Data were unavailable for a few races, so the total number of races is slightly less than 1,080.

from September 13 to December 13, 1981, and February 8 to March 27, 1982, at Keystone Race Track in Bensalem, Pennsylvania. These data were generously supplied to us by Jerry Rosenwald of Havertown, Pennsylvania. The favorite to win is determined for each race. Then using the Exhibition Park regression equations (4.3) and (4.4), the expected value of a \$1 bet to place and show is estimated, based on the final tote board values. These are categorized as 0.85 or less, 0.86–0.9, and so on, all the way to 1.40–1.45, and 1.46 or more. Recall that 1.40 means that one expects to receive \$1.40, or 40¢ profit for each dollar wagered according to these formulas.

The table shows that if you make place or show bets on horses with an expected value of 1.00 or less, you will have losses of about 16.5%. Since Keystone is in Pennsylvania, its track take is 17%. Keystone's 5¢ breakage—that is, their rounding down to the nearest 10¢ on each \$2 bet—amounts to about another 1.5% for favorites. Thus bets on favored horses with an expected value of 1.00 or less gain about 2% (18.5% − 16.5%) above the average bet made by the crowd. Bets on horses with an expected value between 1.01 and 1.17 lose about 8%, or are about 10.5% (18.5% − 8%) better than chance. Betting on every favorite results in losses of 13.1% to place and 7.8% to show, or an average of 10.5%. This is an improvement of about 8% (18.5% − 10.5%) over chance. Thus the underbetting-of-favorites bias for place and show betting is similar to that for win bets.

If, however, you stick to place and show bets where the expected value is 1.18 or more, then you can make substantial *profits*. Indeed, over this 120-day racing period, there were forty-one such place bets that returned an average profit of 22.4% and 107 show bets that returned an average profit of 27.0%. In total, the 149 bets returned an average profit of 25.8%. The value of 1.18 for the cutoff maximizes total profits; this value is typical for a "medium-quality" track such as Keystone.

Notice that bets are not placed on each race. In fact, only one or two bets of this type are made on a typical day. The horses bet on are all favorites; thus they will be coming in the money about 60%–70% of the time. This strategy is a very safe, conservative approach, and you do not need a large fortune to make relatively sizable bets. Of course, these extra bets would depress the odds to place and show slightly, so actual winnings would be a little less than the 25.8% profit rate. For example, starting with a bankroll of \$1,500 and making bets of \$250 on each of these horses would result in a profit of about (\$250)(149)(0.258) = \$9,610. This is a handsome profit, considering that you are taking very little risk. In fact, the chance of ever losing the \$1,500 during an entire season of betting is only about 4% if we assume that favorites are in the money about 65% of the time.* That

*As experts in probability theory will note, this value is obtained by summing the binomial probabilities that consider all the possible sequences of wins and losses that lead to ruin.

4% represents a chance of about one in twenty-five. This compares very favorably with random betting, where you almost certainly will lose the entire $1,500. If you bet $25 per race with a bankroll of $150, then your expected profit will be $961 and the chance of losing the entire $150 will still be 4%.

The $250 we just cited is a typical betting amount for a serious application of such a system. Individuals might wish to bet more or less in each race. The more you bet, the larger your total profits will tend to be. However, because large bets will reduce the payoff in a parimutuel system, the individual payoffs per dollar bet will decrease and the risk of losing your bankroll will increase.

In the basic Dr. Z system advocated in this book, you make bets on horses other than the favorite using charts that have been provided to indicate the size of the optimal bet. Nevertheless, as the data in Table 13.1 indicate, a flat bet on the favorite to place or show when the place or show odds are favorable is a very good strategy.

Betting Extreme Favorites: The Ballerina, Exhibition Park, October 11, 1982

Horses that go off at odds of about 1—2 or less may be classified as extreme favorites. Betting on such horses to win may seem quite risky, since they must win at least two of every three races to break even. However, they often are outstanding place or show bets.

The eighth running of The Ballerina, a $50,000 added feature race at Exhibition Park on October 11, 1982, provides such an example. The field of eleven contained two long-shot entries and a large group of strong horses. Davette was a late scratch. The invader from Longacres in Renton, Washington, Belle of Rainier, completely outclassed the field. Belle of Rainier had twelve wins and fifteen in-the-money finishes in eighteen career races against very high caliber competition. His advantageous post position, number 1, and the reliability of his steady jockey, D. Sorensen, seemed to overcome his high weight assignment of 126 pounds. Belle of Rainier was the top pick of all the *Daily Racing Form's* experts. He was the day's best bet of four of the five experts and the consensus best bet with a rating of 33 out of a possible 35.

Daily Racing Form **EXPERTS' SELECTIONS**

Consensus Points: 5 for 1st (best 7), 2 for 2d, 1 for 3d. Best in CAPITALS.

Trackman, Tim Toon — EXHIBITION PARK — Selections Made for Fast Track

RACE	TRACKMAN	HERMIS	HANDICAP	ANALYST	SWEEP	CONSENSUS	
9	BELLE OF RAINIER Okan Dee Select Brief Grief	BELLE OF RAINIER Okan Dee Select Miss Zulu Gold	BELLE OF RAINIER Au Printemps Okan Dee Select	BELLE OF RAINIER Okan Dee Select Au Printemps	Belle of Rainier Indellare Miss Zulu Gold	BELLE OF RAINIER Okan Dee Select Au Printemps	33 7 3

9

1 1/8 MILES

About 1800 Meters

EXACTOR FEATURE

SWEEP SIX F

THE 8th RUNNING OF "THE BALLERINA" — $50,000-added. A handicap for fillies and mares three-year-olds and upward. by subscription of $100 each, $300 to pass the entry wicket and $100 to start. With $50,000 added of which $31,500 to the winner, $10,000 to second, $5,000 to third, $2,500 to fourth and $1,000 to fifth. All nomination, entry and starting fees to be divided: 70% to the winner, 20% to second and 10% to third. Weights to be announced Monday, October 4th. Starters to be named through the entry wicket Friday, October 8th by 8:30 a.m. Closed with 11 nominations.

SELECTIONS: 3—9—6

ASK FOR HORSE BY THIS NUMBER	OWNER	TRAINER	Post Position / Jockey / Morning Line
1	Irene Reed Blue, gold trim, "MIR" on back **DREAM DISTURBER** Ch m 6. Winning Shot—Seldom Dreams	Pat Jarvis 112	P.P. 2 Joel Mena 30
1A	Mr. & Mrs. A. Jarvis Lilac, green trim, "J" on back **DAVETTE** Roan f 4. No Back Talk—Yukon Belle	A. Jarvis 113	P.P. 4 D. J. Zook 30
2	M. & W. Bowes & F. Reichelt Green, gold trim, gold sash front & back **CHEMAINUS BELLE** Roan f 4. Keep Your Promise—Satin Sue	W. Bowes 113	P.P. 3 Danny Williams 30
2B	Norland Stable Green, yellow & orange hoops **BLUSHING MINSTREL** Dk b/br f 4. Borrower—Taos Trail	E. Sams 112	P.P. 12 Ray Creighton 30
3	Al Benton Royal blue, white V front and back **BELLE OF RAINIER** Ro f 3. Windy Tide—Lap Wing	William Findlay 126	P.P. 1 Danny Sorenson 8/5
4	Tri Star Stable, Bowie & D. Bowman Red, gold trim, 3 stars on back **AU PRINTEMPS** B f 3. Dancing Champ—*Lorgnette II	D. Forster 116	P.P. 5 Brian Johnson 8
5	Mrs. B. Dahl Light & dark blue vertical stripes **OKAN DEE SELECT** Dk b/br f 3. Docile Boy—Marnie Dee	B. Dahl 120	P.P. 6 Mark Patzer 6
6	B.C. Interior Stock Farm Yellow, black diamonds, "BCI" on back & sleeves **CINDERS SHADOW** Dk b/br m 6. Ship Leave—Shy Shadow	Frank Barroby 116	P.P. 7 Joan Phipps 6
7	J. Diamond Blue, white diamonds on back & sleeves **SALT TREATY** B f 4. Bold Reason—Gay Gusher	H. Johnson 112	P.P. 8 Chad Hoverson 20
8	Elmbrook Stables Yellow, green trim, emblem on back **INDELLARE** B f 4. Indefatigable—Emellare	A. May 119	P.P. 9 Chris Loseth 12
9	Poor Four Stable White, red flames, emblem on back **MISS ZULU GOLD** Ch f 3. Zulu Tom—Norm's Choice	H. Belvoir 117	P.P. 10 Sam Krasner 6
10	Connie Guindon All red **BRIEF GRIEF** Ch m 5. Sandy Fleet—Good Grief Mama	T. Taylor 120	P.P. 11 Victor Mercado 8

No. 1 & 1A—Dream Disturber and Davette, coupled

No. 2 & 2B—Chemainus Belle and Blushing Minstrel, coupled

DECLARED — Lady Of York

9th Exhibition

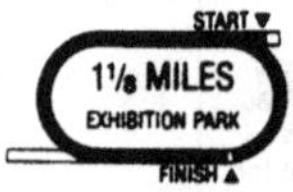

1⅛ MILES. (1.48⅖) 8th Running THE BALLERINA HANDICAP. $50,000 Added. Fillies and Mares, 3-year-olds and upward. By subscription of $100 each, $300 to pass the entry wicket and $100 to start. With $50,000 added of which $31,500 to the winner, $10,000 to second, $5,000 to third, $2,500 to fourth and $1,000 to fifth. All nomination entry and starting fees to be divided 70% to the winner, 20% to second and 10% to third.

Belle of Rainier *

Ro. f. 3, by Windy Tide—Lap Wing, by Donut King
Br.—Benton A (Wash) — 1982 9 6 0 0 $132,615
Own.—Benton A — **126** — **Tr.—Findlay William A** — 1981 9 6 2 1 $142,066
Lifetime 18 12 2 1 $274,681

26Sep82-9Lga	1$\frac{3}{16}$	:48	1:14^1	2:01^{4}sl	*1	121	1$^{3\frac12}$	1^2	1$^{3\frac12}$	1^2	SrnsD^6 ⒻB Roberts H	61	Belle of Rainier, Gi Gi, Latrone	14
4Sep82-9EP	1$\frac{1}{16}$	:47^4	1:13	1:46^{2}m	*3-4	127	1^1	1$^{1\frac12}$	1$^{1\frac12}$	1^3	SrnsnD^1 ⒻSenorita H	79	BllofRnr,APrntmps,Chftn'sCmmnd	9
29Aug82-9Lga	1⅛	:46^4	1:10^4	1:49^{2}ft	*3-4	124	1$^{1\frac12}$	2^{hd}	1^3	1^4	SrnsD^1 ⒻSacajawea H	86	BellofRinir,OknDSlct,MissZuluGold	6
15Aug82-9Lga	1$\frac{3}{16}$	:46^3	1:11^3	1:58^{1}ft	4	118	2^{hd}	1$^{\frac12}$	4$^{5\frac12}$	5^{11}	SrnsnD^6 Lga Derby H	68	Cassaleria,FlyingJudgement,GlArry	9
31Jly82-9Lga	1$\frac{1}{16}$	:46^1	1:11	1:43^{4}ft	*2-3	123	1$^{3\frac12}$	1^3	1^2	1$^{2\frac12}$	SrnsnD^8 ⒻM Donohoe	80	BellofRinir,OknDSlct,NoMorLmons	9
10Jly82-9Lga	1	:45^3	1:10	1:34^{4}ft	*2-3	120	1$^{1\frac12}$	1^2	1^3	1$^{5\frac12}$	SornsnD^2 ⒻB. Ross H	95	BllofRnr,NoMorLmons,MssZulGold	9
19Jun82-9Lga	6½f	:21^3	:44^3	1:16^{4}ft	*3-5	123	5$^{4\frac34}$	5^5	6$^{6\frac12}$	4$^{2\frac12}$	SornsnD^8 ⒻMs Stakes	82	NoMorLmons,EsyTrmph,SddnWnds	8
22May82-9Lga	6f	:22	:45	1:09^{2}ft	*4-5	120	2^2	2$^{1\frac12}$	1$^{\frac12}$	1^5	SornsnD^1 ⒻIngenue H	89	BellofRinir,NoMorLmons,RoylTurn	6
28Apr82-9Lga	5½f	:21^3	:45^2	1:05 gd	*3-5	118	2^{hd}	1$^{\frac12}$	2^{hd}	6$^{6\frac34}$	SornsonD^8 ⒻⓈSeafair	80	MssZuluGold,HYuLulu,BrroomBby	12
30Oct81-8BM	6f	:22	:47^4	1:10^{3}ft	*4-5	120	2^3	2$^{1\frac12}$	2^{hd}	1^3	SrnsnD^3 ⒻBurlingame	87	BellofRinir,GoldnPlum,AuPrintmps	9

Dream Disturber *

Ch. m. 6, by Winning Shot—Seldom Dreams, by Mr Mustard
Br.—O'Connor H R (BC-C) — 1982 11 2 0 0 $11,853
Own.—Reed Mrs I — **112** — **Tr.—Jarvis Pat** — 1981 13 2 4 2 $20,271
Lifetime 45 11 5 5 $50,890

20Oct82-8EP	1$\frac{1}{16}$	:47^4	1:14^3	1:48 m	2½	114	3^4	4^5	3$^{6\frac12}$	4$^{6\frac14}$	JohnsnBG^5 ⒻAw10000	65	LdyofYork,BlushingMinstrel,Indellr	8
17Sep82-9EP	1$\frac{1}{16}$	:47	1:12	1:45^{2}ft	*3-2	113	1^{hd}	1$^{2\frac12}$	1$^{2\frac12}$	1$^{2\frac12}$	Johnson B G^1 Ⓕ 40000	84	DrmDisturbr,DncingProud,BonnLos	7
27Aug82-7EP	6½f	:22^1	:45^3	1:16^{3}ft	6½	113	6$^{7\frac34}$	6$^{3\frac14}$	1^2	1^8	Johnson B G^2 Ⓕ 32000	95	DrmDsturbr,Ldd'sLss,MdmSplndor	7
13Aug82-9EP	6½f	:22^3	:46	1:19^{4}m	21	110^5	7^{12}	7^{15}	5^{12}	4$^{5\frac12}$	Adcock T^7 Ⓕ 32000	73	CrftyMdm,MdmSplndor,WdmntClr	7
23Jly82-9EP	1$\frac{1}{16}$	:48	1:13	1:45^{3}ft	17	109^5	3$^{1\frac12}$	6$^{2\frac14}$	7$^{5\frac34}$	5$^{7\frac34}$	Adcock T^4 Ⓕ 32000	75	Bonnie Lois, Tru Talk, Struckup	9
18Jun82-9Lga	1$\frac{1}{16}$	:47	1:12^4	1:44^{4}ft	16	117	4^7	8$^{6\frac12}$	7^9	6^{17}	Loseth C^1 ⒻAw8800	58	ThreeMisses,TniMoro,EsterFredom	8
12Jun82-9Lga	1$\frac{1}{16}$	:47	1:12^1	1:45^{1}ft	34	116	4^9	6$^{5\frac34}$	4^5	5$^{6\frac14}$	Loseth C^2 ⒻAw11000	67	LovelyWine,PrunePickr,ConniCoco	8
31May82-7Lga	1$\frac{1}{16}$	:48^1	1:13^1	1:44^{3}ft	16	113	4$^{5\frac12}$	4^2	5^7	7^{12}	Frazier B^6 ⒻAw11200	64	Bbe'sJoy,ConnieCoco,PrunePicker	7
26May82-9Lga	6½f	:22	:45^3	1:17^{1}ft	32	117	7^6	8$^{8\frac12}$	7$^{8\frac34}$	7^{13}	Frazier B^1 ⒻAw7200	70	Shoot It Out, Serageous, TaniMoro	8
5May82-9Lga	6f	:22	:45^3	1:09^{3}ft	14	117	8$^{5\frac34}$	6^7	6$^{7\frac34}$	6^{10}	Baze M B^9 ⒻAw9000	78	Mondolu,GoldRunLdy,Blw'sLittlSis	9

Sep 28 EP 4f ft :49 h   Sep 16 EP 3f ft :36^2 b   Sep 7 EP 4f ft :48^1 h

Chemainus Belle

Ro. f. 4, by Keep Your Promise—Satin Sue, by Roman Note
Br.—Reichelt Faye L (BC-C) — 1982 9 1 0 2 $13,465
Own.—Bowes M & W & Reichelt — **113** — **Tr.—Bowes Wilf A** — 1981 13 2 2 2 $12,306
Lifetime 31 3 4 5 $29,205

19Sep82-8Lga	1	:45^3	1:10^3	1:36^{4}ft	75	120	5^7	5^4	5^7	3$^{5\frac12}$	HoversonC^9 ⒻAw12000	79	Flmme,ExpressSuccss,ChminusBll	10
12Sep82-9Lga	1⅛	:47^1	1:12^3	1:52^{4}sy	44	116	6^8	11^{16}	12^{33}	12^{21}	Hoverson C^5 ⒻAlki H	48	BriefGrief,ExprssSuccss,Mondolu	12
28Aug82-8EP	1$\frac{1}{16}$	:47	1:12^1	1:45^{1}ft	25	115	6^8	6$^{6\frac14}$	7^{11}	7^{14}	Adcock T^2 ⒻAw12000	71	HomeRunGl,Struckup,CindrsShdow	9
31Jly82-9EP	1$\frac{1}{16}$	:47	1:11^3	1:44^{2}ft	24	113	6^{10}	6$^{7\frac12}$	7^{10}	6^{11}	KplG^3 ⒻⓈWVncouver	78	HomRunGl,CindrsShdow,BonniLois	8
21Jly82-9EP	1$\frac{1}{16}$	:47^3	1:12^2	1:45^{1}ft	14	115	8^7	8$^{6\frac34}$	6$^{9\frac34}$	6^{13}	Kipling G^2 ⒻAw12000	72	CindersShadow,Dvette,HomeRunGl	8
3Jly82-9EP	1$\frac{1}{16}$	:48^1	1:13^3	1:47^{3}sy	6½	118	8$^{8\frac34}$	9$^{9\frac14}$	8^{14}	7^{14}	Kipling G^4 ⒻVanity H	59	ThreeLeders,Dvette,CindersShdow	10
18Jun82-9EP	1$\frac{1}{16}$	:46^2	1:12	1:46^{1}ft	27	115	7^{12}	6$^{4\frac12}$	1^2	1^3	KplnG^8 ⒻCover Girl H	80	ChmnusBll,MdmosllB,CndrsShdow	9
9Jun82-8EP	1$\frac{1}{16}$	:47	1:12^1	1:46 ft	14	115	6^{12}	6$^{9\frac14}$	5$^{8\frac12}$	3$^{5\frac12}$	Kipling G^6 ⒻAw8000	75	Davette,BonnieLois,CheminusBelle	7
26May82-9EP	6½f	:22^3	:46^2	1:18^{3}ft	40	115	4$^{4\frac12}$	5^4	4$^{4\frac12}$	4^3	Kipling G^3 ⒻAw8500	82	JmmedFlight,TrctbleTrdrop,SltTrty	7
26Sep81-7EP	1⅛	:46^4	1:12^3	1:52^{3}ft	80	115	12^{10}	10$^{8\frac34}$	9^{17}	9^{14}	Carter G^4 ⒻB. C. Oaks	65	Dvette,JmmedFlight,Michel'sBest	12

●Oct 5 EP 6f gd 1:15^2 h   Sep 3 EP 5f ft 1:00^3 h   Aug 27 EP 2f ft :23^4 h   Aug 23 EP 5f ft 1:03 h

Davette

Ro. f. 4, by No Back Talk—Yukon Belle, by Akimbo
Br.—Jarvis Mr-Mrs A (BC-C) — 1982 13 1 4 1 $20,585
Own.—Jarvis Mr-Mrs A — **113** — **Tr.—Jarvis Albert** — 1981 15 3 0 1 $46,910
Lifetime 37 6 8 3 $100,076

20Oct82-8EP	1$\frac{1}{16}$	:47^4	1:14^3	1:48 m	3	115	2^{hd}	2^4	5$^{8\frac12}$	8^{13}	Zook D J^1 ⒻAw10000	58	LdyofYork,BlushingMinstrel,Indellr	8
11Sep82-8EP	1$\frac{1}{16}$	:47^2	1:12^4	1:46^{3}m	9½	114	2^{hd}	2^2	5$^{6\frac12}$	8^{10}	Zook DJ^3 ⒻB Belles H	68	HomeRunGl,CindersShdow,SltTrty	10
28Aug82-8EP	1$\frac{1}{16}$	:47	1:12^1	1:45^{1}ft	8½	115	1^2	2^{hd}	3^6	5^{12}	Zook D J^8 ⒻAw12000	73	HomeRunGl,Struckup,CindrsShdow	9
14Aug82-9EP	6½f	:22^3	:46^3	1:19^{4}m	8¼	116	1^{hd}	1^{hd}	3$^{1\frac12}$	2^6	Zook D J^1 ⒻMilady	73	OknDeeSelect,Dvette,MdmoisllBu	10
31Jly82-9EP	1$\frac{1}{16}$	:47	1:11^3	1:44^{2}ft	4½	116	1$^{\frac12}$	2^{hd}	4^7	7^{11}	ZDJ^8 ⒻⓈWVancouver	78	HomRunGl,CindrsShdow,BonniLois	8
21Jly82-9EP	1$\frac{1}{16}$	:47^3	1:12^2	1:45^{1}ft	9½	115	1^1	1^2	2$^{\frac12}$	2^6	Zook D J^6 ⒻAw12000	79	CindersShadow,Dvette,HomeRunGl	8
3Jly82-9EP	1$\frac{1}{16}$	:48^1	1:13^3	1:47^{3}sy	4	114	1^3	1$^{1\frac12}$	2$^{2\frac12}$	2^6	Zook D J^8 ⒻVanity H	67	ThreeLeders,Dvette,CindersShdow	10
18Jun82-9EP	1$\frac{1}{16}$	:46^2	1:12	1:46^{1}ft	3½	115	1^3	1^2	2^2	5$^{5\frac12}$	ZkDJ^5 ⒻCover Girl H	74	ChmnusBll,MdmosllB,CndrsShdow	9
9Jun82-8EP	1$\frac{1}{16}$	:47	1:12^1	1:46 ft	*2¾	114	1^2	1^4	1^6	1$^{4\frac12}$	Zook D J^7 ⒻAw8000	81	Davette,BonnieLois,CheminusBelle	7
29May82-9EP	1$\frac{1}{16}$	:47^2	1:13^2	1:47^{2}ft	7¾	115	3$^{1\frac12}$	4$^{1\frac12}$	6^{12}	6^{16}	ZkDJ^7 ⒻVancouver H	58	MdemoiselleBeu,SernLdyB,ThrLdrs	7

Sep 30 EP 3f ft :36^2 h   Sep 20 EP 4f ft :51^1 b   Sep 10 EP 2f gd :26^1 b   ●Sep 6 EP 4f ft :49 h

Au Printemps — B. f. 3, by Dancing Champ—Lorgnette II, by High Hat

Own.—Bowie&Bowman&TriStrStble 116

Br.—Livestock Consultants Inc (Md) 1982 8 3 1 1 $47,555

Tr.—Forster Dave 1981 8 2 4 1 $26,108

Lifetime 16 5 5 2 $73,663

24Sep82-9EP	1⅛	:47^1	1:12^2	1:52 gd	¾	115	3^{1½}	3^{1½}	2^{hd}	2^{hd}	JhsBG^1	ⒻB C oaks H	82	‡MssZlGld,APrntmps,ChftnsCmnd	8
24Sep82—Placed first through disqualification															
11Sep82-8EP	1$\frac{1}{16}$	:47^2	1:12^4	1:46^{3}m	3½	113	3^{2½}	4^{3½}	9^{15}	9^{15}	JhnsBG^1	ⒻB Belles H	63	HomeRunGl,CindersShdow,SltTrty	10
4Sep82-9EP	1$\frac{1}{16}$	:47^4	1:13	1:46^{2}m	6¾	115	5^3	3^{2½}	2^{1½}	2^3	JhnsBG^9	ⒻSenorita H	76	BllofRnr,APrntmps,Chftn'sCmmnd	9
20Aug82-9EP	1$\frac{1}{16}$	:47^4	1:13	1:45^{2}ft	*2-3e	116	5^{3¾}	3^2	1^{hd}	1^1	WillimsDR^7	ⒻAw12000	84	AuPrintmps,MiniChillo,EsyTriumph	7
4Aug82-9EP	6½f	:22^3	:46^1	1:17^{4}ft	*7-5	116	9^{6½}	6^5	4^{4¼}	3^{7¼}	WllsDR^8	ⒻQueenChrlo	82	MissZuluGold,LdyCeJy,AuPrintmps	9
24Jly82-3EP	6½f	:23	:46^1	1:17^{1}ft	4¾	116	4^3	3^1	1^{hd}	1^{2½}	WilliamsDR^5	ⒻAw8000	92	AuPrintemps,LdyCeJy,EsyTriumph	7
23Jun82-8EP	1$\frac{1}{16}$	:47^1	1:12^2	1:45^{1}ft	2¼e	116	5^3	4^{4½}	4^9	5^{12}	WilliamsDR^4	ⒻAw7000	73	OkanDeeSelect,HeavyHeart,Cedarly	8
4Jun82-8EP	6½f	:22^4	:46^4	1:19^{3}ft	2¼	120	4^3	4^2	4^{2¾}	4^{5¼}	WilliamsDR^2	ⒻAw6500	75	D.W.'sDrm,RockinHwk,AutumSpirit	9
26Dec81-8BM	1$\frac{1}{16}$	:47^1	1:12^4	1:46^{2}ft	*2¼	112	8^{4½}	3^{4½}	1^1	2^{nk}	JhnsBG^2	ⒻBm Lassie	67	BlmyDys,AuPrintmps,CountrftCon	14
4Dec81-6BM	1	:46^3	1:12^2	1:39^{1}ft	*2	114	7^9	3^1	1^2	1^{¾}	JohnsnBG^9	ⒻAw11000	73	Au Printemps, Hazel Too, Dini K.	10

Sep 22 EP 4f ft :47^3 h   Sep 1 EP 5f ft :59^4 h   ●Aug 17 EP 5f ft :59^4 h

Okan Dee Select — Dk. b. or br. f. 3, by Docile Boy—Marni Dee, by Cecil County

Own.—Dahl Beatrice E 120

Br.—Hochsteiner Gail (BC-C) 1982 12 6 3 0 $83,285

Tr.—Dahl Beatrice 1981 6 2 2 0 $11,072

Lifetime 18 8 5 0 $94,357

24Sep82-9EP	1⅛	:47^1	1:12^2	1:52 gd	*2¼	125	4^{2½}	4^3	4^3	5^{2¾}	PtzrM^8	ⒻB C oaks H	79	‡MssZlGld,APrntmps,ChftnsCmnd	8
11Sep82-8EP	1$\frac{1}{16}$	:47^2	1:12^4	1:46^{3}m	*7-5	120	6^{6¼}	5^{3½}	3^{5½}	6^{6¾}	PatzerM^9	ⒻB Belles H	71	HomeRunGl,CindersShdow,SltTrty	10
29Aug82-9Lga	1⅛	:46^4	1:10^4	1:49^{2}ft	9-5	120	3^{1½}	1^{hd}	2^3	2^4	PtzrM^5	ⒻSacajawea H	82	BellofRinir,OknDSlct,MissZuluGold	6
14Aug82-9EP	6½f	:22^3	:46^3	1:19^{4}m	5¼	118	7^{5¾}	4^{3¼}	1^{1½}	1^6	Patzer M^8	ⒻMilady	79	OknDeeSelect,Dvette,MdmoisllBu	10
31Jly82-9Lga	1$\frac{1}{16}$	:46^1	1:11	1:43^{4}ft	3½	121	5^{7½}	2^3	2^2	2^{2½}	BzeMB^2	ⒻM Donohoe	77	BellofRinir,OknDSlct,NoMorLmons	9
17Jly82-8EP	1$\frac{1}{16}$	:47^3	1:12^3	1:46^{1}ft	2	122	1^{hd}	1^{hd}	1^{hd}	1^1	PtrM^8	Ⓕ[S]LibertionH	80	OknDeeSelect,Cdrly,BoldUndrwritr	8
1Jly82-7EP	1$\frac{1}{16}$	:47^3	1:12^2	1:44^{4}ft	*7-5	119	8^{6¾}	3^2	2^{hd}	1^{nk}	PtzerM^2	ⒻNanaimo H	87	OknDeeSelect,BoldUndrwritr,Cdrly	9
23Jun82-8EP	1$\frac{1}{16}$	:47^1	1:12^2	1:45^{1}ft	*6-5	111^5	4^3	1^{1½}	1^2	1^{1¾}	Patzer M^6	ⒻAw7000	85	OkanDeeSelect,HeavyHeart,Cedarly	8
9Jun82-9EP	1$\frac{1}{16}$	:47^3	1:13^2	1:45^{4}ft	17	111^5	4^{9½}	1^{hd}	1^4	1^6	Patzer M^2	ⒻAw12000	82	OknDeeSlct,CollnCrig,EsyTriumph	10
24May82-8EP	1$\frac{1}{16}$	:48	1:14	1:47^{3}ft	6½	117	4^3	3^{1½}	6^9	7^{16}	PtrM^7	ⒻButn &BowH	57	BorrowdMid,Rgl'sFncy,EsyTriumph	9

●Sep 19 EP 5f ft 1:01^3 h   ●Aug 25 EP 5f ft :59^2 h

Cinders Shadow * — Dk. b. or br. m. 6, by Ship Leave—Shy Shadow, by Merger

Own.—Hall R M 116

Br.—Hall R M (BC-C) 1982 14 3 2 3 $37,259

Tr.—Barroby Frank 1981 5 1 0 1 $5,950

Lifetime 48 11 6 7 $73,930

2Oct82-8EP	1$\frac{1}{16}$	:47^4	1:14^3	1:48 m	*2½e	117	6^{6¾}	5^7	6^9	5^8	Phipps J^8	ⒻAw10000	63	LdyofYork,BlushingMinstrel,Indellr	8
26Sep82-9Lga	1$\frac{3}{16}$	:48	1:14^1	2:01^{4}sl	52	119	9^{13}	10^{9¾}	11^{19}	9^{13}	PppsJ^{11}	ⒻB RobertsH	48	Belle of Rainier, Gi Gi, Latrone	14
11Sep82-8EP	1$\frac{1}{16}$	:47^2	1:12^4	1:46^{3}m	30	115	4^{2¾}	3^{2½}	2^{1½}	2^1	PhippsJ^4	ⒻB Belles H	77	HomeRunGl,CindersShdow,SltTrty	10
28Aug82-8EP	1$\frac{1}{16}$	:47	1:12^1	1:45^{1}ft	3¾	115	3^{4½}	4^{3½}	2^6	3^{8½}	HoversonC^3	ⒻAw12000	76	HomeRunGl,Struckup,CindrsShdow	9
14Aug82-9EP	6½f	:22^3	:46^3	1:19^{4}m	8½	116	6^{5¾}	7^{8¾}	7^{7¼}	5^{7¼}	Hoverson C^5	ⒻMilady	72	OknDeeSelect,Dvette,MdmoisllBu	10
31Jly82-9EP	1$\frac{1}{16}$	:47	1:11^3	1:44^{2}ft	*1	118	3^{4½}	3^4	2^5	2^5	HrsC^1	Ⓕ[S]WVncouver	84	HomRunGl,CindrsShdow,BonniLois	8
21Jly82-9EP	1$\frac{1}{16}$	:47^3	1:12^2	1:45^{1}ft	8¼	113	2^1	2^2	1^{½}	1^6	HoversonC^1	ⒻAw12000	85	CindersShadow,Dvette,HomeRunGl	8
9Jly82-9EP	6½f	:22^2	:46	1:18^{2}ft	3	117	4^{4½}	4^{2½}	1^{1½}	1^{2½}	Hoverson C^1	ⒻAw8000	86	CindersShdow,SltTrety,BonnieLois	7
3Jly82-9EP	1$\frac{1}{16}$	:48^1	1:13^3	1:47^{3}sy	13	112	5^{5½}	5^{7½}	3^{9½}	3^{7¾}	HovrsonC^7	ⒻVanity H	65	ThreeLeders,Dvette,CindersShdow	10
18Jun82-9EP	1$\frac{1}{16}$	:46^2	1:12	1:46^{1}ft	6	112	3^6	5^{3½}	7^{3¼}	3^{3¾}	HrsnC^1	ⒻCover Girl H	76	ChmnusBll,MdmosllB,CndrsShdow	9

Sep 24 EP 3f ft :36 h   Sep 18 EP 4f ft :48^3 h   Sep 8 EP 4f ft :49 h   Sep 3 EP 4f ft :48^4 h

Salt Treaty — B. f. 4, by Bold Reason—Gay Gusher, by Tom Rolfe

Own.—Diamond J 112

Br.—Aitken E T & L F (Ky) 1982 10 0 1 2 $7,725

Tr.—Johnson Harry 1981 17 4 5 3 $38,747

Lifetime 32 6 7 5 $53,177

2Oct82-8EP	1$\frac{1}{16}$	:47^4	1:14^3	1:48 m	5¼	113	5^{6¾}	6^{7½}	7^{9¼}	6^{8½}	HoversonC^6	ⒻAw10000	62	LdyofYork,BlushingMinstrel,Indellr	8
11Sep82-8EP	1$\frac{1}{16}$	:47^2	1:12^4	1:46^{3}m	10e	111	7^{11}	7^{5½}	4^{6½}	3^6	HvrsnC^{10}	ⒻB Belles H	72	HomeRunGl,CindersShdow,SltTrty	10
28Aug82-8EP	1$\frac{1}{16}$	:47	1:12^1	1:45^{1}ft	14	114	9^{11}	8^{6¾}	5^{6¾}	4^{9½}	Krasner S^7	ⒻAw12000	75	HomeRunGl,Struckup,CindrsShdow	9
14Aug82-9EP	6½f	:22^3	:46^3	1:19^{4}m	23	113	9^{16}	9^{16}	9^{12}	9^{14}	Krasner S^9	ⒻMilady	65	OknDeeSelect,Dvette,MdmoisllBu	10
2Aug82-4EP	6½f	:23^1	:47	1:17^{3}m	*2	113	4^3	5^{2½}	4^{11}	5^{16}	Krasner S^4	ⒻAw9000	74	BlshngMnstrl,WodmntClr,SrnLdyB	5
21Jly82-9EP	1$\frac{1}{16}$	:47^3	1:12^2	1:45^{1}ft	5½	114	7^{5½}	6^{5¼}	5^{4¾}	4^7	Krasner S^7	ⒻAw12000	78	CindersShadow,Dvette,HomeRunGl	8
9Jly82-9EP	6½f	:22^2	:46	1:18^{2}ft	4¼	114	6^{12}	6^{6¾}	3^{1½}	2^{2½}	Krasner S^2	ⒻAw8000	83	CindersShdow,SltTrety,BonnieLois	7
26May82-9EP	6½f	:22^3	:46^2	1:18^{3}ft	3¾	112^5	7^{14}	6^9	5^{4½}	3^3	Patzer M^5	ⒻAw8500	82	JmmedFlight,TrctbleTrdrop,SltTrty	7
5May82-9EP	6½f	:22^4	:46	1:18^{1}ft	4½	111^5	7^{8¼}	7^{8¼}	4^5	4^{4¼}	Patzer M^7	ⒻAw10000	83	CindersShdow,Dvette,Michel'sBst	10
23Apr82-9EP	6½f	:22^4	:46^4	1:19^{1}ft	5	120^5	9^9	6^{5½}	4^6	4^6	Patzer M^1	ⒻAw12000	76	ThreeLdrs,MdmoisllBu,Michl'sBst	10

Oct 1 EP 2f ft :24^1 b   Sep 25 EP 7f gd 1:32^1 h   Sep 18 EP 5f ft 1:00 h   Sep 10 EP 2f gd :24^1 h

Indellare — B. f. 4, by Indefatigable—Emellare, by Czar Alexander
Br.—Elmbrook Stable (Alb–C) 1982 13 3 1 2 $56,613
Own.—Elmbrook Stables 119 Tr.—May Alan 1981 15 4 7 3 $39,030
Lifetime 35 9 8 7 $101,483

20ct82-8EP 1 1/16 :474 1:143 1:48 m 7½ 117 79¾ 811 48½ 36 Skinner K3 ⒻAw10000 65 LdyofYork,BlushingMinstrel,Indellr 8
26Sep82-9Lga 1 3/16 :48 1:141 2:014sl 32 121 1013 1414 1327 1321 LsthC8 ⒻB Roberts H 40 Belle of Rainier, Gi Gi, Latrone 14
11Sep82-8EP 1 1/16 :472 1:124 1:463m 6¼ 120 1023 1018 813 78¾ RycrftD2 ⒻB Belles H 69 HomeRunGl,CindersShdow,SltTrty 10
29Aug82-9StP 6f :23 :462 1:111ft 4¼ 118 78½ 76¾ 76¾ 78½ Hedge R6 ⒻLilac H 82 Tyrosong, Fair Tania, Lil 'Ol Gal 7
15Aug82-9StP 1 1/16 :463 1:113 1:45 ft 8½ 116 79½ 57¾ 43 1½ HedgR4 ⓈCal Mat'y H 91 Indellare, Regimen, Atlas Wonder 7
9Aug82-9NP 1 3/8 :473 1:38 2:164ft 28 121 914 914 913 49¾ HedgR6 Spd To Spare 90 Rgimn,BlckIsButiful,MirclMmoris 10
2Aug82-9NP 1 1/16 :463 1:123 1:462ft *1e 122 911 98½ 74 21 Hedge R8 ⒻDistaff H 82 TwilightTresure,Indellre,OnThRoll 10
13Jly82-9NP 1 1/16 :47 1:124 1:46 ft 3½e 121 1112 910 73 11 HdR9 ⒻMadamoiselle 85 Indellre,MissJoBy,TwilightTresure 11
22Jun82-9NP 6½f :224 :464 1:19 gd 6¼ 115 68½ 77¾ 85 53¾ MrccMJ1 ⒻCelebrityH 83 SlghtlyShdy,TlghtTrsr,AvlnchEprss 9
11Jun82-7NP 1 1/16 :483 1:134 1:461ft *2-3 118 66½ 66¼ 67 56 MerciecMJ4 ⒻAw9000 78 SlightlyShady,WilliesLdy,AdVlorem 6
Sep 25 EP 2f gd :261 h

Miss Zulu Gold — Ch. f. 3, by Zulu Tom—Norm's Choice, by Bold Combatant
Br.—Owens G (Wash) 1982 12 3 1 2 $50,140
Own.—Poor Four Stable 117 Tr.—Belvoir Howard 1981 6 2 0 0 $8,800
Lifetime 18 5 1 2 $58,940

24Sep82-9EP 1⅛ :471 1:122 1:52 gd 9 118 2½ 2½ 1hd 1hd† LsthC6 ⒻB C oaks H 82 ‡MssZlGld,APrntmps,ChftnsCmnd 8
†24Sep82—Disqualified and placed second
4Sep82-9EP 1 1/16 :474 1:13 1:462m 11 119 21 21½ 35½ 49 KrsnerS3 ⒻSenorita H 70 BllofRnr,APrntmps,Chftn'sCmmnd 9
29Aug82-9Lga 1⅛ :464 1:104 1:492ft 20 117 21½ 33½ 35 34½ BzeG2 ⒻSacajawea H 81 BellofRinir,OknDSlct,MissZuluGold 6
4Aug82-9EP 6½f :223 :461 1:174ft 12 118 32 21 2hd 1nk KrsrS6 ⒻQueenCharlo 89 MissZuluGold,LdyCeJy,AuPrintmps 9
31Jly82-9Lga 1 1/16 :461 1:11 1:434ft 28 114 34½ 58 716 725 Baze G7 ⒻM Donohoe 55 BellofRinir,OknDSlct,NoMorLmons 9
24Jly82-9Lga 1 :452 1:104 1:364ft 22 113 34½ 44 1120 1219 SrnsnD5 ⒻLuella G. H 66 Flamme, Prune Picker, Tani Moro 12
10Jly82-9Lga 1 :453 1:10 1:344ft 21 116 21½ 22 35 312 Baze G7 ⒻB. Ross H 83 BllofRnr,NoMorLmons,MssZulGold 9
30Jun82-9Lga 1 :46 1:113 1:394sy 4¼ 118 56½ 47 49½ 817 DvidsonJR9 ⒻAw11000 53 VitaLark,GreyPaulus,SwitchinBer 10
19Jun82-9Lga 6½f :213 :443 1:164ft 7½ 118 33½ 42½ 87¼ 76¾ DdsnJR1 ⒻMs Stakes 78 NoMorLmons,EsyTrmph,SddnWnds 8
22May82-9Lga 6f :22 :45 1:092ft 2 121 34½ 43 47 513 DdsnJR4 ⒻIngenue H 76 BellofRinir,NoMorLmons,RoylTurn 6

Brief Grief * — Ch. m. 5, by Sandy Fleet—Good Grief Mama, by Jax Up
Br.—Guindon R R (Wash) 1982 9 2 2 1 $29,190
Own.—Guindon Bonnie 120 Tr.—Taylor Roy 1981 12 3 1 0 $35,244
Lifetime 31 7 7 2 $71,743 Turf 1 0 0 0 $729

26Sep82-9Lga 1 3/16 :48 1:141 2:014sl 11 121 23½ 22 614 1016 BazeG1 ⒻB Roberts H 45 Belle of Rainier, Gi Gi, Latrone 14
12Sep82-9Lga 1⅛ :471 1:123 1:524sy 15 120 23 2hd 1hd 1¾ Baze M B10 ⒻAlki H 69 BriefGrief,ExprssSuccss,Mondolu 12
21Aug82-8Lga 6½f :22 :451 1:17 ft 5¾ 119 77¼ 55½ 45½ 48 Baze M B2 ⒻAw10000 76 Ms.DocShdow,Sergous,DimondVill 12
14Aug82-9Lga 1 1/16 :482 1:14 1:48 sl 9½ 117 45¼ 54¼ 49 413 BMB2 ⒻPrimadonnaH 46 Tani Moro, Flamme, Mondolu 9
6Aug82-8Pla 1 :471 1:122 1:381ft *3-4 120 11½ 1½ 11½ 2 Wright D7 ⒻAw2300 86 JustLikMm,BrfGrf,CountryLovsong 7
17Jly82-9Pla 6½f :23 :463 1:18 ft 3¼ 120 21 22 11 11¼ WrhtD6 ⒻLilac City H 95 Brief Grief, Shoot It Out, Misti O. 9
26Jun82-9Pla 6f :224 :463 1:124ft 9-5 118 2hd 2½ 2hd 31½ Wright D1 Aw2200 84 RecklessPlesure,ChifYkim,BrifGrif 7
12Jun82-9Pla 6f :221 :45 1:103ft 3½ 118 21 22 2½ 2hd Wright D5 Aw2200 97 Seakist Charley, Brief Grief,BiPago 7
21May82-9Pla 6f :232 :464 1:122ft 5 118 33 33½ 65 84 WrightD7 Inaugural H 84 MrvinsMoving,HyMount,RibotAgn 10

Blushing Minstrel * — Dk. b. or br. f. 4, by Borrower—Taos Trail, by Black Mountain
Br.—Ca-Ro-Li Farms Ltd (BC–C) 1982 10 2 2 1 $16,020
Own.—Norland Stables 112 Tr.—Sams Edward 1981 13 1 5 3 $18,543
Lifetime 30 4 7 7 $42,461

20ct82-8EP 1 1/16 :474 1:143 1:48 m 9e 114 1hd 14 12½ 2hd Patzer M2 ⒻAw10000 71 LdyofYork,BlushingMinstrel,Indellr 8
17Sep82-8Lga 6½f :213 :443 1:162ft 3½ 117 65¼ 83¾ 97¾ 76¼ DavidsonJR3 ⒻAw8000 81 Fancy Mink,SailOnRoni,Serageous 10
28Aug82-8EP 1 1/16 :47 1:121 1:451ft 6¾ 113 45 76½ 813 816 JohnsnBG4 ⒻAw12000 69 HomeRunGl,Struckup,CindrsShdow 9
14Aug82-9EP 6½f :223 :463 1:194m 2 115 31½ 2hd 41¾ 47 Johnson BG2 ⒻMilady 72 OknDeeSelect,Dvette,MdmoisllBu 10
2Aug82-4EP 6½f :231 :47 1:173m 2¾ 113 21½ 1hd 16 19 Patzer M3 ⒻAw9000 90 BlshngMnstrl,WodmntClr,SrnLdyB 5
23Jly82-9Lga 6½f :22 :451 1:162ft 18 114 98¼ 73¾ 1hd 12 Sorenson D9 Ⓕ 40000 87 BlushingMinstrl,Bdnot,FrnchJwlls 10
18Jun82-9EP 1 1/16 :462 1:12 1:461ft 29 114 68 86¼ 86¼ 86¾ CrtRL4 ⒻCover Girl H 73 ChmnusBll,MdmosllB,CndrsShdow 9
9Jun82-8EP 1 1/16 :47 1:121 1:46 ft 5½ 110 46½ 56¼ 614 613 Krasner S3 ⒻAw8000 68 Davette,BonnieLois,CheminusBelle 7
24May82-7EP 6½f :224 :462 1:183ft 2¾ 1115 22 32½ 22½ 21¾ Patzer M2 Ⓕ 32000 83 Lddi'sLss,BlushngMnstrl,ToscMgc 10
10May82-9EP 6½f :222 :461 1:19 ft 7¾ 1125 67¾ 68 46½ 32½ Patzer M3 ⒻAw8000 80 LddsLss,TrctblTrdrp,BlshngMnstrl 10
●Sep 28 EP 5f ft 1:003 h ●Aug 26 EP 4f ft :464 b ●Aug 13 EP tr.t 2f sl :243 b

A comparison of Belle of Rainier's record with the rest of the field, including the second and third consensus picks, Okan Dee Select and Au Printemps, reveals why the favorite was bet down to 2—5. The mutuel pools were

	Totals	Belle of Rainier
Win	34,414	20,005
Place	19,347	8,105
Show	14,763	5,485

These values yielded expected returns per dollar bet on Belle of Rainier of*

$$\text{EX Show} = 0.543 + 0.369\left(\frac{W_3/W}{S_3/S}\right)$$

$$= 0.543 + 0.369\left(\frac{20{,}005/34{,}414}{5{,}485/14{,}763}\right) = 1.12,$$

and

$$\text{EX Place} = 0.319 + 0.559\left(\frac{W_3/W}{P_3/P}\right)$$

$$= 0.319 + 0.559\left(\frac{20{,}005/34{,}414}{8{,}108/19{,}347}\right) = 1.09.$$

Both the EX Show and the EX Place are low for Dr. Z system bets, but in light of the extreme favorite bias, the show bet is still interesting, while the place bet is marginal.

Belle of Rainier won the race easily, followed by the 90—1 shot Brief Grief and Au Printemps, who went off at 10—1 (as the third favorite of the crowd). The crowd's second pick, Okan Dee Select, went off at nearly 7—1 and finished out of the money.

The chart of the race and the mutuel payoffs were as follows:

9th One and one-eighth miles. Three-year-olds and up, fillies and mares. Handicap. Purse $50,000-added.

Horse	Jockey	Wt	P	1	1¼	Str	Fin	Odds
Belle Of Rainier	Srnsn	126	1	1-1	1-h	2-1	1-1¼	.45
Brief Grief	Mercado	120	10	4-½	3-h	1-h	2-1¼	90.90
Au Printemps	Johnson	116	4	9-1	8-1	3-2½	3-¾	10.20
Indellare	Loseth	119	8	11	11	10-1	4-nk	15.75
Okan Dee Select	Patzer	120	5	10-2	9-3	4-1	5-3	6.60
Dream Disturber	Mena	113	2	3-1	4-4	6-3	6-2	37.15
Salt Treaty	Hverson	113	7	7-1	7-h	7-2	7-3	20.35
Cinders Shadow	Phipps	116	6	6-2½	6-h	9-3	8-nk	18.20
Miss Zulu Gold	Zook	117	9	2-2	2-2	8-1	9-6	18.85
Chemainus Belle	Williams	117	3	8-½	11	10-6	10-7	3.250
Blushing Minstrel	Cghtn	114	11	5-½	5-h	11	11	32.50

Time — :23, :47, 1:12.1, 1:38.1, 1:51.3.

BELLE OF RAINIER	**2.90**	**3.80**	**2.60**
BRIEF GRIEF		**36.00**	**10.80**
AU PRINTEMPS			**4.60**

*The equations for EX Show and EX Place are those for Exhibition Park discussed in Chapter Four. These equations, (4.3) and (4.4), are quite accurate for other tracks as long as their track take is close to Exhibition Park's 17.1%. More accurate regression equations based on differing track takes also appear in Chapter Four, as equations (4.5) and (4.6).

Thus even though EX Show was greater than EX Place, the place bet appeared to be the preferable one when Brief Grief came in second. In fact, the place payoff exceeded the win payoff.

More insight into the relative merits of the win, place, and show bets on Belle of Rainier results from a consideration of the probability of possible finishes. Belle of Rainier's probability of winning was about

$$q_3 = \frac{W_3}{W} = \frac{20{,}005}{34{,}415} = 0.581.$$

Thus with a $2.90 payoff to win, the expected return per dollar bet was about 84¢, or an average loss of 16¢, which is close to the track take. The probability of finishing second was about 0.257; therefore, the probability of placing was 0.581 plus 0.257, or 0.834.* The $3 place payoff yielded an expected return per dollar bet of $1.25, or 25¢ profit. Finally, the probability of finishing third was about 0.107, and showing 0.945. Hence with a $2.60 payoff, the expected return per dollar bet was $1.23, or 23% profit. Thus even with a 90—1 shot finishing second, the show return was nearly as good as the place payoff. These values indicate that the place and show bets were both quite good. But just how unusual were the $3.00 and $2.60 payoffs? With expected values of 1.09 and 1.12 and probabilities of placing and showing of 0.838 and 0.945, you would expect payoffs for $2 bets of $2.46 and $2.66, respectively, or $2.40 and $2.60 with breakage.

To summarize: Bets on extreme favorites to place or show when the expected values qualify as Dr. Z system bets should be treated as such—

*The probability of winning is $q_3 = W_3/W = 20{,}005/34{,}415 = 0.581$. Since Belle of Rainier was an extreme favorite, assume each of the other nine horses had equal chances of winning of $(1 - 0.581)/9 = 0.047$. Then the probability of finishing second was

$$\frac{9q_iq_3}{1-q_i} = \frac{9(0.581)(0.047)}{0.953} = 0.257,$$

and the probability of finishing third was

$$\frac{(9)8q_iq_jq_3}{(1-q_i)(1-q_i-q_j)} = 0.107.$$

Therefore, the probabilities of placing and showing were 0.838 and 0.945, respectively. These estimates are on the conservative side, since, given the favorite–longshot bias, the probability of winning for such an extreme favorite is higher than 0.581.

good bets. Nearly always, such horses will finish in the money and provide modest returns. If one or more long shots come in, the payoffs will be quite substantial, given the low risk. In fact, if the bets on the remaining horses are relatively evenly divided and there are quite a few horses, say eight or more—as there were in The Ballerina—the payoffs on Dr. Z system bets will invariably be quite good. A very high percentage of extreme favorites do turn out to be Dr. Z system bets to place or show, simply because the crowd finds such bets distasteful. You hear all around you, "I do not want to bet on that favorite and get only $2.20." Bettors should not be discouraged by the apparent low odds; such odds represent an excellent investment opportunity with a good return and low risk.

Betting All Extreme Favorites to Place and Show

We now provide you with an idea of how you might expect to do betting on nothing but extreme favorites to place or show. The results from a full season of betting at the major New York State racetracks at Aqueduct, Belmont, and Saratoga in 1980 are summarized in Tables 13.2 and 13.3. By betting all favorites that are even money or less, you lose about 2% to place and 4% to show. For win, using Table 3.7, you lose about 10% (14% track take plus 3% breakage minus 7% bias). As with the win bets, the rate of return rises the lower the odds. Thus favorites are increasingly underbet the more they become certain of finishing in the money. According to the data in Tables 13.2 and 13.3, at odds of 3—10 or less, you actually make 13% to place and 5% to show. The place payoff is larger because of the possibility of payoffs greater than the $2.10 show bets generally provide. Even at 1—5, the place payoff can be $2.40. Both the place and show payoffs are statistically significantly greater than breaking even. Thus it appears that you can make profits by making place or show bets on all favorites going off at 3—10 or less. Of course, we recommend that you sift from these extreme favorites those that actually are Dr. Z system bets. Most of these extreme favorites will be Dr. Z system bets, and you will do better by eliminating the few that are not. Recall also from the discussion of the Kentucky Oaks in Chapter Six, that the minimum payoff in Kentucky is $2.20, so that there your bets on extreme favorites to place and especially to show have an added advantage.

TABLE 13.2 ***Rate of return on place bets for extreme favorites: 732 races in New York in 1980***

Tracks	Total in-the-Money Places/ Total Races	Odds Ranges (in-the-money places/races)									
		1—10	1—5	3—10	2—5	1—2	3—5	7—10	4—5	9—10	1—1
Aqueduct, Belmont Park, and Saratoga[a]	543/732	1/1	4/4	14/14	47/56	60/70	55/67	86/128	98/128	80/136	98/134
Percent in-the-money places	74.2	100	100	100	83.9	85.7	82.1	70.5	76.6	58.8	73.1
Payoff range	2.10–5.00	2.10	2.10–2.40	2.10–2.40	2.10–3.00	2.10–3.00	2.20–3.00	2.20–3.00	2.20–3.40	2.20–5.00	2.20–3.80
Average payoff	2.64	2.10	2.28	2.25	2.38	2.51	2.54	2.54	2.67	2.84	2.86
Rate of return	0.98	1.05	1.14	1.13	1.00	1.08	1.04	0.90	1.02	0.84	1.05
	±0.07[b]	1.13 ± 0.06[b]			1.04 ± 0.04[b]			0.95 ± 0.10[b]			

Note: The data used to construct this table and Table 13.3 were obtained from the *Daily Racing Form's Chart Books* for 1980. Breakage at all three tracks is to the nearest 10¢ per dollar wagered. Thanks are due to Brian Canfield for help in collecting and analyzing the data.

[a]The racing dates for both tables were over 311 days: January 1–March 17, March 19–May 19, and October 15–December 31 at Aqueduct; May 21–July 28 and August 27–October 13 at Belmont; and July 30–August 25 at Saratoga.

[b]The rates of return in both Tables 13.2 and 13.3 are expected values ± two standard deviations. The standard deviation may be estimated by $\sqrt{\Sigma(X_i - \overline{X})^2/(N-1)N}$, where X_i is the return in the ith race out of the N races in each category, and $\overline{X}$ is the average return.

TABLE 13.3 *Rate of return on show bets for extreme favorites: 721 races in New York in 1980*

Tracks	Total in-the-Money Shows/ Total Races	Odds Ranges (in-the-money shows/races)									
		1—10	1—5	3—10	2—5	1—2	3—5	7—10	4—5	9—10	1—1
Aqueduct, Belmont Park, and Saratoga	611/721	1/1	3/3	13/13	50/55	64/69	56/65	102/121	108/126	105/134	109/134
Percent in-the-money shows	84.7	100	100	100	90.9	92.8	86.2	84.3	85.7	78.4	81.3
Payoff range	2.10–3.20	2.10	2.10	2.10	2.10–2.60	2.10–2.40	2.10–2.60	2.10–2.80	2.10–3.20	2.10–3.20	2.10–3.00
Average payoff	2.27	2.10	2.10	2.10	2.12	2.18	2.24	2.23	2.29	2.35	2.39
Rate of return	0.96	1.05	1.05	1.05	0.96	1.01.	0.97	0.94	0.98	0.92	0.97
	±0.04	1.05 ± 0.00			0.98 ± 0.03			0.95 ± 0.13			

Note: See footnote [b] on Table 13.2.

Betting Overwhelming Favorites in Major Stakes and Futurity Races

McCleary (1981) studied the results of betting on favorites to win, place, and show in major stakes and futurity races during 1977, 1978, and 1979. These are events with a gross of $100,000, the top races in North America. All horses carry the same weight in these races. The futurities are races in which the horses are nominated at or before birth. Since such fees accumulate and many horses drop out, the value of such races is very high. His theory was that if the horse was an overwhelming favorite and the conditions were right, the owners, trainers, and jockeys would be trying their utmost to win, and these horses would be good bets. By "overwhelming," he meant that the horse was the *Daily Racing Form's* consensus for the race, the horse was the betting public's favorite, and no other horse was 3—1 or less. By "conditions are right," he meant that the track conditions were the same as when the consensus was formed. His results indicated profits to win, place, and show that were statistically significant in each of these three years. To extend his analysis we added the years 1968, 1976, 1981, and 1982.* For 1968 we used races with grosses of $50,000 since allowing for inflation this amount corresponds to $100,000 races run at present. Table 13.4 summarizes the results of all these races. In addition, in Table 13.5 we restricted these results to situations were the favorite was extreme—less than even money or better.

The results indicate profits for place and show betting and slight losses for win bets; however, the results for 1968, 1976, 1981, and 1982 are not as encouraging as those McCleary found for 1977–1979.

McCleary argued that the overwhelming favorite would be a better bet if there were no logical contenders at 3—1 or better odds. We look into the wisdom of this filter rule in Table 13.6. The results indicate that you cannot reject the hypothesis that it does not matter if there is a contender or not. The only profits are for show bets, and they are modest. Many of the horses will be Dr. Z system bets. It is these we recommend. Skip the others.

*Thanks are due to Brian Canfield for assistance in collecting and analyzing these data, which were obtained from various years of the *American Racing Manual*.

TABLE 13.4 ***Results from bets to win, place, and show on overwhelming favorites in $100,000+ stakes and futurity races in North America during 1968, 1976–79, 1981, and 1982***

Year	Number of Races for Win	Number of Winners	Profit from $10 Bets to Win ($)	Number of Races for Place	Number of Placers	Profit from $10 Bets to Place ($)	Number of Races to Show	Number of Showers	Profit from $10 Bets to Show ($)
1968	58	27	(4.00)	56	43	104.00	54	45	70.00
1976	19	9	(42.00)	18	11	(30.50)	18	13	(23.50)
1977	26	17	116.00	26	21	84.00	25	23	75.50
1978	38	29	63.00	37	35	103.50	35	33	37.00
1979	46	34	52.50	44	42	114.00	43	42	54.00
1981	79	25	(245.00)	68	36	(130.50)	68	38	(98.50)
1982	58	27	(19.00)	58	38	33.00	58	47	42.00
Totals	324	168	(78.50)	307	226	277.50	301	241	156.50
		(51.9%)			(73.6%)			(80.1%)	
Rate of Return			0.98 ± 0.10			1.09 ± 0.07			1.05 ± 0.06

Note: In Tables 13.4 through 13.6, numerals in parentheses represent losses.

TABLE 13.5 ***Results from bets to win, place, and show on overwhelming, even-money-or-better favorites in $100,000+ stakes and futurity races in North America during 1968, 1976–79, 1981, and 1982***

Year	Number of Races for Win	Number of Winners	Profit from $10 Bets to Win ($)	Number of Races for Place	Number of Placers	Profit from $10 Bets to Place ($)	Number of Races to Show	Number of Showers	Profit from $10 Bets to Show ($)
1968	18	9	(64.00)	16	15	22.00	14	14	23.00
1976	13	9	4.00	12	10	14.00	12	11	9.00
1977	11	8	9.00	11	11	36.00	10	10	20.50
1978	34	27	43.00	33	31	68.50	31	29	18.00
1979	40	30	19.50	38	36	74.00	37	36	32.50
1981	48	18	(110.00)	37	23	(58.50)	37	29	(13.50)
1982	29	15	(74.00)	29	21	(25.00)	29	28	38.00
Totals	193	116	(172.50)	176	147	131.00	170	157	129.50
		(60.1%)			(83.5%)			(92.4%)	
Rate of Return			0.91 ± 0.14			1.07 ± 0.07			1.08 ± 0.05

TABLE 13.6 ***Results from bets to win, place, and show on overwhelming, even-money-or-better favorites in $100,000+ stakes and futurity races in North America during 1968, 1976, 1981, and 1982***

Year	Number of Races for Win	Number of Winners	Profit from $10 Bets to Win ($)	Number of Races for Place	Number of Placers	Profit from $10 Bets to Place ($)	Number of Races to Show	Number of Showers	Profit from $10 Bets to Show ($)
Fast/Firm Tracks Only; Rival Horses Not Allowed									
1968	15	9	(34.00)	14	13	17.00	12	12	17.50
1976	10	6	(11.00)	9	7	0.50	9	8	2.50
1981	31	14	(101.00)	30	18	(54.50)	30	24	(4.50)
1982	27	13	(81.00)	27	19	(27.00)	27	26	36.00
Totals	83	42	(227.00)	80	57	(64.00)	78	70	51.50
		(50.6%)			(71.3%)			(89.7%)	
Rate of Return			0.73 ± 0.16			0.92 ± 0.13			1.07 ± 0.08
Fast/Firm Tracks Only; Rival Horses Allowed									
1968	22	12	(57.00)	20	19	31.00	18	18	22.50
1976	20	11	(20.00)	19	14	(6.50)	19	15	(21.00)
1981	39	18	(107.00)	38	25	(44.50)	38	31	(3.50)
1982	42	20	(106.00)	42	29	(44.00)	41	37	32.00
Totals	123	61	(290.00)	119	87	(64.00)	116	101	30.00
		(49.6%)			(73.1%)			(87.1%)	
Rate of Return			0.76 ± 0.14			0.95 ± 0.11			1.03 ± 0.07

The Longacres Mile, Longacres, Renton, Washington, August 21, 1983

A typical overwhelming favorite was Chinook Pass in the Longacres Mile. He was 8—5 in the morning line, with the next highest rated horse, Moonlately at 5—1, the consensus best bet of the day and the favorite of the crowd at 6—5. Chinook Pass broke the world's record at $5\frac{1}{2}$ furlongs and is a dynamite sprinter. The only question in this race was, Could he last for a mile?

Forty-Eighth Running of

The Longacres Mile

1609 34 METERS

NINTH (GR. II)

1 Mile

$150,000 Added

THE LONGACRES MILE (48th Running)

PURSE $150,000 ADDED. FOR THREE-YEAR-OLDS AND UPWARD. By subscription of $150 each, which shall accompany the nomination, $750 to pass the entry box and $1,000 additional to start with $150,000 added, of which $28,500 to second, $21,750 to third and $13,500 to fourth and $3,750 to fifth, with the winner's share guaranteed to be not less than $115,000. All nominations, entry and starting fees to the winner. No penalties. In the event more than 14 horses are entered, at closing time of entries, the 14 highest weighted horses entered will be preferred in the draw for post position 1 through 14; the remaining entries to draw for post positions 15 and upward regardless of their weights. In the event of a scratch or scratches inside the gate, all horses will be advanced in post position order; however, a low-weighted horse may not move into the gate to the exclusion of a higher-weighted horse. No more than two horses representing an individual owner or trainer will be allowed to enter. Starters to be named through the entry box at the time of closing designated by racing secretary. High weights preferred. Closed with 4[illegible] nominations.

Track Record—ALWAYS GALLANT (5) 127—1:33 4/5 ONE MILE

OWNER TRAINER

DiFiore, Hamilton, & Et Al — Eduardo Inda
Lime green & royal blue squares, lime sleeves, lime green & blue cap
1 PEWTER GREY 118
B. c. 4 Grey Dawn II—Young Libby (FL)
P.P. 1 Jockey—**FRANCISCO MENA** 8

Sheree C Orr, Lessee — Steve Goldsmith
Blue, red sleeves, matching cap
2 TOUT OU RIEN 120
B. h. 5 Sham—Yonnie Girl (CAN)
P.P. 2 Jockey—**J. W. MILLS** 12

Sangara Stables — Joe Walls
Red, white trim, white S on back, matching cap
3 EARTHQUACK 118
B g. 4 Quack—Disastrous (FL)
P.P. 3 Jockey—**LARRY PIERCE** 10

R J Bennett — Robert J Anderson
Green, white sleeves, emblem on back, green cap
4 TRAVELLING VICTOR 118
B. c. 4 Hail to Victory—Travelling Round (CAN)
P P 4 Jockey—**CHRIS LOSETH** 6

Les Brainard — Buford Baze
Red & white, matching cap
5 MOONLATELY 120
Ch. g. 6 Philately—Have Faith (WA)
P P 5 Jockey—**GARY BAZE** 5

Hi Yu Stable — Laurie Anderson
Blue, gold shield HI YU on back, blue cap
6 CHINOOK PASS 125
Br. g. 4 Native Born—Yu Turn (WA)
P P 6 Jockey—**LAFFITT PINCAY** 8/5

J Ng & Tri Star Stables — Dave Forster
Red, gold trim, gold stars on back, red cap
7 WANDER KIND 121 Kenneth Skinner (Photo Unavailable)
B. h. 5 Hold Your Peace—Mlle Liebe (FL)
P P 7 Jockey—**KENNETH SKINNER** 6

CLOCKER'S SELECTION: 6-5-7

NINTH RACE CONTINUED

OWNER TRAINER

Joseph Manzi & A. J. Vela — R. A. Meeking
Grey, black sash, grey cap
8 LORD ADVOCATE 117
B. c. 4 Inverness Drive—Tort Lass (KY)
P P 10 Jockey—**GARY STEVENS** 20

Floyd Street & George Skrypnek — Clement St Louis
Red, white sleeves, BS on back, matching cap
9 POCKET DEAL 119 Marcos Malvaez (Photo Unavailable)
Ch. g. 4 Class A—Kapps Bomb (CAN)
P P 11 Jockey—**MARCOS MALVAEZ** 20

B. G. & J. Billan — W. MacDonald
White, red & blue stripes, matching cap
10 FOOLISH OWNERS 119
Br. g. 5 Captain Courageous—Afula (WA)
P P 12 Jockey—**SANDY HAWLEY** 20

Canada West Ranches & A. L. Valliere — Harold Barroby
White, red maple leaf on back, white cap
11 KING ALPHONSE 115
B. c. 3 Ship Leave—Tricheuse (CAN)
P P 14 Jockey—**BRIAN JOHNSON** 20

Goodtime Stable — Richard Wright
Chartreuse, green polka dots, green GTS in horseshoe on back, chartreuse & green cap
12 FLYING JUDGEMENT 116
FIELD Ch. g. 4 Flying Lark—Rimmy's Judge (WA)
P P 8 Jockey—**TIM MALGARINI** 30

A. J. Segale & R. Rosatto — Marion L. Smith
Orange, black RS on back, orange & black cap
12a FABULOUS PATIENT 115
FIELD Br. c. 4 Somethingfabulous—T. V. Patient (WA)
P P 9 Jockey—**MIKE BAZE** 30

Ronald R. Ratcliff — Wayne McDonnell
White, black & red diagonal stripes, matching cap
12b NATIVE SHEIK 112
FIELD Gr. g. 5 Al Hattab—Sheba Sham (KY)
P P 13 Jockey—**JODY DAVIDSON** 30

Declared: IRON BILLY

Numbers 12, 12a, 12b coupled in mutuel field.

The Honorary Steward for the Longacres Mile (48th running will be Senator Warren G. Magnuson and his wife, Germaine.

HORSES. FIELD—WASHINGTON STATE HORSE RACING COMMISSION RULE 399—

When the total number of horses competing in a race exceeds the numbering capacity of the Tote, the highest numbered horse within the capacity of the Tote and all horses of a higher number shall be grouped together and called the Field and a wager on one of them shall be a wager on all of them.

COMMISSION RULE—WAC 260-48-190

If two or more horses in a race are coupled on the same mutuel ticket there shall be no refund unless all the horses so coupled are excused before off-time, or all of the horses so coupled are locked in the gate.

CLOCKER'S SELECTION: 6-5-7

He could; he won the race by five lengths and paid $4.30 to win, $3.60 to place, and $3.10 to show. Since the second- and third-place finishers, Travelling Victor and Earthquack, were leading contenders, it is clear that Chinook Pass was also an excellent Dr. Z system bet.* The chart of the race was as follows:

NINTH RACE
Lga
Aug. 21, 1983

1 MILE. (1:33⅘). FORTY-EIGHTH RUNNING OF THE LONGACRES MILE. Purse, $150,000-added for three-year-olds and up. By subscription of $150 each, which shall accompany the nomination, $750 to pass the entry box and $1,000 additional to start with $150,000-added, of which $28,500 to second, $21,750 to third, $13,500 to fourth and $3,750 to fifth, with the winner's share guaranteed to be not less than $115,000. All nominations, entry and starting fees to the winner. In the event more than 14 horses are entered, at closing time of entries, the 14 highest weighted horses entered will be preferred in the draw for post position 1 through 14; the remaining entries to draw for post positions 15 and upward regardless of their weights. In the event of a scratch or scratches inside the gate, all horses will be advanced in post position order; however, a low-weighted horse may not move into the gate to the exclusion of a higher-weighted horse. No more than two horses representing an individual owned or trainer will be allowed to enter. Closed with 42 nominations. Value of race, $182,500. Value to winner, $115,000; second, $28,500; third, $21,750; fourth, $13,500; fifth, $3,750. Mutuel Pool, $462,260.

Last Raced		Horse	EqtA	Wt	PP	St	¼	½	¾	Str	Fin	Jockeys	Owners	Odds to $1
31Jly 83	^{8}Dmr^{1}	Chinook Pass	4	125	6	1	$1^{2\frac{1}{2}}$	1^{6}	1^{5}	1^{4}	1^{6}	PincayLJr	Hi Yu Stable	1.15
7Aug83	^{9}Lga^{2}	Travelling Victor	4	118	4	2	4^{3}	3^{h}	3^{2}	2^{h}	2no	LosethC	R J Bennett	11.05
4Aug83	^{9}Lga^{2}	Earthquack	4	119	3	11	7^{h}	7^{2}	2^{h}	$3^{3\frac{1}{2}}$	3^{nk}	PierceL	Sangara Stables	6.80
7Aug83	^{8}Lga^{2}	Native Sheik	5	114	13	14	14	14	12^{3}	$6^{2\frac{1}{2}}$	4no	DavidsonJR	R R Ratcliff	f-22.35
7Aug83	^{9}Lga^{6}	Moonlately	6	120	5	8	5^{h}	6^{h}	$4^{1\frac{1}{2}}$	4^{3}	5^{3}	BazeG	L Brainard	5.85
7Aug83	^{9}Lga^{4}	Foolish Owners	5	119	12	9	10^{1}	$8^{1\frac{1}{2}}$	6^{2}	5^{3}	6^{3}	HawleyS	B-G-J Billan	16.80
10Jly 83	^{9}Lga^{4}	Lord Advocate	b4	117	10	13	13^{6}	$12^{\frac{1}{2}}$	9^{1}	7^{5}	$7^{4\frac{1}{2}}$	StevensG	Manzi-Vela	47.70
7Aug83	^{9}EP^{1}	Wander Kind	b5	121	7	5	$6^{\frac{1}{2}}$	9^{1}	$10^{\frac{1}{2}}$	10^{h}	$8^{1\frac{1}{2}}$	SkinnerK	J Ng-Tri Star Stable	9.40
16Jly 83	^{9}NP^{6}	Pocket Deal	4	119	11	6	$8^{\frac{1}{2}}$	4^{1}	5^{1}	11^{2}	9no	MalvaezMG	Street-Skrypnek	43.70
6Aug83	^{8}EP^{1}	King Alphonse	b3	115	14	10	11^{4}	$11^{2\frac{1}{2}}$	$8^{1\frac{1}{2}}$	9^{h}	10no	JohnsonBG	CndaWstRchs-Vallre	21.85
29Jly 83	^{8}Lga^{8}	Flying Judgement	b4	116	8	12	12^{2}	13^{6}	11^{2}	8^{h}	11^{4}	MalgariniT	Goodtime Stable	f-22.35
5Aug83	^{8}Dmr^{6}	Pewter Grey	4	118	1	3	$2^{\frac{1}{2}}$	$2^{1\frac{1}{2}}$	7^{1}	12^{2}	12^{1}	MenaF	Difiore-Hmiltn-Et Al	35.45
7Aug83	^{9}Lga^{3}	Fabulous Patient	b4	118	9	7	9^{1}	$10^{\frac{1}{2}}$	13^{3}	$13^{3\frac{1}{2}}$	$13^{3\frac{1}{2}}$	BazeMB	Segale-Rosatto	f-22.35
7Aug83	^{9}Lga^{1}	Tout Ou Rien	b5	120	2	4	3^{1}	5^{h}	14	14	14	MillsJW	S C Orr	13.60

f-Mutuel field.

OFF AT 6:30. START GOOD. WON EASILY. Time, :22, :44⅘, 1:09⅘, 1:22⅕, 1:35⅘. Track fast.

$2 Mutuel Prices

6—CHINOOK PASS	4.30	3.60	3.10
4—TRAVELLING VICTOR		8.10	6.10
3—EARTHQUACK			4.30

Dk. b. or br. g, by Native Born—Yu Turn, by Turn-To. Trainer, Laurie N. Anderson. Bred by Hi Yu Stable (Wash.).

CHINOOK PASS, away alertly, sprinted clear at once, drew off to a commanding advantage on the backstretch, settled for the drive with a good lead and pulled away in the late stages to win with complete authority. TRAVELLING VICTOR raced within striking distance early, was sent up to offer a bid on the final turn, bumped with EARTHQUACK in the upper stretch and narrowly edged that rival in a stiff drive. EARTHQUACK saved ground while being outrun early, moved through along the rail on the second turn, bumped with TRAVELLING VICTOR entering the stretch and just missed for the place while under brisk pressure. A claim of foul against TRAVELLING VICTOR by the rider of EARTHQUACK was not allowed. NATIVE SHEIK, outrun for six furlongs, moved to the outside for the stretch run and closed with a bold rush. MOONLATELY lacked a closing kick. WANDER KIND raced in good position early, but gave way before going a half mile. POCKET DEAL was sent up to offer his best bid nearing the far turn and faltered. PEWTER GREY was hard hustled from the inside and stopped after a half.

Overweight—Earthquack, 1 pound; Fabulous Patient, 3; Native Sheik, 2. **Scratched—Iron Billy.**

*I did not attend this race, but my colleague Henry Pollacco did and recognized Chinook Pass as a Dr. Z system bet, much to his pleasure. Near post time, the tote board expected values per dollar bets and optimal bets with a betting fortune of $1,000 to place and show were (approximately) as follows:

	Totals	#6 Chinook Pass	Expected Value per Dollar Bet on Chinook Pass ($)	Optimal Bet on Chinook Pass ($)
Odds		6—5		
Win	236,812	91,000		
Place	123,000	35,000	1.13	75
Show	93,000	27,000	1.12	204

Such bets would have returned $135.00 to place and $316.20 to show, for a profit of $172.20.

CHAPTER 14

A Typical Day at the Races: Making the Best Bet in Each Race, Hollywood Park, May 30, 1982

Betting on All the Races

Many, in fact most, visitors to the racetrack and readers of this book will not wish to play only Dr. Z system bets, since these occur only about two to four times each day. To maintain the excitement of the sporting event, they would rather bet on most or all of the races. Our thesis in this book is that if you keep seriously to the Dr. Z system (and do not bet otherwise) it should win for you. What should you do in the races other than those that have Dr. Z system bets?

There are several possibilities. First, we claim no monopoly on winning systems at the racetrack. While we have no specific suggestions other than those made elsewhere in this book, there may well be systems that you could use to make positive profits in these other races. Second, you could make small bets in these other races, on the assumption that the fun will be worth your small losses, at the same time that you reserve bigger bets for the Dr. Z system bets. Finally, you could bet on that horse or horses in each race that are either Dr. Z system bets or have positive expected value. By *positive expected value,* we mean that for each dollar bet you will receive at least a dollar back, *on average.* As we argued in Chapter Nine, positive expected value using our formulas and methods will *not* lead to the maximum profits. In fact, it is probably not good enough for you to be fairly confident of achieving any profits at all. With the approximations and uncertainties involved, you need a higher expected-value cutoff than 1.00. For example, the break-even point for the data in Table 5.1 was 1.02. To make the maximum profits, we recommend 1.14 at tracks such as Santa Anita and Belmont, where there are very large betting pools and superior horses, and 1.18 at other tracks. Recall that an expected value of 1.14 means that, *on average*, you will receive $1.14 for each dollar wagered. Table A.1 in Appendix A indicates the relative sizes of the betting pools at most of the tracks in North America. Those that warrant cutoffs of 1.14 are listed on page 79 in Chapter Five. Nevertheless, if you pick horses with positive expected value you should at least, more or less, break even and do much better than the average bettor. See Table 13.1 in Chapter Thirteen for some values that indicate how you might do if you simply pick the favorite of the crowd to place or show in each race.

Useful Betting Rules

To investigate how such a system might work and to provide you with guidance on what to expect, I went to Hollywood Park in Inglewood, California, on Sunday, May 30, 1982, to try it out.

I used the following rules:

1. Bet $50 on the horse in each race that seems the best bet to place or show.
2. Bet only if the expected value is at least 1.00.
3. Do not bet on horses that have not run recently.
4. Concentrate on the top horses, namely, those favored by the crowd and the *Daily Racing Form's* consensus and those horses that consistently finish in the money in similar quality races.
5. Stick to the top jockeys, especially when the horse has never been ridden by today's jockey (this consideration is not important for horses that have consistently finished in the money with non-top jockeys riding them again today). See jockey and trainer standings in the following tabulations.
6. Bet to place for Dr. Z system bets only. This is because I also decided to concentrate on show bets. By betting each race, the strategy would be risky and show bets would minimize this risk. Since only about 15% of the Dr. Z system bets are to place, you are unlikely to get good enough place bets in each race to warrant the attention they would need unless they were outstanding bets.
7. For Dr. Z system bets for place and show, I would increase my $50 bet to the optimal Kelly criterion amount using my calculator with an expected-value cutoff of 1.14.

Jockey Standings
(through Saturday, May 29, 1982)

Jockey	Mounts	Firsts	Seconds	Thirds	Win (%)	In the Money (%)	Ranking
McCarron, C.	182	52	33	14	28.5	54.4	1
Guerra, W.	164	22	25	25	13.4	43.9	5
Pincay, L., Jr.	135	21	23	27	15.5	52.6	2
Hawley, S.	109	19	19	13	17.4	46.8	4
Delahoussaye, E.	125	18	21	14	14.4	42.4	6
Valenzuela, P.	114	14	13	13	12.3	35.1	8
McHargue, D.	113	13	14	13	11.5	35.4	7
Shoemaker, W.	55	13	9	6	23.6	50.9	3
Castaneda, M.	130	12	12	20	9.2	33.8	10
Olivares, F.	112	12	12	15	10.7	34.8	9

Trainer Standings
(through Saturday, May 29, 1982)

Trainer	Starts	Firsts	Seconds	Thirds	Win (%)	In the Money (%)	Ranking
Frankel, R.	74	9	18	10	12.1	50.0	3
Palma, H.	59	9	7	6	15.2	37.2	13
Vienna, D.	44	9	7	4	20.4	45.4	7
Bernstein, D.	51	8	7	9	15.7	47.1	5
Stute, M.	40	8	7	3	20.0	45.0	8
Whittingham, C.	34	7	4	3	20.6	41.2	11
Gosden, J.	23	7	2	1	30.4	43.5	10
Mitchell, M.	29	7	1	5	24.1	44.8	9
Truman, E.	34	6	9	2	17.6	50.0	3
Russell, J.	33	6	8	3	18.1	51.5	2
Lukas, D. W.	44	6	6	8	13.6	45.5	6
Jones, G.	25	6	4	3	24.0	52.0	1
Mandella, R.	35	6	3	5	17.1	40.0	12

Note: You can find these jockey and trainer standings in your racing program. If you wish to use this information, you need to calculate separately the in-the-money percentages, as we have done here. The program usually gives only the win percentages. Ranking jockeys and trainers by *numbers* of winners, as is done in these program listings, is misleading. The best measure for our purposes is *in-the-money percentage.* The top jockeys of this meeting were Chris McCarron, Laffit Pincay, Jr., and Bill Shoemaker, followed by Sandy Hawley, Walter Guerra, and Eddie Delahoussaye. The trainers were quite evenly matched. It is better not to try to get to the level of detail involved in evaluating trainers in your betting. Leave that to the experts who are establishing fair win odds.

Experts' Selections

Consensus Points: 5 for 1st (today's best 7), 2 for 2nd, 1 for 3rd. Today's Best in Bold Type.

Racing Form

Trackman, Warren Williams **HOLLYWOOD PARK** Selections Made for Fast Track

	TRACKMAN	HANDICAP	ANALYST	HERMIS	SWEEP	CONSENSUS	
1	SO CALLED	MY MASTERPIECE	TRIPLANE	TRIPLANE	TRIPLANE	TRIPLANE	17
	MY MASTERPIECE	SO CALLED	QUALIFICATION	SO CALLED	THE BIG T.	SO CALLED	10
	TRIPLANE	TRIPLANE	SO CALLED	THE METHOD	QUALIFICATION	MY MASTERPIECE	7
2	CITA SOMBRITA	CITA SOMBRITA	ROLLING GIRL	MY DUTCHESS	CITA SOMBRITA	CITA SOMBRITA	15
	MY DUTCHESS	MY DUTCHESS	MY DUTCHESS	ROLLING GIRL	MY DUTCHESS	MY DUTCHESS	13
	OTRA PROMESA	BAD BAD LUCY	NATIVE ITCH	BAD BAD LUCY	ROLLING GIRL	ROLLING GIRL	8
3	COLONEL STU	MESSAGE TO GARCIA	COLONEL STU	SHANTIN	COLONEL STU	COLONEL STU	19
	DOON'S BAY	COLONEL STU	SHANTIN	COLONEL STU	SHANTIN	SHANTIN	11
	SHANTIN	SHANTIN	DOON'S BAY	DOON'S BAY	DOON'S BAY	DOON'S BAY	5
4	B. RICH GEORGE	**MASTER WARRIOR**	B. RICH GEORGE	PERRY CABIN	SALI'S ROYAL DREAM	B. RICH GEORGE	12
	PERRY CABIN	CHAPEL CREEK	CHAPEL CREEK	B. RICH GEORGE	PERRY CABIN	PERRY CABIN	11
	MASTER WARRIOR	PERRY CABIN	PERRY CABIN	SALI'S ROYAL DREAM	MASTER WARRIOR	MASTER WARRIOR	9
5	INSEARCHOF	JET PIRATE	INSEARCHOF	JET PIRATE	DISTANT GEM	JET PIRATE	16
	JET PIRATE	INSEARCHOF	JET PIRATE	INSEARCHOF	JET PIRATE	INSEARCHOF	14
	EXTRA QUICK	CHECKER'S ORPHAN	FAMILIAR TUNE	MURTAZZ	NAT'S PENNY	DISTANT GEM	5
6	SPARKLE CRYSTAL	DYNAMIC GIRL	LEADING ADVOCATE	ASTORIAN	LEADING ADVOCATE	LEADING ADVOCATE	16
	LEADING ADVOCATE	LEADING ADVOCATE	SPARKLE CRYSTAL	LEADING ADVOCATE	ASTORIAN	SPARKLE CRYSTAL	10
	ASTORIAN	SPARKLE CRYSTAL	ASTORIAN	SPARKLE CRYSTAL	SPARKLE CRYSTAL	ASTORIAN	9
7	PIRATE LAW	PIRATE LAW	MOON BALL	ANOTHER REALM	FAST	PIRATE LAW	12
	PATTI'S TRIUMPH	CONFETTI	CONFETTI	MOON BALL	PIRATE LAW	MOON BALL	9
	MOON BALL	FAST	FAST	FAST	MOON BALL	FAST	8
8	REMEMBER JOHN	REMEMBER JOHN	**NEVER TABLED**	NEVER TABLED	**NEVER TABLED**	NEVER TABLED	23
	NEVER TABLED	NEVER TABLED	REMEMBER JOHN	REMEMBER JOHN	REMEMBER JOHN	REMEMBER JOHN	16
	PETRO D. JAY	POMPEII COURT	POMPEII COURT	SHANEKITE	POMPEII COURT	POMPEII COURT	3
9	**HEART BEAT**	HEART BEAT	HEART BEAT	**HEART BEAT**	HEART BEAT	**HEART BEAT**	29
	EL PANCHO ANGEL	PIERRE LA MONT	KUNDALINI	PIERRE LA MONT	EL PANCHO ANGEL	EL PANCHO ANGEL	5
	KUNDALINI	KUNDALINI	PIERRE LA MONT	EL PANCHO ANGEL	KUNDALINI	KUNDALINI	5

SWEEP'S Hollywood Park Graded Handicaps

FIRST RACE — *Probable Post, 1:31*

1 1/16 MILES. 4–Year–Olds and Up. Claiming ($16,000 to $14,000). Purse $13,000.

P.P.	Horse.	Prob. Jockey.	Wt.	Comment.	Prob. Odds.
6	TRIPLANE	Delahoussaye E	118	Back where belongs	5-2
3	THE BIG T.	Ortega L E	115	Threat to tag speed	8-1
10	QUALIFICATION	Hawley S	115	Try runaway tactics	5-1
2	SO CALLED	Hansen R D	115	Question of condition	4-1
4	MY MASTERPIECE	Lipham T	118	Held on real gamely	6-1
9	THE METHOD	Steiner J J	^{5}108	Comes off good sprint	8-1
1	DR. STORK	Pierce D	115	Claimed in comeback	12-1
8	FLEET RULER	Olivares F	115	Eliminated at start	12-1
7	ON EL PASEO	Diaz A L	115	$12,500 Sinne claim	15-1
5	MAGIC STAR	Valenzuela P A	115	Probably needed last	20-1

SECOND RACE — *Probable Post, 2:02*

6 ½ FURLONGS. 4–Year–Olds and Up, Fillies and Mares. Claiming ($20,000 to $18,000). Purse $14,000.

8	CITA SOMBRITA	Castaneda M	115	Sharp gal right now	5-2
7	MY DUTCHESS	McCarron C J	113	Chris stays with her	3-1
5	ROLLING GIRL	Steiner J J	^{5}110	Ran well over oval	9-2
3	ALLARRONES COMET	McHrDG	115	Failed as favorite	6-1
2	NATIVE ITCH	Valenzuela P A	115	Sharpened in north	8-1
1	BAD BAD LUCY	Sibille R	118	Overmatched in last	8-1
6	KATHINKA	Hansen R D	115	Improvement needed	15-1
4	GOLDEN POLICY	Diaz A L	113	Lacked late kick	15-1
9	OTRA PROMESA	Black K	115	Hard to boost	20-1

THIRD RACE — *Probable Post, 2:33*

6 FURLONGS. 3–Year–Olds and Up, Bred in Cal. Allowance. Purse $20,000.

6	COLONEL STU	Delahoussaye E	116	Ready for a smasher	2-1
3	SHANTIN	Valenzuela P A	111	Drilled in :58 3/5	7-2
4	DOON'S BAY	McCarron C J	122	Back with leading man	5-2
1	CROFTED	Pincay L Jr	122	Slow starter on rail	8-1
8	MESSAGE TO GARCIA	CstndM	111	Can't be dismissed	8-1
2	READY REB	Olivares F	114	Last far from best	15-1
5	SEAVOY	Diaz A L	116	Found where wire is	15-1
7	WAR HOUSE	Wellington H K	116	Third in Fresno stakes	30-1
9	WINDY SCOTT	Steiner J J	^{5}109	Figures to weaken	30-1

FOURTH RACE — *Probable Post, 3:04*

7 FURLONGS. 3–Year–Olds and Up. Allowance. Purse $26,000.

5	SALI'S ROYAL DREAM	McCrrCJ	116	Edge in tight fit	4-1
6	PERRY CABIN	Olivares F	116	Bobbled at break	5-2
7	MASTER WARRIOR	Sibille R	116	Comes off game try	7-2
1	B. RICH GEORGE	Pincay L Jr	111	Look who takes over	3-1
3	CHAPEL CREEK	McHargue D G	116	Last more like it	6-1
4	SURPRISE GEORGE	DlhoussyE	116	Prepping for router?	10-1
2	SOME LUTE	Valenzuela P A	116	Made lead on grass	20-1

FIFTH RACE — *Probable Post, 3:35*

6 FURLONGS. 3–Year–Olds. Claiming ($40,000 to $35,000). Purse $18,000.

6	DISTANT GEM	Valenzuela P A	116	Fast works, likes track	5-2
4	JET PIRATE	Sibille R	116	Dropping for this	3-1
8	NAT'S PENNY	Delahoussaye E	114	Tough with these	6-1
3	INSEARCHOF	McHargue D G	116	Must be considered	9-2
11	SPECTACULAR BEE	McCrrnCJ	116	Fits better here	8-1
10	CHECKER'S ORPHAN	Pierce D	116	Faltered in router	12-1
9	GRINGO JIM	Pincay L Jr	116	Steps into claimer	12-1
5	EXTRA QUICK	Castaneda M	116	Back at best distance	15-1
2	FAMILIAR TUNE	Ortega L E	112	Good race to easier	15-1
7	MURTAZZ	Lipham T	116	Well backed in north	30-1
1	RAMBLE ON JOHN	Ramirez O	116	Little to endorse	30-1

Blinkers On: Insearchof.

SIXTH RACE — *Probable Post, 4:07*

1 MILE. 3–Year–Olds and Up, Fillies and Mares. Maiden Special weights. Purse $18,000.

7	LEADING ADVOCATE	PincyLJr	114	Soft graduation spot	2-1
9	ASTORIAN	McHargue D G	114	Promise in New York	3-1
3	SPARKLE CRYSTAL	McCrrnCJ	114	McCarron-Gosden team	5-2
4	DYNAMIC GIRL	Hawley S	114	Puts on blinkers	8-1
6	TELL'S TREASURE	Hansen R D	122	Speed for partways	10-1
2	DELICATE GRACE	ValenzuelPA	114	Caved in early	15-1
8	LOST LOOT	Ortega L E	114	Dull dash return	15-1
5	QUIZZICAL	Steiner J J	^{5}117	Didn't beat a soul	30-1
1	JENNIE'S IMAGE	Lipham T	114	Must do much better	30-1

Blinkers On: Dynamic Girl, Tell's Treasure.

SEVENTH RACE — *Probable Post, 4:40*

1 1/16 MILES.(turf) 4–Year–Olds and Up. Allowance. Purse $40,000.

5	FAST	McCarron C J	114	Winner if ready	5-2
3	PIRATE LAW	Valenzuela P A	114	Ran well over course	3-1
7	MOON BALL	Castaneda M	114	Staged 48-1 surprise	9-2
6	PATTI'S TRIUMPH	Hawley S	118	No excuses last trip	5-1
9	CONFETTI	Pincay L Jr	114	Wide throughout	6-1
1	HAUGHTY BUT NICE	McHrgDG	114	Gave way on lead	10-1
4	SUNNY WINTERS	DelhoussyeE	116	Didn't belong in last	12-1
2	ANOTHER REALM	Gilligan L	114	Surprise package	12-1
8	GOLDEN FLAK	Hansen R D	114	Back from Golden Gate	3-1

Coupled—Pirate Law and Golden Flak.

EIGHTH RACE — *Probable Post, 5:12*

6 FURLONGS. 30th Running of THE LOS ANGELES HANDICAP (Grade III). 3–Year–Olds and Up. . Purse $75,000 Added.

7	NEVER TABLED	McCarron C J	116	Conditions to order	2-1
1	REMEMBER JOHN	DelhoussyeE	115	Just won from rail	5-2
3	POMPEII COURT	Sibille R	116	Always gives his best	9-2
2	SHANEKITE	Hawley S	117	Doesn't look right	6-1
4	PETRO D. JAY	Castaneda M	116	Equalled world mark	6-1
6	BEACH WALK	Steiner J J	113	Game but in tough	12-1
5	COOL FRENCHY	Aragon J	112	Longshot pilot aboard	20-1
8	TERRESTO'S SINGER	VlnzulPA	113	Rider fits him well	20-1

Blinkers Off: Terresto's Singer.

NINTH RACE — *Probable Post, 5:45*

1 1/8 MILES.(turf) 4–Year–Olds and Up. Claiming ($50,000). Purse $28,000.

5	HEART BEAT	Pincay L Jr	116	Spotted for top try	8-5
4	EL PANCHO ANGEL	Lipham T	116	Nosedive in class	3-1
2	KUNDALINI	Valenzuela P A	116	Finished fairly well	6-1
7	WANTAZEE	Delahoussaye E	119	May take to turf	4-1
8	PIERRE LA MONT	Hawley S	116	Weakened in marathon	6-1
6	INGRES	Sibille R	116	Passed tiring horses	12-1
3	BUFFALO HART	Pierce D	116	Outrun by better	20-1
1	FABULOUS REASON	CastnedM	116	View from Century	30-1

ANALYST'S *Hollywood Comment*

THIRD RACE
1—Colonel Stu
2—Shantin
3—Doon's Bay

COLONEL STU, a lightly raced colt, showed grit last trip when runner-up to Rawbone in 1:09 flat. He was 1 1/2 lengths ahead of strong rival DOON'S BAY and will be getting six pounds from that foe. He also gets off the rail and Eddie D. SHANTIN ran gamely behind the swift L'Cap last trip and the sophomore will be dropping eight pounds. He has a bullet work of :58 3/5 on the 23rd and seems strictly on the improve. DOON'S BAY is usally in the thick of contention and will be reunited with McCarron today. Despite his 122 pounds he has enough heart to be a strong factor. WINDY SCOTT should give them all something to run at.

FOURTH RACE
1—B. Rich George
2—Chapel Creek
3—Perry Cabin

B. RICH GEORGE is the likely speed of this contest, and although he couldn't hold off Jet Travel and Dena Jo last trip, he doesn't find that type of competition in this line-up. He should be extremely tough to catch from the rail with Pincay aloft. CHAPEL CREEK moved up dramatically last time at 27-1 and seems to be coming around for Cleveland and may start running to some of his spectacular works. He drilled a bullet 1:25 since his improved race. PERRY CABIN was flying at the finish last trip, being lapped on stakes caliber No No. If the speed falters, he could be along in time. SALI'S ROYAL DREAM usually moves up with McCarron aboard, while MASTER WARRIOR may be able to push the top choice.

FIFTH RACE
1—Insearchof
2—Jet Pirate
3—Familiar Tune

INSEARCHOF ran a fine race last trip when he closed willingly and was beaten a neck by the vastly improved Michelle's Dream. The colt has come around this season for Warren Stute and McHargue was aboard for his maiden win April 20 at Santa Anita. He may be able to rate him a bit better now and blinkers should help. JET PIRATE is back in a league where he might utilize his speed. FAMILIAR TUNE was third to Michelle's Dream last out, beaten a length. It was a fine try for only his fifth lifetime start and the slightest improvement could find him right in the hunt. MURTAZZ has every right to move up here, while DISTANT GEM could flash speed in his return off good a.m. works.

SIXTH RACE
1—Leading Advocate
2—Sparkle Crystal
3—Astorian

LEADING ADVOCATE was bumped at the start last time and didn't duplicate her fine effort behind Trust Us May 1, although she finished a creditable third behind the impressive Miss Elea. Pincay takes over the controls today and they should find the charmed circle. SPARKLE CRYSTAL has some nice works for her debut (:14 3/5, 1:41 4/5 and 1:26 4/5). Look for McCarron to get some run from this Sir Gaylord filly. ASTORIAN, a full sister to Agitate, the 1974 Hollywood Derby and Swaps winner, showed some promise in New York last September and Laz Barrera may have her ready to ramble, although her workout times have been moderate. TELL'S TREASURE, a half sister to Ack's Secret, may like a mile and gets off the rail. She came back to work well and gets blinkers.

SEVENTH RACE
1—Moon Ball
2—Confetti
3—Fast

MOON BALL appears to have found his winning stride off a stunning 48-1 tally last journey over a fine group of turf specialists. There is enough speed here for him to stalk again and looks perfectly placed for a repeat. CONFETTI was fourth to the top horse last out and seems to be acclimating nicely now after racing well in Group races in France in 1981. Pincay will be aboard this Hofmans trainee. FAST makes his comeback today after being on the shelf since 1980. He has been working exceptionally well for Whittingham and McCarron will be aboard. The 5-year-old could be right on edge. ANOTHER REALM has every right to improve, while SUNNY WINTERS is working well at Santa Anita and may enjoy the turf.

EIGHTH RACE
1—NEVER TABLED
2—Remember John
3—Pompeii Court

NEVER TABLED showed he was made of stakes timber last out when he pulled away in the stretch to win the Triple Bend 'Cap in 1:21. He is certainly favorably weighted at 116 and off a :35 blowout Friday he looks fit and ready to continue his winning ways. REMEMBER JOHN, a 3-year-old beat his elders last time, stepping 5 panels in :56, a tick off the track mark. He has the rail here and will likely have to battle PETRO D. JAY, who equalled the world mark of 1:07 1/5 last out at Turf Paradise. These two speedsters could easily kill each other off. POMPEII COURT is very sharp, while SHANEKITE may be tailing off.

NINTH RACE
1—Heart Beat
2—Kundalini
3—Pierre La Mont

HEART BEAT has the difficult task of dropping back off a 1 3/8 miles nose defeat on the turf to 1 1/8 miles, but the Frankel trainee seems to be reaching a higher plateau these days and the 5-year-old may have the class advantage. Pincay gave him a top ride last out and they combine again in this nightcap. KUNDALINI ran third at 21-1 last trip and has enjoyed this turf course in the past. He should be a stronger contender. PIERRE LA MONTE hasn't been showing his flair for speed in recent races, but should clear this field if WANTAZEE, who has never been on the turf, can't keep him company. Hawley could steal the race with PIERRE. EL PANCHO ANGEL drops into a league where he can be dangerous. Lipham has given him some fine rides in the past.

The Results

I arrived for the third race; the first two races featured only cheap claiming horses—that is, those that can be claimed for a small amount of money. The third race was a $20,000 allowance race. Shantin, the second choice in the consensus, had expected values to show in the 1.05–1.10 range and had finished in the money in seven of his ten career starts, mostly against similar-quality opposition. He was also dropping 8 pounds from his last race, when he ran a creditable second with an 89 speed rating. Colonel Stu, the favorite, also ran an 89 in his last race, but he was picking up weight and had only one race in 1982 and two in 1981. Even if the odds were good, which they were not, I would be quite nervous about placing a bet on such a horse. The choice was Shantin.

3rd Hollywood

6 FURLONGS. (1.07⅗) ALLOWANCE. Purse $20,000. 3-year-olds and upward bred in California which have not won a race other than maiden or claiming. Weights, 3-year-olds, 114 lbs.; older, 122 lbs. Non-winners of a race other than claiming since March 15 allowed 3 lbs.; such a race since February 15, 6 lbs.

Crofted — Dk. b. or br. g. 4, by Reflected Glory—Shadycroft Gal, by Bupers
Own.—Sorenson Heather D — **122** — Br.—Sorenson Heather D (Cal) — Tr.—Gregson Edwin
1982 4 1 1 1 $15,300
1981 5 M 1 0 $3,000
Lifetime 9 1 2 1 $18,300

8May82-7Hol	1 1/16	:46	1:103	1:43 ft	5	114	31½	42	713	717	ShoemkerW6	Aw22000	63	‡LittleShah,Wantazee,RomnMjesty	8
20Mar82-4SA	6½f	:214	:443	1:164ft	4	118	63¾	63¾	43½	1½	Shoemaker W9	Mdn	86	Crofted,QuackAttack,RivetsFctor	12
5Mar82-6SA	6½f	:214	:444	1:162ft	8¾	118	42	43¼	33	32	Black K11	Mdn	86	Santir, Rivets Factor, Crofted	12
11Feb82-6SA	6½f	:221	:454	1:182gd	25	117	52¼	53½	21	22½	Black K7	Mdn	75	RegalFalcon,Crofted,RivetsFactor	12
29Dec81-6SA	1 1/16	:46	1:111	1:434ft	11	117	78¾	1216	1220	1224	Sibille R8	Mdn	58	‡Poor John, Garibi, Durban Deep	12
20Nov81-6Hol	6f	:22	:452	1:11 ft	5	120	2hd	1hd	2hd	2no	Sibille R5	Mdn	82	Royal Name, Crofted, Arnold	12
18Apr81-1GG	6f	:214	:45	1:111ft	22	118	42¼	53¾	88¾	87½	Diaz A5	[S]Mdn	75	Inffbl,AristocrticClown,SnowWrror	8
21Feb81-1GG	1 1/16	:464	1:111	1:434ft	14	118	53¾	811	921	932	Diaz A4	Mdn	52	Truxton'sDoubl,NoPcnc,OurGlmour	9
7Feb81-6GG	6f	:221	:452	1:101ft	15	118	79¼	811	711	69¾	Hall D C2	Mdn	78	BoidDrum,VisiblPol.CutiousRobrt	12

●May 23 Hol 6f ft 1:121 h May 17 Hol 4f ft :47 h May 6 Hol 4f ft :502 b ●Apr 26 SA 1 ft 1:41 h

Ready Reb — Gr. c. 3, by Reb's Policy—Tulita, by Tumollo
Own.—Fanning & Harrison — **114** — Br.—Fanning & Harrison (Cal) — Tr.—Fanning Jerry
1982 6 1 0 0 $11,900
1981 0 M 0 0
Lifetime 6 1 0 0 $11,900

14May82-3Hol	7f	:214	:441	1:221ft	12	120	52¼	52¼	711	612	Olivares F5	[S]Aw20000	74	L'Ntty,EnvoysIntrigue,MssgToGrci	7
24Apr82-6Hol	6f	:221	:45	1:093ft	2½	118	21	21	2½	1hd	Olivares F5	Mdn	89	ReadyReb,ElderwoodSpecial,Crlyon	5
31Mar82-4SA	6f	:221	:444	1:094ft	12	118	82½	67½	66½	66¼	Lipham T5	[S]Mdn	83	Sobrehombr,PrincChnnon,LottFlt	10
17Mar82-2SA	6f	:214	:453	1:113sy	2½	118	35	32½	35	46¾	Lipham T3	[S]Mdn	73	WindyScott,LottFleet,ThQuiltdKid	7
17Feb82-6SA	6½f	:214	:443	1:16 ft	4	118	52½	33½	57½	411	Olivares F7	[S]Mdn	79	MssgToGrci,Polly'sRulr,Mrni'sDncr	9
3Feb82-4SA	6f	:214	:451	1:101ft	6½	118	3½	2hd	23	711	Olivares F4	[S]Mdn	76	Shantin, Buckohoy,ForgottenMan	11

May 23 Hol 4f ft :502 h May 9 Hol 5f ft :593 h May 2 Hol 4f ft :52 b Apr 21 SA 5f ft 1:00 h

Shantin * — B. g. 3, by Exalted Rullah—Career, by Poona II
Own.—Kelly & Christianson — **111** — Br.—Christianson C T (Cal) — Tr.—King Hal
1982 7 2 2 1 $31,000
1981 3 M 1 1 $5,350
Lifetime 10 2 3 2 $36,350

9May82-5Hol	6f	:22	:444	1:09 ft	2½	119	42½	43	23½	22½	McCarron C J4	50000	89	L'Cap, Shantin, Can't Be Beat	6
14Apr82-3SA	6f	:214	:443	1:094ft	5	120	41½	32½	31	42½	Asmussen C B3	62500	86	SkiRacer,Smuggler'sGold,ImSizzler	6
18Mar82-9SA	6f	:214	:452	1:12 m	2½	120	45½	42½	2hd	1½	Guerra W A4	50000	78	Shantin, Daily Report, Il Paladino	7
7Mar82-2SA	6½f	:212	:44	1:144ft	7	120	811	914	911	812	CastanedaM5	Aw20000	84	AdvanceMan,GeneralJimmy,L'Ntty	9
21Feb82-2SA	7f	:214	:44	1:22 ft	12	120	2½	2½	2½	33¼	CastanedaM9	Aw20000	87	Prestigious Lad, Le Smirk, Shantin	9
3Feb82-4SA	6f	:214	:451	1:101ft	*2½	118	1hd	1hd	13	1¾	Asmussen C B8	[S]Mdn	87	Shantin, Buckohoy,ForgottenMan	11
22Jan82-6SA	7f	:221	:452	1:234gd	3	118	2hd	3½	25	212	AsmussenCB11	[S]Mdn	69	DeLaGuerra,Shantin,ForgottenMn	12
26Dec81-3SA	6f	:22	:443	1:092ft	*2¼	118	22½	—	—	—	McCarron C J1	[S]Mdn	—	B.RchGorg,OlympcGol,CrystlDrps	11
26Dec81—Lame															
30Sep81-3SA	6f	:214	:451	1:10 ft	4	118	1hd	1½	1hd	2nk	McCarron C J2	[S]Mdn	88	Gaelic'sSport,Shntin,DesertEnvoy	12
4Sep81-6Dmr	6f	:221	:453	1:11 ft	6¼	118	63¾	42	2½	32¾	McCarron CJ12	[S]Mdn	80	PrinceSpellbound,CrystlStr,Shntin	12

●May 23 Hol 5f ft :583 h May 17 Hol 3f ft :36 h May 4 Hol 5f ft :584 h Apr 27 Hol 4f ft :481 h

Doon's Bay — B. g. 4, by Matsadoon—Sinbay, by Bay Ribbon
Br.—Eklund R L (Cal) — 1982 3 1 1 1 $16,350
Own.—Eklund R L — 122 — Tr.—Harte M G — 1981 11 M 6 0 $13,470
Lifetime 14 1 7 1 $29,820

14May82-5Hol	6f	:221	:444	1:09 ft	*2¾	120	2½	2½	34½	34½	Hawley S5	Aw20000	87	Rawbone, Colonel Stu, Doon's Bay	7
5May82-7Hol	6f	:214	:443	1:091ft	6	120	41¾	53¼	33½	22½	McCarronCJ4	Aw20000	88	TonysLndng,Doon'sBy,ChrgAccont	6
17Apr82-6SA	6½f	:22	:444	1:162ft	5¼	118	31	2½	11½	1¾	McCarron C J9	Mdn	88	Doon'sBy,TruceMker,BruinCounty	12
4Dec81-5BM	6f	:23	:463	1:12 ft	*6-5	118	85¼	74	54½	74¾	Diaz A L10	AlwM	75	CldBTff,BrvCmmndr,QckrEnCndy	12
14Nov81-1BM	1	:462	1:111	1:371gd	*1	118	21	2hd	1hd	2hd	Diaz A L4	Mdn	83	Penns Friends, Doon's Bay, StatsU.	9
30Oct81-3BM	1 1/16	:47	1:123	1:451ft	*8-5	116	2½	2hd	33	27	Diaz A L6	Mdn	66	FbulousRson,Doon'sBy,PrciousTim	7
16Oct81-4BM	1 1/16	:461	1:103	1:424ft	*9-5	116	21	11	12	2nk	Diaz A L4	Mdn	85	ArroyoSeco,Doon'sBy,FbulousRson	9
2Oct81-4BM	1 1/16	:453	1:10	1:424ft	*2½	116	47½	24	22	21½	Diaz A L6	Mdn	83	Cinnpo, Doon's Bay, Stats U.	8
23Sep81-6BM	6f	:223	:452	1:103ft	*6-5	116	1hd	2hd	3nk	2no	Diaz A L2	Mdn	87	BoldTatt,Doon'sBy,BrveCommnder	7
10Sep81-7Bmf	6f	:223	:46	1:112ft	15	116	54	31½	21½	2no	Diaz A L11	Mdn	83	Rhythmus, Doon's Bay, HighAgain	12

Apr 29 Hol 5f ft 1:033 h — Apr 10 SA 7f ft 1:27 h — Apr 3 SA 6f ft 1:122 hg

Seavoy — Dk. b. or br. g. 4, by Envoy—Come Sea Me Honey, by Windy Sea
Br.—Pascoe W T III (Cal) — 1982 9 1 2 0 $17,350
Own.—Cmpnlli-Myr-Murphy-Thoms — 116 — Tr.—Stute Melvin F — 1981 1 M 0 1 $2,100
Lifetime 10 1 2 1 $19,450

6May82-6Hol	6f	:214	:452	1:104ft	3½	123	31½	32	1½	12	Pincay L Jr5	M40000	83	Seavoy, Sales Goal, Blow Taps	12
23Apr82-6Hol	6½f	:222	:451	1:17 ft	*2	121	1½	2hd	23	45½	ValenzuelaPA8	M45000	79	DeltaGambler,JsminePrince,Dilville	8
2Apr82-6SA	6f	:214	:45	1:101ft	*2¼	118	2hd	2½	45	79¾	Delahoussaye E4	Mdn	77	NeverTbled,Hwkire,SpnishNugget	10
20Mar82-4SA	6½f	:214	:443	1:164ft	*2½	118	31½	21	32½	52½	Delahoussaye E2	Mdn	83	Crofted,QuackAttack,RivetsFctor	12
5Mar82-6SA	6½f	:214	:444	1:162ft	*9-5	118	3½	3nk	1hd	42¼	Valenzuela P A4	Mdn	86	Santir, Rivets Factor, Crofted	12
20Feb82-3SA	6f	:214	:443	1:091ft	5	117	11½	12½	13	2nk	Valenzuela P A3	Mdn	92	Cad, Seavoy, Exclusive Session	12
11Feb82-6SA	6½f	:221	:454	1:182gd	10	117	1hd	2½	54½	613	Valenzuela P A10	Mdn	65	RegalFalcon,Crofted,RivetsFactor	12
29Jan82-6SA	6f	:212	:442	1:103ft	2½	117	11½	14	1½	2nk	Valenzuela P A7	Mdn	85	Ergo, Seavoy, Peter Jones	12
16Jan82-4SA	6f	:214	:45	1:10 ft	*2	117	43½	33	45½	47¾	Valenzuela P A11	Mdn	80	DrumDrum,RivetsFctor,Cumplnos	12
20Dec81-2Hol	6½f	:223	:45	1:182ft	4	118	1½	1hd	2hd	3nk	Valenzuela P A6	Mdn	78	Jensen'sPrince,Marc'sGleem,Sevoy	8

May 27 Hol 5f ft :592 h — May 21 Hol 4f ft :51 h — May 16 Hol 4f ft :474 h — May 1 Hol 5f ft 1:001 h

Colonel Stu — B. c. 4, by Orbit Ruler—Sarasvati, by Oceanus II
Br.—Williams & Cofer (Cal) — 1982 1 0 1 0 $4,000
Own.—Cofer R S — 116 — Tr.—Cofer Riley S — 1981 2 0 0 0
Lifetime 4 1 1 0 $12,250

14May82-5Hol	6f	:221	:444	1:09 ft	6½	114	52½	31½	22½	23	Guerra W A1	Aw20000	89	Rawbone, Colonel Stu, Doon's Bay	7
29Mar81-2SA	6½f	:213	:443	1:164ft	*3¾	120	42	64¾	78¾	712	EstradaJJr5	[S]Aw21000	74	Airroling,Jeff'sEncore,WickdHittr	11
17Jan81-2SA	6½f	:214	:443	1:163ft	3½	120	2½	1hd	2½	64¾	McCrrnCJ8	[S]Aw20000	82	HeavyHand,TomMack,BeuVitesse	10
26Dec80-3SA	6f	:214	:45	1:102ft	*1	118	61½	42½	1hd	12½	McCarron C J4	[S]Mdn	87	ColonelStu,FoxieDon,HighIndStyl	12

May 24 Hol 5f ft 1:012 h — ●May 10 Hol 5f ft :59 h — May 5 Hol 6f ft 1:133 hg — Apr 28 Hol 5f ft 1:011 h

War House — B. g. 4, by House Committee—Camera Shy, by Dumpty Humpty
Br.—Santoro M D (Cal) — 1982 6 1 0 2 $9,800
Own.—Santoro M — 116 — Tr.—Finelli Charles — 1981 6 1 0 0 $10,725
Lifetime 13 3 0 2 $22,065

8May82-9Fno	6f	:213	:441	1:091ft	15	118	31½	33	34½	36½	WllingtonHK2	Bulldog	87	AmnBrothr,AnswrtoMusic,WrHous	6
14Apr82-1SA	6f	:22	:444	1:10 ft	22	117	107½	97½	63¾	1hd	Wellington HK9	12500	88	WarHouse,TragicBell,AnotherTost	11
19Feb82-1SA	6½f	:213	:441	1:144ft	20	115	42½	57	810	1219	Torres R2	16000	77	RoughRidr,SummrSlor,Goff'sDncr	12
31Jan82-1SA	6f	:213	:441	1:093ft	14	115	1214	1217	1213	86½	Olivares F6	20000	83	BoldBatim,Predilection,HeavyHnd	12
14Jan82-1SA	6f	:214	:45	1:094ft	12	115	52¼	54½	32½	34½	Winland W M4	16000	84	Devon, Qualification, War House	10
3Jan82-1SA	6f	:221	:462	1:124hy	12	115	42	31½	38	618	Winland W M2	16000	56	SuprStrVncnt,OmhMk,EmprorJohn	7
17Aug81-2Dmr	6f	:221	:452	1:112ft	13	115	76¼	88	119¼	107½	Valdivieso H A5	25000	73	PasstheBll,ImmnentIssue,Rosewlk	12
7Aug81-9Dmr	6f	:223	:453	1:102ft	9½	116	11	1hd	21	47¾	Mena F6	25000	78	Garfield County,BubbasKid,Geraldo	6
27Jly81-7Dmr	6f	:221	:444	1:101ft	11	114	44	68½	77½	89¾	Lipham T6	40000	77	GrfldConty,ImportntMmo,MjorDcn	8
12Apr81-6SA	6½f	:214	:45	1:162ft	15	116	1hd	64	811	716	ConnollyR7	[S]Aw22000	72	Sunshine Swag, Rawbone, Iona	8

Message To Garcia — Ch. c. 3, by Messenger of Song—Sisal, by Hillsdale
Br.—Ridder B J (Cal) — 1982 6 1 0 1 $12,350
Own.—Ridder B J — 111 — Tr.—Campbell Gordon C — 1981 0 M 0 0
Lifetime 6 1 0 1 $12,350

14May82-3Hol	7f	:214	:441	1:221ft	17	117	3½	2hd	2½	32	CastnedM3	[S]Aw20000	84	L'Ntty,EnvoysIntrigue,MssgToGrci	7
17Apr82-2SA	6f	:212	:444	1:10 ft	17	120	53¾	32	43¾	64	Lipham T5	Aw19000	84	Polly's Ruler, L'Natty,WindyScott	12
17Mar82-7SA	6f	:213	:444	1:11 sy	7	120	42½	55½	69½	615	McCrrnCJ6	[S]Aw20000	68	GnrlJimmy,Polly'sRulr,EbonyBronz	6
28Feb82-5SA	1 1/16	:454	1:094	1:411ft	16	115	33	49	817	923	Sibille R1	Aw20000	72	JourneyatSea,RoyalCptive,AskMe	12
17Feb82-6SA	6½f	:214	:443	1:16 ft	4	118	21	21	2½	1hd	McCarron C J9	[S]Mdn	90	MssgToGrci,Polly'sRulr,Mrni'sDncr	9
3Feb82-4SA	6f	:214	:451	1:101ft	12	118	76¾	87¼	77¾	69¾	McHargue DG2	[S]Mdn	77	Shantin, Buckohoy,ForgottenMan	11

May 26 Hol 5f ft 1:002 h — May 10 Hol 5f ft 1:002 h — ●Apr 30 Hol 5f ft :591 h — Apr 14 SA 4f ft :482 hg

Windy Scott ✱ **1095** — B. g. 3, by Doc Scott J—Windy Poppy, by Windy Sea

Own.—J K Houssels Sr Estate

Br.—Houssels J K Jr (Cal) 1982 6 1 1 2 $16.400

Tr.—Adams George D 1981 1 M 0 0

Lifetime 7 1 1 2 $16,400

14May82-3Hol	7f	$:21^4$	$:44^1$	$1:22^1$ft	22	120	1½	3^1	$5^{4½}$	$5^{5½}$	Black K[7]	[S]Aw20000	80	L'Ntty,EnvoysIntrigue,MssgToGrci	7
17Apr82-2SA	6f	$:21^2$	$:44^4$	1:10 ft	41	120	1^{hd}	1^{hd}	2^{hd}	3^3	Black K[1]	Aw19000	85	Polly's Ruler, L'Natty,WindyScott	12
3Apr82-5SA	6f	:22	$:45^2$	$1:09^3$ft	20	120	2^{hd}	3½	3^5	6^{12}	VldiviesoHA[6]	Aw20000	78	B.RichGeorg,Polly'sRulr,Accousticl	9
17Mar82-2SA	6f	$:21^4$	$:45^3$	$1:11^3$sy	*2	118	1^1	1½	$1^{3½}$	1^5	McCarron C J[7]	[S]Mdn	80	WindyScott,LottFleet,ThQuiltdKid	7
26Feb82-4SA	6f	$:21^4$	:45	$1:09^4$ft	5½	118	1½	$1^{2½}$	1^1	$2^{1½}$	Carrasco R L[9]	M32000	87	Can'tBeBet,WindyScott,ChiefZero	11
5Feb82-3SA	6½f	$:21^3$	$:44^2$	$1:16^3$ft	29	118	1½	2^{hd}	4^4	3^8	CarrascoRL[7]	[S]M25000	79	FrnchCmndr,HllljhBrthr,WndSctt	12
29Dec81-3SA	6½f	$:21^4$	:45	$1:17^2$ft	25	115	—	—	—	—	VlenzuelPA[2]	[S]M28000	–	Agitto,SuchGentlemn,DistntChrm	12

29Dec81—Bolted

May 26 SA 6f ft $1:15^1$ h May 12 SA 4f sl $:52^4$ h May 6 SA 6f ft $1:18^1$ h Apr 27 SA 5f ft $1:02^4$ h

At post time the tote board read as follows:

	Totals	#3 Shantin
Odds		2—1
Win	169,900	42,181
Show	55,074	11,784

The expected value was 1.04. Not surprisingly, Shantin won the race and Colonel Stu was out of the money. The payoff to show on Shantin was $3.60, which was a handsome sum for a 2—1 shot going off with an expected value of 1.04. The payoff was high because 24—1 and 18—1 long shots finished second and third. My $50 bet returned $90, for a $40 profit.

The chart of the race was as follows:

THIRD RACE
Hollywood
MAY 30, 1982

6 FURLONGS. (1.07⅘) ALLOWANCE. Purse $20,000. 3–year–olds and upward bred in California which have not won a race other than maiden or claiming. Weights, 3–year–olds, 114 lbs.; older, 122 lbs. Non–winners of a race other than claiming since March 15 allowed 3 lbs.; such a race since February 15, 6 lbs.

Value of race $20,000, value to winner $11,000, second $4,000, third $3,000, fourth $1,500, fifth $500. Mutuel pool $309,240. Exacta Pool $473,323.

Last Raced		Horse	Eqt.	A.	Wt	PP	St	¼	½	Str	Fin	Jockey	Odds $1
9May82	^{5}Hol^2	Shantin	b	3	112	3	8	8½	$5^{1½}$	$4^{2½}$	$1^{1½}$	Valenzuela P A	2.40
14May82	^{3}Hol^5	Windy Scott		3	109	9	1	$1^{1½}$	1^3	1^3	2¾	Steiner J J[5]	24.20
8May82	^{9}Fno^3	War House	b	4	117	7	3	5^1	2½	2^1	3½	Wellington H K	18.30
14May82	^{3}Hol^3	Message To Garcia	b	3	115	8	2	6½	4^1	3½	4^{nk}	Castaneda M	7.00
14May82	^{5}Hol^2	Colonel Stu		4	116	6	6	$7^{1½}$	8^3	$6^{2½}$	5^4	Delahoussaye E	1.40
8May82	^{7}Hol^7	Crofted	b	4	122	1	9	9	9	8^1	$6^{1½}$	Pincay L Jr	18.60
14May82	^{5}Hol^3	Doon's Bay	b	4	122	4	4	4½	7½	7½	7^1	McCarron C J	5.80
14May82	^{3}Hol^6	Ready Reb	b	3	114	2	7	2^{hd}	3^2	5^1	$8^{3½}$	Olivares F	22.60
6May82	^{6}Hol^1	Seavoy	b	4	116	5	5	3^{hd}	6^{hd}	9	9	Diaz A L	35.50

OFF AT 2:40. Start good. Won driving. Time, :22, :44⅗, :57⅕, 1:10⅗ Track fast.

$2 Mutuel Prices:			
3-SHANTIN	6.80	4.80	3.60
9-WINDY SCOTT		17.80	9.60
7-WAR HOUSE			6.60

$5 EXACTA 3–9 PAID $271.00.

B. g, by Exalted Rullah—Career, by Poona II. Trainer King Hal. Bred by Christianson C T (Cal).

SHANTIN, slow to find his best stride after the start, rallied strongly on the outside entering the stretch, wore down WINDY SCOTT and was up in the closing yards. The latter darted to the lead at once, opened up a long lead on the turn but gradually weakened in the final furlong. WAR HOUSE, in contention between horses in the second flight to the stretch, lugged out under left-handed pressure in the deep stretch. MESSAGE TO GARCIA, a bit wide to the stretch, rallied between horses in the upper stretch, was floated out a bit by WAR HOUSE, lodged a claim of foul against SHANTIN, alleging interference in the stretch, but it was dismissed. COLONEL STU lacked early speed and did not reach contention with a mild closing rally while drifting in through the final furlong. DOON'S BAY weakened before a half-mile. READY REB tired in the stretch. SEAVOY, in contention between horses to the turn, gradually tired thereafter.

Owners— 1, Kelly & Christianson; 2, J K Houssels Sr Estate; 3, Hemet Hills Farm; 4, Ridder B J; 5, Spelling A; 6, Sorenson Heather D; 7, Eklund R L; 8, Fanning & Harrison; 9, Campanelli-Meyer-Murphy-Thomas.

Overweight: Shantin 1 pound; War House 1; Message To Garcia 4.

4th Hollywood

7 FURLONGS. (1.19⅘) ALLOWANCE. Purse $26,000. 3-year-olds and upward which have not won $2,500 three times other than maiden, claiming or starter. Weights, 3-year-olds, 114 lbs.; older, 122 lbs. Non-winners of two such races since March 1 allowed 3 lbs.; such a race since then, 6 lbs.

B. Rich George

Ch. c. 3, by Don B—Patch It Up, by My Host
Br.—Trickett B H (Cal) 1982 10 1 2 1 $28,180
Own.—Solar Stable 111 **Tr.—Webb George H** 1981 12 1 3 3 $35,475
Lifetime 22 2 5 4 $63,655 Turf 2 0 1 0 $6,000

21May82-7Hol 7f :221 :45 1:223ft 4½ 114 11 11 2hd 33½ Olivares F6 Aw26000 80 Jet Travel, Dena Jo, B. RichGeorge 6
15May82-8Hol 1 1/16 ①:47 1:11 1:403fm 13 114 2½ 1hd 42½ 815 Olivares F3 W Rgrs H 81 GiveMeStrength,AskMe,Accousticl 8
15May82—Run in two divisions, 8th and 9th races.
15Apr82-8SA a6½f ①:214 :4341:144fm 17 119 2½ 2hd 2hd 2hd Mena F7 Aw30000 85 ChuliStreet,B.RichGeorge,Spiritino 9
3Apr82-5SA 6f :22 :452 1:093ft 5½ 120 42½ 2½ 1hd 1½ Mena F8 Aw28000 90 B.RichGeorg,Polly'sRulr,Accousticl 9
21Mar82-4SA 6½f :212 :44 1:152ft 13 120 32 21 23 47½ Mena F4 Aw20000 85 RemembrJohn,ClticSbr,EstrSrmon 6
7Mar82-2SA 6½f :212 :44 1:144ft 11 120 62¾ 66½ 66 47¾ Mena F3 Aw20000 88 AdvanceMan,GeneralJimmy,L'Ntty 9
10Feb82-7SA 6f :214 :45 1:114sy 3½ 120 2hd 23 39 59 Mena F3 Aw19000 70 JtPirt,HowNowDow,StndupComdin 7
30Jan82-7SA 6f :212 :44 1:091ft 3½ 120 21½ 1½ 2½ 66 ValenzuelPA5 Aw19000 86 TimeToExplode,JourneytSe,SrdSpy 8
14Jan82-5SA 6f :213 :443 1:091ft 5 120 1½ 11 2hd 22½ AsmussenCB2 Aw19000 90 Jet Travel, B. RichGeorge,Rise'nFly 9
8Jan82-5SA 6f :213 :444 1:102gd 2½ 120 33 45½ 715 827 McCarronCJ4 Aw19000 59 Unpredictable,Fanjet,HowNowDow 8
May 7 Hol ① 1 fm 1:47 h (d) Apr 26 Hol 4f ft :49 h

*Some Lute

B. h. 5, by Luthier—Some Dame, by Vieux Manoir
Br.—Socd'Elvs&ExploitationAgr (Fra) 1982 2 0 0 0
Own.—Vanian Souken S 116 **Tr.—Perkins Larry** 1981 8 1 0 2 $21,313
Lifetime 21 2 1 4 $51,265 Turf 21 2 1 4 $51,265

13May82-8Hol 1 ①:4521:10 1:34 fm 81 114 1½ 2hd 86½1015 ValenzuelPA9 Aw30000 84 Table Torch, Guarantee, Dhausli 10
29Apr82-8Hol 6f :22 :443 1:082ft 37 115 76 78½ 712 713 Pierce D6 Aw26000 82 LaughingBoy,BeachWalk,Redoutble 7
27Sep81♦4Longchamp(Fra) a1 1:471gd 1-5 126 ① 1010 BdelA Pr du Rond Pt(Gr3) Deltwn,DimondProspect,Redoutbl 10
8Aug81♦7Deauville(Fra) a1 1:422fm 14 127 ① 54½ Badel A Pr de Varaville Tarrago, Wild Idea, Bookman 7
23Jly81♦4MLafitte(Fra) a1 1:361gd 17 121 ① 13 Badel A Pr Messidor(Gr3) Ya Zaman, Daeltown, Spoleto 16
4Jly81♦4Longchamp(Fra) a7f 1:271gd 35 128 ① 76¾ BadelA Pr Porte Maillot(Gr3) Gosport, Mistra, Manjam 13
9Jun81♦5Chantilly(Fra) a1 1:411gd 26 126 ① 31½ BdlA PrChmndFrdNrd(Gr3) Gosport, Moon Ingraver,SomeLute 8
19May81♦5StCloud(Fra) a1 1:474sf 7 121 ① 1nk Badel A Pr Lovelace Some Lute,Thisman,NewGrandame 8
1May81♦4StCloud(Fra) a1 1:411sf 9 119 ① 79¾ StMrtY Pr du Muguet(Gr3) North Jet, Joberan, Confetti 9
12Apr81♦6Longchamp(Fra) a1 1:422gd 12 123 ① 31½ StMrtin Pr Butte Mrtmrt Daeltown, Roll of Power,SomeLute 8
May 26 Hol 4f ft :462 h May 20 Hol 4f ft :473 h May 7 Hol 1 ft 1:403 h Apr 26 Hol 4f ft :483 hg

Chapel Creek

B. c. 4, by Our Native—Spanked, by Cornish Prince
Br.—Conners Mary E (Conn) 1982 6 0 0 1 $4,950
Own.—Loblolly Stable 116 **Tr.—Cleveland Gene** 1981 10 2 1 1 $47,526
Lifetime 22 3 4 2 $73,896 Turf 1 0 0 0

8May82-3Hol 6f :221 :444 1:084ft 27 115 62½ 55 44 32½ McHrgueDG1 Aw26000 90 BeachWlk,MsterWrrior,ChpelCreek 8
29Apr82-8Hol 6f :22 :443 1:082ft 10 115 43 42 53½ 66¾ Hawley S3 Aw26000 88 LaughingBoy,BeachWalk,Redoutble 7
31Mar82-8OP 6f :222 :464 1:14 ft 3 114 88½ 89½ 711 75½ Snyder L6 Aw20000 69 HerefordMan,TryMac,MyDerChrlie 8
20Mar82-8OP 1 70 :47 1:132 1:432ft 6 111 2hd 2hd 716 720 Kaenel J L9 Aw17500 59 VodikaCollins,Dr.Spnky,Rckensck 10
10Mar82-9OP 6f :213 :453 1:123ft 3½ 113 99¾ 710 54 42½ Kaenel J L3 Aw17500 79 BinABttle,Miromn,AvngingGossip 12
4Mar82-9OP 6f :23 :473 1:123ft *6-5 113 95½ 83 75½ 77 Kaenel J L7 Aw20000 75 Lind'sLughin,JoK.Jr.,Contorsionst 10
2Aug81-5Sar 6f :214 :442 1:082ft 19 112 68¾ 66½ 57 69 Maple E4 Aw23000 89 Maudlin, Khartoum, Will Of Iron 7
8Jly81-6Bel 6f :224 :451 1:084ft 15 111 46½ 37 46½ 47½ MacBeth D2 Aw23000 90 Miswaki, Khartoum, Fly North 6
12Jun81-8Bel 1 ①:45 1:09 1:34 fm 24 113 89 1014 1016 1021 Vasquez J4 Aw25000 74 WrofWords,Bucksplshr,ExplosvBd 11
9May81-8Bel 1 :451 1:10 1:364ft 9½ 126 56 78 710 713 Maple E4 Withers 71 Spirited Boy, Willow Hour, A Run 7
● May 22 Hol 7f ft 1:25 h May 16 Hol 5f ft 1:004 h ● Apr 29 SA 6f ft 1:103 h Apr 14 SA 4f ft :461 h

Surprise George

B. c. 4, by Pleasure Seeker—Porterville Bay, by Nigret
Br.—Achterberg G (Cal) 1981 10 2 0 1 $52,800
Own.—Achterberg G 116 **Tr.—Brooks L J** 1980 2 1 1 0 $10,237
Lifetime 12 3 1 1 $63,037 Turf 7 1 0 1 $36,900

9Jly81-9Hol 1 ①:4621:1031:35 fm 3½ 114 68½ 41 3½ 63½ Lipham T4 Westwood 91 Lemhi Gold,RockSoftly,IslandWhirl 7
9Jly81—Run in two divisions, 8th & 9th races.
26Jun81-4Hol 1 1/16 ①:4731:1141:413fm 6½ 117 63¾ 64 77 77½ Lipham T4 Aw30000 83 MinnsotChif,IslndWhirl,MstrThtch 7
7Jun81-8Hol 1 1/16 ①:4511:0931:403fm 15 114 913 45½ 44 44¾ Lipham T7 Cinema H 91 MinnsotChf,Stnchrry,SplnddSpruc 12
23May81-8Hol 1 1/16 ①:4611:1041:412fm 11 115 65½ 62¾ 42½ 32½ LiphamT5 Wl Rgers H 89 SplendidSpruce,Sfood,SurprisGorg 8
1May81-8Hol 1 ①:4641:1041:351fm 4½ 117 99½ 53¾ 33 1nk Lipham T9 Aw28000 93 SurprisGorg,WtrwyDriv,QuntumLp 10
15Apr81-8SA 1⅛ ①:46 1:0931:464fm 8½ 114 43½ 32 23 54½ Lipham T3 La Puente 89 Axe House, Mehmet, Flying Gene 13
1Apr81-8SA a6½f ①:211 :4331:143fm 12 114 87½ 79 65¾ 4nk Lipham T8 Baldwin 86 Descaro, Motivity, Steelinctive 13
21Mar81-6SA 1 1/16 :461 1:111 1:433gd 4½ 115 2hd 1hd 2hd 42½ DelhoussyeE7 Aw28000 80 Seafood, Partez, Table Torch 8
13Mar81-6SA 6½f :212 :441 1:154ft 7 117 611 69½ 46 47½ Lipham T1 Aw30000 84 Litigator, Scotts Bar, Steelinctive 6
28Feb81-2SA 6½f :214 :451 1:173sy 7 114 85 3½ 13 11 Lipham T8 ⓈAw21000 82 SurprisGorg,Ultrchrg,SunshinSwg 11
May 19 Hol 6f ft 1:152 h May 14 Hol 6f ft 1:14 h May 9 Hol 5f ft 1:001 h May 4 Hol 4f ft :473 h

Sali's Royal Dream
B. g. 4, by Blood Royal—Sali Sara, by Nagea
Br.—Gaylord Ann (Ky) 1982 2 0 0 0 $2,600
Own.—Morton Mr-Mrs H D 116 Tr.—Whitby Steve M 1981 9 3 1 2 $45,675
Lifetime 11 3 1 2 $48,275 Turf 1 0 0 0

29Apr82-8Hol	6f :22 :443 1:082ft	4	114	64½	65½	66½	55½	Guerra W A4	Aw26000	90	LaughingBoy,BeachWalk,Redoutble	7
11Apr82-5SA	6½f :22 :451 1:17 sy	8½	114	710	76	54	41½	McCarronCJ3	Aw26000	83	Tellround,Redoutble,He'sSomthing	7
9Dec81-7Hol	6½f :221 :45 1:154ft	8½	114	87¾	77¼	69½	58½	Ramirez O5	Aw25000	82	PompeiiCourt,KngrooCourt,Dorcro	8
27Nov81-7Hol	6½f :223 :453 1:183sy	4½	113	76½	75½	36½	33¼	Hawley S1	Aw25000	74	DndyWit,PompiiCourt,Sli'sRoylDrm	8
15Nov81-5Hol	1 1/16 Ⓣ:4711:1121:414fm	4	112	54	42½	46	69	McCarronCJ9	Aw28000	81	Krassawitz, Vorlaufer, Lucullus	9
6Nov81-9SA	6f :22 :443 1:09 ft	19	119	77	610	56½	31¼	Ramirez O1	Aw30000	92	ShrpHoofer,Inception,Sli'sRoylDrm	7
24Oct81-8SA	1 1/16 :46 1:10 1:414ft	7¾	112	76½	77¾	89¼	611	McCrronCJ1	Alibhai H	81	Native Tactics, Rock Softly, Damas	9
24Aug81-8Dmr	1 :452 1:101 1:363ft	3	113	42½	33½	45	21½	McCarronCJ3	Aw30000	83	AtYourPlesure,Sli'sRoylDrem,Dscro	6
30Jly81-7Dmr	6f :224 :452 1:102ft	4	115	65¼	43½	32½	1hd	McCarronCJ8	Aw18000	86	Sli'sRoylDrem,BondRullh,BronzStr	8
1Jly81-9Hol	6f :213 :45 1:103ft	*2¾	116	75¼	74¾	53½	1no	McCarronCJ6	Aw20000	84	Sl'sRoylDrm,SchoolHr,RllySmbdy	12

May 25 Hol 6f ft 1:131 h May 18 Hol 5f ft 1:00 h May 11 Hol 3f ft :36 h Apr 24 SA 4f ft :47 h

Perry Cabin
B. g. 5, by Arts and Letters—Hester Prynne, by Dedicate
Br.—Headley D A (Ky) 1982 7 2 2 0 $43,450
Own.—Baumbach & King 116 Tr.—Fanning Jerry 1981 21 3 4 3 $91,010
Lifetime 56 10 12 7 $206,198 Turf 15 5 1 0 $82,435

15May82-3Hol	7f :221 :442 1:22 ft	5	119	612	68	45	2¾	Olivares F1	62500	86	No No, Perry Cabin, Philip E.	6
29Apr82-7Hol	1 1/16 Ⓣ:4641:1031:411fm	4½	116	48½	33	52¾	1no	Olivares F7	62500	93	Perry Cabin, Val De Roi, Chriserik	9
11Apr82-3SA	1⅛ :474 1:121 1:494sy	15	116	43	31	11½	12½	Toro F3	50000	88	Perry Cabin, Three Bits, HeartBeat	6
14Mar82-9SA	1 1/16 :464 1:12 1:452sy	11	116	712	714	717	518	Lipham T5	62500	56	TheArgyleKid,BeauMoro,Stingingly	7
24Feb82-5SA	1⅛ Ⓣ:4631:1041:474fm	5½	116	67½	66	89½	812	Lipham T10	62500	76	BadRascal,BeauSoleil,BlueDncerII	10
31Jan82-9SA	1 1/16 :462 1:103 1:421ft	6	116	67½	62¾	32	2nk	Lipham T1	50000	90	Three Bits, Perry Cabin, Geshes	7
1Jan82-5SA	1 1/16 :48 1:133 1:471hy	5¾	116	55½	65½	45½	59½	Lipham T3	50000	55	Alshurouk, Three Bits, Dogo	9
6Dec81-9Hol	1 Ⓣ:4621:1121:354fm	5½	116	67	63¾	56¾	42½	Lipham T2	65000	87	Sosegdo,MisterWilder,DissiptdDollr	8
21Nov81-9Hol	1 :454 1:10 1:351ft	4	118	87½	68½	511	510	Harris W3	65000	80	Black Sulphur, Dogo, Hard to Lee	8
9Nov81-8LA	1 1/16 :441 1:10 1:431ft	2	116	58½	53¾	3½	2½	Harris W2	Aw28000	92	DancynTim,PerryCbin,BlckSulphur	5

May 29 Hol 3f ft :371 b May 23 Hol 5f ft 1:021 h May 14 Hol 3f ft :363 b Apr 26 Hol 5f ft 1:012 h

Master Warrior
Ch. g. 4, by Native Charger—Mia Mood, by Crozier
Br.—Hooper F W (Fla) 1982 7 0 2 0 $14,950
Own.—Hooper F W 116 Tr.—Fenstermaker L R 1981 11 3 0 2 $44,700
Lifetime 20 3 2 2 $59,650 Turf 4 0 0 0 $650

8May82-3Hol	6f :221 :444 1:084ft	22	115	31	21½	2½	2½	Sibille R6	Aw26000	92	BeachWlk,MsterWrrior,ChpelCreek	8
29Apr82-8Hol	6f :22 :443 1:082ft	16	115	53½	52	33	44½	Sibille R7	Aw26000	90	LaughingBoy,BeachWalk,Redoutble	7
14Mar82-7SA	6½f :213 :443 1:182sy	*2½	117	47½	36	25	21½	McCarronCJ6	Aw26000	76	Trrsto'sSngr,MstrWrror,H'sSmthng	6
26Feb82-7SA	6f :22 :444 1:084ft	14	116	2½	2hd	41¾	46	McCarronCJ4	Aw26000	88	MisterWilder,LughingBoy,Tllround	7
14Feb82-5SA	1 1/16 :46 1:10 1:414ft	16	113	2½	3½	86¾	911	Hansen R D1	Aw30000	81	Egg Toss,EarlySettler,MisterWilder	9
28Jan82-7SA	6½f :212 :434 1:153ft	47	116	67½	68	53	53	Hansen R D4	Aw26000	89	Tooovrprim,MistrWildr,Cloonwillin	7
15Jan82-5SA	6f :22 :443 1:082ft	44	116	65½	67	69½	611	Hansen R D7	Aw26000	85	Maxistar, Bond Rullah, Tellaround	8
22Nov81-7Hol	7f :213 :442 1:223ft	18	116	67½	53½	57½	63	Hansen R D4	Aw30000	81	ImportntMmo,KnndyRidg,DustyHul	9
2Nov81-10LA	7f :222 :461 1:242ft	*4-5	112	1½	1hd	11	1hd	Hansen R D4	Aw24000	87	MasterWarrior,Who'sLeder,Prmetti	7
21Oct81-5SA	a6½f Ⓣ:212 :4411:142fm	10	116	42½	33½	64¼	65½	ValenzuelPA3	Aw25000	81	StrRoute,MisterWilder,Prodigious	10

●May 29 Hol 3f ft :34 h May 23 Hol 6f ft 1:15 h May 7 Hol 3f ft :364 h Apr 27 Hol 4f ft :491 h

In the fourth race, one of the consensus favorites and the favorite of the betting crowd was Perry Cabin. Perry Cabin was ridden by Frank Olivares, who had guided him to a first- and a second-place finish in two recent races at Hollywood Park. The expected value for a show bet on Perry Cabin was about 1.05, with a final tote board of

	Totals	#6 Perry Cabin
Odds		2—1
Win	192,676	50,523
Show	40,661	9,824

Perry Cabin won the race and paid $3.00 to show. This was quite a reasonable payoff for a 2—1 shot with only seven horses and a 1.01 final expected value. The payoff was improved when the second favorite finished out of the money. My $50 bet returned $75, for a $25 profit. The chart of the race was as follows:

FOURTH RACE **7 FURLONGS. (1.19$\frac{3}{5}$) ALLOWANCE. Purse $26,000. 3–year–olds and upward which have not won $2,500 three times other than maiden, claiming or starter. Weights, 3–year–olds, 114 lbs.; older, 122 lbs. Non–winners of two such races since March 1 allowed 3 lbs.; such a race since then, 6 lbs.**

Hollywood

MAY 30, 1982

Value of race $26,000, value to winner $14,300, second $5,200, third $3,900, fourth $1,950, fifth $650. Mutuel pool $319,342. Exacta Pool $427,407.

Last Raced	Horse	Eqt.	A.	Wt	PP	St	¼	½	Str	Fin	Jockey	Odds $1
15May82 ^{3}Hol^{2}	Perry Cabin	b	5	116	6	5	6^{5}	5^{2}	3^{1}	1^{nk}	Olivares F	2 20
29Apr82 ^{8}Hol^{5}	Sali's Royal Dream		4	116	5	4	$5^{1\frac{1}{2}}$	3^{1}	$1^{\frac{1}{2}}$	2^{3}	McCarron C J	6.50
21May82 ^{7}Hol^{3}	B. Rich George		3	117	1	6	$1^{1\frac{1}{2}}$	1^{1}	$2^{\frac{1}{2}}$	$3^{1\frac{1}{2}}$	Pincay L Jr	4.00
8May82 ^{3}Hol^{2}	Master Warrior		4	116	7	1	$4^{1\frac{1}{2}}$	2^{hd}	$4^{2\frac{1}{2}}$	4^{1}	Sibille R	2.30
9Jly81 ^{9}Hol^{6}	Surprise George	b	4	116	4	7	7	7	6^{8}	$5^{\frac{3}{4}}$	Delahoussaye E	17.00
8May82 ^{3}Hol^{3}	Chapel Creek		4	116	3	2	2^{hd}	4^{1}	5^{hd}	6^{10}	McHargue D G	5.90
13May82 ^{8}Hol^{10}	Some Lute		5	116	2	3	3^{hd}	6^{3}	7	7	Valenzuela P A	23.90

OFF AT 3:14 Start good. Won driving. Time, :22$\frac{1}{5}$, :44$\frac{3}{5}$, 1:09$\frac{2}{5}$, 1:22 Track fast.

$2 Mutuel Prices:

6–PERRY CABIN	**6.40**	**3.40**	**3.00**
5–SALI'S ROYAL DREAM		**5.60**	**4.20**
1–B. RICH GEORGE			**3.80**

$5 EXACTA 6–5 PAID $92.50

B. g, by Arts and Letters—Hester Prynne, by Dedicate. Trainer Fanning Jerry. Bred by Headley D A (Ky).

PERRY CABIN, unhurried early, saved ground around the turn, found room to rally on the rail through the stretch and was up in the closing yards. SALI'S ROYAL DREAM, never far back, moved to contention inside horses at the far turn, got the lead in the upper stretch but could not quite last. B. RICH GEORGE sprinted to the lead in the opening quarter-mile, but weakened in the final sixteenth. MASTER WARRIOR, in contention while far wide into the far turn, tired in the final furlong. CHAPEL CREEK, in contention between horses to the far turn, gradually weakened after a half-mile. SOME LUTE had only brief early speed.

Owners— 1, Baumbach & King; 2, Morton Mr-Mrs H D; 3, Solar Stable; 4, Hooper F W; 5, Achterberg G; 6, Loblolly Stable; 7, Vanian Souken S.

Overweight: B. Rich George 6 pounds.

The fifth race was for three-year-olds over 6 furlongs for an $18,000 purse. The top choices were Insearchof, Jet Pirate, Extra Quick, Spectacular Bee, and Distant Gem. Insearchof had finished in the money in three of the last four races against similar-quality horses. Jet Pirate was out of the money in the last four races. However, he had run in faster time against higher-quality opposition. Today he was dropping in class. Extra Quick was moving up in class and appeared too weak for this opposition. Spectacular Bee was never in the money in eight 1982 starts and did not impress me. Distant Gem had a similar record. My preference was for Insearchof, and his show bet expected value was 1.08, making it close to a Dr. Z system bet. At post time the tote board stood as follows:

	Totals	#3 In Search Of
Odds		5—2
Win	174,928	41,682
Show	45,568	8,539

5th Hollywood

6 FURLONGS. (1.07⅗) CLAIMING. Purse $18,000. 3-year-olds. Weight, 122 lbs. Non-winners of two races since March 28 allowed 3 lbs.; a race since then, 6 lbs. Claiming price $40,000; for each $2,500 to $35,000 allowed 2 lbs. (Races when entered for $32,000 or less not considered.)

Ramble on John *

B. g. 3, by Speak John—Hicksville, by Tudor Grey
Br.—Palmer R (Ky) 1982 6 1 0 0 $12,120
Own.—Priddy R or Ann 116 Tr.—Priddy Ann $40,000 1981 2 M 0 0
Lifetime 8 1 0 0 $12,120

8Apr82-9SA	1	:46 1:103 1:36 ft	25	118	52¾ 1017 1019 1022	Valenzuela P A8	50000	67	BisonBy,FortyEightFcts,Rconfirm	10
26Mar82-9SA	1	:46 1:103 1:354ft	8	115	63¾ 53¼ 77¼ 712	Valenzuela P A3	55000	78	Tell Don, Bison Bay, King Darius	9
18Mar82-9SA	6f	:214 :452 1:12 m	8¾	1155	69½ 65¼ 52¾ 42¾	Steiner J J1	50000	75	Shantin, Daily Report, Il Paladino	7
7Mar82-6SA	6½f	:213 :442 1:151ft	8¼	120	45 48½ 514 818	ValenzuelPA2	Aw20000	76	TexsCommerce,LeSmirk,Buckohoy	9
10Feb82-7SA	6f	:214 :45 1:114sy	14	120	58½ 58½ 410 44½	Byrnes D5	Aw19000	74	JtPirt,HowNowDow,StndupComdin	7
3Jan82-6SA	6½f	:23 :473 1:224hy	4¾	118	53¾ 21 1½ 1no	Byrnes D6	Mdn	56	Ramble on John,Supron,BlueJester	7
26Dec81-4SA	6f	:213 :443 1:104ft	57	118	32 22½ 44½ 73	Byrnes D9	Mdn	81	Fanjet, Supron, Berbereau	12
8May81-4Hol	5f	:222 :461 :584ft	5¾	116	54½ 76 711 79¾	Valenzuela P A6	Mdn	75	VagabondSong,KhalDve,RpidRebel	8

May 27 Hol 4f ft :472 h May 20 Hol 6f ft 1:143 h May 14 Hol 5f ft :59 h May 8 Hol 4f ft :472 h

Familiar Tune

Dk. b. or br. c. 3, by Prove It—Harpsichord, by Dr Kacy
Br.—Ellsworth Kim R & R C (La) 1982 5 1 0 2 $8,460
Own.—Sugich D or Jane 112 Tr.—Hop Michael D $35,000 1981 0 M 0 0
Lifetime 5 1 0 2 $8,460

22May82-3Hol	6f	:214 :45 1:103ft	14	119	33 32 31 31	Sibille R6	32000	83	Michelle'sDrem,Insrchof,FmilirTun	7
25Apr82-9Hol	1 1/16	:463 1:111 1:443ft	53	116	42 76¼ 815 721	Ortega L E4	50000	51	‡IndinO.,FrenchCommnder,Cn'tBBt	8
16Apr82-7SA	6f	:214 :443 1:10 ft	4½	116	44 55 47 69¼	Asmussen CB8	c40000	79	DlwrExprss,IndnO.,HomCourtRulng	9
7Apr82-6SA	6f	:221 :451 1:102ft	3	118	2hd 1hd 12½ 15½	Asmussen CB7	M32000	86	FamilirTune,King'sPlot,RoringJet	11
12Mar82-9TuP	5½f	:222 :47 1:072m	21	110	67 64¼ 44½ 34	Snyder D3	Aw3100	67	Solid Charge, BayTay,FamiliarTune	8

May 29 Hol 3f ft :344 h ● May 20 Hol 3f ft :334 h May 8 Hol 5f ft :593 h Apr 24 Hol 3f ft :384 h

Insearchof

Dk. b. or br. c. 3, by Windy Sands—Gaelic Toot, by Gaelic Dancer
Br.—Gaskill Lynn & Arlene (Cal) 1982 6 1 2 1 $14,975
Own.—Gaskill-Lewis et al 116 Tr.—Stute Warren $40,000 1981 8 M 1 1 $8,325
Lifetime 14 1 3 2 $23,300

22May82-3Hol	6f	:214 :45 1:103ft	3	119	22 22 2½ 2nk	McHargue D G4	32000	84	Michelle'sDrem,Insrchof,FmilirTun	7
9May82-5Hol	6f	:22 :444 1:09 ft	10	116	52½ 32½ 57 613	McHargue D G3	50000	79	L'Cap, Shantin, Can't Be Beat	6
30Apr82-5Hol	6f	:214 :444 1:10 ft	5½	116	2hd 1hd 11 23	Pierce D7	40000	84	Cn'tBeBet,Inserchof,BetterWithAg	7
20Apr82-4SA	6f	:22 :444 1:094ft	*9-5	118	11 1½ 12½ 13½	McHrguDG12	[S]M32000	89	Insearchof, Leckie, Susanne's Boy	12
15Apr82-3SA	6f	:214 :444 1:101ft	12	118	32½ 43 54½ 55¼	Asmussen C B6	[S]Mdn	82	Konewah, Prince Channon,FastAxe	6
24Mar82-6SA	6f	:22 :45 1:103ft	4½	118	1½ 11 1½ 32	Asmussen CB6	M50000	83	Stream Side, Kanui, Insearchof	8
25Oct81-3SA	1	:454 1:111 1:38 ft	19	118	1hd 3½ 46½ 816	Olivares F8	Mdn	63	Bison Bay, Berbereau, Crystal Star	8
11Oct81-4SA	1	:463 1:114 1:374ft	5½	118	32½ 32 35 48¾	Olivares F2	[S]Mdn	71	RacingIsFun,CrystlStr,AlmoStrnger	7
30Sep81-3SA	6f	:214 :451 1:10 ft	13	118	2hd 2½ 31½ 56¼	Ortega L E4	[S]Mdn	82	Gaelic'sSport,Shntin,DesertEnvoy	12
9Sep81-8Dmr	1	:453 1:111 1:372ft	100	114	76¼ 73¼ 61¾ 87¼	Ortega L E3	Dmr Fut	74	GatoDelSol,TheCaptain,RingProud	10

May 29 Hol 3f ft :374 h May 16 Hol 5f ft 1:023 h May 7 Hol 4f ft :503 h Apr 27 Hol 4f ft :491 h

Jet Pirate *

Dk. b. or br. g. 3, by Tri Jet—Be Victorious, by Stevward
Br.—Schwietert F C (Fla) 1982 6 2 0 0 $21,775
Own.—Cavanagh Mr-Mrs T M 116 Tr.—Carno Louis R $40,000 1981 7 1 1 0 $11,950
Lifetime 13 3 1 0 $33,725

9May82-5Hol	6f	:22 :444 1:09 ft	10	116	21 22 34½ 46½	Sibille R5	50000	85	L'Cap, Shantin, Can't Be Beat	6
14Apr82-3SA	6f	:214 :443 1:094ft	6	120	51¾ 43 43 53¾	Castaneda M6	62500	85	SkiRacer,Smuggler'sGold,ImSizzler	6
7Apr82-3SA	6f	:22 :442 1:084ft	21	120	46 34½ 44½ 55¾	Sibille R3	Aw23000	88	Spiritino, Art Director, Le Smirk	6
25Feb82-7SA	6½f	:221 :45 1:152ft	9	120	1½ 1½ 22½ 612	Sibille R3	Aw22000	81	LuckyLegend,RcingIsFun,GtoDlSol	6
10Feb82-7SA	6f	:214 :45 1:114sy	7¼	115	1hd 13 16 14½	Sibille R2	Aw19000	79	JtPirt,HowNowDow,StndupComdin	7
15Jan82-2SA	7f	:22 :444 1:232ft	3¾e	116	1½ 11½ 13 14	Sibille R7	40000	83	JetPirte,CptinTuffy,OutBeforDwn	12
30Dec81-4SA	6½f	:222 :46 1:193m	2¼e	116	1hd 15 12½ 2¾	Ortega L E1	40000	71	CapturetheSpirit,JetPirate,JamMan	7
25Nov81-5Hol	6f	:221 :452 1:104ft	5½	114	1hd 11 2½ 74¾	Ortega L E6	40000	78	Jet Travel, JamMan,MoodyCaptain	9
30Oct81-3SA	6½f	:22 :451 1:173ft	*9-5	118	1hd 12½ 14 12¾	Ortega L E4	M25000	82	JetPirte,CptinTuffy,OneBoldReson	8
27Aug81-3Dmr	6f	:223 :461 1:12 ft	6½	118	3nk 42 66 912	Ortega L E11	M40000	66	Dena Jo, Smuggler's Gold,SirBoss	12

May 27 Hol 3f ft :361 h May 22 Hol 4f ft :484 h May 17 Hol 5f ft 1:003 h May 7 Hol 4f ft :50 h

Extra Quick

Ro. g. 3, by Messenger of Song—Trishlyn, by Performance
Br.—Humes Mr-Mrs W A (Cal) 1982 5 1 0 0 $6,950
Own.—Four D Stables 116 Tr.—Hartstone George D $40,000 1981 4 1 1 0 $8,900
Lifetime 9 2 1 0 $15,850

15May82-2Hol	1 1/16	:464 1:113 1:44 ft	*2¼	116	2½ 31 33 109¼	McCarron C J1	c32000	66	Jam Man, Carrie's Ten, ClubFlush	11
29Apr82-5Hol	6f	:22 :443 1:094ft	3¼	115	2½ 2hd 1½ 14½	Guerra W A4	20000	88	ExtrQuick,OleKingTuck,Jo'sTribut	10
8Apr82-2SA	6f	:214 :45 1:092ft	35	117	44½ 46 46½ 46	Guerra W A1	[S] 20000	85	Chris's Lad,Vavavavoom,BrightIsle	9
5Mar82-1SA	6f	:214 :444 1:103ft	13	118	54 1215 1219 1212	Sibille R2	20000	73	Mchll'sDrm,Prt'sOvr,Chcr'sOrphn	12
12Feb82-1SA	6f	:222 :453 1:114gd	13	116	41¾ 813 817 925	Sibille R1	32000	54	L'Cap, Ima Sizzler, Supercede	9
11Dec81-2Hol	6½f	:222 :454 1:183ft	3½	117	3nk 2hd 12 11¼	Sibille R7	M25000	77	ExtrQuick,ARoylWlcom,ToughTim	12
27Aug81-3Dmr	6f	:223 :461 1:12 ft	5½	118	1hd 2½ 76 1116	Lipham T4	M40000	62	Dena Jo, Smuggler's Gold,SirBoss	12
19Jun81-4Hol	5f	:22 :464 :593ft	3	116	21 23 2hd 22¼	Lipham T2	Mc32000	79	Subdivide,ExtraQuick,Cpt'nArphy	10
6Jun81-6Hol	5f	:214 :454 :581ft	8¾	116	3½ 34 47½ 511	Lipham T4	[S]Mdn	77	DistntHrt,B.RichGorg,SwtndNturl	10

May 25 Hol 4f ft :48 h May 10 Hol 5f ft 1:03 h Apr 25 Hol 4f ft :47 h Apr 20 Hol tr.t 4f ft :52 h

Distant Gem

Ch. c. 3, by Distant Day—Gypsy Gem, by Aegean Isle
Br.—Marshall F (Cal) 1982 2 0 0 0 $400
Own.—Marshall Mr-Mrs F 116 Tr.—Tinsley J E Jr $40,000 1981 5 1 0 1 $11,400
Lifetime 7 1 0 1 $11,800

20Feb82-2SA 6f :214 :442 1:10 ft *2 118 31 23 47 511 McHargue D G6 40000 77 L'Cap,FrenchCommander,ImSizzler 7
21Jan82-6SA 6f :221 :453 1:11 m 4½ 120 69 612 615 619 McHrgueDG1 Aw19000 64 Speed Broker, Breen, HowNowDow 6
29Dec81-2SA 6f :212 :441 1:101ft 3½ 120 1½ 12½ 11½ 74 Pincay L Jr9 Aw18000 83 WorldRuler,Gelic'sSport,CrystlStr 12
12Dec81-5Hol 6f :213 :443 1:094ft 6½ 118 46 44½ 37½ 516 Ortega L E1 Aw18000 72 Irisher,Unpredictable,CaptainTuffy 6
28Nov81-3Hol 6f :222 :46 1:123m 2½ 118 11½ 1hd 21 35 Ortega L E3 Aw18000 69 ArtDirector,RedCurrent,DistntGem 5
14Nov81-2Hol 6f :22 :45 1:102ft 8½ 118 1½ 1½ 11 11½ Ortega L E5 [S]Mdn 85 DistntGem,FleetEric,NoHoldsBrrd 12
4Sep81-6Dmr 6f :221 :453 1:11 ft 10 118 11 11 52½ 813 Lipham T5 [S]Mdn 70 PrinceSpellbound,CrystlStr,Shntin 12
May 28 Hol 3f ft :344 h May 16 Hol 5f ft :591 h May 9 Hol 6f ft 1:133 hg May 4 Hol 5f ft 1:013 h

Murtazz

B. c. 3, by Exclusive Native—Privileged, by Flying Fury
Br.—Cashman E C (Ky) 1982 2 0 0 0 $400
Own.—Cashman E C 116 Tr.—Sullivan John $40,000 1981 4 1 1 0 $10,356
Lifetime 6 1 1 0 $10,756 Turf 5 1 1 0 $10,756

28Apr82-8GG 1 Ⓣ:4721:1211:374fm 5 114 52½ 42½ 44½ 55 Baze R A1 Aw16000 73 TheBrginHunter,ThreDocs,Cvllrizzo 7
17Apr82-2SA 6f :212 :444 1:10 ft 79 114 96½ 96¾ 87¾ 97½ Diaz A L9 Aw19000 80 Poily's Ruler, L'Natty,WindyScott 12
28Sep81♦5StCloud(Fra) a6½f 1:213gd 38 119 Ⓣ 9 SamaniH Pr Eclipse(Gr3) Pas de Seul, Rollins, Dear Patrick 10
11Sep81♦1Evry(Fra) a5½f 1:044gd 9¾ 128 Ⓣ 13 Gibert A Pr de Lamballe Murtazz, Moondreamer, Valrant 7
19Aug81♦3Vichy(Fra) a5f 1:01 gd 8 118 Ⓣ 21½ Hassine L Pr Tripolette Goulaine, Murtazz, Rolling Mado 10
21Jly81♦7Evry(Fra) a6f 1:114gd 5½ 123 Ⓣ 612 SamaniH Pr Pensbury African Joy, King's Envoy, Cinto 8
May 27 Hol 5f ft 1:014 h May 21 Hol 5f ft 1:04 h Apr 24 SA 3f ft :362 h Apr 15 SA 4f ft :482 h

Nat's Penny

Ch. g. 3, by L'Natural—Quinto Penny, by Catchpenny II
Br.—Warwick G M (Cal) 1982 6 0 2 0 $5,070
Own.—Warwick G M 114 Tr.—West Ted $37,500 1981 9 2 2 1 $23,540
Lifetime 15 2 4 1 $28,610

4May82-6GG 6f :223 :461 1:122ft 15 115 2hd 2hd 3½ 74½ Burkes T7 Aw14000 72 PublicTrdition,SirMcmllon,Pt'sDud 8
31Mar82-6GG 6f :224 :46 1:114sy 11 115 41½ 41½ 22 23 Burkes T1 Aw13000 77 SirMacmillion,Nt'sPenny,Pet'sDude 6
10Mar82-8GG 6f :222 :453 1:102ft 6½ 115 43 53½ 55½ 77½ Burkes T3 Aw14000 80 ThBrginHuntr,WlkPst,HonorblLook 7
9Feb82-8GG 6f :221 :453 1:111ft 16 117 55 77 812 89½ Lawless G5 Gldn Bear 73 DustyTrader,JetTravel,CousinJosh 11
4Feb82-8BM 6f :224 :461 1:111ft *1 114 21 1½ 11 22 Lawless G4 Aw13000 82 SeniorCitizen,Nt'sPnny,CountMrsll 6
9Jan82-8BM 6f :223 :46 1:12 gd 8½ 115 61½ 54 68 88 Burkes T3 Athtn 72 DominntRoni,Shilling,RoylMmory 12
11Dec81-8BM 6f :223 :453 1:11 ft 4½ 115 2½ 42½ 31½ 2¾ Burkes T4 Aw12000 84 Walk Past, Nat's Penny, Ace King 9
15Nov81-10AC 6f :22 :434 1:084ft 6 122 3½ 44½ 64¾ 611 Munoz J4 A C Fut 84 Sari'sDreamer,Tular,B.RichGeorge 12
7Nov81-9AC 6f :22 :44 1:093ft 2½ 120 41¾ 41 42 44½ Munoz J2 Aw5000 87 DlwrExprss,FltPlAllsn,TwStrAdmrl 6
7Aug81-11SR 5½f :22 :443 1:043ft 4½ 122 32 31½ 31 11½† Levine C3 Rdwd Empr 90 ‡Nat'sPenny,Demarday,Tohottocari 9
† 7Aug81—Disqualified and placed fifth
May 27 Hol 3f ft :361 h May 22 Hol 3f ft :37 h May 3 GG 3f ft :371 h Apr 28 GG 5f ft 1:011 h

Gringo Jim *

Dk. b. or br. c. 3, by Gallant Romeo—Zonta, by Dr Fager
Br.—Tartan Farms Corp (Fla) 1982 4 1 0 0 $9,350
Own.—Tartan Stable 116 Tr.—Lukas D Wayne $40,000 1981 0 M 0 0
Lifetime 4 1 0 0 $9,350

3Apr82-5SA 6f :22 :452 1:093ft 42 120 75½ 812 717 818 Lipham T5 Aw20000 72 B.RichGeorg,Polly'sRulr,Accousticl 9
31Jan82-2SA 1 1/16 :454 1:102 1:432ft 28 116 2hd 3½ 79¾ 918 ValenzuelPA9 Aw20000 66 Turbulation, Ask Me, Keno Hill 10
20Jan82-6SA 6½f :22 :454 1:192sy 10 118 21 1½ 12½ 12 McCarron C J5 Mdn 73 Gringo Jim, Idaho, Sir Pele 8
10Jan82-6SA 6f :214 :451 1:094ft 17 118 83½1011 1015 1022 McCarron C J3 Mdn 67 JournytS,Htmoto,ConsciousEffort 10
May 27 Hol 4f ft :512 h May 21 Hol 4f ft :492 h May 14 Hol 3f ft :364 h

Checker's Orphan

Ch. g. 3, by Raise an Orphan—Checker's Honey, by Orbit Ruler
Br.—Downey J (Cal) 1982 6 1 1 1 $13,525
Own.—Crowley & Downey 116 Tr.—Jordan James $40,000 1981 3 1 1 0 $7,500
Lifetime 9 2 2 1 $21,025

16May82-1Hol 1 1/16 :471 1:113 1:431ft 5 116 32½ 3nk 53 69 Pierce D3 50000 70 Duntlss,FltPulAllison,SultnofSwing 8
1May82-1Hol 1 :454 1:104 1:364ft 5½ 116 11 12½ 15 14 Pierce D1 32000 82 Chckr'sOrphn,ClubFlsh,Ed'sDynsty 9
16Apr82-4SA 1 :452 1:103 1:361ft *3-2 116 22½ 11 1hd 22½ McCarron C J4 25000 85 WestCostNtive,Checkr'sOrphn,Bgly 8
5Mar82-1SA 6f :214 :444 1:103ft 7 116 2½ 22 32 32 McHargue DG4 c20000 83 Mchll'sDrm,Prt'sOvr,Chcr'sOrphn 12
12Feb82-1SA 6f :222 :453 1:114gd 7½ 116 62½ 510 411 516 McHargue D G7 32000 63 L'Cap, Ima Sizzler, Supercede 9
14Jan82-5SA 6f :213 :443 1:091ft 61 114 73½ 913 916 824 Black K3 Aw19000 68 Jet Travel, B. RichGeorge,Rise'nFly 9
19Aug81-4Dmr 6f :224 :463 1:123ft *2 118 31 4¾ 12½ 12½ Pincay L Jr7 Mc32000 75 Checker'sOrphn,TrvlingPul,Ris'nFly 9
7Aug81-6Dmr 6f :23 :464 1:123ft 5½ 118 96½ 87¾ 47 25 Pincay L Jr6 M32000 70 Michll'sDrm,Chckr'sOrphn,Grnnng 11
17Jly81-4Hol 6f :221 :454 1:113ft 14 117 1213 1111 1012 913 Pincay L Jr5 M45000 66 AntiquRulr,Kll'sBoy,GillgnsPurchs 12
May 25 Hol 5f ft 1:004 h Apr 24 SA 5f ft 1:00 h ●Apr 9 SA 7f ft 1:24 h

Spectacular Bee

B. c. 3, by Nose for Money—Bee Cane, by Tumble Turbie
Br.—Ball & Newman (Fla) 1982 8 0 0 0 $3,150
Own.—Twin W Stable 116 Tr.—Calascibetta Joseph $40,000 1981 4 1 1 0 $7,490
Lifetime 12 1 1 0 $10,640

12May82-5Hol 6f :214 :44 1:091ft 35 115 54 55 65 54¾ Toro F6 Aw20000 86 JettingPlesure,TellFib,VgbondSong 8
30Apr82-5Hol 6f :214 :444 1:10 ft 19 116 53½ 41½ 53½ 45½ Guerra W A1 40000 82 Cn'tBeBet,Inserchof,BetterWithAg 7
13Mar82-7GP 7f :221 :452 1:24 ft 12 117 31 3½ 65½ 68¾ Soto S B7 Aw12000 75 HauntedLad,Pavarotti,RoiMusique 11
3Mar82-5Hia 6f :223 :453 1:111ft 10 116 21½ 45 58½ 512 Soto S B1 75000 75 Mr. B. B., DirectAnswer,PeterOwen 7
13Feb82-6Hia 6f :222 :452 1:11 ft 14 116 53 55½ 46½ 55¾ Soto S B10 Aw13000 82 Richness, Pathline, Chan Balum 12
30Jan82-5Hia 6f :22 :45 1:103ft 31 116 86¾ 68½ 47½ 44½ Soto S B8 Aw13000 86 ThrAStrw,Compo'sTmpo,GlfordRd 10
23Jan82-5Hia 6f :214 :443 1:10 ft 50 116 32 52¾ 67½ 811 Soto S B1 Aw13000 82 Cut Away,FrankGomez,StarChoice 12
9Jan82-5Hia 6f :222 :46 1:112ft 22 116 2½ 4¾ 76½ 78¾ Smith A Jr7 Aw13000 77 Angel Bike, Cut Away,CourtScene 12
8Jly81-9Crc 5½f :223 :471 1:071ft 3½ 116 2hd 3nk 34 511 Cohen G6 Aw9500 78 SmrtAli,VictorinLine,IntrepidChrgr 6
12Jun81-5Crc 5f :223 :462 :593ft *3-2 117 1hd 2hd 22½ 44½ Beuviere J L2 Aw9500 89 Center Cut, SmartAli,VictorianLine 6
May 25 SA 4f ft :49 h Apr 12 Crc 5f ft 1:032 b Apr 6 Crc 5f ft 1:022 b Apr 1 Crc 4f ft :50 h

Two long shots, Nat's Penny and Gringo Jim, dominated the race and finished one-two when both Insearchof and Jet Pirate, who were vying for the lead at the stretch, faded. Luckily, Insearchof held on for third and paid $3.80 for show. Jet Pirate finished fourth. The $3.80 payoff for show on the 5—2 shot Insearchof was again a combination of two factors: At a 1.08 expected value it was a reasonably good bet, and the one-two finishers in the race went off at 28—1 and 26—1 odds, respectively. My $50 bet returned $95, for a profit of $45. The chart of the race was as follows:

FIFTH RACE
Hollywood
MAY 30, 1982

6 FURLONGS. (1.07⅖) CLAIMING. Purse $18,000. 3-year-olds. Weight, 122 lbs. Non-winners of two races since March 28 allowed 3 lbs.; a race since then, 6 lbs. Claiming price $40,000; for each $2,500 to $35,000 allowed 2 lbs. (Races when entered for $32,000 or less not considered.)

Value of race $18,000, value to winner $9,900, second $3,600, third $2,700, fourth $1,350, fifth $450. Mutuel pool $294,266. Exacta Pool $454,047.

Last Raced	Horse	Eqt.A.Wt	PP	St	¼	½	Str	Fin	Jockey	Cl'g Pr	Odds $1
4May82 ^{6}GG^{7}	Nat's Penny	b 3 115	8	2	8^{hd}	4^{hd}	$3^{1\frac{1}{2}}$	1^{hd}	Delahoussaye E	37500	28.10
3Apr82 ^{5}SA^{8}	Gringo Jim	3 117	9	1	6^{hd}	6^{3}	5^{3}	2^{nk}	Pincay L Jr	40000	26.80
22May82 ^{3}Hol^{2}	Insearchof	b 3 116	3	10	1^{hd}	$2^{\frac{1}{2}}$	$1^{\frac{1}{2}}$	$3^{3\frac{1}{2}}$	McHargue D G	40000	2.50
9May82 ^{5}Hol^{4}	Jet Pirate	b 3 116	4	4	3^{hd}	$3^{2\frac{1}{2}}$	2^{hd}	$4^{1\frac{1}{2}}$	Sibille R	40000	2.30
22May82 ^{3}Hol^{3}	Familiar Tune	3 112	2	9	2^{hd}	$1^{\frac{1}{2}}$	$4^{\frac{1}{2}}$	$5^{1\frac{1}{2}}$	Ortega L E	35000	17.60
8Apr82 ^{9}SA^{10}	Ramble on John	b 3 116	1	7	10	$7^{\frac{1}{2}}$	7^{4}	$6^{\frac{1}{2}}$	Ramirez O	40000	56.70
15May82 ^{2}Hol^{10}	Extra Quick	b 3 116	5	8	9^{7}	5^{3}	$6^{2\frac{1}{2}}$	7^{3}	Castaneda M	40000	8.00
12May82 ^{5}Hol^{5}	Spectacular Bee	b 3 116	10	3	$7^{\frac{1}{2}}$	9^{7}	9^{8}	8^{7}	McCarron C J	40000	3.50
28Apr82 ^{8}GG^{5}	Murtazz	b 3 116	7	5	$4^{\frac{1}{2}}$	8^{hd}	$8^{\frac{1}{2}}$	9	Lipham T	40000	48.00
20Feb82 ^{2}SA^{5}	Distant Gem	b 3 116	6	6	5^{hd}	10	10	—	Valenzuela P A	40000	8.40

Distant Gem, Eased.

OFF AT 3:46 Start good. Won driving. Time, :22⅕, :45⅖, :58⅕, 1:11⅖ Track fast.

$2 Mutuel Prices:

8-NAT'S PENNY	58.20	20.60	10.60
9-GRINGO JIM		20.00	8.40
3-INSEARCHOF			3.80

$5 EXACTA 8–9 PAID $1,433.00

Ch. g, by L'Natural—Quinto Penny, by Catchpenny II. Trainer West Ted. Bred by Warwick G M (Cal).

NAT'S PENNY, never far back, rallied between horses on the turn, challenged outside the leaders in the upper stretch and outfinished rivals in the final sixteenth. GRINGO JIM, in contention while forced to stay wide early, rallied strongly in the middle of the track through the stretch but missed. INSEARCHOF vied for the lead from the outset, continued to respond in the final drive but could not get up. JET PIRATE forced the pace between horses to the final furlong, drifted slightly in behind INSEARCHOF in the stretch and steadied momentarily. The stewards lit the inquiry sign but after reviewing the videotapes of the stretch run, allowed the finish to stand. FAMILIAR TUNE set or forced the early pace inside INSEARCHOF and weakened in the final furlong. RAMBLE ON JOHN, awkward gaining stride after the start, did not reach contention. EXTRA QUICK saved ground to no avail. SPECTACULAR BEE forced to stay wide into the turn, lacked a rally. DISTANT GEM was eased in the final sixteenth.

Owners— 1, Warwick G M; 2, Tartan Stable; 3, Gaskill-Lewis et al; 4, Cavanagh Mr-Mrs T M; 5, Sugich D or Jane; 6, Priddy R or Ann; 7, Four D Stable; 8, Twin W Stable; 9, Cashman E C; 10, Marshall Mr-Mrs F.

Overweight: Nat's Penny 1 pound; Gringo Jim 1.

Distant Gem was claimed by Winning Ways Stable; trainer, Mitchell Mike.

Scratched—Checker's Orphan (16May82 ^{1}Hol^{6}).

The sixth race was among lightly raced maidens, including several horses making their first start. Since there were no standouts (for example, a horse that consistently finished in the money and had done so recently), I decided to avoid the risk and skip this race.

The seventh race was on the turf. The consensus picks were Fast, Pirate Law, and Moonball. However, my preference was for Patti's Triumph, who was the public's fourth choice at 4—1. Patti's Triumph had finished in the money in four of the last five races against similar-quality opposition. His only finish out of the money was in a major handicap race at a longer distance. He had been leading the race, then faded to fourth at the finish. This fading was typical of most of Patti's Triumph's races. Normally, his lead was sufficiently good to compensate for his late fading so that he still finished well. The odds were quite good, with an expected value of 1.12, or nearly a Dr. Z system bet, when I bet with one minute to post time. The final tote board was as follows:

	Totals	#6 Patti's Triumph
Odds		4—1
Win	182,509	28,241
Show	48,202	5,171

indicating an expected value per dollar bet of 1.14.

Patti's Triumph got a poor start and was in the race in second or third position until the stretch. He then faded to fourth. The three favorites finished in the money. I had a $50 loss on this race. The chart of the race was as follows:

SEVENTH RACE Hollywood MAY 30, 1982 **$1\frac{1}{16}$ MILES.(turf). (1.39⅗) ALLOWANCE. Purse $40,000. 4-year-olds and upward. Non-winners of $18,000 twice since July 20. Weight, 121 lbs. Non-winners of $22,000 at a mile or over since April 1 allowed 3 lbs.; such a race of $19,500 since December 5, 5 lbs.; such a race since July 20, 7 lbs. (Claiming and starter races not considered.)**

Value of race $40,000, value to winner $22,000, second $8,000, third $6,000, fourth $3,000, fifth $1,000. Mutuel pool $305,904. Exacta Pool $482,464.

Last Raced	Horse	Eqt.	A.	Wt	PP	St	¼	½	¾	Str	Fin	Jockey	Odds $1
22May82 ^{5}Hol^{2}	Pirate Law	b	5	114	3	4	$4^{1/2}$	$5^{1\frac{1}{2}}$	4^{hd}	$2^{1\frac{1}{2}}$	1^{hd}	Valenzuela P A	a-3.00
28Dec80 ^{8}SA^{3}	Fast	b	6	114	5	6	6^{5}	6^{6}	$5^{2\frac{1}{2}}$	1^{hd}	$2^{1\frac{1}{4}}$	McCarron C J	2.60
14May82 ^{8}Hol^{1}	Moon Ball		6	115	7	8	8^{3}	$8^{1/2}$	8^{10}	$5^{1/2}$	$3^{3/4}$	Castaneda M	4.20
22May82 ^{5}Hol^{3}	Patti's Triumph	b	5	118	6	5	5^{3}	3^{hd}	$2^{1\frac{1}{2}}$	3^{hd}	4^{2}	Hawley S	4.40
16May82 ^{8}Hol^{7}	Sunny Winters	b	5	116	4	9	9	9	6^{hd}	6^{hd}	$5^{3\frac{1}{2}}$	Delahoussaye E	16.20
14May82 ^{8}Hol^{4}	Confetti		5	117	9	7	7^{2}	7^{1}	7^{2}	7^{5}	6^{1}	Pincay L Jr	10.30
22May82 ^{5}Hol^{6}	Haughty But Nice		4	115	1	1	$1^{1/2}$	1^{hd}	1^{hd}	4^{2}	7^{10}	McHargue D G	11.90
23May82 ^{8}GG^{6}	Golden Flak	b	4	114	8	2	$3^{1/2}$	$4^{1\frac{1}{2}}$	3^{hd}	8^{15}	8^{17}	Hansen R D	a-3.00
25Apr82 ^{7}Hol^{7}	Another Realm	b	4	114	2	3	$2^{1/2}$	2^{hd}	9	9	9	Gilligan L	15.90

a-Coupled: Pirate Law and Golden Flak.

OFF AT 4:48. Start good. Won driving. Time, :22, :45⅘, 1:10⅕, 1:34⅘, 1:41 Course firm.

$2 Mutuel Prices:			
1-PIRATE LAW (a-entry)	8.00	3.20	2.20
5-FAST		4.00	2.60
7-MOON BALL			3.00

$5 EXACTA 1-5 PAID $73.50.

B. h, by Ruffled Feathers—Patio II, by Court Martial. Trainer Barrera Lazaro S. Bred by M Pelinger Estate (Fla).

PIRATE LAW saved ground in good position to the far turn, remained on the rail to lodge his bid in the stretch and outfinished FAST in the final sixteenth. The latter lacked early speed, rallied outside horses around the final turn, got the lead a furlong out but could not outfinish the winner. MOON BALL, outrun for six furlongs, rallied wide into the stretch but finished strongly. PATTI'S TRIUMPH, in contention between horses to the stretch, weakened in the final furlong. CONFETTI, never a factor, appeared lame pulling up following the finish. HAUGHTY BUT NICE set or forced the pace to the final furlong and faltered. GOLDEN FLAK was forced wide at the clubhouse turn, remained in contention on the outside to the stretch but tired quickly thereafter. ANOTHER REALM lugged out on both turns.

Owners— 1, Barrera & Jones Mmes; 2, Hunt & Pascoe III; 3, Perdomo & Pulliam; 4, Grutman D S; 5, Tresvant Stable; 6, Mirkin-Mirkin-Pacifica; 7, Daniels Mrs T L; 8, Barrera & Saiden; 9, Goldstein Margaret.

Overweight: Moon Ball 1 pound; Confetti 3; Haughty But Nice 1.

The eighth race was the featured race of the day: the Los Angeles Handicap. The field was headed by Never Tabled and Remember John. Never Tabled had not raced until he was a five-year-old. But in his four career races, all at Santa Anita and Hollywood Park in April and May of 1982, he had had three wins and a second against strong competition with fast times. Remember John had performed brilliantly in his two-year career. This year he had had four wins and a second with speed ratings from 92 to 99. He was coming to the Los Angeles Handicap with four consecutive wins and post position 1. The race also featured such strong horses as Shanekite and Petro D. Jay. Pompeii Court was scratched.

The *Daily Racing Form* consensus and the crowd favored Never Tabled, with Remember John second. My preference was for Remember John if the odds were good. He seemed more proven and reliable. Never Tabled was running with a longer time between starts than he had before. This, plus the post-position disadvantage, and Never Tabled's brief four-race career gave the nod to Remember John.

8th Hollywood

6 FURLONGS. (1.07⅘) 30th Running of THE LOS ANGELES HANDICAP (Grade III). $75,000 added. 3-year olds and upward. By subscription of $100 each, which shall accompany the nomination, $750 additional to start, with $75,000 added, of which $15,000 to second, $11,250 to third, $5,625 to fourth and $1,875 to fifth. Weights Tuesday, May 25. Starters to be named through the entry box by closing time of entries. A trophy will be presented to the owner of the winner. Closed Wednesday, May 19, 1982 with 13 nominations.

Remember John

B. g. 3, by The Irish Lord—Yoweee, by Crozier
Own.—Sheridan Mr-Mrs J **115** **Br.—Valenti P (Cal)** 1982 5 4 1 0 $113,100
Tr.—Vienna Darrell 1981 6 1 2 1 $52,900
Lifetime 11 5 3 1 $166,000

16May82-6Hol	5f	:21^2	:44	:56 ft	6-5	116	1^{hd}	$1\frac{1}{2}$	$1\frac{1}{2}$	$1\frac{3}{4}$	DelhoussyeE^1	Aw37000	99	RemembrJohn,Unlklt,Trrsto'sSingr	7
1May82-7Hol	6f	:22	:44^2	1:08^{3}ft	*3-5	122	2^{hd}	1^{hd}	1^1	$1\frac{1}{2}$	McCrronCJ^4	Debonair	94	RemmbrJohn,ArtDirctor,RingProud	5
31Mar82-8SA	6½f	:21^3	:44^1	1:15^{1}ft	3	117	$1\frac{1}{2}$	1^{hd}	$1\frac{1}{2}$	$1\frac{3}{4}$	DelhoussyeE^1	Baldwin	94	RmmbrJohn,TmToExplod,CrystlStr	7
21Mar82-4SA	6½f	:21^2	:44	1:15^{2}ft	*2-3	115	$1\frac{1}{2}$	1^1	1^3	1^5	DelhoussyeE^1	Aw20000	93	RemembrJohn,CIticSbr,EstrSrmon	6
17Feb82-8SA	6f	:21^2	:43^4	1:08^{3}ft	20	117	1^{hd}	2^1	$2^{2\frac{1}{2}}$	2^3	DlhoussyE^6	Blsa Chca	92	TmToExplod,RmmbrJohn,JornytS	10
9Sep81-8Dmr	1	:45^3	1:11^1	1:37^{2}ft	10	117	1^{hd}	1^{hd}	$5^{1\frac{3}{4}}$	$9^{7\frac{1}{2}}$	McCarronCJ^8	Dmr Fut	73	GatoDelSol,TheCaptain,RingProud	10
26Aug81-8Dmr	1	:45^4	1:10^3	1:36^{4}ft	6½	117	$1\frac{1}{2}$	$1^{1\frac{1}{2}}$	2^{hd}	$5^{5\frac{1}{2}}$	Toro F^6	Balboa	78	TheCaptain,DistantHeart,GtoDelSol	9
12Aug81-8Dmr	6f	:22	:45	1:11 ft	*4-5	120	1^{hd}	$1\frac{1}{2}$	1^{hd}	3^1	McCarronCJ^5	De Anza	82	King'sFinder,Heln'sBu,RmmbrJohn	5
29Jly81-8Dmr	6f	:22^1	:45^2	1:10^{4}ft	*4-5	114	$1\frac{1}{2}$	$1\frac{1}{2}$	$1^{2\frac{1}{2}}$	$1^{1\frac{3}{4}}$	McCrrCJ^5	[S]Gradution	84	RemmbrJohn,King'sFindr,DistntHrt	9
18Jly81-8Hol	6f	:21^3	:44^4	1:10^{2}ft	19	115	2^{hd}	2^{hd}	$1\frac{1}{2}$	2^{hd}	Toro F^{10}	Hol Juv	85	TheCptin,RememberJohn,Hln'sBu	12

May 28 Hol 3f ft :35^2 h **May 23 Hol 5f ft :59^3 h** **May 14 Hol 3f ft :35^3 h** **May 9 Hol 4f ft :47^3 h**

Shanekite

B. c. 4, by Hoist Bar—Win Shane, by Anyoldtime
Own.—Udko Selma **117** **Br.—Udko Selma (Cal)** 1982 6 0 3 0 $40,925
Tr.—Landers Dale 1981 10 6 0 0 $161,000
Lifetime 22 8 5 0 $224,050 Turf 1 0 1 0 $12,000

16May82-6Hol	5f	:21^2	:44	:56 ft	*6-5	119	$5^{7\frac{1}{2}}$	$5^{7\frac{1}{2}}$	$5^{6\frac{1}{2}}$	$5^{5\frac{3}{4}}$	Hawley S^6	Aw37000	93	RemembrJohn,Unlklt,Trrsto'sSingr	7
8May82-8Hol	7f	:21^4	:44	1:21 ft	*1	117	$6^{7\frac{1}{4}}$	$5^{4\frac{1}{4}}$	$3^{1\frac{1}{2}}$	2^2	HwleyS^7	Trple Bend H	90	NeverTbled,Shnekite,PompeiiCourt	7
17Apr82-8SA	a6½f (T)	:21	:43^1	1:13 fm	7½	118	$6^{5\frac{1}{2}}$	$6^{2\frac{3}{4}}$	$3\frac{1}{2}$	$2^{1\frac{1}{2}}$	Hawley S^1	Sn Simn H	92	Shagbark, Shanekite, Belfort	8
24Mar82-8SA	5½f	:21^3	:44^2	1:02^{1}ft	4½	118	—	—	—	—	HawleyS^6	El Conejo H	—	ToB.OrNot,Belfort,Terresto'sSinger	8
24Mar82—Lost rider															
9Jan82-8SA	7f	:21^3	:43^4	1:20^{4}ft	3½	119	$4^{3\frac{1}{2}}$	$4^{1\frac{1}{2}}$	8^9	8^{12}	Hawley S^6	Sn Crlos H	84	Solo Guy,‡King Go Go, Smokite	8
3Jan82-8SA	7f	:22^1	:45^4	1:26 hy	*8-5	120	$5^{1\frac{1}{2}}$	$1\frac{1}{2}$	$2\frac{1}{2}$	2^6	Hawley S^6	Malibu	64	Island Whirl, Shanekite, It'stheOne	8
19Dec81-8Hol	7f	:21^2	:43^4	1:21^{3}ft	*4-5	117	$4^{1\frac{1}{2}}$	$4^{1\frac{1}{2}}$	1^1	$1^{2\frac{1}{2}}$	Hawley S^4	Yuletide H	89	Shanekite, FlyingChick,IslandWhirl	5
28Nov81-8Hol	1	:48	1:13	1:38^{4}m	3½	113	1^{hd}	$1\frac{1}{2}$	$3\frac{1}{2}$	$4^{2\frac{1}{2}}$	Hawley S^4	Ntv Dvr H	69	Syncopate, King Go Go, Wickerr	6
11Nov81-8Hol	6f	:21^3	:44^1	1:08^{1}ft	2¾	114	$5^{2\frac{1}{2}}$	1^1	1^4	$1^{2\frac{1}{2}}$	HawleyS^8	Sprnt Chmp	96	Shanekite,Syncopte,BigPresenttion	8
11Nov81—Run in two divisions, 8th & 9th races.															
29Oct81-7SA	6f	:22	:44^3	1:09 ft	*4-5	118	$2^{2\frac{1}{2}}$	$2^{2\frac{1}{2}}$	2^{hd}	1^5	Hawley S^1	Aw34000	93	Shnekite,ImportntMemo,NtivFishr	7

May 22 Hol 4f ft :47^3 hg **Apr 30 Hol 6f ft 1:14^2 h** **Apr 24 SA 4f ft :49^4 h** **Apr 13 SA (T) 5f yl 1:04 h (d)**

Pompeii Court

Own.—Lewyk & Crowe **116**

B. h. 5, by Tell—Port Damascus, by Damascus
Br.—Keck H B (Ky) 1982 5 2 0 2 $54,300
Tr.—Anderson Laurie N 1981 16 5 5 3 $45,954
Lifetime 25 9 7 5 $105,134

8May82-8Hol	7f	:21^4	:44	1:21 ft	3¼	116	3½	2^1	2^{1½}	3^2	ShmrW^6	Trple Bend H	90	NeverTbled,Shnekite,PompeiiCourt	7
7Mar82-3SA	1	:44^3	1:08^3	1:34^{2}ft	*2½	116	2½	1½	1½	1^{hd}	Hawley S^1	Aw40000	97	PompCort,KngrooCort,SonofDodo	7
18Feb82-7SA	1	:45^1	1:09	1:33^{3}ft	11	114	1½	1^1	1^3	1^{4½}	Hawley S^2	Aw32000	101	PompeiiCourt,QuntumLep,Western	8
5Feb82-7SA	6½f	:21^2	:43^3	1:15 ft	11	115	4^{2½}	4^{2½}	4^3	3^{3¾}	Sibille R^5	Aw32000	91	VictorySmpl,BondRullh,PompCourt	8
20Jan82-5SA	7f	:21^4	:45	1:24^{4}sy	4¾	115	2^{hd}	1^{hd}	1^{hd}	4^2	Sibille R^1	Aw32000	74	Gristle,QuntumLep,AnswertoMusic	5
18Dec81-7Hol	6f	:21^4	:44^3	1:09^{3}ft	9	115	3^{nk}	3^{nk}	3^2	5^5	Sibille R^6	Aw30000	84	Hacwind,BennyBob,CrestoftheWve	7
9Dec81-7Hol	6½f	:22^1	:45	1:15^{4}ft	5½	116	1^{hd}	1½	1^2	1^{1¼}	Sibille R^2	Aw25000	91	PompeiiCourt,KngrooCourt,Dorcro	8
27Nov81-7Hol	6½f	:22^3	:45^3	1:18^{3}sy	*3	115	1^{hd}	1^{1½}	2^{1½}	2¾	Sibille R^4	Aw25000	76	DndyWit,PompiiCourt,Sli'sRoylDrm	8
13Nov81-7Hol	6f	:22	:44^3	1:08^{4}ft	15	115	1^{hd}	2½	2½	3^{4¼}	Sibille R^1	Aw26000	89	Hcwind,KngrooCourt,PompiiCourt	8
17Oct81-8StP	6f	:22^2	:45^1	1:10^{1}ft	*9-5	118	5^{5½}	5^{4½}	3^5	4^4	Garcia C^1	Aw6500	94	Kinlin, Flashys Champ,ThreeforYou	7

May 21 Hol 5f ft 1:00^4 h   May 3 Hol 6f ft 1:13^1 h   Apr 23 SA 6f ft 1:12^1 h   Apr 16 SA 4f ft :48^3 h

Petro D. Jay

Own.—Ottley R **116**

Dk. b. or br. g. 6, by Tudor Grey—Mucho Petro, by Distillate
Br.—Synhorst W (Neb) 1982 5 2 1 0 $13,410
Tr.—Bradshaw Randy K 1981 13 6 2 2 $53,210
Lifetime 29 11 4 2 $85,755

9May82-9TuP	6f	:21^3	:43^2	1:07^{1}ft	*1-5	120	1^{1½}	1^3	1^6	1^{12}	Renteria S^4	Aw3325	101	Petro D. Jay, Pelemise, Jared Fox	5
4Apr82-10TuP	6f	:21^1	:43^1	1:09^{1}ft	*2-5	120	1^1	1^{hd}	1^1	1^{nk}	Powell J P^1	Express H	91	Petro D. Jay, No Pomp, Maui Star	7
13Mar82-7SA	6f	:22^1	:45^2	1:10^{3}gd	12	114	1^{hd}	3^{1½}	6^8	7^{11}	Hulet L^6	Aw35000	74	Belfort, Mad Key, A Run	10
21Feb82-10TuP	6f	:21^2	:43^3	1:09^{1}ft	6¼	112	8^{6½}	6^7	3^6	4^7	Hulet L^3	Phx Gd Cp	84	Imperial Lass, Mad Key, Bold Ego	9
6Feb82-10TuP	6f	:21^2	:43^1	1:08 ft	*1-2	114	1^1	1^1	1^1	2¾	Hulet L^2	Aw3900	96	Mad Key, Petro D. Jay, Bobby Ben	7
13Sep81-11Pom	6f	:21^1	:44^2	1:10^{2}ft	*8-5	117	2^{hd}	2^{hd}	3^1	5^{5½}	Rosales R^4	Gov Cp H	86	MrblCourt,Murrthblurr,AmnBrothr	5
5Sep81-8Sac	5½f	:21^3	:43^4	1:02^{1}ft	*2-3	119	1½	2^{hd}	2½	3^{4½}	Hamilton M^2	HcpO	94	SrPortRulr,GryMoonRnnr,PtroD.Jy	4
1Aug81-11SR	6f	:22	:44^2	1:08^{3}ft	*7-5	118	2^{hd}	1½	1^{hd}	1^{hd}	SrnsnJJ^5	Ernst Fnly H	101	PetroD.Jy,RomnOblisk,SirPortRulr	7
19Jly81-11Sol	5½f	:21^2	:43^3	1:02^{2}ft	*1-2	116	1^{hd}	1½	1^1	2½	Sorenson J J^4	Aw12000	100	SirPortRuler,PetroD.Jay,BeauBlade	6
4Jly81-11Pln	6f	:22	:44^2	1:09^{1}ft	*6-5	121	1^{hd}	2^{hd}	4^{4½}	6^{11}	SrnsJJ^4	Whtng Mm H	87	ThnkYoWlkr's,KnConty,ImSdwndr	6

●May 27 Hol 4f ft :45^3 h   ●May 6 TuP 4f ft :45 h

Cool Frenchy

Own.—Lichlyter Dr or Mrs F E **112**

Dk. b. or br. h. 7, by French Policy—Cool Persian, by Persia
Br.—Lichlyter Mary Ada (Cal) 1982 1 0 0 0
Tr.—Lichlyter Mary A 1981 13 3 2 3 $79,930
Lifetime 45 10 8 5 $201,924 Turf 3 0 0 0 $2,200

16May82-6Hol	5f	:21^2	:44	:56 ft	8¾	109^5	3^{3½}	3^3	4^4	7^{8½}	Garcia J J^3	Aw37000	90	RemembrJohn,Unlklt,Trrsto'sSingr	7
4Jly81-11Pln	6f	:22	:44^2	1:09^{1}ft	8-5	122	3½	3^{1½}	3^4	4^{5½}	BzeRA^5	Whtng Mm H	92	ThnkYoWlkr's,KnConty,ImSdwndr	6
20Jun81-7Hol	6f	:21^4	:44^4	1:09^{3}ft	3¾	114	1^{hd}	1^{hd}	3^1	3^{5¼}	Olivares F^5	Aw36000	84	Rb'sGoldnAl,GrndAllnc,CoolFrnchy	6
11Jun81-8Hol	6f	:21^4	:44^3	1:09 ft	3½	114	1½	1½	1^1	2½	Olivares F^7	Aw36000	91	FlyingChick,CoolFrenchy,ThCrpntr	8
25May81-7Hol	5f	:21^2	:44	:56 ft	10	113	1½	2^{hd}	2^{2½}	4^{3½}	Lipham T^7	Aw40000	95	I'm Smokin,Back'nTime,Syncopate	9
20May81-7Hol	6f	:21^4	:44^2	1:08^{4}ft	2½	114	1½	1^2	2½	5^{4¾}	Mena F^2	Aw36000	88	Destroyer, Shady Fox, Rich Doctor	6
25Apr81-8GG	7½f	Ⓣ:22^4	:46	1:28 fm	5½	117	1^{hd}	1½	2½	5^{4¾}	Toro F^2	Tly Pp Inv H	95	His Honor, Police Inspector,Josher	9
7Apr81-8GG	6f	:22^2	:44^3	1:09^{1}ft	*2-3	120	1^{hd}	1½	1^{1½}	1½	Mena F^5	Aw20000	93	CoolFrenchy,‡LotoCnd,ChrlySutton	5
25Mar81-8SA	5½f	:21^4	:44^1	1:02^{2}ft	11	115	1^2	1^2	2^{hd}	3^{1½}	Mena F^9	El Conejo H	100	ToBOrNot,SmmrTmGy,ColFrnchy	11
10Mar81-8GG	6f	:22	:44^2	1:08^{3}ft	2½	122	1^{1½}	1^1	1^3	1^5	Mena F^2	Aw20000	96	CoolFrenchy,MightyMixup,Mrketti	5

May 26 Hol 6f ft 1:15^2 h   May 12 Hol 5f ft :59^3 hg   ●May 7 Hol 4f ft :46^1 h   May 2 Hol 4f ft :47^2 h

Beach Walk *

Own.—Knapp P R **113**

Ro. g. 5, by Windy Sands—Squishie, by Gaelic Dancer
Br.—Old English Rancho (Cal) 1982 10 2 5 1 $52,890
Tr.—Villagomez Jaime 1981 7 3 1 1 $28,950
Lifetime 32 7 9 3 $100,405

23May82-7Hol	6f	:22	:44^4	1:09^{2}ft	5¼	109^5	2^{hd}	1½	1½	2½	Steiner J J^5	Aw32000	89	ShadyFox,BeachWalk,AmenBrother	7
8May82-3Hol	6f	:22^1	:44^4	1:08^{4}ft	3	109^5	1^1	1^{1½}	1½	1½	Steiner J J^4	Aw26000	93	BeachWlk,MsterWrrior,ChpelCreek	8
29Apr82-8Hol	6f	:22	:44^3	1:08^{2}ft	3	109^5	1^1	1½	2½	2^{2½}	Steiner J J^5	Aw26000	92	LaughingBoy,BeachWalk,Redoutble	7
18Apr82-3SA	6½f	:21^2	:44^1	1:14^{2}ft	7½	109^5	1½	1^{hd}	2^{hd}	2^{1¾}	Steiner J J^5	45000	96	NaynoBay,BeachWalk,Incorporator	6
11Apr82-1SA	6f	:21^4	:45^1	1:09^{4}sy	7	116	1^1	1½	1^{hd}	2^{nk}	Ortega L E^4	40000	89	NaynoBay,BechWlk,SupremeGlow	12
21Mar82-1SA	6f	:21^4	:44^4	1:09^{1}ft	13	114	2^{hd}	2^{hd}	2^2	3^{4½}	Asmussen C B^4	45000	87	Fingal, Incorporator, Beach Walk	8
12Mar82-6SA	6f	:22^4	:47	1:13 sl	3	111^5	1^2	1^{1½}	2½	1^{nk}	Steiner J J^3	32000	73	BeachWalk,Chnnon'sBrother,I'vPet	4
6Mar82-4GG	6f	:22	:44^3	1:09^{3}ft	3¼	114	1^{hd}	2^{hd}	3½	4^{2½}	Meza R Q^4	35000	88	Cross Flags, Ono Bret, Johnny Iver	5
26Feb82-8GG	6f	:22^1	:44^3	1:09^{2}ft	3	115	1^{hd}	3^2	6^6	7^{10}	Burkes T^3	Aw15000	82	Ineffble,FerlessBedeux,TudorGrove	7
5Feb82-8BM	6f	:21^4	:44^1	1:09 ft	13	114	2^{1½}	2^3	2^3	2^{3½}	Meza R Q^7	Aw16000	91	Coyotero,BeachWalk,PleasntPower	7

May 16 Hol 4f ft :48^3 h   Apr 26 Hol 4f ft :49^4 h   Apr 5 SA 5f ft :59^3 h   Apr 1 SA tr.t 4f sy :51 h

Never Tabled

Own.—Wygod M J **116**

Dk. b. or br. h. 5, by Never Bend—Table Flirt, by Round Table
Br.—Wygod M J (Ky) 1982 4 3 1 0 $55,950
Tr.—Mandella Richard 1980 0 M 0 0
Lifetime 4 3 1 0 $55,950

8May82-8Hol	7f	·21^4	:44	1:21 ft	5	112	1½	1^1	1^{1½}	1^2	McCrrCJ^1	TrpleBendH	92	NeverTbled,Shnekite,PompeiiCourt	7
2May82-3Hol	6f	:22^3	:44^4	1:08^{4}ft	*2-5	120	3^{1½}	2^2	2^{2½}	2no	McCarronCJ^2	Aw22000	93	Jenny'sDvid,NeverTbled,StrikItBig	5
15Apr82-7SA	6f	:21^4	:44^4	1:09 ft	*1	120	2½	2^{hd}	1^2	1^{5¼}	McCarronCJ^7	Aw19000	93	Never Tabled, Santir,TonysLanding	9
2Apr82-6SA	6f	:21^4	:45	1:10^{1}ft	2¾	118	3^2	3^1	1^{2½}	1^8	Pincay L Jr^2	Mdn	87	NeverTbled,Hwkire,SpnishNugget	10

May 28 Hol 3f ft :35 h   May 24 Hol 6f ft 1:13^4 h   ●Apr 26 SA 6f ft 1:11^2 h   Apr 11 SA 5f ft 1:02^1 h

Terresto's Singer * Dk. b. or br. g. 5, by Terresto—Sweet Canary, by No Robbery
Own.—Tschudi & Wong 113 Br.—Valenti P (Cal) Tr.—Goodwin Floyd C

Lifetime	18	3	3	4	\$52,300
1982	8	1	1	3	\$34,600
1981	3	1	0	0	\$4,975
Turf	1	0	0	0	

16May82-6Hol	5f	$:21^{2}$	:44	:56 ft	21	115	$4^{5\frac{1}{2}}$	$4^{3\frac{1}{2}}$	3^{3}	$3^{4\frac{1}{4}}$	McHrgueDG^{4}	Aw37000	95	RemembrJohn,Unlklt,Trrsto'sSingr	7
8May82-3Hol	6f	$:22^{1}$	$:44^{4}$	$1:08^{4}$ft	$8\frac{1}{2}$	116	$4^{1\frac{1}{4}}$	$3^{1\frac{1}{2}}$	$5^{5\frac{1}{2}}$	5^{6}	Jin D^{8}	Aw26000	87	BeachWlk,MsterWrrior,ChpelCreek	8
17Apr82-8SA	a$6\frac{1}{2}$f Ⓣ	:21	$:43^{1}$	1:13 fm	47	115	2^{hd}	2^{hd}	7^{5}	8^{19}	Jin D^{4}	Sn Simn H	75	Shagbark, Shanekite, Belfort	8
24Mar82-8SA	$5\frac{1}{2}$f	$:21^{3}$	$:44^{2}$	$1:02^{1}$ft	29	115	3^{nk}	2^{hd}	3^{nk}	$3^{4\frac{3}{4}}$	Jin D^{8}	El Conejo H	96	ToB.OrNot,Belfort,Terresto'sSinger	8
14Mar82-7SA	$6\frac{1}{2}$f	$:21^{3}$	$:44^{3}$	$1:18^{2}$sy	$6\frac{1}{4}$	115	1^{1}	$1^{3\frac{1}{2}}$	1^{5}	$1^{1\frac{1}{2}}$	Jin D^{4}	Aw26000	78	Trrsto'sSngr,MstrWrror,H'sSmthng	6
25Feb82-4SA	6f	$:21^{2}$	$:44^{1}$	$1:09^{1}$ft	26	116	$3^{2\frac{1}{2}}$	3^{2}	2^{hd}	$2^{\frac{1}{2}}$	Jin D^{4}	25000	91	Devon, Terresto's Singer,NaynoBay	7
16Jan82-1SA	6f	$:21^{4}$	$:44^{1}$	$1:09^{2}$ft	21	118	1^{hd}	1^{3}	$2^{2\frac{1}{2}}$	3^{4}	Jin D^{8}	20000	87	Ggntc,Truxton'sDobl,Trrsto'sSngr	12
9Jan82-1SA	6f	$:21^{3}$	$:44^{4}$	$1:09^{2}$ft	25	118	3^{1}	$6^{1\frac{1}{4}}$	$7^{7\frac{1}{2}}$	8^{15}	Jin D^{1}	25000	76	WnwoodHost,Dcodd,ConslorCoony	9
5Dec81-1Hol	6f	:22	$:45^{3}$	1:11 ft	18	119	1^{2}	1^{hd}	2^{3}	4^{11}	Jin D^{9}	25000	71	Decoded, GummoJoe,AlwaysProper	9
7Nov81-9LA	6f	$:21^{3}$	$:44^{3}$	$1:10^{3}$ft	9	120	1^{hd}	$1^{1\frac{1}{2}}$	3^{1}	$8^{9\frac{1}{2}}$	Jin D^{8}	Aw24000	82	Now and Then,BronzeStar,Graben	10

May 28 Hol 3f ft $:34^{4}$ h May 23 Hol 6f ft $1:13^{3}$ h May 6 Hol 3f ft :35 h Apr 25 Hol 6f ft 1:14 h

The show odds on Remember John were quite good throughout the betting period. With one minute to post time the expected value was 1.15, qualifying it as a Dr. Z system bet. The tote board was

	Totals	#1 Remember John
Odds		2—1
Win	386,787	105,775
Show	50,581	9,430

Instead of making my \$50 bet, I made a Dr. Z system bet. I had brought \$2,000 with me to the track. Of this I reserved \$250 for my \$50 bets, so my betting fortune was \$1,750. The optimal Dr. Z system bet was \$121. There was some last-minute betting on Remember John. However, his show odds were nearly the same at post time, with an expected value of 1.12. The tote board at post time read

	Totals	#1 Remember John
Odds		2—1
Win	439,354	121,364
Show	56,794	11,311

It was a very consistent race, as the following chart indicates. Remember John ran a creditable race, always in second position, but he could not catch the long shot, Terresto's Singer. With Never Tabled out of the money, the payoff to show on the Dr. Z system bet on Remember John was a handsome \$3.40. My \$121 bet returned \$205.70, for a profit of \$84.70.

EIGHTH RACE
Hollywood
MAY 30, 1982

6 FURLONGS. (1.07⅗) 30th Running of THE LOS ANGELES HANDICAP (Grade III). $75,000 added. 3-year olds and upward. By subscription of $100 each, which shall accompany the nomination, $750 additional to start, with $75,000 added, of which $15,000 to second, $11,250 to third, $5,625 to fourth and $1,875 to fifth. Weights Tuesday, May 25. Starters to be named through the entry box by closing time of entries. A trophy will be presented to the owner of the winner. Closed Wednesday, May 19, 1982 with 13 nominations.
Value of race $81,550, value to winner $47,800, second $15,000, third $11,250, fourth $5,625, fifth $1,875. Mutuel pool $647,017.

Last Raced	Horse	Eqt.	A.	Wt	PP	St	¼	½	Str	Fin	Jockey	Odds $1
16May82 6Hol3	Terresto's Singer		5	113	7	1	1½	12½	12	1nk	Valenzuela P A	46.60
16May82 6Hol1	Remember John		3	115	1	4	21½	22½	23½	23	Delahoussaye E	2.00
9May82 9TuP1	Petro D. Jay		6	116	3	5	43	43	3hd	3no	Castaneda M	7.20
16May82 6Hol5	Shanekite	b	4	117	2	7	7	7	5hd	4½	Hawley S	5.10
23May82 7Hol2	Beach Walk	b	5	113	5	3	61½	5hd	42½	51	Steiner J J	27.70
8May82 8Hol1	Never Tabled		5	116	6	6	5hd	6½	63	68	McCarron C J	1.00
16May82 6Hol7	Cool Frenchy		7	113	4	2	3½	3½	7	7	Aragon J	49.00

OFF AT 5:19. Start good. Won driving. Time, :21, :43⅘, :55⅘, 1:09⅕ Track fast.

$2 Mutuel Prices:			
8-TERRESTO'S SINGER	95.20	18.00	5.00
1-REMEMBER JOHN		4.20	3.40
4-PETRO D. JAY			4.20

Dk. b. or br. g, by Terresto—Sweet Canary, by No Robbery. Trainer Goodwin Floyd C. Bred by Valenti P (Cal).

TERRESTO'S SINGER outsprinted REMEMBER JOHN from the gate, drew well clear on the turn, then gamely held that one safe through the final sixteenth. REMEMBER JOHN, unable to keep pace with the winner on the turn, rallied gamely under strong handling in the final furlong and was getting to the winner at the end. PETRO D. JAY went evenly and without apparent mishap. SHANEKITE passed tired horses in the stretch. NEVER TABLED stumbled a stride out of teh gate and failed to mount a threat. COOL FRENCHY tired in the stretch.

Owners— 1, Tschudi & Wong; 2, Sheridan Mr-Mrs J; 3, Ottley R; 4, Udko Selma; 5, Knapp P R; 6, Wygod M J; 7, Lichlyter Dr or Mrs F E.

Overweight: Cool Frenchy 1 pound. **Scratched**—Pompeii Court (8May82 8Hol3).

The final race of a day's card often contains a good bet—a top horse who is heavily bet to win but is overlooked to place or show. With the cumulative losses of the day mounting for most bettors, a show bet on such a horse provides little hope of salvaging the day. Heart Beat was such a horse in the ninth race. He was the top choice of all the *Daily Racing Form's* consensus experts and their best bet of the day, with a rating of 29 out of a possible 35. The next-rated horse had a 5! Heart Beat had run recently at Hollywood, finishing second. With Laffit Pincay, Jr. on board again, he looked like an excellent prospect. The crowd bet Heart Beat down to a 6—5 favorite. His show odds were good, with an expected value in the 1.10–1.15 range throughout the betting period—not quite a Dr. Z system bet, but it was close, so I decided to compromise and bet $100 to show on Heart Beat.

9th Hollywood

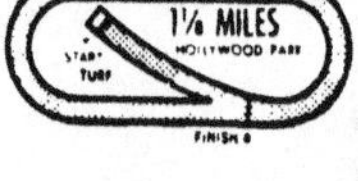

1⅛ MILES. (TURF). (1.46) CLAIMING. Purse $28,000. 4-year-olds and upward. Weight, 122 lbs. Non-winners of two races at a mile or over since March 28 allowed 3 lbs.; such a race since then, 6 lbs. Claiming price $50,000; for each $2,500 to $45,000 allowed 2 lbs. (Races when entered for $40,000 or less not considered.)

Fabulous Reason ✻ — **B. h. 5, by Le Fabuleux—Hail to Nurse, by Hail to Reason**

Own.—Stepp J C — **116** — **Br.—Brookmeade Stable (Ky)** — **Tr.—Moreno Henry** — **$50,000**

1982	9	1	0	1	$15,050
1981	6	1	0	1	$9,550
Turf	7	0	0	1	$4,050

Lifetime 25 2 0 4 $31,825

16May82-9Hol	1⅛ Ⓣ:4621:1021:471fm	74	1095	921	917	917	813	Steiner J J9	Aw24000	81	PetrJons,PrinclyVrdict,MdlofHonor	9
1May82-5Hol	1 1/16 Ⓣ:46 1:0941:404fm	54	117	79½	813	713	712	Black K8	Aw24000	83	CllMeMister,Essenbee,MdlofHonor	8
21Apr82-2SA	1⅛ Ⓣ:4611:1021:473fm	41	118	74¼	93¾	109¾	88½	ValenzuelPA5	Aw25000	80	Disclaim, LordCarnavon,Essenbee	12
8Apr82-5SA	1⅛ Ⓣ:4621:1031:481fm	65	120	77¼	75½	87¾	65¾	CastanedaM1	Aw26000	80	‡Rostropovich,Tom'sSerend.Islndr	12
21Mar82-5SA	1⅛ :461 1:102 1:481ft	24	118	68	56	712	714	AsmussenCB5	Aw27000	74	DurbanDeep,Rostropovich,Disclaim	7
7Mar82-7SA	1⅛ Ⓣ:4541:1041:474fm	21	118	75¾	85½	511	37½	CastanedaM2	Aw27000	80	RasPenng,Essenbee,FbulousReson	10
7Feb82-5SA	1¼ Ⓣ:47 1:3622:004fm	34	121	54½	61¾	64½	65	AsmussenCB6	Aw27000	78	Jurisconsult,CptnGnrl,PrnclyVrdct	11
23Jan82-4SA	1 1/16 :472 1:12 1:444gd	16	121	65¾	76¾	77¼	66¼	Gallitano G5	Aw25000	71	BrillintDouble,CllMeMistr,PocktMn	7
1Jan82-9SA	1 1/16 :491 1:14 1:471hy	16	118	3½	12½	13	1½	Gallitano G3	Aw20000	65	FabulousReason,Stingingly,Clbong	8
8Dec81-6BM	1 1/16 :453 1:094 1:421ft	9¾	117	814	813	716	716	GonzalezRM4	Aw11000	72	Cinnpo, Invective, Court Leader	8

May 22 Hol 6f ft 1:143 h **May 14 Hol 4f ft :50 h** **May 8 Hol 4f ft :513 h** **Apr 27 Hol 4f ft :512 h**

***Kundalini**
B. h. 7, by Snow Track—Karen, by Maporal
Br.—Haras Curiche (Chile) 1982 2 0 0 1 $5,730
Own.—Wright W J 116 Tr.—Brinson Clay $50,000 1981 19 1 2 6 $47,350
Lifetime 61 7 14 11 $96,574 Turf 50 7 11 10 $93,374
20May82-9Hol 1 1/16 Ⓣ:4621:1041:413fm 21 116 75 75¼ 55 33½ Valenzuela P A6 50000 87 Ultracharge, Giriama, Kundalini 8
8May82-3GG 1 Ⓣ:4731:1141:364fm 5½ 113 59 57½ 58 49¼ Anderson JR5 Aw17000 74 KneCounty,UncleBrrydown,MstrAc 7
3Dec81-8Hol 1 Ⓣ:4821:1241:362fm 6½ 116 54 3½ 22 32 ValenzuelPA2 Aw19000 85 First Blade,SpringDigger,Kundalini 9
7Nov81-8BM 1 1/16 Ⓣ:4721:1231:452fm 38 111 1020 1019 1022 1023 CbileroR2 Sbsct Inv H 58 LsAsprs,PolicInspctor,Dggr'sPont 10
17Oct81-8BM 1⅛ Ⓣ:47 1:1111:48 fm 51 112 913 88¼ 88½ 79 Caballero R1 Tan H 99 TheBart,TahitianKing,Dgger'sPoint 9
3Oct81-8BM 1 1/16 Ⓣ:4721:1211:45 gd 16 112 710 79 67½ 35½ CbileroR2 Sn Jqn Iv H 77 Borrego Sun, Les Aspres,Kundalini 7
26Sep81-6BM 1 :454 1:101 1:353ft 6½ 115 58¾ 58½ 411 412 Howell W C5 Aw15000 79 FleetTempo,HeadHawk,BlackSaber 5
19Sep81-11Bmf 1 1/16 Ⓣ:4621:1041:434fm 17 112 811 66½ 67 36 Meza R Q8 Sn Mtn H 83 Hoedown'sDy,BorregoSun,Kundlini 8
7Sep81-9Dmr 1 1/16 Ⓣ:4641:1121:424fm 7¼ 116 721 713 57½ 44¼ Pierce D3 50000 91 GreatGrndson,Spinoz,HostileKnight 8
27Aug81-8Dmr 1⅛ Ⓣ:5021:1411:502fm 5 117 76 76 56½ 55¼ CastanedaM2 Aw18000 81 PocketMn,ChncyBiddr,MusiclBoyII 7
May 19 SA 3f ft :353 h May 6 GG 4f ft :494 h Apr 28 SA 7f ft 1:274 h Apr 21 SA 7f ft 1:261 h

Buffalo Hart ✻
B. c. 4, by Buffalo Lark—To My Lady, by Amber Morn
Br.—Madden P (Ky) 1982 8 1 0 0 $21,625
Own.—Rogers Red Top Farm 116 Tr.—Sullivan John $50,000 1981 17 1 0 1 $15,878
Lifetime 28 3 0 2 $44,613 Turf 6 0 0 0 $2,964
20May82-8Hol 1 Ⓣ:4641:1011:333fm 110 118 85½ 88 811 813 Pierce D7 Aw35000 88 Piperhill, Faiz, Quantum Leap 8
4Apr82-7SA 1 :452 1:094 1:344ft 57 1155 21 66 79½ 712 Steiner J J6 Aw35000 83 Maxistar, Son of a Dodo, A Run 7
28Mar82-7SA 1 1/16 :451 1:084 1:411ft 44 119 23 48 713 812 AsmussenCB5 Aw35000 83 Sunshine Swag, A Run, RockSoftly 8
21Mar82-3SA 1 1/16 :46 1:10 1:411ft 28 118 611 59½ 510 516 McHrgueDG4 Aw35000 79 Mehmet, Native Tactics, A Run 6
12Mar82-5SA 1¼ :47† 1:40 2:074sl 12 114 1hd 13 13½ 1½ AsmussenCB1 Aw32000 59 Buffalo Hart, Pettrax, Lucullus 5
6Mar82-6SA 1 :442 1:083 1:343ft 34 114 714 79½ 78½ 58¼ Lipham T4 Aw30000 88 Mehmet, Western, Notable Axe 7
13Feb82-7SA 6½f :22 :45 1:152ft 26 114 63½ 65¾ 611 619 Lipham T3 Aw32000 74 KngrooCort,Arstocrtcl,AnswrtoMsc 6
5Feb82-7SA 6½f :212 :433 1:15 ft 70 114 67 65½ 55½ 44¼ Lipham T3 Aw32000 91 VictorySmpl,BondRullh,PompCourt 8
27Dec81-5SA 1 1/16 :454 1:093 1:413ft 37 115 89¾ 812 1011 1021 Pierce D1 Aw30000 72 KngrooCourt,PierrLMont,EggToss 10
26Nov81-5Hol 1 1/16 Ⓣ:4641:1031:41 fm 25 113 67 63½ 88 87¾ Hawley S5 Aw27000 86 Truckload, Vorlaufer, Early Settler 8
May 28 Hol Ⓣ 4f fm :482 h (d) May 13 Hol Ⓣ 7f fm 1:31 h (d) May 7 Hol Ⓣ 7f fm 1:294 h (d) May 2 Hol 5f ft 1:034 h

***El Pancho Angel**
Ch. h. 6, by Tantoul—Doninda, by Cardanil II
Br.—Haras Dadinco (Chile) 1982 5 0 0 0 $2,900
Own.—T 9 0 Ranch 116 Tr.—Fanning Jerry $50,000 1981 11 1 5 1 $56,050
Lifetime 28 6 8 2 $85,686 Turf 22 6 7 2 $77,536
8May82-9Hol 1 Ⓣ:4611:1011:34 fm 6¾ 116 43½ 31 42½ 65½ Olivares F6 80000 93 RghtofLght,Jursconsult,SonofDodo 7
30Apr82-7Hol 1⅛ Ⓣ:47 1:1111:47 fm 3½ 114 511 66 54 66½ Guerra W A9 Aw30000 88 HemphillCounty,TbleTorch,Disclim 9
21Apr82-5SA a6½f Ⓣ:211 :4331:13 fm 6½ 116 86¼ 88¼ 47 43 McHargue DG12 80000 91 Fingal, Tellaround, Gray Dandy 12
11Apr82-5SA 6½f :22 :451 1:17 sy 10 114 53¾ 43 3½ 51½ Lipham T1 Aw26000 83 Tellround,Redoutble,He'sSomthing 7
21Mar82-7SA 6½f :214 :443 1:151ft 18 114 52 41¾ 67¾ 69 Olivares F6 Aw35000 85 DoubleDiscount,Aristocrticl,PirtLw 7
5Sep81-8Dmr 1 1/16 Ⓣ:4811:1211:42 fm 21 114 77¼ 76¼ 87¼ 86 Lipham T1 Escndo H 93 Advocatum,ReglBering,MjorSport 10
3Aug81-8Dmr 1⅛ Ⓣ:4731:1141:494fm 10 119 611 55 41 2¾ Olivares F8 Aw24000 88 Wild Surf, El Pancho Angel, Idyll 9
17Jly81-8Hol 1 1/16 :462 1:10 1:42 ft 6½ 122 68 66¼ 55¼ 58¾ Lipham T5 200000 S 76 Joleg, Fingal, Sham's Fool 7
1Jly81-7Hol 1 Ⓣ:4511:0921:342fm 6¾ 115 615 67½ 42 1hd Lipham T2 Aw40000 97 ElPnchoAngel,Lif'sHop,SonofDodo 8
3Jun81-5Hol 1 1/16 Ⓣ:4631:1041:412fm 6¾ 114 57 44½ 1½ 2¾ Lipham T7 Aw24000 91 Bnfctor,ElPnchoAngl,MstrSurgon 10
May 19 Hol 4f ft :503 h Apr 19 SA 4f ft :471 h Apr 10 SA 3f ft :38 h Apr 4 SA 5f ft :593 h

***Heart Beat**
Dk. b. or br. g. 5, by Hard to Beat—Wampum, by Warfare
Br.—Guest R (Fra) 1982 7 1 2 1 $30,650
Own.—Bacharach B 116 Tr.—Frankel Robert $50,000 1980 9 2 2 2 $28,057
Lifetime 16 3 4 3 $58,707 Turf 10 2 3 2 $33,657
12May82-7Hol 1⅜ Ⓣ:4731:3842:16 fm 3¼ 117 37 52½ 31 2no Pincay L Jr3 50000 75 Phillipic, Heart Beat, Nar 8
11Apr82-3SA 1⅛ :474 1:121 1:494sy *6-5 116 1hd 1hd 21½ 33¼ Shoemaker W1 50000 77 Perry Cabin, Three Bits, HeartBeat 6
2Apr82-5SA 1⅛ :482 1:131 1:512gd 2¼ 115 54 64¾ 44 41¾ Shoemaker W2 60000 70 TheArgyleKid,Ultrchrge,Stingingly 7
20Mar82-5SA 1 1/16 :454 1:10 1:411ft 4 114 32½ 32 43½ 47¼ ShoemkerW1 Aw30000 88 Tell Again, Lucullus, Chriserik 7
14Feb82-9SA 1 :464 1:11 1:354ft 4½ 116 2hd 11 12 11¼ DelahoussayeE5 40000 90 HertBet,AnHeirAboutHim,Decodd 10
24Jan82-4SA 1⅛ :462 1:112 1:504ft 3¼e 116 22½ 21½ 11½ 21½ Ortega L E3 32000 73 Denali Ridge,HeartBeat,PortVelate 6
17Jan82-9SA 6½f :221 :442 1:151ft 6¼e 116 96¼ 912 915 813 Ortega L E3 50000 81 MrblCourt,ThArgylKid,AmnBrothr 12
4Nov80♦4MLaffitte(Fra) a1⅝ 3:04 gd 3-2 123 Ⓣ 32 Head F Px Merlin Multicolore, Vald'Amain,HeartBeat 6
11Oct80♦5CrLaroche(Fra) a1½ : sf — 121 Ⓣ 22 StMrtY Px Rene Wattinne Eternity, HeartBeat,FlingDutchman 8
11Oct80—No time taken.
14Sep80♦6Compiegne(Fra) a1⅛ : gd *1 126 Ⓣ 1hd BtblD Px Imperatrice Eugenie Heart Beat, Bold Gold, Pontois 9
14Sep80—No time taken. Race for lady riders.
May 26 Hol 5f ft 1:003 h May 20 Hol 4f ft :491 h May 9 Hol 6f ft 1:134 h May 3 Hol 6f ft 1:17 h

```
*Ingres                                  B. h. 6, by Djakao—Insulaire, by Aureole
                                         Br.—LaComtesse Orazio Sanjust (Fra)        1982  7  0  0  0      $1,450
Own.—Yank A                       116    Tr.—Perkins Larry              $50,000     1981 10  1  1  0     $33,932
                                  Lifetime   33  2  4  4    $86,229                 Turf 30  2  4  4     $85,479
12May82-7Hol   1⅜(T):473 1:384 2:16 fm  9½ 116   815 810 78¼ 54¼  McHargue D G2  50000 71 Phillipic, Heart Beat, Nar   8
21Apr82-9SA    1¼(T):444 1:342 1:593 fm 55 108   716 109½ 105½ 1011 StinrJJ2 Sn Jacinto H 78 Durban Deep, Monarch, Kilty 10
     21Apr82—Run in two divisions, 8th & 9th races.
 2Apr82-5SA    1⅛:482 1:131 1:512 gd    20 116   78 76¾ 66¼ 54¼  Pierce D4        62500 68 TheArgyleKid,Ultrchrge,Stingingly 7
24Mar82-5SA    1⅛:452 1:092 1:472 ft    56 116   819 815 718 721  Ontiveros J A7   62500 71 Chriserik, BeOnTime,TheArgyleKid 8
10Mar82-5SA    1⅛(T):452 1:101 1:474 fm 79 112   1017 1011 107½ 711 Ontiveros J A7  70000 77 RightofLight,Monico,NoblTrdition 10
24Feb82-5SA    1⅛(T):463 1:104 1:474 fm 54 116   914 1010 1012 914 Gilligan L6      62500 74 BadRascal,BeauSoleil,BlueDncerII 10
13Feb82-5SA    6½f :213 :442 1:161 ft   73 114   1017 1019 1021 1020 Ontiveros JA2 Aw26000 69 Kearney,LaughingBoy,Mari'sBook 10
18Oct81♦4Longchamp(Fra)  a1 11/16 3:434 sf  9 120   (T) 817 BarelliE        Pr Jouvence H  Santa Aquila, Jete Battu, SoMisty 14
13Sep81♦3Longchamp(Fra)  a1 11/16 3:293 gd  6¾ 113  (T) 21½ BarelliE        Pr de Dangu H  Val d'Ajol, Ingres, Veneziano 14
15Aug81♦4Deauville(Fra)  a2¼  4:002 fm  6½ 102    (T) 13 BrlliE   Grand de la Manche H  Ingres, ‡Hartwood, Grey Imperial 23
   May 26 Hol 6f ft 1:184 h     May 11 Hol 3f ft :371 h     May 6 Hol 1 ft 1:45 h     Apr 30 Hol 6f ft 1:15 h

Wantazee                                 Ch. g. 4, by Orbit Ruler—Princess Scott, by Doc Scott J
                                         Br.—Coffman R (Cal)                        1982  6  3  1  0     $35,075
Own.—Giacoppuzzi G                119    Tr.—Cofer Riley S              $50,000     1981  4  1  1  0      $2,570
                                  Lifetime   10  4  2  0    $37,645
 8May82-7Hol   1 1/16 :46 1:103 1:43 ft     *1 114   41¾ 31½ 21 21¼  McCarronCJ3 Aw22000 79 ‡LittleShah,Wantazee,RomnMjesty 8
     8May82—Placed first through disqualification
28Apr82-9Hol   1 1/16 :463 1:103 1:422 ft    3 114   2½ 1hd 2½ 21   McCarronCJ1 Aw22000 82 Fager'sBid,Wantzee,FriendlyRoylty 7
 4Apr82-9SA    1 1/16 :463 1:104 1:414 ft   15 114   2½ 2hd 32 43½  ValenzuelPA7 Aw21000 89 Pal's Lad, Peter Jones,RamBoldly 10
 4Mar82-3SA    1 1/16 :451 1:094 1:422 ft  9-5 117   36 22 53½ 53¾  Pincay L Jr3    c32000 85 CptinOrient,EgleTost,PriorApprovl 6
14Feb82-1SA    1 :451 1:094 1:36 ft         5½ 115   34 21½ 2½ 1¾   ValenzuelaPA5   c20000 89 Wantazee, Embermatic,Bandelaire 10
29Jan82-9SA    1 1/16 :463 1:104 1:43 ft    24 115   1hd 1hd 2hd 1nk Valenzuela P A1  16000 86 Wantazee,ElGtoGrnde,OnYourWy 11
19Dec81-3Hol   1 :464 1:121 1:39 ft         25 114   41½ 52¾ 66 57¼  Valenzuela P A7  22500 64 MjstcCourt,FoxyQllo,AttBoyBrook 7
 9Dec81-3Hol   6f :22 :452 1:104 ft         23 119   76¾ 76¼ 68½ 612 Ontiveros JA3 [S] 20000 71 GrfieldCounty,ImmnntIssu,Ws'sRb 9
15Nov81-3AC    6f :223 :443 1:101 ft        *1 116   1hd 1½ 13 12½  Ontiveros J A3   AlwM 88 Wantazee,SirDvidR.,RhythmRunner 6
 8Nov81-4AC    6f :222 :451 1:102 ft        *1 1097  64½ 64¾ 24 24  Cervantes J L1   AlwM 83 Eds Novel, Wantazee, Valley Flash 7
   May 26 Hol 5f ft 1:00 h     May 20 Hol 5f ft 1:02 h     May 5 Hol 5f ft 1:003 h     Apr 22 Hol 4f ft :484 h

Pierre La Mont                           B. g. 8, by Great Mystery—Two Su Sis, by Andys Glory
                                         Br.—Amlung R (Fla)                         1982  8  1  1  1     $30,275
Own.—Giddings & Wilson            116    Tr.—Landers Dale               $50,000     1981 19  4  5  3     $85,875
                                  Lifetime   74 16 15  8   $250,911                 Turf 46  8 10  8    $135,719
12May82-7Hol   1⅜(T):473 1:384 2:16 fm  6¾ 116   2hd 2hd 44½ 79½  Castaneda M5    50000 66 Phillipic, Heart Beat, Nar   8
20Apr82-5SA    1⅛(T):45 1:091 1:473 fm   5 120   24 22½ 1hd 31½   Castaneda M7    50000 88 NightLegue,SoftMrket,PirrLMont 11
14Mar82-9SA    1 1/16 :464 1:12 1:452 sy  7 120   49 614 616 620   Castaneda M7    62500 54 TheArgyleKid,BeauMoro,Stingingly 7
24Feb82-5SA    1⅛(T):463 1:104 1:474 fm 4½ 120   22½ 22½ 33 45½   Castaneda M9    62500 82 BadRascal,BeauSoleil,BlueDncerII 10
15Feb82-5SA    1⅛(T):473 1:122 1:493 gd 10 118   1hd 1hd 45½ 78½  ValenzuelaPA10  75000 70 Ptti'sTriumph,RightofLight,Gmmt 12
31Jan82-5SA    1⅛(T):472 1:114 1:493 gd 2½ 116   11 11 1hd 44     Valenzuela P A3 75000 75 Serang, Lanarkland, Mr. Mud  9
17Jan82-7SA    1 :451 1:093 1:344 ft    *7-5 115  1hd 2hd 1hd 12¾  ValenzuelPA4 Aw30000 95 PierreLaMont,SirDancer,Mr.Metaxa 9
 6Jan82-4SA    1⅛:49 1:14 1:532 m       *2-3 115  11½ 1½ 25 29½    Valenzuela PA6 A40000 52 TellAgain,PierreLaMont,DenliRidge 6
27Dec81-5SA    1 1/16 :454 1:093 1:413 ft  7¾ 115  11 12 2hd 2½     ValenzuelPA6 Aw30000 92 KngrooCourt,PierrLMont,EggToss 10
16Dec81-7Hol   1 1/16(T):484 1:124 1:424 fm 4¾ 115 11 11 1½ 22     ValenzuelPA3 Aw27000 83 LeDucdeBar,PierreLMont,Lucullus 7
   May 24 Hol 4f ft :50 h     May 3 Hol 4f ft :50 h     Apr 13 SA 3f ft :373 h     Apr 8 SA 5f ft 1:014 h
```

At post time the expected return per dollar bet on Heart Beat to show was 1.12 and the tote board was as follows:

	Totals	#5 Heart Beat
Odds		6—5
Win	171,124	64,610
Show	26,958	7,465

Heart Beat won the race easily. The payoff of $2.60 to show was reasonable, given the fact that Heart Beat did go off as a 6—5 favorite, that the third and fourth picks came in the money, and that there was a substantial breakage. Again, it is clear that the bet on Heart Beat was a reasonable one but not good enough to be a Dr. Z system bet. My $100 bet returned $130, for a $30 profit.

NINTH RACE
Hollywood
MAY 30, 1982

1 ⅛ MILES.(turf). (1.46) CLAIMING. Purse $28,000. 4-year-olds and upward. Weight, 122 lbs. Non-winners of two races at a mile or over since March 28 allowed 3 lbs.; such a race since then, 6 lbs. Claiming price $50,000; for each $2,500 to $45,000 allowed 2 lbs. (Races when entered for $40,000 or less not considered.)

Value of race $28,000, value to winner $15,400, second $5,600, third $4,200, fourth $2,100, fifth $700. Mutuel pool $252,477. Exacta Pool $518,904.

Last Raced	Horse	Eqt.	A.Wt	PP	St	¼	½	¾	Str	Fin	Jockey	Cl'g Pr	Odds $1
12May82 ^{7}Hol^{2}	Heart Beat		5 117	5	2	$5^{2\frac{1}{2}}$	3^{hd}	3^{1}	$1^{1\frac{1}{2}}$	1^{2}	Pincay L Jr	50000	1.20
20May82 ^{9}Hol^{3}	Kundalini		7 116	2	6	$6^{\frac{1}{2}}$	7^{1}	6^{hd}	4^{2}	$2^{2\frac{1}{2}}$	Valenzuela P A	50000	7.90
12May82 ^{7}Hol^{7}	Pierre La Mont	b	8 116	8	1	1^{hd}	1^{hd}	2^{2}	3^{1}	$3^{\frac{1}{2}}$	Hawley S	50000	5.60
8May82 ^{7}Hol^{1}	Wantazee		4 119	7	3	$2^{2\frac{1}{2}}$	$2^{2\frac{1}{2}}$	1^{hd}	2^{hd}	$4^{2\frac{1}{2}}$	Delahoussaye E	50000	11.10
16May82 ^{9}Hol^{8}	Fabulous Reason		5 116	1	4	4^{hd}	6^{1}	$7^{1\frac{1}{2}}$	6^{hd}	5no	Castaneda M	50000	28.70
12May82 ^{7}Hol^{5}	Ingres	b	6 116	6	8	8	8	8	7^{4}	$6^{3\frac{1}{2}}$	Sibille R	50000	12.70
8May82 ^{9}Hol^{6}	El Pancho Angel	b	6 116	4	7	7^{1}	5^{hd}	$5^{1\frac{1}{2}}$	$5^{3\frac{1}{2}}$	7^{5}	Lipham T	50000	3.20
20May82 ^{8}Hol^{8}	Buffalo Hart		4 116	3	5	3^{hd}	4^{3}	4^{hd}	8	8	Pierce D	50000	21.80

OFF AT 5:58. Start good. Won ridden out. Time, :23⅕, :46⅖, 1:10⅘, 1:34⅘, 1:47⅗ Course firm.

$2 Mutuel Prices:			
5-HEART BEAT	4.40	3.40	2.60
2-KUNDALINI		6.00	3.80
8-PIERRE LA MONT			3.60

$5 EXACTA 5-2 PAID $62.00.

Dk. b. or br. g, by Hard to Beat—Wampum, by Warfare. Trainer Frankel Robert. Bred by Guest R (Fra).

HEART BEAT, just outside the leaders while reserved off the early pace, rallied to take command from outside entering the stretch and drew off. KUNDALINI, unhurried for six furlongs, rallied willingly in the middle of the course through the final quarter-mile but did not menace the winner. PIERRE LA MONT outsprinted WANTAZEE for the early lead, then weakened in the final furlong. WANTAZEE lacked the needed rally. EL PANCHO ANGEL failed to threaten.

Owners— 1, Bacharach B; 2, Wright W J; 3, Giddings & Wilson; 4, Giacoppuzzi G; 5, Stepp J C; 6, Yank A; 7, T 9 0 Ranch; 8, Rogers Red Top Farm. **Overweight:** Heart Beat 1 pound.

Summary of betting

Race	Bet ($)	Payoff per $2 Bet ($)	Profit ($)
3	50	3.60	40.00
4	50	3.00	25.00
5	50	3.80	45.00
7	50	0	−50.00
8	113	3.40	84.70
9	100	2.60	30.00
			174.70

In summary, there was only one Dr. Z system bet: Remember John in the eighth. Insearchof in the fifth and Heart Beat in the ninth were close, as was the loser Patti's Triumph in the seventh.

All my bets were to show. Six of the seven horses actually came in the money, so I had a pleasant afternoon with a nice profit. This performance was better than what you can expect on average. Since about two-thirds of all favorites finish in the money, one would expect to win about four or five races out of seven. For this reason, it is best to bet when the odds are good. The payoffs will then be higher to compensate for the bets you lose.

CHAPTER 15

Minus Pools

Eliminating Possible Minus Pools: The Kentucky Oaks at Churchill Downs, May 1, 1981

The payoffs for win, place, and show bets reflect the individual pools, the amounts bet on the in-the-money horses, the track take, and breakage. By law, tracks must always pay a minimum amount on any winning bet. This is generally $2.10 for a $2 bet.* A minus pool occurs when the return to bettors, after the track take has been calculated in, is less than this minimum. Such a pool can occur when a horse (or group of horses coupled as an entry) looks unbeatable. The bet is so large on this one possibility that the track must forego some of its profit or actually lose money in order to pay the $2.10. When such a situation appears likely in a given pool, management is likely to disallow certain betting to avoid a minus pool. Such a situation occurred during the running of the 1981 Kentucky Oaks at Churchill Downs in Louisville, Kentucky. The entry of Heavenly Cause and De La Rose was bet down to 3—2 as the second favorite. Since there were only five alternative bets and two extreme favorites (the entry and the even-money favorite, Truly Bound), there would likely be a minus pool in the show mutuels. Management, therefore, disallowed show betting.

---

*An exception is Kentucky, where the minimum payment is $2.20. See the discussion of the Kentucky Oaks in Chapter Six and further comments made later.

Kentucky Oaks

EIGHTH RACE
Churchill
MAY 1, 1981

1 1/16 MILES. (1.41⅗) 107th Running THE KENTUCKY OAKS (Grade I). $100,000 Added. (Plus $10,000 KTDF). 3–year–old fillies. By subscription of $100 which covers nomination for borth The Kentucky Oaks and the La Troienne. All nomination fees to Kentucky Oaks. $200 to pass entry box, $500 additional to start, $100,000 added, of which with the subscription fees and all starting fees to be divided 65% to the winner, 20% to second, 10% to third and 5% to fourth. Weight 121 lbs. Starters to be named through the entry box Wednesday, April 29 at usual time of closing. If race is divided entries or couplings will be divided. The owner of the winner to receive a silver trophy.
Value of race $124,000, value to winner $79,300, second $26,400, third $12,200, fourth $6,100. Mutuel pool $685,768.

Last Raced	Horse	Eqt.A.Wt	PP	St	¼	½	¾	Str	Fin	Jockey	Odds $1
25Apr81 ^{8}CD^{1}	Heavenly Cause	3 121	4	4	4^{3}	4^{4}	$1^{\frac{1}{2}}$	$1^{1\frac{1}{2}}$	1no	Pincay L Jr	a-1.50
8Apr81 ^{7}Kee^{4}	De La Rose	3 121	3	6	6	5^{1}	5^{4}	2^{1}	2^{5}	Day P	a-1.50
18Apr81 ^{7}Kee^{2}	Wayward Lass	3 121	1	1	$3^{\frac{1}{2}}$	3^{1}	$2^{1\frac{1}{2}}$	3^{1}	3^{3}	Asmussen C B	8.40
18Apr81 ^{7}Kee^{1}	Truly Bound	3 121	2	3	$2^{\frac{1}{2}}$	2^{hd}	4^{1}	4^{5}	4^{4}	Shoemaker W	1.00
17Apr81 ^{8}Aqu^{4}	Real Prize	3 121	6	5	$5^{\frac{1}{2}}$	6	6	5^{2}	$5^{8\frac{1}{2}}$	Fell J	23.00
4Apr81 ^{9}OP^{2}	Nell's Briquette	3 121	5	2	1^{hd}	$1^{\frac{1}{2}}$	3^{hd}	6	6	Lively J	5.00

a–Coupled: Heavenly Cause and De La Rose.
OFF AT 5:30 EDT. Start good, Won driving. Time, :25, :48⅘, 1:13, 1:37⅘, 1:43⅘ Track fast.

$2 Mutuel Prices:			
1–HEAVENLY CAUSE (a–entry)	5.00	5.00	—
1–DE LA ROSE (a–entry)	5.00	5.00	—
2–WAYWARD LASS		—	—
(No Show Wagering)			

Ro. f, by Grey Dawn II—Lady Dulcinea, by Nantallah. Trainer Stephens Woodford C. Bred by Ryehill Farm (Md).

HEAVENLY CAUSE, allowed to settle early, took command on the outside leaving the backstretch, drew clear in upper stretch but was all out to withstand DE LA ROSE with pressure from both sides. The latter, unhurried early, launched a bold bid in the extreme outside when set down for the drive, was also under pressure from both sides in the final furlong and just missed at the wire. WAYWARD LASS just behind the early leaders, had no rally. TRULY BOUND prompted the pace for a half and weakened along the rail leaving the backstretch. REAL PRIZE never launched a serious bid. NELL'S BRIQUETTE made the early pace and gave way.

Owners— 1, Ryehill Farm; 2, deKwiatkowski H; 3, Flying Zee Stable; 4, Windfields Farm; 5, Buckland Farm; 6, Triple L Stables.

Trainers— 1, Stephens Woodford C; 2, Stephens Woodford C; 3, Martin Jose; 4, Delp Grover G; 5, Campo John P; 6, Van Berg Jack.

Heavenly Cause and De La Rose finished one-two and returned $5 to win and also $5 to place. The favorite, Truly Bound, finished fourth, out of the money.

The identical payoffs to win and place meant that, after adjusting for breakage, the percentages bet on the entry in the win and place pools were the same. Hence the entry was not a Dr. Z system bet to place. Indeed, its expected value per dollar bet to place was about 90¢ (amounting to the track's payback plus the adjustment for the entry). Techniques for the selection of Dr. Z system bets with entries are discussed in Chapter Sixteen. When the favorite finished out of the money, the one-two finish provided a good payoff.

An Extraordinary Show Pool: The Coaching Club American Oaks at Belmont, June 27, 1981

The entry of Heavenly Cause and De La Rose was also entered the next month in the Coaching Club American Oaks at Belmont. Their strong one-two finish in the Kentucky Oaks made them a 2—5 favorite. The entry was bet even more heavily for show, so that a minus pool was likely.

Management decided not to eliminate the show pool. The betting public believed that a show bet on the entry of Heavenly Cause and De La Rose was virtually a sure thing. It seemed that at least one of these top horses would beat two of the other four horses in the race and finish in the money. The chart of the race speaks for itself.

Coaching Club American Oaks

EIGHTH RACE
Belmont
JUNE 27, 1981

1 ½ MILES. (2.24) 65th Running COACHING CLUB AMERICAN OAKS (Grade I). Purse $125,000 added. Fillies. 3-year-olds. Weight 121 lbs. By subscription of $250 each, which should accompany the nomination; $1,000 to pass the entry box, with $125,000 added. The added money and all fees to be divided 60% to the winner, 22% to second, 12% to third and 6% to fourth. Starters to be named at the closing time of entries. Trophies will be presented to the winning owner, trainer and jockey and mementoes to the grooms of the first four finishers. A special permanent trophy will be presented to the owner of the winner of the Coaching Club American Oaks if the filly has also won the Acorn and the Mother Goose. (Nominations close Wednesday, June 10, 1981). Closed with 17 nominations.

Value of race $136,250, value to winner $81,750, second $29,975, third $16,350, fourth $8,175. Mutuel pool $469,774, OTB pool $305,150.

Last Raced	Horse	Eqt.A.Wt	PP	¼	½	1	1¼	Str	Fin	Jockey	Odds $1
5Jun81 ^{8}Bel^{4}	[D]Real Prize	3 121	1	5½	6	5½	2^{hd}	1^{1½}	1^{2¼}	Velasquez J	9.80
5Jun81 ^{8}Bel^{1}	Wayward Lass	3 121	2	3^{4}	3^{1}	2^{hd}	3^{4}	2½	2^{2¼}	Asmussen C B	5.00
5Jun81 ^{8}Bel^{3}	Banner Gala	3 121	5	1^{hd}	1^{1}	1^{2}	1^{1½}	3^{10}	3^{13}	Cordero A Jr	3.20
5Jun81 ^{8}Bel^{2}	Heavenly Cause	3 121	4	4^{4}	4^{6}	4^{4}	4^{5}	4^{3}	4^{1¾}	Pincay L Jr	a-.40
5Jun81 ^{8}Bel^{5}	Autumn Glory	b 3 121	6	2^{1½}	2½	3½	5^{5}	5^{8}	5^{7½}	Martens G	35.60
13Jun81 ^{8}Mth^{1}	De La Rose	3 121	3	6	5½	6	6	6	6	Maple E	a-.40

[D]-Real Prize Disqualified and placed second.
a-Coupled: Heavenly Cause and De La Rose.

OFF AT 4:55 EDT. Start good, Won ridden out. Time, :24⅕, :47⅘, 1:11⅘, 1:36⅕, 2:01⅘, 2:28⅕, Track fast.

$2 Mutuel Prices:			
3-(B)-WAYWARD LASS	12.00	7.20	35.40
2-(A)-REAL PRIZE		8.60	61.60
5-(F)-BANNER GALA			51.20

Wayward Lass—Dk. b. or br. f, by Hail the Pirates—Young Mistress, by Third Martini. Trainer Martin Jose. Bred by Luro H A (Fla).

REAL PRIZE, unhurried while outrun to the far turn, settled suddenly after going a mile, angled out to continue her rally approaching the stretch, lugged in interfering with WAYWARD LASS near the final furlong and drew away under intermittent urging. REAL PRIZE was disqualified and placed second following a stewards inquiry and foul claim by the rider of WAYWARD LASS. WAYWARD LASS, close up early while under light restraint, made a run between horses leaving the far turn, was checked behind REAL PRIZE near the final furlong and continued on with good courage to best the others. BANNER GALA took over from AUTUMN GLORY at the first turn, made the pace under good handling, saved ground after sprinting away to a clear lead at the far turn, held a narrow advantage into the stretch and weakened. HEAVENLY CAUSE moved up outside horses to reach contention after entering the backstretch, raced within striking distance for nine furlongs and had nothing left. AUTUMN GLORY saved ground while racing forwardly for a mile and tired badly. DE LA ROSE showed nothing.

Owners— 1, Buckland Farm; 2, Flying Zee Stables; 3, Phipps O; 4, Ryehill Farm; 5, Ruiz E; 6, de Kwiatkowski H.

Trainers— 1, Campo John P; 2, Martin Jose; 3, Penna Angel; 4, Stephens Woodford C; 5, Barrera Guillermo S; 6, Stephens Woodford C.

Scratched—Outlaw Native (13Jun81 ^{8}Pim^{3}).

The possible minus pool from the extremely heavy betting to show on the entry led to two possible show outcomes: (1) $2.10 for all horses finishing in the money if at least one of the entry horses was in the money and (2) very large payoffs for the in-the-money finishers if both of the entry horses were out of the money. Indeed, when both of the entry horses finished out of the money, the show payoffs were astronomical! The winner, Wayward Lass, paid three times as much to show as to win. The second-place finisher, Real Prize, paid about seven times as much to show as it did to place, and five times as much as he would have paid to win if he had won. The third-place finisher, Banner Gala, who was the second favorite in the race at 3—1, paid $51.20 to show.

At first glance, you would think that all these horses were good bets to show. It turns out that only Banner Gala was a Dr. Z system bet; She had an expected value of about $1.24 per dollar bet. Bets on Real Prize and Wayward Lass in fact had expected values *less* than $1; for Real Prize it was 89¢. How could this be? With a possible minus pool, there were three possible outcomes for a show bet on Banner Gala, Real Prize, or Wayward Lass: (1) Our horse and at least one of the entry horses would be in the money—result: $2.10; (2) Our horse finished out of the money—result: 0; and (3) Our horse was in the money and both entry horses were not—result: a high payoff. The difficulty is that possibilities (1) and (2) were the most likely ones, and (3) had a very small chance of occurring. Thus even though the payoff in (3) would be high, it might still be that, on average, you would lose with such a bet. For example, with Real Prize these probabilities were (1) 0.260, (2) 0.720, and (3) 0.020. Hence the expected value per $2 bet on Real Prize was

$$\underbrace{(0.260)(\$2.10)}_{\text{Real Prize and at least one of the entry horses in the money}} + \underbrace{0.720(0)}_{\text{Real Prize out of the money}} + \underbrace{0.020(\$61.60)}_{\text{Real Prize in the money and both of the entry horses out of the money}} = \$1.78$$

or 89¢ per dollar bet!

The situation was better with Banner Gala. The probabilities were (1) 0.617, (2) 0.360, and (3) 0.023. The expected value per $2 bet on Banner Gala was 0.617($2.10) + 0.360(0) + 0.023($51.20) = $2.47, or about $1.24 per dollar bet. Thus an extraordinarily high payoff of $51.20 to show on a relative favorite—recall that Banner Gala was a 3—1 shot—was required to make the bet profitable. The reason for the advantageous bet on Banner Gala was her relatively high odds to win and the extraordinary low amount bet on her to show.

The Coaching Club American Oaks illustrates that an occasion may arise where it is advisable to bet in a possible minus pool. However, we feel it is a rare instance indeed and that, in general, bets should not be made in a

TABLE 15.1 ***Probabilities of various outcomes and expected value of show bets in the Coaching Club American Oaks***

Horse	Win Odds	Probability of Winning	Probability of Finishing Second	Probability of Finishing Third	Probability of Finishing in the Money	Probability of Finishing out of the Money	Percentage of Money Bet to Show	Probability of Finishing in the Money When Both Entry Horses Are out of the Money	Probability of Finishing in the Money with at Least One of the Entry Horses	Expected Value per dollar Bet to Show
Wayward Lass	5.00	0.13	0.15	0.20	0.48	0.52	1.91	0.022	0.458	0.87
RealPrize	9.80	0.07	0.09	0.12	0.28	0.72	1.07	0.020	0.260	0.89
Banner Gala	3.20	0.19	0.20	0.25	0.64	0.36	1.30	0.023	0.617	1.24
Entry	0.40	0.59	0.53	0.39	0.98[a]	0.02	95.22	—	—	1.03
Autumn Glory	35.60	0.02	0.03	0.04	0.09	0.81	0.50	0.008	0.082	0.53
		1.00	1.00	1.00						

Note: The calculations of the probabilities were made using the assumptions described in Chapter Five.
[a]At least one horse.

possible minus pool. This example also demonstrates that the favorite should generally not be bet in a possible minus pool. Table 15.1 shows that even with a 98% probability of being in the money, the expected value per dollar bet to show is only 1.03, a return that certainly does not justify the risk. In fact, the best situation to imagine for a possible minus pool is a horse with a probability of 1.00 of finishing in the money; this would return an expected value per dollar bet to show of 1.05. But by the very nature of the event, no horse can ever have a probability of 1.00 of finishing in the money. For example, John Henry, horse of the year in 1981, had ten starts. Although he won eight of them, he was out of the money in the other two races. So he was in the money only 80% of the time.

The point of all this is clear: In a possible minus pool, where the minimum payoff is $2.10, *do not bet to place or show on any horse.*

A Typical Minus Pool: The San Juan Capistrano Invitational Handicap at Santa Anita, April 18, 1982

The final example in this chapter indicates that in a typical minus pool for place or show (1) it is not advisable to bet any horses to place or show regardless of how promising they might appear to be on the basis of either their past performance (the overbet) or their odds (the underbet); and (2) the only bets that are worth considering are win or features bets on horses other than the extreme favorite.

The San Juan Capistrano Invitational Handicap was run as the eighth race on Santa Anita's card. The race featured the dynamite entry of Exploded ridden by Bill Shoemaker, Captain General with Chris McCarron, and Perrault with Laffit Pincay, Jr. in the irons. Perrault was the consensus best bet of the day, with Exploded a major contender. The chief competition to this seemingly unbeatable field was provided by Lemhi Gold ridden by Walter Guerra. The 15—1 shot, Rainbow Connection, was scratched and the remaining five horses were rated at 20—1 or more in the morning line. The field looked unbeatable to the crowd, who immediately installed it as a 1—5 favorite, the same as its morning line. The place and show betting were even more intense, with about three-quarters of these pools being bet on the entry. The tote board indicated a likely minus pool, with a $2.10 place and show payout for all the horses finishing in the money, as long as at least one of the field came in the money.

EXACTA RACE

ABOUT 2,800 METERS

EIGHTH RACE

SAN JUAN CAPISTRANO

(GRADE I)

$300,000 Invitational Handicap

Four-year-olds and upward. By invitation, with no nomination or starting fees. The winner to receive $180,000, with $60,000 to second, $36,000 to third, $18,000 to fourth and $6,000 to fifth. A trophy will be presented to the owner of the winner.

SAN JUAN CAPISTRANO RECORD—ROYAL LIVING (4) 117 lbs. 1959 2:45⅖

Course Record—ROYAL LIVING (4) 117 March 11, 1959 2:45⅖

OWNER **TRAINER** **JOCKEY**

1 **Bradley, Chandler & C. Whittingham** — **Charles Whittingham** — **2/5**
Red, white tie, red cap
EXPLODED **118** — **William Shoemaker**
P.P. 3 Br.h. '77, Cougar 2nd—Blow Up 2nd, by Abdos
Breeder—Mrs. Mary Bradley, C. Whittingham & Dr. B. Wynne (Ky.)

1A **Lowell T. Hughes (Lessee)** — **Charles Whittingham** — **2/5**
White, royal blue braces, blue "HH", blue bars on sleeves, blue cap
CAPTAIN GENERAL **113** — **Chris McCarron**
P.P. 9 B.h. '77, Vaguely Noble—Charming Alibi
Breeder—N. B. Hunt (Kentucky)

1B **Baron Van Zuylen & Fradkoff** — **Charles Whittingham** — **2/5**
Turquoise, royal blue V-sash, blue stripes on sleeves, turquoise and blue cap
PERRAULT (GB) **129** — **Laffit Pincay, Jr.**
P.P. 10 Ch.h. '77, Djakao—Innocent Air
Breeder—A. D. Shead & F. H. Sasse (Great Britain)

2 **Tara Brianne Sweeney (Lessee)** — **Ted West** — **20**
Hunter green, black cap
LANARKLAND (GB) **116** — **Eddie Delahoussaye**
P.P. 1 Gr.g. '76, Ragstone—Kinharvie, by Abernant
Breeder—Lavinia Duchess of Norfolk (Great Britain)

3 **Saddle Hill Farm & Winick** — **Randy Winick** — **30**
Navy, fuchsia sleeves, navy and fuchsia cap
DESVELO (Chi) **114** — **Fernando Toro**
P.P. 2 Br.h. '77, Decano 2nd—Bronze Gem
Breeder—Haras Tarapaca (Chile)

4 **Aaron U. Jones** — **L. S. Barrera** — **5/2**
White, red cross sashes, red bar on sleeves, white and red cap
LEMHI GOLD **121** — **Walter Guerra**
P.P. 4 Ch.c. '78, Vaguely Noble—Belle Marie
Breeder—Owner (Kentucky)

5 **Longden & Carr Stables** — **John Longden** — **30**
White, purple sash, sleeves and cap
REGAL BEARING (GB) **118** — **Joe Steiner**
P.P. 5 Ch.h. '76, Viceregal—Mia Pola, by Relko
Breeder—S. Niarchos (Great Britain)

6 **Fleetwood Stable & Cameron** — **Gary Jones** — **15**
Burgundy, yellow cross sashes, burgundy and yellow cap
RAINBOW CONNECTION **115** — **Marco Castaneda**
P.P. 6 B.f. '78, Halo—Hangin Round, by Stage Door Johnny
Breeder—Mrs. George T. Coker (Canada)

7 Kjell H. Qvale — Bruce Headley — 20
Flame orange, green oak tree on back, orange bars on green sleeves, orange cap — Danny Winick
SILVEYVILLE 118
P.P. 7 B.c. '78, Petrone—Zurina, by Successor
Breeder—Tanaka & Tanaka (California)

8 Cimarron Stable — R. W. Mulhall — 20
White, green hoops and bars on sleeves, white and green cap — Sandy Hawley
RANKIN (Fr) 117
P.P. 8 Ch.h. '77, Owen Dudley—Cup Cake, by Dan Cupid
Breeder—Mrs. Eric Loder (France)

Nos. 1, 1A & 1B—Bradley, Chandler & C. Whittingham—Lowell T. Hughes (Lessee)—Baron Van Zuylen & Fradkoff entry.

8th Santa Anita

ABOUT 1 ¾ MILES. (TURF). (2.45⅘) 43rd running of THE SAN JUAN CAPISTRANO INVITATIONAL HANDICAP (Grade I). Purse $300,000. 4-year-olds and upward. By invitation, with no nomination or starting fees. The winner to receive $180,000, with $60,000 to second, $36,000 to third, $18,000 to fourth and $6,000 to fifth. Weights to be published Wednesday, April 7. The Los Angeles Turf Club will invite a field of the highest weighted horses to accept. In the event that one or more of these decline, those weighted below them will be invited in weight order to replace them. The field will be drawn by the closing time of entries, Friday, April 16. A trophy will be presented to the owner of the winner.

Coupled—Exploded, Captain General and Perrault.

*Lanarkland

Own.—Sweeney Tara (Lessee) **116**
Gr. g. 6, by Ragstone—Kinharvie, by Abernant
Br.—Lavinia Duchess of Norfolk (Eng) 1982 5 2 1 0 $70,925
Tr.—West Ted 1981 8 0 1 1 $2,677
Lifetime 25 7 3 2 $92,057 Turf 25 7 3 2 $92,057

28Mar82-8SA 1½ Ⓣ:4622:00 2:24 fm 32 126 58½ 57½ 513 520 CastanedM1 Sn Ls Ry 75 Perrault, Exploded, John Henry 5
13Mar82-9SA 1½ Ⓣ:4832:0342:29 gd 5 118 77¾ 42½ 1hd 13½ GuerrWA4 Sn Mrno H 70 Lanarkland, Desvelo,SunshineSwag 8
13Mar82—Run in two divisions, 8th & 9th races.
27Feb82-8SA 1½ Ⓣ:4812:0222:271fm 4¾ 115 98½ 32 43 75 GrrWA10 Sn Ls Obs H 74 RegalBearing,LeDucdeBar,Goldiko 10
14Feb82-7SA 1⅛ Ⓣ:4641:1131:50 gd 6½ 114 65¾ 62½ 2hd 12¾ Guerra W A7 Aw35000 77 Lanarkland,Gonzales,YellowMrmlde 8
31Jan82-5SA 1⅛ Ⓣ:4721:1141:493gd 41 112 55 54 4nk 2½ Guerra W A2 70000 78 Serang, Lanarkland, Mr. Mud 9
6Oct81♦5Brighton(Eng) 1 1:413gd*3-2 118 Ⓣ 7 Reid J Bramber TowerWin,MnInThMiddl,Smckovr 13
21Sep81♦4Bath(Eng) a1¼ 2:133gd 20 125 Ⓣ 53½ Perks S Langridge H Aventura,Blakenor,LadyofCornwll 19
31Aug81♦4Epsom(Eng) 1½ 2:394gd 20 160 Ⓣ 59½ BsttlJ Gntlmn Amtr Rdrs H No Bombs, Gay George, GetStoned 8
27Aug81♦6Brihgton(Eng) 1½ 2:293fm 6½ 140 Ⓣ 616 Reid J Rottingdean H BuncBoy,SkrryDnc,FoolsTstimony 11
5Aug81♦4Brighton(Eng) 1½ 2:263fm 10 133 Ⓣ 38½ Reid J Brghtn Chllng Cp Bunce Boy, Lohengrin, Lanarkland 9
Apr 17 SA Ⓣ 3f fm :35 h (d) ●Apr 13 SA Ⓣ 1 yl 1:424 h (d) Apr 7 SA Ⓣ 4f fm :48 h (d) Mar 24 SA 7f ft 1:263 h

*Desvelo

Own.—Saddle Hill Farm & Winick **114**
Dk. b. or br. h. 5, by Decano II—Bronze Gem, by Tobin Bronze
Br.—Haras Tarapaca (Chile) 1982 5 3 1 1 $58,450
Tr.—Winick Randy 1981 4 0 0 1 $4,725
Lifetime 13 4 2 4 $71,393 Turf 10 4 1 3 $67,867

26Mar82-8SA 1¼ Ⓣ:4641:3622:004fm*7-5 122 55½ 42 3½ 2½ Toro F7 Aw32000 82 ‡CaptainGeneral,Desvelo,NotbleAxe 7
26Mar82—Placed first through disqualification
13Mar82-9SA 1½ Ⓣ:4832:0342:29 gd 2½ 116 1hd 11 2hd 23½ ShomkrW7 Sn Mrno H 66 Lanarkland, Desvelo,SunshineSwag 8
13Mar82—Run in two divisions, 8th & 9th races.
20Feb82-5SA 1¼ Ⓣ:4731:36 2:003fm 3½ 121 11½ 12 14 13¾ Toro F3 Aw27000 84 Desvelo, Chancey Bidder, Dip 8
6Feb82-7SA 1¼ Ⓣ:4521:3522:002fm 4¼ 115 47½ 12½ 12½ 11½ Toro F5 Aw20000 85 Desvelo, Padirac, Flying Gene 9
29Jan82-7SA 1 1/16 :472 1:112 1:423ft 7 115 52½ 42¼ 43 36 Toro F8 Aw20000 82 DurbanDeep,Parson'sLeder,Desvelo 8
18Dec81-5Hol 1⅛ Ⓣ:4811:1211:482fm 3½e 116 1½ 1½ 31 42¾ Hawley S3 Aw19000 85 ‡BlueDncerII,SpringDiggr,Amrpour 8
4Nov81-7SA 1⅛ Ⓣ:47 1:1041:473fm 21 117 42½ 31½ 44 34¼ Gallitano G5 Aw22000 85 Caesr'sProfile,HomeBound,Desvelo 6
21Oct81-2SA a6½f Ⓣ:212 :44 1:14 fm 48 116 64½ 79¼ 79½ 89¼ Gallitano G8 Aw25000 80 AlwysAChnc,NowndThn,MdnghtMn 8
7Oct81-7SA 6½f :22 :443 1:152ft 87 1125 64¾ 79¾ 1012 1117 Schoeller CF1 Aw20000 76 StarRoute,NowndThen,Cloonwillin 11
30Nov80♦9ClubHipico(Chile a1¼ 2:01 fm 11 123 Ⓣ 34½ EscbrO ClFernandoFantiniB Rasputin, Chalotin, Desvelo 7
●Apr 15 SA Ⓣ 4f fm :482 h (d) Apr 10 SA Ⓣ 1 fm 1:422 h (d) Apr 4 SA 4f ft :482 h Mar 23 SA 4f ft :50 h

Exploded — Dk. b. or br. h. 5, by Cougar II—Blow Up II, by Abdos
Br.—Bradley-Whittinghm-Wynne (Ky) 1982 4 0 3 0 $64,875
Own.—Bradley-Chandler-Whittnghm 118 Tr.—Whittingham Charles 1981 16 1 4 2 $213,750
Lifetime 29 3 8 5 $377,375 Turf 18 1 6 3 $234,425
28Mar82-8SA 1½T:4622:00 2:24 fm 8-5e126 45½ 43½ 21 23½ Sibille R2 Sn Ls Ry 92 Perrault, Exploded, John Henry 5
13Mar82-8SA 1½T:4842:0222:272gd*3-2 119 22½ 22½ 25 25 Sibille R3 Sn Mrno H 73 LemhiGold,Exploded,ChnceyBidder 8
13Mar82—Run in two divisions, 8th & 9th races.
28Feb82-3SA 1⅛T:4731:1211:471fm*7-5 115 65 63½ 44 21½ Sibille R1 Aw40000 89 Patti's Triumph, Exploded, Isopach 6
15Feb82-8SA 1⅟16:462 1:10 1:41 ft 4e114 75½ 41½ 44 42½ McCrronCJ7 El Monte 93 WoodlandLad,SirDncer,LemhiGold 10
8Nov81-8SA 1½T:4721:5932:232fm 7½e126 54 65½ 57½ 59½ McCrronCJ2 Oak Tree 88 John Henry, Spence Bay, The Bart 7
25Oct81-8SA 1¼T:48 1:3632:003fm 3e116 85½108 108½ 812 McHrDG5 C F BurkeH 72 SpencBy,ProvidntlII,SuprMomnt 10
9Oct81-8SA 1¼T:4841:37 2:014fm 4 115 75½ 42 43 23½ CastanedaM7 Aw40000 74 SuperMoment,Exploded,BeechGrov 8
7Sep81-8Dmr a1¼:463 1:352 1:572ft 2½e115 812 86½ 89 811 Toro F4 Dmr Inv H 79 Wickerr, Tahitian King,GalaxyLibra 8
16Aug81-8Dmr 1⅛T:4931:14 1:494fm 6 114 76½ 74½ 74½ 52½ CastanedM4 E Read H 86 Wickerr,SuperMoment,MikeFogrty 7
2Aug81-8Dmr 1⅟16:46 1:10 1:41 ft 3½ 115 67½ 44½ 36 34½ CstnedM7 Sn Diego H 90 SummerTimeGuy,Shmgo,Exploded 7
Apr 14 SA T5f fm :594 h (d) Apr 10 SA T7f fm 1:292 h (d) Apr 5 SA T5f gd 1:024 h (d) Mar 21 SA 5f ft 1:003 h

Lemhi Gold — Ch. c. 4, by Vaguely Noble—Belle Marie, by Candy Spots
Br.—Jones A U (Ky) 1982 4 2 1 1 $73,675
Own.—Jones A U 121 Tr.—Barrera Lazaro S 1981 7 2 1 0 $50,070
Lifetime 11 4 2 1 $123,745 Turf 3 3 0 0 $81,305
13Mar82-8SA 1½T:4842:0222:272gd 2½ 119 12½ 12½ 15 15 GuerrWA4 Sn Mrno H 78 LemhiGold,Exploded,ChnceyBidder 8
13Mar82—Run in two divisions, 8th & 9th races.
25Feb82-8SA 1⅛T:4641:1111:48 fm*8-5 113 42 41½ 1½ 11½ Guerra W A8 Aw35000 87 LemhiGold,Fingal'sCave,Essenbee 10
15Feb82-8SA 1⅟16:462 1:10 1:41 ft 3½ 114 43 31½ 33½ 31½ Guerra WA1 El Monte 95 WoodlandLad,SirDncer,LemhiGold 10
6Feb82-6SA 1⅟16:462 1:094 1:41 ft *4-5 114 53½ 33½ 23½ 25½ Guerra W A4 Aw25000 90 Shashy, Lemhi Gold, Call MeMister 7
29Aug81-8Bel 1 :444 1:082 1:331ft 12 117 108½ 913 913 915 VelsquezJ11 Jerome H 87 Noble Nashua, Maudlin, Sing Sing 11
15Aug81-8Sar 1¼:463 1:372 2:034sy 17 126 811 911 923 726 Vasquez J6 Travers 55 WillowHour,PlesntColony,LordAvi 10
2Aug81-8Sar 1⅛:47 1:103 1:491ft 3½ 117 53 33 31½ 2½ CordroAJr6 Jim Dandy 88 WillowHour,LemhiGold,SilvrSuprm 8
9Jly81-9Hol 1 T:4621:1031:35 fm 2½ 114 44 62½ 42 1½ McCrrnCJ6 Westwood 94 Lemhi Gold,RockSoftly,IslandWhirl 7
9Jly81—Run in two divisions, 8th & 9th races.
28Mar81-8SA 1⅟16:46 1:10 1:42 ft *3-2 119 57½ 68 711 58 Pincay LJr6 Sn Flpe H 83 Stnchrry,SplndidSpruc,FlyingNshu 12
19Mar81-7SA 1 :452 1:093 1:351ft *1-5 120 44 44½ 46½ 49 Pincay L Jr5 Aw22000 84 Torso, Native Tactics, El Jebel 5
Apr 15 SA T4f fm :492 h (d) ●Apr 9 SA T1 fm 1:39 h (d) Mar 28 SA 4f ft :482 h Mar 23 SA 3f ft :363 h

***Regal Bearing** * — Ch. h. 6, by Viceregal—Mia Pola, by Relko
Br.—Niarchos S (Eng) 1982 6 2 0 0 $155,225
Own.—Longden & Carr Stables 118 Tr.—Longden John 1981 6 2 1 0 $52,400
Lifetime 30 11 3 0 $309,426 Turf 22 8 3 0 $289,716
3Apr82-8GG 1⅟16:483 1:13 1:46 m 5½ 117 46½ 41½ 12 13½ Baze R A4 G G H 73 RegIBring,VisiblPol,ScorTwntyFour 5
20Mar82-8GG 1 T:48 1:1221:364yl *2½ 121 96½ 75½ 78½ 811 Steiner JJ4 S F Mle H 72 Silveyville, Visible Pole, ASureHit 10
27Feb82-8SA 1½T:4812:0222:271fm 3½e114 43 2hd 12½ 13½ SteinrJJ5 Sn Ls Obs H 79 RegalBearing,LeDucdeBar,Goldiko 10
15Feb82-8SA 1⅟16:462 1:10 1:41 ft 26 114 95½ 85½ 912 814 Gilligan L10 El Monte 82 WoodlandLad,SirDncer,LemhiGold 10
7Feb82-7SA a6½f T:213 :4341:133fm 5e118 74½ 65½ 712 813 Steiner J J2 HcpO 78 Mr.PrimMinistr,TrmmlLuck,PirtLw 8
31Jan82-7SA 6f :213 :442 1:084ft 13 1115 68 68 67½ 57½ Steiner J J3 Aw35000 86 Mr.PrmMnstr,Emprr'sKy,FlngChck 6
9Oct81-8SA 1¼T:4841:37 2:014fm 3½ 122 11 2hd 2½ 45½ ShoemkerW5 Aw40000 73 SuperMoment,Exploded,BeechGrov 8
2Oct81-8SA 6½f:22 :45 1:152ft 9-5 122 66½ 67 511 411 ShoemkerW5 Aw34000 82 BigPrsnttion,TonUp,ExcutivCounsl 6
5Sep81-8Dmr 1⅟16T:4811:1211:42 fm *3½ 121 55½ 63½ 54½ 22 ShomkrW10 Escndo H 97 Advocatum,ReglBering,MjorSport 10
26Aug81-7Dmr 1⅟16:464 1:104 1:414ft *2-3 117 1hd 2hd 1hd 1nk ShoemkerW3 Aw32000 91 Regal Bearing, Damas, I'llStandPat 6
Apr 14 SA T7f fm 1:264 h (d) Mar 29 GG 5f sy 1:063 b (d) Mar 17 SA tr.t 5f sy 1:01 h Mar 13 SA 6f sl 1:151 h

Silveyville — B. c. 4, by Petrone—Zurina, by Successor
Br.—Tanaka & Tanaka (Cal) 1982 5 1 1 0 $76,075
Own.—Qvale K H 118 Tr.—Campbell E L 1981 11 6 1 2 $207,130
Lifetime 17 7 3 2 $285,155 Turf 7 4 1 0 $243,250
3Apr82-8GG 1⅟16:483 1:13 1:46 m 8-5 122 2½ 1hd 47 414 Winick D5 G G H 59 ReglBring,VisiblPol,ScorTwntyFour 5
20Mar82-8GG 1 T:48 1:1221:364yl 3 121 11½ 12 13 16 Winick D6 S F Mle H 83 Silveyville, Visible Pole, ASureHit 10
21Feb82-8SA 1¼T:4341:34 1:591fm 11 120 31½1115 1127 — OlivresF11 Sra Nvda H — HighCounsel,HndsomeOn,IrishHrt 11
21Feb82—Eased
10Feb82-8SA 1¼T:4731:3812:043yl 8½ 117 11½ 2½ 21½ 25 Olivares F6 Arcadia H 59 Perrault, Silveyville, Le Duc de Bar 7
17Jan82-8SA 1⅛:452 1:092 1:473ft 17 123 77½ 89 911 715 Winick D7 Sn Frndo 76 It's the One, Princelet, Rock Softly 9
12Dec81-8BM 1⅛T:4841:1341:533sf 7½ 120 14 1hd 31½ 43 Winick D8 B M H 69 SuperMoment,TahitianKing,TheBrt 8
28Nov81-8BM 1⅟16T:4821:1321:481sf 3½ 120 12 1½ 11½ 1½ Winick D5 B M Dby H 67 Silveyvill,SunshinSwg,Tmpo'sTigr 10
15Nov81-9Hol 1⅛T:4621:1031:481fm 27 122 11 11½ 11 1no Winick D1 Hol Dby 89 Silveyville,FrenchSssfrs,WtrwyDriv 8
15Nov81—Run in two divisions, 8th & 9th races.
24Oct81-8BM 1⅟16T:4711:1241:451fm 19 111 13 21 2½ 1nk Winick D7 Ascot H 82 Silveyville,LordTrendy,WterwyDriv 7
9Oct81-8BM 1⅟16:451 1:101 1:412ft 3 114 1hd 31½ 48½ 512 Winick D1 Rnd Tbl H 80 Chiaroscuro,FairShast,Productivity 7
●Apr 14 GG T7f fm 1:31 b (d) ●Mar 13 GG 6f gd 1:12 h Mar 6 GG 6f ft 1:134 h Feb 18 SA 4f ft :474 h

***Rankin** — Ch. h. 5, by Owen Dudley—Cup Cake, by Dan Cupid
Br.—Loder Mrs E (Fra) — 1982 3 1 0 0 $23,000
Own.—Cimarron Stable 117 — Tr.—Mulhall Richard W — 1981 4 0 1 0 $14,532
Lifetime 17 4 3 1 $152,286 — Turf 17 4 3 1 $152,286

4Apr82-8SA 1⅛Ⓣ:4721:1131:483gd 21 117 44½ 41½ 2½ 1¾ Pincay L Jr5 Aw40000 84 Rankin, Patti's Triumph, Glenorum 8
27Mar82-3SA 1⅛Ⓣ:46 1:0941:462fm 8¼ 117 2½ 31½ 43 57½ Pincay L Jr2 Aw40000 87 Falamoun, Pirate Law,CaptainNick 9
24Feb82-7SA a6½f Ⓣ:22 :4431:14 fm 11 115 86¾ 97¼ 911 99¼ McCarronCJ3 Aw35000 79 Kangroo Court, Belfort, Jimsel 9
4Jun81♦3Epsom(Eng) 1½ 2:442gd 33 126 Ⓣ 5 StrkG Coronation Cup(Gr1) Master Willie, Prince Bee, Vielle 5
1May81♦4Newmarket(Eng) 1½ 2:38 gd 4 119 Ⓣ 422 StrkyG Jockey Club(Gr3) MasterWillie,KingsRide,FenneyMill 6
25Apr81♦3Sandown(Eng) 1¼ 2:112gd 2½ 120 Ⓣ 21½ StrkeyG Westbury(Gr3) Hard Fought, Rankin, Vielle 7
15Apr81♦2Newmarket(Eng) 1⅛ 1:542gd 3 122 Ⓣ 49 StrkyG Earl of Sefton(Gr3) HrdFought,Moryshire,PlyboyJubile 9
18Oct80♦2Newmarket(Eng) 1¼ 2:053gd 14 122 Ⓣ 42½ StrkyG Champion(Gr1) Cairn Rouge, Master Willie,Nadjar 13
29Jly80♦4Goodwood(Eng) 1½ 2:38 gd 2¾ 128 Ⓣ 413 StrkeyG Gordon(Gr3) PrinceBee,FingalsCave,LightCavlry 6
28Jun80♦3Curragh(Ire) 1½ 2:434yl 12 126 Ⓣ 79½ StrkG Irish Sweeps Dby(Gr1) Tynavos, Prince Bee, Ramian 13
Apr 12 SA 1 gd 1:413 h ●Mar 25 SA 4f ft :452 h Mar 20 SA 7f ft 1:264 h Mar 6 SA Ⓣ 1 fm 1:421 h (d)

Captain General — B. h. 5, by Vaguely Noble—Charming Alibi, by Honeys Alibi
Br.—Hunt N B (Ky) — 1982 5 0 1 0 $11,775
Own.—Hughes L T (Lessee) 113 — Tr.—Whittingham Charles . — 1981 5 1 1 0 $48,225
Lifetime 17 2 3 1 $75,425 — Turf 8 1 1 0 $54,625

8Apr82-5SA 1⅛Ⓣ:4621:1031:481fm*4-5 114 98¾ 87 54½ 42½ McCarronCJ3 Aw26000 83 ‡Rostropovich,Tom'sSerend,Islndr 12
26Mar82-8SA 1¼Ⓣ:4641:3622:004fm 9-5 114 67½ 31 4¾ 1½ † McCarronCJ5 Aw32000 83 ‡CaptainGeneral,Desvelo,NotbleAxe 7
†26Mar82—Disqualified and placed fourth
27Feb82-8SA 1½Ⓣ:4812:0222:271fm 4¾ 113 1016 1016 89 86 VlnzlPA7 Sn Ls Obs H 73 RegalBearing,LeDucdeBar,Goldiko 10
20Feb82-5SA 1¼Ⓣ:4731:36 2:003fm*4-5 115 814 67½ 57½ 46¾ ValenzuelPA4 Aw27000 77 Desvelo, Chancey Bidder, Dip 8
7Feb82-5SA 1¼Ⓣ:47 1:3622:004fm*9-5 115 1010 51¾ 31 2hd ValenzuelPA9 Aw27000 83 Jurisconsult,CptnGnrl,PrnclyVrdct 11
9Apr81-8SA 1¼Ⓣ:4641:35 1:591fm 5 116 713 76½ 78½ 64½ VlenzulPA7 Grg Ryl H 86 RustyCanyon,BeechGrove,Catermn 7
14Mar81-8SA 1½Ⓣ:4622:0022:244fm 22 113 97¾ 94½ 55 1no VlnzulPA6 Sn Mrno H 91 CaptainGeneral,Aliyoun,‡Catermn 12
25Feb81-7SA 1⅛:47 1:104 1:483ft *9-5 117 711 77½ 76½ 56 ShoemkerW2 Aw23000 88 Defince,RoyllyTrue,MsterCermonis 7
12Feb81-9SA 1⅛:464 1:103 1:484ft 3½ 117 717 613 51½ 22 ShoemkerW3 Aw24000 83 ChuckyBby,CptinGenerl,HerbgerLd 7
16Jan81-5SA 1⅛Ⓣ:4531:1031:482fm 8¼ 117 819 87½ 85 52 Pierce D10 Aw22000 83 Viking, Macdon, ‡Benefactor 10
16Jan81—Placed fourth through disqualification
Apr 16 SA 3f ft :352 h Apr 5 SA 6f ft 1:134 h Mar 21 SA 6f ft 1:134 h Mar 8 SA Ⓣ 5f fm 1:004 h (d)

***Perrault** — Ch. h. 5, by Djakao—Innocent Air, by Court Martial
Br.—Sasse & Shead (Eng) — 1982 3 2 1 0 $263,900
Own.—Baron de Zuylen & Fradkoff 129 — Tr.—Whittingham Charles — 1981 8 3 2 1 $283,566
Lifetime 20 7 5 3 $556,442 — Turf 19 7 4 3 $456,442

20Mar82-8SA 1½Ⓣ:4622:00 2:24 fm 8-5e 126 11½ 11½ 11 13½ Pincay L Jr5 Sn Ls Ry 95 Perrault, Exploded, John Henry 5
7Mar82-8SA 1¼:45 1:342 1:59 ft 4½e 126 57 41½ 1½ 1no† Pincay L Jr4 S A H 94 ‡Perrault, John Henry, It'stheOne 11
† 7Mar82—Disqualified and placed second
10Feb82-8SA 1¼Ⓣ:4731:3812:043yl *8-5 124 44½ 1½ 11½ 15 Pincay LJr7 Arcadia H 64 Perrault, Silveyville, Le Duc de Bar 7
8Nov81-8SA 1½Ⓣ:4721:5932:232fm 7¾e 126 42½ 55½ 711 715 St Martin Y5 Oak Tree 83 John Henry, Spence Bay, The Bart 7
4Oct81♦4Longchamp(Fra) a1½ 2:351sf 27 130 Ⓣ 42¾ SmnH Arc de Triomphe (Gr1) Gold River, Bikala, April Run 24
30Aug81♦4Deauville(Fra) a1⅝ 2:583fm*6-5 131 Ⓣ 1hd StMrtY GrndPrixdeDeuville(Gr2) Perrault, Castle Keep, Glenorum 11
14Jly81♦6StCloud(Fra) a1⅝ 2:382gd*6-5 130 Ⓣ 12½ StMrtY PrixMuricedeNieul(Gr2) Perrault,RoiGuillume,DomMenotti 10
23May81♦5Evry(Fra) a1½ 2:423gd 6½ 124 Ⓣ 2hd StMrtY Gr Pr d'Evry (Gr2) Lancastrian, Perrault, Kelbomec 12
10May81♦6Longchamp(Fra) a1½ 2:492sf *2½ 123 Ⓣ 1hd StMrtY La Coupe(Gr3) Perrult,SonofLove,MonsiurDgobrt 10
20Apr81♦2Longchamp(Fra) a1½ 2:332gd 2¾ 121 Ⓣ 31½ StMrtnY Prix d'Hedouville Lancastrian, En Calcat, Perrault 10
●Apr 14 SA Ⓣ 5f fm :59 h (d) Apr 10 SA Ⓣ 1 fm 1:464 h (d) Apr 5 SA Ⓣ 5f gd 1:073 h (d) Mar 27 SA Ⓣ 3f fm :361 h (d)

Analyst's Comment

EIGHTH RACE

1—Perrault
2—Lemhi Gold
3—Exploded

PERRAULT has done just about everything asked of him this winter and won't have arch rival John Henry to battle today. This import ran a winning race at just about this distance in France under 131 pounds, which suggests he'll have no problems with 129 pounds, although this race has been a jinx for topweights. LEMHI GOLD has found his calling on the turf and has won all three of his grass starts in good style. However, this is an exacting distance and he's second topweight at 121. EXPLODED loves a distance and was second to Obraztsovy in this fixture last year. LANARKLAND is better than his last and he could be the upsetter under 116 pounds and leading rider Eddie D.

SWEEP'S Santa Anita Graded Handicaps

EIGHTH RACE ***Probable Post, 4:45***

ABOUT 1 ¾ MILES.(turf) 43rd running of THE SAN JUAN CAPISTRANO INVITATIONAL HANDICAP (Grade I). 4-Year-Olds and Up. . Purse $300,000.

10	PERRAULT	Pincay L Jr	129	Field at his mercy	1-5
4	LEMHI GOLD	Guerra W A	121	Going great for Laz	5-1
3	EXPLODED	Shoemaker W	118	Runs best against best	1-5
5	REGAL BEARING	Steiner J J	118	Won Golden Gate 'Cap	12-1
7	SILVEYVILLE	Winick D	118	Dangerous early speed	15-1
9	CAPTAIN GENERAL	McCrrnCJ	113	Flopped at odds-on	1-5
1	LANARKLAND	Delahoussaye E	116	Last in San Luis Rey	20-1
8	RANKIN	Hawley S	117	Rang bell at 21-1	20-1
6	RAINBOW CONNECTION	CstdM	115	Look for improvement	20-1
2	DESVELO	Toro F	114	Good try to easier	20-1

Coupled—Perrault, Exploded and Captain General.

Racing Form **EXPERTS' SELECTIONS**

Consensus Points: 5 for 1st (best 7), 2 for 2d, 1 for 3d. Best in CAPITALS.

Trackman, Warren Williams — **SANTA ANITA** — Selections Made for Fast Track

	TRACKMAN	HANDICAP	ANALYST	HERMIS	SWEEP	CONSENSUS	
8	PERRAULT	PERRAULT	PERRAULT	PERRAULT	PERRAULT	PERRAULT	27
	EXPLODED	EXPLODED	LEMHI GOLD	REGAL BEARING	LEMHI GOLD	LEMHI GOLD	7
	LEMHI GOLD	LEMHI GOLD	EXPLODED	LEMHI GOLD	EXPLODED	EXPLODED	6

The tote board was as follows:

	#1 Entry of Exploded, Captain General, and Perrault	#4 Lemhi Gold	Totals
With nine minutes to post time			
Odds	1—5	3—1	
Win pool	86,716	26,684	138,011
Place pool	76,728	13,277	103,643
Show pool	68,451	4,796	83,830
With seven minutes to post time			
Odds	2—5	5—2	
Win pool	92,620	31,028	152,377
Place pool	88,450	14,921	118,856
Show pool	73,009	5,954	91,464
With three minutes to post time			
Odds	2—5	5—2	
Win pool	107,936	41,934	189,118
Place pool	95,831	17,551	134,935
Show pool	84,990	6,994	109,578
With one minute to post time			
Odds	2—5	5—2	
Win pool	117,171	45,591	205,973
Place pool	101,114	18,762	143,313
Show pool	97,604	7,483	124,437
Yield of last-minute surge of betting			
Odds	1—2	5—2	
Win pool	141,334	50,790	238,741
Place pool	108,593	19,610	153,673
Show pool	107,094	8,643	136,568
At post time			
Odds	2—5	3—1	
Win pool	154,169	52,104	253,952
Place pool	116,750	19,820	157,537
Show pool	112,441	8,753	142,689

Throughout the betting period, about a fifth of the win pool was bet on Lemhi Gold, consistent with his 5—2 or 3—1 odds. But only about one-sixteenth of the show pool was bet on Lemhi Gold. After correction for the track take of 15%, one minute before post time the expected value of a dollar bet to show on Lemhi Gold was a whopping 1.97! (This expected value was about the same throughout the betting period.) This would normally be an outstanding Dr. Z system bet on a very top horse, a most enviable position to be in. Further analysis, however, showed this to be a smoke screen. The minus-pool betting on the field made a show bet on Lemhi Gold or any other horse an unattractive proposition.

To establish this conclusion we utilized the data with one minute to post time, when one would normally be doing the final calculations concerning a possible bet. The probability that Lemhi Gold would win the race was about 0.221, and the probability that he would come in second 0.204, and third 0.182. At these odds he would be in the money about 60.7% of the time.

There were three possible outcomes: (1) Lemhi Gold and at least one of the entry horses would finish in the money with a show payoff of $2.10; (2) Lemhi Gold would finish out of the money with a show payoff of zero, which would occur with a probability of 0.393;* and (3) Lemhi Gold would finish in the money and all the entry horses would finish out of the money, in which case the payoff for show would be quite high.

If Lemhi Gold came in without any of the entry horses, he would have to pay $23.80 to show for the bet to be a fair proposition. In fact, from the

---

*The probability that Lemhi Gold would win was $q_{LG} = W_{LG}/W = 45{,}591/205{,}973 = 0.221$. The probability that each of the three entry horses would win was about $q_E = 117{,}171/(205{,}973)3 = 0.190$. The probabilities that the other five long-shot horses would win were about $q_{LS} = 0.210/5 = 0.0420$. The probability that Lemhi Gold would be second was then about

$$q_{LG} \times \left\{ \frac{3q_E}{1 - q_E} + \frac{5q_{LS}}{1 - q_{LS}} \right\} = 0.204$$

and third,

$$q_{LG} \times \left\{ 3\frac{2q_E^2}{(1 - q_E)(1 - 2q_E)} + \frac{5q_E q_{LS}}{(1 - q_E)(1 - q_{LS} - q_E)} + 5\frac{2q_E q_{LS}}{(1 - q_{LS})(1 - q_{LS} - q_E)} + \frac{4q_{LS}^2}{(1 - q_{LS})(1 - 2q_{LS})} \right\} = 0.182.$$

Thus the place probability was 0.425, the show probability 0.607, and the probability that Lemhi Gold would be out of the money was $1 - 0.607 = 0.393$.

final tote board values, Lemhi Gold would have paid only \$9.80.* The \$9.80 would have been quite a good payoff in its own right, given that Lemhi Gold went off at 3—1.

Thus the minus pool makes all show bets poor betting opportunities, regardless of how good they might look.

The only bet in this race that made any sense was Lemhi Gold to win. If Lemhi Gold's chances of winning were 25% or better, then the bet was reasonable. I thought so and bet it accordingly. It turned out to be a wise investment.

The final result was an easy victory for Lemhi Gold. Perrault, heavily weighted at 129, was unable to mount a late charge and finished third. Exploded took second. The chart of the race was as follows:

---

*The probability that Lemhi Gold would be in the money with none of the triple entry horses was

$$\underbrace{\frac{q_{LG}(5)(4)q_{LS}^2}{(1-q_{LS})(1-2q_{LS})}}_{\text{Lemhi Gold third}} + \underbrace{\frac{q_{LG}(5)(4)q_{LS}^2}{(1-q_{LS})(1-q_{LS}-q_{LG})}}_{\text{Lemhi Gold second}} + \underbrace{\frac{q_{LG}(5)(4)q_{LS}^2}{(1-q_{LG})(1-q_{LS}-q_{LG})}}_{\text{Lemhi Gold first}} = 0.0335.$$

The probability that Lemhi Gold would be in the money was 0.607. Thus the probability that Lemhi Gold would be in the money with at least one of the entry horses was $0.607 - 0.0335 = 0.574$.

To break even on a show bet on Lemhi Gold, the expected profit must be equal to zero:

$$0 = -1(0.393) + 0.05(0.574) + O_{LG}(0.0335).$$

Solving for the show odds, $O_{LG} = 10.875$, or a payoff of \$23.75 or \$23.80 with breakage. The actual O_{LG} was

$$\frac{QS - (S_{LG} + 2S_{LS})}{3S_{LG}} = \frac{(1-0.15)(142{,}689) - [8{,}753 + 2(4{,}299)]}{3(8{,}753)} = 3.958$$

which yielded a payout after breakage of \$9.80.

San Juan Capistrano Handicap

EIGHTH RACE
Santa Anita
APRIL 18, 1982

ABOUT 1 ¾ MILES.(turf). (2.45⅗) 43rd Running THE SAN JUAN CAPISTRANO HANDICAP (Grade I). Purse $300,000. Invitational Handicap. 4-year-olds and upward. By invitation, with no nomination or starting fees. The winner to receive $180,000, with $60,000 to second, $36,000 to third, $18,000 to fourth and $6,000 to fifth. Weights to be published Wednesday, April 7. The Los Angeles Turf Club will invite a field of the highest-weighted horses to accept. In the event that one or more of these decline, those weighted below them will be invited in weight order to replace them. The field will be drawn by the closing time of entries, Friday, April 16. A trophy will be presented to the owner of the winner.
Value of race $300,000, value to winner $180,000, second $60,000, third $36,000, fourth $18,000, fifth $6,000. Mutuel pool $554,178, Minus place pool $4,378.03, Minus show pool $5,968.06. Exacta Pool $401,828.

Last Raced	Horse	Eqt.A.Wt	PP	St	1	1¼	1½	Str	Fin	Jockey	Odds $1
13Mar82 $^{8}SA^{1}$	Lemhi Gold	4 121	4	4^{2}	3^{2}½	2^{4}	1^{hd}	1^{2}½	1^{7}	Guerra W A	3.10
28Mar82 $^{8}SA^{2}$	Exploded	5 118	3	9	8^{1}	6^{hd}	4^{1}	3^{2}	2^{1}¾	Shoemaker W	a-.40
28Mar82 $^{8}SA^{1}$	Perrault	b 5 129	9	2^{1}	2½	1½	2^{1}	2^{6}	3^{2}½	Pincay L Jr	a-.40
8Apr82 $^{5}SA^{4}$	Captain General	5 113	8	8^{1}	7½	7^{1}	6^{1}½	5^{1}½	4^{nk}	McCarron C J	a-.40
4Apr82 $^{8}SA^{1}$	Rankin	5 117	7	6^{1}	5^{1}½	5^{1}	3^{1}½	4^{3}	5^{3}½	Hawley S	19.60
28Mar82 $^{8}SA^{5}$	Lanarkland	6 116	1	7^{hd}	9	9	7^{2}	6^{7}	6^{13}	Delahoussaye E	14.00
3Apr82 $^{8}GG^{4}$	Silveyville	4 118	6	1^{1}½	1^{5}	3½	8^{hd}	8^{1}	7½	Winick D	36.70
26Mar82 $^{8}SA^{1}$	Desvelo	5 115	2	3^{1}	4^{2}½	4^{1}	5^{1}	7^{2}	8^{nk}	Castaneda M	27.10
3Apr82 $^{8}GG^{1}$	Regal Bearing	6 118	5	5^{5}	6½	8^{1}½	9	9	9	Steiner J J	21.80

a-Coupled: Exploded, Perrault and Captain General.
OFF AT 5:23 Start good, Won easily. Time, :23, :46, 1:09⅕, 1:33⅘, 1:58⅘, 2:45⅗, Course firm.

$2 Mutuel Prices:				
	4-LEMHI GOLD	8.20	2.10	2.10
	1-EXPLODED (a-entry)		2.10	2.10
	1-PERRAULT (a-entry)		2.10	2.10
	$5 EXACTA 4-1 PAID $33.00.			

Ch. c, by Vaguely Noble—Belle Marie, by Candy Spots. Trainer Barrera Lazaro S. Bred by Jones Aaron U (Ky).
LEMHI GOLD, taken in hand after the start, raced in good position while reserved off the pace through the first mile, moved to closer contention outside of PERRAULT on the front stretch, was roused a bit to stay alongside that one when PERRAULT moved strongly to the lead on the backstretch, got the advantage on the stretch turn and quickly drew off when set down in the upper stretch. EXPLODED, unhurried until after 10 furlongs, rallied when set down but could not reach close contention. PERRAULT, reserved off the early pace and moved strongly to the lead early on the backstretch, matched strides with the winner to the stretch then weakened in the final furlong. CAPTAIN GENERAL failed to threaten.
Owners— 1, Jones Aaron U; 2, Bradley & Chandler & Whittingham; 3, Fradkoff & Van Zuylen; 4, Hughes L T; 5, Cimarron Stable; 6, Sweeney Tara Brianne; 7, Qvale K H; 8, Savoca & Winick; 9, Longden-Carr Stable.
Trainers— 1, Barrera Lazaro S; 2, Whittingham Charles; 3, Whittingham Charles; 4, Whittingham Charles; 5, Mulhall Richard W; 6, West Ted; 7, Headley Bruce; 8, Winick Randy; 9, Longden John.
Overweight: Desvelo 1 pound.
Scratched—Rainbow Connection (3Apr82 $^{8}SA^{5}$).

My win bet provided a handsome payoff, and the rest of the tote board's $2.10s reflected the minus pools. An even more outstanding bet was the 4—1 exacta, which paid $33 for a $5 bet, or $6.60 per dollar bet, considerably more than the $4.10 per dollar bet in the win pool.

The conclusion of the analysis is this: When there is a minus pool with a minimum payoff of $2.10, do not bet to place or show on any horses, regardless of how attractive a bet on one of them appears to be. The only bets that are of possible interest are in the win or features pools. The decision to bet on such latter situations should be based on handicapping estimates that the probability of winning exceeds the odds estimate of the horses' chances. In localities such as Kentucky where the minimum payoff is $2.20, it may on occasion be advantageous to bet in a race with a minus pool. In this case, you should use an analysis like that described in Chapter Six for the Kentucky Oaks to determine the expected value per dollar bet.

CHAPTER 16

Refinements to the Basic Dr. Z System

Dangers to Look For, When Not to Bet and Horses to Avoid, Conservative versus Risky Use of the Dr. Z System, and Hints on Good Betting Techniques at the Racetrack

In Chapter Five we discussed the steps needed to apply the Dr. Z system. There we considered important topics such as horses to avoid and dangers to look for. Now that you have gone through our various applications of the Dr. Z system to real races, let us consider these matters again. Reread that section. Remember not to bet on off-tracks, in minus pools, on long shots, and on "Silky Sullivans." Be careful betting on horses coming off a long layoff and on first-time starters. Bet them only if you feel very confident about their prospects of being in the money. Be sure you can both watch the tote board and wager near the end of the betting period. Don't bet too early! Also try to estimate if there are many Dr. Z system bettors at your track and if their presence is greatly affecting the quality of your bets. If so, read the appropriate section in Chapter Seventeen. Learn how to quickly use the detachable charts to determine when and how much to bet by practicing before you bet, both at home and at the track. Or get one of the calculators discussed in Chapter Five. Decide in advance if you are a strict Dr. Z system bettor or if you prefer to bet most races. If you want to stick closely to the Dr. Z system, then keep your betting fortune for these bets separate from your fun bets or those based on other systems. Don't bet unless the horse in question really does meet the suggested cutoffs: 1.10 (for Derby Day–type events), 1.14 for top tracks, and 1.18 for other tracks. If you want to increase your chances of being sure to come out ahead, bet less than the optimal Kelly amount by using one of the fractional-Kelly strategies discussed in Chapter Five. By chopping the bet to half you will still get about 73% of the maximum growth and you will substantially increase your chances of doubling, tripling, or quadrupling your initial betting fortune before losing half of it. If you want to bet every race, then follow the advice in Chapter Fourteen. Try more or less to break even on your non–Dr. Z system bets by betting small amounts and by wagering more as the bet becomes more advantageous, with higher expected value per dollar bet and higher probability of winning. Wager the optimal amount for your Dr. Z system bets out of your Dr. Z system betting wealth, reserving your additional betting wealth for your other bets. If you think you can handicap better than $q_i = W_i/W$, then modify your betting by using the analysis later in this chapter and in Chapter Seven. Learn how to use the Harville formulas if you do this. Above all, be careful and enjoy the sport!

Regression Equations Based on Differing Wealth Levels and Track Handle

Betting-wealth level and the track handle are both very important factors in determining the optimal bet size. Certainly the larger our betting wealth, the more we will tend to bet, and since our bets affect the odds more at a small track than at a large one, we will generally bet less at the small track. Table 16.1, on optimal place betting, accounts for these factors by reporting optimal place-bet regression equations for four different wealth levels ($50, $500, $2,500, $10,000) and three different place pools ($2,000, $10,000, $150,000). By averaging these equations, we can determine the optimal place bet for *any* wealth level and place pool. This is accomplished in Table 16.2, which indicates which equation from Table 16.1 to use and its corresponding weights for any wealth level and place pool. Tables 16.3 and 16.4 perform the same tasks for show betting. One further qualification: These regression equations were calibrated for a track payback proportion Q of 0.829. For Q's other than 0.829, a correction factor in the optimal bet size must be included. This factor is discussed in the following section.

To illustrate the use of these equations, let us study the Triple Bend Handicap at Hollywood Park on May 8, 1982, that was presented in Chapter Six. The tote board one minute before post time was

	Totals	#8 Shanekite	Expected Value per Dollar Bet on Shanekite
Odds		1—1	
Win	398,851	155,321	
Show	59,163	14,585	1.18

TABLE 16.1 *The optimal place bet for various betting-wealth levels and place-pools sizes*

Place Pool ($)	w_0 = \$50	w_0 = \$500	w_0 = \$2,500	w_0 = \$10,000
2,000		$P2 = 261q + 256q^2 + 180q^3 - \left(\frac{199qP_i}{qP - 0.70P_i}\right)$	$P5 = 426q + 802q^2 - \left(\frac{459qP_i}{qP - 0.60P_i}\right)$	$P8 = 487q + 901q^2 - \left(\frac{521qP_i}{qP - 0.60P_i}\right)$
10,000	$P1 = 39q + 52q^2 - \left(\frac{25qP_i}{qP - 0.75P_i}\right)$	$P3 = 375q + 525q^2 - \left(\frac{271qP_i}{qP - 0.70P_i}\right)$	$P6 = 1{,}307q + 1{,}280q^2 + 902q^3 - \left(\frac{993qP_i}{qP - 0.70P_i}\right)$	$P9 = 2{,}497q + 1{,}806q^2 + 2{,}073q^3 - \left(\frac{2{,}199qP_i}{qP - 0.60P_i}\right)$
150,000		$P4 = 505q + 527q^2 - \left(\frac{386qP_i}{qP - 0.60P_i}\right)$	$P7 = 2{,}386q + 2{,}668q^2 - \left(\frac{1{,}877qP_i}{qP - 0.60P_i}\right)$	$P10 = 7{,}072q + 10{,}470q^2 - \left(\frac{5{,}273qP_i}{qP - 0.70P_i}\right)$

TABLE 16.2 ***Weighting factors to determine the optimal place bet for any betting-wealth level and place-pool size***

Place Pool ($)	w_0 0–50	w_0 51–500	w_0 501–2,500
0–2,000	$\left(\frac{w_0}{50}\right)\left(\frac{P}{2{,}000}\right)[P1]$	$\left(\frac{500-w_0}{450}\right)\left(\frac{P}{2{,}000}\right)[P1]$ $+\left(\frac{w_0-50}{450}\right)\left(\frac{P}{2{,}000}\right)[P2]$	$\left(\frac{2{,}500-w_0}{2{,}000}\right)\left(\frac{P}{2{,}000}\right)[P2]$ $+\left(\frac{w_0-500}{2{,}000}\right)\left(\frac{P}{2{,}000}\right)[P5]$
2,001–10,000		$\left(\frac{500-w_0}{450}\right)[P1]$ $+\left(\frac{w_0-50}{450}\right)\left(\frac{10{,}000-P}{8{,}000}\right)[P2]$ $+\left(\frac{w_0-50}{450}\right)\left(\frac{P-2{,}000}{8{,}000}\right)[P3]$	$\left(\frac{2{,}500-w_0}{2{,}000}\right)\left(\frac{10{,}000-P}{8{,}000}\right)[P2]$ $+\left(\frac{2{,}500-w_0}{2{,}000}\right)\left(\frac{P-2{,}000}{8{,}000}\right)[P3]$ $+\left(\frac{w_0-500}{2{,}000}\right)\left(\frac{10{,}000-P}{8{,}000}\right)[P5]$ $+\left(\frac{w_0-500}{2{,}000}\right)\left(\frac{P-2{,}000}{8{,}000}\right)[P6]$
10,001–150,000	$\left(\frac{w_0}{50}\right)[P1]$	$\left(\frac{500-w_0}{450}\right)[P1]$ $+\left(\frac{w_0-50}{450}\right)\left(\frac{150{,}000-P}{140{,}000}\right)[P3]$ $+\left(\frac{w_0-50}{450}\right)\left(\frac{P-10{,}000}{140{,}000}\right)[P4]$	$\left(\frac{2{,}500-w_0}{2{,}000}\right)\left(\frac{150{,}000-P}{140{,}000}\right)[P3]$ $+\left(\frac{2{,}500-w_0}{2{,}000}\right)\left(\frac{P-10{,}000}{140{,}000}\right)[P4]$ $+\left(\frac{w_0-500}{2{,}000}\right)\left(\frac{150{,}000-P}{140{,}000}\right)[P6]$ $+\left(\frac{w_0-500}{2{,}000}\right)\left(\frac{P-10{,}000}{140{,}000}\right)[P7]$

TABLE 16.2 *(continued)*

Place Pool ($)	w_0 2,501–10,000	w_0 10,001 +
150,001 +	$\left(\frac{500 - w_0}{450}\right)[P1] + \left(\frac{w_0 - 50}{450}\right)[P4]$	$\left(\frac{2{,}500 - w_0}{2{,}000}\right)[P4] + \left(\frac{w_0 - 500}{2{,}000}\right)[P7]$
0–2,000	$\left(\frac{10{,}000 - w_0}{7{,}500}\right)\left(\frac{P}{2{,}000}\right)[P5] + \left(\frac{w_0 - 2{,}500}{7{,}500}\right)\left(\frac{P}{2{,}000}\right)[P8]$	$\left(\frac{P}{2{,}000}\right)[P8]$
2,001–10,000	$\left(\frac{10{,}000 - w_0}{7{,}500}\right)\left(\frac{10{,}000 - P}{8{,}000}\right)[P5] + \left(\frac{10{,}000 - w_0}{7{,}500}\right)\left(\frac{P - 2{,}000}{8{,}000}\right)[P6] + \left(\frac{w_0 - 2{,}500}{7{,}500}\right)\left(\frac{10{,}000 - P}{8{,}000}\right)[P8] + \left(\frac{w_0 - 2{,}500}{7{,}500}\right)\left(\frac{P - 2{,}000}{8{,}000}\right)[P9]$	$\left(\frac{10{,}000 - P}{8{,}000}\right)[P8] + \left(\frac{P - 2{,}000}{8{,}000}\right)[P9]$

TABLE 16.2 *(continued)*

Place Pool ($)	w_0 2,501–10,000	w_0 10,001 +
10,001–150,000	$\left(\frac{10{,}000 - w_0}{7{,}500}\right)\left(\frac{150{,}000 - P}{140{,}000}\right)[P6]$ $+ \left(\frac{10{,}000 - w_0}{7{,}500}\right)\left(\frac{P - 10{,}000}{140{,}000}\right)[P7]$ $+ \left(\frac{w_0 - 2{,}500}{7{,}500}\right)\left(\frac{150{,}000 - P}{140{,}000}\right)[P9]$ $+ \left(\frac{w_0 - 2{,}500}{7{,}500}\right)\left(\frac{P - 10{,}000}{140{,}000}\right)[P10]$	$\left(\frac{150{,}000 - P}{140{,}000}\right)[P9]$ $+ \left(\frac{P - 10{,}000}{140{,}000}\right)[P10]$
150,001 +	$\left(\frac{10{,}000 - w_0}{7{,}500}\right)[P7]$ $+ \left(\frac{w_0 - 2{,}500}{7{,}500}\right)[P10]$	$[P10]$

TABLE 16.3 *The optimal show bet for various betting-wealth levels and show-pool sizes*

Show Pool ($)	w_0 = \$50	w_0 = \$500	w_0 = \$2,500	w_0 = \$10,000
1,200		$S2 = 9 + 994q^3 - 464q^2 - \left(\frac{150qS_i}{qS - 0.80S_i}\right)$	$S5 = 13 + 1{,}549q^2 - 901q^3 - \left(\frac{303qS}{qS - 0.60S_i}\right)$	
6,000	$S1 = 10 + 183q^2 - 135q^3 - \left(\frac{11S_i}{qS - 0.80S_i}\right)$	$S3 = 86 + 1{,}516q^2 - 968q^3 - \left(\frac{90.7S_i}{qS - 0.85S_i}\right)$	$S6 = 53 + 5{,}219q^2 - 2{,}513q^3 - \left(\frac{934qS_i}{qS - 0.70S_i}\right)$	$S8 = 58 + 7{,}406q^2 - 4{,}211q^3 - \left(\frac{1{,}359qS_i}{qS - 0.65S_i}\right)$
100,000		$S4 = 131 + 2{,}150q^2 - 1{,}778q^3 - \left(\frac{150S_i}{qS - 0.70S_i}\right)$	$S7 = 533 + 9{,}862q^2 - 7{,}696q^3 - \left(\frac{571S_i}{qS - 0.80S_i}\right)$	$S9 = 1{,}682 + 28{,}200q^2 - 16{,}880q^3 - \left(\frac{1{,}769S_i}{qS - 0.85S_i}\right)$

TABLE 16.4 ***Weighting factors to determine the optimal show bet for any betting-wealth level and show-pool size***

Show Pool ($)	w_0 0–50	w_0 51–500	w_0 501–2,500
0–1,200	$\left(\frac{w_0}{50}\right)\left(\frac{S}{1{,}200}\right)[S1]$	$\left(\frac{500 - w_0}{450}\right)\left(\frac{S}{1{,}200}\right)[S1]$	$\left(\frac{2{,}500 - w_0}{2{,}000}\right)\left(\frac{S}{1{,}200}\right)[S2]$
		$+ \left(\frac{w_0 - 50}{450}\right)\left(\frac{S}{1{,}200}\right)[S2]$	$+ \left(\frac{w_0 - 500}{2{,}000}\right)\left(\frac{S}{1{,}200}\right)[S5]$
1,201–6,000		$\left(\frac{500 - w_0}{450}\right)[S1]$	$\left(\frac{2{,}500 - w_0}{2{,}000}\right)\left(\frac{6{,}000 - S}{4{,}800}\right)[S2]$
		$+ \left(\frac{w_0 - 50}{450}\right)\left(\frac{6{,}000 - S}{4{,}800}\right)[S2]$	$+ \left(\frac{2{,}500 - w_0}{2{,}000}\right)\left(\frac{S - 1{,}200}{4{,}800}\right)[S3]$
		$+ \left(\frac{w_0 - 50}{450}\right)\left(\frac{S - 1{,}200}{4{,}800}\right)[S3]$	$+ \left(\frac{w_0 - 500}{2{,}000}\right)\left(\frac{6{,}000 - S}{4{,}800}\right)[S5]$
			$+ \left(\frac{w_0 - 500}{2{,}000}\right)\left(\frac{S - 1{,}200}{4{,}800}\right)[S6]$

Show Pool ($)	w_0 0–50	w_0 51–500	w_0 501–2,500
6,001–100,000	$\left(\frac{w_0}{50}\right)[S1]$	$\left(\frac{500-w_0}{450}\right)[S1]$ $+\left(\frac{w_0-50}{450}\right)\left(\frac{100{,}000-S}{94{,}000}\right)[S3]$ $+\left(\frac{w_0-50}{450}\right)\left(\frac{S-6{,}000}{94{,}000}\right)[S4]$	$\left(\frac{2{,}500-w_0}{2{,}000}\right)\left(\frac{100{,}000-S}{94{,}000}\right)[S3]$ $+\left(\frac{2{,}500-w_0}{2{,}000}\right)\left(\frac{S-6{,}000}{94{,}000}\right)[S4]$ $+\left(\frac{w_0-500}{2{,}000}\right)\left(\frac{100{,}000-S}{94{,}000}\right)[S6]$ $+\left(\frac{w_0-500}{2{,}000}\right)\left(\frac{S-6{,}000}{94{,}000}\right)[S7]$
100,001 +		$\left(\frac{500-w_0}{450}\right)[S1]$ $+\left(\frac{w_0-50}{450}\right)[S4]$	$\left(\frac{2{,}500-w_0}{2{,}000}\right)[S4]$ $+\left(\frac{w_0-500}{2{,}000}\right)[S7]$

TABLE 16.4 *(continued)*

Show Pool ($)	w_0 2,501–10,000	w_0 10,001 +
0–1,200	$\left(\frac{S}{1{,}200}\right)[S5]$	
1,201–6,000	$\left(\frac{6{,}000 - w_0}{4{,}800}\right)[S5]$ $+ \left(\frac{10{,}000 - w_0}{7{,}500}\right)\left(\frac{S - 1{,}200}{4{,}800}\right)[S6]$ $+ \left(\frac{w_0 - 2{,}500}{7{,}500}\right)\left(\frac{S - 1{,}200}{4{,}800}\right)[S8]$	$\left(\frac{6{,}000 - S}{4{,}800}\right)[S5]$ $+ \left(\frac{S - 1{,}200}{4{,}800}\right)[P8]$
6,001–100,000	$\left(\frac{10{,}000 - w_0}{7{,}500}\right)\left(\frac{100{,}000 - S}{94{,}000}\right)[S6]$ $+ \left(\frac{10{,}000 - w_0}{7{,}500}\right)\left(\frac{S - 6{,}000}{94{,}000}\right)[S7]$ $+ \left(\frac{w_0 - 2{,}500}{7{,}500}\right)\left(\frac{100{,}000 - S}{94{,}000}\right)[S8]$ $+ \left(\frac{w_0 - 2{,}500}{7{,}500}\right)\left(\frac{S - 6{,}000}{94{,}000}\right)[S9]$	$\left(\frac{100{,}000 - S}{94{,}000}\right)[S8]$ $+ \left(\frac{S - 6{,}000}{94{,}000}\right)[S9]$
100,001 +	$\left(\frac{10{,}000 - w_0}{7{,}500}\right)[S7]$ $+ \left(\frac{w_0 - 2{,}500}{7{,}500}\right)[S9]$	[S9]

Suppose our betting wealth is \$400. We refer to the show Table 16.4 with w_0 = \$400 and S = \$59,163. This indicates that the show regression equations needed from Table 16.3 are $S1$, $S3$, and $S4$. The $S1$ equation is weighted by $(500 - w_0)/450 = (500 - 400)/450 = 0.222$ and the $S3$ equation is weighted by

$$\left(\frac{w_0 - 50}{450}\right)\left(\frac{100{,}000 - S}{94{,}000}\right) = \left(\frac{400 - 50}{450}\right)\left(\frac{100{,}000 - 59{,}163}{94{,}000}\right) = 0.338,$$

and the $S4$ equation is weighted by

$$\left(\frac{w_0 - 50}{450}\right)\left(\frac{S - 6{,}000}{94{,}000}\right) = \left(\frac{400 - 50}{450}\right)\left(\frac{59{,}163 - 6{,}000}{94{,}000}\right) = 0.440.$$

The sum of the weights is one: 0.222 + 0.338 + 0.440 = 1.000. From Table 16.3 with w_0 = \$400, S = \$59,163, S_i = \$14,585, and $q = W_i/W = 155{,}321/398{,}851 = 0.389$, equation $S1$ is

$$10 + 183q^2 - 135q^3 - \frac{11S_i}{qS - 0.80S_i} = 10 + 183(0.389)^2 - 135(0.389)^3 - \frac{11(14{,}585)}{(0.389)(59{,}163) - (0.80)(14{,}585)}$$
$$= 10 + 27.7 - 7.9 - 14.1 = \$16.$$

For simplicity, we write q rather than q_i in these formulas.

Similarly, equation $S3$ is

$$86 + 1{,}516q^2 - 968q^3 - \frac{90.7S_i}{qS - 0.85S_i}$$
$$= 86 + 229.4 - 57.0 - 124.6 = \$134,$$

and equation $S4$ is

$$131 + 2{,}150q^2 - 1{,}778q^3 - \frac{150S_i}{qS - 0.70S_i}$$
$$= 131 + 325.3 - 104.7 - 170.9 = \$181.$$

From the calculated weightings, the optimal show bet is

$$(0.222)(16) + (0.338)(134) + (0.440)(181) = \$128.$$

Since California has $Q = 0.85$, we must include a correction factor for Q different from 0.829. We will return to our example after discussing this correction factor.

Adjusting the Optimal Bet Size for Differing Track Paybacks

An increase in the track payback Q is beneficial to the bettor, since it will mean larger payoffs on winning tickets. This is illustrated in Figure 9.4, which shows how a change in Q can have a surprisingly large effect on long-run profits. To account for differing Q's, we must be able to calculate expected values per dollar bet and optimal bet sizes for any Q. Equations (4.5) and (4.6) accomplish the former, and in this section we discuss how to adjust the optimal betting results of Tables 16.1 to 16.4, since they were calibrated for $Q = 0.829$. The adjustment steps follow:

1. Use Tables 16.1 and 16.2 to calculate the optimal place bet p^* or Tables 16.3 and 16.4 to calculate the optimal show bet s^* for a track payback of 0.829.
2. To p^* add the adjustment factor

$$(Q - 0.829)(3.16p^* + 0.0351w_0), \tag{16.1}$$

or to s^* add the adjustment factor

$$(Q - 0.829)(3.16s^* + 0.0351w_0). \tag{16.2}$$

These steps result in the correct optimal bet size. For Q larger than 0.829, the adjustment factor is positive; for Q less than 0.829, it is negative.

To illustrate, let's return to the Triple Bend Handicap example. Step 1 gave $s^* = \$128$. Since $w_0 = \$400$ and $Q = 0.85$ in California, step 2 indicates that the correct optimal show bet is

$$128 + (0.85 - 0.829)[(3.16)(128) + (0.0351)(400)] = 128 + 9 = \$137.$$

Adjustments for Coupled Entries

Occasionally, two or more horses are run as a single coupled entry, or simply entry, because (1) an owner or a trainer has two or more horses in the same race, or (2) there are more horses than the tote board can accommodate. The latter case is more commonly called a field. The entry wins, places, or shows if any of the horses wins, places, or shows. If the horses in the entry come first and second, all the place pool goes to the place tickets on the entry. If two of three of the in-the-money horses are from the entry, then two-thirds of the show pool goes to the tickets on the entry (rather than the usual third).* Finally, if all the in-the-money horses are from the entry, then the entire show pool goes to the show tickets on the entry.

Because of the possibility that the entry will collect the whole place pool or a major portion, or even all, of the show pool, the expected value per dollar bet to place or show on the entry is higher than if the entry were just one horse. Equations (4.7) and (4.8) indicated how to adjust the expected-value formulas for coupled entries. Here we describe the steps we took to adjust the optimal betting for coupled entries.

Place betting on horse i

1. Set $q = W_i/W$.
2. Let

$$\tilde{q} = 0.991q + 0.1378q^2 + 3.47 \times 10^{-7}w_0. \tag{16.3}$$

3. Use $\tilde{q}$, w_0, P, P_i in Tables 16.1 and 16.2.

Show betting on horse i

1. Set $q = W_i/W$.
2. Let

$$\tilde{q} = 1.07q + 4.13 \times 10^{-7}w_0 - 0.00663. \tag{16.4}$$

3. Use $\tilde{q}$, w_0, S, S_i in Tables 16.3 and 16.4.

This method does not attempt the difficult task of setting up a new set of tables similar to Tables 16.1 to 16.4, but specifically designed for coupled entries. Rather, it simply increases q to $\tilde{q}$, where $\tilde{q}$ is the single-horse entry probability that leads you to bet the optimal amount when q is a two-horse entry probability.

There is still greater advantage to a three-or-more-horse entry or field. The additional benefits, however, become very small once you move beyond accounting for the entry as two horses. For this reason we suggest the

*In some locales the split is 50-50, as each betting opportunity shares the profit equally.

simplification of considering all coupled entries or fields as two-horse entries.

Also, if the Dr. Z system underestimates the value of a bet on an entry (before we perform the adjustments), then it stands to reason that it overestimates the value of a bet on a single horse running against an entry. While this is true, tests have shown that this overestimation is very small, and that for all practical purposes we may ignore it.

Adjustments for Making More Than One Bet

The optimal-bet equations assume that you are making only one place bet or one show bet in a race. If the expected-value equations indicate that there is more than one Dr. Z system bet in the race, then it is *not* correct to calculate each of the optimal bets using the regression equations and then wager those amounts. If you did, you would often be overbetting—although often, for diversification reasons, you would be underbetting. This should indicate why accounting mathematically for multiple bets is difficult. The most common multiple bet is a Dr. Z system place bet and a Dr. Z system show bet on the same horse. We have carefully analyzed this situation.

If the expected-value formulas from Chapter Four, accounting for any necessary adjustment factors, indicate making a Dr. Z system bet to both place and to show on a horse, then the recommended procedure is as follows:

1. Use Tables 16.1 to 16.4 to determine the suggested place bet p^* and show bet s^*.
2. Make any necessary adjustments on p^* and s^* for $Q \neq 0.829$ or for a coupled entry.
3. Let the ***true*** optimal place bet $\tilde{p}^*$ be

$$\tilde{p}^* = \min\{p^*, 1.59p^* - 0.639s^*\} \tag{16.5}$$

and the true optimal show bet $\tilde{s}^*$ be

$$\tilde{s}^* = 0.907s^* - 0.134p^*. \tag{16.6}$$

4. Wager the amounts $\tilde{p}^*$ and $\tilde{s}^*$.

*Flow Chart of the Betting Rules for a Single Bet to Place or Show**

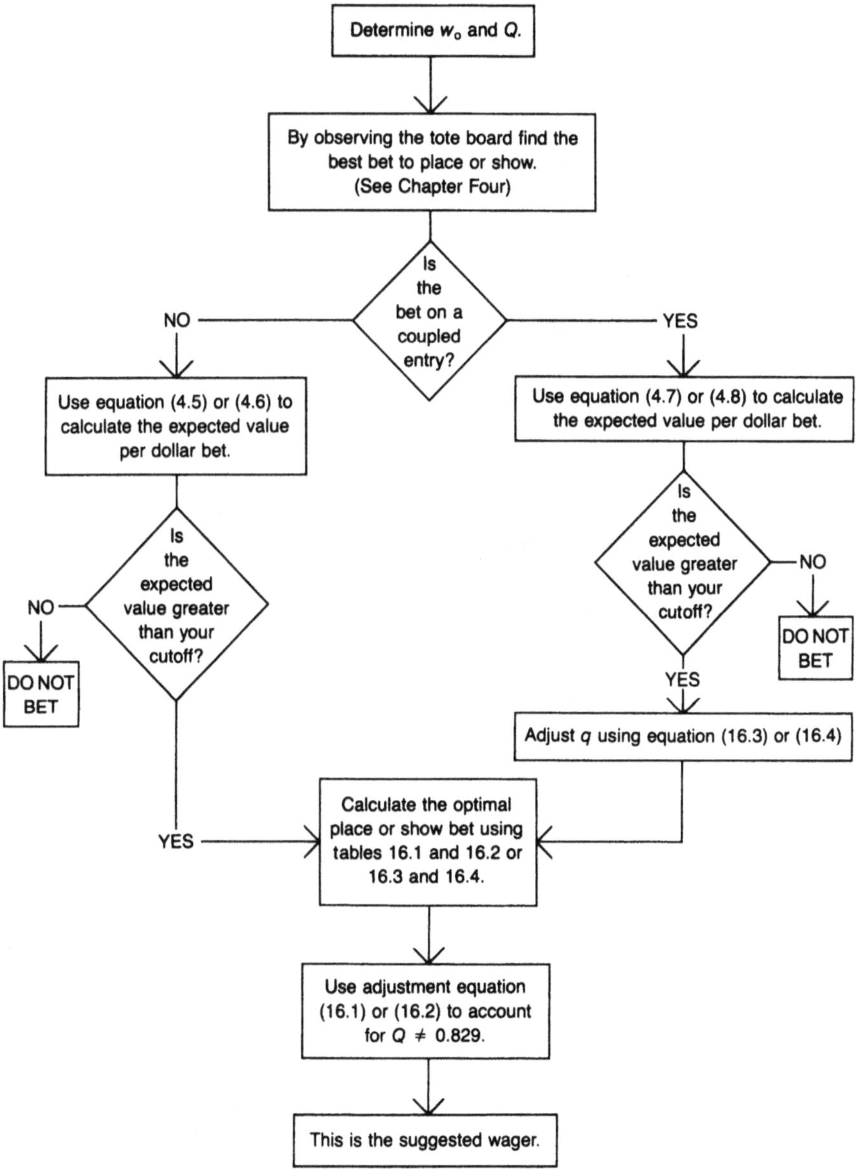

*For place and show bets on the same horse, follow this flow chart for each bet and then adjust the place- and show-betting amounts using equations (16.5) and (16.6).

Warning: The equations in Tables 16.1 and 16.3 are the result of statistical regressions using data with (1) q between 0.1 and 0.7; and (2) EX Place and EX Show (equations [4.3] and [4.4], respectively) between 1.05 and 1.40. Therefore the equations in Tables 16.1 and 16.4 should be used only when these conditions are met. However, we can deal with cases that do not meet these conditions as follows.

1. If q is less than 0.1 we recommend no wagering since the long-shot bias, presented in Table 3.1 and Figure 3.2, is working against you.

If q is greater than 0.7 it is possible to use Tables 16.1 to 16.4 by pretending q is 0.7 and scaling down the other data inputs. The procedure is:

If $q > 0.7$ then let (i) $\tilde{q} = 0.7$

(ii) $\tilde{P}_i = (0.7/q)P_i$

(iii) $\tilde{S}_i = (0.7/q)S_i$

(iv) input $\tilde{q}, \tilde{P}_i, P, \tilde{S}_i$, and S.

2. If EX Place or EX Show is less than 1.10, we recommend no wagering; even with corrections for differing Q it is unlikely that the adjusted expected value would meet the suggested cutoffs.

If EX Place or EX Show is greater than 1.40, another scaling down procedure is suggested to use Tables 16.1 to 16.4:

Let (i) $\tilde{P}_i = qP/1.93$

(ii) $\tilde{S}_i = qS/2.32$

(iii) input $q, \tilde{P}_i, P, \tilde{S}_i$, and S.

An example of this procedure is Viendra in the Matinee Handicap at Hollywood Park discussed in Chapter Six. Both of the scaling down procedures indicate a lower bet than is optimal, but usually it is close to optimal.

One final warning: For horses with a very low probability of winning and a very low expected-value-per-dollar-bet, the betting equations will indicate a negative bet. Obviously in these cases the optimal bet is zero.

Using Fundamental Information to Improve the Dr. Z System

Throughout this book we have emphasized that the win market is efficient: That is, a good estimate of the probability of horse i to win is $q_i = W_i/W$. However we have also mentioned that there are some expert handicappers who have the ability, over the long run, to calculate better win probabilities than the crowd. That is, they can determine their own q_i values. Can you, as such a handicapper, use the Dr. Z system? The answer is yes and the adjustments are very easy:

1. In the expected-value formulas of Chapter Four, use your q_i instead of W_i/W.
2. In the optimal-bet-size equations of this chapter use your q_i instead of the crowd's $q = W_i/W$.

What we are suggesting here is very similar to what we discussed in Chapter Seven. There we looked at the 1982 Belmont Stakes, which provided for other-track betting at many tracks across the United States. While each track had its own q_i estimates, we believed that since the home-track Belmont crowd had access to more information, their q_i estimates were the best. That meant that if we were at one of the other tracks, we would prefer to use the Belmont track win odds over our own track's win odds when calculating expected values and optimal bet sizes. This would be possible if our track presented the betting mutuels at Belmont on the infield screen or over the closed-circuit TVs, and this is something that is sometimes actually done. Handicappers with their own q_i estimates would use them in a similar way.

Recommended Handicapping Books

> The raw material of handicapping is contained in the past-performance pages, official result charts, jockey and trainer standings, workout reports, and columns of news and commentary published in the *Daily Racing Form*. Individual methods of interpreting and evaluating this material vary widely, but the substance of handicapping is far more significant than the procedures devised by its practitioners. No matter what his school of thought may purport to be, and no matter how elaborate the gadgetry, graphs, tabulations and worksheets he may use, the handicapper's effectiveness remains below par until he applies his skills to the full range of available information (*American Racing Manual,* 1983, p. 714.)

Handicapping is still, and perhaps will remain, an art. Statistical and computer methods that combine the myriad factors that make up a race to generate the probability of a given horse's winning have, so far, met with limited success. The difficulty is that there are so many relevant factors, and these factors interact in different ways as circumstances change. The *Amer-*

ican Racing Manual's statement on the fundamentals of handicapping considers the most important basic factors to be class, form, consistency, distance, pace, speed, weights, rider, mud, turf, post position and paddock, and post parade. Each of these basic factors are compositions of a number of subfactors. Trying to put them together is a stimulating challenge. Good advice to help you in this regard can be found in the following:

Tom Ainslie, *Ainslie's Complete Guide to Thoroughbred Racing* (New York: Simon and Schuster, 1968).
Andrew Beyer, *Picking Winners*, (New York: Houghton Mifflin, 1975).
Andrew Beyer, *The Winning Horseplayer* (New York: Houghton Mifflin, 1983).
Steven Davidowitz, *Betting Thoroughbreds: A Professional's Guide for the Horseplayer* (New York: Dutton, 1977).
Bonnie Ledbetter and Tom Ainslie, *The Body Language of Horses* (New York: Morrow, 1980).

Each of these authors is an extremely knowledgeable and successful handicapper with over twenty years of experience. Their books are also written in a very lucid style. They are all currently active as handicappers and have written other books or are currently writing new books.

A useful recent book is

James Quinn, *The Literature of Thoroughbred Handicapping, 1965–1982*. (Las Vegas: Gamblers Book Club Press, 1983).

Quinn provides compact "abstracts" to give you the main ideas of many of the important contributions made to handicapping since 1965.

Finally, a bibliography listing many of the existing handicapping books through 1979 with brief comments on their contents is

Jack Gardner, *Gambling: A Guide to Information Sources* (Gale Research Company, Book Tower, Detroit, Michigan 48226, 1980).

These books are probably available at your local library.

Good luck! Remember that to break even on bets to win, you will need to be about 23.5% better than the average bettor, who establishes probabilities of winning for horse i of W_i/W.

CHAPTER 17

Epilogue

Why Are We Making the Dr. Z System Public?

I am frequently asked why I don't quit my job as a university professor and make more money betting on the horses full time. People are shocked that I give lectures, usually without honorariums, to academics and others on the Dr. Z system and its development. They believe that I should have a whole army of Dr. Z system players betting at major North American racetracks and reap a substantial share of the profits. You may be wondering about this as well, so here's my explanation.

Academics by their very nature are inquiring people. I have more interests and demands on my time that I ever dreamed possible. For me, it's exciting to be involved in research in various areas, such as portfolio theory and management and other areas of finance, optimization under uncertainty—my true academic love, how to make decisions in an uncertain world, energy policy, and my special hobbies of Oriental rugs and the mathematics of gambling. Professors like to share their findings with colleagues all over the world—that's the academic way.

This academic jet-setting life style aside, why are Don and I making the Dr. Z system public? I'm convinced that the benefits of doing so exceed the satisfaction and profits from keeping the Dr. Z system secret. First, we shall still be able to play the Dr. Z system when we wish to join in with all the others. Second, a best-selling book brings a number of attendant benefits to the authors. Besides the royalties, it opens doors to new books, consulting and lecture activities, and other useful contacts. The exposure and attention are fun and rewarding as well. Third, the process of developing the Dr. Z system and writing this book taught us a lot about the subject of horse racing and efficient betting markets. This will certainly be useful to us. Fourth, it is a supreme intellectual challenge to beat the races, and we wanted to present our full evidence to our critics, as well as to the general public. We believe that the evidence is quite convincing. The Dr. Z system actually works. Obviously, more evidence will be forthcoming. Many academics and serious horse players will be skeptical at first. Among other things, our whole approach of exploiting the inefficiencies in betting markets is very likely to be new to many, if not most, people. We hope this book is thorough enough to allay such skepticism. Fifth, there is a great threat of rediscovery. Several articles that we mentioned in Chapter One had ideas that are consistent with our approach. After publishing the paper "Efficiency of the Market for Racetrack Betting" in *Management Science* in November 1981, and after giving numerous talks to academic groups, as well as appearing on radio and TV talk shows, we found that our ideas are getting around. If we had not written this book, someone else probably would have. We felt it should be us.

Will the Market Become Efficient: How Much Can Be Bet by All Dr. Z System Bettors?

Naturally, as more people learn about and utilize the Dr. Z system, the place- and show-betting markets will tend to become more efficient. We would like to know the answers to two basic questions: How many people can play the Dr. Z system and still allow it to provide the kind of profits we have obtained in this book? and How many people need to be playing before their bets make the place- and show-betting markets so efficient that the profit margins of all Dr. Z systems players will shrink to virtually zero? We need also to ask how likely is the latter situation to occur, how can you recognize it, and what should you do about it?

Let's look first at the initial question and try to assess how many people can play the Dr. Z system and have it still provide the 10%–20% return on investment we have described. One way to analyze this is to determine how much additional money can be bet on a particular horse to place or show before the expected value per dollar bet reaches the suggested cutoffs for good betting opportunities. Figures 17.1, 17.2, and 17.3 give you the information to calculate this amount for place bets for cutoffs of 1.10, 1.14, and 1.18, respectively. Similarly, Figures 17.4, 17.5, and 17.6 provide this same information for show bets. Recall that 1.10 was suggested when the very highest quality horses and large pools were available at events such as the

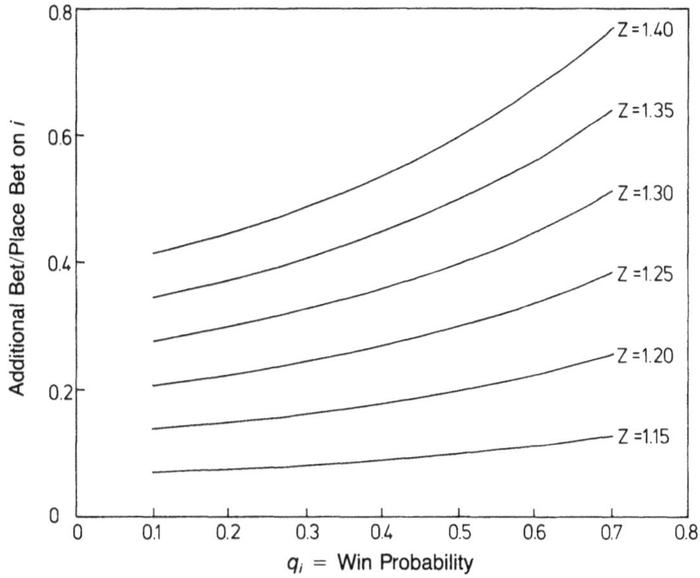

Figure 17.1 How much can be bet, B, by Dr. Z system bettors relative to the crowd's place bet P_i on horse i to lower the expected value to place on i from Z to 1.10 when the track take is 17.1%

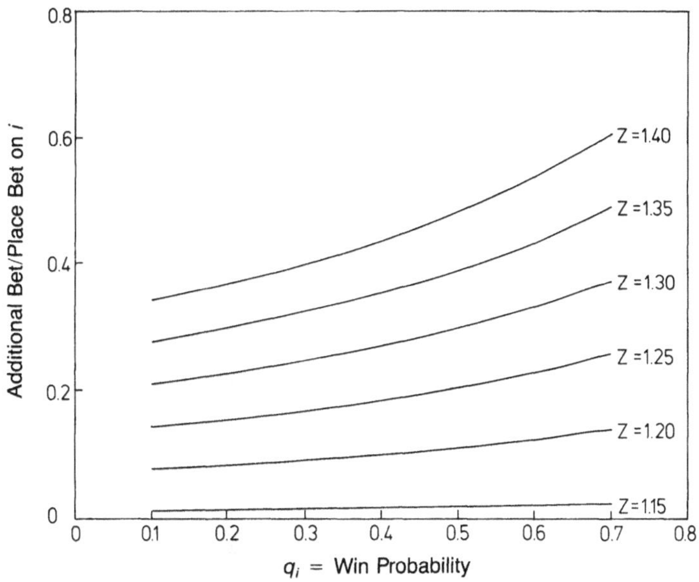

Figure 17.2 How much can be bet, B, by Dr. Z system bettors relative to the crowd's place bet P_i on horse i to lower the expected value to place on i from Z to 1.14 when the track take is 17.1%

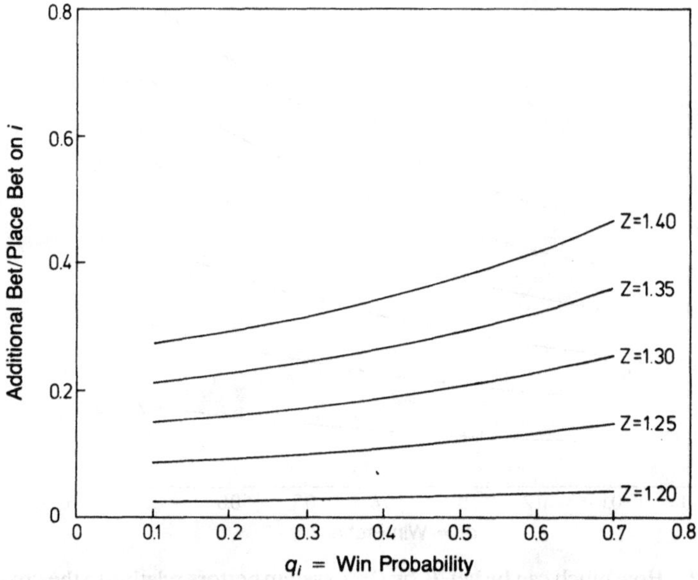

Figure 17.3 **How much can be bet, *B*, by Dr. Z system bettors relative to the crowd's place bet P_i on horse *i* to lower the expected value to place on *i* from *Z* to 1.18 when the track take is 17.1%**

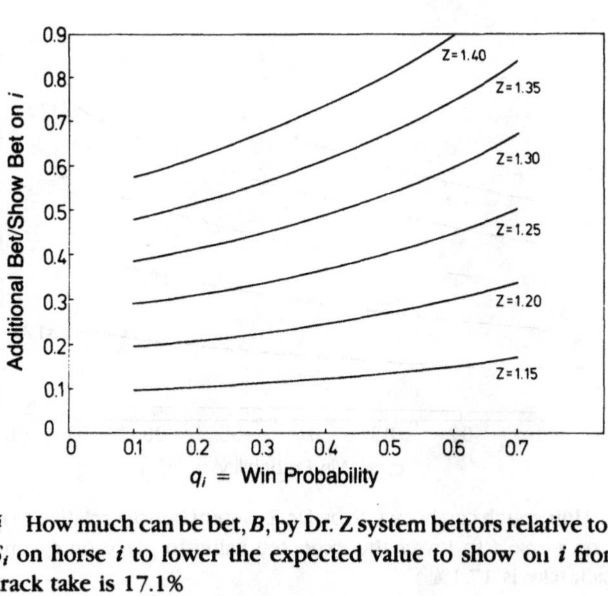

Figure 17.4 **How much can be bet, *B*, by Dr. Z system bettors relative to the crowd's show bet S_i on horse *i* to lower the expected value to show on *i* from *Z* to 1.10 when the track take is 17.1%**

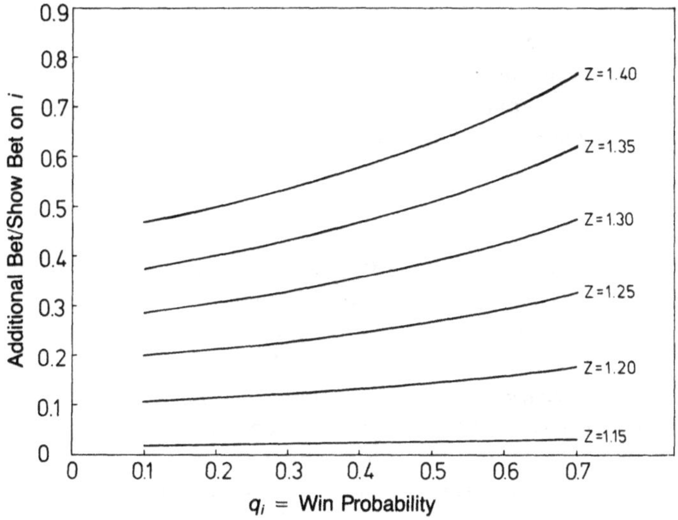

Figure 17.5 How much can be bet, B, by Dr. Z system bettors relative to the crowd's show bet S_i on horse i to lower the expected value to show on i from Z to 1.14 when the track take is 17.1%

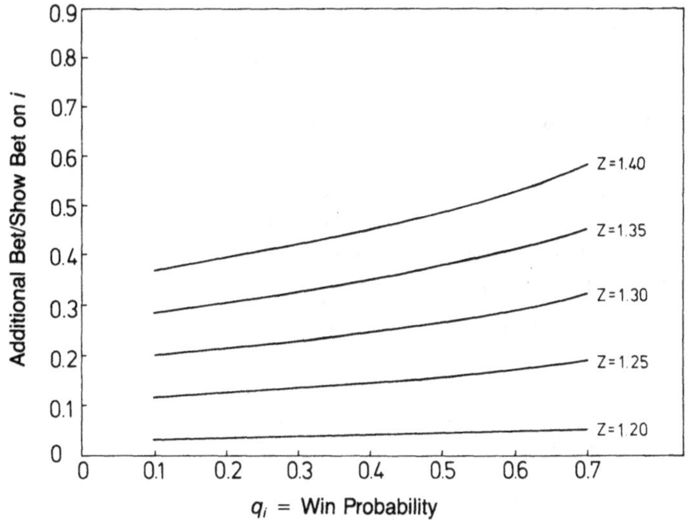

Figure 17.6 How much can be bet, B, by Dr. Z system bettors relative to the crowd's show bet S_i on horse i to lower the expected value to show on i from Z to 1.18 when the track take is 17.1%

Kentucky Derby Day, 1.14 for top-quality tracks on ordinary days, and 1.18 at other tracks. These figures are based on a track take of 17.1%. To use these figures, determine the present expected value per dollar bet using equations (4.5) for place bets and (4.6) for show bets. Then, using the probability of winning for the horse in question, read off the additional fraction of the current place or show pool that can be bet on the vertical axis.

Table 17.1 provides guidance concerning our two basic questions and addresses an additional point. In this table we made the following experiment: For each potential Dr. Z system bettor, we posited that he or she computes his optimal bet about one minute to post time. Then, using the final tote board values, we can compute how many Dr. Z system bettors there can be before the expected value per dollar bet drops to the suggested cutoff, or to 1.06, or to 1.02. At an expected value of 1.06, we still should expect to make a rate of return on our bets of about 5% based on the data in Table 5.1. Finally at 1.02, we would expect simply to break even. This experiment is close to what might happen in practice, except for the fact that we or any other Dr. Z bettors who now bet on these races would not be counted, so to be fair one might add these bettors to those in Table 17.1. Also, Dr. Z system bettors following the Kelly criterion make hefty bets, so if many bettors are following a fractional-Kelly criterion, even more people can bet.

The number of Dr. Z bettors that you can have depends upon four factors: the size of the place- or show-betting pools, the expected value per dollar bet, the probability that the horse wins the race, and the betting wealth of the Dr. Z system players. We have used examples with expected-value cutoffs of 1.10 and 1.14. They have a variety of expected values per dollar bet to place or show, ranging from a low of 1.14 to a high of 1.47. They also have various probabilities of winning that vary from 0.127 to 0.406. The total amount that can be bet in the three categories, based on likely average rates of return of 10%–20%, 5%, and 0%, ranges from \$1,411 to \$19,323, \$1,923 to \$41,175, and \$2,264 to \$68,409, respectively. At the 10%–20% level, the number of Dr. Z system bettors ranges from fifty-three to 1,757 bettors with \$200 fortunes all the way to seven to 201 bettors with \$2,000 fortunes. At the 5% level, the ranges are eighty-seven to 3,743 bettors with \$200 and thirteen to 429 bettors with \$2,000. Finally, we reach the 0% level, where there are between 103 to 6,219 bettors with \$200 and eighteen to 713 bettors with \$2,000.

Advice and Conclusions

(1) When the bet is good and the track mutuels are large, it will usually take quite a few Dr. Z system bettors to make the market efficient. (2) A

few very big bettors can certainly do the others in, so you must keep an eye out for them. (3) If you think such bettors are at your track, simply watch the tote board and don't bet or bet modestly. If the bet has an expected value of 1.20 with two minutes to post time, and it's 1.00 at post time, your worst fears have been realized. (4) Don't despair. Take a few weeks' holiday, then try it again; the big bettors may have gone away. (5) Remember that at tracks with small mutuel pools the effect of large bettors will be even greater. At such tracks, however, there are proportionally fewer people betting, and any Dr. Z system bettor bets less as well, since his or her bets will influence the odds. (6) Our experience with inefficiences in other areas, such as blackjack and options markets, shows that it takes quite a while before the inefficiency is wiped out; the same will probably be true here. (7) People are greedy and like to brag. That will not change! Sooner or later, they will go back to their old bets and you will be able to apply the Dr. Z system successfully again, even if the market does become efficient temporarily.

TABLE 17.1 *Amount that can be bet by and number of Dr. Z system bettors to drop the expected value per dollar bet to the Dr. Z system bet cutoff, to a 5%-return-on-investment level, or the break-even point*

Name of Horse	Type of Bet	Expected Value per Dollar Bet at Post Time	Win Pool at Post Time ($)	Win Bet on *i* at Post Time ($)	Probability of Winning	Show or Place Pool at Post Time ($)
C'est Moi Cheri Hollywood Park Chapter Five, pp. 93–95	Show	1.29	335,698	136,125	0.406	56,841
Sunny's Halo Churchill Downs Chapter Twelve, pp. 239–51	Show	1.14	3,143,669	745,524	0.237	1,099,990
John Henry Santa Anita Chapter Eight, pp. 152–58	Place	1.22	425,976	149,879	0.352	122,847
	Show	1.34	425,976	149,879	0.352	79,645
Viendra Hollywood Park Chapter Six, pp. 133–37	Show	1.47	129,233	16,353	0.127	27,488

TABLE 17.1 *(continued)*

Show or Place Bet on i at Post Time ($)	Recommended Expected-Value Cutoff	Total Amount That Can Be Bet by All Dr. Z System Bettors before the Expected Value per Dollar Bet Reaches the Cutoff ($)	Optimal Dr. Z System Bets with Betting Wealths (using data up to 1 minute to post time) of $200	$500	$1,000	$2,000
12,284	1.14	4,814	91	227	383	694
179,758	1.10	19,323	11	31	52	96
27,894	1.14	3,909	14	33	70	143
14,007	1.14	6,916	68	173	311	587
1,149	1.14	1,411	22	56	72	106

Number of Dr. Z System Bettors Who Can Make the Usual Gains with Betting Wealths of $200	$500	$1,000	$2,000	Total Amount That Can Be Bet by All Dr. Z System Bettors before the Expected Value per Dollar Bet Becomes 1.06 ($)	Number of Dr. Z System Bettors Needed to Drop the Expected Value per Dollar Bet to 1.06, so All Bettors Will Still Have Modest Profits with Betting Wealths of $200	$500	$1,000	$2,000
53	21	13	7	9,229	101	40	24	13
1,757	623	372	201	41,175	3,743	1,328	792	429
279	118	56	27	8,925	637	270	127	62
102	40	22	12	12,029	177	70	39	20
64	25	20	13	1,923	87	34	27	18

Total Amount That Can Be Bet by All Dr. Z System Bettors before the Expected Value per Dollar Bet Becomes 1.02 ($)	Number of Dr. Z System Bettors Needed to Drop the Expected Value per Dollar Bet to 1.02, so All Bettors Will Simply Break Even with Betting Wealths of $200	$500	$1,000	$2,000
12,417	136	54	32	18
68,409	6,219	2,207	1,316	713
12,077	862	366	173	84
15,654	230	90	50	27
2,264	103	40	31	21

Using the Dr. Z System for Harness Racing

Although this book has been concerned with thoroughbred racing, the Dr. Z system can be used in the same way at harness races. As we saw in Figure 3.3 and Table 3.3, the win market at harness tracks is efficient. It shows the usual favorite–long-shot bias. You can make profitable place and show bets.

To test the Dr. Z system, I went to Cloverdale Raceway near Vancouver on Saturday, February 12, 1983. The program contains the past performances, driver standings, post-position statistics, percentage of winning favorites, etc. The track take for straight bets is 16.1%; it's 3% higher, or 19.1%, for the features. The driver standings report the in-the-money finishes and win-place percentages. But you need to compute the in-the-money percentages, as I have done below. Harness races generally have eight or fewer horses and standouts dominate, so top jockeys have very high in-the-money percentages. A guide for reading the racing information and a list of the major harness racing tracks in North America appear as well.

Driver standings

Up to and Including Saturday, February 5/83
Minimum 1 Drive per Day (75 drives to qualify)

	Starts	First	Second	Third	Win and Place (%)	In the Money (%)
1. Keith Linton	281	83	45	43	45.6	60.9
2. Joe Hudon	339	90	59	50	44.0	58.7
3. John Glen	95	22	20	8	44.2	52.6
4. Mike Evans	112	24	21	16	40.2	54.5
5. Bill Davis	171	38	26	23	37.4	50.9
6. Dave Jungquist	171	25	21	37	26.9	48.5
7. Mike Stymest	86	16	20	18	41.9	62.8
8. Paul Megens	236	34	37	26	30.1	41.1
9. Sten Ericsson	202	30	27	26	28.2	41.1
10. Jim Wiggins	243	28	42	27	28.8	39.9
11. Bill Babineau	81	10	7	7	21.0	29.6
12. Bob Cameron	85	7	12	19	22.4	44.7
13. Keith Quinlan	300	29	48	44	25.7	40.3
14. Brent Beelby	206	23	25	32	23.3	38.8
15. Howard Portelance	176	22	14	31	20.5	38.1
16. Denis Linford	174	19	22	24	23.6	37.4
17. Ed Stewart	86	8	13	12	24.4	38.4
18. Phil Coleman	138	11	22	22	23.9	39.9
19. Clark Beelby	99	13	11	7	24.2	31.3
20. Al Bowman	82	9	11	8	24.4	34.1
21. Leonard Hill	113	12	14	13	23.0	34.5

WINNING POST POSITIONS

Up to and including Sat., Feb. 5, 1983 – 75 Race Days, 751 Races

	1	2	3	4	5	6	7	8
No. of Starts	751	751	751	751	748	723	635	630
No. of Wins	134	108	97	145	84	60	43	82
	dead heat	dead heat		dead heat		dead heat		

% OF WINNING FAVORITES

Up to and including Sat., Feb. 5, 1983 – 75 Race Days, 751 Races

Order of finish of favorite	1	2	3	4	5	6	7	8
No. of Wins of Favorite	286	140	108	62	48	49	28	30
% of Wins of Favorite	38%	19%	14%	8%	6%	6%	4%	5%

71% in the money

OF EVERY $1 WAGERED AT CLOVERDALE RACEWAY . . .

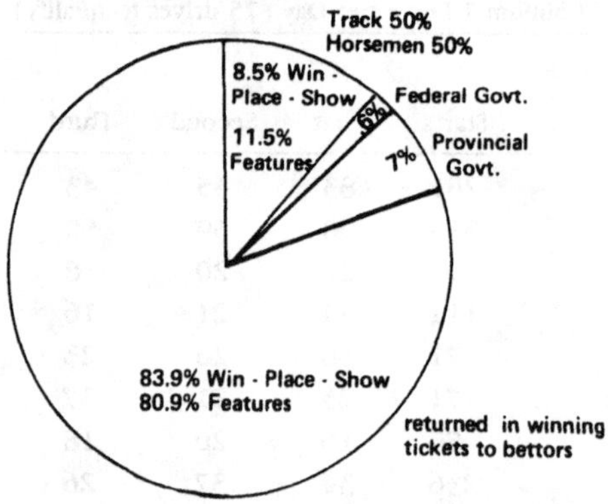

HORSEMEN'S SHARE:
Distributed in the form of purses.

TRACK'S SHARE:
Used for operating costs and capital improvements.

FEDERAL GOVERNMENT SHARE:
Used to defray supervision costs.

PROVINCIAL GOVERNMENT SHARE:
3.5% General Revenue
3.5% horse racing improvement fund, as follows:
1.0% B.C. Bred Purse Suppl.
.9% Purse & Stake Suppl.
.6% Sire Stakes
.5% Broodmare program
.4% Filly & Mare program
.1% Reserve Fund

*Note: These supplements are NOT included in the advertised purse in the program.

HOW TO READ THE RACING INFORMATION

1		2	3	4		
BARON NUFF		B. g.	1976,	Goodnuff — Baroness Brenna — Baron Hanover		
	5	Hudon Stables, Surrey, B. C.			1983 1 0 0 1 $ 600	8
Joe Hudon, A, 165, blue, orange	11 / 10	Tr. J. Hudon	Time 1:59^{3}M,5, (6)	Earn. to 1983 $87,300 (7)	1982 2:02^{3}H 4 2 1 0 $ 6,150	9

1. **BARON NUFF. This is the name of the horse.**
2. **B. g. This indicates the color and sex of the horse. Here the "B" is an abbreviation for Bay and the "g" means he is a gelding.**
3. **1976. This is the year the horse was foaled. He is now a seven year old.**
4. **Goodnuff — Baroness Brenna — Baron Hanover. In order these are the names of the horse's father (sire), mother (dam), and the sire of the dam.**
5. **Hudon Stables, Surrey, B. C. This is the owner and his address.**
6. **Time 1:59.4F,4. This is the best winning time ever for Baron Nuff. His mark of 1:59.4 was taken on a five-eights track as a four-year old.**
7. **Earnings to 1983 $87,300. This is a record of the total amount he has won in purses to December 31, 1982.**
8. **1983 1 0 0 1 $600 . This is his performance recap from this year (to Jan.20). He started once and finished third for total earnings of $600.**
9. **1982 2:02.3H 4 2 1 0 $6,150. This is his performance recap from last year. His best winning time was 2:02.3 and he started 4 times, had 2 wins and 1 second for earnings of $6,150.**
10. **Tr. J. Hudon. J. Hudon trains the horse.**
11. **JOE HUDON, A, 165, BLUE, ORANGE. This the name of the driver, his license classification, weight and the color of his silks.**

PAST PERFORMANCE LINE

Date of Race — Track — Race Number — Track Condition — Condition — Purse — Distance — Leader's time at ¼ — Leader's time at ½ — Leader's time at ¾ — Winner's time — Post Position — Pos. & lengths at ¼ — Pos. & lengths at ½ — Pos. & lengths at ¾ — Pos. & lengths at Stretch — Pos. & lengths at Finish — Horse's actual time — Dollar Odds — Driver — Winner — Second Horse — Third Horse — Temperature — No. of starters

Mr21^{1}Clv^6 ft Inv 6000 m:29^2 1:01 1:31^3 2:00^4 3 1$^1\frac{1}{2}$ 1$^1\frac{1}{2}$ 1^1 1^2 1$^3\frac{1}{2}$ 2:00^4 *.45 J.Hudon BaronNuff SengaRoly Jodana 15^4

Track ratings are determined from individual times made by horses at one track compared with times made by the same horses at other tracks during comparable seasons of the year, over tracks rated "fast", without breaks or parkouts and at the standard mile distance.

AC (5/8)	Atlantic City, N.J.	2:03.2
AP (1)	Arlington Park	2:04.1
Aur (1/2)	Aurora Downs, Ill.	2:07
Bal (1/2)	Balmoral Park, Ill.	2:03.1
BaR (1/2)	Barrie Raceway, Ont.	2:05.3
Bat (1/2)	Batavia Downs, N.Y.	2:05.1
BB (5/8)	Blue Bonnets, Que.	2:03.1
BgR (1/2)	Bangor Raceway, Main	2:07.1
Blm (1/2)	Bloomsburg, Pa.	2:06.1
Blv (1/2)	Belleville, Que.	2:06.4
BM (1)	Bay Meadows, Calif.	2:04
BR (1/2)	Buffalo Raceway, N.Y.	2:05.1
Brd (5/8)	Brandywine Raceway, Del	2:02.3
Cen (1/2)	Centennial Park, Colo	2:05.2
Cls (1/2)	Carlisle, Pa.	2:05
Cka (3/4)	Cahokia Downs, Ill	2:04.1
Cltn (1/2)	Clinton Raceway, Ont	2:06
Col (1/2)	Columbus, Ohio	2:05.1
Clv (1/2)	Cloverdale Raceway, B.C.	2:06.2
Cum (1/2)	Cumberland Raceway	2:06.1
Conn (1/2)	Connaught Park, Que.	2:05.3
DD (5/8)	Dover Downs, Del	2:04.2
Del (1/2)	Delaware, Ohio	2:04.3
Dres (1/2)	Dresden Raceway, Ont	2:05.3
DuQ (1)	Du Quoin, Ill	2:01.1
Elm (1/2)	Elmira Raceway, Ont	2:05.4
FD (5/8)	Frontenac Downs, Ont	2:04.2
Fhld (1)	Freehold Raceway, N.J.	2:04
FlmD (1/2)	Flamboro Downs, Ont	2:04.4
FP (1)	Fairmount Park, Ill	2:03.3
GCy (5/8)	Garden City, Ont.	2:03.3
GG (1)	Golden Gate Fields, Calif	2:03.1
Gor (1/2)	Gorham Raceway	2:06.1
Gos (1/2)	Goshen, N.Y.	2:05
GMP (1)	Green Mountain Park	2:04.3
GrR (5/8)	Greenwood Raceway, Ont	2:04.2
Har (1/2)	Harrington Raceway, Del.	2:05.2
Haw (1)	Hawthorne Park, Ill	2:03.4
Haz (5/8)	Hazel Park, Mich.	2:04
Hin (1/2)	Hinsdale Raceway, N.H.	2:06.1
Hnvr (1/2)	Hanover Raceway, Ont	2:05.5
HP (1)	Hollywood Park, Calif	2:01.4
Ind (1)	Indianapolis, Ind.	2:01.4
Jac (1/2)	Jackson Raceway, Mich	2:05
KD (5/8)	Kawartha Downs, Ont	2:04.3
LA (5/8)	Los Alamitos, Calif	2:03.4
Lat (1/2)	Latonia, Kentucky	2:03
Lau (5/8)	Laurel Raceway, Maryland	2:03.1
LB (5/8)	Liberty Bell, Penn	2:02.3
Lea (1/2)	Leamington Raceway, Ont	2:05.1
Leb (1/2)	Lebanon Raceway, Ohio	2:06.2
Lew (1/2)	Lewiston Raceway, Me	2:05.2
Lex (1)	Lexington Trots, Kentucky	2:01.2
Lon (1/2)	Western Fair Raceway, Ont	2:05.1
LouD (1/2)	Louisville Downs, Kentucky	2:05.2
May (1/2)	Maywood Park, Ill.	2:04
Mea (5/8)	The Meadows, Penn	2:03
Mid (1/2)	Midwest Raceway, Kty	2:05.3
Mlds (1)	Meadowlands, N.J.	2:01.2
Moh (5/8)	Mohawk Raceway, Ont	2:04
MqD (5/8)	Marquis Downs, Sask	2:04.2
MR (1/2)	Monticello Raceway, N.Y.	2:03.1
NEn (5/8)	New England, Mass.	2:03
Nfld (1/2)	Northfield Park, Ohio	2:04.3
Nor (1/2)	Northville Downs, Mich.	2:05
NP (5/8)	Northlands Park, Alta.	2:04.2
OcD (1/2)	Ocean Downs, Md	2:04.3
Orn (1/2)	Orangeville Raceway, Ont	2:06.2
OwnS (1/2)	Owen Sound, Ont.	2:06.4
PcD (5/8)	Pocono Downs, Penn	2:03.1
PPk (5/8)	Pompano Park, Fla	2:03.2
PVR (5/8)	Pre Vert Raceway, Que	2:06
QcD (5/8)	Quad City Downs, Ill.	2:04
Que (1/2)	Quebec City, Que	2:04.4
RC (5/8)	Rideau Carlton, Ont	2:04
Reg (1/2)	Exhibition Track, Sask	2:05.3
Ric (1/2)	Richelieu Park, Que	2:04
Roc (1/2)	Rockingham Park, N.H.	2:04.4
RoR (1/2)	Rosecroft Raceway, Md	2:03.3
RP (5/8)	Raceway Park, Ohio	2:03.3
RR (1/2)	Roosevelt Raceway, N.Y.	2:03.2
Sac (1)	Cal Expo, Sacramento, Calif	2:03.2
Sca (1/2)	Scarborough Downs, Me	2:05.3
San (5/8)	Sandown Raceway, B.C.	NR
ScD (5/8)	Scioto Downs, Ohio	2:02.2
Sem (1)	Seminole Downs, Fla	2:03.2
Spk (5/8)	Sportsman's Park, Ill	2:02.4
Spr (1)	Springfield, Ill	2:01
Stga (1/2)	Saratoga Raceway, N.Y.	2:03.2
StP (5/8)	Stampede Park, Alta.	2:04.2
Sud (1/2)	Sudbury Downs, Ont	2:05.3
TrR (1/2)	Hippodrome Trois-Riv., Que	2:05
VD (3/4)	Vernon Downs, N.Y.	2:01.4
Was (1)	Washington Park, Wash	2:03.1
Wdsk (1/2)	Woodstock Raceway, Ont.	2:06.1
Wol (1)	Wolverine Raceway	2:01.2
WR (5/8)	Windsor Raceway, Ont	2:04
YR (1/2)	Yonkers Raceway, N.Y.	2:03.3

3rd race

BLACK SADDLE CLOTH

1 MILE PACE
VIP Tavern Feature

EXACTOR

SUPER 6

EXACTOR

PURSE $2300 — Claiming Handicap — Claiming Prices $3500 to $4000 plus allowances.

HANDICAP SELECTIONS: 5 — 1 — 6

ASK FOR HORSE BY THIS NUMBER

```
Date Tk. Cond. Class   Purse Dis. Leaders Times            Post 1/4 1/2 3/4 Str. Fin. Time Odds Driver   1st/2nd/3rd   Temp./Starters

$3500  1  7-2
DECK HAND                                   B. g. 1972, Shadow Wave — Rhonda Byrd — Poplar Byrd
                                            S. Petrachuk, Surrey, B. C.                          1983             6  0  1  1 $    950
Steve Petrachuk, A, 160, blue, white        Tr. S. Petrachuk   Time 2:01M,4, Earn. to 1983 $81,417   1982  2:03^3F 51  6  9 10 $10,068
Fb10^3Clv^6 sy 3500    2000 m:32^3 1:05^3 1:38^1 2:10^1 7  8^10  7^6    7^5¼   6^5½   6^5    2:11^1  34.00 S.P'chuk  Moore.Dick Marg.Misty PilotFrost 8^8
Fb2^3 Clv^7 ft 3500    2000 m:31^1 1:02^4 1:34^3 2:07   3  4^4   6^4¼   °5^3¼  4^5    4^3¼   2:07^2  15.65 S.P'chuk  NorLeaSue JimTheBear Rad.General 6^7
Ja26^3Clv^2 gd 3500hp  2200 m:31^1 1:03^3 1:36^3 2:08^3 2  5^4   5^2½   °5^3   7^7    7^5    2:09^3  11.35 S.P'chuk  Beth.Blazet Rad.General PilotFros. 9^8
Ja19^3Clv^5 gd 3500    2000 m:32^1 1:06^3 1:39^1 2:10^4 8  6^7   6^5    °6^4   6^5½   3^2    2:11     6.50 S.P'chuk  BraveBullet GypsyBlue DeckHand 9^8
Ja13^3Clv^6 ft 3000    1800 m:31^1 1:02^1 1:34^4 2:05^4 5  7^11  6^6    °5^2½  2^4    2^3¼   2:06^2  13.25 S.P'chuk  GypsyBlue DeckHand Wint.PrinceA 6^8
Ja7^3 Clv^2 sy 3500hp  2000 m:31^2 1:04^1 1:37 2:08^4   5  7^6   °6^4   °7^4   3^3    5^7    2:10^1  19.65 S.P'chuk  DustyBreeze PanawaBay Sen.Lytton 13^8

$3500  2  6-1
GYPSY BLUE                                  Ch. g. 1970, Thor Hanover — Koala Red — Flight Commander
                                            J. Palmer, Vancouver, B. C.                          1983  2:05^4H  6  2  2  1 $ 3,055
Glen White, C, 150, red, white              Tr. D. Linford     Time 2:04F,10, Earn. to 1983 $81,552  1982  2:04^4F 45  6 10  7 $10,988
Fb5^3 Clv^4 ft c3000   1800 m:32^3 1:04^2 1:36^1 2:07^2 4  4^4½  °3^2   °°3^1¼ 4^4    5^6    2:08^3   3.10 K.Quinlan Moore.Dick CooksChas. JimTheBear 7^7
Ja29^3Clv^7 ft 3000    1800 m:30^2 1:02^3 1:34^3 2:06^2 4  6^5½  5^4    °2^1½  1^nk   1½     2:06^2   2.20 K.Quinlan GypsyBlue MrKeith AndysDean 10^8
Ja24^3Clv^9 gd 3500hp  2000 m:31^2 1:04 1:36^1 2:09     7  8^11  8^6½   °8^5   6^3½   3^2    2:09^1   9.25 P.Megens  BethanyOdd Shad.D'less GypsyBlue 10^8
Ja19^3Clv^5 gd 3500    2000 m:32^1 1:06^3 1:39^1 2:10^4 2  5^6   4^3½   °4^2   3^2½   2½     2:10^4   2.40 P.Megens  BraveBullet GypsyBlue DeckHand 9^8
Ja13^3Clv^6 ft 3000    1800 m:31^1 1:02^1 1:34^4 2:05^4 3  5^4   5^4½   °2½    1^4    1^3¼   2:05^4   3.55 K.Quinlan GypsyBlue DeckHand Wint.PrinceA 6^8
Ja6^3 Clv^2 sy 3000    1700 m:30^3 1:01^4 1:33^4 2:07   2  3^2   °3^1   °1^hd  1^1    2^ns   2:07^1  *2.60 K.Quinlan Hol.Hero GypsyBlue SimplyGrand 7^8

$3500  3  10-1
SHADOWS DAUNTLESS                           Br. g. 1978, Invincible Shadow — Lucinda Goose — Brown Prince
                                            A.Gatey,M.Lebaron,W.Terry, Prince George,B.C.Alta.   1983  2:08^1H  6  1  2  1 $ 1,889
Dave Smith, A, 180, red, white              Tr. N. Clarkson *  Time 2:03F,4, Earn. to 1983 $17,163   1982  2:03F   53  3  8  7 $ 9,935
Fb9^3 Clv^6 sy 4500    2400 m:33 1:05^3 1:37^1 2:09     7  6^7½  5^5    5^5    x7^8½  7^17   2:12^2  16.80 D.Smith   RomanJoe T'tahiRidge Ch.Dominion 10^8
Fb3^3 Clv^6 ft 4000    2200 m:30^3 1:03^4 1:36^1 2:08^4 6  8^10½ °5^3¼  °3^1½  3^2¼   3^1    2:08^4  16.35 D.Smith   Yarver RomanJoe ShadowsDauntless 4^8
Ja28^3Clv^9 ft 4500hp  2600 m:30^4 1:02^1 1:34 2:07^1   5  6^8½  6^7    °5^3   6^4¼   6^4½   2:07^4  15.60 D.Smith   Mich.Hall Chel.Domin. Blk.StormA 8^7
Ja24^3Clv^9 gd c3000hp 2000 m:31^2 1:04 1:36^1 2:09     3  °2^1½ °2^1   °2^nk  2^hd   2^1    2:09    12.65 C.Sibiga  BethanyOdd Shad.D'less GypsyBlue 10^8
Ja20^3Clv^3 ft c2500   1500 m:32 1:04^4 1:36^3 2:08^1   4  1^1½  1^1½   1½     1^2    1^1½   2:08^1  *1.55 D.Smith   Shad.D'less SurdaleAlex Ch.Poncho 9^8
Ja14^3Clv^1 ft 2500    1500 m:30^3 1:02^1 1:35^3 2:08^1 6  5^6½  °5^8   °3^1½  2^2½   2^2    2:08^3   9.25 D.Smith   Damuraz Shad.Dauntless KingKoil 4^8

$3500  4  10-1
FERR CHER                                   Br. m. 1976, Ferric Hanover — Lassie Tar — Cole Tar
                                            D. Weinert, B. White, Vancouver, Surrey, B. C.       1983  2:07^4H  6  1  2  0 $ 1,855
Bruce White, B, 170, red, white             Tr. B. White       Time 2:05H,4, Earn. to 1983 $19,376   1982  2:06^1H 47  1  9  8 $ 6,432
Fb5^3 Clv^4 ft 3000    1800 m:32^3 1:04^2 1:36^1 2:07^2 7  7^8   6^6    °6^4½  5^4½   4^5    2:08^1  18.35 B.White   Moore.Dick CooksChas. JimTheBear 7^7
Fb3^3 Clv^10ft 3000    1800 m:30^3 1:02 1:34^2 2:07^1   5  6^6½  °7^4½  °2^1   2^1½   2^nk   2:07^1  14.05 G.White   AndysDean FerrCher PanawaBay 4^8
Ja29^3Clv^7 ft 3000    1800 m:30^2 1:02^3 1:34^3 2:06^2 3  5^4   °4^3   7^4½   6^7½   6^7    2:07^4   6.25 B.White   GypsyBlue MrKeith AndysDean 10^8
Ja21^3Clv^4 ft 2500    1500 m:31 1:03^2 1:35^4 2:07^4   2  3^2½  3^1½   °1½    1^3    1^3    2:07^4  *1.45 B.White   FerrCher Assin.Brave HustlingHall 5^8
Ja10^3Clv^1 gd c2500   1500 m:33 1:06^1 1:37^2 2:09^1   4  5^6   °6^5   °4^3½  4^3    2^1    2:09^2   3.25 S.P'chuk  GunsmokeN FerrCher ReyOGrattan 12^8
Ja3^3 Clv^9 sy 3000    1700 m:31^4 1:04^3 1:37^1 2:09^4 2  3^2½  4^3½   6^4    5^4    4^3½   2:10^2  14.40 S.P'chuk  MicroH'over BudsChamp Fr.Memory 10^8
```

$3500 **5** **3-1**

CEFFYL DU

Blk. g. 1971, Toreador Hanover — Black Maggie — Johnny Globe
B. Ashcroft, Surrey, B. C. 1983 2:07^2H 4 1 0 3 $ 1,572
Mike Evans,A,170,white,brown,orange Tr. J. Richards Time 2:01M,10, Earn. to 1983 $35,802 1982 2:$05^2$F 42 3 5 2 $ 5,715
Fb5^3 Clv^3 ft c3000 1800 m:31 1:$03^2$1:$36^2$2:09^1 7 $^o4^{3\frac{1}{2}}$ $4^{3\frac{1}{2}}$ $^o3^2$ 3^2 3^2 2:09^3 3.30 P.Coleman CountForce BraveBullet CeffylDu 7^8
Ja27^3Clv^6 gd c3000 1800 m:$31^7$1:$02^4$1:$34^4$2:07^1 3 $6^{8\frac{1}{2}}$ $^o5^7$ $^o5^3$ $5^{3\frac{1}{2}}$ $3^{3\frac{1}{4}}$ 2:07^4 *.95 M.Evans W.PrinceA PanawaBay CeffylDu 9^8
Ja10^3Clv^6 gd 3000 1800 m:$31^4$1:$04^2$1:$35^2$2:07^2 8 $3^{2\frac{1}{2}}$ $^o2_{\frac{1}{2}}$ 1^2 1^3 1^3 2:07^2 *1.05 M.Evans CeffylDu CavalierN JimTheBear 12^8
Ja6^3 Clv^6 sy 4000 2000 m:$31^3$1:$04^1$1:$36^1$2:08 5 $6^{6\frac{1}{2}}$ $^o5^{4\frac{1}{2}}$ $^o6^3$ $6^{4\frac{1}{4}}$ 3^1 2:08^1 2.45 M.Evans DandyCola SatinSatan CeffylDu 7^8
Dc31^2Clv^6 ft 4000hp 2000 m:$30^3$1:$02^4$1:$35^1$2:07^4 7 $^o6^{4\frac{1}{4}}$ $^o4^{2\frac{1}{4}}$ $^o3^2$ $3^{1\frac{1}{4}}$ $2_{\frac{1}{2}}$ 2:07^4 17.45 M.Evans Kings.Hanover CeffylDu Dus.Breeze 1^8
Dc22^2Clv^1 gd 4000 2000 m:$31^2$1:03 1:$34^2$2:06^2 8 $3^{2\frac{1}{2}}$ $^o3^2$ $^o3^2$ $3^{2\frac{1}{4}}$ 1^1 2:06^2 3.45 M.Evans CeffylDu Kings.Hanover Ethnic 6^7

$4000 **6** **9-2**

HUGGY

Blk. m. 1976, Brother Christie — Richalon Scott — Dr. Scott Hal Volo
G. Phair and C. Salamanchuk, High River and Calgary, Alta. 1983 5 0 0 0 $ 421
Todd Beelby,C,150,lt.blue,dk.blue Tr. C. Beelby Time 2:03^3F,5, Earn. to 1983 $20,756 1982 2:$06^4$F 39 2 11 6 $13,686
Ja31^3Clv^7 ft 4000hp 2400 m:$30^2$1:$02^2$1:$34^2$2:06^1 8 4^5 $^o3^{2\frac{1}{2}}$ $^o2^{1\frac{1}{2}}$ 3^3 $5^{3\frac{1}{2}}$ 2:06^4 9.50 B.Beelby DustyBreeze ArdenBret SatinSatan 8^8
Ja24^3Clv^6 gd 4000 2200 m:32 1:03 1:$35^4$2:08^1 3 $^o1^k$ $^o2^1$ $^o2^{hd}$ 3^2 4^4 2:08^4 4.65 C.Beelby Spec.Game MichiganHall JimTheB. 10^8
Ja21^3Clv^6 ft 4000cd 2500 m:31 1:$03^3$1:36 2:08 5 2^1 2^1 4^3 5^6 5^7 2:09^3 8.75 C.Beelby Dus.Breeze Rad.General PilotFrost 5^6
Ja14^3StP^2 ft 4000 1700 m:$30^1$1:$03^3$1:$33^3$2:05^4 2 1^1 $1^{1\frac{1}{2}}$ $2_{\frac{1}{2}}$ $2^{1\frac{1}{2}}$ $6^{5\frac{1}{4}}$ 2:06^4 7.15 R.Hennessy Spring.Crocus Kara.Beau Su.Adios -3^8
Ja2^3 StP^3 ft 5500 2200 m:$29^1$1:$01^2$1:$32^4$2:05^3 7 2^1 2^1 3^3 $6^{7\frac{1}{2}}$ $7^{18\frac{1}{4}}$ 2:09^1 22.95 G.McQuaid Lilloet SepoyNatel MarubaPicky 2^8
Dc12^2StP^3 ft 5500 2400 m:$29^2$1:$00^2$1:32 2:05 5 1^1 1^1 $1_{\frac{1}{2}}$ $3^{1\frac{1}{2}}$ $8^{6\frac{1}{4}}$ 2:06^1 9.15 EdTracey SepoyNatel WarCloud TedTheGreat 10^8

$4000 **7** **6-1**

KINGSLEY HANOVER

B. g. 1971, Hondo Hanover — Little Kim — Hundred Proof
P. Megens, Surrey, B. C. 1983 2:07^3H 5 1 0 0 $ 1,516
Paul Megens, A, 160, red, white Tr. P. Megens Time 2:00^4M,10, Earn. to 1983 $49,052 1982 2:$00^4$M 33 10 6 3 $14,047
Fb3^3 Clv^6 ft 4000 2200 m:$30^3$1:$03^4$1:$36^1$2:08^4 2 x4^4 $^o3^2$ $^o2^1$ 2^2 4^3 2:09^2 *1.95 P.Megens Yarver RomanJoe ShadowsDauntless 4^8
Ja26^3Clv^2 gd 4000hp 2200 m:$31^1$1:$03^3$1:$36^3$2:08^3 6 $^o3^2$ $^o3^{1\frac{1}{4}}$ $^o4^2$ 5^6 $6^{4\frac{1}{2}}$ 2:09^2 3.25 P.Megens Beth.Blazet Rad.General PilotFros.9^8
Ja21^3Clv^9 ft 5000cd 2800 m:$32^2$1:05 1:$36^3$2:07^4 5 $6^{6\frac{1}{2}}$ $^o5^4$ 6^5 7^{13} 7^{13} 2:10^1 3.90 P.Megens MightyTyrosA PerleBlue Keesno 5^7
Ja14^3Clv^6 ft 5000hp 2800 m:$31^3$1:$02^1$1:$34^2$2:05^2 3 $^o1^1$ 2^1 $4^{1\frac{1}{2}}$ $5^{5\frac{1}{2}}$ 5^5 2:06^2 *2.10 P.Megens Beth.Pegas. Hol.GoSkip LTWohcaz 4^8
Ja7^3 Clv^7 sy 5000 2400 m:$31^3$1:$04^2$1:$35^4$2:07^3 1 $2^{1\frac{1}{2}}$ $2^{2\frac{1}{2}}$ $3^{1\frac{1}{2}}$ $2^{1\frac{1}{2}}$ 1^k 2:07^3 2.95 P.Megens Kings.Hanover Daub.Comm. Ethnic 13^8
Dc31^2Clv^6 ft 4000hp 2000 m:$30^3$1:$02^4$1:$35^1$2:07^4 6 $^o5^{3\frac{1}{4}}$ $^o2^1$ $^o2^1$ 1^k $1_{\frac{1}{2}}$ 2:07^4 6.25 P.Megens Kings.Hanover CeffylDu Dus.Breeze 1^8

$3500 **8** **8-1**

HOLRIDGE HERO

Br. g. 1977, Skip Away — Du Du Byrd — Du Boy *B.C. Bred*
W. Waples, Surrey, B. C. 1983 2:07H 6 2 0 0 $ 1,990
Wendell Waples, A, 150, gold, blue Tr. W. Waples Time 2:02^2F,4, Earn. to 1983 $15,922 1982 2:$07^1$H 25 4 4 3 $ 6,923
Ja29^3Clv^7 ft 3000 1800 m:$30^2$1:$02^3$1:$34^3$2:06^2 8 $3^{2\frac{1}{2}}$ $3^{2\frac{1}{2}}$ $3^{2\frac{1}{2}}$ $5^{5\frac{1}{2}}$ $5^{6\frac{1}{2}}$ 2:07^3 8.30 W.Waples GypsyBlue MrKeith AndysDean 10^8
Ja24^3Clv^9 gd 3000hp 2000 m:$31^2$1:04 1:$36^1$2:09 5 7^9 6^4 6^3 $7^{4\frac{1}{2}}$ 5^4 2:09^3 6.00 W.Waples BethanyOdd Shad.D'less GypsyBlue 10^8
Ja19^3Clv^5 gd 3500 2000 m:$32^1$1:$06^3$1:$39^1$2:10^4 4 1^k $1^{1\frac{1}{2}}$ 1^k 1^1 $5^{2\frac{1}{2}}$ 2:11 3.35 W.Waples BraveBullet GypsyBlue DeckHand 9^8
Ja13^3Clv^6 ft c3000 1800 m:$31^1$1:$02^1$1:$34^4$2:05^4 6 $^o2^{hd}$ $^o2^1$ $^o3^{1\frac{1}{2}}$ 5^7 6^8 2:07^2 2.95 S.Ericsson GypsyBlue DeckHand Wint.PrinceA 6^8
Ja6^3 Clv^2 sy 3000 1700 m:$30^3$1:$01^4$1:$33^4$2:07 7 $^o4^{2\frac{1}{4}}$ $^o1^{hd}$ 2^{hd} 2^1 1^{ns} 2:07 15.65 S.Ericsson Hol.Hero GypsyBlue SimplyGrand 7^8
Ja1^3 Clv^4 gd 3000 1700 m:$32^1$1:06 1:$39^2$2:12^1 2 2^1 $^o2^1$ 2^k 1^2 1^4 2:12^1 *2.15 S.Ericsson Hol.Hero SimplyGrand SallyStreak. 4^8

*Denotes Assistant Trainer

In the third race, horse number 3, Shadows Dauntless, was a Dr. Z system bet. Near post time the tote board was as follows:

	Totals	#3 Shadows Dauntless	Expected Value per Dollar Bet on Shadows Dauntless
Odds		4—1	
Win	6,257	1,065	
Show	2,147	202	1.24

The mutuel pools at Cloverdale are quite small, so I used a betting fortune of $200. The optimal bet was then $8. It proved very easy to bet just before post time. The favorite, Ceffyl Du, won the race, Shadows Dauntless took second, and Gypsy Blue was third. Shadows Dauntless's $4.20 show payoff returned $16.80 on my $8 bet, for an $8.80 profit. The mutuel payoffs were as follows:

5	6.60	4.10	2.70
	3	5.50	4.20
		2	3.20

Pardner Jove, the number 6 horse, was a Dr. Z system bet in the eighth race. Pardner Jove was the favorite at 6—5 for his sixth race in succession.

With one minute to post time the tote board was as follows:

	Total	#6 Pardner Jove	Expected Value per Dollar Bet on Pardner Jove
Odds		6—5	
Win	9,093	3,264	
Show	2,476	560	1.16

I bet $33. At post time the odds were

	Total	#6 Pardner Jove	Expected Value per Dollar Bet on Pardner Jove
Odds		6—5	
Win	9,410	3,387	
Show	2,609	621	1.13

8th race

BLUE SADDLE CLOTH

1 MILE PACE

EXACTOR SUPER 6 | **SUPER 6** EXACTOR

PURSE $3200 — Claiming — Claiming Price $7000 plus allowances.

HANDICAP SELECTIONS: 6 — 4 — 8

ASK FOR HORSE BY THIS NUMBER

1 HERE BY CHANCE

$7000 — 8-1

B. g. 1975, Adios Pick — Actress Abbe — Actor Abbe *B.C. Bred*
F. Rasmussen, C. Pedersen, Vanc., B. C.
Howard Portelance,A,140,grey,bl,orange Tr. T. Brown * Time 2:03F,7, Earn. to 1983 $31,901
1983 8 0 1 3 $ 2,684
1982 2:03F 40 1 10 4 $ 9,534

Date	Tk.	Cond.	Class	Purse	Dis. Leaders Times	Post	1/4	1/2	3/4	Str.	Fin.	Time	Odds	Driver	1st/2nd/3rd	Temp./Starters
Fb5^3	Clv^5	ft	7000hp	3200	m:30^{2}1:02^{2}1:33^{3}2:05^1	1	$4^{4\frac{1}{2}}$	4^4	7^5	$4^{7\frac{1}{2}}$	$3^{6\frac{1}{2}}$	2:06^2	5.70	H.P'lance	HHClipper MacLobellA HereByChance	7^8
Ja29^3	Clv^5	ft	7000hp	3200	m:30^{1}1:02^{1}1:34 2:06^2	4	$6^{7\frac{1}{2}}$	$6^{4\frac{1}{2}}$	8^4	$7^{3\frac{1}{2}}$	2^{nk}	2:06^2	18.80	H.P'lance	Wind.Andy H.ByChance TakeAStart†	10^8
Ja26^3	Clv^{10}	sy	7000	3000	m:31^{3}1:03^{4}1:36^{1}2:08^1	6	$6^{7\frac{1}{2}}$	$7^{7\frac{1}{2}}$	$^{\circ}7^6$	$7^{4\frac{1}{2}}$	4^2	2:08^2	14.75	H.P'lance	Rich.Dauber Nor.Roddy Daub.Com.	9^8
Ja22^3	Clv^6	ft	7000hp	3200	m:31^{1}1:03^{1}1:34^{1}2:06^3	2	$2^{1\frac{1}{2}}$	$^{\circ}2^{nk}$	$^{\circ}1^{hd}$	3^2	5^3	2:07^1	6.15	H.P'lance	SengaPayne Nor.Roddy Com.Osborne	8^8
Ja15^3	Clv^{10}	gd	7000hp	3000	m:32 1:05 1:37^{4}2:09^2	4	6^6	$8^{6\frac{1}{2}}$	$^{\circ}7^{4\frac{1}{2}}$	$7^{4\frac{1}{2}}$	4^2	2:09^4	3.45	H.P'lance	Wind.Andy Nor.Roddy Com.Osborne	6^8
Ja12^3	Clv^7	gd	7000	3000	m:31^{1}1:02^{3}1:34^{3}2:06^2	3	$4^{4\frac{1}{2}}$	$4^{3\frac{1}{2}}$	$^{\circ}3^{1\frac{1}{2}}$	$4^{2\frac{1}{2}}$	$3^{1\frac{1}{2}}$	2:06^4	3.85	H.P'lance	Inv.Strip Daub.Comm. H.B.Chance	10^7

2 HICRIDGE APOLLO †

$7000 — 6-1

B. g. 1972, Army Hanover — Bertha Breeze — Mighty Medium
W. Dobie, Surrey, B. C.
Mike Evans,A,170,white,brown,orange Tr. J. Richards Time 2:02F,6, Earn. to 1983 $91,230
1983 2:06^{2}H 5 1 0 1 $ 2,098
1982 2:05^{3}F 35 9 3 7 $14,495

Date	Tk.	Cond.	Class	Purse	Dis. Leaders Times	Post	1/4	1/2	3/4	Str.	Fin.	Time	Odds	Driver	1st/2nd/3rd	Temp./Starters
Fb5^3	Clv^5	ft	7000hp	3200	m:30^{2}1:02^{2}1:33^{3}2:05^1	4	$7^{8\frac{1}{2}}$	$7^{6\frac{1}{4}}$	$^{\circ}8^{5\frac{1}{2}}$	$7^{8\frac{1}{2}}$	4^9	2:06^4	5.55	M.Evans†	HHClipper MacLobellA HereByChance	7^8
Ja28^3	Clv^{10}	ft	6000cd	2800	m:30^{4}1:01^{4}1:34 2:06^2	1	$1^{1\frac{1}{2}}$	1^{hd}	$1^{1\frac{1}{2}}$	1^2	1^5	2:06^2	*2.10	M.Evans†	Hic.Apollo† FracoDoc Sur.Princess	8^8
Ja19^3	Clv^6	gd	5000	2600	m:31^{1}1:02^{2}1:34^{2}2:06	3	$3^{1\frac{1}{4}}$	3^3	$5^{3\frac{1}{2}}$	$4^{4\frac{1}{2}}$	$3^{1\frac{1}{4}}$	2:06^1	2.90	M.Evans†	JohnHanoverN Hol.GoSkip H.Apollo†	9^8
Ja7^3	Clv^6	sy	6000	2600	m:30^{1}1:00^{4}1:33^{1}2:05^2	7	7^{13}	7^{15}	$7^{8\frac{1}{2}}$	7^{13}	6^{13}	2:08^1	7.85	M.Evans†	Rich.Dauber HippocampusC Chatter	13^8
Ja3^3	Clv^5	sy	6000hp	2600	m:32^{1}1:05^{3}1:36^{2}2:07^3	5	6^7	$^{\circ}6^{4\frac{1}{2}}$	$^{\circ}4^5$	$4^{6\frac{1}{2}}$	$5^{7\frac{1}{4}}$	2:09	*2.35	M.Evans†	Com.Osborne Rich.Daub. Daub.Comm.	10^8
Dc27^2	Clv^7	gd	6000	2600	m:30^{3}1:03 1:35^{2}2:06^3	1	4^3	$^{\circ}3^2$	$^{\circ}1\frac{1}{2}$	1^2	1^{hd}	2:06^3	4.20	M.Evans†	Hic.Apollo† MarkDoc LTWohcaz	3^8

3 UFLEX

$7000 — 10-1

Blk. g. 1972, Springflex — U Love — U Scott
M. Graham, D. Tough, G. Lum, Surrey, Vancouver, B. C.
Paul Megens, A, 160, red, white Tr. G. Abbott Time 2:00^{1}M,7, Earn. to 1983 $107,139
1983 6 0 0 1 $ 856
1982 2:05^{4}H 34 9 4 4 $18,444

Date	Tk.	Cond.	Class	Purse	Dis. Leaders Times	Post	1/4	1/2	3/4	Str.	Fin.	Time	Odds	Driver	1st/2nd/3rd	Temp./Starters
Fb5^3	Clv^5	ft	7000hp	3200	m:30^{2}1:02^{2}1:33^{3}2:05^1	6	3^3	$3^{2\frac{1}{2}}$	3^3	5^8	$7^{10\frac{1}{2}}$	2:07^1	43.65	P.Megens	HHClipper MacLobellA HereByChance	7^8
Fb2^3	Clv^2	ft	7000	3000	m:30^{4}1:03^{1}1:34^{2}2:05^4	4	2^1	$3^{1\frac{1}{4}}$	$7^{3\frac{1}{4}}$	$5^{6\frac{1}{2}}$	4^6	2:07	6.75	P.Megens	Rich.Dauber Com.Osborne J.Indigo	6^8
Ja27^3	Clv^9	gd	8000	3200	m:31 1:03 1:34 2:06^2	1	$4^{3\frac{1}{2}}$	$^{\circ}4^{2\frac{1}{4}}$	$^{\circ}6^3$	$7^{3\frac{1}{2}}$	5^3	2:06^4	11.00	P.Megens	S.Chettsal Lang.Charm Nor.Martin	9^8
Ja20^3	Clv^9	ft	8000	3200	m:30^{1}1:01^{3}1:34^{2}2:06	7	8^7	7^7	$^{\circ}7^5$	7^9	7^{10}	2:08	11.30	P.Megens	Pard.Jove Sw.Angie LangleyCharm	9^8
Ja14^3	Clv^9	ft	10000hp	4000	m:29^{3}1:01^{2}1:33 2:05	3	4^5	$4^{4\frac{1}{2}}$	$5^{4\frac{1}{2}}$	6^5	$6^{7\frac{1}{4}}$	2:06^3	9.65	P.Megens	CallNRaise HHClipper RossN	4^6
Ja7^3	Clv^9	sy	10000hp	3800	m:31^{4}1:05^{1}1:36^{2}2:08	2	$2^{1\frac{1}{2}}$	$2^{1\frac{1}{2}}$	$3^{1\frac{1}{2}}$	$3^{1\frac{1}{2}}$	3^2	2:08^2	17.35	P.Megens	GritN PrairieJean Uflex	13^6

4 CHATTER

$7000 — 7-2

Blk. h. 1976, Speedy Count — Noccalula — Spectator
B. Hirsch, Surrey, B. C.
Jim Wiggins, A, 150, green, gold Tr. B. Hirsch Time 2:01F,4, Earn. to 1983 $23,605
1983 2:07H 4 1 0 2 $ 2,048
1982 2:01^{2}F 37 12 3 4 $13,044

Date	Tk.	Cond.	Class	Purse	Dis. Leaders Times	Post	1/4	1/2	3/4	Str.	Fin.	Time	Odds	Driver	1st/2nd/3rd	Temp./Starters
Fb4^3	Clv^7	ft	6000	2800	m:30^{2}1:02^{1}1:34^{2}2:07	7	8^{10}	$8^{6\frac{1}{2}}$	$^{\circ}8^6$	7^4	1^2	2:07	22.90	J.Wiggins	Chatter Invinc.Strip Spec.Game	4^8
Ja28^3	Clv^{10}	ft	6000cd	2800	m:30^{4}1:01^{4}1:34 2:06^2	7	7^7	$^{\circ}6^{5\frac{1}{4}}$	$^{\circ}7^{4\frac{1}{2}}$	$8^{8\frac{1}{4}}$	8^{17}	2:09^3	3.35	K.Linton	Hic.Apollo† FracoDoc Sur.Princess	8^8
Ja17^3	Clv^7	gd	6000cd	2800	m:31^{2}1:02^{1}1:33^{4}2:05^2	5	6^5	$^{\circ}5^{6\frac{1}{2}}$	$^{\circ}5^{4\frac{1}{4}}$	5^7	$3^{5\frac{1}{2}}$	2:06^3	3.80	J.Wiggins	FortDean DantePatch Chatter	10^8
Ja7^3	Clv^6	sy	6000	2600	m:30^{1}1:00^{4}1:33^{1}2:05^2	6	6^{11}	6^{10}	$^{\circ}5^{2\frac{1}{2}}$	3^4	$3^{4\frac{1}{4}}$	2:06^2	3.05	K.Linton	Rich.Dauber HippocampusC Chatter	13^8
Dc29^2	Clv^8	ft	7000	2800	m:31^{4}1:03^{2}1:35^{3}2:06^4	3	$6^{6\frac{1}{2}}$	$6^{5\frac{1}{2}}$	$^{\circ}5^5$	$5^{4\frac{1}{2}}$	$5^{3\frac{1}{4}}$	2:07^2	9.00	J.Wiggins	CannyBretN BwanaByrd North.Martin	0^8
Dc20^2	Clv^{10}	sy	6000	2600	m:31^{2}1:03^{2}1:35^{2}2:07^2	2	2^1	$^{\circ}1^1$	1^1	$1^{1\frac{1}{2}}$	$1^{1\frac{1}{2}}$	2:07^2	3.20	J.Wiggins	Chatter Com.Osborne RedBerryN	6^8

```
$7000  FLASH FIRE                                 B. m. 1976, Dexter Hanover — Stonegate Taretta — Tarport Count
  5                                               J. and L. Kositsky and J. Plottel, Vancouver, B. C.      1983              6  0  1  0 $ 1,245
 10-1  Wendell Waples, A, 150, gold, blue         Tr. J. Kositsky.   Time 2:03F,4, Earn. to 1983 $44,661    1982  2:06^2H 31  3  2  6 $ 9,013
Fb5^3 Clv^5 ft 7000hp  3200 m:30^2 1:02^2 1:33^3 2:05^1 5  2^1 1/2  2^1  2^2  3^6  8^11  2:07^1 17.25 D.J'quist HHClipper MacLobellA HereByChance 7^8
Ja29^3Clv^5 ft 7000hp  3200 m:30^1 1:02^1 1:34 2:06^2 1  2^1 1/2  3^1 1/4  3^1 1/2  3^1 1/4  5^2 1/4  2:06^4  6.80 D.J'quist Wind.Andy H.ByChance TakeAStart† 10^8
Ja19^3Clv^7 gd 8000hp  3200 m:31^3 1:04 1:35^2 2:05^4 5  5^6  5^5  5^5  5^7 1/2  5^8 1/4  2:07^3 *1.75 D.J'quist Nor.Martin Jam.Indigo Rich.Dauber 9^5
Ja13^3Clv^10 ft 8000   3200 m:30 1:03^2 1:35^3 2:05^3 4  1^1  1^1  1^nk  2^4  6^7 1/2  2:07  3.15 D.J'quist Jim.N'nuff Lang.Charm Nor.Martin 6^8
Ja8^3 Clv^7 gd 8000hp  3000 m:29^4 1:02^3 1:34^2 2:06^3 6  2^1 1/2  2^1 1/2  °2^hd  1 1/2  2 1/2  2:06^3  3.35 D.J'quist PrimaGavel FlashFire H.ByChance 6^8
Ja3^3 Clv^7 sy 9000hp  3500 m:31^1 1:05^3 1:38^3 2:09^2 3  1^1  1^1  1 1/2  2^2  5^3 1/2  2:10^1  5.15 S.Ericsson Booz.Delight Comm.Jove Pr.Jean 10^7
```

```
$7000  PARDNER JOVE                               B. g. 1974, Tar Duke — Lady Jane Grey — Lon Tass                                  *B.C. Bred*
  6                                               Hudon Stables, Surrey, B.C.                               1983  2:06H    4  1  1  0 $ 2,791
 3-1   Joe Hudon, A, 165, blue, orange            Tr. J. Hudon       Time 2:02^3F,8, Earn. to 1983 $61,734  1982  2:02^3F 39 10  8  7 $23,397
Ja28^3Clv^6 ft 10000   3700 m:29^3 1:00^4 1:32^2 2:04^3 2  4^5 1/2  4^4 1/2  6^4 1/4  6^7  5^5  2:05^2 *2.40 J.Hudon LaurelWayGB ServingYou JamesGem 8^7
Ja20^3Clv^9 ft 8000    3200 m:30^1 1:01^3 1:34^2 2:06 2  4^3  3^2 1/2  °1^1  1^1 1/2  1^1  2:06 *1.30 J.Hudon Pard.Jove Sw.Angie LangleyCharm 9^8
Ja13^3Clv^10 ft 8000   3200 m:30 1:03^2 1:35^3 2:05^3 3  6^4 1/2  °2^1  °2^nk  3^5 1/2  4^7  2:07 *1.45 J.Hudon Jim.N'nuff Lang.Charm Nor.Martin 6^8
Ja6^3 Clv^10 sy 8000   3000 m:30^1 1:01^3 1:33^2 2:05^3 8  4^3 1/2  °4^2 1/2  °2^2 1/2  2^2  2^2  2:06 *1.95 J.Hudon Sen.Chettsal Pard.Jove Nor.Martin 7^8
Dc27^2Clv^10 gd 9000cd 3300 m:31^3 1:04^3 1:36^2 2:08^2 7  i4^4 1/2  °3^1 1/2  °2 1/2  3^2  4^3  2:09 *1.50 J.Hudon Uflex JustDuke PrimaGavel 3^8
Dc17^2Clv^8 sy 10000hp 3800 m:30^2 1:02^1 1:36 2:08^2 5  6^5 1/2  °5^9  5^5 1/2  6^6 1/2  6^8  2:10 *1.65 J.Hudon Prair.Jean Wing.Lead.† S.Chettsal 6^8
```

```
$7000  MAC LOBELL A                               B. g. 1977, Smart Lobell — Narooma Gift — Free Fight
  7                                               A. Peterson, R. Acheson and J. Glen, Surrey, B. C.        1983              3  0  1  0 $   950
 8-1   Mike Stymest,A,150,orange,green,white      Tr. J. Glen        Time 2:00^4F,4, Earn. to 1983 $24,743  1982  2:02^2F 15  1  4  3 $ 6,685
Fb5^3 Clv^5 ft 7000hp  3200 m:30^2 1:02^2 1:33^3 2:05^1 8  5^5 1/2  5^5  5^3 1/2  2^2  2^3  2:05^3  9.25 J.Glen HHClipper MacLobellA HereByChance 7^8
Fb2^3 Clv^2 ft 7000    3000 m:30^4 1:03^1 1:34^2 2:05^4 3  8^8  °6^3  °3^1 1/4  3^3  5^6 1/4  2:07  5.50 J.Glen Rich.Dauber Com.Osborne J.Indigo 6^8
Ja21^3Clv^8 ft 10000hp 4000 m:31^4 1:04 1:35^4 2:06^3 1  3^2  5^3  6^3 1/2  7^5 1/2  8^8 1/2  2:08^1  7.80 J.Glen RossN GritN KawarthaOshawa 5^8
Ja13^3Clv^1 ft Qua      Nil m:30^3 1:01^4 1:34^3 2:05^4 5  4^7 1/2  4^13  3^3 1/2  3^3  3^2 1/4  2:06^2  NB J.Glen Hol.Iroqua BaronNuff MacLobellA 5^5
Ja6^3 Clv^4 sy Qua      Nil m:34 1:08 1:41^3 2:13^2 6  6^7  7^7 1/2  5^4  4^2  2 1/2  2:13^2  NB J.Glen GunsmokeA MacLobellA BabyKhan 7^7
Ag21^2Reg^9 gd wo1000L6 1500 m:31^3 1:03^3 1:35^2 2:06^3 5  °1^1  2^2  2^2  2^1 1/4  5^12  2:09  2.55 J.Glen SirMedicine M.Majestic IrishCom. 28^6
```

```
$7000  BWANA BYRD                                 B. g. 1976, Baron Duane — Birdie Bright Eyes — Tar Duke
  8                                               B. Babineau, Surrey, B. C.                                1983  2:07^3H  5  1  0  1 $ 1,932
 9-2   Bill Babineau,A.160,r.bl,lt.bl,white       Tr. B. Babineau    Time 2:02F,5, Earn. to 1983 $26,427    1982  2:03^1F 50 14 11  7 $18,283
Fb7^3 Clv^6 gd 5000hp  2600 m:30^2 1:02^2 1:35 2:07^3 6  fog  8^8  fog  3^2  1^1  2:07^3  4.60 B.Babineau BwanaByrd RedBerryN Yarver 5^8
Fb3^3 Clv^7 ft 8000    3200 m:30^1 1:02^1 1:35^2 2:06^4 7  8^14  8^6  °7^3  7^6  7^5 1/2  2:07^3 21.35 B.Babineau Lang.Charm FortDean North.Martin 4^8
Ja13^3Clv^8 ft 8000cd  3400 m:30^1 1:01^3 1:33^2 2:04^3 4  5^4 1/2  °5^4  °4^3 1/2  4^6  3^7 1/4  2:06  5.10 B.Babineau TributeN Hoatu BwanaByrd 6^7
Ja8^3 Clv^7 gd 7000hp  3000 m:29^4 1:02^3 1:34^2 2:06^3 2ix°4^4 1/2  °3^2 1/2  8^8  8^12  8^15  2:09^3 *2.15 B.Babineau PrimaGavel FlashFire H.ByChance 6^8
Ja1^3 Clv^7 sl 7000cd  2800 m:32^2 1:06^2 1:39 2:11^2 6  7^8 1/2  °6^5 1/2  °6^4  7^5 1/2  4^4 1/2  2:12^1  3.25 B.Babineau TributeN BaronsLass Hoatu 4^7
Dc29^2Clv^8 ft 7000    2800 m:31^4 1:03^2 1:35^3 2:06^4 2  5^4  5^4  °4^4  2^1  2^ns  2:06^4  3.15 B.Babineau CannyBretN BwanaByrd North.Martin 0^8
```

ALSO ELIGIBLE: THIS HORSE WILL ONLY START IN THE EVENT OF A SCRATCH

```
$7000  DAUBERS COMMAND                            Br. h. 1978, Hank The Dauber — Gladys Command — Take Command                      *B.C. Bred*
  9                                               W. and T. Smith, Surrey, B. C.                            1983              7  0  2  2 $ 2,448
(P.P. .....) Dave Smith, A, 180, red, white       Tr. N. Clarkson *  Time 2:03^4F,4, Earn. to 1983 $19,226  1982  2:03^4F 31  8  8  2 $11,169
Fb9^3 Clv^7 sy 7000cd  3000 m:31^4 1:03^3 1:35^4 2:06^4 2  1^1  1^nk  4^2 1/4  7^10  7^15  2:09^4  5.55 D.Smith Jim.N'nuff Arm.Almond B'sFancy† 10^8
Ja31^3Clv^10 ft 6000cd 3400 m:30^3 1:02 1:33^4 2:05^1 1  2^1 1/2  2^1 1/2  3^1 1/4  3^2  5^3  2:05^3  6.00 D.Smith DiabloN KinaJ EastwindStar 8^8
Ja26^3Clv^10 sy 7000   3000 m:31^3 1:03^4 1:36^1 2:08^1 2  1^1 1/2  1^1 1/2  1^1  1 1/2  3^1 1/2  2:08^2 10.10 D.Smith Rich.Dauber Nor.Roddy Daub.Com. 9^8
Ja19^3Clv^7 gd 7000hp  3200 m:31^3 1:04 1:35^2 2:05^4 2  1^1 1/2  1 1/2  2 1/2  3^4  4^7 1/2  2:07^2  3.15 J.Wiggins Nor.Martin Jam.Indigo Rich.Dauber 9^5
Ja12^3Clv^7 gd 7000    3000 m:31^1 1:02^3 1:34^3 2:06^2 2  1^1  1^1 1/2  1 1/2  1^1 1/2  2^1  2:06^3  8.75 J.Wiggins Inv.Strip Daub.Comm. H.B.Chance 10^7
```

*Denotes Assistant Trainer

Chatter won the race. Pardner Jove took second, followed by Here By Chance. Pardner Jove paid \$2.80, so my \$33 bet returned \$46.20, for a \$13.20 profit. The mutuel payoffs were as follows:

4	14.00	5.20	3.20
	6	3.30	2.80
		1	3.30

Using the Dr. Z System in England

The parimutuel system of betting utilizing electric totalizator boards is the dominant method of betting at North American racetracks. Las Vegas and the other legal sports books may set odds on particular betting situations, but these fixed odds are not available at racetracks. In England, and in other Commonwealth countries, such as Australia and Hong Kong, and in other European countries, such as Italy and France, odds betting against bookies is the prevalent wagering scheme. The bookies set odds that you can *lock in* by buying a ticket. These odds do change over time, largely so that the bookies can balance their books to ensure themselves of a profit no matter which horse wins. You therefore have the chance to bet on different horses at different times, so you can hedge your bets. If you play it right, you either never or rarely lose, while making a sizable return all or most of the time.*

Table 17.2 lists the rates of return in British flat racing for thoroughbreds for different odds levels set by the bookmakers. As you can see, to get action on the favorites, they have to set the odds at levels that allow you to make a profit betting on these horses. Notice also, that they have the usual favorite–long-shot bias. They make their profits on the medium- and longer-priced horses, in particular on the long shots over 18—1, where they return an average of only about 20%–40% of the amount bet. The total average take by the bookies, including government taxes of 4% on course and 8.5% off course, is 10% on course and 19% off course. You have the option of paying the tax when you bet or when you win. For example, with a bet of £100 on course, you can pay the £4 in advance, or pay 4% of your winnings. Suppose the payoff is £3 per pound bet. The tax is then £4 if paid in advance, but £12 if you win and have not prepaid the tax. In the long run, if you

---

*Lest you think we've just invented a method for shaking the money out of the trees, let me tell you that this is pretty tricky. But see Lane and Ziemba (October 1983) for some preliminary research on this problem in the context of Mexican team Jai Alai, whose odds are set in a similar fashion.

TABLE 17.2 *Rates of return for different odds ranges in British flat racing before taxes*

	Rate of Return				
Odds Ranges	1950	1965	1973	1975	1976
1—100 to 2—5	97.2	108.1	108.5	112.1	107.0
4—9 to 2—5	98.8	89.4	109.7	108.4	107.8
8—11 to 1—1	94.8	88.4	93.6		
21—20 to 3—2	96.5	87.2	88.6		
13—8 to 9—4	90.4	95.9	83.6		
95—40 to 4—1	95.5	95.0	95.5		
9—2 to 9—1	90.1	89.5	89.1		
19—2 to 18—1	64.5	64.9	66.5		
larger than 18—1	23.8	37.3	23.2		

Sources: Figgis (1974) and Lord Rothschild (1978).
Note: Taxes on course of 4% and off course of 8.5% must be subtracted to determine the actual net rate of return. These rates of return are based on the assumption that every horse in each odds range was bet to return 100.

are more or less breaking even on your bets, the tax collected is about the same by either method. However, if you are winning on average, it is better to prepay the tax and if you are losing on average, it is better to pay the tax only when you win.

A parimutuel betting system using the tote board, although less popular in England, is available for betting on course as well as off course. As in North America, the odds are flashed periodically, but the betting pools are not shown. The odds are quoted on the payoff per £1 bet with a minimum payoff of £1. Forget about betting on superhorses—all you will get is your money back. Also the odds are quoted in terms of total return, so if the odds are shown as 3.1—1, you get £3.1 per pound bet if the horse wins, not £4.1 as would be the case in North America.

Instead of the North American parimutuel system of win, place, and show, the bets are to win and place. By "place" the British mean "finish in the money." This is much like what North Americans call show. There is, however, one important difference. The number of horses that can place in a particular race is dependent on the number of starters. This works as follows:

NUMBER OF HORSES THAT PLACE	NUMBER OF STARTERS
One: the winner	four or fewer
Two: winner and second	five, six, or seven
Three: winner, second, and third	eight to fifteen
Four: winner, second, third, and fourth	sixteen or more

The place pools are not shown on the tote board, but the current payoffs for place bets for each horse are flashed on the screen. Bookies, on the other hand, simply pay a percentage of the win odds, as shown in Table 17.3.

TABLE 17.3 *Bookmakers payoff for place bets*

Number of Runners	Type of Race	Fraction of Win Odds Paid on Place Element	Horses Regarded
Two to five		No place betting	
Six or seven	Any	$\frac{1}{4}$	First and second
Eight or more	Any except handicaps involving twelve or more runners	$\frac{1}{5}$	First, second, and third
Twelve to fifteen	Handicaps	$\frac{1}{4}$	First, second, and third
Sixteen to twenty-one	Handicaps	$\frac{1}{5}$	First, second, third, and fourth
Twenty-two or more	Handicaps	$\frac{1}{4}$	First, second, third, and fourth

Source: Lord Rothschild (1978).

There are many types of exotic bets as well, as shown on page 350. The tote jackpot corresponds to what North Americans call the pick six or sweep six. The tote placepot bet has no analogue in North America. The average rates of return on the various bets on and off course against a bookmaker or the tote are listed in Table 17.4. Of particular interest to us is the fact that the track take is 5% larger in the place pool than in the win pool. The tote take is larger than what the bookies make on average, and on-course betting takes are much less than off-course takes.

Your tote Betting Guide

MINIMUM STAKE: £1 on Win, Place, Dual Forecast and Daily Double pools; 50p for Jackpot, Placepot and Daily Treble pools, but 10p Jackpot lines accepted for permutations of not less than £5 in value.

HOW TO BET: Win, Place and Dual Forecast tickets on sale at all windows marked 'SELL' or 'BET HERE' Please use racecard numbers when placing your bet, e.g. "£1 each way number four". At some meetings SELL AND PAY will be handled at the same window. Special windows in each enclosure sell Jackpot, Placepot, Daily Double and Treble tickets.

WIN: In the Win pool, payout is on the first horse subject to the 'weighed-in'.

PLACE: Place dividends are paid on the first, second, third and fourth in handicaps of 16 or more runners coming under starter's orders; on the 1,2,3 in other races of 8 or more runners coming under orders and on the 1 and 2 in races of five, six or seven runners coming under orders. When a place pool is operating and the number of runners is reduced to four or less before coming under starter's orders, a place dividend will be declared on the winner only.

DUAL FORECAST: Dual Forecasts in which you nominate the first and second to finish in either order are available in every race with three or more runners.

PLEASE RETAIN YOUR TICKETS UNTIL THE 'WEIGHED-IN' HAS BEEN ANNOUNCED

TOTE DAILY DOUBLE: Pick the winners of the third and fifth races on the card. Winning tickets on the first leg must be exchanged for tickets on the second leg of the Double.

TOTE DAILY TREBLE: Pick the winners of the second, fourth and sixth races on the card. Winning tickets must be exchanged after each of the first two legs.

TOTE JACKPOT: Pick the winners of races 1,2,3,4,5 and 6. If there is no all-correct entry, the gross pool is carried forward.

TOTE PLACEPOT: To win the Placepot you must nominate a horse on which a place dividend is declared in Races 1,2,3,4,5 and 6 (see PLACE paragraph above). If there are 4 or less runners you must name the winner.

NON-RUNNERS: If a horse is withdrawn without coming under starter's orders a refund is made to holders of tickets nominating a non-runner in the Win, Place and Forecast pools. In the Jackpot, Placepot, Daily Double and Daily Treble, non-runners are put on the S.P. favourite. If there is more than one favourite, the backer is on the one with the lowest racecard number. Winning tickets in any one leg of the Double or Treble which have not been exchanged for a selection in the next leg will be invested on the favourite.

LATE PAY: Pay windows will remain open until 30 minutes after the last race. Tickets can be cashed on any subsequent day of the same meeting or sent for payment by post to Horserace Totalisator Board (Dept T), Tote House, 74 Upper Richmond Road, London SW15 2SU.

TABLE 17.4 *Rates of return on different types of bets in England on thoroughbred and greyhound racing*

Type of Bet	Rate of Return (%)
On-course bookmaker	90
Off-course bookmaker	81
Single bet to win with off-course bookmaker	85
Double bet to win with off-course bookmaker	78
Treble bet to win with off-course bookmaker	72
ITV Seven bet to win with off-course bookmaker	70–75
Computer straight forecast with off-course bookmaker	65
Greyhound forecast with off-course bookmaker	76
Greyhound forecast double with off-course bookmaker	58
Place element of each-way with off-course bookmaker	80
Ante-post betting with off-course bookmaker	96
Horse race tote win pool (on course)	80
Horse race tote win pool (off course)	77
Horse race tote place pool (on course)	75
Horse race tote place pool (off course)	72
Horse race tote daily double pool (on course)	74
Horse race tote daily double pool (off course)	71
Horse race tote daily treble pool (on course)	70
Horse race tote daily treble pool (off course)	67
Horse race tote daily forecast pool (on course)	70
Horse race tote daily forecast pool (off course)	67
Horse race tote jackpot pool (on course)	70
Horse race tote jackpot pool (off course)	67
Horse race tote placepot pool (on course)	70
Horse race tote placepot pool (off course)	67
Greyhound tote pool betting, average	83.5

Source: Lord Rothschild (1978).

In June 1983, I was in Europe participating in conferences on risk and capital and Oriental rugs and finishing up a project at a research institute. I had a free day in London on Thursday, June 9, and took the special train from Paddington to the Newbury Race Course, where six races were being featured that day. The races in England are on the turf for distances of generally at least a mile, except for some shorter races for two-year-olds. The season in southern England is unique in that races are run for about three days at each race course. The jockeys, trainers, and so forth then move on to a new course. After a month or so they return to the same course. Handicapping is very sophisticated in England. It has to be, with little information easily accessible (they have no analogue of the *Daily Racing Form*, although some past performances are available in newspapers) and all that moving from course to course. The first race in the program is shown on page 352. It featured twenty-one horses.* The mutuel payoffs to win and place were

1	7.80	1.80
	25	2.00
	88	2.00
	28	1.00

With more than sixteen starters, four horses placed. Horse number 28, Tower Win, at 3.90—1 to win paid £1 for a fourth in-the-money place finish, namely a return of one's money. Since I bet on Tower Win, that was one easily learned feature of English betting.

The method of computing the place payoffs in England differs from that used in North America. In both locales, the net pool is the total amount wagered minus the track take. In North America, the cost of the winning in-the-money tickets is first subtracted to form the profit. This profit is then shared equally among the in-the-money horses. Holders of winning tickets receive a payoff consisting of the original stake plus their proportionate share of the horse's profits. This means that the amount of money wagered on the other horses in the money greatly affects the payoff. In England, the total net pool is divided equally among the horses that finish in the money. This means that the payoff on a particular horse depends upon how much is bet on this horse to place but *not* on how much is bet on the other horses. Since the minimum payoff is £1 per £1 wager, management is able to keep a control on betting for particular favorites. Once this minimum level is reached, it does not pay to wager on a given horse. This occurs whenever the percentage of the place pool that is bet on a given horse becomes as large as Q_p, which is the track take for place, divided by m, which is the number of in-the-money horses. In a race with 8–15 starters, if Q_p is about 0.735, and $m = 3$, the just-get-your-money-back point is reached when the bet on a particular horse to place becomes 24.5% of the total place pool: $0.735/3 = 24.5\%$. Hence in England you will often see

*The second race had twenty-seven starters. These are huge fields compared to the typical six to twelve in North America.

First Race

1 MILE, STRAIGHT COURSE START

One Mile, Straight Course, for Three Yrs Old and Upwards

2.00 The Polar Jest Apprentice Stakes (Handicap)

£2000 added to stakes
Distributed in accordance with Rule 194 (iii) (b)
for three yrs old and upwards — Rated 0-35
ONE MILE, Straight Course
£4 to enter, **£16** extra if declared to run

Lowest weight 7st 7lb
Penalties, after May 18th, a winner 7lb
To be ridden by Apprentices who have not ridden more than 3 winners
Allowances: Riders who have not ridden a winner 3lb
(Apprentice races in all cases included)
THE BILLY HIGGS MEMORIAL WHIP will be presented to the winning rider
This is given in his memory by his son, Mornington I. Higgs

A **SS**

Weights raised 1lb and Rule 94 (iii) (c) complied with where applicable

98 entries, 65 at £4 and 33 at £20. — Closed 18th May, 1983.

Owners Prize Money. Winner £1556; Second £476; Third £228.
(Penalty Value £2024.00)

Form		Trainer	Age	st	lb	Draw
	1 SOCKS UP		6	9	10	(17)
	Ch g Sharpen Up — Mrs Moss					
24640-2	**Mr R.F. Johnson Houghton**					
		(R.F. Johnson Houghton, Didcot)				D. Price
	BUFF, BLUE sleeves, MAUVE cap.					
	2 MASSINO		4	9	8	(12)
	B c Blakeney — Never a Fear					
041210-	**Mr Peter S. Winfield**	**(P.D. Cundell, Newbury)**				J. Kennedy
	ROYAL BLUE and RED (quartered), WHITE sleeves, BLACK cap.					
	5 SMILING LAUREL		4	9	2	(19)
	Ch c Young Emperor — Tom's Delight (USA)					
4030-	**Mr P. Terry**	**(Mrs Barbara Waring, Malmesbury)**				S. Keightley
	RED and WHITE check, DARK BLUE sleeves, RED and BLUE quartered cap.					
	8 SWIFT PALM		6	8	0	(7)
	B g Some Hand — March Stone					
6-0400	**Nimrod Company**	**(P.D. Cundell, Newbury)**				
	YELLOW, BLACK seams, BLACK cap with YELLOW star.					
	9 WESTGATE STAR		4	8	8	(16)
	B g He Loves Me — Sea Swallow (FR)					
34360-4	**Mr G. Harwood**	**(P. Calver, Ripon)**				
	YELLOW and RED (halved horizontally), BLACK 'H', BLACK and RED halved sleeves, quartered cap.					
	10 ON THE SPOT		4	8	6	(11)
	Gr g Town Crier — Creolina					
4650-00	**Mrs G.E. Maloney**	**(C.E. Brittain, Newmarket)**				S. Gilmour
	Mrs C.E. Brittain					
	BLACK and ORANGE stripes.					
	11 POLO BOY		3	8	5	(14)
	Ch g Red Alert — Bermuda					
6003-60	**Mrs A. Herbage**	**(G.B. Balding, Weyhill)**				
	GREEN and ORANGE (quartered), ORANGE sleeves, GREEN cap.					
	15 OPTIMISTIC DREAMER		4	8	3	(18)
	B g Full of Hope — La Crima					
0560-42	**Mr Jeff Goodman**	**(A. Bailey, Newmarket)**				
	MAROON, GREY spots.					
	16 COFFEE HOUSE		8	8	2	(10)
	Br g Silly Season — Village Gossip					
46/0050	**Mrs I.A. Balding**	**(I.A. Balding, Kingsclere)**				A. Watkins
	GREEN and GOLD stripes					

Form		Trainer	Age	st	lb	Draw
	17 SOLEROF		5	8	2	(1)
03460/0-	B g Averof — Solhoon **Mr M.C. Lawrence (J. Thorne, Bridgwater)** **LIGHT and DARK GREEN (halved), sleeves reversed, LIGHT GREEN cap, DARK GREEN star.**					
	18 NO SALE		4	8	1	(5)
5606-00	B c Nonoalco (USA) — Salote (USA) **Mr J.D. Riddell (R.A.L. Atkins, Elstead)** **RED, BLACK star, BLACK cap, RED star.**					
	20 MARDI GRAS		4	8	0	(15)
00450-0	Gr g Martinmas — Miss Pimm **Mrs H.G. Cambanis (B. Hobbs, Newmarket)** **BLACK, WHITE spots on body and sleeves.**				J. Brown	
	21 MATCH MASTER		4	8	0	(8)
325325-	Ch g Roman Warrior — Giglet **Mr J.B. Stafford (C.R. Nelson, Upper Lambourn)** **Mrs N.G. Stafford** **DARK BLUE, LIGHT BLUE sleeves, YELLOW cap with DARK BLUE stripes.**					
	22 ACUSHLA MACREE		6	8	0	(20)
2140-00	Ch m Mansingh (USA) — Cannie Cassie **Mr R.F. Johnson Houghton** **(R.F. Johnson Houghton, Didcot)** **BUFF, BLUE sleeves, MAUVE cap.**				Sherry Cooper	
	25 DANCER'S EMULATION		3	7	10	(13)
0000-6	Gr c Dancer's Image (USA) — Mossinella **Mr Jim Horrocks (M.J. Masson, Lewes)** **PURPLE and BEIGE stripes.**					
	26 SCOTTISH GREEN		5	7	10	(3)
50/5020-	Ch g Scottish Rifle — Nuque (CHI) **Mr B.E. Green (P.J. Makin, Marlborough)** **BROWN, LIGHT GREEN hoop, YELLOW cap.**					
	28 TOWER WIN		6	7	8	(4)
64130-4	Ch h Tower Walk — Takawin **Mr D. Turner (C.J. Benstead, Epsom)** **BROWN and EMERALD GREEN diamonds, GREEN sleeves, YELLOW cap.**					
	29 SWEET DIPPER		6	7	7	(9)
000000-	Br g Golden Dipper — Sharp And Sweet **Mrs Andrew Normand (W.G.R. Wightman, Upham)** **PINK, BLACK sleeves and cap, PINK spots.**					
	30 DARTCAN		4	7	7	(21)
0400-0	Ch f Streak — Canamour **Mr W.N. Pooley (D.C. Tucker, Frome)** **ROYAL BLUE and MAUVE (quartered), WHITE sleeves, MAUVE hoops, WHITE cap, ROYAL BLUE hoops.**					
	31 LADY CYNARA		5	7	7	(6)
000/045	B m Starch Reduced — Golden Perch **Mr William Ivin (C.P. Wildman, Salisbury)** **YELLOW, RED diamond, RED cap, YELLOW star.**					
	33 RIVERHILL BOY		5	7	7	(2)
030/0-00	B g Manacle — My Grace **Mr A.G. Marriott (C.P. Wildman, Salisbury)** **PINK, LIGHT GREEN sash, armlets and cap.**					

NUMBER OF DECLARED RUNNERS **21** (DUAL FORECAST)

BLINKERS WILL BE WORN BY No. **11,17,18,22,26 30,33**

1st .... 2nd .... 3rd .... 4th ....

Time: .... Distance: ....

Standard Time: 1 min. 38.2 secs.

1982 Winner: **Fandangle**, 4-9-6, M. Rogan, 11-4 (fav), A. J. Tree 11 ran horses whose place payoffs are £1 or just slightly higher. This method of sharing the place pool tends to favor longer-priced horses at the expense of the favorites.

The current track take to win is about 20.6% and to place is 26.5%, and the breakage is of the 10¢ variety, or more properly 10p, for pence.* These track takes are much higher than those in North America.

---

*We can calculate these track takes as follows: The payoff on horse i if it wins is $Q_w W/W_i$, but the pools are not made public. So let $q_i = W_i/W$, the efficient-market assumption. Let B be the average breakage, namely, 4.5p. Since breakage can be 0,1,2, . . . ,9 pence, its average is 4.5p. Then the payoff on i is $Q_w/q_i - B$, which equals the odds O_i, since the odds are based on total return (not return plus original stake as in North America). So $q_i = Q_w/(B + O_i)$. Summing over all n horses gives

$$\sum_{i=1}^{n} q_i = 1 = Q_w \sum_{i=1}^{n} \left(\frac{1}{B + O_i}\right),$$

since some horse must win. Hence

$$Q_w = \frac{1}{\sum_{i=1}^{n} (B + O_i)}.$$

For place, there are one, two, three, or four horses that are in the money, depending upon the number of starters. So

$$Q_p = \frac{m}{\sum_{i=1}^{n} (B + O_i)},$$

where $m = 1, 2, 3,$ or 4.

In the third race, the eight starters had win odds O_i and place odds PO_i as follows:

Horse Number	O_i	$1/(O_i + B)$	PO_i	$1/(PO_i + B)$
1	2.80	0.35149	1.10	0.87336
3	10.00	0.09955	1.50	0.64725
4	6.60	0.15049	1.90	0.51414
6	2.70	0.36430	1.60	0.60790
7	6.50	0.15279	1.80	0.54201
8	17.70	0.05635	3.10	0.31797
9	22.10	0.04516	3.30	0.29895
12	23.80	0.04194	3.50	0.28209
		1.25922		4.08367

Hence $Q_w = 1/1.25922 \cong 0.794$, and $Q_p = 3/4.0836 \cong 0.735$.

Since the track paybacks to win and place are different, we call the former, $Q_w = 0.794$, and the latter, $Q_p = 0.735$.

It is easy to apply the Dr. Z system in Great Britain, although with its much-higher track takes, there may not be as many Dr. Z system bets. We will utilize the simple substitution that

$$q_i = \frac{Q_w}{O_i} \tag{17.1}$$

where Q_w is the track payback to win and O_i are the odds to win on the horse under consideration.

At Newbury, $Q = 0.794$, so equation (17.1) becomes

$$q_i = \frac{0.794}{O_i}. \tag{17.2}$$

We developed new equations and figures to compute the expected value per pound bet to place, which may be used with your cutoff to determine when to bet.

The expected value per pound bet to place on horse i is

$$\begin{aligned} \text{EX Place} &= (\text{probability of placing})(\text{place odds}) \\ &= (\text{Prob})(PO_i). \end{aligned} \tag{17.3}$$

In equation (17.1), PO_i refers to the odds to place on horse i. Prob, the probability of placing, is determined as follows:*,†

With $n = 5$ to 7 horses, the first 2 horses place and

$$\text{Prob} = 0.0667 + 2.37q - 1.61q^2 - 0.0097n. \tag{17.5}$$

---

*These equations were developed using the 1981/82 Aqueduct data to relate probability of in-the-money finishes to q, the probability of winning, and n, the number of horses. Equations (17.5), (17.6), and (17.7) had R^2's of 0.991, 0.993, and 0.998, respectively. These equations are valid when q ranges from 0 to 0.6 for (17.5), from 0 to 0.45 for (17.6), and 0 to 0.3 for (17.7), which should be the case in most instances. However, Figures 17.7, 17.8, and 17.9 are valid for any q.

†In a race with $n = 2$, 3, or 4 horses, only one horse places, the winner. Such races are rare. Also, it is unlikely that the win and place pools would then become so unbalanced as to yield a Dr. Z system bet. However, one would occur when PO_i/O_i was at least 1.44, for a track payback of 0.794 and an expected-value cutoff of 1.14, since 1.14/0.794 is 1.44. In such a case, one would have a good bet.

With n = 8 to 15 horses, the first 3 horses place and

$$\text{Prob} = 0.0665 + 3.44q - 3.47q^2 - 0.0049n. \tag{17.6}$$

With n = 16 or more horses, the first 4 horses place and

$$\text{Prob} = 0.0371 + 4.47q - 6.29q^2 - 0.00164n. \tag{17.7}$$

You may use Figures 17.7, 17.8, and 17.9 to determine Prob directly using only O_i, the win odds on the horse in question. You read off the graph corresponding to the number of horses in the race. Figure 17.7 corresponds to equation (17.5) and applies when there are five, six, or seven horses. Figure 17.8 corresponds to equation (17.6) and applies when there are eight to fifteen horses. Finally, Figure 17.9 corresponds to equation (17.7) and applies when there are sixteen or more horses.

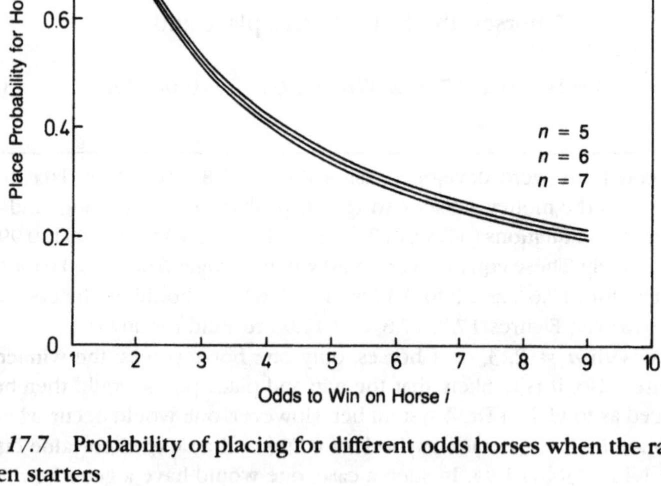

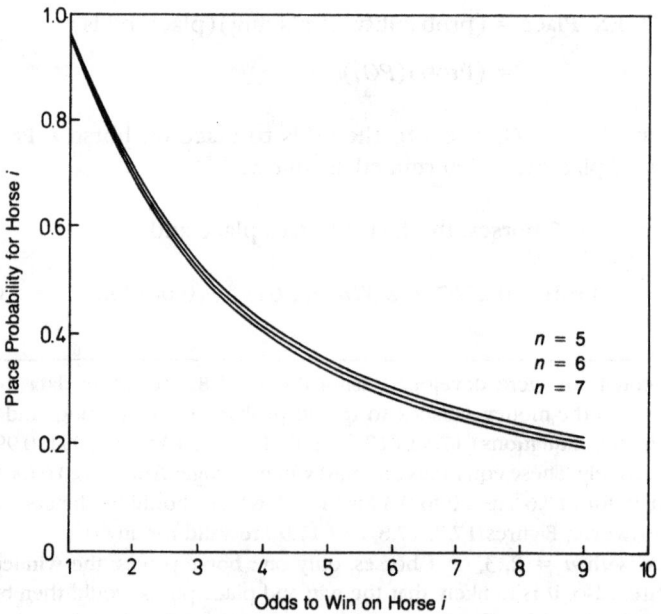

Figure 17.7 Probability of placing for different odds horses when the race has five to seven starters

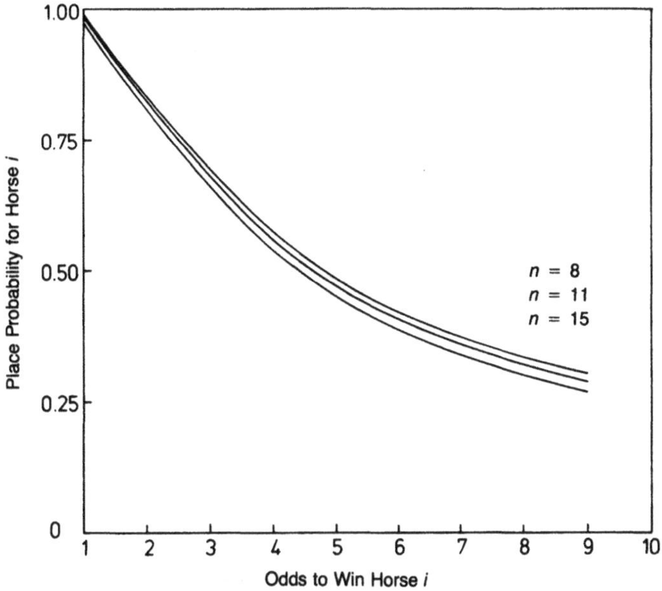

Figure 17.8 Probability of placing for different odds horses when the race has eight to fifteen starters

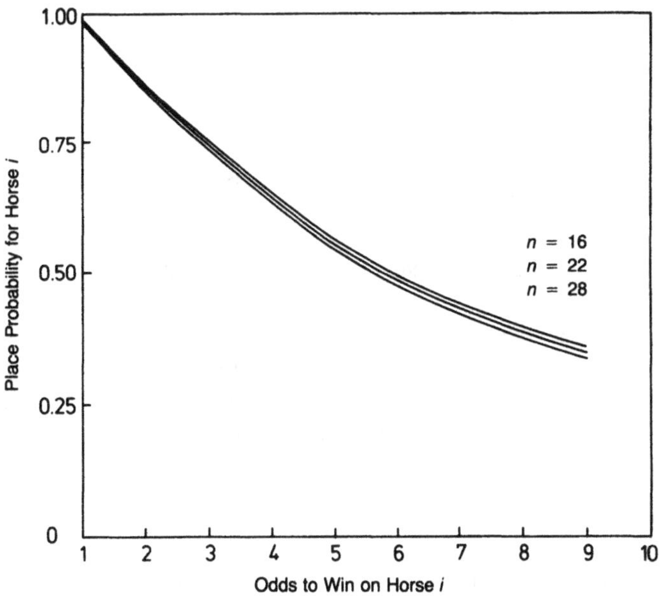

Figure 17.9 Probability of placing for different odds horses when the race has sixteen or more starters

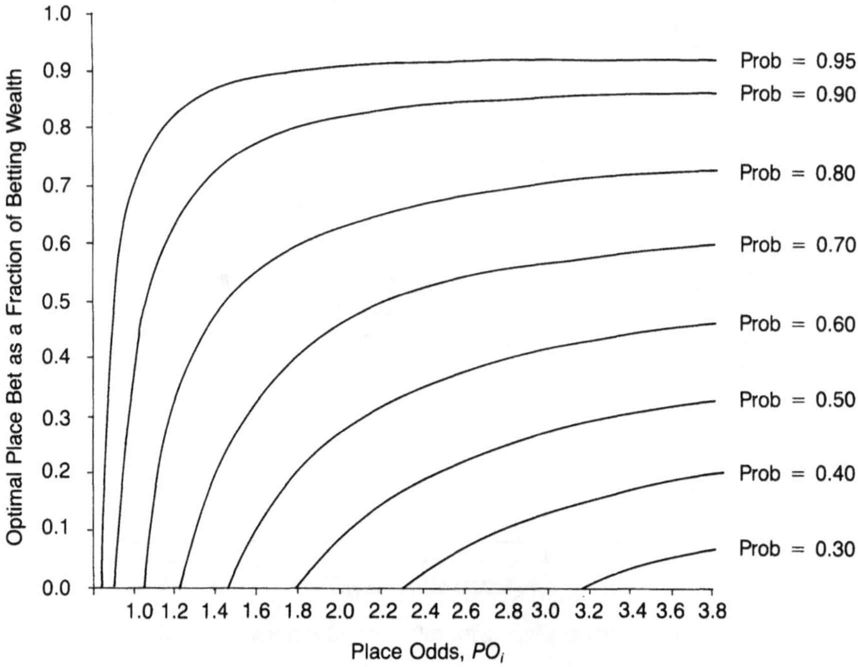

Figure 17.10 The optimal bet when the probability of placing is Prob and the place odds of the horse in question is PO_i

The optimal Kelly-criterion bet is then*

$$\text{Optimal bet} = \left(\frac{\text{Prob } PO_i - 1}{PO_i - 1}\right)(\text{betting wealth}). \qquad (17.8)$$

So you wager (Prob $PO_i - 1)/(PO_i - 1)$ percent of your betting wealth.

You can determine the optimal fraction of your wealth to bet indicated by equation (17.8) using Figure 17.10.

The fourth race was the Kingsclere Stakes for two-year-old fillies over 6 furlongs. The field had seven starters, which meant that only two horses could place. The favorite of the crowd at odds of 2.20—1 to win was

*We have assumed that your bets will be small and hence will not affect the odds very much. Thus to determine the optimal bet b for betting wealth w_0, you maximize Prob $\log[w_0 + (PO_i - 1)b] + (1 - \text{Prob})\log(w_0 - b)$, whose solution is equation (17.8).

Valkyrie. She was ridden by the legendary jockey Lester Piggott, England's answer to America's Bill Shoemaker. Near post time, the place odds on Valkyrie were 1.90—1. Hence by equation (17.2),

$$q = \frac{0.794}{2.20} = 0.361.$$

So Valkyrie had a 36.1% chance of winning the race. Her chance of placing, using equation (17.5) or Figure 17.7, was

$$\begin{aligned}\text{Prob} &= 0.0667 + 2.37(0.361) - 1.61(0.361)^2 - 0.0097(7)\\ &= 0.646.\end{aligned}$$

Hence, Valkyrie's chance of placing was 64.6%. The expected value per pound bet to place on Valkyrie from equation (17.3) was

$$\text{EX Place} = (\text{Prob})(PO_i)$$

$$\text{EX Place} = (0.646)(1.90) = 1.23.$$

Thus we should expect to make a 23% profit betting on Valkyrie to place.

My betting fortune was £100, so from Figure 17.10 or equation (17.8), my optimal bet was £25. Pebbles won the race, followed by Refill, with Valkyrie taking third. I lost my £25 bet (see pages 360 and 361).

The fifth race was the Kenneth Robertson Stakes for three-year-olds over one mile and 3 furlongs. There were eight starters, so three horses would place. With three minutes to post time the tote board read as follows:

	Horse						
	#1	#2	#4	#8	#9	#10	#11
Win odds	7.20	4.70	3.50	5.50	5.90	7.70	15.40
Place odds	1.70	2.70	1.40	1.20	1.60	1.80	3.60

Near the end of the betting period the tote board was

	Horse						
	#1	#2	#4	#8	#9	#10	#11
Win odds	7.30	4.80	3.60	4.30	6.90	9.10	17.20
Place odds	1.90	1.80	1.70	1.20	2.00	1.90	3.40

Fourth Race
TOTE TREBLE

Six Furlongs, for Two Yrs Old Fillies Only

3.30 The Kingsclere Stakes

£6000 added to stakes
Distributed in accordance with Rule 194 (iii) (a)
(Includes a fourth prize)
for two yr old fillies only
SIX FURLONGS
£12 to enter. **£48** extra if declared to run
Weights 8st 8lb each

6 FURLONG START

Penalties, a winner of a race value £2500 .... 4lb
Maidens allowed 3lb

The winner of this race, if qualified under Rule 195, will receive a Fillies' Premium of £2400

FP A SS

72 entries, 54 at £12 and 18 at £60. — Closed 18th May, 1983.

Owners Prize Money. Winner £3817; Second £1253; Third £596; Fourth £268.
(Penalty Value £4963.20)

Form	No.	Horse / Breeding / Owner / Colours	Trainer	Age	st	lb	Draw	Jockey
1	**1**	**BLANCHE NEIGE** Gr f Forlorn River — La Magna **Mrs Paulette Meynet** **PINK, PURPLE diamonds, PURPLE sleeves, hooped cap.**	**(M.A. Jarvis, Newmarket)**		**8**	**8**	**(3)**	B. Raymond
41	**2**	**VALKYRIE** B f Bold Lad (IRE) — Sarissa **Lord Howard de Walden** **APRICOT.**	**(H. Cecil, Newmarket)**		**8**	**8**	**(4)**	L. Piggott
32	**5**	**DAMKINA** Gr f Hittite Glory — Charter Island **Mrs Peter Hastings** **PRIMROSE, BLACK hoop, armlets and cap.**	**(R. Sheather, Newmarket)**		**8**	**5**	**(6)**	
	8	**ISLAND MILL** B f Mill Reef (USA) — Siliciana **Mrs I.A. Balding** **GREEN and GOLD stripes.**	**(I.A. Balding, Kingsclere)**		**8**	**5**	**(2)**	J. Matthias
0	**10**	**PEBBLES** Ch f Sharpen Up — La Dolce **Capt M. Lemos** **ROYAL BLUE, WHITE hoop on body, striped cap.**	**(C.E. Brittain, Newmarket)**		**8**	**5**	**(5)**	P. Robinson
2450	**11**	**POUSDALE-TACHYTEES** B f Tachypous — Teesdale **Lord Oakley Ltd** **DARK GREEN, YELLOW chevron and armlets, hooped cap.**	**(Mrs C.J. Reavey, Wantage)**		**8**	**5**	**(7)**	
	13	**REFILL** Br f Mill Reef (USA) — Regal Twin (USA) **Mr E.N. Kronfeld** **DARK BLUE, WHITE cross-belts and sleeves, PINK cap.**	**(I.A. Balding, Kingsclere)**		**8**	**5**	**(1)**	Pat Eddery

NUMBER OF DECLARED RUNNERS 7 **(DUAL FORECAST)**

1st .... 2nd .... 3rd .... 4th ....

Time .... Distance: ....

Standard Time: 1 min. 12.6 secs.

1982 Winner: **Bright Crocus (USA)**, 8-5, L. Piggott, 4-9, H. Cecil 9 ran

The Horserace Betting Levy Board Prize Money Scheme provides for the inclusion of £486,810 added money at this racecourse of 1983

Fifth Race
DAILY DOUBLE

One Mile and Three Furlongs, for Three Yrs Old Only

4.00 The Kenneth Robertson Stakes (Handicap)

£3000 added to stakes
Distributed in accordance with Rule 194 (iii) (b)
for three yrs old only — Rated 0-50
ONE MILE AND THREE FURLONGS
£6 to enter, **£24** extra if declared to run

1 MILE 3 FURLONG START

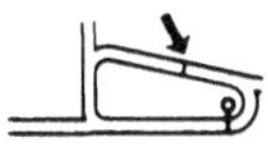

Lowest weight 7st 7lb
Penalties, after May 18th, a winner 6lb
SS

Weights raised 7lbs and Rule 94 (iii) (c) complied with where applicable

55 entries, 43 at £6 and 12 at £30. — Closed 18th May, 1983.
Owners Prize Money. Winner £1923; Second £585; Third £277.
(Penalty Value £2502.60)

Form — Trainer — Age — st — lb — Draw

1 ORANGE REEF .... **9 7 (5)**
Ch c Mill Reef (USA) — Carrot Top
515 **Beckhampton Ltd (A.J. Tree, Marlborough)** Pat Eddery
PINK, BLACK and WHITE striped sleeves, WHITE cap.

2 EQUANAID .... **9 7 (2)**
B c Dominion — Jungle Queen
010-12 **Mr V. Kilkenny (C.R. Nelson, Upper Lambourn)**
DARK GREEN and YELLOW (quartered), YELLOW sleeves, check cap.

4 GAELIC JEWEL .... **9 3 (8)**
Br f Scottish Rifle — Red Ruby
0-13 **Lavinia Duchess of Norfolk (J.L. Dunlop, Arundel)**
SKY BLUE, SCARLET quartered cap.

8 MOON JESTER .... **8 11 (4)**
Gr c Comedy Star (USA) — Castle Moon
41-2622 **Mr T.C. Marshall (M.D.I. Usher, Lambourn)** D McKay
ORANGE and WHITE (halved), sleeves reversed, striped cap.

9 MISINSKIE (USA) .... **8 11 (6)**
B f Nijinsky (CAN) — Kankakee Miss (USA)
4233- **Mr S.S. Niarchos (P.T. Walwyn, Lambourn)** J Mercer
DARK BLUE, LIGHT BLUE cross-belts, striped sleeves, WHITE cap.

10 HARBOUR BRIDGE .... **8 8 (7)**
B c Blakeney — Solar
030-015 **Mrs R.B. Kennard (W.G.R. Wightman, Upham)** B. Rouse
PALE BLUE and ORANGE stripes, BLUE cap, ORANGE diamond.

11 CAPTAIN WEBSTER .... **8 2 (3)**
Ch c Sandford Lad — Maynooth Belle
01-6416 **Mr J. Woodman (S. Woodman, Chichester)** W. Newnes
Mr S.R. Deveson
BROWN, YELLOW seams, hooped cap.

12 KWA ZULU (USA) .... **7 11 (1)**
Ch c Naskra (USA) — Sweet Nothings (USA)
055-5 **Mr D.I. Scott (G.H. Hunter, East Ilsley)**
Mr G.H. Hunter
BLACK, WHITE Maltese cross and cap, RED sleeves.

NUMBER OF DECLARED RUNNERS 8 **(DUAL FORECAST)**

1st .... 2nd .... 3rd .... 4th ....

Time: .... Distance: ....

Standard Time: 2 mins. 18 secs.

1982 Winner: **Khairpour,** 9-1, J. Reid, 11-10, R. F. Johnson Houghton 9 ran

The best bet was on Gaelic Jewel, the number 4 horse. From equation (17.2)

$$q = \frac{0.794}{3.60} = 0.221.$$

So Gaelic Jewel's chance of winning was 22.1%. His chance of placing, using equation (17.6) or Figure 17.8, was

$$\begin{aligned} \text{Prob} &= 0.0665 + 3.44(0.221) - 3.47(0.221)^2 - 0.0049(8) \\ &= 0.616. \end{aligned}$$

Hence, Gaelic Jewel would be in the money 61.1% of the time. The expected value per pound bet to place on Gaelic Jewel from equation (17.3) was then

$$\text{EX Place} = (0.616)(1.70) = 1.05.$$

This low expected value signalled caution. A bet of £5 was suggested from Figure 17.10 or equation (17.8).

$$\begin{aligned} \text{Optimal bet} &= \frac{(0.616)(1.70) - 1}{(1.70 - 1)} \text{(betting wealth)} \\ &= (0.07)(\pounds 75) \\ &= \pounds 5. \end{aligned}$$

Moon Jester won the race. Gaelic Jewel took second, and Orange Reef was third. My £5 bet returned £8.50, for a £3.50 profit.

In summary, the Dr. Z system is easy to apply in England, France, Italy, Germany, Australia, Hong Kong, and the other countries that utilize a win-and-place betting scheme. First determine Prob using one of Figures 17.7, 17.8, or 17.9. Then multiply Prob by PO_i to determine the expected value per pound bet to place. If this value exceeds the cutoff—we recommend 1.14—then use O_i in Figure 17.10 to determine the optimal bet. We have not done enough research to determine how often Dr. Z system bets will occur in England. With the higher track take, however, there will likely be fewer than in North America.

APPENDIX A

Thoroughbred Racetracks in North America: Seasons, Purses, Betting, and Track Takes

At the end of this appendix is a map that shows you the locations of the major thoroughbred racetracks in North America. More detailed information on the typical seasons, days, attendance, mutuel handle, races run, number and percentage of winning crowd favorites at these racetracks in 1982 appears in Table A.1. Information about racing in the United States appears in Tables A.2–A.5. Table A.2 shows the number of racing days by state for the twenty-four states that have thoroughbred racing. Oklahoma, Minnesota, and Iowa are likely to add racing soon, and New Hampshire's Rockingham Park is due to reopen soon. Delaware no longer has thoroughbred racing, now that Delaware Park has been closed. California has the most racing days, with large purses at Del Mar, Hollywood Park, and Santa Anita; medium purses at Bay Meadows and Golden Gate Fields; and small purses at the fair meetings.

The daily average gross purses by state in 1982 are shown in Table A.3. New York, which features Aqueduct, Belmont, and Saratoga and both on-track and off-track betting has the largest purses, averaging $151,000 per racing day. California and Arkansas have purses nearly as great. Arkansas rates so high because the only racing is at Oaklawn Park, one of the nation's top tracks. In 1982, purses in the United States averaged 6.8% of the money bet. The daily average betting in 1982, by state, appears in Table A.4. New York has the highest figure, followed by California and Arkansas, New Jersey, and Florida, each of which averaged over $1 million per day. The total betting per year appears in Table A.5. New York and California swamp the other states, with totals of $2.2 and $1.5 billion, respectively. Surprisingly, Louisiana is third, higher than wealthier states such as Illinois, Florida, New Jersey, and Pennsylvania, and the famous racing state of Kentucky.

The track takes that are set by state in the United States and by province in Canada appear in Table A.6.

TABLE A.1 *Typical seasons, attendance, mutuel handle, and percentage of winning favorites of the crowd at major North American racetracks in 1982*

Track	Dates	Days	Attendance	Mutuel Handle	Races Run	Winning First Choices	Percentage Winning Favorites
Agua Caliente, Mexico	Jan. 1 to Dec. 31	100	650,500	40,429,519	1,079	397	.35
Ak-Sar-Ben, Nebr.	Apr. 27 to July 26	67	1,006,636	115,941,609	613	170	.27
Albuquerque, N.M.	Sep. 10 to Sep. 26	17	194,994	16,190,449	150	43	.27
Arlington Park, Ill.	May 17 to Sep. 30	121	1,284,981	176,654,761	1,099	402	.35
Aqueduct, N.Y.	Jan. 1 to Mar. 15	59	784,749	148,109,394	519	158	.30
	Mar. 17 to May 17	52	860,543	171,566,282	468	162	.33
	Oct. 13 to Dec. 31	68	965,872	195,433,702	612	193	.31
Assiniboia Downs, Man.	Apr. 23 to Oct. 11	108	430,821	40,529,870	1,001	352	.34
Atlantic City, N.J.	May 27 to Sep. 4	72	473,379	45,904,747	656	206	.30
Atokad Park, Nebr.	Apr. 30 to July 25	40	66,686	3,796,533	356	140	.38
	Nov. 12 to Dec. 12	14	24,454	2,491,321	123	55	.43
Belmont Park, N.Y.	May 19 to Aug. 2	70	1,289,698	221,472,820	630	227	.36
	Sep. 1 to Oct. 11	36	617,416	110,060,017	324	101	.30
Beulah Park, Ohio	Mar. 6 to Apr. 25	36	153,289	18,264,991	339	111	.32
	Sep. 25 to Nov. 28	46	183,862	22,089,733	434	116	.25
Billings, Mont.	Aug. 11 to Oct. 3	33	124,080	5,063,825	334	121	.34
Bay Meadows, Calif.	Jan. 1 to Feb. 6	27	253,668	47,983,101	247	74	.29
	Sep. 22 to Oct. 24	25	252,181	44,045,016	225	67	.29
	Oct. 26 to Dec. 31	49	467,237	85,710,533	449	120	.26
Bay Meadows Fair, Calif.	Sep. 6 to Sep. 19	12	110,979	19,099,266	108	27	.24
Balmoral, Ill.	May 21 to Aug. 22	67	199,537	25,031,368	620	230	.36
Boise, Idaho	May 11 to Aug. 22	50	150,939	6,465,564	346	122	.34
Bowie, Md.	Jan. 1 to Mar. 12	57	434,503	59,256,971	513	151	.29
	Sep. 7 to Oct. 18	36	253,555	33,764,538	324	114	.34
Churchill Downs, Ky.	Apr. 24 to June 26	55	719,278	75,316,479	496	169	.32
	Nov. 1 to Nov. 27	24	242,855	30,039,099	216	68	.31

Coeur d'Alene, Idaho	Apr. 4 to May 16	14	21,113	1,763,472	118	39	.32
Centennial, Colo.	May 1 to Sep. 26	96	313,805	30,638,584	963	324	.32
	Sep. 29 to Nov. 7	24	53,166	5,330,636	120	47	.38
Columbus, Ohio	Sep. 1 to Oct. 3	26	90,800	8,512,210	224	68	.29
Commodore, Pa.	May 1 to Sep. 12	78	168,047	12,778,543	780	272	.33
Calder, Fl.	Jan. 1 to Jan. 7	6	64,102	8,900,284	60	24	.39
	May 17 to Nov. 10	130	1,072,291	134,487,479	1,299	436	.32
	Nov. 11 to Dec. 31	44	385,357	52,316,043	440	146	.32
Charlestown, W.V.	Jan. 8 to Mar. 31	52	163,894	17,334,892	505	147	.28
	Apr. 1 to June 30	65	265,559	24,828,104	633	207	.31
	July 1 to Sep. 30	68	302,370	26,477,994	665	223	.33
	Oct. 1 to Dec. 11	51	202,980	21,263,573	504	176	.34
Delta Downs, La.	Jan. 1 to Mar. 28	49	154,177	22,757,751	490	155	.31
	Sep. 10 to Dec. 31	57	165,980	23,335,873	350	120	.33
Delaware, Del.	May 29 to Sep. 6	73	380,434	41,294,062	672	224	.32
Detroit, Mich.	July 13 to Oct. 24	90	436,577	59,215,287	843	293	.33
Del Mar, Calif.	July 21 to Sep. 8	43	842,062	133,798,260	387	114	.28
Ellis Park, Ky.	July 1 to Sep. 6	59	302,915	34,437,823	553	149	.26
Exhibition Park, B.C.	Apr. 12 to Oct. 16	109	1,106,037	146,837,394	1,089	340	.31
Evangeline Downs, La.	Apr. 1 to Sep. 6	94	356,416	47,626,656	898	300	.32
Fort Erie, Ont.	May 8 to Aug. 2	37	181,896	17,917,624	318	114	.35
	Aug. 4 to Sep. 3	22	128,622	30,382,121	206	60	.28
Ferndale, Calif.	Aug. 12 to Aug. 21	9	31,563	1,190,743	51	28	.50
Fair Grounds, La.	Jan. 1 to Apr. 4	69	540,638	94,665,569	690	253	.35
	Nov. 25 to Dec. 31	27	245,864	35,286,225	270	81	.30
Finger Lakes, N.Y.	Mar. 28 to Apr. 18	8	28,422	2,992,195	72	23	.31
	Apr. 23 to June 27	48	155,092	16,246,723	434	144	.32
	June 29 to Sep. 1	48	187,765	18,099,973	442	160	.35
	Sep. 3 to Nov. 9	49	149,064	15,998,158	444	145	.32
Fresno, Calif.	May 7 to May 31	18	66,245	7,749,026	104	35	.32
	Oct. 4 to Oct. 16	12	82,476	9,018,714	108	40	.36

TABLE A.1 *(Continued)*

Track	Dates	Days	Attendance	Mutuel Handle	Races Run	Winning First Choices	Percentage Winning Favorites
Fairmount Park, Ill.	Mar. 26 to Nov. 6	155	804,119	83,702,594	1,570	502	.31
Great Barrington Fair, Mass.	Sep. 17 to Sep. 26	10	51,658	5,555,324	100	43	.42
	Oct. 1 to Oct. 11	10	34,488	3,015,452	100	43	.40
Great Falls, Mont.	July 28 to Aug. 8	12	—	1,032,426	107	43	.41
Golden Gate, Calif.	Feb. 9 to May 12	67	679,792	120,252,239	605	193	.31
	May 13 to June 27	35	377,245	68,866,904	317	100	.30
Gulfstream Park, Fla.	Mar. 8 to May 15	60	647,995	88,397,226	600	180	.29
Greenwood, Can.	Mar. 22 to May 1	33	321,811	46,249,144	283	105	.36
	Nov. 1 to Dec. 9	34	287,286	42,854,757	304	98	.32
Grants Pass, Ore.	June 11 to July 5	13	19,696	1,349,859	74	40	.51
Hawthorne, Ill.	Jan. 1 to Jan. 2	2	22,340	3,225,973	18	3	.16
	Oct. 1 to Dec. 31	79	686,878	102,084,166	711	243	.33
Hialeah, Fla.	Jan. 8 to Mar. 6	50	614,090	92,769,564	503	168	.32
Hollywood Park, Calif.	Apr. 23 to July 19	66	1,796,686	335,255,438	595	213	.35
	Nov. 3 to Dec. 23	38	837,687	152,081,677	342	98	.27
Hazel Park, Mich.	Mar. 6 to July 10	99	532,875	77,799,438	919	306	.32
Jefferson Downs, La.	Apr. 8 to Sep. 18	105	484,906	59,867,648	939	321	.33
	Sep. 22 to Nov. 13	32	136,018	17,907,835	296	91	.29
Keeneland, Ky.	Apr. 2 to Apr. 23	15	183,335	17,952,311	120	47	.38
	Oct. 9 to Oct. 30	16	204,767	19,099,494	129	44	.33
Keystone, Pa.	Jan. 1 to Jan. 8	7	53,730	6,841,068	63	14	.21
	Feb. 2 to Feb. 24	14	99,826	12,887,595	126	37	.29
	Feb. 26 to Mar. 24	24	185,828	24,716,067	216	66	.29

	Mar. 26 to May 12	38	280,085	38,445,543	343	86	.24
	May 14 to May 31	16	127,898	14,977,609	145	43	.29
	June 1 to June 23	17	102,354	12,621,770	153	49	.31
	June 25 to Aug. 11	35	227,017	27,682,378	315	101	.30
	Aug. 13 to Sep. 15	26	185,777	21,902,649	235	77	.31
	Sep. 17 to Nov. 6	44	296,922	39,696,249	396	125	.30
	Nov. 7 to Dec. 31	46	302,711	41,378,098	414	122	.28
Los Alamitos, Calif.	Oct. 25 to Nov. 8	13	108,343	17,871,269	104	38	.35
Louisiana Downs, La.	May 7 to Oct. 17	115	1,299,868	208,198,136	1,092	303	.27
La Mesa Park, N.M.	May 1 to Oct. 3	59	107,043	13,711,177	389	116	.29
Latonia, Ky.	Jan. 1 to Apr. 1	69	255,603	32,286,430	662	204	.30
	Sep. 9 to Oct. 7	25	112,079	12,929,652	227	70	.30
	Nov. 28 to Dec. 31	29	116,033	15,082,852	269	91	.32
Longacres, Wash.	Apr. 28 to Oct. 25	131	1,235,682	160,650,188	1,310	352	.26
Lincoln State Fair, Neb.	July 28 to Aug. 29	25	169,826	19,487,108	238	81	.33
	Oct. 6 to Nov. 7	25	100,007	11,558,966	219	90	.40
Laurel, Md.	May 24 to July 19	49	319,365	40,999,337	441	150	.33
	Oct. 19 to Dec. 31	61	497,636	67,531,290	541	178	.32
Marquis Downs, Can.	July 9 to Oct. 16	57	97,464	9,999,606	570	178	.30
Meadowlands, N.J.	Sep. 6 to Dec. 31	95	1,501,475	204,330,278	974	305	.30
Marshfield Fair, Mass.	Aug. 20 to Aug. 28	8	48,284	3,336,207	80	32	.40
Monmouth Park, N.J.	Apr. 30 to Sep. 4	110	1,124,113	145,181,452	1,037	338	.32
Northampton Fair, Mass.	Sep. 3 to Sep. 12	10	54,847	5,462,528	100	46	.45
Northlands Park, Alta.	Apr. 9 to Aug. 9	85	505,738	73,233,797	839	296	.35
Oaklawn Park, Ark.	Feb. 5 to Apr. 10	56	1,296,635	159,195,877	538	168	.30
Penn National, Pa.	Jan. 1 to Mar. 3	37	148,681	15,600,459	342	106	.30
	Mar. 5 to July 23	99	487,578	45,619,549	912	294	.31
	July 24 to Dec. 19	101	461,625	44,884,216	953	303	.30

TABLE A.1 ***(Continued)***

Track	Dates	Days	Attendance	Mutuel Handle	Races Run	Winning First Choices	Percentage Winning Favorites
Pimlico, Md.	Mar. 13 to May 22	60	583,182	72,482,503	540	175	.31
Park Jefferson, S.D.	July 31 to Oct. 10	23	31,949	2,296,009	199	72	.34
Playfair, Wash.	May 21 to Oct. 11	82	331,683	25,645,858	820	268	.32
Pleasanton, Calif.	June 28 to July 11	12	132,134	17,435,726	108	36	.31
Portland Meadows, Ore.	Jan. 2 to Apr. 25	61	288,116	28,208,340	537	176	.31
	Oct. 30 to Dec. 31	33	147,639	12,840,923	294	90	.29
Pomona, Calif.	Sep. 9 to Sep. 26	18	246,370	34,173,163	164	43	.25
Prescott Downs, Ariz.	May 29 to Sep. 6	34	64,828	4,141,970	201	61	.29
River Downs, Ohio	Apr. 24 to June 27	56	264,846	31,017,129	534	152	.27
	June 28 to Sep. 6	61	311,259	37,260,594	589	203	.33
Regina, Sask.	May 7 to July 3	34	46,309	4,870,059	334	122	.36
Rillito, Ariz.	Jan. 1 to Apr. 11	32	38,887	2,892,758	167	58	.33
Ruidoso, N.M.	May 8 to Sep. 6	66	360,737	41,612,788	450	162	.34
Santa Anita Park, Calif.	Jan. 1 to Apr. 21	81	2,518,942	415,047,491	729	247	.32
	Sep. 29 to Nov. 1	27	778,185	120,664,811	243	79	.31
	Dec. 26 to Dec. 31	5	180,284	26,232,290	45	17	.36
Sacramento, Calif.	Aug. 24 to Sep. 6	14	135,511	11,308,763	126	48	.36
Salem, Ore.	Aug. 28 to Oct. 24	30	97,300	6,108,357	257	98	.36
Sandown Park, B.C.	Oct. 21 to Nov. 21	19	41,087	3,434,149	162	57	.33
Saratoga, N.Y.	Aug. 4 to Aug. 30	27	678,059	75,030,078	243	89	.36
Santa Fe, N.M.	May 7 to Sep. 6	69	253,614	27,468,451	556	185	.32
Solano, Calif.	July 13 to July 25	12	131,886	13,114,915	108	38	.34
Sportsman's Park, Ill.	Feb. 17 to May 15	74	718,410	105,998,674	666	236	.34
Santa Rosa, Calif.	July 26 to Aug. 7	12	116,749	12,791,008	108	26	.23

Stockton, Calif.	Aug. 9 to Aug. 21	12	63,348	8,892,122	108	34	.31
Stampede Park, Alta.	Aug. 13 to Nov. 8	66	289,275	46,736,507	660	201	.30
Suffolk Downs, Mass.	Jan. 1 to Aug. 15	161	1,108,697	148,705,932	1,622	529	.31
	Aug. 30 to Dec. 31	89	567,952	77,370,040	899	294	.31
Sunland Park, N.M.	Jan. 1 to May 2	53	176,436	20,872,868	444	160	.35
	Oct. 15 to Dec. 31	30	81,231	9,435,332	227	83	.35
Tampa Bay, Fla.	Jan. 1 to Apr. 5	68	291,203	25,278,194	683	227	.32
	Dec. 3 to Dec. 31	14	54,240	5,038,666	140	50	.34
Thistledown, Ohio	Mar. 19 to May 23	46	209,639	28,037,694	434	151	.34
	May 26 to Aug. 1	51	254,513	31,623,508	482	164	.33
	Aug. 4 to Oct. 10	50	239,799	30,049,728	471	155	.31
	Oct. 13 to Dec. 13	44	179,979	24,941,092	425	129	.29
Timonium, Md.	July 20 to Sep. 6	42	231,717	25,851,655	386	139	.35
Turf Paradise, Ariz.	Jan. 1 to Mar. 5	46	291,254	27,987,932	506	137	.26
	Mar. 6 to May 28	58	279,837	27,855,443	590	189	.31
	Oct. 13 to Dec. 31	58	364,956	25,896,826	552	168	.29
Waterford Park, W.V.	Jan. 1 to Mar. 31	58	111,949	13,616,503	602	194	.31
	Apr. 1 to June 30	67	153,778	15,771,067	706	230	.32
	July 1 to Sep. 30	66	166,355	16,221,754	708	233	.32
	Oct. 1 to Dec. 31	55	108,260	11,854,079	574	179	.30
Woodbine, Ont.	May 2 to Aug. 2	68	700,559	104,933,274	618	202	.32
	Sep. 4 to Oct. 31	44	411,093	70,549,204	415	140	.33
Yakima Meadows, Wash.	Feb. 13 to Apr. 25	25	71,886	7,093,925	250	81	.32
	May 1 to May 31	11	24,311	1,940,825	46	11	.23
	Aug. 28 to Oct. 3	13	32,829	2,138,872	50	20	.38
	Oct. 9 to Nov. 28	24	48,579	4,958,798	240	88	.36
Grand Totals		7,729	57,050,085	7,723,476,101	71,516	23,412	.32

Source: The American Racing Manual, 1983; The *Daily Racing Form.*

TABLE A.2 *Thoroughbred racing days in the United States in 1982*

1.	California	607	13.	Massachusetts	288
2.	Pennsylvania	587	14.	New Jersey	279
3.	Louisiana	548	15.	Nebraska	237
4.	Illinois	498	16.	Arizona	228
5.	West Virginia	482	17.	Michigan	189
6.	New York	466	18.	Oregon	137
7.	Ohio	390	19.	Colorado	120
8.	Florida	372	20.	Delaware	73
9.	Maryland	311	21.	Idaho	64
10.	Washington	308	22.	Arkansas	56
11.	Kentucky	295	23.	Montana	45
12.	New Mexico	294	24.	South Dakota	23

Source: American Racing Manual, 1983, and Hollingsworth (1983).

TABLE A.3 *Daily average gross purses at all thoroughbred tracks in various U.S. states in 1982 in dollars*

1.	New York	151,000	13.	Pennsylvania	51,000
2.	California	145,000	14.	Nebraska	43,000
3.	Arkansas	143,000	15.	Ohio	41,000
4.	New Jersey	101,000	16.	Washington	36,000
5.	Florida	87,000	17.	New Mexico	29,000
6.	Maryland	79,000	18.	Arizona	27,000
7.	Delaware	73,000	19.	Colorado	24,000
8.	Illinois	73,000	20.	West Virginia	24,000
9.	Kentucky	73,000	21.	Oregon	18,000
10.	Louisiana	69,000	22.	Montana	12,000
11.	Massachusetts	55,000	23.	South Dakota	10,000
12.	Michigan	52,000	24.	Idaho	9,000

Source: American Racing Manual, 1983, and Hollingsworth (1983).

TABLE A.4 *Daily average betting in the United States in 1982 in dollars*

1.	New York	4,786,350	13.	Washington	638,827
2.	California	3,348,967	14.	Pennsylvania	617,550
3.	Arkansas	2,844,569	15.	Ohio	572,524
4.	New Jersey	1,412,202	16.	Delaware	565,672
5.	Florida	1,106,731	17.	Oregon[a]	442,171
6.	Illinois	998,941	18.	New Mexico[a]	417,527
7.	Maryland	978,735	19.	Arizona[a]	392,356
8.	Massachusetts	851,208	20.	Colorado	319,152
9.	Louisiana[a]	838,080	21.	West Virginia	305,743
10.	Kentucky	812,137	22.	Idaho[a]	87,500
11.	Michigan	721,130	23.	Montana[a]	85,190
12.	Nebraska[a]	666,503	24.	South Dakota[a]	71,980

Source: National Association of State Racing Commissioners and Hollingsworth (1983).
[a]Includes quarter-horse racing.

TABLE A.5 *Thoroughbred betting in the United States in 1982 in dollars*

1. New York	2,228,000,000	13. Nebraska[a]	187,000,000
2. California	1,547,000,000	14. Arkansas	159,000,000
3. Louisiana[a]	503,000,000	15. West Virginia	147,000,000
4. Illinois	498,000,000	16. Michigan	137,000,000
5. Florida	398,000,000	17. New Mexico[a]	129,000,000
6. New Jersey	395,000,000	18. Arizona[a]	86,000,000
7. Pennsylvania	360,000,000	19. Oregon[a]	50,000,000
8. Maryland	300,000,000	20. Delaware	41,000,000
9. Massachusetts	243,000,000	21. Colorado	31,000,000
10. Kentucky	237,000,000	22. Montana	11,000,000
11. Ohio	223,000,000	23. Idaho	10,000,000
12. Washington	205,000,000	24. South Dakota[a]	4,000,000

Source: National Association of State Racing Commissioners and Hollingsworth (1983).
[a]Includes quarter-horse racing.

TABLE A.6 *Track takes in various states and provinces in 1982*

State	Track Take (%)	State	Track Take (%)
Arizona	18	Nebraska	15
Arkansas	16	New Hampshire Harness	19
California	15	New Jersey	17
Harness and fair track	16.75	New Mexico	18.75
Colorado	17	New York	17
Florida	17.6	Harness	17
Harness	19	Ohio	17.50
Quarter horse	18	Oregon	16
Idaho	17	Pennsylvania	17
Illinois	17	South Dakota	18.25
Kentucky	15	Washington	16
Harness	18	West Virginia	17.25
Quarter horse	17		
Louisiana	17	PROVINCE	
Maryland	15	Alberta	15.1
Fair tracks	16	British Columbia	16.3
Steeplechase	18	Manitoba	17.6
Massachusetts	19	Ontario	14.8
Michigan	16.25	Saskatchewan	22.1
Montana	20		

Source: The *Daily Racing Form.* Your local Jockey Club can advise you of any changes in these rates.

Locations of North American Thoroughbred Tracks

MAP KEYS

1 Ak Sar-Ben
2 Albuquerque
3 Aqueduct
4 Arlington Park
5 Assiniboia Downs
6 Atlantic City
7 Atokad Park
8 Balmoral
9 Bay Meadows
10 Belmont Park
12 Beulah Race Track
14 Bowie Race Course
16 Calder Race Course
17 Caliente
18 Centennial Race Track
19 Charles Town
20 Churchill Downs
21 Coeur D'Alene
22 Columbus
23 Commodore Downs
25 Delaware Park
26 Del Mar
27 Delta Downs
28 Detroit Race Course
29 James C. Ellis Park
30 El Comandante
31 Evangeline Downs
32 Exhibition Park
33 Fair Grounds
34 Fairmount Park
35 Ferndale
36 Finger Lakes
38 Fonner Park
39 Fort Erie
40 Fresno
41 Golden Gate Fields
42 Great Barrington
44 Greenwood
45 Gulfstream Park
46 Hawthorne
47 Hazel Park
48 Hialeah Park
49 Hipodromo de las Americas
50 Hollywood Park
51 Jefferson Downs
52 Juarez Race Track
53 Keeneland
54 Keystone Race Track
55 La Mesa Park
56 Latonia
57 Laurel Race Course
58 Les Bols Park
59 Lethbridge
60 Lincoln State Fair
61 Longacres
62 Los Alamitos
63 Louisiana Downs
64 Marquis Downs
65 Marshfield Fair
66 The Meadowlands
67 Monmouth Park
68 Northampton
69 Northlands Park
70 Oaklawn Park
71 Park Jefferson
72 Penn National Race Course
73 Pimlico Race Course
74 Playfair
75 Pleasanton
76 Pocono Downs
77 Pomona
78 Portland Meadows
79 Prescott Downs
80 Regina
81 Rillito Race Track
82 River Downs
83 Rockingham Park
84 Ruidoso Downs
85 Sacramento
86 Salem Fairgrounds
87 Sandown Park
88 Santa Anita Park
89 Sante Fe
90 Santa Rosa
91 Saratoga
93 Solano
94 Sportsman's Park
95 Stampede Park
96 Stockton
97 Suffolk Downs
98 Sunland Park
99 Tampa Bay Downs
100 Thistledown
101 Timonium
102 Turf Paradise
103 Waterford Park
104 Woodbine
105 Yakima Meadows

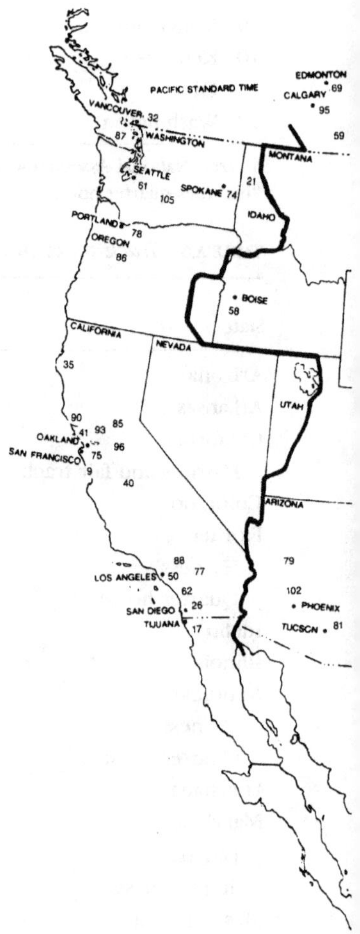

MOUNTAIN STANDARD TIME
64
CENTRAL STANDARD TIME
EASTERN STANDARD TIME
CANADA
80
WINNIPEG
5
NORTH DAKOTA
MINNESOTA
SOUTH DAKOTA
WYOMING
WISCONSIN
MICH
MICHIGAN
CANADA
MAINE
VT
NH
83
TORONTO
44
104
ROCHESTER
36
39
BUFFALO
91
ALBANY
SALEM
97
MASS
BOSTON
68
65
RI
PAWTUCKET
NEW YORK
42
CONN
10
76
66
NEWARK
3
WINDSOR
DETROIT
28
23
ERIE
PENNSYLVANIA
WILKES BARRE
CLEVELAND
PHILADELPHIA
47
100
PITTSBURGH
HARRISBURG
72
54
67
IOWA
71
SIOUX CITY
7
NEBRASKA
ILLINOIS
4
94
CHICAGO
INDIANA
OHIO
AKRON
103
COLUMBUS
12
BALTIMORE
101
25
6
MD
WILMINGTON
19
57
73
14
46
8
22
38
OMAHA
60
1
MISSOURI
82
CINCINNATI
WASHINGTON
COLORADO
DENVER
18
KANSAS
EVANSVILLE
LOUISVILLE
56
LEXINGTON
WEST VIRGINIA
VIRGINIA
34
ST LOUIS
20
53
HENDERSON
29
KENTUCKY
NORTH CAROLINA
NEW MEXICO
OKLAHOMA
TENNESSEE
SANTA FE
89
55
TEXAS
ARKANSAS
ALBUQUERQUE
2
MISSISSIPPI
ALABAMA
GEORGIA
S CAROLINA
HOT SPRINGS
70
84
63
SHREVEPORT
LOUISIANA
98
EL PASO
52
FLORIDA
31
33
MEXICO
BEAUMONT
27
51
NEW ORLEANS
99
TAMPA
45
HALLANDALE
48
MIAMI
16
SAN JUAN
30
PUERTO RICO
MEXICO CITY
49

APPENDIX B

Mathematics of the Dr. Z System*

The basic assumptions of the Dr. Z model are (1) the efficiency of the win market; (2) the validity of the Harville formulas, which along with (1) provide good estimates of the probability of all possible in-the-money finishes; and (3) the Kelly-criterion capital-growth model for determining the optimal bet size.

If q_i is the probability that horse i wins, then assumption (1) is

$$q_i = \frac{W_i}{W} \tag{B1}$$

where $i = 1, \ldots, n$ horses and W_i is the amount bet to win on horse i out of a total win pool of W.

The Harville formulas then estimate the probability that horse i is first and j is second as

$$q_{ij} = \frac{q_i q_j}{1 - q_i} \tag{B2}$$

for all i and j running from 1 to n. Similarly, the probability that horse i is first, j is second, and k is third is

$$q_{ijk} = \frac{q_i q_j q_k}{(1 - q_i)(1 - q_i - q_j)} \tag{B3}$$

for all i, j, and k running from 1 to n.

*This appendix is highly mathematical and is intended for those readers who would like a more detailed development of the Dr. Z system. The results given here were adapted from Hausch, Ziemba, and Rubinstein (1981) and Hausch and Ziemba (October 1983).

Equations B1–B3 can be used to calculate the expected value per additional dollar bet to place, EXP_l, and show, EXS_l on any given horse l as follows:

$$EXP_l =$$

$$\sum_{\substack{j=1\\ j\neq l}}^{n}\left(\frac{q_l \times q_j}{1-q_l}\right)\left\{1+\frac{1}{20}\text{INT}\left[\left(\frac{Q(P+1)-(1+P_l+P_j)}{2}\right)\left(\frac{1}{1+P_l}\right)20\right]\right\}$$

$$+\sum_{\substack{i=1\\ i\neq l}}^{n}\left(\frac{q_i q_l}{1-q_i}\right)\left\{1+\frac{1}{20}\text{INT}\left[\left(\frac{Q(P+1)-(1+P_i+P_l)}{2}\right)\left(\frac{1}{1+P_l}\right)20\right]\right\}$$

(B4)

$$EXS_l =$$

$$\sum_{\substack{j=1\\ j\neq l}}^{n}\sum_{\substack{k=1\\ k\neq l,j}}^{n}\frac{q_l q_j q_k}{(1-q_l)(1-q_l-q_j)}$$

$$\times\left\{1+\frac{1}{20}\text{INT}\left[\left(\frac{Q(S+1)-(1+S_l+S_j+S_k)}{3}\right)\left(\frac{1}{1+S_l}\right)20\right]\right\}$$

$$+\sum_{\substack{i=1\\ i\neq l}}^{n}\sum_{\substack{k=1\\ k\neq i,l}}^{n}\frac{q_i q_l q_k}{(1-q_i)(1-q_i-q_l)}$$

$$\times\left\{1+\frac{1}{20}\text{INT}\left[\left(\frac{Q(S+1)-(1+S_i+S_l+S_k)}{3}\right)\left(\frac{1}{1+S_l}\right)20\right]\right\}$$

$$+\sum_{\substack{i=1\\ i\neq l}}^{n}\sum_{\substack{j=1\\ j\neq l,i}}^{n}\frac{q_i q_j q_l}{(1-q_i)(1-q_i-q_j)}$$

$$\times\left\{1+\frac{1}{20}\text{INT}\left[\left(\frac{Q(S+1)-(1+S_i+S_j+S_l)}{3}\right)\left(\frac{1}{1+S_l}\right)20\right]\right\}$$

(B5)

In these formulas Q is the track payback; P_i and S_i are the place and show bets on horse i, respectively; $P = \sum_{i=1}^{n} P_i$ and $S = \sum_{i=1}^{n} S_i$ are the place and show pools, respectively; and $\text{INT}(Y)$ means the largest integer not exceeding Y. The expressions involving INT assume here that the breakage is of the 5¢ variety. For 10¢ breakage replace 20 by 10 in equations (B4) and (B5). These equations were used to compute the expected values per dollar bet in Table 5.1.

The Kelly criterion is equivalent to maximizing the expected logarithm of final wealth after the public's bets in each race are known. Considering the effect of all possible i, j, k finishes on the possible payoffs and the fact that our bets influence these odds, we have the following model for determining our optimal place and show bets, which we denote by p_l and s_l.

$$\underset{\{p_l\}\ \{s_l\}}{\text{Maximize}} \sum_{i=1}^{n} \sum_{\substack{j=1 \\ j \neq i}}^{n} \sum_{\substack{k=1 \\ k \neq i,j}}^{n} q_{ijk} \log \left[\begin{array}{l} \dfrac{Q(P + \Sigma_{l=1}^{n} p_l) - (p_i + p_j + P_i + P_j)}{2} \\ \times \left(\dfrac{p_i}{p_i + P_i} + \dfrac{p_j}{p_j + P_j} \right) \\ + \dfrac{Q(S + \Sigma_{l=1}^{n} s_l) - (s_i + s_j + s_k + S_i + S_j + S_k)}{3} \\ \times \left(\dfrac{s_i}{s_i + S_i} + \dfrac{s_j}{s_j + S_j} + \dfrac{s_k}{s_k + S_k} \right) \\ + w_0 - \displaystyle\sum_{\substack{l=1 \\ l \neq i,j,k}}^{n} s_l - \sum_{\substack{l=1 \\ l \neq i,j}}^{n} p_l \end{array} \right] \tag{B6}$$

such that

$$\sum_{l=1}^{n} (p_l + s_l) \leq w_0, \qquad p_l \geq 0, s_l \geq 0, l = 1, \ldots, n.$$

Model (B6) assumes that any horse i can win, followed by any horse j (except i), and any horse k can finish third (except i or j). This event has probability q_{ijk}. The expression inside the brackets has three parts: returns received from possible place bets, and from possible show bets, and money left over because the place and show bets made are less than the bettor's fortune w_0.

The only data needed to compute the optimal place and show bets in any given race using (B6) are Q, the track payback; the place and show bets P_i and S_i, respectively, on each horse i; the total place and show pools P and S, respectively; and the investor's wealth w_0.

Although model (B6) lacks some desirable concavity properties—see Kallberg and Ziemba (1981)—it is easy to solve on a computer. Calculations for thousands of races have routinely been made on the University of British Columbia's AMDAHL 470V6 Model II computer, using a code for the generalized reduced gradient algorithm.

Development of the Dr. Z System for Use at the Track

Since phones are not generally available at racetracks and since even portable computers are cumbersome, while the time when you need to act is so short, we have used multiple regression approximations to the solutions to (B6). These equations, such as the expected-value-per-dollar-bet equations in Chapter Four and the optimal-betting-amount equations in Chapter Five and Sixteen, were developed by solving (B6) for many many races and then regressing the results on the variables of interest. In all cases, the regression's independent variables are functions of only the simplest input data, namely, Q, w_0, W, W_i, P, P_i, S, and S_i for horse i.

In developing the Dr. Z system for very general use, several factors had to be considered: different track sizes, different betting-wealth levels, different track paybacks, coupled entries, and multiple betting. These factors are discussed below.

Track Size and Betting-Wealth Level

Track size and wealth level do not affect the expected-value equations, since (B4) and (B5) involve only the relative size of the public's bets and the track take. However, track size and wealth level are both important factors in determining the optimal bet sizes in (B6). To account for them, (B6) was solved for a broad range of wealths and track sizes. Regressions were determined for four different wealth levels (\$50, \$500, \$2,500, \$10,000), three different place pools (\$2,000, \$10,000, \$150,000), and three different show pools (\$1,200, \$6,000, \$100,000). These twelve pairs of wealth and place pools resulted in the twelve optimal place regressions in Table 16.1, and these twelve pairs of wealth and show pools resulted in the twelve optimal show regressions in Table 16.3. Then Tables 16.2 and 16.4 used interpolation of these 24 regressions to account for *any* betting wealth and place- or show-pool size. The R^2 values for these regressions were extremely good, varying from 0.982 to 0.995.

Track Payback

Both the expected-value equations (B4) and (B5) and the optimal bet sizes from (B6) are nondecreasing functions of Q, the track payback. As was demonstrated in Figure 9.4, a change in Q can have a very large effect on long-run profits. This section therefore develops modifications of the basic regression equations for use at tracks with differing paybacks.

Regression equation (4.3) for the expected value per dollar bet to place was calculated with $Q = 0.829$. Equation (B4) gives the exact expected value. If we neglect breakage for simplicity, it is

$$\text{EXP}_i = \sum_{j \neq i} \left(\frac{q_i q_j}{1 - q_i} + \frac{q_i q_j}{1 - q_j} \right) \left[1 + \frac{QP - (P_i + P_j)}{2P_i} \right].$$

Note that EXP_i is linear in Q and

$$\frac{\partial \text{EXP}_i}{\partial Q} = \frac{q_i P}{2P_i} \left[1 + \sum_{j \neq i} \left(\frac{q_j}{2 - q_j} \right) \right]. \qquad \text{(B7)}$$

Thus the appropriate adjustment factor for equation (4.3) to account for a $Q \neq 0.829$ should involve an approximation to (B7). From 124 Exhibition Park races with EXP_i in the range 1.16 and greater, the true $\partial \text{EXP}_i / \partial Q$ was regressed against q_i

$$\frac{\partial \text{EXP}_i}{\partial Q} = 2.22 - 1.29 q_i \qquad R^2 = 0.861, \quad SE = 0.0548, \qquad \text{(B8)}$$

both coefficients highly significant.

Therefore when the track payback is Q, the expected value per dollar bet to place can be approximated by adjusting equation (4.3) to

$$\text{EXP} = 0.319 + 0.559 \left(\frac{W_i / W}{P_i / P} \right) + \left[2.22 - 1.29 \left(\frac{W_i}{W} \right) \right] (Q - 0.829).$$

This is equation (4.5). A similar procedure for expected value to show results in equation (4.6) from equation (4.4).

The regression equations in Chapter Sixteen were calibrated for $Q = 0.829$. Since the optimal bet size is nondecreasing in Q, which will vary from track to track, we must adjust the optimal bets at tracks with $Q \neq 0.829$. To study this effect, optimization model (B6) was run on a number of Exhibition Park examples to compute the optimal place or show bets at several different initial wealths, several track sizes, and several different Q's (from 0.809 to 0.859). The results indicated that $\Delta p^* / \Delta Q$ and $\Delta s^* / \Delta Q$ were independent of Q over this short range of Q's. Therefore with a ΔQ of 0.01, $\Delta p^* / \Delta Q$ and $\Delta s^* / \Delta Q$ were regressed on p^*, w_0, P_i, P, and s^*, w_0, S_i, S respectively. The analysis for $\Delta p^* / \Delta Q$ showed that p^* and w_0 were very significant independent variables but that neither P_i nor P was significant; similar results for $\Delta s^* / \Delta Q$ were observed.

The regressions were

$$\frac{\Delta p^*}{\Delta Q} = 0.0316p^* + 0.000351w_0$$

$R^2 = 0.948$, $SE = 2.23$, $n = 56$.

$$\frac{\Delta s^*}{\Delta Q} = 0.0316s^* + 0.000351w_0$$

Therefore, if p^* and s^* are the optimal place and show bet sizes from Tables 16.1 to 16.3, then the true optimal place bet $\tilde{p}^*$ and true optimal show bet $\tilde{s}^*$ for a racetrack with a track payback Q are

$$\tilde{p}^* = p^* + (Q - 0.829)(3.16p^* + 0.0351w_0) \tag{B9}$$

and

$$\tilde{s}^* = s^* + (Q - 0.829)(3.16s^* + 0.0351w_0). \tag{B10}$$

Coupled Entries

As mentioned in Chapter Sixteen, because of the possibility that an entry will collect the whole place pool or a major portion of the show pool, the expected value per dollar bet to place or show is underestimated, as is the optimal bet size. The formula for correcting this underestimation is presented here.

Suppose the coupled entry has number 1 and let $q_1 = W_1/W$. Then q_1 estimates the probability that one of the horses in the entry will win the race. Suppose further that q_{1A} and q_{1B} (with $q_{1A} + q_{1B} = q_1$) are the correct winning probability estimates of the two horses in the entry. Calculating the probability to place using q_1 for one horse, and using q_{1A} and q_{1B} for two horses, results in the same probabilities. This suggests that the only reason the one-horse expected-value equations are underestimates of the true two-horse expected-value equations is the possibility of 1A-1B and 1B-1A finishes. To make a correction for this, the true expected value per dollar bet was calculated for the one-horse case of q_1 and for the two-horse case of q_{1A} and q_{1B}.* The difference between these two expected values, call it ΔC_i, was then regressed on (W_i/W) and (P_i/P). Again, Exhibition Park† data were used and

$$\Delta C_i = 0.867(W_i/W) - 0.857(P_i/P). \tag{B11}$$

Adding this correction factor for coupled entries changes equation (4.5) to (4.7). A similar procedure yields equation (4.8) from (4.6).

*It is generally the case that the two horses in the entry are not of equal ability. It is assumed that $q_{1A} = (\frac{2}{3})q_1$ and $q_{1B} = (\frac{1}{3})q_i$. The results are quite robust to the weighting however.

†The data used were for cases where the expected value was at least 1.16, that is, the cases of interest. For instances with a low expected value, the correction factor is not accurate.

The regression equations in Chapter Sixteen underestimate the true optimal bets on a coupled entry. To understand this phenomenon (1) many Exhibition Park examples were run on the optimization model (B6) assuming the data were for one horse, then (2) the same examples were run again using (B6) supposing the entry was two horses (the formulation was adjusted to consider the possibility of the two horses finishing first and second and then receiving a high payoff), but the win bet on the entry was lowered, using an iterative scheme, until the optimal bet was the same as the optimal bet from (1). This procedure gave pairs of $\tilde{q}_i^p$ and q_i, where $\tilde{q}_i^p$ was the probability of entry i's winning in (1), that is, thinking of the entry as one horse; and q_i was the adjusted probability that gave the same optimal bet in (2) as was observed in (1), that is, thinking of the entry as two horses. Since the regression equations in Chapter Sixteen give the optimal place bet when the horse's probability of winning is q_i, then using the slightly higher $\tilde{q}_i^p$ in those regressions would give the approximate optimal place bet when the entry's probability of winning is q_i.

The regression relating $\tilde{q}_i^p$ and q_i is

$$\tilde{q}_i^p = 0.991q_i + 0.137q_i^2 + 3.471 \times 10^{-7}w_0$$

$$(R^2 = 0.9998, SE = 0.00161). \qquad \text{(B12)}$$

The examples from which the data were derived spanned many wealth levels and pool sizes. While the wealth level was a very significant independent variable, the pool size was found to be statistically insignificant. Therefore, to compute the optimal place bet on coupled entry i use the following procedure:

1. Set $q_i = W_i/W$.
2. Determine $\tilde{q}_i^p$.
3. Use $\tilde{q}_i^p$, w_0, P, and P_i in regression equations in Tables 16.1 and 16.2.

Use the same procedure for the optimal show bet on coupled entry i:

1. Set $q_i = W_i/W$.
2. Determine

$$\tilde{q}_i^s = 1.07q_i + 4.13 \times 10^{-7} w_0 - 0.00663$$

$$R^2 = 0.999, SE = 0.00298, \text{ all coefficients highly significant.}$$

3. Use $\tilde{q}_i^s$, w_0, S, and S_i, in the regression equations in Tables 16.3 and 16.4.

Multiple Betting

The optimal bet equations in Tables 16.1 and 16.3 were calibrated assuming only one place bet or one show bet in a race. Sometimes, however, there is more than one Dr. Z system bet in a race (see Chapter Sixteen). It is not correct to calculate each of the optimal bets using the regression equations and then wager those amounts. In some instances it would result in overbetting; in others, for reasons of diversification, it would result in underbetting.

In what follows we have accounted for the most common multiple-betting situation—Dr. Z system bets to place and show on the same horse. Ninety-eight cases of place and show betting on the same horse were analyzed over a wide range of track handles, q_i's, and w_0's. Using the optimization model (B6) resulted in the quadruples (p_T^*, s_T^*, p_A^*, s_A^*). The p_T^* and s_T^* are the optimal pair of place and show bets when they are considered together. The p_A^* is the optimal place bet assuming it is the only good bet in the race and s_A^* is the optimal show bet supposing it is the only good bet in the race—namely, the values obtained using the regressions in Tables 16.2 and 16.4. Then p_T^* was regressed on p_A^*, s_A^*, w_0, P_i, P, and q_i. The only statistically significant independent variables were p_A^* and s_A^*, leading to the regression equation

$$\tilde{p}_T^* = 1.59p_A^* - 0.639s_A^*.$$

(R^2 = 0.967, SE = 73.7, all coefficients highly significant.)

A similar procedure for s^* yields

$$\tilde{s}_T^* = 0.907s_A^* - 0.134p_A^*.$$

(R^2 = 0.992, SE = 72.6, all coefficients highly significant.)

Exploitation of Inefficiencies or Chance?

These are equations (16.5) and (16.6), respectively.

An important question concerns the reliability of the results: Are the results true exploitations of market inefficiencies or could they be obtained simply by chance? This question is investigated utilizing the following simple model. The first application is concerned with an estimate of the probability that the Dr. Z system's theory is vacuous and, indeed, the observations conform to specific favorable samples from a random betting population. The second application estimates the probability of not making a positive profit. The calculations utilize the 1980 Exhibition Park data; those appear in Table 9.3.

Let π be the probability of winning a bet in each trial and

$$X_i = \begin{cases} 1 + w & \text{if the bet is won,} \\ 0 & \text{otherwise} \end{cases}$$

be the return from a $1 bet in trial i. In n trials, the probability of winning at least $100y\%$ of the total bet is

$$\Pr\left[\frac{1}{n}\left(\sum_{i=1}^{n} X_i\right) - 1 > y\right]. \tag{B13}$$

Assume that the trials are independent. Since the X_i are binomially distributed, (B13) can be approximated by a normal probability distribution as

$$1 - \phi\left\{\frac{\sqrt{n}\,[y - (1 + w)\pi + 1]}{(1 + w)\pi\sqrt{(1 - \pi)/\pi}}\right\} \tag{B14}$$

where ϕ is the cumulative distribution function of a standard $N(0, 1)$ variable. The observed probability of winning a bet, weighted by size of bet made from the 1980 Exhibition Park bets according to Table 9.5, yields 0.771 as an estimate of π. If the system's theory were vacuous and random betting were being made, then $(1 + w)\pi$ would equal 0.83, since the track's payback is approximately 83%. The twenty-two bets made totalled $5,304 and resulted in a profit of $1,216, for a rate of return of 22.9%. Using the equation with $n = 22$, gives 3×10^{-5}, which is negligible, as the probability of making 22.9% through random betting.

Suppose that the 1980 Exhibition Park results represent typical Dr. Z system behavior, then $\pi = 0.771$ and $(1 + w)\pi = 1.229$. In n trials the probability of making a nonpositive net return is

$$\Pr\left[\frac{1}{n}\left(\sum_{i=1}^{n} X_i\right) - 1 < 0\right]$$

which can be approximated as

$$\phi\left[\frac{\sqrt{n}(1 - (1 + w)\pi)}{(1 - w)\pi\sqrt{(1 - \pi)/\pi}}\right] = \phi(-0.342\sqrt{n}).$$

For $n = 22$, this probability is only 0.054. Thus in twenty-two races, the chance is only 5.4% that you are behind simply by chance. For $n = 50$ or 100, the probabilities are 0.008 and 0.0003, respectively. Thus it is reasonable to suppose that the results from the 1980 Exhibition Park data (as well as the 1978 Exhibition Park, 1973/74 Santa Anita, and 1981/82 Aqueduct data, with their larger samples) represent true exploitation of a market inefficiency.

Bibliography

Ainslie, Tom. *Ainslie's Complete Guide to Thoroughbred Racing.* New York: Simon & Schuster, 1968. A very thorough guide to handicapping fundamentals by its most distinguished student.

———. *Ainslie's Encyclopedia of Thoroughbred Handicapping.* New York: Morrow, 1978. Brief abstracts about many horse-racing topics.

Ali, Mukhtar M. "Probability and Utility Estimates for Racetrack Bettors," *Journal of Political Economy* 85 (August 1977): 803–15. A technical article concerned with the efficiency of win markets and the favorite–long-shot bias in harness racing.

American Racing Manual, Daily Racing Form. Chicago: Triangle Publications, published annually. The definitive year-by-year source of information concerning all aspects of racing.

Asch, Peter; Malkiel, Burton G.; and Quandt, Richard E. "Racetrack Betting and Informed Behavior," *Journal of Financial Economics* 10 (1982): 187–94. A demonstration that late bettors are better informed than the general public.

Bell, Robert M. and Cover, Thomas M., "Competitive Optimality of Logarithmic Investment," *Mathematics of Operations Research* 5 (May 1980): 161–166. They show that the Kelly criterion is optimal even for single bets.

Beyer, Andrew. *Picking Winners.* New York: Houghton Mifflin Co., 1975. An excellent source of information on speed handicapping.

———. *My $50,000 Year at the Races.* New York: Harcourt Brace Jovanovich, Inc., 1978. Colorful story of this well-known handicapper's attempts to beat the races over a full season.

———. *The Winning Horseplayer.* New York: Houghton Mifflin Co., 1983. An introduction to trip handicapping written in the author's entertaining style.

Bolton, Ruth N. and Chapman, Randall, G. "Searching for Positive Returns at the Track: A Multinomial Logic Model for Handicapping Horse Races." Mimeographed. Edmonton: University of Alberta, Faculty of Business, July 1983. A method for estimating win probabilities with a statistical model.

Canfield, Brian; Fauman, Bruce; and Ziemba, William T. "Efficient Market Adjustment of Odds Prices to Reflect Track Biases." Vancouver: University of British Columbia, Faculty of Commerce Working Paper No. 973, September 1983. A look at the wisdom of betting on favorable post positions.

Chernoff, H. "An Analysis of the Massachusetts Numbers Game." Technical Report No. 23. Cambridge, Mass.: MIT, Department of Mathematics, November 1980. A clever analysis of how statistical methods can be used to attempt to isolate numbers sufficiently unpopular so that they are profitable bets. The conclusions are easy to follow despite the highly mathematical analysis.

Cootner, Paul, ed. *The Random Character of Stock Market Prices.* Cambridge, Mass.: The MIT Press, 1964. Important collection of papers dealing with random walk ideas in security markets.

Copeland, Thomas E. and Weston, J. Fred. *Financial Theory and Corporate Policy.* 2d ed. Reading, Mass.: Addison-Wesley, 1982. A standard business-school textbook describing modern financial analysis.

Daily Racing Form. Chicago: Triangle Publications, published daily. The definitive source of current racing information.

Davidowitz, Steven. *Betting Thoroughbreds.* New York: Dutton, 1979. Informative and entertaining tips by one of the nation's top handicappers.

Dowie, J. "On the Efficiency and Equity of Betting Markets." *Economica* 43 (May 1976): 139–50. Shows that the win market in England is efficient.

Epstein, Richard A. *Theory of Gambling and Statistical Logic.* 2d ed. New York: Academic Press, 1977. The definitive source of information on the mathematics of gambling.

Ethier, S. and Tavare, S. "The Proportional Bettor's Return on Investment." *Journal of Applied Probability,* 1983. This article and those by Finkelstein-Whitley and Griffin listed below are mathematical studies concerned with win rates using the Kelly criterion.

Fabricand, Burton F. *Horse Sense.* New York: McKay, 1965. This and the author's other book present an interesting theory of horse-race betting based on rules of similarity.

———. *The Science of Winning.* New York: Van Nostrand Reinhold, 1979.

Fama, Eugene F. "Efficient Capital Markets: A Review of Theory and Empirical Work." *Journal of Finance* 25 (May 1970): 383–417. A survey of research on random walks of security prices.

Figgis, E. L. "Rates of Return from Flat Race Betting in England in 1973." *Sporting Life* 11 (March 1974). Estimates of track takes by bookies and totalizator betting in England.

Finkelstein, Mark and Whitley, Robert. "Optimal Strategies for Repeated Games." *Advances in Applied Probability* 13 (1981): 415–28.

Friedman, Joel H. "Understanding and Applying the Kelly Criterion." Mimeographed. 1981. The article that introduced fractional-Kelly strategies to a wide audience.

Griffin, Peter A. "Different Measures of Win Rate for Optimal Proportional Betting." Mimeographed. Sacramento: California State University, Mathematics Department, 1983.

Griffith, R. M. "Odds Adjustment by American Horse Race Bettors." *American Journal of Psychology* 62 (April 1949): 290–94. An early study of the favorite–long-shot bias.

Harville, David A. "Assigning Probabilities to the Outcomes of Multi-Entry Competitions." *Journal of American Statistical Association* 68 (June 1973): 312–16. Presentation of the formulas that bear his name for computing the probabilities of all possible in-the-money finishes.

Hausch, Donald B. and Ziemba, William T. "Transactions Costs, Extent of Inefficiency, Multiple Bets, and Entries in a Racetrack Betting Model." Vancouver: University of British Columbia, Faculty of Commerce Working Paper No. 974, October 1983.

———. "Optimal Strategies for Multiple Track Betting on Major Stakes Races." Vancouver; University of British Columbia, Faculty of Commerce Working Paper No. 975, December 1983. A mathematical article concerned with cross-track hedging and Kelly betting on races such as the Preakness and Belmont Stakes, which are bet on at many tracks with the aid of closed-circuit TV coverage.

Hausch, Donald B.; Ziemba, William T.; and Rubinstein, Mark. "Efficiency of the Market for Racetrack Betting." *Management Science* 27 (December 1981): 1435–52. This and the October 1983 study by Hausch and Ziemba are the technical articles that form the basis of the Dr. Z system.

Herbert, Ivor. *Horse Racing: The Complete Guide to the World of the Turf.* New York: St. Martin's Press, 1980. Lavish coffee-table book with useful information concerning the sport of kings.

Hollingsworth, Kent. "The States of Racing." *THE BLOOD-HORSE,* July 30, 1983, pp.5230–33. A summary of the current status of racing in America.

Humber, Larry, "You Don't Have to Lose at the Races." In *The Big Winner's System Book,* edited by L. Miller. Hollywood, Calif.: Gambling Times Publications, 1981. Argues that place and show betting may be profitable.

Isaacs, Rufus. "Optimal Horse-Race Bets." *American Mathematical Monthly* (May 1953): 310–15. A mathematical article showing the effect of bet sizes on the win odds.

Kallberg, Jerry G. and Ziemba, William T. "Generalized Concave Functions in Stochastic Programming and Portfolio Theory." In *Generalized Concavity* in *Optimization and Economics.* Edited by S. Schaible and W. T. Ziemba. New York: Academic Press, 1981, pp. 719–67. A technical article concerned with mathematical properties of the Dr. Z system.

Kelly, John L., Jr. "A New Interpretation of the Information Rate." *Bell System Technical Journal,* July 1956, pp. 917–26. The article where the Kelly criterion system of wagering was first presented.

King, A. P. "Market Efficiency of a Multi-Entry Competition." MBA essay, Graduate School of Business, University of California, Berkeley, June 1978. An early analysis of the predictive effect of the Harville formulas.

Lane, Daniel and Ziemba, William T. "Jai Alai Hedging Strategies." Vancouver: University of British Columbia, Faculty of Commerce Working Paper No. 974, October 1983. The development of exact and approximate winning hedge strategies for the game of Mexican team Jai Alai.

McCleary, James. "Blue Chip Investments in Horse Racing" and "Blue Chip Investments in Horse Racing: An Update." In *The Big Winner's Systems Book,* edited by L. Miller. Hollywood, Calif.: Gambling Times Publications, 1981. Shows that betting on overwhelming favorites in major stakes and futurity races may be profitable.

McGlothlin, W. H. "Stability of Choices Among Uncertain Alternatives." *American Journal of Psychology* 69 (December 1956): 604–15. An early article on the favorite–long-shot bias.

McLean, Leonard; Ziemba, William T.; and Blazenko, George. "Growth Versus Probability of Ruin Strategies in Gambling and Risky Investment Situations." Mimeographed. Vancouver: University of British Columbia, September 1983. A technical article concerned with fractional-Kelly betting strategies.

McNeill, Stuart. "This Math Whiz Knows How to Pick the Winners." *Vancouver Sun,*

January 6, 1983, p. B4. This and the next article give an account of how I showed that you can beat the Quebec Hockey sports pool, to the tune of $70,000.

Malkiel, Burton G. *A Random Walk Down Wall Street.* 2d ed. New York: W. W. Norton & Co., Inc., 1981. Lucid account of modern financial theories and their use in evaluating stocks and other securities.

Miller, David. "Successful Bets a Sure Thing for B. C. Professor." *Toronto Sunday Star,* January 16, 1983, p. A14.

Quinn, James. *The Literature of Thoroughbred Handicapping: 1965–1972.* Las Vegas: Gamblers Book Club Press, 1983. Useful essays on major handicapping ideas.

Ritter, Jay R. "Racetrack Betting: An Example of a Market with Efficient Arbitrage." Term paper, Finance 432-433, University of Chicago, March 3, 1978. An early paper on the wisdom of wagering on overlooked place and show bets.

Rothschild, Lord. *Royal Commission on Gambling. Vols. I and II.* Presented to Parliament by Command of Her Majesty, July 1978. The definitive source of information on gambling activities and practices in England.

Sharpe, William, F. *Investments.* 2d ed. Englewood Cliffs, N. J.: Prentice-Hall, 1981. A leading business-school text discussing modern investment ideas by the co-inventor of the capital asset pricing model.

Snyder, Wayne W. "Horse Racing: Testing the Efficient Markets Model." *Journal of Finance* 33 (September 1978): 1109–18. A summary of research on the favorite–long-shot bias for win bets.

Thorp, Edward O. *Beat the Dealer.* New York: Random House, 1966. The book that changed the rules of blackjack by presenting the first winning card-counting system.

———. "Portfolio Choice and the Kelly Criterion." In *Stochastic Optimization Models in Finance,* edited by William T. Ziemba and Raymond G. Vickson. New York: Academic Press, 1975, pp. 599–619. A lucid technical account of the major properties of the Kelly system of betting.

Thorp, Edward O. and Kassouf, Sheen T. *Beat the Market.* New York: Random House, 1967. The development of a profitable strategy for warrant hedging.

Vergin, R. C. "An Investigation of Decision Rules for Thoroughbred Race Horse Wagering." *Interfaces* 8 (1977): 34–45. Shows that sets of ad hoc filter rules may lead to profitable betting schemes.

Yass, Jeffrey. "An Econometric Strategy for Winning at the Track." *Gambling Times,* January 1980, pp. 46–48. Argues that place and show bets may be advantageous if they are sufficiently underbet.

Ziemba, William T. "Dr. Z on Horseracing." *Lottery News and Gaming Review,* Monthly Columns, July 1983–. In these and my "Mathematics of Gambling" columns, I discuss topics of current interest, with the emphasis on turning wagers into investments with positive expectations.

———. "The Favorite–Long-shot Bias in Hockey: Betting on the 1982 Stanley Cup Playoffs." Mimeographed. Vancouver: University of British Columbia, Faculty of Commerce, March 1984. Shows that Las Vegas odds are constructed to have the favorite–long-shot bias in sports-betting situations.

Ziemba, William T. and Vickson, Raymond G., eds. *Stochastic Optimization Models in Finance.* New York: Academic Press, 1975. Technical articles concerned with the mathematics of the Kelly criterion and other financial topics.

INDEX

Place Bet

EXPECTED-VALUE CUTOFF: 1.14

BET: if the values meet on or below the line
DO NOT BET: if the values meet above the line

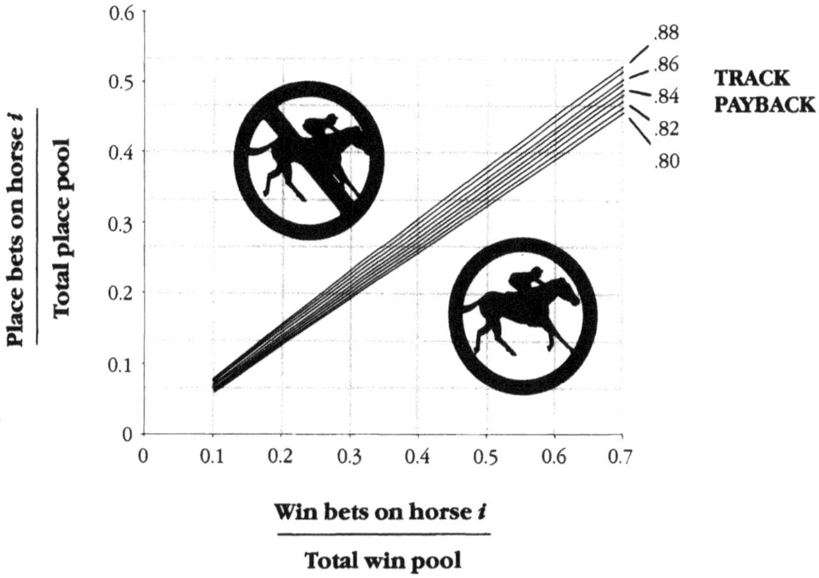

Show Bet

EXPECTED-VALUE CUTOFF: 1.14

BET: if the values meet on or below the line
DO NOT BET: if the values meet above the line

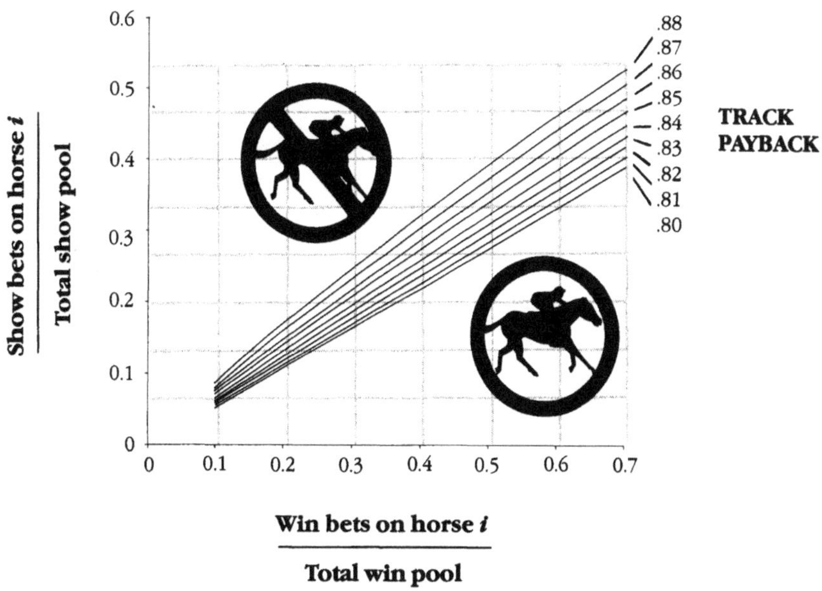

Optimal Place Bet for Various Probabilities of Winning

1. when the expected return is 1.14
2. when the total place pool is Small ($2,000– $9,999)

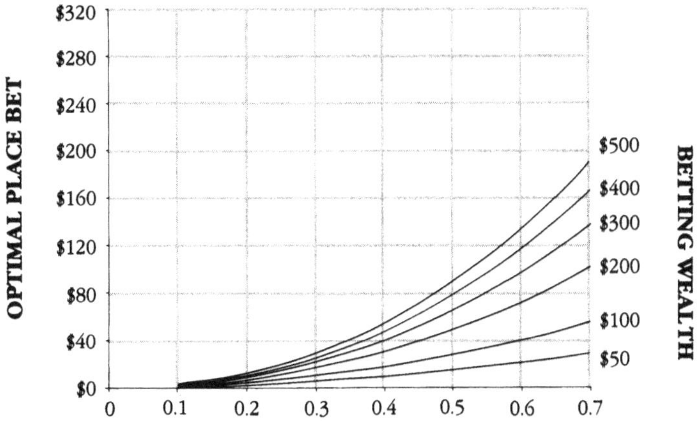

$\frac{\text{Win bets on horse } i}{\text{Total win pool}}$ (= probability of winning)

Optimal Show Bet for Various Probabilities of Winning

1. when the expected return is 1.14
2. when the total show pool is Small ($1,200– $5,999)

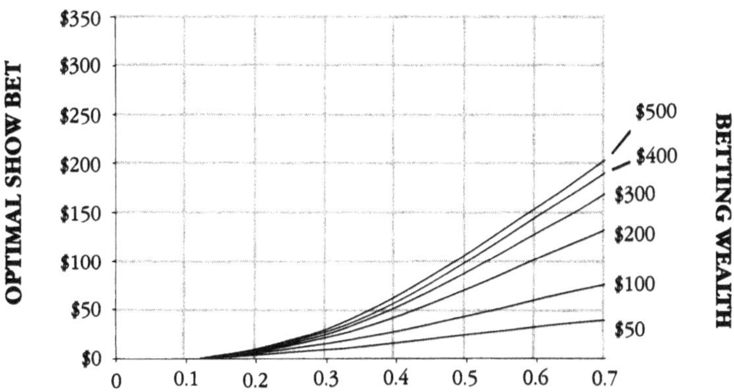

$\frac{\text{Win bets on horse } i}{\text{Total win pool}}$ (= probability of winning)

Optimal Place Bet for Various Probabilities of Winning

1. when the expected return is 1.14
2. when the total place pool is Medium ($10,000– $49,999)

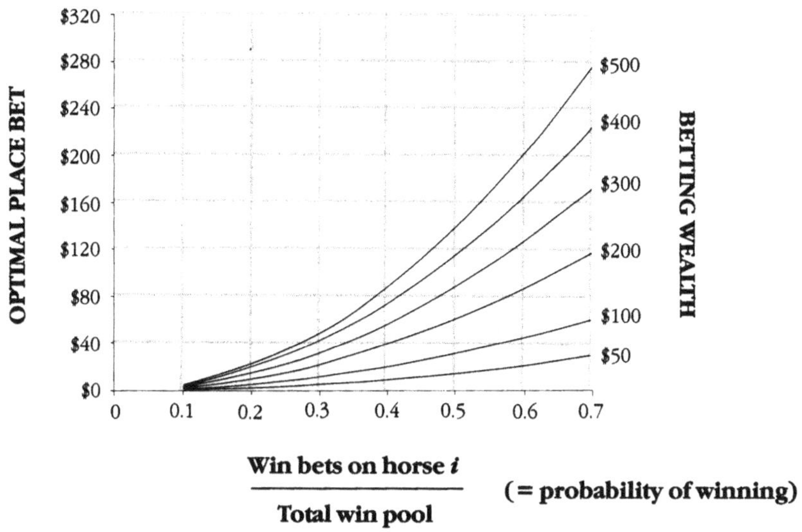

Optimal Show Bet for Various Probabilities of Winning

1. when the expected return is 1.14
2. when the total show pool is Medium ($6,000– $29,999)

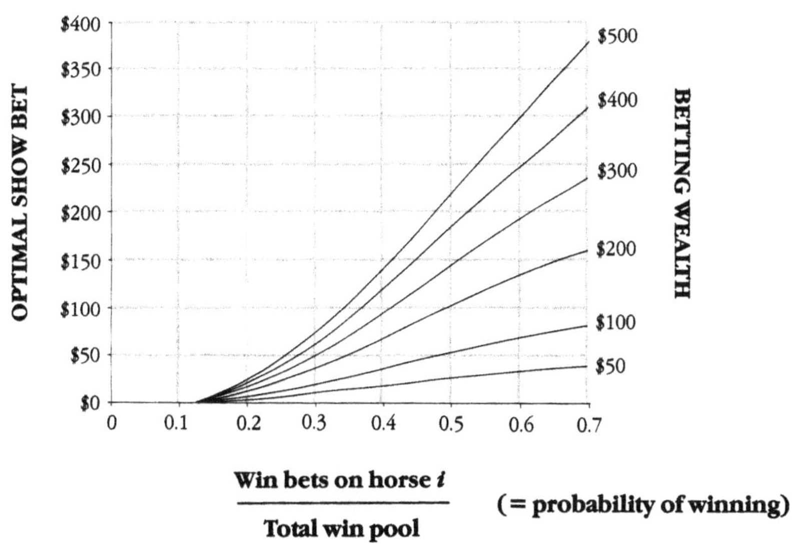

Optimal Place Bet for Various Probabilities of Winning

1. when the expected return is 1.14
2. when the total place pool is Large ($50,000+)

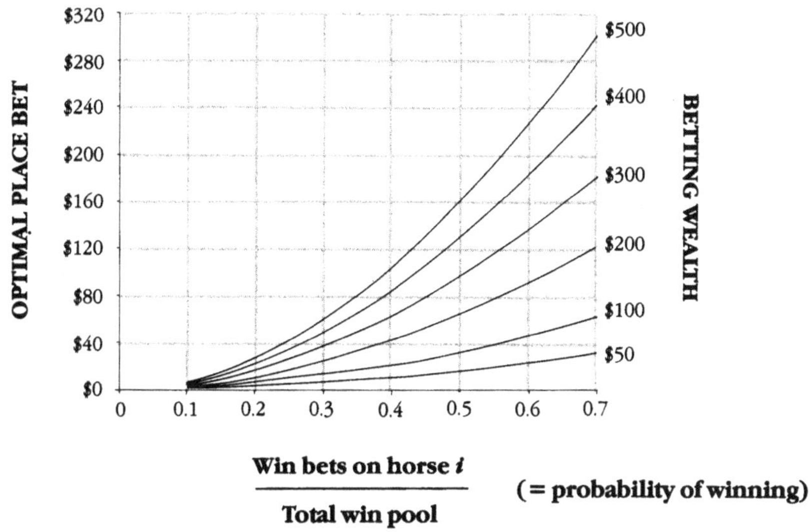

Optimal Show Bet for Various Probabilities of Winning

1. when the expected return is 1.14
2. when the total show pool is Large ($30,000+)

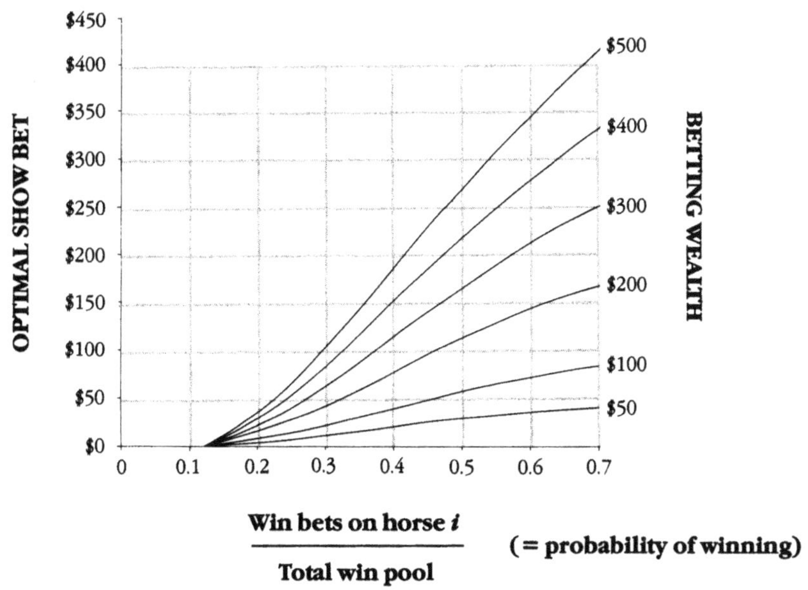

Place Bet

EXPECTED-VALUE CUTOFF: 1.18

BET: if the values meet on or below the line
DO NOT BET: if the values meet above the line

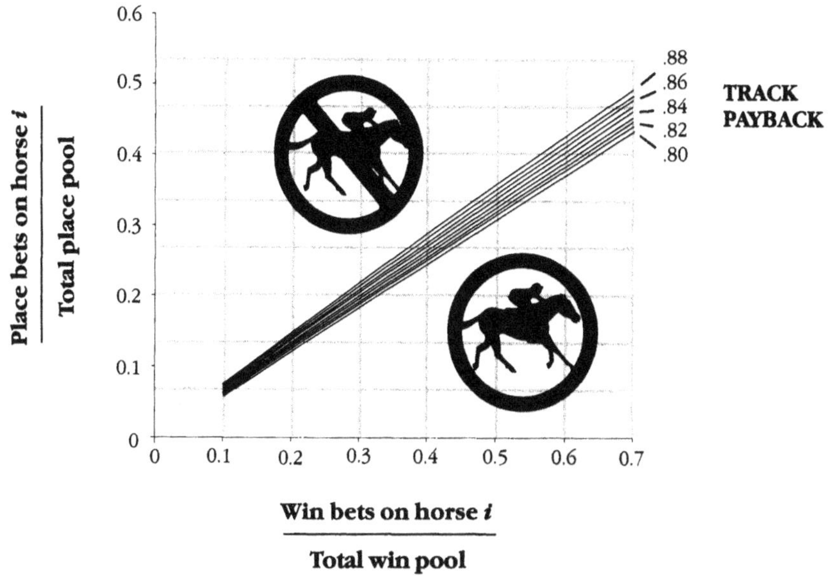

Show Bet

EXPECTED-VALUE CUTOFF: 1.18

BET: if the values meet on or below the line
DO NOT BET: if the values meet above the line

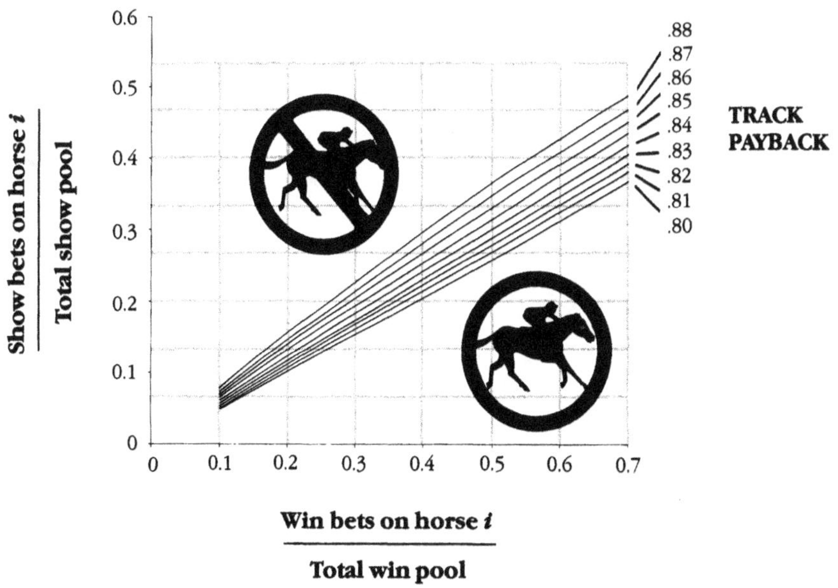

Optimal Place Bet for Various Probabilities of Winning

1. when the expected return is 1.18
2. when the total place pool is Small ($2,000– $9,999)

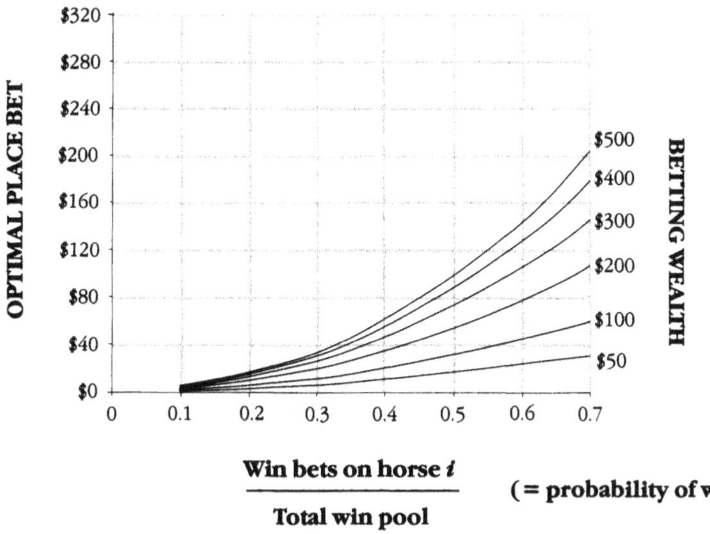

Optimal Show Bet for Various Probabilities of Winning

1. when the expected return is 1.18
2. when the total show pool is Small ($1,200– $5,999)

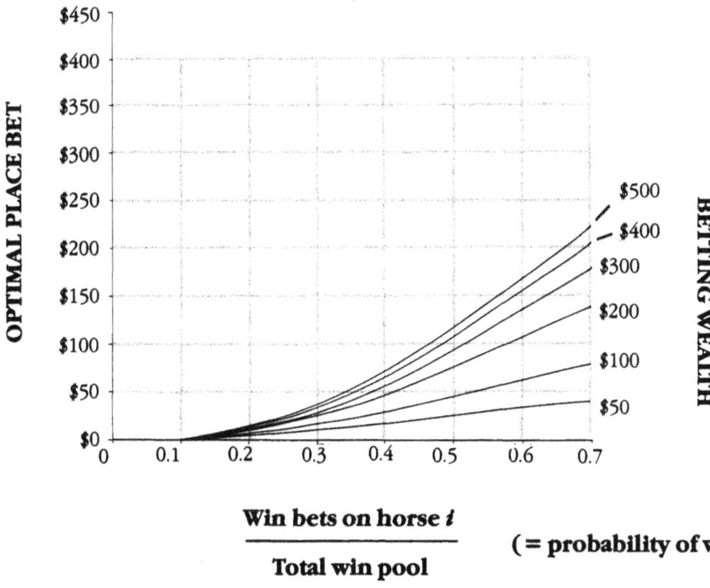

Optimal Place Bet for Various Probabilities of Winning

1. when the expected return is 1.18
2. when the total place pool is Medium ($10,000– $49,999)

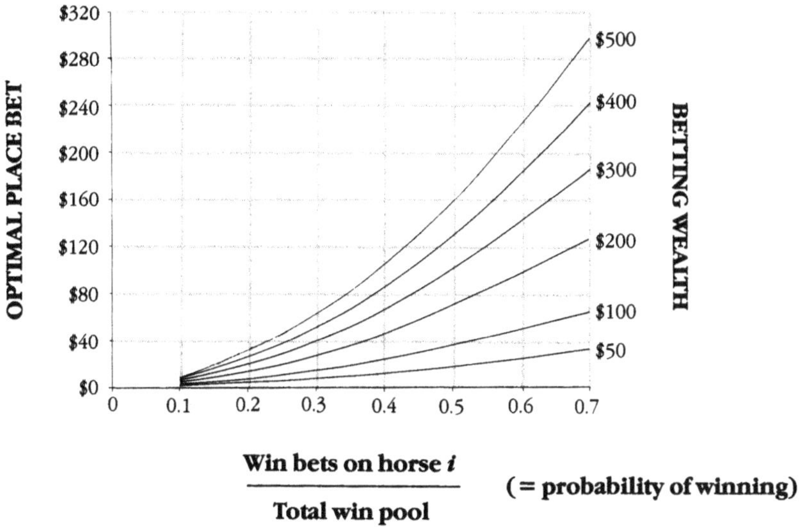

Optimal Show Bet for Various Probabilities of Winning

1. when the expected return is 1.18
2. when the total show pool is Medium ($6,000– $29,999)

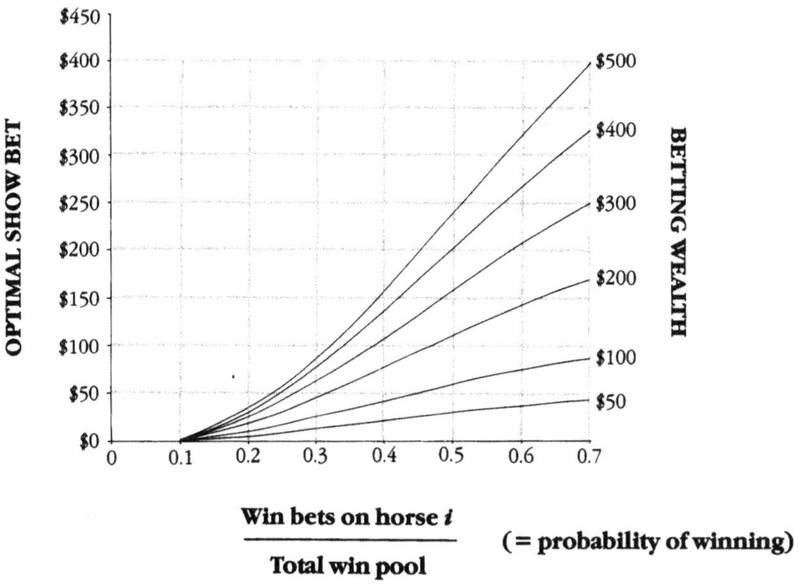

Optimal Place Bet for Various Probabilities of Winning

1. when the expected return is 1.18
2. when the total place pool is Large ($50,000+)

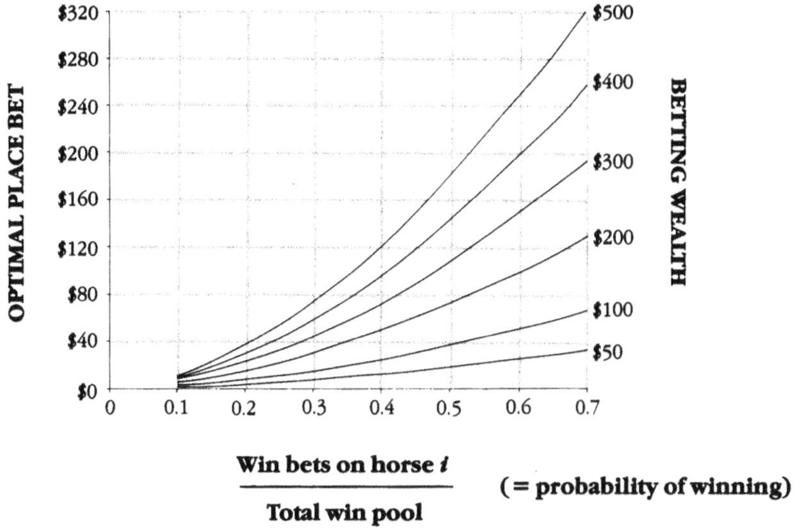

Optimal Show Bet for Various Probabilities of Winning

1. when the expected return is 1.18
2. when the total show pool is Large ($30,000+)

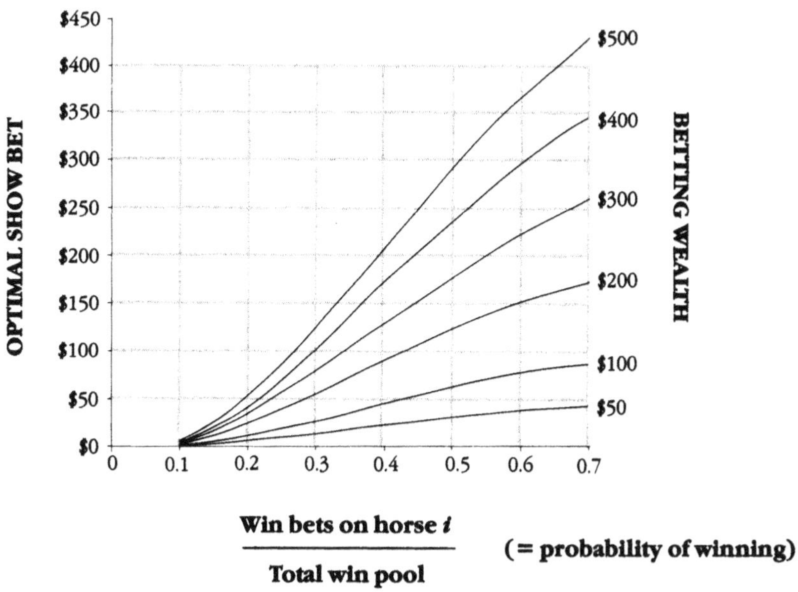

www.ingramcontent.com/pod-product-compliance
Lightning Source LLC
Chambersburg PA
CBHW050247170426
43202CB00011B/1593
* 9 7 8 1 6 3 5 6 1 7 4 4 3 *